CLASSICAL AND MEDIEVAL LITERATURE CRITICISM

Guide to Gale Literary Criticism Series

For criticism on	Consult these Gale series
Authors now living or who died after December 31, 1959	*CONTEMPORARY LITERARY CRITICISM (CLC)*
Authors who died between 1900 and 1959	*TWENTIETH-CENTURY LITERARY CRITICISM (TCLC)*
Authors who died between 1800 and 1899	*NINETEENTH-CENTURY LITERATURE CRITICISM (NCLC)*
Authors who died between 1400 and 1799	*LITERATURE CRITICISM FROM 1400 TO 1800 (LC)* *SHAKESPEAREAN CRITICISM (SC)*
Authors who died before 1400	*CLASSICAL AND MEDIEVAL LITERATURE CRITICISM (CMLC)*
Black writers of the past two hundred years	*BLACK LITERATURE CRITICISM (BLC)*
Authors of books for children and young adults	*CHILDREN'S LITERATURE REVIEW (CLR)*
Dramatists	*DRAMA CRITICISM (DC)*
Hispanic writers of the late nineteenth and twentieth centuries	*HISPANIC LITERATURE CRITICISM (HLC)*
Native North American writers and orators of the eighteenth, nineteenth, and twentieth centuries	*NATIVE NORTH AMERICAN LITERATURE (NNAL)*
Poets	*POETRY CRITICISM (PC)*
Short story writers	*SHORT STORY CRITICISM (SSC)*
Major authors from the Renaissance to the present	*WORLD LITERATURE CRITICISM, 1500 TO THE PRESENT (WLC)*

ISSN 0896-0011

Volume 21

CLASSICAL AND MEDIEVAL LITERATURE CRITICISM

Excerpts from Criticism of the Works of World
Authors from Classical Antiquity through the
Fourteenth Century, from the First Appraisals
to Current Evaluations

Daniel G. Marowski
Editor

GALE

DETROIT • NEW YORK • TORONTO • LONDON

STAFF

Daniel G. Marowski, *Editor*

Dana Ramel Barnes, Jelena Krstović, James E. Person, Jr., *Contributing Editors*
Gerald Barterian, *Associate Editor*
Michelle Lee, *Assistant Editor*
Aarti D. Stephens, *Managing Editor*

Susan M. Trosky, *Permissions Manager*
Kimberly F. Smilay, *Permissions Specialist*
Sarah Chesney, *Permissions Associate*
Steve Cusack, Kelly A. Quin, *Permissions Assistants*

Victoria B. Cariappa, *Research Manager*
Laura C. Bissey, Julia C. Daniel, Tamara C. Nott, Michele P. Le Meau,
Tracie A. Richardson, Cheryl Warnock, *Research Associates*
Alfred Gardner, *Research Assistant*

Mary Beth Trimper, *Production Director*
Deborah Milliken, *Production Assistant*

Pamela A. Reed, *Photography Coordinator*
Randy Bassett, *Image Database Supervisor*
Mikal Ansari, Robert Duncan, *Imaging Specialists*

This book is printed on acid-free paper that meets the minimum requirements of American National Standard for Information Sciences—Permanence Paper for Printed Library Materials, ANSI Z39.48-1984.

Library of Congress Catalog Card Number 88-658021
ISBN 0-7876-1125-5
ISSN 0896-0011
Printed in the United States of America

10 9 8 7 6 5 4 3 2 1

Contents

Preface   vii

Acknowledgments   xi

Marcus Porcius Cato 1
Roman statesman and orator

Epicurus 59
Greek philosopher

Kojiki 216
Japanese historical compilation

Richard Rolle 270
English religious writer

Literary Criticism Series Cumulative Author Index   405

Literary Criticism Series Cumulative Topic Index   487

CMLC Cumulative Nationality Index   495

CMLC Cumulative Title Index   497

CMLC Cumulative Critic Index   517

Preface

Since its inception in 1988, *Classical and Medieval Literature Criticism* has been a valuable resource for students and librarians seeking critical commentary on the writers and works of these periods in world history. Major reviewing sources have assessed *CMLC* as "useful" and "extremely convenient," noting that it "adds to our understanding of the rich legacy left by the ancient period and the Middle Ages," and praising its "general excellence in the presentation of an inherently interesting subject." No other single reference source has surveyed the critical reaction to classical and medieval literature as thoroughly as *CMLC*.

Scope of the Series

CMLC is designed to serve as an introduction for students and advanced readers of the works and authors of antiquity through the fourteenth century. The great poets, prose writers, dramatists, and philosophers of this period form the basis of most humanities curricula, so that virtually every student will encounter many of these works during the course of a high school and college education. By organizing and reprinting an enormous amount of commentary written on classical and medieval authors and works, *CMLC* helps students develop valuable insight into literary history, promotes a better understanding of the texts, and sparks ideas for papers and assignments. Each entry in *CMLC* presents a comprehensive survey of an author's career, an individual work of literature, or a literary topic, and provides the user with a multiplicity of interpretations and assessments. Such variety allows students to pursue their own interests; furthermore, it fosters an awareness that literature is dynamic and responsive to many different opinions.

CMLC continues the survey of criticism of world literature begun by Gale's *Contemporary Literary Criticism (CLC)*, *Twentieth-Century Literary Criticism (TCLC)*, *Nineteenth-Century Literature Criticism (NCLC)*, *Literature Criticism from 1400 to 1800 (LC)*, and *Shakespearean Criticism (SC)*. For additional information about these and Gale's other criticism series, users should consult the Guide to Gale Literary Criticism Series preceding the title page in this volume.

Coverage

Each volume of *CMLC* is carefully compiled to present:

- criticism of authors and works which represent a variety of genres, time periods, and nationalities

- both major and lesser-known writers and works of the period (such as non-Western authors and literature, increasingly read by today's students)

- 4-6 authors or works per volume

- individual entries that survey the critical response to each author, work, or topic, including early criticism, later criticism (to represent any rise or decline in the author's reputation), and current retrospective analyses. The length of each author or work entry also indicates relative importance, reflecting the amount of critical attention the author, work, or topic has received from critics writing in English, and from foreign criticism in translation.

An author may appear more than once in the series if his or her writings have been the subject of a substantial amount of criticism; in these instances, specific works or groups of works by the author will be covered in separate entries. For example, Homer will be represented by three entries, one devoted to the *Iliad*, one to the *Odyssey*, and one to the Homeric Hymns.

Starting with Volume 10, *CMLC* will also occasionally include entries devoted to literary topics. For example, *CMLC*-10 focuses on Arthurian Legend and includes general criticism on that subject as well as individual entries on writers or works central to that topic—Chrétien de Troyes, Gottfried von Strassburg, Layamon, and the Alliterative *Morte Arthure*.

Organization of the Book

An author entry consists of the following elements: author heading, biographical and critical introduction, principal English translations or editions, excerpts of criticism (each preceded by a bibliographic citation and an annotation), and a bibliography of further reading.

- The **Author Heading** consists of the author's most commonly used name, followed by birth and death dates. If the entry is devoted to a work, the heading will consist of the most common form of the title in English translation (if applicable), and the original date of composition. Located at the beginning of the introduction are any name or title variations.

- A **Portrait** of the author is included when available. Many entries also feature illustrations of materials pertinent to the author or work, including manuscript pages, book illustrations, and representations of people, places, and events important to a study of the author or work.

- The **Biographical and Critical Introduction** contains background information that concisely introduces the reader to the author, work, or topic.

- The list of **Principal Works** and **English Translations** or **Editions** is chronological by date of first publication and is included as an aid to the student seeking translated versions or editions of these works for study. The list will focus primarily on twentieth-century translations, selecting those works most commonly considered the best by critics.

- **Criticism** is arranged chronologically in each entry to provide a useful perspective on changes in critical evaluation over the years. All titles by the author featured in the critical entry are printed in boldface type to enable the user to ascertain without difficulty the works being discussed. Also for purposes of easier identification, the critic's name and the publication date of the essay are given at the beginning of each piece of criticism. Anonymous criticism is preceded by the title of the journal in which it appeared. Publication information (such as publisher names and book prices) and parenthetical numerical references (such as footnotes or page and line references to specific editions of works) have been deleted at the editors' discretion to provide smoother reading of the text. Many critical entries in *CMLC* also contain translations to aid the users. Footnotes that appear with previously published pieces of criticism are reprinted at the end of each essay or excerpt. In the case of excerpted criticism, only those footnotes that pertain to the excerpted text are included.

- A complete **Bibliographic Citation** provides original publication information for each piece of criticism.

- Critical excerpts are also prefaced by **Annotations** providing the reader with information about both the critic and the criticism, the scope of the excerpt, the growth of critical controversy, or changes in critical trends regarding an author or work. In some cases, these notes include cross-references to excerpts by critics who discuss each other's commentary. Dates in parentheses within the annotation refer to a book publication date when they follow a book title, and to an essay date when they follow a critic's name.

- An annotated bibliography of **Further Reading** appears at the end of each entry and lists additional secondary sources on the author or work. In some cases it includes essays for which the editors could not obtain reprint rights. When applicable, the Further Reading is followed by references to additional entries on the author in other literary reference series published by Gale.

Topic Entries are subdivided into several thematic rubrics in which criticism appears in order of descending scope.

Cumulative Indexes

Each volume of *CMLC* includes a cumulative **author index** listing all authors who have appeared in Gale's Literary Criticism Series, along with cross references to such biographical series as *Contemporary Authors* and *Dictionary of Literary Biography*. For readers' convenience, a complete list of Gale titles included appears on the page prior to the author index. Useful for locating an author within the various series, this index is particularly valuable for those authors who are identified with a certain period but who, because of their death date, are placed in another, or for those authors whose careers span two periods. For example, Geoffrey Chaucer, who is usually considered a medieval author, is found in *Literature Criticism from 1400 to 1800* because he died after 1399.

Beginning with the tenth volume, *CMLC* includes a cumulative index listing all topic entries that have appeared in the Gale Literary Criticism Series *Classical and Medieval Literature Criticism, Contemporary Literary Criticism, Literature Criticism from 1400 to 1800, Nineteenth-Century Literature Criticism,* and *Twentieth-Century Literary Criticism.*

Beginning with the second volume, *CMLC* also includes a cumulative nationality index. Authors and/or works are grouped by nationality, and the volume in which criticism on them may be found is indicated.

Title Index

Each volume of *CMLC* also includes an index listing the titles of all literary works discussed in the series. Foreign language titles that have been translated are followed by the titles of the translations—for example, *Slovo o polku Igorove (The Song of Igor's Campaign).* Page numbers following these translated titles refer to all pages on which any form of the title, either foreign language or translated, appears. Titles of novels, dramas, nonfiction books, and poetry, short story, or essay collections are printed in italics, while those of all individual poems, short stories, and essays are printed in roman type within quotation marks. In cases where the same title is used by different authors, the author's name or surname is given in parentheses after the title, e.g. *Collected Poems* (Horace) and *Collected Poems* (Sappho).

Critic Index

An index to critics, which cumulates with the second volume, is another useful feature of *CMLC*. Under each critic's name are listed the authors and/or works on whom the critic has written and the volume and page number where criticism may be found.

A Note to the Reader

When writing papers, students who quote directly from any volume in the Literary Criticism Series may use the following general forms to footnote reprinted criticism. The first example pertains to material drawn from a periodical, the second to material reprinted from books.

Rollo May, "The Therapist and the Journey into Hell," *Michigan Quarterly Review,* XXV, No. 4 (Fall 1986), 629-41; excerpted and reprinted in *Classical and Medieval Literature Criticism,* Vol. 3, ed. Jelena O. Krstović (Detroit: Gale Research, 1989), pp. 154-58.

Dana Ferrin Sutton, *Self and Society in Aristophanes* (University of Press of America, 1980); excerpted and reprinted in *Classical and Medieval Literature Criticism,* Vol. 4, ed. Jelena O. Krstović (Detroit: Gale Research, 1990), pp. 162-69.

Suggestions Are Welcome

Readers who wish to make suggestions for future volumes, or who have other comments regarding the series, are cordially invited to write or call the editors (1-800-347-GALE, Fax: (313) 961-6815).

Acknowledgments

The editors wish to thank the copyright holders of the excerpted criticism included in this volume and the permissions managers of many book and magazine publishing companies for assisting us in securing reproduction rights. We are also grateful to the staffs of the Detroit Public Library, the Library of Congress, the University of Detroit Mercy Library, Wayne State University Purdy/Kresge Library Complex, and the University of Michigan Libraries for making their resources available to us. Following is a list of the copyright holders who have granted us permission to reproduce material in this volume of *CMLC*. Every effort has been made to trace copyright, but if omissions have been made, please let us know.

COPYRIGHTED EXCERPTS IN *CMLC*, VOLUME 21, WERE REPRODUCED FROM THE FOLLOWING PERIODICALS:

ELH, v. 40, Spring, 1973 for "Biblical *Imitatio* in the Writings of Richard Rolle," by John A. Alford. Copyright © 1973 by The Johns Hopkins University Press. All rights reserved. Reproduced by permission.--*Monumenta Nipponica: Studies in Japanese Culture,* v. 43, no. 4, Winter, 1988. Edited by Michael Cooper. Sophia University, 1988. Reproduced by permission.--*The Month,* v. 23, January, 1960. Reproduced by permission.

COPYRIGHTED EXCERPTS IN *CMLC*, VOLUME 21, WERE REPRODUCED FROM THE FOLLOWING BOOKS:

Annas, Julia. From *Hellenistic Philosophy of Mind.* University of California Press, 1992. Copyright © 1992 by the Regents of the University of California. Reproduced by permission.--Astin, Alan E. From *Cato the Censor.* Oxford at the Clarendon Press, 1978. Copyright © Oxford University Press 1978. Reproduced by permission.--Bailey, Cyril. From *The Greek Atomists and Epicurus.* Oxford at the Clarendon Press, 1928. Reproduced by permission.-- Coleman, T. W. From *English Mystics of the Fourteenth Century.* The Epworth Press, 1938. Reproduced by permission.--Comper, Frances M. M. From *The Life of Richard Rolle.* J.M. Dent & Sons Limited, 1928. Reproduced by permission.--Conte, Gian Biagio. From *Latin Literature: A History.* The Johns Hopkins University Press, 1994. All rights reserved. Reproduced by permission.--DeWitt, Norman Wentworth. From *Epicurus and His Philosophy.* University of Minnesota Press, 1954. Copyright © 1954 by the University of Minnesota. All rights reserved. Reproduced by permission.--Fantham, Elaine. From *Roman Literary Culture.* The Johns Hopkins University Press, 1996. Copyright © 1996 The Johns Hopkins University Press. All rights reserved. Reproduced by permission.--Farrington, Benjamin. From *The Faith of Epicurus.* Weidenfeld and Nicolson, 1967. Copyright © 1967 Benjamin Farrington. Reproduced by permission.--Festugiere, A. J. From *Epicurus and His Gods.* Translated by C. W. Chilton. Basil Blackwell, 1955. Reproduced by permission.--Hadas, Moses. From *A History of Latin Literature.* Copyright © 1952 by Columbia University Press. Reprinted with permission of the publisher.--Irwin, Terence. From *A History of Western Philosophy: I Classical Thought.* Oxford University Press, 1989. Copyright © 1989 by Terence Irwin. Reproduced by permission.--Janson, Tore. From *Latin Prose Prefaces: Studies in Literary Conventions.* Almqvist & Wiksell, 1964. Reproduced by permission.--Knowles, Dom David. From *The English Mystics.* Burns Oates & Washbourne Ltd., 1927. Reproduced by permission.--Knowlton, Sister Mary Arthur. From *The Influence of Richard Rolle and of Julian of Norwich on the Middle English Lyrics.* Mouton, 1973. Copyright © 1972 Mouton & Co., Publishers. Reproduced by permission of Mouton de Gruyter, a division of Walter de Gruyter & Co.--Kotanski, Wieslaw. From "The Belief in *Kotodama* and Some Earlier Misinterpretations of *Kojiki,*" in *European Studies on Japan.* Edited by Ian Nish and Charles Dunn. Paul Norbury Publications, 1979. Copyright © Paul Norbury Publications Ltd. 1979. Reproduced by permission.--Long, A. A. From *Hellenistic Philosophy: Stoics, Epicureans, Sceptics.* University of California Press, 1974. Copyright © 1974, 1986 A. A. Long. All rights reserved. Reproduced by permission.--Scullard, H. H. From *Roman Politics: 220-150 B.C..* Oxford at the Clarendon Press, 1973. Reproduced by permission.--Vannovsky, Alexander. From *Volcanoes and the Sun.* Bridgeway Press, 1960. Copyright in Japan, 1960. All rights reserved. Reproduced by permission of Charles E. Tuttle Co., Inc. (Boston).--Watson, Nicholas. From *Richard Rolle and the Invention of Authority.* Cambridge

University Press, 1991. Copyright © Cambridge University Press 1991. Reproduced by permission of Cambridge University Press and the author.--Woolf, Rosemary. From *The English Religious Lyric in the Middle Ages.* Oxford at the Clarendon Press, 1968. Copyright © Oxford University Press 1968. Reproduced by permission.--Yaku, Masao. From *The* **Kojiki** *in the Life of Japan,* translated by G. W. Robinson. The Centre for East Asian Cultural Studies, 1969. Copyright © 1969. Reproduced by permission.

PHOTOGRAPHS AND ILLUSTRATIONS APPEARING IN *CMLC,* VOLUME 21, WERE RECEIVED FROM THE FOLLOWING SOURCES:

Cato, Marcus Porcius, engraving. Archive Photo/Popperfoto. Reproduced by permission.--Cato, Marcus Porcius, line drawing. Archive Photo/Popperfoto. Reproduced by permission.--Cato, Marcus Porcius, photograph. Stock Montage, Inc.. Reproduced by permission.--Epicurus, photograph. Archive Photo/Popperfoto. Reproduced by permission.--Rolle, Richard, a manuscript painting. The British Library. Reproduced by permission.--The Kojiki, photograph. Maeda Ikutoku-kai Foundation. Reproduced by permission.

Marcus Porcius Cato

234 B.C.-149 B.C.

(Also known as Cato the Censor, Cato Major, and Cato the Elder. Roman statesman, orator, and author of nonfiction prose.)

INTRODUCTION

A roman soldier, estate-owner, and statesman, Cato has for many centuries exemplified the values of the Roman republic: honesty, fortitude, asceticism, determination, and simplicity. As a censor—an elected official who monitored the moral conduct of the ruling class—he became known for fulfilling his duties with incorruptible rigor. Cato also excelled at the oration required by his work; his style not only won many cases but also garnered praise from later writers, including Cicero and Livy. His writing constituted a second career, which he began after he reached the status of censor. Despite lacking formal trainng in composition, Cato developed a genuinely national prose literature for Rome. Where Greek ideals had previously set the standard for writing, Cato produced the first works of prose in Latin, including the landmark history, the *Origines*.

Biography

Cato was born in 234 B.C. into a family of Sabine landowners—prosperous, non-aristocratic farmers who belonged to the Roman middle class. Cato grew up on a farm in Tusculum, not more than ten miles from Rome, and received a practical education that prepared him to run an estate and to serve as a citizen and a soldier. He fought in the war against Hannibal and served as military tribune in Sicily when he was only twenty years old. By 191 B.C. he was filling the same post, along with an aristocratic mentor named Lucius Valerius Flaccus, at some of the most important cities in Greece, including Athens. By this time, however, his military career had taken second place to his political career, also sponsored by Valerius Flaccus. Cato's first political position was as a quaestor, or financial administrator, in Sicily and Africa. By 199 B.C. he became plebeian aedile, an administrator of public works. He assumed a specifically judicial role as a minor magistrate or praetor of Sardinia in 198 B.C. In 195 B.C., he reached the summit of his judicial career, becoming one of Rome's two censors, or chief magistrates; he again shared the honor with Valerius Flaccus. Cato pursued his new position with zeal, developing the political capacity for which he became known: to check the excesses of the aristocracy in order to advance the prosperity of the republic.

Cato's judicial career was quite active from this point forward; he was often the primary prosecutor in cases involving the powerful circle of aristocrats led by Africanus Maior Scipios. He was known as a defender of Roman virtue and tradition, which he saw embodied in the public life of Rome, rather than in the individual achievements of its noble families. In his promotion of Roman values he also became a vocal critic of Greek culture, which he saw as individualistic, indulgent, and morally degenerate. Many of the influential speeches for which he was celebrated addressed these topics; in 155 B.C., for example, he was responsible for securing the expulsion from Rome of Greek philosophers who had come as ambassadors.

Cato pursued farming alongside his military and political careers, building a plantation that quickly eclipsed the small holding his father had owned. His devotion to hard work, frugality, and stern management facilitated the economic success of his estate. Writing constituted something of a sideline for him; he probably began only after achieving the status of censor. Critics have speculated that his writing might have grown out of domestic need—educational manuals for his son, farm management manuals for the running of his estate—or out of boredom, pursued in depth once his civic duties tapered off late in life. Whatever the motivation, all of his writings bear strong evidence of his practical nature and his efforts to check the influence of Greek culture in Rome.

Major Works

Many sayings attributed to Cato survive, preserved by his later admirers, and one of the most invoked of these is his advice regarding composition: *rem tene, verba sequentur,* or "have the contents clear, and the words will come of themselves." This rejection of deliberate art in writing—a specifically Greek value—manifests itself clearly in his major works, all of which are known for their simplicity and directness. He is probably most celebrated for the *Origines,* since this was the first history of Rome and Italy composed in Latin prose. This work occupies seven books, the first several of which describe the nation's origins and the last three of which are devoted to recent history. Cato unabashedly used the work as a vehicle for his political agenda, dotting it throughout with his speeches. It also portrays the Rome he believed in, one built by the people rather than by individual heroes and aristocratic families.

Cato's other two significant written works were practical manuals. *De agricultura* addresses farm management, while *Ad filium* was designed for his son's education. The first has enjoyed considerable critical attention, largely because it is the only work of Cato's that has survived in a complete form. Although scholars have discerned evidence of Cato's political perspective in the volume, it is on the surface a purely instructional work, providing advice specifically for the non-aristocratic landowner. Ranging from guidelines for labor management to recipes, the writings reflect Cato's values, specifically his commitment to hard work, leadership, ambition, and unsentimental virtue. The *Ad filium* apparently addressed a broader range of topics in a similar fashion, providing information on rhetoric and medicine, among other concerns, for the sake of his son's education. Critics disagree about whether it was one volume or a set of volumes, maybe constituting the first Roman encyclopedia.

Unlike his written works, Cato's orations were the product of his skill and training. Scholars estimate that there were 150 of his speeches in print after his death—a number they determine mostly from the

evidence of Cicero, who made an effort to find copies of these speeches in his own day, recording some of them and many of their titles in his own works. The speeches fulfilled immediate purposes—usually military or judicial—but were carefully styled for persuasive effect. Cato was noted for the function of humor as a primary element in his speeches, and he was also known for his aphorisms, which were apparently collected in a few volumes, including *Apophthegmata* and *Carmen de moribus.*

Textual History

Little of Cato's work has survived in any form. Scholars rely on references in the works of other writers and the manuscript fragments that occasionally surface. Without Cicero, whose portrayals of Cato were based on sources that vanished sometime around the fourth century, very little would be known of Cato's speeches. The *Origines,* one of the primary works of Latin historiography, remains only in a few fragments. Only *De agricultura* survives in a complete manuscript, although critics cannot be certain how true it is to Cato's original; centuries of readers scribbled commentary in manuscript margins, and the manuscripts that followed may have been revised accordingly.

Critical Reception

Cato's earliest commentators, including Cicero, Livy, and Gellius, praised his style, gleaned primarily from his speeches. While Cato's untainted reputation as a Roman citizen has persisted through the centuries, the estimation of his writing has not enjoyed such unequivocal estimation. Modern scholars have tended to note the obvious absence of compositional training in his education, commenting on the lack of art and even coherence in his written works. J. W. Mackail charges the *Origines* with an "absence of method," and John Dunlop refers to the "total want of arrangement." Late twentieth-century critics, however, have begun to discern organizing strategies—albeit not immediately apparent—in, for example, *De agricultura.*

Cato's value to modern scholars has been mostly as an innovator of Latin prose literature. Their opinions about why he took this step, however, are varied. Two issues dominate discussion of Cato's work: audience and motivation. Regarding audience, critics are divided about how public Cato meant his works to be, some arguing that the *Origines* and *De agricultura,* like *Ad filium,* are simple notes written for use in his own home, while others maintain that he desired publication. The disagreement regarding motivation rests on the sincerity of Cato's hatred for Hellenism. Most critics have perceived him as driven by the threat of Greek influence, for which he wanted to create a wholly native alternative. The *Origines* and *Ad filium* constitute the usual material for this argument, since both compete with Greek traditions—one in historiography and the other in education—on which Romans depended. This argument relies on a long-standing assumption that Cato was unremittingly hostile to Greek culture. Later in the twentieth century, however, some critics began to soften that view, pointing to the Greek echoes in Cato's work, including the *Origines* and *De agricultura*. Michael Grant contends that "Cato, while anti-Hellenic, was also a Hellenist." According to this perspective, Cato's anti-Greek stance was a pose determined by his desire to see a specifically Roman culture come to fruition, with his own Latin prose as a significant contribution.

PRINCIPAL WORKS

Ad filium (educational tract[s])
De agricultura (handbook)
Carmen de moribus (aphorisms)
Origines (history)

PRINCIPAL ENGLISH TRANSLATIONS

Cato the Censor. On Farming. (translated by Ernest Brehaut) 1993
On Agriculture (translated by William Davis Hooper) 1935

CRITICISM

Marcus Tullius Cicero (essay date 46 B.C.)

SOURCE: Marcus Tullius Cicero, "The Brutus: The Importance of Oratory," in *On Government*, translated by Michael Grant, Penguin Books, 1993, pp. 221-334.

[*Cicero referred to Cato in many of his works, often making the earlier orator a character in ethical dialogues. In the excerpt below, Cicero praises Cato's skills as an orator.*]

Cato's speeches are almost as numerous as those of the Athenian (to whom, however, I believe that some are wrongly attributed). I call Lysias Athenian because he was certainly born and died at Athens, although Timaeus,[1] by a sort of Licinian and Mucian law,[2] ascribes him to Syracuse instead. Between Lysias and Cato there is a certain resemblance. Both are penetrating, elegant, clever and concise. But as regards reputation the Greek has been considerably more fortunate. He has a very definite body of supporters. They are men who cultivate a slim rather than an ample oratorical structure and, within the bounds set by good health, even favour leanness. True, Lysias himself often displays an effective muscular vigour. Yet his style as a whole belongs to the plain variety. And, as I have said, he has his admirers, who derive satisfaction from this stark style.

As for Cato the elder, surely none of our orators today reads him, or knows anything about him at all. And yet, heavens above, what a man! To Cato as citizen, senator, general, I am not now referring. All we are considering here is Cato the orator. I can think of no one who deals out a more impressive compliment, whose words of censure, conversely, are more biting, who expresses what he thinks more penetratingly, who presents a demonstration or an explanation with greater acuteness. He delivered more than a hundred and fifty speeches—judging by those that I myself have discovered and read. Both in style and content, they are packed with brilliance. Choose from them the passages that seem to you most worthy of note and praise. You will find in them everything that is best in an orator. And take his **Origins,** too: they display every ornament and splendour of eloquence that you could wish. Yet Cato is short of admirers. Many centuries ago, the same was true of Philistus of Syracuse,[3] and even of Thucydides. For they displayed an epigrammatic and sometimes too pointedly concise brevity which became eclipsed by the lofty, high-flown manner of Theopompus.[4] The same thing had happened to Lysias, whom Demosthenes superseded. And in just the same way the excessively elevated diction of subsequent writers has overshadowed Cato.

Some people find the early period of Greek literature deeply satisfying, and admire its simplicity, which they describe as Attic. That the same quality is to be found in Cato, however, they are completely unaware. Their models are Hyperides[5] and Lysias. Excellent, but why do they not model themselves on Cato? Their admiration for the Attic style makes excellent sense—though I only wish they imitated its life-blood, and not just its bones! However, their intention deserves praise. But I still say, why, in that case, do they adore Lysias and Hyperides, while they know nothing about Cato at all? True, his phraseology is rather archaic, and some of the words he uses are somewhat uncouth. Yes, because that is how people spoke in those days. Change that—which he could not have done at his time—insert rhythm, and rearrange his words and fasten them together to make what he has to say run more smoothly (which even the early Greeks never managed to do), and you will not be able to find anyone whom you can set above Cato.

The Greeks believe that language is beautiful if you modify your terminology by what they call "tropes", and employ the forms of epigrammatic expression which they describe as figures of speech. Now Cato was quite remarkably rich and distinguished in both these kinds of ornament. Certainly, I realize that he did not yet possess the polish an orator ought to have, and that a higher degree of perfection has to be aimed at. Nor is that so remarkable, seeing that from the standpoint of our own epoch he is so outstandingly antique that nothing of an earlier date which is worth reading exists at all. But the fact is that in ancient periods every other form of art was held in greater honour than this single art of eloquence. . . .

Notes

[1] Timaeus of Tauromenium (*c.* 356-260), Greek historian.

[2] The *Lex Licinia Mucia* of Lucius Licinius Crassus and Quintus Mucius Scaevola Pontifex (95) set up an inquiry into aliens who were claiming to be citizens, relegating to the place of their birth non-Roman Italians who by long residence had assumed Roman citizen rights.

[3] Historian (*c.* 430-356).

[4] Historian from Chios (born *c.* 378).

[5] Athenian orator (389-322).

Livy (essay date c. 17)

SOURCE: Livy, "Book XXXVIII," in *Livy*, Vol. XI, translated by Evan T. Sage, Cambridge, Mass.: Harvard University Press, 1965, pp. 217-400.

[*In the following excerpt Livy briefly summarizes Cato's reputation, commending him to the reader's highest admiration. Because the exact date of composition is not known, Livy's death date is used to date this essay*].

[Among] all the patricians and plebeians of the most illustrious houses, Marcus Porcius Cato stood out most conspicuously. In this man there was such force of mind and character that in whatever station he had been born it seemed that he would have made his fortune for himself. No art of conducting either private or public business was lacking to him; he was equally skilled in affairs of the city and of the farm. Some men were advanced to the highest offices by knowledge of the law, others by eloquence, others by military reputation: his comprehensive genius was so adapted to everything alike that you would say that whatever he was doing was the one thing for which he was born: in war he was the bravest of fighters and was famous for many remarkable battles, and after he attained to the highest offices, he was likewise a consummate commander; the same man in peace was, if you asked advice on law, most skilled therein, if there was a case to be pleaded, most eloquent, nor was he merely one whose tongue was potent while he lived but left no record of his eloquence: rather, he lives and flourishes by his eloquence, enshrined in books of every kind. There are many orations, both for himself and for and against others; for he wore down his enemies not only by accusing them but also by pleading his own cause. Feuds in excessive numbers pursued him and he himself pursued them; nor could you easily say whether the nobility worked harder to suppress him or he to irritate the nobility. Without question he had a stern temper, a bitter tongue and one immoderately free, but he had a soul unconquerable by appetites, an unwavering integrity, and a contempt for influence and wealth. In his economy, in his endurance of toil and danger, he was of almost iron-like body and mind, and his mind not even old age, which weakens everything, could break down, since at the age of eighty-six he pleaded a case, spoke and wrote in his own defence, and in his ninetieth year brought Servius Galba to trial before the assembly.

Plutarch (essay date c. 120)

SOURCE: Plutarch, "Marcus Cato," in *Plutarch's Lives*, pp. 516-42.

[*Plutarch's life of Cato has supplied the definitive biography, relied upon by centuries of scholars. Although certain details have been disputed, the comprehensiveness of the account furnishes a very full portrait of Cato's character. Plutarch's death is used to date this essay, since the exact composition date is not known.*]

Marcus Cato, we are told, was born at Tusculum, though (till he betook himself to civil and military affairs) he lived and was bred up in the country of the Sabines, where his father's estate lay. His ancestors seeming almost entirely unknown, he himself praises his father Marcus, as a worthy man and a brave soldier, and Cato, his great-grandfather, too, as one who had often obtained military prizes, and who, having lost five horses under him, received, on the account of his valour, the worth of them out of the public exchequer. Now it being the custom among the Romans to call those who, having no repute by birth, made themselves eminent by their own exertions, new men or upstarts, they called even Cato himself so, and so he confessed himself to be as to any public distinction or employment, but yet asserted that in the exploits and virtues of his ancestors he was very ancient. His third name originally was not Cato, but Priscus, though afterwards he had the surname of Cato, by reason of his abilities; for the Romans call a skilful or experienced man *Catus*. He was of a ruddy complexion and grey-eyed; as the writer, who, with no good-will, made the following epigram upon him lets us see:—

> Porcius, who snarls at all in every place,
> With his grey eyes, and with his fiery face,
> Even after death will scarce admitted be
> Into the infernal realms by Hecate.

He gained, in early life, a good habit of body by work-ing with his own hands, and living temperately, and serving in war; and seemed to have an equal proportion both of health and strength. And he exerted and prac-tised his eloquence through all the neighbourhood and little villages; thinking it as requisite as a second body, and an all but necessary organ to one who looks for-ward to something above a mere humble and inactive life. He would never refuse to be counsel for those who needed him, and was, indeed, early reckoned a good lawyer, and, ere long, a capable orator.

Hence his solidity and depth of character showed itself gradually more and more to those with whom he was concerned, and claimed, as it were, employment in great affairs and places of public command. Nor did he merely abstain from taking fees for his counsel and pleading, but did not even seem to put any high price on the honour which proceeded from such kind of combats, seeming much more desirous to signalise himself in the camp and in real fights; and while yet but a youth, had his breast covered with scars he had received from the enemy: being (as he himself says) but seventeen years old when he made his first compaign; in the time when Hannibal, in the height of his success, was burning and pillaging all Italy. In engagements he would strike boldly, without flinch-ing, stand firm to his ground, fix a bold countenance upon his enemies, and with a harsh threatening voice accost them, justly thinking himself and telling others that such a rugged kind of behaviour sometimes terri-fies the enemy more than the sword itself. In his marches he bore his own arms on foot, whilst one servant only followed, to carry the provision for his table, with whom he is said never to have been angry or hasty whilst he made ready his dinner or supper, but would, for the most part, when he was free from mili-tary duty, assist and help him himself to dress it. When he was with the army, he used to drink only water; unless, perhaps, when extremely thirsty, he might mingle it with a little vinegar, or if he found his strength fail him, take a little wine.

The little country house of Manius Curius, who had been thrice carried in triumph, happened to be near his farm; so that often going thither, and contemplating the small compass of the place, and plainness of the dwelling, he formed an idea of the mind of the person, who being one of the greatest of the Romans, and

having subdued the most warlike nations, nay, had driven Pyrrhus out of Italy, now, after three triumphs, was contented to dig in so small a piece of ground, and live in such a cottage. Here it was that the ambassa-dors of the Samnites, finding him boiling turnips in the chimney corner, offered him a present of gold; but he sent them away with this saying; that he, who was content with such a supper, had no need of gold; and that he thought it more honourable to conquer those who possessed the gold, than to possess the gold itself. Cato, after reflecting upon these things, used to return and, reviewing his own farm, his servants, and house-keeping, increase his labour and retrench all superflu-ous expenses.

When Fabius Maximus took Tarentum, Cato, being then but a youth, was a soldier under him; and being lodged with one Nearchus, a Pythagorean, desired to understand some of his doctrine, and hearing from him the language, which Plato also uses—that plea-sure is evil's chief bait; the body the principal calam-ity of the soul; and that those thoughts which most separate and take it off from the affections of the body most enfranchise and purify it; he fell in love the more with frugality and temperance. With this exception, he is said not to have studied Greek until when he was pretty old; and in rhetoric, to have then profited a little by Thucydides, but more by Demosthenes; his writings, however, are considerably embellished with Greek sayings and stories; nay, many of these, translated word for word, are placed with his own apophthegms and sentences.

There was a man of the highest rank, and very influ-ential among the Romans, called Valerius Flaccus, who was singularly skilful in discerning excellence yet in the bud, and also much disposed to nourish and advance it. He, it seems, had lands bordering upon Cato's: nor could he but admire when he understood from his servants the manner of his living, how he laboured with his own hands, went on foot betimes in the morning to the courts to assist those who wanted his counsel; how, returning home again, when it was winter, he would throw a loose frock over his shoul-ders, and in the summer time would work without anything on among his domestics, sit down with them, eat of the same bread, and drink of the same wine. When they spoke, also, of other good qualities, his fair dealing and moderation, mentioning also some of his wise sayings, he ordered that he should be invited to supper; and thus becoming personally assured of his fine temper and his superior character, which, like a plant, seemed only to require culture and a better situation, he urged and persuaded him to apply him-self to state affairs at Rome. Thither, therefore, he went, and by his pleading soon gained many friends and admirers; but, Valerius chiefly assisting his pro-motion, he first of all got appointed tribune in the army, and afterwards was made quæstor, or treasurer.

And now becoming eminent and noted, he passed, with Valerius himself, through the greatest commands, being first his colleague as consul, and then censor. But among all the ancient senators, he most attached himself to Fabius Maximus; not so much for the honour of his person, and the greatness of his power, as that he might have before him his habit and manner of life, as the best examples to follow; and so he did not hesitate to oppose Scipio the Great, who, being then but a young man, seemed to set himself against the power of Fabius, and to be envied by him. For being sent together with him as treasurer, when he saw him, according to his natural custom, make great expenses, and distribute among the soldiers without sparing, he freely told him that the expense in itself was not the greatest thing to be considered, but that he was corrupting the frugality of the soldiers, by giving them the means to abandon themselves to unnecessary pleasures and luxuries. Scipio answered, that he had no need for so accurate a treasurer (bearing on as he was, so to say, full sail to the war), and that he owed the people an account of his actions, and not of the money he spent. Hereupon Cato returned from Sicily and, together with Fabius, made loud complaints in the open senate of Scipio's lavishing unspeakable sums, and childishly loitering away his time in wrestling matches and comedies, as if he were not to make war, but holiday; and thus succeeded in getting some of the tribunes of the people sent to call him back to Rome, in case the accusations should prove true. But Scipio demonstrating, as it were, to them, by his preparations, the coming victory, and, being found merely to be living pleasantly with his friends, when there was nothing else to do, but in no respect because of that easiness and liberality at all the more negligent in things of consequence and moment, without impediment, set sail toward the war.

Cato grew more and more powerful by his eloquence, so that he was commonly called the Roman Demosthenes; but his manner of life was yet more famous and talked of. For oratorical skill was, as an accomplishment, commonly studied and sought after by all young men; but he was very rare who would cultivate the old habits of bodily labour, or prefer a light supper, and a breakfast which never saw the fire, or be in love with poor clothes and a homely lodging, or could set his ambition rather on doing without luxuries than on possessing them. For now the state, unable to keep its purity by reason of its greatness, and having so many affairs, and people from all parts under its government, was fain to admit many mixed customs and new examples of living. With reason, therefore, everybody admired Cato, when they saw others sink under labours and grow effeminate by pleasures; and yet beheld him unconquered by either, and that not only when he was young and desirous of honour, but also when old and grey-headed, after a consulship and

triumph; like some famous victor in the games, persevering in his exercise and maintaining his character to the very last. He himself says that he never wore a suit of clothes which cost more than a hundred drachmas; and that, when he was general and consul, he drank the same wine which his workmen did; and that the meat or fish which was bought in the meat-market for his dinner did not cost above thirty *asses*. All which was for the sake of the commonwealth, that so his body might be the hardier for the war. Having a piece of embroidered Babylonian tapestry left him, he sold it; because none of his farmhouses were so much as plastered. Nor did he ever buy a slave for above fifteen hundred drachmas; as he did not seek for effeminate and handsome ones, but able sturdy workmen, horse-keepers and cow-herds: and these he thought ought to be sold again, when they grew old, and no useless servants fed in the house. In short, he reckoned nothing a good bargain which was superfluous; but whatever it was, though sold for a farthing, he would think it a great price, if you had no need of it; and was for the purchase of lands for sowing and feeding, rather than grounds for sweeping and watering.

Some imputed these things to petty avarice, but others approved of him, as if he had only the more strictly denied himself for the rectifying and amending of others. Yet certainly, in my judgment, it marks an over-rigid temper for a man to take the work out of his servants as out of brute beasts, turning them off and selling them in their old age, and thinking there ought to be no further commerce between man and man than whilst there arises some profit by it. We see that kindness or humanity has a larger field than bare justice to exercise itself in; law and justice we cannot, in the nature of things, employ on others than men; but we may extend our goodness and charity even to irrational creatures; and such acts flow from a gentle nature, as water from an abundant spring. It is doubtless the part of a kind-natured man to keep even worn-out horses and dogs, and not only take care of them when they are foals and whelps, but also when they are grown old. The Athenians, when they built their Hecatompedon, turned those mules loose to feed freely which they had observed to have done the hardest labour. One of these (they say) came once of itself to offer its service, and ran along with, nay, and went before, the teams which drew the waggons up to the acropolis, as if it would incite and encourage them to draw more stoutly; upon which there passed a vote that the creature should be kept at the public charge even till it died. The graves of Cimon's horses, which thrice won the Olympian races, are yet to be seen close by his own monument. Old Xanthippus, too (amongst many others who buried the dogs they had bred up), entombed his which swam after his galley to Salamis, when the people fled from Athens, on the top of a cliff, which they call the Dog's Tomb to this day. Nor are we to use living creatures like old shoes or dishes, and throw them away when they are worn out or broken with service; but if it were for nothing else, but by way of study and practice in humanity, a man ought always to prehabituate himself in these things to be of a kind and sweet disposition. As to myself, I would not so much as sell my draught ox on the account of his age, much less for a small piece of money sell a poor old man, and so chase him, as it were, from his own country, by turning him not only out of the place where he has lived a long while, but also out of the manner of living he has been accustomed to, and that more especially when he would be as useless to the buyer as to the seller. Yet Cato for all this glories that he left that very horse in Spain which he used in the wars when he was consul, only because he would not put the public to the charge of his freight. Whether these acts are to be ascribed to the greatness or pettiness of his spirit, let every one argue as they please.

For his general temperance, however, and self-control he really deserves the highest admiration. For when he commanded the army, he never took for himself, and those that belonged to him, above three bushels of wheat for a month, and somewhat less than a bushel and a half a day of barley for his baggage-cattle. And when he entered upon the government of Sardinia, where his predecessors had been used to require tents, bedding, and clothes upon the public account, and to charge the state heavily with the cost of provisions and entertainments for a great train of servants and friends, the difference he showed in his economy was something incredible. There was nothing of any sort for which he put the public to expense; he would walk without a carriage to visit the cities, with one only of the common town officers, who carried his dress, and a cup to offer libation with. Yet though he seemed thus easy and sparing to all who were under his power, he, on the other hand, showed most inflexible severity and strictness in what related to public justice, and was rigorous and precise in what concerned the ordinances of the commonwealth; so that the Roman government never seemed more terrible, nor yet more mild than under his administration.

His very manner of speaking seemed to have such a kind of idea with it; for it was courteous, and yet forcible; pleasant, yet overwhelming; facetious, yet austere; sententious, and yet vehement; like Socrates, in the description of Plato, who seemed outwardly to those about him to be but a simple, talkative, blunt fellow; whilst at the bottom he was full of such gravity and matter, as would even move tears and touch the very hearts of his auditors. And, therefore, I know not what has persuaded some to say that Cato's style was chiefly like that of Lysias. However, let us leave those to judge of these things who profess most to distinguish between the several kinds of oratorical style in Latin; whilst we write down some of his memorable sayings; being of the opinion that a man's character appears much more by his words than, as some think it does, by his looks.

Being once desirous to dissuade the common people of Rome from their unseasonable and impetuous clamour for largesses and distributions of corn, he began thus to harangue them: "It is a difficult task, O citizens, to make speeches to the belly, which has no ears." Reproving, also, their sumptuous habits, he said it was hard to preserve a city where a fish sold for more than an ox. He had a saying, also, that the Roman people were like sheep; for they, when single, do not obey, but when altogether in a flock, they follow their leaders: "So you," said he, "when you have got together in a body, let yourselves be guided by those whom singly you would never think of being advised by." Discoursing of the power of women: "Men," said he, "usually command women; but we command all men, and the women command us." But this, indeed, is borrowed from the sayings of Themistocles, who, when his son was making many demands of him by means of the mother, said, "O woman, the Athenians govern the Greeks; I govern the Athenians, but you govern me, and your son governs you; so let him use his power sparingly, since, simple as he is, he can do more than all the Greeks together." Another saying of Cato's was, that the Roman people did not only fix the value of such and such purple dyes, but also of such and such habits of life: "For," said he, "as dyers most of all dye such colours as they see to be most agreeable, so the young men learn, and zealously affect, what is most popular with you." He also exhorted them that, if they were grown great by their virtue and temperance, they should not change for the worse; but if intemperance and vice had made them great, they should change for the better; for by that means they were grown indeed quite great enough. He would say, likewise, of men who wanted to be continually in office, that apparently they did not know their road; since they could not do without beadles to guide them on it. He also reproved the citizens for choosing still the same men as their magistrates: "For you will seem," said he, "either not to esteem government worth much, or to think few worthy to hold it." Speaking, too, of a certain enemy of his, who lived a very base and discreditable life: "It is considered," he said, "rather as a curse than a blessing on him, that this fellow's mother prays that she may leave him behind her." Pointing at one who had sold the land which his father had left him, and which lay near the seaside, he pretended to express his wonder at his being stronger even than the sea itself; for what it washed away with a great deal of labour, he with a great deal of ease drank away. When the senate, with a great deal of splendour, received King Eumenes on his visit to Rome, and the chief citizens strove who should be most about him, Cato appeared to regard him with suspicion and apprehension; and when one that stood by, too, took occasion to say that he was a very good prince and a great lover of the Romans: "It may be so," said Cato; "but by nature this same animal of a king is a kind of man-eater;" nor, indeed, were there ever kings who deserved to be compared with Epaminondas, Pericles, Themistocles, Manius Curius, or Hamilcar, surnamed Barcas. He used to say, too, that his enemies envied him because he had to get up every day before light and neglect his own business to follow that of the public. He would also tell you that he had rather be deprived of the reward for doing well than not to suffer the punishment for doing ill; and that he could pardon all offenders but himself.

The Romans having sent three ambassadors to Bithynia, of whom one was gouty, another had his skull trepanned, and the other seemed little better than a fool, Cato, laughing, gave out that the Romans had sent an embassy which had neither feet, head, nor heart. His interest being entreated by Scipio, on account of Polybius, for the Achæan exiles, and there happening to be a great discussion in the senate about it, some being for, and some against their return, Cato, standing up, thus delivered himself: "Here do we sit all day long, as if we had nothing to do but beat our brains whether these old Greeks should be carried to their graves by the bearers here or by those in Achæa." The senate voting their return, it seems that a few days after Polybius's friends further wished that it should be further moved in the senate that the said banished persons should receive again the honours which they first had in Achæa; and to this purpose they sounded Cato for his opinion; but he, smiling, answered, that Polybius, Ulysses like, having escaped out of the Cyclops' den, wanted, it would seem, to go back again because he had left his cap and belt behind him. He used to assert, also, that wise men profited more by fools, than fools by wise men; for that wise men avoided the faults of fools, but that fools would not imitate the good examples of wise men. He would profess, too, that he was more taken with young men that blushed than with those who looked pale; and that he never desired to have a soldier that moved his hands too much in marching, and his feet too much in fighting; or snored louder than he shouted. Ridiculing a fat, overgrown man: "What use," said he, "can the state turn a man's body to, when all between the throat and groin is taken up by the belly?" When one who was much given to pleasures desired his acquaintance, begging his pardon, he said he could not live with a man whose palate was of a quicker sense than his heart. He would likewise say that the soul of a lover lived in the body of another: and that in his whole life he most repented of three things; one was, that he had trusted a secret to a woman; another that he went by water when he might have gone by land; the third, that he had remained one whole day without doing any business of moment. Applying himself to an old man who was committing some vice: "Friend," said he, "old age has of itself blemishes enough; do not you add to it the deformity of vice." Speaking to a tribune, who was

reputed a poisoner, and was very violent for the bringing in of a bill, in order to make a certain law: "Young man," cried he, "I know not which would be better, to drink what you mix, or confirm what you would put up for a law." Being reviled by a fellow who lived a profligate and wicked life: "A contest," replied he, "is unequal between you and me: for you can hear ill words easily, and can as easily give them: but it is unpleasant to me to give such, and unusual to hear them." Such was his manner of expressing himself in his memorable sayings.

Being chosen consul, with his friend and familiar Valerius Flaccus, the government of that part of Spain which the Romans called the Hither Spain fell to his lot. Here, as he was engaged in reducing some of the tribes by force, and bringing over others by good words, a large army of barbarians fell upon him, so that there was danger of being disgracefully forced out again. He therefore called upon his neighbours, the Celtiberians, for help; and on their demanding two hundred talents for their assistance, everybody else thought it intolerable that even the Romans should promise barbarians a reward for their aid; but Cato said there was no discredit or harm in it; for, if they overcame, they would pay them out of the enemy's purse, and not out of their own; but if they were overcome, there would be nobody left either to demand the reward or to pay it. However, he won that battle completely, and after that, all his other affairs succeeded splendidly. Polybius says that, by his command, the walls of all the cities on this side the river Bætis were in one day's time demolished, and yet there were a great many of them full of brave and warlike men. Cato himself says that he took more cities than he stayed days in Spain. Neither is this a mere rhodomontade, if it be true that the number was four hundred. And though the soldiers themselves had got much in the fights, yet he distributed a pound of silver to every man of them, saying, it was better that many of the Romans should return home with silver, rather than a few with gold. For himself, he affirms, that of all the things that were taken, nothing came to him beyond what he ate and drank. "Neither do I find fault," continued he, "with those that seek to profit by these spoils, but I had rather compete in valour with the best, than in wealth with the richest, or with the most covetous in love of money." Nor did he merely keep himself clear from taking anything, but even all those who more immediately belonged to him. He had five servants with him in the army; one of whom called Paccus, bought three boys out of those who were taken captive; which Cato coming to understand, the man, rather than venture into his presence, hanged himself. Cato sold the boys, and carried the price he got for them into the public exchequer.

Scipio the Great, being his enemy, and desiring, whilst he was carrying all things so successfully, to obstruct him, and take the affairs of Spain into his own hands, succeeded in getting himself appointed his successor in the government, and, making all possible haste, put a term to Cato's authority. But he, taking with him a convoy of five cohorts of foot and five hundred horse to attend him home, overthrew by the way the Lacetanians, and taking from them six hundred deserters, caused them all to be beheaded; upon which Scipio seemed to be in indignation, but Cato, in mock disparagement of himself, said, "Rome would become great indeed, if the most honourable and great men would not yield up the first place of valour to those who were more obscure, and when they who were of the commonalty (as he himself was) would contend in valour with those who were most eminent in birth and honour." The senate having voted to change nothing of what had been established by Cato, the government passed away under Scipio to no manner of purpose, in idleness and doing nothing; and so diminished his credit much more than Cato's. Nor did Cato, who now received a triumph, remit after this and slacken the reins of virtue, as many do, who strive not so much for virtue's take, as for vainglory, and having attained the highest honours, as the consulship and triumphs, pass the rest of their life in pleasure and idleness, and quit all public affairs. But he, like those who are just entered upon public life for the first time, and thirst after gaining honour and glory in some new office, strained himself, as if he were but just setting out; and offering still publicly his service to his friends and citizens, would give up neither his pleadings nor his soldiery.

He accompanied and assisted Tiberius Sempronius, as his lieutenant, when he went into Thrace and to the Danube; and, in the quality of tribune, went with Manius Acilius into Greece, against Antiochus the Great, who, after Hannibal, more than any one struck terror into the Romans. For having reduced once more under a single command almost the whole of Asia, all, namely, that Seleucus Nicator had possessed, and having brought into obedience many warlike nations of the barbarians, he longed to fall upon the Romans, as if they only were now worthy to fight with him. So across he came with his forces, pretending, as a specious cause of the war, that it was to free the Greeks, who had indeed no need of it, they having been but newly delivered from the power of king Philip and the Macedonians, and made independent, with the free use of their own laws, by the goodness of the Romans themselves: so that all Greece was in commotion and excitement, having been corrupted by the hopes of royal aid which the popular leaders in their cities put them into. Manius, therefore, sent ambassadors to the different cities; and Titus Flamininus . . . suppressed and quieted most of the attempts of the innovators, without any trouble. Cato brought over the Corinthians, those of Patræ and Ægium, and spent a good deal of time at Athens. There is also an oration of his said to be extant which he spoke in Greek to the people; in which he

expressed his admiration of the virtue of the ancient Athenians, and signified that he came with a great deal of pleasure to be a spectator of the beauty and greatness of their city. But this is a fiction; for he spoke to the Athenians by an interpreter, though he was able to have spoken himself; but he wished to observe the usage of his own country, and laughed at those who admired nothing but what was in Greek. Jesting upon Postumius Albinus, who had written an historical work in Greek, and requested that allowances might be made for his attempt, he said that allowance indeed might be made if he had done it under the express compulsion of an Amphictyonic decree. The Athenians, he says, admired the quickness and vehemence of his speech; for an interpreter would be very long in repeating what he expressed with a great deal of brevity; but on the whole he professed to believe that the words of the Greeks came only from their lips, whilst those of the Romans came from their hearts.

Now Antiochus, having occupied with his army the narrow passages about Thermopylæ, and added palisades and walls to the natural fortifications of the place, sat down there, thinking he had done enough to divert the war; and the Romans, indeed, seemed wholly to despair of forcing the passage; but Cato, calling to mind the compass and circuit which the Persians had formerly made to come at this place, went forth in the night, taking along with him part of the army. Whilst they were climbing up, the guide, who was a prisoner, missed the way, and wandering up and down by impracticable and precipitous paths, filled the soldiers with fear and despondency. Cato, perceiving the danger, commanded all the rest to halt, and stay where they were, whilst he himself, taking along with him one Lucius Manlius, a most expert man at climbing mountains, went forward with a great deal of labour and danger, in the dark night, and without the least moonshine, among the wild olive-trees and steep craggy rocks, there being nothing but precipices and darkness before their eyes, till they struck into a little pass which they thought might lead down into the enemy's camp. There they put up marks upon some conspicuous peaks which surmount the hill called Callidromon, and, returning again, they led the army along with them to the said marks, till they got into their little path again, and there once made a halt; but when they began to go further, the path deserted them at a precipice, where they were in another strait and fear; nor did they perceive that they were all this while near the enemy. And now the day began to give some light, when they seemed to hear a noise, and presently after to see the Greek trenches and the guard at the foot of the rock. Here, therefore, Cato halted his forces, and commanded the troops from Firmum only, without the rest, to stick by him, as he had always found them faithful and ready. And when they came up and formed around him in close order, he thus spoke to them: "I desire," he said, "to take one of the enemy alive, that so I may understand what men these are who guard the passage; their number; and with what discipline, order, and preparation they expect us; but this feat," continued he, "must be an act of a great deal of quickness and boldness, such as that of lions, when they dart upon some timorous animal." Cato had no sooner thus expressed himself, but the Firmans forthwith rushed down the mountain, just as they were, upon the guard, and, falling unexpectedly upon them, affrighted and dispersed them all. One armed man they took, and brought to Cato, who quickly learned from him that the rest of the forces lay in the narrow passage about the king; that those who kept the tops of the rocks were six hundred choice Ætolians. Cato, therefore, despising the smallness of their number and carelessness, forthwith drawing his sword, fell upon them with a great noise of trumpets and shouting. The enemy, perceiving them thus tumbling, as it were, upon them from the precipices, flew to the main body, and put all things into disorder there.

In the meantime, whilst Manius was forcing the works below, and pouring the thickest of his forces into the narrow passages, Antiochus was hit in the mouth with a stone, so that his teeth being beaten out by it, he felt such excessive pain, that he was fain to turn away with his horse; nor did any part of his army stand the shock of the Romans. Yet, though there seemed no reasonable hope of flight, where all paths were so difficult, and where there were deep marshes and steep rocks, which looked as if they were ready to receive those who should stumble, the fugitives, nevertheless, crowding and pressing together in the narrow passages, destroyed even one another in their terror of the swords and blows of the enemy. Cato (as it plainly appears) was never oversparing of his own praises, and seldom shunned boasting of any exploit; which quality, indeed, he seems to have thought the natural accompaniment of great actions; and with these particular exploits he was highly puffed up; he says that those who saw him that day pursuing and slaying the enemies were ready to assert that Cato owed not so much to the public as the public did to Cato; nay, he adds, that Manius the consul, coming hot from the fight, embraced him for a great while, when both were all in a sweat; and then cried out with joy that neither he himself, no, nor all the people together, could make him a recompense equal to his actions. After the fight he was sent to Rome, that he himself might be the messenger of it: and so, with a favourable wind, he sailed to Brundusium, and in one day got from thence to Tarentum; and having travelled four days more, upon the fifth, counting from the time of his landing, he arrived at Rome, and so brought the first news of the victory himself; and filled the whole city with joy and sacrifices, and the people with the belief that they were able to conquer every sea and every land.

These are pretty nearly all the eminent actions of Cato relating to military affairs: in civil policy, he was of opinion that one chief duty consisted in accusing and indicting criminals. He himself prosecuted many, and he would also assist others who prosecuted them, nay, would even procure such, as he did the Petilii against Scipio; but not being able to destroy him, by reason of the nobleness of his family, and the real greatness of his mind, which enabled him to trample all calumnies under foot, Cato at last would meddle no more with him; yet joining with the accusers against Scipio's brother Lucius, he succeeded in obtaining a sentence against him, which condemned him to the payment of a large sum of money to the state; and being insolvent, and in danger of being thrown into jail, he was, by the interposition of the tribunes of the people, with much ado dismissed. It is also said of Cato, that when he met a certain youth, who had effected the disgrace of one of his father's enemies, walking in the market-place, he shook him by the hand, telling him, that this was what we ought to sacrifice to our dead parents—not lambs and goats, but the tears and condemnations of their adversaries. But neither did he himself escape with impunity in his management of affairs; for if he gave his enemies but the least hold, he was still in danger, and exposed to be brought to justice. He is reported to have escaped at least fifty indictments; and one above the rest, which was the last, when he was eighty-six years old, about which time he uttered the well-known saying, that it was hard for him who had lived with one generation of men, to plead now before another. Neither did he make this the least of his lawsuits; for, four years after, when he was fourscore and ten, he accused Servilius Galba: so that his life and actions extended, we may say, as Nestor's did, over three ordinary ages of man. For, having had many contests, as we have related, with Scipio the Great, about affairs of state, he continued them down to Scipio the younger, who was the adopted grandson of the former, and the son of that Paulus who overthrew Perseus and the Macedonians.

Ten years after his consulship, Cato stood for the office of censor, which was indeed the summit of all honour, and in a manner the highest step in civil affairs; for besides all other power, it had also that of an inquisition into every one's life and manners. For the Romans thought that no marriage, or rearing of children, nay, no feast or drinking-bout, ought to be permitted according to every one's appetite or fancy, without being examined and inquired into; being indeed of opinion that a man's character was much sooner perceived in things of this sort than in what is done publicly and in open day. They chose, therefore, two persons, one out of the patricians, the other out of the commons, who were to watch, correct, and punish, if any one ran too much into voluptuousness, or transgressed the usual manner of life of his country; and these they called Censors. They had power to take away a horse, or expel out of the senate any one who lived intemperately and out of order. It was also their business to take an estimate of what every one was worth, and to put down in registers everybody's birth and quality; besides many other prerogatives. And therefore the chief nobility opposed his pretensions to it. Jealousy prompted the patricians, who thought that it would be a stain to everybody's nobility, if men of no original honour should rise to the highest dignity and power; while others, conscious of their own evil practices, and of the violation of the laws and customs of their country, were afraid of the austerity of the man; which, in an office of such great power, was likely to prove most uncompromising and severe. And so, consulting among themselves, they brought forward seven candidates in opposition to him, who sedulously set themselves to court the people's favour by fair promises, as though what they wished for was indulgent and easy government. Cato, on the contrary, promising no such mildness, but plainly threatening evil livers, from the very hustings openly declared himself, and exclaiming that the city needed a great and thorough purgation, called upon the people, if they were wise, not to choose the gentlest, but the roughest of physicians; such a one, he said, he was, and Valerius Flaccus, one of the patricians, another; together with him, he doubted not but he should do something worth the while, and that by cutting to pieces and burning like a hydra all luxury and voluptuousness. He added, too, that he saw all the rest endeavouring after the office with ill intent, because they were afraid of those who would exercise it justly, as they ought. And so truly great and so worthy of great men to be its leaders was, it would seem, the Roman people, that they did not fear the severity and grim countenance of Cato, but rejecting those smooth promisers who were ready to do all things to ingratiate themselves, they took him, together with Flaccus; obeying his recommendations not as though he were a candidate, but as if he had had the actual power of commanding and governing already.

Cato named, as chief of the senate, his friend and colleague Lucius Valerius Flaccus, and expelled, among many others, Lucius Quintius, who had been consul seven years before, and (which was greater honour to him than the consulship) brother to that Titus Flamininus who overthrew King Philip. The reason he had for his expulsion was this. Lucius, it seems, took along with him in all his commands a youth whom he had kept as his companion from the flower of his age, and to whom he gave as much power and respect as to the chiefest of his friends and relations.

Now it happened that Lucius being consular governor of one of the provinces, the youth setting himself down by him, as he used to do, among other flatteries with which he played upon him, when he was in his cups, told him he loved him so dearly that, "though there was a show of gladiators to be seen at Rome, and I," he said, "had never beheld one in my life; and though

I, as it were, longed to see a man killed, yet I made all possible haste to come to you." Upon this Lucius, returning his fondness, replied, "Do not be melancholy on that account; I can remedy that." Ordering therefore, forthwith, one of those condemned to die to be brought to the feast, together with the headsman and axe, he asked the youth if he wished to see him executed. The boy answering that he did, Lucius commanded the executioner to cut off his neck; and this several historians mention; and Cicero, indeed, in his dialogue *de Senectute,* introduces Cato relating it himself. But Livy says that he that was killed was a Gaulish deserter, and that Lucius did not execute him by the stroke of the executioner, but with his own hand; and that it is so stated in Cato's speech.

Lucius being thus expelled out of the senate by Cato, his brother took it very ill, and appealing to the people, desired that Cato should declare his reasons; and when he began to relate this transaction of the feast, Lucius endeavoured to deny it; but Cato challenging him to a formal investigation, he fell off and refused it, so that he was then acknowledged to suffer deservedly. Afterwards, however, when there was some show at the theatre, he passed by the seats where those who had been consuls used to be placed, and taking his seat a great way off, excited the compassion of the common people, who presently with a great noise made him go forward, and as much as they could tried to set right and salve over what had happened. Manilius, also, who, according to the public expectation, would have been next consul, he threw out of the senate, because, in the presence of his daughter, and in open day, he had kissed his wife. He said that, as for himself, his wife never came into his arms except when there was great thunder; so that it was for jest with him, that it was a pleasure for him, when Jupiter thundered.

His treatment of Lucius, likewise the brother of Scipio, and one who had been honoured with a triumph, occasioned some odium against Cato; for he took his horse from him, and was thought to do it with a design of putting an affront on Scipio Africanus, now dead. But he gave most general annoyance by retrenching people's luxury; for though (most of the youth being thereby already corrupted) it seemed almost impossible to take it away with an open hand and directly, yet going, as it were, obliquely around, he caused all dress carriages, women's ornaments, household furniture, whose price exceeded one thousand five hundred drachmas, to be rated at ten times as much as they were worth; intending by thus making the assessments greater, to increase the taxes paid upon them. He also ordained that upon every thousand *asses* of property of this kind, three should be paid, so that people, burdened with these extra charges, and seeing others of as good estates, but more frugal and sparing, paying less into the public exchequer, might be tired out of their prodigality. And thus, on the one side, not only those were disgusted at

Cato who bore the taxes for the sake of their luxury, but those, too, who on the other side laid by their luxury for fear of the taxes. For people in general reckon that an order not to display their riches is equivalent to the taking away of their riches, because riches are seen much more in superfluous than in necessary things. Indeed this was what excited the wonder of Ariston the philosopher; that we account those who possess superfluous things more happy than those who abound with what is necessary and useful. But when one of his friends asked Scopas, the rich Thessalian, to give him some article of no great utility, saying that it was not a thing that he had any great need or use for himself, "In truth," replied he, "it is just these useless and unnecessary things that make my wealth and happiness." Thus the desire of riches does not proceed from a natural passion within us, but arises rather from vulgar out-of-doors opinion of other people.

Cato, notwithstanding, being little solicitous as to those who exclaimed against him, increased his austerity. He caused the pipes, through which some persons brought the public water into their houses and gardens, to be cut, and threw down all buildings which jutted out into the common streets. He beat down also the price in contracts for public works to the lowest, and raised it in contracts for farming the taxes to the highest sum; by which proceedings he drew a great deal of hatred upon himself. Those who were of Titus Flamininus's party cancelled in the senate all the bargains and contracts made by him for the repairing and carrying on of the sacred and public buildings as unadvantageous to the commonwealth. They incited also the boldest of the tribunes of the people to accuse him and to fine him two talents. They likewise much opposed him in building the court or basilica, which he caused to be erected at the common charge, just by the senate-house, in the marketplace, and called by his own name, the Porcian. However, the people, it seems, liked his censorship wondrously well; for, setting up a statue for him in the temple of the goddess of Health, they put an inscription under it, not recording his commands in war or his triumph, but to the effect that this was Cato the Censor, who, by his good discipline and wise and temperate ordinances, reclaimed the Roman commonwealth when it was declining and sinking down into vice. Before this honour was done to himself, he used to laugh at those who loved such kind of things, saying, that they did not see that they were taking pride in the workmanship of brass-founders and painters; whereas the citizens bore about his best likeness in their breasts. And when any seemed to wonder that he should have never a statue, while many ordinary persons had one, "I would," said he, "much rather be asked, why I have not one, than why I have one." In short, he would not have any honest citizen endure to be praised, except it might prove advantageous to the commonwealth. Yet still he had passed the highest commendation on himself; for he tells us that those

who did anything wrong, and were found fault with, used to say it was not worth while to blame them, for they were not Catos. He also adds, that they who awkwardly mimicked some of his actions were called left-handed Catos; and that the senate in perilous times would cast their eyes on him, as upon a pilot in a ship, and that often when he was not present they put off affairs of greatest consequence. These things are indeed also testified of him by others; for he had a great authority in the city, alike for his life, his eloquence, and his age.

He was also a good father, an excellent husband to his wife, and an extraordinary economist; and as he did not manage his affairs of this kind carelessly, and as things of little moment, I think I ought to record a little further whatever was commendable in him in these points. He married a wife more noble than rich; being of opinion that the rich and the high-born are equally haughty and proud; but that those of noble blood would be more ashamed of base things, and consequently more obedient to their husbands in all that was fit and right. A man who beat his wife or child laid violent hands, he said, on what was most sacred; and a good husband he reckoned worthy of more praise than a great senator; and he admired the ancient Socrates for nothing so much as for having lived a temperate and contented life with a wife who was a scold, and children who were half-witted.

As soon as he had a son born, though he had never such urgent business upon his hands, unless it were some public matter, he would be by when his wife washed it and dressed it in its swaddling clothes. For she herself suckled it, nay, she often too gave her breast to her servants' children, to produce, by suckling the same milk, a kind of natural love in them to her son. When he began to come to years of discretion, Cato himself would teach him to read, although he had a servant, a very good grammarian, called Chilo, who taught many others; but he thought not fit, as he himself said, to have his son reprimanded by a slave, or pulled, it may be, by the ears when found tardy in his lesson: nor would he have him owe to a servant the obligation of so great a thing as his learning; he himself, therefore (as we were saying), taught him his grammar, law, and his gymnastic exercises. Nor did he only show him, too, how to throw a dart, to fight in armour, and to ride, but to box also and to endure both heat and cold, and to swim over the most rapid and rough rivers. He says, likewise, that he wrote histories, in large characters, with his own hand, that so his son, without stirring out of the house, might learn to know about his countrymen and forefathers; nor did he less abstain from speaking anything obscene before his son, than if it had been in the presence of the sacred virgins, called vestals. Nor would he ever go into the bath with him; which seems indeed to have been the common custom of the Romans. Sons-in-law used to avoid bathing with fathers-in-law, disliking to see one another naked; but having, in time, learned of the Greeks to strip before men, they have since taught the Greeks to do it even with the women themselves.

Thus, like an excellent work, Cato formed and fashioned his son to virtue; nor had he any occasion to find fault with his readiness and docility; but as he proved to be of too weak a constitution for hardships, he did not insist on requiring of him any very austere way of living. However, though delicate in health, he proved a stout man in the field, and behaved himself valiantly when Paulus Æmilius fought against Perseus; where when his sword was struck from him by a blow, or rather slipped out of his hand by reason of its moistness, he so keenly resented it, that he turned to some of his friends about him, and taking them along with him again, fell upon the enemy; and having by a long fight and much force cleared the place, at length found it among great heaps of arms, and the dead bodies of friends as well as enemies piled one upon another. Upon which Paulus, his general, much commended the youth; and there is a letter of Cato's to his son, which highly praises his honourable eagerness for the recovery of his sword. Afterwards he married Tertia, Æmilius Paulus's daughter, and sister to Scipio; nor was he admitted into this family less for his own worth than his father's. So that Cato's care in his son's education came to a very fitting result.

He purchased a great many slaves out of the captives taken in war, but chiefly bought up the young ones, who were capable to be, as it were, broken and taught like whelps and colts. None of these ever entered another man's house, except sent either by Cato himself or his wife. If any one of them were asked what Cato did, they answered merely that they did not know. When a servant was at home, he was obliged either to do some work or sleep, for indeed Cato loved those most who used to lie down often to sleep, accounting them more docile than those who were wakeful, and more fit for anything when they were refreshed with a little slumber. Being also of opinion that the great cause of the laziness and misbehaviour of slaves was their running after their pleasures, he fixed a certain price for them to pay for permission amongst themselves, but would suffer no connections out of the house. At first, when he was but a poor soldier, he would not be difficult in anything which related to his eating, but looked upon it as a pitiful thing to quarrel with a servant for the belly's sake; but afterwards, when he grew richer, and made any feasts for his friends and colleagues in office, as soon as supper was over he used to go with a leathern thong and scourge those who had waited or dressed the meat carelessly. He always contrived, too, that his servants should have some difference one among another, always suspecting and fearing a good understanding between them. Those who had committed anything worthy of death, he punished

if they were found guilty by the verdict of their fellow-servants. But being after all much given to the desire of gain, he looked upon agriculture rather as a pleasure than profit; resolving, therefore, to lay out his money in safe and solid things, he purchased ponds, hot baths, grounds full of fuller's earth, remunerative lands, pastures, and woods; from all which he drew large returns, nor could Jupiter himself, he used to say, do him much damage. He was also given to the form of usury, which is considered most odious, in traffic by sea; and that thus:—he desired that those whom he put out his money to should have many partners; when the number of them and their ships came to be fifty, he himself took one share through Quintio his freedman, who therefore was to sail with the adventurers, and take a part in all their proceedings, so that thus there was no danger of losing his whole stock, but only a little part, and that with a prospect of great profit. He likewise lent money to those of his slaves who wished to borrow, with which they bought also other young ones, whom, when they had taught and bred up at his charges, they would sell again at the year's end; but some of them Cato would keep for himself, giving just as much for them as another had offered. To incline his son to be of his kind or temper, he used to tell him that it was not like a man, but rather like a widow woman, to lessen an estate. But the strongest indication of Cato's avaricious humour was when he took the boldness to affirm that he was a most wonderful, nay, a godlike man, who left more behind him than he had received.

He was now grown old, when Carneades the Academic, and Diogenes the Stoic, came as deputies from Athens to Rome, praying for release from a penalty of five hundred talents laid on the Athenians, in a suit, to which they did not appear, in which the Oropians were plaintiffs and Sicyonians judges. All the most studious youth immediately waited on these philosophers, and frequently, with admiration, heard them speak. But the gracefulness of Carneades's oratory, whose ability was really greatest, and his reputation equal to it, gathered large and favourable audiences, and ere long filled, like a wind, all the city with the sound of it. So that it soon began to be told that a Greek, famous even to admiration, winning and carrying all before him, had impressed so strange a love upon the young men, that quitting all their pleasures and pastimes, they ran mad, as it were, after philosophy; which indeed much pleased the Romans in general; nor could they but with much pleasure see the youth receive so welcomely the Greek literature, and frequent the company of learned men. But Cato, on the other side, seeing the passion for words flowing into the city, from the beginning took it ill, fearing lest the youth should be diverted that way, and so should prefer the glory of speaking well before that of arms and doing well. And when the fame of the philosophers increased in the city, and Caius Acilius, a person of distinction, at his own request, became their interpreter to the senate at their first audience,

Cato resolved, under some specious pretence, to have all philosophers cleared out of the city; and, coming into the senate, blamed the magistrates for letting these deputies stay so long a time without being despatched, though they were persons that could easily persuade the people to what they pleased; that therefore in all haste something should be determined about their petition, that so they might go home again to their own schools, and declaim to the Greek children, and leave the Roman youth to be obedient, as hitherto, to their own laws and governors.

Yet he did this not out of any anger, as some think, to Carneades; but because he wholly despised philosophy, and out of a kind of pride scoffed at the Greek studies and literature; as, for example, he would say, that Socrates was a prating, seditious fellow, who did his best to tyrannise over his country, to undermine the ancient customs, and to entice and withdraw the citizens to opinions contrary to the laws. Ridiculing the school of Isocrates, he would add, that his scholars grew old men before they had done learning with him, as if they were to use their art and plead causes in the court of Minos in the next world. And to frighten his son from anything that was Greek, in a more vehement tone than became one of his age, he pronounced, as it were, with the voice of an oracle, that the Romans would certainly be destroyed when they began once to be infected with Greek literature; though time indeed has shown the vanity of this his prophecy; as, in truth, the city of Rome has risen to its highest fortune while entertaining Grecian learning. Nor had he an aversion only against the Greek philosophers, but the physicians also; for having, it seems, heard how Hippocrates, when the king of Persia sent for him, with offers of a fee of several talents, said, that he would never assist barbarians who were enemies to the Greeks; he affirmed, that this was now become a common oath taken by all physicians, and enjoined his son to have a care and avoid them; for that he himself had written a little book of prescriptions for curing those who were sick in his family; he never enjoined fasting to any one, but ordered them either vegetables, or the meat of a duck, pigeon, or leveret; such kind of diet being of light digestion and fit for sick folks, only it made those who ate it dream a little too much; and by the use of this kind of physic, he said, he not only made himself and those about him well, but kept them so.

However, for this his presumption he seemed not to have escaped unpunished; for he lost both his wife and his son; though he himself, being of a strong, robust constitution, held out longer; so that he would often, even in his old days, address himself to women, and when he was past a lover's age, married a young woman, upon the following pretence: Having lost his own wife, he married his son to the daughter of Paulus Æmilius, who was sister to Scipio; so that being now a widower himself, he had a young girl who came privately to visit him, but the house being very small, and a daughter-in-law also in it, this practice was quickly discovered; for the young woman seeming once to pass through it a little too boldly, the youth, his son, though he said nothing, seemed to look somewhat indignantly upon her. The old man perceiving and understanding that what he did was disliked, without finding any fault or saying a word, went away, as his custom was, with his usual companions to the market: and among the rest, he called aloud to one Salonius, who had been a clerk under him, and asked him whether he had married his daughter? He answered no, nor would he, till he had consulted him. Said Cato, "Then I have found out a fit son-in-law for you, if he should not displease by reason of his age; for in all other points there is no fault to be found in him; but he is indeed, as I said, extremely old." However, Salonius desired him to undertake the business, and to give the young girl to whom he pleased, she being a humble servant of his, who stood in need of his care and patronage. Upon this Cato, without any more ado, told him he desired to have the damsel himself. These words, as may well be imagined, at first astonished the man, conceiving that Cato was as far off from marrying, as he from a likelihood of being allied to the family of one who had been consul and had triumphed; but perceiving him in earnest, he consented willingly; and going onwards to the forum, they quickly completed the bargain.

Whilst the marriage was in hand, Cato's son, taking some of his friends along with him, went and asked his father if it were for any offence he brought in a stepmother upon him? But Cato cried out, "Far from it, my son, I have no fault to find with you or anything of yours; only I desire to have many children, and to leave the commonwealth more such citizens as you are." Pisistratus, the tyrant of Athens, made, they say, this answer to his sons, when they were grown men, when he married his second wife, Timonassa of Argos, by whom he had, it is said, Iophon and Thessalus. Cato had a son by this second wife, to whom, from his mother, he gave the surname of Salonius. In the meantime, his eldest died in his prætorship; of whom Cato often makes mention in his books, as having been a good man. He is said, however, to have borne the loss moderately and like a philosopher, and was nothing the more remiss in attending to affairs of state; so that he did not, as Lucius Lucullus and Metellus Pius did, grow languid in his old age, as though public business were a duty once to be discharged, and then quitted; nor did he, like Scipio Africanus, because envy had struck at his glory, turn from the public, and change and pass away the rest of his life without doing anything; but as one persuaded Dionysius, that the most honourable tomb he could have would be to die in the exercise of his dominion; so Cato thought that old age to be the most honourable which was busied in public affairs; though he would, now and then, when he had leisure, recreate himself with husbandry and writing.

And, indeed, he composed various books and histories; and in his youth he addicted himself to agriculture for profit's sake; for he used to say he had but two ways of getting—agriculture and parsimony; and now, in his old age, the first of these gave him both occupation and a subject of study. He wrote one book on country matters, in which he treated particularly even of making cakes and preserving fruit; it being his ambition to be curious and singular in all things. His suppers, at his country-house, used also to be plentiful; he daily invited his friends and neighbours about him, and passed the time merrily with them; so that his company was not only agreeable to those of the same age, but even to younger men; for he had had experience in many things, and had been concerned in much, both by word and deed, that was worth the hearing. He looked upon a good table as the best place for making friends; where the commendations of brave and good citizens were usually introduced, and little said of base and unworthy ones; as Cato would not give leave in his company to have anything, either good or ill, said about them.

Some will have the overthrow of Carthage to have been one of his last acts of state; when, indeed, Scipio the younger did by his valour give it the last blow, but the war, chiefly by the counsel and advice of Cato, was undertaken on the following occasion. Cato was sent to the Carthaginians and Masinissa, King of Numidia, who were at war with one another, to know the cause of their difference. He, it seems, had been a friend of the Romans from the beginning; and they, too, since they were conquered by Scipio, were of the Roman confederacy, having been shorn of their power by loss of territory and a heavy tax. Finding Carthage, not (as the Romans thought) low and in an ill condition, but well manned, full of riches and all sorts of arms and ammunition, and perceiving the Carthaginians carry it high, he conceived that it was not a time for the Romans to adjust affairs between them and Masinissa; but rather that they themselves would fall into danger, unless they should find means to check this rapid new growth of Rome's ancient irreconcilable enemy. Therefore, returning quickly to Rome, he acquainted the senate that the former defeats and blows given to the Carthaginians had not so much diminished their strength, as it had abated their imprudence and folly; that they were not become weaker, but more experienced in war, and did only skirmish with the Numidians to exercise themselves the better to cope with the Romans: that the peace and league they had made was but a kind of suspension of war which awaited a fairer opportunity to break out again.

Moreover, they say that, shaking his gown, he took occasion to let drop some African figs before the senate. And on their admiring the size and beauty of them,

he presently added, that the place that bore them was but three days' sail from Rome. Nay, he never after this gave his opinion, but at the end he would be sure to come out with this sentence, "ALSO, CARTHAGE, METHINKS, OUGHT UTTERLY TO BE DESTROYED." But Publius Scipio Nasica would always declare his opinion to the contrary, in these words, "It seems requisite to me that Carthage should still stand." For seeing his countrymen to be grown wanton and insolent, and the people made, by their prosperity, obstinate and disobedient to the senate, and drawing the whole city, whither they would, after them, he would have had the fear of Carthage to serve as a bit to hold the contumacy of the multitude; and he looked upon the Carthaginians as too weak to overcome the Romans, and too great to be despised by them. On the other side, it seemed a perilous thing to Cato that a city which had been always great, and was now grown sober and wise, by reason of its former calamities, should still lie, as it were, in wait for the follies and dangerous excesses of the overpowerful Roman people; so that he thought it the wisest course to have all outward dangers removed, when they had so many inward ones among themselves.

Thus Cato, they say, stirred up the third and last war against the Carthaginians: but no sooner was the said war begun, than he died, prophesying of the person that should put an end to it who was then only a young man; but, being tribune in the army, he in several fights gave proof of his courage and conduct. The news of which being brought to Cato's ears at Rome, he thus expressed himself:—

> The only wise man of them all is he,
> The others e'en as shadows flit and flee.

This prophecy Scipio soon confirmed by his actions.

Cato left no posterity, except one son by his second wife, who was named, as we said, Cato Salonius; and a grandson by his eldest son, who died. Cato Salonius died when he was prætor, but his son Marcus was afterwards consul, and he was grandfather of Cato the philosopher, who for virtue and renown was one of the most eminent personages of his time.

Lorenzo Valla (essay date 1433)

SOURCE: Lorenzo Valla, "Book II" and "Book III," in *On Pleasure (De voluptate)*, translated by A. Kent Hieatt and Maristella Lorch, Abaris Books, Inc., 1977, pp. 132-227, 228-327.

[*Valla, an Italian intellectual, served as the Librarian of the Vatican. His* De vero bono, *or* On Pleasure, *takes the form of a letter in which the writer, who identifies himself as an Epicurean, refutes the arguments of a friend who advocates stoicism. Cato ap-*

pears in this work as an example of the stoic person-
ality; in the excerpts below, Valla criticizes Cato in
order to promote Epicureanism.]

Here . . . [you] may meet my argument with authoritative instances (not being able to do so by reason), for
we see that many besides those whom you mentioned
believed that for the sake of virtue no pain should be
avoided. Most outstanding among these are Cato,
Scipio, and, above all, Lucretia. However, these examples certainly do not affect me, and, in addition, I
am able to censure the behavior of these three according to the law of the Stoics.

Can you really believe that someone seems to me to
have acted with courage who has tolerated adversities, and who has not only failed to refuse death when
it was offered to him but has even offered himself to
it? Who tolerates more adversities than pirates, who
are never far from danger; or than bandits, who join
day to night in fear; or than the worst slaves, who
prefer to be torn to pieces each day rather than yield
to corrections?

In order not to delay our progress with many instances
on the subject of those who inflicted death upon themselves, I shall content myself with one: the law according to which whoever turned his hand against himself
should be left unburied, unless the cause of his suicide
was first reported to the Senate. We are given to understand by this law that many committed suicide for
the wrong reason, among whom perhaps, if we examine the matter carefully, are the three people just mentioned. But I don't want to take this line, lest I seem
to be asking that they be exhumed and left without
burial, and lest I seem to offend such great names. Yet
for those who have ceased to exist, what injury is there
in not being buried?

What, then, should be said of these three? Did they
desire death for the sake of virtue? Not at all, but for
the sake of pleasure. "How can this be?" you ask.
Because someone who cannot aspire to pleasure
chooses as his next best course to escape from pain.
Thus Cato and Scipio understood, each for himself,
how painful it would be (note their weakness of character) to see Caesar ruling in Rome, since he was the
enemy of both of them, and how painful it would be
to see not only him but also his followers in positions
of the greatest power and invested with the highest
dignities, and, on the other hand, to see the followers
of Pompey, of whom they themselves were easily the
principal ones, suffering in defeat and servitude the
insolence of the victors.

Demosthenes seems to me to have plainly understood
his teacher Plato to have meant this when he said,
"Whoever believes himself to be a son of his mother
country will give himself over to death rather than see

her enslaved." Note the reason given: "More than death,
he will fear the outrage and disgrace that have to be
borne in one's native land when it is enslaved." Therefore, fearing this pain of Fortune, Cato and Scipio
preferred the comfort of death to life. And how bravely,
I have already said—for in my opinion they would
have done better not to turn their backs to Fortune but
rather to fight her as she raged against them, even
though many make their own misfortune themselves.
Vergil puts it excellently: "Wherever the Fates pull
and push us, let us follow; whatever is to be, every
fortune is to be conquered by being borne." And:

> Do not yield to evils, but go out against them more
> boldly, as fortune calls.

Similarly, in another passage, he reproaches those who
have innocently killed themselves:

> Whoever in innocence wrought their own death and,
> loathing the light, flung away their lives—how
> gladly now, in the air above, would they bear want
> and harsh distress!

Brutus himself, a great authority among the prime ones
in philosophy, also shows in his book *Of the Happy
Life* that he disapproves of Cato's dying in this way;
Cato was Brutus's uncle and father-in-law, and Brutus
considered him the greatest of men and so described
him. Notwithstanding all this, I do not reproach everyone who commits suicide, since, to be sure, the very
law that I have cited empowers men to take their own
lives if they have first reported their motive in the
Senate. I was referring exclusively to Cato and Scipio.

. . . . .

Was Cato overly harsh, unbending, too gloomy? Sometimes he was, but not always. I shall briefly compare
his right and wrong actions. For he was not always at
fault in this way, as I have said. Do you not remember
what kind of opinion Cato had on the subject of the
conspirators, and how the majority of the Senate followed it? And how much Sallust praised him for the
very austerity of which you disapprove, and how much
Lucan praised him? I neglect to quote their statements
because they are somewhat long and very well known,
and thus all of you will concede, without quotation,
the truth of what I have said. If Cato was unbending,
he was far removed from the fault of inconstancy; that
is, he was often serious, which ought to be said of all
of us.

I do not speak at this point of those who are infamous
for their evil. As there are some who are near to being
divine, so there are some who hardly differ from brutes,
as you claimed Catilina to be—deformed by contrary
vices. I shall give you a brief answer on this subject:
either those vices were not contrary, as I have shown,

or he could have had as many virtues as vices; that is, there are as many soldiers on our side as on the other, an equality that you felt was lacking.

I realize that I am not proceeding with this argument as I should. Cato was blamed by some, but can we say that this blame was necessarily just? Do we not know that this field of bitter struggles is common to all orators and most frequented by them? The same thing is affirmed by one to be cruelty, by another to be strictness; or one says "stinginess," another "thrift"; or I say "popularity-seeking," you say "magnificence." These controversies turn upon definition of motives and upon syllogistic or logical procedures. Thus it needs to be understood that to every virtue is assigned its proper vice, not its excess and deficiency. Controversy never arises, for instance, over whether a particular deed was characterized by strictness or by mildness or weakness, but it may arise over whether this deed was characterized by strictness or by cruelty, which, as I have said, are opposed to each other.

But let us return to the point. The virtues and vices are so close together that it is not easy to distinguish them. And thus most individuals are inclined to judge exactly according to their natures or feel according to their kind of life, as Horace says:

> The sad hate the cheerful man, and the merry hate
> the sad; the swift hate the quiet man, and the inactive
> hate the active and energetic man.

Thus it happened that to some people Cato seemed too hard, Cicero too soft—when perhaps the former really acted with appropriate strictness and the latter with courtesy, both of which modes are praiseworthy. . . .

John Dunlop (essay date 1824)

SOURCE: John Dunlop, "Marcus Porcius Cato," in *History of Roman Literature, From Its Earliest Period to the Augustan Age*, Longman, Hurst, Rees, Orme, Brown and Green, 1824, pp. 13-31.

[*In the following excerpt from his history of Rome, Dunlop emphasizes Cato's devotion and skill as a farmer. He also summarizes Cato's works, giving an extensive synopsis of the* De agricultura, *here called* De Re Rustica.]

Marcus Porcius Cato, better known by the name of Cato the Censor, wrote the earliest book on husbandry which we possess in the Latin language. This distinguished citizen was born in the 519th year of Rome. Like other Romans of his day, he was brought up to the profession of arms. In the short intervals of peace he resided, during his youth, at a small country-house in the Sabine territory, which he had inherited from

his father. Near it there stood a cottage belonging to Manius Curius Dentatus, who had repeatedly triumphed over the Sabines and Samnites, and had at length driven Pyrrhus from Italy. Cato was accustomed frequently to walk over to the humble abode of this renowned commander, where he was struck with admiration at the frugality of its owner, and the skilful management of the farm which was attached to it. Hence it became his great object to emulate his illustrious neighbour, and adopt him as his model. Having made an estimate of his house, lands, slaves, and expenses, he applied himself to husbandry with new ardour, and retrenched all superfluity. In the morning he went to the small towns in the vicinity, to plead and defend the causes of those who applied to him for assistance. Thence he returned to his fields; where, with a plain cloak over his shoulders in winter, and almost naked in summer, he laboured with his servants till they had concluded their tasks, after which he sat down along with them at table, eating the same bread, and drinking the same wine. At a more advanced period of life, the wars, in which he commanded, kept him frequently at a distance from Italy, and his forensic avocations detained him much in the city; but what time he could spare was still spent at the Sabine farm, where he continued to employ himself in the profitable cultivation of the land. He thus became, by the universal consent of his contemporaries, the best farmer of his age, and was held unrivalled for the skill and success of his agricultural operations. Though everywhere a rigid economist, he lived, it is said, more hospitably at his farm than in the city. His entertainments at his villa were at first but sparing, and seldom given; but as his wealth increased, he became more nice and delicate. "At first," says Plutarch, "when he was but a poor soldier, he was not difficult in anything which related to his diet; but afterwards, when he grew richer, and made feasts for his friends, presently, when supper was done, he seized a leathern thong, and scourged those who had not given due attendance, or dressed anything carelessly." Towards the close of his life, he almost daily invited some of his friends in the neighbourhood to sup with him; and the conversation at these meals turned not chiefly, as might have been expected, on rural affairs, but on the praises of great and excellent men among the Romans.

It may be supposed, that in the evenings after the agricultural labours of the morning, and after his friends had left him, he noted down the precepts suggested by the observations and experience of the day. That he wrote such maxims for his own use, or the instruction of others, is unquestionable; but the treatise **De Re Rustica,** which now bears his name, appears to have been much mutilated, since Pliny and other writers allude to subjects as treated of by Cato, and to opinions as delivered by him in this book, which are nowhere to be found in any part of the work now extant.

In its present state, it is merely the loose unconnected journal of a plain farmer, expressed with rude, sometimes with almost oracular brevity; and it wants all those elegant topics of embellishment and illustration which the subject might have so naturally suggested. It solely consists of the dryest rules of agriculture, and some receipts for making various kinds of cakes and wines. Servius says, it is addressed to the author's son; but there is no such address now extant. It begins rather abruptly, and in a manner extremely characteristic of the simple manners of the author: "It would be advantageous to seek profit from commerce, if that were not hazardous; or by usury, if that were honest: but our ancestors ordained, that the thief should forfeit double the sum he had stolen, and the usurer quadruple what he had taken, whence it may be concluded, that they thought the usurer the worst of the two. When they wished highly to praise a good man, they called him a good farmer. A merchant is zealous in pushing his fortune, but his trade is perilous and liable to reverses. But farmers make the bravest men, and the stoutest soldiers. Their gain is the most honest, the most stable, and least exposed to envy. Those who exercise the art of agriculture, are of all others least addicted to evil thoughts."

Our author then proceeds to his rules, many of which are sufficiently obvious. Thus, he advises, that when one is about to purchase a farm, he should examine if the climate, soil, and exposure be good: he should see that it can be easily supplied with plenty of water,—that it lies in the neighbourhood of a town,—and near a navigable river, or the sea. The directions for ascertaining the quality of the land are not quite so clear or self-evident. He recommends the choice of a farm where there are few implements of labour, as this shews the soil to be easily cultivated; and where there are, on the other hand, a number of casks and vessels, which testify an abundant produce. With regard to the best way of laying out a farm when it is purchased, supposing it to be one of a hundred acres, the most profitable thing is a vineyard; next, a garden, that can be watered; then a willow grove; 4th, an olive plantation; 5th, meadow-ground; 6th, corn fields; and, lastly, forest trees and brushwood. Varro cites this passage, but he gives the preference to meadows: These required little expense; and, by his time, the culture of vines had so much increased in Italy, and such a quantity of foreign wine was imported, that vineyards had become less valuable than in the days of the Censor. Columella, however, agrees with Cato: He successively compares the profits accruing from meadows, pasture, trees, and corn, with those of vineyards; and, on an estimate, prefers the last.

When a farm has been purchased, the new proprietor should perambulate the fields the day he arrives, or, if he cannot do so, on the day after, for the purpose of seeing what has been done, and what remains to be accomplished. Rules are given for the most assiduous

employment without doors, and the most rigid economy within. When a servant is sick he will require less food. All the old oxen and the cattle of delicate frame, the old waggons, and old implements of husbandry, are to be sold off. The sordid parsimony of the Censor leads him to direct, that a provident *paterfamilias* should sell such of his slaves as are aged and infirm; a recommendation which has drawn down on him the well-merited indignation of Plutarch. These are some of the duties of the master; and there follows a curious detail of the qualifications and duties of the *villicus,* or overseer, who, in particular, is prohibited from the exercise of religious rites, and consultation of augurs.

It is probable that, in the time of Cato, the Romans had begun to extend their villas considerably, which makes him warn proprietors of land not to be rash in building. When a landlord is thirty-six years of age he may build, provided his fields have been brought into a proper state of cultivation. His direction with regard to the extent of the villa is concise, but seems a very proper one;—he advises, to build in such a manner that the villa may not need a farm, nor the farm a villa. Lucullus and Scævola both violated this golden rule, as we learn from Pliny; who adds, that it will be readily conjectured, from their respective characters, that it was the farm of Scævola which stood in need of the villa, and the villa of Lucullus which required the farm.

A vast variety of crops was cultivated by the Romans, and the different kinds were adapted by them, with great care, to the different soils. Cato is very particular in his injunctions on this subject. A field that is of a rich and genial soil should be sown with corn; but, if wet or moist, with turnips and raddish. Figs are to be planted in chalky land; and willows in watery situations, in order to serve as twigs for tying the vines. This being the proper mode of laying out a farm, our author gives a detail of the establishment necessary to keep it up;—the number of workmen, the implements of husbandry, and the farm-offices, with the materials necessary for their construction.

He next treats of the management of vineyards and olives; the proper mode of planting, grafting, propping, and fencing: And he is here naturally led to furnish directions for making and preserving the different sorts of wine and oil; as also to specify how much of each is to be allowed to the servants of the family.

In discoursing of the cultivation of fields for corn, Cato enjoins the farmer to collect all sorts of weeds for manure. Pigeons' dung he prefers to that of every animal. He gives orders for burning lime, and for making charcoal and ashes from the branches or twigs of trees. The Romans seem to have been at great pains in draining their fields; and Cato directs the formation both of open and covered drains. Oxen being employed in ploughing the fields, instructions are added for feeding and taking due care of them. The Roman plough has been a subject of much discussion: Two sorts are mentioned by Cato, which he calls *Romanicum,* and *Campanicum*—the first being proper for a stiff, and the other for a light soil. Dickson conjectures, that the *Romanicum* had an iron Share, and the *Campanicum* a piece of timber, like the Scotch plough, and a sock driven upon it. The plough, with other agricultural implements, as the *crates, rastrum, ligo,* and *sarculum,* most of which are mentioned by Cato, form a curious point of Roman antiquities.

The preservation of corn, after it has been reaped, is a subject of much importance, to which Cato has paid particular attention. This was a matter of considerable difficulty in Italy, in the time of the Romans; and all their agricultural writers are extremely minute in their directions for preserving it from rot, and from the depredations of insects, by which it was frequently consumed.

A great part of the work of Cato is more appropriate to the housewife than the farmer. We have receipts for making all sorts of cakes and puddings, fattening hens and geese, preserving figs during winter; as also medical prescriptions for the cure of various diseases, both of man and beast. *Mala punica,* or pomegranates, are the chief ingredient, in his remedies, for Diarrhœa, Dyspepsia, and Stranguary. Sometimes, however, his cures for diseases are not medical recipes, but sacrifices, atonements, or charms. The prime of all is his remedy for a luxation or fracture.—"Take," says he, "a green reed, and slit it along the middle—throw the knife upwards, and join the two parts of the reed again, and tie it so to the place broken or disjointed, and say this charm—'Daries, Dardaries, Astataries, Dissunapiter.' Or this—'Huat, Hanat, Huat, Ista, Pista, Fista, Domiabo, Damnaustra.' This will make the part sound again."

The most remarkable feature in the work of Cato, is its total want of arrangement. It is divided, indeed, into chapters, but the author, apparently, had never taken the trouble of reducing his precepts to any sort of method, or of following any general plan. The hundred and sixty-two chapters, of which his work consists; seem so many rules committed to writing, as the daily labours of the field suggested. He gives directions about the vineyard, then goes to his corn-fields, and returns again to the vineyard. His treatise was, therefore, evidently not intended as a regular or well-composed book, but merely as a journal of incidental observations. That this was its utmost pretensions, is farther evinced by the brevity of the precepts, and deficiency of all illustration or embellishment. Of the style, he of course would be little careful, as his *Memoranda* were intended for the use only of his family and slaves. It is therefore always simple,—sometimes even rude; but it is not ill adapted to the subject, and suits our notion of the severe manners of its author, and character of the ancient Romans.

Besides this book on agriculture, Cato left behind him various works, which have almost entirely perished. He left a hundred and fifty orations, which were existing in the time of Cicero, though almost entirely neglected, and a book on military discipline, both of which, if now extant, would be highly interesting, as proceeding from one who was equally distinguished in the camp and forum. A good many of his orations were in dissuasion or favour of particular laws and measures of state, as those entitled—"Ne quis iterum Consul fiat—De bello Carthaginiensi," of which war he was a vehement promoter—"Suasio in Legem Voconiam,—Pro Lege Oppiâ," &c. Nearly a third part of these orations were pronounced in his own defence. He had been about fifty times accused, and as often acquitted. When charged with a capital crime, in the 85th year of his age, he pleaded his own cause, and betrayed no failure in memory, no decline of vigour, and no faltering of voice. By his readiness, and pertinacity, and bitterness, he completely wore out his adversaries, and earned the reputation of being, if not the most eloquent, at least the most stubborn speaker among the Romans.

Cato's oration in favour of the Appian law, which was a sumptuary restriction on the expensive dresses of the Roman matrons, is given by Livy. It was delivered in opposition to the tribune Valerius, who proposed its abrogation, and affords us some notion of his style and manner, since, if not copied by the historian from his book of orations, it was doubtless adapted by him to the character of Cato, and his mode of speaking. Aulus Gellius cites, as equally distinguished for its eloquence and energy, a passage in his speech on the division of spoil among the soldiery, in which he complains of their unpunished peculation and licentiousness. One of his most celebrated harangues was that in favour of the Rhodians, the ancient allies of the Roman people, who had fallen under the suspicion of affording aid to Perseus, during the second Macedonian war. The oration was delivered after the overthrow of that monarch, when the Rhodian envoys were introduced into the Senate, in order to explain the conduct of their countrymen, and to deprecate the vengeance of the Romans, by throwing the odium of their apparent hostility on the turbulence of a few factious individuals. It was pronounced in answer to those Senators, who, after hearing the supplications of the Rhodians, were for declaring war against them; and it turned chiefly on the ancient, long-tried fidelity of that people,—taking particular advantage of the circumstance, that the assistance rendered to Perseus had not been a national act, proceeding from a public decree of the people. Tiro, the freedman of Cicero, wrote a long and elaborate criticism on this oration. To the numerous censures it contains, Aulus Gellius has replied at considerable length, and has blamed Tiro for singling out from a speech so rich, and so happily connected, small and insulated por-

An artist's rendering of Cato.

tions, as objects of his reprehensive satire. All the various topics, he adds, which are enlarged on in this oration, if they could have been introduced with more perspicuity, method, and harmony, could not have been delivered with more energy and strength.

Both Cicero and Livy have expressed themselves very fully on the subject of Cato's orations. The former admits, that his "language is antiquated, and some of his phrases harsh and inelegant: but only change that," he continues, "which it was not in his power to change—add number and cadence—give an easier turn to his sentences—and regulate the structure and connection of his words, (an art which was as little practised by the older Greeks as by him,) and you will find no one who can claim the preference to Cato. The Greeks themselves acknowledge, that the chief beauty of composition results from the frequent use of those forms of expression, which they call tropes, and of those varieties of language and sentiment, which they call figures; but it is almost incredible with what copiousness, and with what variety, they are all employed by Cato." Livy principally speaks of the facility, asperity, and freedom of his tongue. Aulus Gellius has

instituted a comparison of Caius Gracchus, Cato, and Cicero, in passages where these three orators declaimed against the same species of atrocity—the illegal scourging of Roman citizens; and Gellius, though he admits that Cato had not reached the splendour, harmony, and pathos of Cicero, considers him as far superior in force and copiousness to Gracchus.

Of the book on Military Discipline, a good deal has been incorporated into the work of Vegetius; and Cicero's orations may console us for the want of those of Cato. But the loss of the seven books, *De Originibus,* which he commenced in his vigorous old age, and finished just before his death, must ever be deeply deplored by the historian and antiquary. Cato is said to have begun to inquire into the history, antiquities, and language of the Roman people, with a view to counteract the influence of the Greek taste, introduced by the Scipios; and in order to take from the Greeks the honour of having colonized Italy, he attempted to discover on the Latian soil the traces of ancient national manners, and an indigenous civilization. The first book of the valuable work, *De Originibus,* as we are informed by Cornelius Nepos, in his short life of Cato, contained the exploits of the kings of Rome. Cato was the first author who attempted to fix the era of the foundation of Rome, which he calculated in his *Origines,* and determined it to have been in the first year of the 7th Olympiad. In order to discover this epoch, he had recourse to the memoirs of the Censors, in which it was noted, that the taking of Rome by the Gauls, was 119 years after the expulsion of the kings. By adding this period to the aggregate duration of the reigns of the kings, he found that the amount answered to the first of the 7th Olympiad. This is the computation followed by Dionysius of Halicarnassus, in his great work on Roman antiquities. It is probably as near the truth as we can hope to arrive; but even in the time of Cato, the calculated duration of the reigns of the kings was not founded on any ancient monuments then extant, or on the testimony of any credible historian. The second and third books treated of the origin of the different states of Italy, whence the whole work has received the name of *Origines*. The fourth and fifth books comprehended the history of the first and second Punic wars; and in the two remaining books, the author discussed the other campaigns of the Romans till the time of Ser. Galba, who overthrew the Lusitanians.

In his account of these later contests, Cato merely related the facts, without mentioning the names of the generals or leaders; but though he has omitted this, Pliny informs us that he did not forget to take notice, that the elephant which fought most stoutly in the Carthaginian army was called Surus, and wanted one of his teeth. In this same work he incidentally treated of all the wonderful and admirable things which existed in Spain and Italy. Some of his orations, too, as we learn from Livy, were incorporated into it, as that for giving freedom to the Lusitanian hostages; and Plutarch farther mentions, that he omitted no opportunity of praising himself, and extolling his services to the state. The work, however, exhibited great industry and learning, and, had it descended to us, would unquestionably have thrown much light on the early periods of Roman history and the antiquities of the different states of Italy. Dionysius of Halicarnassus, himself a sedulous inquirer into antiquities, bears ample testimony to the research and accuracy of that part which treats of the origin of the ancient Italian cities. The author lived at a time which was favourable to this investigation. Though the Samnites, Etruscans, and Sabines, had been deprived of their independence, they had not lost their monuments or records of their history, their individuality and national manners. Cicero praises the simple and concise style of the *Origines,* and laments that the work was neglected in his day, in consequence of the inflated manner of writing which had been recently adopted; in the same manner as the tumid and ornamented periods of Theopompus had lessened the esteem for the concise and unadorned narrative of Thucydides, or as the lofty eloquence of Demosthenes impaired the relish for the extreme attic simplicity of Lysias.

In the same part of the dialogue, entitled *Brutus,* Cicero asks what flower or light of eloquence is wanting to the *Origines*—"Quem florem, aut quod lumen eloquentiæ non habent?" But on Atticus considering the praise thus bestowed as excessive, he limits it, by adding, that nothing was required to complete the strokes of the author's pencil but a certain lively glow of colours, which had not been discovered in his age.— "Intelliges, nihil illius lineamentis, nisi eorum pigmentorum, quæ inventa nondum erant, florem et colorem defuisse."

The pretended fragments of the *Origines,* published by the Dominican, Nanni, better known by the name of Annius Viterbiensis, and inserted in his *Antiquitates Variæ,* printed at Rome in 1498, are spurious, and the imposition was detected soon after their appearance. The few remains first collected by Riccobonus, and published at the end of his Treatise on History, (Basil, 1579,) are believed to be genuine. They have been enlarged by Ausonius Popma, and added by him, with notes, to the other writings of Cato, published at Leyden in 1590.

Any rudeness of style and language which appears either in the orations of Cato, or in his agricultural and historical works, cannot be attributed to total carelessness or neglect of the graces of composition, as he was the first person in Rome who treated of oratory as an art, in a tract entitled *De Oratore ad Filium.*

Cato was also the first of his countrymen who wrote on the subject of medicine. Rome had existed for 500 years without professional physicians. A people who as yet were strangers to luxury, and consisted of farmers and soldiers, (though surgical operations might be frequently necessary,) would be exempt from the inroads of the "grisly troop," so much encouraged by indolence and debauchery. Like all semi-barbarous people, they believed that maladies were to be cured by the special interposition of superior beings, and that religious ceremonies were more efficacious for the recovery of health than remedies of medical skill. Deriving, as they did, much of their worship from the Etruscans, they probably derived from them also the practice of attempting to overcome disease by magic and incantation. The Augurs and Aruspices were thus the most ancient physicians of Rome. In epidemic distempers the Sibylline books were consulted, and the cures they prescribed were superstitious ceremonies. We have seen that it was to free the city from an attack of this sort that scenic representations were first introduced at Rome. During the progress of another epidemic infliction a temple was built to Apollo; and as each periodic pestilence naturally abated in course of time, faith was confirmed in the efficacy of the rites which were resorted to. Every one has heard of the pomp wherewith Esculapius was transported under the form of a serpent, from Epidaurus to an islet in the Tiber, which was thereafter consecrated to that divine physician. The apprehension of diseases raised temples to Febris and Tussis, and other imaginary beings belonging to the painful family of death, in order to avert the disorders which they were supposed to inflict. It was perceived, however, that religious processions and lustrations and *lectisterniums* were ineffectual for the cure of those complaints, which, in the 6th century, luxury began to exasperate and render more frequent at Rome. At length, in 534, Archagatus, a free-born Greek, arrived in Italy, where he practised medicine professionally as art, and received in return for his cures the endearing appellation of *Carnifex.* But though Archagatus was the first who practised medicine, Cato was the first who wrote of diseases and their treatment as a science, in his work entitled ***Commentarius quo Medetu Filio, Servis, Familiaribus.*** In this book of domestic medicine—duck, pigeons, and hare, were the foods he chiefly recommended to the sick. His remedies were principally extracted from herbs; and colewort, or cabbage, was his favourite cure. The recipes, indeed, contained in his work on agriculture, show that his medical knowledge did not exceed that which usually exists among a semi-barbarous race, and only extended to the most ordinary simples which nature affords. Cato hated the compound drugs introduced by the Greek physicians—considering these foreign professors of medicine as the opponents of his own system. Such, indeed, was his antipathy, that he believed, or pretended to believe, that they had entered into a league to poison all the barbarians, among whom they classed the Romans.—"Jurârunt inter se," says he, in a passage preserved by Pliny, "barbaros necare omnes medicinâ: Et hoc ipsum mercede faciunt, ut fides iis sit, et facile disperdant." Cato, finding that the patients lived notwithstanding this detestable conspiracy, began to regard the Greek practitioners as impious sorcerers, who counteracted the course of nature, and restored dying men to life, by means of unholy charms; and he therefore advised his countrymen to remain stedfast, not only by their ancient Roman principles and manners, but also by the venerable unguents and salubrious balsams which had come down to them from the wisdom of their grandmothers. Such as they were, Cato's old medical saws continued long in repute at Rome. It is evident that they were still esteemed in the time of Pliny, who expresses the same fears as the Censor, lest hot baths and potions should render his countrymen effeminate, and corrupt their manners.

Every one knows what was the consequence of Cato's dislike to the Greek philosophers, who were expelled the city by a decree of the senate. But it does not seem certain what became of Archagatus and his followers. The author of the *Diogene Moderne,* as cited by Tiraboschi, says that Archagatus was stoned to death, but the literary historian who quotes him doubts of his having any sufficient authority for the assertion. Whether the physicians were comprehended in the general sentence of banishment pronounced on the learned Greeks, or were excepted from it, has been the subject of a great literary controversy in modern Italy and in France.

Aulus Gellius mentions Cato's **Libri quæstionum Epistolicarum,** and Cicero his ***Apophthegmata,*** which was probably the first example of that class of works which, under the appellation of *Ana,* became so fashionable and prevalent in France.

The only other work of Cato which I shall mention, is the **Carmen de Moribus**. This, however, was not written in verse, as might be supposed from the title. Precepts, imprecations, and prayers, or any set *formulæ* whatever, were called *Carmina.* I do not know what maxims were inculcated in this *carmen,* but they probably were not of very rigid morality, at least if we may judge from the "Sententia Dia Catonis," mentioned by Horace:

> Quidam notus homo cùm exiret fornice, Macte
> Virtute esto, inquit sententia dia Catonis. . . .

Charles Thomas Cruttwell (essay date 1878)

SOURCE: Charles Thomas Cruttwell, "Chapter IX," in *A History of Roman Literature: From the Caliest Period to the Death of Marcus Aurelius,* fourth edition, Charles Griffin and Company, 1878, pp. 87-103.

[*Dubbing Cato "the perfect type of an old Roman," Cruttwell proceeds, in the excerpt below, to attribute the character of genuinely Roman letters to Cato's style and values. Cruttwell also espouses the traditional view of Cato's motivation for writing: his hostility to Greek culture.*]

The creator of Latin prose writing was CATO (234-149 B.C.). In almost every department he set the example, and his works, voluminous and varied, retained their reputation until the close of the classical period. He was the first thoroughly national author.

The character of the rigid censor is generally associated in our minds with the contempt of letters. In his stern but narrow patriotism, he looked with jealous eyes on all that might turn the citizens from a single-minded devotion to the State. Culture was connected in his mind with Greece, and her deleterious influence. The embassy of Diogenes, Critolaus, and Carneades, 155 B.C. had shown him to what uses culture might be turned. The eloquent harangue pronounced in favour of justice, and the equally eloquent harangue pronounced next day against it by the same speaker without a blush of shame, had set Cato's face like a flint in opposition to Greek learning. "I will tell you about those Greeks," he wrote in his old age to his son Marcus, "What I discovered by careful observation at Athens, and how far I deem it good to skim through their writings, for in no case should they be deeply studied. I will prove to you that they are one and all, a worthless and intractable set. Mark my words, for they are those of a prophet: whenever that nation shall give us its literature, it will corrupt everything."

With this settled conviction, thus emphatically expressed at a time when experience had shown the realization of his fears to be inevitable, and when he himself had so far bent as to study the literature he despised, the long and active public life of Cato is in complete harmony. He is the perfect type of an old Roman. Hard, shrewd, niggardly, and narrow minded, he was honest to the core, unsparing of himself as of others, scorning every kind of luxury, and of inflexible moral rectitude. He had no respect for birth, rank, fortune, or talent; his praise was bestowed solely on personal merit. He himself belonged to an ancient and honourable house [so he himself asserted; but they had not held any Roman magistracy.], and from it he inherited those harsh virtues which, while they enforced the reverence, put him in conflict with the spirit, of the age. No man could have set before himself a more uphill task than that which Cato struggled all his life vainly to achieve. To reconstruct the past is but one step more impossible than to stem the tide of the present. If Cato failed, a greater than Cato would not have succeeded. Influences were at work in Rome which individual genius was powerless to resist. The ascendancy of reason over force, though it were the noblest form that force has ever assumed, was step by step establishing itself; and no stronger proof of its victory could be found than that Cato, despite of himself, in his old age studied Greek. We may smile at the deep-rooted prejudice which confounded the pure glories of the old Greek intellect with the degraded puerilities of its unworthy heirs; but though Cato could not fathom the mind of Greece, he thoroughly understood the mind of Rome, and unavailing as his efforts were, they were based on an unerring comprehension of the true issues at stake. He saw that Greece was unmaking Rome; but he did not see that mankind required that Rome should be unmade. It is the glory of men like Scipio and Ennius, that their large-heartedness opened their eyes, and carried their vision beyond the horizon of the Roman world into that dimly-seen but ever expanding country in which all men are brethren. But if from the loftiest point of view their wide humanity obtains the palm, no less does Cato's pure patriotism shed undying radiance over his rugged form, throwing into relief its massive grandeur, and ennobling rather than hiding its deformities.

We have said that Cato's name is associated with the contempt of letters. This is no doubt the fact. Nevertheless, Cato was by far the most original writer that Rome ever produced. He is the one man on whose vigorous mind no outside influence had ever told. Brought up at his father's farm at Tusculum, he spent his boyhood amid the labours of the plough. Hard work and scant fare toughened his sinews, and service under Fabius in the Hannibalic war knit his frame into that iron strength of endurance, which, until his death, never betrayed one sign of weakness or fatigue. A saying of his is preserved—"Man's life is like iron; if you use it, it wears away, if not, the rust eats it. So, too, men are worn away by hard work; but if they do no work, rest and sloth do more injury than exercise." On this maxim his own life was formed. In the intervals of warfare, he did not relax himself in the pleasures of the city, but went home to his plough, and improved his small estate. Being soon well known for his shrewd wit and ready speech, he rose into eminence at the bar; and in due time obtained all the offices of state. In every position he made many enemies, but most notably in his capacity of censor. No man was oftener brought to trial. Forty-four times he spoke in his own defence, and every time he was acquitted. As Livy says, he wore his enemies out, partly by accusing them, but still more by the pertinacity with which he defended himself. Besides private causes, he spoke in many important public trials and on many great questions of state: Cicero had seen or heard of 150 orations by him; in one passage he implies that he had delivered as many as Lysias, *i.e.* 230. Even now we have traces, certainly of 80, and perhaps of 13 more. His military life, which had been a series of successes, was brought to a close 190 B.C., and from this time until his death, he appears as an able civil administrator, and

a vehement opponent of lax manners. In the year of his censorship (184 B.C.) Plautus died. The tremendous vigour with which he wielded the powers of this post stirred up a swarm of enemies. His tongue became more bitter than ever. . . .

Here, at 85 years of age, the man stands before us. We see the crisp, erect figure, bristling with aggressive vigour, the coarse, red hair, the keen, grey eyes, piercingly fixed on his opponent's face, and reading at a glance the knavery he sought to hide; we hear the rasping voice, launching its dry, cutting sarcasms one after another, each pointed with its sting of truth; and we can well believe that the dislike was intense, which could make an enemy provoke the terrible armoury of the old censor's eloquence.

As has been said, he so far relaxed the severity of his principles as to learn the Greek language and study the great writers. Nor could he help feeling attracted to minds like those of Thucydides and Demosthenes, in sagacity and earnestness so congenial to his own. Nevertheless, his originality is in nothing more conspicuously shown than in his method of treating history. He struck a line of inquiry in which he found no successor. The ***Origines,*** if it had remained, would undoubtedly have been a priceless storehouse of facts about the antiquities of Italy. Cato had an enlarged view of history. It was not his object to magnify Rome at the expense of the other Italian nationalities, but rather to show how she had become their greatest, because their truest, representative. The divisions of the work itself will show the importance he attached to an investigation of their early annals. We learn from Nepos that the first book comprised the regal period; the second and third were devoted to the origin and primitive history of each Italian state; the fourth and fifth embraced the Punic wars; the last two carried the history as far as the Praetorship of Servius Galba, Cato's bold accusation of whom he inserted in the body of the work. Nepos, echoing the superficial canons of his age, characterises the whole as showing industry and diligence, but no learning whatever. The early myths were somewhat indistinctly treated. His account of the Trojan immigration seems to have been the basis of that of Virgil, though the latter refashioned it in several points. His computation of dates, though apparently exact, betrays a mind indifferent to the importance of chronology. The fragments of the next two books are more copious. He tells us that Gaul, then as now, pursued with the greatest zeal military glory and eloquence in debate. His notice of the Ligurians is far from complimentary. "They are all deceitful, having lost every record of their real origin, and being illiterate, they invent false stories and have no recollection of the truth." He hazards a few etymologies, which, as usual among Roman writers, are quite unscientific. Graviscæ is so called from its unhealthy climate (*gravis aer*), Praeneste from its conspicuous position on the mountains (*quia montibus praestet*). A few scattered remarks on the food in use among different tribes are all that remain of an interesting department which might have thrown much light on ethnological questions. In the fourth book, Cato expresses his disinclination to repeat the trivial details of the Pontifical tables, the fluctuations of the market, the eclipses of the sun and moon, &c. He narrates with enthusiasm the self-devotion of the tribune Caedicius, who in the first Punic war offered his life with that of 400 soldiers to engage the enemy's attention while the general was executing a necessary manœuvre. "The Laconian Leonides, who did the same thing at Thermopylae, has been rewarded by all Greece for his virtue and patriotism with all the emblems of the highest possible distinction—monuments, statues, epigrams, histories; his deed met with their warmest gratitude. But little praise has been given to our tribune in comparison with his merits, though he acted just as the Spartan did, and saved the fortunes of the State." As to the title **Origines,** it is possible, as Nepos suggests, that it arose from the first three books having been published separately. It certainly is not applicable to the entire treatise, which was a genuine history on the same scale as that of Thucydides, and no mere piece of antiquarian research. He adhered to truth in so far as he did not insert fictitious speeches; he conformed to Greek taste so far as to insert his own. One striking feature in the later books was his omission of names. No Roman worthy is named in them. The reason of this it is impossible to discover. Fear of giving offence would be the last motive to weigh with him. Dislike of the great aristocratic houses into whose hands the supreme power was steadily being concentrated, is a more probable cause; but it is hardly sufficient of itself. Perhaps the omission was a mere whim of the historian. Though this work obtained great and deserved renown, yet, like its author, it was praised rather than imitated. Livy scarcely ever uses it; and it is likely that, before the end of the first century A.D. the speeches were published separately, and were the only part at all generally read. Pliny, Gellius, and Servius, are the authors who seem most to have studied it; of these Pliny was most influenced by it. The Natural History, especially in its general discussions, strongly reminds us of Cato.

Of the talents of Cato as an orator something will be said in the next section. His miscellaneous writings, though none of them are historical, may be noticed here. Quintilian attests the many-sidedness of his genius: "M. Cato was at once a first-rate general, a philosopher, an orator, the founder of history, the most thorough master of law and agriculture." The work on agriculture we have the good fortune to possess; or rather a redaction of it, slightly modernized and incomplete, but nevertheless containing a large amount of really genuine matter. Nothing can be more characteristic than the opening sentences. We give a transla-

tion, following as closely as possible the form of the original: "It is at times worth while to gain wealth by commerce, were it not so perilous; or by usury, were it equally honourable. Our ancestors, however, held, and fixed by law, that a thief should be condemned to restore double, a usurer quadruple. We thus see how much worse they thought it for a citizen to be a moneylender than a thief. Again, when they praised a good man, they praised him as a good farmer, or a good husbandman. Men so praised were held to have received the highest praise. For myself, I think well of a merchant as a man of energy and studious of gain; but it is a career, as I have said, that leads to danger and ruin. But farming makes the bravest men, and the sturdiest soldiers, and of all sources of gain is the surest, the most natural, and the least invidious, and those who are busy with it have the fewest bad thoughts." The sententious and dogmatic style of this preamble cannot fail to strike the reader; but it is surpassed by many of the precepts which follow. Some of these contain pithy maxims of shrewd sense, *e.g.* "Patrem familias vendacem non emacem esse oportet." "Ita aedifices ne villa fundum quaerat, neve fundus villam." The Virgilian prescription, "Laudato ingentia rura: exiguam colito," is said to be drawn from Cato, though it does not exist in our copies. The treatment throughout is unmethodical. If left by the author in its present form it represents the daily jotting down of thoughts on the subject as they occurred to him.

In two points the writer appears in an unfavourable light—in his love of gain, and in his brutal treatment of his slaves. With him farming is no mere amusement, nor again is it mere labour. It is primarily and throughout a means of making money, and indeed the only strictly honourable one. However, Cato so far relaxed the strictness of this theory that he became "an ardent speculator in slaves, buildings, artificial lakes, and pleasure-grounds, the mercantile spirit being too strong within him to rest satisfied with the modest returns of his estate." As regarded slaves, the law considered them as chattels, and he followed the law to the letter. If a slave grew old or sick he was to be sold. If the weather hindered work he was to take his sleep then, and work double time afterwards. "In order to prevent combinations among his slaves, their master assiduously sowed enmities and jealousies between them. He bought young slaves in their name, whom they were forced to train and sell for his benefit. When supping with his guests, if any dish was carelessly dressed, he rose from table, and with a leathern thong administered the requisite number of lashes with his own hand." So pitilessly severe was he, that a slave who had concluded a purchase without his leave, hung himself to avoid his master's wrath. These incidents, some told by Plutarch, others by Cato himself, show the inhuman side of Roman life, and make it less hard to understand their treatment of vanquished kings and generals. For the other sex Cato had little respect. Women, he says, should be kept at home, and no Chaldaean or soothsayer be allowed to see them. Women are always running after superstition. His directions about the steward's wife are as follows. They are addressed to the steward:—"Let her fear you. Take care that she is not luxurious. Let her see as little as possible of her neighbours or any other female friends; let her never invite them to your house; let her never go out to supper, nor be fond of taking walks. Let her never offer sacrifice; let her know that the master sacrifices for the whole family; let her be neat herself, and keep the country-house neat." Several sacrificial details are given in the treatise. We observe that they are all of the rustic order; the master alone is to attend the city ceremonial. Among the different industries recommended, we are struck by the absence of wheat cultivation. The vineyard and the pasture chiefly engage attention, though herbs and green produce are carefully treated. The reason is to be sought in the special nature of the treatise. It is not a general survey of agriculture, but merely a handbook of cultivation for a particular farm, that of Manlius or Mallius, and so probably unfit for wheat crops. Other subjects, as medicine, are touched on. But his prescriptions are confined to the rudest simples, to wholesome and restorative diet, and to incantations. These last have equal value assigned them with rational remedies. Whether Cato trusted them may well be doubted. He probably gave in such cases the popular charm-cure, simply from not having a better method of his own to propose.

Another series of treatises were those addressed to his son, in one of which, that on medicine, he charitably accuses the Greeks of an attempt to kill all barbarians by their treatment, and specially the Romans, whom they stigmatise by the insulting name of *Opici*. "I forbid you, once for all, to have any dealings with physicians." Owing to their temperate and active life, the Romans had for more than five hundred years existed without a physician within their walls. Cato's hostility to the profession, therefore, if not justifiable, was at least natural. He subjoins a list of simples by which he kept himself and his wife alive and in health to a green old age. And observing that there are countless signs of death, and none of health, he gives the chief marks by which a man apparently in health may be noted as unsound. In another treatise, on farming, also dedicated to his son, for whom he entertained a warm affection, and over whose education he sedulously watched, he says,—"Buy not what you want, but what you must have; what you don't want is dear at a farthing, and what you lack borrow from yourself." Such is the homely wisdom which gained for Cato the proud title of *Sapiens,* by which, says Cicero, he was familiarly known. Other original works, the product of his vast experience, were the treatise on eloquence, of which the pith is the following: "Rem tene: verba sequentur;" "Take care of the sense: the sounds will

take care of themselves." We can well believe that this excellent maxim ruled his own conduct. The art of war formed the subject of another volume; in this, too, he had abundant and faithful experience. An attempt to investigate the principles of jurisprudence, which was carried out more fully by his son, and a short *carmen de moribus* or essay on conduct, completed the list of his paternal instructions. Why this was styled *carmen* is not known. Some think it was written in Saturnian verse, others that its concise and oracular formulas suggested the name, since *carmen* in old Latin is by no means confined to verse. It is from this that the account of the low estimation of poets in the early Republic is taken. Besides these regular treatises we hear of letters, and ἀποφθέγμᾶτᾶ, or pithy sayings, put together like those of Bacon from divers sources. In after times Cato's own apophthegms were collected for publication, and under the name of *Catonis dicta,* were much admired in the Middle Ages. We see that Cato's literary labours were encyclopædic. . . .

J. W. Mackail (essay date 1895)

SOURCE: J. W. Mackail, "Cato," in *Latin Literature*, Frederick Ungar Publishing Company, 1895, pp. 31-2.

[*In the following excerpt, Mackail praises Cato as "the founder" of Roman prose, while also describing his influence as "somewhat narrow and harsh." He briefly summarizes each of the major works.*]

In the history of the half-century following the war with Hannibal, Cato is certainly the most striking single figure. It is only as a man of letters that he has to be noticed here; and the character of a man of letters was, perhaps, the last in which he would have wished to be remembered or praised. Yet the cynical and indomitable old man, with his rough humour, his narrow statesmanship, his obstinate ultra-conservatism, not only produced a large quantity of writings, but founded and transmitted to posterity a distinct and important body of critical dogma and literary tradition. The influence of Greece had, as we have already seen, begun to permeate the educated classes at Rome through and through. Against this Greek influence, alike in literature and in manners, Cato struggled all his life with the whole force of his powerful intellect and mordant wit; yet it is most characteristic of the man that in his old age he learned Greek himself, and read deeply in the masterpieces of that Greek literature from which he was too honest and too intelligent to be able to withhold his admiration. While much of contemporary literature was launching itself on the fatal course of imitation of Greek models, and was forcing the Latin language into the trammels of alien forms, Cato gave it a powerful impulse towards a purely native, if a somewhat narrow and harsh development. The national prose literature, of which he may fairly be called the founder, was kept up till the decay of Rome by a large and powerful minority of Latin writers. What results it might have produced, if allowed unchecked scope, can only be matter for conjecture; in the main current of Latin literature the Greek influence was, on the whole, triumphant; Cato's was the losing side (if one may so adapt the famous line of Lucan), and the men of genius took the other.

The speeches of Cato, of which upwards of a hundred and fifty were extant in Cicero's time, and which the *virtuosi* of the age of Hadrian preferred, or professed to prefer, to Cicero's own, are lost, with the exception of inconsiderable fragments. The fragments show high oratorical gifts; shrewdness, humour, terse vigour and controlled passion; "somewhat confused and harsh," says a late but competent Latin critic, "but strong and vivid as it is possible for oratory to be." We have suffered a heavier loss in his seven books of **Origines,** the work of his old age. This may broadly be called an historical work, but it was history treated in a style of great latitude, the meagre, disconnected method of the annalists alternating with digressions into all kinds of subjects—geography, ethnography, reminiscences of his own travels and experiences, and the politics and social life of his own and earlier times. It made no attempt to keep up either the dignity or the continuity of history. His absence of method made this work, however full of interest, the despair of later historians: what were they to think, they plaintively asked, of an author who dismissed whole campaigns without even giving the names of the generals, while he went into profuse detail over one of the war-elephants in the Carthaginian army?

The only work of Cato's which has been preserved in its integrity is that variously known under the titles **De Re Rustica** or **De Agri Cultura**. It is one of a number of treatises of a severely didactic nature, which he published on various subjects—agricultural, sanitary, military, and legal. This treatise was primarily written for a friend who owned and cultivated farms in Campania. It consists of a series of terse and pointed directions following one on another, with no attempt at style or literary artifice, but full of a hard sagacity, and with occasional flashes of dry humour, which suggest that Cato would have found a not wholly uncongenial spirit in President Lincoln. . . .

William Davis Hooper (essay date 1935)

SOURCE: William Davis Hooper, in an introduction to *Marcus Porcius Cato on Agriculture, Marcus Terentius Varro on Agriculture,* translated by William Davis Hooper, Harvard University Press, 1935, pp. ix-xxii.

[*In the introduction, excerpted below, to his translation of Cato's* De agricultura, *Hooper provides a synopsis of the work and a brief sketch of Cato's biography.*]

Marcus Porcius Cato (234-149 B.C., known also as the Orator, the Censor, Cato Major, or the Elder, to distinguish him from his great-grandson Marcus Porcius Cato Uticensis, was born of an old plebeian family at Tusculum, an ancient town of Latium, within ten miles of Rome. His youth was spent on his father's farm near Reate, in the Sabine country. Here he acquired early in life those qualities of simplicity, frugality, strict honesty, austerity, and patriotism for which he was regarded by later generations as the embodiment of the old Roman virtues. His native ability and shrewdness, says Plutarch, gave him the surname Cato ("the shrewd") replacing the earlier name of Priscus. Love of the soil, implanted in him in his youth, remained throughout his life; though not content with the agricultural limitations of a Sabine farmer he became in later years the owner of great plantations worked by slave labour.

Entering upon a military career at the age of seventeen, Cato served with distinction in the Second Punic War, and devoted the following twenty-six years of his life to military affairs. He accompanied Tiberius Sempronius as his lieutenant in his expedition into Thrace. He went with Manius Achilius Glabrio into Greece against Antiochus the Great in 191, in the capacity of tribune. As commander of the Roman army in Hither Spain during his consulship he won many victories and was a successful ruler, but noted for his cruelty to his defeated enemies. Always active in the affairs of the state, he showed himself an obstinate and vigorous opponent of the nobility, of luxurious living, and of the invasion into Italy of Greek culture; though it is said that he himself was taught Greek late in life by the poet Ennius. Political offices came to him in due succession, a quaestorship in Sicily and Africa in 204, an aedileship in 199, a praetorship in Sardinia in 198, the consulship in 195 with Hither Spain as his province, and the censorship in 184. His innumerable speeches, political and judicial, delivered before the senate or popular assembly, were marked by eloquence, earnestness, and pungent wit, not without vainglory and narrowness of view. Always the champion of the common people, he stood out as the relentless foe of aristocratic factions. The vigour and severity with which he applied himself to the duties of the censorship, with his strict revision of the senatorial lists, gained for him the surname *Censorius*. Sent into Carthage on an official mission in 175, he conceived such hatred for the Carthaginians, upon noting their obvious recovery from the effects of the Punic wars, that from that time on he closed every speech in the senate with the words *delenda est Carthago,* regardless of the occasion. The words of Cato became the policy of the senate and in 149, the year of Cato's death, the Third Punic War began.

Quintilian speaks of the great versatility of Cato as general, philosopher, orator, historian, and outstanding expert in jurisprudence and agriculture. Cicero bears witness to the breadth of his learning and the variety of his writings. He is praised by Pliny as "the master of all good arts"; and is said by Columella to have been the first to teach Rome to speak Latin. In the field of literary composition, for which he affected contempt, Cato was prolific. He was the first Roman to write out and publish on a large scale his own speeches, of which Cicero professed to have known and read more than one hundred and fifty. He was the first Roman to leave to us prose writings of any consequence, and is regarded as the father of Latin prose as Ennius is the father of Latin poetry. He rebelled against the prevailing annalistic treatment of history as written to flatter the vanity of the nobles, and omitted the names of all such from his account of the Second Punic War, preferring rather to sing the praises of a certain Surus, bravest elephant of the Carthaginian army. He paved the way in the field of encyclopaedic learning so dear to the Romans, and was the first of a group of Roman writers on husbandry. Yet of the great bulk of his writings comparatively little has been preserved to us in anything like completeness. The speeches were familiar to Servius as late as the fourth century of our era, but are known to us only through scattered references and occasional quotations. The same fate has overtaken the seven books of *Origines,* a work begun in his old age, dealing with the ethnology, antiquities, and history of Italy from the founding of Rome down to the year 149, and deriving its title from its attempt to trace the origins of various Italian tribes. His greatest didactic work, an encyclopaedic handbook for his son, containing precepts on morals, sanitation, oratory, military science, agriculture, and other subjects, has perished, as has also a collection of aphorisms and witty sayings of others; what now passes under the name of *Catonis Disticha* is a collection of moral maxims in verse, perhaps spurious imitations of Cato, which circulated in the latter period of the Empire. The only work now surviving to represent Cato in its complete form is a miscellaneous collection of agricultural precepts which appear in the manuscripts under the name *De Agri Cultura,* and in the earlier printed editions as *De Re Rustica.*

The *De Agri Cultura* constitutes our earliest extant specimen of connected, if often loosely connected, Latin prose. The work, with its notable lack of systematic arrangement, can hardly pass as literature. It resembles rather a farmer's notebook in which the author had jotted down in random fashion all sorts of directions for the care of the farm, for his own private use or for the benefit of his friends and neighbours. Based on the writer's own first-hand experience and probably intended as a practical

manual on the subject of husbandry, it contains all sorts of authoritative directions for the farm overseer. The work in its present form has lost in great measure its archaic diction, but the spirit of the stern old Roman remains. In its haphazard arrangement and abrupt Catonian style, a style best characterized by Aulus Gellius as perhaps open to improvement in matters of clearness and fullness of expression, yet forceful and vigorous, it falls far short of the more finished work of Varro and the fluent, methodical treatise of Columella. So, too, it proved inadequate for the husbandmen of later generations; but Cato blazed the trail for his more eloquent successors in the field, and is often quoted by them as an authority. The work, despite its confused text, its difficulty of interpretation, and its problems still unsolved, is readable. Its greatest charm to-day lies in its severe simplicity, and its chief value in the picture which may be drawn from it of old Roman life in the best days of the Republic.

Moses Hadas (essay date 1952)

SOURCE: Moses Hadas, "Pre-Ciceronian Prose," in *A History of Latin Literature*, Columbia University Press, 1952, pp. 58-68.

[*In the following excerpt, Hadas stresses the importance of Cato's contribution to Roman historiography. In his discussion of Cato's career, however, Hadas attributes "more than a touch of demagoguery" to the orator's political and literary style.*]

In history as well as oratory Cato is a pioneer. Various priestly and other chronicles must have been kept from the earliest organization of the state, but it was only when Rome entered the main stream of Mediterranean history in the Second Punic War that awareness of self and of other peoples provided impulse to historiography of the Greek type. It was natural, in the absence of Latin models and with knowledge of Greek general in the selected audience whom the aristocratic early historians addressed, that the first works of this category should be written in Greek. But the nationalist note which characterizes all Roman historiography and constitutes its principal divergence from the Greek becomes apparent at once. Indeed, a collateral motive for the use of Greek was probably a desire to impress upon Greek readers the high dignity of the Roman state and the irresistible prowess of Roman arms. So Fabius Pictor, the earliest literary historian of Rome, is criticized by Polybius for his Roman bias, though Polybius respects him sufficiently to use him. He is also cited with respect by Livy and Dionysius of Halicarnassus. Fabius fought in the Second Punic War, and was a member of the embassy to Delphi after the disaster at Cannae. It was not only Rome that Fabius favored, but his own senatorial class, and the same was doubtless true of the other senatorial writers of Roman history in Greek—L. Cincius Alimentus, P.

Cornelius Scipio, A. Postumius Albinus, and C. Acilius. Cincius Alimentus also fought in the Second Punic War, and was captured by Hannibal in Sicily in 209 B.C. Scipio was the elder son of Scipio Africanus and adoptive father of the Africanus who destroyed Carthage. Postumius Albinus was consul in 151 B.C. Polybius and Cicero speak well of him, but Cato ridiculed his modest deprecation of his inadequate Greek: apology for awkward use of a language not one's own, said Cato, (Gellius 11.8.2), is appropriate only if a man had been compelled by the Amphictyons to write in that language. C. Acilius was interpreter for the three Greek philosophers who came to Rome as ambassadors in 155 B.C. Both his Roman and his senatorial bias are seen in the anecdote reported from him in Livy 35.14.5. In conversation with his conqueror Scipio, Hannibal rated the three greatest generals of the world, in order, as Alexander, Pyrrhus, and himself. When Scipio asked what Hannibal would have said if he had beaten him, Hannibal replied that he would then have put himself ahead of both Alexander and Pyrrhus. The reaction against these noble writers of Greek, and against the rising tide of Hellenism in general, was led by Cato, who is our earliest writer of Latin prose.

Marcus Porcius Cato, called "the Elder" or "the Censor" to distinguish him from his great-grandson Marcus Porcius Cato "of Utica," was born of an old plebeian family at Tusculum, about ten miles from Rome, in 234 B.C. He too fought in the Second Punic War, and thereafter in Thrace, in Greece, and in Spain. He was quaestor in Sicily and Africa in 204, aedile in 199, praetor in Sardinia in 198, consul in 195, and censor in 184. His strictness in the latter office gives "censorious" its connotation. In politics he was the leader of the opposition to the aristocratic group headed by the Scipios, and he defended his nationalist and "popular" position with ruthlessness, scathing wit, constant glorification of ancient Roman austerity and dignity, no little personal pride, and a measure of theatricality. A decree ordering the expulsion of Greek philosophers and rhetoricians from Rome in 161 B.C. testifies to the political strength of Cato's party. When, in 155 B.C., the Greeks sent to the senate an embassy composed of Carneades the Academic, Diogenes the Stoic, and Critolaus the Peripatetic, it was Cato who insisted that their business be dispatched at once, so that they should not linger in Rome to corrupt the youth. He insisted that Greek physicians were in a conspiracy to kill their Roman patients. When the question of releasing the thousand Achaean hostages (of whom Polybius was one) was brought up, Cato said it little suited the senate's dignity to debate whether Greek or Roman undertakers should bury the derelicts. He struck a senator from the roll for kissing his wife in broad daylight, and he left behind the horse that had carried him through his campaign in Spain because he refused to put Rome to the charge of transporting the animal. After a mission to Carthage in 157 he concluded his

every speech in the senate, regardless of the occasion, with *delenda est Carthago*. When he died in 149 B.C. he was already a legend.

Actually the conflict between Cato and his noble adversaries was not a struggle between liberal and conservative views, but rather a rivalry within conservative ranks, with rather more enlightenment on the side of the nobles. For all their philhellenism Scipio's friends too cherished Roman values, and they too were concerned over moral deterioration. Cato's assumed monopoly of morality, like his scorn of Hellenism, had more than a touch of demagoguery. But his eminent merits and his striking personality made him, in succeeding generations, the Jefferson or Jackson or Lincoln of his party. Pamphlets doubtless embellished his known proclivities to make political capital. Hence, though we have *Lives* of Cato by Nepos and Plutarch, as well as the *Cato Maior* of Cicero and numerous other characterizations, the total picture which emerges is something of a caricature. He cannot have been ignorant of Greek until he was an octogenarian, for we know that he negotiated with Greeks in his prime. Whether his hatred of Greek was genuine or a sham, Cato's sponsorship of Ennius, who did more than any other man to introduce Hellenism to Latin literature, is a wry joke on the leading opponent of Hellenism in Rome.

In any case it was not education that Cato opposed, but Greek education, and to supply the place of Greek treatises he wrote practical handbooks on all the subjects of the curriculum except philosophy. We know that he dealt with medicine, rhetoric, and agriculture, and it seems likely that he included military science and law also. Apparently these works were combined into a kind of encyclopedia, entitled *Ad filium.* When his son was still a child he wrote for him a history of Rome "in large letters" with his own hand, and when the boy grew older he dedicated to him these various treatises. All were imbued with Roman ideals and traditions; the fragments reveal an oracular manner. An orator is *vir bonus dicendi peritus,* "a good man skilled in speech"; and in rhetoric the main principle is *Rem tene, verba sequentur,* "Hold fast to the matter, the words will come." Gellius (11.2) also ascribes to Cato a *Carmen de moribus,* from which he cites characteristic moralizing saws, but in prose.

Besides the encyclopedia for his son Cato also wrote independent treatises on various subjects. The surviving *De agricultura* or *De re rustica* is the oldest extant prose work in Latin; the language of his treatise underwent modernization in antiquity, but the tone remains authentically archaic. Beginning with a statement of the advantages of agriculture over commerce and banking, Cato proceeds to describe the best location for a farm, the duties of the owner and of his steward, and various principles of farm management. Interspersed with instructions on farm economy are prescriptions for medicaments, recipes for cooking, religious formulae, and other matters. The disorder of the book is further confused by interpolations and repetitions. Throughout the tone is a hard and cheerless drive for profit; there is nothing about the compensations of the rural life, nothing of the joys of living and cooperating with nature, or of sentimental attachment between master and slaves and livestock. "Sell worn-out oxen, blemished cattle, blemished sheep, wool, hides, an old wagon, old tools, an old slave, a sickly slave, and whatever else is superfluous. The master should have the selling habit, not the buying habit" (2.7). "The overseer must lend to no one seed grain, fodder, spelt, wine, or oil. He must have two or three households, no more, from whom he borrows and to whom he lends" (5.3). "When you issue the tunic or blanket [every second year] first take up the old one and have patchwork made of it" (59). We are told where equipment of various sorts may be bought, and the proper prices: "Lucius Tunnius of Casinum and Gaius Mennius, son of Lucius Mennius of Venafrum, make the best press ropes" (135.3). The recipes seem generous enough; the veterinary medicine has a strong admixture of superstition. "Both the sick ox and he who administers the [prescribed] medicine must stand, and both be fasting" (71). For mending a dislocated limb the split reeds to serve as splints must be joined to the accompaniment of a chant: *Motas uaeta daries dardares astataries dissunapiter;* and after they are applied the officiant must duly pronounce the charm: *Huat haut haut istasis tarsis ordannabou dannaustra* (160).

But the proper vehicle for communicating the gospel of Rome was history; and the fact that Roman history had already been written by senatorial historians and in Greek made it inevitable that Cato should turn his hand to the history. Nepos (*Cato* 3.3) tells us:

> When he was an old man Cato began to write history, of which he left seven books. The first contains an account of the kings of the Roman people; the second and the third, the origin of all the states of Italy—and this seems the reason he called the whole *Origines*. Then in the fourth book we have the first Punic war, and in the fifth the second. All this is told in summary fashion, and he treated the other wars in the same manner down to the praetorship of Servius Galba, who plundered the Lusitanians. In his account of all these wars he did not name the leaders, but related the events without mentioning names. In the same work he gave an account of the noteworthy occurrences and sights in Italy and the Spains; and in it he showed great industry and carefulness, but no learning.
>
> —*J. C. Rolfe*

The latter four books seem to have been joined on to the first three after Cato's death and the title *Origines* then applied to the whole.

But it was in his speeches that Cato gave fullest expression to his national Roman program and most effectively influenced the course of Roman literature. He spoke his mind vigorously on every political issue, and participated in numerous judicial trials; Cicero (*Brutus* 17.65) knew a hundred and fifty speeches of Cato, and the titles of some eighty have come down. Ancient critics find fault with his roughness, but all admit his torrential vigor. Many terse apophthegms drawn from his speeches testify to his scathing wit and his gift for epigram. One specimen must suffice: "Thieves who steal from individuals spend their lives in prison and chains; thieves who steal from the commonweal, in purple and gold." Cicero and Plutarch refer to Cato's letters to his son Marcus; perhaps letters addressed to others were also collected. Ennius had pioneered in various forms of verse and endowed each with a distinctive Roman color; Cato pioneered in various forms of prose, and his Roman coloring was much more vivid. In subsequent Latin prose the Roman note regularly rings clearer than in poetry.

Tore Janson (essay date 1964)

SOURCE: Tore Janson, "Agricultural Handbooks," in *Latin Prose Prefaces: Studies in Literary Conventions*, Almqvist & Wiksell, 1964, pp. 83-94.

[*In the excerpt that follows, Janson examines the rhetorical structure of Cato's preface to the* De agricultura. *Its sentence structure, Janson argues, reveals a social and economic purpose at odds with the professed moral purpose of the work.*]

The entire preface to Cato's book on agriculture is devoted to a comparison between different ways of earning a living, with on the one hand agriculture and on the other trade and banking.[1] The disposition of this brief preface requires some clarification.[2] In his first sentence Cato states that trade and banking could be (economically) preferable (to agriculture), were it not for their riskiness and dishonesty respectively. The plan of the rest of the preface is clearly to deal first with banking, then with trade and finally with agriculture. The second sentence obviously approves the custom of "our ancestors" of condemning a thief to double fine, a *fenerator* to quadruple. After this discouraging dismissal of the banking world, the writer does not continue at once with the merchant but—since he has now mentioned the Romans of old—takes the opportunity of describing their attitude to agriculture in a passage that is worth quoting:

> (Cato *Agr.* pref. 2) Et uirum bonum quom laudabant, ita laudabant, bonum agricolam bonumque colonum. Amplissime laudari existimabatur qui ita laudabatur.

Then follows a sentence on merchants, paying tribute to their energy but summing up their occupation with a repetition of what has already been said of its risks. Finally comes the writer's own assessment of agriculture:

> (*Agr*. pref. 4) At ex agricolis et uiri fortissimi et milites strenuissimi gignuntur, maximeque pius quaestus stabilissimusque consequitur minimeque inuidiosus, minimeque male cogitantes sunt qui in eo studio occupati sunt.

The preface then concludes with a brief transitional phrase.

In this preface are interwoven two different types of argument in favour of agriculture, the ethical and the economic. In order to clarify Cato's manner of argument we must distinguish as far as possible between them.

The ethical argument aims to show that the farming life is morally better than any other. Two lines of thought are presented. The first comprises a reference to the view of the Romans of old. In a society as enormously bound by tradition as that of the Republic it was of the greatest importance to be able to quote the opinions of the men of old. Cato himself was also a traditionalist of the purest water. Emotionally, he knew of nothing more strongly attractive than what he felt to be a heritage from the early Romans.

The other moral argument is of a more practical nature. From the farming class come the bravest men and the best soldiers, and persons in this occupation are the most upright (*minime male cogitantes*).

These two arguments are naturally interrelated. In Cato's view, the reason why the Romans of old valued the life of the farmer so highly was above all its beneficent effect on the character (even if he does not expressly say this). Cato follows the ideology of the old Italian farming class. His ideal was the type probably represented by his own father,[3] farmers who looked after their estates, took part in war and were active in political life.[4]

If we confront these views on the merits of the agricultural life with the reality that is reflected in the work that follows,[5] the result is somewhat surprising. In fact, there is no place at all for a farmer on the sort of holding that is described. Cato rather describes a small estate, looked after by a *uilicus,* a steward. The owner himself is not assumed to live on the estate for more than brief periods.[6] It is hard to conceive how this occasional visitor could be fostered by country life to be *fortis* or *strenuus*. Even more difficult, however, would it be to conceive Cato as meaning that it was the persons living on the farm, the *uilicus* and his subordinates, who were blessed with these outstanding qualities. Cato's entire view of life is patriarchal. There is no doubt but that he regarded people of his own

social class as in all respects the most important, and that it was them he was addressing in his work. It is hardly reasonable to suppose that he would have consciously portrayed these people as morally inferior to their subordinates.

One is also struck by the type of farm Cato chooses to describe. Its most important products by far are wine and olives.[7] In the very detailed descriptions of the staff and equipment needed for the olive grove and vineyard[8] he departs from the idea of a farm of 100 *iugera* and a varied production as hinted in the first chapters, and assumes instead exclusive cultivations of olives on 240 *iugera* and wine on 100 *iugera*.[9] These cultivations are conceived as equipped with presses of what—to judge from the exhaustiveness of the description—must have been a quite unusual size and kind.[10] This is a far cry from the type of farm we can imagine as run by a *bonus agricola bonusque colonus* of the old Italian farmer class. What would he have done with such quantities of wine and oil? He could never have disposed of them either to his neighbours or in the market.[11]

The reality portrayed in Cato's book thus chimes very badly with the moral argument presented in the preface. On the other hand it fits the economic arguments very well indeed. The picture of Cato and his environment that emerges when we study the introduction from this aspect is most interesting.

Cato is concerned to show that from agriculture there comes *maxime pius quaestus stabilissimusque,* as compared with trade and banking. He ought therefore, in all reason, to be writing for people who had some possibility of choosing between these different forms of livelihood. To carry out the dangerous trading activities that Cato envisaged it would be necessary to live in a port. Both merchants and moneylenders must obviously have abundant access to cash. The circle for whom Cato was writing and to which he himself belonged[12] was thus in a situation as unlike as possible that of the resident farmer. They were capitalists in a Rome that had already started to develop into a commercial metropolis of Hellenistic type, with a good flow of capital and markets for large volumes of desirable products. The majority of these men were without doubt landowners by inheritance, if not by purchase, but their interest in land was not that of the farmer, only that of the owner.

The two lines of argument interwoven in Cato's preface thus have no real connexion in fact. Cato's moral arguments presuppose conditions that no longer existed—at least not in the type of agriculture with which Cato was concerned. This is not to say that they were meaningless. They are presented in the preface to assure to agriculture the high renown accorded by the traditional Roman standards. The ancestors—the old

Roman farmers—are mobilized as revered ghosts to give prestige to an economic investment. The economic arguments, on the other hand, are aimed to recommend a realistic and so far as we can judge advantageous form of financial investment.[13] Such arguments should have aroused the interest of the persons at whom they were directed.[14]

Notes

[1] As Klingner (*Cato Censorius* [1934] p. 254) has pointed out, Cato most certainly took the actual idea of writing a preface with this type of content from the Greeks.

[2] Leeman analyses this preface in *Orationis Ratio* [1963] pp. 22 f. He there points out a fact of great importance, namely that the division of the arguments for agriculture into one line concerning its freedom from *periculum* and another concerning its *honestas* has its background in rhetorical theory. For in the *genus deliberatiuum* the arguments for the usefulness of something are divided thus: *Vtilitas in duas partes in ciuili consultatione diuiditur: tutam, honestam (Rhet. Her.* 3.2.3). This has no direct bearing on Cato's factual reasons for the composition of the preface, which is what I treat here, but is extremely interesting as a proof of rhetorical influence in an author where one would least expect it.

[3] See Klingner, *Cato Censorius* pp. 243 f.

[4] Cf. Frank [*Rome and Italy of the Republic,* 1933] p. 162.

[5] Frank gives a survey of the conditions of agricultural economics implied by Cato's work (pp. 160-172) with a wealth of quotations but unfortunately few comments.

[6] See Chap. 2.1. In Chap. 4 the owner is urged to build himself a good *uilla urbana* on his estate, to entice him there more often.

[7] See in particular Chap. 1.7, though Cato reverts to the cultivation of these two products throughout the entire book.

[8] Chaps. 10 and 11 respectively.

[9] It is beyond my competence to judge how far this and many other inconsistencies in the construction of the book can be explained by the hypothesis put forward by Hörle. This scholar maintains that the book preserved is a compilation of a number of smaller works, originally entirely independent of each other, with short sections inserted in between.

[10] Chaps. 12-13, 18-22.

[11] Frank pp. 171 f.: "Cato's book shows the beginnings of specialized farming with slave gangs on a relatively large scale."

[12] A wealth of literature is available on Cato's personality, social position and political convictions. Consideration has been paid in the present study above all to Klingner and Kienast [*Cato der Zensor,* 1953] who represent largely opposing views. The former sees Cato above all as a farmer's son from the land of the Sabines, a champion of the farming population of Italy and the sworn enemy of the senatorial aristocracy. The latter regards him as an upstart who had quickly allied himself to the ruling class and become the central figure in the majority side of the senatorial aristocracy, in opposition only to the few leading families, the Scipios and others. The plentiful but often contradictory sources permit both interpretations (and perhaps others). The picture gained from the book on agriculture fits Kienast's view rather than Klingner's. Naturally, however, it is impossible to assume without further argument a direct connexion between Cato's political activities—which is what Kienast is primarily discussing—and his private financial position and transactions. Politically it is perfectly possible for a capitalist in Rome to have represented the Italian farming population. It is clear enough, on the other hand, that it is the economist and capitalist who is speaking in the work under discussion here.

[13] See the calculations on the profitability of the olive plantation put forward by Frank, p. 171.

[14] It should be noted how Cato has selected the forms of livelihood to be contrasted with agriculture. Moneylending and its shamefulness provide an effective foil to agricultural *pietas* in the moral argument. The dangers of being a merchant are set off against the security of the farm in the economic argument. Plutarch postulates in fact that Cato devoted himself to both trade and usury. His source is probably a pamphlet aimed against Cato (see Kienast p. 24) and this information should therefore perhaps be viewed with greater scepticism than is shown by Klingner (p. 256) and Kienast (pp. 35 f.).

H. H. Scullard (essay date 1973)

SOURCE: H. H. Scullard, "Cato's Censorship," in *Roman Politics: 220-150 B.C.*, Oxford at the Clarendon Press, 1973, pp. 153-64.

[*In the excerpt that follows, Scullard explains Cato's position in Roman politics, describing both his historical influence and the bureaucratic context in which a censor functioned.*]

Cato's censorship is remarkable less for any positive reforms than for the spirit in which it was conducted and the impression which it made upon Roman tradition. Censors had more arbitrary and personal influence than other regular magistrates, because they did not have to account for their acts;[1] since they were not appointed strictly to administer the law,[2] they had far greater latitude than, for instance, praetors, who were limited by the *edictum perpetuum*. On entering office immediately after the elections, normally held in April, they held a *contio* in the Campus Martius preparatory to the *census* proper, or registration of the citizens. Here they announced the moral principles by which they proposed to exercise their *censoria potestas,* explained any novelties which they intended to introduce into their edict, and remarked on any new evils which they thought might be endangering the state.[3] They then published in the form of a written edict the chief arrangements for the census.

Their main administrative duties were the assessment of the property of citizens and the assignment of them to their proper tribes, classes, and centuries; the revision of the lists of senators and knights, which involved an estimation of the moral fitness of individuals to exercise their functions in the State (*regimen morum*); leasing the public revenues and maintaining public property; and a final purification (*lustrum*) of the People. It is not generally possible to trace the precise order in which they performed their tasks, many of which might be tackled concurrently, but after their preliminary proclamation of policy the *lectio Senatus* would be among their first duties.

From one aspect Cato's censorship was a landmark in Rome's history: it epitomized the clash between the old and the new. Cato stands forth as the representative of the older type of Roman, of that solid core of countrymen who had defeated Hannibal. Cautious, shrewd, hard-headed and hard-hearted, unimaginative and unadaptable, endowed with excessive respect for the more rigid ancestral qualities of the Roman People, distrustful of Greek influences although not so ignorant of them as tradition sometimes suggests, Cato championed the last real attempt of the old-fashioned Romans to re-establish a more austere manner of life in face of the social and moral decline which was resulting from Rome's expansion in the Mediterranean world and her contacts with the East. He wished his censorship to accomplish a real purification of the people, not merely a ritual *lustrum*. Hence, unlike his predecessors, he acted harshly, and the natural result was much bitterness: 'nobilis censura fuit simultatiumque plena'.[4]

Cato wished to restrain all elements in Roman life, the Senate, Equites, and People, the Latins and Italians, and to keep them within the traditional mould which history had hitherto prescribed for them. His ideal was not ignoble and the example which he set in his private life might appeal to some, but the result was bound to be failure: he could neither stop, still less put back, the clock, nor by a few legislative measures and personal example induce widespread moral regeneration. True, he was no fool, although in face of the suave Hellenized nobles the *novus homo* aggressively played the part of a countryman, thereby gaining self-confidence and at the same time partly hiding his wide knowledge and interests, but he was more concerned with symptoms than causes and failed to get to grips with the vital problems of the day. Only by a thoroughgoing programme of reform, based on a keen appreciation of the fundamental needs of Rome and Italy, could the senatorial government and the Republic itself be saved from ultimate destruction. Rome was entering upon a new epoch; much hard thinking and unselfish action were required to effect a healthy union between the institutions and traditions of the past and the wider demands of the present. Cato might point to some of the needs, but his reactionary attitude towards others involved his ultimate failure to redeem Roman society.

Grounds there certainly were for his severity, to which point was given by the recent Bacchanalian Conspiracy. Although Livy has drawn a lurid picture of the crime, immorality, and disorder which attended it, he has merely heightened the colours; in sober fact, the public conscience was severely shocked and the Senate regarded the movement as a challenge to law and order which threatened the government. The realization that the worshippers were organized in secret societies, that the movement arose among slaves and freedmen and spread among the plantations and ranches that were springing up in Etruria, Campania, and Apulia, that the cult itself derived from Greece, and that its mystical rites were highly suspect—such factors even apart from the public disorders which the conspiracy evoked would be sufficient to render it a public menace in the estimation of many Romans besides Cato. But despite the prompt and sensible counter-measures, which avoided persecuting the cult as such and the consequent risk of creating a body of religious martyrs, the evil was not eradicated in 186, since renewed inquiries had to be undertaken until 181.

Other symptoms of public unrest were a widespread conspiracy of slave herdsmen in Apulia, where they took to brigandage on a considerable scale in 185, and cases of poisoning in 184 and 180 which demanded investigation.[5] Even the army had on occasion shown discontent at its terms of service, and lack of discipline resulted. There had been a mutiny in Greece in 198 and insubordination in 190, while even Cato had difficulty with his cavalry in Spain in 195; the complaints of the soldiers were supported by the tribunes in 193;

Vulso had to bribe his troops by granting donations and relaxing discipline in 189; there was discontent in the Spanish army in 184.[6] Even more urgent, because it was ever flaunting itself in the capital, was the problem of luxury and personal display which increased rapidly as a result of the Eastern wars.

To such questions Cato devoted his attention, doubtless hoping that if he could restore a more austere manner of life other problems would settle themselves. But the need to adjust the constitution to new claims, to infuse fresh blood and ideals in the Senate, to define the political activities of the business classes, to awaken the People to their political responsibilities, to modify relations with the Latins and Italians, to face the economic upheavals caused by the influx of capital and slave labour, to shape a comprehensive foreign policy which should balance the claims of East and West, of Rome and the provinces, such problems were either neglected or tackled half-heartedly. The senatorial nobility was entering upon an era of tolerably efficient government, but was blind to the needs of the future or too selfish to try to envisage them. Some sought reform by reaction, others by greater liberalism, but a political genius who could analyse all the needs of his day, formulate practical solutions, and win sufficient moral backing to carry them through did not arise until the body of the Roman Republic had become too rotten to be revivified. Cato, like his great rival Scipio, could not justly claim the title of statesman, but at least he tried to re-establish that widespread sense of duty and moral responsibility which was the prerequisite of any far-reaching reforms. Unfortunately for Rome he looked backwards rather than forwards.

The new measures which Cato proposed to take against luxury were outlined at the preliminary *contio*. As consul he had vainly opposed the repeal of the lex Oppia; as censor he intended to answer this repeal by edict. He imposed a tax, equivalent to at least 3 per cent., on ornaments, women's clothing, certain vehicles, and luxury slaves,[7] and he indignantly told the People, perhaps on this occasion, that no better proof could be shown of the degeneracy of the State than that good-looking slaves should cost more than a farm, or a jar of pickled fish more than a carter.[8] Statues and other *objets d'art,* a by-product of Rome's Eastern conquests, were also made liable to a luxury tax.[8a] In denouncing these Cato probably took the opportunity to condemn the increasing practice of erecting public statues to famous men, and even to Roman ladies in the provinces, presumably that is to the wives of provincial governors.[9] His denunciation was doubtless sharpened by his hatred of the increasing importance of women in public life; and the man who suppressed the names of outstanding generals in his *Origines* would hardly welcome the individual glory which men sought by the erection of statues. He used to boast that 'his own image was borne about in the hearts of his fellow-

citizens', and that he would prefer that men should ask why he had no statue, rather than why he had one. He changed his tune, however, when the people erected a statue in honour of his censorship in the temple of Health, with an inscription which recorded, not his military commands or his triumph, but that when the Roman State was tottering he was made censor and by helpful guidance, wise restraints, and sound teachings restored it once again.[9a]

Another form of self-display was for soldiers to place their war-spoils in the most conspicuous places in their houses.[10] Some might go farther and exhibit trophies which they had obtained by other less honest means, since the possession of such spoils, genuine or fictitious, had a certain political as well as social value: Buteo in 216 had added to the Senate some 'qui spolia ex hoste fixa domi haberent'.[10a] In a speech *Ne spolia figerentur nisi de hoste capta* Cato probably denounced the abuse of this practice and may have suggested that some generals did not stop despoiling their opponents as soon as peace was made.[11]

In revising the list of the Senate Cato did not at first have to appoint a new *princeps senatus*: Scipio Africanus did not suffer the final indignity of having his name struck off the list. After his death, however, early in 183, Cato placed his friend and colleague, Valerius Flaccus, at the head of the list. It had been customary to appoint the senior surviving patrician ex-censor, but this procedure had been set aside in 209 in favour of Fabius (p. 70) and Scipio himself had become *princeps senatus* when still well under 40; seniority had yielded to outstanding merit and service to the State. Now Cato disregarded the claims of Cornelius Cethegus, censor of 194 (if, as is probable, he was still living: the latest reference to him is in 193), and of T. Flamininus, the patrician censor of 189, who had both seniority and service to commend him, in order to honour Flaccus.

Before this, however, in 184 Cato had conducted the ordinary *lectio senatus* with exceptional severity: he expelled seven men including a consular and at least one praetorian. This action appeared unduly harsh partly by contrast with his predecessors' greater leniency, but more because only junior members normally were expelled.[12] The consular was L. Quinctius Flamininus, brother of the victor of Cynoscephalae, who during his campaign against the Boii in 192 had got drunk at a banquet and, in order to please a favourite Carthaginian boy, with his own hand had cut down a Boian noble who had come with his children to seek Roman protection.[13] Hitherto he had avoided punishment because the crime had been committed within the sphere of his military authority (*militiae*) and against an enemy (*hostis*), but he did not escape the moral condemnation of Cato who was often aroused by acts of cruelty or oppression against Rome's allies or subjects.

Censorial procedure was to place a mark (*nota*) in the register against the name of anyone considered unworthy. The reason need not be communicated to the man himself or be given when the revised list of the Senate was read aloud to the People from the Rostrum, although it was usually stated in the document which the censors deposited in the archives (*subscriptio censoria*). Thus a censor could act solely on the basis of his arbitrary power, and the first knowledge that Flamininus may have received of his disgrace would be when he heard the revised list being read aloud (*recitatio*). But men as influential as the Flaminini could seek an explanation in the *contio* by appealing to public opinion; this they did.[14] Cato replied by delivering a damning speech in which he must have castigated Flamininus' neglect of the *mos maiorum* and the *fides populi Romani,* and pointed to the demoralizing effects of Greek standards of sexual morality and to the conditions prevailing in the military quarters of the generals of the nobility. Cato then challenged him, if he denied the charges, to a formal trial with monetary securities (*sponsio*), but Flamininus remained silent and Cato won a striking moral and political victory. Titus Flamininus, whose relations with his brother were very close,[15] would be involved in the disgrace. Thus Cato avenged his defeat by Titus at the censorial elections of 189, exposed the moral weakness of some of the Hellenizing nobles, and later was able to pass over the superior claims of Titus and appoint his own colleague, Valerius Flaccus, as *princeps senatus.*

Cato also expelled from the Senate a certain Manilius (or Manlius) who had good prospects for the consulship, because, it is said, he kissed his own wife in the presence of his daughter![16] If this anecdote, which at any rate illustrates Cato's rigidly doctrinaire outlook, is to be regarded with any seriousness, the offence must have lain in so acting in front of a child. Cato had high ideals of a father's duties: he himself taught his son to read because he thought that the child should not be indebted to a slave for such a priceless thing as education, while he declared that his son's presence put him on guard against indecencies of speech.[17]

The censors then had to review the knights.[18] The nucleus of the equestrian order comprised 1,800 cavalrymen aged 18 to 45 (*equites equo publico*), enrolled in 18 centuries; men over 45 with the necessary property qualifications could remain knights though not for active service, while another group consisted of men under 45 who provided their own horses. Before the time of the Gracchi senators appear to have retained their public horse and their privileged position in the 18 centuries; even after this period sons of senators continued to be enrolled among the junior *equites* until they became magistrates and senators or until they reached the age of 45. The censors reviewed the *equites equo publico* in the Forum, where the whole corps filed past, each man leading his horse by the bridle

when his name was called by a herald. The censor then either passed ('traduc equum') or discharged him ('vende equum'). Discharge was either *sine ignominia* or an act of censure. In the former case the reason would be the completion of the normal period of service, in the latter some moral weakness in the knight's character or failure to look after his horse properly. As a penalty the censors could impose a further period of service on the knight at his own expense.[19] They also had to fill up any gaps in the centuries.

Cato began with an astonishing example: he expelled L. Cornelius Scipio Asiaticus.[20] Lucius may have been over 45 and perhaps not fit for cavalry service, and Cato may have wished to abolish the practice of allowing ageing senators to retain their horses, but the fact that Cato started with his old political rival was scandalous. True, the discharge was not marked by *ignominia,* as Asiaticus was not expelled from the Senate also, but this was a public insult, which would not strengthen the idea that Cato's reforming zeal in the interests of a sound body of cavalry was entirely disinterested. Cato's second victim, expelled with *ignominia,* was a certain L. Veturius, perhaps the son of the consul of 206 and a member of a family which was friendly with the Scipionic group. Two reasons were given: first, that Veturius had neglected some private religious rites of his *gens,* and secondly, that he was too fat for cavalry service.[21]

Cato, however, was genuinely concerned about the cavalry. He had seen how in the Hannibalic War Rome had suffered defeats through its inefficiency and insufficiency and how this defect had been remedied less by using Roman resources than by reliance upon allied cavalry; then as consul in Spain he had to face a panic among his own cavalry. He probably wished to see the *equites* become an effective body of cavalrymen instead of a privileged aristocratic corps of young noblemen: hence his attempt to weed out the physically and morally unfit. Further, he proposed to raise the number of equestrian centuries and in a speech to the Senate urged an increase from 1,800 to 2,200 men.[22] But here he challenged the vested interests of the nobility, who for voting purposes were mainly enrolled in the 18 centuries. They were unwilling to share their privileges with others and no doubt thought that if the number of *equites* attached to the legions needed to be increased this could be done by drawing on the men who possessed the equestrian census but not the *equus publicus;* by this means they would safeguard their class interests and save the State from the burden of providing horses and upkeep for a greater number. Thus Cato failed in his attempt to increase the number and fighting efficiency of the Roman cavalry—and to increase his own political influence, since as censor he would have been responsible for selecting and enrolling the new *equites* who would then have been in his debt.

The censors performed some other tasks which in origin were not an integral part of the census and in the exercise of which they were more subject to supervision by the Senate or People. These comprised financial duties, such as leasing taxes and contracts for *opera publica,* the upkeep of public property, and the administrative jurisdiction which these tasks involved.[23] In arranging State-contracts the censors had wide discretionary powers, but when once the contracts had been fixed any revision could be granted only by the Senate. Although these more material activities were supplementary to the moral work of the censors, Cato carried them out in the same rigid spirit.

Finding evidence of abuse and speculation in connexion with the public water-supply, Cato cut off the pipes by which people drew water from the State aqueducts for use in their private houses, gardens, or fields.[24] Tapping the public supply presumably was illegal or at any rate subject to payment.[25] To drive home the lesson Cato delivered a public speech in which he apparently charged a certain L. Furius with having bought up badly irrigated fields cheaply and using the public water-supply to increase their fertility and value; Cato further explained his views on the *regimen aquarum* and the responsibility of the officials involved. This Furius may have been Purpureo, the consul of 196 and Cato's competitor for the censorship, but even if he was only a lesser member of his *gens,* Cato would be glad to find a victim in the ranks of a family associated with the Scipios.[26]

Another abuse which stimulated Cato's reforming zeal was the erection of private buildings up against public buildings or on public ground: these had to be demolished within thirty days.[27] Public opinion must normally have tolerated this misuse of public land, since men would hardly have invested capital in such buildings unless they had a sanguine hope that they would remain undisturbed. He also perhaps cleared away some private buildings that were encroaching on some shrines,[28] and removed some statues from public ground.

The victims of Cato's measures probably were offered help by a tribune M. Caelius who threatened to use his veto. This was legally possible because in the exercise of their duties relating to *opera publica* (which could in fact have been carried out by any of the higher magistrates) censors were subject to possible supervision; consuls, whose *potestas* was less than the censors', could not intervene, but tribunes could. Cato replied to this threat by delivering a speech against Caelius in which he soundly trounced him as a babbling clown and a corrupt tribune. Caelius did not press his point, but probably returned to the attack later.

Cato's handling of the public contracts (*censorum locationes*) provoked further discontent. The censors may have started by issuing an edict which excluded some unreliable contractors from undertaking any new contracts.[29] This is suggested by the fragment of a speech of Cato against a certain Oppius, who had undertaken to supply wine for the public sacrifices, presumably under a contract granted by the censors of the previous *lustrum*.[30] Oppius had put down only a small guarantee, and perhaps as the result of a bad harvest and high prices he preferred to forfeit his deposit rather than to continue to supply wine at a loss. Cato appears to have excluded him from seeking any further contracts and probably developed his own views on the responsibilities of private contractors towards the State. After this warning the censors farmed the taxes to the highest bidders, and let out the contracts to those offering the lowest tenders.[31] The capitalists were annoyed and began to agitate. This was feasible because although the censors allocated the contracts, the Senate had considerable control over their subsequent working.[32] Censors imbued with a good senatorial outlook doubtless had some regard for vested interests, and Cato's neglect of these in an effort to strike a hard bargain for the benefit of the State caused much dissatisfaction. This was voiced in the Senate by Titus Flamininus, who seized the chance to attack the man who had expelled his brother from the Senate.[33] The violent discussion which followed was probably the occasion of Cato's delivering a speech in which besides defending his action he explained his ideas of duty in a State where prosperity had led to laxity of administration. He was, however, overruled by the Senate which, yielding to financial interests, annulled his arrangements and ordered the contracts to be relet.[34] Cato answered the Senate's decree with an edict which forbade those contractors who had treated the earlier contracts with contempt to make new bids.[35] With his colleague he then signed fresh contracts for everything on slightly easier terms. The Senate had asserted its authority, but Cato yielded more in the letter than spirit.

Flamininus and his supporters pressed home their advantage by inciting some tribunes to call Cato to account before the People and fine him two talents.[36] The precise ground of accusation is unknown, but it probably arose from his previous quarrel with the tribune Caelius, who may now have joined in the attack. The trial must have been stopped by the veto of another tribune, since it is unlikely that the Senate intervened, as it did in 204; Cato at any rate was not condemned.

The building programme of Cato and Valerius Flaccus was conceived on generous lines. Censors received a fixed grant from the Senate for the preservation and construction of public buildings; the amount would be determined after their plans had been discussed by the Senate. Cato's proposal to construct a basilica in the Forum provoked some opposition, but he got his way, and the Basilica Porcia was built, perhaps the first basilica to be constructed in Rome.[37] That Cato, the anti-Hellenist, should instigate the erection of a building that was Greek in name and form may seem strange, but he must have seen in south Italy and Greece how much more useful a covered building was than an open forum for the transaction of business. While the Hellenized Roman nobility might indulge their individual and self-advertising tastes by constructing luxurious private buildings in Hellenistic style, Cato followed a good Roman tradition by erecting a building for public utility. Further, it was probably built not in the new Hellenistic manner with stone architraves and ornamental stucco friezes but in the old Tuscan style with timber architraves covered with terra-cotta revetments like most of Rome's ancient and venerated temples.

But the censors' greatest constructional work was even more useful and at the same time more typically Roman: the overhauling of Rome's sewage system.[38] The details were probably keenly debated in the Senate where Cato justified his policy.[39] The scale of this work has not perhaps been adequately emphasized by Livy, who regarded the Tarquins as the chief architects of Rome's drainage system, but it becomes clear, if we accept the almost contemporary evidence of the annalist Acilius, that the censors spent 1,000 talents (6,000,000 *denarii*) upon it.[40] This is a staggering sum (the annual war indemnity from Carthage was only 200 talents, that from Antiochus 1,000) and is seen in its right proportion when contrasted either with the expenditure of the censors in a more normal year (e.g. in 179 B.C. the total building programme was probably under 500,000 *denarii*) or with the cost of the Basilica Porcia (a single item among the censors' contracts) which may be put at some 25,000 *denarii*.[41] If the figure of six million *denarii* is correct, Cato's scheme must have been much more thorough than is elsewhere suggested. No doubt most of Rome's open drainage channels, some of which dated from the regal period, were covered in and the whole system was widely extended. Well might the Roman People erect a statue in Cato's honour in the temple of Health: while attempting to restore their moral health, he promoted their physical well-being by his insistence upon sanitation.[42]

The completion of a censorship was marked by a formal purification of the people (*lustratio*), more probably when the censors went out of office than when the strict *census* had been completed. An ox, sheep, and pig (*suovetaurilia*) were led around and then sacrificed on behalf of the whole assembled army in the Campus Martius. Although there is no evidence that censors made a formal speech on such occasions, Cato delivered a speech *De lustri sui felicitate*.[43] This fact and the discontent that his censorship had aroused render it probable that someone challenged the *felicitas* and validity of his *lustrum,* and that he vindicated his

actions in this speech.[44] The attack may well have been launched by L. Minucius Thermus, who was probably a son of the consul of 193 who had been one of Cato's victims in 190; he will have welcomed the chance to criticize the administration of his father's opponent.[45] In his defence Cato enlarged upon his Spartan youth, military service, diplomatic activity, perseverance, and self-abnegation.[46] Such a catalogue of the more austere Roman virtues might well come from a speech in which he expatiated on the *felicitas* of his censorship.

Such, then, was the range of Cato's activities.[47] A censor who spent more than six million *denarii* on public works cannot be said to have accomplished nothing, but in relation to the problems of the day Cato's work was disappointing. His attempt to enforce a programme of moral rearmament by legislation and personal example was too rigidly conceived and too narrowly based. The Romans of his day were not the Romans of the Pyrrhic War, nor were their problems identical: not all Cato's moral forcefulness and wishful thinking could bring back the past. Although he may have deliberately exaggerated his anti-Hellenic attitude, partly as the shield of a *novus homo* against the darts of a proud nobility in an attempt to show that the outsider was a truer Roman than the nobles themselves, yet it must be admitted that the general trend of his policy was too reactionary and that the real value of his censorship lay less in what he accomplished than in the impression which it made upon later generations: in Cato they saw the true nature of the Roman censorship, *sanctissimus magistratus.*

Notes

[1] Dion. Hal. xix. 16: ἀρχὴ ἀνυπεύθυνος. Cf. Varro, *LL,* v. 81. This immunity from control is attested in a senatorial decree of 204 B.C. (L. xxix. 37. 17; Val. Max. vii. 2. 6).

[2] Cf. Varro, *LL,* vi. 71: 'quod tum et praetorium ius ad legem et censorium iudicium ad aequum existimabatur.'

[3] On this aspect of their activity see E. Schmähling, *Die Sittenaufsicht der Censoren* (1938).

[4] L. xxxix. 44. 9.

[5] L. xxxix. 29. 9; 38. 3; 41. 5-7; xl. 19. 9; 37. 1-7.

[6] L. xxxii. 3. 2-7; xxxvii. 32. 11-14; Cato, frg. 20-1 M; L. xxxiv. 56. 9; xxxviii. 23. 4; 44. 9-50; xxxix. 6. 3-7. 5; 38. 6-12. Cf. A. H. McDonald, *CHJ,* 1939, 129, 132. Such conditions may have helped to extort the concession which a lex Porcia granted: that citizens on military service should have the right of appeal against punishment in the field. This law, however, can only be dated between 198 and 134 and may have been

carried during the Spanish Wars of 150-135: cf. A. H. McDonald, *JRS,* 1944, 19 f.

[7] L. xxxix. 44; Plut. *Cato,* 18; Nepos, *Cato,* 2. 3; cf. p. 260. On the question of the taxation see Mommsen, *Staatsr.* ii. 395 n. 7; Fraccaro, *St. Stor.* 1911, 91-7; De Sanctis, III. ii. 624. The tax applied to slaves worth more than 10,000 *asses;* since the normal price of a slave was some 5,000 *asses,* the purpose of the tax will have been to limit the influx into Roman homes of highly trained Greeks whose morals and views might be harmful, rather than to help the small farmer by trying to check the spread of slave labour.

[8] P. xxxi. 25.

[8a] Cato delivered a speech *De signis et tabulis.* . . .

[9] Pliny, *NH,* xxxiv. 6. 31. This custom must have been increasing, because a law of 215 had forbidden the erection of women's statues in open places. For the base of a statue to Cornelia, daughter of Scipio Africanus, to which Pliny refers in this passage, see *Inscr. Ital.* XIII, *fasc.* iii (*Elogia*), p. 53. Statues to two Greek cooks aroused Cato's wrath in a speech against a certain Lepidus. . . . A gilded statue of Acilius Glabrio, the friend of Scipio Africanus, the first of its kind in Rome, was placed in the temple to Pietas which he had vowed at the battle of Thermopylae in 191 and which his son had dedicated in 181 (L. xl. 34. 4; Val. Max. ii. 5. 1).

[9a] Plut. *Cato,* 19.

[10] P. vi. 39. 10.

[10a] L. xxiii. 23. 6.

[11] See p. 261.

[12] The censors of 199, 194, and 189 had expelled none, three, and four respectively. But in 252 B.C. 16 senators had been expelled, 8 in 209, 7 in 204, 9 in 174, 7 in 169 (32 in 115 and 64 in 70 B.C.). But even in the severe year 174, when a praetor, a praetorian, and the brother of the censor were expelled, the consulars remained immune. Cf. P. Fraccaro, *Stud. Stor.* 1911, 99-100.

[13] Livy's account (xxxix. 42-3) was based (not necessarily directly, but possibly through Nepos) on a speech by Cato. . . . Versions of the episode by Valerius Antias and Plutarch (*Cato,* 17; *Flam.* 16) tone down some details of the crime. See further, Fraccaro, *Stud. Stor.* 1911, 9 ff., 14 ff.

[14] Plut. *Flam.* 19. 1 is more correct than Plut. *Cato,* 17. 5 where it is stated that T. Flamininus appealed to the People. There could be no question of a *provocatio*

against the censor's authority. Fraccaro, *Stud. Stor.* 1911, 22, rejects the view of Mommsen, *Staatsr.* ii³. 386 (based on Cic. *Pro Cluent.* 120), that the question was referred to the People in another form.

[15] L. xl. 12. 17. According to Plut. *Cato,* 17. 6, Lucius soon regained popular favour.

[16] Ibid. 17. 7. The name Manilius is doubtful. If he had good hopes of the consulship he must presumably have been of praetorian standing, but no Manilius is contained in the praetorian fasti of 218-179. The name may be a corruption of Mamilius or Manlius. No Mamilius figures among the praetors, but there are several Manlii. Of these A. Manlius Vulso (*cos.* 178) is possible; true, his name is not among the praetors, but it is very improbable that he reached the consulship without having been praetor and Willem's suggestion (*Sénat,* i. 324) that he was *praetor suffectus* of 189 may be accepted. If ejected from the Senate by Cato, he will have been restored by the censors of 179 (who, as will be seen, were friendly to the Manlii); he gained the consulship of 178 with the help of the consuls of 179, L. Manlius Acidinus and Q. Fulvius Flaccus. . . . An alternative is P. Manlius, praetor in Spain with Cato in 195; it may be have been there that he incurred Cato's hatred. He held a second praetorship in 182, by which he would regain entry into the Senate.

Cato's care for the proprieties of married life is seen in his punishment of a certain Nasica for an untimely jest about his wife (Aul. Gell. iv. 20. 3-6; Cic. *De orat.* ii. 260). This Nasica can scarcely have been a man of note, but Cato's hatred of the Scipios was not apparently confined to the famous.

Another of the seven expelled senators was probably a Claudius Nero, but his identity is uncertain. . . .

[17] Cato, however, retained the services of an accomplished slave named Chilo, a γραμμᾰτιστής, who 'taught many boys' (Plut. *Cato,* 20. 3). Cato apparently was less concerned with the corrupting influence of a Greek slave upon his neighbours' children, since he allowed Chilo to teach others and presumably himself took the profit.

[18] See A. H. J. Greenidge, *Roman Public Life,* 224 ff.; P. Fraccaro, *Stud. Stor.* 1911, 106 ff.

[19] L. xxvii. II. 14 (209 B.C.).

[20] L. xxxix. 44. I; Plut. *Cato,* 18. 1.

[21] On this second point Cato made merry. . . .

[22] One hundred of the 400 additional *equites equo publico* would presumably have been attached to each

of the four consular legions (at Cannae the number of cavalry attached to each legion had been raised by 100: see L. xxii. 36. 3), but it is not clear how they would have been arranged in the electoral centuries. Mommsen supposed that Cato would have raised the number in each of the 18 centuries from 100 to 120, thus making a total of 2,160 men (*Staatsr.* iii. 260); but it is difficult to believe that the figure 2,200 given in Cato's speech is only a round number. More probably Cato envisaged an increase of the equestrian centuries from 18 to 22. . . .

[23] Private individuals also who neglected their lands and crops were apparently subjected to Cato's censorial *nota* and relegated to the *aerarii:* see Gellius, iv. 12. 1.

[24] L. xxxix. 44. 4; Plut. *Cato,* 19. 1.

[25] Frontinus, *De aqu.* 94. . . .

[26] The argument of P. Fraccaro (*Stud. Stor.* 1911, 39, 51) against the identification with Purpureo does not seem very cogent. Cato would doubtless choose as eminent an offender as he could find. The imposition of a fine would not necessarily involve expulsion from the Senate, especially if the *lectio Senatus* had already been completed, i.e. there is no reason (with Fraccaro) to reject Purpureo because he still remained a member of the Senate. Q. Minucius Thermus, who had incurred far more serious accusations in 190, had served on an official commission immediately afterwards.

[27] L. xxxix. 44. 4.

[28] . . . On similar activity by the censors of 179 see L. xl. 51. 8. . . .

[29] L. xliii. 16. 2. Cf. P. Fraccaro, *Stud. Stor.* 1911, 121 ff.

[30] On this censorial function see Mommsen, *Staatsr.* ii. 62 f. Oppius is otherwise unknown; as he was a *publicanus* or *eques* he cannot be identified with Q. Oppius, the tribune of 191. . . .

[31] L. xxxix. 44. 7. Cf. Plut. *Cato,* 19. 1.

[32] P. vi. 17.

[33] Plut. *Cato,* 19. 2. . . .

[34] De Sanctis, IV. i. 602, suggests that the Senate's action may have been unconstitutional and Cato could have disregarded it: in any case he was unwilling to provoke a constitutional crisis.

[35] Alternatively to the view expressed above, this might have been the occasion of Cato's speech against Oppius.

[36] Plut. *Cato,* 19. 2. . . .

[37] Opposition: Plut. *Cato,* 19. 2. . . . There was no basilica in 210 (L. xxvi. 27. 3). To obtain the site, Cato had to buy up some property (L. xxxix. 44. 7).

[38] L. xxxix. 44. 5.

[39] This may be inferred from two unassigned fragments of Cato's speeches . . .

[40] *Apud* Dion. Hal. iii. 67. 5. This stupendous sum is accepted, apparently without qualms, by Tenney Frank (*Econ. Survey,* i. 144, 184), although neither expensive material nor much skilled labour would be needed.

[41] For these estimates see T. Frank, *Econ. Survey,* i. 153. The cost of the Basilica Aemilia is reckoned at 25,000 *denarii:* the Porcia would be about the same.

[42] Plut. *Cato,* 19. 3. Pliny's statement (*NH,* 19. 23) that Cato wished to pave the Forum with sharp stones in order to discourage loungers need not be taken seriously. On the loiterers see Plautus, *Curc.* 476 ff. On further building activity see L. xxxix. 44. 6.

[43] So Eumenius (a rhetorician of the Constantinian period), *Gratiarum act. Const. Aug.* 13. . . .

[44] Unpropitious acts which could mar the *felicitas* of a *census* include a censor's seeing a corpse or the changing of the appointed day without augural permission. A later example of such a challenge is when Claudius Asellus in 139 challenged the *felicitas* of the *lustrum* of Scipio Aemilianus.

[45] Thermus will have been the tribune of 183 and may be identified with the legate of Fulvius Flaccus in Spain in 181-180 and the legate of the consul Manlius Vulso in Istria in 176. He is probably the same man as he whom Cato accused in 154.

[46] These points come from a speech *De suis virtutibus contra Thermum* which is probably to be identified with *In Thermum post censuram* and *De lustri sui felicitate.* . . .

[47] References to two other speeches, which were probably censorial, attest but do not illuminate other activities of Cato. . . .

Alan E. Astin (essay date 1978)

SOURCE: Alan E. Astin, "The De agricultura and Other Writings," in *Cato the Censor,* Oxford at the Clarendon Press, 1978, pp. 182-210.

[*Astin's* Cato the Censor *is the first extensive biography of Cato since Plutarch's* Lives *and the only in-depth study to date in English. The chapter excerpted below summarizes all of the writings, provides an extensive discussion of* De agricultura, *and examines Cato's development and purpose as an author. Astin ultimately deems Cato's influence on Roman prose "a considerable imaginative achievement."*]

1. Cato's writings

'His eloquence lives and flourishes, enshrined in writings of every kind.'[1] If Livy has here allowed enthusiasm to outweigh precision, if his claim has too wide a sweep, the overstatement is at least understandable. The motivations and purposes which induced Cato to write, the range, the forms, the quality, even the basic nature of his compositions may all be subject to debate; but the magnitude of his achievement is beyond question. He was virtually the founder of Roman prose literature. Nor is his achievement in any way diminished by the recognition that, like all who make original contributions, he was not working in a vacuum, that his writings were related to, and developed from, what others had done. Other Romans had written historical works in prose, but in Greek, not in Latin. Others had created literary works in the Latin language, but in verse, not in prose. Other Romans must have noted down practical information and assembled 'books' for private use, but Cato was the first to prepare such books with a view to circulation, to their use by a 'public'. And if the scope and sophistication of his compositions has sometimes been overestimated, still they unquestionably display a remarkable breadth of interest and variety. A summary survey will illustrate this and provide a basis for more detailed discussion.

1. . . . Although [the speeches] proved to be of great significance in the development of Roman literature it is unlikely that Cato himself thought of them in such terms. Whether he himself 'published' any, apart from those included in the *Origines,* is uncertain, though the balance of probability inclines slightly against.

2. Two 'books' not intended for publication and probably never published:

(*i*) A history which, according to Plutarch, Cato stated he himself wrote 'with his own hand in big letters, so that his son might have in his home an aid to the understanding of the old Roman traditions'. It was presumably written *c.* 185-180. Despite occasional conjectures to the contrary it is generally agreed that this work is to be distinguished from the *Origines,* except in so far as the experience of writing it could have been one of the factors encouraging the later decision to write a major historical work.[2]

(*ii*) A *commentarius* or notebook in which Cato collected prescriptions for the treatment of illnesses in his household. He mentioned this *commentarius* in his *Ad filium,* adding an indication, probably very brief, of the general nature of his treatments. Occasional modern attempts to identify this book either with part of the *Ad filium* itself or with the extant *De agricultura* are certainly erroneous.[3]

3. Writings addressed to his elder son, M. Porcius Cato Licinianus:

(*i*) The *Ad filium.* This has often been envisaged as a set of books, probably conceived as a single project, written to assist with the education of Cato's son, each book dealing with a separate topic, and including at least agriculture, medicine, and rhetoric; in fact the first Roman 'encyclopaedia'. However, there are grave objections to such a reconstruction. The most likely interpretation of the evidence is that Cato addressed to his son a collection, probably in only one book, of precepts, exhortations, and observations, many of them pithily expressed, on a variety of topics and with a marked emphasis on practical affairs. Since the son was almost certainly born in 192 or 191 such a work would probably have been put together during the 170s. Subsequently copies of the work passed into circulation, so that it was known to Pliny, Plutarch, and others, and several fragments survive. There is nothing to indicate whether Cato himself was in any way responsible for the 'publication', but in any event it is unlikely that the *Ad filium* was written with a view to this.

(*ii*) A letter from Cato to his elder son, congratulating him on his bravery at the battle of Pydna in 168. This is presumably the same letter as the one in which Cato, having heard that his son had received his discharge from the army, warned him against engaging in combat unless he was first formally re-enlisted. A few other very brief fragments, including at least one usually assigned to the *Ad filium,* may come from this letter and could be taken to suggest that its contents were rather wide-ranging. That would help to account for its subsequent publication and survival until at least the time of Cicero. There is no good evidence for the survival of other letters, either to the son or to others. The letter is most unlikely to have been written originally with a view to 'publication'; whether Cato himself was in any way responsible for its passing into circulation is unknown.[5]

4. Three specialized monographs. The interpretation of the *Ad filium* as an 'encyclopaedia' gave rise to questions about the relationship between that work and these monographs. With the interpretation of the *Ad filium* adopted in this book these questions no longer arise.

(*i*) *De agricultura.* The only one of Cato's works to survive intact, this will be discussed in detail below. It consists of a single book.

(*ii*) **De re militari**. Fifteen different fragments are preserved in eighteen citations, and the work is explicitly mentioned in three further passages. There is little doubt that the correct title is **De re militari**, though other phrases are found, such as *De militari disciplina*. Despite one reference to 'books' the work virtually certainly consisted of a single book. It cannot be dated but a fragment from its preface shows that it was not merely a private notebook but was written for publication. Material drawn from it was incorporated in later military writings and transmitted as far as the *Epitoma rei militaris* of Vegetius, who refers to Cato by name, though it is virtually certain that he did not have direct access to Cato's work. There is good reason to believe that Vegetius has significantly more Catonian material than the three fragments positively established, but attempts to identify further specific passages are in varying degrees insecure.[6] The fifteen fragments of Cato's work suggest that it was a handbook of practical information about Roman military practices and methods, especially on the tactical level, ranging through such matters as the taking of *auspicia,* details of internal organization, methods of maintaining discipline, formations on the march and in battle, and the uses of specialist troops such as archers. Probably the points were exemplified by accounts of particular events.[7]

(*iii*) A work dealing with aspects of civil law, perhaps more specifically with augural and pontifical law. In this case special difficulties arise because Cato's elder son, who predeceased him, wrote books on law which were evidently more extensive and more authoritative than Cato's own, the references to which are all rather indirect. It is likely that most of the citations from 'Cato' in the *Digest* and Justinian's *Institutes* are from the son's work (though at least one is probably a corruption of 'Capito').[8] The same could be true of the one fragment which is usually assigned to Cato's own work, though more probably Festus, who preserved it, and may be supposed to have taken it from the Augustan scholar Verrius Flaccus, would have added some qualification if he had believed any other Cato to have been the author.[9] The most explicit evidence is a passage of the *De senectute* in which Cicero represented Cato as busying himself in old age with various literary occupations, including, 'I am dealing with the civil law of the augurs and pontifices.'[10] Though this is not reliable evidence for the date of composition, read in its context it does show that Cicero believed Cato to have written such a work. That is implied also in not a few other references to Cato's expertise in law, several of them in lists of his skills which clearly correspond to his principal writings.[11] The paucity of fragments is presumably because this work was quickly outdated by the flood of voluminous and authoritative legal writings which followed.

5. **Carmen de moribus**. This work is known only from a single passage of Gellius (a later reference by Nonius is almost certainly taken from Gellius), whose initial interest is in the use of the word *elegans* in a particular quotation, though he is led on to recall two further quotations.[12] He explicitly terms it 'the book of Cato which is entitled **Carmen de moribus**', and he twice more refers to it in the singular. Of the three fragments Gellius makes it clear that the second really consists of several (three?) separate quotations he has brought together. Although the term *carmen* has inspired a variety of suggestions regarding metrical form, the very diversity of conclusions encourages the belief that it was a prose work of markedly didactic tone.[13] Such a tone is certainly suggested by the fragments, though such limited material is a slender basis on which to make assertions about the book as a whole. Nevertheless they suggest that, as is only to be expected, it was concerned with *mores* not in a theoretical or philosophical sense but in the practical terms of actual behaviour. The first two fragments contrast certain features of contemporary conduct with the practice of earlier generations, by implication to the disadvantage of the former, while the third uses a simile to moralize about deterioration consequent upon idleness. It is a reasonable assumption, but no more than that, that the work was written for the purpose of circulation—rather than, for example, as a further preceptual guide for Licinianus—and that it was some kind of public exhortation to higher standards of conduct, as Cato conceived them to be.

6. A collection of 'sayings'. Cicero in the *De officiis* speaks explicitly of 'many witty sayings by many people, like those which were collected by the old Cato', 'multa multorum facete dicta, ut ea, quae a sene Catone collecta sunt'. A passage in the *De oratore,* though not quite explicit, is beyond reasonable doubt another reference to the same collection and shows that Cicero drew several of his examples from it.[14] Presumably the compilation of such a work was primarily a reflection of Cato's own sense of humour and fondness for aphorism. It would be rash to assume that it was compiled for the express purpose of circulation, but supposing it to have been made initially for private purposes it is easy to envisage Cato allowing copies to be made and the collection quickly passing into circulation. Cicero's reference to the 'old' Cato, *senex,* is not adequate evidence that Cato compiled the collection towards the end of his life, for Cicero often applies the word to Cato as a distinguishing epithet rather than as an indication of time. It is obviously possible, though undemonstrable, that the collection was built up over a considerable period. The only dictum certainly from the collection was spoken by a certain C. Publicius about a P. Mummius. It is highly probable however that the collection is the source of a dictum (quoted twice by Cicero) addressed by Q. Fabius Maximus Cunctator to M. Livius Macatus after the

capture of Tarentum in 209, and possibly also of a remark by Scipio Africanus which Cicero in the *Republic* says was reported by Cato.[15] Several other remarks in the second book of the *De oratore* must have been drawn from the collection. There are about ten possibilities, but no means of establishing that any particular one of them was taken from this source.

Inevitably there has been speculation as to whether Cato included in this collection any sayings of his own. The question has been complicated by Plutarch's statement that 'many literal translations [sc. from Greek] are included among his sayings and maxims'. . . .[16] This however is almost certainly a different matter. Plutarch means that there were many such translations among the sayings attributed to Cato, and by Plutarch's time there were available collections of such sayings independent of Cato's own collection. One such collection was manifestly the basis of chapters 8 and 9 of Plutarch's *Life*. Moreover a number of sayings in general circulation, including some of Greek origin, were posthumously attached to Cato's name and included in such collections; indeed there are a number of such spurious attributions among the ***Apophthegmata*** preserved in the Plutarch corpus.[17] Not that Cato himself is likely to have been shy of using sayings translated from Greek: he was evidently quite prepared to borrow a sentence from Xenophon for the Preface to the ***Origines***.[18] However that may be, it is clear that the Plutarch passage probably has no direct connection with Cato's own collection.

Nor is much help to be got from the survival of a large number of sayings attributed to Cato. Many of these, probably the majority, were culled from his speeches and other writings, and some from Polybius. There are others which could not easily be envisaged in such works, but it is perfectly possible that they were incorporated in a collection by someone else soon after—or even before—Cato's death. On the other hand it is by no means inconceivable that Cato included some of his own *dicta* in his own collection. The suggestion that they would no longer have had meaning or interest for him apart from the original circumstances is as much—and as little—applicable to other people's *dicta* as to his own. He unquestionably made a collection of the former; and he was not a man inhibited by modesty. The conclusion must be that while it is possible he included *dicta* of his own, it remains quite uncertain whether he actually did so.

7. ***Origines***. This was a major historical work, the first in Latin, written with a view to circulation among a reading public. About 125 fragments survive from its seven books. The first book dealt with the origins and very early history of Rome, the second and third books with the origins of many other Italian peoples. The remaining four books covered the history of Rome from at least as early as the First Punic War literally down

Cameo of Cato.

to Cato's own day: the last book included the speech against Ser. Sulpicius Galba which he delivered only shortly before his death. . . .

Such is the range of Cato's writings, so far as they are known. The very list highlights his remarkable versatility and the vigour with which he pursued a variety of interests. At the same time it raises fundamental questions about such matters as Cato's motives in writing, his debt to his predecessors, his methods of working, and the level of his artistry. The starting-point must be the ***De agricultura,*** not for its special merits—for some of the works of which only fragments remain were certainly of higher literary and intellectual quality—but because it is the only work which has survived to be judged as a full text.

2. The De agricultura[19]

Cato's ***De agricultura*** is a book of moderate length—just over one hundred pages in a modern critical edition—which despite its title deals with only some aspects of agriculture.[20] It is not—and makes no pretension to be—a comprehensive treatment of the different types of agricultural production and organization. In particular it does not deal with either cereal production or animal raising as topics of central importance, according them only cursory mention as auxiliary items on farms the primary function of which was to produce wine or olive oil. Indeed, although Cato also dealt briefly with horticulture in the neighbourhood of a city, it was clearly wine and oil production that he had in the forefront of his mind as he wrote. Yet although in this sense the scope of his work is limited, in places it extends beyond strictly agricultural matters to include a number of medicinal treatments and even cooking recipes. Strongly didactic in character, with the imperative form predominating throughout, it offers little in the way of theory and generalization but a great deal of practical instruction, much of it on matters of detail, even of minute detail. With very few exceptions each of the 162 chapters deals with a single quite specific topic—such as a particular operation on the farm or a particular recipe—and this is basically true even of a few chapters, mostly in the earlier part of the book, in which the topics are rather broader and more complex. Indeed in the manuscript tradition through which the work has been preserved the point was emphasized by the rubrics indicating the contents of the individual chapters—though there is uncertainty as to whether these rubrics, which usually reproduce or paraphrase the opening words of the chapter, were part of the original work.

Stylistically the *De agricultura* is plain in the extreme, consisting largely of short uncomplicated sentences and making only limited use even of a narrow range of simple conjunctions and particles. The rare flash of more vivid language and the occasional aphorism provide a tenuous link with the fragments of the speeches and other works,[21] but by the very contrast which they create these also emphasize the simple, unadorned directness which prevails. In short, Cato here employs the language of direct practical instruction, without effort to achieve literary effect or linguistic elegance. The striking exception to this is the Preface, which, whatever may be thought of its intellectual content, was manifestly composed with considerable care in order to achieve an elevated and artistic effect. It has even been suggested that its style and structure were strongly influenced by Greek rhetorical principles, but in fact its characteristics are those of the native Latin tradition, with its use of synonyms, of parallelism, of repetitions—sometimes for deliberate effect, sometimes because there was no attempt to avoid them—and the emphasis on the opening and closing elements in sentences of relatively simple structure.[22]

It has often been observed that the Preface contrasts with the main body of the work in another respect also; for it makes explicit reference to the type of the *colonus,* the peasant farmer working his own farm, whereas the book itself is not directed at all to this form of farming. Instead, although not a little of the detailed practical information would be applicable within any kind of farm organization, Cato clearly has in mind larger units belonging to, and managed on behalf of, an owner who is not normally resident on the farm.

There is no firm evidence as to when the *De agricultura* was composed. One of the early chapters contains a hint that it was probably written later than 198, but since Cato did not die until 149 that does little to help.[23] If the most literal interpretation is placed upon Cato's assertion that up to his seventieth year none of his villas was plastered and also upon the full implications of the instructions in chapter 128 'for plastering a dwelling', that chapter should have been written after 164;[24] but a date inferred only from the literal implications of such details is scarcely a reliable basis for further argument and interpretation. That the *De agricultura* was composed in Cato's later years is certainly plausible but is not securely established.

Nevertheless this book is not only the first work on agriculture to have been written by a Roman;[25] it is also the earliest prose work in Latin to have survived and was among the earliest written. Consequently it is of exceptional interest in several different respects, including textual criticism, the history of Latin language and idiom, Roman religion, and the practical aspects of Roman agriculture; and it has also received much attention as a social and economic document. In the present study attention is focused especially on two aspects: the characteristics, methods, and processes of composition, which are considered in this chapter; and the light which the work may throw on Cato's personality and especially upon his attitudes to various social and economic matters. . . .

Two striking features of the *De agricultura* have prompted numerous discussions about the time and manner of its composition, its publication, and possible subsequent modification. They are the seemingly disorderly presentation of the material and the occurrence of 'doublets'.

The appearance of disorder is obvious to any reader. Items appear to be introduced casually, following no systematic plan, sometimes intruding between chapters which are related to each other, sometimes in a bewildering succession of apparently disconnected individual points. Closer examination has led to a fairly widespread recognition that the first twenty-two chapters are associated with the broad theme of purchasing, managing, and developing a farm, and that the next thirty or so are based upon a calendar of farm operations beginning with the vintage and extending through to the tasks of the following summer. Yet even within these broad themes there is a general impression of interruptions and digressions and of very loose construction. In the remaining two-thirds of the book, although two or three or even more chapters in succession may be loosely connected around a single topic and in a few cases a more extended sequence can be distinguished, as in the case of the cooking recipes, the over-all impression is almost universally agreed to be that there is a lack of system, a largely haphazard arrangement, and no unifying theme. Even the person addressed is not always the same. Usually it is the owner, the *dominus,* but in at least one section and possibly in others the *vilicus,* the slave who manages the farm, is addressed in the second person.[26] In many chapters instructions are given in an 'impersonal' second person form for tasks which the owner is most unlikely to carry out in person; and although the imperatives which predominate throughout the book are most often in the second person, quite frequently there is a change into the third.

This sense of disorder is heightened by the occurrence within this short work of a number of 'doublets', that is to say items, in some cases whole chapters, which occur twice, usually with very little variation in content or even in wording. Not all repetitions are to be regarded as doublets or in need of special explanation; and sometimes the reckoning has perhaps been on the generous side. In some cases only a few words or a single sentence are repeated, and quite a number of doublets are merely another aspect of the relatively limited amount of over-all planning in the book. These are items which occur in two different contexts to both of which they are equally relevant and appropriate, and it is arguable that such repetitions could have been eliminated only if the organization of the material had been planned in advance with meticulous care and attention to detail, and perhaps even then only with the aid of a number of cross-references. Nevertheless several striking and apparently unnecessary doublets remain.[27] Thus instructions for the propagation of trees by layering are given first in chapters 51 and 52 and again, with only minor variations, in 133. Recommendations about the lengths of various ropes, reins, and straps given in 63 are repeated with slight differences in 135. 4, in the midst of other recommendations of the same kind. Chapters 91 and 129 are virtually identical in content and closely related (though not identical) in wording, and the relationship between 92 and 128, though not quite so close, is similar. Chapter 115 gives instructions for the preparation of a laxative wine differing only slightly from those just given in 114, without any reference back or mention that an alternative is being set out; and another prescription is found twice, with almost identical vocabulary and differing only in grammatical structure, first in 156. 5 and then in 157. 9, both of these unusually long chapters being concerned with the uses of cabbage.

Although these features have been exciting discussion for more than a century, it has been observed with some plausibility that the numerous explanations which have been offered, despite their variations in detail,

fall into two principal categories: (*i*) that Cato's original text has been distorted by subsequent revisions and interpolations; (*ii*) that the text is largely as Cato left it (except that at some stage the spelling was 'modernized') and that its disorderliness reflects the manner in which it was compiled and published.[28] However, these two approaches to the problem are not necessarily mutually exclusive, nor indeed have they always been treated as such. Moreover the second of these categories perhaps imposes a misleading unity on what are really several separate categories of argument. It would be more accurate to say that there have been four main types of explanation which, as well as varying in detail within themselves, have been brought together in a variety of combinations.[29]

(*i*) It has been argued that the **De agricultura** was substantially revised and interpolated after Cato's death, though probably before the time of the elder Pliny, who seems to have known the work in its present form.[30] One suggestion is that at a particular time, perhaps in the Augustan period, the text was subjected to a wholesale and incompetent revision which included the insertion of much material from some other work. The form of revision more frequently postulated is that because it was a practical handbook in constant use its users were inclined to add notes and glosses which sometimes were additional material, sometimes slightly modified versions of Cato's instructions, and that in due course these became incorporated in the text. A practical handbook, it is thought, would have been particularly liable to that kind of interpolation, though it perhaps occurred less in the earlier, more coherent sections, where the author's personality had imposed itself more strongly.

(*ii*) It is likely that Cato obtained at least some of his material for the **De agricultura** from 'notebooks' or *commentarii* in which useful practical information had been collected, such as a 'calendar' of farm operations, a number of cooking recipes, and various other grouped or miscellaneous notes. (Again there has been much variation in modern assessments, ranging from a simple recognition of such underlying documents as the calendar and some inventories through to a highly complex theory which seeks to identify the basic documents and the manner of their synthesis in considerable detail.[31]) It has therefore been suggested that the disorder springs partly from the unsystematic character of such notebooks, partly from a failure to integrate properly material drawn from a number of such sources. The origin of the doublets might have been that the same particulars had been recorded in more than one notebook.

(*iii*) A further suggestion is that the process of composition, especially perhaps of the later part of the book, was spread over a long period. Cato simply went on adding individual chapters or groups of chapters from time to time, when appropriate items happened to come to his attention. Hence the arrangement was haphazard, lacking theme and structure. Some information was put in twice, either by accident or because Cato did not bother to delete the earlier version when he put in a modified version. The sporadic nature of the process, perhaps spread over many years (as many as forty have been suggested), resulted in some loss of the sense of relevance and purpose, so that among the miscellaneous items added could be such items as the cookery recipes.

(*iv*) Lastly, it has been held that the book was unfinished at Cato's death. Consequently he had not completed the work of revising and rearranging a rough draft which in places may have consisted of little more than a collection of notes. Subsequently by allowing copies of the draft to be made someone in effect published it more or less in the rough unfinished state in which Cato had left it. Unfulfilled intentions might also account for the rather tenuous relationship between the Preface and the body of the work. (A variant on this, that Cato compiled the work in a rough and ready way because he did not envisage it being published, is incompatible both with the existence of the Preface and with the content of the earlier chapters.[32])

These various hypotheses certainly contain some valid points. In particular it cannot reasonably be doubted that Cato drew a great deal of material from private notes and documents which were kept for practical purposes. Indeed it is highly probable that the specific recommendations given in respect of farms of different types and sizes—a suburban garden, a vineyard, and at least two farms devoted to olive-production—are based on the inventories and other particulars of actual farms belonging to Cato. The material drawn from such sources includes the inventories of farm equipment, the sample contracts, the religious formulas, the instructions on cypress trees and on brooms attributed to particular persons, and many other detailed instructions.[33] Presumably some of the sequences of closely related items, such as the cooking recipes, were obtained in this way rather than from Cato's memory, but the process was by no means wholly mechanical, even in the later sections. In the middle of chapter 157, which is certainly based on some special source, Cato's personal control of the material is revealed by the phrase 'if you use cabbage as I advise'; and the impress of his personality is particularly evident in chapters 54, 61, and 142-3, as well as in many of the earlier chapters. Similarly the possibility of intrusive glosses in a work of this kind is certainly to be taken seriously. It is, for example, the most plausible explanation for the bare statement in chapter 124 that 'dogs should be shut away during the day so that they may be keener and more watchful at night', which occurs totally unexpectedly in the middle of a sequence of chapters devoted to wine-based medicinal prescriptions. Nevertheless it is

not so easy to envisage this kind of interpolation on such a scale that it was a major factor in bringing about the seeming disorder of the whole work.

Indeed, when the effort is made to envisage in detail what is actually supposed to have happened, physically, to Cato's text it may be doubted whether any of the four kinds of hypothesis outlined above is a satisfactory explanation or can account for more than a few details. A revision so incompetent that it distorted and disrupted the whole sequence and coherence of Cato's work is itself something which would require a special explanation, especially when it is supposed to have happened not at the hands of an uncomprehending medieval scribe but in the age of Caesar or Augustus; yet a less dramatic revision which had not done this could not afford an explanation of the peculiarities of the *De agricultura*. Again, while it is easy to admit the possibility that the work is unfinished in the sense that Cato might have intended to add more material at the end, it is much less easy to envisage what kind of process of compilation and drafting would, in ancient conditions, have left the incomplete work awaiting major rearrangement and revision, yet in a sufficiently coherent form, presumably in one manuscript, for it to have been possible for it to pass into circulation. Yet if Cato was not contemplating such drastic revision a failure to finish would not itself be the explanation of the peculiarities; and if Cato left simply a collection of drafts and notes, presumably on waxed tablets, the decision to copy them into a single manuscript for publication as a book is also in need of special explanation. There is more to be said for the view that the later parts of the work were compiled without reference to any clear-cut plan or structure, in a manner which might be better described as accumulation than as composition. Whether such a process took place sporadically over a substantial period of time is more doubtful. At any rate, a sense of continuity is apparent in chapter 142, where there is an unmistakable reference back to the instructions to the *vilicus* set out in chapter 5. Moreover it is necessary to account also for the fact that the progression of thought is frequently erratic and surprising even in the earlier sections of the book, where a broad plan is observable. For these sections the explanation of sporadic accumulation is neither helpful nor probable.

Nevertheless, the view of the *De agricultura* as characterized by a lack of systematic planning is helpful in two respects. Up to a point it is valid in itself, and it points to a fifth type of explanation, one which is sometimes briefly stated or implied but which is deserving of fuller consideration, namely that the origin of the peculiarities is to be sought not so much in the mechanics of compilation or transmission as in Cato's own attitudes and preconceptions. It has been recognized, for example, that chapter 34 reveals a tolerance of digressions which would be thought inept in a modern writer, for with the words 'I return to the matter of planting' Cato resumes a topic from which he had strayed several chapters earlier and at the same time shows that the digression was his own and not a subsequent interpolation.[34] In fact the emphasis on disorder and fragmentation in the **De agricultura** has perhaps been slightly misplaced. Although there is no strong over-all structure or rigid discipline of relevance, neither the earlier nor even the later sections are quite as fragmented as has often been supposed. A distinction must be drawn between disciplined thought and continuity of thought. Definite—though undisciplined—sequences of thought can be found more extensively and with fewer sharp breaks than has usually been assumed. Frequently, however, the sequential element does not take the form of a coherent exposition or development of a central theme. It will be as well to examine this in more detail before returning to the question of Cato's attitude in a more general sense.

In some cases the continuity of thought is simply a matter of a series of individual points which are related to each other, at times only loosely, by a particular concept or a particular farm product. In others it takes the form of a type of progression which paradoxically both establishes and tends to obscure the element of continuity: there is a tendency when a particular topic is being discussed to pick up something which has been mentioned in a subordinate or indirect manner and to make a comment directly upon this without any further direct relevance to the topic from which it sprang. In such cases there is sometimes a speedy return to the initial topic, as in chapter 3. There, in logical sequence to comments on the need for adequate buildings, there is mention of the need for good presses 'so that the work can be done well', which inspires a digression about the importance of doing the pressing as quickly as possible and the reasons why gatherers and press-operators are tempted to delay; but after a few short sentences Cato returns to the details of the pressing-equipment required.[35] The digression mentioned above which ends with the 'I return to planting' of chapter 34 is similar in kind but on a larger scale. In some other cases an earlier topic is picked up in a way which suggests not so much a resumption after a digression as the addition of an afterthought.[36]

As for groups of passages which centre on a particular theme, some are obvious enough, such as the inventories, the cookery recipes, the religious formulas, and the sample contracts. Others however are set out in such a way that the common element is not presented to the reader as a prominent feature. Thus chapters 91-101 at first sight seem to consist of a number of miscellaneous recipes and prescriptions for widely differing purposes, each introduced by reference to its purpose: e.g. 'To make a threshing-floor . . . If an olive tree is sterile . . . To keep caterpillars off vines . . . To keep scab from sheep . . . If you intend to store oil in

a new jar . . .' On closer examination however all these items are found to involve the use of *amurca,* olive-lees, so that the whole group could have been entitled 'On the uses of *amurca*'. Several similar groups can be identified. Although there are some breaks in continuity where Cato changes to a completely different topic, these breaks are not as frequent as some modern accounts might suggest. In particular chapters 104 to 127, excepting only the intrusive injunction about dogs in 124, are linked together by the concept of the uses and applications of various other products of the farm; and it is likely that this idea really governs the whole block from 91 to 130, opening with uses of *amurca* and coming back to this in the last three chapters with supplementary material. Apart from the dogs in 124, only chapter 102 (a prescription for treating oxen and other animals bitten by snakes) seems to fit awkwardly into such a sequence; and for that a reasonable explanation can be conjectured if these lists were at least in part specially compiled by Cato himself. That this was so is indeed probable, for it would be surprising if in the normal course of running a farm there had been occasion to assemble a miscellany of very varied uses of, for example, *amurca,* and it seems more likely that these were brought together from other notes arranged on a different basis.

The fundamental explanation for the lack of system and the lack of disciplined thought in the **De agricultura** is to be found precisely in Cato's role as the virtual founder of Latin prose literature, a role which is invariably recognized but the implications of which are easily overlooked. It is all too easy to forget how different was Cato's background and experience in this field from that of modern scholars and writers, almost all of whom have from childhood been trained and disciplined in techniques of composition; whose education and literary environment alike have constantly instilled ideals of relevance, consistency, clear and logical exposition, and avoidance of repetition; who take it for granted that the satisfactory presentation of a complicated and technical topic requires a high degree of organization and preliminary planning, not to mention the repeated revision of drafts, and who have had plenty of opportunity to observe the consequences of an insufficiency of such organization and planning. Cato had received no such training, did not live in an environment which constantly inculcated such ideals and techniques of composition, and had had little previous experience of constructing books and equally little opportunity to benefit from the experience of others. Experience and skill in the composition of speeches he certainly did have, but that is a different kind of composition, presenting different problems which are of limited relevance to the **De agricultura**. A speech was not only a relatively short composition; the very circumstances which called it into being gave it a strong inherent unity and direction, in effect imposed a kind of plan and coherence—just as chronological sequence has often provided a basic framework for historical writings. Even so Gellius' comments suggest that the Rhodian speech, however forceful and vigorous, was by no means notable for disciplined thought or for clear, logical, and well-organized exposition of the arguments.[38] The Preface to the *De agricultura* does display a care and coherence in composition which may well be related to Cato's experience with speeches; but the Preface is brief and it could be argued that even within this short passage the arrangement of material is in one respect determined less by logic than by the kind of progression of ideas which was discussed above.[39] Similarly experience gained from writing the other works which may have been earlier than the *De agricultura* would have been with much simpler material. In particular the *Ad filium* was probably only a miscellany of precepts, and it is easy to imagine the *Carmen de moribus* as rather similar, loosely assembled about the theme indicated by its title. The composition of an extended didactic work devoted to a single topic and containing a mass of interrelated practical information was a much more demanding task.

It may be objected that Cato had had the literary experience of reading Greek works, often works of high quality; but this too is of doubtful relevance. In the first place his acquaintance with Greek literature by no means necessarily implies that he read it with serious attention to techniques of composition and organization. In the second place Cato is most likely to have come across works of quality, hence unlikely to have been confronted with instructive examples of glaring faults which sprang from inadequate planning and discipline. Nor is it by any means certain that he even had the opportunity to examine work similar to his own; for there is doubt as to whether there were available Greek predecessors for the type of practical agricultural handbook he was attempting to write.[40] In any event, despite the few chapters which bear traces of being derived, directly or indirectly, from Greek sources, there are few clear signs of Greek influence in the work, and even if the idea of writing it was directly inspired by a Greek predecessor, its peculiarities make it almost impossible to believe that it was closely modelled upon any earlier work.

The *De agricultura* was probably not the first of Cato's writings. Although most of his books cannot be dated with confidence it is likely that he had already written others, such as the *Ad filium* and perhaps the *Carmen de moribus,* both of which were strongly didactic in tone (and much easier to compose). Probably encouraged by these experiments and not a little pleased with his achievements, it then occurred to him, in the same didactic spirit, to make available in writing more of his own expertise, only this time in the form not of precepts addressed to his son but of a work on a particular topic for a wider public: he would write a practical instructional book on agriculture, drawing upon his own personal knowledge and *commentarii* relating to his own properties. He commenced composition with only a sketchy and rudimentary scheme in mind, not thought out either in particular detail or at sufficient length to carry him more than a limited way through the book. He simply intended to give advice on the selection, general management, and equipment of a farm, and, since he believed it important for the owner to have sufficient knowledge to carry out frequent detailed inspections, he would supply a great deal of specific information about the tasks of the farm; probably the 'calendar' of operations through the year was envisaged as part of the initial plan. It is improbable that it ever occurred to him to think out with any precision who were his potential readers, or to put himself imaginatively in their place in order to assess what would be useful or appropriate to them. No attempt was made to relate the carefully composed Preface closely to the substance of the work—indeed the relationship is so loose that the Preface neither states nor implies the purpose of the book, while its references to *coloni* and soldiers have no relationship at all to the type of farming actually described. Contrasting the merits of agriculture as a source of income with the hazards of trade and the disrepute of usury, Cato mentions a traditional attitude that to be 'a good farmer and a good *colonus*' was the height of excellence, then states the advantages of agriculture to be that 'from farmers come both the bravest men and the most energetic soldiers, the income is especially respectable and secure and the least likely to provoke resentment, and those who are engaged in that occupation are least inclined to contemplate wrongdoing.' The underlying idea is that a book on agriculture is a worthy project because agriculture itself has such merits; but this is conceived in such general terms, drawing no distinction between different types of farming or of farmer, that it was clearly not thought out with close attention either to the purpose or to the substance of the book itself.[41] In short, it is a brief self-contained essay, and it probably never occurred to Cato to take account of the specific material which was to follow, about which his ideas at this stage were in any case still for the most part rather general and vague. Then, untroubled by powerful preconceptions about the desirability of system, discipline, and strict relevance, he pressed ahead with topics largely as they came to mind, the sequence determined in part by a simple association of ideas and in the earlier sections loosely controlled by his sketchy plan.

Particularly in the later sections of the book much of the material gleaned from *commentarii,* especially the recipes and prescriptions, was reproduced more or less as it stood, without rephrasing to bring out its relationship to the new context, and in some cases the same item was found to be appropriate in more than one place. Occasionally an item was introduced into an irrelevant context because it was copied along with an adjacent item which was relevant and with which it was linked in a *commentarius* (this is almost certainly the explanation of the doublet in chapter 133, and probably of the ill-fitting chapter 102). Such features point to a lack of concern for or of interest in careful choice of words to create a sense of unity; they may also reflect a brisk and rather impatient manner of work, and possibly even that Cato did not actually copy out the passages with his own hand but instructed a secretary to do it.[43] Moreover when Cato came across additional information appropriate to some theme which he had dealt with previously his lack of a strong concern about relevance allowed him to insert such material at the point he had now reached in his manuscript, without deleting what had intervened or attempting an insertion into the earlier section. Probably he composed a continuous text in a single manuscript, so that such an insertion would have been difficult; but it is also probable that it never occurred to him that it would be desirable to attempt it.

The heavy reliance on *commentarii* and personal knowledge had another consequence. It both reflected and powerfully reinforced the markedly particularist tendencies in Cato's attitudes, his frequent failure to distinguish details which were applicable to his own situation from information which had general validity and utility. Thus recommendations as to places at which to purchase materials, statements of prices, and even calculations of cost linked with the number of days required for transportation are expressed in terms which could not have been applicable generally.[44] Similarly particular details of Cato's own properties are transformed into general recommendations, and he really deals only with those forms of agriculture which happened to concern him at the time—even though it is certain that he did have experience of other forms, at least at some stage in his career.[45] Hence too—almost certainly—the extraordinary piece of advice that an owner should commence building on his farm only from the age of thirty-six.[46]

The application of such attitudes and such methods to a mass of detailed material, not infrequently interrelated and interdependent, inevitably resulted in a degree of unevenness and disorder and an erratic progression of ideas which can only be bewildering to readers habituated to orderliness and relevance and to whom these are, quite properly, major criteria in the assessment of instructional works. The peculiarities of the *De agricultura* are the consequence of major shortcomings in method and concept; but those shortcomings must be seen and indeed can be satisfactorily understood only in the context of Cato's pioneering role in the development of Roman prose writing. They reflect not carelessness or a lack of imagination but the novelty of the situation, the lack of relevant training and experience, in short the absence of an established literary culture such as Cato himself was helping to initiate. In such a context it was a considerable imaginative achievement to have conceived of such a work, all the more so if there were no Greek models for this particular type of handbook; and for all the peculiarities and omissions it was probably also a considerable practical achievement to assemble this mass of detailed material.

3. Other writings in relation to De agricultura

Since the **De agricultura** is the only one of Cato's works to have survived, the scope for detailed comparison and general assessment of his writings is severely limited. The meagre fragments of the lost works offer little or no opportunity to pursue many of the questions which over the years have been so intensively studied in the **De agricultura**. The **Origines,** which is more extensively attested than the others in both *testimonia* and fragments, affords slightly greater opportunity; but since it is clearly distinctive in a number of respects and poses several problems of its own, it will be reserved for the next chapter. There it will be possible to consider how far it does or does not conform with such general conclusions as may be reached regarding Cato's other writings; for, in spite of all the limitations, certain points do seem to emerge.

Perhaps the most obvious characteristic is that so far as can be seen all the works which came into circulation, with the probable exception of the collection of witticisms, were essentially didactic. Admittedly this is only an assumption in the cases of the **Carmen de moribus** and the book on law, but it is an assumption which is difficult to avoid. Closely allied to the didactic aspect is the markedly practical, almost utilitarian emphasis. That was evidently the case even with the **Carmen de moribus** which, as was noted earlier, seems to have been concerned with *mores* not in a theoretical sense but in the practical terms of actual behaviour. Again, only the collection of witticisms was probably an exception.

If in some respects attention focuses naturally on characteristics which Cato's writings share in common, from other points of view these writings fall readily into distinguishable groups. One such group consists of the three works devoted respectively to agriculture, warfare, and law—each concerned with a single topic, each written with the intention of publication, and each envisaged as a kind of practical instructional handbook. Again it must be admitted that the latter two points are only assumptions—though assumptions which can scarcely be avoided—in respect of the book on law, about which it is possible to say nothing further. The **De re militari** however does offer some interesting points of comparison. As with the **De agricultura** its subject-matter was directly related to Cato's personal experience. Indeed the Preface contained a clear allusion to the relevance of that experience: 'I know that if what has been written is made public there will be many who will bring pettifogging criticisms, but for the most part they are people quite devoid of true distinction. I have allowed their pronouncements to flow past me.'[47] Such a personal declaration, condemning in advance any who might venture to disagree, is certainly different from anything in the *De agricultura*. (It is tempting to see it as a reaction to earlier criticism, hence as evidence that the *De re militari* was a relatively late work, probably later than the *De agricultura*.) On the other hand two other fragments strongly suggest that the Preface, similarly to that of the *De agricultura* but perhaps in a manner more directly related to the book itself, argued the importance of the topic;[48] and marked stylistic effects in all three fragments indicate that in this Preface too some effort was devoted to creating an impressive and high-sounding effect. In general the stylistic characteristics are such as are to be expected: sentences short and simple, with instances of asyndeton and antithesis—one of the latter particularly striking—two neologisms,[49] an epigrammatic touch, and a bold, perhaps even grandiloquent, use of the word *orationes* to indicate the pronouncements of possible critics. Most of these occur in the three fragments which are probably from the Preface. Of the remaining fragments three use the second person, which again suggests an approach similar to that of the *De agricultura*.[50] Also, though most of the fragments are such short extracts that they must be judged with caution, it does look as if the treatment was in general plain and straightforward; and one fragment heavily links together five nouns by using *aut* four times in succession.[51] It is perhaps significant that the one instance of *atque* is in a fragment which appears to be part of a narrative, where Cato may have thought it appropriate to seek a more elevated or dramatic effect.[52]

Like the *De agricultura* the *De re militari* was the first Latin book of its kind; but whereas in the case of the former there is uncertainty about the earlier existence of Greek handbooks of comparable type, there is no doubt that there were a considerable number of practical military treatises and manuals, mostly written in the Hellenistic period.[53] In view of Cato's particular interests, general curiosity, and at least moderate familiarity with Greek writings, it is scarcely conceivable that he did not know of at least some of these manuals; and it would therefore be unreasonable to suppose that there was no connection between these and his decision to write his own military book, at least to the extent of prompting the general idea of doing so. It is much less likely, however, that he followed any of them closely as a model. Much of the detail in them would have been irrelevant to Roman military practices, and both the fragments and the use made subsequently of Cato's work indicate that it dealt very specifically with Roman methods and practices. Cato, who in the *De agricultura* is so unconcerned about structure, is scarcely likely to have attempted to

fit these Roman details into a pattern taken over from a Greek manual. It is impossible to tell, however, to what extent the *De re militari* exhibited the same attitudes as the *De agricultura* towards matters of composition, coherence, relevance, and structure, though the very nature of the military material may be expected to have encouraged a rather firmer structure.

Other writings contrast with the three practical handbooks in various ways. The *Ad filium* and perhaps the collection of witticisms are distinctive in probably not having been written with a view to publication, and neither they nor the *Carmen de moribus* were concerned with the exposition of a single topic. The *Ad filium* was evidently a collection of precepts and exhortations covering a wide range of subjects, while a book about *mores* was scarcely dealing with a single topic in the same sense as a book of practical instruction on agriculture or warfare. In fact the *Carmen* as well as the *Ad filium* may well have been predominantly 'preceptual' in character, and in both cases, though there was no doubt a tendency for topics to occur in groups roughly determined by topic, the nature of the subject-matter probably meant that there was even less constraint to think about structure. The nature of the material explains also why striking stylistic features are more in evidence in the fragments of these works, though the features themselves are much the same as in other writings: a marked epigrammatic quality, as is only to be expected, together with brevity and succinctness, asyndeton and assonance, antitheses and paradox.[54]

4. The development of Cato's literary activity

There remains the most basic of the questions about Cato's writings: why did he write them? Clearly no single comprehensive answer could completely and sufficiently explain such a diversity of works. It is obvious that in an important sense the considerations which lay behind a book of miscellaneous guidance for Cato's son differed from those behind a book on agriculture intended for general circulation, and similarly in the case of each individual book. The *De agricultura* in particular, no doubt partly because it alone survives, has from time to time been seen (implausibly) as a kind of propaganda tract, usually in the sense of seeking to encourage the spread of the type of agriculture Cato describes.[55] Yet it is not sufficient to fragment the question by considering the motivation for each book separately and in isolation; there is a more general question to be answered. For Cato was an innovator, not merely in the sense of being the first Roman to write books about these particular topics but in the much more fundamental sense of being the first to write prose books in Latin about any topic at all. An explanation is required not simply for his choice of topics but for the fact that he wrote at all.

Answers to this question have been very largely along the lines that he was attempting to create a Latin prose literature as a response to the Romans' rapidly growing awareness of Greek literature—though within this general concept it is possible to discern two rather different emphases, as well as numerous variations in detail. Usually stress is laid on Cato's supposed hostility to Greek culture, or at least to certain aspects of it. Alarmed at the dangers with which he judged Rome to be threatened, yet conscious of the power of Greek literature to fascinate, not only on account of its brilliance and intellectual content but because an extensive literature was in itself an exotic novelty in Rome, he deliberately set out to create a Latin literature as an alternative. Between such an interpretation and the apparent theme of the *Carmen de moribus* it is possible to envisage a positive relationship, thus adding to the coherence of the picture; but it is the *Ad filium* which has bulked largest in such discussions. Almost universally believed to have been a kind of 'encyclopedia', in the form of a set of books with each book dealing with a separate topic, this is usually supposed to have been an attempt to provide a specifically Roman version of Greek educational programmes. Sometimes, and particularly in more recent studies, the motive for attempting to provide such an alternative has been seen not so much in outright alarm at the influence of Hellenic culture, as in a rational appraisal that certain features of Greek educational programmes were unsuited to Roman requirements and also that these programmes lacked a number of topics needed by Romans. That approach shades off into the other main category of interpretation, that Cato was not so much anxious to combat Greek literature as fired by a patriotic zeal that Rome be given a literature of its own: consciousness of cultural and literary inferiority was hurtful to the pride of the conquering Romans and was a deficiency which must be remedied. Others had already been at work in the field of verse—among them, Ennius, initially sponsored by Cato himself—and now Cato would attempt to create a prose literature.

In what follows it must be borne in mind that no account has yet been taken of the *Origines,* which has featured significantly in such assessments; but at least it is not easy to see that work, to which Cato was still making additions in the last year of his life, as having an initial or a primary role in the development of his literary activity. For the other works enough has been seen both about them and about Cato's attitudes to the Greeks for it to be evident that the type of explanation outlined above is not satisfactory.[57] Cato's attitude to the Greeks and their culture, ambivalent though it was and in certain respects strongly prejudiced, was not such as would naturally have led him into attempting to create a substitute for Greek literature. It is misleading to take his hostile comments about Greek culture literally or in isolation from the other evidence which compels a different and more complex view; and it is far from clear that

he was troubled by a sense of cultural inferiority, let alone afflicted with a sense of doom because he believed the fascinations of Hellenic literature threatened to hypnotize the Romans into a blind acceptance of all the worst along with the best in Greek life and culture. Profound though his dislike was of certain features of that culture, most of his writings had little or no relevance to those features. Indeed the topics about which he wrote are for the most part wholly unconvincing and implausible as the basis of a literature intended to rival that of the Greeks. So also are the unsystematic attitudes and methods displayed in the composition of the *De agricultura,* suggestive of a confident self-reliance that simply gave no thought to the Greeks, far more than of an anxious concern to produce a work that could be compared in merit. Neither does it seem likely that in these works Cato was closely following Greek models, either in detail or in structure. Above all the *Ad filium,* which for over a century has been a central feature of most discussions, has been incorrectly interpreted and was not a full-scale Latin version of a Greek educational programme. Instead it was probably simply a collection of precepts and exhortations for the guidance of Cato's son, and in the first instance was probably assembled for that purpose alone.

The question 'Why did Cato write?' is deceptively simple. It appears to invite an explanation of a particular event, and thereby an answer which would almost certainly be too static, too monolithic, expressed in terms of an event rather than the growth of an idea. For it is improbable that Cato's authorship can be explained in terms of a single decision, a single moment, or even a single attitude or a single overriding purpose. It is better understood as emerging and developing, and doing so in response to his circumstances and his experience. There was a background to Cato's composition of prose works in Latin. Familiarity with the concept of books had been growing for a considerable time. Well before Cato wrote it had reached the point where some books originated in Rome and dealt with Roman subject-matter. Already the dramatists and poets, above all Ennius, had notable achievements to their credit, while Fabius Pictor and Cincius Alimentus with their histories in Greek had at least set the precedent for books to be written by Romans of high social standing. Furthermore the actual use of writing in Latin was of great antiquity and was certainly familiar for a wide variety of practical uses, including domestic records and communications. It is a reasonable guess that Cato's first prose books were not envisaged at all as books for a public but were intended for purely domestic, practical purposes. Possibly the 'history in big letters' written to aid the education of his elder son— itself an imaginative idea—was one of the earliest experiments and led him on to others. In due course the same basic idea of instructing his son through the medium of writing, linked with an awareness of his own talent for aphorism, produced the further development of a collection of precepts and exhortations. By its very nature, however, this was a vehicle which encouraged Cato to display his facility in the use of language, so that a work almost certainly written for the guidance of an individual could arouse sufficient interest for copies to be made and in due course for it to pass into circulation. Such experiments are likely to have stimulated not only pleasure in their success but an interest in further ventures; so increasing enthusiasm led Cato on to new and more elaborate ideas, including that of devoting a whole book to a single topic of instruction. It is indeed plausible that as he went on he was encouraged by a certain patriotic pride, for he can scarcely have been unconscious that what he was doing was novel in Rome and hitherto had been in the province of the Greeks; but the obvious relationship of his topics to his personal experience and interests suggests that his thoughts were not so much concerned with the literary background or with possible comparisons as centred on what he himself was doing as, so to speak, a self-contained activity.

If Cato's authorship did develop in some such manner as this, the question of motivation takes on a different aspect. No longer is it necessary to seek some powerful overriding purpose. That does not mean that the writing of the books was simply an end in itself, a pastime without purpose. Particular motives for individual works there must have been, perhaps especially for the **Carmen de moribus;** and linking almost all the works one with another is their common didactic character. Cato wrote his books for the purpose of instruction, probably thought automatically in those terms without seriously considering alternatives, and perhaps had a heightening sense of usefulness—and of self-importance—as he applied the concept to topic after topic. It is much less likely, however, that the purpose was carefully and precisely thought out on each occasion, or that his authorship was inspired in the first place by a burning desire to instruct the community.

If this explanation is broadly correct—and any explanation can be only a matter of interpretation and hypothesis—it may appear at first sight to somewhat diminish Cato's achievement. Unsystematic in method, deficient in discipline, relevance, and order, his initiative in Latin prose literature is no longer seen either as a sudden, dramatic step or as inspired by some great patriotic or social purpose. Furthermore, seen in the wider pattern of the development of Roman literature as a whole, the emergence of prose writings in Latin at about this time seems inevitable. Is it then little more than an accident that it was Cato who did what someone was bound to do anyway before long?

To present Cato's contribution in such subdued terms would unquestionably be misleading. What the histo-rian, viewing in retrospect a whole historical movement, sees as an inevitable development may not have been so obvious and predictable in the contemporary context: fulfilment of the inevitable often requires an agent gifted with exceptional initiative and inventiveness. It is surely no accident that in this instance the agent was one of the most forceful, vigorous, and versatile personalities of the time. What was said before about the **De agricultura** may be said of Cato's writings in general: his innovation has to be viewed in the light of the absence of an established literary culture, with all that implies in terms of the lack of training in techniques of composition and in terms of an environment in which various concepts and standards were not yet familiar norms. In such a context Cato's contribution was a considerable imaginative achievement, no less so if it was a step-by-step development, extending and elaborating a modest initial idea, rather than a single momentary inspiration. . . .

Notes

[1] Livy, 39. 40. 7.

[2] Plut. *Cato Mai.* 20. 7. Cf. Peter, *HRR* i², pp. cxxix f.; Helm, *RE,* s.v. *Porcius,* no. 9, col. 146; Kienast's view, p. 107, that the composition of this work shows that Cato was probably already collecting material for the *Origines* goes further than the facts warrant. It is possible that Plutarch's words τῶν παλαιῶν καὶ πατρίων reflect an original reference to *mores maiorum.*

[3] Pliny, *Nat. hist.* 29. 15; Plut. *Cato Mai.* 23. 5. . . . Mazzarino, *Introduzione,* chs. II and III, *passim,* esp. pp. 31 ff. . . .

[5] Plut. *Cato Mai.* 20. 11; *Quaest. Rom.* 39; Cic. *De off.* 1. 36 and 37; Cugusi, *Epistolographi latini minores* i. 1, pp. 67 ff., i. 2, pp. 34 ff.; cf. Jordan, pp. 83 f., *Epistulae* frs. 1 ff. Schmidt, 'Catos Epistula ad M. filium', *Hermes,* 100 (1972), 568 ff., argues for a wide-ranging didactic letter and also against the survival of more than one letter. Festus, p. 280L and Diom. *Gramm.* 1. 366. 13K are not good evidence for more and both passages are probably to be emended.

[6] Veget. 1. 8; 2. 3; 3. 20. A sentence in this last chapter, with no mention of Cato, is identical with a sentence cited by Nonius, p. 301, 32L, as from Cato's *De re militari,* and it is probable that the whole of Veget. 3. 20 follows Cato closely. For discussion of Cato as a source for Vegetius see esp. Schenk, *Flavius Vegetius Renatus, Klio,* Beih. 22; Neumann, *RE,* Suppb. X, s.v. *Vegetius,* cols. 1005 ff., esp. 1014 f.

[7] Jordan, pp. 80 ff., *De re mil.* frs. 1-15. Barwick, 'Zu den Schriften des Cornelius Celsus und des alten Cato', *WJA* 3 (1948), 126 f., is not convincing when he seeks

to explain the plural *in libris* in Veget. 1. 15 (= fr. 7) by the hypothesis that in addition to the separate monograph Cato included another *in libris ad filium*. Apart from the relationship to Vegetius the monograph has aroused only slight modern interest. See Köchly and Rüstow, *Griechische Kriegschriftsteller* ii. 61 ff.; Nap, 'Ad Catonis librum de re militari', *Mn* 55 (1927), 79 ff.; Spaulding, 'The Ancient Military Writers', *CJ* 28 (1933), 660 f.

[8] Just. *Inst.* 1. 11. 12; *Dig.* 1. 2. 2. 38; 21. 1. 10. 1; 24. 3. 44 pr. (prob. Capito); 45. 1. 4. 1; cf. 34. 7; Gell. 13. 20. 9; *RE*, s.v. *Porcius*, no. 14, col. 168.

[9] Festus, p. 144, 18L, s.v. *mundus:* 'sic refert Cato in commentaris iuris civilis.'

[10] Cic. *De sen.* 38. It is conceivable that Cato's complaint recorded in Cic. *De divin.* 1. 28 = *HRR* i², fr. 132 that auguries had been lost as a result of neglect by the college is a fragment of this work, though this is not the only possible source.

[11] Livy, 39. 40. 5 f.; Nepos, *Cato* 3. 1; Quintil. *Inst.* 12. 11. 2; also Cic. *De orat.* 1. 171; 3. 135; Val. Max. 8. 7. 1; Quintil. *Inst.* 12. 3. 9. Cic. *De orat.* 2. 142 perhaps refers to the son.

[12] Jordan, pp. 82 f., *Carmen* frs. I-3 = Gell. 11. 2. 1 ff.; Nonius, p. 745, 15L. Helm, *RE,* s.v. *Porcius*, no. 9, cols. 146 f., suggests that another possible fragment is in Column. *De re rust.* 11. 1. 26. A further possibility is Jordan, p. 110, *Dict. mem.* 76 = Sen. *Epist.* 122. 2; cf. Cic. *De fin.* 2. 23; Column. *De re rust.* I pr. 16.

[13] Helm, *RE,* s.v. *Porcius,* no. 9, cols. 146 ff., referring to *TLL* iii. 463, 51. For a recent argument that it was in saturnians, Pighi, 'Catonis carmen de moribus', *Latinitas,* 14 (1966), 31 ff.

[14] Cic. *De off.* 1. 104; *De orat.* 2. 271.

[15] Fabius: Cic. *De orat.* 2. 271; 2. 273, cf. *De sen.* 11; *Rep.* 1. 27. Africanus: Quintil. *Inst.* 6. 3. 105, which Jordan, p. 83, cites as *Apophth.* fr. 1.

[16] Plut. *Cato Mai.* 2. 6. See esp. Rossi, 'De M. Catonis dictis et apophthegmatis', *Athenaeum,* n.s. 2 (1924), 174 ff.; Della Corte, *Catone censore²,* pp. 246 ff.

[17] Nachstädt, Teubner edn. of Plut. *Moralia,* ii. 1, p. 81. It has been generally recognized that this collection cannot be the one used by Plutarch. Though it has sometimes been suggested that it was compiled by extracting dicta from Plutarch's *Life,* this too is incorrect: the order of the common items differs too much, and there are too many striking sayings in the *Life,* especially in chs. 8 and 9, which are not in the collection and which would scarcely have been omitted if the latter had been based

on the former. Yet there is a definite relationship between the two, indicated by some correspondence in order and in a number of cases by exact correspondence in much of the wording. It looks as if somewhere in the antecedents of both works there was a common list, that the version available to Plutarch was more comprehensive (as shown (*a*) by chs. 8 and 9, (*b*) by sayings which are in both the *Life* and the *Moralia* but not in the *Apophthegmata*), and that the *Apophthegmata* was based on part of the same material but drew also upon other— and spurious—material.

[18] *HRR* i², fr. 2; cf. Xen. *Sympos.* I. I.

[19] Useful surveys of the extensive literature regarding the *De agricultura* will be found in Schanz-Hosius, *Gesch. der röm, Literatur* i⁴. 184 ff.; Helm, *RE,* s.v. *Porcius,* no. 9, cols. 147 ff.; Mazzarino, *Introduzione, passim;* White, 'Roman Agricultural Writers', in Temporini, *Aufstieg und Niedergang* i. 4, pp. 439 ff. Marmorale, *Cato Maior²,* p. 162 n. 36, has a major bibliographical list; see also Zuccarelli, 'Rassegna bibliografica . . . (1940-1950)', *Paideia,* 7 (1952), 213 ff. On the aspects of the work discussed in this chapter see also esp. Gummerus, *Der röm. Gutsbetrieb, Klio, Beih.* 5 (1906), 15 ff.; Leo, *Gesch. der röm. Literatur* i. 270 ff.; Birt, 'Zum Proöm und den Summarien', *BPhW* 29 (1915), cols. 922 ff.; Hörle, *Catos Hausbücher,* §§I and II; Brehaut, *Cato the Censor. On Farming,* pp. xiii ff.; Della Corte, *Catone censore²,* pp. 100 ff.; Thielscher, *Belehrung, passim.* For bibliography more esp. concerned with social and economic aspects see p. 240 n. 1. On the agricultural material from a practical point of view see esp. White, *Roman Farming;* Brehaut, *Cato the Censor. On Farming.*

[20] The correct title is almost certainly *De agricultura,* despite the occasional occurrence of *De re rustica:* Schanz-Hosius, op. cit. p. 184; Marmorale, op. cit., p. 163. Helm, op. cit., cols. 147 ff., links the question too closely with the issue of whether Cato himself published the book.

[21] e.g. *De agr.* 2. 7; 4 ('frons . . . est'); 39. 2 ('cogitato . . . etc.'); 61. 1. Note also several vigorous sequences, markedly rhetorical in character, in ch. 2, dealing with the owner's inspection of the farm and his discussion with the *vilicus*.

[22] Leeman, *Orationis Ratio,* pp. 21 ff., suggests Greek influence, but see Kappelmacher, 'Zum Stil Catos im De re rustica', *WS* 43 (1922/3), 168 ff.; von Albrecht, *Meister röm. Prosa,* pp. 15 ff.

[23] *De agr.* 3. 1, with the injunction to build only at thirty-six years of age.

[24] Thielscher, *Belehrung,* pp. 14 f., who however places too much confidence in the inference. Pliny, *Nat. hist.*

14. 45, is clearly not to be taken literally as secure evidence for composition in Cato's old age, though it has sometimes been quoted to that effect.

[25] Colum. *De re rust.* 1. 1. 12; cf. Pliny, *Nat. hist.* 14. 47.

[26] *De agr.* 143; cf. 5. 6 ff., where it is not clear whether the *vilicus* or the *dominus* is addressed, though the latter is perhaps more probable. Elsewhere many of the second-person imperatives would have been directed most appropriately to the *vilicus,* but they may have been thought of rather as 'impersonal' directions.

[27] See esp. Mazzarino, *Introduzione,* pp. 69 ff. Doublets are examined in great detail by Hörle, *Catos Hausbücher,* esp. pp. 5 and 127 ff. Thielscher, *Belehrung,* in his commentary sets out many of the passages concerned in a form which greatly facilitates comparison.

[28] See esp. Schanz-Hosius, *Gesch. der röm. Literatur* i⁴. 184 ff.; Helm, *RE, s.v. Porcius,* no. 9, cols. 152 ff.; Mazzarino, *Introduzione, passim*; White, 'Roman Agricultural Writers', in Temporini, *Aufstieg und Niedergang* i. 4, pp. 439 ff., esp. 447 ff.

[29] e.g. Mazzarino, *Introduzione,* esp. p. 57, combines three of the approaches set out below: that Cato was adapting material in *commentarii* to a literary form, that the task was incomplete at his death, and that when this unfinished work passed into circulation it was modified by annotations.

[30] So, rightly, Helm, *RE, s.v. Porcius,* no. 9, col. 152, citing esp. Pliny, *Nat. hist.* 19. 147. In 15. 44 and 46 Pliny states that Cato did not discuss plum-trees. On the basis of this Mazzarino, *Introduzione,* pp. 69 ff., argued that Pliny's copy of Cato's book did not include the list given in *De agr.* 133, which does mention the plum, but only the version in 8. 2, which is similar but without the plum; from which he infers that only the version of layering given in 51-2 is original, the version of layering in 133 being a gloss unknown to Pliny. He does not however account for Pliny, *Nat. hist.* 17. 96, which seems fatal to the argument, since it clearly quotes Cato's instructions on layering from the version in 133, including the reference to plums: cf. Münzer, *Beiträge zur Quellenkritik,* pp. 14 f. (though Münzer's principal argument is that much of Pliny's Catonian material is at second hand). Furthermore comparison of the sequence of ideas in 50-2 and 131-3 suggests a different explanation and that both sections are original: see Appendix 10. Aside from this question *Nat. hist.* 18. 34 seems to be the only one of the many unequivocally agricultural passages attributed by Pliny to Cato which does not correspond reasonably well to a passage in the *De agricultura.* Among a great number of quotations this is such a striking

exception that the correctness of the attribution must be suspect.

[31] Hörle, *Catos Hausbücher,* I and II.

[32] Hauler, *Zu Catos Schrift,* p. 6.

[33] Thielscher, *Belehrung,* pp. 5 ff., though he applies this type of interpretation too extensively, inferring from the text much more than is justified in the way of biographical detail concerning Cato.

[34] Leo, *Gesch. der röm. Literatur* i. 272; cf. Helm, *RE, s.v. Porcius,* no. 9, col. 152; Brehaut, *Cato the Censor. On Farming,* p. xix; Marmorale, *Cato Maior²,* p. 164, cf. p. 184, who regards the work of planning as the simple and complete explanation.

[35] Some other examples: *De agr.* 6. 3-4, on the planting of reeds; 7-8, on fruits; 15-18, digressing from building to lime-burning and thence to woodcutting, then back to building. Note also how reference to a general activity several times provokes a digression into detailed instructions: 39 (mending pots); 40 (suitable sites for trees leads to instructions for grafting); and other instances through to 49.

[36] e.g. 128-30, uses of *amurca,* picking up from 103. . . .

[38] pp. 137 ff. and 151 f.

[39] Cato begins by contrasting trade and usury unfavourably with agriculture as sources of income. After indicating briefly the disadvantages of the two former he begins to expand his points by emphasizing the hostility of the *maiores* to usury. Mention of the *maiores,* however, leads him into a report of their high opinion of farming, after which he returns to the disadvantages of trade, and finally takes up again the merits of farming. Evidently the mention of the *maiores* led him to introduce at once an idea which from the point of view of orderly presentation would have been better placed after the account of the disadvantages of trade; for as it is it makes the sequence of ideas in the Preface more awkward and complicated to follow. Cf. Janson, *Latin Prose Prefaces,* p. 84.

[40] On Hellenistic agricultural writings see Susemihl, *Gesch. der griech. Lit. in der Alexandriner-Zeit* i. 829 ff.; cf. Schmid-Stählin, *Gesch. der griech. Lit.* ii. i⁶, pp. 289 ff.; White, *Roman Farming,* pp. 15 f. Many Greek authors are named by Varro, *De re rust.* 1. 1.7 ff. and Columella, *De re rust.* 1. 1.7. It is clear that some of these works were scientific and theoretical rather than practical (the majority of the authors named by Varro are termed philosophers), and that others were specialized monographs, e.g. on bee-keeping or viticulture; but about many nothing is known, though

Susemihl conjectures that there was a preponderance of specialized monographs. No practical handbook comparable to Cato's is known, though it would be rash to insist that none existed. The nearest is perhaps Xenophon's *Oeconomicus,* but that differs in many major respects.

⁴¹ Janson, *Latin Prose Prefaces,* pp. 84 ff., distinguishes two lines of argument interwoven in the Preface: a moral argument, which is not relevant to the book, and economic arguments with which the book fits well. It is certainly the case that there is a loose, rather general relationship in so far as Cato alludes in the Preface to an income from farming of such a kind that it could be compared with an income from trade or usury; for that is the type of farming with which the book is concerned. Nevertheless by presenting Cato's treatment in terms of the interweaving of two distinct lines of argument and by overestimating the element of economic argument Janson creates the impression of a closer and more positive relationship than actually exists. Only in one point— that an income from agriculture is more secure than one from trade—can the argument be termed economic; and in the sentence just quoted in the text that point is so closely joined to 'moral' arguments that even in this respect it seems less a case of interweaving different kinds of arguments than of failing to draw a distinction. . . .

⁴³ Such a procedure would fit well with the form in which many of the items are given. Cato certainly had secretaries (cf. Plut. *Cato Mai.* 24. 3) and the passage relating to the composition of the speech *De sumptu suo* (*ORF*³, fr. 173; see pp. 135 f.) suggests that he may not so much have read his *commentarii* as had them read to him; for the idea of a scribe copying a passage, note in the same fragment the words *noli, noli scribere, inquam, istud.* It is a hypothesis to be approached with caution and the general interpretation set out in this chapter is not dependent upon it; for Cato's personal touch is apparent at various points even in the later parts of the *De agricultura.* Nevertheless the fragment from the *De sumptu suo* does suggest that Cato sometimes composed by dictation. Possibly Cato's own explicit statement that the 'history in big letters' was written with his own hand (Plut. *Cato Mai.* 20. 7) also indicates that this was out of the ordinary and that he often dictated. However it is also possible that the significance of this lies rather in the emphasis on Cato's personal intervention as opposed to the use of slave tutors, which is certainly the point being made a few lines before.

⁴⁴ Esp. *De agr.* 21. 5; 22. 3 f.; 135; 136. Brehaut, *Cato the Censor. On Farming,* pp. xiv f., rightly observes that despite these particularistic items Cato's intention was undoubtedly to write a book of general guidance with much wider reference.

⁴⁵ The Sabine inheritance. Note also the enthusiasm for pasturing reported in Cic. *De off.* 2. 89 = Jordan, p. 108, *Dicta mem.* 63, with other references. Thielscher, *Belehrung,* p. 272, wrongly rejects the authenticity of this on the ground of its similarity in form to *De agr.* 16. 1.

⁴⁶ *De agr.* 3. 1. So Thielscher, *Belehrung,* pp. 9 f. and 187, and others. Leeman, 'Cato, De Agricultura 3, 1', *Helikon,* 5 (1965), 534 ff., suggests that it may have reference to an old Greek or Etruscan belief that life is to be divided into seven-year periods. Brehaut, op. cit., p. 8, note ad loc., seeks a rational explanation in the suggestion that by that age most Romans would be approaching the end of their liability for military service.

⁴⁷ Jordan, p. 80, *De re militari* fr. 1 = Pliny, *Nat. hist. praef.* 30. In the remainder of this chapter the fragments of this work will be indicated by the number only.

⁴⁸ Frs. 2 and 3.

⁴⁹ Fr. 1, *vitilitigent;* fr. 14, *disciplinosus;* said to be neologisms by Pliny, *Nat. hist. praef.* 32 and Gell. 4. 9. 12 respectively, evidently correctly in both cases. Cf. Till-Meo, *La lingua di Catone,* pp. 81, 90, 128 f.

⁵⁰ Frs. 9, 11, and 13.

⁵¹ Fr. 11.

⁵² Fr. 6: 'inde partem equitatus atque ferentarios praedatum misit.'

⁵³ Schmid-Stählin, *Gesch. der Griech. Literatur* ii. 1⁶, pp. 286 ff.; Kromayer-Veith, *Heerwesen und Kriegführung,* p. 13.

⁵⁴ Jordan, pp. 82 f., *Carmen* frs. 1-3 = Gell. 11. 2. 1 ff.; see further p. 186 n. 12. Jordan, pp. 77-80, assigns sixteen fragments to the *Ad filium,* though five (10, 11, 13, 15, 16) have no indication that they actually belong.

⁵⁵ For the question of social and economic attitudes in the *De Agricultura* see Ch. 11. Della Corte, *Catone censore²,* pp. 99 ff., takes the initial purpose to have been political, an attempt by Cato to restore his 'peasant image' after he had been prosecuted *de sumptu suo.* . . .

⁵⁷ Ch. 8, *passim,* esp. pp. 178 ff. . . .

Abbreviations

HRR i² H. W. G. Peter, *Historicorum Romanorum Reliquiae,* Leipzig, 1914.

RE Pauly-Wissowa-Kroll, *Real-Encyclopadie der classichen Altertumswissenschaft.*

Kienast D. Kienast, *Cato der Censor,* Heidelberg, 1954.

Titles of periodicals are abbreviated in accordance with the system used in *L'Année philologique.*

Gian Biagio Conte (essay date 1987)

SOURCE: Gian Biagio Conte, "Cato," in *Latin Literature: A History,* The Johns Hopkins University Press, 1994, pp. 85-91.

[*Conte's authoritative text on Latin literature,* first published in Italian in 1987, provides a brief summary of Cato's life and work. *He emphasizes the significance of the* Origines, *the* De agricultura, *and Cato's attitude to Greek culture, which Conte contends to have been less hostile than usually described.*]

Life

Marcus Porcius Cato was born in 234 at Tusculum, near what is today Frascati, to a plebeian family of prosperous farmers. He fought in the war against Hannibal, and in 214 he was military tribune in Sicily. The aristocrat Lucius Valerius Flaccus aided him in his political career. In 204 Cato was quaestor, accompanying Scipio to Sicily and Africa, in 199 plebeian aedile, and in 198 praetor in charge of governing Sardinia. In 195 the *homo novus* Cato was consul with Valerius Flaccus. While in office he opposed revoking the *lex Oppia,* a sumptuary law that limited the expenditures particularly of women from wealthy families. Spain was assigned as his province, where he acted harshly towards the Spanish tribes and enhanced his own reputation for efficiency and frugality.

In 191 B.C., as military tribune with Valerius Flaccus under the command of the consul Acilius Glabrio, he fought at Thermopylae and carried out an important diplomatic mission at Athens and other Greek cities. From 190 onwards he was prosecutor in a series of political trials against members of the dominant faction of the Scipios. In 184 he was censor along with Valerius Flaccus. In that office he presented himself as the champion of the ancient Roman virtues against moral degeneration and against the spread of a tendency towards individualism that was influenced in part by Hellenistic culture. In addition, and in parallel to his polemic against the extravagance of private citizens, Cato glorified the wealth and power of the state, as must have been evident to all: as censor, he promoted a vast program of public construction. The censorship of Cato remained famous on account of the intransigence with

which he performed his duties, giving vent to his moral rigor. Afterwards, too, his attitude won him many enemies, and he was often involved in trials, as accuser as well as defendant. In 181 he opposed the revoking of another sumptuary law, the *lex Orchia,* and in 169 supported the *lex Voconia,* which limited women's rights of inheritance. In 167 he opposed the war against Rhodes (fragments remain of his *Oratio pro Rhodiensibus,* which Cato himself had reported in his **Origines**): before the Third Punic War he, along with a part of the ruling class, may have been thinking of the possibility of a balance among the Mediterranean powers, and for this reason he may have opposed ending Rhodian independence and favored the independence of Macedon.

In 155 Cato spoke against the philosophers whom Athens had sent to Rome as ambassadors . . . , and he secured their expulsion. Probably his conservative nature caused him to fear that they, in particular Carneades, with his antilogies on justice, might lead educated Romans to entertain doubts about the validity of the traditional ethics. In 153, on a visit to Carthage, which after its defeat in the Second Punic War was beginning to flourish again, Cato became persuaded that Rome's survival depended on the destruction of its ancient rival. He therefore urged the Third Punic War, but, dying in 149, did not live to see the destruction of the enemy city.

Works

Speeches: Cicero knew more than 150 speeches of Cato. Today we know the titles and the circumstances of about 80 of them, about 20 of which go back to the year of his censorship. We also possess various fragments.

Origines, a historical work in seven books, written in old age; some fragments survive.

A treatise **De Agri Cultura,** which is preserved, the earliest Latin prose text that has come down to us entire; it consists of a preface and 170 short chapters.

Carmen de Moribus, probably a work in prose; the term *carmen* would seem to indicate rhythmic prose.

Apophthegmata, a collection of memorable sayings or anecdotes that went under Cato's name, some of which are cited by such authors as Cicero or Plutarch.

Sources

Plutarch's *Life of Cato;* Cornelius Nepos's *Life of Cato;* Cicero's *Cato Maior de Senectute;* sections of Livy, books 29, 32, 34, 36, 38-39, 43, and 45.

1. The Beginnings of Senatorial Historiography

Cato wrote the **Origines** in old age, thus starting historiography in Latin; he scorned and derided Roman annals in Greek, such as those of Aulus Postumius Albinus. . . . From its beginning, as we saw, Roman historical writing had felt the effects of being produced primarily by members of the senatorial elite, even though often not by the politically most eminent figures. The case of Cato, a politician of the first rank who wrote history, was fated to remain practically unique in Latin culture; autobiographical *commentarii* such as those of Sulla or Caesar are evidently different.

Its being produced by members of the ruling class, which sees in it a dignified way of filling its own *otium,* lends to the nascent Roman historiography a robust political engagement. In Cato's historical work much space is given to his own concerns over the rampant moral corruption and to his personal battles, waged in the name of public solidarity, against the emergence of notable figures with marked tendencies towards individualism and the cult of personality; some such individuals were found in the Scipionic circle, chief among them Africanus Maior. For this reason Cato allowed his political polemics a place in the **Origines** and reported his own speeches, for example, those in behalf of the Rhodians or against Sulpicius Galba; indeed, it has been thought, and it is not unlikely, that a part of Cato's historical work was a sort of self-celebration. Moreover, he tended to privilege contemporary history, to which he dedicated about half (three books out of seven) of a work that reached far back, to the very origins of Rome.

The first book of the **Origines** was devoted to the founding of Rome, the second and third to the origins of the Italian cities. The title of the work properly applied only to these first three books. The fourth book told of the First Punic War, the fifth of the Second, the sixth and seventh of events down to the praetorship of Servius Sulpicius Galba, in 152 B.C. The proportions of the individual book grew as the work approached the present: the last two books covered a period of less than fifty years and were a detailed contemporary history.

In attempting to kill at birth the charismatic cult of the great personalities, Cato worked out a conception of Roman history that emphasized above all the gradual formation of the state and its institutions over the generations and the centuries, a conception that would be partially taken up by Cicero in the *De Re Publica:* the creation of the Roman state was seen as the collective work of the *populus Romanus* around the senatorial ruling class. Thus Cato, probably breaking with the traditional annals often composed by members of the noble families, did not give the names of commanders, neither Romans nor foreigners; Hannibal himself, as we see from a preserved frag-

ment, was called *dictator Carthaginiensium.* The *novus homo* from Tusculum probably aimed at dimming the renown of the *gentes* in favor of the *res publica.* In their stead Cato seems to have brought into the light of history the names of rather obscure persons, heroes of less elevated rank, who precisely for this reason deserved to be hailed as symbols of the collective heroism of the Roman people; thus Cato dedicated a certain amount of space to the account of the valiant deeds of a certain Quintus Caedicius.

In other directions, the **Origines** showed a notable broadening of horizons. Perhaps the origins of the *novus homo* Cato outside the city helped give him a lively interest, shown in books 2 and 3, in the history of the Italian populations, emphasizing their contributions to the greatness of Rome and to the creation of the traditional ethical model. He boasted, for example, of the moral uprightness of his own people, the Sabines, and their parsimony, which were due in the first place to their alleged Spartan origins and strengthened by their strong relation to the land. But Cato also showed an almost ethnographic interest in foreign peoples, for instance, in certain customs of the African and Spanish peoples; the particulars that he furnished probably went back to direct observations, since in the course of his political and military career he had been in direct contact with these peoples.

2. The Treatise on Agriculture

The **De Agri Cultura** has no place for literary ornaments or for philosophical reflections on the farmer's life and fate of the sort found in a large number of the subsequent Latin treatises on agriculture; the work consists mostly of a series of precepts laid down in dry, schematic fashion, but sometimes very effectively. The tone of the sententious precepts must have been especially dear to Cato, since it shaped such works as the *Praecepta ad Filium* (on various subjects, but the title and structure are uncertain) and the **Carmen de Moribus,** a collection of lapidary sayings on moral subjects. For grasping the purpose and intended audience of the **De Agri Cultura** the proem is important, in which Cato shows that agriculture is more than anything an acquisitive activity; various social considerations make it preferable to others, for instance, to lending money at interest, which is immoral, or to trading by sea, which is too risky. Agriculture is more secure and more honorable; moreover, it is by farmwork that good citizens and good soldiers are formed.

The type of farm that Cato describes probably represents the passage from the small family holding to the much vaster estates that were based upon the concentration and intense exploitation of slaves, whom overseas conquests had begun to make available to the Romans in large numbers. Cato, the *homo novus* who had absorbed the aristocracy's values, strives to set the aristocracy's domination upon sturdier economic and ideological bases. In the period when farming by slaves was expanding, he demonstrates to the nobility and the sectors dominated by them how to find great profits in those landholdings that were the traditional inheritance of the ruling class, without needing to resort to more dynamic, but also more dangerous, forms of investment—which, to be sure, Cato did not eschew: we know of an involvement of his in maritime commerce. Remaining attached to the land, the ruling class remained attached also to the ethical-political values which formed the ideological foundation of their power.

The *De Agri Cultura* is a collection of general precepts on how the landowner should behave. In the role of *pater familias* he, in accordance with the patriarchal tradition, should be present on his own estate as much as possible, in order to supervise the punctual carrying out of all tasks. The style is spare and concise but enlivened by bits of rustic folk wisdom, which find ready expression in figurative proverbial formulations. The patina of archaism contributes to the effect: alliteration, homoeoteleuton, and repetition are found in abundance in the *De Agri Cultura*. Yet it would be a mistake to imagine that one is dealing with a kindhearted, patriarchal agricultural civilization. The brutality of slave exploitation is manifest in several passages: Cato recommends selling, like scrap metal, a slave who is old or ill and thus incapable of work. It should also be kept in mind that in the *De Agri Cultura* farming is regarded as an enterprise conducted on a vast scale: the landowner ought to have huge storehouses in which to keep the produce while waiting for prices to rise, and he ought to buy as little as possible and sell as much as possible; that is, he ought to have the outlook of a producer, not a consumer. Hence one can infer the salient features of the Catonian ethic, which are the same ones that the late Republic would come to regard as making up the *mos maiorum*: virtues such as *parsimonia, duritia, industria,* the disdain for riches, and resistance to the seductiveness of pleasure show how Catonian severity is not the practical wisdom of an ingenuous, uncorrupted peasant, but represents rather the ideological implication of a genuinely practical requirement: deriving economic advantage from farming, or rather increasing the productivity of the slave labor employed in it.

3. Cato's Political-Cultural Battle

Cato's oratorical style, as far as we can gather from the fragments of his speeches, was lively and full of movement, certainly much less reserved and archaizing than the style of the treatise on agriculture. A famous maxim, transmitted as part of the *Praecepta ad Filium,* seems to express concisely Cato's notions about rhetoric: *rem tene, verba sequentur* ("have the contents clear, and the words will come of themselves"), an ostenta-

tious rejection of *ars,* the Greek rhetorical *techne,* which is also attested in several anecdotes about the Censor. This rejection of stylistic elaboration needs to be interpreted in the light of Cato's unceasing polemic against the penetration of Greek morals and culture, in their various forms, at Rome. In fact Cato was not so ignorant of Greek literature as he is made out to have been by the traditional account, according to which only in advanced age did he approach the study of that language. The *De Agri Cultura* avails itself frequently of Greek agricultural science; the influence of the Greek historian Timaeus upon the *Origines* can perhaps be felt; and even in the speeches Greek rhetorical technique is not so much absent as cleverly concealed, so as to give the audience the impression of lively immediacy and not the scent of midnight oil.

Personally imbued with Greek culture, Cato fought not so much that culture itself as certain of its enlightened features, in particular its criticism of traditional social values and relations, which had been the inheritance of sophistic thought. The enlightened elements of Greek culture may have been for Cato a corrosive agent working upon the ethical-political basis of the Republic and the aristocratic regime. These concerns probably explain the successive expulsions of Greek philosophers and intellectuals from Rome, beginning perhaps in 173. At the same time there was the risk that imitating certain Hellenizing customs could endanger the unity and internal cohesion of the aristocracy by elevating the status of charismatic personalities above the others. From this point of view one can understand Cato's battle in favor of the sumptuary laws, which limited consumption by the wealthy aristocrats and also the pomp and ostentation on the part of individual families. Moreover, by trying to prevent inherited family wealth from being dissipated in such displays of status, the sumptuary laws were also concerned to prevent excessive economic imbalances within the ruling class, which were dangerous since they could undermine its stability.

In his literary work Cato probably aimed at creating a culture that could maintain firm roots in the Roman tradition but also accept Greek contributions, yet without openly propagandizing on their behalf. We know that Cato, who had fought Scipio Africanus, was on good terms with him; this notice is nearly a presage of the destiny of Latin culture. Through the intellectuals of Aemilianus's circle Greek culture, penetrating into Rome, would henceforth go beyond the bounds that the Roman aristocracy wanted to set for it. It would allow a little rationalism to enter, perhaps more than Cato would have tolerated, but still it would stay within the limits of political-social conservatism. It would lead to a new synthesis of the *mos maiorum* with the mitigated forces of enlightenment, which in its turn would become the basis of Cicero's ethical and political thought.

4. Literary Success

Cato the Censor: the name freezes him in his function as censor and declares his transformation from a person into a symbol, a symbol of the rigid custodian of tradition and conservatism. And as a figure who summarizes in himself the fundamental virtues of the Rome of the past—austerity, parsimony, devotion to work, moral rigor—he was idealized by Cicero in the *De Re Publica* and then especially in the famous dialogue *Cato Maior de Senectute*. Cicero, however, attempting to restore unity to the ideological contrasts of the past, mitigated the harsher aspects of his character and the more intransigent features of his aversion to the phil-Hellenic nobility.

The figure of Cato would be honored with various biographies, those of Cornelius Nepos (age of Caesar) and Plutarch (first-second centuries A.D.) and the one contained in the anonymous work *De Viris Illustribus* (fourth century A.D.).

Livy appreciated his gifts but did not refrain from criticizing the intransigent uprightness of a man who seemed to him "a ferocious mastiff set upon the nobility." The highest estimation of his qualities as a writer came from the archaizers of the second century, Gellius, Fronto, and the emperor Hadrian, the last two putting him ahead of Cicero himself. But after the fourth century the firsthand knowledge of his works beings to disappear (a collection of moral maxims in verse circulated under his name, the so-called *Disticha* or *Dicta Catonis*). Only the ***De Agri Cultura*** would survive in its entirety, on account of its technical nature and utility.

Elaine Fantham (essay date 1996)

SOURCE: Elaine Fantham, "Ennius and Cato, Two Early Writers," in *Roman Literary Culture*, The Johns Hopkins University Press, 1996, p. 11.

[*In the following excerpt, Fantham sketches Cato's literary influence, presenting it in relation to the poet Ennius.*]

Rome's earliest literary culture can be exemplified in the intersecting careers of two famous men, born within five years of each other, Q. Ennius (239-169) and M. Porcius Cato (234(?)-149). Between them they wrote in every known genre of Latin prose and verse, and their long lives—Ennius reached seventy and Cato either eighty-five or ninety—witnessed the full expansion of Roman imperial conquest and both public and private wealth. Cato was born into a family of Sabine landowners and owed his early career to the patronage of a noble family. He met Ennius when he was returning from his quaestorship (he would be about thirty

years old) and brought the poet back to Rome.[1] While the Calabrian Ennius was trilingual, in Greek, Oscan, and Latin, and a professional poet, the Sabine Cato is said to have learned Greek late in life (but "late" might only mean after the age of formal education), and turned to writing only after he had carried his political career to the summit of the censorship.

Ennius, who affirmed his artistic standards by claiming the Greek title of *poeta* or "maker," wrote successful tragedies and less successful comedies, but achieved his lasting fame for his national epic of Rome, the *Annales* or "Chronicles." This was originally intended to cover Rome's history from Romulus to the defeat of Hannibal, but was continued by the poet into the wars of his own maturity. He is known to have written not only the public poetry of the drama but the lesser genres of fashionable epigram and a didactic poem on gastronomy adapted from the work of a Sicilian Greek, Archestratus of Gela. He wrote a kind of verse called *satura* on miscellaneous topics, without the social criticism or invective of Lucilian or Horatian satire; he is even credited with adapting into Latin prose the debunking history of the Olympian gods by Euhemerus, but evidence for this sophisticated product is insecure. In later life Ennius found other patrons, the Scipios (both Africanus and Nasica) and Fulvius Nobilior, the conqueror of Aetolia, whose son bestowed Roman citizenship on the poet.[2] This was a man who gave learned readings and interpretations of poetry, who lived in his own house on intimate terms with the Cornelii Scipiones, and received a statue in their family monument.

The other, complementary, side of Roman literature was developed by his former patron, Cato, who after Ennius's death composed the first history of Rome and Italy in Latin. Cato included in his history some of his own political speeches on major foreign and domestic issues, and left behind him separate texts of some 150 published speeches of every kind.[3] He even composed a manual of agriculture for his own class and an encyclopedia written in large letters for the education of his son. Each of the works I have mentioned might be said to have a different audience, according to its genre, but in their persons these two extraordinary men provided Rome with the full range of literature, omitting only philosophy and prose fiction.

Notes

[1] Nepos's *Life of Cato* (1.4) makes Cato bring Ennius from Africa: but Silius Italicus (12.390) more plausibly has Ennius fighting in Sardinia where we know Cato served as quaestor.

[2] It was always easier for a Roman master to convert his slave into a citizen by emancipation, than for a patron of a foreign national to bestow citizenship upon

him. This seems to have been a privilege limited to military commanders, who could give citizenship to individuals or units as a reward for active service.

[3] The evidence comes from Cic. *Brut.* 65, but Cicero makes it clear that he had personally sought out these texts. It is not to be thought that they were commonly available. . . .

***

FURTHER READING

Copley, Frank O. "Early Prose, Cato." In *Latin Literature from the Beginnings to the Close of the Second Century A.D.* Ann Arbor: University of Michigan Press, 1969, pp. 56-65.

　Considers Cato's influence on Latin prose in the context of the development of Latin prose literature in general.

Grant, Michael. "Cato the Censor and After." In *The Ancient Historians.* New York: Charles Scribner's Sons, 1970, pp. 167-80.

　Assesses Cato's contribution to Roman historiography, emphasizng in particular his reaction against Greek influences.

Grenier, Albert. "The New Spirit and the Old Ideal: Scipio Africanus and the Cato the Censor." In *The Roman Spirit in Religion, Thought, and Art.* London: Kegan Paul, Trench, Trubner & Co., Ltd., 1926, pp. 138-53.

　Presents Cato as a hero of Roman culture, leading the resistence against Greek influence and promoting the values of ordinary citizens against the excesses of the nobility.

Kienast, D. *Cato der Zensor.* Heidelberg, 1954.

　Authoritative German study; portrays Cato as an ambitious political maneuverer who allied himself with most of the Roman aristocracy.

Leeman, A. D. "Rhetoric in the Archaic Period." In *Orationis Ratio: The Stylistic Theories and Practice of the Roman Orators, Historians, and Philosophers.* Amsterdam: Adolf M. Hakkert, 1963, pp. 19-42.

　Claims for Cato the status of Rome's "true creator of oratorical and historical prose," substantiated with close readings of *De agricultura.*

Montanelli, Indro. "Cato." In *Romans without Laurels.* Trans. Arthur Oliver. New York: Pantheon Books, 1959, pp. 109-15.

　Frames a portrait of Cato with a description of the Roman political scene.

Till, R. *Die Sprache Catos.* Leipzig, 1936.

　Standard, extended, German study of Cato's style.

Von Albrecht, Michael. "The Beginnings of Literary Prose: M. Porcius Cato (234-149 B.C.)." In *Masters of Roman Prose: From Cato to Apuleius.* Trans. Neil Adkin. Leeds, England: Francis Cairns, 1989, pp. 1-32.

　Delves into three selections of Cato's writings for detailed study of his prose style; provides translations of selected passages.

Epicurus

341 B.C.-270 B.C.

Greek philosopher.

INTRODUCTION

Epicurus contributed significantly to Greek, Roman, and ultimately European philosophy, science, ethics, and political science. He was the master of his philosophical school, known as the Garden, roughly contemporaneous with Plato and Aristotle, the propounders of Socratic philosophy, and with the Stoic school founded by Zeno. Generally at odds with both the Stoic and the Socratic philosophy, Epicurean philosophy had its supporters for another six centuries after its founder's death but receded into stigmatized obscurity with the rise of Christianity. Nonetheless, the impact of Epicurus's thought has been wide-ranging. Its strange history manifests itself in English words—such as "epicure" and "Epicurean"—and their attendant ideas of taste, hedonism, and even debauchery. Those words reflect Epicurus's values less than they suggest Renaissance and post-Renaissance distortions of his thought. English-speaking scholars have only recently begun committing the kind of in-depth analysis and explanation necessary to redefine with some accuracy the meaning of Epicureanism.

Biographical Information

What we know of Epicurus' life we owe mainly to the efforts of Diogenes Laertius, who included Epicurus in his *Lives of Philosophers* (c. 221-235 B.C.). Epicurus was born in 341 B.C. at Samos, a colony of Athens. His youth in Samos provided the standard Greek education, which Epicurus supplemented with his own investigations into philosophy. Historians have speculated that when Epicurus went to Athens at age eighteen for a standard two years of military service, he may also have anticipated a philosophical education in the city; any such plans, however, were disrupted by political changes that forced his family to move from Samos to Colophon in Asia minor. Epicurus followed in 321 B.C., continuing his philosophical studies on his own and as teachers were available.

Epicurus became a teacher himself around the time he turned thirty. He established a school at Mytilene in 310 B.C. and moved it to Lampsacus a few years later, with his reputation and following growing all the while. By 307 B.C. he was ready to move the new school of Epicureanism to Athens. He bought a house—the gar-

den of which would lend its name to his school—to shelter his community of disciples. Here he taught, thought, wrote, and mentored the works of the followers who lived with him. Both the teacher and his students wrote prolifically, explaining and defending the Epicurean creed. Ensconced in the city with the devout core of his followers, Epicurus immersed himself in his philosophical pursuits, remaining disengaged from the social and political life of the city, which at that time observed obsequious subservience to Demetrius Polioscetes. Despite the community's isolation, politics in a sense still came after them. Rival philosophical schools—particularly the Stoic—slandered the Garden, depicting it as a hotbed of amoral self-indulgence. Ironically, Garden life was in fact decidedly simple; meals, for example, generally consisted of bread and water, with cheese only to celebrate special occasions. The life of the Garden's "brotherhood" became in itself an investigation of human nature and society, embodying a kind of ideal fraternity. Upon his death in 270 B.C., Epicurus left his estate to the students who had lived with him.

Major Works

Scholars have determined that Epicurus must have composed about 300 scrolls, comprising at least twenty books. To approach this breadth of work manageably, Diogenes Laertius divided Epicurus's thought into three parts—methodological, physical, and ethical—a standard that most criticism has since followed. The first, apparently of less concern to Epicurus than it was to other Greek philosophers, addresses the epistemological question, "How do we know?" Essentially, Epicurus asserts that one knows through sensation so that, for example, abstract concepts emerge from an aggregation of physical experiences. Several works sketch Epicurus's epistemological thought, including *Principal Doctrines*, the *Letter to Herodotus*, and the *Canon*. The forty aphorisms that make up *Principal Doctrines* apparently served as a catechism (some scholars refer to it as such) of Epicurus's thought, providing the basic education to new disciples. Epicurus detailed his view of the physical world in one of his major works, *On Nature*, thought to have originally comprised almost forty scrolls.

Most critics suggest that, while issues of epistemology and physics are fundamental to the Epicurean treatment of ethical issues, they are also ultimately less important. Epicurus addressed the significance of human action, of choices made, to a greater or lesser degree in nearly all of his works. Primary among these are *Lives, The Purpose of Life, On Choice and Avoidance,* and his letters. Epicurus contended that all human action depends on pleasure and pain, always directed toward one and away from the other. Reason and virtue play a definitive role in the Epicurean notion of pleasure, always leading the wise man to choose a simple life and rational action above excess and self-indulgence. Similarly, Epicurus advocated the necessity of freedom from prejudice, superstition, and extremes of emotion in the pursuit of happiness. The apparent simplicity of this formula allowed detractors to misinterpret Epicurus, depicting him as debauched, hedonistic, anarchistic, and atheistic.

Textual History

Of the many titles attributed to Epicurus—treating topics from the gods to the senses, from music to government—only a few of his letters are extant today in any kind of complete form. Diogenes Laertius copied the *Letter to Herodotus, Letter to Menoeceus, Letter to Pythocles* (of dubious authorship), and *Principal Doctrines* into his biography. The other scraps that are available are very fragmented, either because of the condition of the manuscripts when they were found or because they were quoted with little sense of context in other writers' works. Some significant pieces of *On Nature* came to light in the eighteenth century, when a large cache of papyrus rolls was unearthed at Herculaneum. One other manuscript, maintained at the Vatican, presents a relatively extensive collection of Epicurus's aphorisms, apparently similar in purpose to *Principal Doctrines*. In 1926 Cyril Bailey published the most extensive English translation of Epicurus's works; this volume has since been considered the standard English edition.

Aside from these resources, scholars depend on the works of other Epicureans, either contemporary with their master or living in the following centuries, to fill out the picture of Epicurus's thought. Primary among these are Philodemus, who authored most of the papyrus rolls at Herculaneum; Diogenes of Oenoanda, who left an inscription dated c. 200 A.D.; and Lucretius. The latter's long poem from c. 43 B.C., *On the Nature of Things*, articulates Epicurean philosophy at length and in greater detail than any other source.

Critical Reception

Epicureanism as a movement gathered strength before its founder's death and continued for another seven centuries, waxing and waning, inciting both popular enthusiasm and sharp criticism. Many philosophers of the ancient world allied themselves with the school, devoting themselves to what they perceived to be the path to true happiness. Both Lucretius (99-44 B.C.) and Diogenes of Oenoanda (c. 200 A.D.) were products of this discipleship. Other prominent figures experimented with Epicureanism at some time in their lives without becoming committed to it. Horace and Vergil were both Epicureans in their youth but distanced themselves in later years. Also among these was Cicero (106-43 B.C.), who would become one of the most outspoken Roman detractors of Epicureanism. He expressed his contempt for Epicurus's moral philosophy and theology in many of his works, including *De Finibus* and *De Natura Deorum*. Epicurus's popularity in Rome was deemed dangerous to the populace, since it suggested skepticism in religious matters at a time when the government maintained control in part through superstition. Both Plutarch and Seneca carried on the criticism in the first century A.D.; while Seneca adopted a somewhat more approving stance, he still invoked the traditional debate between Epicurean and Stoic and pronounced that Stoicism prevailed in virtue.

Epicureanism spread through the ancient world in a manner that prefigured Christianity, with individual disciples traveling and preaching to win converts to their doctrine. Such similarities between Epicureanism and Christianity caused the two movements often to be lumped together by common enemies. By the end of the second century, however, as Christianity began to prevail in the ancient world, Epicureanism was on its wane. By the Middle Ages, Epicureanism had reached a level of distortion that allowed critics to use it as a representation of everything un-Christian, including atheism, hedonism, and materialism. Christian debate about Epicurus did, however, have two sides. Some Christian writers praised Epicurus for his rejection of superstition and his religious skepticism at a time when Christianity was not yet an option.

The earliest hints of a shift away from prevailing anti-Epicureanism emerged in the work of Lorenzo Valla, whose *On Pleasure* (1433) resurrected the ancient debate between Epicurean and Stoic in order to defend the former. A virtual Epicurean vogue occurred in seventeenth-century France, catalyzed largely by Pierre Gassendi, a theologian and religious leader who sought to recapture the virtue of Epicurus's thought in three books devoted to the topic. Although frequently unnamed as such, Epicureanism played a significant role in the thought of modern Europe, contributing to rationalism, science, and conceptions of the modern secular state. Epicurus or his shadow appears everywhere from the works of Thomas Hobbes and Jeremy Bentham to a young Karl Marx's vision of a wholly free society.

Some hints of the continental revival of Epicureanism drifted across to England and America, but a puritan heritage generally kept that interest in check, even through the nineteenth century. While Victorian England experienced a revival of interest in the classics—initiated by curricular changes at Oxford—this development afforded only marginal attention to Epicurus, since Plato and Aristotle constituted its core. Even into the twentieth century, this aversion to Epicurus often took a specifically masculinist turn, as commentators deemed him "effeminate" and "decadent" even when not misconstruing his doctrines. Some landmark works of the early twentieth century did, however, dismantle some of the age-old prejudices against Epicurus—such as Cyril Bailey's 1928 argument for Epicurus's originality and significance, which countered a long-standing charge that Epicurus simply reproduced Democritus's atomic theories. By the second half of the twentieth century, scholars were able to be less defensive about Epicurus, gradually reaching the point where serious and in-depth discussions did not require an initial vindication of their subject.

PRINCIPAL WORKS

On Nature (essay)
On Atoms and Void (essay)
Against Theophrastus (essay)
Letter to Herodotus (letter)
Letter to Menoeceus (letter)
Letter to Pythocles (letter)
Principal Doctrines (aphorisms)
Canon (essay)
On Choice and Avoidance (essay)

PRINCIPAL ENGLISH TRANSLATIONS

Epicurus: The Extant Remains (translated by Cyril Bailey) 1926

The Philosophy of Epicurus (translated by George K. Strodach) 1963

The Epicurus Reader (translated by Brad Inwood and L. P. Gerson) 1994

CRITICISM

Marcus Tullius Cicero (essay date c. 50 B.C.)

SOURCE: Marcus Tullius Cicero, "The Testimony of Cicero," in *The Epicurus Reader: Selecting Writings and Testimonia*, translated and edited by Brad Inwood and L. P. Gerson, Hackett Publishing Company, Inc., 1994, pp. 47-64.

[*The following excerpts from Cicero range from the most judicious of Cicero's critiques of Epicurus, when he engages details of Epicurus's ideas, to his most vehement manifestations of dislike.*]

TEXT 14: *On Goals* 1.18-20

18. Epicurus generally does not go far wrong when he follows Democritus . . . but these are the catastrophes which belong to Epicurus alone. He thinks that these same indivisible and solid bodies move down in a straight line by their own weight and that this is the natural motion of all bodies. 19. Then this clever fellow, when it occurred to him that if they all moved directly down and, as I said, in a straight line, it would never come about that one atom could make contact with another and so . . . he introduced a fictitious notion: he said that an atom swerves by a very little bit, indeed a minimal distance, and that in this way are produced the mutual entanglements, linkages, and cohesions of the atoms as a result of which the world and all the parts of the world and everything in it are produced. . . . The swerve itself is made up to suit his pleasure—for he says that the atom swerves without a cause . . . —and without a cause he tore from the atoms that straight downward motion which is natural to all heavy objects (as he himself declared); and by so doing he did not even achieve the goal he intended when he made up this fiction. 20. For if all the atoms swerve, none will ever cohere in a compound; but if some swerve and some move properly by their own impetus, this will amount, first of all, to assigning different spheres of influence, so to speak, to the at-

oms, some to move straight, others to move crookedly; and second, that very same confused concourse of atoms (and this is the point which Democritus too had trouble with) will not be able to produce the orderly beauty of this world.

TEXT 15: *On Fate* 18-48 (selections)

18. If it were stated thus, "Scipio will die by violence at night in his room", that would be a true statement. For it would be a statement that what was going to occur actually was going to occur; and one ought to know that it was going to occur from the fact that it did happen. And "Scipio will die" was no more true than "he will die in that manner", nor was it any more necessary that he die than that he die in that manner; nor was [the statement that] "Scipio was killed" any more immune from a change from truth to falsehood than [the statement that] "Scipio will be killed".

And the fact that these things are so does not mean that Epicurus has any reason to fear fate and seek aid from the atoms by making them swerve from their paths, and so at one time to burden himself with two unsolvable difficulties: first, that something should occur without a cause, which means that something comes to be from nothing (and neither he nor any other physicist believes that); second, that when two atoms move through the void one goes in a straight line and the other swerves.

19. Epicurus can concede that every proposition is either true or false and still not fear that it is necessary that everything occur by fate. For it is not in virtue of eternal causes derived from a necessity of nature that the following proposition is true: "Carneades will go down to the Academy"; but neither is it uncaused. Rather, there is a difference between causes which just happen to precede [the event] and causes which contain in themselves a natural efficacy. So it always was true that "Epicurus will die at the age of seventy-two in the archonship of Pytharatus", but there were not any fated causes why it should occur like this; rather, what happened certainly was going to happen as it [indeed did] happen. 20. And those who say that what is going to occur is immutable and that a true future statement cannot be converted into a false one are not in fact asserting the necessity of fate, but merely indicating what our words mean. But those who introduce an eternal series of causes are the ones who strip the human mind of free will and bind it by the necessity of fate.

But so much for this; let us move on. Chrysippus reasons thus. "If there is a motion without a cause, not every proposition, which the dialecticians call an *axioma,* will be either true or false. For what will not have effective causes will be neither true nor false. But every proposition is either true or false. Therefore, there

is no motion without a cause. 21. And if this is so, everything which happens happens in virtue of prior causes; and if this is so, all things happen by fate. So it is shown that whatever happens happens by fate."

First of all, if I here chose to agree with Epicurus and deny that every proposition is either true or false, I would rather accept that blow than approve of the claim that all things happen by fate. For that claim is at least subject to debate, but this latter is intolerable. And so Chrysippus exerts all his efforts to persuade us that every *axioma* is either true or false. Just as Epicurus fears that if he should concede this, he must concede that whatever happens happens by fate (for if one of the two is true from eternity, it is also certain, and if certain, then necessary too: that is how he thinks that necessity and fate are confirmed), so Chrysippus feared that, if he did not maintain that every proposition was either true or false, he could not maintain that everything happened by fate and as a result of eternal causes of future events.

22. But Epicurus thinks that the necessity of fate can be avoided by the swerve of an atom. And so a third kind of motion appears, in addition to weight and collision, when an atom swerves by a minimal interval (he calls it an *elachiston* [smallest]); and he is forced to concede, in fact if not in his words, that this swerve is uncaused. For an atom does not swerve because it is struck by another atom. For how can one be struck by another if the atomic bodies are moving, owing to their weight, downward in straight lines, as Epicurus thinks? It follows that, if one atom is never displaced by another, then one atom cannot even contact another. 23. From which it is also concluded that if an atom exists and it does swerve, it does so without cause. Epicurus introduced this line of reasoning because he was afraid that if an atom always moved by its natural and necessary heaviness, we would have no freedom, since our mind would be moved in such a way that it would be compelled by the motion of atoms. Democritus, the founder of atomism, preferred to accept that all things happened by necessity than to tear from the atomic bodies their natural motions.

Carneades was even more acute and showed that the Epicureans could defend their case without this fictitious swerve. For since they taught that there could be a voluntary motion of the mind, it was better to defend that claim than to introduce the swerve, especially since they could not find a cause for it. And if they defended this [the possibility of a voluntary motion of the mind] they could easily resist Chrysippus' attack. For although they conceded that there was no motion without a cause, they did not concede that everything which occurred occurred by antecedent causes. For there are no external and antecedent causes for our will. 24. Thus we [merely] exploit the common linguistic convention when we say that someone wills or does not will something without cause. For we say "without cause" in order to indicate "without external and antecedent cause," not "without any cause at all"; just as when we refer to an "empty jar" we do not speak as the physicists do, who do not believe that there is a genuinely empty space, but to indicate that the jar is without water or wine or oil, for example. Thus when we say that the mind is moved without cause, we say that it is moved without an external and antecedent cause, not without any cause at all. It can even be said of the atom itself that it moves without a cause when it moves through the void because of weight and heaviness, since there is no external cause.

25. But again, to avoid being mocked by the physicists if we say that anything occurs without a cause, one must make a distinction and say that the nature of the atom itself is such that it moves because of weight and heaviness and that exactly this is the cause of its moving the way it does. Similarly, no external cause is needed for the voluntary motions of the mind; for voluntary motion itself contains within it a nature such that it is in our power and obeys us, but not without a cause. Its very nature is the cause of this fact.

37. . . . But from all eternity this proposition was true: "Philoctetes will be abandoned on the island", and this was not able to change from being true to being false. For it is necessary, when you have two contradictories—and here I call contradictories statements one of which affirms something and the other of which denies it—of these, then, it is necessary that one be true and the other false, though Epicurus disagrees. For example, "Philoctetes will be wounded" was true during all previous ages, and "he will not be wounded" was false. Unless, perhaps, we want to accept the view of the Epicureans, who say that such propositions are neither true nor false, or, since they are ashamed of that, say what is [in fact] even more outrageous: that disjunctions of such contradictories are true, but that neither of the propositions contained in them is true. 38. What an amazing audacity and what a wretched ignorance of logic! For if in speech there is something which is neither true nor false, certainly it is not true. But how can what is not true not be false? Or how can what is not false not be true? So the principle defended by Chrysippus will be retained, that every proposition is either true or false. Reason itself will require that certain things be true from all eternity, that they not have been bound by eternal causes, and that they be free from the necessity of fate. . . .

46. This is how this matter should be discussed, rather than seeking help from wandering atoms which swerve from their [natural] course. He says, "an atom swerves." First of all, why? Democritus had already given them another kind of force, that of collision, which he called a "blow"; and you, Epicurus, had given them the force of heaviness and weight. What new cause, then, is

there in nature which would make the atom swerve? Or surely you don't mean that they draw lots with each other to see which ones will swerve and which not? Or why do they swerve by the minimal interval, and not by a larger amount? Or why do they swerve by one minimal interval, and not by two or three? This is wishful thinking, not argument. 47. For you do not say that the atom moves from its place and swerves because it is struck from outside, nor that there is in the void through which the atom moves any trace of a cause for it not to move in a straight line, nor is there any change in the atom itself which would cause it not to maintain the natural motion of its weight. So, although he adduced no cause to produce that swerve, he still thinks that he is making sense when he makes the claim which everyone's mind rejects and recoils from. 48. And I do not think that there is anyone who does more to confirm, not just fate, but even a powerful necessity governing all things, or who has more effectively abolished voluntary motions of the mind, than [Epicurus], who concedes that he could not have resisted fate in any other way than by taking refuge in these fictitious swerves. For even supposing that there were atoms, which can in no way be proven to my satisfaction, nevertheless, those swerves will remain unexplained. For if it is by natural necessity that atoms move [downwards] owing to their weight, since it is necessary that every heavy body should move and be carried along when there is nothing to prevent it, then it is also necessary for certain atoms (or, if they prefer, all atoms) to swerve, . . . naturally . . .

TEXT 16: *On the Nature of the Gods* 1.43-56

43. . . . For he [Epicurus] is the only one who saw, first, that the gods exist, because nature herself has impressed a conception of them on the souls of everyone. For what people or race of men is there which does not have, even without being taught, a basic grasp of the gods, which is what Epicurus calls a *prolepsis,* i.e., a kind of outline of the thing [in question], which is antecedently grasped by the mind, and without which nothing can be either understood or investigated or debated? We have learned the force and utility of this line of inference from that divine book of Epicurus on the canon or standard [of truth]. 44. You see, then, that the point which is the foundation of this investigation has been laid very well indeed. For since the opinion is established not on the basis of some convention or custom or law, but is and remains a solid and harmonious consensus of all men, it is necessary to understand that there are gods, because we have implanted, or rather innate, conceptions of them. For what all men by nature agree about must necessarily be true. So one must concede that the gods exist. Since this point is accepted by virtually everyone, philosophers and laymen alike, let us admit that the following point too is established, that we have this basic grasp, as I said before, or preconception about the gods—for new

names must be assigned to new things, just as Epicurus himself referred to a *prolepsis,* which no one had previously designated by this term—45. we have, then, this basic grasp, that we consider the gods to be blessed and immortal. And the same nature which gave us an outline of the gods themselves has also inscribed in our minds the notion that they are eternal and blessed. And if this is so, that was a true maxim expounded by Epicurus, that what is blessed and eternal neither has any troubles of its own nor provides them to others, and so is subject to neither anger nor gratitude, since everything of this nature is weak.

Enough would have been said already, if all we were looking for were pious worship of the gods and freedom from superstition; for the excellent nature of the gods would be worshipped by pious men because of that nature's blessedness and eternity (for whatever is excellent is justifiably the object of reverence), and all fears of the anger or power of the gods would have been expelled (for it is understood that anger and gratitude are banned from a blessed and immortal nature, and when these are removed no fears about the beings above hang over us). But in order to confirm this opinion, the mind enquires into the form of god, the kind of activity which characterizes his life, and the mode of operation of his intellect.

46. Nature tells us part of what we need to know about the form of the gods, and the rest is the instruction of reason. For by nature all of us, men of all races, have no other view of the gods but that they have human form; for what other form ever appears to anyone either waking or sleeping? But so that every point will not be referred to the primary notions, reason herself reveals the same thing. 47. For it seems appropriate that the most excellent nature, excellent either for its blessedness or for its eternity, should also be the most beautiful. So what configuration of the limbs, what arrangement of features, what shape, what general appearance can be more beautiful than the human? . . . 48. But if the human shape is superior to the form of all living things, and a god is a living thing, then certainly he has that shape which is most beautiful of all. And since it is agreed that the gods are most blessed, but no one can be blessed without virtue, nor can virtue exist without reason, nor can reason exist except in a human form, one must concede that the gods have human appearance. 49. But that appearance is not [really] a body, but a quasi-body, nor does a god have blood, but quasi-blood.

Although Epicurus was so acute in the discovery of these truths and expounded them so subtly that not just anyone could grasp them, still I can rely on your intelligence and expound them more briefly than the subject matter actually demands. Epicurus, then, who not only has a mental vision of hidden and deeply abstruse matters but even manipulates them as though

they were tangible, teaches us that the force and nature of the gods is as follows. First, they are perceived not by the senses but by the intellect, and not in virtue of some solidity or numerical identity (like those things which because of their resistance he calls *steremnia*), but rather because the images [of the gods] are perceived by virtue of similarity and transference; and since an unlimited series of very similar images arises from innumerable atoms and flows to the gods, our intellect attends to those images and our intelligence is fixed on them with the greatest possible pleasure, and so it grasps the blessed and eternal nature [of the gods]. 50. It is most worthwhile to reflect long and hard on the tremendous power of infinity, which we must understand is such as to make it possible that all [classes of] things have an exact and equal correspondence with all other [classes of] things. Epicurus calls this *isonomia,* i.e., equal distribution. In virtue of this it comes about that if there is such and such a number of mortal beings, there is no less a number of immortal beings, and if there is an innumerable set of forces which destroy, there ought also to be an infinite set of forces which preserve.

Balbus, you [Stoics] often ask us what the life of the gods is like and how they pass their time. 51. Well, they spend their time in such a manner that nothing can be conceived which is more blessed or better supplied with all kinds of good things. For a god is idle, is entangled with no serious preoccupations, undertakes no toilsome labour, but simply rejoices in his own wisdom and virtue, being certain that he will always be in the midst of pleasures which are both supreme and eternal. 52. This god we could properly call blessed, but your [i.e., the Stoic] god is assigned to very hard labour. For if god is the world itself, what can be less restful than to be revolving around the heaven's axis at amazing speed, with not even a moment of rest? But nothing is blessed if it is not at rest. But if there is some god *in* the world to rule and guide it, to maintain the orbits of the heavenly bodies, the changes of the seasons and the ordered variations of [natural] events, to oversee land and sea to ensure that men have lives full of advantages, then surely that god is entangled with burdensome and laborious obligations. 53. But we claim that happiness is a matter of freedom from disturbance in the mind and leisure from all duties. For the same person who taught us the rest [of this theory] also taught us that the world was produced by nature and that there was no need for someone to make it, and that the task which you say cannot be carried out without divine wisdom is so easy that nature has produced, is producing and will produce an unlimited number of worlds. Since you do not see how nature can do so without [the use of] intelligence, you take refuge like tragedians in [the agency of] god when you cannot work out the conclusion of the plot. 54. You would certainly not need the assistance of god if you realized the unlimited magnitude of space which is unbounded in all directions; the intellect casts itself into and contemplates this [infinity] and travels so far and wide that it can see no final boundary at which it might stop. So, in this immense length, breadth, and height there flies about an infinite quantity of innumerable atoms, which (despite the interspersal of void) cling to each other and are linked together by their mutual contacts. From this are produced those forms and shapes which you think cannot be produced without the use of a veritable blacksmith's shop! And so you have burdened us with the yoke of an eternal master whom we are to fear by day and by night; for who would not fear an inquisitive and busy god who foresees everything, thinks about and notices everything, and supposes that everything is his own business? 55. This is the origin of that fated necessity which you call *heimarmene,* and which leads you to say that whatever happens has flowed from an eternal [set of] truth[s] and a continuous chain of causes. But how much is your philosophy worth, if it thinks, like old women—and uneducated ones at that—that everything occurs by fate. Your *mantike* follows too, which is called 'divination' in Latin, because of which we would be drenched in such superstition (if we were prepared to listen to you [Stoics]) that we would have to worship the soothsayers and augurs, the oracular priests and the prophets, and even the diviners! 56. We are freed from these terrifying fears by Epicurus; we are liberated from them! We do not fear [gods] whom we know do not create trouble for themselves nor for anyone else, and we worship in piety and holiness their excellent and supreme nature.

TEXT 17: *On the Nature of the Gods* 1.69-76 excerpts

69. You [Epicureans] do this all the time. You say something implausible and want to avoid criticism, so you adduce something which is absolutely impossible to support it! It would be better to give up the point under attack than to defend it in such a brazen manner. For example, when Epicurus saw that, if the atoms moved by their own weight straight down, nothing would be in our power, since the atoms' movements would be certain and necessitated, he found a way to avoid necessity—a point which had escaped Democritus' notice. He says that an atom, although it moves downward in a straight line because of its weight and heaviness, swerves a little bit. 70. This claim is more shameful than the inability to defend the point he is trying to support. He does the same thing in his debate with the dialecticians. They have an accepted teaching to the effect that, in all disjunctions which have the form "either this or not this," one of the two disjuncts must be true; but Epicurus was afraid that if a statement such as "Epicurus will either be alive tomorrow or he will not" were admitted, then one of the two disjuncts would be necessary. So he denied that all statements of the form "either this or not this" were necessary. What could be more stupid than this?

Arcesilaus attacked Zeno because, while he himself said that all sense-perceptions were false, Zeno said that some were false, but not all. Epicurus was afraid that, if one sense-perception were false, none would be true; so he said that all sense-perceptions were messengers of the truth. None of these cases shows great cleverness; in order to ward off a minor blow, he opened himself up to a more serious one.

71. He does the same thing with the nature of the gods. While trying to avoid saying that [the gods are] a dense compound of atoms, so that he will not have to admit that they perish and dissipate, he says that the gods do not have a body, but only a quasi-body, and that they do not have blood, but only quasi-blood. It is taken to be remarkable if one soothsayer can see another without laughing, but it is even more remarkable, that you [Epicureans] can restrain your laughter when you are by yourselves. "This is not a body, but a quasi-body"; I could understand what this would be like if we were talking about waxen images and earthenware figurines. But I cannot understand what quasi-body and quasi-blood are supposed to be in the case of a god. And neither can you, Velleius, but you don't want to admit it. . . .

. . . 73. Now, what do you understand by that quasi-body and quasi-blood? 74. Not only do I concede that you understand them better than I, but I am even happy about it. But when the idea is expressed in words, what reason is there that Velleius should be able to understand it and Cotta should not? So I know what body is and what blood is; but in no way do I understand what quasi-body is or what quasi-blood is. Yet you do not hide [your view] from me, as Pythagoras used to hide his views from outsiders, nor do you deliberately speak in riddles like Heraclitus; rather, to speak frankly between ourselves, you yourself do not understand. 75. I am aware that you contend that there is a kind of image of the gods which has nothing solid or dense about it, no definite shape, no depth, but is refined, light, and translucent. So we will speak of it as we do of the Venus on Cos: it is not a body but like a body, and the blush blended with pallor which suffuses [her skin] is not blood but a sort of semblance of blood. In the same way Epicurean gods are not real things but semblances of real things.

But suppose that I believe in things which I cannot even understand. Now show me the outlines and shapes of those shadowy gods of yours! 76. Here you suffer from no lack of arguments designed to show that the gods have human form. First [is the argument that] our minds contain an outline and basic grasp of such a nature that when a man thinks about a god, a human form appears to him; second, that since the divine nature is better than everything else, it ought also to have the most beautiful form, and none is more beautiful than the human form; the third argument you adduce is that no other shape can house an intellect.

TEXT 18: *On the Nature of the Gods* 1.103-110

103. Let us suppose it true, then, as you wish, that god is an image and semblance of man: what home, what dwelling, what place does he have? what, indeed, are his activities? in virtue of what is he, as you claim, happy? For he who is going to be happy ought to both use and enjoy his own goods. And even inanimate natures have each their own proper place; for example, earth occupies the lowest place, water floods the earth, air is above it, and the highest reaches [of the cosmos] are set aside for the fires of the heavens. Some animals are terrestrial, some aquatic, some are 'double', as it were, living in both environments; there are even some which are thought to be born in fire and which often appear flying about in blazing furnaces! 104. So I ask, first, where does this god of yours live? next, what cause motivates him to move spatially—if, that is, he ever does move? then, since it is characteristic of animals that they pursue what is adapted to their nature, what does god pursue? to what, pray tell, does he apply his mind and reason? finally, *how* is he happy, *how* is he eternal?

Whichever of these issues you touch on, it is a weak spot. A theory with such a bad foundation cannot come to a successful conclusion. 105. You claimed that the appearance of god is perceived by thought, not the senses; that it has no solidity and is not numerically identical over time; that the visual image of it is such that it is discerned by similarity and transference; that there is an unfailing supply of similar [images] from the infinite atoms; and that this is why our mind, when directed at these things, believes that their nature is blessed and eternal. Now, in the name of the very gods we are talking about, what sort of a claim is this? For if they are only valid for thought and have no solidity or depth, then what difference does it make whether we think about a centaur or a god? The rest of the philosophers call that sort of mental condition an 'empty motion [of the mind]', but you claim that it is the approach and entry of images into the mind. 106. So when I seem to see Tiberius Gracchus making a speech on the Capitol and bringing out the voting-urn for the verdict on Marcus Octavius, I say that is an empty motion of the mind; but you say that the images of Gracchus and Octavius, which arrived at the Capitol and came to my mind, persist—and that the same thing happens in the case of god (by whose image our minds are frequently struck) and that this is why the gods are thought of as blessed and eternal.

107. Suppose that there are images which strike our minds; it is still only a certain appearance put before us and not also a reason for it to be happy and eternal. What are these images of yours, and where do they come from? Of course, this free-wheeling idea came from Democritus. But he has been criticized by many, and you [Epicureans] cannot find a way out. The whole theory wobbles and limps. For what could

be less plausible than that my mind is struck by images of Homer, Archilochus, Romulus, Numa, Pythagoras, and Plato, let alone by images faithful to the original people! So how do those people [come to my mind]? And whose images are these? Aristotle holds that the poet Orpheus never existed and the Pythagoreans claim that the surviving Orphic poem was written by a certain Cercon. But Orpheus, i.e., on your theory his image, often comes into my mind. 108. And what about the fact that your mind and mine receive different images of the same man? What about the fact that we get images of things which never existed at all and never could have, like Scylla and Charybdis? What about the fact that we get images of people, places, and cities which we have never seen? What about the fact that an image is instantly available as soon as I feel like it? What about the fact that images come unbidden, even to those who are asleep. Velleius' whole theory is nonsense! But you [Epicureans] impose these images not just on our eyes, but on our minds too—that's how recklessly you blather on! 109. And how careless it is. 'There is a steady succession of flowing visual images so that the many produce the appearance of one.' I would be ashamed to admit that I don't understand this, if you yourselves, who defend this stuff, really understood it. For how do you prove that the images move continuously, or if they do move continuously, how are they eternal? 'The infinity of atoms keeps the supply up,' he says. So does the same 'infinity of atoms' make everything eternal? You take refuge in 'equal distribution' (let us use this term for *isonomia,* if you will) and say that, since there exists a mortal nature, there must also exist an immortal nature. By that reasoning, since men are mortal, there should be some immortal men too, and since they are born on land, they should also be born in water. 'And because there are forces of destruction, there must also be forces of preservation.' Of course there are. But they preserve things which exist; but I don't think those gods exist. 110. Anyway, how do all your images of things arise from the atomic bodies? Even if they existed, which they don't, they might perhaps bump into each other and be shaken up by their collisions; but they could not impart form, shape, colour, and life. Therefore you [Epicureans] utterly fail to show that there is an immortal god.

TEXT 19: *Tusculan Disputations* 3.41-42

41. . . . Are these your words, [Epicurus,] or not? In the book which sums up your entire teaching you say this (and here I merely translate, so that no one will think that I am making this up): "Nor do I know what I could understand that good to be, if I set aside the pleasures we get from sex, from listening to songs, from looking at [beautiful] shapes, from smooth motions, or any other pleasures which affect any of man's senses. Nor, indeed, can it be said that only mental

rejoicing is [to be counted] among the goods; for this is my understanding of mental rejoicing: it lies in the expectation that our nature will avoid pain while acquiring all those things I just mentioned." 42. That is exactly what he said, so that anyone can grasp what kind of pleasure Epicurus recognizes. Then a bit later: "I have often asked," he says, "those who are called wise, what they would have left [to put] in the category of goods if they removed those things—unless they were willing to emit empty sounds. I was able to learn nothing from them. And if they wish to burble about virtues and wisdom, they will be referring to nothing except the means by which those pleasures which I mentioned above are produced."

TEXT 20: *Tusculan Disputations* 3.47

The same man says that pleasure does not increase once pain is removed, but that the greatest pleasure lies in not being in pain. . . .

TEXT 21: *On Goals* 1.29-33

29. . . . First, then, he said, I will handle the subject in the manner approved of by the founder of this school: I will settle what it is that we are talking about and what qualities it has, not because I think that you do not know, but so that my discourse might proceed in an orderly and systematic fashion. So, we are asking what is the final and ultimate good, which according to the view of all philosophers ought to be what everything should be referred to, but which should itself be referred to nothing else. Epicurus places this in pleasure, which he claims is the highest good and that pain is the greatest bad thing. And the beginning of his teaching about this is as follows.

30. As soon as each animal is born, it seeks pleasure and rejoices in it as the highest good, and rejects pain as the greatest bad thing, driving it away from itself as effectively as it can; and it does this while it is still not corrupted, while the judgement of nature herself is unperverted and sound. Therefore, he says that there is no need of reason or debate about why pleasure is to be pursued and pain to be avoided. He thinks that these things are perceived, as we perceive that fire is hot, that snow is white, that honey is sweet. None of these things requires confirmation by sophisticated argumentation; it is enough just to have them pointed out. For there is a difference between the rational conclusion of an argument and simply pointing something out; for the former reveals certain hidden and, as it were, arcane facts, while the latter indicates things which are evident and out in the open. Moreover, since there is nothing left if you deprive man of his sense-perception, it is necessary that nature herself judge what is natural and what is unnatural. And what does nature perceive or judge, with reference to what does she decide to pursue or avoid something, except pleasure and pain?

31. There are, however, some members of our school [Epicureans] who want to teach a more subtle form of this doctrine, and they say that it is not sufficient to let sense-perception judge what is good and what is bad, but that the intellect and reason can also understand that pleasure by itself is worth pursuing for its own sake and that pain by itself is to be avoided for its own sake. And so they say that we have this conception, which is, as it were, naturally implanted in our souls, and that as a result of this we perceive that the one is to be pursued and the other to be rejected. But there are other Epicureans too, men with whom I agree, who do not think it right for us to be too sure of our case, since so many philosophers say so much about why pleasure ought not to be counted as a good thing and pain ought not to be counted as a bad thing; they think that one must argue and debate with great care, and employ well researched lines of argument in the dispute about pleasure and pain.

32. But so that you will see the origin of the mistake made by those who attack pleasure and praise pain, I shall open up the whole theory and explain exactly what was said by that discoverer of the truth [Epicurus], who was a kind of architect of the happy life. No one rejects or dislikes or avoids pleasure itself just because it is pleasure, but rather because those who do not know how to pursue pleasure rationally meet with great pains as a result. Nor again is there anyone who loves, pursues, and wants to acquire pain just because it is pain, but rather because sometimes circumstances of such a nature occur that he can pursue some great pleasure by means of effort and pain. To cite a minor instance: who among us undertakes any demanding regimen of physical training except in order to get some sort of benefit from it? Who, moreover, could justifiably criticize either a man who wished to have the sort of pleasure which is followed by no pains or a man who avoids a pain which serves to produce no pleasure?

33. But we do attack and indeed find most worthy of justified hatred those who are seduced and corrupted by the allures of present pleasures and, being blinded by desire, do not foresee the pains and troubles which they are bound to incur; similarly to blame are those who abandon their duties because of moral weakness, i.e., a tendency to avoid efforts and pains. The distinction here is simple and clear enough. For at a moment of free time, when we have an unrestricted opportunity to select and there is no hindrance to our doing what will be most pleasing to us, [in such circumstances] every pleasure is to be accepted and every pain rejected. But at certain other times, because of the press of responsibilities or the obligations imposed by circumstances it will often happen that pleasures are to be turned down and pains are not to be rejected. And so the wise man sticks with this [principle of] of choos-

ing, that he either acquires greater pleasures by rejecting some of them, or that he avoids worse pains by enduring some of them.

TEXT 22: *On Goals* 1.37-38

37. . . . Now I will explain what pleasure is and what it is like, to remove any misunderstandings which inexperienced people may have and to help them to understand how serious, self-controlled, and stern our doctrine is, though it is commonly held to be hedonistic, slack and soft. For we do not just pursue the kind [of pleasure] which stimulates our nature itself with a kind of smoothness and is perceived by the senses with a sort of sweetness, but rather we hold that the greatest pleasure is that which is perceived when all pain is removed. For since when we are freed from pain we rejoice in this very liberation from and absence of annoyance, and since everything in which we rejoice is a pleasure (just as everything which irritates us is a pain), then it is right to call the absence of all pain pleasure. Just as when hunger and thirst are driven out by food and drink, the very removal of annoyance brings with it a resulting pleasure, so in every case too the removal of pain brings with it a consequent pleasure. 38. So Epicurus did not think that there was some intermediate state between pleasure and pain; for that state which some people think is an intermediate state, viz. the absence of all pain, is not only pleasure but it is even the greatest pleasure. For whoever perceives the state which he is in must in fact be in pleasure or in pain. But Epicurus thinks that the limit for the greatest pleasure is set by the absence of all pain; and though later [i.e., after all pain has been eliminated] pleasure can be varied and adorned, it cannot be increased or augmented.

TEXT 23: *On Goals* 1.55-57

55. I shall give a brief account of what follows from this firm and well established view. There is no possibility of mistake about the limits of good and bad themselves, that is about pleasure and pain; but people do make mistakes in these matters when they are ignorant of the means by which they are produced. Moreover, we say that the pleasures and pains of the mind take their origin from the pleasures and pains of the body (and so I concede the point which you were making recently, that any Epicurean who disagrees is abandoning his case—and I know that there are many who do so, but they are inexperienced); moreover, although mental pleasure and pain do produce good and bad feelings, nevertheless both of them have their origins in the body and take the body as their point of reference; nevertheless, the pleasures and pains of the mind are much greater than those of the body. For with the body we can perceive nothing except what immediately affects it in the present, but with the mind

we can also perceive past and future. Even granted that when we feel pain in the body our pain is equal [to what we feel in the mind], still there can be a very large increase [in this pain] if we think that there is some eternal and unlimited bad thing hanging over us. And you may transfer the point to pleasure, so that it is greater if we are not afraid of some such thing. 56. But this point, at any rate, is already clear, that the greatest pleasure or annoyance in the mind makes much more difference to the production of a blessed or wretched life than either one of them would if they lasted an equally long time in the body. But we do not think that pain immediately follows as soon as pleasure is removed, unless by chance a pain should move into the place of the pleasure; on the other hand we are delighted when pains are eliminated even if no pleasure of the kind which stimulates the senses moves into their place; and from this one can understand just how great a pleasure it is to be free of pain.

57. But just as we are thrilled by the expectation of good things, so too we are pleased by the recollection of good things. But fools are tortured by the recollection of bad things, while wise men enjoy past goods kept fresh by a grateful recollection. For it is a deeply rooted part of human nature to bury in virtually eternal oblivion things which go badly and to recall with satisfaction and contentment things which go well. But when we contemplate past events with a keen and attentive mind, then we feel distress if what we recall was bad, and joy if it was good.

TEXT 24: *On Goals* 2.98

You have often said that no one rejoices or feels pain except because of the body . . . you deny that there is any joy in the mind which is not referred to the body.

TEXT 25: *Tusculan Disputations* 5.93-96

93. You realize, I believe, how Epicurus divided the kinds of desires, perhaps not in a very sophisticated fashion, but usefully at any rate. Some are natural and necessary, some natural and not necessary, some neither [natural nor necessary]. The necessary can be satisfied with next to nothing; for nature's riches are easily acquired. He holds that the second type of desires is not difficult, either to acquire or to do without. The third type he thought should be utterly rejected, since they are clearly vain and not only unnecessary but also unnatural. 94. At this point the Epicureans make a number of arguments and make excuses one by one for the pleasures of the types which they do not condemn, but which they <do not> seek an abundance of. For they say that even obscene pleasures, which they spend quite a bit of time talking about, are easy, common, and readily available; and that if nature does require them they must be evaluated not with reference to family background, social station, or rank, but only

but only with respect to beauty, age, and figure; and it is not at all difficult to refrain from them, if that is required by poor health, duty, or concern for one's reputation; and in general, that this type of pleasure is to be chosen, if it does not do any harm, but that it never actually benefits anyone. 95. The upshot of his entire discussion of pleasure is this. He holds that pleasure itself should always be wished for and pursued for its own sake because it is pleasure, and that by the same reasoning pain should always be avoided, just because it *is* pain; and so the wise man will employ a principle of compensation, and will avoid pleasure if it will produce a greater pain and will endure pain if it produces a greater pleasure; and that all pleasing feelings are to be referred to the mind, although they are actually judged by bodily senses. 96. As a result the body is pleased for only so long as it perceives a present pleasure, while the mind perceives a present pleasure just as much as the body does, but also foresees a pleasure which is coming in the future and does not let a past pleasure slip from its grasp. So the wise man will always have a continuous and interconnected [set of] pleasures, since the expectation of hoped-for pleasures is linked to the memory of pleasures already perceived.

TEXT 26: *On Goals* 1.65-70

65. There remains a topic which is especially important for our present debate, that is friendship. You [the critics] claim that if pleasure is the greatest good there will be no friendship at all. Epicurus indeed says this on the topic: that of all the things which wisdom has contrived which contribute to a blessed life none is more important, more fruitful, or more pleasing than friendship. And he proved this not just in his discourse, but much more clearly by his life and deeds and character. The fictitious tales told by the ancients make it clear how important it is; but in all those stories, so many and so varied and drawn from the most remote periods of antiquity, you could hardly find three pairs of [true] friends, starting with Theseus and finishing up with Orestes. But in just one household—and a small one at that—Epicurus assembled such large congregations of friends which were bound together by a shared feeling of the deepest love. And even now the Epicureans do the same thing.

But let us get back to the point; we do not need to speak of individuals. 66. I see that the question of friendship has been dealt with in three ways by our school. Some say that our friends' pleasures are not in themselves as worthy of pursuit as are our own (a doctrine which some think undermines the stability of a friendship), but nevertheless they do defend this claim and easily, as I think, get themselves out of their difficulties. Just as we said about the virtues somewhat earlier, so for friendship: they deny that it can be separated from pleasure. For since a solitary life without

friends is full of dangerous traps and fear, reason herself advises us to get some friends; and when we do so our mind is reassured and becomes indissolubly linked to the expectation that pleasures will thereby be acquired. 67. And just as hatred, envy, and contempt are inimical to pleasures, so friendships are not only the most trustworthy supports for our pleasures, but they also produce them, as much for our friends as for ourselves. We enjoy friends not only while they are present with us, but we are also elated by our expectations for the immediate and for the more distant future. Because we cannot possibly secure a stable and long-lasting pleasantness in our life without friendship, and cannot maintain friendship itself unless we cherish our friends just as much as we do ourselves, it follows both that this kind of thing does occur in friendship and that friendship is linked with pleasure. For we rejoice at our friends' joys just as much as at our own, and grieve just as much for their anguish. 68. That is why a wise man will have the same feelings for his friend as for himself and will undertake the same labours for the sake of a friend's pleasure as he would undertake for the sake of his own.

What we said about the way the virtues are always found to be essentially connected to pleasures must also be said about friendship. For Epicurus made a splendid declaration, in almost exactly these words: One and the same doctrine has reassured our minds that there is no eternal or even long-lasting bad thing to fear and has also seen that in this present span of life the most reliable source of protection lies in friendship.

69. There are, however, some Epicureans who are more timid in the face of your abusive criticisms, but are nevertheless pretty sharp-witted; they are afraid that if we believe that friendship is to be pursued for the sake of our own pleasure, all of friendship might seem to be crippled. So they say that people first meet, pair up, and desire to form associations for the sake of pleasure, but that when increasing experience [of each other] has produced the sense of a personal bond, then love flowers to such a degree that even if there is no utility to be gained from the friendship the friends themselves are still loved for their own sake. Indeed, if we typically come to love certain locations, temples, cities, gymnasia, playing fields, dogs, horses, public games (whether with gladiators or animals) just because of familiarity, how much easier and more fitting is it for this to happen in the case of human familiarity?

70. There are also those who say that there is a kind of agreement between wise men, to the effect that they will not cherish their friends less than themselves. We know that this can happen, and that it often does happen; and it is obvious that nothing can be discovered which would be more effective for the production of a pleasant life than this sort of association.

From all of these considerations one can draw the conclusion that not only is the case of friendship not undermined if the highest good is located in pleasure, but also that without this no firm basis for friendship could possibly be discovered.

Plutarch (essay date c. 1st to 2nd century)

SOURCE: Plutarch, "The Polemic of Plutarch," in *The Epicurus Reader*, translated and edited by Brad Inwood and L. P. Gerson, Hackett Publishing Company, Inc., 1994, pp. 68-74.

[*In the following excerpt from* Against Colotes, *Plutarch seeks out logical contradictions and inconsistencies in Epicurean philosophy, focusing largely on ideas of sensation and sense perception.*]

(1109a) . . . Anyway, he [Colotes] who even held that nothing is any more like this than like that, is using Epicurus' doctrine that all presentations received through the senses are true. (1109b) For if when two people speak and one person says that the wine is dry and the other says that it is sweet, and neither is wrong about his sense-perception, how can the wine be dry rather than sweet? And again, you can see that some people treat a bath as though it were hot and that others treat the same bath as though it were cold. For some ask for cold water to be poured in and others ask for hot. They say that a lady from Sparta came to see Berenike, the wife of Deiotaurus, and when they got close to each other they both turned away, the one nauseated by the [smell of] perfume, the other by the [smell of] butter. So if the one sense-perception is no more true than the other, it is likely both that the water is no more cold than hot and (1109c) that the perfume and the butter are no more sweet-smelling than foul-smelling. For if someone says that the same object of presentation is different for different people, he has missed the fact that he is saying that [the object] is both [at once].

And the much discussed symmetries and harmonies of the pores in the sense organs and the compound mixtures of seeds which they say produce different sense-perceptions of quality in different people by being distributed in all flavours and odours and colours, do these not immediately force things into being 'no more [this than that]' for them? For they reassure those who think that sense-perception deceives on the grounds that they see the same things having opposite effects on perceivers, and instruct them [as follows]: (1109d) since everything is combined and blended together and since different things are designed by nature to fit into different [pores], it is not possible for everyone to touch and grasp the same quality; nor does the object [of sense-perception] affect everyone the same way with all of its parts, but all of them only experience those

parts [of an object] with which their sense-organs are symmetrical; so they are wrong to quarrel about whether the object is good or bad or white or not white, supposing that they are supporting their own sense-perceptions by undermining those of other people; but one must not quarrel with even one sense-perception, since all sense-perceptions make contact with something, (1109e) each drawing what is compatible and suitable to itself from the compound mixture as though from a spring; and must not assert [things] about the whole when one is in contact with [mere] parts, nor think that everyone has the same experience, but that different people have different experiences according to the differing qualities and powers of it.

So is it time to consider which men do more to inflict 'no more [this than that]' on things than those who proclaim that every sensible object is a blend of all sorts of qualities—'mixed like new wine in the filter'—and who agree that their canons [of truth] would perish and their criterion would completely vanish if they left any object of perception whatsoever pure [and simple] and they did not leave each and every one of them a plurality?

Notice, then, what Epicurus has had Polyaenus (in the *Symposium*) say to him about the heating power of wine. (1109f) For when he said, "Epicurus, do you deny that there are heating properties in wine?" he answered, "What need is there to show that wine has heating properties?" And a bit further on: "For wine seems in general not to have heating properties, but a given quantity could be said to have a heating effect on this individual person."

And again, suggesting the cause [for this], he attributed it to (1110a) compactions and dispersions of atoms and to commixtures of and linkages with other atoms in the mixture of wine with the body; and then he adds: "that is why one must not say that wine has heating properties in general, but that a given quantity has a heating effect on a nature of this type which is in this sort of condition, or that a given amount could have a cooling effect on this [other] nature. For in such an aggregate [as wine] there are also the sort of natures from which coolness might be produced, or which being linked appropriately with other natures, would produce the nature of coolness. Hence, people are deceived, some into saying that wine in general has cooling properties, others that it has heating properties."

But he who says that the majority are deceived when they suppose that what heats things has heating properties, or that what cools things has cooling properties, is himself deceived, (1110b) unless he believes that it follows from what he says that each thing is no more like this than like that. And he adds that wine often does not enter the body with heating or cooling properties, but that when the mass has been set in motion and the rearrangement of bodies has occurred, sometimes the atoms which produce heat assemble in one place and by their numbers produce heat and fever in the body, and sometimes they are expelled and [so] chill it.

It is obvious that these arguments can be used against everything which is generally said or believed to be bitter, sweet, purgative, soporific, or bright, on the grounds that nothing (1110c) has its own independent quality or power when it is in bodies, nor is it active rather than passive, but rather takes on different features and mixtures in various bodies.

For Epicurus himself, in book two of his *Against Theophrastus,* says that colours are not natural properties of bodies, but are produced by certain orderings and positions [of the atoms] relative to our vision; yet he says that, by this argument, body is no more colourless than it is coloured. And earlier he had written this, word for word: "but even without this part [of my theory] I do not know how one can say that those things which are in the dark have colour. And yet, when there is a dark cloud of air [i.e., fog] evenly wrapped around things, (1110d) it is often the case that some men perceive differences in colours while others do not because of the dullness of their vision; again, when we go into a dark house we do not see colours, but after we have stayed for a while we do." Therefore, no body will be said to have colour rather than not to have it.

And if colour is relative, so too will white and blue be relative, and if these, so too sweet and bitter; consequently it will be true to predicate of every quality that it no more exists than does not exist: for the object will be like this for people in one condition, but not for those who are not. (1110e) So Colotes ends up pouring over himself and his master the very mud and confusion in which he says those people wallow who assert that things are 'no more this than that'.

So is this the only place where this fine fellow shows that he "teems with sores though he tries to heal others"? Not at all. In his second accusation [Colotes] fails even more miserably to notice how he drives Epicurus, along with Democritus, outside, the pale of normal life. For he claims that Democritus' dicta, "colour is by convention and sweet is by convention" and compounds are by convention and so forth, but "in truth there are void and atoms," are opposed to sense perception; and that anyone who clings to and uses this theory could not even think of himself as human or as alive.

I have no criticism to make of this argument, and I claim that these [Democritean] views are as inseparable from Epicurus' opinions as they themselves say

the shape and weight are from the atom. For what does Democritus say? that substances infinite in number, indivisible and indestructible and, moreover, qualitiless and impassible, are scattered about and move in the void; (1111a) and when they approach one another or collide or get tangled up with each other they appear, because they are aggregated, as water, fire, a plant, or a man; and that everything is what he calls atomic 'forms' and is nothing else. For there is no coming-into-being from what-is-not, and from what-is nothing could come to be since atoms can neither suffer nor change due to their solidity. Hence colour does not exist, [for it would have to be] made up of colourless things, nor do nature and soul exist, [for they would have to be] made up of qualitiless and impassive things.

So Democritus is to be criticized not for conceding what follows from his principles, but for assuming principles from which these conclusions follow. (1111b) For he ought not to have posited that the primary entities were unchangeable, but having made this postulate he ought to have seen that he has eliminated the genesis of all qualities. The most brazen position of all is to see the absurdity and to deny it. So Epicurus makes the most brazen claim, saying that he posits the same principles but does not say that "colour is by convention" and [so too] sweet and bitter and the qualities. If "does not say" means "does not admit," then he is up to his old tricks. For while destroying divine providence he says that he leaves piety intact, and while choosing friendship for the sake of pleasure he says that he would suffer the greatest pains for the sake of his friends, and he says that he postulates that the totality is unlimited but that he does not eliminate up and down. This sort of behaviour is not right even when one is joking over a drink: (1111c) to take a cup and drink as much as one wants and then to give back what is left. In argument one must recall this wise maxim: the beginnings may not be necessitated, but the consequences are. So it was not necessary to postulate—or rather to steal [the doctrine] from Democritus—that the principles of the universe are atoms; but when once he postulated the doctrine and prided himself on its superficial plausibility, then he ought to have drained its difficulties to the last drop too, or showed us how bodies which have no qualities produced most varied qualities just by coming together in a compound. For example, where did you get what is called hot and how did it come to be an attribute of your atoms, (1111d) which neither came [into the compound] already having heat, nor did they become hot by their conjunction? For the former is characteristic of something which has a quality, and the latter of something which is naturally prone to be affected; but you say that neither of these is appropriate for your atoms because they are indestructible.

. . . (1112e) . . . When Epicurus says, "the nature of existing things is bodies and place," should we interpret him as meaning that nature is something distinct from and in addition to the existing things, (1112f) or as referring just to the existent things and to nothing else? just as, for instance, he is in the habit of calling the void itself 'the nature of void' and, by Zeus, the totality [of things] the 'nature of the totality'.

. . . (1114a) Yet by saying that the totality is one he somehow prevented us from living. For when Epicurus says that the totality is unlimited and ungenerated and indestructible and neither grows nor shrinks, he discourses about the totality as though it were some one thing. In the beginning of his treatise [*On Nature*] he suggests that the nature of existing things is bodies and void, and though it is one nature, he yet divided it into two. One of these is really nothing, but you call it intangible and void and incorporeal.

. . . (1118d) . . . For if, as they think, a man is the product of both, a body of this sort and a soul, then he who investigates the nature of soul is investigating the nature of man by way of its more important principle. And let us not learn from Socrates, that sophistical boaster, that the soul is hard to understand by reason and ungraspable by sense-perception, but rather let us learn it from these wise men who get only as far as the corporeal powers of the soul, by virtue of which it provides the body with warmth and softness and tension, (1118e) when they cobble together its substance out of something hot and something breathlike and something airy, and they do not get to the most important part, but give up. For that in virtue of which it judges and remembers and loves and hates and in general the intelligent and reasoning part, this they say comes to be from a kind of 'nameless' quality.

. . (1119f) . . . Who makes worse mistakes in dialectic than you [Epicureans], who completely abolish the class of things said [*lekta*], which give substance to discourse and leave only [mere] utterances and the external things, saying that the intermediate class of 'signified things' (by means of which learning, (1120a) teaching, basic grasps, conceptions, impulses, and assents all occur) does not exist at all? . . .

Diogenes Laertius (essay date c. 250)

SOURCE: Diogenes Laertius, "Excerpts From the Life of Epicurus," in *The Philosophy of Epicurus*, Northwestern University Press, 1963, pp. 101-12.

[*More than anyone, Diogenes Laertius was responsible for preserving details of Epicurus's life; most later scholarship has depended on his biography of the philosopher. The following excerpt begins with summaries of accounts meant to discredit Epicurus—accounts that portray the Epicurean life as de-bauched. After refuting these attacks, Diogenes Laertius walks his reader through the basics of Epicurean philosophy.*]

[1]The Stoic Diotimus, who bore Epicurus ill will, slandered him most cruelly by publishing fifty lascivious letters under his name, and so did the person who compiled the love letters that are supposedly Epicurus' but are traceable to Chrysippus, not to mention Posidonius the Stoic and his followers. . . . They claimed that he went around to houses with his mother, reading off chants of purification, and that he taught grammar school with his father for a miserable fee; also that one of his brothers was a pimp and had relations with the hetaera Leontion; and that Epicurus passed off Democritus' atomic theory and Aristippus' pleasure theory as his own. . . .

In his letters to Pythocles,[2] who was then in the bloom of his youth, he wrote, "I shall sit down and await your beauteous, godlike advent." . . . And they claim that he wrote to many other hetaerae, especially Leontion, of whom Metrodorus was also enamored. And in the essay **The Purpose of Life** he supposedly wrote, "As far as I am concerned, I do not know how I can think of the good if I subtract the pleasures of taste and the pleasures of sex, sound, and form." In a letter to Pythocles he said, "Hoist sail, happy youth, and speed far from all book learning."

Epictetus,[3] too, called him a "foul-mouthed bastard" and abused him savagely. And even Timocrates, the brother of Metrodorus and a student of Epicurus' who later quit the school, says in a book entitled *The Amenities* that Epicurus vomited twice a day because of his high living, and he explains that he himself hardly had the strength to escape those nightly colloquia on philosophy and the mystic brotherhood. Also that Epicurus was ignorant in many ways about his subject and even more about life; that his body was in pitiable condition, so that for many years he was unable to get out of his sedan chair; also that he spent a mina[4] every day on his table, as he himself mentioned in a letter to Leontion . . . , and that there were other hetaerae living with him and Metrodorus, named Mammarion, Hedeia, Erotion,[5] and Nicidion. . . .

. . . . .

But these critics are all crazy. The man Epicurus has plenty of witnesses to his unparalleled benevolence toward all: his country, which honored him with bronze statues; his friends, so many in number that they could not even be counted by whole cities; his intimates, all of whom remained bound to him by the siren call of his teachings. . . . [6] Then there is the continuity of the school, which lasted on and on after almost all the others had ceased to exist and which produced countless leaders, chosen one after another from among the "friends."[7] And there is his gratefulness to his parents, his generosity to his brothers, and his kindness to his house slaves, as is evident from the provisions of his will and from the fact that they participated in the discussions on philosophy. The outstanding example is Mys, previously mentioned.[8] We have, in short, his humanity toward all. It is impossible to describe his attitude of reverence for the gods[9] and his love of country; it was because of his excessive reasonableness that he did not engage in politics. And though very difficult conditions prevailed in Greece at that time, he lived out his life there and crossed over to Ionia only two or three times to see his friends in various places. But they came to him from everywhere and lived with him in the Garden (as Apollodorus[10] tells us) on a very frugal and plain diet. In fact, they were satisfied with a half pint of cheap wine and usually drank water. Epicurus did not think it right for them to deposit their property in a common fund, as did Pythagoras (who had said, "The property of friends is common property"), because this was the way of people who distrust each other, and if people are distrustful they are not friends. Epicurus himself remarked in his letters that he was satisfied with just water and plain bread. "Send me a small pot of cheese," he wrote, "so that I can have a costly meal whenever I like." This was the man who gave it as his opinion that pleasure is life's goal. . . .

Apollodorus tells us in his *Annals* that Epicurus was born in the third year of the 109th Olympiad in the magistracy of Sosigenes[11] . . . , seven years after Plato's death. At the age of thirty-two he first established a school at Mitylene and Lampsacus[12] and ran it for five years; after that he moved over to Athens. There he died at the age of seventy-two, in the second year of the 127th Olympiad in the magistracy of Pytharatus. Hermarchus of Mitylene, son of Agemortus, took over the school. Epicurus died of a stone that blocked his urine, as Hermarchus also tells us in his letters, after an illness of fourteen days. Hermippus relates that he got into a bronze tub filled with hot water, called for straight wine, and swallowed it. He then exhorted his friends to remember his teachings and passed away. . . .

As he was dying he wrote the following letter to Idomeneus: "On this happy day, which is also the last day of my life, I write the following words to you. The symptoms of my strangury and dysentery are continuing and have not lost their extreme seriousness. But offsetting all this is the joy in my heart at the recollection of the conversations we have had. Take charge of the children of Metrodorus,[13] as behooves one who from boyhood on has been attached to me and to philosophy."

. . . . .

Epicurus was an extremely productive writer and surpassed all other philosophers in the number of his works, of which there are upwards of 300 rolls. There is not one reference in these to outside authorities—nothing but Epicurus' own words. . . . [14] The best of his works are the following: *On Nature,* 37 rolls; *Atoms and Space; On Love; . . . Problems; Leading Doctrines; On Choice and Aversion; The Purpose of Life; The Criterion, or Canon; . . . On the Gods; Religion; . . . Lives,* 4 books; *. . . Symposium; . . . On Vision; . . . Atomic Films; Perception; . . . On Music; Justice and the Other Virtues; . . . Letters.*

I shall now attempt to set forth the teachings contained in these works by laying before you three of his letters,[15] in which he provided a summary of his entire philosophy; . . . but I shall first say a few words about the divisions of his philosophy.

It is divided into three parts—the normative, the physical, and the ethical. The normative contains the methodology of the system and is found in the single work entitled *The Canon*.[16] The physics contains his whole theory of nature and is found in the 37 books of *On Nature* and, in elementary form, in his letters.[17] The ethical part has to do with acts of choice and aversion and is found in the treatises entitled *Lives* and *The Purpose of Life* and also in his letters.[18] The Epicureans, however, ordinarily group the normative part with the physical, claiming that it deals with fundamental criteria and the elements of the system. Physics, on the other hand, has to do with the generation and destruction of worlds and with nature as a whole; ethics, with things to be chosen or avoided, with different ways of life, and with the purpose of life.

They reject dialectic as deceptive, because (they say) it is enough for the natural philosopher to proceed according to the names of things.[19] In *The Canon* Epicurus says that sensations, concepts, and feelings are the criteria of truth, and his followers add direct perceptions of the mind.[20] [Epicurus says as much in the *Letter to Herodotus* and in *Leading Doctrines*.]

1. Sensation is completely irrational and incapable of memory; it is not activated by itself, nor when activated by something else can it add anything or subtract anything.[22]

2. Nor is there anything capable of refuting sensations, because a sensation of one class cannot refute another of the same class, since they are of equal authority; nor can sensations of different classes refute each other, since they do not pass judgment on the same objects.[23]

3. Nor, again, can reason refute sensation, since it is wholly dependent on the sensations.[24]

4. Nor can one sensation refute another, since we give our attention to them all.

5. Furthermore, the existence of our apperceptions is a guarantee of the truth of the sensations.[25]

6. Our seeing and hearing are actualities, just as much as our experience of pain.

7. Thus it is necessary to draw inferences from phenomena regarding things that are not perceived.[26]

8. All ideas take their rise from sensations through processes of coincidence, analogy, resemblance, and combination, with reflection contributing something also.[27]

9. The mental images of madmen and dream images are realities, since they activate the mind, whereas the nonexistent does not thus activate it.

10. By "concept" the Epicureans mean "an apprehending," "correct opinion," "a thought" or "universal idea" deposited in the mind—in other words, a remembering of something frequently given in sensation from the external world. For example, take the expression, "X is a man." As soon as "man" is pronounced, we immediately think of a typical human being in line with the concept formed from antecedent sensory data. Hence the original meaning assigned to any word is clear and distinct evidence of truth. Furthermore, we could not look into what we want to investigate if we did not have prior knowledge of it. For example, the question "Is that thing in the distance a horse or an ox?" implies that we must have some conceptual knowledge of the appearance of a horse or an ox. We could not even have named anything without having first learned of its appearance through the concept. Hence concepts are clear and distinct evidences of truth.[29]

11. In addition, matters of belief rest on clear antecedent evidence, to which we refer when expressing them (e.g., How do we know if this is a man?). Beliefs are also known as assumptions, and they may be true or false. They are true if verified or not contradicted, but false if they are not verified or if they are contradicted. It was for this reason that the principle of "the problem awaiting verification" was introduced—for example, waiting to get close to the tower and find out how it looks close up.[30]

12. The feelings are two in number, according to the Epicureans, pleasure and pain. They are found in all animals, and the former is congenial, the latter naturally foreign. It is by means of these that acts of choice and aversion are decided upon.[31]

13. Some investigations have to do with actualities, others with mere verbiage. . . . .[32]

Let us review what Epicurus and those who came after him thought about the wise man.[33]

1. Men inflict injuries from hatred, jealousy, or contempt, but the wise man masters all these passions by means of reason.

2. Once he has become wise, he no longer experiences the opposite state, nor does he voluntarily feign to. He will be more affected by feelings of pleasure and pain, but this will be no hindrance to wisdom.

3. A man cannot become wise in any and every bodily condition or in every nationality.

4. Even if the wise man is tortured he is happy. Nonetheless he will moan and groan under those conditions.

5. The wise man alone will show his gratitude and will continue to speak well of his friends, whether they are present or absent.

6. The wise man will not have intercourse with any woman with whom it is legally forbidden, as Diogenes tells us in his digest of Epicurus' ethical teachings.[34]

7. Nor will he punish his house slaves; he will show them mercy and grant pardon to any that are conscientious.

8. The Epicureans do not think that the wise man will fall in love, or worry about his burial.

9. Love is not divinely sent, Diogenes tells us.

10. The wise man will not make high-flown speeches in public.

11. Intercourse never helped any man, and it's a wonder that it hasn't hurt him.

12. In addition, the wise man will marry and beget children, as Epicurus tells us in **Problems** and his work **On Nature;** but he will marry according to his station in life, whatever it may be.

13. He will avoid certain persons and certainly not make a fool of himself when drinking, as Epicurus remarks in the **Symposium**.

14. Nor will he meddle in politics (**Lives,** Bk. I), nor play the dictator, nor live like a Cynic[35] and beg alms (**Lives,** Bk. II).

15. Even if he goes blind he will still take part in life (*ibid.*)

16. He will likewise grieve,[36] as Diogenes tells us in Bk. V of his *Excerpts.*

17. He will plead his own case at law.

18. He will leave written works behind him, but not make set speeches in public.

19. He will be prudent about his property and provide for the future.

20. He will love country life.

21. He will confront adversity, because no one can count on the friendship of Lady Luck.

22. He will be careful about his good name to the extent of not losing public respect.

23. He will take greater pleasure than others in the festivals.[37]

24. He will set up likenesses of others but will be indifferent as to whether he has any of himself.

25. Only the wise man could talk properly about music and poetry, but he would not actually compose poetry.

26. One sage is no wiser than another.[38]

27. He will make money if he stands in need of it, but only by his profession.

28. He will, on occasion, wait upon a sovereign.

29. He will gloat over another's troubles—but only as a means of setting him straight.

30. He will assemble a school but not for demagogic purposes; he will lecture publicly but not of his own free will; and he will speak dogmatically without skeptical reservations.[39]

31. He will be the same asleep or awake.[40]

32. Sometimes he will die for a friend.

The Epicureans teach:

That faults are not equal in importance;[41]

That health is a value for some persons but a matter of indifference to others;

That courage does not arise naturally but from utilitarian considerations;

That friendship arises because of its advantages; that there must be a starting point, of course, just as we sow seed in the ground, but that friendship is consolidated by the communal living of those who have attained the full complement of pleasure;[42]

That happiness has two senses: supreme happiness, like that of the deity, which cannot be intensified, and the happiness that has to do with the increase and decrease of pleasure. . . .

In other works Epicurus rejected divination, e.g., in *The Minor Epitome*. "Divination is nonexistent," he says, "and even if it did exist, events are to be regarded as things not within our control."[43] So much for the practical considerations that he has treated in greater detail elsewhere.

Epicurus differs from the Cyrenaics[44] regarding pleasure, in that they sanction only dynamic pleasure and not static, whereas Epicurus sanctions both types in the soul and in the body, as he tells us in *On Choice and Aversion, The Purpose of Life,* Book I of *Lives,* and in his letter to his friends in Mytilene. Similarly Diogenes in Bk. 17 of his *Excepts* and Metrodorus in the *Timocrates* write that pleasure is conceived as both dynamic and static. And Epicurus says in *On Choice and Aversion* that "freedom from mental and bodily pain is a static pleasure, whereas joy and merriment are looked upon as dynamic, active pleasures."

Epicurus also differed from the Cyrenaics in that they taught that bodily pains are worse than mental and pointed out that offenders undergo bodily punishment, whereas Epicurus held that pains of the mind are worse, since the body is afflicted only momentarily in the present, but the mind in the past, present, and future. Similarly the pleasures of the mind are greater. As proof that pleasure is the purpose of life he adduces the fact that all animals from birth on are well content with pleasure but recoil from pain naturally and nonrationally. Our own experience, then, is the reason we avoid pain. . . .

And the virtues are chosen not for themselves but for their pleasurable consequences. . . . Virtue is the only thing inseparable from pleasure; other things, such as food, are separable. . . .

Notes

[1] These selections are drawn from the tenth book of Diogenes Laertius' *Lives of the Philosophers,* a compilation of the second century A.D. The work is of uneven merit and reliability, although the biography of Epicurus happens to be the best single life of a philosopher that we have from antiquity.

Epicurus was a very affectionate man and a great letter writer. The effusive language of some of his personal letters could easily be interpreted erotically by those who wished to do so, and apparently there were many malicious and cynical persons who did. Furthermore, the walled Garden in Athens was the habitat of a number of Epicurean "friends" of both sexes—male disciples such as Metrodorus and Hermarchus and female followers such as the free woman Themista and the three slave hetaerae, Leontion, Nicidion, and Mammarion ("Baby Lion," "Little Conquest," and "Sweet Mamma," respectively).

The hetaerae were not only high-grade "call girls" but also semieducated professional entertainers, roughly comparable to the Japanese geishas. The price of this (apparently) innocent and high-minded experiment in communal living was the inevitable charge of promiscuous sexual relations leveled by foes and rivals in the outside world. The opening selections give us a sordid picture of the backbiting and vilification that were undoubtedly current in all the philosophical schools of the time, including the Epicurean. In true journalistic fashion Diogenes first gives us "the dirt" about his subject, then quickly takes pains to correct this impression by showing us the real Epicurus. The biography ends with a disjointed and choppy account of what Epicurus taught, some parts of which are nonetheless quite valuable and throw additional light on the meager remains of this prolific writer.

2 The recipient of the (second) letter bearing his name.

3 None other than the famous Stoic philosopher, who happened to live more than three centuries after Epicurus! The brickbats exchanged by the Greek schools remind us of the snide comments made by the various Christian sects about each other over the years.

4 Almost twenty dollars.

5 Hedeia and Erotion were both common names in the trade, meaning "Sweetie" and "Lovey," respectively.

6 The language is fanciful, but the claim is not. The loyalty of successive generations of Epicureans to the person and teachings of the master was remarkable and a well-known fact in ancient times. Lucretius, who lived two centuries after Epicurus and was a non-Greek, is a prime example. "Deviationists" were almost unknown. This probably testifies to the strong religious feeling of the Epicurean communities, which made for solidarity among the "friends" as well as for philosophical purity.

7 The school had a continuous life of some five centuries, but by the time Diogenes wrote his biography it had already begun to assimilate itself, both in doctrine and membership, to the surrounding communities of Stoics and Christians, who were far better organized for survival. See DeWitt, *op. cit.,* Chap. XV, "Extension, Submergence, and Revival."

8 This name means "The Mouse."

9 The gods in question were the deities of the state religion, purified and redefined. . . .

10 A famous disciple who had the nickname of "Despot of the Garden." He is mentioned later in the biography

(sect. 25) as having more than four hundred rolls, or books, to his credit, one of which was *Annals,* a history of the school.

11 I.e., at the end of 342 B.C. or the beginning of 341 B.C. His death occurred in 270 B.C. An Olympiad was the four-year period between the celebration of the Olympic games.

12 Two cities of northwestern Asia Minor. Geography is of some importance here because it was in the coastal cities of Ionia further to the south that Greek materialism had its beginnings, rather than in Greece proper. Democritus, the founder of atomism, had lived and taught for many years at Abdera in Thrace, the district northwest of the Hellespont and not far distant from Mitylene and Lampsacus.

13 A favorite disciple who died seven years before Epicurus.

14 Epicurus always insisted that he was self-taught and owed no philosophical debts, even to Democritus. He denied that Leucippus, Democritus' predecessor, had ever lived (sect. 13). This dishonest or, at the least, disingenuous attitude was no doubt intended to magnify his own originality and authority, but it only succeeded in calling forth numerous changes of plagiarism. Professor DeWitt excuses Epicurus on the ground that he was a moral reformer and hence felt himself "absolved from debts of gratitude."

15 Diogenes interspersed his biography with the *Letter to Herodotus, Letter to Pythocles,* and *Letter to Menoeceus* as well as the important collection of ethical aphorisms entitled *Leading Doctrines.* We would have little or no knowledge of these works otherwise.

16 This is what we today would call his epistemology, which emphasizes the empirical basis of knowledge and the various tests for truth (sensation, direct mental perception, universal concepts, and the feelings of pleasure and pain) as against the dialectical or purely logical methods favored by Plato and other rationalists. . . .

17 E.g., the *Letter to Herodotus.*

18 I.e., his personal letters, of which we have fragments, and also the *Letter to Menoeceus.*

19 Two important points:

1. Epicurus rejected the dialectic of Plato, i.e., the method of logical argument that aimed at universal definitions (What is piety? What is justice? etc.) and at the discovery of eternal archetypes or Ideas

(Piety, Justice, etc.). The Epicureans of course used deductive logic in building their system as much as anybody else, but they anchored it firmly to empirical data and never allowed it to become a free-floating, speculative method. Epicurus believed that if logic were divorced from fact it became mere verbalizing and led to "inconceivable" entities such as the Platonic Ideas, which to him were "empty words." The root cause of his break with Plato lay in the fact that in a "salvation" philosophy the purpose of knowledge is necessarily practical and therapeutic and not theoretical or speculative. . . .

2. "The names of things" (e.g. "horse," "ox," "man") immediately evoke their corresponding concepts, which have been generated in the mind by repeated sensory experience (of horses, oxen, and men). The point of this obscure remark is that it is unnecessary and misleading to engage in a long search for definitions, in Platonic fashion, since our experience of natural objects already provides us with clear and distinct mental images. Cf. *Herod.* 37-38: "We must grasp the meanings associated with the word sounds in order . . . to avoid leaving matters in a state of confusion by expounding terms *ad infinitum* or by using meaningless verbiage. We must therefore look to the primary concept in the case of each word and not require exposition. . . ." See also sect. 33 of this biography. . . .

[20] The numbered items following in the translation are snippets from *The Canon,* or theory of knowledge, a treatise now lost. Note the order that they follow: sensations, concepts, feelings. This is one of the more important sections of the biography.

[22] I.e., sensation is self-evident in its truth value and does not need proof. Every sensation is autonomous and self-contained, and neither gains nor loses by comparison with another, except when the mind misinterprets what is given in sensation—as in the case of a mirage, where something is added.

[23] E.g., taste cannot refute taste. A says, "This martini is very dry"; B says, "It isn't dry at all." This apparent contradiction doesn't destroy the reliability of the senses, as the Skeptics claimed, but shows their relativity to the perceiver and makes each sensation authoritative. In the second case, one sense cannot contradict another; e.g., A says, "This martini *tastes* of juniper berries," and B, "It *looks* like water." Obviously. What is not mentioned here is the important fact that sensations are often misinterpreted by the mind, in which case we need to "refute" them by closer inspection. . . .

[24] Reason was an ancillary tool and was never listed as a primary test for truth. Cf. Lucr. 4.482-85, "What should we consider as having greater validity than sensation? Will reasoning that takes its rise from 'false' sensation have power to contradict the senses when it

originates wholly from them? If they are not true, all reasoning likewise becomes false." Professor DeWitt (*op. cit.,* p. 136) strongly denies that this means that "the whole content of consciousness is derived from the sensations," and for this and other reasons refuses to regard Epicurus as an empiricist.

[25] I.e., the fact that our sensations are not merely passively registered but actively cognized and fitted into the existing content of consciousness, witnesses to their truth.

[26] There are two classes of material events that are not open to direct perception: (1) atoms and their behavior and (2) remote celestial phenomena such as comets and solar eclipses. In both cases our knowledge is inferential and derived from the "signs" that observed phenomena provide. Reason enables us to draw such inferences, but it is not the primary source of truth. Much the same attitude is seen today in statements such as "Science is a mental construct resting on the evidence of the senses."

[27] This passage is discussed and illustrations provided in Introduction V.2.d. Professor DeWitt (*op. cit.,* p. 136) unconvincingly writes off this testimony of Diogenes as unreliable, although it is obviously part of a context extracted from Epicurus' lost treatise on the theory of knowledge. He would translate the Greek noun for "ideas" as "secondary or inferential ideas," i.e., ideas that are logically derived rather than built up from sense experience. In other words, DeWitt has strong prejudices against calling Epicurus an empiricist. On the other hand, it is certainly obvious that Diogenes was in error, or at least inexcusably vague, in saying that *all* our ideas "take their rise from sensation." For example, the proposition that "worlds are infinite in number" (*Herod.* 45) is clearly not given in sensation, but logically derived from the first principle that "the totality is infinite both in the quantity of atomic bodies and in spatial magnitude" (*Herod.* 42). Perhaps we should give Diogenes the benefit of the doubt by saying that by the term "ideas" he meant "universals" such as "man," "horse," "ox"; but DeWitt is not willing to concede even this (*op. cit.,* 112-13).

[29] Cf. Lucr. 4.478-79: "You will find that the concept of truth arose first from the senses and that the senses cannot be refuted." . . . Professor DeWitt again writes off Diogenes' account of the empirical origin of concepts as the testimony of a two-bit hack. He attempts to reverse the generally accepted opinion on this point and by using a battery of arguments both good and bad (*op. cit.,* pp. 142-8), tries to prove that, far from being empirical in origin, Epicurus' "concepts" were *a priori* or innate ideas provided by nature as effective guides for thinking—just as it has provided the feelings of pleasure and pain as effective guides for the moral life. One of the pieces of evidence seemingly in favor of

this view is the fact that the Greek noun for "concept" (*prolepsis*) means "anticipation"; hence "if an idea precedes or anticipates something, this can hardly be anything but experience" (p. 145). Thus, for example, nature has provided us with an innate idea of justice, so that when we mature we may be able to distinguish just acts from unjust. But if so, nature is a purposeful agent, and . . . ideas of purpose are utterly foreign to a materialism such as Epicureanism. It would seem, rather, that Diogenes has provided us with the correct interpretation of "anticipation": "We could not look into what we want to investigate *if we did not have prior knowledge of it.*" A concept is anticipatory in the sense of being a precondition to our identifying new occurrences of individuals of given classes (e.g., Is that a horse or an ox?) or as a preexisting means of delimiting some field of investigation (e.g., how could one write a book on baroque art without first having some conception of the meaning of "baroque," gained through hearing baroque music and seeing baroque painting and architecture?). Both these meanings of "anticipatory" are compatible with the empirical origin of concepts.

In all fairness it must be admitted that other arguments adduced by DeWitt are very persuasive, among them the testimony of Cicero that the true conceptions of the gods were inborn. The question of the status of concepts in Epicurus is closely connected with the larger question of whether he was an empiricist, and DeWitt wages a concerted campaign on several fronts against the widely accepted opinion that he was. If he is right, then Epicurus was an intuitionalist and not an empiricist at all as far as the nature of concepts is concerned. But even so, the other two important criteria of truth—sensations and feelings—are unaffected and constitute major evidence for the empiricist side of the argument. In any case DeWitt's arguments must remain inconclusive, since the word for "concept" appears only four times in the extant writings of Epicurus, which is too slender a basis for decision, and because we lack an all-important document, Epicurus' *Canon,* or theory of knowledge.

[30] . . . Some beliefs are open to direct verification (e.g., Is that tower round or square?). Others are not, especially when they involve the causes of remote celestial phenomena (e.g., What is the cause of the rising and setting of the sun?). In the latter case, plural hypotheses are set up, and the principle of noncontradiction comes into play: Any hypothesis that is not contradicted by our terrestrial experience may be regarded as probable. . . .

[31] I.e., decisions for or against various courses of action. . . .

[32] Epicurus is contrasting his own empirical methods with the dialectical methods of the Platonists. See note 19, above.

[33] What follows is a scrapbook of Epicurus' views on "the wise man," or ideal Epicurean. The recurring "will" is usually equivalent to "ought to." Everything is disjointed and run together, and the reader gets the impression that Epicurus was no better than a cracker-barrel moralist. Numbering has been introduced into this melange to give a semblance of order. This section is capped by the *Letter to Menoeceus.*

[34] Not the biographer, but Diogenes of Tarsus.

[35] The "beat" philosophers of antiquity, who flouted all civilized conventions and lived like street dogs (whence their name).

[36] Unlike the rival Stoic sage, who disciplined himself not to feel emotion, including grief at the loss of a child or friend.

[37] Oddly enough, Epicurus was very punctilious in his own observance of the rites of the state religion and urged his followers "to sacrifice piously and properly." Whether his motives were defensive, hypocritical, or pious cannot be properly ascertained, but Professor DeWitt (*op. cit.,* 280-81) holds that they were completely sincere and gives good reasons for so believing.

[38] It is suggested by Ettore Bignone, an Italian editor, that since Epicureanism was a closed, dogmatic system any idea of progress or of one Epicurean thinker advancing beyond another was automatically ruled out.

[39] The Epicureans considered it a virtue and not a vice to have arrived at a complete system of positive dogmas about nature and human nature. This closed body of teachings they regarded as the only "true philosophy," in contradistinction to the speculative uncertainties of Platonism and the crippling excesses of Skepticism. Their dogmatism can be justified only in the light of their over-all aim—the cure of souls in an age of anxiety. . . .

[40] I.e., equally unperturbed.

[41] The Stoics, contrariwise, held that they are equal, since conduct is either moral or immoral, with no possible middle ground of partly moral, partly immoral.

[42] I.e., by professional Epicureans who live the simple life of *ataraxia* in a group; cf. *L.D.* 40. "Those who have attained the full complement of pleasure" is a technical phrase for "perfect Epicureans." It may anticipate a similar technical phrase in St. Paul's Epistles (cf. Ephesians 3.19: "To know the love of Christ which passeth knowledge, that ye may be filled unto all the fullness of God," i.e., become perfect Christians).

[43] I.e., it is impossible to read the future by supernatural means. Even if it were possible, things happen deterministically, and we can do nothing about them.

[44] A fifth-century school founded by Aristippus of Cyrene, a student of Socrates'. Since it antedated the Epicurean school by more than a century and also taught that pleasure is the moral good, Epicurus was accused of plagiarizing from Aristippus (sect. 4 of Diogenes' biography). But the two conceptions of pleasure differed radically. Epicurus taught that pleasure was neutral and largely static, consisting in freedom from pain in body and mind, whereas Aristippus held that pleasure is positive and dynamic, consisting in the immediate, intense enjoyments of the moment, whatever they may be; also that there is no difference between "lower" and "higher" pleasures (e.g., sex and Brahms), because all pleasures are bodily states. The moral life consisted in rational regulation of our actions, with a view to maximizing the positive balance of pleasure over pain. In other words, Cyrenaicism was what Epicureanism has always tended to become in the hands of its lay practitioners . . . Nevertheless it was fundamentally different from the sectarian practice of the Garden.

St. Augustine (essay date c. 413-26)

SOURCE: St. Augustine, "Book VIII," in *The City of God against the Pagans*, translated by David S. Wiesen, Harvard University Press, 1968, pp. 1-146.

[*In the following excerpt from Book VIII of* The City of God, *St. Augustine includes Epicureanism in his castigation of philosophies that value materialism above religious faith.*]

Thus not only the doctrines of both theologies, mythical and political alike, must give way to the philosophy of the Platonists, for they have said that the true God is the author of all things, the illuminator of truth, and the bestower of happiness, but so must the other philosophers too who have adopted a belief in the material elements of nature because their own minds are subservient to the body give way to these great men who recognize so great a God. Such were Thales with his moisture, Anaximenes with his air, the Stoics with their fire, Epicurus with his atoms, that is, very minute bodies which are indivisible and imperceptible, and any others that there are whom we need not stop to enumerate, whether they named bodies simple or compound, animate or inanimate, as the cause and primary substance of everything, as long as they named bodies. For some of them, like the Epicureans, have believed that living things could originate from things without life, while others have held that both living and lifeless objects come from what is living, yet still that these are bodies produced

from bodily matter. For instance, the Stoics have held that fire, one of the four material elements of which the visible universe is composed, is endowed with life and wisdom and is the creator both of the universe and of everything within it, and that such fire is in the fullest sense god.

They and the others like them have not been able to imagine anything more than the fabrications of their own wit, confined as it is in the bonds of their fleshly senses. Note that they had within themselves what they did not see, and they pictured inwardly what they had seen externally, even when they did not see it but only had it in their mind. Now the representation that appears to that sort of mental scrutiny is no longer a body but only the likeness of a body, and the faculty by which this likeness of a body is seen within the soul is neither a body nor the likeness of a body. Moreover, the faculty that sees and judges whether the likeness is beautiful or ugly is assuredly superior to the actual likeness on which such a judgement is passed. Now that faculty is the human mind and the substance of a rational soul, and it is certainly not material, if even the likeness of a body, when seen and judged in the mind of one who is engaged in thinking, is not itself material. It is, then, neither earth nor water nor air nor fire, of which four materials, or elements as they are called, we see the material universe to have been composed. Furthermore, if our mind is not material, how can God, the mind's creator, be material?

So, as we have said, these philosophers must make way for the Platonists . . .

Lorenzo Valla (essay date 1433)

SOURCE: Lorenzo Valla, "Book III," in *On Pleasure (De voluptate)*, translated by A. Kent and Maristella Lorch, Abaris Books, Inc., 1977, pp. 228-327.

[*Valla, an Italian intellectual, served as the Librarian of the Vatican. His* Devero bono, *or* On Pleasure, *takes the form of a letter in which the writer, who identifies himself as an Epicurean, refutes the arguments of a friend who advocates stoicism. The excerpts that follow exemplify the speaker's stance on Epicureanism.*]

I believe that if this dispute about the comparative worths of pleasure and virtue should come to the vote of the people, that is, of the world (for this is a worldly contest), and if the issue were whether the primacy in wisdom should be awarded to either the Epicureans or the Stoics, then the vote for our side would be so large that you would seem to have been not only rejected but also branded with the ultimate disgrace. I pass over the mortal danger that you would run with such an abundance of enemies. For by the gods and also by men, what is the point of temperance, thrift, and continence unless we get something useful from such actions? Otherwise, the resultant condition is mournful, hideous, similar to constant illness, displeasing to human bodies, hateful to the ears, and, finally, something that ought to be harried out of all states into deserts and the farthest solitudes. . . .

On this account, I can afford to take less trouble in considering the other half of our present discussion, that is, the matter of what the Stoics call tranquillity of mind, maintaining as they do that it is a kind of diadem for the virtuous soul. I cannot see why this mental or spiritual tranquillity should not fit the goal that we have established. For as contemplation generates joy in the mind, so tranquillity and safety keep passion or trouble from entering: they open the way to pleasure, so to speak, and preserve what pleasure has been received. It does not escape me how much some people are raising this argument, and how often they repeat that nothing is more disturbed, anxious, and unhappy than a depraved mind. They mention many people in this connection and describe their loves at length: Phalaris,[132] Dionysius [of Syracuse], and others like them. . . .

How much better a man Epicurus was in this respect is sufficiently expressed by his having considered the day of his death to be a happy day by virtue of the memory of his wellspent and happy previous life. This was not the way with Vergil's Dido or Lucan's Caesar: they hoped for fame based on their deeds, which will never confer advantage upon the dead. On the contrary, that old man of Quintilian's is made to say: "I confess that as my son was dying I received some solace from the circumstance that the unhappy boy had lived just as he wished, for his short life was cheerful and happy." Because this kind of consolation cannot alter, it is more genuine than fame, which can. There are those who mock the good consciences and mental peace and tranquillity of us Epicureans, as though, after the fashion of Orestes, the unremitting firebrands of the Furies had a permanent seat in our countenances and stood ready for battle in our eyes, although in fact these critics can see in an Epicurean the serene heart of a man who gives thanks for his past life, regards the advancing Fates with calm and cheerful eye, and is not any more hostile to death than to the shades of night after sunset. This, I say, is to live well, to live happily; this is a good and happy death. . . .

Perhaps you now ask me to speak of Pythagoras' and Plato's doctrine of the transmigration of souls from one body to another, which Vergil followed in these words:

That they may start wishing to return again to the body.

Neither Porphyry nor Apuleius, two of the greatest Platonists, dared to support this doctrine against the philosophers who railed at it. A little later, Macrobius, also one of the greatest Platonists, who borrowed many things from Plato's *Timaeus* and from Plotinus, discussed this doctrine so anxiously and hesitantly that he seems almost to be walking on tiptoe through thorns. Marcus Terentius Varro had previously argued against the doctrine, speaking as in a dream in the fashion of the prophet Tiresias, as Horace says:

Whatever I predict either will happen or will not. . . .

According to my Epicurus, however, nothing remains after the dissolution of the living being, and in the term "living being" he included man just as much as he did the lion, the wolf, the dog, and all other things that breathe. With all this I agree. They eat, we eat; they drink, we drink; they sleep, and so do we. They engender, conceive, give birth, and nourish their young in no way different from ours. They possess some part of reason and memory, some more than others, and we a little more than they. We are like them in almost everything: finally, they die and we die—both of us completely. But we shall have knowledge of this—or rather we shall have no knowledge—when we have departed from this life. As for now, however, let us serve what we know and what is the only good in life, pleasure. . . .

Jean Francois Sarasin (essay date c. 1645)

SOURCE: Jean Francois Sarasin, "An Essay in Vindication of Epicurus, and his Doctrine," in *Epicurus's Morals*, 1712.

[*Although mistakenly attributed to St. Evremond for some decades, the essay on Epicurus's morals was actually composed by Sarasin, a seventeenth-century French intellectual and cardinal. His piece, reprinted many times in French and translated into English in 1712, represents one of the significant French attempts to revive Epicurus's reputation, particularly by reminding readers of the simplicity of his philolosophy.*]

Our Modern Philosophers are very industrious to lessen the Reputation of *Epicurus,* they explode his Doctrine, not only as unworthy of a Philosopher, but as dangerous to the State; imagining that a Man must necessarily be vicious as soon as he becomes one of his Disciples. They take all Occasions to brand his Opinions as opposite to good Manners, and load his Name with

Infamy and Reproach. Yet some among the Stockis who were his greatest Enemies have not used him thus roughly; their Praises agree not with the Modern Aspersions; they have attacked, but not vilified him, and the Writings they have left us, still speak in several Passages, the great Veneration and Esteem they had for him.

From whence then proceeds this so mighty Difference, and why are we no longer of Opinion with the Philosophers of Old? The reason is plain, we do not act like them, we make no enquiry, we do not sift Matters, we only adhere to what is told us, without instructing our selves in the true Nature of Things: We esteem those best which have the greatest Number of Approvers, and do not follow Reason, but the Resemblance of it. We hug our Errours, because they are justified by those of other Men, we had rather believe than judge, and are so unjust that we defend against Reason the spurious Opinions which have been handed down to us. Through this Infirmity hath *Epicurus* fallen under a general Aversion, and ignorant Men who know not his worth, have endeavoured to strike him out of the List of Philosophers; they have condemned him unknown, and banished him unheard, they never enquired into the Merits of his Cause, and seem to be afraid of his making his Defence, lest they should become Converts to the Superiour Excellence of his Divine Precepts.

The first and only reasonable pretence that Men had to slight his Doctrine was, the Lives of some Vicious Wretches, who abusing the Name of this Great Man, gave their Vices the Inscription of his Vertue; and thus fathering their Defects upon the Principles of his Philosopy, lessened the Reputation of his Sect. Multitudes flock'd to Places where they understood that Pleasure was commended, but the Misfortune was, they neither apprehended that Pleasure, nor understood the Praises bestowed upon it; they rested satisfied with the Name in general, not doubting, under the Authority of so great a Man, to screen their Debaucheries and Palliate the Lewdness of their Lives; so that, instead of Profiting in his School, and correcting their loose Inclinations, by the Good Instructions and Vertuous Example of that Philosopher, they even lost that which could only be left them the shame of Tripping, and proceeded so far as to extol Actions at which they blushed before, and to Glory in those Vices which they had formerly concealed. In short, following the bent of their own Vicious Appetites, they publickly, without Shame indulg'd themselves in the Pleasure they brought along with them, and not in that which their Great Master inculcated into them. However, the World judging by Appearances, and seeing Persons who styled themselves Philosophers thus extremely dissolute, that they made a Publick profession of their Failings, and cited *Epicurus* to countenance their Impurity, Laziness, Gluttony and

Drunkenness, made no difficulty to pronounce this Philosophers Doctrine most pernicions and scandalous; and to compare his Disciples to the vilest Animal in Nature; *Epicuri de grege Porcum,* was a Sarcastick Expression of a Poet, reflecting upon the Followers of *Epicurus,* and representing them as Persons wallowing like Swine in all manner of sensuality, and more than beastly Pleasures. The Zeal of our Philosophers Adversaries hath so confounded his Opinion, with the Errors of his Disciples, that it is highly Criminal, with the generality of Mankind, to attempt his Vindication; though the greatest of his Enemies fix no greater Crime upon him than what he hath in common, with the rest of the Philosophers: Nay, even Christianity it self, suffers under the like Misfortune, and is disgraced by the scandalous Lives of base pretending Hypocritical Professors.

Thus unreasonably do ignorant Pretenders treat *Epicurus,* and set his Morals in a very bad Light, but the Wiser and more judicious sort, who (separating themselves from that Multitude, which hath ever been an Enemy to Wisemen; and which, upon a groundless Opinion, condemned the Divine *Socrates,* though approved of by the Gods) have taken a nearer and more perfect View of our Philosophers Life and Doctrine, not giving Credit to common Fame, or taking things upon Trust, but searching to the bottom, have upon the result of their Inquiry, given large and honourable Testimonies of his exalted Vertue and sublime Precepts. They have fully proved his Pleasure to be as severe as the Stoicks Vertue, that though his Title be soft and delicate, his Precepts are difficult; and that to be debauched like *Epicurus,* a Man must be as sober as *Zeno.*

And certainly it is very ridiculous and inconsistent to suppose, that our Philosopher should propagate Lewdness, or instruct his Disciples in the Practice of Vice; if we consider that his Friends and chief Followers were Rulers in the Grecian Cities; that his Reverence for the Gods, Love to his Country, Piety to his Parents, Liberality to his Countrymen, and gentleness to his Slaves, were so remarkably Eminent; that his Country, to reward such exemplary Vertue, erected Statues in his Honour. His Modesty kept him from engaging in Affairs of State; and his Temperance was so great, that his ordinary Diet was nothing but Bread and Water.

However, This Great Man apprehending that the Title he bestowed upon his Doctrine, might be made use of to countenance the sensual Inclinations of some, and others thereby induced to calumniate his Pleasure; as if he had foreseen the unjust Censure of succeeding Ages, and the Vicious Lives of his pretended Followers, hath prevented the World with a sufficient Justification of his Pleasure, and fully explained the same to be sober and severe. He banished from his Garden, where the Philosophiz'd with his Friends, all such as abused the Name of Pleasure, and considered Vice as the sovereign Good of Man, and Tranquillity of Life. For Proof whereof, I will produce you one of his Letters written *to Menetaus;* wherein he speaks thus,

Notwithstanding that we assert Pleasure to be the end of Man, we do not mean vile and infamous pleasure; such as proceeds from Taste and Gluttony: This is an unlikely Opinion of Persons that are Ignorant of, or oppose our Precepts; they wrest them to an ill sense, and we separate our selves from their Company.

Thus you see, how careful he was to defend himself against Ignorance and Misconstruction, which he foresaw were the only two things capable to prejudice the World against him. His Life, though Innocent, Sober and Discreet, hath not, however, been free from Invectives and Detraction, which have been sufficiently answered and resulted, by learned and judicious Writers, who have taken the Pains to write our Philosophers Life, in which they have not failed, with clearness of Judgment and sound Reason, to vindicate his Reputation against the trifling Cavils of weak and partial Enemies. But, as it is not my Design to entertain you with a Detail of his Actions, but to defend his Pleasure; I shall refer you to *Diogenes Laertius Gassendus,* and others, for the relation of his Life; and Philosophise with you a while upon the Nature of that which hath so many Enemies; and enquire whether it be such as will exclude those who defend and follow it out of the Rank of Good and Wise Men.

Epicurus placeth the Felicity of Man in Pleasure, and esteemeth that Life happiest which is attended with an indolence of Body, and transquillity of Mind. And wherein can a Wiseman better place his Happiness than in a Serene and undisturb'd Mind? All the Motions of our Soul center in Pleasure, and those who condemn it must consequently condemn Nature, and accuse her of Faults in all her Works; for this Wise Mother hath mingled Delight with all our Actions, and by an admirable piece of Wisdom hath so ordered it, that as those Things which are most necessary, are the meanest, so they are most pleasing; and certainly had she not found out this innocent Slight, the World had perished long ago, and Man who is the noblest part thereof, neglecting his own Preservation, had left it a Prey to Wild Beasts. Who would trouble himself with eating, did not Pleasure as well as necessity invite him to it? Who would endure that Sleep should benum his Senses, take from him the use of Reason, and make him exchange Life with the image of Death; did not the sweetness of her Poppies allure him, and make the remedy as charming as it is shameful? So necessary is Pleasure to us, that the Indigence of our Nature contributes to it.

Pleasure is so interwoven in our Nature, that she stands not in need of an Advocate, and so prevalent are the Charms of her Beauty, that when she appears, all Opposition falls before her; and when absent, she is the Object of our Desires. The Stoicks vainly endeavour to enslave the Body to the Tyranny of the Soul. The Peripateticks wrangle much about what they do not understand, and are great Lovers of Wealth; the Academicks are Proud, Conceited and Vainglorious Pretenders to Universal Knowledge and Wisdom, but it is *Epicurus* alone that hath found out that Soveraign good, which is the Complement of an happy Life, and those only that follow his Steps are Rich, Powerful and Wise, and at once enjoy whatever is desireable.

The true Felicity of Life, and the Government of our Passions (from the Disorder of which none can absolutely and at all times defend themselves) hath been the Subject upon which Philosophers have chiefly employed their Studies, and is that part of Moral Philosophy which hath been oftnest enquired into; yet no one Point of the whole Body of Philosophy hath been treated of with greater Ostentation, and to less satisfaction. Some have taken great Pains to describe the Passions to us, and to discover their Causes and Effects, but never instructed us how to regulate and govern them; very careful they were to let us know our Disease, but unskillful or negligent in applying Remedies to Cure the same. Others of less Judgment but greater Zeal, have confounded them with Vices, and made no difference between the Motions of the Sensitive Appetite, and the Misgovernment of the Will, so that according to them, a Man cannot be passionate without being Criminal. Their Discourses which should have been Instructions to Vertue, were only so many Invectives against Vice, and hurried by a mistaken Zeal; they made the Distemper greater than it was, and the Cure less Practicable: Others again, vainly puft up with Pride, have pretended to stifle Passion, and to raise Man to the Condition of Angels. They have not feared to debase their Gods that they might exalt their Wiseman, and have often times made him happier than their *Jupiter.* They have given him the upper Hand of Fortune and Destiny, and make his Happiness to depend entirely upon his own Free Will; Pain and Pleasure they represent as imaginary Distractions, that Passions are the Sickness of the Soul, and that a Man must renounce his Liberty if he obey such insolent Masters. Thus they have framed a Wiseman only in Idea, and whilst they have endeavoured to make him equal or superiour to the Gods, they have made him less than Man.

Thus did these vain Pretenders to Wisdom busie themselves in a blind and eager pursuit after Happiness; but the more hast they made in a wrong way, the more Labor and Pains they took to be further from their Journies end. And though Wisdom and Happiness was the sole aim and drift of every one of them; yet they all took a different way to attain the desired End; and notwithstanding, amongst such different Opinions, one only could be in the right; each of them pretended to be that only one which could give access to Vertue, and put its Followers into the right way, passing by the rest as leading them astray and beside the Mark. In this, however, they unanimously agreed to explode the Doctrine of *Epicurus,* and to represent his Pleasure as Voluptuousness, his Philosophy as Vanity, and his Precepts such as plunged Men into all manner of Dissoluteness, but upon a due enquiry into the matter, we shall evidently find that these their heavy Censures of *Epicurus,* proceeded more from Pride and Ignorance, than from Knowledge and sound Judgment.

The Stoicks and all other Philosophers agree with *Epicurus* in this; that the true Felicity of Life is to be free from Perturbations, to understand our Duty towards God and Man to enjoy the Present, without any anxious Dependance upon the future, not to amuse our selves either with Hopes or Fears, to curb and restrain our unruly Appetites, to rest satisfied with what we have, which is abundantly sufficient; For he that is content wants nothing. He that can look Death in the Face and bid it Welcome, open his Door to Poverty, and bridle his Appetites, he is the Man (they all agree) whom Providence hath established in the Possession of consummate Happiness. The difference between them is this, the Stoicks and the other Philosophers deny the Passions, and rank them among things which are not *in rerum Natura; Epicurus* on the other Hand asserts them to be necessary to the Soul, that they are Seeds of Vertue, and that Joy must perfect that Felicity which desire hath begun. Their Happiness is purely Speculative, but that of *Epicurus* is practical.

But as there is no Beauty without some Moles, no Chrystal without some Specks; neither is *Epicurus* without his Imperfections, which (tho' it is not my Design to justifie are) however, easily pardonable if we consider the dark time he lived in, when there was scarce any Religion but sottish Idolatry, more Gods than Nations, and no other Light by which to steer his Course, than the dim Lamp of Nature. He seems rather to be honoured for coming so near to the Knowledge of the true God, than condemned for coming no nearer; rather to be admired for having such agreeable Conceptions of some of the Divine Attributes, than reproached for not comprehending them all, especially if we compare his Notions relating to the Gods, with those of the Elder *Grecian* Philosophers and Poets, as well as the common and received Opinions of those Days.

Who can blame our Philosopher, who sway'd by the highest Reason, trac'd Nature in her Primitive Innocence, and not only taught but practic'd Vertue to such an Excellence, as few in these days, to our Shame be it spoken, tho' we enjoy the glorious Sunshine of the Gospel, can equal? The Bounds Nature hath prescrib'd,

are those of Justice and Equity; Avarice came not from Nature, she hath concealed Gold in the lowest Bowels of the Earth, and we have torn it from thence, Nature was not the Cause of Ambition, which torments us, she brought us into the World, and with Equality sends us out of it; we only differ from one another in as much as we corrupt her. We all equally enjoy Liberty, and the Sun; Servitude was introduc'd by Violence, and the first Kings were Tyrants. Is it Nature, think you, which incites to Luxury? The Poets, themselves, who have foisted Defects into the very Heavens, to screen their own Follies with Celestial Examples, and made *Jupiter* Wicked that they might be so themselves, durst not own such a Thought. In their Description of the Golden Age, they tell you, that Acorns were then Mens Food, that Rivers quenched their Thirst, that they dwelt in Caves, that they had no Cloaths to defend them against the Injuries of the Weather, and that they followed Nature in all their Actions. I readily grant, that there never was such a Constitution of Human Affairs; and that Mankind was never reduc'd to such a Level with Brutes: The Poets have indeed carried the Fiction too far, but their Design was to instruct us; that Excess proceedeth not from Nature; she doth not Prompt or Encourage us to it; Experience plainly teacheth, that the Necessities of Nature may be plentifully satisfied with slender and easily provided Fare. Hear how the incomparable Mr. *Cowley,* our English *Pindar,* expresses himself on the occasion.

> When Epicurus to the World had taught,
>   That Pleasure was the chiefest Good,
> (And was perhaps i'th' Right, if rightly
>   understood)
>   His Life he to his Doctrine brought,
> And in a Garden's Shade that Sovereign
>   Pleasure sought;
>   Whoever a true Epicure would be,
>   May there find cheap and vertuous Luxury.
> Vitellius's Table which did hold
>   As many Creatures as the Ark of old:
>   That Fiscal Table, to which ev'ry day
>   All Countries did a constant Tribute pay,
>   Could nothing more delicious afford,
>   Than Nature's Liberality,
>   Help'd with a little Art and Industry,
>   Allows the meanest Gard'ners board.
> The wanton Taste no Fish or Fowl can
>   choose,
> For which the Grape or Melon she would
>   loose,
>   Though all th' Inhabitants of Sea an Air
>   Be listed in the Gluttons Bill of Fare;
>   Yet still the Fruits of Earth we see
>   Plac'd the third Story high in all her Luxury.
>   Cowley's Garden to J. Evelyn, Esq;

In short, 'tis we that abuse the Gifts of Heaven, and the Advantages it confers upon us, since those things without which Nature cannot subsist are very compendious, and may be obtained with great Ease, without the violation of Justice, Liberality or Tranquillity. How then doth Nature require that a Man should abstain from those things which are submitted to him, and over which she hath made him Lord? No, We ought rather to use them, provide we use them according to Nature. We must so use things as that we may be without them, we must be their Masters, and not their Slaves; we must not be impatient for them, nor dejected at their Loss, enjoy them peaceably as occasion offers, and not pursue them with disquiet and fatigue.

There is no Condition of Life but may become a Wise Man, a Philosopher is not to be blamed for dwelling in a Palace, but in not having the Power to be contented with a Cottage; I shall not be scandalized at seeing him in his Robes, if he have not the Ambition of a King. Let *Aristippus* possess the Riches of *Cræsus,* what matter? He will throw them away when they incommode him. Let *Plato* be at *Dionysius* the Tyrants Table, yet in the midst of that abundance of Delicacies, he will feed only on Olives; the possession of Goods is not to be condemned, but our Slavery and Subjection to them; it is not Poverty will make us Wise, it may take from us, indeed, the Opportunity of committing some Faults; but there are others which it cannot remedy. The Cynicks Rags contribute not the least to Tranquillity or Moderation: Ambition dwelt with *Diogenes* in his Tub, and there it was he had the Insolence to insult *Alexander,* the haughtiest of all Mankind.

Undoubtedly, there is more difficulty to follow Nature in Affluence than in Necessity; the Spurs which our Delights make use of to try our Moderation, are much more keen than those which Adversity employs for that purpose; but the greater the Difficulty the more Glory in surmounting it, and the loss of false Joys secures to us a much better Possession of real ones. We are not sensible of a Felicity which costs us nothing, and for which we are indebted to chance, it must be given us by Wisdom and Prudence, if we would have a true Relish of it, and Pain must sometime usher us to pleasure: Suppose a Man should enter the Lists at the Olympick Games, with a Design to try his Strength and Skill; if no body encountred him, he might possibly be crowned; but nevertheless, that would not render him Victorious. Skilful Pilots gain their Reputation from Storms and Tempests. If *Penelope*'s Chastity had not been try'd, the envious World would have said she only wanted Corrupters. Wherefore, let us not fly the World, nor fly the Court; let us not sculk in Deserts, from whence Philosophy fetch'd the primitive Mankind; let us possess Riches, and refuse not the administration of Publick Offices; if we are Wise, we may enjoy these Things without any Danger to our Ease and Tranquillity; we may fail happily amidst these Rocks, and view all with an unconcerned Eye. If we be stript of them by our not looking back, we may testify our Contempt, and that we were not wedded to them. It is shameful for a Wiseman to be weaker than those Desires, which as they are unnatural so are they vain and unnecessary, only in Opinion. This is *Epicurus*'s Pleasure, this is what he calls living according to Nature, this is his Doctrine, and these his Sentiments.

Consider then, whether this Opinion deserves to be ill treated, and see whether we have Reason to despise it; whether this Pleasure pimps to Debauchery and Excess, and whether any thing can be more Sober or Chast. If you ask *Epicurus* what it is to live pleasantly, he will answer you, *That it consists not in a Fondness for worldly Concerns, but in resisting corrupt Affections and Inclinations, contemning Honour, getting the mastery of Fortune; and in a Word, possessing an absolute Peace and Tranquillity of Mind.* To this Point are all his Precepts leveled, in this you meet with Pleasure; and in this, indeed, we ought to seek it, not in the satisfaction of the Senses, nor in giving a loose to our Appetites. This Pleasure is too pure to depend upon the Body, it depends on the intellectual Part; Reason is its Mistress, Reason is its Rule, the Senses are only its Ministers: Besides, Whatever Delights we may hope for by indulging the Palate in Pleasures of the Sight, in Musick or Perfumes; if we do not receive them with a serene Mind we are deceived, we fall under the delusion of a false Joy, and take the Shadow of Pleasure for the real Substance. We will burn, if you please, the most costly Perfumes, we will Closet up our selves with *Venus,* we will Riot our selves upon *Nectar* and *Ambrosia,* and enjoy the utmost Pleasure the Poets have imagined, yet all will prove bitter if our Minds be disquieted and in spight of these Delights, sorrow will appear manifestly upon our Brows.

I will give you one Instance to prove this Assertion, and demonstrate to you how incapable that Man is of Pleasure, whose Mind is discomposed. You have read, no doubt, of that Feast which *Tigellinus* made for *Nero,* and may remember that great Debauch, the Noise whereof hath lasted to our Age; it seems to have been the utmost Effort of Prodigality, Art and Luxury, which succeeding Ages have not been able to rival, much less exceed. *Agrippa*'s Pond was the Place pitch'd upon for this extravagant Repast; it was made upon a stately Bark, which being drawn by a great many others, seem'd insensibly to move. All the Barges were adorned with Gold, and inlay'd with Ivory; the Rowers were so many lovely Youths habited like Cupids. The Taste knew no Fowl, which it was not furnished with at that Entertainment; the Ocean provided it with Fish, and the Provinces of the Empire with diversity of Flesh. In short, every thing was there in Plenty and Perfection. I omit those infamous Houses erected on the Banks, which were stock'd with Women of the best Quality, and stark naked, Courtezans. The Night itself contributed to the Pleasure of his Debauch; its Shades were dissipated by an infinity of Lights, and its Silence agreeably disturb'd by the harmonious Consort of several Kinds of Musick. Would you know what delight *Nero* took in all these things, and whether he departed satisfied from this Entertainment? Consider only, that he carried with him thither, the Memory of his Crimes, and the sting of a bad Conscience, and you will readily conclude, that he had no real Satisfaction throughout the whole Entertainment; that he there felt the penitential Whip, and that though he appear'd outwardly gay and brisk, yet he was inwardly tormented with Horror and Despair. If he had any Joy, it was that of the *Menades;* he was obliged to his Drunkenness for that little Pleasure he enjoyed, and his Happiness encreased with the Diminution of his Reason. I conclude his whole Retinue under the same Circumstances; for, I conceive, neither *Seneca,* nor *Thraseas Pœtus,* nor *Bareas Soranus,* were of the number of the Guests; they lived according to Nature, admist the corruption of a most profligate and degenerate Age, and were consequently improper Company for such a Crew of Debauchees; doubtless such only were present, as endeared themselves to his Conversation by a Congruity of Manners, such as spurr'd him on in his Crimes, and pimp'd to his Lusts; before such, he had no Opportunity to blush, where an eager desire to excel each other in Vice, had stified all manner of Shame. Certainly, such vile Wretches were far from being Happy; there was no finding a sound Man in the whole Company, Pleasure could get no admittance into those Breasts which Lewdness had so entirely possessed. They were entirely govern'd by those Passions which destroy the Tranquillity of the Mind; and by consequence, were not in a Condition to relish that Pleasure we so much approve. Had our Philosopher been present at this Debauch, he would have declared the Truth before *Nero,* and in the Face of the whole World, he would not have feared Death, which he held indifferent, but would have boldly expressed his Mind after the following Manner.

Unhappy Prince! How wretchedly are you deceived in believing Pleasure is to be found in these Excesses! It is as far distant from them as you are from Lifes truest Happiness. You drag your Misery along with you, in all Places, wheresoever you go; and do what you will, you cannot hide your self one Moment from your Conscience. Cover your Table with Meats yet more delicious than those it now abounds with, add the richest Wines of *Greece* and *Italy,* or the whole World; Nay, heap up all that Luxury and Lust can think on or invent, yet you will find nothing in all these things to afford you Satisfaction, for tho' your Body be satiated, your Mind will still be in search after Pleasure. These are not the Things which render Life happy, it is prudence alone which directs you to the soveraign Good; it is she only, which will teach you to regulate your Desires according to Nature; and in this Rule it is that you will meet with what you cannot find in your Disorders; if any thing be wanting, turn

your Eyes towards that common Mother, and she will give you, easily, wherewith to be content. Are you Thirsty? She hath every where placed Rivers and Springs where you may quench your Thirst. Hungry? Places where you will find Fruits to live on. If you are not satisfied with these things, you will never be satisifed with all your Excesses; consult your Hunger, and your Thirst, they will find Delights for you in the simplicity of Nature, and Bread and Water will serve you instead of the best Dish upon Earth you can call to mind, when you are in Necessity: But now you are not, so you give no time to your Stomach to digest your Meat; your Intemperance daily contracts Crudities, and accelerates the Hour of that Death which terrifies you with such dismal Apprehensions. Thus you make Feasts which afford you no Pleasure, because you strain Nature, forcing it to obey your Desires. But know this, your Desires interfere with your Nature, and the Errors of your Mind darken the Light of your Reason; wherefore flatter not your self with tasting Pleasure as you fondly imagine. There is nothing bounded but in Nature, whatever is repugnant to Nature is infinite, and consequently above us. Ambitious Subjects aspire to Crowns, if they became Kings, they would aim at being sole Monarchs of the Earth; if Monarchs, they would wish for Incense and Sacrifices: And the Fable of the Gyants informs us, that the Earth hath dared to contend with Heaven for its Dominion. It is the same with other Evil Appetites, none can be Happy but he that knows how to govern them, and as it belongs only to a Wise Man to undertake that Province, so it only belongs to him to sway the Universe. He only can extract Pleasure out of all these things; he alone uses Delights soberly, and possesseth them in their true Perfection. For your part, you dishonour the Race of *Augustus,* and are the Infamy of Mankind, over whom the Anger of the Gods hath given you the Command; but do what you please, you will be always Miserable, your Grief will harrass you at all times, and in all Places; you will never steal one *Moment* from your Conscience, and in the midst of all your Good Cheer, you will drink no Wine but what shall represent to you the Blood of those Innocents which your Cruelty hath shed on one base Pretence or other.

Thus would *Epicurus* have delivered himself, thus would he have justified his Philosophy, and thus reprov'd that Emperor's most abominable Vice and Folly: But as it is impossible that the *Mind* should truly *relish* Pleasure, if her Companion, the Body, labour under any Affliction. *Epicurus,* or rather Truth it self teaches, that Privation of corporal Pain is a very necessary Composition in that Supreme Good or Felicity of Life which Pleasure doth produce; and in truth, there is so close an Alliance between the Body and the Mind, that their Pleasures and their Sufferings are inseparable, the Mind cannot be entirely happy whilst Pain afflicts the Body; neither can the Body retain its Vigour if the Mind be afflicted and disturbed. Hence it evidently appears, that the Sum of all Pleasure consists only in the amotion of Pain, or in that State which follows upon that amotion; for where-ever Pleasure is, there can be nothing of Anxiety or Pain; and consequently it must be a great Pleasure not to be in Pain; for a further Proof whereof, if any Man doubt, let him consult those who have been tormented with the Gout, Cholick, Strangury, or any other acute Disease. Let the Stoicks boast as much as they please of the insensibility of their Sect, and that rigorous Vertue which makes a mock of Pain; one fit of the Stone, or such like Distemper, will fully convince them that their Bodies do not center with their Opinion, and that their Discourses, tho' most eloquent and sublime, are neither agreeable to Truth nor Humane Nature.

It will not be amiss to illustrate this Assertion with a suitable Example, and the same shall not be taken from the Crowd of pretending Philosophers. I will make use of a Name the Stoicks themselves shall not scruple to admit, and pitch upon a Person whose Vertues they never doubted of; *Hercules* shall bear witness to the Truth of what I assert; that *Hercules* whose Labours have gain'd him a Seat amongst the Gods, and rendred him so glorious to Men, that the Poets have always made choice of him as a perfect instance of the Force and Power of Wisdom. We will take a view of this Hero dying, and consider him in the last Actions of his Life; this invincible Man's *Exit,* we expect, should be like his Entrance, illustrious in performing something worthy of his Character, that he should say nothing which would sully his Noble Actions, or seem unworthy of his former Vertue. But alas, we are deceived, the strength of his Pain gets the Mastery of his Courage, his Constancy yields to the Heat of that Poyson which devours him; he does not only Complain, he Weeps, he Cries, he Howls; and it is with the utmost Effects of Rage and Despair, that he quits this Life to take his place among the Gods. Let not the Stoicks then rattle any longer of their Insensibility, nor pretend, that a Wise man may be happy in the midst of Tortures; neither let them despise Pain, to which *Hercules* himself was forced to yield, after so many Victories.

But if the Stoicks, in favour of this their darling Hero, reject the Authority of Poets, and the consent of Theatres, as representing *Hercules* contrary to the Truth: *Possidonius,* Master to *Cicero,* and by him stiled, the greatest of the Stoicks, will serve as an illustrious Example to prove the Truth of my assertion; here we shall see a main Pillar of the Porch stagger'd, and by consequence, the whole Fabrick ready to fall; *Pompey the Great,* understanding that this famous Philosopher lay grievously tormented with the Gout, made him a Visit, to see whether so great a Master was able to bear that Pain with the same Ease, now when aflicted, as he contemned and despised it by his florid Harangues, when in Health. The Philosopher was surprized at the Presence of so noble and unexpected a Guest;

and judging that the true cause of his coming was something more than a friendly Visit, he bore the violence of his Pain with the utmost uneasiness; and tho' the extreme Agony thereof, made sweat trickle from him, in abundance; yet obstinately resolving not to contradict his former Doctrine, either by Words or Groans, before so great a Witness; in the midst of his Pain, cries out, *I ne'er will own you to be an Evil;* by which Expression, he only confirm'd his Noble Guest in his former Opinion: That the Doctrine of the Stoicks consisted more in haughty and vain glorious Expressions, than a right conformity to Truth and Reason. *Cicero* comes in as a full Proof of this Wiseman's Weakness: and Inconsistency; *I have seen,* says he, Possidonius *the Greatest of the Stoicks, have as little power to undergo the Pains of the Gout, as my Host* Nicomachus; a Person whom *Tully* accounted an ordinary sort of Fellow.

As I have given an Instance of *Hercules* in his last Moments, that I may fully dispatch this Point: I will examine that grand Question of the Stoicks. What think you of *Hercules* and *Theseus,* whose Lives were one continued Series of glorious Labours, which if they had not undertaken, the Earth had been over-run with Monsters and Injustice? By which Question, it is undeniably evident, that the Stoicks are nothing more than vain ignorant Pretenders, and blind Guides, who lead their Admirers on in a Wildgoose Chace, from which they have reaped nothing but Confusion, and made themselves ridiculous to all Ages. For, had they understood the Matter right, or had they not been blinded with Pride and Arrogance, they would readily have perceived that the Actions of these brave Men were so many shining Proofs of the Truth and Excellency of the *Epicurean* Doctrine; for as much as all their great and glorious Labours were undertaken and performed by them, in order to obtain that Pleasure, which our Philosopher, with so much Reason, affirms to be the Soveraign Good, and true Felicity of Life. Nature hath dispersed Pleasure through all her Actions; she useth it as a Motive and Assistance to us, in doing every thing that is Good and Commendable, and its recompence, when done, according to that received and approved Axiom, *Vertue is its own Reward.* Man's Life is full of Misery, and were not our Passions to be sweetned with Pleasure, they would end in Grief or Despair; we should be pressed to Death under the Load of our Misfortunes; and losing all hope of conquering our Enemies: We should likewise lose the Desire of resisting them. To heighten our Courage therefore, this wise Mother solicits us by Pleasure, and proposing that to us as a full recompence of all our Labours, encourageth us to despise Difficulties, and banish Fear; for though the Mind of Man be naturally ambitious; yet would she not attempt to obtain Vertue, and subdue Vice, were there not as much Pleasure as Glory in the Action; or to speak more properly, were there not an inward, excellent, and inexpressible Pleasure attending every such Glorious Attempt.

The Pleasure which our Philosopher recommends, is, the enjoyment of a real pleasing Good; such as fills the Soul with Content; swallows up Desire in Fruition, and banisheth Sorrow and Fear, so that he excludes from thence all those false Delights which spring from Indigence, or end in Sorrow, for as they are desired with so much Anxiety as far exceeds the Pleasure they promise; they are such Enemies likewise to our Peace, that it is impossible to taste of them, without disordering our Nature; they wound, at once, both our Soul and Body, they weaken the one, and corrupt the other; they are worse Remedies than the Evils they would Cure; they are constantly attended with Repentance, Sorrow and Shame, and dare not appear to publick View; for being conscious that they lessen our Reputation, they seek out Shade, and court Solitude and Silence; they would blush, were they forced to discover themselves, and Confusion would so overwhelm them, that all their Joy would be turned into bitterness and mourning. The solid Pleasures are those of the Mind; and Man cannot enjoy Peace and Tranquillity, unless that which is the noblest Part, whereof he is composed, be Happy; the Knowledge of Truth, and Practice of Vertue, ought to be his chief Delight; he must remember that the Body is the Souls Slave, and that in choice of Pleasures it is reasonable that the Soveraign have the Preference. Those which the Soul relisheth, are the truest; and if any Man be of another Opinion, we may conclude him void of Reason, Sense, and Understanding. The Pleasures of the Senses are limitted, whereas those of the Soul have no Bounds; the Pleasures of the Body are Strangers, those of the Soul are Natural; the former may be taken from us without great Difficulty, but Death itself cannot deprive us of the latter, which tho' it rob us of our Riches, cannot rob us of our Vertues; the Pleasures of the Body are Transitory and Dangerous, but the Tranquillity of the Mind produceth true and solid Content, and is a Permanent and Essential Good.

Now, though we do esteem Pleasure as a real Good, and Pain to be a real Evil; yet we do not affirm that we ought always to pursue the one, and avoid the other: For it may be convenient for us, at sometimes, to suffer Pain, that we may, afterwards, enjoy more abundant and satisfactory Pleasure, and to abstain from some Pleasures, lest they draw upon us more grievous Pain, for some things there are, which tho' they yield some Pleasure, yet they are of such a Nature as to occasion Pains much greater than themselves. It was this Maxim that made *Regulus* put himself again into the Hands of his enraged Enemies, where the Cruelties of his Tormenters were less painful to him than his Remorse would have been, had he broke his Faith and Promise. It was this Maxim that made *Fabricius* despise the offered Treasures of the King of *Epirus,* whereby he lost also those Evil Desires which attend the Possession of Riches, and preserved to himself that repose of

Mind, which is the chief of Pleasures, and Supreme Good. To this Maxim may be referred all those great Deeds, and commendable Actions, done by the Heroes of former Ages; you will find that if they at any time embraced Pain, it was to avoid a much greater, or if they refused some Pleasures, it was by such abstinence to obtain others much more solid and satisfactory. For to what other Motive can we ascribe those their illustrious Actions. They would not have turned their Backs upon Riches, embraced Poverty, or hunted after Enemies, Difficulties, and Pain; had they not found therein that Pleasure which is the only solid Good, and Complement of a Happy Life. *Hercules* and *Theseus* had never done such great Things for Mankind, had they not taken Pleasure in doing Good, tho' it were attended with Pain and Labour. *Regulus* had never returned to *Carthage,* had he not rightly considered that breach of Faith would have tormented his Mind with more exquisite and durable Pains, than any his Body could endure. Neither had *Fabricius* rejected the Royal *Epirot*'s Profer, had not Wisdom convinced him that there was more Pleasure in an honest undefiled Poverty, than was consistent with such Riches as were to be gained by sacrificing his Honour to the Enemy of his Country.

These great Men, it is true, were not, as we can find, the professed Disciples of *Epicurus;* but it is sufficient, that whatsoever is Praise worthy in their Examples, is to be found in the Doctrine of our Philosopher; and the World may know, that it was not Vertue alone which was the motive to their glorious Actions; or at least, what they called Vertue, ought more rightly to be called Pleasure. And yet, out of our Wiseman's School have proceeded Spirits truely Heroick; who in the midst of a corrupt Age, have performed Actions as highly Honourable as any we have or can mention. Under the Reign of *Nero,* the World as much admired the Death of *Petronius,* as that of *Seneca.* The Emperor's Tutor gained no Glory by Dying, which was not equally bestowed upon the Arbiter of his Pleasures; and the general Opinion was, that the Stoick who had always preached up a Contempt of Life, did not quit it more generously, or with a braver Resolution, than *Petronius,* who had courted all its Pleasures.

I will not omit, therefore, for the Honour of *Epicurus;* to give you a short account of the Life and Death of this his great Disciple; who without Offence, may be Rank'd amongst the Bravest and most Illustrious of Men. *Petronius* became a Courtier under the Reign of the Emperor *Claudius;* where following the Methods of the Court, he became insensibly Luxurious; tho' at the same time, it was observed, that he took no delight in the brutal pleasures of Love, like *Mesalina;* nor in those of the Table and Drunkenness, like *Claudius;* only in a gallant and delicate manner, took a Relish of both, rather to gratifie his Curiosity than indulge his

Senses. In this manner, he employed a part of the Day in Sleeping, and dedicated the Night to Business and Pleasure. His House was the Rendezvous of the better sort of the People of *Rome,* with whom he spent his time, agreeably in the most charming Pleasures; not like a Prodigal, or Debauchee; but like a nice and learned Artist in the Science of Voluptuousness. Having thus pass'd away his Youth, in a Life of Softness and Tranquillity, he resolved to convince those that doubted of his Abilities, that he was capable of the weightiest Affairs in Government: For putting a stop to his Pleasures, he accepted the Office of Proconsul of *Bithynia,* went into that Province, where he discharged all the Duties of his Place, with Applause; and having finished his employ, upon his return to *Rome,* was by the Emperor *Nero,* in Recompence of his Services, made Consul. This new Dignity gave him a ready Access to the Emperor, who at first honoured him with his esteem, and afterwards, with his Friendship, in acknowledgment of the Sumptuous Entertainments, he sometimes gave that Prince, to refresh him, when fatigued with the Toil of State Affairs. The Consulate of *Petronius* being expired, without quitting the Court, he re-assumed his first manner of Living; and whether it proceded from his own inclination, or a desire to please *Nero;* he soon became one of the Emperors Confidents, who could find nothing agreeable to his Humour, but what was approved by *Petronius;* thus being possessed of the Authority of deciding what might be acceptable, he gained the Sirname of *Arbiter,* as Master and Comptroler in those Affairs. *Nero,* in the first part of his Reign, acted like a prudent wise Prince, and applied himself with care to the management of the State. However *Petronius* observed that he was naturally inclined to Lust and Sensuality, and therefore, like an able Politician, being in Possession of his Princes Mind, he seasoned it with honest delights; and procured him all the innocent Charms imaginable, in order to remove the thought of seeking after others; which would have been more irregular, and of worse consequence to the Common Wealth. Things continued in this Posture, while the Emperor kept himself within the bounds of Moderation; and so long *Petronius* acted chearfully under him, as Intendant of his Pleasures.

But the Emperor, sometime after, complying with his Nature, changed his Conducct, not only in respect to the Publick Affairs of the Empire, but in relation, also to his more private and Domestick Affairs; to his Sports and Recreations. He listened to others, rather than to *Petronius;* and insensibly plunging himself into Debauchery, he abandoned himself to his Passions; and became as Monstrous in his Pleasures, as before he had been Nice, and Delicate. The high advancement of *Petronius* drew upon him the Envy of all those who courted the Princes Favour, and of all others *Tigellinus* Captain of the *Petrorian* Guards, was a most dangerous Rival. This Man, from an obscure Birth, had in a short time, by his corrupt Manners, gained an absolute

sway over the Emperors Temper; and as he knew his blind-side perfectly well, he set himself seriously to bring about the ruin of his Competitor; and by such means as very much endangered the Ruine of the Empire. The curious Artful Pleasures invented by *Petronius,* were of a more refined Nature, than the gross Debauches of *Tigellinus;* who foreseeing that the Credit *Pecronius,* thereby, gained with the Emperor, would always be an Obstacle to his Designs; endeavoured therefore, to possess himself, entirely, of the Princes Heart, and engage him in the foulest Brutalities. For *Nero,* no sooner, hearkned to the Perswasions of *Tigellinus,* but he fignalized his Power by the Deaths of *Sylla* and *Rubellius Plautus,* Persons dreaded by them, for their eminent Vertues, and in great Esteem and Favour with the People; thus proceeding from one Degree of Infamy to another, arrived, at last, to such an Excess, that all manner of Crimes were perpetrated by him. Our ancient Favourite thus supplanted in his Employment, by the Artifices of a new one, and highly disgusted at the horrible Actions he had seen, gave way to his Successor; withdrew from Court, indulged himself in the Pleasures of a Retired Life; and then wrote that incomparable Satyr, in which he so exactly represents the Nature and Character of *Nero,* and under feigned Names of Lewd and Vicious Persons, exposed the Vices of that infamous Prince and Court. Whilst *Petronius* thus lived in a retired Tranquillity, *Tigellinus* laboured with all his Power to destroy him, and to establish his own Fortune upon the Ruine of his Rival; for he greatly feared, that if *Petronius* were once reinstated in his Masters Favour, he might, by the Means of honest Pleasures, have restored *Nero* to himself, to the great Blessing of all Honest Men, and the Confusion of *Tigellinus,* and others, his most flagitious Pimps and Panders; Knowing, therefore, that the Prince was naturally inclined to Cruelty; he insinuates that *Petronius* was too familiar with *Stevinus,* not to be concerned in *Piso*'s Conspiracy, and having suborned one of *Petronius*'s Slaves to swear against his Master, to deprive him of all Means to justifie himself, he sends the greatest part of his Domesticks to Prison. *Nero* was well enough pleased to find an Opportunity of parting with a Man who was become a check to his Affairs; for the Vicious cannot endure the presence of such whose Sight reproaches them with their abominable Practices; he readily received the Accusation against *Petronius,* and ordered him to be apprehended at *Cumes,* when the Emperor made a Voyage thither, and *Petronius* should be one of the Company; but as it required time to deliberate, whether they ought to put a Man of his Figure to Death, without clear proof of the Crimes he stood charged with: *Petronius* perceiving that his Life was a burthen to his Prince, and that he only wanted some colourable Pretext to take it away; that he might no longer be the sport of Slaves and Villains, he resolved to die. However, that he might not give himself a Precipitate Death, he opened his Veins, then closed them again, that he might have time to converse with his Friends, who came to see him, in his last Moments, which he spent not in Discourses of the Immortality of the Soul, and those celebrated Axioms which the Pride of Philosophers had invented to acquire Glory, and a Vain Opinion of Constancy, but with the recital of curious Pieces of Poetry; and to convince the Spectators that he did not die, but only cease to live, He continued his ordinary Functions, took a particular Account of the Behaviour of his Domesticks, punished some, and rewarded others; sate, as usual, at his Table; and slept very quietly; insomuch, that he rather seemed a Man in perfect Health, than one that was Dying; at length, perceiving the time draw near of shaking off Mortality, after using a little Exercise, he fell into a calm and gentle Slumber; so that his Death, tho' violent, appeared to his Friends as if it had been natural. Thus fell the Great, the Voluptuous *Petronius* a Sacrifice to the Ingratitude of *Nero,* and the Ambition of *Tigellinus.* Boast no more then of the Divine *Socrates,* and that constancy and firmness of Mind wherewith he drank the Poison; *Petronius* yields not to him in the least particular: Nay, *Petronius* may claim the advantage of having quitted a Life infinitely more delicious than that of the Greek Philosopher, with the same serenity of Mind, and the same equality of Countenance.

But there remains one Objection still, against *Epicurus;* his asserting the lawfulness and expediency of Self-Murther: This is certainly a very heavy Charge, but it is plain, that in this as in all other, his Enemies have had more regard to the weight, than the Truth of the Crime they charge him with, not considering that at the same time the weight of the Objection lay fuller upon themselves. Self-murther is undoubtedly a very heinous and abominable Crime; if we consider it, either as a Christian or a Philosopher; it is a Violation of the Law of Nature; and expresly repugnant to the Law of God. That we may not therefore seem to justifie that in our Philosopher, which God, the Church, nay, moral Philosophy itself, so highly Condemns: Let us compare the Doctrine and Practice of *Epicurus,* with the Doctrine and Practice of those, who so vehemently exclaim against him; and if I cannot fully clear him in this point, I shall at least prove, that he was not single in his Opinion; and that his Enemies were much more guilty herein than himself. *Every Man ought,* says *Epicurus, to make it his care so to Live, that Life may not be a burthen to him; and not to be willing to part with Life, till either Nature, or some intolerable Case call upon him to surrender it; and in that Case, we are to weigh seriously, whether it be more commendable for us to stay till Death come to us, or to go and meet it; for though it be an Evil indeed for us to live in Necessity, yet there is no Necessity for us to live in necessity: Since Nature hath been so kind, to give us though but one Door into the World, yet many Doors out of it. But although there be some Cases so extream, that in respect of them, we are to hasten and fly to the Sanctuary of Death; yet we are not to attempt any thing in that kind, but when it may be done Opportunely and Commendably.* Thus you see in what limited Sense our Philosopher delivered this Doctrine; it is not to be pursued, unless *some intolerable Case require it;* nor then neither, *except it may be done Opportunely and Commendably.* And what is this intolerable Case, which may justifie a Man Voluntarily to leap over the Battlements of Life? Do his Precepts any where shew it? No. Poverty it cannot be, for Wise and Bountiful Nature hath so provided against that; that those things which are necessary are easie to be procured; whereas those things which are unnecessary, are hard to come by. *If you live according to Nature, you shall never be Poor; if according to Opinion, you shall never be Rich; Nature desires little, Opinion is never Satisfied.* Neither can it be when any Pain whatsoever afflicts the Body. *No Pain is both intolerable and perpetual;* for if it be long, it must be light, and if great, short; it is either determined of itself, and succeeded, if not by an absolute Indolence, yet by a very great Mitigation; or it is determined by Death, in which there can be no Pain. Neither can it be when the Mind is loaded or oppressed; for *discontent of Mind is not grounded upon Nature, but upon meer Opinion of Evil; and it is Reason alone which makes Life Happy and Pleasant; by expelling all such false Conceits or Opinions, as may any way disturb the Mind.* Why then doth *Epicurus* so highly extol that Person, who when some intolerable Case calls upon him to surrender his Life, leaps over the Battlements of Life bravely? To this I answer, Our Philosopher was of a Modest, Humble Temper and Disposition; not positive and Dogmatical as his Enemies generally were; and therefore tho' he had fully answered all the Arguments which have ever yet been made use of to justifie that abominable Crime, and had plainly demonstrated that it was Ridiculous for a Man out of a Weariness of Life, to fly to Death as a Sanctuary; when his own Imprudence and Irregular Course of Life, is the only Cause of that Weariness. But as our Philosopher would not positively determine, but that such extream Case, might at some time or other happen; for which Philosophy could find no other or more proper remedy than Death; then and then only he encourages *to dispatch, and leap over the Battlements of Life bravely; for neither is it fit for him, who thinks of flight to Sleep; nor are we to despair of a happy Exit, even from the greatest difficulties; in Case we neither hasten before our Time, nor let it slip when it comes.* And the Practice of *Epicurus,* fully evinces that he was very careful, not to hasten before his time; for he endured the Tormenting Pains of the Stone in the Bladder, and other most acute Diseases for many Years together, with a most admirable patience, and invincible Courage; and waited till extream old Age gently put out his Lamp of Life.

On the contrary, if we enquire into the Doctrine and Practice of other Philosophers; we shall soon find that the Stoicks not only approved of it, but strictly enjoyned Men to Embrace Death Voluntarily; and from their own Hands. The Doctrine you have from *Cicero*, who in his Treatise *De Legibus*, implicitely Commends it in these Words: *I judge that Man worthy of Condemnation, who kills himself; if he do it neither by order of State, nor Compelled by any intolerable or inevitable chance of Fortune; nor Oppressed by any Ignominy of a Poor and Miserable Life;* and in his *2d Tusculan* Question, he expresly enjoyns it in these Words: *That Rule ought to be observed in Life, which prevails in the Grecian Feasts; either let a Man drink, or let him leave the Company; because a Man should drink with the same Freedom as others do, or go away, least being Sober, he should be abused by his drunken Companions; so if you cannot bear the Injuries of Fortune, you ought to avoid them by Flight.* Agreeable hereunto was their Practice; for thus *Zeno*, Father of the Stoicks, a Man of the most Spotless Character of any of the Philosophers, having by a fall bruised one of his Fingers, interpreted it as a Summons to the Grave, went presently home and Hanged himself, and was therefore by *Diogenes Laertius*, honoured with this Elogy *: A most happy Man who safe, sound, and without Disease, departed this Life.* Thus *Demosthenes,* to prevent being beholding to any one, but himself, either for his Life or Death, drank mortal Poison out of that Quill, which had given him immortal Life long before. Thus also *Democles* to prevent his Pollution, by the unnatural heat, of a lustful Greek Tyrant; who attempted to force him, leaped into a Copper of Scalding Water: And thus *Cleanthes, Chrysippus,* and *Empedocles* brake open the Gates of Death, and forced their Passage into another World. To these we may add the Memorable Examples, of that Prince of Roman Wisdom, (as *Lactantius* calls him) *Cato,* who with his own Hands and Sword, opened a Flood-gate in his Bowels, to let his Life flow out, having the Night before, prepared himself to fall bravely, by reading *Plato*'s Discourse on the Immortality of the Soul, and of the Famous *Cleombrotus,* who upon no other inducement, than *Plato*'s Reasons in the same Discourse, threw himself from a Precipice, as if he went instantly to experiment the Truth of what he had so lately Read.

From all that hath been said, we may at length conclude, that *Epicurus* was a Person of a Sublime Wit, and profound Judgment; a great Master of Temperance, Sobriety, Continence, Fortitude, and all other Vertues, no Patron of Impiety: Gluttony, Drunkenness, Luxury, or any other Intemperance; that he was the greatest of all Philosophers, that the Doctrine which he Taught, was of all others the most Conducible to a happy Life; and such as none besides himself ever Taught, by the pure light of Nature, unassisted by Grace: Nay, though *Epicurus* and his Doctrine, have been Exploded and Rejected; through the Ignorance of some, and the Malice of others; I will not be afraid to say, *that Good and Pious Christians, are the the truest Epicureans;* they only have a right Notion of that undeniable Truth, which he so Strenuously inculcates, *viz. That all Felicity consists in Pleasure;* they only know, that *to exercise one self, to have a Conscience void of Offence, both towards God, and towards Man,* is a Practice full of Pleasure, in this Life; and will be rewarded with Inexpressible and Eternal Joys in the World to Come. Whereas on the other Hand, the Consciousness of an ill spent Life, is a constant and inseparable Tormentor, which perpetually haunts and afflicts the Guilty in this World, and will be a never dying, ever gnawing Worm of Misery to them in the next. In short, if we do not with *Epicurus* Place our Happiness, in Pleasure, and run that Race which is set before us, with Cheerfulness; it will be vain for us to expect to hear at the last Day, that joyful Salutation of our Great Captain and Saviour; *Well done thou good and faithful Servant, enter thou into the Joy of thy Lord.*

Walter Charleton (essay date c. 1656)

SOURCE: Walter Charleton, "An Apologie for Epicurus," in *Epicurus's Morals: Collected and Faithfully Englished*, Peter Davies, 1926, pp.

[*Charleton's "Apology" for the mid-seventeenth-century English edition of Epicurus's writings attempts to redeem the philosopher's reputation, especially regarding religious attitude. Like Sarasin, Charleton argues that Epicurus's religious skepticism was appropriate to his pre-Christian context and that his ethical simplicity prefigured Christian morals.*]

Sir,

Your beloved EPICURUS, having lately learn'd English, on purpose to converse more familiarly with you; comes now at length to wait upon you, and at your vacant hours to entertain you with grave Discourses touching the Happiness of Man's life, and the right means of attaining it, Wisdom. I have no reason to doubt of his welcome and kind reception by you, considering that he comes not, but upon your frequent, and (I am confident) hearty invitations of him; your own ingenious and commendable desire to be intimately acquainted with his Principles, and Doctrine of Morality, and to hear him speak his own Thoughts purely and sincerely, having been the only occasion and motive to my assistance of him in his Travels from Greece into this Country, and my accommodation of him with such an Equipage, as might be exactly suitable as well to your wishes, as to his own mind. Nay more, I have reason to presume, that a few days conversation will create in you a very great dearness towards him, as well because I am assured you will soon find him what you expect, a sublime Wit, a profound Judgment, and a great Master of Temperance, Sobriety, Continence, Fortitude and all other Virtues, not a Patron of Impiety, Gluttony, Drunkenness, Luxury and all kinds of Intemperance, as the common people (being misinform'd by such learned men as either did not rightly understand, or would not rightly represent his opinions) generally conceive him to be; as because I have perceived him not only to give strong and lively hints to sundry of those sublime speculations, wherewith your thoughts are sometimes delightfully employed; but also solidly to assert many of those Tenents which I have often heard you defend, with the like Reasons, and which indeed nothing but the voluntary and affected Ignorance of Superstition will deny. So that, if the Rule hold, that Similitude of Opinions is an Argument of Similitude in Affections, and Similitude of Affections the ground of Love and Friendship, certainly I am not altogether destitute of support for my conjecture, and consequently that you will soon admit him into your Bosom, and treat him with all the demonstrations of respect due to so excellent a Companion.

But, as there is no Beauty without some moles, no Chrystal without some specks; so is not our EPICURUS *without his imperfections, and you will discover in him some things which cannot escape your reprehension; and yet I expect, that your censure of him should be much more moderate and charitable, than that of the ignorant and scarce humane Multitude hath been for many ages together. And therefore I ask leave to state the Nature of his guilt unto you, and afterwards to give you my Judgment thereupon; in the mean time humbly leaving you to the Liberty of your own more judicious sentiments of both the one and the other. For, my design therein, is not to possess your breast with my thoughts concerning the crimes usually charged upon this Philosopher, but to dispossess it of an opinion that I might have the same indignation against him in respect of some unjustifiable positions of his, as not only the common people, but even the greatest number of Scholars, have for many hundred of years, entertain'd. And what I shall say to that purpose I humbly desire you will be pleas'd to understand to be intended as an* Exercitation, *to take off from his memory the greatest part of that unjust Odium, and Infamy which envy and malice on one hand, and Ignorance and Inhumanity on the other, have cast upon it, to the eclipsing even of all his excellent merits from the Commonwealth of Philosophy, and not as a defence of any unreasonable or dangerous Errour, whereof he is found really guilty. Which was more perhaps then was needful for me to advertise you of, who well understand the difference betwixt a* Vindication *and an* Excusation; *that it is one thing to mitigate a too severe and rash sentence, and another to justifie the Offender. And therefore without any further Apologizing for my short Apology for* EPICURUS, *I directly address to my Province.*

The Opinions, which, being asserted by him in this Treatise concerning Ethicks, *have so much incens'd the world against him, are principally these three.* (1.) That the Souls of men are mortal, and so uncapable of all, either happiness or misery after death. (2.) That Man is not obliged to honour, revere, and worship God, in respect of his beneficience, or out of the hope of any Good or Fear of any evil at his hands, but merely in respect of the transcendent Excellencies of his Nature, Immortality, and Beatitude. (3.) That Selfhomicide is an Act of Heroick Fortitude in case of intolerable or otherwise inevitable Calamity. *These, I confess, are Positions to be rather wholly condemned and abominated, than in the least measure patroniz'd by us Christians, whose understandings (thanks be to the mercy of the Fountain of Wisdom) are illuminated by a brighter light than that of Nature; and yet notwithstanding when I remember, that our Philosopher was a meer Naturalist, born and educated in times of no small Pagan darkness, and consider that neither of these Tenents will be found upon due Examination so destitute of all support of Reason, as rash and unexamining heads have apprehended, I profess I cannot but think it an argument of much more inhumanity than judicious zeal in any man, upon this account alone, to invade him with the crimination of superlative* Impiety, Blasphemy, *and absolute* Atheism. *For,*

As to the FIRST, viz. *That the humane soul doth not survive the funerals of the body, but absolutely perish in the instant of death; as I need not tell you, how uncomfortable an Opinion it is to all Virtuous Persons, and how manifestly repugnant to Christianism, and indeed to the fundamental Reason of all Religions beside (if I may be admitted to use that improper phrase of the vulgar, while I well know that there can be but one Religion truly so called, and that all the rest are more properly called Superstitions) so I need not advertise you how highly difficult it is to refute it, by satisfactory and convincing Arguments desumable from meer Reason. For, to suspect the light of Nature, is scarce strong enough by its own single force, to dispel all those thick mists of difficulties, that hinder our discernment of the full nature of the humane soul, and scarce bright enough clearly to demonstrate the immortality of that noble Essence, so, as to leave no room for diffidence or contradiction; I hope it can be no Heresie in any man, because no disparagement to either his Faith or Reason. You have, Sir, I presume, attentively perused that so worthily commended Discourse of* Plato, *touching the immortality of Mans soul, and acquainted your self moreover with all those mighty Arguments, alledged by Saint* Thomas, Pomponatius *(who will hardly be out-done in subtlety, touching the same Theam, by any that comes after him, and yet he was forced to conclude himself a Sceptick, and leave the Question to the decision of some other bolder Pen)* Des Cartes, *our noble friend Sir* Kenelm Digby, *and divers other great Clerks, to prove the Soul of Man to be a substance distinct from, and independent upon that of the body, and to have eternal existence a parte post; and yet if I were not assured, that your perswasion of its immortality is founded upon a much more firm basis, than that of the most seemingly apodictical of all their Reasons, I might well doubt of the impregnability thereof. And this I may say somewhat the more freely and boldly, both because I my self, having with all possible attention, and equity of mind, examined the validity of most of those Arguments, for the immortality of mens souls, which their Authors have presented as perfect Demonstrations thereof, cannot find any of them to make good that glorious Title, or satisfie expectation to the full; and because I have observed many learned men, Divines, and others, who have long laboured their thoughts in the same Disquisition, to concur with me in opinion,* That to believe the Soul of Man to be immortal, upon Principles supernatural, is much more easie, then to demonstrate the same by Reasons purely Natural. Now, if for the most sublime Wits, even of our times (wherein the Metaphysicks have, doubtless, received a very great encrease of clearness, and mens Speculations seem to be highly refined, in regard of sundry lively and fruitful hints, that are inspersed upon the leaves of sacred Writ, concerning as well the Original and Nature of the Soul, as the state of it after death) it be so hard a task to erect a firm perswasion of the immortality of the humane soul, upon a foundation of Natural Reason alone; I appeal to every imprejudicate man, with what justice our Epicurus *is so highly condemned, for being ignorant of that unattainable Truth, when he could steer the course of his judgment and belief by no other Star, but that remote and pale one of the Light of Nature, that bright North-Star of Holy Scripture appearing not at all to the Horizon of* Greece, *till many Ages after his death.*

Again, EPICURUS *is not the only man amongst the Ancients that is to be accused, for entertaining and divulging erroneous conceptions of the nature and condition of the reasonable soul after death, it being well known, that most of the Grecian Philosophers did indubitate the incorruptibility thereof, either implicitly and upon consequence, or immediately, and in direct terms. This perhaps may seem a Paradox to you, and therefore I ask leave to make it good. The Grecian Scholiarchs may all be divided into two Classes, in reference to this subject; the First consisting of those who* Asserted, *the other of such as expresly* Denied *the Immortality of Man's Soul, the former containing the greater, the latter the lesser number. And among all those that are on the Affirmative part, you shall not find one that is not (more or less) tainted with that so common Errour, of the* Refusion *of all mens Souls after death, into the* Anima Mundi, *or general Soul of the Universe, which is upon consequence, That, they cease to exist, per se, or to be what they were before, so soon as they are separated from the body. for your further satisfaction of this unfrequent Truth, be pleased*

to observe, that, as they generally conceived the soul of every individual man, to be a certain particle of the Mundane, or universal soul, immitted into the body at its conception, and therein contained during life, as a drop of water is contained in a Glass Phial; so did they also conceive, that the same soul, upon the breaking of the Glass, or dissolution of the Body, doth flow forth, and again return and unite it self to the universal soul, from whence it was at first desumed. Thus Plutarch (4 Placit. 9.) *expresly tells us, that* Pythagoras *and* Plato *maintained, that Mans Soul having taken its farewel of the body . . .* in congeniam sibi animam Mundi concedere, *doth return to the soul of the world, which is of the same substance and nature with it. Now by this common soul of the world, it is manifest, that they sometimes meant* God, *in respect they acknowledged him to be the supreme Intelligence, or Mind, which disposeth and ordereth all parts of the body; and sometimes the* Heavens, *because as Heaven is the most pure and noble part of the Universe, so is the soul the most pure and noble part of Man.*

This considered, you have here an opportunity (at least, if a short and pertinent digression may be opportune) of taking notice in what sence we are to understand some remarkable passages in their Writings, touching the humane soul, which are often mentioned, but seldom rightly interpreted.

First, we may hence collect what their true meaning was, when they said, Animam esse divinae aurae Particulam, *that the Soul is a particle of Divine breath, or as* Cicero *speaks (in* Cato Major) Ex Divina mente universa delibutos animos habemus: *We have our souls derived from the Universal Divine Mind; And again, when they affirmed, that our Souls were taken from Heaven, and to return thither again after their emancipation from the body: All which the Prince of Poets elegantly insinuateth in these Verses;*

> —Deum namque ire per omnes
> Terrasque tractusque maris, cœlumque
>   profundum;
> Heinc homines, armenta, viros, genus omne
>   ferarum,
> Quemque fibi tenues nascentem arcessere
>   vitas,
> Scilicet huc reddi deinde ac resoluta referri
> Omnia, nec morti esse locum; sed viva evolare
> Sideris in numerum, atque alto succedere
>   cœlo.

Secondly, we may hence learn the sence of Empedocles, *as well in that saying quoted by* Plutarch (de exilio) Præsentem vitam esse exilium, e quo tandem animus sit in pristinam sedem demigraturus, *That this present life is a banishment of the soul, from which it is at length to be recall'd to its primitive place; as in that mentioned by* Clem. Alexandrinus (Lib. 4. Stromat. 2.

hypotypos. 24.) Animos sapientum Deos fieri, *That the souls of Wise-men become Gods.*

Thirdly, we may hence know how to understand the true sence of Plato's *opinion, that all Learning is only Reminiscence. For supposing the Soul of the Universe to be omniscient, and each particle thereof to be of the same nature and faculties with the whole; he thereupon infers, that the soul of each man being a particle of that Universal and omniscient soul, must be likewise omniscient, though in the moment, when it is immers'd into the body, it becomes dim and beclouded, so that as if it had been made drunk with* Lethe, *or the Waters of Oblivion, it forgets all its Original knowledge, and must recollect and call to mind the notions of particular things, by the help and mediation of the senses.*

Lastly, why Pythagoras *and* Plato, *to this opinion of the Souls Remigration to the Universal Soul, connected that their other so famous one of the* Transmigration *of Souls from body to body successively. For, having imbibed this latter errour of the Souls transmigration, in their conversation with some Egyptian Priests, as* Stobæus *informs us (in Eccl. Physic.) they strived to accommodate the same to their own former opinion, of the souls being a particle of the* Anima mundi; *insomuch as it might thence follow, that the soul being exhal'd from its first body, and wandring up and down in quest of its Fountain, the universal soul, might probably enough light upon some other body then in the act of Conception, and being united thereunto, animate it, or being by inspiration attracted into some living creature, unite it self to the soul præexistent therein, and so become one with it, especially if the body it meet with be of the same, or like conditions and affections with the former, which it bath so lately forsaken. True it is, nevertheless, that they delivered this Doctrine of the Transmigration of souls, very obscurely, and wrapt up in Fables and Allegories, but their design herein was to make men more mansuete and mild in their dispositions, by bringing them to put a greater value upon the lives of Animals (for, according to this Doctrine, who would kill a Beast, when for ought he knew, his Fathers Soul might animate that Beast?) and a greater degree of horrour against shedding of Blood, that so having devested them of all savageness and cruelty, they might have a greater detectation against Homicide, and preserving the peace and safety of Societies.*

Nor can the Stoicks *be exempted from the same Errour, of the* Refusion *of all souls into the Universal one; insomuch as it was their constant tenent, that the world was animated by a certain fire, which they called* Jupiter; *that mens souls were particles derived from that fire, and should again be reunited thereunto, some sooner, others later, but all in that general Conflagration of the Universe, when all things shall be (as they dreamt) sublimed into* Jove *again.*

Now if we look narrowly into the business, we shall discover even Aristotle *himself to be in some measure guilty of the very same delusion, as well in respect of his* Animal Heat, *which, discoursing of the Generation of Animals (Lib. 2. Cap. 3.) he affirms to be respondent in some proportion to the Element of Celestial bodies, and wherewith all things in the world are impregnated, as of his* Intellectus Agens, *which he teacheth to be diffused through the whole world, after the same manner as the light of the Sun is diffus'd through the air, and so apply'd and conjoyned to the* Intellectus Patiens, *or proper soul of every man, as the eternal light is applyed and conjoyned to the eye; and as the eye by the conjunction of eternal light comes to see visible objeccts, so doth the proper passive Intellect of every man, by the illustration of the general active Intellect, come to understand intelligible Objects. Adding thereunto, that the Intellect passive is separable, corruptible, and capable of utter dissolution; but the Active, inseparable, incorruptible, immortal. For, thus much may be collected from several places of his Books* de Anima, *and thus are those places explained by the best of his Greek interpreters,* Alexander, *and the best of the Arabians,* Averrhoes, *whose opinion of the* Unity of the Intellect *in all the world, is sufficiently known.*

And thus much of the Philosophers of the former Classis, *who though they seem to affirm, do yet in reality, upon natural consequence, deny the Immortality of the Humane Soul, in that they all concur in that contradictory Errour of the Refusion thereof into the* Anima mundi. *For, the proper Notion of Immortality, is,* the eternal existence of a thing in the self same nature, and *per se; and therefore, if a thing be devested of its own proper nature, so, as to become invested with that of another, and to have no existence or subsistence, but what is dependent upon its union with that other, to which it is assimilated and identified; for my part, truly, I cannot understand how it can be said to be immortal without manifest contradiction. And whether it be not as gross an absurdity to say, that the soul of a man shall be for ever the same (i.e.) the soul of a man, and yet that it shall be identified, or made the same with the soul of the world; as to say, that such a thing shall be for ever the same, and not the same, is no hard matter to determine.*

As for those of the latter, *who in downright terms denied the Immortality of the soul, they subdivide themselves into two different Sects, some having contended for the total* destruction, *or absolute annihilation, and others for only the* exsolution *and dispersion of it into the* matter *or principles of which it was composed.*

To the former *of these Sects we may justly annumerate all such, who conceived the soul of man to be only a certain harmony, not of Musical sounds, but a contemperation of parts, humours, and qualities; and consequently, that as of Musical Harmony, nothing can remain after the sounds are vanished, so of the soul nothing can remain, after death bath once destroyed that harmonious Contemperation of parts, humours, and qualities, from whence it did result. And this purely was the opinion of not only those ancienter Greeks,* Dicæarchus, Aristoxenus, Andræas, *and* Asclepiades, *all which are thereof strongly accused by* Plato (in Phaed.) *and* Aristotle (Lib. I. de Anima. Cap. 5.) *but also our Master* Galen, *who was positive and plain in his definition of the soul, to be a certain Temperament of Elementary Qualities. In the same list may we also inscribe the names of all those, who imagining the soul to be nothing else but a certain* Act, *or* Form, *or* Quality inseparable *(i.e.)* a certain special Modification *of* Matter, *have accordingly concluded, that as the* Figure, *or special* Mode *of a thing must inevitably vanish, immediately upon the immutation or change of the thing figurate, so must the soul, being only a special Mode of the Matter, necessarily vanish immediately upon the immutation of that Mode by death. Which* Origen, Justine, Theodoret, *and some other* Fathers, *understanding to have been the Tenent of* Aristotle, *have written sharp investives against him, as an assertor of the souls mortality, and this so justly, that if his Zealous Disciple, honest Mr.* Alexander Rosse, *were alive again, he would never be able to discredit that their charge.*

To the latter *we are to refer all such, as held the soul to be* Corporeal. *For, as they would have it to be composed of* material principles, *so would they also have it to be, by death, again resolved into the same material principles; so that in their sence, the extinction of the Soul is no other, but the dissipation thereof into those very corporeal particles, of which it was composed. And this seems to be the true meaning of Demonax in Lucian, when being interrogated whether he thought the Soul to be immortal, he answered,* mihi videtur, sed ut omnia; *it seems to me to be immortal, but no otherwise than all things are immortal, i.e. as to the matter only, or component Principles of it, which are incapable of Annihilation. In this Catalogue we may worthily place* Marcus Antoninus, *in regard of his saying* (Lib. 4.) Animas hominum dispergi in auras, *that mens souls are dispersed into Aer: and* Seneca, *for his* Animam hominis magno pondere extriti permeare non posse, & statim dispergi, quia non fuerit illi exitus liber; *as also* Democritus *and* Epicurus, *who equally contested, that the soul was nothing but very* Atoms, *in such a special order, in such a special position, &c. contempered, and Death nothing but a discomposure of that determinate Contecture, and a Resolution of the soul into separated Atoms again; and therefore are they always conjoined by the good* Lactantius (Lib. 3. cap. 7. & lib. 9. cap. 8. & 13.) *as confederates in the Doctrine of the Dissolution of Souls.*

And thus, Sir, you may at once plainly perceive the justice *of my Attainder of the most, and most eminent of the antient Grecian Philosophers, with the guilt of having been (either obliquely or directly) Impugners of the Souls Immortality; and the great* Injustice *of their Sentence, who more particularly condemn* Epicurus *for the same Errour, when so many others were equally culpable with him therein.*

As to the SECOND, viz. *That man is not obliged to honour, revere, and worship God upon the motive of his Beneficence, or upon the account of either Good or Evil expected from him; but only out of a sentiment of the superlative Excellencies of his Nature, and chiefly of his Immortality and Beatitude. I might well plead for him, that living in a time, when there was scarce any Religion, but sottish Idolatry, when there were more Gods then Nations, yea, then Temples; and when all Devotion was absurd and ridiculous Superstition: He seems rather to be honour'd, for that he came so neer to the knowledge of the true God, then condemned for coming no neerer; rather to be admir'd for having so clear and genuine an apprehension of some of the Divine Attributes, then reproached for not comprehending them all. Especially, when I should not infringe the Law of charity, to doubt, that among us Christians, and even such as think themselves not a little vers'd in Theologie, there may be some, who, if they were put to give but an Adumbration of that mysterious piece, the Divine Nature, would discover themselves to have as imperfect an Idæa thereof, as* EPICURUS *had. But this excuse would be too general for his particular vindication, from the imputed crime of perfect* Atheism, *and therefore we shall fix only on such Reasons as are more properly accommodate to that purpose.*

First, I dare say, his Piety, *in deriding the incompetency of those Conceptions, that men in his time commonly entertained of the supreme Essence (for they ascribed generally unto it, all the self same passions and affections, which they perceived to be in themselves, and so copied out an imperfect Divinity, by the infinitely disproportionate Original of Humanity) was much greater than his* Impiety *could be, in teaching, that the Diety was of so transcendently excellent a nature, as to be wholly unconcern'd in any thing but it self, and far above all sentiments whatever, besides those of its own eternal and compleat Felicity; and consequently, that it was to be reverenc'd and worshiped solely and purely for its own sake, without the least mixture of self-Reflection. For, as by the one, he judiciously attempted to subvert the false and unreasonable Religion, or (rather) Superstition, in the worship of* Bacchus, *and other the Imaginary Deities, wherewith his Country swarmed in his days (there being no better way to alienate mens minds from the Veneration of False Gods, than to acquaint them with notions comprehending the Essential and Incommunicable attributes of the true God) so by the other, he seems to have laid a very firm foundation for the true Religion, in that he would have the Right or Justice of all Divine worship to be founded wholly and entirely upon the Excellency of the Divine Nature. How far therefore he was from being a Professor and Seminary of down-right Atheism, as some (whose Zeal may well be thought to have been much greater than their knowledge, as to that particular) have represented him to the World; every man, who hath but so much reason, as to under-stand, that* Polytheism *is the greatest* Atheism, *may easily judge.*

In the next place, I can hardly allow him to deserve the odious Epithete of, Most highly Impious, *which most men brand him withall, upon the account of this latter Doctrine only, because I meet with not a few, nor contemptible Reasons, that incline my judgment to more moderation. In particular, you well know, Sir, how highly unreasonable it is, for any man to expect, from* EPICURUS, *the knowledge of the true and legiti-mate worship of God, when that was by God himself prescribed only to the ancient Hebrews, and professed only by their Posterity, and no other Nation in the World; if so, why should more be expected from Him, than from* Plato, Zeno, Socrates, Aristotle, *or any other of the elder Grecian Philosophers, they being all equally benighted with Paganism? why should he be so severely sentenc'd, and all the rest pass unques-tioned, one and the same charge of invincible igno-rance of the true Religion lying against each of them? Besides, Humane Justice will hardly permit, that any man should suffer meerly for wanting that, which, without supernatural means, was impossible for him to obtain; and he that will adventure to determine, whether or no, at the Tribunal of Divine Justice, any one shall be condemned simply upon that score, must have dived very deep into that fathomless gulf of Prædestination.*

You likewise know, that our Christian Doctors as-sign only Two causes, *or Fundamental Consider-ations, why men should worship God: The* one *they teach to be the transcendent Excellency of the Na-ture of God, which singly, and without any respect to our own Utility or Advantage, doth justly claim the highest veneration of our minds. The* other, *they admit to be the benefits, we either have received, or (which is the stronger motive of the two) hope to receive at his hands. Hereupon, if any man be in-duced to revere and worship the Divine Majesty solely and simply upon the* former *motive, they say that he bears a* Filial *respect and affection to God; and if only by the* latter, *a meer* servile *or merce-nary. Now though the servile or mercenary love of God, be not altogether to be disliked, in regard it is a kind of gratitude due to him as a Benefactor; yet I conceive no man will gainsay, but the filial and free love is much the nobler and more acceptable, insomuch as it hath no other than the noblest of Objects, God Himself. And sure I am (however) that*

the most Learned, most Pious, and most Religious of our School Divines, have been earnest in their advisoes to us, to extract all selfness from our love of God, and (as much as our frailties will admit of) to fix all our affections entirely upon Him, as he is infinitely Good, and Amiable in Himself.

Moreover, you may remember, Sir, that Cicero *in his Book touching the nature of the Gods, hath these very words,* Quid est cur Deos ab hominibus colendos dicas, cum dii ipsi non modo homines non colant, sed omnino nihil curent? Et quæ porro Pietas ei debetur, a quo nihil acceperis? Aut quid omnino, cujus nullum meritum sit, ei deberi potest? *By which it is evident, that he would exclude all other inducements to Religion, besides a meer mercenary and servile respect: And yet I dare say, that you do not remember, that ever you heard him accounted Impious for that opinion. Why therefore should* EPICURUS *have such hard measure, as to be stigmatiz'd with the name of* Atheist, Impious wretch, Secretary of Hell, Enemy to all Religion, &c? *and all for asserting, that man ought to be induc'd to a reverence and venera-tion of the Divine Majesty, only by the Sentiments of a Filial* Piety *(not supernatural Piety, arising from Grace justifying, and by which we are made the Sons of God, but a pure Natural one) such as* Right Reason *had suggested unto him? Certainly, of the two opinions,* Epicurus's *will appear much more venial, to an Equi-table Arbiter. Sundry other arguments there are, which might be advantagiously alledged on our Authors be-half, in this case. But, considering that these few al-ready urged, are of importance enough, to evince the temerity of his Accusers judgment, and that the prolixity of this discourse, hath long since, given you just occa-sion to question, by what right I call it a Letter; I per-ceive my self obliged in good manners, no longer to exercise your patience, then while I briefly express my sentiments of the* LAST *Article of his Charge.*

Which is, His asserting of Self-Homicide, *in case of intolerable, and otherwise inevitable Calamity. This, as a Christian, I hold to be a bloody and detestable opinion, because expresly repugnant to the* Law *of* God; *and yet in the person of a meer* Philosopher, *I might, without being unreasonably Paradoxical, adventure to dispute, whether it be so highly repugnant to the Law of* Nature, *as men have generally conceived. For,*

First, if all the precepts of the Law of Nature concenter in this one point; Fly Evil, pursue Good; *as those who have most laboured to conduct our understanding out of that intricate Labyrinth, the ambiguous Sence of the word,* Law of Nature, *have unanimously determined; certainly, that man assumes no very easie task, who undertakes to prove, that in case of insupportable dis-tress, and where all other hopes [fail] of evading, or ending that misery (than which there can be no greater Evil) for a man to free himself from that extremity of Evil, and seek the* Good *of ease and quiet, by taking away his own life, which chiefly makes him subject to, and only sensible of that misery, is an infringement of the Law of* Nature.

Again, if we understand Self-preservation *(which all men allow to be the foundation of Natural Law in General) to be no other, but an innate Love, or Natural affection to Life, as a* Good, *when Life ceaseth to be a* Good, *and degenerates into an* Evil, *as commonly it doth to men, in cruel torments of the body, or high discontent of mind, (the more desperate affliction of the two by much) and when all the Stars of hope and comfort are set in the West of black desperation, why should not the force or obligation of that Law also, cease at the same time? Or rather, why should not self-homicid, in such cases, be an absolute accomplishment of the Law of Self-preservation, it being manifest, that we are by the tenour of that Law, obliged to use such means, as conduce to our preservation from the greatest* Evil; *and as manifest, that to free ones self from misery, which cannot otherwise be avoided, but by breaking asunder the Ligaments of Life, is a pursuance of the only means we can discover, to be conducible to our end: that is, to preservation from more sufferings, and to* Indolency, *which in Death we propose to our selves as a* Good?

But lest we seem to give any encouragement to that, which God, *the* Church, *and the* Civil *Power so highly condemn; let us grant, that Self-murther, in whatsoever case, is a violation of the Law of Nature, and yet we shall have one consideration left, that seems strong enough to refract the violence of their malice, who exclaim against* EPICURUS, *as the grand abettor of self-assasination; and that is, that he was not single, nor most vehement in the justification of it. For, if we look upon the* Doctrine *of other Philosophers, we shall soon perceive, that the* Stoicks *generally, 'not only approved thereof, but strictly enjoyned men to embrace death voluntarily, and from their own hands; That* Cicero *doth* (Lib. de Legibus) *implicitly allow of it in these words,* Eum damnandum esse censeo qui seipsum interficit, si neque ex decreto Civitatis fecerit, neq; ullo Fortunæ casu intolerabili inevitabæliq; coactus, neque obrutus ullâ pauperis, miseræq; vitæ ignominia; *and expresly confirms it* (in 2. Tusculan.) *in these,* Eam in vita servandam Legem quæ in Græcorum conviviis obtinet, Aut bibat, aut abeat; quoniam ut oportet aliquis fruatur pariter cum aliis voluptate potandi, aut ne sobrius in violentiam vinolentorum incidat, ante discedat; sic injurias Fortunæ quas ferre nequeas, defugiendo relinquas. *And if their* Practice, *we shall assoon find many of them to have laid violent hands upon themselves, and that in cases of far less moment, than that of insupportable and inevitable* Calamity, *to which only* EPICURUS's *precept is limited; while He, leaving others to become examples of that* Rule, *with admirable patience, and invincible magnanimity, endured the tortures of the Stone in the Bladder, and other most excruciating Diseases, for many years*

together, and awaited, till extreme old age gently put out the Taper of his life. Thus Zeno, *a man of the most spotless fame of any Philosopher among the Antients, having by a fall bruised one of his fingers against the ground, and interpreting that to be a summons of him to the earth, went presently home and hanged himself, and was therefore by* Diogenes Laertius *honoured with this Elogie;* Mira felicitate vir, qui incolumis, integer, sine morbo e vivis excessit. *Thus* Demosthenes, *you know, to prevent his being beholding to any man but himself, either for his life or death, drank mortal poyson out of his own Quill, which had given him immortality long before. Thus also* Democles, *to prevent his pollution, by the unnatural heat of a certain lustful Greek Tyrant, who attempted to force him, leaped into a Furnace of boyling Water. And thus* Cleanthes, Chrysippus, *and* Empedocles, *all brake open the Gates of Death, and forced themselves into the other World. To these you may please to add the memorable Examples of that Prince of* Roman *wisdom (as* Lactantius *calls him)* Cato, *who with his own hands and Sword, opened a flood-gate in his Bowels, to let his life flow forth, having all the night before prepared himself to fall boldly, with the Lecture of* Plato's *Discourse, of the Immortality of the soul; and of the famous* Cleombrotus, *who, upon no other incitement, but* Plato's *reasons in the same Discourse, threw himself from a precipice, as if he went instantly to experiment the truth of what he had newly read; and though* Aristotle *would not admit, that he did it upon any other account, but that of* Pusillanimity *and* Fear, *yet Saint* Augustine (De Civit. Dei, Lib. I.

Jonathan Swift comments on what he sees to be the weaknesses in Epicurus's philosophy:

Epicurus . . . had no notion of justice but as it was profitable; and his placing happiness in pleasure, with all the advantages he could expound it by, was liable to very great exception; for although he taught that pleasure did consist in virtue, yet he did not any way fix or ascertain the boundaries of virtue, as he ought to have done; by which means he misled his followers into the greatest vices, making their names to become odious and scandalous even in the heathen world.

Quoted in Epicurus in England (1650-1725), *by Thomas Franklin Mayo, Southwest Press, 1934.*

---

cap. 22.) *ascribes it altogether unto* Greatness of mind, *his words being these;* When no Calamity urged him, no Crime, either true or imputed, nothing but greatness of mind moved him to embrace death, and dissolve the sweet bonds of life. *And* Lactantius, *who was severe enough in his censure, both of the* Act, *and the* Book *that occasion'd it, says of him;* Præcipitem se dedit nullam aliam ob causam nisi quod Platoni *credidit.*

Sir,

By this time you are satisfied, both of the injuries done to the memory of the Temperate, Good, *and* Pious Epicurus, *and of my willingness and devoir to redress them. And my dull and unequal Apology for him being now ended, I should begin another for* my self, *in that I have rather disturbed, than either delighted or informed you. But this being much the greater difficulty of the two, I think it safer for me, to put my self upon your mercy for an absolute forgiveness, than to trust to my own wit, to make excuses for my failings herein, especially, since your patience cannot but be already overcome by the tediousness of*

Your very Humble Servant,

W. Charleton.

E. Zeller (essay date 1879)

SOURCE: E. Zeller, "The Moral Science of the Epicureans: General Principles" and "The Epicurean Ethics Continued: Special Points," in *The Stoics, Epicureans and Sceptics*, Russell & Russell, Inc., 1962, pp. 472-93.

[*A professor at the University of Heidelberg, Zeller first published his landmark work on Epicurus in German. The following excerpt presents an overview of Epicureanism as a meeting of scientific and moral thought.*]

The Moral Science of the Epicureans. General Principles.

Natural science is intended to overcome the prejudices which stand in the way of happiness; moral science to give positive instructions as to the nature and means of attaining to happiness. The speculative parts of the Epicurean system had already worked out the idea that reality belongs only to individual things, and that all general order must be referred to the accidental harmony of individual forces. The same idea is now met with in the sphere of morals, individual feeling being made the standard, and individual well-being the object of all human activity. Natural science, beginning with external phenomena, went back to the secret principles of these phenomena, accessible only to thought. It led from an apparently accidental movement of atoms to a universe of regular motions. Not otherwise was the course followed by Epicurus in moral science. Not content with human feelings alone, nor with selfishly referring everything to the individual taken by himself alone, that science, in more accurately defining the conception of well-being, ascertained that the same can only be found by rising superior to feelings and purely individual aims, and by that very process of referring consciousness to itself and its universal being, which the Stoics declared to be the only path to happiness.

It is for us now to portray this development of the Epicurean platform in its most prominent features.

The only unconditional good, according to Epicurus, is pleasure; the only unconditional evil is pain. No proof of this proposition seemed to him to be necessary; it rests on a conviction supplied by nature herself, and is the ground and basis of all our doing and not doing. If proof, however, were required, he appealed to the fact that all living beings from the first moment of their existence pursue pleasure and avoid pain, and that consequently pleasure is a natural good, and the normal condition of every being. Hence follows the proposition to which Epicurus in common with all the philosophers of pleasure appealed, that pleasure must be the object of life.

At the same time, this proposition was restricted in the Epicurean system by several considerations. In the first place, neither pleasure nor pain are simple things. There are many varieties and degrees of pleasure and pain, and the case may occur in which pleasure has to be secured by the loss of other pleasures, or even by pain, or in which pain can only be avoided by submitting to another pain, or at the cost of some pleasure. In this case Epicurus would have the various feelings of pleasure and pain carefully estimated, and in consideration of the advantages and disadvantages which they confer, would under circumstances advise the good to be treated as an evil, and the evil as a good. He would have pleasure forsworn if it would entail a greater corresponding pain, and pain submitted to if it holds out the prospect of greater pleasure. He also agrees with Plato in holding that every positive pleasure presupposes a want, i.e. a pain which it proposes to remove; and hence he concludes that the real aim and object of all pleasure consists in obtaining freedom from pain, and that the good is nothing else but emancipation from evil. By a Cyrenaic neither repose of soul nor freedom from pain, but a gentle motion of the soul or positive pleasure was proposed as the object of life; and hence happiness was not made to depend on man's general state of mind, but on the sum-total of his actual enjoyments. But Epicurus, advancing beyond this position, recognised both the positive and the negative side of pleasures, both pleasure as repose, and pleasure as motion. Both aspects of pleasure, however, do not stand on the same footing in his system. On the contrary, the essential and immediate cause of happiness is repose of mind—ἀταραξία. Positive pleasure is only an indirect cause of ἀταραξία in that it removes the pain of unsatisfied craving. This mental repose, however, depends essentially on the character of a man's mind, just as conversely positive pleasure in systems so materialistic must depend on sensuous attractions. It was consistent, therefore, on the part of Aristippus to consider bodily gratification the highest pleasure; and conversely Epicurus was no less consistent in subordinating it to gratification of mind.

In calling pleasure the highest object in life, says Epicurus, we do not mean the pleasures of profligacy, nor, indeed, sensual enjoyments at all, but the freedom of the body from pain, and of the soul from disturbance. Neither feasts nor banquets, neither the lawful nor unlawful indulgence of the passions, nor the joys of the table, make life happy, but a sober judgment, investigating the motives for action and for inaction, and dispelling those greatest enemies of our peace, prejudices. The root from which it springs, and, therefore, the highest good, is intelligence. It is intelligence that leaves us free to acquire possession thereof, without being ever too early or too late. Our indispensable wants are simple, little being necessary to ensure freedom from pain; other things only afford change in enjoyment, by which the quantity is not increased, or else they rest on a mere sentiment. The little we need may be easily attained. Nature makes ample provision for our happiness, would we only receive her gifts thankfully, not forgetting what she gives in thinking what we desire. He who lives according to nature is never poor; the wise man living on bread and water has no reason to envy Zeus; chance has little hold on him; with him judgment is everything, and if that be right, he need trouble himself but little about external mishaps. Not even bodily pain appeared to Epicurus so irresistible as to be able to cloud the wise man's happiness. Although he regards as unnatural the Stoic's insensibility to pain, still he is of opinion that the wise man may be happy on the rack, and can smile at pains the most violent, exclaiming in the midst of torture, How sweet! A touch of forced sentiment may be discerned in the last expression, and a trace of self-satisfied exaggeration is manifest even in the beautiful language of the dying philosopher on the pains of disease. Nevertheless, the principle involved is based in the spirit of the Epicurean philosophy, and borne out by the testimony of the founder. The main thing, according to Epicurus, is not the state of the body, but the state of the mind; bodily pleasure being of short duration, and having much about it to unsettle; mental enjoyments only being pure and incorruptible. For the same reason mental sufferings are more severe than those of the body, since the body only suffers from present ills, whilst the soul feels those past and those to come. In a life of limited duration the pleasures of the flesh never attain their consummation. Mind only, by consoling us for the limited nature of our bodily existence, can produce a life complete in itself, and not standing in need of unlimited duration.

At the same time, the Epicureans, if consistent with their principles, cannot deny that bodily pleasure is the earlier form, and likewise the ultimate source, of all pleasure, and neither Epicurus nor his favourite pupil Metrodorus shrunk from making this admission; Epicurus declaring that he could form no conception of the good apart from enjoyments of the senses; Metrodorus asserting that everything good has reference to the belly. Still the Epicureans did not feel themselves thereby driven to give up the pre-eminence which they claimed for goods of the soul over those of the body. Even the Stoics, notwithstanding the grossness of their theory of knowledge, never abated their demand for a knowledge of conceptions, nor ceased to subordinate the senses to reason, notwithstanding their building a theory of morals on nature. But all character has vanished from their joys and their pains. Their only distinctive feature can be found in the addition either of memory, or of hope, or of fear to the present feeling of pleasure or pain; and their greater importance is simply ascribed to the greater force or duration belonging to these ideal feelings as compared with the attractions which momentarily impress the senses. Only accidentally is the remembrance of philosophic discourses mentioned as a counterpoise to bodily pain; properly speaking, mental pleasures and pains are not different from other pleasures in kind, but only in degree, by reason of their being stronger and more enduring. Accordingly Epicurus cannot escape the admission that we have no cause for rejecting gross and carnal enjoyments if these can liberate us from the fear of higher powers, of death, and of sufferings; and so the only consolation he can offer in pain is the uncertain one that most violent pains either do not last long, or else put an end to our life; and the less violent ones ought to be endured since they do not exclude a counterbalacing pleasure. Hence victory over the impression of the moment must be secured, not so much by a mental force stemming the tide of feeling, as by a proper estimate of the conditions and actions of the senses.

In no other way can the necessity of virtue be established in the Epicurean system. Agreeing with the strictest moral philosophers, so far as to hold that virtue can be as little separated from happiness as happiness from virtue, having even the testimony of opponents as to the purity and strictness of his moral teaching, which in its results differed in no wise from that of the Stoics; Epicurus, nevertheless, holds a position strongly contrasted with that of the Stoics as to the grounds on which his moral theory is based. To demand virtue for its own sake seemed to him a mere phantom of the imagination. Those only who make pleasure their aim have a real object in life. Only a conditional value belongs to virtue as a means to happiness; or, as it is otherwise expressed, Not virtue taken by itself renders a man happy, but the pleasure arising from the exercise of virtue. This pleasure the Epicurean system does not seek in the consciousness of duty fulfilled, or of virtuous action, but in the freedom from disquiet, fear, and dangers, which follows as a consequence from virtue. Wisdom and intelligence contribute to happiness by liberating us from the fear of the Gods and death, by making us independent of immoderate passions and vain desires, by teaching us to bear pain as something subordinate and passing, and by pointing the way to a more cheerful and natural life. Self-control aids in that it points out the attitude to be assumed towards pleasure and pain, so as to receive the maximum of enjoyment and the minimum of suffering; valour, in that it enables us to overcome fear and pain; justice, in that it makes life possible without that fear of Gods and men, which ever haunts the transgressor. To the Epicurean virtue is never an end in itself, but only a means to an end lying beyond it—a happy life—but withal a means so certain and necessary, that virtue can neither be conceived without happiness, nor happiness without virtue. Little as it may seem to be required, still even he would ever insist that an action to be right must be done not according to the letter, but according to the spirit of the law, not simply from regard to others, or by compulsion, but from delight in what is good.

The same claims were therefore advanced by Epicurus on behalf of his wise man as the Stoics had urged on behalf of theirs. Not only was a control over pain attributed to him, in nothing inferior to the Stoic insensibility of feeling, but he endeavoured himself to describe his life as most perfect and satisfactory in itself. Albeit not free from emotions, and being in particular susceptible to the higher feelings of the soul, such as compassion, he yet finds his philosophic activity in no wise thereby impaired. Without despising enjoyment, he is altogether master of his desires, and knows how to restrain them by intelligence, so that they never exercise a harmful influence on life. He alone has an unwavering certainty of conviction; he alone knows how to do the right thing in the right way; he alone, as Metrodorus observes, knows how to be thankful. Nay, more, he is so far exalted above ordinary men, that Epicurus promises his pupils that, by carefully observing his teaching, they will dwell as Gods among men; so little can destiny influence him, that he calls him happy under all circumstances. Happiness may, indeed, depend on certain external conditions; it may even be allowed that the disposition to happiness is not found in every nature, nor in every person; but still, when it is found, its stability is sure, nor can time affect its duration. For wisdom—so Epicurus and the Stoics alike believed—is indestructible, and the wise man's happiness can never be increased by time. A life, therefore, bounded by time can be quite as complete as one not so bounded.

Different as the principles, and different as the tone of the systems of the Stoics and of Epicurus may be, one and the same endeavour may yet be observed in both. It is the tendency which characterises all the post-Aristotelian philosophy—the wish to place man in a position of absolute independence by emancipating him from connection with the external world, and by awakening in him the consciousness of the infinite freedom of thought.

The Epicurean Ethics Continued: Special Points.

The general principles already laid down determine likewise the character of particular points in the moral science of the Epicureans. Epicurus, it is true, never developed his moral views to a systematic theory of moral actions and states, however much his pupils, particularly in later times, busied themselves with morality and special points in a system of morals. Moreover, his fragmentary statements and precepts are very imperfectly recorded. Still, all that is known corresponds with the notion which we must form in accordance with those general views. All the practical rules given by Epicurus aim at conducting man to happiness by controlling passions and desires. The wise man is easily satisfied. He sees that little is necessary for supplying the wants of nature, and for emancipating from pain; that imaginary wealth knows no limit, whereas the riches required by nature may be easily acquired; that the most simple nourishment affords as much enjoyment as the most luxurious, and is at the same time far more conducive to health; that therefore the restriction of wants rather than the increase of possessions makes really rich; and that he who is not satisfied with little will never be satisfied at all. He therefore can with Epicurus live upon bread and water, and at the same time think himself as happy as Zeus. He eschews passions which disturb peace of mind and the repose of life; considering it foolish to throw away the present in order to obtain an uncertain future, or to sacrifice life itself for the means of a life, seeing he can only once enjoy it. He therefore neither gives way to passionate love, nor to forbidden acts of profligacy. Fame he does not covet; and for the opinions of men he cares only so far as to wish not to be despised, since being despised would expose him to danger. Injuries he can bear with calmness. He cares not what may happen to him after death; nor envies any for possessions which he does not himself value.

It has been already seen how Epicurus thought to rise above pains, and to emancipate himself from the fear of the Gods and death. And it has been further noticed that he thinks to secure by means of his principles the same independence and happiness which the Stoics aspired to by means of theirs. But whilst the Stoics thought to attain this independence by crushing the senses, Epicurus was content to restrain and regulate them. Desires he would not have uprooted, but he would have them brought into proper proportion to the collective end and condition of life, into the equilibrium necessary for perfect repose of mind. Hence, notwithstanding his own simplicity, Epicurus is far from disapproving, under all circumstances, of a fuller enjoyment of life. The wise man will not live as a Cynic or a beggar. Care for business he will not neglect; only he will not give himself too much trouble therewith, and will prefer the business of education to any and every other. Nor will he despise the attractions of art, although he can be content when obliged to dispense with them. In short, his self-sufficiency will not consist in *using* little, but in *needing* little; and it is this freedom from wants which will add flavour to his more luxurious enjoyments. Nor is his attitude towards death a different one. Not fearing death, rather seeking it when he has no other mode of escaping unendurable suffering, still, the cases in which he will resort to suicide will be rare, since he has learnt to be happy under all bodily pains. The Stoic's recommendation of suicide finds no favour with the Epicurean.

Fully as the wise man can suffice for himself, still Epicurus would not separate him from connection with others. Not, indeed, that he believed with the Stoics in the natural relationship of all rational beings. Yet even he could form no idea of human life except in connection with human society. He does not, however, assign the same value to all forms of social life. Civil society and the state have for him the least attraction. Civil society is only an external association for the purpose of protection. Justice reposes originally on nothing but a contract entered into for purposes of mutual security. Laws are only made for the sake of the wise, not to prevent their committing, but to prevent their suffering injustice. Law and justice are not, therefore, binding for their own sake, but for the general good; nor is injustice to be condemned for its own sake, but only because the offender can never be free from fear of discovery and punishment. There is not, therefore, any such thing as universal, unchangeable justice. The claims of justice only extend to a limited number of beings and nations—those, in fact, which were able and willing to enter into the social compact. And the particular applications of justice which constitute positive right differ in different cases, and change with circumstances. What is felt to be conducive to mutual security must pass for justice; and whenever a law is seen to be inexpedient, it is no longer binding. The wise man will therefore only enter into political life in case and in as far as this is necessary for his own safety. The sovereign power is a good, inasmuch as it protects from harm. He who pursues it, without thereby attaining this object, acts most foolishly. Private individuals living as a rule much more calmly and safely than statesmen, it was therefore natural that the Epicureans should be averse to public affairs; public life, after all, is a hindrance to what is the real end-in-chief—wisdom and happiness. Their watchword is therefore Λάθε βιώσς. To them the golden mean seemed by far the most desirable lot in life. They only advise citizens to take part in affairs of state when special circumstances render it necessary, or when an individual has such a restless nature that he cannot be content with the quiet of private life. Otherwise they are far too deeply convinced of the impossibility of

pleasing the masses to wish even to make the attempt. For the same reason they appear to have been partisans of monarchy. The stern and unflinching moral teaching of the Stoics had found its political expression in the unbending republican spirit, so often encountered at Rome. Naturally the soft and timid spirit of the Epicureans took shelter under a monarchical constitution. Of their political principles so much at least is known that they did not consider it degrading for a wise man to pay court to princes, and under all circumstances they recommended unconditional obedience to the powers that be.

Family life is said to have been deprecated by Epicurus equally with civil life. Stated thus baldly, this is an exaggeration. So much, however, appears to be established, that Epicurus believed it to be generally better for the wise man to forego marriage and the rearing of children, since he would thereby save himself many disturbances. It is also quite credible that he declared the love of children towards parents to be no inborn feeling. This view is, after all, only a legitimate consequence of his materialism; but it did not oblige him to give up parental love altogether. Nay, it is asserted of him that he was anything but a stranger to family affections.

The highest form of social life was considered by Epicurus to be friendship—a view which is distinctive in a system regarding the individual as the atom of society. Such a system naturally attributes more value to a connection with others freely entered upon and based on individual character and personal inclination, than to one in which a man finds himself placed without any choice, as a member of a society founded on nature or history. The basis, however, on which the Epicurean friendship rests is very superficial, regard being had mainly to its advantages, and in some degree to the natural effects of common enjoyments; but it is also treated in such a way, that its scientific imperfection has no influence on its moral importance. Only one portion of the School, and that not the most consistent, maintained that friendship is pursued in the first instance for the sake of its own use and pleasure, but that it subsequently becomes an unselfish love. Moreover, the assumption that among the wise there exists a tacit agreement requiring them to love one another as much as they love themselves, is clearly only a lame shift. Still, the Epicureans were of opinion that a grounding of friendship on motives of utility was not inconsistent with holding it in the highest esteem. Friendly connection with others affords in short so pleasant a feeling of security, that it entails the most enjoyable consequences; and since this connection can only then exist when friends love one another as themselves, it follows that self-love and the love of a friend must be equally strong.

Even this inference sounds forced, nor does it fully state the grounds on which Epicurus's view of the value of friendship reposes. That view, in fact, was anterior to all the necessary props of the system. What Epicurus requires is primarily enjoyment. The first conditions of such enjoyment, however, are inward repose of mind, and the removal of fear of disturbances. But as to trusting his own powers for satisfying these conditions, Epicurus was far too effeminate and dependent on externals. He needed the support of others, not only to obtain their help in necessity and trouble, and to console himself with this view for the uncertainty of the future, but still more, to make sure of himself and his principles by having the approval of others, thus obtaining an inward satisfaction which he could not otherwise have had. Thus, the approval of friends is to him the pledge of the truth of his convictions. In sympathy with them his mind first attains to a strength by means of which it is able to rise above the changing circumstances of life. General ideas are for him too abstract, too unreal. A philosopher who considers individual beings as alone real, and perceptions as absolutely true, cannot feel quite happy and sure of his ground, unless he finds others go with him. The enjoyment which he seeks is the enjoyment of his own cultivated personality; and wherever this standard prevails, particular value is attached to the personal relations of society, and to friendship.

Hence Epicurus expresses himself on the value and necessity of friendship in a manner far exceeding the grounds on which he based it. Friendship is unconditionally the highest of earthly goods. It is far more important in whose company we eat and drink, than what we eat and drink. In case of emergency the wise man will not shrink from suffering the greatest pains, even death, for his friend.

It is well known that the conduct of Epicurus and his followers was in harmony with these professions. The Epicurean friendship is hardly less celebrated than the Pythagorean. There may be an offensive mawkishness and a tendency to weak mutual admiration apparent in the relations of Epicurus to his friends, but of the sincerity of his feelings there can be no doubt. One single expression, that referring to the property of friends, is enough to prove what a high view Epicurus held of friendship; and there is evidence to show that he aimed at a higher improvement of his associates.

In other respects Epicurus bore the reputation of being a kind, benevolent, and genial companion. His teaching, likewise, bears the same impress. It meets the inexorable sternness of the Stoics by insisting on compassion and forgiveness, and supersedes its own egotism by the maxim that it is more blessed to give than to receive. The number of such maxims on record is, no doubt, limited; nevertheless, the whole tone of the Epicurean School is a pledge of the humane and generous character of its moral teaching. To this trait the Epicurean School owes its greatest importance in his-

tory. By its theory of utility it undoubtedly did much harm, partly indicating, partly helping on the moral decline of the classic nations. Still, by drawing man away from the outer world within himself by teaching him to look for happiness in the beautiful type of a cultivated mind content with itself, it contributed quite as much, after a gentler fashion, as Stoicism by its sterner tone, to the development and the extension of a more independent and more universal morality.

William Wallace (essay date 1880)

SOURCE: William Wallace, "General Aspect of the System" and "The Chief Good," in *Epicureanism*, Society for Promoting Christian Knowledge, 1880, pp. 85-94, 125-69.

[*Wallace, a British scholar who taught at Oxford, published his extensive volume on Epicureanism as the philosopher's reputation was beginning to revive after some centuries of general rejection in England. The excerpt that follows provides, first, a synopsis of Epicureanism in general and, second, a delineation of Epicurus's notion of ethics. Wallace begins with a refutation of myths and misperceptions; he concludes with an image of Epicurus as "modern" in his notion of the individual's relationship to the state.*]

General Aspect of the System.

The popular conception of an Epicurean has varied at different times, but at no time has it been either very fair or very favourable. To the writers of the Roman classical period the charges against Epicureanism were drawn from its denial of the divine providence, its open proclamation of pleasure as the chief good, its opposition to a merely literary and intellectual culture, its withdrawal of its followers from political interests and occupations, and the grotesque features in some of its physical and physiological speculations. Its unscientific character, and its studied indifference, and even hostility, to the prevailing literary and logical as well as mathematical investigations of that epoch, were probably the chief charges in the count. During the ages of theological supremacy which succeeded the downfall of the Empire, Epicurean became synonymous with atheist and unbeliever; it meant a follower of the lusts of the flesh, with whom there was no fear of God to terrify, no ideal aspirations to ennoble, no belief in immortality to check or cheer. Irreligion, freethinking, scepticism, infidelity, on the side of divine affairs: and on the human side, a selfish devotion to one's own ease and comfort, with no care for country or kindred, were the chief ideas connoted by Epicureanism. If we come down to more modern times, the Epicurean of Hume's essays is "the man of elegance and pleasure." He refuses to be bound by the arbitrary restraints which philosophers impose in seeking to "make us happy by reason and rules of art": he alternates his hours between the "amiable pleasure" and "the gay, the frolic virtue"; "forgetful of the past, secure of the future," he enjoys the present: the sprightly muses are the companions of his cheerful discourses and friendly endearments; and, after a day spent in "all the pleasures of sense, and all the joys of harmony and friendship," the shades of night bring him "mutual joy and rapture," with the charming Celia, the mistress of his wishes.[1]

A cloud hangs, and has hung, over Epicureanism; and though we can say with confidence that much of the obloquy is undeserved, there will apparently always be a good deal in its teachings on which certainty, or even intelligence, is unattainable. The unbiassed documentary evidence for exposition which we possess is fragmentary, obscure, and does not extend to every part of the philosophic field. On the other hand, from a variety of causes, misconstruction and misrepresentation have made it their victim. It has been treated as an enemy and an interloper by the statesman, the priest, and the philosopher. It has shared the common fate of every system which attacks either of these great powers, the State, the Church, and the republic of arts and letters, and does so without relying on the support of one member or other of the triumvirate against the others. Science and literature, politics and religion, each and all found themselves assailed by the system of Epicurus. That system came forward as a philosophical system, and yet it turned a hostile front to the customary views of education and of culture, and to the accepted methods and results of the sciences.[2] Whilst other philosophical doctrines either supported or did not interfere with the claims and projects of the political world, Epicureanism openly preached a cosmopolitan and humanitarian creed, which taught the citizen to stand aloof from patriotic and national obligations, and to live his own life as a human being amongst others, in the realm of nature and not of statecraft.[3] As to religion, the case was much the same as it was with the State. The gods, like the government of the State, disappeared at the flat of Epicureanism from their commanding position above nature, to become part and parcel of the great natural process in which they, like all other things, live and move and have their being.[4] Above the intellectual structures of science and art, above the gods of religious faith, above the laws of political convention, rose man, the real individual man, seeking in voluntary association with his fellow-men to live his own life to the fullest of his capacity and with fullest satisfaction.

Of Epicureanism, as of all philosophy, it may be said, that it aims at emancipation, liberation, freedom. But scarcely anywhere was the emancipation carried to the same length as in Epicureanism. Generally speaking, emancipation has meant and means the substitution of an ideal for a material or sensuous sovereignty. We are freed from the dominion of the passions and the flesh by being handed over as subjects to the spirit and the reason. We are taken out of the bondage of this world by taking upon ourselves the yoke of the other world. The heavenly frees from the earthly, and the intellectual from the sensual. Epicureanism professes to impose no yoke or obligation. It agrees with other philosophies in distinguishing between the intellect and the senses (or what it calls the flesh), and, even in a way, in subordinating the latter to the former. But the man of Epicureanism is no abstraction—a reason struggling in the bonds of an alien flesh, which in Pythagorean, and occasionally in Platonic language, forms its prison. Man was not held to be a merely "rational animal," as he was defined by the Stoics. The reason or understanding in Epicureanism is neither the prisoner *de facto,* nor the lord *de jure* of the body or flesh. The flesh, in the view of Epicurus, is our unenlightened, the understanding our enlightened self. The reason is the light which shows us the complete nature which we unwittingly are, and in which we blindly and ignorantly live; which tells us those laws and limits of our existence of which the fleshly nature is unaware, and ignorance whereof breeds vain and inevitably baffled hopes. Naturally, or in our flesh, we are like children stranded in the darkness of night, with no idea of our true position in the world, and inclined to fancy terrors in the gloom which surrounds us.[5] Hence arises the need of philosophy; which, said Epicurus, is an activity that by doctrine and reasoning prepares the way for the happy life.[6]

The main problems of philosophy are, therefore, two in number; or, Epicureanism falls into two parts. The first is a theory of man and of the universe, explaining his position therein, his constitution, and natural powers. This is the physiology . . . , or philosophy of nature. The other is the practical application of the knowledge so acquired to the regulation of conduct. This is the practical or ethical part of the system. It is at the same time evident that the two parts cannot be completely separated. The theoretical examination has its course limited by the practical need: it is knowledge, not for the sake of knowledge, but for the sake of action, and the rule of conduct. Scientific investigation is permitted only so far as it lays down the true place and position of man in the world of things.

And this exclusion of extraneous considerations may be presented under another aspect. If there are any sciences which deal with words and ideas rather than things—and the sciences of rhetoric, grammar, and mathematics come in different ways under this description—then application to their study can only be held to be waste of time. They divert attention from the one thing needful. The human soul cannot find nourishment in mere words: it craves for realities. Epicurus, following up certain ideas which Socrates had emphasized, asks of every science, Does it deal with facts?

and is it useful to me as a human being? If it does not, it may possibly be the pastime of an idle hour; but it should never claim the devotion of a life, because it makes a man miss his true good. It should never be forgotten, therefore, that the natural philosophy of Epicurus is the foundation of his ethics; its *raison d'ätre is, that it renders possible a theory of conduct.*

Besides these two parts of the system, however, there is another, which may be styled introductory. It deals with the general principles on which we are entitled to assert anything. This is the Canonic, the doctrine of the canons, or grounds of evidence. But the Canonic can scarcely be said to form an independent part of Epicureanism: it goes little beyond a few general and preliminary remarks on the question, "What right have we to believe or affirm?" It is, in short, a protest against the scepticism which declares that every statement is uncertain, and science only a probability; and which maintains that, in these circumstances, the only thing left for man is to keep himself free and unshackled from all onesided adherence. The Canonic is thus the beginning of a logic, dealing, not with the grounds for inferring one proposition from another, but with the more fundamental question: On what ultimate grounds is a statement of fact based?

The three parts of Epicureanism are, then, Logic, Physics, and Ethics, if we apply to Epicureanism the distinction which had been applied by the Stoics to the doctrines of their own school. But, at the same time, the terms are infinitely misleading when so applied. Of logic, in the sense in which the term was understood by Aristotle and the Stoics, there was none in Epicureanism. Nor was this all. The Epicureans regarded it as folly, as unnecessary trifling with useless questions. Still less, again, is there a distinction between the Epicurean physics and ethics as independent or parallel branches of inquiry.

The case stands thus: The Epicurean school professes, in the first instance, to be founded on the senses and the feeling, to be based on reality, as popularly understood. It appeals to our immediate perception and feeling, and declares that these must never be recklessly set aside. What we immediately feel and perceive, that is true; what we directly find ourselves to be, that is what we ought to do. Act what thou art is its motto, and sense and feeling tell thee with sufficient distinctness what thou art. But the promise thus held out is certainly not kept to the letter. What we supposed to be our feelings and sensations turn out to be less trustworthy than we had been, up to this point, led to suppose. The greater number of our beliefs and opinions are due to hasty and erroneous inferences. What seemed to be perception was really reasoning. We must, therefore, get back to our original perceptions. We were told originally that we must believe nothing for which we have not the evidence of the senses and the feeling.

It becomes apparent that that evidence does not go so far as we had supposed. Our senses and our feelings seem to mislead, and yet, if we reject all sense and feeling, knowledge is made impracticable.

In other words, the world is not as it seems: all our perceptions cannot, without examination or qualification, be relied upon. This, however, is only because in our perceptions there constantly intrudes an element which is not sense. The other element, which is truly sense, is infallible.[7] All our sensations are witnesses to reality, only liable to be misinterpreted. Above all, there is a great deal which is inaccessible to direct observation altogether. But though it is unknown, the human mind cannot let it alone. Hence arises the need of a canon of inference, which is given as follows:—Everything that is supposed to happen in the sphere beyond knowledge must follow the same laws of operation as what is known to occur within the range of our experience. Whether it happen in what is beneath the range of the senses (*i.e.,* in the microscopic world, and what lies beyond the power of the microscope), or beyond the range of the senses (*i.e.,* in the telescopic world, and what lies beyond the reach of the telescope), it is governed by the same laws as regulate the occurrences visible to unaided sense.

The canonic thus justifies those inferences which go beyond sense. It is right and just to affirm about the unknown, either what is confirmed and witnessed by the known, or what at least is not witnessed against by the known.[8] But, at the same time, it is well to note in which sense the reason is here said to go beyond the sense. It goes beyond simply quantitatively: it carries us further and deeper, but there is a general likeness between the one case and the other. The atoms, *e.g.,* which are intellectually perceived, have precisely the same qualities as the bodies which are sensibly perceived, when we deduct from the latter all which can be shown to be the effect of a combination of circumstances. The intellect is only a subtler and more far-seeing sense, and the sense is a short-sighted and grosser intellect. In Epicurean phraseology, in fact, the particles which constitute the one are said to be finer and more ethereal than those which constitute the other; and for that reason, and that reason only, they are susceptible to minute influences, to which the grosser particles composing the senses are stolidly insensible.[9]

The Epicurean logic, then, if logic it can be called, is in the direction of inductive logic. It lays down the senses as the first, and, we may say, the ultimate court of appeal as a criterion of reality. They never can be mistaken, though the mind may be wrong in the inferences it draws from them. This is the first principle; and the second is, that the unknown is regulated by the same laws as the known: that is to say, the operations in the world invisible to the senses follow on a larger or less scale the same principles as govern the operations of the visible world. We do not, in the intelligible world, find ourselves lifted into a world where new categories and higher conceptions prevail. Thirdly, language in the Epicurean logic is subjected to scrutiny. Every word, if it is to pass muster in argument, must be *en rapport* with a clear and distinct conception, which again must finally be based upon one clear and distinct perception.[10] These are the three main principles of Canonic: that sensation is the only guarantee of reality, that language must be able to recall distinct images, and that reasoning must employ known and familiar processes to make unknown and mysterious facts explicable. . . .

The Chief Good.

We may now pass on to what would, in ordinary parlance, be described as the moral theory or ethical system of Epicurus. On this topic we get little help from Lucretius, whose poem breaks off before it has even completed the theory of natural phenomena. But in Diogenes Laertius, in Cicero and Seneca, there are a number of fragmentary statements, and even of tolerably connected passages, which help us to form in outline at least a conception of the Epicurean Ethics. But we must not expect too much from this title. We shall find no code of duties, no principle of obligation, no abstract standard of morals; and still less any discussion of the moral faculties. In morals we are referred as elsewhere to the guidance of feeling. In feeling, properly interpreted, we have our rule; and we have only to use our intellect to see that we are not led astray from obedience to its voice. Our feeling unequivocally tells us the general character of what we should pursue, viz., pleasure. It is the business of our reason to prevent this object being lost by injudicious pursuit, or by mistaking a less pleasure for a greater. Pleasure always is our aim; the natural aim of every living being, the end or law of nature. It needs some care, however, to discriminate real pleasure from pretended. We are corrupted, we inherit a perverse taste; and it is the office of philosophy to purify our feelings, to make our taste for pleasure true.

As an introduction, we may take a letter of Epicurus in which he presents a summary of his theory of life and conduct; it is given by Diogenes Laertius[11]:—

EPICURUS *to* MENŒCEUS.

Be not slack to seek wisdom when thou art young, nor weary in the search thereof when thou art grown old. For no age is too early or too late for the health of the soul. And he who says that the season for philosophy has not yet come, and that it is passed and gone, is like one who should say that the season for happiness has not yet come, or that it has passed away. Therefore, both old and young ought to seek wisdom, that so a man as age comes over him may be young in good things, because of the grace of what has been, and while he is young may likewise be old, because he has no fear of the things which are to come. Exercise thyself, therefore, in the things which bring happiness; for verily, while it is with thee thou wilt have everything, and when it is not, thou wilt do everything if so thou mayest have it.

Those things which without ceasing I have declared unto thee, those do and exercise thyself therein, holding them to be the elements of right life. First, believe that God is a being blessed and immortal, according to the notion of a God commonly held amongst men; and so believing, thou shalt not affirm of him aught that is contrary to immortality or that agrees not with blessedness, but shalt believe about him whatsoever may uphold both his blessedness and his immortality. For verily there are gods, and the knowledge of them is manifest; but they are not such as the multitude believe, seeing that men do not uphold steadfastly the notions they currently believe. Not the man who denies the gods worshipped by the multitude, but he who affirms of the gods what the multitude believes about them, is truly impious. For the utterances of the multitude about the gods are not true preconceptions, but false assumptions; according to which the greatest evils that happen to the wicked, and the blessings which happen to the good, are held to come from the hand of the gods. Seeing that, as they are always most familiar with their own good qualities, they take pleasure in the sight of qualities like their own, and reject as alien whatever is not of their kind.

Accustom thyself in the belief that death is nothing to us, for good and evil are only where they are felt, and death is the absence of all feeling: therefore, a right understanding that death is nothing to us makes enjoyable the mortality of life, not by adding to years an illimitable time, but by taking away the yearning after immortality. For in life there can be nothing to fear to him who has thoroughly apprehended that there is nothing to cause fear in what time we are not alive. Foolish, therefore, is the man who says that he fears death, not because it will pain when it comes, but because it pains in the prospect. Whatsoever causes no annoyance when it is present causes only a groundless pain by the expectation thereof. Death, therefore, the most awful of evils, is nothing to us, seeing that when we are, death is not yet, and when death comes, then we are not. It is nothing, then, either to the living or the dead, for it is not found with the living, and the dead exist no longer. But in the world, at one time men seek to escape death as the greatest of all evils, and at another time yearn for it as a rest from the evils in life. The mere absence of life is no object of fear, for to live is not set in view beside it, nor is it regarded as an evil. And even as men choose of food, not merely and simply the larger lot, but the most pleasant, so the wise seek to enjoy the time which is most pleasant, and not merely that which is longest. And he who admonishes the young men to live well, and the old men to make a good end, speaks foolishly, not merely because of the desirableness of life, but because the same exercise at once teaches to live well and to die well. Much worse is he who says that it were best not to be born, but when once one is born, to pass with greatest speed the gates of Hades. If he, in truth, believes this, why does he not depart from this life? There is nothing to hinder him, if he has truly come to this conclusion. If he speaks only in mockery, his words are meaningless among people who believe in them not.

Thou must remember that the future is neither wholly ours, nor wholly not ours, so that neither may we wholly wait for it as if it were sure to come, nor wholly despair as if it were not to come.

Thou must also keep in mind that of desires some are natural, and some are groundless; and that of the natural some are necessary as well as natural, and some are natural only. And of the necessary desires, some are necessary if we are to be happy, and some if the body is to remain unperturbed, and some if we are even to live. By the clear and certain understanding of these things we learn to make every preference and aversion, so that the body may have health and the soul tranquillity, seeing that this is the sum and end of a blessed life. For the end of all our actions is to be free from pain and fear; and when once we have attained this, all the tempest of the soul is laid, seeing that the living creature has not to go to find something that is wanting, or to seek something else by which the good of the soul and of the body will be fulfilled. When we need pleasure, is, when we are grieved because of the absence of pleasure; but when we feel no pain, then we no longer stand in need of pleasure. Wherefore we call pleasure the alpha and omega of a blessed life. Pleasure is our first and kindred good. From it is the commencement of every choice and every aversion, and to it we come back, and make feeling the rule by which to judge of every good thing.

And since pleasure is our first and native good, for that reason we do not choose every pleasure whatsoever, but ofttimes pass over many pleasures when a greater annoyance ensues from them. And ofttimes we consider pains superior to pleasures, and submit to the pain for a long time, when it is attended for us with a greater pleasure. All pleasure, therefore, because of its kinship with our nature, is a good, but it is not in all cases our choice, even as every pain is an evil, though pain is not always, and in every case, to be shunned. It is, however, by measuring one against another, and by looking at the conveniences and inconveniences, that all these things must be judged. Sometimes we treat the good as an evil, and the evil, on the contrary, as a good; and we regard independence of outward goods as a great good, not so as in all cases to use little, but so as to be contented with little, if we have not much, being thoroughly persuaded that they have the sweetest enjoyment of luxury who stand least in need of it, and that whatever is natural is easily

procured, and only the vain and worthless hard to win. Plain fare gives as much pleasure as a costly diet, when once the pain due to want is removed; and bread and water confer the highest pleasure when they are brought to hungry lips. To habituate self, therefore, to plain and inexpensive diet gives all that is needed for health, and enables a man to meet the necessary requirements of life without shrinking, and it places us in a better frame when we approach at intervals a costly fare, and renders us fearless of fortune.

When we say, then, that pleasure is the end and aim, we do not mean the pleasures of the prodigal, or the pleasures of sensuality, as we are understood by some who are either ignorant and prejudiced for other views, or inclined to misinterpret our statements. By pleasure, we mean the absence of pain in the body and trouble in the soul. It is not an unbroken succession of drinking feasts and of revelry, not the pleasures of sexual love, not the enjoyment of the fish and other delicacies of a splendid table, which produce a pleasant life: it is sober reasoning, searching out the reasons for every choice and avoidance, and banishing those beliefs through which greatest tumults take possession of the soul. Of all this, the beginning, and the greatest good, is prudence. Wherefore, prudence is a more precious thing even than philosophy: from it grow all the other virtues, for it teaches that we cannot lead a life of pleasure which is not also a life of prudence, honour, and justice; nor lead a life of prudence, honour, and justice which is not also a life of pleasure. For the virtues have grown into one with a pleasant life, and a pleasant life is inseparable from them.

Who then is superior, in thy judgment, to such a man? He holds a holy belief concerning the gods, and is altogether without fears about death; he has diligently considered the end fixed by nature, and has understood how easily the limit of good things can be satisfied and procured, and how either the length or the strength of evils is but slight. He has rejected fate which some have introduced as universal mistress, no less than chance, in respect of what is due to human agency, for he sees that fate destroys responsibility, and that fortune is inconstant; as for our actions, there is no lord and master over them, and it is to them that blame and praise naturally ensue. Better were it, indeed, to believe the legend of the gods, than be in bondage to the destiny taught by the physical philosophers; for the theological myth gives a faint hope of deprecating divine wrath by honouring the gods, while the fate of the philosophers is deaf to all supplications. Nor does he hold chance to be a god, as the world in general does, for in the acts of God there is no disorder, nor to be a cause, though an uncertain one, for he believes that good or evil is not given by it to men so as to make life blessed, though it supplies the starting-point of great good and great evil. He believes that the misfortune of the wise is better than the prosperity of the fool. It is better, in short, that what is well-judged in action should not owe its successful issue to the aid of chance.

Exercise thyself in these and kindred precepts day and night, both by thyself and with him who is like unto thee; and never, either in waking or in dream, wilt thou be disturbed, but wilt live as a god amongst men. For in nothing does he resemble a mortal creature, the man who lives in immortal blessedness.

Thus unequivocally does Epicureanism proclaim pleasure to be the end of nature—the first good, common to the whole race of man. The announcement of such a doctrine naturally gave rise to a chorus of reproving and protesting voices. Even if it be true that we are irresistibly urged towards pleasure by an impulse of our nature, it is our duty, say the objectors, to guard against the temptations thus arising. We have nobler aims to live for then mere pleasure. Honour and duty demand our allegiance: obligations bind us to our family and friends and to our country. Pleasure is of the earth, but virtue calls us to make ourselves worthy of heaven. A mere pleasure-seeker is of all beings the most miserable: his search is hopeless: and the fruits he plucks are but as apples of Sodom and turn into ashes between his teeth. The man of pleasure must inevitably, it is said, cry out, Vanity of vanities: all is vanity. Worse than this: his pleasures will become more and more sensual, degrading, and animal. As life goes on, his jaded sensibilities require more poignant excitements to ward off the attacks of ennui. A life of pleasure hardens the heart, and the sense of enjoyment comes to find a peculiar delight in the sight of others suffering. Domitian at Rome and Catherine the Second of Russia are pointed out as the examples warning against lawless lust for pleasures. That Epicureanism should inculcate a lesson which bears such fruits seems argument enough to condemn it.

In all of this the truth is marred by exaggeration. There is a long interval between the statement that pleasure is the natural law, and the recommendation to pursue pleasures everywhere and above all things. The former can hardly be disputed, when explained; the latter is unwise and, possibly, impracticable advice. To do justice to the doctrine of Epicurus we should never forget that it is to a large extent the reaction and protest of an opposition. Its statements to be understood must be taken in connection with the doctrines to which they are antagonistic. Every thesis loses half its meaning, and almost all its truth, when completely dissevered from its antithesis. The expression of a dogma in such a case is misleading. The author, strong in his sense of a correction to be made, hardly gives full place to the large and important body of doctrine which he accepts without correction. His exposition is fragmentary and unbalanced, and requires to be interpreted with caution. Because something is passed over in silence, we

must not infer that it is denied. Every revelation of new truth, every attempt at reform, always and necessarily assumes and tacitly embodies with itself much that was old.

Epicureanism need not be assumed, therefore, to abolish or contradict the old morality altogether, although it proposes to put it upon a new foundation, and denies the especial principles on which the virtues were sometimes said to be founded. In the moral systems of Plato and Aristotle a very subordinate and undignified place was assigned to pleasure. When Aristotle in his "Ethics" attempts to find the characteristic mark of virtue, he sees it in the circumstance that the end or aim of the action is [*tò kalòn*].[12] The beautiful—the idea of an objective perfection and symmetry which is to be maintained—the entirely ideal motive of correspondence with an existent law of rectitude,—the desire to reflect a moral beauty in our individual conduct—that is the sunlight which elevates acts out of mechanical obedience into conscious actualization of an ethical world or moral cosmos. The presupposition here, as in Plato, is that of an order which exists before us, of an ideal perfection which we do not make, and can but approximate to. Of the origin and authority of this fundamental idea of his ethical system Aristotle can scarcely be said to render any account. What the "beautiful" is, and how it comes to sway our conduct, is rather removed from his range. Nor can Plato be said to carry more conviction when he asserts, what in its way is true enough, that these conceptions are the very ante-natal dower of the soul—the ideas which mind has been familiar with before it sank into the darkness of this sense-world in which we live. The interesting question still remains how we as human beings come to shake off the confusing influences of nature, and learn to see the idea of goodness in its very truth. But Plato, though he attacks this question, does not answer it. He discusses an analogous question, viz., how the statesman is to be equipped for his duties; and to the statesman thus formed and perfected he entrusts the task of telling the ordinary human being what is to be done and what is not to be done. And a like criticism may be passed on Aristotle. They both had in view an objective order and system which stood above the likes and feelings of men; and a willing conformity to this order was the aim which they assigned to the legislator in his normative action in society. So long as there was a tolerable agreement between this ideal order and the actual constitutions under which men lived, so long their theory might be accepted. But when even the blindest eye could no longer refuse to see in the existing political forms only a tissue of vice, injustice, and baseness, then the ideal order, bereft of its sensuous vicegerent, the State, must collapse or find another support.

The ancient sages before Epicurus had condemned pleasure, and opposed it to virtue. A few of them went so far as to carry out the implication, and to assert the absolute incompatibility of pleasure and virtue. Aristotle had not been so extravagant. In pleasure he recognised the sign that the capacity and tendency to good which habit and discipline had produced had at length become a second nature.[13] He had spoken of pleasure as the accompaniment of such action as combined the fullest expansion of a natural power in the agent with the most satisfactory condition of the objects in which it found room for its exercise. Pleasure was the concomitant of action when the perfect agent found a perfect medium for his action. But the character of the active power made a profound difference in the estimate to be formed of the pleasure. There were higher pleasures, and there were lower pleasures. This distinction of the worth or worthlessness of different pleasures rests upon the presumption that there is a hierarchical system of ends in life, that some acts or things are intrinsically worth more than others, quite apart from the pleasure which individuals may derive from them. It rests on a belief in ideas and on ideal truth: on the faith that man is only a member of a great order, an everlasting realm of truth and goodness, which receives him when he comes into the world, and which connects him with the past and the future, as well as with his contemporaries in the present.

Such an order Epicureanism ignores. It isolates a man from his membership of the body politic; it cuts him off from anything beyond this life by the doctrine of man's absolute mortality. For Epicureanism man is a sentient being, capable of pleasure and pain, and possessed of an intelligence which enables him to take forethought for both. Around him are other sentient beings similarly circumstanced, with whom it is often necessary, and sometimes convenient, that he should come into contact and relationship. But these connections are lax, accidental, and temporary; the unions so formed are transient, and owe their existence and maintenance to the convenience of individuals. They have no subsistence in themselves, no rights as against individuals, no powers to enforce obligations or require duties. The individual being, susceptible to pains and pleasures, is the starting-point and the standard. Nothing exists outside him which should thwart and check the claims of his person to enjoyment, nothing of an ideal kind, at any rate. To some extent, however, the bond which is thus taken off is reimposed as the easier and lighter yoke of friendship.

Antiquity is almost unanimous in the praises it bestows upon the friendly affection which prevailed in the communities of Epicureans.[14] Friendship enhances the charm of life; it helps to lighten sorrows and to heighten joys by fellowship. In itself, the fact of friendship bears witness to something beyond the mere individual, perhaps—but it speaks only imperfectly and indistinctly. Reflection seems to show that all friendship has a selfish basis, and is built upon util-

ity. In every union of affection the cynical observer is able to point to something which may be interpreted into the presence of an earthly element, a self-regarding consideration. Nor is the cynical observer to be pronounced in error. The self-regarding cannot be entirely absent from anything human; the absolutely and wholly unselfish is the divine. But the cynical observer is wrong in emphasizing this fact to the exclusion of another side. The prophet and the reformer are not to be regarded as hypocrites because even in their holiest fervours and their purest counsels the absence of self is never perfect and undisputed. Rather were it well to note the different contents and structure of the self which is operative in different individuals. There is a wide interval between the self which excludes all others in antagonism and the self which includes them in love.

Yet for an ordinary world, the cynicism which reminds us that utility is the creator of law and morality is not altogether without its value. Harsh as it may sound against more ideal or more sentimental principles, the assertion of utilitarianism has at least the advantage of fighting against an unreasoning conservatism adhering to the past with blind tenacity. Even if utility be not an adequate formula to account for the existence of the organization of human society on its present basis, it at least affords a mark for the reformer, and suggests ameliorations. In the great words in which Plato proclaimed the rights of reason against authority and tradition,[15] there is not and never will be finer phrase than this:—Only the useful is truly beautiful and noble, only the harmful truly unsightly and bad.

But the basis of utilitarianism may be different, as the doctrine itself varies. It may rest on a philanthropic sentiment, a humanitarian feeling. Such a foundation must to Epicurus have seemed vague and uncertain; and he builds his creed accordingly on a more solid foundation; more solid, that is, if we compare sentiment with sentiment. He bases it on the natural feeling of pleasure, and on the general gravitation of all human kind towards pleasure. No more than other writers is Epicurus able to give a definition of pleasure. To know what is meant by being pleased we must go to consciousness, to feeling. "The state of pleasure," says Professor Bain, "is an ultimate, indefinable experience of the mind. The fact itself is known to each person's consciousness: the modes, varieties, degrees, collaterals, and effects of it, may be stated in propositions."[16] In a sense, it is quite true that every one does understand what is meant by pleasure. Unfortunately, however, the word pleasure, like all words of this 'abstract' description, easily becomes ambiguous. It denotes not merely the abstract and general relation in virtue of which an act or object is termed pleasant, but also the particular objects or acts themselves which give pleasure to some, or perhaps to the majority of mankind. Like other abstract terms, it is interpreted and defined by the habits and experience of each individual. It is specified into various concrete pleasures, and identified with certain things which produce pleasure. Every man has pleasures of his own, and the cases are rare where the same thing gives pleasure to everybody.

The phrase "pursue pleasure," is therefore somewhat elliptical. Strictly speaking, we do not and cannot pursue pleasure; which is as great an abstraction as the pursuit of truth, perhaps even a greater; for the latter, at least, is in some degree objective and abiding, whereas pleasure is transient and subjective. What we pursue are certain objects of desire, the attainment of which causes pleasure. Pleasure in itself, if we may use such an expression, is neither one thing nor another: what it is depends entirely on the nature of the person, and the character of the object. No so-called pleasure has the power of producing pleasure, inevitably and in all circumstances. Yet for this reason, it may be said what we desire is not a thing, but rather an action. It is the eating, and not the food, which gives pleasure to the hungry.

There is a controversy, in some respects verbal, raised on this point. It may be said, that the object of a desire is not pleasure, but some special thing or act. "All particular appetites and passions," says Bishop Butler,[17] "are towards external things themselves, distinct from the pleasure arising from them." Action, which should have in view no particular object but only the general end of pleasure, would be so indefinite and vague as to be unreal. The actual appetites of the actual human being go straight at their specific ends. It is only with reflection and thought that the voluptuary who pursues pleasure for pleasure's sake becomes in any degree possible. A mere liking for pleasant things does not make a voluptuary, or few would escape the name. To become a voluptuary, a human being must care for and desire nothing in these pleasant things but the pleasure which they bring to his individual self. Every concrete reality fades away into nothingness in his eyes except his own consciousness, and the honey which can be extracted by him from the vast world, for whose intrinsic existence and fortunes he has no interest whatever. To such a person, if he can be said anywhere to exist in full-fledged reality, the doctrine that pleasure is the sole object of desires may be applied.

No such assertion does Epicurus, however, make. The end of nature, he says, is pleasure. Pleasure, and not pain, is the end towards which all things in the world tend as their natural and normal condition. But what are pleasure and pain? It is necessary to look at them together. No doubt it may be said that there is a third or neutral state, which is neither pleasure nor pain. There are certainly many states of consciousness, which we should not in ordinary language describe as either pleasant or painful. But whether that gives a ground for asserting that these states are absolutely

without such quality, are wholly indifferent, is a question which seems difficult to answer in the affirmative. It may, however, be convenient to assume the existence of some such point of transition and indifference as a terminus from which we ordinarily measure the degree of pleasure or of pain, or as an average level of no very definable character, and liable to divergence on two sides.

According to Plato, however, there are two categories of pleasures ordinarily so called.[18] There are pleasures which rest, to some extent, upon an illusion; they seem pleasant, that is, when set in contrast with a background of pain. In themselves they are nothing positive: they are no more than the absence or the removal of uneasiness. They presuppose an antecedent pain: they are the satisfaction of a want. Of this kind, for example, is the pleasure derived from eating by the hungry man. These pleasures are unreal and untrue. On the other hand, there are pleasures,—as an instance, Plato gives the pleasures of smell,—which are preceded by no pain. They accompany certain exertions of activity or certain states of susceptibility: they come unsought, and leave no sense of want behind them. Such pleasures are positive and real.

It may be doubted if this distinction rests on wholly satisfactory ground. The sense of want or desire which accompanies certain pleasures as their condition, is probably to be explained by their close connection with our nature and character, whether original or acquired. The pleasures of smell, to take Plato's instance, excite no previous desires in most cases, because they have little connection with our well-being; and the pleasure they do produce may, perhaps, be due directly or indirectly to an association with life-giving and beneficial function. Perhaps, too, the facility with which certain pleasures may be represented by imagination in the objects which habitually cause them, has something to do with the feeling of uneasiness which Plato alludes to. At any rate, all pleasures seem to be, at least in the case of those who feel them most acutely, attended by the sense of want. But, of course, there is a difference of another origin which has a bearing upon the point. The pleasures of the sensualist are much less within his own power than those of the intellectualist. The former is in a large degree dependent on the favour of external circumstances, and thus inevitably he must occasionally be deprived of a favourite gratification, must suffer want and pain. The intellect carries its own resources, at least, to a large extent, and is less dependent on external help. But even in the case of intellectual delights, the absence of intellectual exercise would be felt as a pain and loss, and a man would put himself to pain and trouble to recover his mental ease and freedom. The various conditions under which pleasure is experienced seem to point in the direction of the relativity of pleasure and pain. Whether as the removal of an obstruction, the conquest of a difficulty, the replenishment of a void, the satisfaction of an uneasiness, the re-establishment of an equilibrium, the enlargement of an imprisoned force, pleasure presupposes something of its opposite.

It is in this sense that Epicurus defines pleasure: "When once the pain arising from deficiency has been removed, the pleasure in the flesh admits of no further augmentation, but only of variation: and similarly the limit of the pleasure of the mind is reached, when the causes of our principal mental fears have been removed."[19] The limit of pleasure, according to the stock phrase, was the eradication of everything painful. When so much has been gained, no further increase in the amount of the pleasure is possible. Subsequently, of course, variety may be introduced by more costly appliances, but the net result will be the same as that gained by simpler methods. And for that reason it is a wise precaution to find out experimentally the simplest and least expensive mode of gratifying our wants, not with any ascetic intention, but simply to prepare for a state of affairs when the more costly means is not at our command. If it be said that the variety and vicissitude of luxuries also satisfies what is to many a real want, Epicurus replies by instituting a distinction between our wants. Of the desires, some are pronounced to be natural and necessary; others to be natural, but not necessary; a third class includes desires which are neither natural nor necessary, but due merely to fancy and fashion. This division of desires and pleasures into the natural and the artificial comes from older sources: it is laid down, for example, by the Cynics. But it is in the application of the distinction to hedonism that the important point lies for Epicureanism. Epicurus, like the Stoics in his own time, and like Rousseau and his adherents in the last century, tries to find in nature a help against fashion and civilization. It is nothing to have cast away the rags of superstition, if we still retain the artificial vestments of human culture. Avoid all culture, was the advice of Epicurus.[20] He is at war with the artificialities of life. Nature had made man upright, but he had sought out many inventions. An exclusive literary training was leading men away from the perception of the truth of life, to spend their days in a hollow world of unreality, filled with æsthetic vanities, with political pomps, with religious anxieties. To the doctrine that poetry and art had a useful end, the Epicureans opposed a denial; poetry might be justified on some grounds, but certainly not for its utility.[21] If the hard-worked statesman, said Epicurus in his work **on Kingdom,**[22] desires relaxation, let him seek it in the tales of war, or even in rough common jesting, but not in æsthetic discussions, on topics of music and poetry; let him seek his amusement in spectacles and pageants, in the drama and the concert, but not in critical or philological investigations of the principles of art. Epicurus is impatient of the nebulous regions which only exist, according to him, for highly sensitive and sentimental souls.

In this way Epicureanism seems to approach to a point of view at the opposite pole of opinion, viz. Cynicism or Stoicism. "Man needs but little here," is its assertion. "Riches, according to nature, are of limited extent, and can easily be procured; but the wealth craved after by vain fancies knows neither end nor limit." "He who has understood the limits of life, knows how easy to get is all that takes away the pain of want, and all that is required to make our life perfect at every point. In this way he has no need of anything which implies a contest."[23] Thus Epicurus can scarcely be identified with the ordinary advocates of pleasure. His hedonism is of a sober and reflective kind. It rests on the assumption that pleasure is the end or natural aim, but, it adds, that the business of philosophy is to show within what limits that end is attainable. Thus, if, on one hand, it declares against the philosophers that pleasure is the law of nature, and that ideal ends ought to promote the welfare of humanity, it declares on the other against the multitude that the ordinary pursuit of pleasure, and the common ideas of its possibilities, are erroneous. To the ordinary vision the search for pleasure is endless: one beckons after another: illimitable vistas of new delights seem to extend before the ravished eyes. All this is a delusion, says Epicurus. True pleasure is satisfaction, and not a yearning, which, though momentarily stilled, bursts forth again.

It would almost seem a misnomer to call this pleasure. As true politeness, so-called, often differs widely with what is usually understood by politeness, so true pleasure seems far apart from pleasure in its vulgar meaning. A body free from pain, and a mind released from perturbations, is the ideal of Epicurean life. The prominent point, in short, is not the doctrine that pleasure is the natural end. That Epicurus asserts as a universal law of animated existence. But what he emphasizes is rather the conditions under which this end is possible for man. He seems, at first sight, to describe pleasure, as Schopenhauer, as a merely negative state, as the absence of pain. It would, however, be a grave mistake were we to suppose that because this condition is negatively described, it was a mere abstraction or negation. The imperturbability of the Epicurean was not an ascetic or an insensate withdrawal from all life and action. But it certainly introduced a rational and reflective aspect into the doctrine of hedonism, as it had been practised or taught by Aristippus of Cyrene. The Cyrenaic preached enjoyment of the present moment: he took pleasure as he found it scattered all over the earth. He did not balance pleasure against pleasure. His theory was, that as pleasure is the one thing desirable, the main aim of education should be to fit men to enjoy with all their heart, to give them that strength of mind and body, which enables them to take pleasure in anything. He said, Learn to enjoy: at each moment the absolute good of life is before you, and you ought to attain it. You need not wait for the lapse of time, so as to see how it has turned out upon the whole. Comparison and reflection are the foe of pleasure. You must be able to throw yourself wholly into what this moment presents, as if this moment were eternity with no before or after. When another moment comes, you treat it in like manner. Thus, while you enjoy each in its turn to the full, you remain detached from its control, you are still your own master, your action creates no obligation, you are equally free to enjoy what comes next.

To all of this the reply of the Epicurean is that such a doctrine, if practicable at all, is only possible under exceptional circumstances. To carry it out implies a previous training and reflection on life as a whole, on its capacities and its needs, on the laws of nature, and the relations of men to one another. A happy tact, a natural taste, may, in peculiarly gifted natures, and in favourable circumstances, enable a man to enjoy, without running upon the shoals and quicksands which beset the course of the pleasure-seeker. But in the vast majority of cases, where no æsthetic instincts guide the decision, the search for pleasure proves a chase after a phantom, which allures only to deceive. For "the flesh takes the limits of pleasure to be endless, and an endless time would be needed to provide it; but the mind, having learned the limit and the end of the flesh, and having cast away fears about the distant future, has made for us life perfect and adequate, and we no longer need infinite time. And yet it has not been an exile from pleasure, and when the time comes to depart from life, it closes with no sense of having fallen short of felicity."[24] In other words, if we really and truly enjoy the moment, we can only do so by having taken, some time or other, a view beyond the moment, and having learned to see each moment in the light of the whole life, of our nature as a whole. We must refer each action to the end and aim of nature, and not throw ourselves blindly into what promises pleasure.

"No pleasure is evil in itself, but the objects productive of certain pleasures may lead to annoyances many times greater than the pleasure."[25] Hence the place of prudence or reflection in the Epicurean system, as the chief of the virtues. But it must not be supposed that the function of φραυησις is in Epicurus any more than in Aristotle, merely to weigh pleasure against pleasure, so as to choose the heavier. Prudence, here as there, means the intelligent conception of human nature, as a whole, in its limits and its powers. It is not a fitful and casual agent, interfering with the natural bent towards pleasure, and exhorting it to hear reason, but a deep-settled and permanent character—the second nature of the Epicurean sage—which acts like an instinct to preserve from extravagance and excess. If reflection, indeed, were employed to choose amongst pleasures with a conscious reasoning at every moment, such a process would certainly be a kill-joy. But this is only the case with the learner, who is endeavouring

to correct his natural errors. As he advances in the path of perfection, the feeling of opposition between the habitual tendency fostered by evil influences and the rational law of nature grows fainter, till at last, in the character of the ideal sage, it disappears altogether. Once for all, the wise man has counted the cost, and learnt the real worth, of various enjoyments; he has learned to discriminate apparent from real pleasures, and can turn away without a single sigh of regret from many entertainments which the world esteems highly.

This, then, is one point of contrast between pleasure, as understood by the Cyrenaics and Epicureans. With the former it was the pleasure of the moment, of action and excitement: life, as a whole, did not enter into the account—it was taken as a series of moments, and each moment deemed an eternity. With the latter it was the pleasure of a life, in which the pleasures of the several moments took their place in a system and modified each other. The pleasure of the Cyrenaics was a keen sensation—in motion, κίνησις, as the technical phrase described it: that of the Epicureans was more tranquil and sedate—an habitual and permanent rather than a changeful and temporary enjoyment.[26] With the Cyrenaic it was the pleasure of the healthy and vigorous natural man; with the Epicurean, of the philosopher, and, perhaps, to some extent, of the weakly valetudinarian. Epicureanism could thus appeal to the many, whilst Cyrenaic theories could only find an echo in specially-endowed personalities. Few in any age can stand for a portrait like that drawn by Cicero,[27] of M. Thorius Balbus. "This man was a citizen of Lanuvium. He lived in such a way as to miss none of the finest pleasures; for in all kinds of pleasure he was an amateur, connoisseur, and adept. So free was he from superstition that he treated with scorn many of the sacred places and religious rites of his country: and yet so fearless of death that he fell on the battle-field fighting for his fatherland. He limited his desires, not at the point fixed by Epicurus, but by his own satiety: yet never so as to injure his health. His exercise was arranged so as to make him come hungry and thirsty to dinner; his food was at once calculated to please the palate and promote digestion, and his wine was selected of such quality as to give pleasure and produce no injury. As for the other enjoyments which Epicurus declares to be an essential part of the conception of happiness, he tasted them, too. He did not suffer from pain; yet when it did come he bore it manfully, trusting perhaps more to a physician than a philosopher. He had a splendid colour, sound health, great popularity; in a word, his life was brimful of every variety of pleasure." But people with all these advantages are on the whole rare, and a gospel for their benefit is scarcely needed. Epicureanism addressed itself to a frailer and humbler multitude, who neither in circumstances nor in personal endowments were equal to making the world comport itself to their demands. It proposed to enable them, by discipline, to gain all that the others acquired by wealth, position, and innate force. It preached that pleasure was not restricted to the rich or to the mighty, but was equally attainable by the poor and the lowly. It levelled all ranks and equalized men, by showing that it is the variety and superficial glitter of pleasure and not its essence which imposed upon the powerful and their admirers. Epicurus thus took from Cynicism its representation of the difference between artificial and natural pleasures and desires; but he employed the distinction for different purposes, and with other presuppositions. He did not, like them, allow the means to become an end.

It is sometimes put as another difference between Epicurus and his Cyrenaic predecessors, that while the latter put the bodily pleasures highest, the former gave preference to the pleasures of the mind. It may, of course, be said that as the mind, whether as *animus* or as *anima* (to adopt a Lucretian distinction[28]), is, according to Epicurus, only a species of body or matter, any distinction between the mental and bodily in such a system can be of little importance. This, however, would be to confuse the explanation of a difference with the difference itself. To the Epicureans, as to everybody else, the distinction between body and mind was an important one, however it was accounted for in terms of their especial creed. But the ground on which the mental is put higher than the corporeal in its capacity for enjoyment or misery is not based on abstruse considerations, but simply on the fact that while the flesh simply felt in the moment, and for the moment, the mind could be under the combined influence of past, present, and future. The flesh, σάρξ, as Epicurus terms the blind, natural, and unconscious self in us, looks neither before nor after; it pines for nothing, and has no prospects of coming joy. It is buried in itself. The mind, on the contrary, the intelligent self, has a larger range, both in its pleasures and its pains. Yet it might be urged that this consideration tells both ways: the mind can relieve its pain by the prospect of deliverance, and can damp a joy by the reflection on future or contemporaneous pains.

Yet it would be a foolish mistake to suppose that when Epicurus thus advocates the primacy for mind, he is doing more than asserting that the pains and pleasures of the intelligent man have an intensity and vigour exceeding those of the mere boor. He has no idea of pleasures which exclude the body from all share. On this point we have a sentence which his adversaries have quoted and misconstructed to their own delight. "I am unable," he says, "to form any conception of good, from which have been eliminated the pleasures of eating and drinking, the pleasures of sexual love, the pleasures of music and eloquence, and the pleasures of shape and pleasant movements."[29] Of course this does not mean that pleasure merely lies in these things. But it does assert that a pleasure from which they have all been excluded as unreal and incompat-

ible, is to Epicurus an impossible and fanciful conception—a mere dream of the idealist. And it is to be looked at in that light, as a protest against a school of ethics which regarded bodily pleasure as something unworthy and degrading, and held that the true and real pleasure was intellectual or mental. It is here that Epicurus is directing his remarks against the idealist philosophers, who made their heaven a life of intellectual vision of truth. Such a one-sided view of human nature as a mere spirit or reason is what Epicureanism constantly and rightly denies. But, as we have seen, it equally on the other hand refuses to acknowledge the supremacy of the mere flesh. It never flinches from the difficult task of emphasizing the complete constitution of human nature—as flesh and spirit.

In the same way we have this double edge of Epicureanism presented in the statement that, "It is impossible to live pleasantly without living wisely, and well, and justly, and it is impossible to live wisely and well, and justly, without living pleasantly."[30] The path of virtue and the path of pleasure coincide. "It is my belief," says Seneca, "however much my fellow-Stoics may disagree with me, that the teaching of Epicurus is holy and right; pleasure with him is reduced to something small and slender, and the very law which we impose on virtue he lays down for pleasure: he bids it obey nature. And, therefore, I shall not say, like many of the Stoics, that the sect of Epicurus is a guide to vice; but this I say, it has a bad name, an ill-repute, and that undeservedly. Its countenance gives room for such stories, and suggests wrong expectations. It is like a brave man dressed as a woman."[31] But Epicurus was denied the credit, and even the right, of making this identification between true virtue and true happiness. Words of his were quoted to the effect that "we should honour virtue and goodness and the like, if they produce pleasure, but not otherwise;" or that "he scorned virtue and its foolish admirers when it produced no pleasure."[32] To understand these statements and give them no exaggerated sense, it is well to recollect against whom they are directed. They are no abstract enunciations, but polemical remarks directed against exaggeration on the opposite side. And that exaggeration is found in certain forms of Stoical and Cynical doctrine, which make virtue an end in itself, not merely irrespective of the amount of pleasure it may bring to the individual on a special occasion, but without any consideration of its utility to mankind at large. These enthusiastic friends of virtue have confounded its accidental divergence from pleasure, in the lower sense, when it takes its colour from sensuality, with a divergence from pleasure in its higher sense, when pleasure means the blissful feeling of well-being. The whole character of the dispute reminds us vividly of Bentham's assaults upon the ascetic moralists—as those who "have gone so far as to make it a matter of merit and of duty to court pain."[33] Of course, Epicureanism is a great deal more than utilitarianism.

It is a theory of life and nature as a whole, and not a mere hypothesis to explain the existence of moral distinctions. Epicureanism is an attempt to afford human souls a guide amid the perplexities of life: it is as much a religion as a scientific theory. Its end is practice, and not mere doctrine. It speaks for the benefit of the individual man as a being for whom life is pregnant with possibilities of pain and pleasure, while utilitarianism is mainly engaged with a speculative problem. Yet, in some ways the drift of Epicureanism would be made clear if it were described as an assertion of the "principle of utility." When Bentham says that "A man may be said to be a partizan of the principle of utility when the approbation or disapprobation he annexes to any action or to any measure is determined by and proportioned to the tendency which he conceives it to have to augment or to diminish the happiness of the community," he at least expresses one side of Epicureanism. But he does not afford equally adequate expression to the personal, practical, and inward aspects. The ethics of the individual, according to Epicurus are not merely and wholly determined by the interests of the community. Man has a right and a law of his own, the right to enjoy existence, and the duty to secure his own full and free development. The rights of society over the individual, the subordination of the individual to the laws and institutions of the State, are in this theory supplementary and derivative.

It is in its remarks on justice and the political virtues that Epicureanism comes nearest to the standpoint of English utilitarianism. "It was not because sovereignty and dominion were intrinsically good that men sought for fame and glory in society, but in order to fence themselves round from their fellowmen."[34] Political life is a *pis aller,* or at any rate the current forms and institutions of political life have only a relative and subsidiary value. The school of political philosophy to which Epicurus, Hobbes, Hume, and Rousseau in very different ways belong, insists upon an original compact between the individual members of society as the origin of its establishment. It is probably possible at the present day to acknowledge the amount of truth contained in this doctrine without committing one's self to its absurdities. It is no doubt true that society as it exists upon the face of the earth is largely due to the operation of natural causes, with which purpose or deliberation has exceedingly little to do. The necessities of procuring the means of subsistence, the exigencies of the sexual passion, and the natural force of kindred in the human race, will always and inevitably form societies of differing character and extent. But it is a long way from such animal and natural unions to the mature forms of family and civic life. The operations of instinct only go a small way to explain the rise of domesticity and political associations. The influence of the family instinct, if unaided, seldom goes beyond a narrow circle; and, if the world had to depend on that alone, the race of men would

be broken up into an endless number of miniature societies. But other agencies step in to complete the work, and to resist the disintegrating tendencies of selfishness. On one hand tradition—the reverence for what is, the might of the existent to maintain itself,—prevents change, and keeps up old unities. Thus even children's children bow to the supremacy of the family chief. And on another hand the necessities of self-defence and the pressure of war check the separatist forces of individualism.

In what sense, then, it may be asked, are the family and the State due to a contract? Their comparative indissolubility seems to put a great separation between them and other contracts. They are not, as Kant in one instance supposed,[35] mere partial contracts for a special purpose and a special function. Their will and tendency are to claim the whole human being, to demand an undivided and a perpetual allegiance. It is against such a sweeping universal claim that the theory of contract has a certain relative justification. It is thereby declared that the rights of the individual, though for the time they may be put in abeyance, are not wholly annihilated. The rights of the individual are in a sense paramount over those of the community. Such, at least, is the assertion of Epicureanism, and such seems to be the direction in which, even in many modern communistic schemes, the thought of the world is moving. The old Greek theory of an omnipotent State and the Catholic dogma of indissoluble wedlock are set aside. In their stead modern legislation tends more and more to emancipate the members of the family from the bonds of *status;* and modern politics tend more and more to found Government on a constitutional compact between the rulers and the subjects. Here as in many other places Epicurus is practical, realistic, and modern.

Undoubtedly, neither side of the relationship can be ignored. To sacrifice the interests of the individual bars the way to reform. To put these interests forward in a one-sided way is to banish the very possibility of order and permanence. And, unquestionably, Epicurus was in harmony with the general feeling and opinion of his time. Man the individual, is the only *real* unit of social life: all other unities are so far *ideal* and fictitious, and are due to the combined effort of individual wills. They are entered upon with certain presuppositions; should they continue, when these presuppositions are no longer fulfilled? At any rate, when the State and the family cease to be mere natural unions, due solely to the instincts of sex and of self-defence, steadied and perpetuated by the influence of imitation and authority, there must be some sort of understanding or compact, tacit or formal, in the shape of a common law or customary right, accepted by the members of a community as binding upon them all. Not that such a compact is an arbitrary act, depending entirely on the will either of the majority or of a natural aristocracy. The customary law is an attempt to give expression to the principles which are required in order to make human society possible; to state, so far as individual bias or prejudice on the part of the expositors will allow, the conditions and relations which must be maintained if a society is to flourish and its several members reap the full advantage of its constitution. Such is the profession made by law; unfortunately, law, in its actual shape, represents seldom the relations of the community regarded as an organic whole, but more frequently the relations imposed upon a community from the point of view afforded by the privileged position of some one class or caste of men in the body politic.

The point especially emphasized by Epicurus is, that law was made for man, and not man for law. Law has no intrinsic or abstract claim on the obedience of men except in so far as its precepts and its sanctions have the welfare of humanity for their aim. It is not, in short, because it has been legislatively declared and enacted that a law has obligatory force, but because it is right and expedient. Epicurus is at one with Hume, who says that, "Public utility is the sole origin of justice, and reflections on the beneficial consequences of this virtue are the sole foundation of its merit."[36] "Natural justice," says the former,[37] "is a contract of expediency, so as to prevent one man doing harm to another. Those animals which were incapable of forming an agreement to the end that they neither might injure nor be injured are without either justice or injustice. Similarly, those tribes which could not or would not form a covenant to the same end are in a like predicament. There is no such thing as an intrinsic or abstract justice."

So far there is not, perhaps, much practical objection to be taken to the theory. The case seems different when we hear that, "Injustice is not in itself a bad thing: but only in the fear arising from anxiety on the part of the wrong-doer that he will not always escape punishment."[38] This anxiety, according to Epicurus, inasmuch as it never can be annihilated, but always lingers on in an evil conscience, is a sufficient deterrent from criminal actions. If we interpret this doctrine, after the example of some of the ancients, to mean that any wrong-doing would be innocent and good, supposing it escaped detection, we shall probably be misconstruing Epicurus. What he seems to allude to is rather the case of strictly legal enactments, where previously to law the action need not have been particularly moral or immoral: where, in fact, the common agreement has established a rule which is not completely in harmony with "the justice of nature." In short, Epicurus is protesting against the conception of injustice which makes it consist in disobedience to political and social rules, imposed and enforced by public and authoritative sanctions. He is protesting, in other words, against the claim of the State upon the citizens for their complete obedience; against the old

ideas of the divine sanctity and majesty of law as law; against theories like that maintained by contemporaries of Socrates, that there could be no such thing as an unjust law.[39]

The Epicurean accepts the existence of an orderly society as a condition of a satisfactory life, but he does not admit that it has a right to demand his services. "When safety on the side of man has been tolerably secured, it is by quiet and by withdrawing from the multitude that the most complete tranquillity is to be found." "A wise man will not enter upon political life unless something extraordinary should occur." "The free man," says Metrodôrus, "will laugh his free laugh over those who are fain to be reckoned in the list with Lycurgus and Solon."[40] A man ought not to make it his aim to save his country, or to win a crown from them for his abilities. Political life, which in all ages has been impossible for those who had not wealth, and who were unwilling to mix themselves with vile and impure associates, was not to the mind of Epicurus. If he be condemned for this, there are many nobler and deeper natures in the records of humanity who must be condemned on the same account. But it is hard to see why he should be charged with that as a fault which is the common practice of mankind, and which in a period of despotism, of absolute monarchy, is the course of obvious wisdom. And, above all, it is not the duty of a philosopher to become a political partisan, and spend his life in the atmosphere of avaricious and malignant passions.

For politics, Epicurus substituted friendship. "Of all the things which wisdom procures for the happiness of life as a whole, by far the greatest is the acquisition of friendship."[41] We have already spoken of the friendship of the Epicureans: a characteristic which did not disappear down to the latest times of the sect. But here, too, Epicurus is true to his realistic and non-mystical creed. Friendship is based upon utility mutually enjoyed: only some one must begin the career of service-rendering, just as we must sow the ground in hopes of a future harvest. Or, as Professor Bain puts it[42]:—"The giver should not expect compensation, and should, nevertheless, obtain it." The same realistic tone is apparent in Epicurus's views on sexual love: where he rejects altogether what in modern times has received the somewhat misleading conventional name of Platonic love.[43] Love, as he remarks, and as Cicero approves, is in the strict sense of the term, not accidentally, but essentially different from affection or friendship. The former is a passion or instinct. The latter is a rational and reflective relation of one human being to another. It is in friendship, freely formed and imposing no inalienable obligation, no binding impersonal law, that man, according to Epicurus, finds his true home. The only duties which he recognises are those voluntarily accepted on reasonable grounds, and not from natural instincts or through the compulsion of circumstances. The family and the State impose permanent checks and obligations which to him seemed to diminish the independence of man, and to make him a slave of external powers. Thus, the principle of community, rejected in its more stable forms, is accepted in its laxest and most flexible shape, where it is maintained solely by participation in pleasures in common. To leave it to such attraction alone seems to expose the communion of man and man too much to chance: it seems to provide too weak a safeguard against the inconstancy and inequality so characteristic of most human feelings. Yet, on the other hand, to maintain an association when it is only a form or bond, and not the genuine birth of a free spirit, seems to be dangerous and immoral. And perhaps Epicurus is right in holding that the best security of permanence in attachment is given not by imposing a yoke on unwilling or at least varying tempers, but by so unifying all the nature of man that his choices and appetencies will not change from day to day, but maintain a uniform tenor through all varieties of circumstance.

In the ethics of the post-Aristotelian schools the sage or wise man plays a prominent part. In his full perfection he is the property of the Stoics, and represents their ideal of what the perfect man ought to be. The Epicureans, however, seem to have followed their example and drawn up an ideal picture, in which the main features exhibit an intentional contrast to the demands of the opposite sect. The wise man, they said, cannot arise in any race whatever, and must possess a well-ordered constitution, for virtue is not enough without certain natural endowments. Once he has attained that rank, he never loses it: once wise, he is wise for ever. But there are various degrees of wisdom, and not one hard-and-fast line of distinction between wise and unwise. The sage is not inaccessible to feelings: he will feel pain, and will cherish compassion. But though pain affects him, it will not deprive him of his happiness: he will moan when put to torture, but still retain his superiority to fate and circumstance. When his dependents misbehave, he will chastise, yet not as if without pity. All sins are not in his eyes of like magnitude: there are degrees in vice, as in virtue. He will not be over-anxious to figure in the public eye even in his own special department as a philosophic teacher. Though he set up a school, he will not care to draw crowds of pupils: it will only be by constraint that he will read in public, and he will rather leave what he has to teach, in his writings, than try to proclaim it in places of general resort. He will not be indifferent to secure for himself a capital for his subsistence, but will keep aloof from commerce, except when in poverty he may be able to earn something by his teaching. The wise man will never fall in love with women, for such love is not heaven-sent. He will neither take a wife nor become the father of a family, except in very special circumstances; nor will he take part in the business of the State, nor seek for fame, except to avoid contempt.

But we need not complete the list of what the sage will or will not do—a list which is full of confusion as it stands, and largely unintelligible. Its last words are:— "He will dogmatize, and not merely raise difficulties. He will be like himself in sleep, and a time may come when he will die for a friend." This incongruous assortment is a specimen of the system and manner with which Diogenes Laertius tells his tale.[44]

We may conclude the remarks on the Ethics of Epicurus by quoting a few of his sayings, mainly taken from Seneca:—

> If you live by nature, you will never be poor: if by opinion, you will never be rich.
>
> Cheerful poverty is an honourable thing.
>
> Great wealth is but poverty when matched with the law of nature.
>
> I said this not to many persons, but only to you: we are a large-enough theatre, one for the other.
>
> You must be a bondman to philosophy, if you wish to gain true freedom.
>
> If any one thinks his own not to be most ample, he may become lord of the whole world, and will yet be wretched.
>
> We ought to select some good man and keep him ever before our eyes, so that we may, as it were, live under his eye, and do everything in his sight.
>
> It is an evil to live in necessity, but there is no necessity to live in necessity.
>
> Among the other ills which attend folly is this: it is always *beginning* to live.
>
> He enjoys wealth most who needs it least.
>
> A foolish life is restless and disagreeable: it is wholly engrossed with the future.
>
> With many the acquisition of riches is not an end to their miseries, but only a change.
>
> We ought to look round for people to eat and drink with, before we look for something to eat and drink: to feed without a friend is the life of a lion and a wolf.
>
> Trust me, your words will sound grander in a common bed and a rough coverlet: they will not be merely spoken then, they will be proved true.
>
> Some people leave life as if they had just entered it.
>
> It is troublesome to be always commencing life.
>
> It is absurd to run to death from weariness of life, when your style of life has forced you to run to death. What so absurd as to court death, when you have made your life restless through fear of death?
>
> Do everything as if Epicurus had his eye upon you. Retire into yourself chiefly at that time when you are compelled to be in a crowd.
>
> Learn betimes to die, or if it like thee better, to pass over to the gods.

The knowledge of sin is the beginning of salvation.

I never wished to please the people: for what I know, the people does not approve; and what the people approves, that I know not.[45]

We are born once: twice we cannot be born, and for everlasting we must be non-existent. But thou, who art not master of the morrow, puttest off the right time. Procrastination is the ruin of life for all; and, therefore, each of us is hurried and unprepared at death.

If thou wilt make a man happy, add not unto his riches, but take away from his desires.[46]

He who is least in need of the morrow will meet the morrow most pleasantly.[47]

Notes

[1] Hume's Essays: "The Epicurean."

[2] Cicero, *De Fin.,* I.7, 26; Plutarch, 1094 E.; Athenæus, XIII. 588.

[3] Seneca, *Epist.,* 90, 35; Plutarch, 1125 C.-1127; Epictetus, *Dissertat.,* II, 20, 20; III. 7, 19.

[4] Seneca, *De Benefic.,* IV. 19.

[5] Lucretius, II.55.

[6] Sext. Emp. *adv. Ethic,* 169.

[7] Cicero, *De Finibus,* I. 7, 22; *Acad.,* II. 29; Diogenes, X. 31.

[8] Diogenes Laertius, X. 24, 51; Ibid., 25, 88.

[9] Lucretius, III, 180.

[10] Diogenes Laertius, X. 24, 38; Lucretius, IV. 478.

[11] Diogenes Laertius, X. 122-135.

[12] Arist., Ethics, IV. 2, &C.

[13] Arist., *Ethics,* II. 2.

[14] Cicero, *Acad. Pr.,* II. 115; *De Fin.,* I. 20 65.

[15] Plato, *Republic,* V. 457.

[16] "The Emotions and the Will," p. 12.

[17] Sermon XI. (On the Love of our Neighbour.)

[18] Plato, *Republic,* IX. 584.

[19] Diogenes Laertius, X. 144. . . .

[20] Diogenes Laertius, X. 6; Plutarch, *Non posse suav.,* XIII. 1.

[21] Sextus Empir., *Adv. Musicos,* c. 27.

[22] Plutarch, *Non posse suav.,* XIII. 1.

[23] Diogenes Laertius, X. 144, 146.

[24] Diogenes, X. 145.

[25] Diogenes, X. 141.

[26] Diogenes Laertius, X. 136.

[27] Cicero, *De Fin.,* II. 20, 63.

[28] The *animus* (Lucret. III. 136 seq.) or *mens* is the reason or intellect; it is superior, and seated in the breast: the *anima,* or sentient soul, is dispersed throughout the body. Both are atomic and corporeal.

[29] Athenæus, VII. 279; Cicero, *De Fin.,* II. 10, 29.

[30] Diogenes, X. 140.

[31] Seneca, *Dialog.,* VII. 12-13.

[32] Athenæus, XII. 546.

[33] "Introduction to the Principles of Morals and Legislation," ch. II. sec. 6.

[34] Diogenes Laertius, X. 140.

[35] "Rechtslehre," 24.

[36] *Inquiry Concerning the Principles of Morals,* III. 1.

[37] Diogenes Laertius, X. 150.

[38] Ibid., X. 151; Plutarch, *Non posse suav.,* XXV. 33.

[39] Cf. Plato, *Crito.;* Xenophon, *Memorab.,* IV. 4.

[40] Plutarch, *Adv. Colot.,* XXXIII. 8.

[41] Diogenes Laertius, X. 148.

[42] *The Emotions and the Will,* p. 299.

[43] *Tuscul, Disp., IV. 70.*

[44] Diogenes Laertius, X. 117-121.

[45] Seneca, *Ep.* 16, 7; 2, 5; 4, 10; 7, 11; 8, 7; 9, 20; 11, 8; 12, 10; 13, 16; 14, 17; 15, 10; 17, 11; 19, 10; 20, 9; 22, 14; 23, 9; 24, 22; 25, 5; 25, 6; 26, 8; 28, 9; 29, 10.

[46] Stobæus, *Florilegium: De Parsimon.*, 28; *De Contint.*, 24.

[47] Plutarch, *De Tranquil. Anim.*, 16.

A. E. Taylor (essay date 1911)

SOURCE: A. E. Taylor, "The Life of Epicurus" and "The Salvation of Man," in *Epicurus*, Constabel & Company Ltd., 1911, pp. 35-79, 80-96.

[*In the following excerpt from his* Epicurus, *Taylor first places Epicurus's biography in the context of Greek culture and history and then presents his view of Epicurus's ethics. Refuting the myth of Epicurus's debauchery, Taylor instead charges the philosopher with "timidity" and "a lack of moral robustness." His biography ends with a summary of the connection between Epicureanism and early Christianity. In his discussion of Epicurean ethics, Taylor contends that they were uniquely democratic, made accessible to the layperson as well as the ruling elite.*]

The Life of Epicurus

When we turn from Plato and Aristotle, the great constructive thinkers of the fourth century before Christ, to the study of the new sects or schools,— that of Epicurus was, in date of foundation, slightly older than the others,—which came into being early in the third century, under the successors of Alexander, we feel at first as if we had passed into a new moral atmosphere.

Philosophy seems to have dwindled from the magnificent attempt to arrive at scientific knowledge of God, man, and nature into a mere theory of conduct, and, in the theory of conduct itself, the old conception of the individual man as essentially a member of a community freely banded together to live the 'good life,' in virtue of which Plato and Aristotle could treat what we call 'ethics' as a mere part of the wider study of society, its aims and institutions (*Politics*), to have given place to a purely individualistic doctrine of morals which has lost the sense of the inseparable union of the civilised man with the civilised society. So keenly has this difference of tone been felt that writers on philosophy have almost always adopted the death of Aristotle as one of those historical land-marks which indicate the ending of an old era, and the beginning of a new, like the English Revolution of 1688 or the French Revolution of 1789. The cause of so great a change has been variously sought in the special conditions of life in the third century. Under the hard pressure of the Macedonian dynasts, it has been said, Philosophy naturally became identical with the theory of conduct, because, in such untoward times, the effort to understand the

world had to be abandoned for the task of making life bearable. The theory of statesmanship shrank into a mere doctrine of morals because with the battle of Chaeronea the free life of the independent city-states came once for all to an end. Others, again, have seen the key to the developments of Philosophy in the third century in a return of Greek thought from the 'idealism' of Plato and Aristotle into the materialism, which, as is alleged, was natural to it. There is an element of truth in these views, but they are none the less, as they stand, thoroughly unhistorical.

It is true, to be sure, that under the Macedonian rulers the ordinary man was cut loose from the immediate participation in public affairs of moment which had been characteristic of the life of the sovereign city-state, and that individualism in ethics is the natural counterpart of cosmopolitanism in public life. It is also true that both the Epicurean and the Stoic systems regarded the theory of the chief good for man and the right rule of life as the culminating achievement of Philosophy, and that both tended, in their doctrine of nature, to revert to views which are curiously reactionary as compared with those of Plato and Aristotle. But it is false to suppose that the death of Aristotle or the appearance of Epicurus as a teacher really marks any solution of historical continuity. From the time of Pythagoras at least Philosophy had always been to the Greek mind what personal religion is to ourselves, a 'way of life,' that is a means to the salvation of the soul, and this conception is no less prominent in Plato and Aristotle, when they are rightly read, than in Epicurus and Zeno. And, with regard to the alleged effects on Philosophy of the disappearance of the old life of the free city-state, it is important to recollect that Aristotle composed his *Politics* under the Macedonian régime, and that the Athens of Pericles had ceased to exist, except as a mere shadow of its former past, before Plato wrote the *Republic*. If any single date can be taken as signalising the end of the old order, it should rather be that of the surrender of Athens to Lysander, or even that of the defeat of Nicias before Syracuse, than that of the collapse of the anti-Macedonian agitation of Demosthenes and Hypereides on the field of Chaeronea.

Similarly the cosmopolitanism and individualism of the Epicurean and Stoic ethics is no new departure, nor even a reaction to the attitude of the 'Sophists' of the fifth century, but a direct continuance of traditions which had never died out. Epicurus is directly connected by a series of discernible though little known predecessors with Democritus, just as Zeno is with Antisthenes and Diogenes. Nor is it true that the third century was a period of intellectual stagnation. It is the age of the foundation of the great Museum and Library at Alexandria, of the development of literary criticism into a craft, of the creation of the organised and systematic study of history and chronology, and the compilation of full and exact observations of natural history in the widest sense of the term. Above all, it is the time to which belong the greatest of the Greek mathematicians, and astronomers, Eudoxus, Euclid, Eratosthenes, Aristarchus of Samos, Apollonius of Perga, Archimedes.

The notion that a century so full of original scientific work was one of intellectual sterility is probably due to a simple historical accident. For the most part the writings of the successors of Plato and Aristotle, as well as those of the early Stoics, happen not to have been preserved to us. Hence we readily tend to forget that the scientific and philosophical work of the Academy and Lyceum was vigorously propagated all through the period in which the new schools were seeking to establish themselves, and that the Stoics, the most important of the new sects, were not merely keenly interested in 'Physics,' but were also devoted to minute researches into Formal Logic, much of which, in the shape in which the Middle Ages have handed it down to us, has been inherited directly from them. Hence we come to look on the indifference to logic and scientific Physics which was characteristic of the temperament of Epicurus as if it was a universal feature of 'Post-Aristotelian' thought, and falsely ascribe to the age what is really true of the man. Of the age it would be much more true to say that it was one of devotion to the advancement of special sciences rather than to the elaboration of fresh general points of view in Philosophy. In this respect it is closely parallel with the middle of our own nineteenth century, when the interest in philosophical speculation which had culminated in the 'absolute Philosophy' of Hegel gave place to absorption in the empirical study of Nature and History.

Having said so much to guard ourselves against a common misunderstanding we may proceed to consider what is known of the personal life and habits of Epicurus. Our chief source of information is the so-called *Life of Epicurus* which forms the last section of the ill-digested serap-book known as the *Lives of the Philosophers* by Laertius Diogenes. (Of additional matter from other sources we have little beyond one or two unimportant letters of Epicurus himself which have been preserved, along with much later Epicurean materials, under the lava which overwhelmed the city of Herculaneum). In its present form the work of Diogenes only dates from the middle of the third century A.D., and, indeed, hardly deserves to be called a 'work' at all, since it can be shown to contain notes which must have been made by generations of successive readers, and seems never to have been subjected to the final revision of a single editor. Its value, for us, depends on the fact that it is largely made up of notices drawn from much more ancient authorities who are often quoted

by name. This is particularly the case with the *Life* of Epicurus which is, in the main, drawn from the statements of Epicurus himself, his intimate friends, and his contemporary opponents, . . . and may thus be taken as, on the whole, a fair representation of what was known or inferred about him by the Alexandrian writers of 'Successions,' or Handbooks to the history of Philosophy, the earliest of whom date from the latter part of the third century B.C. For this reason, and for the sake of giving the reader a specimen of the biographical material available in the study of ancient Philosophy in a specially favourable case, I proceed to give a complete rendering of the strictly biographical part of Diogenes' account of Epicurus from the text of Usener.

'Epicurus, an Athenian, son of Neocles and Chaerestrata, of the township of Gargettus, and of the house of the Philaidae, according to Metrodorus in his work *On Good Birth*. Heracleides, in the *Epitome of Sotion,* and others say that he was brought up in Samos, where the Athenians had made a plantation, and only came to Athens at the age of eighteen when Xenocrates was conducting his school in the Academy and Aristotle at Chalcis (*i.e.* 323/2 B.C.). After the death of Alexander of Macedon and the expulsion of the Athenians by Perdiccas, he followed his father (they say) to Colophon. He spent some while there and gathered disciples round him, and then returned to Athens in the year of Anaxicrates. For a time he pursued Philosophy in association with others; afterwards he established the special sect called by his name and appeared on his own account. He says himself that he first touched Philosophy at the age of fourteen. But Apollodorus the Epicurean says in Bk. I. of his *Life of Epicurus,* that he was led to Philosophy by dissatisfaction with his schoolmasters who had failed to explain to him Hesiod's lines about Chaos. Hermippus says that he had been an elementary schoolmaster himself but afterwards fell in with the books of Democritus and threw himself at once into Philosophy, and that this is why Timon says of him:—

> From the island of Samos the loudest and last
>   Of the swaggering scientists came;
> 'Twas a dominie's brat whose defects in *bon
>   ton*
>   Might have put the creation to shame.

His brothers, too, were converted by him and followed his Philosophy. There were three of them, and their names were Neocles, Charidemus, and Aristobulus, as we are told by Philodemus the Epicurean in his *Compendium of Philosophers,* Bk. x. Another associate was a slave of his called Mys, as Myronianus says in his *Summary of Historical Parallels.* Diotimus the Stoic, who hated him, has calumniated him savagely by producing fifty lewd letters as the work of Epicurus. So has he who collected under the name of Epicurus the correspondence ascribed to Chrysippus. Other calumniators are Poseidonius the Stoic, Nicolaus and Sotion in the twelve books entitled *An Answer to Diocles,* which deal with the observance of the twentieth day of the month, and Dionysius of Halicarnassus. They actually say that he used to accompany his mother on her rounds into cottages, and recite her spells for her, and that he helped his father to teach children their letters for a miserable pittance. Nay, that he played the pimp to one of his brothers, and kept Leontion the courtesan. That he gave out as his own the atomic theory of Democritus and the Hedonism of Aristippus. That he was not a true born Athenian citizen, as we learn from Timocrates and the work on *The Early Years of Epicurus* by Herodotus. That he heaped shameful adulation on Mithres the intendant of Lysimachus, addressing him in correspondence as Gracious Preserver, and My very good Lord. Nay, he even bestowed the same sycophantic flatteries on Idomeneus, on Herodotus, and on Timocrates, who exposed his secret abominations. In his correspondence he writes to Leontion, 'Gracious God, darling Leontion, how your sweet letter set me clapping and cheering when I read it'; and to Themista, the wife of Leonteus, 'If you do not both pay me a visit, I shall prove a very stone of Sisyphus to roll at a push wherever you and Themista invite me'; and to Pythocles, then in the bloom of his youth, 'Here I shall sit awaiting your delightful and divine advent.' In another letter to Themista, according to Theodorus in Bk. IV. of his work *Against Epicurus,* he calls her 'Queen and huntress chaste and fair.'

He corresponded, they allege, with a host of courtesans, particularly with Leontion, with whom Metrodorus also fell in love. Further, in the work **On the Moral End,** he writes: 'For my part I can form no notion of the good if I am to leave out the pleasures of taste and sex, of hearing and of form.' And (they say) in the **letter to Pythocles** he writes, 'For God's sake, crowd on sail and away from all "culture"!' Epictetus calls him a lewd writer and reviles him in round terms. Nay, worse, Timocrates, the brother of Metrodorus, a disciple who had deserted the School, says in his *Paradise of Delights* that Epicurus used to vomit twice a day in consequence of his riotous living, and that he himself escaped by the skin of his teeth from the 'midnight lore' and 'mystical fellowship.' Further, that Epicurus was grossly ignorant of science and even more ignorant of the art of life; that he fell into so pitiable a habit of body as not to be able to rise from his litter for years on end; that he spent a mina a day on his table, as he writes himself to Leontion and to the philosophers at Mytilene. That he and Metrodorus enjoyed the favours of Mammarion, Hedeia, Erotion, Nicidion and other courtesans. That in the thirty-seven books of his treatise on **Nature** he is nearly always repeating himself and transcribing the ideas

of others, especially of Nausiphanes, and says in so many words, 'But enough of this; the fellow's mouth was always in labour with some piece of sophistic bragadoccio, like those of so many others of the slaves.' And Epicurus is charged with having said himself of Nausiphanes in his letters, 'this threw him into such a passion that he started a personal polemic against me, and had the face to call me his scholar.' Indeed he used to call Nausiphanes a 'mollusc,' a 'boor,' a 'quack,' and a 'strumpet.' The Platonists he called 'Dionysius' lickspittles,' and Plato himself 'that thing of gold.' Aristotle, he said, was a rake who ran through his patrimony and then turned mountebank and druggist. Protagoras was styled 'the Porter' and 'Democritus' scrivener,' and reproached with being a village dominie. Heracleitus he called 'the Muddler,' Democritus 'Dumb-ocritus,' Antidorus 'Zany-dorus,' the Cynics 'the national enemy,' the dialecticians 'a general pest,' Pyrrho 'Block' and 'Boor.'

Now all this is stark madness. There are abundant witnesses to his unsurpassed goodwill to all mankind: his native city, which honoured him with statues of bronze; his friends, who were too numerous to be reckoned by whole cities; his followers, who were all held spellbound by the charms of his doctrine—except Metrodorus of Stratonice, who deserted to Carneades, perhaps because he was depressed by his master's unrivalled merits; his school, which has maintained an unbroken existence, though almost all others have had their seasons of eclipse, and has been under a succession of innumerable heads, all of them faithful to the persuasion; his gratitude to his parents, beneficence to his brothers, and the humanity to his servants which may be seen from his will, and from the fact that they shared in his Philosophy, the most notable of them being the aforesaid Mys; in a word, his universal benevolence. As for his piety towards the gods and his native land, words cannot describe them. 'Twas from excess of conscientiousness that he would not so much as touch political life. Consider, too, that though Hellas had then been overtaken by most troublous times, he spent his whole life at home, except that he made one or two flying visits to Ionia to see his friends in that quarter, who, in their turn, flocked from all parts to share the life in his Garden, as we are told particularly by Apollodorus, who adds that he payed eighty minae for the site. The life they led there, so says Diocles in Bk. III. of his *Brief Relation,* was of the simplest and plainest. They were amply content, so he says, with half a pint of *vin ordinaire;* their regular drink was water. Epicurus, he says, disapproved of the community of goods sanctioned by the saying of Pythagoras, 'what belongs to friends is common.' Such a system, he thought, implies distrust, and where there is distrust there can be no true friendship. He says himself in his letters that he can be satisfied with water and coarse bread. And again, 'Pray send me part of a pot of cheese, that I may be able to enjoy a varied table when I am in the mind.' Such was the character of the man who made 'Pleasure the end' an article of his creed. So Athenaeus celebrates him in the following epigram:—

> Alas, we toil for nought; the woful seed
> Of strife and wars is man's insatiate greed:
> True riches harbour in a little space,
> Blind Fancy labours in an endless chase;
> This truth Neocles' deep-considering son
> From heavenly Muse or Pytho's tripod won.

We shall see the truth of this still better, as we proceed, from his own writings and sayings.

Among the ancients, says Diocles, his preference was for Anaxagoras, though he controverted him on some points, and for Archelaus the teacher of Socrates. He says further that he trained his followers to learn his compositions by heart. Apollodorus says in his *Chronology* that he had heard Nausiphanes and Praxiphanes, but he himself denies it in his letter to Eurylochus, where he says he had no master but himself. He even declares (and Hermarchus agrees with him), that there never was any such philosopher as Leucippus whom Apollodorus the Epicurean and others speak of as the teacher of Democritus. Demetrius of Magnesia adds that Epicurus had heard Xenocrates.

His style is plain and matter of fact, and is censured by the grammarian Aristophanes as very tame. But he was so lucid that in his **Rhetoric** he insists on no stylistic quality but lucidity. In correspondence he used 'Farewell' and 'Live worthily' in place of the customary formula of salutation.

Antigonus says in his *Life of Epicurus* that he copied his **Canon** from the *Tripod* of Nausiphanes, and that he had heard not only Nausiphanes but Pamphilus the Platonist in Samos. That he began Philosophy at the age of twelve, and became head of his school at thirty-two.

According to the *Chronology* of Apollodorus he was born in Olympiad 109/3, in the archonship of Sosigenes, on the 7th of Gamelion, seven years after Plato's death. That he first collected a school in Mytilene and Lampsacus at the age of thirty-two. This lasted for five years, at the end of which he migrated, as said, to Athens. His death fell in Olympiad 127/2, in the year of Pytharatus, at the age of seventy-two. He was followed as head of the School by Hermarchus of Mytilene, son of Agemortus. The cause of death was strangury due to calculus, as Hermarchus, too, says in his correspondence. The fatal illness lasted a fortnight. Hermarchus further relates that he entered a brazen bath filled with hot water, called for some neat wine which he took off at a draught, enjoined his friends not to forget his doctrines, and so came to his end. I have composed the following lines upon him:—

> Farewell, my friends; be mindful of my lore;
> Thus Epicurus spoke,—and was no more:
> Hot was the bath, and hot the bowl he
>   quaffed;
> Chill Hades followed on the after-draught.

Such then was the tenour of his life, and the manner of his end. His will runs as follows. [The main provisions are that the 'Garden and its appurtenances' are to be held in trust for the successors of Epicurus, and their associates. A house in the suburb Melite is to be inhabited by Hermarchus and his disciples for the former's lifetime. Provision is made for the due performance of the ritual for the dead in memory of the parents and brethren of Epicurus, for the regular keeping of his birthday, for the regular festival of the twentieth of each month, and for annual commemoration of his brothers and his friend Polyaenus. The son of Metrodorus and the son of Polyaenus are to be under the guardianship of the trustees on condition that they live with Hermarchus and share his Philosophy. The daughter of Metrodorus is to receive a dowry out of the estate on condition that she behaves well and marries with the approval of Hermarchus. Provision is to be made for an aged and needy member of the community. The 'books' of Epicurus, *i.e.* presumably the manuscripts of his works, are bequeathed to Hermarchus. If Hermarchus should die before the children of Metrodorus come of age, they are to be under the guardianship of the trustees. Mys and three other slaves are to receive their freedom.]

The following lines were written to Idomeneus on the very point of death: 'I write these lines to you and your friends as I bring to a close the last happy day of my life. I am troubled with strangury and dysentery in unsurpassable degree, but I can confront it all with a joy of mind due to remembrance of our past discussions. To you I leave the injunction to take care of the children of Metrodorus as befits your lifelong association with me and Philosophy.'

'He had numerous disciples. Specially distinguished were Metrodorus of Lampsacus, son of Athenaeus, (or Timocrates) and Sande, who never left him after making his acquaintance except for one six months' visit to his birthplace, whence he returned to him. He was an excellent man in all respects, as is attested by Epicurus himself in sundry Dedications and in the **Timocrates,** Bk. III. With all these excellences he bestowed his sister Batis on Idomeneus, and took Leontion the Athenian courtesan under his protection as a morganatic wife. He was imperturbable in the face of troubles and death, as Epicurus says in his **Metrodorus,** Bk. I. They say he died in his fifty-third year, seven years before Epicurus. Epicurus himself implies that he had predeceased him by the injunction in the aforesaid will to care for his children. Another was the aforesaid Timocrates, a worthless brother of Metrodorus. [Here follows a list of the works of M.]

'Another was Polyaenus of Lampsacus, son of Athenodorus, according to Philodemus an upright and amiable man. Also Hermarchus of Mytilene, son of Agemortus, who succeeded to the headship of the school. He was born of poor parents, and originally a teacher of rhetoric by profession. The following admirable works are ascribed to him. [The list follows.] He was an able man and died of a palsy.

'*Item,* Leonteus of Lampsacus and his wife Themista, the same with whom Epicurus corresponded. *Item,* Colotes and Idomeneus, both of Lampsacus. These are the most eminent names. We must include Polystratus who followed Hermarchus, and was succeeded by Dionysius, and he by Basileides. Apollodorus, the 'despot of the Garden,' who composed over four hundred books, is also a man of note. Then there are the two Ptolemies of Alexandria, the dark and the fair; Zeno of Sidon, a pupil of Apollodorus and a prolific author; Demetrius, surnamed the Laconic; Diogenes of Tarsus, the author of the *Selected Essays*; Orion; and some others whom the genuine Epicureans decry as Sophists.

'There were also three other persons of the name Epicurus: (1) the son of Leonteus and Themista, (2) an Epicurus of Magnesia, (3) a *maître d'armes*. Epicurus was a most prolific author.' [Follows a list of his works, and the writer then proceeds to give a summary of his doctrine.]'

The proceding pages have given us a fairly full account of the life and personality of Epicurus as known to the students of antiquity. I may supplement it with a few remarks intended to make the chronology clear, and to call attention to one or two of the salient points in the character which it discloses to us.

First as to chronology. Of the authorities used in the *Life* far the best is Apollodorus, whose versified *Chronology* embodied the results of the great Eratosthenes. His data make it clear that Epicurus was born on the 7th of Gamelion (*i.e.* in our January) 341 B.C., and died in 270 B.C. They also enable us to fix his first appearance as an independent teacher in Mytilene and the neighbourhood, approximately in 310, and his removal to Athens in 306/5 B.C. We may take it also as certain, from other sources as well as from the evidence of Timon, that the place of Epicurus' birth was the island of Samos, where a colony or plantation was established by the Athenians in the year 352/1, Neocles, the father of Epicurus, being, as we learn from Strabo, one of the settlers. When the Athenians were expelled from Samos by the regent Perdiccas in 322, Neocles for unknown reasons preferred emigrating to the Ionian town of Colophon to returning to Athens, and Epicurus

followed him. The assertion of his enemies that he was no true Athenian citizen (this would be *their* way of explaining his lifelong abstention from public affairs), may have no better foundation than the fact of his birth at a distance from Athens, or, again, may be explained by supposing that Neocles had some special connection with the Ionic cities of the Asiatic coast. In any case the salient points to take note of are that Epicurus must have received his early education in Samos (itself an Ionian island), and that his philosophical position had been definitely settled before he left Asia Minor to establish himself at Athens. This will account for the attitude of aloofness steadily maintained by the society of the 'Garden' towards the great indigenous Athenian philosophical institutions, and also for the marked Ionicisms of Epicurus' technical terminology. It is clear from the narratives preserved by Diogenes that the family of Neocles was in straitened circumstances, but there is no more ground to take the polemical representation of Neocles and his wife as a hedge dominie and village sorceress seriously than there is to believe the calumnies of Demosthenes on the parents of Aeschines. That Neocles was an elementary schoolmaster may, however, be true, since it is asserted by the satirist Timon, who belongs to the generation immediately after Epicurus, and the schoolmaster, as we see from the *Mimes* of Herodas, was not a person of much consideration in the third century. With regard to the date of the establishment of Epicurus at Athens one should note, by way of correcting erroneous impressions about 'Post-Aristotelian Philosophy,' that when Epicurus made his appearance in the city which was still the centre of Greek intellectual activity, Theophrastus, the immediate successor of Aristotle, had not completed half of his thirty-four years' presidency over the Peripatetic school, and Xenocrates, the third head of the Academy, and an immediate pupil of Plato, had only been dead some eight years. The illusion by which we often think of the older schools as having run their course before Epicurus came to the front may be easily dispelled by the recollection that Epicurus's chief disciples, Metrodorus, Hermarchus, Colotes, all wrote special attacks on various Platonic dialogues, and that Hermarchus moreover wrote a polemic against Aristotle and Epicurus himself one against Theophrastus, while, as we shall see later, we still possess a 'discourse of Socrates' in which an anonymous member of the Academy sharply criticises Epicurus as the author of superficial doctrines which are just coming into vogue with the half-educated.

With regard to the personal character of Epicurus one or two interesting things stand out very clearly from the conflicting accounts of admirer like the original writer of the main narrative which figures in Diogenes, and again Lucretius, and enemies, like the detractors mentioned by Diogenes, or unfriendly critics like Plutarch and his Academic authorities. We may disregard altogether the representation of Epicurus and his associates as sensualists who ruined their constitutions by debauchery. There is abundant testimony, not solely from Epicurean sources, for the simplicity of the life led in the Garden, not to say that most of the calumnious stories are discredited by the fact that the worst of them were told by personal or professional enemies like Timocrates, the Judas of the society, and the Stoic philosopher who palmed off a fictitious 'lewd correspondence' on the world under the name of Epicurus. Abuse of this kind was a regular feature of controversy, and deserves just as much credit as the accusations of secret abominations which Demosthenes and Aeschines flung at each other, that is to say, none at all. What we do see clearly is that Epicurus was personally a man of clinging and winning temperament, quick to gain friendship and steadfast in keeping it. There is something of a feminine winsomeness about his solicitude for the well-being of his friends and their children, and the extravagant gratitude which the high-flown phrases quoted from his letters show for the minor officers of friendship. At the same time Epicurus and his 'set' exhibit the weaknesses natural to a temperament of this kind. Their horror of the anxieties and burdens of family life, their exaggerated estimate of the misery which is caused in human life by fear of death and the possibilities of a life to come . . . testify to a constitutional timidity and a lack of moral robustness. The air of the Garden is, to say the least of it, morally relaxing; one feels in reading the remains of Epicurus and Metrodorus that one is dealing with moral invalids, and that Nietzsche was not far from the truth when he spoke of Epicurus as the first good example in history of a 'decadent.' Partly we may explain the fact by the well-attested physical invalidism of the founders of the school. Epicurus, as we see from Diogenes, though he lived to a decent age, was for years in feeble health, and it is significant that Metrodorus and Colotes, two of his chief disciples, died before him at a comparatively early age. We shall probably find the key at once to the Epicurean insistence on the life of simple and homely fare, and to the violence with which, as we shall see, he and his friends insisted on the value of the 'pleasures of the belly,' to the great scandal of their later critics, in the assumption that they were life-long dyspeptics. (The ancients simply inverted the order of causation when they observed that the bad health of Epicurus and Metrodorus might be regarded as God's judgment on the impiety of their tenets.)

The ugliest feature in the character of Epicurus, as revealed in his life and remains, is his inexcusable ingratitude to his teachers, and his wholesale abuse of all the thinkers who had gone before him. This tone of systematic detraction was taken up by his friends; the quotations given in Plutarch's Essay against Colotes are a perfect mine of scurrilities directed against every eminent thinker of the past or the present who had in any way strayed from the path of rigid orthodoxy as understood by Epicurus. There can be no doubt that the object of all this abuse was to make Epicurus appear, as he claimed to be, no man's pupil but his own, the one and only revealer of the way of salvation. And yet it is quite clear, as we shall see, that Epicurus is in every way the least independent of the philosophers of antiquity. There is no reason to doubt that he had originally been instructed in Samos by a member of the Platonic school, and the bitterness with which the Academy afterwards attacked his character and doctrines may, as has been suggested, have been partly due to the sense that he was, in some sort, an apostate from the fold. His treatment of the teachers from whom he had learned the Atomism which has come to be thought of as his characteristic doctrine is absolutely without excuse.

We shall see [later] that the whole doctrine is a blundering perversion of the really scientific Atomism of a much greater man, Democritus, and that Epicurus had undoubtedly derived his knowledge of the doctrine from Nausiphanes, a philosopher whose importance we are only now beginning to learn from the Herculaneum papyri. Yet both Democritus and Nausiphanes are, on the showing of Epicurus' own admirers, covered by him with the coarsest abuse, and one may even suspect that we have to thank Epicurean anxiety to conceal the dependence of the adored master on his teacher for the fact that until Herculaneum began to yield up its secrets, Nausiphanes was no more than an empty name to us. This vulgar self-exaltation by abuse of the very persons to whom one is indebted for all one's ideas distinguishes Epicurus from all the other Greek thinkers who have made a name for themselves, Plato is almost overanxious to mark his debt to his Pythagorean teachers, and the way in which he does so, by putting discoveries of his own into the mouth of the Pythagorean astronomer Timaeus, has played sad havoc with the histories of Greek science. Aristotle has undoubtedly rather more self-importance then is good for most men, but even he stops short at regarding his own system as the final philosophy towards which his predecessors were unconsciously progressing. It was reserved for Epicurus to put forward a clumsy amalgam of inconsistent beliefs, and to trust to bluster to conceal the sources of his borrowings.

A few words may be said here as to the amount of the extant remains of Epicurean literature, and the later fortune of the School. Of the actual works of Epicurus the whole has perished, apart from scattered fragments preserved in quotations of later authors, mostly unfriendly. We possess, however, two undoubtedly genuine letters, one to Herodotus on the general principles of Epicurean Atomism, and another to Menoeceus containing a summary of ethical teaching, both inserted in Diogenes' *Life*. The *Life* also contains two other documents, purporting to be by Epicurus, (1) a **letter to Pythocles** on astronomy and meteorology, and (2) a set of . . . *Select Apophthegms* forming a brief catechism of the main points of the doctrine.

The accuracy of the first of these is evinced by its close agreement with what we are told by later authors of the physical doctrine of Epicurus, particularly with the corresponding sections of the poem of Lucretius. This letter cannot possibly be a genuine work of Epicurus, and we know from Philodemus that even in his own time (first century B.C.) its authenticity was doubted. It is pretty certainly an excerpt made by some early Epicurean from the voluminous lost work on *Physics* and thrown into epistolary form in imitation of the two genuine letters. As to the second document, it was known to Philodemus and Cicero under its present title, and appears, as Usener holds, to be an early compendium made up of verbal extracts of what were considered the most important statements in the works of Epicurus and his leading friends. There are also a large number of moral apophthegms either quoted as Epicurean or demonstrably of Epicurean authorship embedded in Cicero, Seneca, Plutarch, Porphyry, the Anthology of Stobaeus and elsewhere. Usener has shown that the chief source of these sayings must have been an epitome of the correspondence between Epicurus and his three chief friends, Metrodorus, Polyaenus, and Hermarchus, the four recognised καθηγεμανες or 'doctors' of the sect. From later Epicureans we have the great poem of Lucretius who can be shown in general to have followed his master very closely, though in what strikes a modern reader as his highest scientific achievement, his anticipations of the doctrine of the evolution of species, he is probably reproducing not Epicurus but his own poetical model Empedocles. The excavation of Herculaneum, and the subsequent decipherment of the papyri found there, has also put us in possession of a great deal of very second-rate stuff from the hand of Philodemus.

A word as to the subsequent fate of the School. The two chief characteristics of the sect, as remarked by the ancients, were the warmth of the friendship subsisting between its members, and their absolute unity of opinion, which last, however, had its bad side, since, as the ancients complain, the chief reason of the absence of controversies is that the Epicureans read nothing but the works of Epicurus and the καθηγεμανες, and treat them as infallible scriptures, even being expected to learn the *Catechism* by heart. A third peculiarity was the almost idolatrous adoration paid to the founder who, as we see from Lucretius, was regarded as all but divine, as the one and only man who had redeemed the race from universal misery by pointing out the path to true happiness.

It has been remarked that the Epicurean society in many ways is more like the early Christian Church than it is like a scientific school. Thus (1) it is not so much a band of thinkers as a group of persons united by a common rule of life. (We must remember, however, that this 'religious' side to the association between the members of a 'school' belong equally to Pythagoreanism and Platonism.) (2) Like the Christians, the Epicureans are primarily united by the 'love of the brethren,' and by a common devotion to a personal founder who is regarded rather as a Redeemer from misery than as an intellectual teacher (though here, too, we must not forget that Pythagoras was equally to his early disciples a divine or semidivine Redeemer, with the difference that with them it was largely by revealing scientific truth that he was believed to have effected the redemption). (3) Like the Church, the Epicurean society is indifferent to differences of nationality, sex, social status. (4) As Wallace says, the correspondence of Epicurus and his friends mixes up high speculative theories with homely matters of every-day life, such as the regulation of diet, in a way which is equally characteristic of the New Testament. (5) Epicureanism has also its analogue to the Christian 'love-feasts' in the monthly common meals which are provided for by Epicurus in his will. Similarly his concern for the children of Metrodorus and for the support of needy and aged brethren reminds us of the care of the early Christians for the 'poor saints,' the widows, and the orphans. The two societies also correspond on their unfavourable side, in what has always been the great intellectual sin of the Church, undue readiness to treat its formulae as infallible and exempt from all examination. The Epicurean who read nothing but the καθηγεμανες is the prototype of those modern Christians who read nothing but the Bible and the approved commentaries, and regard criticism and free inquiry as the work of the devil. If the Philosophy of the Garden had ever become a widely diffused and influential theory of conduct, it must necessarily have plunged the ancient world into the same conflict between 'science' and 'religion' of which we hear too much today.

These analogies—though most of them can be to some extent found in other philosophical schools—make it all the more interesting to note that the Epicureans and the Christians, though representing diametrically opposite types of thought, met on common ground as being the only sects who openly repudiated the established religion and scoffed at its apparatus of public ceremonial. The Sceptic avoided the collision easily enough. Precisely because he held that unreasoning faith is involved in all judgements he felt no call to deny the theological belief of his fellows. The Platonist and the Stoic stood to a large extent on common ground with popular religion in their devotion to their belief in Providence and the moral government of the world, to which the Platonist added a fervid faith in Theism and immortality: like Broad Churchmen to-day, they could always acquiesce in the details of popular religion by putting a non-natural interpretation on everything which, in its plain sense, seemed objectionable or absurd. But the Epicurean was cut off from these expedients by the fact that it was one of his cardinal doctrines that 'the gods' exercise no influence on human affairs, as the Christian was by his belief that they were 'idols' or even devils who could not be worshipped without blasphemy against the true God. Not that the Epicureans, like the Christians, refused to take part in the public ceremonial of worship. Philodemus expressly appeals to the exemplary conduct of Epicurus himself on this point. But they made no secret of their scorn for the popular belief in Providence, prayer, and retribution, and hence no amount of external compliance could clear them from the charge of atheism with persons for whom religion was a vital affair. Lucian (second century A.D.) illustrates the point amusingly in his account of the ritual instituted by the charlatan Alexander of Aboni Teichos who set up an oracle which gained great repute and was even once formally consulted by the Emperor Marcus. Among other things, Alexander started a mystical ceremonial from which he used formally to exclude all 'infidels, Christians, and Epicureans.' In the course of the worship he used to cry, 'Away with the Christians!' the congregation giving the response, 'Away with the Epicureans!' the Christians and Epicureans being the two bodies who were persistently infidel from Alexander's point of view. Lucian adds that Alexander solemnly burned the works of the objectionable teacher, and that it was an Epicurean who first exposed the fraudulent trickery of his oracle, and narrowly escaped being lynched by the devout mob for doing so.

Much earlier, probably about 200 B.C., there appear to have been actual persecutions, and perhaps even martyrdoms, of Epicureans in various Greek cities, and we know that works were published in the style of the religious tracts of our own day, relating the judgments of Heaven on Epicureans and their miraculous conversions.

As to the internal history of the sect there is not much to be said, since, as we have seen, they were too indifferent to speculation to make any important innovations on the original teaching of the 'doctors,' though, as we have yet to see, there was at least some attempt to lay the foundations of an Inductive Method in logic. The School continued to flourish as a distinct sect well down into the third century after Christ. The names of a number of prominent Epicureans of the first century B.C. are well known to us from Cicero, who had himself attended the lectures of two of them, Phaedrus and Zeno of Sidon. (It should be mentioned that before Cicero's time the house of Epicurus in Melite had fallen into ruins and the gardens of the philosophical sects had been ruined in the cruel siege of Athens by Sulla.)

When Greek philosophy began to make its appearance in Rome itself the first system to be so transferred was the Epicurean. Cicero mentions as the first Latin writers on Epicureanism Gaius Amafinius (*Tusculan Disputations,* iv. 6) and Rabirius (*Academics,* i. 5), and speaks vaguely of their being followed by many others. He finds much fault both with the literary style of these writers and with the want of arrangement in their works, but says that the doctrine made rapid headway owing to its unscientific character and apparent simplicity. It is not clear whether these Latin prose works were earlier or later than the great poem of Lucretius. Lucretius, according to St. Jerome, lived from 94 to 53 B.C., wrote his poem in the intervals of an insanity brought on by a love-potion, and ended by his own hand. The poem was polished up by Cicero. A comparison with Donatus's *Life of Virgil* shows that Jerome's dates are a few years out, and that the real dates for the poet's birth and death should probably be 99/98-55 B.C. The meaning of the remark about Cicero is probably that Cicero edited the poem for circulation after the author's death. Munro has shown that the Cicero meant is pretty certainly the famous Marcus, and the fact of his connection with the work is made all the more likely since the only contemporary allusion to it occurs in a letter from Marcus to his brother Quintus, then serving on Caesar's staff in Britain and Gaul, written early in the year 54 (*Epp. ad Quintum Fratrem,* ii. 11). The 'editing' cannot have been at all carefully done, as the poem is notoriously in a most disjointed state. According to the manuscripts Cicero tells his brother that it is a work exhibiting both genius and art (which is, in fact, the case), but most modern editors make him underrate the poem by inserting a negative with one or other of the two clauses. The influence of Lucretius on the poets of the Augustan age, such as Virgil, Ovid, Manilius, belongs to the history of literature, not to that of philosophy.

To the same general period as Lucretius belongs Philodemus from whom so many fragments have been discovered in the rolls brought from Herculaneum, and who lived under the protection of Cicero's enemy L. Calpurnius Piso, the father-in-law of Caesar. Another well-known Roman Epicurean is Titus Pomponius Atticus, the life-long friend and correspondent of Cicero. Gaius Cassius Longinus, the real author of the conspiracy against Caesar, is also said to have belonged to the sect, to which, it must be owned, he did no credit. Horace's profession of Epicureanism is well known, though we may be sure that his interest in the system was confined to its ethical side. A later and greater writer who, without being a member of any sect, was largely in sympathy with the spirit of the Epicureans and shared their veneration for Epicurus as the deliverer of mankind from degrading superstition, is Lucian of Samosata (second century A.D.). There is some evidence that the popularity of the doctrine was augmented in the second century of our era. Plutarch and Galen, in this century, found it worth while to revive the polemic against Epicurus which had been originated in his own lifetime by Plato's Academy, and steadily kept up until it took a Latin dress in the ridicule which Cicero's Academic and Stoic characters are made to pour on the School in his philosophical dialogues. When the Emperor Marcus endowed the chairs of Philosophy at Athens at the expense of the state, Epicureanism, as well as Platonism, Aristotelianism and Stoicism figured among the state-supported doctrines.

Naturally enough, as the Christian Church became more powerful and more dogmatic, it found itself in violent conflict with the anti-theological ideas of Epicurus, and such writers as Lactantius (end of third century A.D. made him a special object of invective, thereby unconsciously contributing to increase our stock of Epicurean fragments. By the middle of the fourth century the School had fallen into oblivion, and the Emperor Julian (reigned 360-363 A.D.) congratulates himself on the fact that most even of their books are no longer in circulation. Towards the end of the century St. Augustine declares that even in the pagan schools of rhetoric their opinions had become wholly forgotten. (*Epist.*, 118, 21).

. . . . .

The Salvation of Man

We come now to the central citadel of Epicurean doctrine, the part which, as Epicurus holds, gives all the rest its value—the theory of human conduct, variously styled by him the doctrine of *Lives,* of *Ends,* of *Choice and Avoidance*. Here again we shall find the attempt to replace high and difficult ideals by some more homely and apparently more easily compassed end of action. Epicurus wants a principle of conduct which is not for the elect few only, but can be immediately understood and felt by the common man. Like many moralists before and after him, he thinks he finds what he wants in the notion of pleasure as the only good and pain as the only evil. The Platonic conception of life as 'becoming like unto God,' the Aristotelian identification of the best life with one in which, by means of science, art, religious contemplation, we put off the burden of our mortality, may be inspiring to the chosen few, but to the plain average man these are noble but shadowy ideas. And for what is shadowy the prosaic Epicurus has no taste. 'The consecration and the poet's dream' are to him empty nothings. 'I call men,' he writes in one letter, 'to continual pleasures, not to empty and idle virtues which have but a confused expectation of fruit' (*Fr.* 116); and in another place, 'I spit on the noble and its idle admirers, when it contains no element of pleasure' (*Fr.* 512). But pleasure and pain are things we all know by immediate experience, and what could seem a simpler basis for conduct than the rule that pleasure is good and pain bad? So Epicurus seeks once more to bring down moral philosophy from

heaven to earth by reverting to Hedonism. The naturalness of the view that pleasure is the only ultimate good, says Epicurus, borrowing an argument from Plato's pupil Eudoxus, is shown by the spontaneity with which all animals seek it. 'His proof that pleasure is the end is that animals delight in it from their birth and object to pain spontaneously, independently of any process of education.' Like other Hedonists, he has been roundly abused for degrading morality by his doctrine, but some of the abuse at least may be pronounced undeserved. When we consider how many philosophies and religions have done their best to make life miserable by representing the tormenting of ourselves and others as admirable in itself, we may feel that some credit is owing to any man who is not afraid to maintain that happiness is itself a good thing, and that to be happy is itself a virtue. And, as we shall see, Epicurus does not in the least mean that the best life is that of the voluptuary. He taught and enforced by his example the doctrine that the simple life of plain fare and serious contemplation is the true life of pleasure, and in the main, with one great exception, the practical code of action he recommends does not differ much from that of the ordinary decent man. The main objection to his Hedonism is a theoretical one; as he regards the feeling of pleasure as the only good, he is bound to deny that virtue or beauty has any moral value except as a necessary means to pleasure, and thus his ethics, while demanding an innocent and harmless life, can afford no inspiration to vigorous pursuit of Truth or Beauty, or strenuous devotion to the social improvement of man's estate. The air of the Garden is relaxing; it is a forest of Arden where nothing more is required than to 'fleet the time carelessly.' There is a touch of moral invalidism about the personality of a teacher who could declare that 'the noble, the virtuous, and the like should be prized if they cause pleasure; if they do not, they should be left alone' (*Fr.* 70). To be more precise, in saying that pleasure is the good, Epicurus is not telling us anything new. Hedonism as a moral theory is dealt with in Plato's *Protagoras,* had been advocated by Democritus, and expressly put forward within the Academy itself by Eudoxus.

What does look at first sight more original is the way in which Epicurus conceives of the highest pleasure attainable by man. He holds the curious view that, though pleasure is a positive thing not to be confounded with mere absence of pain, yet the moment pain is entirely expelled from the mind and body we have already attained the maximum degree of pleasure. Any further increase in the pleasure-giving stimulus, according to Epicurus, can only make pleasure more variegated, not increase its intensity. 'The (upper) limit of pleasures in magnitude is the expulsion of all pain. Where pleasure is present, and so long as it is present, pain and grief are, singly and conjointly, non-existent' (*Catechism*, 3). 'Pleasure receives no further augmentation in the flesh after the pain of want has once been expelled; it admits merely of variegation' (*ib.* 18). The source of this pessimistic estimate of the possibilities of pleasure is patent; the doctrine comes from Plato's *Philebus*. Plato had taught that the satisfactions of appetite are never purely pleasurable; they are 'mixed' states, half-pleasurable, half-painful. They depend for their pleasantness upon a pre-existing painful state of want, and the process of satisfaction only continues so long as the pain of the want is not completely assuaged, but still remains in the total experience as a stimulus to go on seeking more and more satisfaction. The 'true' pleasures—*i.e.* those which do not depend for their attractiveness on the concealed sting of unsatisfied want—belong to the mind, not to the body. It is to meet this depreciation of the everyday pleasures of satisfying bodily appetite that Epicurus declares the complete expulsion of pain and want to be already the maximum attainable degree of pleasure, and denies the existence of the 'mixed' experiences. The *alma voluptas* of his school thus comes to mean a life of permanent bodily and mental tranquillity, free from disquieting sensations and from the anticipation of them—a view which he has merely taken over from Democritus, who spoke of εὐθυμία, 'cheerfulness of temper,' as the true end of life. What he has done is simply to express the Democritean theory in a terminology specially intended to mark dissent from the Platonic and Aristotelian doctrine. His own words are: 'The end of all our actions is to be free from pain and apprehension. When once this happens to us, the tempest in the soul becomes a calm, and the organism no longer needs to make progress to anything which it lacks, or to seek anything further to complete the good for soul and body. For we only need pleasure so long as the absence of it causes pain. As soon as we cease to be in pain we have no need of further pleasure. This is why we call pleasure the beginning and end of the happy life. It is recognised by us as our primal and connatural good, and is the original source of all choice and avoidance, and we revert to it when we make feeling the universal standard of good. [*Eudoxus.*] Now it is *because* this is our primal and connatural good that we do not choose to have every pleasure, but sometimes pass by many pleasures when a greater inconvenience follows from them, and prefer many pains to pleasures when a greater pleasure follows from endurance of the pain. Every pleasure then is a good, as it has the specific character of the good [*i.e.* to attract us for its own sake], but not every pleasure is to be chosen; so also every pain is an evil, but not every pain should be always avoided' (*Ep.* iii., p. 62, Usener). Hence he differs from his Cyrenaic contemporaries, who preached a robuster type of Hedonism, in three points. (1) The *end* of the individual action is not the pleasure of the *moment,* but a permanent lifelong condition of serene happiness. So, unlike Aristippus, he does not accept the doctrine of taking no thought for the morrow, but says 'we must remember that the future is neither

wholly our own, nor wholly not our own, that we may neither await it as certain to be, nor despair of it as certain not to be' (*Ep.* iii., Usener, p. 62). (2) Epicurus insists strongly that pleasures are not all 'transitions' from one condition to another; besides the pleasures of transition there are κατᾱστημᾱτικαὶ ἡδοναί, pleasures of repose, a point which had already been made by Plato and Aristotle. He says: 'Freedom from mental disquietude and from pain are pleasures of repose; joy and delight we regard as activities of change' (*Fr.* 2). Hence he is often wrongly classed among those who regard *mere* freedom from pain as the highest good. (3) He definitely gives the preference to pleasures of mind over pleasures of body, arguing that 'in bodily pain the flesh is tormented merely by the present, but in mental pain the soul is distressed on account of the present, the past, and the future. Similarly mental pleasures are greater than bodily' (*Fr.* 452). They are greater, that is, because they include the memory of past and the anticipation of future happiness. Indeed, Epicurus carried this doctrine to the point of paradox, saying that a 'sage' would be happy on the rack, since his pleasant recollections of the past would outweigh his bodily sufferings (*Fr.* 601). Later writers like Seneca are never tired of making merry over the Epicurean 'sage' who must be able to say, even while he is being roasted alive, 'How delightful this is! How I am enjoying myself!' Epicurus, as we have seen, illustrated the doctrine practically by the serenity of his last painful days. But, as the Academic critics are careful to remind us, we must recollect that all the mental pleasures of memory and anticipation, to which Epicurus attributes such value, are resoluble into the recollection or anticipation of pleasurable experiences which are themselves analysable into sensations, and therefore corporeal.

As we should expect, Epicurus is never tired of denouncing all ascetic views about the pleasures of bodily appetite. He insists *ad nauseam* that man has a body as well as a soul, and that the happy life is impossible if we neglect the claims of the body. He and his friends often put the point in coarse and vigorous language, which scandalised persons of refined turn of mind. Metrodorus said in a letter to his brother Timocrates, 'The doctrine of nature is wholly concerned with the belly' (*Fr.* 39), and Epicurus that 'the beginning and root of all good is the pleasure of the belly, and even wisdom and culture depend on that' (*Fr.* 67). Metrodorus, probably using a formula devised by his master, asks 'what else is the good of the soul but a permanent healthy condition of the flesh, and a confident expectation of its continuance?' (*Fr.* 5), a definition which is a perpetual subject for denunciation by the Academic critics. The real meaning of sayings like these is more innocent than it looks to be. Epicurus is, after all, only saying in exaggerated language, that even a philosopher cannot afford to neglect his digestion. The fact that both he and Metrodorus were confirmed dyspeptics goes far to explain the vehemence of their language about the 'pleasures of the belly.' Carlyle might easily have said the same sort of thing, and Dr. Johnson, who was far from being a voluptuary, actually did.

More open to attack was Epicurus' trick of abstracting from the whole concrete experience of the satisfactions of virtuous action, and asserting that the pleasure which accompanies the right act is the end to which the act itself is merely a means. This leads him to the utilitarian view that if you could only escape the painful consequences which attend on indulgence in a pleasant vice, the vice would no longer be bad. 'If the things which give rise to the pleasures of the profligate could deliver our understanding from its fears about celestial portents, and death, and future suffering, and could also teach us to limit our desires, we should have no reason left to blame them' (10 of the *Catechism*). This is, of course, a conscious contradiction of the famous Platonic doctrine, that to have a bad soul is itself the worst penalty of sin. Epicurus, however, holds that this separation of vice from its attendant consequences is not actually possible. The pleasures of sin are always attended by the fear of detection and punishment, and often by other disagreeable consequences. Also they cannot teach us to limit our desires, and thus escape the torment of unsatisfied passion. Nor can they, like science, dispel the fear of death or divine judgment. This, and not any inherent badness in them, is why they must not be admitted into our lives. The true conditions of a happy life are two: (1) the assurance that all consciousness ends with death, and that God takes no interest in our doings; (2) the reduction of our desires to those which cannot be suppressed and are most easily satisfied; the simple life. Epicurus accordingly recognises that there are three classes of pleasures: (1) those which are natural and necessary, *i.e.* those which come from the satisfaction of wants inseparable from life, such as the pleasure of drinking when thirsty; (2) those which are natural but not necessary, *e.g.* the pleasures of a variegated diet, which merely diversify the satisfaction of our natural appetites; (3) those which are neither necessary nor natural, but created by human vanity, such as the pleasure of receiving marks of popular esteem, 'crowns' and 'garlands,'—as we might say, knighthoods and illuminated addresses. The wise man despises the last class, he needs the first, the second he will enjoy on occasion, but will train himself to be content without them. (The basis of this classification is Plato's distinction, in the *Philebus,* between 'necessary' and 'unnecessary' bodily pleasures. The sensualism of Epicurus compels him to take no account of Plato's 'pure' or 'unmixed' pleasures, such as those which arise from the performance of noble deeds, or the pursuit of beauty and truth for their own sakes.)

Epicurus, then, looks on the simple diet not as necessary in itself to happiness, but as useful by keeping us from feeling the lack of delicacies which cannot be procured. 'We regard self-sufficiency as a great good, not that we may live sparingly in all circumstances, but that when we cannot have many good things we may be content with the few we have, in the fixed conviction that those who feel the least need of abundance get the greatest enjoyment out of it' (*Ep.* iii., Usener, p. 63). Thus in practice the Epicurean ideal comes to be satisfaction with the simplest necessaries of life, and Epicurus could say (*Catechism,* 15), 'natural riches are limited in extent and easy to procure, while those of empty fancy are indefinite in their compass'; and again (*Fr.* 602), 'give me plain water and a loaf of barley-bread, and I will dispute the prize of happiness with Zeus himself.' So enemies of the theories of the school often praise its practical counsels. As Seneca says, 'my own judgment, however distasteful it may be to the adherents of our school [*i.e.* the Stoics], is that the rules of Epicurus are virtuous and right, and, on a clear view, almost austere; he reduces pleasure to a small and slender compass, and the very rule we prescribe to virtue he prescribes to pleasure; he bids it *follow Nature.*' Even of the tortures of disease he holds that they cannot disturb true happiness. If severe, they are brief; if prolonged, they are interrupted by intervals of relief.

In practice, then, though not in theory, Epicurus refuses to separate pleasure and virtue. 'You cannot live pleasantly without living wisely and nobly and justly, nor can you live wisely and nobly and justly without living pleasantly. Where any one of these conditions is absent pleasurable life is impossible' (*Catechism,* 5).

In respect of the details of his scheme of virtues, Epicurus is enough of a true Greek to give the first place to φρανησις, *wisdom, reasonable* life. 'He who says that it is not yet time for Philosophy, or that the time for it has gone by, is like one who should say that the season for happiness has not yet come, or is over. So Philosophy should be followed by young and old alike: by the old that in their age they may still be young in good things, through grateful memory of the past; by the young that they may be old in their youth in their freedom from fear of the future' (*Ep.* iii., Usener, p. 59). 'When we say that pleasure is the end, we do not mean the pleasures of the profligate, nor those which depend on sensual indulgence, as some ignorant or malicious misrepresenters suppose, but freedom from bodily pain and mental unrest. For it is not drinking and continual junketing, nor the enjoyments of sex, nor of the delicacies of the table which make life happy, but sober reasoning which searches into the grounds of all choice and avoidance, and banishes the beliefs which, more than anything else, bring disquiet into the soul. And of all this the foundation and chiefest good is wisdom. Wisdom is even more precious than Philosophy herself; and is the mother of all other intellectual excellences' (*Ep.* iii., Usener, p. 64).

Of all the fruits of Philosophy the chief is the acquisition of true friendship. 'Of all that Philosophy furnishes towards the blessedness of our whole life far the greatest thing is the acquisition of friendship' (*Catechism,* 27). The solitary life is for Epicurus, as for Aristotle, no life for a man who means to be happy. He would have agreed with some recent writers that the highest good we know is to be found in personal affection. We have already seen how closely analogous the Epicurean organisation, bound together by no tie but the personal affection of its members, was to the early Christian Church, in which also love for the brethren replaces the old Hellenic devotion to the 'city' as the principle of social unity. Hence it is not surprising that Epicurus, like Our Lord, is credited with the saying that it is more blessed to give than to receive. In his attitude towards the State Epicurus naturally represents a view antithetic to that of Plato and Aristotle, who insisted upon common service to the 'city' as the basis of all social virtue. Unlike Aristotle, who teaches that man is by his very constitution a 'political animal,' a being born to find his highest good in the common life provided by the community into which he comes at birth, Epicurus revives the old sophistic distinction between the 'natural' and the 'conventional,' taking the purely conventional view as to the origin of political society and the validity of its laws. Societies are merely institutions created by compacts devised by men to secure themselves against the inconveniences of mutual aggression. 'Natural justice,' he says, 'is an agreement based on common interest neither to injure nor to be injured.' 'Injustice is not an evil in itself, but because of the fear caused by uncertainty whether we shall escape detection by the authorities appointed to punish such things.' 'It is impossible for one who has secretly done something which men have agreed to avoid, with a view to escaping the infliction or reception of hurt, to be sure that he will not be found out even if he should have gone undetected ten thousand times' (*Catechism,* 31, 34, 35).

Law, then, has no deeper foundation in human nature than agreement based on considerations of utility. It is only when such an agreement has been made that an act becomes unjust. Hence Epicurus holds that brutes have no rights because, from their lack of language, they can make no agreements with one another. The personal friendship of the 'brethren' is a thing which goes infinitely deeper and is more firmly rooted in the bed-rock of human nature, though even friendship is held to be founded in the end on mere utility. Of Plato's conception of law as the expression of the most intimately human, and, at the same time, the most divine element in our personality, Epicurus has no comprehension. So though his doctrine, as preserved in the *Catechism,* is that the 'wise man' will in general conform to the laws, since some of them are obviously based on sound utilitarian considerations, and even the breaking of those that are not is likely to have unpleasant consequences, Epicurus definitely refuses to say that the wise man will never commit a crime. His words, as reported by Plutarch, are: 'Will the wise man ever do what the laws forbid, if he is sure not to be found out? It is not easy to give an unequivocal answer to the question.' Plutarch interprets this to mean, 'He will commit a crime if it brings him pleasure, but I do not like to say so openly.' It must be allowed that on Epicurus' own showing his 'wise man' would have no motive for refraining from a pleasant crime if he really could be secure of impunity. The 'sage' is not a person whom one would care to trust with the 'ring of Gyges.'

It was a consequence as much of the age as of the Epicurean ideal that Epicurus dissuaded his followers from taking part in public life. They were to leave the world to get on by itself, and devote themselves to the cultivation of their own peace of soul by plain living and anti-religious reasoning. This separation of personal conduct from service to society is the point on which the Epicureans lay themselves most open to attack as representing an ethics of selfishness and indolence. We may plead in palliation that their 'quietism' may be regarded as partly a necessary consequence of the substitution of large monarchies for the old city-states. In such monarchies, even when their code of public morality does not keep men of sensitive conscience out of public life, it is inevitable that the direction of affairs of moment shall be confined to a few practised hands. Yet it must also be remembered that not a few philosophers, Academics, Stoics and others did play a prominent part in the public affairs of the age without soiling their garments. It is impossible to acquit Epicurus and his friends altogether of a pitiable lack of wholesome public spirit. It was only reasonable that a noble temper like that of Plutarch should be outraged by the insults they heaped on the memory of such a statesman and patriot as Epameinondas because he preferred wearing himself out in the service of his country to taking his ease at home. In practice, however, as the ancient critics observed, the apparently contradictory maxims of Epicurus and Zeno were not so far apart as they seem. Epicurus said that the 'sage' should not engage in politics except for very pressing reasons; Zeno that he should, unless there were special reasons against doing so. But in actual life an Epicurean with a bent for politics, or a Stoic with a taste for retirement, could always find that the reason for making the exception existed in his own case.

By following the rules of life thus laid down the Epicureans hold that any man, without need of special good fortune or high station or intellectual gifts, may learn to lead a life which is free from serious pain of body or trouble of mind, and therefore happy. The 'sober reasoning' which teaches him to limit his wants to the necessities of life, to banish fear of God from his mind, to recognise that death is no evil, and to choose always the course of action which promises to be most fruitful of pleasure and least productive of pain, will, in general, leave him with very few pains to endure. And if there are inevitable hours of suffering to be gone through, and if death is the common doom of all, the 'wise man' will fortify himself in his times of suffering and on his deathbed by dwelling in memory on the many pleasant moments which have fallen to his share. Thus prepared, says Lucretius, he will leave the feast of life, when his time comes to go, like a guest who has eaten his full at a public banquet, and makes way without a grumble for later comers; Metrodorus adds, that he will not forget to say 'grace after meat,' and thank 'whatever gods there be' that he has lived so well (*Fr. 49*).

W. T. Stace (lecture date 1919)

SOURCE: W. T. Stace, "The Epicureans, Physics, Ethics," in *A Critical History of Greek Philosophy*, Macmillan & Co., Limited, 1960, pp. 354-60.

[*The excerpt below, originally delivered as a lecture in 1919, encapsulates the Epicurean system, which Stace finds "amiable and shallow," and also ascribes to the general view that Epicurus was a kind of ancient decadent. Stace concludes that Epicureans are "gentle and lovable," but "lacking the stern stuff of heroes."*]

Epicurus was born at Samos in 342 B.C. He founded his school a year or two before Zeno founded the Stoa, so that the two schools from the first ran parallel in time. The school of Epicurus lasted over six centuries. Epicurus early became acquainted with the atomism of Democritus, but his learning in earlier systems of philosophy does not appear to have been extensive. He was a man of estimable life and character. He founded his school in 306 B.C. The Epicurean philosophy was both founded and completed by him. No subsequent Epicurean to any appreciable extent added to or altered the doctrines laid down by the founder.

The Epicurean system is even more purely practical in tendency than the Stoic. In spite of the fact that Stoicism subordinates logic and physics to ethics, yet the diligence and care which the Stoics bestowed upon such doctrines as those of the criterion of truth, the nature of the world, the soul, and so on, afford evidence of a genuine, if subordinate, interest in these subjects. Epicurus likewise divided his system into logic (which he called canonic), physics, and ethics, yet the two former branches of thought are pursued with an obvious carelessness and absence of interest. It is evident that learned discussions bored Epicurus. His system is amiable and shallow. Knowledge for its own sake is not desired. Mathematics, he said, are useless, because they have no connexion with life. The logic,

or canonic, we may pass over completely, as possessing no elements of interest, and come at once to the physics.

Physics.

Physics interests Epicurus only from one point of view—its power to banish superstitious fear from the minds of men. All supernatural religion, he thought, operates for the most part upon mankind by means of fear. Men are afraid of the gods, afraid of retribution, afraid of death because of the stories of what comes after death. This incessant fear and anxiety is one of the chief causes of the unhappiness of men. Destroy it, and we have at least got rid of the prime hindrance to human happiness. We can only do this by means of a suitable doctrine of physics. What is necessary is to be able to regard the world as a piece of mechanism, governed solely by natural causes, without any interference by supernatural beings, in which man is free to find his happiness how and when he will, without being frightened by the bogeys of popular religion. For though the world is ruled mechanically, man, thought Epicurus in opposition to the Stoics, possesses free will, and the problem of philosophy is to ascertain how he can best use this gift in a world otherwise mechanically governed. What he required, therefore, was a purely mechanical philosophy. To invent such a philosophy for himself was a task not suited to his indolence, and for which he could not pretend to possess the necessary qualifications. Therefore he searched the past, and soon found what he wanted in the atomism of Democritus. This, as an entirely mechanical philosophy, perfectly suited his ends, and the pragmatic spirit in which he chose his beliefs, not on any abstract grounds of their objective truth, but on the basis of his subjective needs and personal wishes, will be noted. It is a sign of the times. When truth comes to be regarded as something that men may construct in accordance with their real or imagined needs, and not in accordance with any objective standard, we are well advanced upon the downward path of decay. Epicurus, therefore, adopted the atomism of Democritus *en bloc*, or with trifling modifications. All things are composed of atoms and the void. Atoms differ only in shape and weight, not in quality. They fall eternally through the void. By virtue of free will, they deviate infinitesimally from the perpendicular in their fall, and so clash against one another. This, of course, is an invention of Epicurus, and formed no part of the doctrine of Democritus. It might be expected of Epicurus that his modifications would not be improvements. In the present case, the attribution of free will to the atoms adversely affects the logical consistency of the mechanical theory. From the collision of atoms arises a whirling movement out of which the world emerges. Not only the world, but all individual phenomena, are to be explained mechanically. Teleology is rigorously excluded. In any particular case, however, Epicurus is not interested to know what particular causes determine a phenomenon. It is enough for him to be sure that it is wholly determined by mechanical causes, and that supernatural agencies are excluded.

The soul being composed of atoms which are scattered at death, a future life is not to be thought of. But this is to be regarded as the greatest blessing. It frees us from the fear of death, and the fear of a hereafter. Death is not an evil. For if death is, we are not; if we are, death is not. When death comes we shall not feel it, for is it not the end of all feeling and consciousness? And there is no reason to fear now what we know that we shall not feel when it comes.

Having thus disposed of the fear of retribution in a future life, Epicurus proceeds to dispose of the fear of the interference of the gods in this life. One might have expected that Epicurus would for this purpose have embraced atheism. But he does not deny the existence of the gods. On the contrary, he believed that there are innumerable gods. They have the form of men, because that is the most beautiful of all forms. They have distinctions in sex. They eat, drink, and talk Greek. Their bodies are composed of a substance like light. But though Epicurus allows them to exist, he is careful to disarm them, and to rob them of their fears. They live in the interstellar spaces, an immortal, calm, and blessed existence. They do not intervene in the affairs of the world, because they are perfectly happy. Why should they burden themselves with the control of that which nowise concerns them? Theirs is the beatitude of a wholly untroubled joy.

> Immortal are they, clothed with powers,
>   Not to be comforted at all,
> Lords over all the fruitless hours,
>   Too great to appease, too high to appal,
>   Too far to call.
>   A. C. Swinburne's *Felise.*

Man, therefore, freed from the fear of death and the fear of the gods, has no duty save to live as happily as he can during his brief space upon earth. We can quit the realm of physics with a light heart, and turn to what alone truly matters, ethics, the consideration of how man ought to conduct his life.

Ethics.

If the Stoics were the intellectual successors of the Cynics, the Epicureans bear the same relation to the Cyrenaics. Like Aristippus, they founded morality upon pleasure, but they differ because they developed a purer and nobler conception of pleasure than the Cyrenaics had known. Pleasure alone is an end in itself. It is the only good. Pain is the only evil. Morality, therefore, is an activity which yields pleasure. Virtue has no value on its own account, but derives its value from the pleasure which accompanies it.

This is the only foundation which Epicurus could find, or desired to find, for moral activity. This is his only ethical principle. The rest of the Epicurean ethics consists in the interpretation of the idea of pleasure. And, firstly, by pleasure Epicurus did not mean, as the Cyrenaics did, merely the pleasure of the moment, whether physical or mental. He meant the pleasure that endures throughout a lifetime, a happy life. Hence we are not to allow ourselves to be enslaved by any particular pleasure or desire. We must master our appetites. We must often forgo a pleasure if it leads in the end to greater pain. We must be ready to undergo pain for the sake of a greater pleasure to come.

And it was just for this reason, secondly, that the Epicureans regarded spiritual and mental pleasures as far more important than those of the body. For the body feels pleasure and pain only while they last. The body has in itself neither memory nor fore-knowledge. It is the mind which remembers and foresees. And by far the most potent pleasures and pains are those of remembrance and anticipation. A physical pleasure is a pleasure to the body only *now*. But the anticipation of a future pain is mental anxiety, the remembrance of a past joy is a present delight. Hence what is to be aimed at above all is a calm untroubled mind, for the pleasures of the body are ephemeral, those of the spirit enduring. The Epicureans, like the Stoics, preached the necessity of superiority to bodily pains and external circumstances. So a man must not depend for his happiness upon externals; he must have his blessedness in his own self. The wise man can be happy even in bodily torment, for in the inner tranquillity of his soul he possesses a happiness which far outweighs any bodily pain. Yet innocent pleasures of sense are neither forbidden, nor to be despised. The wise man will enjoy whatever he can without harm. Of all mental pleasures the Epicureans laid, perhaps, most stress upon friendship. The school was not merely a collection of fellow-philosophers, but above all a society of friends.

Thirdly, the Epicurean ideal of pleasure tended rather towards a negative than a positive conception of it. It was not the state of enjoyment that they aimed at, much less the excitement of the feelings. Not the feverish pleasures of the world constituted their ideal. They aimed rather at a negative absence of pain, at tranquility, quiet calm, repose of spirit, undisturbed by fears and anxieties. As so often with men whose ideal is pleasure, their view of the world was tinged with a gentle and even luxurious pessimism. Positive happiness is beyond the reach of mortals. All that man can hope for is to avoid pain, and to live in quiet contentment.

Fourthly, pleasure does not consist in the multiplication of needs and their subsequent satisfaction. The multiplication of wants only renders it more difficult to satisfy them. It complicates life without adding to happiness. We should have as few needs as possible. Epicurus himself lived a simple life, and advised his followers to do the same. The wise man, he said, living on bread and water, could vie with Zeus himself in happiness. Simplicity, cheerfulness, moderation, temperance, are the best means to happiness. The majority of human wants, and the example of the thirst for fame is quoted, are entirely unnecessary and useless.

Lastly, the Epicurean ideal, though containing no possibility of an exalted nobility, was yet by no means entirely selfish. A kindly, benevolent temper appeared in these men. It is pleasanter, they said, to do a kindness than to receive one. There is little of the stern stuff of heroes, but there is much that is gentle and lovable, in the amiable moralizings of these butterfly-philosophers.

Cyril Bailey (essay date 1928)

SOURCE: Cyril Bailey, "Atoms and Space," in *The Greek Atomists and Epicurus*, Oxford at the Clarendon Press, 1928, pp. 274-99.

[*Bailey's work on Epicurus has often been cited by fellow scholars as fundamental to the field—particularly his 1926 translation of the philosopher's works. The following chapter from his well-respected* The Greek Atomists and Epicurus *concentrates on Epicurus's concept of the atom. Bailey elucidates the originality of Epicurus's system, countering claims by earlier critics that he simply lifted Democritus's thought.*]

In passing from Leucippus to Democritus the atomic theory . . . [grows] in consistency and harmony: with Epicurus the change is even more marked. It is now felt to be a system of interrelated parts: the connexion of one proposition with another has been thought out and the various conceptions involved in Atomism ordered and organized on fundamental principles. This impression is due in some degree, no doubt, to the form in which our information has reached us: the theories of the earlier Atomists have to be pieced together from scattered fragments, the accounts of the doxographers and the detached criticisms of later philosophers; for Epicurus we have the compressed and rather confused, though far better ordered, account in his own **letter to Herodotus**, and the continuous commentary of the poem of Lucretius. But there is much more than this: Epicurus had the master mind, which would not rest content with a mere 'adoption' of Democritus' Atomism, as hasty critics have been too ready to suppose, but insisted on development, modification, and improvement, and above all on the correlation of the whole system under the central principle of the infallibility of sense-perception. No account can do justice to Epicurus' physics which does

not attempt to grasp it as a whole, to emphasize the interdependence of its parts and the constant control of the principles of the **Canonice**. It is from this point of view that I shall attempt in the following pages to describe it.

Epicurus makes his start, like Democritus, from the principle of causality and permanence: 'nothing is created out of the non-existent', but unlike his predecessor he does not leave the principle as an *ex cathedra* assumption, but supports it by argument. Here we are dealing with perceptible and imperceptible alike; the problem is universal and cannot be solved directly by the senses: we must ask whether the senses give us any 'indication' to support the principle or whether they in any way contradict it. Such an 'indication' Epicurus finds in the ordered generation of things in the perceptible world: 'nothing is created out of the nonexistent; for, if it were, everything would be created out of everything with no need of seeds'. Lucretius follows the same argument and brings it out with a wealth of illustration. The proof is tersely put, but is clearly on the lines demanded by the **Canon**. Critics have proclaimed it unsatisfactory on the ground that Epicurus, to put it in modern phraseology, is arguing against 'spontaneous generation' by denying 'sporadic creation'. The truth is surely that he proves more than he need: all it was necessary for him to show was that every created thing was sprung from an antecedent something, was created of substance which already existed. Epicurus has gone beyond this and pointed out that not merely is there always preexisting substance, but in each case substance in a particular form, a 'seed', which can only produce one particular thing and nothing else. Suppose for a moment that the opposite were true, that things could suddenly come into existence without being formed from pre-existing substance? What is the evidence of phenomena? That things require definite 'seeds' for their creation. The evidence of sensation interposes its veto . . . , and the supposition is untenable: it must be true that 'nothing is created out of the non-existent'. There is no confusion in the argument: it is, if anything, gratuitously specific. It may be noticed that it has a double application: (1) the sum total of things is never increased by new additions, (2) every material thing has a material cause.

The second principle—the complement of the first—is next stated and proved. 'If that which disappears were destroyed into the non-existent, all things would have perished, since that into which they were dissolved would not exist.' The statement here is less lucid, principle and proof being run into one: Lucretius puts the principle more clearly: 'nature breaks up each thing again into its own first-bodies, nor does she destroy ought into nothing', nothing, in other words, ceases entirely to exist: as nothing is added to the sum of things, so nothing is entirely taken from it. The proof again is from phenomena: if things were utterly destroyed, and by the first principle nothing new could be added, the sum total of the universe must gradually be diminished, and ultimately would pass out of existence altogether. But this is not the evidence of the senses: we do indeed see things perish, cease, that is, to be what they were before, but this perishing means only the assumption of another form. Change we see all around us, but not the absolute cessation of existence. Lucretius is fond of using this principle as an axiom in the converse form, 'whatever changes and departs from its own limits is straightway the death of that which was before'. Once again there is a double implication in the principle: (1) the sum of matter is never decreased by absolute loss—this is the modern idea of the 'permanence of matter', (2) no individual thing is utterly destroyed, but only resolved into its component atoms.

There follows a third principle: 'the sum of things always was such as it is now and always will be the same'. This is in part a direct deduction from the other two: if nothing is added, the universe cannot increase; if nothing perishes, it cannot decrease. But Epicurus adds other arguments: 'there is nothing into which it changes: for outside the universe there is nothing which could come into it and bring about the change'. This is the reference to sense-experience. Among phenomena two conditions are always required for change, (1) something for the original 'thing' to change into, something which it may become, (2) some external agent to effect the change—by means, as Epicurus held, of a blow. But by 'mental apprehension', by 'looking at' the concept we have already formed of the universe, we can see that neither of these conditions can in its case be fulfilled: the universe cannot change into something else, for there is nothing else which it could become, nor is there anything external to it, which could effect the change. The argument is put in a more elaborate form by Lucretius in a passage probably based on the Greater Epitome. He seems to imply three possibilities by which the universe might change, (1) if there were anything outside it into which any part of it might escape, (2) if there were anywhere from which a new force might come into the universe and alter it, (3) if change could be caused by internal-rearrangement. Epicurus in the **letter to Herodotus** seems to have the first two of these causes most prominently in his mind. The third might at first sight seem to be at work in the universe in the constant dissolution and recomposition of the atomic compounds, but Epicurus' answer would lie in his conception of equilibrium . . . ; the atoms have long ago entered into all possible combinations and cannot create anything new which could alter the sum total. The universe then cannot change for there is nothing for it to change into and no external or internal force to change it. It is birthless, deathless, and immutable.

In these three primary principles themselves there is nothing new: they were practically implied in the Parmenidean conception, they were enunciated by Empedocles and Anaxagoras and explicitly stated by Democritus. But Epicurus has done more than 'adopt' them: he has adduced proof for them, and in doing so has linked them directly to the base principles of his whole system. The proofs from phenomena and the trust in sensation which they involve are the new and characteristic addition.

In what form then does this eternal universe exist? 'In the form of body (or matter) and space (or, as Epicurus here says, "place").' That body exists is testified by universal sensation: all men through all their senses are made conscious of matter. That space exists is shown by the existence and motion of matter: 'if there were not that which we term void and place and intangible existence . . . bodies would have nowhere to exist and nothing through which to move, as they are seen to move.'

At this point certain difficulties arise, though rather from a modern than an ancient point of view. In the first place it is true that the sensation of matter is universal, but that has not hindered philosophers from calling in question the objective reality of the external world, or asking what meaning, if any, can be attached to the statement of its existence as apart from a percipient intelligence. But, if we are inclined to raise this objection, we must bear in mind that it is essentially a modern difficulty, unknown to the ancient world, and secondly that Epicurus spoke here, as always, as the average man of common sense. To him, as to the modern man of science, the existence of matter is sufficiently testified and its properties sufficiently made known by the sense. Once again he is content to take as his starting-point what 'common sense' would say, without any attempt to get behind it.

The difficulty connected with the syllogistic argument by which Epicurus inferred space from the fact of motion is more serious, for it was a problem which antiquity had very fully discussed. Parmenides and the Eleatics had, as has been seen, in order to preserve the unity of the world, denied both space and motion: the world was a single corporeal *plenum,* compact 'body' without space, and the appearance of motion was merely a delusion of the senses. As against this theory Epicurus was justified, indeed impelled, by his own first principles to reassert the evidence of the senses: we perceive motion, therefore motion is a reality. But is it necessary to infer from this the existence of void? Some modern scientists, holding the hypothesis of ether, would answer in the negative, and a very similar solution was put forward by Epicurus' contemporaries, the Stoics. They, under the stress of their desire to assert the divine unity of the world, maintained that the whole world was but one primary substance, which however was elastic and capable of existing in various degrees of tension; under the greatest strain it appeared as fire, with less tension as air, with less again as water, and with least of all as earth. Motion, on this view, then is but an interchange of parts, much as one might move about the various portions of a piece of putty without causing a break, or as one sees changes of position in a kaleidoscope. With this possibility Epicurus does not concern himself, though it must have been current at the time of the writing of his letter, but that it did become a real question to the later Epicureans, we may infer from the fact that Lucretius consents to deal with it. His main answer is, in effect, simply the restatement of the common-sense view: there must be empty space in order that there may be a beginning of motion; a thing cannot begin to move unless there is 'room' for it to move into. His second argument is an illustration from experience—if you clash two broad bodies, e.g. boards, together and then quickly draw them apart, the air rushes round to fill up the space between them: but there must be an interval of time in which that space is empty or 'void'. That Epicurus' own answer would have been on these lines may safely be inferred from the fact that in the controversial passages about the Epicurean view of space the examples are drawn from such illustrations as the interior of a cask or a vessel—not of course that Epicurus would have denied that they were filled with air; but would have argued rather that they afforded an 'indication' of that real empty space which lay between atom and atom. More cogent is Lucretius' third argument that the 'elasticity' of the primary substance, its power to condense and rarify, must itself imply the existence of void. The Stoic view, Epicurus would have maintained, is not that immediately suggested by sensation: it is an 'addition of the mind' which the 'clear facts' of sensation refute. Once again 'common sense' is good enough. Matter then and space are the sole independent existences: 'and besides these two nothing can be thought of . . . such as could be grasped as whole existences and not spoken of as the accidents or properties of such existences'.

We must ask then next how are we to conceive these two existences, 'body' and space? 'Among bodies', Epicurus proceeds, 'some are compounds . . . and others those of which compounds are formed'. This is little more than a verbal explanation: the term 'body' is in itself ambiguous, for it may be applied alike to the 'bodies' or 'things' which we perceive by sensation or to the ultimate bodies of which they are composed. But the confusion is only momentary and does not produce any serious difficulty either in Epicurus or in Lucretius, who follows him in making the distinction: for as soon as the character of these ultimate bodies has been determined, there will be other descriptive names to apply to them in order to distinguish them from the bodies of sensation. What then

are they? 'These latter', says Epicurus, 'are indivisible . . . and unalterable . . . (if, that is, all things are not to be destroyed into the non-existent, but something permanent . . . is to remain behind at the dissolution of compounds): they are completely solid . . . in nature and can by no means be dissolved in any part. So it must needs be that the first-beginnings are indivisible corporeal existences. . . .' Here then is the first statement of the atomic position. The argument by which it is supported is put very briefly in the parenthesis and requires examination. It rests on the Atomic contention that there must be a limit to the divisibility of matter, but this is put both negatively and positively. In the first place Epicurus appears to maintain that, unless there were such a limit, things would pass out of existence altogether, which would be a contradiction of the principle that 'nothing is destroyed into the non-existent'. The idea is that if it were possible to go on dividing and dividing you would ultimately find that matter had disappeared and you had reached 'nothing'. Strictly this is of course a fallacy: it is theoretically possible, apart from such a physical barrier as Epicurus supposes, to go on dividing and subdividing to infinity and yet to reach only smaller and smaller particles of matter. And it is improbable that Epicurus would seriously have maintained the point: it is rather a popular way of putting what he meant. For the stress of the argument lies on the other, the positive, side: 'something permanent (or "strong") must remain'. Here the argument is independent of the fallacy of ultimate resolution into nothing. For if infinite division were possible, all particles of matter however small would be compound bodies, for they could always be separated into smaller particles. But the compound body on Epicurus' view is always a mixture of matter and void, and the presence of void is a source of weakness: for it means the possibility of destruction by external blows. If, then, however low one may go in the scale of minuteness, nothing indestructible is ever reached, matter as we know it in external things could not exist; for there could be no solid and permanent substratum— 'nothing strong'—to hold it together and to resist the shocks of collision.

The argument recurs in two other contexts in the letter, which will throw some light upon it. In the first Epicurus is arguing that the atoms have none of the 'secondary qualities', which we associate with things: 'for every quality changes; but the atoms do not change at all, since there must needs be something which remains solid and indissoluble at the dissolution of compounds, which can cause changes'. Just then as there must be indestrucible particles to explain the creation and the destruction of phenomena, so to explain their changes, there must be something unchanging: and this can be nothing else than the atom, the hard body without the admixture of void, which alone can resist the attacks of external blows. The second passage is more directly connected with our argument, for Epicurus is there proving that the atoms must have a definite size, they cannot be 'infinitely small'. 'We must', he says, 'do away with division into smaller and smaller parts to infinity in order that we may not make all things weak and so in the composition of aggregate bodies be compelled to crush and squander the things that exist into the non-existent.' Again the idea is the same: if there is no limit to the smallness of particles, there is no permanent strength in the substratum; things become weak and can be whittled away past the limits of material existence. A more striking and interesting form of the same proof occurs in a difficult passage of Lucretius, which has been clearly explained by Giussani. If there were no *minimum,* the poet maintains, but the infinite division of matter were possible, then, because the process of dissolution is quicker than that of creation, all things, i.e. perceptible things, must long ago have ceased to exist. Let us suppose, for instance, that the process of dissolution is twice as quick as that of creation, and that it takes ten years to create a living creature and bring it to its maturity: then in five years it can be dissolved into particles of the size from which it started, and in ten, if there is no limit to division, the particles will be as much smaller again. If out of these particles a similar creature is now to be formed, it will require twenty years, and on the next occasion forty and so on. In all the ages which have passed since the creation of the world, the powers of destruction would have so got the upper hand that by now no perceptible things would be left. Again, division cannot go on to infinity: there must be some permanent *minimum* 'with strength' to resist the influences of destruction. The passage is unusually interesting and throws considerable light on the general Epicurean argument.

This, as I understand it, is the contention of Epicurus for the existence of indivisible particles as the permanent substratum of matter: not that, without them, matter would cease altogether to exist—for however minutely divided, it must still continue to be matter—but that without a limit to division, it is impossible to arrive at anything completely solid, and so sufficiently strong to resist the attacks of destruction, in other words, the blows of other particles. The result would be continuous destruction and no formation: in this sense 'all things would be dissolved into the non-existent', for there would be no power to keep existing things as they were, or to create similar new ones.

The atom then is a necessary postulate for the existence of the world as we know it. How is it to be conceived? Certain characteristics follow immediately from its definition as an 'indivisible existence'. It must be completely solid, completely compact, and entirely without void: it is, that is to say, pure body without any intervals. From this it immediately follows that it is 'unchangeable': for change is due to the alteration of the position of parts and that can only be brought

about in compound bodies, in which there is an admixture of void. What then are the properties of this indissoluble, unalterable body? They are according to Epicurus, three in number, size, shape, and weight.

The question of the size of the atom was already, as we have seen, a problem with a history in the Atomic theory. Leucippus wishing to insist on their extreme minuteness had stated that they were 'without parts' . . . : Democritus, seeing that it might then also be said that they were without magnitude, i.e. without material existence, had denied this and gone so far as to maintain that some of them were even 'very large'. Epicurus dealt with the question in a more systematic and philosophic manner.

> 'We must not suppose', he says, 'that every size exists among the atoms, in order that the evidence of phenomena may not contradict us, but we must suppose that there are some variations of size. . . . The existence of atoms of every size is not required to explain the differences of qualities in things, and at the same time some atoms would be bound to come within our ken and be visible: but this is never seen to be the case, nor is it possible to imagine how an atom could become visible.'

Here then is the answer to Democritus: sense-perception is against his theory: there must be an upward limit of magnitude, otherwise atoms could be seen. What of the downward limit? It follows of course from the very definition of an atom, as a limit of division, that it cannot be of infinite smallness, but Epicurus proceeds to treat the question in a subtle and very characteristic argument. This argument must be studied in the original and compared with the rather more lucid, but less far-reaching version of Lucretius. I shall here attempt to give the gist of it in as simple a form as possible. Epicurus appeals as usual to the facts of sensation: and the appeal involves the expression of strong controversial views with regard to area and extension. 'Not merely can we not admit infinite division, but we cannot suppose an 'infinite progression from less to less. . . .' His contention here is directed primarily against the geometrical view of surface or area, which held that surface was perfectly continuous, and that it was possible, in considering for instance a line to pass continually to smaller and smaller sections to infinity: the idea is clearly expressed in the well-known story of Achilles and the tortoise. As against this theory Epicurus upholds the view of common sense based upon the experience of sensation. If we take any object and try by looking at it to analyse its surface, we find that we may indeed proceed from smaller to smaller parts for a long distance: but ultimately we come to a point—not a geometrical but a material point—which is the smallest visible thing. If we attempted to see any smaller part, we should pass out of the range of the perceptible altogether. Indeed, this point itself is only visible as a part of a larger whole: it is 'distinguishable, but not perceptible by itself' . . . , and if we try to look at its 'right-hand or left-hand part', we shall find that our eye has in reality wandered to the next similar point. We have then in this point reached something from which further progression to anything smaller is impossible . . . : in other words, surface is not continuous and does not permit of infinite progression, but is a series of discrete *minima*. Further, these 'least parts' (*minimae partes*) afford a standard of measure: as we pass from one of them to another, we can—or could, if we had patience—go on till we reached the last point, then count them up and so from their number reckon the size of the object. This, Epicurus holds, is the only view of surface which is warranted by the 'clear vision of perception', and the opposite view is due to the contamination of the sense-perception by the false addition of opinion. Yet, if we pass from the world of sensation to the world of thought, we know that even these 'points', the 'least parts' for perception, are themselves aggregates . . . of infinitely smaller particles: in thought division may still be carried on. But in the world of thought the analogy still holds: ultimately we come to the 'least possible' . . . , the *minima* of extension. They similarly are not separable: they can only exist as parts of the atom. They never come together to form it, they are not parted in it by void, they could themselves have no 'powers', but they may in thought be distinguished. They too are 'boundary marks' . . . and by their number the size of the atom which they compose may in thought be calculated. The world of thought corresponds exactly . . . to the world of sense: in the world of sense we have the visible body composed of 'distinguishable' points, in the world of thought the atom composed of 'inseparable' parts. This imaginative analogy has then given us the answer to Leucippus and his critics and to Democritus: the atoms are not 'without parts' . . . in the sense that they have magnitude and parts 'distinguishable' by thought; they are on the other hand without parts in the sense that they are not formed of parts which could be separated. In other words the atom has size, i.e. measurable extension, but it remains an 'indivisible existence'. The size of the atom then is neither 'very great' nor infinitely small: it is extremely minute but with a lower as well as an upper limit.

Furthermore there are some variations in the sizes of atoms: 'for if this be the case, we can give a better account of what occurs in our feelings and sensations'. As will be seen later, difference in the size of the component atoms is a large factor in producing difference of qualities in things. That the atoms will have shape is manifest from the fact that they have size, but now that we have the theory of the least parts, we can go farther: for it is obvious that the shape of the atom varies according to the number and disposition of the 'least parts'. An ingenious critic [Brieger, *Fahrbuch Fleck.*, 1875] has worked out some of these differ-

ences. If, for instance, we suppose the *minimae partes* to be cubes of exactly the same size, then, if an atom contains two only, it can have but one shape . . . ; if it contains three, two shapes . . . ; if four, five shapes on one plane, . . . and two more in two planes, according as one of the parts in the last figure be placed on top either of one of its neighbours, or of that at the opposite corner: with five or six parts the possibilities are very largely increased. Are we to suppose then that this process of variation may be infinitely continued, or is there a limit to the possible varieties? Epicurus' answer is again carefully thought out: the number of different atomic shapes is indefinitely great . . . , but not infinite. It must be 'inconceivably great': 'for it is not possible that such great varieties of things should arise from the same (atomic) shapes, if they are limited in number'. Phenomena, as usual, give the 'indication': the varieties of compound bodies are very largely due to the difference of shape in the component atoms, and it would not be possible to account for these varieties, if we conceived of any comparatively small number of atomic shapes. Why then is there a limit to the number? Epicurus does not himself give us any reason, but Lucretius suggests two proofs, so characteristically Epicurean that they must represent the regular tradition of the school. The first is an argument suggested by 'mental apprehension': variety of shape, as we have seen, can only be obtained by supposing an increase in the number of least parts: or, in other words, an increase of size. If this process were infinitely continued, we should again arrive at atoms so large as to be perceptible to the senses: we should be guilty of the fallacy of Democritus. The second is based on the 'indications' of phenomena: varieties of quality in things are caused by varieties of atomic shape: yet even the varieties of things are limited; there is an extreme of beauty and ugliness, just as there is of hot and cold. But if there were infinite varieties of atomic shape, there could be no such limitation of qualities: all that we find most beautiful and most hideous would long ago have been surpassed. We must conclude then that these varieties of shape in the atoms are indefinitely great, yet not infinite. On the other hand the number of atoms of each particular shape is infinite, for if it were not so (the reason is again given by Lucretius), the sum total of atoms would itself be limited—which is not the case. The ideas connected with the shape of the atoms are not so penetrating as those relating to their size, but are particularly well thought out and form an interesting example of the application of the principles of the Canon.

Thirdly, the atoms have weight. The question whether weight is a property of the atoms has, as has already been seen, a very perplexing history in the Atomic theory. Leucippus makes no mention of weight and it may be taken for certain that he did not assign weight to the atoms. Over the attitude of Democritus controversy still rages, but we have seen reason to think that he did not regard it as an absolute property of the atoms, but only as a derivative from their size which comes into action in the cosmic 'whirl'. We might therefore naturally suppose that the idea was introduced into the system by Epicurus himself in order to account for the 'downward' motion of the atoms in space. This conclusion is however made improbable by a passage in Lucretius in which, evidently following Epicurus, he argues against the idea that variation in weight was the cause which enabled the atoms to meet in the downward fall, on the ground that in the void, which offers no resistance, all bodies, whatever their weight, must fall at an equal 'atomic' pace. It is true that Lucretius puts this idea as a supposition, but it is hard to believe that he is not arguing against some definite suggestion on these lines, and if so, the idea of weight as the absolute property of the atoms and the cause of downward motion must have been introduced by some one into the atomic theory before Epicurus— possibly by Nausiphanes. In view of the history of the discussion it is certainly strange that we find no argument on the question in Epicurus. He is content with the mere mention of weight together with size and shape as one of the properties of the atoms. Lucretius assumes it all through, and it is only in a passage of the *Placita* that we find any kind of proof recorded, a proof, as might be expected, from the fact of motion: 'it must needs be, says Epicurus, that the bodies (i.e. the atoms) are moved by the blow of their weight: for otherwise they will not move'. That this was Epicurus' own argument is clear, apart from the testimony of Plutarch, from the passages in which he speaks of the 'natural downward motion of the atoms owing to their weight'. There are reasons too which may be suggested for the absence of explicit argument on the subject. On the one hand the weight of the atoms is an immediate deduction from their size: solid matter, having size, must also have weight: demonstration is hardly needed as soon as the idea of 'weight' had become explicit. On the other hand—a more subtle consideration— though differences of size and shape in the atoms were productive of important results, difference of weight is not effective. For to the atoms, always moving in the void at an equal rate, difference of weight does not produce difference of motion, and in compound bodies where difference of weight first begins to tell, it is not the weight of individual atoms that matters, but the weight of the aggregate of matter compared with the aggregate of void. The atoms then have weight, and since they are solid matter with no admixture of void, their weight varies directly with their size: their weight is moreover the cause of their natural 'downward' motion, but difference of weight has no effect so far as rate of motion is concerned.

Size, shape, and weight are thus proved to be properties of the atoms, but beyond these they have no other qualities. Here it might seem that the evidence of sensation was against such a conclusion: all things that we can perceive have other qualities, colour, smell, sound, cold, heat, and so on: we might reasonably conclude that the atoms too were similarly endowed, that white things were made of white atoms, black of black, and so forth. But this would be a false assumption. For all qualities are susceptible of change: the wave which was green one moment becomes white the next; the colours on the peacock's tail are always shifting, as the light strikes it: but the atoms cannot change. They are, as has been proved, unalterable and we must not attribute to them qualities which imply alteration. How then can we account on an atomic basis for the changing qualities of things? The unchangeable atoms are themselves the cause of change: 'there must be something which remains solid and indissoluble . . . which can cause changes: not changes into the non-existent or from the non-existent, but changes effected by the shifting of position of some particles, and by the addition or departure of others'. All the qualities of things are thus due to their atomic conformation: their original qualities are given them by the size and shape and arrangement of the atoms which compose them, the change in their qualities is caused by the mutual change of position and order among the atoms, and in some cases because some of the original atoms break off or new ones are added. Nor is this difficult to conceive, when we remember that the atoms inside compound bodies are continually in motion, ever clashing against one another and starting off in new directions, so that in every perceptible moment of time their position and arrangement is altered: the marvel is rather on Epicurus' view that the qualities of things should remain as constant as they do. Here we are once more on the lines of atomic tradition: the differences of quality are due to the three 'differences' of the atoms originally postulated by Leucippus, the differences of shape, position, and arrangement. Epicurus of course is not contented with mere tradition, but as usual appeals to phenomena: even in things perceptible which change their shape by a mutual rearrangement of their parts, we see that other qualities are altered, but the shape of the parts remains the same. So then in all changes; the atoms with their unchangeable shapes cause the differences and alterations in the qualities of things. The idea is greatly elaborated by Lucretius, who adduces a series of proofs to show that the atoms are without colour and then conscientiously applies the same notion to the qualities perceptible by the other senses. We need not consider his arguments in detail, but we must here notice a very important addition, which is not suggested in Epicurus' more summary treatment. Not merely are the atoms without qualities, but they are also without sensation: here again analogy might lead us astray and we might suppose that those atoms which compose our 'soul' are themselves endowed with sensation. But this is not the case: all atoms are completely without sensation and sensation and consciousness in us are due merely to particular movements on the part of a particular combination of atoms: as arrangement results in qualities, so movement may produce sensation. It is manifest that this position will prove of great importance, when we come to consider the Epicurean psychology.

This denial of qualities to the atoms by Epicurus was the subject of considerable criticism in antiquity. In the first place the critics asked how could atoms without qualities merely by 'coming together' create things with qualities. In the second they argued that Epicurus' theory was in effect a denial of the reality of quality: if quality did not belong to the atoms—the only real material existences—it was in things a delusion: Democritus was right when he said that qualities existed only in appearance . . . : the senses were mistaken in attributing them to things, and were not therefore infallible. Both criticisms are discerning and important, but both rest on a failure to appreciate Epicurus' true view of the nature of a compound body. If a compound body were a mere aggregate of atoms—a collection of atoms, as it were, arbitrarily separated off from the hosts of surrounding atoms (much as the old astronomers separated off a 'constellation' from the surrounding stars), then these criticisms would hold true: the atoms could acquire no new powers in the compound body and must remain as they ever were. But this was by no means Epicurus' view: the compound body to him was not a mere aggregate, but a new entity, an 'organism' almost . . . , or, as Lucretius calls it again and again, a *concilium*. In the organism of the whole the atoms did collectively acquire new properties and characteristics which as detached individuals they could never possess: no number of independent atoms could have colour, but unite them in the new entity of the whole, and it acquired colour. The idea is important and fruitful and we shall meet it again in the Epicurean kinetics and psychology. Moreover this whole is a reality, not a delusion: its reality for sense is as great as the reality of the atoms for thought: it is directly grasped by sense-perception, as the atoms are by 'mental apprehension'. And this carries with it the reality of its qualities: indeed, it is by the perception of its qualities that a thing's existence is known. To argue then that no quality which is not possessed by the individual atoms is 'real' in the compound, is to misunderstand fundamentally the Epicurean position. There are two worlds, or rather two departments of the same world, the one known by sense, the other by 'mental apprehension'; both are equally real, and in passing from the one to the other, matter acquires new qualities. The notion is in reality, as we have seen, underlying the Canonice, and to lose sight of it in the physical theory is to misconstrue Epicurus all through.

We must turn now to Epicurus' conception of space, for, although from the nature of the case it is not so complicated as that of the atoms, it involves certain difficulties which cannot be disguised. The syllogistic argument by which he inferred the existence of

space from the fact of motion has been discussed already: we must now inquire more closely what it was that he meant by space. The mathematical conception of space as extension may be put out of court: it is impossible that Epicurus should have meant that for several reasons; (1) it would have been inconsistent with his whole attitude to the mathematical point of view, (2) it would have clashed with his theory of area as a succession of discrete *minima,* (3) it is sufficiently contradicted by the many synonyms which he employs to describe it, and particularly with its definition as 'intangible existence'. Space is an 'existence' just as much as body, it is not mere measurement or extension: it is a 'thing', but a thing whose sole property is that it cannot touch or be touched, it can offer no sort of resistance to body. Here then is his answer to the difficulties of the earlier Atomists: he does not trouble himself with their subtle discussions as to whether space is 'nothing' . . . , or 'non-existent' . . . ; he simply affirms, with the same meaning but much closer precision, that it is an 'intangible existence'. The conception is not abstract but concrete: it is derived from that of body by a negation of its properties.

Yet considerable difficulty remains. Are we to conceive space as absolutely continuous and universal, coextensive with the universe itself, or as discrete and consisting only of the intervals between bodies? In other words, is there space in a place which is occupied by body, or is there not? does he mean 'place' or 'empty space'? The question is a very difficult one to decide and there seem many indications on either side. If we consider the synonyms which Epicurus uses, we see that two of them, 'place' . . . and 'room', . . . are in favour of the former view, that by space he means occupied as well as empty space—a continuous whole: the same conclusion may be drawn from the definition of space as that 'in which things exist and through which they move', and possibly (though I think it need not be interpreted in this sense) the contention that space is infinite in extent: for if there is no space, where bodies are, then there is a limit to space. On the other side, we have the fourth synonym, 'the empty' . . . , which clearly suggests only unoccupied space, and the frequent reference to the void in compound bodies as 'intervals' . . . between the component atoms. Most of the ancient commentators too seem to interpret Epicurus in this sense, and among their comments is the express statement of Simplicius that the Epicureans regarded space as 'the interval between the boundaries of that which surrounds it'. A consideration of the main passages in Epicurus and Lucretius, where space is mentioned, seems to show that they both oscillate between the two conceptions. Are we then to leave this difficulty—so fundamental in the system—as a point which Epicurus never really thought out? I believe that it arises largely from the fact that we are not easily able to approach Epicurus with a sufficiently concrete conception. Giussani, in one of the most interesting of his Essays, has very largely cleared the matter up. He points out that we must think of Epicurus' notion primarily in relation to the ideas which he was combatting. The Parmenideans, for instance, would readily admit the conception of space in the sense of 'extension', but they would maintain that there is matter everywhere, there is no such thing as empty space. In strong opposition to this view Epicurus wished to maintain not merely that there was empty space between portions of matter, but that empty space was a necessary presupposition to that of matter: there must be empty space in order that things may exist at all; otherwise there would be 'nowhere for them to be and nothing through which they might move'. 'Void' then is the fundamental notion always in the mind of Epicurus and his disciple, and therefore he is most often apt to think of it as completely empty space, or the intervals between matter. Yet even where matter is present, he can still speak of 'place' or 'room', and think not of something which has ceased to be void, but rather of potential void: it is indeed empty space which happens temporarily to be occupied. Space then does mean to Epicurus primarily 'empty space', but he is not inconsistent when at times he includes in it the 'place' which matter is for the moment filling. The two ideas are significantly combined in another passage of Simplicius, where he says that the Atomists say that 'empty space is infinite, and exceeds bodies in infinity (i.e. of extension), and for this reason can admit different things in its different parts'. Here the conception works outwards, as it were, from the notion of 'interval' to that of omnipresence. But the unity of the two conceptions is made very much more intelligible, if we remember that in Epicurus' idea matter is in perpetual motion: the atoms even in compound bodies are never still. Consequently the occupation of empty space by matter is never more than instantaneous: for no two consecutive instants is the same space occupied by the same atom. The idea then of occupied space becomes almost an abstraction: it is an attempt to take a static view of what is always kinetic. Our difficulty thus arises in great part from the fact of our approaching the question with the presupposition of a world of (mostly) stationary objects: if we can put ourselves back in thought to Epicurus' world of ever-moving atoms, the contradiction between the two views of space very largely disappears. Space thus means 'void', any portion of which may momentarily, but not more, be occupied by an atom.

We come back then to the original conception of the Universe as atoms moving in space and we must ask finally whether this universe and its two constituents are or are not infinite. Epicurus gives the traditional answer of the atomic school, but once again supports it with argument. 'The universe is boundless. For that which is bounded has an extreme point: and the extreme point is seen against something else. So that as it has no extreme

point, it has no limit; and as it has no limit it must be boundless and not bounded.' Lucretius puts the proof rather more lucidly: 'it is seen that nothing can have an extreme point, unless there is something beyond to bound it, so that there is seen to be a spot farther than which the nature of our sense cannot follow it. As it is, since we must admit that there is nothing outside the whole sum, it has not an extreme point, it lacks therefore bound and limit.' The appeal is then once again to phenomena: the condition of limitation there, the existence of something else beyond, is one which cannot be applied to our mental conception of the universe. Lucretius brings out his point by the famous illustration of the hurling of the spear. 'Go, if you can, he challenges the doubter, to the extreme limit of the universe and hurl a spear: either it will be stopped or it will go on: if it is stopped, there will be matter beyond, if it goes on there will be empty space: in either case you did not start from the end of the universe. The same will happen wherever you take your stand.' The universe then cannot have a limit.

Moreover the two constituents are also infinite, though in different senses, the atoms in number and the void in extent. For, as Lucretius argues, in order that the sum total, the universe, may be unlimited, either both or one or other of its constituents must be infinite. Epicurus then deals with the two questions separately. 'If the void were boundless, and the bodies limited in number, the bodies could not stay anywhere, but would be carried about and scattered through the infinite void, not having other bodies to support them and keep them in place by means of collisions.' The statement is careful and precise: the condition of the creation of things is the constant collision of atoms and their crowding together in such numbers as to be able to enter into the combined existence of a compound, which in its turn is kept together and held in its place by the external blows of other countless atoms. That this may occur in an infinite universe, it is necessary that there should be an infinite supply of matter: otherwise the comparatively few collisions which would take place would just send individual atoms wandering far out into space, where they would have no chance of meeting their fellows. Lucretius elaborates the idea with a fine imaginative description of the chaos which must ensue.

Similarly, space is infinite in extent: for 'if the void were limited, the infinite bodies would have no room wherein to take their place'. Lucretius' argument here is rather different and perhaps less satisfactory: 'if space were limited, the atoms through the downward motion due to weight would all have sunk to the bottom and there remained in an inert mass: it is because there is no bottom that they are still kept in eternal restlessness'. The limitation of space would in fact preclude the ceaseless motion of the atoms which is an essential part of the atomic conception. The argument is more esoteric and less likely than Epicurus' own to convince a non-Epicurean. It is simpler and more cogent to maintain that unless space were infinite, there would not be room for infinite atoms.

The idea of the infinity of space raises again the question of the conception of space and presents the same difficulty. One is inclined to ask: does not the existence of the infinite number of atoms really preclude the infinity of space: for each atom, inasmuch as it is not itself empty space, is really a limitation to it? This question requires a careful answer. It is tempting to argue that the instantaneous occupation of any 'piece' of space by an atom does not interfere with the conception of space as continuous and infinite 'place', in which the atoms have their momentary station. But there is a good reason against this: if this were the Epicurean conception, then space would itself be co-extensive with the universe, whereas Epicurus always speaks of the universe as 'body plus void': the sum total of matter, divided though it is into infinite particles in ceaseless motion has to be added to infinite void to make the sum total of the infinite universe. Similarly it is significant that in this section space is spoken of throughout as 'the void' . . . and not 'place' . . . as before. It would probably be a more correct solution of the difficulty to say that this 'internal' limitation of space, if it may be so described, was not here present to Epicurus' mind. He was thinking rather, as he clearly was when speaking of the infinity of the universe, of an 'external' limit. . . . In extension outward space is unlimited . . . , even though internally it might be thought of as limited by the presence of atomic matter. Once again the notion of 'empty space' seems to be uppermost and that from which Epicurus started: the kinetic view of matter helps to an understanding of his point of view, but the particular difficulty would not have troubled him.

We have then at last reached the traditional atomic conception of an infinite universe, consisting of atoms infinite in number moving in space infinite in extent. The conception has not varied since Democritus, but in its gradual unfolding in Epicurus it seems almost to have changed its nature. Each step in the argument has now been thought out under the definite rules of the Canonice: the detached notions about the character of the atoms have been correlated into a self-dependent whole: a universe seems not to have been assumed but created in thought. There has been occasion here and there to point out weak points in the argument or possibly hazy and ill-defined conceptions. But the result is one worthy of a great thinker: it is no mere wholesale adoption of the theory of Democritus—in certain places it has been seen to differ conspicuously from it: nor is it the work of a preacher, who hastily patched together some kind of physical theory to act as a basis for his moral teaching. With all its limitations, it is the construction of a master-mind, working on definite lines and with a deep and penetrating interest in his subject for its own sake. . . .

A. J. Festugière (essay date 1946)

SOURCE: A. J. Festugière, "The Religion of Epicurus," in *Epicurus and His Gods*, translated by C. W. Chilton, Basil Blackwell, 1955, pp. 51-65.

[*Originally published in France in 1946, Festugière's* Epicurus and his Gods *quickly became standard criticism in discussions of Epicurean theology. In the excerpt below, Festugière looks at Epicurus—both as an Athenian citizen and as a philosopher—in the context of his culture's religious thought.*]

Ever since men in Greece had believed in the existence of gods—and this belief seems to go back to an unfathomable antiquity—they had thought also that the gods rule human affairs. These two aspects of faith are connected; for this very faith in the existence of superior powers, whose favour we must win and whose anger we must turn aside, is born of the observation, a thousand times repeated, that most of our actions do not achieve their object, that almost of necessity there remains a gap between our best laid plans and their fulfilment, and that as a result our being is circumscribed by doubt, whose offspring is hope and fear. By the same psychological law, human conjectures about the attitude of the gods varied according as men enjoyed prosperity or suffered misfortune. When our projects succeed we readily believe that the gods take notice of us, that they are good, and that they love us; but when we suffer a reverse, we imagine that the gods are far away, indifferent, or hostile. On this point Greek religion is no different from any other; it is one of the sentiments most deeply rooted in the heart of man and can be found alike in all peoples and in all times.

If there were any need to demonstrate the strength of these beliefs in Greece itself we should only have to dip into literature from the time of Homer. Let me quote but one example, exactly contemporary with Epicurus. When in September 290 Demetrius Poliorcetes and his new wife Lanassa made their solemn entry into Athens as gods made manifest (Demetrius and Demeter), the city instituted a contest of paeans in honour of the divine couple. Now this is what we read in the paean of Hermocles, who carried off the prize: 'As to him (Demetrius), he appears with a kindly face . . . , as befits a god, and he is fair and full of joy . . . The other gods are far away, or they have no ears, or they do not exist, or they pay not the least attention to us: but you we see face to face, not in wood or in stone but in truth and reality.' What could be more obvious? If the old gods are left on one side it is because they no longer concern themselves with the affairs of Athens and because for the last fifty years (since Chaeronea 338) Athens had lived under foreign domination. The gods of Athens are far away, or they have no ears: or even, since they are no longer active, they do not exist. Demetrius on the other hand appears as a smiling conqueror: it is he who is the god. Traditional expressions show how usual it was to link in this way the existence of the gods with their activity. A man could not succeed except 'with the gods' . . . , he got nothing without them. These expressions were so common that Epicurus did not hesitate to use them in his private letters. In the archonship of Charinus (308-7) he wrote to a friend: 'Even if war comes it will bring us nothing dreadful if the gods are favourable . . .', and again, 'Thanks to the gods . . . I have lived and intend to live a pure life in the company of Matro alone' (fr. 99 Us[ener, *Epicure,* 1887]).

As long as men ascribed to the gods the entire government of earthly matters they could not help but live in permanent anxiety. Theophrastus has given us a good example in his portrait, hardly overdrawn, of the *deisidaimōn,* that is to say, not of the 'superstitious man' as it is usually translated, but of the man who lives in perpetual fear of divine powers. 'Undoubtedly,' he begins, '*deisidaimonia* would seem to be a feeling of constant terror . . . in regard to the divine power; and here is a picture of the *deisidaimōn.*' There follows a series of instances the accumulation of which certainly gives us the impression that such a man exaggerates, but each instance taken by itself shows nothing at all abnormal in Greek religion. Our *deisidaimōn* celebrates the Feast of Pitchers (16, 2); we shall soon see that Epicurus also took part in this feast without distinguishing himself in any way from the good people of Athens . . . fr. 169 Us.). On the fourth and twenty-fourth days of the month, the *deisidaimōn* gives himself a holiday, has warm wine prepared, and spends his time garlanding the statues in his house (16, 10): Epicurus used to banquet with his friends on the twentieth day in each month. Every month the *deisidaimōn* betakes himself with his children and his wife (or, in her place, the nurse) to the *Orpheotelestai* to renew his initiation (16, 11): we are told that Epicurus had himself initiated 'into the mysteries of the city—no doubt the Eleusinian mysteries—and into other (initiations?)'. The *deisidaimōn* as such is distinguished by the keenness which makes him repeat the ceremony indefinitely, as though the first time did not afford him a sufficient guarantee. To shun the pollution brought by contact with a tombstone, a corpse, or a woman in childbed (16, 9) was, so to speak, one of the most rigid dogmas of Greek religion. Equally there was nothing more common than the fear of bad omens (16, 3, 6, 8), the need to have an explanation of one's dreams (16, 11), the belief in the purificatory virtues of the olive (16, 2), of sea-water (16, 12), of garlic and the sea-leek (16, 13), the panic caused by the sight of a madman or an epileptic (16, 14), or the veneration felt towards a snake that has glided into the house (16, 4). We

must not, therefore, think that the *deisidaimōn* of Theophrastus is an exception: at the time of Epicurus, and much later still, he had thousands of brothers in all parts of the Greek world.

It is clear, then, that for an infinite number of people religion remained a bondage which weighed heavily on their souls. No doubt in educated circles it was possible to banish the fear of the Olympians by denying their existence. It is also perfectly true that doubt and indifference as regards the civic gods had made great progress at the end of the fourth century; hence the parallel efforts on the one hand of Lycurgus and Demetrius of Phalerum to revive the official cults, on the other, earlier still, of Plato, of the author of the *Epinomis,* and of Aristotle . . . to introduce the new religion of the astral gods. But these well-educated men, more in the public eye perhaps and in any case better known to us because they were writers, are far from representing the masses. They remained attached to their gods, and so imprisoned in fear and hope; in fear, because they always had to dread that by an omission, even involuntary, of some ritual observation they might have offended the divinity; in hope, because it was always possible to believe that by purifications, sacrifices, and offerings the heart of the gods might be touched.

There is any amount of positive proof that these sentiments were thoroughly implanted in the pagan soul quite apart from the proof by implication provided by Lucretius' eloquent protest against the terrors of the over-devout. In the third century of our era one of the commonest motives for the popular hatred felt towards Christians was the belief that, neglecting the sacrifices themselves and encouraging others to do likewise, they had aroused the fury of the gods against the Empire. In 410, after the capture of Rome by Alaric and his Goths, this prejudice still had such power that St. Augustine was compelled to answer it; in the first ten books of the *City of God* he is engaged in showing that the Christians were not responsible for Rome's misfortunes. Let us simply recall, to cut the matter short, Plutarch's little essay on *deisidaimonia.* Plutarch opposes atheism—by which he means the Epicurean doctrine—to an excessive fear of the gods. But the latter evil seems to him worse than the former. Atheism may well be a false idea (C.1., . . . C.2), but at least it does not cause any unrest of soul; far from doing that, it steeps a man in a state of insensibility (. . . C.2) and as a result drives out fear (. . . C.2). On the other hand *deisidaimonia* does untold harm. There is no peace any more for a man once he regards the gods as spiteful and given to doing harm (. . . C.2); the Divinity is everywhere, it can pursue him even in sleep and beyond the grave.

No doubt not everything is original in this little work of Plutarch. Certain features were probably stock themes in the school of Epicurus since they are found both in Lucretius and Philodemus; Plutarch must have borrowed them from Epicurean literature. Nevertheless when we read his finely drawn analyses we are very soon convinced that they are not merely a statement of commonplaces but are the result of observation and experience. Take for example chapter 7 where Plutarch is contrasting the feelings of the atheist and the *deisidaimōn* when things are not going as they would like. . . . If the atheist is a moderate man he keeps silent and seeks his consolation within. If he has a peevish disposition he blames Chance or Fortune; accustomed to thinking that all is confusion here below, his own plight confirms him in that belief. In any event the atheist escapes more or less unharmed. It is otherwise with the *deisidaimōn*. 'If he suffers the most trivial misfortune he loses heart and builds upon his grief painful and serious afflictions from which he will be unable to rid himself; of his own accord he fills himself with fears and terrors, suspicions and worries, never ceasing to wail and groan. He blames neither man, nor chance, nor circumstances, nor himself but the sovereign Creator, God; it is from God, he would have us believe, that these tempestuous billows of heaven-sent malediction unfurl upon him. *According to him it is not because he is unfortunate but because the gods hate him that he is punished by them; that is why he submits to expiation and he is convinced that he deserves and has brought on himself everything he suffers.*' This passage, and what follows, could have been written by the most modern spiritual director. The reason is that excessive fear of God is a malady which is always with us, and one of the most difficult to cure, as Plutarch notes. It is congenital with religious emotion and grows *pari passu* with that emotion because it is in proportion to the degree of faith. If we really believe that, giving no scope to secondary causes, God intervenes himself, directly, in the smallest incidents in our life, and if we are really conscious of the impurity of our being in comparison with the divine being, we are not far from being convinced that all our misfortunes have as their cause some sin or, more likely, that permanent state of sin which is the peculiar lot of man and which gives him his essential character in the eyes of God. Hence comes a continuous vexation of the Divinity because we never cease offending against him. 'How can one speak to the *deisidaimōn*? What means is there of helping him? He sits outside his house muffled in a miserable sack or girt in hideous rags. He often rolls naked in the mud *confessing at the top of his voice certain faults, certain omissions of which he is guilty,* crying out that he has drunk this and eaten that, or that he has followed such and such a course without the permission of his Guardian Spirit'. Plutarch invents nothing; epigraphy confirms what he says. We possess such public confessions carved upon stone.

This fear of the gods did not afflict men for this life only, it made them anticipate an eternity of punishment. No doubt generalization must be avoided, for the sentiments of the ancients on this subject admitted of infinite variation, especially perhaps in the Hellenistic age, from complete scepticism to a sincere disquiet which drove a man to become initiated in all the oriental Mysteries so as to obtain a surer guarantee of immortality. The belief in punishment beyond the grave had a long history in Greece, where the *Nekyia* of Homer, which all knew by heart, had popularized it, and it appears in fourth-century literature. A client of Lysias declares herself ready to take the oath and, to give it more weight, recalls the punishments which are reserved in Hell for perjurors. Cephalus, the father of Lysias, admits that ever since he became an old man he has been tormented by the fear of having to expiate in Hades the faults which he might have committed during his long life. 'Demosthenes says that the author of a detestable law should be condemned to death so that he might administer his law to the impious in Hell. Elsewhere, he assumes that a base informer will one day be hurled by the infernal gods into the place where the impious are.' The punishments of Hell were a favourite subject with painters; an archaic vase as early as the sixth century depicts them, Polygnotus in the fifth had drawn them in the Lesche at Delphi, and a line from the *Captivi* of Plautus, a play imitated from a Greek original, is witness for the spread of these representations. Finally, if the celebrated text in the *Republic* does not mean that a man could seek purification in the place of his dead parents so as to rescue them from their pains, it does at least prove that many had recourse to certain sacrifices in order to obtain pardon for their crimes both during life and also after death.

So fear of the gods, fear of their anger towards the living and of their vengeance on the dead, played a great part in Greek religion. Perhaps Epicurus had experienced it himself. Perhaps he had undergone a crisis of conscience from which he had emerged victorious. If that is so we can understand better his unfailing certitude. He was convinced, at any rate, that *deisidaimonia* prevailed all about him, and as he had reached the haven of safety and, in a sentiment of universal benevolence, wished to lead others into it, he felt it to be his first care to banish this fear which utterly prevents peace of mind (*ataraxia*).

Now the whole of this evil comes from a false notion about the gods. The remedy for the evil, that is to say, a true notion about the gods, will be furnished by the first principles themselves of the doctrine of *ataraxia*. The system of Epicurus is perfectly coherent on this subject, and the solution which it provides is not without elegance in its simplicity.

Freed from all anxiety by the limitation of his desires the Sage, in this world, finds peace of soul and thereby blessedness. But is it credible that the gods do not enjoy an equal happiness—the gods whom the Greek had always been accustomed to regard as immortal and happy beings par excellence so much so that this double privilege of immortality and happiness is the very thing that essentially distinguishes the god from wretched, mortal man? Surely, if man can attain to happiness, so can the gods; and that which constitutes happiness for humans must also be the substance of the happiness enjoyed by the gods. Now human happiness consists of the absence of worry or, at least, this absence of worry is its first condition. It is to avoid being worried that a man restricts himself to the simplest mode of life, gives up the comforts of wealth, and lives apart from the world, politics, and affairs, thereby cutting off at the source all the causes of passion which might spoil his peace. The same considerations apply to the gods. It is absurd, then, to imagine that the gods constantly concern themselves with the government of the Universe and human affairs. That would run counter to the perfect serenity which is the basis of their happiness. 'Furthermore, we must not believe that the movement of the heavenly bodies, their turnings from one place to another, their eclipses, their risings and settings, and all such phenomena are brought about under the direction of a being who controls or will always control them and who at the same time possesses perfect happiness together with immortality; for the turmoil of affairs, anxieties, and feelings of anger and benevolence do not go with happiness, but all that arises where there is weakness, fear and dependence on others' (*Ep.*, I, 76-77). 'Blessed and immortal Nature knows no trouble herself nor does she cause trouble to anyone else, so that she is not a prey to feelings either of anger or benevolence; for all such things only belong to what is weak' (*k.d.*, 1). 'In the first place believe that god is a living being, immortal and blessed, exactly resembling the common idea of the divine being that is engraved in us, and do not attribute to him anything that is alien to immortality or ill suited to blessedness, but consider that he possesses everything which can preserve his happiness and immortality. Certainly the gods exist—the knowledge that we have of them is clear vision—but these gods are not as the vulgar believe them to be. For the vulgar do not know how to keep unblemished the idea they have of the gods. And it is not the man who denies the gods of the vulgar who is impious, but he who attaches to the idea of god the false opinions of the vulgar. For the assertions of the vulgar about the gods are not concepts born of sensation . . . but erroneous suppositions. Hence it comes about that the worst injuries are inflicted on the wicked by the doing of the gods, as also the greatest benefits are conferred <on the good>. These latter, in fact, having through their own excellence been familiar during their whole life with the true nature of the gods gladly receive into their souls the gods who are like themselves, while they regard as foreign to the divine nature everything which is

not such' (*Ep.*, III, 123-124). 'From their indestructibility (i.e. the gods') it follows that they are strangers to all suffering; nothing can cause them any joy or inflict on them any suffering from outside' (fr. 99 Us. = Philod., . . . p. 125 G.).

In this situation, then, what was the religion of Epicurus likely to be? To begin with, there was no question of denying the gods: 'The gods exist, the knowledge which we have of them is clear vision' (*Ep.*, III, 123). Far from reckoning Epicurus among the sceptics or the indifferent whose numbers were increasing at the end of the fourth century we must on the contrary regard him as one of those who reacted against the growing unbelief. He himself believed in the gods and in the benefits of religion. He was punctilious in performing the traditional acts of worship and was, in short, a pious man in the sense in which the ancients understood that word. That he must have received, in his childhood in Samos, the religious education of a young citizen of Athens goes without saying—even without giving currency to the story spread about by his enemies, 'that he used to go round with his mother from house to house so as to read the formulae for purification'. Nor is it necessary, in order to be convinced of his piety, to note the use he makes of the language of the Mysteries, for that might well be merely a literary borrowing. It is enough to hear him speak: '<That the civic gods must be honoured>', declares Philodemus, 'was not only the teaching of Epicurus but it is clear from his conduct also that he loyally observed all the traditional feasts and sacrifices. In the archonship of Aristonymus, when writing to Phyrson about one of his fellow citizens, Theodotus, he says that he has joined in all the festivals . . . that he has celebrated with the people the festival of Pitchers . . . on the 2nd day of Anthesteria) and has been initiated into the Mysteries of the city as well as other (initiations?).' In another letter quoted by Philodemus, Epicurus writes, 'As for us, let us piously and fittingly sacrifice on the proper days, and let us perform all the other acts of worship according to custom, without letting ourselves be in any way troubled by common opinions in our judgments about the best and most august beings. Besides, let us remain also observant of custom for the reason I have mentioned; for it is thus that we may live in conformity with nature . . . ' According to Philodemus again, in the second book *On the kinds of Life* Epicurus says that the Sage 'will show marks of respect to the gods', and Philodemus adds a little later: 'Furthermore it will appear that Epicurus loyally observed all the forms of worship and enjoined upon his friends to observe them, not only because of the laws but for reasons in conformity with the nature of things . . . Indeed, he says, in the book *On the kinds of Life*, Prayer is proper to wisdom, not because the gods would be annoyed if we did not pray, but because we see how much the nature of the gods is superior to us in power and excellence.' Finally let me add the evidence of one of the ancients who was not a member of the School, Cicero, in his *De Natura Deorum:* 'Certainly Epicurus holds that the gods exist and indeed I have never seen a man so afraid of things which, according to himself, he ought not to fear, I mean death and the gods.'

These texts are enough, and there is not the least reason for interpreting the facts they report as evidence of hypocrisy. That charge is part of the usual collection of insults and calumnies that one sect hurled against another in antiquity. The Stoics used it against Epicurus and Plutarch repeats it after them. Philodemus in turn throws it in the teeth of the Stoics. In the same way, relying on the *De Mundo* which they wrongly attributed to him, the Fathers of the Church charged Aristotle with impiety, and it is well known how often the crime of ἀθεατης has been imputed to the Christians. Such accusations, coupled most often with that of immorality, are usually worthless. In the case of Epicurus it can be seen at once how easily they could arise from a misunderstanding of the Sage's thought.

Sincere in his fidelity to the civic cults Epicurus was not less so in the use he made in his writings of those interjections in which the name of the gods is called as witness. 'It would be laughable to mention that they sanctioned the use of oaths,' remarks Philodemus, 'since their philosophic works are full of them. It is right, however, to say that Epicurus urged them to keep the faith pledged by these and other oaths, and particularly to respect the emphatic oath by the name of Zeus himself. For he is not the man to write, "In the name of . . . — but what shall I say? How can I speak piously?" And he counsels Colotes to pay attention always to the regard for oaths and to the proper use of the name of the gods.

Epicurus, then, observed the forms of the State religion not only so as to 'obey the law' but from genuine feeling. Nevertheless his religion was not that of the common people. It differed from it in two ways.

In the first place, Epicurus' gods, being without cares like the Sage, take no interest in human affairs. Let us go over this essential dogma once again with the help of some quotations. 'In his treatise **On Holiness** he (Epicurus) calls the life of the Divinity infinitely pleasant and happy, and he considers that we must remove all impurity from the notion we have about the divine, understanding the conditions of such a kind of life (i.e. that of the gods) so that we adapt everything which happens to us to the manner of living which befits divine felicity. It is thus, thinks Epicurus, that holiness is made complete while at the same time common traditions are carefully preserved. But those people that we call "smitten with 'religious' dread", into what unsurpassable impiety do they not hurl

themselves? He is not impious, who upholds the immortality and the supreme blessedness of God, together with all the privileges that we attach to those two. Rather he is pious who holds both opinions about the divine (i.e. that the divine is immortal and happy). And he who sees also that the good and ill sent us by God come without any unhealthy anger or benevolence, shows clearly that God has no need of human things, but enjoys all good in full realization.' And again, 'Let it suffice to say now that the divine needs no mark of honour, but that it is natural for us to honour it, in particular by forming pious notions of it, and secondly by offering to each of the gods in turn the traditional sacrifices.' '<If we admit that the gods take care of the world> we must then admit that they toil in an unsurpassable fashion, and not only for a limited time. For to say that we are convinced that the gods, being endowed with prudence, cannot enter into the category of bunglers, any more than zealous men here below, is, according to our doctrine, to destroy their serenity. Therefore to speak correctly we must assert that the gods know neither toil nor fatigue.'

On the other hand, since the gods are indescribably happy, to praise them in prayer, to draw near to them on those solemn occasions when the city offers them a sacrifice, and to rejoice with them at the annual festivals is to take part in their happiness. That is why the disciple of Epicurus would be faithful to the prescriptions of religion. If the feasts at Athens were an occasion of merriment for all, the Epicurean had a still better reason for rejoicing. Was he not the equal of Zeus? As long as he suffered neither hunger nor thirst nor cold, as long as he was provided with a little barley-cake and water—easy things to obtain—he could rival Zeus himself in happiness. That is why, also, the Epicurean sage did not scruple to call upon the name of the gods: 'He appeals to the Completely Happy so as to strengthen his own blessedness.'

The Sage would perhaps have been surprised to hear it said, nevertheless it remains true that this religion of Epicurus is related to Plato's. Both put the goal of religious activity in the contemplation of beauty, and in so doing show themselves to be true sons of Greece. For them, as for all Greeks, the divine being, whatever its essence, is a being of perfect beauty who lives a life of harmony and serenity. Thus the Divine Universe of the *Timaeus* is a work of finished beauty which the Demiurge 'the best of artists', has lovingly chiselled; and this theme of beauty constantly recurs as the *leitmotiv* in every reference to the fabric of the Universe. Likewise the gods of Epicurus are filled with beauty; 'We must start from the nature of man so as to deduce, by analogy, the nature of the gods, and to assert, as a result, that the Divinity is a being living for ever and imperishable, and that it is totally filled with blessedness. Yet there is this reservation, that it does not admit of the fatigues of man or of the evils relating to death, to say nothing of the punishments after death, that we cannot attribute to it any of the things which make us suffer, but rather all good things, and that it possesses beauty in plenitude.' So again, following the Greek tradition, the Divine Universe of the Timaeus is completely self-sufficient and needs nothing. The same applies to the gods of Epicurus. However, to quote from Plato, these blessed gods who lack nothing 'have taken pity on the human race doomed by nature to suffer. They have therefore instituted, as moments of relief from our troubles, the festivals in which men hold converse with the gods, and they have given us as companions in the festivals the Muses, Apollo Musagetes, and Dionysus so that, associating with the gods in these meetings we might set right once again our way of living . . . Hence come rhythm and harmony. For the gods who have thus been given to us as companions in the dance make us feel pleasure when we perceive rhythm and harmony. It is they who, instructing us to move ourselves in order and making themselves our leaders, unite us one to another by a mixture of dances and songs and have called these exercises *choirs* . . . from the joy which we feel in them. . . . Philodemus in his turn says, 'It is principally through the gods that pleasure springs up in the heart of man (*voluptatem in homine a deo auctore creatam adserit principaliter*).' As Diels has well seen, this remark refers to religious festivals. The gods have instituted these festivals to give us a share in their everlasting joy. No doubt a man can taste of the happiness of the gods at other times as well, whenever he receives into his soul the blessed emanations which flow from the persons of the gods. But it is on festal days, when we approach the altar of sacrifice or contemplate the divine statue, that the influence of the gods makes itself more strongly felt and produces the greatest joy. 'That', says Epicurus, 'is the most essential thing and the one which is, as it were, pre-eminent. For every wise man has pure and holy opinions about Divinity and believes that its nature is noble and august. But it is particularly in festivals that he, progressing in the perception of its nature whilst having its name on his lips the whole time, comes by a more vivid sensation to understand (or, "to possess") the immortality of the gods.' '<The Sage addresses prayers> to the gods, he admires their nature and condition, he strives to come near to it, he aspires, so to speak, to touch and live with it, and he calls wise men friends of the gods, and the gods friends of wise men.'

All these elements of the Epicurean religion are brought together in a letter written by the Sage to an unknown friend; discovered in an Egyptian papyrus, recognized as belonging to Epicurus and carefully edited by Diels, this precious document will form a fitting conclusion to our analysis. In it we meet again, of course, the dogma of the *ataraxia* of the gods and, therefore, that of their indifference towards human affairs. But in it we see also that this dogma, far from abolishing religion, should purify it; the

truly pious man does not approach the gods to appease them or to obtain some favour from them, but to unite himself to them by contemplation, to rejoice in their joy, and so to taste for himself, in this mortal life, their unending happiness.

'<It is no proof of piety to observe the customary religious obligations—though the offering of sacrifices> on suitable occasions may be, as I have said, in keeping with nature—nor is it, by Zeus, when someone or other goes about repeating, "I fear all the gods, and honour them, and want to spend all my money in making sacrifices and consecrating offerings to them." Such a man is perhaps more praiseworthy than other individuals, but still it is not thus that a solid foundation for piety is laid. You, my friend, must know that the most blessed gift is to have a clear perception of things; that is absolutely the best thing that we can conceive of here below. Admire this clear apprehension of the spirit, revere

---

In his poem *On the Nature of Things*, Lucretius portrays Epicurus as an epic hero:

When before our eyes man's life lay
  groveling, prostrate,

Crushed to the dust under the burden of
  Religion

(Which thrust its head from heaven, its
  horrible face

Glowering over mankind born to die),

One man, a Greek, was the first mortal who
  dared

Oppose his eyes, the first to stand firm in
  defiance.

Not the fables of gods, nor lightning, nor the
  menacing

Rumble of heaven could daunt him, but all
  the more

They whetted his keen mind with longing to
  be

First to smash open the tight-barred gates of
  Nature

His vigor of mind prevailed, and he strode far

Beyond the fiery battlements of the world.

Raiding the fields of the unmeasured All.

Our victor returns with knowledge of what
  can arise.

What cannot, what law grants each thing its
  own

Deep-driven boundary stone and finite scope.

Religion now lies trampled beneath our feet.

And we are made gods by the victory.

On the Nature of Things, *edited by Anthony M. Esolin, Johns Hopkins University Press, 1995.*

this divine gift. After that, <you should not honour the gods because you think thus to gain their favour>, as people will think when they see you performing acts of piety, but only because, in comparison with your own happiness, you see how the condition of the gods is infinitely more august, according to our doctrine. And certainly, by Zeus, <when you practise> this doctrine—the doctrine most worthy of belief, <as your reason should tell you—it is of course open to you to offer sacrifices to the gods. By doing so you perform> an act which gives confidence and is a pleasure to see, if it is done at the proper time, because you honour your own doctrine by enjoying those pleasures of the senses which befit such occasions and besides you conform in some sense to religious traditions. [Only be careful that you do not permit any admixture of fear of the gods or of the supposition that in acting as you do you are winning the favour of the gods.]

'For indeed, in the name of Zeus (as men affect to say) what have you to fear in this matter? Do you believe that the gods can do you harm? Is not that, on any showing, to belittle them? How then will you not regard the Divinity as a miserable creature if it appears inferior in comparison to yourself? Or will you rather be of the opinion that by sacrificing thousands of oxen you can appease God if you have committed some evil deed? Can you think that he will take account of the sacrifice and, like a man, remit at some time or another a part of the penalty?

'No doubt men tell each other that they should fear the gods and honour them with sacrifices so that, restrained by the tribute they receive, the gods will not attack them; as a result they think that if their surmise is correct they will altogether escape injury and if it is not, all will be well because they pay homage to the power of the gods. But if these close relations <between gods and men were really to exist it would be a great misfortune, for the effect would make itself felt even beyond the grave>, after the funeral ceremonies, as soon as a man was cremated. For then men would suffer injury even beneath the earth and everyone would have to expect punishment. Moreover, I need not describe how men would have to beg for signs of favour from the gods in their fear of being neglected by them (for they would think to induce the gods in this way to communicate with them more readily and come down into their temples), any more than I can tell of the diversity and number of the methods they would employ because of their fear of harm and so as to guard against punishment. For to speak the truth all this seems a pure illusion of these people when compared with the doctrine of those who think that a life of happiness exists for us in this world and do not admit that the dead live again—a marvel not less unlikely than those which Plato imagined.'

Norman Wentworth DeWitt (essay date 1954)

SOURCE: Norman Wentworth DeWitt, "A Synoptic View of Epicureanism," in *Epicurus and His Philosophy*, University of Minnesota Press, 1954, pp. 3-35.

[*The following excerpt, arranged according to Epicurus's own principles of education, sketches DeWitt's view of Epicurus, ranging from his life and philosophy to his reputation and historical influence. DeWitt makes it his explicit goal "to create the proper attitude for a sympathetic understanding of the man and his work."*]

This book attempts to present for the first time a fairly complete account of the life and teachings of Epicurus. At the very outset the reader should be prepared to think of him at one and the same time as the most revered and the most reviled of all founders of thought in the Graeco-Roman world.

His was the only creed that attained to the dimensions of a world philosophy. For the space of more than seven centuries, three before Christ and four afterward, it continued to command the devotion of multitudes of men. It flourished among Greeks and barbarians alike, in Greece, Asia Minor, Syria, Judaea, Egypt, Italy, Roman Africa, and Gaul. The man himself was revered as an ethical father, a savior, and a god. Men wore his image on finger-rings; they displayed painted portraits of him in their living rooms; the more affluent honored him with likenesses in marble. His handbooks of doctrine were carried about like breviaries; his sayings were esteemed as if oracles and committed to memory as if Articles of Faith. His published letters were cherished as if epistles of an apostle. Pledges were taken to live obedient to his precepts. On the twentieth day of every month his followers assembled to perform solemn rites in honor of his memory, a sort of sacrament.

Throughout these same seven centuries no man was more ceaselessly reviled. At his first appearance as a public teacher he was threatened with the fate of Socrates. In Athens he never dared to offer instruction in a public place but confined himself to his own house and garden. His character and his doctrines became the special target of abuse for each successive school and sect, first for Platonists, next for Stoics, and finally for Christians. His name became an abomination to orthodox Jews. The Christians, though by no means blind to the merit of his ethics, abhorred him for his denial of divine providence and immortality.

Throughout this book certain devices of procedure will be employed which were worked out and practiced by Epicurus himself. One of these has been exemplified in the preceding paragraphs. He laid special stress upon the importance of the diathesis or the attitude to be chosen at the beginning. For instance, in the very first of his forty Authorized Doctrines the disciple is informed that the gods are not to be feared, because "the incorruptible being is immune to feelings of anger or gratitude." If only the disciple could maintain this attitude, it was felt that he would be rightly disposed to receive all subsequent instruction about the nature of the gods. On this same principle the hope is here entertained that, if the reader habituates himself from the outset to think of Epicurus as both the most revered and the most reviled of all ancient philosophers, he will be rightly prepared to judge with impartiality the course of his life and the true structure of his doctrine.

Another device consistently practiced by Epicurus was to begin with the synoptic view. He thought of his writings as maps drawn to larger and smaller scales. The process of learning was regarded as a progression from general maps with few details to regional maps, as it were, with a proportionate increase of detail.

The procedure was regularly from the general to the particular. The truths of Physics were reduced to Twelve Elementary Principles. These corresponded to a general map, affording a panoramic view of the nature of things. Of the Twelve Principles the most important was the third: "The universe consists of atoms and void." Since the void is incapable either of delivering or receiving a stimulus, it followed that the soul, which is capable both of stimulating and being stimulated, must be corporeal by nature, composed of atoms. Hence vision and the other sensations must be explained by the impact of matter upon matter. In this way one detail of truth after another was deduced from the general principle.

From the point of view of logic this progression from the general to the particular constituted a sort of chain argument, a device in which Epicurus had great faith. He looked upon truth in terms of the whole and the part, the integer and the details. The details seemed to him so linked with one another that, if only the beginning was rightly made, one truth after another would infallibly reveal itself until perfection of knowledge should be attained. As Lucretius expressed it: "One point will become clear from understanding another; nor will blind night ever rob you of the path and prevent you from peering into the ultimate realities of nature; so surely will understanding of one thing kindle a gleam to illuminate the next."

The first text to be placed in the hands of the beginner was the Little Epitome, which is extant as the letter addressed to Herodotus. This is contained in a mere twenty pages of print and offers what Epicurus called "the condensed view of the integrated survey of the whole." This too corresponds to a general map. Only the main features of the system are sketched in, the atoms and their qualities, the nature of attributes, such as color, the soul, sensation, the evolution of society and culture, heavenly phenomena. At the same time the objective of study is stressed, which is ataraxy, the quiet of mind that arises from faith in the certainty of knowledge. Incidentally, faith was recognized for the first time as a factor in happiness.

When the student had mastered the Little Epitome, which was, as it were, a First Reader, he would progress to the Big Epitome. This Second Reader, though written earlier, served as an amplification of the Little Epitome and is represented for us by the poem of Lucretius *On the Nature of Things*. The only new topic was the nature of the gods, planned for the seventh book but never written, which leaves the worst gap in our knowledge. The six extant books merely add what seems to us an abundance of detail to the topics already adumbrated in the Little Epitome. This increase of detail, however, is illuminating for the educational procedure involved. The bald outline of doctrine must first be mastered and thereafter the task of the student is "to incorporate all the particulars into it." He might even go on from the Big Epitome to the encyclopedic treatment in the thirty-seven books on Physics but the procedure was always the same, adding details to details until at last perfection of detail should be attained.

In harmony with this method a synoptic view of Epicurus and his philosophy will now be presented in the form of dogmatic general statements. These will be amplified at once by a sparing addition of details in preparation for the yet larger amplification along with footnotes in the chapters that follow. The immediate objectives are two in number. The first has three aspects: to show where Epicurus belongs in the succession of philosophers, how his thought is related to the cultural context in which it arose, and how it survived in the cultural context into which it was finally absorbed. The second objective has two aspects: so to orientate the reader at the outset as to create the proper attitude for a sympathetic understanding of the man and his work; and not less to warn the reader against the disparagement and prejudice that abound in all the secondary literature.

Unhappily this warning will call for frequent emphasis and repetition. All that we possess of the original texts of Epicurus is comprised in a booklet of sixty-nine pages, though supplemented by the poem of Lucretius. The secondary literature, on the contrary, is abundant and for the greater part hostile. If this were received uncritically we should be thinking of the man as a brawling Thersites in the camp of the philosophers, as an ingrate, an ignoramus, a dullard, a scorner of all culture, a sensualist, and an atheist. The ancient critics who originated these slanders were declared by Diogenes Laertius, whose excellent biography of Epicurus is our chief authority, "to be out of their minds." In spite of this fact our modern scholars prefer to hunt with the pack and with lighthearted disdain for the evidences they denounce Epicurus as a quietist, a friend of anarchy, an incoherent thinker, a moral invalid, and an egoistic hedonist, enlarging the vocabulary of detraction from the armories of modern philosophy.

In the case of these false opinions also it will be convenient to follow a practice employed by Epicurus. It was his way to oppose true opinions to false opinions. For example, it was a true opinion to believe the gods immune to feelings of anger or gratitude, a false opinion to fear them as venal and vindictive. Again, it was a true opinion to believe that happiness was to be found in the simple life and retirement, a false opinion to think it lay in wealth, power, or glory. After this same fashion the false opinions concerning Epicurus and his philosophy will here be paired with judgments based upon the evidences. In some instances, it may be mentioned, the mistakes of scholars are not false opinions but examples of oversight; to particularize, they fail to recognize Epicurus as an acute critic of Platonism. For convenience, however, errors of all kinds will be listed under the heading of false opinions.

True Opinions: False Opinions

In the succession of philosophers the place of Epicurus is immediately after Plato and Pyrrho the skeptic. Platonism and skepticism were among his chief abominations. The false opinion is to think him opposed to Stoicism. The traditional order of mention, Stoics, Epicureans, and Skeptics, is the exact reverse of the chronological succession. The philosophy of Epicurus was an immediate reaction to the skepticism of Pyrrho and it was offered to the public as a fully developed system before Zeno the founder of Stoicism even began to teach.

Epicurus was an erudite man and a trained thinker. He made the rounds of the contemporary schools, Platonic, Peripatetic, and Democritean, and he devoted several years to reading and study before offering himself as a teacher. The false opinion is to think him an ignoramus and an enemy of all culture.

Historians persist in judging him only as a philosopher, but to be rightly understood he must be recognized also as a moral reformer. The fallacy consists in damning him as an ingrate and in failing to discern that reformers are rebels and as rebels feel themselves absolved from debts of gratitude.

As a man of science Epicurus returned to the tradition of the Ionian thinkers, which had been interrupted by Socrates and Plato. The chief positive influence on his thinking was Ionian, the chief negative influence Platonic. The error in this instance consists in the failure to recognize Epicurus as an Antiplatonist and a penetrating critic of Platonism.

As a philosopher Epicurus belongs in the class of thinkers who have attempted a synthesis of philosophical thought, and his modern analogues are Herbert Spencer and Auguste Comte. He surveyed the whole field of previous thought and either wrote critiques of his predecessors himself or delegated the task to his colleagues. This aspect of the activity of his school has been completely overlooked.

He was the first to promulgate a dogmatic philosophy, actuated by a passion for certainty and a detestation of skepticism, which he imputed even to Plato. The distinction of being a dogmatist was naturally not denied him, because it was deemed a demerit, the renunciation of inquiry.

He exalted Nature as the norm of truth, revolting against Plato, who regarded Reason as the norm and hypostatized it as a divine existence. The fallacy consists in classifying Epicurus as an empiricist in the modern sense; he never declared sensation to be the source of knowledge; much less did he declare all sensations to be trustworthy.

As an educator Epicurus adopted the procedures of Euclid, parting company with both Plato and the Ionian scientists. The chief mistake in this instance is to foist upon him the method of inductive reasoning; his chief reliance was upon deduction. As for the influence of Euclid, it is regularly overlooked.

Epicureanism was the first missionary philosophy. The mistake is to look upon Epicurus as an effeminate and a moral invalid; by disposition he was combative and by natural gifts a leader, organizer, and campaigner.

Epicureanism was the first world philosophy, being acceptable to both Greek and barbarian. The mistake is to think of Epicurus as an egoistic hedonist, ruled solely by self-interest. He was an altruistic hedonist.

Epicureanism served in the ancient world as a preparation for Christianity, helping to bridge the gap between Greek intellectualism and a religious way of life. It shunted the emphasis from the political to the social virtues and offered what may be called a religion of humanity. The mistake is to overlook the terminology and ideology of Epicureanism in the New Testament and to think of its founder as an enemy of religion.

Epicureanism presented two fronts to the world, the one as repellent as the other was attractive. Its discouragement of the political career was repellent to the ambitious, its denial of divine providence to pious orthodoxy, and its hedonism to timorous respectability. Its candor, charity, courtesy, and friendliness were attractive to multitudes of the honest and unambitious folk.

The influence of Epicureanism, though anonymous, has been persistent in literature, ethics, and politics. In literature and ethics it has survived by amalgamation with Stoicism, chiefly through Seneca and Marcus Aurelius. In politics it fathered the doctrine that the least government is the best government, which was espoused by John Locke and popularized in North America by Thomas Jefferson. All these aspects of influence have been overlooked because of the usual anonymity. It was the fate of Epicurus to be named if condemned, unnamed if approved.

The Cultural Context

Epicurus was born in 341 B.C. This mute fact will take on significance if it be recalled that barely seven years had passed since the death of Plato and only seven were to elapse before Alexander crossed the Hellespont for the conquest of Persia. The childhood and adolescence of the man were destined to be separated from his adult life by the bold dividing line between the introverted world of Greek city-states and the extroverted world of far-flung Macedonian monarchies. Only a few dividing lines in history are so distinctly drawn.

Boyhood and adolescence were passed in the last years of the so-called great age of Greece, which produced philosophy and eloquence as its final fruitage. Platonism was still dominant in the field of higher education and Athens abounded in gifted orators as at no other time. From Platonism and the political career Epicurus turned away with so passionate a revulsion that this became the chief single factor in shaping his tactics as an educator and his thought as a philosopher. At the same time there were other factors in the cultural context which exercised an active influence. These may be associated with the names of Isocrates, Euclid, Diogenes, Aristotle, and writers such as Aristobulus, Nearchus, and the first Ptolemy, who reported the explorations and campaigns of Alexander. This statement calls for immediate, though brief, amplification.

Isocrates, a great teacher, had inaugurated a shift of emphasis from artistic speech for the benefit of listeners to artistic writing for the benefit of readers and his example was followed up by his admirer Praxiphanes, who became the teacher of Epicurus. The young man seems to have fallen under this spell for a time, and his extant **letter to Menoeceus** is artfully composed in the Isocratean manner. This fashion, however, was subsequently abandoned in favor of the bald style of Euclid, of which the sole merit was clarity. Along with this unadorned style came the adoption of the textbook form and the deductive procedures. Euclid himself, of course, was merely bringing to perfection a technique of book-making which had gradually taken shape in the circle of geometers. His name is here used to stand for a trend which

Epicurus manifestly followed. The school textbook was just beginning to emerge as a distinct type.

In the domain of ethics the influence of the men called Cynics is unmistakable. Diogenes, known as the Dog, was still alive when Epicurus arrived in Athens for his required military training; his pupil Crates was a closer contemporary. These Cynics were staging a riotous rebellion against the conventional smugness and hypocrisy and they affected to make absolute honesty their ideal. Epicurus wholeheartedly endorsed the quest of honesty but repudiated their insolence and vulgarity. He insisted that honesty be joined with courtesy and decorum. His criticism of society was sympathetic and urbane and links the school not only with the better exemplars of the contemporary New Comedy, especially Menander, but also with the best tradition of satire as a literary form. Horace, Juvenal, and Petronius were all communicants of the Epicurean fellowship.

In his approach to the problem of knowledge Epicurus plainly owed an unacknowledged debt to the later Aristotle. One of the latter's innovations was to switch attention from inorganic to organic life; he founded the sciences of botany and zoology. This meant the revelation of a new order of Nature, a terrestrial order as opposed to the celestial order, and in the light of this discovery Epicurus rejected the hypostatized Reason of Plato as the norm of truth and looked instead to Nature as furnishing the norm.

This revolution in the approach to knowledge was fortuitously promoted and confirmed by the simultaneous extension of the geographical horizon by the explorations of Alexander. During the youth of Epicurus Greece was deluged by the new wealth of information concerning the geography, the flora and fauna, and the divergent wisdoms of Persia and India. Even the works of Megasthenes, written under Seleucus, Alexander's successor, were available before Epicurus launched his philosophy. It is consequently not surprising that his new canon of truth was based upon earthly rather than heavenly phenomena nor that his social and political outlook transcended even the Panhellenism of Isocrates and took cognizance of Greeks and barbarians alike, however sundered from the motherland of city-states and parochial politics.

While these positive influences are under survey it should still be remembered that the chief negative influences were Platonism and oratory. The characteristic shared in common by Platonism and oratory was the political obsession. The aim of Demosthenes and his party was to preserve the Greek world of city-states: the political teachings of Plato may justly be appraised as a theoretical extension of the political experience represented by the city-state. It was the assumption of philosopher and orator alike that the happiness of the individual was inseparable from his life as a citizen. The truth of this assumption was destined to be tested in the very presence of the young Epicurus; he was in Athens performing his required military service when the orator Hypereides and others were put to death and Demosthenes escaped a like fate by suicide. The futility of the political career and the folly of continuing to marry ethics with politics could hardly have been more objectively demonstrated.

The result for Epicurus was a violent revulsion from the spirit of the past, though it must not be inferred that this was followed quickly by a reasoned adjustment to the challenge of the new world in the process of becoming. There was an interval of several years consumed in study and in brooding. Even if by disposition the individual be inclined toward rebellion, the obstinate factors of a complicated problem refuse to disengage themselves at once from the pattern of the old to rearrange themselves into the pattern of the new. When this process had at length completed itself, however, it was manifest that Epicurus was determined to divorce ethics from politics and prepared to promulgate a philosophy adapted to the new world of Màcedonian monarchs and universal rather than parochial Hellenism.

The promulgation of the new philosophy was bound to mean the declaration of war upon the whole program of Platonic education, not only because it was the system then dominant in the schools but also for the reason that more than others it stood for the tight combination of ethics with politics which disqualified philosophy for universal acceptance.

It was this opposition to Platonism that chiefly determined the shape of Epicureanism; more than half of its forty Authorized Doctrines are flat contradictions of Platonism. It is the mistake of historians to oppose Epicurus to Stoics. This is an anachronism; it comes of throwing back into the lifetime of Epicurus a hostility that arose only after his death. The error is chiefly due to the writings of Cicero, who matches Epicureans and Stoics as if rival schools of gladiators.

Already in 311 B.C. Epicurus was offering a neatly integrated body of doctrine to the youth of Mytilene. At that date the founder of Stoicism, Zeno of Citium in Cyprus, was a new arrival in Athens about twenty-one years of age. In contrast to the precocious Epicurus he was a late beginner and a slow learner. Many years were to elapse before he began to address himself to the people of Athens in the Painted Porch. The assumption of hostility between the two is unsupported even by a scrap of evidence. It was Chrysippus, the second founder of Stoicism, who began the feud and he was a mere lad of nine years living in his native Soli of Cilicia when Epicurus passed away. Stoicism is consequently to be written off absolutely as an influence in the life of Epicurus.

Epicurus as Man of Erudition

It should not be necessary to defend Epicurus against the charge of being an ignoramus and an enemy of all culture, but the slanders of ancient and modern writers render refutation obligatory.

As a precocious boy and the son of a schoolmaster it is certain that he received the usual elementary education and that too in advance of his years. Even the scant and fragmented tradition preserves the item that as a mere schoolboy he cornered his teacher over the problem of chaos in Hesiod. In an extant work he denounces the pessimism of Theognis. He is said to have quoted Sophocles in proof of the principle that pain is an evil. He cited Homer as authority for the doctrine that pleasure is the telos or goal of living. He is also reported to have declared the teachings of the poets on the subject of morals to be a hodgepodge, which is true. All of this evidence points to the customary training and some of it to the early manifestation of a bold spirit and an inquisitive mind.

It is inconceivable that he escaped the Platonic training in geometry, dialectic, and rhetoric. He is known to have studied with Pamphilus, a Platonist, in the city of Samos, probably for four years. His extant **letter to Menoeceus** is composed according to the rules of rhythmical prose and certain excerpts from other writings afford hints of his possessing this skill. There is even reason for believing that he gave instruction in rhetoric for a time.

He declared dialectic a superfluity but was able to criticize Plato with great acumen and he wrote against the Megarians, the contemporary experts in logic. He rejected geometry as having no bearing upon problems of conduct but adopted the procedures of Euclid in the composition of his own textbooks. He refuted the assumption of the mathematicians that matter is infinitely divisible, rightly insisting that the result would be zero. This is not the thinking of an ignoramus.

He also exhibits great familiarity with the writings of Plato and he distributed among members of his school the work of refuting or ridiculing his various dialogues. His own classification of the desires is developed from a Platonic hint and he begins to erect his structure of hedonism from the point where this topic was left by Plato. A paragraph is extant in which he warns his disciples against the Platonic view of the universe as described in the *Timaeus,* and elsewhere he pokes a little satirical fun at that famous opus. More than half of his forty Authorized Doctrines are direct contradictions of Platonic teachings.

The closeness of the relationship between Epicurus and Aristotle may be judged from the fact that two volumes on the subject have been published by the eminent Italian scholar Ettore Bignone. Leaving aside for the moment the undoubted contentions of the two schools, it may be said that common to both founders was the direct analytical approach to problems as opposed to the circuitous analogical approach adopted by Plato. The main difference was that the attitude of Aristotle was analytical while that of Epicurus was analytical and pragmatic at the same time. His injunction "to neglect no opportunity to disseminate the doctrines of the true philosophy" finds no analogue in Aristotle's *Nicomachean Ethics*. On the other hand there is no better preparation for the ethics of Epicurus than a perusal of that treatise and especially of the sections on Friendship, the Magnanimous Man, and Happiness. Many anticipations of his teachings may there be identified: for example, the possibility of man's attainment to a life that in respect of quality may be called immortal or divine.

The debt of Epicurus to Aristotle the biologist is equally manifest for those who are interested in observing it. The mere fact that he rejected Reason from his Canon of truth and set up Nature as the norm is a tacit recognition of Aristotle's discovery of the order in organic life. In its proper place the suggestion will be made that Aristotle's study of the embryo seems to have given rise to the doctrine of innate ideas or Anticipations, as Epicurus styled them, which forecast adult understanding just as the venous system of the embryo prefigures the adult organism. Another subject of interest to both our philosophers was animal behavior, upon which Epicurus based in large part his theory of pleasure and his definition of justice.

The later schooling of Epicurus was also such as to lay the foundations for a broad erudition. After his exciting cadetship there is good evidence for believing that he studied with the acidulous Praxiphanes in Rhodes, a Peripatetic who shared the partiality of his school for literary criticism, while owning "good writing" for a special interest. It is certain that Epicurus spent a longer time in Teos with the Democritean Nausiphanes, who in spite of his indolence was an able, versatile, and original thinker. He gave his ungrateful pupil a fruitful suggestion about a canon of truth.

After tiring of teachers, to none of whom he afterward acknowledged any debt, Epicurus must have devoted himself to an extensive program of reading and study, because a few years later he planned a series of critiques of all previous thinkers, assigning the sophists, dialecticians, and physicians to his trusted Metrodorus, while Empedocles was turned over to the less agile Hermarchus. He chose himself to write against the physicists, among whom he expressed a preference for Anaxagoras and Archelaus, an example of discriminating judgment. He also reserved to himself, as mentioned above, the task of refuting the disputative Megarians, because this school was active and to combat it was an urgent necessity.

When all these facts are added up, the conclusion must follow that Epicurus was not only a man of comprehensive learning but also an ambitious organizer of knowledge. It is doubtful whether any other philosopher made a more earnest attempt to survey the whole field. It should also be borne in mind that those who would have him an enemy of all culture are sometimes driven to emend the texts in order to save their prejudices.

Epicurus as Moral Reformer

Special abuse has been heaped upon Epicurus because of his alleged ingratitude to teachers. There is some injustice in this charge and a notable lack of discrimination. If he felt no gratitude—and this seems to have been the case—it is unfair to demand the profession of it. The lack of discrimination consists in failing to recognize his double role as philosopher and moral reformer. These two roles may be combined in one person but their respective motivations are quite different and the one role is bound to dominate the other.

Reformers, whether moral or political, feel themselves absolved from debts of gratitude. Epicurus, having become conscious of himself as belonging in this class, denied all obligations to teachers, and this in spite of the fact that he had made the rounds of the schools and acquired the knowledge and skills respectively offered by them. To ascribe this conduct to him as a vice is on a par with vituperating Martin Luther for not proclaiming his gratitude to the Roman Catholic instructors whose skills he had acquired.

The attitude displayed by Epicurus is to a certain degree comparable to that assumed by St. Paul, who declared himself an apostle "not from men neither through man"; he wished the Galatians to know "that the gospel preached by him was not according to man, for he did not receive it from man, neither was he taught it." At this point the similarity ends, and Epicurus and Paul part company as being respectively Greek and Jew. Paul claimed authority by virtue of revelation through Jesus Christ and God the Father, qualifying himself as a prophet, which was a concept familiar to his race. Epicurus declared himself to be "self-taught" and he arrogated to himself the title of Sage or Wise Man, a concept familiar to the Greeks. He could not claim inspiration, because he denied all participation of the gods in human affairs. He was capable, however, of claiming perfection of knowledge, because he had approximated to the life of the gods. Thus to him his wisdom was not a revelation, though it was such to his disciples. Paul's gospel, on the contrary, was a revelation both to himself and to his disciples.

The presumptuous attitude of Epicurus was not only excusable as befitting a rebel and a reformer; it was also virtually imperative for him as the founder and head of a sect. Self-assuredness and even arrogance is rather demanded of a leader by his disciples than resented, however exasperating it becomes to his rivals. The acrimony of rivals really defeats itself, because their very malice and vociferousness operates as an exciter to keep alive and invigorate the loyalty of disciples. In the fourth century A.D., when the Christians fell to attacking one another instead of Epicureanism, this kindly creed began to fade. It had thriven so long as it was under fire.

Epicurus as Man of Science

While it was in the role of moral reformer that Epicurus felt himself absolved from the duty of reverence for his predecessors, it was in the role of natural scientist that he became the antagonist of Platonism in particular. It was his choice to revive the tradition of Ionian science, which had been interrupted by Socrates and Plato.

A few details will suffice to amplify this statement. Greek philosophy had made its advances in two separate areas and exhibited two general trends; the earlier was confined to cities of the Aegean Sea, the later to cities of southern Italy. The former trend was observational and speculative, the latter mathematical and contemplative. The Aegean Greeks were familiar with all the industrial techniques of the time, such as spinning, felting, fermentation, ceramics, and metallurgy, and they were acute observers of seasons, climates, winds, waters, and storms. Obsessed by the phenomenon of universal change combined with permanence of the whole, they devoted themselves to the task of discovering the unchanging something that underlay all changing things. After propounding and rejecting or improving one solution after another, they finally arrived at the belief that the ultimate existences were invisible and indivisible bodies, which they called atoms. It was this atomic theory that Epicurus espoused and revived.

The Greeks of Italy, on the contrary, were not greatly interested in physical change or in natural processes. They were addicted to the sitting posture. In art they are represented as comfortably seated with a slender rod or radius in the hand, with which they draw figures on a sanded floor. Counters and writing tablets were also at hand. The advances made by them were in the domains of geometry and arithmetic and these advances were so remarkable as to capture the imagination of the contemporary world and to overshadow for a time the progress which had been made by their Ionian brethren. Geometry in particular, though itself a positivistic study, inspired in the minds of men a new movement that was genuinely romantic.

It was the romantic aspect of the new knowledge that captivated Plato, who was no more than up-to-date as a mathematician himself. In geometry he seemed to see absolute reason contemplating absolute truth, perfect precision of concept joined with finality of demonstration.

He began to transfer the precise concepts of geometry to ethics and politics just as modern thinkers transferred the concepts of biological evolution to history and sociology. Especially enticing was the concept which we know as definition. This was a creation of the geometricians; they created it by defining straight lines, equilateral triangles, and other regular figures. If these can be defined, Plato tacitly reasoned, why not also justice, piety, temperance, and other virtues? This is reasoning by analogy, one of the trickiest of logical procedures. It holds good only between sets of true similars. Virtues and triangles are not true similars. It does not follow, therefore, because equilateral triangles can be precisely defined, that justice can be defined in the same way. Modern jurists warn against defining justice; it is what the court says it is from time to time.

The deceptiveness of analogy, however, does not prevent it from flourishing, and Plato committed himself to the use of it unreservedly. In this he was abetted by a happy coincidence. The method of analysis by question and answer, developed by Socrates recently before, commended itself as the very technique that was needed for the quest of definitions in the domain of ethics. By disposition Socrates was a gifted actor, staging semiprivate theatricals before small groups. As for Plato, in an earlier age he might have become a dramatist. Thus it is not astonishing that the fruit of their joint invention was the dramatization of logic which is called dialectic, best exemplified by the Platonic dialogues.

Yet this was only the beginning. One false step invites another. The quest of a definition, of justice, for example, presumes the existence of the thing to be defined. If equilateral triangles did not exist, they certainly could not be defined. Assume that justice can be defined and at once it is assumed that justice exists just as equilateral triangles exist. Hence arose Plato's theory of ideas. The word *idea* means shape or form and he thought of abstract notions as having an independent existence just as geometrical figures exist, a false analogy.

The theory of ideas was rejected as an absurdity by the young Epicurus, because he was a materialist and denied all existences except atoms and space. The theory once rejected, the instrument became useless; scientists have no use for dramatized logic; they depend chiefly upon their senses.

Plato became guilty of another error upon which the sharp-eyed Epicurus did not fail to place a finger. From

Pythagoras was inherited the belief in the repeated rebirth or transmigration of souls. Along with this went the belief that the body was a tomb or prison-house, which blurred the vision of reason and prevented perfection of knowledge. All that the human being perceived was the transient appearance of things as opposed to the eternal ideas. This to Epicurus was virtually skepticism.

This error, moreover, was compounded and also aggravated. Closely allied to geometry was the study of astronomy. The latter, in turn, required the observation of heavenly bodies. Thus Plato was in the position of assuming the validity of sensation in the case of the remoter phenomena and denying it in the case of the nearer terrestrial phenomena. This was a glaring inconsistency.

The aggravation consisted in the belief that circular motion, which was in those days ascribed to heavenly bodies, was the only perfect and eternal motion and identifiable with Reason itself. Reason, in turn, was identified with the divine nature. Therefore the planets were declared to be gods. This seemed both shocking and absurd to Epicurus: shocking because it meant having more gods to fear, absurd because august gods were assumed to become hurtling balls of fire.

These criticisms, plainly explicit or implicit in the writings of Epicurus, were as stinging and penetrating as any to be urged against Platonism in antiquity, and to men of the Academy they seemed nothing short of blasphemy. Violent measures were taken to repress the brash heretic. Learning caution from this painful experience, the chastened Epicurus abandoned as futile the fighting in the streets, withdrew to the security of his own house and garden, and confined himself to the task of disseminating the true philosophy. As a propagandist he soon began to exhibit a marked superiority.

It is remarkable that this man, who exhibited so much acumen in discerning the errors and inconsistencies of Plato, should be denounced today as an incoherent thinker himself. Any thinker, of course, will seem incoherent to a rival of another school; a modern pragmatist seems incoherent to a Thomasite or a logical positivist. Every thinker, however, has a right to be judged within the structure of his own system. If Epicurus be judged within the structure of his Canon, Physics, and Ethics, he will be found to exhibit an admirable coherence of thought.

Epicurus as Philosopher

Of all false opinions concerning Epicurus the most preposterous is that which would dismiss him as a dullard or even as a charlatan. If correctly appraised he will be seen to have attempted a genuine synthesis of philosophy.

He came upon the scene when a great corpus of speculative writings had accumulated, which is precisely the circumstance that invites to a synthesis. A certain progress in this direction had been made by Plato and Aristotle but neither of these was a conscious synthetizer and neither of them was interested in creating an encyclopedic digest of philosophic thought for public use, much less for the amelioration of human life and the increase of happiness. This is precisely what Epicurus attempted. His aim was to survey the whole course of Greek creative thought, to criticize, to cull it, to organize it and make the results available in the form of useful and understandable handbooks.

Insofar as he aspired to become a synthetizer of philosophy his true affinity is with Herbert Spencer or Auguste Comte but more particularly with the latter, and this in spite of their respective contempt and esteem for mathematical studies. The three stages of development recognized by Comte, the theological, metaphysical, and positive, were clearly recognized also by Epicurus, though it was impossible for him so to denominate them. The first stage was represented by the popular religion and mythology, according to which the universe and the destinies of man seemed to be ruled by the gods, by Fate or Necessity, forces external to humanity.

What Comte called the metaphysical stage was for Epicurus represented by Plato and in part by Aristotle. Phenomena were separated from matter and regarded as separate entities. Form was separated from substance and in Plato's theory of ideas was esteemed as the real existence. This meant, as Epicurean ridicule tauntingly insisted, that "horseness" was a real existence but horses were mere apparitions. It seemed less unreasonable, perhaps, to think of justice as existing apart from conduct, public or private. On the physical level the difference between this stage of thought and the next is aptly exemplified in the case of color. Theophrastus believed it to have a separate existence while Epicurus explained it as arising from the arrangement and motions of the atoms comprising the compound, being close to the truth, as so often.

Epicurus was at one with Comte in believing that progress consisted in advancement from the theological and metaphysical stages to the positive. In point of fact he placed these two stages on a par, denominating the first as the age of mythology and the Platonic stage as a new kind of mythology, equally objectionable. Lacking a background of specialized studies such as physics and chemistry, he was unable to formulate a gradation of sciences, but he did subordinate his Ethics to his Physics and in so doing he adumbrated that same direction of logical procedure which prompted Comte to place sociology at the opposite extreme from mathematics and physics.

Epicurus was also in accord with Comte in linking human behavior with animal behavior, because he recognized a rudimentary justice of Nature in the organization of certain animal herds.

A third point of agreement between Epicurus and Comte was the recognition that some form of religion was indispensable. In point of fact it is somewhat startling to observe into how many details this agreement extended itself. The new religion of Epicurus, stressing piety and reverence while excluding divine government of the universe, may aptly be described in Comte's terminology as a Religion of Humanity. Both systems exhibited a vigorous distrust of regimentation and political mechanisms; both renounced force in favor of persuasion; and both allowed a generous latitude for the play of human feeling. Finally, they both stressed altruism as opposed to self-love, and neither of them shrank from recognizing at the same time the utilitarian motive or calculus of advantage.

As a last item of similarity it may be mentioned that both men were among the most provoking thinkers who ever lived. In the thought of both there was so much that was exasperating combined with so much that was true and penetrating that no subsequent thinker could ignore them. Total dissent was just as impossible as total agreement. The careers of the two men mark parallel stages in the onward march of philosophic thought, which is an endless progression.

The First Dogmatic Philosophy

Although men contemporary with Epicurus were incapable of recognizing him as a moral reformer, they were quick enough to know him for a dogmatist, which counted for a demerit and a reproach. The modern scholar, however, being long habituated to observe historical processes and laws of development, will easily discern that moral reform and dogmatism are logically related. The moral reformer cannot afford to be a doubter. Epicurus is definitely on record as having said, "The wise man will not be a doubter but will dogmatize," and in this he was implying that the wise man is bound to be more than a speculative thinker. He must make his philosophy useful for the increase of happiness; this, in turn, is impossible without faith, and faith is impossible without certainty. Therefore philosophy must be dogmatic.

If appeal be made to the historical process, it will become clear that skepticism and dogmatism are also related by the logic of cause and effect. The man who denies the possibility of knowledge is challenging others to declare that knowledge is possible. This challenge had never been seriously taken up before the time of Epicurus, because to speculative thinkers skepticism is merely another way of thinking and escapes

notice as a menace or a danger. Neither could this aspect of it have presented itself to Epicurus before he became aware of a passion for the increase of human happiness. This passion once awakened, however, he speedily developed a special acumen for discerning even latent skepticism, as in the teachings of his own Democritus, not to omit those of Plato and Aristotle. His later critiques of preceding philosophies stressed this feature.

He was first alerted to this danger by his last teacher, Nausiphanes. This able man had been a pupil of Pyrrho of Elis, who in the company of Anaxarchus, a follower of Democritus, had accompanied Alexander the Great on his eastern campaigns. In the course of these journeys Pyrrho made acquaintance with the wise men of Persia and India, who were not less self-confident than the wise men of Greece. The result for him was the loss of all faith in the certainty of knowledge, reason and sensation seeming alike untrustworthy.

Both Nausiphanes and the young Epicurus admired the placidity of Pyrrho but rebelled against his skepticism. This reaction resulted in the erection of a criterion of truth, which Nausiphanes called his Tripod, obviously so named because capable of standing firmly on its three legs. Subsequently Epicurus quarreled violently with his teacher, seemingly on moral grounds, and feeling himself thereafter absolved from all gratitude he published his own Canon with a threefold basis, Sensations, Anticipations, and Feelings. By the Sensations was meant the evidences furnished by the five senses. The Anticipations were innate ideas, such as that of justice, which exist in advance of experience and so anticipate it. The Feelings are pleasure and pain, Nature's educators, her Go and Stop signals.

Insofar as this system was presented as the true and ultimate philosophy Epicurus laid himself open to the charge of discouraging all further inquiry. It must be allowed that he seemed to favor the confinement of research to the discovery of truth that would contribute to human happiness. It must further be admitted that he made it one of his chief objectives to immunize the minds of his disciples against all teachings other than his own. Some justice may even be allowed to the allegation that his disciples read no writings other than those of their own school.

As a clarification of these criticisms it should be recognized that Epicurus, like Plato, entertained a clear distinction between the talented minority of men and the multitude. He knew also that for the multitude dogmatism, which to Plato was "right opinion" as opposed to rational understanding, was sufficient. Unlike Plato, however, he recognized no need of deception. Since his creed was nonpolitical and his society classless there was no call to institute one training for rulers and another for the ruled. He insisted that his teachings were the same for all men, assuming that each would benefit by them to the limit of his capacities and opportunities.

Individual disciples were conscious of no imposed limitations. Each was free to follow his tastes and his talents. Some even became expert mathematicians. Lucretius was none the less a good Epicurean because of the breadth of his reading. One Asclepiades, an Epicurean physician contemporary with him in Rome, made a notable impact upon the theory and practice of medicine. Epicurus himself knew the true joy of the researcher and gave apt expression to it: "In all other activities the joy comes after laborious completion but in philosophy the pleasure keeps pace with understanding, for enjoyment does not come after learning but learning and enjoyment are simultaneous." His system of thought resembled what is called an open-end plan of investment; it was not a closed but an open-end variety of dogmatism.

The New Order of Nature

Especially conspicuous in the **Canon** of Epicurus is the omission of Reason as a criterion of truth. Only the Sensations, Anticipations, and Feelings are recognized as direct contacts between man and his physical and social environment. By virtue of being direct contacts, they acquire a priority over Reason and in effect exalt Nature over Reason as affording a norm of truth.

How this revolution came about may be explained by recalling a few details. The Ionian scientists had studied nature chiefly in her terrestrial aspects, taking reason for granted as a faculty. The Italian Greeks had ignored the terrestrial aspects of nature and exploited the faculty of reason. This procedure led from arithmetic and geometry to astronomy, and by astronomy was revealed the celestial order of nature. This inflexible celestial order captivated the imagination of Plato, who was a romantic, and it was this he was imitating when he proposed in his *Republic* and his *Laws* a rigidly regimented polity, of which a travesty now flourishes in Soviet Russia.

After this Platonic interruption the Ionian tradition was revived by the later Aristotle, but he switched the emphasis from inorganic to organic nature. The sciences of zoology and botany were founded by him. In the course of these studies he arrived at the conclusion "that Nature does nothing at random." Of this discovery he did not realize the importance. It signified that organic nature is governed by laws. In reality it marks the discovery of a new order of nature, the terrestrial order, as contrasted with the celestial order of Plato's grandiose cosmogony.

It was the lead of Aristotle that Epicurus chose to follow. He looked to organic nature as furnishing the norm just as Plato had looked to reason. This divergence resulted in two opposing interpretations of the phrase "living according to Nature." To the Stoics, who hitched their wagon to Plato's star, it signified the imitation of the inflexible celestial order by a rigid and unemotional morality. To Epicurus and Epicureans, "living according to Nature," though they never made a slogan of it, signified living according to the laws of our being. Of this being the emotions were recognized as a normal and integral part, undeserving of suspicion or distrust.

How the new terrestrial order of nature and the older celestial order operate as points of departure for inferential truth may be illustrated simply in the case of justice. For Epicurus the Feelings are the criterion. Injustice hurts and justice promotes happiness. Therefore human beings make a covenant with one another "not to injure or be injured." Justice is this covenant. It is of Nature. No dialectic is necessary to discover the fact; it is a matter of observation. The sense of justice is innate; it is an Anticipation or Prolepsis existing in advance of experience and anticipating experience. Even certain animals possess it; elephants, for example, the bulls excepted, do not injure one another and they marshal the herd to protect one another against injury from outside.

Plato, on the contrary, taking his departure from the analogy between geometry and ethics and politics, requires a definition; dialectic is invoked as the instrument and the ten books of the *Republic* are devoted to the quest. In the background are the mathematical notion of ratio and the musical notion of harmony. Thus at long length the conclusion is reached that justice is a harmony of the three constituents of the soul, reason, passion, and desire. Justice in the state is a harmony of the constituent classes.

Plato was complicating philosophy for the few who find self-gratification in complexity. Epicurus was simplifying philosophy for the many who were willing to live by their philosophy. Platonic justice seemed to him a specious pretense. In Vatican Collection 54 he wrote: "We should not pretend to philosophize but philosophize honestly, because it is not the semblance of health we need but real health."

Epicurus analyzed human nature just as the later Aristotle analyzed ethics and politics, like a student of natural science observing the ways of plants and animals. It was this method he was following when he scrutinized human nature in action and reduced the direct contacts between man and his physical and social environment to Sensations, Anticipations, and Feelings. It was the same method he followed when he classified human desires as "natural and necessary, natural but not necessary and neither natural nor necessary." After the same fashion he scanned the behavior of man in society and concluded "that the injuries inflicted by men are caused by hatred or by envy or by contempt."

The best evidence of a certain validity in the *Canon* was the ridicule heaped upon it; ridicule is available when arguments are lacking. A tacit tribute to its validity is the fact that the idea of the Prolepsis or Anticipation, the innate idea, was adopted by the Stoics and appears as an accepted commonplace in Cicero's thought. The Sensations were seized upon as the weakest leg of the canonic tripod and in this instance misrepresentation scored a victory. The fallacy that Epicurus declared all sensations to be true and hence trustworthy still flourishes. This would mean that vision informs us no more correctly about a cow at twenty paces than at half a mile.

Equally fallacious was the allegation that the *Canon* had been set up as a substitute for logic. To make such a claim is on a par with asking a trial lawyer to criticize a chemist, or, as Epicurus might have said, to ask the ears to pass judgment on the nose; the phenomena of which they are competent judges would not fall in the same class. The function of ancient logic was to score points and make opponents wince but no adversaries or witnesses were needed for the use of the *Canon*; solitude was sufficient. The modern scientist in his laboratory follows a like method. He depends upon the sensations as Epicurus did. The researcher works on the basis of an hypothesis, which he puts to the test of experiment, that is, of the senses, and these, exactly as Epicurus said, "confirm or fail to confirm" the truth of the proposition. Even the theory of Einstein, that rays of light from distant stars are bent in passing the sun, was tested by photographs taken during an eclipse, and photographs are merely extensions of vision.

Epicurus as an Educator

When Epicurus is considered as an educator—and he took himself very seriously in this role—a double paradox presents itself. Plato, while stressing the study of geometry, rejected the bald style of exposition proper to that branch and employed instead a very artistic prose. Epicurus, on the contrary, while rejecting geometry, adopted and recommended the bald style as employed by Euclid, who happens to have been a contemporary. Plato rejected also the textbook form as developed by the geometricians and favored the dramatic dialogue. Epicurus took over the textbook form along with certain subsidiary features that consorted with it.

In adopting the bald style familiar to us from Euclid, Epicurus was looking to Nature as a teacher. He even went so far as to say that it was she who revealed the true meanings of words and the right kind of style.

The physicist, he asserted, should be content to take words as he found them, in their literal meanings; the sole requisite of writing was clarity. To express this differently, he was denying that Nature was either a dialectician or a rhetorician. With equal justice he might have denied that Nature was a poet, because he was no less rejecting the didactic poetry of Empedocles and his kind than the artistic language of Plato. Indeed he is on record as saying "that the wise man would not compose poems, though he would be the best judge of poetry."

Along with the adoption of the bald style and the textbook form was taken over the demand for memorization. The practice of committing poetry to memory had long prevailed among the Greeks, but with the vogue of geometry there was a new and different necessity for memorization. The new necessity was one of logic. The theorems could not be mastered unless the student had memorized the axioms and learned "to handle them smartly," as Epicurus said of his Elementary Principles. It was just as necessary for the beginner in Epicureanism to have at the tip of his tongue the Principle "The universe consists of atoms and void," or the Authorized Doctrine "Justice is a sort of covenant not to injure or be injured," as it was for the beginner in geometry to know by heart "Things which are equal to the same thing are equal to one another."

The adoption of the Euclidean textbook as a model involved, of course, the procedure by deductive reasoning. The Twelve Elementary Principles were first stated and then demonstrated like theorems. Each theorem, in turn, once demonstrated, became available as a major premise for the deduction of subsidiary theorems. The truth of this subsidiary theorem is then confirmed by the evidence of the Sensations, which operate as criteria. The mistake of believing Epicurus to be an empiricist must be avoided; it is not his teaching that knowledge has its origin in sensation. The status of the Sensations is that of witnesses in court and is limited to confirming or not confirming the truth of a given proposition.

Another innovation demanded by the adoption of the textbook model was the institution of graded texts. For example, the extant *Little Epitome* is a mere syllabus of selected truths. Next above it stood the *Big Epitome*, probably in seven rolls, as seems to be indicated by the six of Lucretius and the promised sequel on the gods. Above this in turn stood the famous thirty-seven books *on Physics* and other special treatises. Similarly, the *Authorized Doctrines* are to be appraised as a beginner's book in Ethics. From this the disciple would move on to special treatises *on Piety, on the Gods, on the End or Telos,* and *on Justice and the other Virtues,* to mention a few. It may be added that an order of procedure was prescribed. For instance, the lore of the gods was placed last in the list and reserved for advanced students.

It deserves to be known also that Epicureans set up their own schools and developed a pedagogical method based upon their own kindly ethics. A good description of their procedures is extant in a Herculanean papyrus containing the treatise of Philodemus entitled *On Frankness of Speech*. It is better preserved than some others and makes clear the essential rules, among which may be mentioned the requirement that the teacher should conceal his own annoyances and be actuated solely by the good of the instructed.

The First Missionary Philosophy

Epicureanism was the first and only real missionary philosophy produced by the Greeks. So foreign was such a concept to the thought of the earlier philosophers and the sophists that they failed even to found schools in the sense that Plato's Academy became a school; much less did they found sects. As Epicurus rightly discerned, human institutions arise from the evolution of the unintended. Just as Nature, according to him, is the sole creatrix in the physical world, so Nature, working through the joint and cumulative experience of mankind, is the sole creatrix in the social and political spheres. Language for example, was an innovation of Nature; men merely improved upon her beginnings. On this principle, it must be deemed incredible that Plato's conscious purpose was to found a school in perpetuity when he chose the Academy as his place of instruction; no model as yet existed. The lack of a model, according to Epicurus, would even have prevented the gods from creating a universe.

One model the Greeks did possess and this was the city-state, itself an exquisite specimen of the evolution of the unintended, and by this model their minds were obsessed. It was a city-state that Pythagoras essayed to found upon philosophical principles. The project failed and a scattering of his followers survived like displaced persons. Their creed was exclusive and incapable of evangelism.

Epicurus was not the first to escape the political obsession. The Cynics had preceded him in this, and Diogenes was dubbed the Dog because he advocated a life of vagrancy, absolved from all social and political decencies and ties. This excess, like others of the blatant school, repelled the decorous Epicurus. He knew that a certain modicum of governmental control was a necessity but he rejected utterly the doctrine of Protagoras, Plato, and Aristotle that the state was in the place of a parent and that the laws were educators.

If any model whatever was in his mind when he took up residence in Athens, this is more likely to have been the school of Aristotle, which from the first exhibited the aspect of a research institution and was less a one-man enterprise than Plato's Academy. It must be remembered that Epicurus brought with him three colleagues who were conceded almost equal rank with himself and that even members who remained behind in Lampsacus continued to cooperate in the business of writing under his aegis.

It is, however, to the Hippocratic medical fraternity that we must look for the undoubted model. As a zealot for the increase of human happiness Epicurus was bound to make a pragmatic interpretation of the analogy between philosophy and medicine, which had long flourished as an idle and unctuous figure of thought. If philosophy was to heal the maladies of the soul, the necessity for its involvement with politics was nonexistent. If all human beings stood in need of health of soul as of health of body, then the healing philosophy must be framed for all mankind and offered to all mankind. It was his resolve "to issue the kind of oracle that would benefit all men, even if not a soul should understand him."

The motive that sparked his missionary zeal was likewise of Hippocratic origin: "Where there is love of mankind there will be love of healing." It is true that the power of love or friendship had long been exploited in Greek institutions. Pythagoras had thought of his ideal state as a unit bound together by friendship along with a mandatory pooling of resources, but this friendship was confined to members of the community. Epaminondas had utilized friendship to build up a spirited military force, but this too was a local and limited phenomenon, love of Thebans for Thebans. It was Epicurus who first extended brotherly love to embrace mankind and exalted it as the impelling motive for revealing to men the way to happiness.

As a missionary enterprise the activity of Epicureanism was not confined to the school premises. Every convert everywhere became a missionary. In the view of Epicurus philosophy should begin at home and be disseminated from the home. It was his injunction to his disciples "to apply it in their own households, to take advantage of all other intimacies and under no circumstances to slacken in proclaiming the sayings of the true philosophy." This feature of the creed possessed the advantage of rendering it independent of schools and tutors; it was able to infiltrate itself into small towns and villages where no schools existed and even into rural areas. It was capable also of winning adherents in social groups untouched by more strictly intellectual systems.

In ancient times Epicurus was denounced as effeminate, and in modern times this reproach has been phrased as moral invalidism. Neither can it be denied that a certain plausibility attaches to the imputation in view of his ill health, the espousal of pleasure as the goal of living, his retired life, and his discouragement of the political career. In reality, however, the accusation is a shallow one. Many a spirited enterprise has been directed from a sickbed. Caesar Augustus, the founder of the Roman Empire, was the least robust of the men of his court and plagued by recurrent illnesses. Ill health is even capable of intensifying the tenacity of the invalid. It was so with Epicurus. In his own circle he was a master mind and alone of all the founders of schools he built up and dominated an organization for the dissemination of his creed. As Seneca said, "In that famous fellowship every word that was spoken was uttered under the guidance and auspices of a single individual." The battle is not always to the strong. Inherent in Epicureanism was a quiet crusading spirit which quickly extended it over the contemporary world and endowed it with a tenacity unequaled by rival creeds; it flourished for almost seven centuries. The vogue of Stoicism as a militant creed lasted a mere two centuries.

The First World Philosophy

It is no more inevitable that a missionary philosophy should be a world philosophy than it is that a missionary religion should be a world religion. Christianity was first intended for the Jews alone. In the case of Epicureanism it is possible that a similar limitation was followed by a similar extension. From the first, however, it was nonpolitical. Unlike the philosophy of Plato, it was not restricted to adolescent youth nor to males nor even to citizens. By virtue of the analogy between the healing of the soul and the healing of the body the new creed became applicable to women as well as to men and to human beings of all ages, whether slave or free. The political contract was superseded by the social contract. It is significant that in the writings of Epicurus the word *neighbor* is almost as frequent as in the Gospels.

When Epicurus established himself in Athens it was no part of his plan to offer education to the Athenian youth. To forestall persecution he took the precaution of confining his instruction to the house and garden registered in title deeds in his own name. His chief reason for taking up residence there was the renown of the city as the cultural capital of the contemporary world. He wished to have the prestige of the city as a recommendation for the merit of the new philosophy being offered to the public at large.

The time as well as the location was advantageous. His philosophy was being launched just as the whole Orient was thrown open for Greek exploitation by the conquests of Alexander the Great. The migrations that ensued while new cities were being founded all the way from Egypt and Syria to distant Bactria attained the dimensions of a diaspora. His philosophy rode this

tide. It had reached Alexandria even before his arrival in Athens. By the second century it was flourishing in Antioch and Tarsus, had invaded Judaea, and was known in Babylon. Word of it had reached Rome while Epicurus was still living, and in the last century B.C. it swept over Italy. Both Greeks and barbarians were becoming Epicureans.

For this ambitious program of expansion the school was prepared as no Greek school had ever been or ever would be. Not only was every convert obligated to become a missionary; he was also a colporteur who had available a pamphlet for every need. "Are you bloated with love of praise? There are infallible rites," wrote Horace, "which can restore your health if only you will read a pamphlet three times with open mind." "Send him a pamphlet," cried Cicero in the senate-house, taunting the Epicurean Piso about the ambition of his son-in-law Julius Caesar. Could better evidence be cited to prove that Epicureans were pamphleteers?

The system of handbooks was carefully planned and diligently maintained. Not only was Epicurus an industrious writer himself; his three colleagues and other members of the school were encouraged to emulate his example. Nor was this activity confined to the parent school; the new schools in Antioch and Tarsus adapted the writings to meet the needs of the changing times. In Rome the pen of Philodemus was busy interpreting the creed afresh for the age in which he lived. For those whose tongue was Latin a certain Amafinius had made translations, and his services were supplemented by those of Catius, an abler man. The evangelical zeal of Lucretius was characteristic of the sect and exceptional only because of its surpassing fervor. The objective was to awaken men to the blessedness of the Epicurean way of life.

As a design for living Epicureanism is patently suggestive of modern hominism or humanism or pragmatism. It was centered in man and not in the state or in theology. The breadth of its humanity is well expressed by one of its later devotees, who wrote "that the whole earth is just one country, the native land of all, and the whole world is just one household." The most potent single sentiment in the development of modern social theory is Epicurean as well as Menandrian: *Homo sum; humani nihil a me alienum puto.* This sentence has suffered a variety of English translations, but the substance is, "I am a man; I deem nothing that concerns mankind to be a matter of indifference to me."

In the light of this manifesto it is astonishing to find Epicurus coldly classified in modern times as an "egoistic hedonist." This mistaken judgment can be traced to the total honesty of Epicurus. It was because of this honesty that he did not shrink from choosing the suspected name of pleasure as the designation of the goal of life. Because of this same forthright honesty he dared to base friendship upon advantage. He knew that human motives are mixed and he possessed the courage to face the fact. This outspokenness laid him open to the charge of basing conduct upon expediency or self-interest, even though he declared "that, if need be, a friend will die for a friend." Consequently, when in the nineteenth century a distinction was made between egoistic and universalistic hedonism, the pleasure of tagging him as an egoistic hedonist was too tempting to be resisted.

This imputation can be disproved by the doctrines, but recourse to them is superfluous. A point of logic will serve the same purpose. When a philosopher chooses the role of missionary and launches a campaign "to awake the world to the blessedness of the happy life," he may still be a hedonist, but he ceases to be egoistic. If correctly described, he must be seen as an altruistic hedonist. This is not a contradiction in terms, but a higher hedonism.

Preparation for Christianity

By virtue of its spirit, its procedures, and certain of its doctrines Epicureanism served as a preparation for Christianity in the Graeco-Roman world. The similarity between the one and the other has long been evident to friend and foe. To the scornful Nietzsche the teaching of Epicurus seemed to be "a pre-existing Christianity," because in his judgment both creeds had been framed for the weak and timorous. To a sympathetic scholar it seemed "like the twilight between the beliefs that were passing away and that which rose on the world after his time."

The first missionary philosophy was a natural preparation for the first missionary religion. The one had been detached from Greek politics and the other was to be detached from Jewish politics. Both creeds were framed for men of peace, militant only for the increase of human happiness. Both offered healing and comforting beliefs for both sexes and all ages of men. Both based their ethics on love and friendliness. The fellowship cultivated by the Epicureans was comparable to the communion of saints as fostered by the Christians. Both stressed the social virtues, mutual helpfulness, forbearance, and forgiveness.

Epicurus distinguished clearly between the inner life and the external life of circumstance; these corresponded to the spiritual life and the worldly life in Christian thought. Both creeds spoke of ignorance as darkness and knowledge as light. Both essayed to deprive death of its sting. Both spoke of the narrow way and warned of the deceitfulness of wealth, power, and glory.

The two sects were singular in taking their names from their leaders and in pledging loyalty to those leaders;

both spoke of following in the steps of those leaders. Both rejected the conventional education and founded their own schools, providing new textbooks. The texts provided by the Epicureans anticipated the texts composed by the Christians. The biographies of the beloved Epicurus, whose life "compared with that of other men would be considered a myth," corresponded to the Gospels; he was revered as nothing short of a god; he was called savior. The affectionate memoirs of his colleagues were comparable to the Acts of the Apostles. The letters of Epicurus to various communities of friends were like the Epistles. Even in their style of writing the two literatures resembled each other, aiming only at clarity.

It should also be carried in mind that the adherents of both sects belonged to the lower and middle classes of society; they practiced in common a voluntary sharing of goods; they were alike in holding their meetings in private houses and in having common meals at regular intervals; in the will of Epicurus provision was made for certain rites to be performed in memory of himself, which reminds us of the Eucharist. It would have been singularly easy for an Epicurean to become a Christian.

As a last word on this topic it may be mentioned that the custom prevailed among Epicureans of carrying about with them small images of their founder; they also had likenesses done in marble or painted on wooden panels to adorn their homes or lodgings. His features are well known to this day from surviving portrait busts and exhibit an expression singularly Christlike. In this connection it is remarkable that the beardless Christ so often seen on Christian sarcophagi down to the fourth century gave way to the bearded form which is now traditional. Since the two sects lived side by side for three centuries, it is by no means impossible that in this particular the practice of the one was a preparation for the practice of the other.

The Two Fronts

Epicureanism presented two fronts to the world, the one repellent, the other attractive. Both the repulsion and the attraction were keenly experienced by St. Augustine, who declared that he would have awarded it the palm had it not been for the denial of immortality and judgment after death. It was chiefly the ethical creed that attracted men, based upon love or friendship and all the kindly social virtues that make for peace and good companionship. It was chiefly the eschatology that offended, arousing in succession the hostility of Platonists, Stoics, and Christians.

Another repellent aspect of the creed was its hedonism. The very name of pleasure is quick to accumulate a semantic load of disapproval. This was well expressed by Cicero when he declared that no one dare proclaim the creed "in the senate, in the forum or in the camp." It is not this name of pleasure, however, that alone divorced the sect from the political life; Epicurus discouraged the political career as a surrender of the happiness of the individual to the whim of mobs and monarchs. For two reasons, therefore, the creed became abhorrent to that minority of mankind which is ruled by worldly ambition and in particular to those breeds who, like Cicero, set their hearts upon high office under democracies or, like Platonists and Stoics, prized court appointments under monarchies or patronage under aristocracies. By the same tokens the unambitious creed made itself attractive to the innumerable majority of men who could never aspire to the seats of the mighty or to move in the public eye.

The effect of these opposing aspects of Epicureanism was to win for it the most numerous, the most ubiquitous, and most enduring of all followings among ancient philosophies and to have adverse to it at all times a rancorous and vociferous minority. The written tradition is hostile for the greater part and sometimes malicious, with which the modern scholar too often concurs. Against this tendency to malign and misrepresent it is well that the unsuspecting layman and the candid inquirer should be warned repeatedly.

Survival

It is hardly possible for a philosophy to perish utterly so long as the continutiy of its cultural context remains unbroken. Each philosophy rises to its peak of popularity, fulfills its appointed role in the historical process, and yields place to its successor. Yet certain strands of it will weave their way into the succeeding pattern of the continuous context. Philosophies are not exempt from the law declared by Lucretius: "One thing will never cease to be born from another and life is given to none in fee simple but only in usufruct." Epicureanism in particular, because of its repellent front, has been especially susceptible to this anonymous absorption. It survives anonymously to this day in literature sacred and profane.

When Christian people assemble for the last tribute of affection to a departed friend and the preacher reads, "The dead shall be raised incorruptible" and "O death, where is thy sting?" and "The sting of death is sin and the strength of sin is the law," only the word *sin* and the idea of the resurrection are here strange to the language and thought of Epicurus. These two new ideas were being presented in a context of Epicurean terminology and ideology so as to make them acceptable to Epicurean listeners. Epicurus had taught that the bodies of the gods were incorruptible. Paul is holding out to the convert the hope of being raised in this very incorruption. Epicurus had essayed to deprive death of its sting by reconciling men to mortality; Paul would deprive death of its sting by holding out the assurance of immortality.

Epicureanism was the prevailing creed among the Greek populations to which Paul addressed himself and, in harmony with his avowed practice of making himself all things to all men that he might save some, he here makes himself an Epicurean to Epicureans. He is shuffling the familiar components of that creed so as to erect a new matrix of meanings. It is just as if the older monument were being demolished in order to yield stones for the wall of the new edifice.

In rabbinical literature the name of Epicurus became a synonym for unbeliever and survives in this meaning. In both ancient and medieval art he was depicted as a type of sensualist, sometimes along with Sardanapalus, a notorious oriental voluptuary. In Dante's Inferno a whole section was set aside for a unique punishment for men of his creed. In the seventeenth century his doctrines experienced a tardy renaissance in France and were carried to England in the period of the Restoration, where they enjoyed a high but fleeting vogue, only to be driven once more into anonymity by paritan condemnation. In the nineteenth century the revival of the study of Greek philosophy in learned circles was too exclusively concerned with Plato and Aristotle to accord him more than grudging consideration, subject to an actual exaggeration of ancient prejudices.

As for political teachings, those of Plato have enjoyed the greatest notoriety and those of Epicurus have been steadily despised or ignored. Yet the latter have affected the direction of political thought in the Western world for three hundred years. Epicurus rebelled against the highly regimented polity of Plato's *Republic* and the *Laws* and advocated instead a minimum of government. The function of government, he believed, was to guarantee the safety of the individual. This doctrine was anonymously revived by John Locke and espoused by Thomas Jefferson, who was an avowed Epicurean. It is consequently not surprising that Safety and Happiness, catchwords of Epicurus, should be named in the Declaration of Independence as the ends of government. Neither is it surprising that the same document should mention Life, Liberty, and the Pursuit of Happiness; these concepts also are Epicurean. . . .

Since classical scholarship, until recent years, has accorded to Epicurus only condescending and prejudiced notice, it is not astonishing that in other circles the neglect has been almost total. This oversight is but natural; nothing else could be expected in view of the anonymity to which the man's acceptable teachings have been condemned because of his unacceptable doctrines. The hidden tradition has been continuous nevertheless. In the main stream of prose and poetry it often survives under Stoic labels. In the terminology and thought of religion it survives in spite of the obliviousness of New Testament scholars. In politics it has been a dominant, though nameless, influence ever since the succession of modern philosophers was started by Thomas Hobbes and John Locke during the brief vogue of Epicureanism in the Restoration period. In North America the Epicurean doctrine that the least government is the best government was virtually made to order for the circumstances of the Revolution, even if not a single Jeffersonian democrat was ever aware of its origin.

Benjamin Farrington (essay date 1967)

SOURCE: Benjamin Farrington, "Friendship versus Justice," in *The Faith of Epicurus*, Weidenfeld and Nicolson, 1967, pp. 20-32.

[*In his* Faith of Epicurus *Farrington stresses the centrality of friendship in Epicurean doctrine. The excerpt that follows fills out his thesis, explaining the significance of context, and, especially, of Plato "just city."*]

In what remains of the writings of Epicurus we have nothing intellectually comparable to the splendid edifices raised by Plato in the *Republic* and the *Laws*. What we have of Epicurus is three letters and a handful of sayings. It is true that the more closely these are studied the clearer it becomes that they are expressions of a firmly articulated system. [G.] Arrighetti [*Epicurus Opere*, 1960] is right to maintain that the scientific language of the school is so technical and strict that translation is difficult because every term recalls a doctrine and requires a note. Still we must not assume that in the lost 'three hundred scrolls' were literary masterpieces comparable to those of Plato. However that may be, what is certain is that the sayings of Epicurus, as they are, represent a protest from a man of different temperament, sensibility, and aims; and that they cut so deep and proved so effective that Epicureanism, rightly judged, is found to be an historical phenomenon as important as Platonism.

It is the clash of these two temperaments, these two sensibilities, that is symbolized by the terms Friendship and Justice. The divergence produced more than a battle of the books. Both Plato and Epicurus aimed at a reconstruction of Greek life, and each in his own way was a man of action. When Epicurus founded his society of friends and forbade his adherents to partake in politics he was challenging both the theory and the practice of Plato. The Epicurean movement was designed to spread by personal contact, by example and persuasion, as a kind of leaven. There is no other way in which friendship can be spread. But the just city of Plato was to be established, if opportunity offered, by force.

If Plato did not enter the political arena in his native city, it was for the reason he put into the mouth of Socrates in the *Apology*. His chance of survival would have been slight. But in 367 BC (two years after the founding of Megalopolis in Arcadia, just to remind ourselves what politics in this age was like) Plato, being sixty years of age, accepted an invitation from Dionysius II of Syracuse, a city in which democracy had been overthrown, to advise and assist in the plan to synoecize Western Sicily as a means of strengthening the Greek presence in the island against the pressure from Carthage. The project did not go well, and, after a few months, Plato was back in Athens. But he returned to Syracuse on the same errand six years later, working on the draft constitution for the synoecism, and stayed for almost a year. Soon the involvement of the Academy in the affairs of Syracuse was to become more dramatic and direct. Dionysius was not in the eyes of Plato and his followers a suitable ruler; and in 357, Plato being then too old to participate personally, Dion, a friend of Plato and a member of the Academy, having whipped up support in the Peloponnese, made a dash across the Ionian Sea and captured Syracuse by a surprise assault. Many young members of the Academy were in the expeditionary force, among them Aristotle's friend Eudemus, who fell at the moment of success. The victorious Dion established a narrow oligarchy, but soon ran into trouble. Having fallen foul of his admiral, he liquidated him, and was then himself treacherously killed by another Academician, Callippus, who made himself tyrant.

Such activities were not isolated but rather typical of the role the Academy aspired to play in public affairs. Shortly before Plato's death, at the other end of the Greek world, a gifted adventurer, Hermias of Atarneus in the Troad, who had been in Athens and liked Plato's views, carved a small kingdom for himself out of territories nominally at least under Persian way. He built himself a new capital, Assos, and, if the *Letters* of Plato can be accepted as genuine, it was with Plato's support that he assembled a small cabinet of Academicians to guide him in his task. These in the end amounted to five—Erastus, Coriscus, Xenocrates, Aristotle, and Theophrastus. As the purpose of the Syracusan project had been to contain Carthage, so the kingdom of Assos was to provide a bridgehead for the invasion of Persia now being planned by Philip of Macedon. But the Persians tumbled to what was going on, seized the person of Hermias, interrogated him under torture, and crucified him.

These and other incidents of the same kind gave the Academy its reputation as a centre of political activity not stopping short of military violence. The activity and the reputation persisted down to the life-time of Epicurus. . . . [A] Platonist, Evaeons, had just been ejected from his position as tyrant of Lampsacus when Epicurus came upon the scene. The role of the philosopher in politics was a burning topical issue, and when Epicurus laid it down as a rule that such activity was to be eschewed in the Garden as incompatible with the life of friendship, he was consciously breaking away from the example of the older school.

There is, in fact, a certain brutality about Plato that must have been offensive to Epicurus. For instance in the *Republic* (IX, 578) he discusses the dangerous isolation of the tyrant and does it in this way: Rich individuals in cities have many slaves and yet live securely. But this is because the whole citizen body is leagued together for the protection of each individual. But imagine one of these slave-owners, say with fifty slaves, carried off by some god into the wilderness with his family and property where there are no freemen to help him. Will he not be in an agony of fear lest he and his wife and children should be put to death by the slaves? Well, such is the situation of the tyrant who isolates himself.

This placid acceptance of the city as a league of masters to protect themselves against their slaves is exhibited again in the *Laws* (VI, 777-8). Here the correct management of slaves is the topic. Plato gives two main rules. First, the slaves should be recruited from different countries so that they will share no common speech. Second, while they must not be unjustly punished they must not be allowed to forget that they are slaves. This result will be achieved, if every word addressed to them is a command, if the slightest pleasantry is absolutely excluded, and if correction is always physical chastisement, not a verbal rebuke, as if they were free.

How in God's name should Epicurus, whose rule was not to punish slaves, but to pity and forgive (Diogenes Laertius, *Life of Epicurus,* 118), really take kindly to this man? Even Aristotle, who knew and loved him, was put out of patience. For Aristotle, as for Epicurus, happiness was the highest good. He examines the regulations made by Plato for the realization of the ideal city. Control of the city is to be in the hands of a small class of Guardians, and to ensure that they shall not be selfish he deprives them of all the means by which selfhood is normally achieved. His Guardians are to have their wives, children and property in common so as to be uninfluenced by any but public motives. Aristotle protests, 'The Guardians must be unhappy, being bereft of wives, children, and property. And if *they* are not happy, who will be? Surely not the exponents of the arts and crafts, nor the mass of manual workers.' (*Politics,* 1264b.)

'The bird a nest, the spider a web, man friendship', says William Blake. This conception of friendship as the very essence of man, and also indeed of God, is the heart of what Epicurus has to say to his age. With this message he swept the ancient world as Rousseau did eighteenth-century Europe. 'It is surely a wonderful thing,' says Rousseau, 'to have got men into a

situation in which they cannot live together without outwitting, supplanting, deceiving, betraying, and destroying one another.' This too Plato deplored; but his solution was the imposition of a 'just' constitution by a small élite of trained metaphysicians on a rigidly stratified State. For Epicurus this remedy was worse than the disease. He sought, not an external order, but a voluntary acceptance of a contract of friendship, in this also anticipating Rousseau.

The question, then, arises, whether Epicurus was an anarchist. The answer must be No. Anarchism, understandably, was not without its representatives in Athens at this time. The Cynics, some of them men of noble character, were in revolt against the very conception of civil society. They advocated a return to nature without drawing any clear distinction between animal and human nature. Hence a certain flouting of public decency, which was, indeed, the origin of their name. But for the Epicureans the cure for the ills of the time was not a return to nature but to human nature, human nature being defined by its possession in the highest degree of the capacity for friendship.

Here a comparison with Rousseau can help. Rousseau, like Epicurus, thought that man at a certain point in his development had lost the true path. What that point was Emile Faguet [*La Littérature Fraçdise,* 1715-18, 1896] well defines:

> It was the day on which humanity abandoned patriarchal life, the life in which goods are held in common, well-being is universal, riches are unknown, and luxurious pleasures, arts, and vices are still undreamed of. This, not savagery, is what Rousseau meant by the state of nature. This half-pastoral, half-rustic stage, the stage which excludes great nations, great towns, and property, he calls the state of nature, not because he thought it primitive but because he thought it most natural to man. It was to this he would recall mankind.

The State which Faguet describes is identical with Plato's First or Simple City, before the Luxurious State arose. This had had the benediction of Socrates; and this, as A. E. Taylor remarks [in *Plato, the Man and his Work,* 1926], 'is already on the right side of the line which separates civilization from barbarism'.

To enable us to transport the argument back into the conditions of ancient life in Attica we are not lacking in information. The rapid changes in the fortunes of Athens and, it must be added, the astonishing clarity with which from the time of Solon and Cleisthenes the underlying economic, political, and social realities had been grasped, combined to produce a pageant of historical development unique at so early a period. The political philosopher had much material at hand. Philochorus, the greatest of the historians of Attica, who in the year that Epicurus founded the

Garden, held the posts of seer and diviner at Athens, took as his subject the constitutions, festivals, and ceremonies of Athens and was able to bring his history down from the stage when the inhabitants of Attica were shepherds living in scattered villages till Athens had become an oligarchy, or plutocracy, in which the effective control of public life was in the hands of the 12,000 men who were rich enough to share the burden of the liturgies.

The details of this long political evolution escape us, but the main fact is clear. In its original state the population of Attica was organized in four tribes with their constituent groups, the phratries or brotherhoods. They prided themselves on their equality, calling themselves by such names as 'feeders from the same crib', 'sharers of the bran-tub', 'suckled on the same milk'. They had no tradition of submerged groups of inferiors, serfs, plebeians within their ranks. The equality, of course, did not last. In the pseudo-Xenophontine *Constitution of Athens,* which dates a little before the outbreak of the Peloponnesian War in 431 BC, the population is already divided into the wealthy, the noble, the good, the few, the fortunate, the landowners, on the one hand; and the poor, the commoners, the inferior, the bad, and anyone connected with the sea, on the other. But the memory of the old tradition remained strong.

As we have already seen in our quotation from Thucydides, right down to 431 BC, 'the bulk of the Athenian citizens were living on the very estates with land, house, and shrine which their families had held continuously since before even the time of Theseus'. (N. G. L. Hammond, *Land Tenure in Athens* etc, *Journal of Hellenic Studies,* 1961, 76-98.) Even the ancient festival of the phratries, the Apatouria, had survived, with its worship of Apollo Patröus and Zeus Herkeios, its communal meal, and its country jollifications. If, then, we want to inform ourselves what Plato was thinking about when he drew his contrast between the Simple and the Luxurious City, and of that better state of society Epicurus had in mind when he recommended abstention from politics and affairs, it is foolish to look elsewhere than to the idyllic past of Attica itself.

It was to the gods of this idyllic past that the Antigone of Sophocles appealed when she found that the law of the city asked her to love one of her brothers and hate the other. Zeus for her was Zeus Herkeios, the patron god of the phratries. Aristotle discusses the passage when he makes his distinction between particular law and universal law. 'Universal law is the law of nature. For there really is, as everyone by some intuition of the divine dimly discerns, a natural justice that is binding on all even without formal covenant with each other. This is clearly what Antigone means when she claims that the burial of Polyneices was a just act in spite of the prohibition. She means that it was just by nature, being, as she says, one of 'the unwritten and unfailing statutes

of the gods, the life of which is not of today nor yesterday, but from all time, and no man knows when they were first put forth'. (*Rhetoric,* 13, 1-2.)

For Epicurus, brooding on the same problems, the commandments are reduced to one, 'Believe in the immortality and blessedness of god, for this is the image of god engraved on the mind of every man.' (TM [*Epistle to Menoeceus*], 123.) Blessedness, the attribute of the immortal nature, is synonymous with love or friendship (*philia*). 'Of all the good things wisdom provides for life-long blessedness the chief is the acquisition of friendship.' (PD [*Principal Doctrines*], xxlvii.) 'The noble nature dedicates itself to wisdom and friendship, of which the first is a mortal good, the second immortal.' (VF [*Vatican Fragments*], lxxviii.) Here friendship is called immortal because it is the way of life of the gods, while wisdom is only the path by which mortals may discover the blessedness of friendship. Then the conclusion of the whole matter, 'Meditate on these things day and night, both by yourself and with one like yourself, and you shall live like a god among men. For a man who lives amidst immortal blessings is not like a mortal man.' (TM, 135.)

This religion of friendship had its roots in the current idealization of primitive life, seen not as a form of savagery but as a state of civilization congenial to the true nature of man. In arriving at this conception Epicurus was indebted to many of his predecessors but to none more deeply than to Aristotle, with whom the topic of friendship received an astonishing development. To understand what Epicurus owed to Aristotle in this matter, and where he broke with him, will be our concern in the rest of this chapter.

In his *Politics* Aristotle accepts justice as the basis of the State, and the State itself as natural:

> Man is intended by nature to be part of a political whole and is driven by an inward impulse to such an association. Accordingly the man who first constructed such an association was the greatest of benefactors. For man, when perfected, is the best of animals; but without law and justice he is the worst of all . . . Justice is the basis of the *polis,* and the constitution of a political association is the same thing as the decision of what is just. (*Politics,* 1253a.)

Epicurus was by no means blind to the force of this argument. But he thought it needed correction. Only the simple form of the State was 'natural', for this was held together by the natural impulse of friendship. The fully-developed State, with its code of laws enforced by external sanctions, was not natural to man.

This point of view was clearly expressed in a remarkable document drafted even before the School had left

Lampsacus for Athens. Epicurus had been admitted to Lampsacus by the representative of the Macedonian overlord, Lysimachus. This must have encouraged the school to expect favour also with the Macedonian overlord of Egypt. Accordingly Colotes, as we have said, addressed to the first Ptolemy a defence of the Epicurean school against all others. In it he attempts an explanation of the reform aimed at by his Master, a portion of which has been preserved by Plutarch. It might have been written as a supplement and correction to the argument of Aristotle quoted above:

> Those who have established laws and ordinances and instituted monarchies and other forms of government in towns and cities, have placed human life in great repose and tranquillity and delivered it from many troubles; and if anyone should go about to abolish this, we should live the life of wild beasts and be ready to devour one another when we met. But we are to treat now of *how a man may best keep and preserve the end of nature, and how he may from the very beginning avoid entering of his own freewill upon offices of magistracy and government over the people*. (Plutarch, *Against Colotes,* 30 and 31.)

The italicized words define the limit of the form of association Epicurus thought natural for man.

So much for the *Politics* of Aristotle. When, however, he wrote his Ethics, he saw things from a somewhat different angle. The last two books of the *Nicomachean Ethics* are wholly devoted to friendship. The treatment is thorough. And in this extensive discussion almost everything which survives in the scanty remains of Epicurus is anticipated. The debt of Epicurus is open and undisguised. If it is not also acknowledged this is because, in the last analysis the spirit which animates the philosophy of the two men, is so very different.

In his treatise on the *Generation of Animals* (753a) Aristotle notes how the capacity of animals for love of their young is proportionate to their practical intelligence:

> Nature seems to wish to implant in animals the sense of care for their young. In the lower animals it lasts only to the moment of giving birth to an incompletely developed animal. In others it lasts till the development is complete. In all the more intelligent it covers the bringing up of the young also. And in those which have the greatest share of practical intelligence we find familiarity and love shown also towards the young when fully grown, as with men and some quadrupeds.

Then in the *Ethics,* when he begins the discussion of friendship, he harks back to this natural association between love and intelligence:

> Parent seems by nature to feel it for child and child for parent, not only among men but among birds and most animals. Creatures of the same kind are drawn together; and this is especially true of men, so that we bestow praise on men who love their fellows. That this is true of mankind as a whole we see when we travel. Every man is a friend to every man. Moreover friendship seems to hold States together, and law givers set more store by friendship than they do by justice. For concord seems to be akin to friendship, and when men are friends there is no need of justice. On the other hand, even just men need the impulse of friendship to bring them together in the first place. Indeed justice in its fullest sense is friendship. Nor is friendship only a means. It is also an end. For we praise those who love their friends, and regard the possession of many friends as a noble thing. In short we identify goodness and friendship. (1155a.)

If there were not so much else that differentiated Epicurus from Aristotle, this magnificent paragraph might be accepted as the foundation-charter of the Garden. To a man of the temper of Epicurus it was an invitation and a challenge to base an ecumenical movement on the philosophy of friendship. For friendship is shown to be rooted in nature, to be proportionate to the degree of intelligence, to be the common possession of all men everywhere, to be prior to justice both in the order of time and of logic, to be a self-sufficient principle of concord in society, and an end in itself. In a word, friendship is virtue in practice.

How deeply rooted this ideal was in the school of Aristotle is exemplified by what remains of the writings of his pupil Dicaearchus, a slightly older contemporary of Epicurus, to whom Aristotle had assigned the task of writing a history of civilization in Greece. 'Men at the first stage of civilization,' writes Dicaearchus, 'were near the gods, best by nature, and lived the best life. They did not know war, and their chief blessings were freedom from the compulsion of necessity, health, peace, and friendship.' (Porphyry, *De Abstinentia,* IV, 2; Cicero, *De Officiis* II, 5.16.)

Apart from the agreement between the Lyceum and the Garden on the great fundamentals touched upon above, there is agreement also on points of detail. We have noted, for instance, that Epicurus admitted his slaves to his society of friends. It might be thought that this was a point on which Aristotle gave no lead to the practice of the Garden. In fact Aristotle discusses the question, and, in spite of his well-known insistence that slaves are so by nature, by a characteristic distinction he opens the door for Epicurus. There can be no friendship, he says, with a slave *qua* slave. But a slave is also a man, and there can be friendship with him in so far as he is a man. (*Nicomachean Ethics,* 1161a.)

Other points on which Epicurus was to insist are that under certain circumstances a man will die for his friend, and that the value of a life is to be judged not by its duration but by its quality. Aristotle anticipates both opinions. 'The good man does many things for his friend, and if need be dies for him . . . , since he would prefer a short period of intense pleasure to many years of humdrum existence.' (*Nicomachean Ethics*, 1169a.)

Finally Aristotle stresses the importance for friendship of the life together. The argument is elaborate and characteristic of the emergence at this period of a greatly increased consciousness of the inner life. Animals, says Aristotle, have sense-perceptions, men alone are conscious of the fact that they have them. In the technical language of the time, their *aisthesis* is accompanied by *synaisthesis*. Self-consciousness accompanies not only their sensations but their thoughts. We think, and we are conscious that we think. This is the source of the good man's pleasure in himself. When he thinks about himself, he can approve himself. He has a good conscience. But his friend is to him another self, and to share with a friend the awareness each has of the other's goodness is the specific pleasure of friendship. The beasts of the field can share only the pleasure of feeding on the same pasture. Sharing for men means sharing their thoughts and words (1170 a-b).

What is there left for Epicurus to tell us about friendship? Not very much, it might seem, except that for Aristotle friendship was the stepping-stone to political life, while for the Epicureans politics were the destruction of friendship. 'They fled from the *polis*,' says Plutarch, 'because they held it to be the ruin and confusion of blessedness.' (*Life of Pyrrhus*, xx.) Philodemus, the head of the Garden at Naples, explains why:

> If a man were to undertake a systematic enquiry to find out what is most destructive of friendship and most productive of enmity, he would find it in the regime of the *polis*. Witness the envy felt for those who compete for its prizes. Witness the rivalry that necessarily springs up between the competitors. Witness the division of opinion that accompanies the introduction of fresh legislation and the deliberate organization of faction fights which set not only individuals but whole peoples by the ears. (Sudhaus, *Volumina Rhetorica* ii, 158-9.)

Nor do we lack direct evidence in his own words of what Epicurus thought about Aristotle's political writings. The nub of Epicurus's complaint is that at the end of his life Aristotle deserted philosophy for political theory, and thus he became (writes Epicurus, in words that plainly survive in a very damaged manuscript) 'a more damaging adversary of the blessed and wholesome life than those who actively engage in politics.' (Sudhaus, *Volumina Rhetorica*, ii, 56-64.) The astonishing thing is that so uncompromising a creed should have met with wide success. 'Friendship,' cried Epicurus, 'goes dancing round the world bidding us all awake and pass on the salutation of blessedness.' (VF, iii.)

It is not easy to understand the appeal of the Epicurean gospel of friendship unless we remember that it was addressed to a very sick society. For a gospel it was, as well as a severe intellectual discipline for those who were capable of such mental exertion. In one of the writings of William Tyndale we read, 'Evangelion (that we call the gospel) is a Greek word; and signifieth good, merry, glad and joyful tidings, that maketh a man's heart glad, and maketh him sing, dance, and leap for joy.' Epicurus, too, was an evangelist and thought of himself as such, as did also his disciples. The mood of disillusionment with politics was not to last for ever, but it lasted a long time. More than two hundred years later Lucretius was celebrating the man who set friendship above politics in these terms:

> Who can avail by might of mind to build a song to match the majesty of truth and these discoveries? Who has such skill in speech that he can fashion praises to match the deserts of him who has left us such treasures, conceived and won by his genius? It is beyond the skill of mortal man. For if we are to speak as befits the majesty of the truth now known to us, then we must say that he was a god, a god I say, who first disclosed that principle of life we now call wisdom, and who by his skill rescued us from the seas that engulfed us and the thick darkness and brought us into still waters and a clear light. (*On the Nature of Things*, v, 1-11.)

A. A. Long (essay date 1974)

SOURCE: A. A. Long, "Epicurus and Epicureanism," in *Hellenistic Philosophy: Stoics, Epicureans, Sceptics*, University of California Press, 1974, pp. 14-74.

[Long offers a broad view of Epicurus's thought in the excerpt below, moving from biography and history to epistemology, and culminating with his ethical teachings.]

It has often been said that Epicurus was primarily a moralist, and if by this we mean someone who strives by theory and practice to advocate a particular way of life the description is appropriate. Epicurus thought that he could trace the causes of human unhappiness to mistaken beliefs in his society, beliefs about the gods, the destiny of the soul, and the objects in life which are truly valuable. Ultimately all his teaching has the aim of discrediting such beliefs and replacing them with those which he holds to be true. By his adherents Epicurus was regarded as a 'saviour', as the bringer of 'light', words which we naturally associate with Judaism and Christianity. But Epicurus was not a preacher, even if he sometimes preaches. He wished ardently to persuade, and to convince; it would be quite wrong to try to make him into a purely academic philosopher. But he was a philosopher. Arguments and evidence are the instruments by which he hoped to persuade those who would listen, and it is with the theory rather than the practical aspects of Epicureanism that I shall be concerned here. Beginning, after some introductory remarks, with Epicurus' theory of knowledge I propose to consider the details of his system in an order which seems to be both coherent and representative of his own methodology. Ethics proper is dealt with last, for other topics have ethical implications which can be noted *en passant* and moral conclusions are the ultimate goal of Epicurus' philosophy.

(i) Life and works

Epicurus was born on the island of Samos in 341 B.C. (D.L. [Diogenes Laertius] x 14). His father, who held Athenian citizenship, had settled there some ten years earlier. The first philosophical influence on Epicurus may have come in Samos itself from Pamphilus, a Platonist (Cic. *N.D.* [*De natura deorum*] i 72; D.L. x 14). But Epicurus' own philosophy is strikingly at odds with Platonism, and perhaps while still an adolescent he began an association with Nausiphanes on the neighbouring island of Teos (Herculaneum papyrus 1005) which nipped in the bud any positive allegiance to Plato. Nausiphanes was a Democritean (D.L. i 15; Cic. *N.D.* i 73), and it is likely that Epicurus first became acquainted with the basic principles of atomism through the teaching of Nausiphanes. In later life Epicurus denounced Nausiphanes in highly vitriolic language (D.L. x 7-8). It is not clear what prompted these attacks, but they are typical of Epicurus' attested attitudes towards other philosophers.

At the age of eighteen Epicurus went to Athens to do his two years of military and civilian service alongside the comic poet Menander (Strabo xiv 638). We know little in detail of his activities during the next fifteen years. He may have taught for some time as an elementary school teacher in Colophon, a small town to the north-west of Samos on the Persian mainland, where his family had now taken up residence (D.L. x 1; 4). Later he established his own philosophical circle first in Mytilene (on Lesbos) and then in Lampsacus (D.L. x 15), a port near the site of ancient Troy, returning to Athens at the age of thirty-four in 307/6. Here he remained for the rest of his life. The return to Athens indicates that Epicurus was now confident of attracting followers in the main centre of philosophy. Between Athens and Piraeus Epicurus bought a house the garden of which came to stand as the name of the Epicurean school.

The community which Epicurus founded differed in important respects from the Academy and Lyceum. Its modern analogue is not a college or research institution but a society of friends living according to common principles, in retreat from civic life. Friendship has particular ethical significance in Epicureanism, and the Garden provided a setting for its realization. Women and slaves were admitted, and scraps of several private letters are preserved in which Epicurus expresses deep affection for his friends and followers. It is doubtful whether the Garden during Epicurus' lifetime offered much that might be called formal training to would-be Epicureans. Those who committed themselves to Epicurus were not so much students 'reading for a course' as men and women dedicated to a certain style of life. Seneca quotes the revealing maxim: 'Act always as if Epicurus is watching' (*Ep.* 25, 5). The similarity to George Orwell's 'Big brother is watching you' could scarcely be more misleading. Epicurus clearly inspired the strongest regard in his associates and personified the values of his own philosophy. But if the Garden lacked the formal curriculum of the Academy we can safely assume that its members devoted much time to reading and discussing Epicurus' books; his **Principal doctrines** (see below) were probably learnt by heart; some members must have been engaged in the preparation and copying of works both for internal consumption and for dissemination to Epicureans outside Athens; and Epicurus' chief adherents, such as Metrodorus, will have engaged in advanced study with the master himself.[1] Book xxviii of Epicurus' **On Nature** refers to Metrodorus in the second person, and the fragments which survive record parts of a discussion between the two philosophers on problems of language and theory of knowledge. Epicurus kept in touch with his followers outside Athens by correspondence, and the opening of his **Letter to Pythocles** is worth quoting for the attitudes it reveals of Epicurus himself and one of his disciples:

> Cleon brought me a letter from you in which you continue to show good-will towards me matching my own love for you. You are trying not ineffectively to memorize the arguments which are directed at a life of sublime happiness, and you ask me to send you a brief summary of the argument about astronomical phenomena so that you can easily get it by heart. For you find my other writings difficult to remember even though, as you say, you are always using them. I was delighted to receive your request and it caused me joyous expectations.[2]

Consistent with these principles Epicurus preferred the company of a few intimates to popular acclaim (Sen. *Ep.* 7, 11). He did not however withdraw completely from civic life. In a letter cited by Philodemus Epicurus says that he has participated in all the national festivals (Us[ener,] 169); his slogan 'live quietly' was not a revolutionary denunciation of contemporary society but a prescription for attaining tranquillity. Opponents of Epicureanism vilified the founder as a libertine and voluptuary, but this is inconsistent both with his teaching on pleasure, as we shall see, and with his own professed attitudes. He claimed to derive great pleasure from a subsistence diet which cheese would turn into a feast (Us. 181f.). On his death in 271 B.C., Epicurus bequeathed his house and garden to his follower, Hermarchus, for the benefit of the Epicurean community, and succeeding heads of the school probably nominated their own successor. On the twentieth of every month Epicurus' memory and that of Metrodorus were celebrated at a festival within the Garden. This and other arrangements which are recorded in Epicurus' will (D.L. x 16-21) throw an interesting light on the character of the man himself.

Epicureanism has rightly been called 'the only missionary philosophy produced by the Greeks'.[3] Before he took up residence at Athens, Epicurus had established a following in Lampsachus and Mytilene, and his disciples helped to propagate the Epicurean gospel throughout the Mediterranean world. Antioch and Alexandria are two major cities in which Epicureanism established itself at an early date. Later, it spread widely into Italy and Gaul. Cicero in the middle of the first century B.C. could write, and it gave him no pleasure to do so, 'The [Roman] Epicureans by their writings have seized the whole of Italy' (*Tusc.* iv 6-7). This was a time when Epicureanism briefly claimed the allegiance of some prominent Romans including Calpurnius Piso and Cassius. Julius Caesar may have been sympathetic and Cicero's Atticus was an Epicurean. The fortunes of the movement fluctuated. Political opposition was not unknown, but the main antagonists were first rival philosophers, especially Stoics, and later Christianity.

In the Roman world Epicureanism seems to have been at its strongest immediately before the fall of the Republic. But it suffered no sudden decline. Seneca quotes with approval many Epicurean moral maxims; Lucian's *Alexander,* written in the second century A.D., gives a fascinating account of Epicurean and Christian reactions to persecution in the area south of the Black Sea. And most remarkable of all, about A.D. 200 in the interior of modern Turkey, at a place called Oenoanda in antiquity, an old man named Diogenes had erected a huge philosophical inscription carved on a great stone wall. Between 1884 and the present day many fragments of his work have been recovered, and it constitutes a summary of Epicurus' teaching which Diogenes bestowed on his countrymen and humanity at large for their happiness.[4] Apart from adding valuable information to our knowledge of Epicureanism, Diogenes' inscription proves the vitality of Epicurus' gospel five hundred years after the foundation of the Garden.

Epicurus himself was a prolific writer. Diogenes Laertius, who records forty-one titles of Epicurus' 'best

books', says that his writings ran to three hundred rolls (x 26), and that he exceeded all previous writers 'in the number of his books'. Many of these consisted of short popular tracts and letters. Epicurus' major work was the series of thirty-seven books *On Nature,* a treatise *On the criterion* or *kanôn,* and a collection of ethical books which included *On lives; On the goal; On choice and avoidance.* He also wrote polemical works *Against the physicists, Against the Megarians,* and *Against Theophrastus.* Many of the letters, as we know from our own evidence, summarized points of doctrine or discussed these in some detail. Of all this writing only a small fraction has survived. Three letters are preserved which Diogenes Laertius included in his Life of Epicurus. The longest and most important of these, *To Herodotus,* gives a compressed and difficult summary of the main principles of atomism. Astronomical phenomena are the subject of the *Letter to Pythocles,* and the third letter, *To Menoeceus,* presents a clear if somewhat over-simplified account of Epicurean moral theory. In addition to these letters, Diogenes gives us a collection of forty *Kuriai doxai, 'Principal doctrines',* and a further set of maxims (*Vaticanae sententiae*) survives in a Vatican manuscript. Excavation at Herculaneum during the eighteenth century brought to light many charred rolls of papyrus which originally formed the library of some wealthy Roman. He was probably an adherent of Epicureanism, since most of the papyri which have been unrolled and read are fragmentary works by Philodemus of Gadara, an Epicurean philosopher and poet contemporary with Cicero. The rolls also contain fragments of some of the books of Epicurus *On Nature.* These are formidably difficult to read and reconstruct, but an invaluable supplement to earlier knowledge. Much work remains to be done on them.[5]

For our information about details of Epicurus' doctrine we are heavily dependent upon secondary sources. The most important of these is the Roman poet Lucretius, who wrote more than two hundred years after Epicurus' death. It is perhaps misleading to describe Lucretius as a secondary source. His poem, *De rerum natura,* is a work of genius which preceded the *Aeneid* and challenges it as a literary masterpiece. Lucretius, whose life and character are virtually unknown to us, was a fervid proponent of Epicureanism who presents Epicurus' teaching as the only source of human salvation. But Lucretius is no mere panegyrist. His six books set out in great detail Epicurean arguments concerning the basic constituents of things, the movement of atoms, the structure of body and mind, the causes and nature of sensation and thought, the development of human culture, and natural phenomena. At the same time, there is no reason to regard Lucretius himself as an original thinker. His work amplifies and explains points that we can find in Epicurus' own writings. Even where Lucretius reports theories, for instance the swerve of atoms (ii 216-93), which cannot be checked against

Epicurus' own words, he was probably drawing on original sources which we cannot recover. Epicurus' own immediate successors were not noted for any major innovations. Certain refinements were doubtless made, and Philodemus' treatise *On signs* (preserved partially on papyrus) incorporates logical work by Zeno of Sidon (*c.* 150-70 B.C.) which may well go beyond anything worked out by Epicurus himself. But for the most part Epicurus' own writings remained canonical throughout the history of the school.

After Lucretius the best secondary sources are Diogenes Laertius, Cicero, Seneca and Plutarch. Cicero and Plutarch intensely disliked Epicureanism, and their criticism is of interest for understanding the adverse reception which the school often encountered. Seneca, though officially a Stoic, concludes most of his first *Moral letters* with an Epicurean maxim which he recommends to his correspondent, Lucilius. Sextus Empiricus, to whom Epicureanism was the most congenial of the dogmatic schools of philosophy, provides a useful supplement to our direct knowledge of Epicurean empiricism. Finally, as I have already mentioned, we have substantial fragments from the inscription of Diogenes of Oenoanda.

(ii) The scope of Epicurus' philosophy

Epicurus' philosophy is a strange mixture of hard-headed empiricism, speculative metaphysics and rules for the attainment of a tranquil life. There are links between these aspects of his thought, some of which are clearer than others. But one thing which certainly unites them is Epicurus' concern to set the evidence of immediate sensation and feeling against the kind of logical analysis which is characteristic of Platonic and Aristotelian methodology. Epicurus rejected many of the fundamental principles in terms of which Plato and Aristotle described the world. But more important than his disagreement concerning what is to be said about the world is his dismissal of certain logical and metaphysical concepts which are basic to Plato and Aristotle. Epicurus recognized the distinction between universal and particular; but he did not regard universals as having existence in their own right, like Plato; nor apparently was he interested, as Aristotle had been, in classifying things under genera and species. He did not set up principles such as Plato's *same* and *different,* or Aristotle's *substrate* and *form,* for the analysis of objects and their properties. Philosophers who proceed in this way, he held, are merely plying with words, setting up empty assumptions and arbitrary rules. He did not deny that philosophy uses language and logic as its tools (Us. 219). But he vehemently rejected the view that linguistic analysis by itself can tell us anything about the world which is true or relevant to a happy life. The value of words is to express those concepts which are clearly derived from sensations and feelings. These latter give us our only hold on facts and the only secure foundation for language.

One might suppose from this that Epicurus would have dispensed with metaphysics altogether. In fact, his account of what exists does not stop short at the objects of which we are made aware by immediate sensations and feelings. Our senses report to us things which we call sheep, grass, cats etc., but for Epicurus all such things are compounded out of atoms and void, neither of which is something that we can sense or feel. In asserting atoms and void to be the ultimate entities which constitute the world, Epicurus is making a metaphysical statement. This is not something which he can prove or verify directly from sensations with or without the help of experiment. He has to establish it by setting up certain axioms and assuming the validity of certain methods of inference.

The first atomist explanation of things was advanced more than a century before Epicurus began his philosophical career. Epicurus clearly believed it to be a theory for which he could offer new and improved proof. But while providing an elegant and economical answer to such questions as 'What is the structure of physical objects?' or 'How are bodies able to move?', the atomist theory attracted Epicurus on other than purely theoretical grounds. If all events and all substances are ultimately explicable by reference to atoms necessarily moving in empty space, both divine causation as popularly conceived and its sophisticated equivalents—Plato's Forms and Demiurge or World-Soul, Aristotle's Prime Mover and Heavenly Intelligences—become superfluous. Epicurus held that beliefs in divine management of the cosmos and of human destiny were a major cause of human failure to live a tranquil life. On an atomist analysis of the world, supposing this to be demonstrable, consequences would follow which could not fail to affect beliefs about a man's own place in the world.

Epicurus often asserts that philosophy has no value unless it helps men to attain happiness. This applies with particular force to his moral theory, but there is no necessary connexion between atomism and hedonism. The claim that pleasure is the only thing which is good as an end is compatible with all manner of metaphysical hypotheses. Epicurus has various ways of establishing his hedonism, none of which draws direct support from atoms and void. In this he differs markedly from the Stoics whose moral theory is intrinsically related to their metaphysics. But Epicurus thought he could show the validity of hedonism by appeal to immediate experience which, less directly, he held to support atomism. If labels can be usefully applied to a philosopher, Epicurus should be called an empiricist. That at least is what he would like to be remembered as, and empiricism provides the clearest internal connexion between his different ideas.

(iii) Theory of knowledge

> If you fight against all sensations, you will have nothing by reference to which you can judge even those which you say are deceptive (**K.D. [Kuriai doxai/Principal doctrines]** xxiii).

The foundation of Epicurus' theory of knowledge is sense-perception. He starts from the fact that all men have sensations (*aisthêseis*), and asserts, without proof, that these must be caused by something other than themselves (D.L. x 31). It does not of course follow from this assertion that sensations are caused by things external to the percipient, and Epicurus would acknowledge that a feeling such as hunger (a *pathos* in his terminology) has an internal cause. But he takes it as self-evident that sensations of colour, sound, smell etc. must be caused by actual objects which possess these properties. 'We must suppose that it is when something enters us from things which are external that we perceive . . . their shapes' (**Ep. Hdt. [Letter to Herodotus]** 49). This statement at once raises questions which the Sceptics did not hesitate to ask about mirages, hallucinations and the like. But Epicurus has an answer to put forward, as we shall see later.

Suppose we accept that sensations cannot lie concerning their causes: in other words, that if I have the sensation of hearing there must be something sounding which causes my sensation. Does this support the further proposition that there is some object like a motor-car horn or a train whistle which corresponds precisely to the content of my sensation? For Epicurus the inference may or may not be warranted. That about which our sensations cannot deceive us is not a motor-car horn but a sense-impression (*phantasia*). What enters me from things outside is not a motor-car horn, if that is what I do genuinely hear, but a cluster of atoms (*eidôla*) thrown off the outer surface of such objects. Provided that these 'effluences', as we may call them, enter the sense organ without experiencing any change of structure the impression they produce on us will be an accurate image of the object.[6] If on the other hand their structure is disrupted in transit, the effluences will cause us to sense something which corresponds not to some actual characteristic of the object itself but to their own modified structure.

Sensations therefore are necessarily good evidence only of effluences. This raises the problem of how we can distinguish between those sensations which report to us accurately about objects and those which do not. For we cannot get at objects independently of effluences. Epicurus tackles this problem in an interesting way. He distinguishes sharply between the sense-impressions itself and judgments, or the identification of sense-impressions with objects (**Ep. Hdt.** 50-1). Our sense-impressions are not judgments, nor are they de-

pendent upon reason. We are not to say that this sense-impression is reliable, that one untrustworthy, for to do so presupposes an object which can test the validity of sensation, and our sole knowledge of objects is derived from sensations. Considered as an item of information about that which affects our senses every impression is of equal validity (D.L. x 31-2).

Nevertheless, sense-impressions can be distinguished from one another in terms of clarity or vividness. Sounds may be sharp or faint, visual images both clear and blurred. Epicurus was also aware of the fact that as we move away from the apparent source of many sensations our impressions change, and may decrease in clarity. Putting these facts together he concluded that sensations provide reliable evidence about objects if and only if they are characterized by clear and distinct impressions (*enargeia*, **Ep. Hdt.** 52, cf. **K.D.** xxiv). Other impressions 'await confirmation' by those which are clear. This conclusion could also seem to derive some support from Epicurus' explanation of the physical processes by which sensation takes place.

If we are near the ultimate source of our sensations the effluences which affect us are less likely to encounter disruption. It is only from a distance, supposedly, that the tower which is square looks round (Us. 247).

Epicurus does not specify conditions which establish the clarity of a sense-impression. He probably regarded this as something which would entail an infinite regress. He could take it as a datum of experience that we do distinguish within limits between that which is clear and that which is blurred or obscure. Clarity however is not a sufficient guarantee that we see things as they really are. Epicurus was grossly misled by 'clear views' when he argued that the sun is about the same size as it is seen to be (**Ep. Pyth. [Letter to Pythocles]** 91).

Close attention to clear impressions is the first stage in acquiring knowledge. But Epicurus did not regard it as sufficient by itself. However clear our sense-impressions may be they do not constitute knowledge. They do not tell us what something is. Before judgments about objects can be made, our sense-impressions must be classified, labelled and so marked off from one another. Epicurus proposed to satisfy these conditions by what he called *prolêpseis*, 'Preconceptions'[7]. These are general concepts or mental pictures produced by repeated sense-impressions which are both clear and similar in kind. They persist after particular sensations cease and constitute a record of our experience of the world. We acquire a concept or *prolêpsis* of man by repeated and remembered experience of particular men. Hence we are able to interpret new sensations by comparing them with preconceptions, and all our judgments about objects are made on this basis of recorded experiences, which we classify by using language (D.L. x 33). Epicurus agreed broadly with Aristotle who asserted that 'science comes to be when out of many ideas born of experience a general concept which is universal arises concerning things that are similar' (*Met.* [*Metaphysics*] A 981a5 ff.). For Epicurus, preconceptions are the foundations of judgments and language. "We should not have named anything unless we had previously learnt its form by a preconception' (D.L. ibid.). Language is a method of signifying those preconceptions which seem to us to fit the present object of experience. Because preconceptions themselves are supposed to possess 'clarity', they establish, in association with the appropriate new sense-impressions, what it is that we see, hear and so on.[8] Error arises when we use words which signify a preconception that does not correspond with the phenomenon (*De nat.* [*De natura/On Nature*] xxviii fr. iv col. 3). This may happen through confusing unclear with clear impressions, and Epicurus also recognized that the ambiguity of many words can be a cause of misassociating sense-impressions and preconceptions.[9]

Epicurus probably thought that all other concepts, including those which have no empirical reference, are derived from preconceptions. Preconceptions can be combined with one another, or they can be used as basis for inference (see D.L. x 32). But, with a few exceptions, preconceptions seem to be direct derivatives of sensation, and Epicurus recommended that the meaning of words should always be established by reference to 'the first mental image' (*Ep. Hdt.* 37). In this way he hoped to forge a firm bond between statements and immediate experience, though he gave no sufficient reasons why people's preconceptions should be regarded as similar and therefore identifiable by the same words.

So far Epicurus can claim to be a rigorous empiricist. But we must now note a number of curious exceptions to the principle that our ideas about the world are all derived ultimately from sense-impressions. Apart from those effluences which cause our sense-impressions, Epicurus also supposed that there are 'images' which somehow bypass the sense organs and penetrate directly to the mind. In nature these too are atomic clusters, but their density is much finer than the effluences which affect our senses. They are *tenuia simulacra*, as Lucretius called them (iv 722ff.), and account both for dream-images, phantoms, visions of the dead, and for such ordinary objects of thought as lions. Such 'images' may be direct effluences from the surface of an object. But many of them are simply chance combinations of individual atoms; others may consist of real effluences which are compounded and then produce images of Centaurs and monsters (*Ep. Hdt.* 48; Lucret. iv 130-42). Instead of accounting for dreams and hallucinations by reference to images entirely created or brought to consciousness by some psychological fac-

ulty, Epicurus supposed that dreams and hallucinations too are explicable by the mind's contact with atoms that enter it from outside.

If we ask how dreams and visions are to be distinguished from sense impressions, the answer is not entirely clear. Lucretius looks for a distinction in terms of continuity. 'Real' sense-impressions are produced by a steady stream of effluences; but the mind can be moved by a single 'image' (iv 746), and thus presumably catch a momentary vision. Also, dream-images are said to move by a series of effluences perishing one after another; Lucretius' description makes one think of the staccato movement of early cinema. Clearly such criteria are inadequate for Epicurus' purpose. In effect he is saying that a hallucinated person really does see something which is there, but mistakenly takes it to correspond with an actual solid object (cf. Us. 253).

The gods are a further object of direct mental perception. Postponing for the present consideration of their physical structure, we may observe here that Epicurus posits a series of fine effluences from the gods which penetrate directly to the mind. The texts which describe these divine 'images' are difficult; Epicurus put forward theoretical reasons, as well as the evidence of such visions, to justify his claims about the divine nature (Cic. *N.D.* i 43-55). But he seems to have given no adequate arguments in favour of divine 'images'. It is no help to this queer thesis to invoke the supposed universality of human belief in gods. The real difficulty is however that of the grounds for verification. By the concept of 'clear' view Epicurus has a standard for verifying perceptual judgments which has some claims to be called objective. Only in a special philosophical sense could people's perception of dogs be said to depend on their beliefs. How we may conceive of gods, on the other hand, is something which cannot be assimilated to perception of empirical objects. Epicurus' theory of divine 'images' puts religious belief in the same category as empirical observation.

Some scholars have argued that Epicurus posited a special mental faculty, 'apprehension by intellect' (*epibolê tês dianoias*), which somehow guarantees the veracity both of impressions of the gods and the validity of scientific concepts. If Epicurus had held such a theory he would have been an intuitionist in much of his philosophical activity. This interpretation was defended at great length by Cyril Bailey, whose work on Epicurus and Lucretius has held authority in the English-speaking world. According to Bailey, Epicurus supposed that the 'clear' sense-impression, of which I have already spoken, is obtained by the 'attention of the senses', and correspondingly, clear visions of the gods and clear concepts concerning, for instance, atoms and void, are obtained by the 'attention' of the mind. If Bailey were merely arguing that we cannot be aware of any object or thought unless we 'attend' to something, he would be ascribing nothing remarkable to Epicurus. But Bailey meant much more than this. On his interpretation, Epicurus supposes that 'the concepts of science are built up step by step by the juxtaposition of previous concepts, each in their turn grasped as "clear" . . . by the immediate apprehension of the mind'.[10]

Epicurus' use of the expression 'apprehension by intellect' does not justify Bailey's view. Any explanation of Epicurus as an intuitionist is on quite the wrong tack. Probably what he means by 'apprehension', whether by the mind or the senses, is concentration or attention: we need to concentrate, if we are to grasp the images which can be received by the sense organs or the mind. I shall return to this subject in the discussion of Epicurean psychology.

In order to use the evidence of the senses as material for establishing true propositions about the world, Epicurus assumed the validity of certain axioms. One of these has been stated already: 'Sense-impressions which are "clear" provide accurate information about the external appearance and properties of objects.'[11] These sense-impressions *confirm* or *bear witness against* the truth of judgments about objects which we may make provisionally on evidence lacking the requisite clarity. But Epicurus also allowed a weaker form of confirmation, 'lack of contrary evidence'. And this we may state as a further axiom: 'Judgments about non-evident objects are true if they are consistent with clear sense-impressions.' This second axiom is of the utmost importance to Epicurus. If positive confirmation by clear impressions were the sole ground for true objective statements, Epicurus would be unable to advance beyond the description of sensible objects. As it is, he assumes that the validity of clear impressions is such that they provide indirect evidence of things which are imperceptible, or for which a clear view is unobtainable in the nature of the case. Here is an example preserved by Sextus Empiricus (cited n. 21): If void does not exist (something non-evident) then motion should not exist since *ex hypothesi* all things are full and dense; so that since motion does exist the apparent does not contradict the judgment about that which is non-evident. (As stated, of course, the argument is invalid since it assumes that void is a necessary condition of movement, having fullness as its contradictory.)

Epicurus associates the axiom concerning non-contradiction with a further proposition (X), which may be treated as an implication of the second axiom: If more than one explanation of non-evident phenomena is consistent with observation then all such explanations are to be treated as equally valid (*Ep. Pyth.* 87). Let us state this more formally. Suppose that *p* is an evident fact, *q* a problem requiring explanation which cannot be solved directly by reference to *p*, and *s, t, u* three different statements about *q* which are all consistent with *p*. Then, independently of any other criterion or axiom, it follows from proposition *X* that *s, t,* and *u* are all equally acceptable explanations. This argument is formally valid, and Epicurus applied it rigorously to all statements concerning astronomical phenomena. In order to reject any of the hypotheses *s, t* and *u* it would be necessary to introduce some further principle of verification over and above the second axiom. Epicurus declined to do this on the grounds that it would be a departure from that which is definitely knowable, that is, the state of objects as given by clear sense-impressions.

Epicurus applies this principle regularly in the ***Letter to Pythocles,*** as the following excerpt shows (94):

> The repeated waning and waxing of the moon may come about owing to the rotation of this celestial body; equally it may be due to configurations of air; or again by reason of the interposition of other bodies; it may happen in any of the ways in which things manifest to us invite us to account for this phenomenon, provided that one does not become so attached to a single explanation that one rules out others for no good reason, failing to consider what it is possible for a man to observe and what impossible, and therefore desiring to discover the indiscoverable.

Up to a point this is admirable as a scientific principle. One thinks of the current debate concerning different explanations of the origin of the universe (big bang, steady state etc.) which has not yet been resolved by empirical data. Epicurus could argue, with considerable justification, that the astronomy of his own day claimed to know more than its source of evidence, the naked eye, justified. What he seems to have wholly failed to appreciate is the valid check on immediate observations which some astronomers were already trying to make by reference to systematic records and by mathematical calculations.

In application to celestial phenomena, Epicurus' use of the axiom of non-contradiction has the largely negative function of leaving open a plurality of possible explanations. But the Epicureans used the principle positively as grounds to support general statements arrived at by induction. Philodemus records this example: from the proposition 'Men in our experience are mortal' we infer that 'men everywhere are mortal'. The general statement is based on the empirical fact that we know no exception to it *and therefore* it is consistent with experience (*On signs* col. xvi). The Stoics objected to this kind of reasoning on the grounds that it presupposes the non-evident (unobserved men) to be similar in kind to the evident. The Epicureans replied that their inference does not make a presupposition that all men are mortal. It is the absence of any man known to be immortal which justifies the general inference about human mortality.

Epicurus assumes, as any scientist must, that there are certain uniformaties in nature which hold for what is evident and non-evident alike. Of course, it does not follow by the second axiom that a proposition which is consistent with some evident phenomenon *must* also be true concerning something non-evident. But science cannot operate merely by propositions which are necessarily true. It must proceed by empirical generalizations which are rejected as and when new evidence refutes previous hypotheses. The Stoics held that all inferences must be established by arguments which are deductively valid. But deductive reasoning by itself can never be sufficient to establish a scientific statement. For the premises which entail a deductive conclusion about observable data must either be empirical generalizations, or be ultimately based upon statements of this form. At some point the scientist must make an inductive inference on the basis of evidence, and for Epicurus that point is reached when observation seems to support the belief that no instances are likely to be found which will contradict a general statement.

Epicurus and Lucretius often appeal to 'analogy' or 'similarity' to support an inference from the visible to the invisible. Thus Epicurus takes the (allegedly) observed fact that no parts can be distinguished in the smallest visible magnitude to support the inference that the same is true of the smallest invisible magnitude, the minimum part of an atom (***Ep. Hdt***. 58f.). The main subject of Philodemus' *On signs* is 'analogical inference', and we might suppose that this requires a further axiom for its justification. None of our secondary sources nor Epicurus himself gives any independent discussion of 'analogy', and it is not needed. The justification for inference by analogy is provided by the two axioms already discussed.[12] By the first axiom we are justified in asserting that 'clear impressions' give evidence that men are mortal. All the men of whom we have reliable experience are similar in respect of mortality. From this positive evidence Epicurus infers that men of whom we have no experience are equally similar in respect of mortality. The inference is justified by the second axiom which allows us to assert *p* if there is no evidence against it. Philodemus even states that it is 'inconceivable' that there should be something which possesses nothing in common with empirical evidence (*On signs* col. xxi 27ff.). The Epicurean test of the 'conceivable' is sense-perception and the problematic mental 'images' already discussed.

Epicurus' method of indirect proof can be illustrated by copious passages from Lucretius. It is the poet's regular practice to refute a proposition by appeal to what is clear, what we actually see, and thus infer the contradictory of the rejected proposition. I give just one example. In Book i Lucretius argues towards the atomist thesis by stages. He begins by dismissing the proposition 'Something can be created from nothing'.

For, if this were so, every type of thing could be produced out of anything; nothing would require a seed. But we see (*videmus*) that cultivated land produces better yield than uncultivated land, which proves the existence in the soil of primary bodies stirred to birth by the plough. 'If there were no primary bodies you would see (*videres*) each thing coming to birth much more successfully of its own accord' (159-214).

Like this Lucretian argument Epicurus' methodology seems imprecise and informal when judged by the criteria of stricter logic. I have no doubt that it is proper to describe as 'axioms' the two principles concerning confirmation and non-contradiction. But Epicurus does not *call* them axioms. He almost certainly knew Aristotle's *Analytics,* if a fragment of Philodemus has been correctly deciphered.[13] But although Aristotle's inductive methodology may have been an influence on Epicurus, the later philosopher did not share Aristotle's interest in logic for its own sake; and he seems to have thought that any kind of demonstrative science, based upon deductive reasoning, was mere word-play. Since most of Aristotle's *Analytics* is concerned with the analysis of deductive argument in the form of syllogisms and with specifying the sufficient conditions of necessary truths, Epicurus cannot have liked what he read. Above all, he rejected any kind of logical inquiry which was not applied to the understanding of empirical data. He did not, apparently, see that empirical science, if it is to be well-grounded, cannot advance very far solely on the guidance of 'clear' sense-impressions.

The reader will be able to extend the criticism of Epicurus' methodology for himself. What should be added is a warning against taking at face value offhand remarks in ancient writers, which would imply that Epicurus had no interest in logic and scientific method. These views are to be found in many modern hand-books and they are incorrect. Epicurus, in order to shock, sometimes writes as if he despised all learning; but this is rhetoric, an expression of contempt for what he regarded as pedantic and positively harmful in the culture of his own day. Fortunately, sufficient of the twenty-eighth book of ***On Nature*** survives to give us a glimpse of Epicurus when he is not merely summarizing or exhorting. In this work Epicurus discussed induction, using Aristotle's technical term *epagôgê,* problems of meaning and ambiguity, the distinction between universal and particular, problems connected with the designation of individuals, and linguistic puzzles of the sort propounded by the Megarians. Unfortunately the text is too badly damaged to let us see how he treated all of these subjects in detail.[14] But it gives us sufficient evidence to judge that parts of the following statement by Cicero are grossly misleading: 'Epicurus rejects definitions [he did not]; gives no instruction concerning division [classification into genus and species]; fails to show how an argument is to be constructed; does not point out how sophisms are to be resolved nor how ambiguities are to be distinguished' (*Fin. [Definibus]* i 22). It is salutary to remember that Epicurus wrote thirty-seven books *On Nature,* and that we can observe Cicero's prejudice by studying fragments from just one of these.

(iv) The structure of things

> The nature of the universe is bodies and void (*On Nature* i).

Epicurus claimed to be self-taught, but atomism was more than a century old in Greece by the time he re-asserted its central principles. First Leucippus and then Democritus, in the second half of the fifth century, had argued that what really exists is ultimately reducible to two and only two kinds of thing: the full (indivisible bodies) and the empty (space). How such a thesis came to be propounded is itself a fascinating story, but it belongs to the history of Presocratic philosophy. I will touch on it here only in so far as it is essential to understanding Epicurus' atomism.

Our starting-point is once again the *Letter to Herodotus*. There, in a few paragraphs of highly succinct argumentation, Epicurus discloses the essential features of the atomist theory (38-44). The problem which that theory purports to solve may be stated as follows: What principles derived from empirical evidence are necessary and sufficient to account for the physical world as it presents itself to our senses? The answer is highly economical: an infinite number of indivisible bodies moving in infinite empty space.

Epicurus arrives at this answer by a series of metaphysical propositions, which he then uses to support inferences about the underlying structure of the changing objects of experience. (A) Nothing can come out of nothing. (B) Nothing can be destroyed into nothing. (C) The universe never was nor will be in a condition which differs from its present one.[15] The first two propositions are established indirectly by what I have called the second axiom. It would controvert experience to suppose that nothing pre-exists or survives the objects which we observe to grow and decay. Things are seen to grow *out of* something; they do not just emerge at random. Secondly, there *is* something *into* which things pass away. Otherwise there would be no limit to destruction and everything would have perished into non-being. The third proposition (C) is treated by Epicurus as analytic. Since the universe embraces all that there is, nothing exists outside the universe which could cause it to change. (He does not consider the possibility that any internal cause of change might bring about different conditions of the universe as a whole at different times.)

From (C) it follows that any explanation of things in general which holds now is eternally valid.

It is an evident fact that bodies exist; empty space must therefore also exist, since bodies must be *in* something and have something through which to move.[16] Epicurus next asserts that apart from bodies and void nothing can be conceived of as an independent entity: all things must be reducible to body and mind. Bodies are of two kinds, compounds and the units out of which compounds are formed. From (B) it follows that one class of bodies, non-compounds, must be limited with respect to change and destruction. Epicurus expresses this thus: 'And these bodies [*sc.* non-compounds] are indivisible and changeless, if all things are not to be destroyed into *non*-being but are to persist secure in the dissolution of compounds; they are solid in nature and cannot be divided at any place or in any manner. Hence the first principles must be bodies which are indivisible' (*Ep. Hdt.* 39-41).

Question-begging though this argument is, in Epicurus' abbreviated formulation, its main points are wholly clear. We do not see atoms, but what we see, birth and death, growth and decay, is taken to require the existence of bodies which are themselves changeless and wholly impenetrable.

What else is to be said about atoms and empty space? Epicurus proceeds to argue that the universe is 'unlimited' in itself and also in the number of atoms which it contains, and in the extent of empty space. If the universe were limited it would have extremities; but there is nothing to limit the universe. And if the universe itself is unlimited its constituents must also be unlimited. For a limited number of atoms in infinite empty space would not be sufficient to hold one another together; they could not form the plurality of compounds which we experience; and an unlimited number of atoms could not be accommodated in limited space (*Ep. Hdt.* 41-2).

Since all the objects of experience are compounded out of atoms and void, Epicurus held that the atoms themselves must have innumerable, though not infinitely, different shapes, in order to account for the variety of things. Besides shape, all atoms are necessarily subject to continuous movement, a fact which will require further discussion shortly. They also possess weight, and of course bulk or mass. All other properties of which we have experience are accounted for by the arrangements which come into being when a plurality of atoms and void combine. Atoms as such are not hot or cold, coloured or resonant, and so forth (*Ep. Hdt.* 42-4; 68-9).

It is now time to consider in more detail what Epicurus meant by the 'indivisibility' of the atom. As has been shown already, the concept of an atom is arrived at by elimination of a contradictory hypothesis, that bodies are ultimately divisible into *non*-being. If Epicurus supposed that the infinite divisibility of a body must lead to its reduction to nothing at all he was guilty of an elementary fallacy. Infinite divisibility implies nothing about reduction to sheer non-existence. Lucretius however sets out an argument for indivisible bodies which avoids this fallacy, and which, we may presume, goes back to Epicurus himself.

The argument runs thus: body and empty space are mutually exclusive, otherwise there would not be *two* kinds of real things (i.e. all things could be reduced to either body or empty space). Body therefore cannot include as part of itself empty space. Anything which does include as part of itself empty space must be bounded by that which is solid—body. Created things are of this kind, that is, compounds of body and empty space. But the particular bodies which help to form such compounds must consist of that which is wholly solid and indivisible. For nothing can be divided unless it contains within itself empty space. And nothing can contain within itself empty space unless it has components which are themselves wholly indivisible (Lucret. i 503-35).

The force of this argument turns on the assumption that empty space is a necessary condition of divisibility. The earlier atomists had spoken of empty space as 'non-being' and of body as 'being': empty space is non-body. If we take Epicurus' reference to *non*-being as a legacy of this earlier usage his argument becomes compatible with the passage summarized from Lucretius. Just as what-is cannot be ultimately reduced to what-is-not, so body cannot be reduced to non-body, i.e. empty space.

The Epicurean atoms cannot be split into smaller bodies. They are physically indivisible. But they are not the smallest units of extension. The atom itself consists of minimal parts which are not merely physically unsplittable but indivisible in thought: nothing beyond these *minima* can be conceived of. Epicurus supposed that there is a finite number of such minimal parts for every atom. Atoms vary in size, and their size is determined by the number of their minimal parts. Again, atoms vary in shape and their shape is determined by the arrangement of their minimal parts.

This doctrine of minimal parts raises many difficulties and will only be discussed briefly here. Epicurus apparently regarded each atom as something composed of minimum units of magnitude which are not separable from one another, and therefore not separable from the whole atom which they compose (*Ep. Hdt.* 56-9).[17] The notion is obscure and may be clarified by a concrete analogy. Suppose we take a cubic centimetre of solid metal and mark it off in three dimensions by millimetres. Then, the minimal parts stand to the atom as each cubic millimetre to the whole cube of metal, with this proviso: each square millimetre must be taken

as the smallest unit which can be distinguished on any surface of the whole cube. The Epicurean atom is the smallest magnitude which can exist as a discrete independent body. Epicurus seems to have thought that this left something to be accounted for—namely, the atom's boundary points, or the fact, to put it another way, that the atom is a three-dimensional object and as such possesses shape. He sought an explanation by reference to its having minimal parts.

In giving the atoms minimal parts Epicurus almost certainly modified earlier atomism. The atoms of Leucippus and Democritus were physically indivisible but also, in all probability, without parts, and therefore theoretically indivisible as well. Simplicius, the Aristotelian commentator, distinguishes Epicurus from the earlier atomists thus: Epicurus, he says, appealed merely to the changelessness of his primary bodies, whereas Leucippus and Democritus also referred to their smallness and lack of parts (Us. 268).

Our knowledge of early atomism is largely derived from Aristotle. Modern research has shown that he was right to connect the fifth-century atomists with the slightly older Eleatic philosophers, Parmenides and Zeno.[18] This is not the place to offer any detailed account of the Eleatics. Very briefly, Parmenides, in his poem *The way of truth,* had set out arguments of quite remarkable subtlety concerning what can be said about that which exists. He concluded that the following predicates are inadmissible: subject to creation and destruction, subject to divisibility, subject to change of place, and change of quality; what exists is 'whole, immobile, eternal, all together, one and continuous'. Zeno reinforced Parmenides' arguments by seeking to show that the proposition 'Things are many and subject to motion' leads to insoluble dilemmas. Zeno's puzzles turn chiefly on the notion of partition or divisibility. The interpretation of them is extremely difficult and controversial. One point only concerns us here. Zeno argued that if a unit of magnitude can be divided at all it must be infinitely divisible. This conclusion was unpalatable to the early atomists who wished to give an explanation of the world which would be compatible, as far as possible, with Parmenides' logic. Hence they adopted as their primary bodies partless, and therefore indivisible, units of magnitude, which satisfied most of the predicates deduced by Parmenides to belong to what really exists. Lacking parts, the atoms of Democritus would not even be theoretically divisible.

Epicurus modified this doctrine by ascribing parts to the atom but making these parts themselves *minima,* i.e. physically and theoretically indivisible. He seems to have supposed that it is a necessary condition of the atom itself, the minimum discrete body, that it possesses parts—but parts which rule out theoretical divisibility to infinity for the atom itself. Minimal parts satisfied this condition, and they also provided a means of accounting for differences in the shape, size and weight of particular atoms. Lucretius asserts that 'things which are not augmented by parts do not have the diversities of properties which creative matter must have' (i 631-3). Finally, Aristotle had pointed out a number of difficulties in the notion of a partless atom which Epicurus' new thesis may have been intended to resolve (*Physics* vi 231b25-232a17; 240b8-241a6). We shall come back to minimal parts in the next section.

(v) The motion of atoms and formation of compound bodies

One modification of earlier atomism by Epicurus has just been discussed. He also differed from Democritus concerning the motion of atoms. Both agreed that the atoms are always in motion, but Democritus almost certainly supposed that the course which any one atom takes relative to any other is wholly random.[19] In fact, most of our evidence for the motion of Democritus' atoms clearly refers to motion derived from collisions with other atoms, and we can only speculate about what he might have said of the original motion of an atom. He probably did not attribute weight to the atom, and if so, cannot have used weight as a cause of motion. Furthermore, it is unlikely that he would have thought it proper to ascribe any direction to the movement of atoms since he said of infinite void that it has neither top nor bottom, centre or extremity (Cic. *Fin.* i 17). Void provided Democritus with a condition which he certainly regarded as necessary for motion, and he may have simply taken it as a fact about the atom that it does necessarily move in the void.

Against Democritus Epicurus held that weight is a necessary property of the atom. His reasons for this assertion cannot be established by any direct testimony, but they are almost certainly founded on the hypothesis that a weightless body cannot move. Aristotle devoted considerable attention to the analysis of weight as a determining factor of motion. Indeed, in the *De caelo* Aristotle defines heavy and light as 'the capacity for a certain natural motion' (307b32), and a little later says: 'There are certain things whose nature it is always to move away from the centre, and others always towards the centre. The first I speak of as moving upwards, the second downwards' (308a14). Now Epicurus recognized that in an infinite universe one cannot strictly speak of a centre, nor of up and down (*Ep. Hdt.* 60). But the thought that one could speak of up and down relative to some fixed point, and that in this relative sense the natural motion of atoms is downwards as a consequence of their weight. Any other motion than perpendicular fall requires other factors than weight alone to account for it. In all probability, Aristotle's discussion of weight as a determinant of movement influenced Epicurus' modification of Democritus.

If an atom is unimpeded by collision with other atoms its speed and direction of motion are invariant. Epicurus grasped the important fact that differences of weight make no difference to the velocity of bodies falling in a vacuum: 'When they are moving through the void and encounter no resistance the speed of the atoms must be equal. Neither will heavy ones travel faster than light ones . . .' (*Ep. Hdt.* 61). At what speed then do free-falling atoms move? Epicurus sometimes expresses this in the graphic phrase 'as quick as thought'. But that does not help us very much. In fact, he seems to have supposed that time, like extension, is not infinitely divisible. Just as the atom is the minimum discrete body and consists of minimal parts, so time is divisible into 'minimum continuous periods' which themselves consist of indivisible temporal units, 'times distinguishable only in thought' (*Ep. Hdt.* 62). Epicurus probably supposed that the time which an atom takes to move the minimum distance, that is the minimum of extension, is the minimum temporal unit. This temporal unit, being indivisible, is not such that a movement can take place *during* it. 'Has moved' not 'is moving' is the relation which a moving body has to the indivisible units that constitute time and space (Us. 278). As Aristotle saw, such a theory turns movement into a series of jerks (*Phys.* vi 231b25—232a17). The atom has to hop, as it were, from one set of spatial units into the next. For there is no time or space in which its progression from one unit into the next can be said to occur. The minimum distance by which an atom can alter its location at any moment is the measure of any one minimal part.

Epicurus could have avoided these consequences if he had seen that the infinite divisibility of any *quantum,* whether of space or time, can be asserted without its entailing the consequence that these *quanta* are, as a matter of fact, divisible into infinite parts. He chose instead to predicate physical indivisibility of the atom and a limit to the theoretical division of its parts. Having wrongly concluded that the extremities of the atom must be accounted for by positing minimal spatial units, he accepted as a corollary the indivisibility of time and movement as well. He countered Aristotle's objection, that this makes differences of speed impossible, by arguing that apparent differences in the speed of the compound bodies which we see can be explained as a function of the collective movements at constant speed of individual atoms within each compound; the speed of a moving compound is determined by the collisions which occur between its internal atoms. The more its atoms tend to move in the same direction over a short period of time the greater the speed of the compound body. If the movement of some atoms in one direction is balanced by a movement of others in a different direction the compound body will be stationary (*Ep. Hdt.* 47; 62).[20]

Let us now return to consider the falling atom in more detail. Given that this fall is at constant speed for any atom, and in the same direction, how can a world be formed which consists of atoms in conjunction, atoms which have collided and formed compound bodies? Oddly enough, no word of the answer to this problem survives by Epicurus himself. But his theory can be reconstructed from Lucretius and other later writers. Lucretius writes as follows: 'At this point I wish you to learn this too: when bodies are being carried straight down through the void by their own weight, at an undetermined time and at undetermined places they push a little from their course—only as much as you might call a change of direction. If they were not accustomed to swerve, all things would fall down through the deep void like raindrops, nor could collision come about nor would the atoms experience blows. And so nature would never have created anything' (ii. 216-24).

This swerve which atoms make at no determined time or place has always intrigued the readers of Lucretius. It apparently builds into the universe, as Epicurus conceives of this, a principle of relative indeterminacy. The movements of an atom, and therefore any consequences of its movement, are not entirely predictable. Our further information about the swerve in this context merely confirms Lucretius' words, and they must be taken at face value.[21] It follows then that an atom, independently of any secondary motion which may result from collisions, has both a unidirectional movement and an unpredictable tendency to deviate from this.

The atomic swerve is also important to Epicurus' theory of human action. But that will require discussion later. The effect of the swerve with which we are concerned here is the collision between two or more atoms which it may bring about. Since every atom is solid through and through, the effect of a collision between atoms is a momentary check on atomic movement followed by a rebound (at the same speed), and hence a further change of direction. But it may sometimes happen that colliding atoms in spite of their tendency to rebound become intertwined and form a temporary and apparently stable compound. The compound so formed is in fact a dynamic entity, a collection of atoms moving both in their normal downward manner and from the effect of blows or swerves. But it will often present the appearance of something stable. Lucretius reports that the different densities of objects are determined by the relation between the atoms and void which they contain. Iron consists of close-packed atoms which are unable to move and rebound any great distance. Air, on the other hand, is composed of atoms which are interspersed with large areas of void (ii 100-8).

We have seen that for Epicurus all properties of things beyond size, shape, weight and movement are secondary. That is to say, they are properties which cannot be predicated of atoms but only of the compound bodies which atoms may form. This does not mean that colour, sound etc. are merely human ways of ordering and interpreting sense-impressions. Democritus had argued thus, but Epicurus did not agree (*Ep. Hdt.* 68-71). His discussion of secondary qualities is condensed and obscure, but seems basically to amount to this: colour, sound etc. cannot exist independently of bodies, nor are they 'parts' out of which compound bodies arise. Rather, any secondary property which is a permanent attribute of some object (compound body) is a *constituent* of the object in the sense that the object would not be what it is without this attribute. We might illustrate this point by saying that a man does not arise out of a combination of hands, legs, colour and so forth. He arises from a combination of atoms and void. But the effect of this combination is the production of hands, legs, pink or black colour etc., and these, or some of them, are necessary attributes of any man.

Although Epicurus' basic distinction between bodies is the simple disjunction, atom or compound, he may have supposed that certain compounds function as molecules or basic complexes which serve as 'seeds' for the production of more complex things.[22] Lucretius writes of 'seeds of water' or 'seeds of fire', and though he may mean simply 'that out of which water or fire is composed' the specific property of water or fire is something which only arises through the combination of atoms. It is probable, though not certain, that Epicurus would have regarded a pool of water as a compound of smaller compounds—molecules of water. If the molecule were broken down we should of course be left only with atoms and void. Epicurus firmly rejected the four-element theory which persists through Greek philosophy in various forms from Empedocles to Neoplatonism.

I have called the compound body a dynamic entity. This description applies not merely to its internal atoms but also to those atoms which constitute its surface. An object which persists over any length of time does not retain the same atoms throughout that time. Epicurus supposed that atoms are constantly leaving the surface of objects and having their place taken by further atoms which bombard the object and may then get caught up on its structure.[23] The notion that atoms are constantly leaving the surface of objects is fundamental to the explanation of sensation. As observed already, we sense something when effluences enter our sense organs. If these are 'real' images they are simply the outer surface or skin of objects which is 'sloughed off', to use a Lucretian metaphor, in a continuous stream of 'films'.

Epicurus took over his fundamental principles of atoms and void from earlier atomists but we have seen that he was no slavish imitator. The atomist system seemed to him to provide an explanation of the structure of things which was both compatible with empirical data and psychologically comforting, in that it did away with the need for divine causation and any form of teleology. Whether or not men find it more or less comforting to suppose that the world is determined by a supernatural being or beings, seems to be very much a matter of personal temperament. Lucretius praises Epicurus for delivering mankind from 'the weight of religion' (i 62ff.). He means popular religion, superstitious beliefs in the gods as direct arbiters of human destiny and fears of divine anger as expressed in thunder and lightning. But Epicurus cannot have taken popular superstitions as his only target. He was also concerned to reject the sophisticated theology of Plato and probably Aristotle too.

How he did so and what he put in its place will be the subject of the next few pages. Before discussing this, however, we should notice how Epicurus rejects out of hand the method of teleological explanation which bulks so large in Plato and Aristotle. Plato makes Socrates complain that Presocratic thinkers fail to show why it is best for things to be as they are (*Phaedo* 99a-d).[24] What Socrates is alleged to have found a defect—the concentration on mechanical explanations—Epicurus regarded as a positive merit. Things are not 'good for anything', he argued; this is merely a piece of learned superstition. There is no purpose which the world as a whole or things in particular are designed to fulfil. For design is not a feature of the world; it is manifestly imperfect.[25] Given the fact that the number of atoms is infinite and that their shapes are immensely various, it is not remarkable that similar combinations of things arise. Indeed, Epicurus held that the number of worlds is infinite, some of which are like our own while others vary (*Ep. Hdt.* 45). All of them however are ultimately explicable by reference to the purposeless combination and separation of discrete and inanimate physical entities moving in empty space.

Epicurus' cosmology denies the foundation of the Platonic and Aristotelian world-picture. The fossilized Aristotelianism of the schoolmen came under attack in the Renaissance, and Epicurean atomism was given a new relevance by the French mathematician and opponent of Descartes, Pierre Gassendi. The history of later science has amply vindicated Epicurus' rejection of final causes. But it is arguable that Epicurus' renunciation of teleology, in its historical context, went too far. His principle of explanation in terms of accidental arrangement of atoms will hardly serve to account adequately for such phenomena as biological reproduction. Why, to give the question an Aristotelian tone, does man produce man? Lucretius, it is true, offers an answer to this question: the characteristics of a species are transmitted to the offspring through its own seed (iii 741ff.), and he repeatedly emphasizes that each

thing has its own fixed place; that there are natural laws determining biological and other events (i 75-7; ii 700ff.; iii 615ff. etc.). But the basis of these laws does not seem to rest firmly on anything implied by Epicurus' atomist principles. His physical theory has to explain too much by too little. These complaints are legitimate if we judge Epicurus by Aristotelian standards. But in making them it is necessary to remember that Epicurus did not set out to be a purely disinterested investigator of things. According to his own words, 'the purpose of studying nature is to gain a sharp understanding of the cause of those things which are most important' (*Ep. Hdt.* 78). By 'most important' he means fundamental to human well-being.

The two subjects on which he thought it most important to have correct beliefs were theology and psychology. Having now discussed Epicurus' basic physical principles I turn to consider how he applied these to his treatment of the gods and the human mind.

(vi) The gods of Epicurus

> That which is sublimely happy and immortal experiences no trouble itself nor does it inflict trouble on anything else, so that it is not affected by passion or partiality. Such things are found only in what is weak (*K.D.* i).

Nothing disquieted Epicurus more profoundly than the notion that supernatural beings control phenomena or that they can affect human affairs. That there are gods he did not deny. But he repeatedly and vociferously rejected the belief that gods are responsible for any natural events. His rejection of this belief is expressed most pointedly in contexts concerning astronomical phenomena.

> Moreover we must not suppose that the movement and turning of the heavenly bodies, their eclipses and risings and settings and similar movements are caused by some being which takes charge of them and which controls or will continue to control them, while simultaneously enjoying complete bliss and immortality. For occupation and supervision, anger and favour, are not consistent with sublime happiness. . . . Nor again must we suppose that those things which are merely an aggregate of fire possess sublime happiness and direct these (celestial) movements deliberately and voluntarily (*Ed. Hdt.* 76-7).

The object of Epicurus' polemic in these lines is any theology which ascribes divine control to the heavenly bodies. By denying the survival of the personality in any form after death Epicurus thought he could remove the source of one basic human anxiety—fear of divine judgment and eternal punishment. And I will discuss this feature of his philosophy in the next section. But he held that it was equally false and disturb-

ing to credit gods with any influence over human affairs here and now. Thereby he denied the foundations
of popular Greek religion. The notion that human well-
being and adversity are dispensed by the gods was
fundamental to popular Greek religion. Language reflected the belief: a happy man was *eudaimôn,* 'one
who has a favourable deity'; *kakodaimôn,* 'unhappy',
literally means 'having a harmful deity'. For the majority perhaps, belief in the gods of mythology had
generally been a matter of civic or private ritual rather
than any inner experience. But many Greeks, educated
and uneducated alike, subscribed to mystery cults which
promised salvation to the initiated, and fears of pollution and divine intervention remained strong.
Theophrastus' portrait of the Superstitious Man, overdrawn though it is, would lose all point if it had no
basis in everyday experience.[26]

But Epicurus' attack on divine management of the
cosmos was more specifically directed, we may suppose, against the cosmology of Plato and Aristotle.
Plato, in his later works, constantly refers to the regularity of celestial movements as evidence of intelligent
direction by divine beings. In the *Timaeus* we are told
that the purpose of sight for men is to observe the
'revolutions of intelligence in the heavens, so that we
may use their regular motions to guide the troubled
movements of our own thinking'; we are to 'imitate
the invariant movements of God' (47b-c.) This concept of divine ordination of the heavens was developed by Plato with much more detail in the *Laws,* his
last major work.[27] There he defends the thesis that the
heavenly bodies have as their cause virtuous souls or
gods (x 899b). Their virtue is proved by the regularity
of the movements which they cause. Disorderly movements, whether in the heavens or on earth, must be
accounted for by a soul which is bad (897d).

Not only, according to Plato, are the stars directed by
gods. Mankind and the universe as a whole are the
'possessions' of the gods (902b-c). In the *Laws* Plato
emphasizes that the control which gods exercise over
men is providential. But he states equally strongly that
it is absolute. Plato thought he could legislate for a
reformed religion by banishing the discreditable gods
of tradition and replacing them with new gods whose
excellence was manifested in the mathematical perfection of celestial physics. But to Epicurus Plato's astral
gods were quite as repugnant as the traditional Olympian pantheon. His refusal to regard the movements of
the stars as a consequence of divine intentions is an
explicit rejection of Plato's own language. In the
Epinomis, the title of which means 'after the laws',
astronomy is made the key to this new theology.[28] The
heavenly bodies are there said to be the source of our
knowledge of number, which itself is the foundation of
intelligence and morality. This queer assertion is put
forward in all seriousness, and it leads to a reiteration
of the divinity of the stars. These beings possess won-

drous powers of mind; they know our own wills; they
welcome the good and loathe the bad (984d-985b).

Epicurus regarded such beliefs as a prime source
of human anxiety. To him they seemed to compound old superstitions and to make the heavenly
bodies, with their watching brief over human affairs, an object of utter terror. He can have been
little less disquieted by Aristotle's theology. For
Aristotle too regarded the heavenly bodies as intelligent, divine beings whose movements are voluntary. We know that Aristotle expressed such views
in an early work designed for popular consumption.[29] It is also true that Aristotle's views about
celestial movements developed during his lifetime
and that he does not in any extant treatise make the
heavenly bodies personal arbiters of human destiny. But it is a basic doctrine of his *Metaphysics*
that all movement and life are ultimately dependent upon the Unmoved Mover, pure Mind or God,
whose activity of eternal self-contemplation promotes desire and motion in the heavenly bodies,
each governed by its own intelligence. Aristotle
approved of popular beliefs in the divinity of the
heavens, even though he denied their traditional
mythological trappings (*Met.* 1074a38ff.). The
Unmoved Mover, like Epicurus' own gods, is not
personally concerned with the universe. But unlike
Epicurus' gods the Unmoved Mover is the prime
cause of all things. He does not determine human
affairs by his own fiat. They are none the less
dependent upon events, such as the sun's diurnal
rotation and seasonal change, of which he is the
ultimate cause.[30]

Epicurus rejects divine management of the world by an
argument based upon the meaning and implications of
the words 'sublimely happy' and 'immortal'. He accepts that these predicates, traditionally ascribed to the
gods, express real attributes of divine beings (***Ep. Men.***
123). But he denies that sublime happiness and immortality are compatible with any involvement in 'our affairs' (Cic. *N.D.* i 51-2). In his view happiness, whether
human or divine, requires for its full realization a life of
uninterrupted tranquillity or freedom from pain. For the
moment we must accept this concept of happiness as a
dogmatic assertion, for its full analysis belongs to the
field of ethics. Epicurus' argument concerning the gods'
indifference to the world picks up this concept of happiness, applies it to the gods and thereby removes from
them any actions or feelings which take account of
human affairs. Seneca summarizes this position: 'Hence
god dispenses no benefits; he is impregnable, heedless
of us; indifferent to the world . . . untouched by benefits
and wrongs' (Us. 364).

The argument makes three assumptions. First, that there
are gods. Secondly, that the gods are sublimely happy
and immortal. Thirdly, that their happiness consists in

uninterrupted tranquillity. We must now consider how Epicurus justified these assumptions.

Since he was disposed to combat all beliefs about divine control of the world it may seem surprising that Epicurus accepted even the existence of supernatural beings. For, if the gods could be shown to be fictions, all activities associated with them would necessarily also be ruled out. Epicurus argued however that the universal beliefs of mankind establish the fact that gods exist. 'What people or race is there which lacks an untaught conception of gods?' (Cic. *N.D.* i 43). The argument claims that *a* belief in gods exists independently of institutionalized religion or custom. It is therefore something *natural*. Of course the belief might be natural and false. But Epicurus uses a basically Aristotelian premise (*E.N. Nicomachean ethics* 1172b35) to reject this objection: 'That about which all agree must be true.'

The same principle, *consensus omnium,* is used to establish the properties of the gods. All men are also said to have a natural belief that the gods are immortal, sublimely happy and of human shape.[31] Epicurus held that these common beliefs are 'preconceptions' derived from experience—visions which people have when awake and all the more when asleep. He argued that these visions must, like all sensations, be caused by something real, that is to say atomic configurations or images (effluences) which come from the gods themselves and which penetrate to our minds. The theory is naïve and fails to take account of other factors which might have led men to believe in gods. If as a matter of fact human beliefs about gods were as consistent with each other and as similar as Epicurus claims, the hypothesis of mental perception of divine images would offer a reason for the *consensus omnium:* we are all acted upon by the same kind of external images. But Epicurus assumes the *consensus omnium,* and then seeks to explain it in psychophysical terms.

According to Lucretius the properties of sublime happiness and immortality were inferred by men from their mental images of the gods:

> They endowed the gods with eternal life, because images of the gods were constantly supplied with unchanging form, and also because they believed that beings possessed of such strength could not be vanquished by any chance force. And they supposed that the gods enjoyed supreme happiness because no fear of death troubled any of them, and because in dreams the gods were seen to do many remarkable things without any expenditure of effort (v 1175-82).

Lucretius proceeds to argue that early men, having acquired a belief in gods, supposed them to be the agents of astronomical and meteorological phenomena through ignorance of the real cause of these things. Elsewhere

he argues at length that the gods cannot have had any desire or ability to create the universe, the imperfections of which are clear evidence that it is not under divine direction (v 156-94). The gods, like true Epicureans, dwell in *sedes quietae* ('tranquil resting-places') enjoying a life free of all trouble (iii 18-24).

Besides the natural conceptions of mankind Epicurus himself gave other reasons for justifying his account of the gods' nature. He defended their anthropomorphic appearance by the argument that this is the most beautiful of all shapes and therefore the shape which belongs to beings whose nature is best (Cic. *N.D.* i 46-9). Not all of his statements about the gods can be reduced to the supposed evidence of natural conceptions.[32] But while recognizing that the images which men receive from the gods are 'insubstantial' and difficult to perceive, he clearly hoped to show that primary knowledge of the gods is something similar in kind to the direct acquaintance with physical objects which we obtain through our sense organs.

How is the physical structure of the gods to be conceived of and what manner of life do they lead? The evidence which bears on these questions is difficult and must be dealt with summarily here. The basic problem is the everlasting existence of the gods. Atoms and void are imperishable, for atoms possess a solidity which is impervious to all 'blows' and void is unassailable by 'blows' (Lucret. iii 806-13). But the ordinary objects of experience, because they are compounded out of atoms and void, are not of a kind to resist destruction indefinitely. So Lucretius writes:

> By (natural) law they perish, when all things have been made weak by outflow (of atoms) and give way to the blows which come from outside (ii 1139-40).

Epicurus sought to avoid this difficulty by introducing a mode of being which is not a compound body in any ordinary sense. Our main evidence is a difficult text of Cicero. After observing that the gods are perceived by the mind and not the senses, Cicero writes that they do not possess 'solidity' nor 'numerical identity', like the ordinary objects of perception, but 'an unlimited form of very similar images arises out of the innumerable atoms and flows towards the gods' (*N.D.* i 49, cf. 105). Elsewhere the gods are perhaps spoken of as 'likenesses' and some gods (or all of them from one point of view) are 'things which exist by similarity of form through the continuous onflow of similar images which are brought to fulfilment at the same place' (Us. 355).[33] Scholars have questioned the accuracy of these statements on the grounds that they make the atoms which flow *towards* the gods 'images'. But these doubts may be misplaced. 'Image' (or *eidôlon* in Epicurus' terminology) is distinguished from 'solid body'. There can be 'images' in this sense which are merely patterns of fine atoms lacking the density to constitute a solid body. We may perceive Centaurs in virtue of such 'images', but they are not images contrasted with a real Centaur; for there is no solid body corresponding to a Centaur. Similarly, there is no solid body which emits images of the gods. For the gods do not possess a solid body. They are called 'likenesses', in all probability, because their nature is continuously reconstituted by a moving stream of 'images', discrete arrangements of fine atoms which possess *similar* form.

The gods then have no numerical identity. If their substance were that of an ordinary compound body they would be subject to an irreplaceable loss of atoms and hence destructible by external 'blows'. Their identity is 'formal', a consequence of the constant arrival and departure of similar forms at the points in space occupied by the gods. It has sometimes been aptly compared with the nature of a waterfall the shape of which is determined by continuous flow. Epicurus does not explain why there should be a continuous supply of atoms patterned in the right way to constitute the form of the gods. If pressed he would probably have argued that in a universe which contains an infinite number of atoms this is not impossible in principle and that our experience of the gods—the fact that we can have more than momentary visions of them—proves the continuity of their form, and therefore the supply of appropriate atoms. Moreover we think of them as immortal.

Does this strange notion of the gods' physical structure imply that they themselves make no contribution to their own unceasing existence? The evidence discussed so far could imply that the gods are simply happy beneficiaries of a constant supply of atoms which replace those they have lost. Some scholars have adopted such a view. But Philodemus, who wrote a work *On the gods* (as did Epicurus himself), parts of which are preserved on a Herculaneum papyrus, seems to have argued that the gods' own excellence and powers of reason secure them from destructive forces in the environment.[34] It should not be supposed that this is a laborious activity for the gods. On the contrary, all our sources stress the fact that the gods enjoy an existence completely free of toil. They are able, in virtue of their nature, to appropriate the atoms which preserve their existence and to ward off atoms of the wrong kind. This seems to have been Philodemus' view, and we may reasonably credit it to Epicurus himself.

The gods' tenuity of structure is explained by the 'images' which form their bodies, a theory ridiculed by ancient critics (*N.D.* i 105). We may now see why the gods are not said to have body but quasi body, not blood but quasi blood (Cic. *N.D.* i 49). They are seen above all in dreams and are themselves dreamlike in substance, insubstantial like the 'images' which make up their being. It may seem strange that Epicurus should have credited such creatures with perfect happiness, but this becomes less odd when we study what their happiness consists in. It is something negative rather than positive. The gods have no occupations, they can be affected by no pain, they are liable to no change. They dwell in no world but in the spaces which separate one world from another (*intermundia*, Cic. *N.D.* i 18). And since it is Epicurus' claim that absence of pain is the highest pleasure, and pleasure is the essence of happiness, the gods are perfectly happy. In the later Epicureanism of Philodemus more positive things are said about the gods, including the fact that they speak Greek! But Epicurus, so far as we know, did not go in for such crude anthropomorphism.

> . . . The Gods, who haunt
> The lucid interspace of world and world,
> Where never creeps a cloud, or moves a wind,
> Where never falls the least white star of snow,
> Nor ever lowest roll of thunder moans,
> Nor sound of human sorrow mounts to mar
> Their sacred everlasting calm![35]

Human affairs are no concern of the gods. But are the gods, or should they be, any concern of men? Epicurus seems to have held that certain forms of ritual and private devotion are appropriate because, although the gods cannot be touched by prayers or sacrifices, they provide men with a model of beatitude. Whether or not a man is benefited by the gods depends upon his state of mind when he apprehends divine 'images'. If he himself is tranquil he will attain to the right view of the gods (Lucret. vi 71-8), and a passage in the *Letter to Menoeceus* (124) is perhaps to be interpreted along the same lines: those whose disposition is already akin to that of the gods can appropriate and gain benefit from divine 'images'. It is in the same spirit that Philodemus writes: 'He [*sc.* Epicurus] appeals to the completely happy in order to strengthen his own happiness' (Diels, *Sitz. Berl.* 1916, p. 895).

(vii) The soul and mental processes

> Death is nothing to us; for that which has been dissolved lacks sensation; and that which lacks sensation is no concern to us (*K.D.* ii).

The first thing which Epicurus strove to establish in his psychological theory was the complete and permanent loss of consciousness at death. All his philosophy has the ultimate aim of removing human anxiety, and the therapeutic aspect of his psychology is a most conspicuous example of this. By denying any kind of survival to the personality after death, Epicurus hoped to show that beliefs in a system of rewards and punishments as recompense for life on earth were mere mythology. It is difficult to assess precisely the strength and prevalence of such beliefs in Epicurus' own time.

But apart from his vehement desire to undermine them, which must be evidence that they were not uncommonly held, we find independent confirmation in literature and the popularity of 'mystery cults'.

Traces of such beliefs are already to be found in fifth-century writers. It is not likely that they declined during the fourth century. Plato, in the *Republic,* writes scathingly of those who provide books of Musaeus and Orpheus, and try to persuade 'whole cities as well as individuals' to absolve themselves from their crimes by performing certain rituals. Such men hoodwink people into believing that they will reap benefits in this world and the next, while those who fail to observe the rituals will be confronted with 'terrible things' (*Rep.* ii 364e). Cephalus, the old man who figures at the beginning of the *Republic,* is portrayed as someone who has been tormented by fears of having to expiate his offences in Hades. Plato himself condemns the quacks who try to exploit such fears by offering absolution at a fee. But he ends the *Republic* with a myth which has judgment of the dead and rewards and punishments for earthly existence as its central feature. Similar myths are used by him in the *Phaedo* and the *Gorgias.* Both the pre-existence and the survival of the soul, after death, are central Platonic doctrines which he combines with the theory of metempsychosis.

The fear of death is common to all peoples at all times. Epicurus may have exaggerated the psychological disturbance he attributed to explicit beliefs in a destiny for the soul after death. But he did not confine his diagnosis of the fear of death to eschatological dogmas. As he himself writes (**Ep. Hdt.** 81), and as Lucretius writes at greater length, men also fear death who believe that it is the end of all sensation. Lucretius uses an argument to remove such fear which simply asserts that this is a true belief and *therefore* no grounds for anxiety: events which took place before we were born did not disturb us, for we did not *feel* them. By parity of reasoning, nothing can disturb us when we cease to be conscious of anything (iii 830-51). A little later he goes on:

> If there is to be any trouble and pain for a man he too must exist himself at that time in order that ill may affect him. Since death removes this and prevents the existence of him to whom a mass of misfortunes might accrue, we may be assured that there is nothing to be feared in death and that he who no longer exists cannot be troubled (iii 861-8).

For Epicurus birth and death are limits which contain the existence of a person. *I* have not existed in another body prior to this life, nor am *I* liable to experience a further incarnation following this life. There is such a thing as *psychê,* soul, the presence of which in a body causes that body to possess life. Here Epicurus agreed with philosophical and popular conceptions. But he

also insisted against Plato and other dualists that the soul cannot exist independently of the body, and that a living being must be a union of the body and the soul. Disrupt this union and life ceases. His view bears comparison with that of Aristotle who defined soul as 'the first actuality of an organic natural body' (*De an. [De anima/On the soul]* ii 412b5). For Aristotle too, most functions of the soul are necessarily related to the body, though Aristotle made an exception of intellect. We should not however press this comparison. Aristotle's treatment of soul proceeds by very different steps from Epicurus'. It calls for distinctions between form and matter and between potentiality and actuality which are quite foreign to Epicurus' way of thinking; in Aristotle soul is not a kind of physical substance, as it is for Epicurus. That on which they broadly agree is the mutual dependence of body and soul.

What then did Epicurus say about the soul? Or, to put the question another way, how did he explain life? The first point is that life must be accounted for by reference to something corporeal. For that which is not body is void, and void cannot *do* anything nor *be affected* by anything (**Ep. Hdt.** 67). The grounds for denying that soul is incorporeal show that Epicurus regards the capacity to act and to be acted upon as a necessary condition of that which animates a living being. More specifically, soul consists of atoms which act upon and are affected by the atoms constituting the body itself.

'Soul is a body, the parts of which are fine, distributed throughout the whole aggregate. It resembles most closely breath mixed with heat' (**Ep. Hdt.** 63). Lucretius enables us to amplify this description. The atoms which form the soul, he tells us, are very small and they are also round. Roundness is inferred from the speed of thought: the soul atoms can be stirred by the slightest impulse (iii 176ff.). Furthermore, breath and heat (Lucretius adds air as well) are not sufficient to account for soul. That soul is warm and airy is clear from the fact that warmth and breath are absent from a corpse. But breath, heat and air cannot create the movements which bring sensation (iii 238-40). Something else is needed—a 'fourth nature', consisting of atoms which are smaller and more mobile than anything else which exists. They have no name.

How are we to conceive of the relation between the different kinds of atoms which constitute soul? As I observed earlier when discussing compound bodies, fire, breath and so forth are things which can only arise when certain kinds of atoms are combined. We are probably therefore to suppose that the atoms which can, in appropriate combinations, create the substances specified by Lucretius are in the soul combined in such a way that they form a body which is analysable as a *mixture* of fire, breath, air and the unnamed element. But the soul will not be divisible into these things.

Lucretius says explicitly that 'no single element [of the soul] can be separated, nor can their capacities be divided spatially; they are like the multiple powers of a single body' (iii 262-6).[36]

This body, in virtue of the unnamed element, can produce the movements necessary to sensation. It is the unnamed element which gives the soul its specific character. Life and vital functions in general are thus explained by reference to something which cannot be analysed fully into any known substances. Epicurus wants to avoid the objection that life has been simply reduced to an appropriate mixture of familiar substances. Life requires these and something else as well. Given the primitive notions which the Greeks had of chemistry, Epicurus was wise to refrain from attempting to explain life purely in terms of the traditional four elements.

The soul then, so constituted, is the 'primary cause of sensation'. But soul by itself cannot have or cause life. It must be contained within a body. That is to say, a living being can be constituted neither out of soul alone nor out of body alone. Placed within a body of the right kind, the soul's vital capacities can be realized. From the soul the body acquires a derivative share in sensation; there is physical contact, naturally, between the body and the soul, and the movements of atoms within the body affect and are affected by those of the soul. Epicurus illustrated the relation of body and soul by considering the case of amputation (*Ep. Hdt.* 65). Loss of a limb does not remove the power of sensation; but loss of the soul removes all vitality from the body, even if the body itself remains intact. By insisting that soul must be contained in the body, Epicurus denied any prospect of sensation and consciousness surviving death.

In Lucretius (iii 136ff.) and some other sources a spatial distinction is drawn between the *animus* (rational part) and the *anima* (irrational part). The *animus* is located in the chest; the rest of the soul, though united with the *animus,* is distributed throughout the other regions of the body. These two parts of the soul do not undermine its unity of substance; they are introduced to explain different functions. That in virtue of which we think and experience emotion is the *animus,* the mind. This governs the rest of the soul. Epicurus had no knowledge of the nervous system, and we may most easily think of the *anima* as fulfilling the function of nerves—reporting feelings and sensations to the *animus* and transmitting movement to the limbs. If Epicurus had known of the nerves and their connexion with the brain he would probably have been fully prepared to accept the notion that the brain is equivalent to the *animus.*[37]

Lucretius' account of the soul inspired some of his finest poetry. It also shows much acute observation of

behaviour. Before considering further aspects of Epicurean psychology, we may pause over one or two passages in which Lucretius calls attention to the relations between body and soul:

> If the vibrant shock of a weapon, forced within and opening to view bones and sinews, falls short of destroying life itself, yet faintness follows and a gentle falling to the ground, and on the ground there ensues a storm of the mind, and moment by moment an unsteady desire to stand up. Therefore it must be the case that the mind is corporeal in substance, since it suffers under the blow of bodily weapons (iii 170-6).

> Furthermore we perceive that the mind comes into being along with the body, develops with the body and grows old with it. Just as young children totter whose body is frail and soft, so too their powers of judgment are slight. Then, when maturity has developed bringing hardy strength, their judgment too is greater and their strength of mind increased. Later, after their body has been assailed by the tough force of age and their limbs have failed with their strength blunted, the intellect grows lame, the tongue raves, the mind stumbles, all things fail and decline at the same time. And so it is appropriate that all the substance of vitality should be dissolved like smoke into the lofty breezes of the air (iii 445-56).

> Again, if the soul is immortal and can feel when separated from our body we must, I believe, cause it to be equipped with the five senses. There is no other way in which we can imagine to ourselves souls wandering below in the realm of Acheron. And so painters and former generations of writers have presented souls endowed with the senses. But neither eyes nor nostrils nor hand nor tongue nor ears can exist for the soul apart from the body. Therefore souls on their own cannot feel, nor even exist (iii 624-33).

The psychological function on which we have most copious information is sense-perception. This is due no doubt to its importance in Epicureanism as a whole. In discussing the theory of knowledge I have already described Epicurus' concept of effluences or images from external objects which enter the sense organs, or which penetrate directly to the mind, and thereby cause our awareness of something. Perception is thus ultimately reducible to a form of touch, physical contact between the atoms of the percipient and atoms which have proceeded from objects in the external world (cf. Lucret. ii 434f.). It will not be possible in this context to discuss the treatment of specific problems of optics and other matters which Lucretius deals with at great length in Book iv. But some more general aspects of the theory need consideration.[38] In particular, it would be desirable to know how we are to conceive of the 'sense-bearing movements' which the soul bestows on the body. Lucretius states that it is not the mind which sees through the eyes, but the eyes themselves (iii 359-69), and the same holds good for the other sense organs. The eye is an organ of the body. When it is struck by a stream of effluences which have the appropriate size, we are probably to suppose that this sets up a movement of the adjoining soul atoms, which then cause sensation in the eye itself. The same internal processes will account for feelings—burns, itches and so forth. Lucretius traces a series of movements beginning with 'the stirring of the unnamed element' which passes via the other elements in the soul to the blood, the internal organs and finally the bones and marrow (iii 245-9). These stages represent an increasing disturbance of 'everything' and life cannot be maintained if the movements or sensations penetrate beyond a certain point. But 'generally the movements come to an end on the surface of the body' (252-7).

All of this still leaves the notion of sensation or consciousness very obscure. Is it simply a kind of movement, or is it rather something which supervenes as an epiphenomenon upon a kind of movement? Epicurus and Lucretius leave us in the dark here, and no wonder! For no one has yet succeeded in giving a purely mechanistic explanation of consciousness.

The treatment of thought raises further problems. In Epicurus' *Letter to Herodotus* (49-50) and in Lucretius, thought is assimilated to sense-perception so far as its objects and causes are concerned:

> Come now, learn what things stir the mind, and hear in a few words the source of those things which enter the understanding. First of all, I declare that many likenesses of things wander in many ways in all regions in all directions; they are fine in texture and easily become united with one another in the air when they meet.... They are much finer than those things which seize hold of the eyes and rouse vision, since they pass right through the vacant spaces of the body and stir the fine nature of the mind within and rouse its awareness (Lucret. iv 722-31).

Lucretius proceeds to illustrate these statements by reference to the perception of monsters and the dead. From this we might suppose that he is describing only certain kinds of mental perception. But he goes on to argue that the thought of a lion is also produced, like the sight of a lion, by *simulacra leonum* ('images of lions'). He also asks the question, 'How is that we are able to think of things at will?' The answer which he suggests is curious:

> In a single period of time which we perceive, that is, the time it takes to utter a single word, many times escape notice which reason discovers; and so it happens that in any time all the images are available, ready in every place. So great is their power of movement, so great the supply of them.... Because they are fine the mind can only distinguish

sharply those on which it concentrates. Therefore all except those for which it has prepared itself pass away. The mind prepares itself and expects that it will see what follows on each thing; therefore this comes about (iv 794-806).

We should expect thought to be explained by reference to data, images, or what not which are somehow already present in or created by the mind. But that is not what Lucretius says. He clearly implies that the 'supply' of images is external, and that the mind apprehends just those images to which its attention is directed. Thinking, on this interpretation, is analogous to noticing something which falls within the scope of vision.

Many scholars have been reluctant to take this passage at its face value. They have presumed that Epicurus must have envisaged an internal store of images in terms of which some thought at least and memory are to be explained. It has been suggested that the effluences which are received by the sense organs or the mind cause a change in the movements of the soul atoms, and this new pattern of movement persists as a memory or thought-image. But if Epicurus held such a view no evidence about it has survived, and it is not presupposed in the theory recorded by Lucretius. According to this theory, thought is a kind of internal film-show in which the mind controls the images which it permits to enter the body. Not only thought but volition also requires the consciousness of appropriate images. Lucretius observes that we walk when 'images of walking fall upon the mind' (iv 881). Then the will rouses itself, and passes on movement to the rest of the soul so that finally the limbs are activated. In dreaming, too, passages are open in the mind through which images of things can enter (iv 976-7).

We must suppose that this is Epicurus' own theory, and it is quite consistent with the strange idea that images of the gods possess objective status. But if memory is not explicable by a storehouse of images how is it to be accounted for? The few texts which bear upon this question suggest that memory is a disposition, produced by repeated apprehension of images of a certain kind, to attend to such images as continue to exist after the previously experienced object which produced them may have perished or changed in other ways. Hence we can remember the dead.

Although Lucretius' account of thought should be given full weight as orthodox Epicurean doctrine, certain forms of thinking must have been explained in other ways. There are no images of atoms and void; there is no image of the principles of confirmation and non-contradiction. Yet these are things which cannot be grasped except by thought. Epicurus himself distinguished between what he called 'the theoretical part', and 'apprehension' whether by the senses or the mind.[39] I have already discussed 'apprehension', and rejected Bailey's claim that it guarantees the clarity of an image. What it does involve, I suggest, is the *direct* apprehension of some image. In other words, 'apprehension' covers awareness of all data, whether of the senses or the mind, which possess objective existence because they are in origin images which enter us from outside. 'The theoretical part' refers to thinking which may be presumed to function purely by internal processes. That is to say, it involves inference about things like atoms and void which are unable to be apprehended directly. How such thinking takes place in detail, and whether or not it involves images, are questions which we cannot answer categorically. It almost certainly must make use of 'preconceptions', general concepts arrived at by repeated observation of particular objects. Preconceptions however cannot be reduced to external images for there are no 'generic' images existing objectively. These must be constructions of the mind, which can be utilized in the formation of new non-empirical concepts. Epicurus may have explained them as patterns of movement in the soul, but his words on this subject, if he described it in detail, have not survived.

(viii) Freedom of action

Our next subject is one of the most interesting and controversial problems in Epicureanism. According to Lucretius and other later writers, the 'swerve' of atoms has a part to play in the explanation of 'free will' (*libera voluntas*). But what part? The answer must be sought, if anywhere, from a difficult passage of Lucretius. It is the second argument which he uses to prove that atoms sometimes deviate from the linear direction of their downward movement through the void:

> If every movement is always linked and the new movement arises from the old one in a fixed sequence, and if the primary bodies do not by swerving create a certain beginning of movement which can break the bonds of fate and prevent cause from following cause from infinity, how comes it about that living things all over the earth possess this free will, this will, I say, severed from fate, whereby we advance where pleasure leads each man and swerve in our movements at no fixed time and at no fixed place, but when and where our mind has borne us? For undoubtedly each man's will gives the beginning to these movements, and it is from the will that movements are spread through the limbs.

> You see, do you not, that when the barriers are opened at an instant of time, the horses for all their strength and eagerness cannot burst forward as promptly as their mind desires. This is because the whole stock of matter throughout their whole body has to be set in motion, so that having been roused through all the frame it may make an effort and follow the desire of the mind. So you can see that a beginning of movement is engendered by the heart, and it comes forth first from the mind's volition and then is dispatched throughout the whole body and limbs.

> It is not the same as when we move forward under the pressure of a blow from the mighty strength and strong constraint of another man. For then it is clear that the whole matter of the body in its entirety moves and is seized against our will, until the will restrains it throughout the limbs. So now you surely see that although an external force pushes many men and often compels them to go forward against their will and be driven headlong, yet there is something in our breast which can fight back and resist. At its direction too the stock of matter is at times compelled to change direction through all the limbs, and although pushed forward is checked and comes to rest again.

> Therefore you must admit the same thing in the atoms too; that another cause of motion exists besides blows and weights which is the source of this power innate in us, since we see that nothing can arise out of nothing. For weight prevents all things happening by blows, by external force as it were. But a tiny swerve of the atoms at no fixed time or place brings it about that the mind itself has no internal necessity in doing all things and is not forced like a captive to accept and be acted upon (ii 251-93).

This is our only detailed evidence for the relation between the swerve and 'free' will in Epicurean literature.[40] No explicit word about the swerve from Epicurus himself has so far been discovered. We know however that he attacked 'the destiny of the natural philosophers' for its 'merciless necessity' (***Ep. Men.*** 134). And he discussed the causes of human action in a book which is partially preserved on papyrus from Herculaneum.[41] The text contains so many gaps and defective lines that it is difficult to grasp a clear train of thought; more work may yield positive advances in our understanding of it. But Epicurus certainly distinguished sharply in this book between 'the cause in us' and two further factors, 'the initial constitution' and 'the automatic necessity of the environment and that which enters' (i.e. external 'images'). These distinctions should be borne in mind when one approaches Lucretius' text.

The first thing to notice is his context. Lucretius' main subject at this stage of his work is not psychology but the movement of atoms. He offers no formal argument to defend the 'freedom' of the will. Rather, he assumes it, exemplifies it by examples, and uses the assumption and examples to prove that atoms sometimes swerve.

The logical structure of the first paragraph might be expressed like this: (A) If all movements are so causally related to each other that no new movements are created by a swerve of atoms, then there could be no such thing as 'free will'. (B) For 'free will' entails the creation of a new movement at no fixed time and at no fixed place. (C) But there is such a thing as 'free will'. (D) Therefore the atoms sometimes create new beginnings by swerving.

In the next two paragraphs (as I have set out the text) Lucretius gives his examples to show that the will can create new beginnings of movement. First, he considers the case of the race-horses. When the barriers are raised they are free of any external constraint to move forward; and they do move forward (fulfil their desire to move) as soon as their will has had time to activate the limbs. This example is used to show that there is some faculty within the horses which enables them to initiate movement freely.

In his second example Lucretius considers a different case. Unlike the horses, which require a brief interval of time for their will's action to have an external effect, men may be pushed forward immediately by outside pressures; and such *involuntary* movements require no internal movements in the men before they occur. But men have something within them which can resist external pressures. This is a power to cause atoms within the body to change their enforced direction of movement. In this case, the will initiates movement when the body is already undergoing compulsory movement. But the power which is exercised is the same as that faculty for initiating movement exemplified by the horses.

It seems clear to me that both examples are intended to illustrate 'free will', from different starting-points. And what are we to make of the 'blows' and 'weights' mentioned in the last paragraph? Lucretius does not exclude these as necessary conditions of a 'free' action. He denies only that they are sufficient to bring it about. We have already seen that the 'will' to walk requires 'images', that is, 'blows from outside', and nothing weightless could act or be acted upon in Epicurus' system. The weight of the mind's atoms affects its reaction to external blows. But an action caused solely by blows and weights could not be 'free'. The horses' movement and the men's resistance were 'free' in virtue of an additional third factor which Lucretius calls *voluntas,* 'will'. The will, it should be noted, is not treated as equivalent to desire. Desire is prompted by the awareness of some pleasurable object. Lucretius, I think, regards the will as that in virtue of which we seek to fulfil our desires (cf. ii 258, 265).

If we ask where the swerve features in all this, the answer seems to be that the swerve is a physical event which presents itself to consciousness as a 'free' will to initiate a new movement. Consciousness during waking states is normally continuous. But our external bodily movements are not wholly continuous. Nor are our intentions. Lucretius, I suggest, treats some animal actions as if they were relatively discontinuous events initiated by the 'will'. But they are not wholly discontinuous. Memory, reflection, habit, these and other dispositions are not ruled out as causal factors by anything which Lucretius says. A swerve among the soul atoms need not be supposed to disrupt all or even any character traits. The swerve is not treated in a context which enables us to place its precise function in the whole history of living things. But what does seem clear is its rôle as an initiator of new actions.

Once it is recognized that other causes besides the swerve are necessary to the performance of a voluntary act, certain difficulties observed by one recent writer become less acute. If the swerve, which by definition is something random and unpredictable, were sufficient by itself to explain voluntary actions, then the bonds of fate could seem to have been broken at the expense of making actions purposeless and wholly indeterminate. Sensing this difficulty, David Furley has suggested that the swerve need not be supposed to feature in the explanation of *every* voluntary action.[42] Its function, he argues, is rather to free the disposition from being wholly determined by heredity and environment. For this purpose he suggests that a single swerve of a single atom in an individual's *psyche* would be sufficient.

Furley's interesting arguments cannot be surveyed in detail here. But it is my own opinion that Lucretius' text is easier to interpret on the assumption that a swerve is at work in the freedom of particular actions. The theoretical single swerve which Furley postulates can hardly suffice to explain the 'beginnings of motion' which characterize each act of 'free' will. But Furley is right to object to interpretations which treat the swerve by itself as a sufficient condition. We know from Diogenes of Oenoanda that the swerve was held to be necessary by Epicureans if moral advice is to be effective (fr. 32 col. iii). But moral advice cannot be effective if it is to depend entirely on the possible occurrence of a swerve in the soul of the man being advised. I think we are to suppose that the swerve of a single atom is a relatively frequent event. It may occur when one is asleep or when one is awake, without having any observable or conscious effect. If however a man's natural disposition to seek pleasure or to avoid pain is roused by external or internal causes, and if at such times he is in a physical condition which makes it possible for him to act then, depending upon the kind of man he is, any swerve(s) among the atoms of his mind constitutes a free decision to act. If he is untrained in Epicurean philosophy he may decide to pursue objects which in the event cause more pain than pleasure. The true Epicurean's atoms may also swerve at a time when he walks down a Soho street, but having learnt that freedom from pain is more pleasurable than momentary sensations of pleasure he does not follow his companions into the night-club. Swerves help him to initiate new actions in the pursuit of tranquillity.

Before concluding this subject two general observations may be made. First, it may be asked whether the use of the swerve which I attribute to Epicurus is historically plausible. Furley believes not, but he omits one point which seems to me important. The so-called problem of 'free will' arises primarily out of two conceptions—beliefs in God's omniscience and predetermination, and beliefs in the absolute continuity of physical causation. There is every reason to attribute the second of these to Zeno, the founder of Stoicism, and probably the first as well. Zeno and Epicurus were active in Athens together for thirty years, and I find it unlikely that Epicurus developed his opposition to determinism quite independently of Stoic theories. Those theories provide conditions which favour the emergence of a concept of volition which is not completely dependent upon the state of things at the preceding instant. I conjecture that Epicurus used the swerve to defend such a concept.

Secondly, the random nature of the swerve is a difficulty for Epicurus whatever its rôle in human psychology. But it seems to me logically possible to suppose that the swerve of a soul atom is not random so far as the consciousness of the soul's owner is concerned. And Epicurus attempted to solve that problem, so I think, by making the swerve a constituent of the 'will'. If it is not part of the will or cognitive faculty, but a random event which disrupts the soul's patterns of atoms from time to time, are not the consequences for mortality which trouble Furley still more serious? He wants the swerve to free inherited movements of atoms and make character adaptable. But this raises new problems. A man of good Epicurean character will live in fear of an unpredictable event which may change him into a Stoic or something worse. I find it easier to posit some discontinuity between the antecedent conditions of an action and the decision to do it than discontinuity between movements on which character depends.

To conclude, Epicurus used the swerve of atoms in the soul to explain situations where men are conscious of doing what they want to do. Obscurities persist, and we cannot rule them out in order to make the theory more palatable or convincing. I pass now to a less controversial subject. Epicurus' theory of pleasure has already been referred to, and we must now consider its full ethical significance.

(ix) Pleasure and happiness

Epicurus was not the first Greek philosopher whose ethics can be called hedonist. In [an earlier chapter] I referred briefly to the earlier hedonism of Aristippus whose conception of the pleasant life differs sharply from Epicurus'. Unlike Aristippus, who regarded absence of pain as an intermediate condition, Epicurus claimed that the removal of all pain defines the magnitude of pleasure (***K.D.*** iii), and his interest in specifying the conditions which establish a life free of trouble may well have been roused by Democritus. The earlier atomist probably had no systematic ethical theory, but he is credited with a conception of happiness which consists above all in peace of mind (D.L. ix 45). It was Epicurus' primary concern to show how this state can be attained.

Pleasure was also a topic which received considerable attention from Plato, Aristotle and the Academy in general. It is highly probable that Epicurus was familiar with ideas which Plato discusses in the *Philebus,* and he may also have been influenced by some Aristotelian notions, most notably the distinction between pleasure 'in movement' and pleasure 'in rest' (*E.N.* 1154b28). The great difference between Plato and Aristotle on the one hand and Epicurus on the other turns on the relation they posit between happiness and pleasure. All three philosophers are concerned in their ethics with specifying the necessary conditions of happiness, but only Epicurus identifies happiness with a life full of pleasure. Some pleasures for Plato and Aristotle are good, and make a contribution to happiness; others are bad. For Epicurus no pleasure in itself can be anything but good since the good means that which is or causes pleasure. The fundamental constituent of happiness for Plato and Aristotle is virtue, excellence of 'soul', which manifests itself in the exercise of those activities appropriate to each faculty of the personality and in moral action. (The differences between Plato and Aristotle are less important for my present purpose than the similarities.) But for Epicurus virtue is necessary to happiness not as an essential ingredient but as a means to its attainment. This is the most significant difference between Epicurus and his major predecessors:

> We say that pleasure is the starting-point and the end of living blissfully. For we recognize pleasure as a good which is primary and innate. We begin every act of choice and avoidance from pleasure, and it is to pleasure that we return using our experience of pleasure as the criterion of every good thing (***Ep. Men.*** 128-9).

Subjective experience is a 'test of reality' for Epicurus, and it is on this evidence that he based his doctrine of pleasure.

> All living creatures from the moment of birth take delight in pleasure and resist pain from natural causes independent of reason (D.L. x 137).

The goodness of pleasure needs no demonstration. Epicurus takes it as an obvious fact that men, like all living things, pursue pleasure and avoid pain. The attractiveness of pleasure is treated as an immediate datum of experience comparable to the feeling that fire is hot (Cic. *Fin.* i 30). We learn from Aristotle that his contemporary Eudoxus also inferred that pleasure is 'the good' from the allegedly empirical fact that all creatures pursue it (*E.N.* x 1172b9). Now it does not follow from the fact, if it is a fact, that men pursue pleasure that pleasure is what they ought to pursue. As G. E. Moore argued at great length in *Principia Ethica,* that which is desired is not equivalent to that which is desirable. Some scholars have indeed claimed that Epicurus is not concerned with what 'ought' to be or what is 'fitting', but only with what is.[43] But this claim is at best a half-truth. It would be a correct description of his view to say that we are genetically programmed to seek what will cause us pleasure and to avoid what will cause pain. And he probably held that no living creature whose natural constitution is unimpaired *can* have any other goals. But there is a place for 'ought' in his system because the sources of pleasure and pleasure itself are not uniform. What we ought to do is to pursue that which will cause us the greatest pleasure. 'Ought' here of course does not signify what we are obliged to do by any purely moral law. It signifies that which needs to be done if we are successfully to attain our goal, happiness or the greatest pleasure. It applies to means and not to ends:

> Since pleasure is the good which is primary and innate we do not choose every pleasure, but there are times when we pass over many pleasures if greater pain is their consequence for us. And we regard many pains as superior to pleasures when a greater pleasure arises for us after we have put up with pains over a long time. Therefore although every pleasure on account of its natural affinity to us is good, not every pleasure is to be chosen; similarly, though every pain is bad, not every pain is naturally always to be avoided. It is proper to evaluate these things by a calculation and consideration of advantages and disadvantages. For sometimes we treat the good as bad and conversely the bad as good (*Ep. Men.* 129-30).

In order to grasp the implications of this important passage, we need to consider in more detail what Epicurus meant by pleasure and how he proposed to use pleasure as a guide to action. The most striking feature of his hedonism is the denial of any state or feeling intermediate between pleasure and pain. Pleasure and pain are related to one another not as contraries but as contradictories.[44] The absence of the one entails the presence of the other. If all pleasure is regarded as a sensation of some kind, this relationship between pleasure and pain makes no sense. For clearly most of us pass a large part of our waking lives with-

out having either painful or pleasing sensations. But the periods of our waking life in which we could describe ourselves as neither happy nor unhappy, or neither enjoying nor not enjoying something, are much smaller. Epicurus' view of the relationship between pleasure and pain should be interpreted in this light. He has, as we shall see, a way of distinguishing the pleasures of bodily sensations and feelings of elation from pleasures which cannot be so described; absence of pain is not, he thinks, an adequate description of the former. Epicurus' mistake is a failure to see that indifference characterizes certain of our moods and attitudes towards things.

His analysis of pleasure rests on the assumption that the natural or normal condition of living things is one of bodily and mental well-being and that this condition is *ipso facto* gratifying. This is the meaning of the statement quoted above: 'Pleasure is the good which is primary and innate.' It is possible in English to speak of 'enjoying' good health, and we may also call this something gratifying, or something a man rejoices in. Epicurus' use of the word pleasure to describe the condition of those who enjoy good physical and mental health is not therefore purely arbitrary. In physical terms this pleasure is a concomitant of the *appropriate* movement and location of atoms within the body. If these are disturbed pain follows. In other words, pain is a disruption of the natural constitution. Pleasure is experienced when the atoms are restored to their appropriate position in the body (Lucret. ii 963-8).

The idea that pain is a disturbance of the natural state was not invented by Epicurus. We find it in Plato's *Philebus* along with the notion that pleasure is experienced when the natural state is 'replenished' (31e-32b). Plato however argued that pleasure is only experienced during the process of restoring the natural condition. According to his theory, pleasure and pain are movements or processes. There is also, however, a 'third' life in which any bodily processes produce no consciousness of pleasure or pain. This 'intermediate' condition cannot be regarded as pleasurable or painful (42c-44a).

It is interesting to find Plato attacking the theory that absence of pain can be identified with pleasure. Epicurus of course would not accept Plato's specification of an intermediate life. Like Plato, however, Epicurus holds that the process of removing pain results in pleasurable sensations. He calls this pleasure 'kinetic'. Suppose that a man is hungry: he desires to eat and the act of satisfying this desire produces 'kinetic' pleasure. If he succeeds in fully satisfying the desire for food he must have wholly allayed the pangs of hunger. From this complete satisfaction of desire, Epicurus argues, a second kind of pleasure arises. This is not an experience which accompanies a process, but a 'static' pleasure. It is characterized by complete absence of pain and enjoyment of this condition. Torquatus, the Epicurean spokesman in Cicero's *De finibus,* expresses the distinction between pleasures thus:

> The pleasure which we pursue is not merely that which excites our nature by some gratification and which is felt with delight by the senses. We regard that as the greatest pleasure which is felt when all pain has been removed (*Fin.* i 37).

'Static' pleasure follows the complete satisfaction of desire. Desire arises from a sense of need, the pain of lacking something. In order to remove this pain, desire must be satisfied, and the satisfaction of desire is pleasurable. 'Kinetic' pleasure is thus (or so I think) a necessary condition of at least some 'static' pleasure, but it is not regarded by Epicurus as equivalent in value to 'static' pleasure.[45] For if freedom from pain is the greatest pleasure, we should satisfy our desires not for the sake of the pleasurable sensations which accompany eating, drinking and so on, but for the sake of the state of well-being which results when all the pain due to want has been removed:

> When we say that pleasure is the goal we do not mean the pleasures of the dissipated and those which consist in the process of enjoyment . . . but freedom from pain in the body and from disturbance in the mind. For it is not drinking and continuous parties nor sexual pleasures nor the enjoyment of fish and other delicacies of a wealthy table which produce the pleasant life, but sober reasoning which searches out the causes of every act of choice and refusal and which banishes the opinions that give rise to the greatest mental confusion (*Ep. Men.* 131-2).

Epicurus, in this passage, is not denying that drink, eating good food, sex, and so on are sources of pleasure. He is asserting that the pleasures which such activities produce are to be rejected as goals because they do not constitute a calm and stable disposition of body and mind. It is freedom from pain which measures the relative merits of different activities. This is the basis of Epicurus' hedonist calculus. His criticism of luxury and sexual indulgence is not grounded in any puritanical disapproval:

> If the things which produce the pleasures of the dissipated released the fears of the mind concerning astronomical phenomena and death and pains . . . we should never have any cause to blame them (***K.D.*** x).

He holds that the greatest pain is mental disturbance produced by false beliefs about the nature of things, about the gods, about the soul's destiny. Any pleasure therefore which fails to remove the greatest pain is ruled out as an ultimate object of choice by application of the rule—absence of pain establishes the magnitude

of pleasure. Furthermore, the pleasure which arises from gratifying the senses may have a greater pain as its consequence. A man may enjoy an evening's drinking or the thrill of betting, but the pleasure which he derives from satisfying his desires for drink and gambling must be set against the feeling of the morning after and the anxiety of losing money.

Epicurus' concept of pleasure is closely related to an analysis of desire:

> We must infer that some desires are natural, and others pointless; of natural desires some are necessary, others merely natural. Necessary desires include some which are necessary for happiness, others for the equilibrium of the body and others for life itself. The correct understanding of these things consists in knowing how to refer all choice and refusal to the health of the body and freedom from mental disturbance since this is the goal of living blissfully. For all our actions are aimed at avoiding pain and fear. Once we have acquired this, all the mind's turmoil is removed since a creature has no need to wander as if in search of something it lacks, nor to look for some other thing by means of which it can replenish the good of the mind and the body. For it is when we suffer pain from the absence of pleasure that we have need of pleasure (***Ep. Men.*** 127-8).

Epicurus' analysis of desires is consistent with the principle that freedom from pain is the greatest pleasure. The desire for food and clothing is natural and necessary. Failure to satisfy this desire is a source of pain. But, Epicurus argues, it is neither necessary nor natural to desire this food or clothing rather than that, if the latter is sufficient to remove the pain felt by absence of food or clothing (Us. 456). Hence Epicurus becomes an advocate of the simple life, on the grounds that we cause ourselves unnecessary pain if we seek to satisfy desires by luxurious means. Necessary desires, he holds, can be satisfied simply, and the pleasure which we thus experience is no less in quantity even if it differs in kind. Moreover, those who seek pleasure in luxuries are likely to suffer pain unnecessarily either as a direct consequence of luxurious living or through an inability to satisfy a desire:

> We regard self-sufficiency as a great blessing, not that we may always enjoy only a few things but that if we do not have many things we can enjoy the few, in the conviction that they derive the greatest pleasure from luxury who need it least, and that everything natural is easy to obtain but that which is pointless is difficult. Simple tastes give us pleasure equal to a rich man's diet when all the pain of want has been removed; bread and water produce the highest pleasure when someone who needs them serves them to himself. And so familiarity with simple and not luxurious diet gives

us perfect health and makes a man confident in his approach to the necessary business of living; it makes us better disposed to encounter luxuries at intervals and prepares us to face change without fear (*Ep. Men.* 130-1).

Time and again in his *Principal doctrines* Epicurus asserts that pleasure cannot be increased beyond a certain limit.[46] So far as sensual gratification is concerned, this limit is reached when the pain which prompted desire has ceased; thereafter pleasure can be 'varied'—by 'kinetic' pleasure—but not augmented. This is something which needs to be grasped by the intellect, since the flesh itself recognizes no limits to pleasure (*K.D.* xviii; xx). The mind has its own pleasures the 'limit' of which is reached with the ability to calculate correctly the pleasures of sensual gratification and to assess the feelings which cause mental disturbance. Ancient critics familiar with Plato's distinction between the soul and the body criticized Epicurus for failing to draw a sharp distinction between bodily pleasures and the 'good' of the soul (Us. 430, 431). But when Epicurus distinguishes body and soul in statements about pleasure he has nothing like Platonic dualism in mind. Body and mind are in physical contact with one another; pleasurable sensations are 'bodily' events but they also give rise to pleasure or joy in the mind (Us. 433, 439). Unlike the body however the mind is not confined for its objects of pleasure to the experience of the moment:

> The body rejoices just so long as it feels a pleasure which is present. The mind perceives both the present pleasure along with the body and it foresees pleasure to come; and it does not allow past pleasure to flow away. Hence in the wise man there will always be present a constant supply of associated pleasures, since the anticipation of pleasures hoped for is united with the recollection of those already experienced (Us. 439).

The memory of past pleasures can 'mitigate' present sufferings (Us. 437), and the same holds for the anticipation of future pleasures. Unlike the Cyrenaics who regarded bodily pleasures of the moment as the greatest, Epicurus is reported by Diogenes Laertius to have argued that the mind's capacity to look forward and back entails that both its pleasures and its pains are greater than those of the body (x 137).

The distinction between 'kinetic' and 'static' pleasures applies to both body and mind (D.L. x 136). Corresponding to the 'kinetic' pleasure of satisfying a desire for food, drink and the like, the mind can experience 'joy' when, say, meeting a friend or solving a problem in philosophy. This pleasure, consisting in motion, is to be distinguished from the 'static' pleasure of 'mental repose' which corresponds to the body's pleasure in freedom from pain.

Since pleasure is the only thing which is good in itself, prudence, justice, moderation and courage, the traditional four 'moral virtues' of Greek philosophy, can have value only if they are constituents of or means to pleasure. Epicurus settled for the second alternative. Torquatus puts his position succinctly, opposing the Epicureans to the Stoics:

> As for those splendid and beautiful virtues of yours, who would regard them as praiseworthy or desirable unless they produced pleasures? Just as we approve medical science not for the sake of the art itself but for the sake of good health . . . so prudence, which must be regarded as the 'art of living', would not be sought after if it achieved nothing. In fact it is sought after because it is the expert, so to speak, at discovering and securing pleasure. . . . Human life is harassed above all by an ignorance of good and bad things, and the same defect often causes us to be deprived of the greatest pleasures and to be tormented by the harshest mental anguish. Prudence must be applied to act as our most reliable guide to pleasure, by removing fears and desires and snatching away the vanity of all false opinions (Cic. *Fin.* i 42-3).

Moderation, on the same principle, is desirable because and only because 'it brings us peace of mind'. It is a means to attaining the greatest pleasure since it enables us to pass over those pleasures which involve greater pain. Similarly, Torquatus finds the value of courage in the fact that it enables us to live free of anxiety and to rid ourselves, as far as possible, of physical pain. Justice and social relationships are analysed in the same way, but I will say a little more about Epicurus' treatment of these at the conclusion of this chapter.

Although Epicurus regarded the virtues as means and not as ends, he held that they are necessary to happiness and inseparably bound up with the hedonist life:

> Of sources of pleasure the starting-point and the greatest good is prudence. Therefore prudence is something even more valuable than philosophy. From prudence the other virtues arise, and prudence teaches that it is not possible to live pleasurably without living prudently, nobly and justly, nor to live prudently, nobly and justly, without living pleasurably. For the virtues are naturally linked with living pleasurably, and living pleasurably is inseparable from them (*Ep. Men.* 132).

This association between virtue and pleasure is striking, but it should not be interpreted as giving an independent value to prudence and the other virtues. The necessary connexion between pleasure and the virtues is due to the notion that pleasure requires for its attainment a reasoned assessment of the relative advantages and disadvantages of a particular act or state of affairs, a capacity to control desires the satisfaction of which will involve pain for the agent, freedom from fear of punishment and the like. The pleasure which men should seek is not Bentham's 'greatest happiness of the greatest number'. Epicurus never suggests that the interests of others should be preferred to or evaluated independently of the interests of the agent. The orientation of his hedonism is wholly self-regarding.

(x) *Justice and friendship*

> Natural justice is a pledge of expediency with a view to men not harming one another and not being harmed by one another (*K.D.* xxxi).

> Of all the things which wisdom secures for the attainment of happiness throughout the whole of life, by far the greatest is the possession of friendship (*K.D.* xxvii).

Aristotle asserted that 'man is naturally a political animal', and Plato held that the true good of the individual is also the good of the community to which he belongs. Epicurus took a very different view, which, though less forcefully than the Cynics, challenged fundamental values of Greek society. In his opinion human beings have no 'natural' leanings towards community life (Us. 523). Civilization has developed by an evolutionary process of which the determinants have been external circumstances, the desire to secure pleasure and to avoid pain, and the human capacity to reason and to plan. Learning by trial and error under the pressure of events, men have developed skills and formed social organizations which were found to be mutually advantageous. The only details of this process which survive in Epicurus' own words concern the origin and development of language (*Ep. Hdt.* 75-6). But Lucretius treats the whole subject at some length in Book v. Following the invention of housing and clothing, the discovery of how to make fire, and the introduction of family life, he writes, 'neighbours began to form friendships desiring neither to do nor to suffer harm' (1019-20). From this supposed historical stage in human culture Epicurus traces the origins of justice.

He describes justice as 'a kind of compact not to harm or be harmed' (*K.D.* xxxiii), prefacing this statement with the words: 'It is not anything in itself', an implicit attack on Plato's theory of the autonomous existence of moral values. Several longer statements on justice are preserved in the *Principal doctrines,* and a selection of these will serve to illustrate Epicurus' position:

> Injustice is a bad thing not in itself, but in respect of the fear and suspicion of not escaping the notice of those set in authority concerning such things (*K.D.* xxxiv).

> It is not possible for one who secretly acts against the terms of the compact 'not to harm or be harmed', to be confident that he will not be apprehended. . . . (*K.D.* xxxv).

> Evidence that something considered to be just is a source of advantage to men, in their necessary dealings with one another, is a guarantee of its justice, whether or not it is the same for all. But if a man makes a law which does not prove to be a source of advantage in human relationships, this no longer is really just. . . . (*K.D.* xxxvii).

> The just man is most free from trouble, but the unjust man abounds in trouble (*K.D.* xvii).

This concept of justice, which recalls Glaucon's analysis in Plato (*Rep.* ii), is not the 'social contract' of Rousseau. Epicurus is not saying that people have an obligation to act justly because of an agreement entered into by their remote or mythical ancestors. The 'contractual' element in his concept of justice is not advanced as a basis of moral or social obligation. Epicurus' justice requires us to respect the 'rights' of others if and only if this is advantageous to all parties concerned. Justice, as he conceives of it, does imply recognition of the interests of others besides oneself. But the basis of this recognition is self-interest. The 'compact' of which he speaks has self-protection as its basis. It is an agreement to refrain from injuring others if they will refrain from injuring oneself.

Epicurus' comments on the fears of apprehension which beset the unjust man show clearly that justice is desirable for the freedom which it brings from mental distress as well as physical retaliation. This is wholly consistent with his calculus of pleasures and pains. Injustice is bad not in itself but because of the painful consequences which it involves for the unjust man. In a book of *Problems* Epicurus raised the question: 'Will the wise man do anything forbidden by the laws, if he knows that he will escape notice?'; and he replied, 'The simple answer is not easy to find' (Us. 18). Epicurus' comments in *K.D.* xxxv imply that the problem is a purely academic one. No one in practice *can* be confident that his injustice will be unnoticed; as Lucretius puts it, 'fear of punishment for crimes during life' is the real hell, and not the Acheron of myth (iii 1013-23). Realizing this the wise man acts justly in order to secure tranquility of mind.

In Epicurus' eyes political life is a rat-race or 'prison' from which the wise man will keep well clear (*Sent. Vat.* lviii).[47] He diagnoses political ambition as a 'desire for protection from men', and argues that this in fact can only be secured by a quiet life in retirement from public affairs (*K.D.* vii, xiv). But Epicurus' rejection of political life as a context for the attainment of happiness was not based upon misanthropy. On the contrary, he held that friendship is 'an immortal good' (*Sent. Vat.* lxxviii). So today, 'opting out' *and* communal life are practised by many who find society at large 'alienated'. Torquatus, in Cicero's *De finibus,* asserts that 'Epicurus says that of all the things which prudence has provided for living happily, none is greater or more productive or more delightful than friendship' (i 65). Once again we notice that the value of something other than pleasure or happiness is referred to this end. But Epicurus, when writing of friendship, uses almost lyrical language at times, as when he says: 'Friendship dances round the world, announcing to us all that we should bestir ourselves for the enjoyment of happiness' (*Sent. Vat.* lii).

There is no doubt that Epicurus practised what he preached. The Garden was a community of friends, and Epicurus clearly derived intense happiness from friendship. We are told that he was famous for his 'philanthropy' to all (D.L. x 10), and on the day of his death, when racked by pain, he wrote to Idomeneus that he was happy, with the joyous memories of their conversations (Us. 138). Some of Epicurus' remarks about friendship might imply that it is compatible with altruism and self-sacrifice. But the basis of friendship, like justice, is self-interest, though Epicurus in the same breath says that it is 'desirable for its own sake' (*Sent. Vat.* xxiii). There is probably no inconsistency here. 'He is not a friend who is always seeking help, nor he who never associates friendship with assistance' (*Sent. Vat.* xxxix). One can enjoy or derive pleasure from helping a friend independently of any tangible benefit which this brings. When Epicurus writes of the 'benefits' of friendship he does not mean the pleasure which may come from helping others but the actual practical help which friends provide for each other. Apart from this, however, friendship is desirable because 'it is more pleasant to confer a benefit than to receive it' (Us. 544). One again we are brought back to pleasure as the sole criterion of value.

There is an elegant simplicity to Epicurus' ethics, a refreshing absence of cant, and also much humanity. He was born into a society which, like most societies, rated wealth, status, physical attributes and political power among the greatest human goods. It was also a slave-based society which reckoned men as superior to women and Greeks as superior to all other peoples. The good for man which Epicurus prescribes ignores or rejects these values and distinctions. Freedom from pain and tranquillity of mind are things which any sane man values and Epicurus dedicated his life to showing that they are in our power and how we may attain them. His ethics is undeniably centred upon the interests of the individual, and some have, with justification, praised the nobility of Epicurus more highly than his moral code. Yet we must see it in its social and

historical context. No Greek thinker was more sensitive to the anxieties bred by folly, superstition, prejudice and specious idealism. At a time of political instability and private disillusionment Epicurus saw that people like atoms are individuals and many of them wander in the void. He thought he could offer them directions signposted by evidence and reason to a way of being, a way of relating to others, other individuals. Negative, self-centred, unstimulating we may regard it; we cannot say priggish or self-indulgent, and in antiquity many found liberation and enlightenment in Epicureanism. For a modern reader too there is much philosophical interest in the consistency with which Epicurus applies his basic principles. What he has to say about family life and sexual love is entirely based on the proposition that the greatest good is freedom from pain in body and mind. But consistency can be purchased too dearly; a few criticisms of Epicurus' hedonism will show this.

First, it may be objected that Epicurus misapplies the factual observations with which he starts. Unless pleasure is used analytically to mean merely that which is desired, it is difficult to agree that pleasure is the object of every desire. But such a usage of pleasure tells us nothing about what is desired or desirable, and Epicurus does not use pleasure in this empty way. He is claiming that the desire to attain a state of consciousness which we find gratifying is sufficient to explain all human action. And this seems to be patently false. Secondly, Epicurus can fairly be charged with failure to grasp the complexity of the concept of pleasure. As we say, one man's meat is another man's poison, but Epicurus seems to think that he can classify by reference to absence of pain the magnitude of any man's pleasure. This may often be good advice, but many will argue from their own experience that Epicurus' claims have no basis in fact. They will also reject his assertion that sharp pains are short and long pains mild.

Ancient critics complained that Epicurus has united under the term pleasure two quite different *desiderata,* positive enjoyment and the absence of pain (Cic. *Fin.* ii 20), and there is some grounds for the complaint. Such remarks as 'The beginning and root of all good is the pleasure of the stomach' (Us. 409) are much more naturally interpreted in the former sense, even if Epicurus did not intend this. In particular, it is difficult to make sense of the notion that absence of pain entails that pleasure can only be varied and not increased. If I derive pleasure from smelling a rose at a time when I am suffering no pain, it seems perverse to say that my pleasure is merely varied. For what I experience is something *sui generis,* a new sense of gratification which is more than a variation of my previous state of consciousness. Even if it is reasonable to call tranquillity of mind a kind of pleasure it is straining language and common sense to call it the greatest pleasure. That procedure leaves us no way to take account of experiences which cannot be assimilated to tranquillity and which do cause us intense gratification without pain.

Thirdly, under 'static' pleasure Epicurus seems to have classified two quite different things. The pleasure which follows from the satisfaction of desire is normally related closely in time to the desire. When I leave hospital, restored to health, it makes sense to say 'You must be pleased to be better'. But it makes much less sense to say this a long time later. The mental equilibrium enjoyed by an Epicurean of ten years' standing seems to be something quite different.

These and other observations could be prolonged. I have confined my comments to Epicurus' own theories, and it is hardly necessary to dwell on some of the obvious objections to egoistic hedonism as a 'moral' theory. But in this book Epicurus should have the last word, and it is eloquently expressed by his great disciple and admirer, Lucretius:

> When the winds are troubling the waters on a mighty sea it is sweet to view from the land the great struggles of another man; not because it is pleasant or delightful that anyone should be distressed, but because it is sweet to see the misfortunes from which you are yourself free. It is sweet too to watch great battles which cover the plains if you yourself have no share in the danger. But nothing is more pleasing than to be master of those tranquil places which have been strongly fortified aloft by the teaching of wise men. From there you can look down upon other men and see them wandering purposelessly and straying as they search for a way of life— competing with their abilities, trying to outdo one another in social status, striving night and day with the utmost effort to rise to the heights of wealth and become masters of everything. Unhappy minds of men, blind hearts! How great the darkness, and how great the dangers in which this little life is spent. Do you not see that nature shouts out for nothing but the removal of pain from the body and the enjoyment in mind of the sense of joy when anxiety and fear have been taken away. Therefore we see that for the body few things only are needed, which are sufficient to remove pain and can also provide many delights. Nor does our nature itself at different times seek for anything more pleasing, if there are no golden status of youths in the entrance halls holding in their right hands fiery torches so that evening banquets may be provided with light, or if the house does not gleam with silver and shine with gold and a carved and gilded ceiling does not resound to the lute, when, in spite of this, men lie on the soft grass together near a stream of water beneath the branches of a lofty tree refreshing their bodies with joy and at no great cost, particularly when the weather smiles and the time of the year spreads flowers all over the green grass (ii 1-35).

Notes

[1] Epicurus probably first encountered Metrodorus, his junior by about ten years, at Lampsachus, the latter's native town.

[2] The authenticity of this letter has been questioned, but there is no reason to doubt its reliability as a statement of Epicurus' attitudes and doctrine.

[3] N. W. De witt, *Epicurus and his Philosophy* (Minneapolis 1954) p. 329. The last chapter of this book should be consulted for a survey of the later fortunes of Epicureanism.

[4] For the evidence see Bibliography.

[5] Nearly all the Herculaneum papyri belong to the Biblioteca Nazionale of Naples; but the British Museum has substantial fragments of Epicurus *On Nature* Book ii.

[6] Epicurus did not invent the 'effluence' theory of sense-perception. It goes back to Democritus and still earlier, in a different form, to Empedocles.

[7] Cicero (*N.D.* i 44) says that Epicurus was the first to use the word *prolêpsis* in this sense.

[8] Clement of Alexandria (Us. 255) reports Epicurus as saying that 'it is impossible for anyone to investigate . . . or to form a judgment . . . independently of preconception'.

[9] For further evidence and discussion see my article in *Bulletin of the Institute of Classical Studies* 18 (1971) 114-33.

[10] *The Greek Atomists and Epicurus* (Oxford 1928) p. 570.

[11] Formal statements of these 'axioms' are to be found in Sextus Empiricus, *Adv. math.* vii 212-13 (Us. 247). Epicurus writes of them more informally in *Ep. Hdt.* 51 and *K.D.* xxiv.

[12] See Philodemus, *On signs* col. xvi ed. Ph. and E. A. De Lacey (Pennsylvania 1941).

[13] *Adversus sophistas* frs. 1, 3 ed. Sbordone (Naples 1947).

[14] For more details see the article cited in n. 2.

[15] Lucretius develops (A) and (B) at length, i 159-264; he deals with (C) at ii 294-307.

[16] For Lucretius' arguments concerning void, see i 329-97. Aristotle denied the necessity of void to explain motion, as did the Stoics.

[17] See also Lucretius i 599-634.

[18] The most penetrating study of Democritean and Epicurean atomism is by D. J. Furley, *Two Studies in the Greek Atomists* (Princeton 1967). His first study deals with the notion of minimal parts.

[19] This is supported by Aristotle's words, quoted by Simplicius (DK 68 A 37); cf. W. K. C. Guthrie, *History of Greek Philosophy* vol. ii (Cambridge 1965) pp. 400-2.

[20] For a detailed treatment, to which I am much indebted, see Furley, *Two Studies in the Greek Atomists,* pp. 111-30.

[21] The gist of what Lucretius says is repeated by Cicero, *Fin.* i 18-20.

[22] Good arguments in favour of this have been advanced by G. B. Kerferd, *Phronesis* 16 (1971) 88-9.

[23] See in particular *Ep. Hdt.* 48. The regular replenishment of 'lost' atoms explains why objects are not (normally) seen to diminish in bulk.

[24] Plato himself attacks purely mechanistic theories of causation, probably with Democritus in mind, in the tenth book of his *Laws* 889b.

[25] Lucretius attacks 'final' causes at length, v 195-234.

[26] The reference is especially relevant because it is a contemporary one. Theophrastus' *Characters* are a set of short vignettes of character types: complaisance, boorishness, miserliness etc.

[27] The development of Plato's theology is a complex subject; for a well-balanced account see F. Solmsen, *Plato's Theology* (Ithaca, N.Y. 1942).

[28] Doubts about the Platonic authorship of this work have been expressed from antiquity onwards. If not by Plato himself, which is likely enough, it should be ascribed to a younger contemporary Academic, perhaps Philip of Opus (D.L. iii 37).

[29] Cic. *N.D.* ii 42-4. Comparison with Book i 33 of Cicero's treatise suggests the reference may be to Aristotle's third book 'On philosophy'. On Aristotle's theology see W. K. C. Guthrie, *Classical Quarterly* 27 (1933) 162-71; 28 (1934) 90-8.

[30] It was clearly Epicurean practice to attack all theological views which differed from their own; cf. Cic. *N.D.* i *passim*. Epicurus must have found much to object to in the writings of Plato's successor, Xenocrates, whose theology contained 'daimons' as well as celestial divinities and who foreshadowed the Stoics in referring the names of certain gods to natural substances.

[31] Cic. *N.D.* i 45-6; see also *Ep. Men.* 123-4 which refers to the false conceptions of the 'many' about gods.

[32] See further, K. Kleve, *Symbolae Osloenses,* suppl. xix. Epicurus (Cic. *N.D.* i 50) also inferred that there must be divine beings equal in number to mortals by the principle of 'equal balance' or 'reciprocal distribution' (*isonomia*). 'From this,' we are told, 'it follows that if the number of mortals is so many there exists no less a number of immortals, and if the causes of destruction are uncountable the causes of conservation must also be infinite.'

[33] The word 'brought to fulfilment' (*apotetelesmenôn*) should not be emended with Kühn and Usener to *apotetelesmenous:* it is the 'images' not the gods which are brought to fulfilment; cf. *Ep. Pyth.* 115, 'by the meeting of atoms productive of fire'.

[34] *De dis* iii fr. 32a p. 52 Diels. For further discussion of Philodemus' evidence and theories based upon it, cf. W. Schmid, *Rheinisches Museum* 94 (1951) 97-156, K. Kleve, *Symbolae Osloenses* 35 (1959), who attributes the gods' self-preservation to the exercise of free will.

[35] Tennyson, *Lucretius,* based on Lucret. iii 18-23, itself a translation of Homer.

[36] See further Kerferd, *Phronesis* 16 (1971) 89ff.

[37] The nervous system was discovered by the medical scientists, Herophilus and Erasistratus, during the first half of the third century B.C.

[38] Epicurus himself writes about seeing, hearing and smell, *Ep. Hdt.* 49-53. Lucretius also discusses taste, iv 615-72.

[39] *De nat.* xxviii fr. 5 col. vi (sup.), col. vii (inf.), ed. A. Vogliano, *Epicuri et Epicureorum scripta in Herculanensibus papyris servata* (Berlin 1928).

[40] Cic. *De fato* 22 and *N.D.* i 69 also show that the swerve was supposed to save 'free will'. See also Diogenes of Oenoanda fr. 32 col. iii Chilton.

[41] This is found in Arrighetti's edition, *Epicuro Opere* 31 [27] 3-9. It is just possible that the swerve is implied at 31 [22] 7-16.

[42] 'Aristotle and Epicurus on Voluntary Action' in his *Two Studies in the Greek Atomists.* My brief remarks here cannot do justice to the importance of Furley's wide-ranging treatment. Much of his argument turns on similarities he has detected between Aristotle and Epicurus.

[43] So Bailey, *Greek Atomists,* p. 483, followed by Panichas, *Epicurus* (N.Y. 1967) p. 100.

[44] cf. Cic. *Fin.* ii 17, 'I assert that all those who are without pain are in a state of pleasure.'

[45] This interpretation of the relation between 'kinetic' and 'static' pleasure seems to me to suit the evidence best and to make the best sense. It has also been argued that 'kinetic' pleasure serves only to 'vary' a previous 'static' pleasure; see most recently J. M. Rist, *Epicurus* (Cambridge 1972) ch. 6 and pp. 170ff.

[46] e.g. *K.D.* iii, ix, xviii, xix, xx.

[47] See also D.L. x 119 and Lucretius' brilliant denunciation of *ambitio,* iii 59-77, related to the fear of death.

Terence Irwin (essay date 1989)

SOURCE: Terence Irwin, "Epicureanism," in *A History of Western Philosophy: I Classical Thought*, Oxford University Press, 1989, pp. 145-63.

[*In the following excerpt, Irwin places Epicurean thought in the context of Greek political and intellectual history. He investigates the movement's doctrine using the tools of logic.*]

i. The Hellenistic world[1]

The 'Hellenistic Age' (a term coined by modern historians, not by the Greeks) begins with the death of Alexander the Great in 323, and ends with the end of the Roman Republic and the victory of Octavian (later Augustus) in 31 BC. Alexander conquered the empires of Persia and Egypt, and his successors ruled over them until they were incorporated in the Roman Empire under Augustus.

Alexander's conquests extended the Greek-speaking world. Greek cities (Alexandria in Egypt being the most famous) were founded throughout his empire; and they made the Greek language and culture familiar and dominant far beyond mainland Greece and Ionia.[2] Though Greek culture spread over a wide area, however, it did not penetrate very deeply; for the new Greek cities remained sharply separated from the surrounding rural areas, where native language, culture, and religion survived, and Greek speakers were an alien elite.[3] Still, Greek became the primary language of the Eastern Roman Empire, and remained so until AD 1453, when the last Byzantine emperor was deposed. Because Greek was the dominant language, the Hebrew scriptures were translated into Greek (the 'Septuagint', from the seventy-two translators traditionally supposed to have produced it), and the Christian scriptures were originally composed in Greek.[4]

Alexander succeeded his father Philip as king of Macedon; and the Macedonians became the dominant power in Greece even before their Asian conquests. From then on, the major Greek states, including Athens (Sparta was now a minor power), no longer enjoyed their previous degree of autonomy. The Athenian orator Demosthenes (384-322) was one of those who regarded the coming of the Macedonians as the end of Greek freedom; and he urged resistance to Philip and Alexander.[5] Not everyone, however, thought the Macedonians were so dangerous to freedom. Two centuries later the historian Polybius (*c.* 200-after 118 BC, vigorously defended the other side of the case, in his argument for the pro-Macedonians in the Peloponnese:

> By inducing Philip into the Peloponnese, and by humiliating the Spartans, they allowed all the Peloponnesians to draw new breath, and to form the thought of freedom; further they [the Peloponnesians] recovered the territories and cities that the Spartans had, during their prosperity, taken from them . . . and undoubtedly strengthened their own states.

Nor did Macedonian domination completely transform the political life of Greek cities. When new Greek cities were founded across Alexander's empire, a similar pattern of political life was to some degree repeated.[6]

The condition of the Greek cities in the Hellenistic world helps to explain some new developments in Greek intellectual life. The foundation of the Museum and Library in Alexandria, as centres of study and research, helped to make that city the main focus of natural science, medicine, and literary studies. Athens remained the centre of philosophy. This division tended to encourage some separation of philosophical from scientific studies. This was not a sharp division. Theophrastus (*c.*370-*c.*287) and Straton (died 269), for instance, two of Aristotle's successors in his school the Lyceum, continued his strong interest in empirical scientific research and theory. But the Lyceum lost influence and vigour, and no other philosophical school arrested the tendencies to specialization—and these were in any case a natural result of the development and elaboration of philosophy.

In Athens distinct schools of philosophy formed, arguing with each other, and competing for the attention of students. Stoics, Epicureans, Sceptics, and Peripatetics (i.e. Aristotelians) formulated their own doctrines and strategies. This tendency was a predictable result of developments in philosophy; but the concentration of these schools in Athens (in contrast to the early fifth century) also reflected the place of that city in Greek culture and higher education. Both

Athens and other cities began to require some philosophical instruction as part of the course of training (originally military) for young men of the upper classes. The Athenian philosophical schools therefore influenced some of the content of higher education for the ruling classes.[7]

Athens eventually became an international centre of philosophical study not just for the Greek world, but also for the whole Roman Empire; and it retained this position for at least six centuries. In 146 BC the Romans completed the conquest of Greece, with the sack and destruction of Corinth; but, as the Roman poet Horace, (65 BC-AD 8) remarks, 'Greece took its brutish captor captive and introduced the arts into rustic Latium'. From then on the Roman ruling class cultivated Greek literary and philosophical studies, with increasing success.[8]

ii. Epicurus: general aims

For Epicurus (341-271), as for Socrates, philosophy is a way to reform our lives. We conduct our lives badly because we fear death; and we fear death because we fear punishment after death. Cephalus' remarks at the beginning of Plato's *Republic* illustrate the fears that Epicurus has in mind:

> When a man begins to realize he is going to die, he is filled with apprehension and concern about matters that previously did not occur to him. <He remembers> the stories (*muthos*) that are told about Hades and how the men who have done injustice here must pay the just penalty there; and though he may have ridiculed them hitherto, they now begin to torture his soul with the fear that they may after all be true.

According to Cephalus, wealth is some protection against these fears, since it removes the temptation to cheat people, and allows us to make lavish offerings to the gods—two ways to avoid punishment after death. Hence the fear of death stimulates the desire to accumulate wealth.

Epicurus thinks that fear of death underlies all the acquisitive and competitive aspects of our lives; indeed, he thinks it explains our tendency to accept a Homeric outlook. Fearing death, we try to assure ourselves of security and protection against other people. The search for security leads us to pursue power, wealth, and honour, and makes us constantly afraid of losing them. We seek posthumous fame and honour, as Achilles did, because we refuse to admit to ourselves that we will not be present to enjoy it; and our fear of death explains why we refuse to admit that we will not be present. We occupy ourselves in constant activity and competition, to conceal our fear of death from ourselves. We do not

realize that fear of death is our basic motive; each of us 'flees from himself'; we need occupations to divert us from the oppressive awareness of ourselves and our fears, but we do not know why we find the awareness of ourselves so oppressive.[9]

Epicurus' diagnosis of human fears and ambitions is his reason for studying the nature of the universe. As Lucretius (? 94-55), a Roman poet and Epicurean, says:

> We must disperse this terror of the mind, this darkness, not by the sun's rays and the day's gleaming shafts, but by nature's face and law.

Epicurus himself claims that this is the only reason that we need to study nature:

> If we had never been troubled by suspicions about the heavens, or that death might be something to us, or by ignorance of the limits of pains and appetites, we would have had no need to study nature (*phusiologia*).[10]

To remove our fears, both the known and the unacknowledged, we need an account of the universe that gives us no reason to fear death. We free ourselves from fear once we believe that the universe is not controlled by gods who determine or modify natural processes for their own purposes, and that we do not survive death. If we have reason to believe this, then (in Epicurus' view) we have no reason to think death does any harm to us; hence we have no reason to fear death; hence we will no longer fear death.

iii. The challenge of Scepticism

To find a theory of the universe that dissolves our fear of death and the gods, Epicurus turns to the Atomism of Leucippus and Democritus. Aristotle attacks Atomism in so far as he insists on the reality of form and the truth of teleological explanations; and Epicurus presents a defence of Atomism against Aristotle's attacks.

On one important point, however, he is closer to Aristotle than to Democritus. In Democritus' view, the atomic theory depends on principles that are evident to reason, but contrary to the testimony of the senses; the world revealed by reason is quite different from anything that the senses show us. The conflict between sense and reason leads Democritus some way towards scepticism, and forces him to ask where he will find the evidence for his theory if he disregards the senses.[11] Not surprisingly, Aristotle criticizes Atomism for its conflicts with the appearances. Epicurus, however, starts from an epistemological position quite close to Aristotle's and argues, against both Aristotle and Democritus, that this position actually supports Atomism.

Epicurus has good reason to reconsider Democritus' epistemological position, not only because of Aristotle's criticism, but also because of the revival of scepticism after Aristotle. A central Sceptical question concerns the problem of the 'criterion' (or 'standard'; Greek *kritêrion,* from *krinein,* 'judge' or 'discriminate') to be used in discriminating true appearances from false ones. The Sceptic argues that we have no reliable standard. Appearances conflict; different things appear true to different people; even if we confine ourselves to sensory appearances, these conflict; and hence we cannot rely on the senses as a criterion. How, in any case, do we know we have found a criterion? We can justifiably treat some principle or method P1 as a criterion only if we know that P1 gives us true answers; but apparently we cannot know that without appealing to some further principle P2 to serve as a criterion for deciding about P1; but we can ask the same question about P2, leading us to a further principle P3; and now we face an infinite regress, giving us no answer to our original question.[12]

The Sceptic facing arguments of apparently equal strength for conflicting conclusions finds no basis for choosing between the conclusions, suspends judgement about their truth, and thereby claims to achieve tranquillity (*ataraxia*)—freedom from fear and anxiety. This Sceptical claim suggests a further challenge to Epicurus. For he and the Sceptic seem to agree that tranquillity is the right goal; and the Sceptic seems to offer a short cut to it by suspension of judgement. Why should Epicurus pursue tranquillity by the more laborious route of a dogmatic theory about the world?

Epicurus rejects this Sceptical solution. If we are Sceptics, he thinks, we will be full of indecision and, therefore, of disturbance. If we cannot decide between two views, our indecision will leave us worried and agitated; we therefore need some basis for judgement and decision. The Sceptic admits that it is simply a matter of good luck that tranquillity follows suspension of judgement. Epicurus suggests that the Sceptic is foolishly optimistic in hoping for tranquillity rather than anxiety.[13]

iv. The appeal to the senses

In reply to Scepticism, Epicurus thinks we must trust the senses: 'If you fight with all your perceptions, you will have nothing to refer to in your judgement of whichever ones of them you say are false.' He relies on the argument that Democritus offers on behalf of the senses; we have no more confidence in anything than we have in the senses, and so if we lose confidence in them, we lose it in everything else as well. Trust in the senses is the only alternative to scepticism, since it is the only way out of complete suspension of judgement about everything.

This argument claims that we cannot *totally* reject the senses, and must accept *some* of their reports. But Epicurus accepts *all* their reports, and so claims that all perceptions are true. In developing a sceptical argument, Descartes argues that 'it is sometimes proved to me that these senses are deceptive, and it is wiser not to trust entirely to anything by which we have once been deceived'. Epicurus takes this sceptical doubt further, arguing that any doubt about any sensory report requires general doubt about all sensory reports, and hence total suspension of judgement.[14]

This total confidence in the senses appears to expose them to a different attack. For we might think that if we accept every report of the senses, we will have to accept conflicting reports (e.g. the stick appears bent when I see it in water, and straight when I pull it out); then we will have to admit conflicting appearances (the stick appears both bent and straight); since we are not allowed to choose between them, and both cannot be true of the same object, we cannot say how the object is. This argument drove Democritus to scepticism about the senses.

In reply Epicurus denies any conflict between the two appearances of the stick, and appeals to the Atomic theory. The appearance of the bent stick is true, in so far as it corresponds to a bent configuration of atoms thrown off by the stick and eventually hitting the eyes. The appearance of the straight stick is true, in so far as it corresponds to a straight configuration of atoms. We are usually wrong if we expect the bent-stick-in-water appearance to be followed by a bent-stick-out-of-water appearance. But the error lies with us and our hasty inferences and false beliefs, not in the senses themselves.

If Epicurus is right, then our appearance of a chair is an accurate presentation of a chair-shaped configuration of atoms. But this answer does not undermine sceptical doubts about our belief in such things as chairs. For chair-shaped configurations may be momentary and short-lived, and further beliefs are needed for the inference that the configuration belongs to the longerlasting configuration that is a chair. We avoid scepticism only if we can show that these inferences are warranted. Sometimes we explain our chair-shaped appearances as the products of dreams or hallucinaitons, even though, in Epicurus' view, they result from some external chair-shaped configuration. Why should this not always be so?[15]

Epicurus defends the senses by restricting our normal view of what they say, and hence rejecting our belief that sensory reports may conflict. But since sensory reports, as he construes them, tell us so little, his defence of their accuracy does not answer a Sceptical doubt about common beliefs that are based on the senses. Epicurus has not shown that he has good reason for believing in the ordinary external world of persisting objects. Though he defends the truth of the purely sensory appearances, he does not defend the appearances that matter most for the construction of a scientific theory.

v. Sense and science

In Democritus' view, the atomic theory is the product of reason superseding the senses; the conflicting appearances of sense show that reality cannot consist of things with colour, taste, and so on, but must consist of indestructible atoms. Since Epicurus insists on the senses as the criterion of truth, he cannot use Democritus' argument. He must argue that the evidence of the senses themselves supports atomism. For this purpose we must allow that Epicurus has answered sceptical threats to our belief in an objective world; and we must see whether he can argue from this belief to the truth of the atomic theory.

Some examples suggest the strategy. Atomism tells us (*a*1) the atoms are in constant motion, and (*a*2) they lack colour. The senses, however, seem to tell us (*b*1) there are stable bodies not in constant motion, and (*b*2) bodies are coloured. The evidence of the senses, then, seems to conflict with atomism, because we cannot understand how (*c*1) apparently stable bodies are simply collections of moving constituents, or how (*c*2) apparently coloured bodies are simply collections of colourless constituents.

Lucretius, however, argues that the senses provide us with examples of (*c*), and hence do not commit us to (*b*) against (*a*). He describes two cases: (*c*1) We see a flock of sheep on a distant hill; though from a distance they appear still, we see, when we come closer, that they are moving. (*c*2) We tear a red rag into smaller and smaller pieces, and gradually lose the colour. Attention to these examples supports the claims in (*c*); and so trust in the senses does not conflict with (*a*). When we think the evidence of the senses requires the truth of (*b*), we are looking carelessly at ill-chosen examples. In fact the evidence of the senses tells us to accept the atomic theory, not to reject it.[16]

Epicurus concludes, against Democritus, that atomists need not reject the senses; they need only attend carefully and without prejudice to what the senses really tell us. Aristotle assumes that judgements such as (*b*) are among the appearances that a theory should vindicate; but Epicurus replies that these are common beliefs, not genuine sensory appearances, and that the genuine sensory appearances do not commit us to (*b*).

His attempted defence raises a general difficulty about all the numerous and elaborate arguments for the atomic theory. In Epicurus' view, some questions allow only

one answer that is consistent with the evidence of the senses, whereas other questions allow several answers that are consistent with such evidence. Questions of the second type (e.g. about the size of the sun) arise because the relevant observations are not available. These cases allow many 'empirically equivalent' theories and explanations, all equally consistent with the evidence of the senses; an Epicurean does not choose between them.[17]

It is important for Epicurus to show that the atomic theory answers a question of the first type, so that he has reason to believe in it as opposed to rival theories. His arguments, however, seem to show only that it is consistent with observation; he hardly shows that it is the only theory of this sort. It seems easy to imagine a non-atomist account of the world that is consistent with the evidence of the senses. We argued, indeed, that the Homeric view could easily show itself to be consistent with any observations; that was why the naturalists could not hope to refute Homer by a simple appeal to the senses.[18] If this is true, then the atomic theory does not answer questions of the first type, since such questions do not seem decidable by the test of mere consistency with observations. The atomic theory seems to be only one of a number of empirically equivalent theories, and Epicurus' own principles forbid us to prefer it over rival theories that are equally consistent with observations.

This difficulty for Epicurus is parallel to one we raised at a more elementary level, in arguing that he fails to rule out the suggestion that our purported experience of an objective world is really a dream or hallucinaiton. In each case the view that Epicurus chooses may well be the most reasonable; but his demand for mere consistency with the senses does not support his choice.

vi. Atomism and the soul

Epicurus wants to show that the soul is a collection of atoms, just as trees and chairs are, and therefore is just as certain to decay and dissolve into its constituents. If Epicurus is right about this, then Plato cannot be right to believe in an immaterial and immortal soul. If we do not believe in immortality, we will not believe that we can suffer harm after death, and therefore, Epicurus thinks, we have no reason to fear death and will not fear death.

Lucretius collects a series of twenty-nine Epicurean arguments for the mortality of the soul; but most of them show the characteristic weakness of Epicurean empiricism. Lucretius finds abundant evidence to show that the soul is affected by what happens to the body: a blow on the head causes me pain, my mind decays with my body, and so on. One possible explanation of these facts will say that the soul is material and destructible, and depends on the body for its existence. But that is only one possible explanation, and someone who agrees with Plato that the soul is immaterial and immortal can offer other explanations.[19]

To rule out these other explanations, a materialist might claim that only material bodies can be affected by material bodies. If this claim is true, the soul cannot be immaterial; but how do we know it is true? Epicurus will hardly convince us that no other view is consistent with the evidence of the senses; to justify his materialism he must rely on a claim that is not warranted by his empiricism. Since he believes that a claim about reality is illegitimate unless it is warranted by his empiricism, his argument faces grave objections, on purely Epicurean grounds.

Epicurus' treatment of the soul raises a broader question about the extent of his disagreement with Aristotle. He wants to show not only that the soul is mortal, but also that it is simply a collection of atoms. He therefore argues for eliminative atomism, rejecting the claims of form (and therefore of soul) to be anything distinct from the collection of atoms. He speaks of compounds of atoms, roughly corresponding to macroscopic objects as ordinarily conceived; but their status is obscure. He thinks every change in a compound implies its destruction, probably because he follows Heraclitus in accepting a compositional principle of identity; in that case he cannot recognize the persistent substances that Aristotle recognizes.[20] Though Epicurus' conception of the world leaves no room for Aristotelian substance and form, he hardly justifies their exclusion.

vii. The gods

Plato's *Laws* contains a discussion of different types of unsound views about the gods. After replying to a complete atheist, Plato turns to the person who believes in the gods but is so impressed by the apparent imperfections of the world that he concludes that the gods have no concern for it. This is Epicurus' view; and whereas Plato condemns it as a threat to religion and morality, Epicurus thinks we need it for a sound attitude to death, and therefore to our lives.

To show that the gods are not concerned with the world, Epicurus attacks a particular teleological doctrine. Plato and the Stoics argue that the order in individual organisms depends on the larger order that maintains them, and that this order is plausibly explained as the product of intelligent design. The order in the world supplies an argument for the existence of a designing god.

In reply Epicurus holds that the disorder in the world tells against the existence of any designing gods. Natural disasters and other apparent imperfections suggest that only non-purposive forces could control the processes in the world—unless the gods are remarkably stupid, malicious, or incompetent. The flaws in the observed character of the world confirm the atomic theory, and undermine belief in gods who care about the world.[21]

These arguments against design do not answer all of Aristotle's reasons for believing in teleology. Aristotle claims that organisms are to be understood and explained teleologically, without claiming that they must be products of design. Epicurus must reject this claim if he rejects the reality of form. But though his commitment to eliminative atomism requires rejection of form, he does not undermine Aristotle's case. His failure to answer Aristotle does not necessarily affect his specific arguments against design; but it may affect his reasons for believing the basic atomist principles.

Though Epicurus denies that the gods design or control the world order, he believes that empiricism requires him to accept gods. For in dreams and visions people claim to be aware of gods; and something external must correspond to their perceptions, since all perceptions are true; but the only external things that could correspond to our perceptions are immortal, intelligent, and blessedly happy beings looking like human beings with human bodies. The gods, like everything else with human or animal bodies, must be composed of atoms; but they are not destroyed in the way other collections of atoms are destroyed, since they live between the words that are subject to destruction, and so avoid the atomic forces that destroy other collections of atoms.[22]

This account of the gods maintains empiricism, and remains strikingly congenial to one element of traditional Greek religious thought. He agrees with Homer's description of the gods as blessedly happy, not vulnerable to the dangers that threaten human beings. By insisting on this aspect of the gods, Epicurus raises a serious question: why should an invulnerable and blessed being interest himself in the world or in us? Plato appeals to the Demiurge's desire to create something that embodies the Forms; but we may wonder how that desire is consistent with the gods' independence. Why should they want to create a world, if they are already completely happy and need nothing more?[23]

viii. Necessity and freedom

In accepting the atomic theory, Epicurus agrees with Democritus' naturalist determinism: all natural processes are the necessary results of atomic movements, with no external interference from gods, and no laws irreducible to laws about atomic movements. The same patterns are repeated in nature because the same atomic forces operate, and their operations necessarily produce the same results.

This belief in necessity, however, seems to conflict with our belief that human beings are free and responsible agents. We suppose that it is up to us how we act, and that we can fairly be praised or blamed for our actions. Moreover, the Epicurean message is addressed to us on the assumption that we have a real choice about how to live our lives. The Epicurean takes control of his life, and frees himself from the fears that preoccupy most people. But if atomist determinism is true, all our actions are nothing but the necessary result of atomic movements, all the way back to the infinitely distant past. How could our belief in responsibility be true, and how could it be up to us to take control of our lives?[24]

Aristotle seems to suggest that I am justly held responsible for my action if certain negative conditions are met—if I am not pushed or otherwise physically forced, and my action is not the result of ignorance. But Epicurus notices that even if Aristotle's conditions are met, my action might still be necessitated by past states of the world beyond my control. Epicurus thinks determination by the past excludes responsibility; indeed, he says it would be better to believe in interfering gods than to believe the philosophers who speak of fate and natural necessity.[25]

Epicurus might well argue that other remarks of Aristotle's support the *incompatibilist* view that responsibility is incompatible with determinism. Aristotle claims that if I am responsible for an action, the action is 'up to me'—I am free to do and not to do it; and 'the origin is in me'—I am the cause. Epicurus implicitly argues:

(1) If determinism is true, events in the distant past make my action inevitable.

(2) If so, then they are the cause, and I am not.

(3) If I am not the cause, it is not up to me, and I am not responsible for it.

(4) Hence, if determinism is true, I am not responsible for my actions.

Steps (1) and (2) spell out the apparent consequences of determinism; Aristotle accepts (3); and so we seem to have no escape from (4).[26]

Since Epicurus is an incompatibilist, but believes we are responsible for our actions, he rejects determinism, and modifies Democritean atomism. He claims that some atoms at some times undergo a random and imperceptible swerve from their normal course. This swerve introduces an uncaused motion; and in so far as our act of choice includes an atomic swerve, it is undetermined. This solution violates (so Epicurus claims) neither our experience of the world nor our firm belief in free will.[27]

The solution is not clearly convincing. If each choice we think is free really is free, then every such choice includes a swerve. If Epicurus thinks the immediate evidence of sensation assures us that we are free, and therefore that there must have been an atomic swerve, he faces the usual difficulty for his empiricism: he does not rule out alternative explanations of the sensations of freedom.

But even if swerves happen on the right occasions, do they imply the sort of freedom that is needed for responsibility? If a choice involves a swerve, it is uncaused, and therefore cannot be caused by my past choices and my states of character. But actions that are unconnected to my past and my character are not the ones we think we are responsible for; indeed, we are more likely to regard them as aberrations allowing us to claim diminished responsibility. Epicurus' view implies, then, that I am no more responsible for any of my 'free' actions than I am for aberrations unconnected with my character; hence he seems to undermine claims of responsibility, not to defend them.

To answer this objection Epicurus needs to show that the inference from indeterminism to absence of causal connexion is unwarranted, or that responsibility does not require causal connexion between my action, my past choices, and my character. Other incompatibilists have taken up the tasks that he leaves unfinished; the issue has not yet been settled in their favour.

Epicurus is an incompatibilist about responsibility partly because he is an eliminative atomist. An alternative approach might say that claims about responsibility apply to Aristotelian souls and forms, not to their constituent matter, and that the eliminative, not the determinist, aspects of Democritus threaten responsibility. This approach is not open to Epicurus; but the Stoics exploit it.[28]

ix. Pleasure, happiness, and virtue

Epicurus' ethical theory rests on his hedonism—his belief that pleasure is the ultimate good, and other things are good only to the extent that they are means to pleasure. Aristotle accepts the common belief that pleasure is *a* good and must be a component of any credible account of *the* good. Epicurus claims that this belief about pleasure is no mere common belief (an 'appearance' in Aristotle's broad sense), but an immediate appearance of sensation, and therefore infallible; and he claims that the infallible appearance recognizes pleasure as *the* good. All animals immediately recognize that pleasure is good, and pursue it as their end; children pursue it spontaneously before they have acquired any other beliefs about what is good.[29]

Epicurus rejects the sensual pleasures that require expanded and demanding desires and abundant material resources. A life of such pleasures would, he concedes, be a happy life if it really maximized pleasure. But it cannot do this; the only way to maximize the balance of pleasure over pain is to eliminate anxiety, but sensual pleasures simply leave us prey to pains, fears, and needs. Dependence on external resources that are not in our control is a source of anxiety to be avoided. The Epicurean is to approach the independence and invulnerability of the gods, secure in his pleasures, and free from the external hazards causing fear and apprehension.[30]

This conception of the good is meant to explain why the Epicurean cultivates the virtues that Plato and Aristotle describe. The Epicurean wants to regulate his desires so that they do not make him dependent on external fortune; he therefore values the results of temperance. He does not fear the loss of worldly goods, since he does not need many; he is therefore not tempted to act like a coward. He finds mutual aid and pleasure in the society of friends, and so he cultivates friendships.[31]

The Epicurean is not greedy for power or domination over others. He finds it a source of severe anxiety and insecurity. Since he understands the benefits of mutual aid and physical security, he follows rules of justice, for the reasons given by Glaucon and Adeimantus in Plato's *Republic*. Since he values freedom from anxiety, he will want to avoid the risk of detection and punishment—a risk that is the inevitable penalty of injustice, even if it leads to no further penalty. The evolution of society is to be explained neither as a product of divine design, nor (following Aristotle) as the expression of the inherently social nature of human beings, but simply as the product of particular responses to insecurity and danger. The needs that cause the formation of the state also give the Epicurean hedonist reason to conform to justice.[32]

In all these ways Epicurus defends the Aristotelian virtues, as he conceives them, by means of quite un-Aristotelian premises. He argues that the pursuit of pleasure, properly understood, actually requires the cultivation of the moral virtues.

x. Questions about Epicurean ethics

Doubts about Epicurus' argument may arise even if we accept hedonism. He argues for a version of hedonism that values freedom and independence from externals; he avoids the excitements of gross sensual pleasures, and of the more subtle pleasures that depend heavily on external resources, because these pleasures are sources of anxiety. But can this preference for independence and security be defended on hedonistic grounds? Epicurus claims that the anxiety, fear, and insecurity resulting from self-indulgence and intemperance are too severe to be tolerated; but it is hard to justify this claim

on purely hedonistic grounds, and any nonhedonistic argument is, for Epicurus, quite worthless.

Hedonism in general faces wider questions about the relation of pleasure to happiness and the human good. Aristotle insists that no one would want to return to the condition of a child, even if he could maximize the sorts of pleasures that a child enjoys.[33] He implies that objective features of my situation—including the nature of the activities I enjoy—make a difference to my well-being and happiness. On Aristotle's view, my subjective attitude to my situation does not by itself determine whether or not I am happy or well off. This objection applies to Epicurus no less than to other hedonists. We could be content and free from anxiety even if we were crippled, our friends and family were being tortured, and we were sold into slavery, as long as we were deceived about these things or did not care about them. But if we apply Aristotle's test for the complete good, we see that we would be better off if all these things were going better. Epicurus does not seem to answer this objection to hedonism in general.

The objection is important if we want to evaluate a central assumption of the whole Epicurean outlook. Epicurus tries to relieve us from the fear of death:

> Get used to thinking that death is nothing to us, since every good and evil is in sensation, and death is deprivation of sensation. Hence correct knowledge that death is nothing to us makes the mortal aspect of life enjoyable, not by adding unlimited time, but by having removed the longing for immortality.[34]

He assumes that being dead would harm us only if it were painful after death. His whole method of removing the fear of death assumes a hedonist conception of a person's good.

Once we challenge hedonism, however, the fear of death may be harder to remove. If we say that a young person who dies before he has fulfilled his striking promise has suffered some harm, we do not mean that he felt or is feeling anything painful; we mean that he would have gained some great benefit if he had lived and that he has lost it because he has died. If death can do us this sort of harm, then we seem to have good reason (in some circumstances) to fear it. In this case Epicurus' theory of the good seems to leave out those goods that underlie some of our reasonable fears of death; for they are goods distinct from pleasure.

His hedonism also seems to threaten his defence of the virtues. He claims that they are simply instrumental to pleasure. Though an Epicurean is free of some temptations to act like a coward, that does not seem to make him brave. For a brave person is normally concerned about some important interest of himself or of other people he cares about; but the Epicurean's indifference to external conditions will apparently make him indifferent to these sorts of interests as well. Though he will not be tempted to shirk danger for the sake of his life, health, or material goods, he seems to have no particular reason to face danger either; when so few things matter to him, he seems to have no positive incentive to be brave.[35]

For similar reasons, we may doubt the Epicurean's commitment to justice and friendship. Even if the threat of punishment deters him from all or most unjust actions, he seems to have no positive reason to care about the good of others for its own sake; for to care about it for its own sake would be to regard it as a good in itself, not simply a means to some other good, whereas a hedonist cannot allow this status to any good except pleasure. If the Epicurean is indifferent to the interest of others as a good in itself, he seems to have no reason for doing any good to them, except when it is instrumental to some further benefit to himself, and ultimately instrumental to his own pleasure.[36]

We may reasonably be unconvinced, then, by Epicurus' efforts to reconcile his hedonism with the commonly recognized virtues that are defended by Plato and Aristotle. The failure of these efforts does not refute his hedonism; it may simply show the falsity of common views about the virtues. If Epicurus has to choose between the common views ('appearances' in the broad sense) and his hedonism (allegedly resting on immediate appearances of sensation), his empiricism requires him to choose hedonism. But is the truth of hedonism so clear that we are right to maintain it against so many of our fairly confident and considered judgements about goods and virtues? If the truth of hedonism is so obvious to sensation, should we perhaps doubt the truth of sensation? If we do that, we challenge the whole basis of Epicurus' system.

xi. The coherence of the system

Epicurus tries to construct a system of simple, coherent, and plausible principles. He is a hedonist who regards the fear of death as the most dangerous source of fear, insecurity, and unhappiness. To avoid insecurity we must trust the senses, since otherwise we will be filled with doubts and anxieties; and the senses assure us of the truth of atomism and hedonism. Each principle seems attractively simple, and they seem to combine into an attractive system. But in fact each is open to doubt, and they are hard to combine satisfactorily.

Epicurus' defence of atomism has often appealed to those who suppose that they take empirical science seriously. It often seems natural to suppose that science is justified by experience and observation. Epicurus takes the empiricist view to extreme lengths, refusing to reject the evidence of the senses on any occasion for any reason. In doing this, however, he prevents himself from justifying any reasonable scientific theory at all.

Epicurus believes we cannot choose between empirically equivalent explanations; and in believing this, he undermines his own empiricist defence of a scientific theory. For sense-perception (as he construes it) cannot rule out the possibility that our perceptions are a consistent hallucination, not matching any external objects; nor can it rule out rivals to the atomic theory. Epicurus' narrow view of sense-perception, and his exclusive trust in consistency with sense-perception as a test of a theory, undermine his argument from empiricism to atomism.

Hedonism in moral philosophy seems to be parallel to empiricism in the theory of knowledge—an intuitively appealing and superficially clear general principle that offers a method of understanding and criticizing other principles. Epicurus claims that it is not merely parallel to empiricism, but actually justified by empiricism, since he thinks we can see the truth of hedonism by appeal to immediate sensation. Like empiricism, hedonism seems easier and more plausible than its more complicated rivals; but once we examine its implications, we see it is neither clear nor plausible.

In antiquity Epicureanism was often brusquely dismissed. Its anti-religious tendencies (real and supposed) aroused suspicion; and its hedonism was sometimes misinterpreted as advocacy of immoral self-indulgence.[37] These dismissals did not rest on any careful criticism of the basic Epicurean principles; and so they did not undermine the appeal of the principles themselves. Brusque dismissal of Epicurus is unwarranted and self-defeating, failing to expose the real difficulties in his position. Exposure of the difficulties, however, has a useful result: it shows us why principles that initially seem simple and attractive are neither simple nor attractive after all.

Notes

[1] Hellenistic philosophy in general: Sedley in Barnes [1980], ch. 1; Long [1974]. Long [1987] is excellent; it contains many of the texts cited in this . . . chapter, and its commentary is a reliable guide to the problems.

[2] An inscription bearing the Delphic advice to know oneself (cf. Plato, *Charmides* 164c-165b) has been found in Afghanistan. See Walbank [1981], 61, Austin [1981], 314f.

3 See Acts of Apostles 14: 11, Jones [1940], 285-90. The later use of 'pagan' (Latin *pagus,* village) for non-Christians indicates this division between city and country.

4 Septuagint: Barrett [1956], 208-16; *ODCC* s. v. Aristeas.

5 Polybius ix. 28-9; Walbank [1981], 91f.

6 Polybius xviii. 14. 6-7. Political life: Jones [1964].

7 Alexandria and Athens: Lloyd [1973], chs. 1-2. Education: Jones [1940], 220-4.

8 Horace, *Epistles* ii. 1. 156-7 (referring to literature).

9 Cephalus: Plato, *Rep.* 330d-e. Security: Diogenes Laertius x. 141. Fame: contrast Plato, *Symposium* 208c-d. Competition: Lucretius ii. 39-54, iii. 1053-75. Underlying fear of death: iii. 1053-6, 1068.

10 Purpose of studying nature: Lucretius ii. 58-60; Diogenes Laertius x. 143. On *phusiologia* see 3 § i.

11 Scepticism: 4 § xii, 6 § ix, 9 § ii.

12 Criterion: Sextus, *P* ii. 14-16; ii. 18-20. The most extreme Sceptics were the Pyrrhonians, following Pyrrhon (*c.* 365-270). The Academic Sceptics took a more moderate line; see 6 § xix, 10 § i, Annas [1986]. Our evidence for this Hellenistic scepticism is largely derived from the later compilation by Sextus Empiricus. I use 'Sceptic' and 'Sceptical' with initial capitals for members or doctrines of these schools; I use small initial letters to refer more generally to this philosophical tendency.

13 Tranquillity: Sextus, *P* i. 12, 25-9. Epicurus: Diogenes Laertius x. 146.

14 Senses: Diogenes Laertius x. 146-7; Sextus, *AM* viii. 9; Diogenes Laertius x. 52. Descartes: *Meditation* i.

15 Epicurus on conflicting appearances: Taylor in Barnes [1980], ch. 5. Dreams etc.: Plato, *Theaetetus* 158b-e.

16 Lucretius, ii. 112-41, 308-32, 826-33.

17 Empirical equivalence: Diogenes Laertius x. 87, 91, 94.

18 Senses: 3 § viii, 7 § ii-iii, xv.

19 Soul: Lucretius iii. 417-829.

20 Compounds: Diogenes Laertius x. 69; Lucretius i. 670-1. See 3 § iv, 7 § v.

21 Gods: Plato, *Laws* 899d-900b. Design: Cicero, *De Natura Deorum* i. 43; Lucretius v. 195-234, 1161-1240.

22 Perceptions of gods: Sextus, *AM* ix. 43-6, Lucretius v. 1169-82. The gods' location: Lucretius v. 146-55, 75-8, Cicero, *De Divinatione* ii. 40.

23 Divine happiness: Diogenes Laertius x. 123, Lucretius iii. 1827, Homer, *Od.* 6. 42-6, Ar. *EN* 1178b8-23. Plato: 6 § xviii.

24 Determinism: see 3 § ix.

25 Aristotle: *EN* 1111a22-4. Fate: Diogenes Laertius x. 134.

26 Aristotle: *EN* 1110a14-18, 1113b3-21.

27 Swerve: Lucretius ii. 251-93; Furley [1967]; Long [1987], 106-12.

28 See 9 § v.

29 Pleasure: Diogenes Laertius x. 126; Cicero, *De Finibus* i. 30; Ar. *EN* 1172b9-25.

30 Sensual pleasure: Diogenes Laertius x. 142; 6 § xiv (Callicles).

31 Virtues: Diogenes Laertius x. 132, 148.

32 Justice: Diogenes Laertius x. 141, 150-1; 4 § vii, 6 § 12. Evolution of society: Lucretius v. 958-61, 988-1027. See 4 § vi, 7 § xiii.

33 See 7 § 10.

34 Death: Diogenes Laertius x. 124; cf. 125-6, Lucretius iii. 830-68. See Nagel [1979], ch. 1.

35 Virtues: Cicero, *De Finibus* ii. 69-71.

36 Some Epicureans try to meet the objection about friendship, by claiming that the wise person will find pleasure in the company of his friend, apart from any further instrumental benefits (Cicero, *De Finibus* i. 65-70). But it is hard to see how, on purely Epicurean grounds, such pleasure can be justified.

37 On Epicureans in politics see 9 § x.

Works Cited

Annas, J., and Barnes, J. [1986] *The Modes of Scepticism,* Cambridge.

Austin, M. M. [1981] *The Hellenistic World,* Cambridge.

Barnes, J. Burnyeat, M. F., and Schofield, M., eds. [1980] *Doubt and Dogmatism,* Oxford.

Barrett, C. K., ed. [1956] *The New Testament Background,* London.

Furley, D. J. [1967] *Two Studies in the Greek Atomists,* Princeton.

Jones, A. H. M. [1940] *The Greek City,* Oxford.

———. [1964] "The Hellenistic Age," *Past and Present* 27 (1964): 1-22.

Lloyd, G. E. R. [1973] *Greek Science after Aristotle,* London.

Long, A. A. [1974] *Hellenistic Philosophy,* London.

Long, A. A., and Sedley, D. N. [1987] *The Hellenistic Philosophers,* Cambridge.

Nagel, T. [1979] *Mortal Questions,* Cambridge.

Walbank, F. W. [1981] *The Hellenistic World,* London.

Julia Annas (essay date 1992)

SOURCE: Julia Annas, "Atomism and Agents," in *Hellenistic Philosophy of Mind,* University of California Press, 1992, pp. 123-56.

[*Below, Annas examines Epicurus's physical theories in order to determine the Epicurean idea of the relationship of the human subject to the physical world, particularly to atoms, the universe, and the body.*]

a) Physicalism and Reductivism

Epicurean and Stoic theories of the soul are often structurally very similar and sometimes also similar in detail. The two theories have very different metaphysical backing: the Stoics have a continuum theory of matter and hold that the universe is animate and runs by laws which reveal the workings of providence, while the Epicureans have an atomic theory of matter and reject all appeal to providence and any kind of teleology. They also have different ethical contexts: the Stoics think that rationality is what is crucially important in our ethical development, while Epicurus holds that our final end is pleasure, and that this is revealed to us directly by our feelings. However, the two theories share a common physicalist framework of thinking about the soul and in many ways have far more in common with each other than either does with a theory like Aristotle's. The chief differences are due to the fact that the Stoics are heavily influenced by contemporary medical and scientific theories, whereas Epicurus is less impressed by scientific results and more reliant on a combination of commonsense folk psychology and straightforward philosophical argument.[1]

"The soul is a body of fine parts, spread over the whole assemblage."[2] Epicurus has one brisk argument for the soul's physicality, which appeals to the principles of Epicurean physics: everything in the world must be explained in terms only of Epicurus' meager ontology of atoms and void.[3] This applies to the soul in just the same way that it applies to everything else. Thus, he says, we cannot conceive of anything existent that is not body, except the void. The void can neither act nor be acted on. But soul clearly does both. The soul therefore must be body. The crucial premise here is that only body (ultimately, atoms) can act or be acted on. Lucretius develops a different argument, from interaction: the soul moves the body, and what happens to the body affects the soul.[4] Hence the soul is a body. Lucretius relies on the more roundabout premise that interaction requires touch and that this requires body.

We have seen the Stoics use versions of these arguments;[5] they are part of shared Hellenistic philosophical currency. They make it clear that Epicurus is a physicalist, as defined in part 1. Study of the soul is part of *phusik* , enquiry into the natural world; Epicurean *phusike* recognizes only two kinds of basic item, atoms and void, so the soul must be accounted for, in some way, in terms of atoms and void.

Epicurus is sometimes thought to have abandoned physicalism (or, alternatively, to have made his version of physicalism untenable) because he modified Democritean atomism by allowing a random "swerve" among the atoms; the swerve is connected in our chief sources with our having freedom of action,[6] and it is often concluded that free human actions are, for Epicurus, due to events which breach regular Epicurean physical laws. . . .

The swerve introduces an indeterminate element into physics, but this is a thesis within physics,[7] not an abandonment of physicalism. It complicates the physical picture but is not a breach of it. It is not defined in terms of solving a problem of free agency; it is just a factor in the physical world, which operates in us, and also enables the production of worlds to get going.

It is often assumed that Epicurus was not only a physicalist but a reductivist. Possibly the tone of some of his writings may have given a handle to this: Epicurus is sometimes aggressively philistine, and we find Sextus asking the Epicureans how pleasure can exist in "the heap of atoms" they call the soul.[8] But it is clear that Epicurus is not a reductivist from a striking passage in book 25 of *On Nature,* fragments of which we possess.[9] Epicurus argues in this passage against the thesis that all events in the world, including our actions and thoughts, come about "of necessity." He allows that the truth about the physical world is given by atomic theory, which is (apart from the swerve, which is not mentioned in this text) determinist. So at the atomic level, events do happen "of necessity." But it is a mistake to conclude from this that, at the macro-level, my actions happen of necessity. It seems as though they must; for my action of arguing, say, *is* atoms moving in various ways which come about of necessity: so how can it not come about of necessity that I am arguing? Against Democritus Epicurus argues that this involves one in a blindness to oneself that lands one in a self-refuting position.[10]

He begins from the fact that we have practices of praise, blame, and the like, which make sense only on the assumption that we are agents capable of choice between perceived alternatives, and not just nodes in causal chains. He contrasts these practices with the way we treat wild animals, which we do not treat as agents but merely handle as best we can.[11] Epicurus then addresses the reductivist opponent who claims that these beliefs and practices are undermined by the truth of deterministic atomism, since all our actions are "merely" movements of atoms, so that even our very praising and blaming are "of necessity." Epicurus maintains that

> such an argument refutes itself [lit. turns itself upside down] and never can establish that everything is such as the things which are said to happen according to necessity. Rather, he combats a person on this very point as though it were because of himself that the person were being silly. And even if he goes on *ad infinitum* saying that the person is doing *that* according to necessity, always from arguments, he is failing to reason in that he ascribes to himself the cause of having reasoned correctly and to his opponent the cause of having reasoned incorrectly.[12] (Arrighetti [34.28]; Sedley 1983, 19; Long and Sedley 1987, 20 C [5]-[6])

Epicurus is using a standard ancient "overturning" argument.[13] It involves what we would call pragmatic self-refutation. There is no formal self-contradiction, but what the person says or puts forward is, it is claimed, undermined by her way of saying it or putting it forward. An example would be proving that there is no such thing as proof. If I prove to you that there is no such thing as proof, then what I prove (that there is no such thing as proof) is pragmatically refuted by the fact that I prove it. If I win, I lose. Epicurus claims here that reductivists like Democritus fall into a trap of this form and that they are "blind to themselves" because they fail to notice this point.

The reductivist holds that because all human actions are movements of atoms, human actions are "necessitated"; thus they are not really up to us, as we suppose them to be, and there is really no such thing as free human acting. If so, of course, there is really no such thing as arguing, criticizing, and so on; what we think to be such is "nothing but" atoms moving in the void

in ways that they have to move. However, the reductivist *argues* against Epicurus to this effect, *states* and *defends* his view, *criticizes* Epicurus for getting it wrong, and so on. And all this undermines his thesis, since it presupposes that the thesis is mistaken. Hence he is landed with a conflict between his thesis and what he is doing in stating and defending his thesis. He can of course retreat, admitting of what he says that it was necessitated. But the retreat can never be quite fast enough; in *admitting* this he is presupposing the falsity of his thesis. As Epicurus points out, at every stage of his retreat what he does is in conflict with the thesis he holds.

Epicurus does not here meet the more sophisticated determinist who claims that the necessitation appropriate to atomic motions is not in conflict with human agency because it is compatible with it. Epicurus is here concerned only with the opponent who tries to undermine our everyday concept or *prolēpsis* of agency. The opponent, he says, is trying to change our concept of what it is to act. But he has not succeeded in doing this unless he can evade the self-refutation argument, and otherwise he is in effect just changing a word by calling "necessitated" what we call free agency, and this is futile, since it makes no real difference.[14]

Epicurus' is the first in a long line of arguments to establish nonreductive physicalism by showing that reductivism (at least in a determinist version) cannot be consistently stated. So, there are facts about atoms and facts about human agency, and each set of facts will be real; it will be wrong to treat the latter as a mere appearance of the former.[15] We should note that this argument does *not* show that Epicurus is not a determinist. It shows that he thinks that, properly understood, determinism must be compatible with our commonsense understanding of ourselves and of the world. The argument is thus more properly antireductivist than antideterminist.[16]

Epicurus is thus justified in distinguishing between what happens by necessity or by chance from what depends on us (*par' hēmas*).[17] It is noteworthy that Epicurus does not claim that things are up to us (*eph' hēmin*) but that they depend on us (*par' hēmas*). He is defending the intuitive idea that we are agents, and seems not to want to defend a very strong and possibly unintuitive version of the idea.[18]

In particular, moral development is real; Lucretius insists that by reasoning the individual can overcome handicaps of inherited temperament.[19] In several unfortunately fragmentary and difficult parts of *On Nature* 25 Epicurus insists that our atomic constitution is to be distinguished from our "development" (*apogegennēmenon*), which depends on us. It depends on me, not just my atoms, how I develop and what kind of a person I become; even though it is a truth of physics that I *am* atoms. This is a defense of common sense: my physical makeup and the experience I have put some constraints on what I can become, but still how I develop depends on me. As Epicurus explains,

> from the first beginning we have seeds directing us, some toward some things, others toward others, others toward both—in every case seeds, which may be many or few, of actions, thoughts, and dispositions.[20] Thus it depends on us at first absolutely what becomes of what is already a development, whether of one or another kind, and the things which of necessity flow in from the environment through the pores depend on us when they come about at some time, and depend on our beliefs that come from ourselves. (Arrighetti [34.26]; Sedley 1983, 36-37; Long and Sedley 1987, 20 C [1])

Epicurus clearly has great reliance on our commonsense view of ourselves as free, developing agents.[21]

In this passage, which is unfortunately both highly technical and very fragmentary, Epicurus talks of, on the one hand, the self ("we") and the development and, on the other, of the atoms, the nature, and the constitution. Sometimes the development seems to depend on the self (as in the above passage), but the text as a whole supports the view that Epicurus is simply talking about an agent who develops. Sometimes the agent is identified with her development, sometimes the development is discussed separately, as being an aspect of the agent as a whole. On the other side, the constitution (sometimes the original constitution) is distinguished from the development. The development changes the original constitution and gets it to change or "grow" in some respect. The nature is simply the nature of the constitution; and likewise the atoms are the atoms of the constitution. There is no implication that the self or the development are nonatomic, but the atoms of the constitution can be contrasted with the atoms which impinge from the outside and help to produce the development.[22]

Epicurus thus sees us, commonsensically enough despite the jargon, as developing agents, indeed as agents who develop ourselves. Although humans are atomic compounds like any other, they differ from other kinds of atomic compounds in that their growth and functioning is not to be explained solely in terms of automatic response to stimuli from outside. How they develop depends to some extent, though not totally, on themselves, on what they do with the information they take in, how they decide to react selectively to it, and what kinds of character and dispositions they build up.[23] Thus Epicurus is concerned to do justice to folk psychology's belief that we are agents who move and develop ourselves. This point on its own does not

determine either the outline or the detail of any metaphysical conception of the self; it is a minimal basis compatible with a number of different kinds of theoretical explanation. As to how such self-development is possible we find in the fragments only the point that we have from the very start "seeds," potentials for developing one way rather than the other. This is taken for granted and not further defended.

The only hint we find in the remains of this book as to how we develop ourselves lies in the reference to the information we take in from the environment depending on the beliefs we have. It is because we have reason and can form beliefs that we develop as agents; this is clear already from the passage from Lucretius which tells us that by developing our reason we can order the rest of our nature and overcome the tendencies we are born with. Reason, however, takes many forms; we shall see in the next section that they are not all limited to humans.

There is one passage of book 25 which seems to suggest something stronger than the commonsense picture:

> Many [developments?][24] which have a nature which is capable of becoming productive of both this and that through themselves do not become productive, and it is not because of the same cause in the atoms and in themselves.[25] These in particular we combat and rebuke . . . in accordance with[26] their nature, which is disturbed from the beginning, as is true of all animals; for in their case the nature of the atoms has contributed nothing to some of their actions, and to the extent of their actions and dispositions, but the developments themselves contain all or most of the cause of some of these things. As a result of that nature some of the atoms' motions are moved in a disturbed way, not in every way through the atoms, but through what enters . . . from the environment into the natural . . . combatting and advising many people together, which is opposed to the necessary cause of the same kind. Thus when something develops which has some distinctness among the atoms[27] in a differential way which is not like that from a different distance,[28] it acquires a cause from itself, then transmits it at once to the primary natures and in some way makes all of it one.[29] (Arrighetti [34.21-22]; Sedley 1983, 36-38; Long and Sedley 1987, 20 B [1]-[6]; Laursen 1988, 17-18)

This passage has been made the basis for claims that Epicurus holds that we are not just agents in the commonsense understanding of self-developers, but selves in a way that transcends atomism altogether.[30] However, it is important to note that this passage concerns *disordered* people, in whom something, though it is not clear just what, has gone wrong. Furthermore, even in these people it is only some of their actions to which the atoms contribute nothing,[31] and even then we are told that the development accounts for all or most of the cause of what they do. This is, therefore, not an account of normal agency, and so cannot give us Epicurus' own view of human agency.

However, it is interesting to us even as an account of deviant agency, and it is a pity that it is so hard to see just what has gone wrong. Epicurus says that the condition of "all animals" is disturbed from the beginning; this may well include humans, and seems to embody the idea that we achieve the desirable Epicurean ethical end of untroubledness (*ataraxia*) as we mature, by imposing order on our initially disorderly nature. What is wrong with the agents here is that they are like immature, disorderly agents. However, this does not seem to be what they are themselves, since the passage suggests that they are perverse or deviant, rather than immature. Perhaps the nearest we can get to a general interpretation of what is going on is that two things are true of these agents. The way they are developing is at odds with their constitution. They are developing, or trying to develop, in ways that do not fit the way they have developed hitherto. Secondly, their constitution is, as a result, disorderly, like the initial state of immature agents.

However we interpret the details of this passage, the overall picture which emerges is that of an Epicurus who is impressed by the fact that humans are a self-moving kind of thing, with potential to develop in diverse ways, but who does not react by abandoning physicalism. We shall see further that he is quite ingenious in working out details of a thoroughly physicalist account of the soul. He is aware that there is a tension between reductive physicalism and our commonsense view of ourselves, which he wants to preserve, and he responds with an argument to show that reductivism cannot, in principle, be true. It is clear even by this point that Epicurus' account is answering to a number of constraints. His philosophy of mind must be physicalist, and in particular must be developed within his version of atomism. It is also, as we shall see, an empiricist account. But it also takes very seriously what we believe about ourselves, and where this conflicts with a possible way for his theory to develop, it is the theory he rejects and not our intuitive picture of ourselves as developing agents. We have to wait until later to find out what makes us *free* agents.

b) Soul in the World

The Stoic cosmos is animate, designed by providence, and permeated by reason. The Epicurean cosmos is none of these things, and this makes a big difference to the place in it of human beings.

The motions of atoms in the void give rise to compounds among which are animate, sensing, beings; but the atoms themselves are inanimate;[32] Epicurus rejects the panpsychist demand that life be present in the ul-

timate constituents of what has life. Hence there is no Epicurean world soul; living beings do not display in themselves the workings of principles of life also at work in the universe as a whole.

Further, Epicurus rejects providence and any teleology, both for the world as a whole and for its parts.[33] Since the world is not an ordered whole, humans have no particular place in it; there is no scale of beings. "The soul is a peculiar kind of thing, like nothing else."[34] For Epicurus there is also nothing like Stoic rationality which permeates the world and gives it (in many senses) significance. Rationality does not cut humans sharply off from animals as it does for the Stoics. Animals as well as humans act freely; at least Lucretius illustrates the existence of free impulse (*libera voluntas*) from the example of horses in a race.[35] Further, a passage in *On Nature* 25 distinguishes between wild and tame animals by the extent to which their reaction is straightforwardly caused by input from the environment, or depends on the animal itself.[36]

The Epicureans in fact have a position strikingly different from the Stoics' on "the reason of animals." Not only does Lucretius talk of horses having *libera voluntas,* he talks of horses and deer as having a mind.[37] However, Hermarchus, an early Epicurean, denies, in a discussion of justice and animals, that animals have *logos* or reasoning. That is, he says; why we can make no contracts with them.[38] Humans, as opposed to animals, have advanced in civilization because they can reason about what is in their interests, whereas animals have only "irrational memory."[39]

Are these mutually contradictory views on the part of different branches of the school? They seem rather to be a matter of differences of emphasis. We find a more nuanced view in a later head of the school, Polystratus.[40] Animals, he says, share broad general features with us but are importantly different. They take in, but do not understand as we do,[41] certain things: prudential concepts (healthy, expedient), ethical concepts (fine, base), religious concepts (sacred, profane), and signs (*sēmeia*). The last amounts to the claim that animals have no inferential reasoning; this explains, for Polystratus, why they cannot foresee problems, learn from the past, assess their own interests, or reflect on their lives as wholes.[42] So animals "do not share in reasoning, or not one like ours."[43] Yet Polystratus thinks it ridiculous to deny that we are in general ways like animals, as the Stoics do.

The obvious way to make all this consistent is to recognize that animals have some reasoning capacities, but not others; in particular, not the ones that distinguish humans, which we inevitably call the higher ones. This is a commonsense conclusion, but it has an important, though overlooked, consequence: for the Epicureans rationality is not a single kind of thing but a cluster of capacities, some of which animals share with us and some not. We shall see that Epicurus frequently falls into difficulties over the status of the rational part of the soul, and much of his philosophy of mind would have benefited from taking more to heart this consequence of denying a sharp cutoff between humans and other animals.[44]

Kuria doxa 32 encapsulates the Epicurean attitude to what divides us from animals: "As for those animals that cannot make contracts about not harming one another or being harmed—toward these there is no just or unjust; and similarly with those nations that cannot or will not make contracts about not harming or being harmed."[45] We do not owe duties of justice to animals; but this is merely because they do not have enough reasoning capacity to make and keep contracts—something true of some humans also. And we can see from book 5 of Lucretius how deeply ambivalent the Epicureans are about the "progress" of civilization and the ways in which we have used our reasoning to differentiate ourselves from animals.

c) The Nature and Structure of the Soul

"The soul consists of the smoothest and roundest atoms, greatly superior [sc. in these respects] to those of fire."[46] The soul animates the entire body without depending on bulk or brute force, merely because of the nature of its composition. "The soul provides nature with the reason for the [presence or absence of] life. For even though it does not possess the same number of atoms as the body, being placed in it with its rational and irrational elements, nevertheless it encompasses the whole body and, being bound by it, binds it in its turn, just as the shortest dash of acid juice curdles a vast quantity of milk."[47]

The soul is a combination of four kinds of soul atom. It is puzzling that Epicurus' own *Letter to Herodotus* 63 so understates the doctrine as to seriously misleading,[48] but we know from other sources that the soul is constituted of atoms of four kinds: firelike, airlike, *pneuma*-like, and nameless.[49] The claim that the first three kinds of atoms are *like* the atoms of fire, air, and so on presumably amounts to something like the following. The soul does not contain just the kind of fire that we find in fireplaces, but something which is like that in basic respects, but more refined (it does not burn the rest of the soul, for example). The idea we have of it comes from our idea of fire, indeed for Epicurus it has to, since he is an empiricist and holds that our concepts are built up from what we encounter in experience. Thus our concept of it is simply something fire*like,* since we have no direct access to it in experience; all we can do is simply extend the experiential conception that we do have.

The basis for this account of the soul's composition is just the commonsense observation that "a certain thin breath mixed with heat leaves the dying, and heat, further, brings air along with it."[50] It is notable here that *pneuma* has retained its commonsense meaning of "breath," in contrast to its dramatic theoretical development in Aristotle and the medical writers. So far is Epicurus from what was to become the scientific mainstream, in which *pneuma* is essentially warm, that his *pneuma* is characteristically cold.[51]

Lucretius develops a theory about differing contributions made by the first three elements.[52] Fierce lions have a preponderance of heat; timid stags illustrate the dominance of cold *pneuma,* and placid cows that of stable air. He goes on to apply the idea to explain differences of temperaments between individual humans; it is not clear whether this is his own contribution, or how it is to be extended from the idea of type differences.

The fourth, nameless element has a privileged position. It greatly exceeds the other elements in the fineness of its parts (*leptomereia*) and "thus is more sensitive to (*sumpathēs*) the entire assemblage."[53] According to Plutarch it is from this nameless element that there comes about "that by which the agent judges and remembers and loves and hates, and in general the intelligence and reasoning."[54] According to Aëtius the fourth element is the only one that can produce sensation.[55] So the fourth atom type seems to be responsible for sensation, thought, emotion, and memory.

Why is the fourth element nameless? Epicurus is hardly reluctant to coin new jargon elsewhere. Here he is constrained by his empiricism about concepts and language. We have some idea of what the firelike atoms in the soul are like from our experiences with fire, which have led us to produce the word "fire"; our concept of the ingredient in the soul works outward from this. But in the case of the fourth kind of atom there is nothing in our experience capable of giving us any, even partial, idea of what it is like. Not only do we never encounter it, we never even encounter anything that stands to it the way fire in fireplaces, stands to the firelike atoms in the soul. The nameless kind of atom is the only purely theoretical entity in Epicureanism. Even in the case of atoms and void we can conceive both by extension from things in our experience which are indivisible and empty.

Many have found the anomalous nature of the nameless atoms an embarrassment. Critics ancient and modern have claimed that here Epicurus is driven back upon a something he knows not what, and that this really amounts to an abandonment of physicalism; for the nameless kind of atom is physical, but, in appealing to something that has no experiential basis whatever, Epicurus is just providing a stand-in for everything that is hard to explain, given a physicalist position.[56] It is undeniable that Epicurus is weakening his empiricism here to a great extent; we have to rely on there being a theoretical entity which does a great deal of work in the theory but of which we have no idea at all from experience. But this need not be seen as objectionable; indeed it can be seen as merely realistic. Our idea of the soul goes far beyond what we can readily extrapolate from the natures of fire, air, and *pneuma*. Nor is there any reason to think that Epicurus is abandoning physicalism, thinking of the fourth kind of atom as in effect a magic addition which will bring to life something that physicalist principles cannot account for.[57]

The role of the fourth element emerges from Lucretius.[58] The motions of the atoms, he says, so interpenetrate that they cannot be separated, nor can their properties be divided off. The atoms (the kinds of atom, presumably) are like the many powers of a single body. A living creature is one thing, although it has many properties like smell, heat, and taste; similarly, the kinds of atom form "a single nature." We are reminded of the comparison of the Stoic unified soul with its different powers to an apple with its different properties. The fourth element is the power that makes the soul into a unity—without it, Lucretius says, the other three kinds of atom would not hold together and be enabled to function as they in fact do in an animate body.[59]

The fourth element is "hidden deepest" in the soul, as the soul is in the body; it is "the soul of the soul" and "runs things in the entire body." Clearly the fourth element is not spatially farthest inside, boxed in by the other three.[60] The soul, after all, is not boxed in by the body. Rather the soul is "hidden" in the sense that we do not encounter it in experience. We see clearly enough the effects of having a soul: it animates and directs the body. But the soul itself is not open to observation. Similarly, the fourth element is what "animates" the soul. Although we cannot observe the soul, we can make inferences as to its nature, and in particular infer the existence of a kind of atom which gets the soul to function as a whole, and which is distinct from the other soul elements whose nature we can partially describe from experience.

Soul and body, as Lucretius says,[61] are mutually dependent: soul is like the scent in a perfume which you cannot remove without destroying the substance. And the fourth element stands to the soul as the soul stands to the body; it and the other soul elements are mutually dependent in that without them it would have nothing to "animate," and without it they would not hold together as a single kind of thing. How does the fourth element do this? It cannot be by operating, in a seemingly magical fashion, on its own. Rather, it must, by its particularly fine nature, enable the other elements to come together in a new sort of compound. It makes the soul a unity in the straightforward sense that its nature forms the necessary basis for the other atom kinds to cohere in a compound that has the properties of a soul. The introduction of the fourth element marks an insistence that there is a *physical* difference between souls and other kinds of body.

In one way this fits well into Epicurean theory: the soul's operations are supposed to involve particularly fine, invisible processes, and the fourth element serves to explain how the soul, though physical, can have a peculiarly fine structure enabling these to occur. But in other ways the move seems undermotivated. Epicurean physics and cosmology operate with atoms and void: atomic motions and the resulting compounds they give rise to are all we have to explain the varied phenomenal world. Faced by a complex and self-reproducing kind of thing like a tree, an Epicurean has to admit that the way it grows and reproduces is accounted for by its pattern of functional organization, which is stable enough to establish trees as things with persisting natures. Given an ontology as meager as that of atoms and void, and a rejection of teleology, patterns of functional organization are required to explain a world where things fall into species with stable behavior. But why will the approach deemed adequate to explain the species-specific behavior of trees not suffice to explain the behavior of people? To reverse the point, if we need a special kind of nameless atom to explain what souls are, why do we not need another kind of atom to explain what trees are?

It may be that Epicurus simply thought that animals and humans are so different in their complexity from things like trees that the same type of explanation would leave something out in their case. More likely, he may have thought that appealing merely to patterns of functional organization in the case of humans to explain what is characteristic of them was problematic from the point of view of atomist methodology. It is all right to say that a tree is the kind of thing it is because its atoms are organized in a particular stably functioning way. But to say this of humans might sound dangerously close to Aristotle, and would verge on recognizing a metaphysical principle like form as being as basic for explanation as matter. If it really provides an explanation to say that I perceive and act because there are stable perceptive, reactive, and so on patterns of functioning which my soul enables my body to carry out, these patterns seem to have a large explanatory role. And we can see why Epicurus would find this problematic; large differences of explanatory role ought, in a physicalist system, to have a physical basis. Thus the nameless atom type, far from signaling a retreat from physicalism, reveals confidence in the adequacy of physicalism as a theory of the soul. There is a physical difference between souls and other kinds of thing; so we do not need anything like Aristotelian forms to explain the way the soul functions.

Is this move successful? Aristotle argues that ignoring the role of form leaves us unable to explain functioning. Is the postulation of a physical difference, a new kind of ingredient, adequate to meet this kind of challenge? We might feel unhappy when we recall that the ingredient is nameless, since theory postulates something of which experience gives us no idea. A successful challenge to Aristotle would rely on achieved science and point to acknowledge complexity of structure to do the explanatory work assigned to form. But not only is Epicurus not in a position to appeal to such science, he is in general not very interested in low-level, working science. He accepts atomism as the best available scientific theory and tends to assume that what is needed can be worked out within atomism, without waiting for actual research. Thus in his appeal to nameless atoms there is a considerable element of faith—the kind of faith in science which philosophers often have who do not do any actual science.

Epicurus' account of the soul tries to interpret common sense in terms of atomic theory. Unlike the Stoics, he does not try to push the interpretation of soul in the direction of the mental. He accounts for much of what we call the mental by the rational soul, but the rational soul is merely a part of the whole soul, and that is clearly taken to be the physical basis of all the functionings of a living thing. We can see from a fragment of Diogenes of Oenonda how closely Epicurus stays to common sense:

> Often when the body has been brought to surrender by a long illness, and reduced to such thinness and wasting that the dry skin is almost adhering to the bones whilst the nature of the inward parts seems empty and bloodless, nevertheless the soul stands its ground, and does not permit the creature to die. And this is not the only indication of supremacy: the severing of hands, and often the removal of whole arms or feet by fire and steel cannot undo the bonds of life. So great is the sway of life held by that part of us which is soul. (Frag. 37, cols. 2-3)[62]

Soul is what makes us alive, and so functioning. This is a commonplace, but Epicureanism stresses the importance of rightly understanding the commonplace.

d) Parts of the Soul

The soul is not uniform; "the rational part" (*to logikon*) is located in the chest, while the rest, "the irrational part," is diffused through the whole body. This part of the theory, surprisingly absent from the ***Letter to Herodotus,*** is well attested in a scholium on the letter and, in the same words, in Diogenes of Oenoanda.[63] Lucretius makes much of it; he calls the parts *animus* and *anima,* elegant Latin which unfortunately loses the point that the *animus* is the rational part and the *anima* the irrational one.

The rational part is responsible not only for reasoning and cognition but for emotions such as "fears and joys." Lucretius says that in it are located both the understanding (*consilium*) and the governing (*regimen*) of life.[64] In fact the irrational soul tends to be thought of as responsible solely for perception, in which role it has some independence: the eyes themselves see, rather than being windows through which the rational soul sees.[65]

There is a clear contrast with the Stoics, who put perception and impulse together as characterizing the whole soul, and who take thinking to be involved in all the soul's activities. In fact, while the Epicurean rational soul is bound to remind us in some ways of the Stoic *hēgemonikon*—it centralizes all the soul's activities, for example—there are striking differences. For the Epicureans sensation is registered in the sensing organ; for the Stoics the sensation is registered in the *hēgemonikon*. Thus the Epicurean rational soul is not involved in all events in the soul in the way that is true of the *hēgemonikon*. And while the Stoics come to use "the *hēgemonikon*" to refer to the soul as a whole, this is not the case with the Epicurean rational soul. In fact Lucretius says explicitly that when he refers to the soul as a whole he will use *anima,* the word for the irrational soul.[66] This is surprising, and in many ways unfortunate. One wonders whether he would have done so as readily had he been using words which reflected the fact that the parts are introduced by Epicurus in ways that make clear their relation to rationality.

The rational soul is located in the chest, because this is the region of emotions.[67] This is reminiscent of Chrysippus' insistence that the *hēgemonikon* is in the chest and not the head. Two interesting fragments of Demetrius Lacon show that later Epicureans had to contend, much as Chrysippus did, with the discovery of the function of the brain and the nervous system[68] Demetrius mentions Epicurus' view that the location of the soul's reasoning part allows of enquiry that is both practical (*pragmatikē*) and rational (*kata logon*). There is a claim that it is obvious that movement and emotion "drag" toward the chest. "Many doctors" are mentioned, who use some inductive reasoning (*sēmeiōsis*) to establish that reasoning is in the head. We seem to have a fragment of a confrontation very similar to the Stoic one.[69] Scientific research points to the role of the brain; but the philosophers refuse to abandon folk psychology.

However, the Epicureans' response differs in two ways. Firstly, they are in general not much impressed by the lower levels of science. Secondly, they do not have Chrysippus' reluctance to divide the soul; for the Epicurean rational soul is not the rational aspect of the whole soul. The whole soul is not rational; the rational soul is a part of the whole, as much a part as is a hand or an eye.[70] It organizes and so dominates the soul's activities, so that it can function as a relatively independent part, while the irrational soul depends on it.[71] It is located in a specific part of the body, and damage there is more destructive to life than damage to other parts.[72]

Two questions suggest themselves. Is the rational soul itself a unity? We have already seen that the conclusion suggested by Epicurean views of humans and animals is that it is more like a cluster of capacities.[73] Rationality is shown in a variety of ways and comes in different kinds.[74] It cannot be said, however, that the Epicureans recognize this point explicitly, as one might expect them to do.

Secondly, how does the division of the soul affect the thesis that it is the fourth, nameless kind of element that makes it function as a unity? This thesis has to be rendered consistent with the partially independent workings of the *animus* and *anima,* and the obvious solution is that the effects of having the fourth element must be differentiated. Since it is associated with the soul's exceptionally fine structure, it is tempting to take it as located primarily in the *animus;* its most prominent activity is thinking, the activity most likely to require fine, rapid processes.

If the fourth element were located only in the *animus,* however, it would be the working of the *animus* that accounted for the unity of the whole soul. This Stoic kind of picture is arguably what Epicurus needs, and what he implicitly assumes much of the time. But it sorts ill with the relative independence of the *anima,* and the state of our sources makes the safest conclusion the disappointing one that Epicurus had not thought the point through. In fact Epicurus faces a difficulty over the unity of the soul. The whole soul is a functional unity; but the only part competent to unify it is not involved in all the soul's activities.

Does this matter? Epicurus is concerned to do justice to common sense; does that take for granted that our whole soul, rational and irrational, is strongly unified? One might think that common sense is actually inclined to deny the unity of the soul; the Stoic theory of the emotions, for example, is commonly taken to be highly counterintuitive, and more generally the Stoics might be taken to flout common sense in holding that information reaching the eyes and damage reaching the foot are registered in the *hēgemonikon* rather than in the eyes or in the foot. So perhaps in making *animus* and *anima* partially independent of each other Epicurus is deliberately answering to folk psychology.[75] This may well be true; certainly the Epicurean soul is much more weakly unified than the Stoic soul, and this may be due to a conscious desire to conform with common sense. However, we also find Epicurean claims that the soul is a unity, rather than two linked systems: Lucretius claims, for example, that rational and irrational soul together form "a single nature," and cannot be separated without mutual destruction.[76] The very fact that Lucretius is content to use *anima* to cover the whole soul suggests that he is not taking really seriously the partial independence of the irrational soul. And in his account of the soul-body relation, and in his arguments about death and its importance, Epicurus seems to be presupposing a unified soul and failing to take due account of the differences between its parts and the ways they function.

e) The Soul-Body Relation

There is a tension in Epicureanism over the soul-body relation. On the one hand the body is emphatically said to be the container or vessel of the soul. Epicurus uses such language repeatedly; Lucretius even bases his first argument for the soul's mortality on the comparison of the body with a vessel.[77] It is the body that holds together the soul and thus enables unified animate functioning—a reversal of the Aristotelian and Stoic view that what makes the agent alive and functioning is the soul's holding the body together.

Such language is, however, surprisingly inappropriate for the soul-body relation as Epicureanism actually develops that idea. Lucretius adds that the soul is the body's "guardian and cause of preservation; for they cling together like common roots and it is seen that they cannot be sundered without destruction." The soul is "in" the body like scent in perfume; it cannot be removed without destroying the substance. "So interwoven are their elements between them from their first beginning; they are endowed with a mutual life."[78] Diogenes of Oenoanda insists that the soul, which is "bound" by the body, "binds" it in turn.[79] Soul and body are two bodies which, in a living thing, are mutually dependent.

Epicurus presses the point for sentience: strictly speaking, it does not belong to the soul alone but is a joint product of soul and body. Lucretius puts this point more elegantly,[80] but here Epicurus' famously rugged Greek reveals an interesting conceptual struggle:

> We should keep in mind that soul has the greatest share in causing (*aitia*) sensation (*aisthēsis*). However, it would not have had this if it had not been enclosed in a way by the rest of the assemblage. The rest of the assemblage, which provides it with this causality, itself has, derived from the soul, a share in just such a property—though not in everything the soul possesses. Hence when the soul departs it lacks sensation. For it did not itself possess this power in itself; something else connate with it provided it, and this, through the power brought about in connection with it depending on movement,

at once achieved for itself a property of sentience and supplied it to the other also, depending on juxtaposition and mutual sensitivity, as I said. Therefore while the soul is indwelling it never lacks sensation through the removal of any other part—whatever of it perishes along with the breaking up of the enclosure, in whole or in part, if it remains, it will have sensation. The rest of the assemblage, whether it survives in whole or in part, will not have sensation when it is gone—that is, whatever quantity of atoms is needed to hold together to constitute the soul's nature. Further, when the whole assemblage is broken up the soul is scattered and no longer has the same powers, or moves; so it does not possess sensation either, for we cannot think of it as sentient unless in this composite and using these movements, when the enclosing and surrounding parts are not such as these in which [the soul] now is and has these movements. (***Ep. Herod.*** 64-66)

The point which Epicurus has such trouble getting across is not that the soul requires the body for sensation, nor that sensation is the product of soul and body interacting, nor even that this is necessarily so. All these claims are quite compatible with dualism. Rather, Epicurean soul and body need each other to exist and to function *as soul and as body*. Without the body, the soul no longer exists or functions as soul, but is just scattered atoms; without the soul, the body no longer exists or functions as a body, but is a mere corpse. Sentience brings this out: it is the product of the mutually dependent soul and body, for the soul needs the body to exist as the soul of a sentient agent, and the body needs the soul to exist as the body of a sentient agent.

Why does Epicurus have such a struggle to express this? The problems are due largely to his clinging to the inappropriate conception of body and soul as vessel and contents.[81] Epicurus often states a thesis in unnecessarily and sometimes misleadingly polemical and crude form; when we examine the thesis we find the crude formulations fail to do it justice. We can only put this down to an imperfect fit between Epicurus' philosophical activity and his pedagogical approach. The latter sometimes requires shock tactics to shake people out of their set views and prejudices. If and when they get involved in studying Epicurean philosophy, they may find that the initially controversial appearance was misleading; but by that time it will probably no longer matter, at least to the convinced Epicurean. Sometimes, however, Epicurus' cruder statements turn out to make trouble for his more sophisticated thoughts.[82]

What brings out the closeness of the soul-body relation is sentience, which characterizes the irrational soul. We find elsewhere, however, that the Epicureans tend to *contrast* soul and body, and that when they do they have a different contrast in mind, namely, that between the body plus the irrational soul on the one hand and the rational soul on the other. "The pains of the soul," for example, "are worse than those of the body; for the flesh suffers only for the present moment, but the soul for past, present, and future. Similarly, the pleasures of the soul are greater."[83] Here "the body" clearly refers to the sentient body, closely linked to the irrational soul, and "the soul" clearly refers to the rational soul.

Further, many themes in Epicurean ethics stress not only this distinction, but the superiority of the soul, which by drawing on past, present, and future experiences can more than counterbalance what happens to the body. The star example here is Epicurus' dying letter to his friends, where he says that his present agonizing pains are more than counterbalanced by the joy in his soul from memories of philosophical activity.[84] Epicureans from Polystratus to Lucretius tirelessly urge on us that only the rational activity of philosophy will make us happy, for we need the exercise of the rational soul in order to organize our lives and make sense of the products of the irrational soul.

There is potentially a tension here. For Epicurus it is crucial that I think of my soul as something dependent for its existence and functioning on the existence and functioning of my body. He has shown this for the irrational soul, the source of sentience. But, given the stress on the importance of our identifying with the rational soul, and the contrast between the rational soul on the one hand and the body with the irrational soul on the other, the question is bound to arise whether Epicurus has adequately shown that the soul as a whole is indissolubly linked with the body. It could be objected, of course, that all he needs to show is that the sentient, irrational soul is indissolubly linked to the body, and the rational soul in turn indissolubly linked to the irrational soul; if the soul's unity is weak anyway, we would not expect an argument to show directly that the rational soul was linked indissolubly to the workings of the body. But, while that is arguably what Epicurus needs, we do not find explicitly either any acknowledgment that this is what is to be shown or any arguments to show it.

f) Survival

A famous and fundamental Epicurean teaching is that "death is nothing to us; for what is broken up has no sensation, and what has no sensation is nothing to us."[85] At greater length:

> Get used to the idea that death is nothing to us, since every good and evil lies in sensation, and death is the deprivation of sensation. . . . So death, the most fearful of all evils, is nothing to us, since when we are, death is not present, and when death is present, then we are not. It is therefore nothing to the living, nor to the dead; for the former it is not, and the latter are no longer. (Epicurus ***Ep. Men.*** 124-25)

Lucretius puts this point forcefully: what happens after I am dead will be of no concern to me, since there will be no me, just as the Punic Wars were of no concern to me when they happened, since there was then no me to be concerned. "And even if the nature of the rational soul and the power of the irrational soul go on having sensation after being torn from our body, still it is nothing to us, who are made into one united compound by the mating and marriage of body and soul."[86] It is possible, he adds, that in the past my soul and body atoms came together in just the way they do now; but any such union was not *me*. *I* could not be around before the conception which brought me into being as an ensouled body, and in the same way *I* cannot be around after the death that breaks up the mutually dependent functioning of soul and body. So what happens after my death is like what happened before my birth—nothing to me.

The argument has raised controversy, ancient and modern. The important point here is the need for the premise that all good and evil lie in sensation. For sensation is, of course, characteristic of the irrational soul; and we have seen that in sentience the body and irrational soul are indeed mutually dependent. But the claim that for us *all* good and evil lie in sentience seems to neglect the role of the rational soul. This comes out in at least two ways. It is because of the activity of the rational soul that we are able to identify our good with projects whose content goes beyond our own personal pleasures, and which may be fulfilled only after our death. Epicurus himself stresses the value of friendship, and concern for friends and their activities for their own sake. But this will involve an agent in perfectly rational concern for projects and activities whose fruition does not depend on her being alive. It is hard to see how death is nothing to such a person just because she knows she will not be aware of these projects: her concern for the projects did not depend on her being aware of them.

Secondly, because the rational soul can, as Epicurus puts it, compare past, present, and future, it is what gives an agent a sense of himself as an agent continuing through time, a being with a whole life. And this means that though death is nothing to me when it arrives, since it removes the agent in question, it is not necessarily irrational to worry about its happening in the future. Both Epicurus and Lucretius deny this: since death will not concern me when it comes, it is irrational for me to worry about it now.[87] But why are they entitled to this? That death is not an evil when it comes does not imply that it is not an evil in someone's life as a whole (by coming sooner rather than later, for example).

It might be urged that these objections come from unfairly pressing Epicurus' language of good and evil lying in *sensation*. Surely he did not mean to limit sensation in this connection to the activity of the irra-

tional soul. Is he not more fairly understood as claiming that nothing is a good or evil for an agent unless that agent can *experience* it—where "experience" is taken to refer to the activity of the whole soul, rational and irrational? It may be that something like this is what Epicurus did mean. But however generously we interpret "sensation" here, we shall not get out of the problem. Death is not an evil at the time it occurs, but this does not show that it is not an evil in one's life as a whole. But the rational soul is what gives the Epicurean a notion of her life as a whole. Nor does it show that death is not an evil in frustrating concerns that go beyond one's life and do not depend on one's experiencing the results. But the rational soul is what gives the Epicurean her concern for projects and activities that go beyond her life and matter whether she experiences the results or not—for example, the concerns and activities of friends.

Epicurus has an answer to these objections. They all involve in some way the claim that death, while it may not be an evil when it occurs, is nonetheless an evil by depriving us of goods which we would otherwise have; for thanks to our rational soul, we have a conception of our lives as wholes, and of projects that go beyond the reach of our own sentience; yet it is just this which enables us to commit ourselves to there being goods which, so it seems, death can deprive us of. Epicurus can say that only a non-Epicurean will be concerned by this, because she has a faulty conception of what these goods are. An Epicurean will realize that our highest good is pleasure and that all the goods that we can reasonably recognize in our lives are means to, or ways of, achieving this pleasure. We even seek friendship, and goals that extend beyond our own lives, for the sake of pleasure. Epicurus' own theory of what this pleasure, rightly conceived, actually is, is complicated, and the evidence difficult, but some things are clear. It is not to be identified with good feeling: it is a condition of "untroubledness" or *ataraxia,* which one achieves by following only natural desires and avoiding courses of action which will predictably lead to worry and trouble.

An important aspect of this is that the Epicurean will have achieved equanimity about goods that can be lost; for what she is after, in seeking *ataraxia,* is not the external results of action, but the inner result, the pleasure that lies in having the right attitude toward things that make other people upset. The pleasure that is our goal of life is radically internalized. One remarkable result of this is the thesis that pleasure is not increased by duration: once you have achieved Epicurean happiness, you have all that you need for happiness, and further time spent doing actions can merely vary what you have, not add to it.[88] Hence death does not deprive the good Epicurean of goods after all.[89]

The limitation of this response is clear: it works only for the committed Epicurean, who already accepts Epicurean ethics in full. It will not convince the non-Epicurean, who has a different idea of what it is rational to consider good. And it seems a weakness that a thesis about the soul should depend so directly on a very controversial ethical thesis. Unless one is an Epicurean on other grounds, therefore, the death arguments contain a gap, one that makes more obvious Epicurus' lack of an explicit discussion of the nature of the soul's unity, and the relations of the rational and irrational parts of the soul.

Epicurus' argument does not depend on the premise that my soul is mortal; as Lucretius makes clear, it would hold even if my soul did survive the breakup of its union with the body—and even if it were immortal, since death is nothing to me even if there will be a qualitatively identical *Doppelgänger* constituted of the very same atoms that constitute me. In principle, the Epicurean soul could be immortal without endangering the survival arguments.

It is therefore surprising that Lucretius prefaces his great declaration that death is nothing to us with nearly thirty arguments to prove that the soul is mortal.[90] Lucretius may be confused.[91] But possibly these arguments are meant to play an important subsidiary role; for the belief that my soul is immortal, while not as crucial as the belief that death is a bad thing for me, does play an important role in the various beliefs that make up fear of death and a negative attitude toward dying. Lucretius' flood of arguments is best understood as a sustained attempt to remove mistakes and to enable us to have a correct *prolēpsis* or conception of the soul. Their unsophisticated nature is deliberate—Lucretius hammers home simple and undeniable facts, such as that disease affects us psychologically as well as physiologically, and brings them into direct conflict with the notion of the soul as immortal. In Epicureanism it is important that we start from a right conception of what we are investigating;[92] in the case of the soul this involves the removal of confusions, and an effective way to do this is to appeal repeatedly to our basic intuitions. For Epicurus our awareness of something clear and concrete in our lives is not likely to be corrupted by bad theory. Diogenes of Oenoanda ridicules belief in survival after death in the same down-to-earth and unsophisticated way.[93]

For Epicurus both the belief that my soul is immortal and the belief that death is a bad thing for me are not just false but unhealthy, pathological. As long as we hold them, we will not be happy, for they deeply corrupt our conception of what we are and how we should live. We will be tempted, for example, to locate the significance of our lives in something supposedly waiting for us after death.[94] Lucretius devotes passionate rhetoric to showing us that this is perverse; the desire to survive death is based on failure to face reality. Those who regret dying are merely rebuked for clinging to immature fantasies.[95]

Notes

[1] Epicurus is clearly influenced in his physics by Aristotle's criticisms of atomism, and we know from a papyrus fragment that he read the *Physics* and *Analytics* (Philodemus *Pap. Herc.* 1005; Arrighetti 1973, 473). But claims that his philosophy of mind and particularly action are heavily influenced by Aristotle seem to me exaggerated (see Diano 1974a; Furley 1967; Englert 1988).

[2] *Ep. Herod.* 63.

[3] For his argument for the soul's physicality see *Ep. Herod.* 67. For some texts on the basic principles of Epicurean physics, see Long and Sedley (1987, 4-13). Texts on the soul can be found on pp. 14 and 15. Some passages discussed in this section, on free agency, are on p. 20.

[4] 3.161-76.

[5] In part 2, chapter 2, section a.

[6] Diogenes of Oenoanda frag. 32; Lucr. 2. 256-60. . . .

[7] And is so introduced by Lucretius (2. 216-93).

[8] *Pyr.* 3. 187.

[9] That this is the number of this book has been argued by Laursen (1987). See also Diano (1946); Sedley (1974, 1983, 1989). The text can be found in Arrighetti [34]; there are sections with translation in Sedley (1983); in Long and Sedley (1987, 2:20 B and C; 1:20 j); and in Laursen (1988). I have had the benefit of seeing Laursen's new readings for much of this book; I am very grateful. A new edition by Laursen of the entire text (which exists in fragments from three papyri) is forthcoming.

[10] Democritus is not named explicitly, but there are Epicurean precedents for seeing him referred to here as "the great man"; see Sedley (1983). For Epicurus' argument see Arrighetti [34.30]; Sedley (1983, 20, 29-30 with n. 28); Long and Sedley (1987, 20 C [13]). This passage has been extensively discussed; see Laks (1981); Gigante (1981, 56-62).

[11] Arrighetti [34.30]; Sedley (1983, 24 n. 18); Long and Sedley (1987, 20 j); Laursen (1988, 17). In contrast to admonition (*nouthetikos . . . tropos*), we exonerate wild animals instead of admonishing them or trying to reform them, or indeed regarding ourselves as retaliating against them. We treat them not as agents

whose developments are up to them, but "conflate their developments (*apogegennēmena*) and their makeup (*sustasis*) alike into a single thing." Elsewhere in the book Epicurus denies that we do this in the case of responsible agents.

[12] *Cf. Vatican Sentence* (hereafter *VS*) 40: "The person who says that everything comes about according to necessity cannot criticize the person who denies it—for he says that this too comes about according to necessity."

[13] For this kind of argument see Burnyeat (1976).

[14] Arrighetti [34.(28)19-(30)7]; Long and Sedley (1987, 20 C [8][12]).

[15] There is also a specifically Epicurean argument; see Arrighetti [34.28-30]; Sedley (1983, 20; cf. 27-28); Long and Sedley (1987, 20 C [8]). If the reductivist claims that talk of "necessity" does not conflict with, but rather has proper application to, what we do "through ourselves," by our own agency, then he is merely changing the word; our "conception" (*prolēpsis*) of our own agency precisely contrasts with being necessitated. This argument also has modern analogues.

[16] As Sedley (1983, 1989) recognizes, though he conflates reductivism with eliminativism and takes the argument to be stronger than it is, claiming that it shows that Epicurus was not only not a determinist but not a physicalist either. Given our total evidence about Epicurus, it is impossible that a breach in his physicalism should have gone unnoticed in the ancient world (see the end of this section), and the argument does not even show that Epicurus is not a determinist; it shows only that if he is (as he seems to be) he must be a compatibilist.

[17] As he does at *Ep. Men.* 133.

[18] Epicurus does not use *epi* with the dative with the meaning "up to the person," an idiom common among other philosophers. He prefers *para,* which has the force of "depending"; there is a parallel in the fourth sceptical Mode (see Annas and Barnes 1985, chap. 7).

[19] 3. 307-22.

[20] The Greek is syntactically ambiguous, and Sedley translates with actions, thoughts, and so on being what the seeds direct us toward, not what they are seeds of.

[21] On the argument of these difficult texts see Sedley (1983, 1989); Laursen (1988); Annas (1991 and forthcoming).

[22] Sedley (1983, 1989) claims that the self is distinct from *all* atoms, and that Epicurus is thus not a physi-

calist (see above n. 16). For arguments against this as a reading of this text see Annas (forthcoming).

[23] The last clause goes beyond anything explicitly in the papyrus, but the opening and concluding fragments make it fairly clear that the book was concerned with ethically right development. . . .

[24] Long and Sedley (1987) take the subject here to be *zōia,* that is, the agents or selves themselves. Laursen (1988) argues that the subjects must be the developments themselves.

[25] The Greek is syntactically ambiguous; Long and Sedley take "through themselves" with "do not become" rather than with "becoming productive."

[26] There is a participle here, but the verb is uncertain. Long and Sedley read "hating them" (*misountes*).

[27] Long and Sedley (1987) read "distinctness *from* the atoms." See Sedley (1983). For the present reading see Laursen (1988, 12-13).

[28] See Sedley (1989, n. 45); on "differential" see Laursen (1988, 13-14).

[29] See Laursen (1988, 14-15) for difficulties in identifying the subject here. Long and Sedley (1987) translate "he," importing a hitherto unmarked subject.

[30] See Sedley (1983, 1989) and the commentary on Long and Sedley (1987, 20 B, C, and j).

[31] The atoms of the constitution, that is. . . .

[32] As Lucretius argues at length (2. 865-990).

[33] Lucr. 4. 823-57.

[34] Philodemus *On Signs* 25. 3-4.

[35] 2. 263-71. Huby (1969) finds this problematic and contrasts the *On Nature* passage about wild and tame animals. But the problem is greatly lessened once we realize that *libera voluntas* is not "free will" but the capacity for free action. . . .

[36] Arrighetti [34.25]; Sedley (1983, 24 n. 18); Long and Sedley (1987, 20 j); Laursen (1988, 17).

[37] Horses: 2. 265, 268 (*mens*), 270 (*animus*). Deer have a *mens* at 3. 299.

[38] Frag. 34 Longo Auricchio (= Porph. *Abst.* 1. 7-12, 26, 4) 12. 5-6.

[39] Hence the rather bleak conclusion that the rise of human society is at the expense of animals, who are

"expelled" from it, and to whom we owe no duties of justice.

[40] In the opening columns (1-8) of his *On Irrational Contempt for Popular Opinions*.

[41] *Sunoran:* they cannot "see them together." It is tempting, though speculative, to connect this with passages in *On Nature,* 25 that talk of thinking of oneself, and seem to be discussing the idea of holding together different experiences as experiences of the same self: Arrighetti [34.14-16].

[42] Polystratus seems to be denying animals some kind of memory; possibly he would allow, with Hermarchus, that they have "irrational" memory.

[43] Polystr. 7. 6-8.

[44] Epicureans are often willing to see specifically human capacities as more developed forms of what we can see in other animals. They hold this for human language (Lucr. 5. 1056-90), sexual desire (4. 1192-1207), and dreams (4. 986-1010).

[45] We find the content of this and associated *Doxai* expanded by Hermarchus, Epicurus' successor, in the work paraphrased by Porphyry in *De abstinentia* 1. 7-12. Cf. Clay (1983).

[46] Schol. in *Ep. Herod.* 66 (= Usener 311); cf. Lucr. 3. 177-230.

[47] Diogenes of Oenoanda frag. 37, col. 1; trans. Chilton, with slight alterations.

[48] Kerferd (1971) ingeniously avoids the problem by denying that the relevant sentence of Epicurus refers to the composition of the soul at all.

[49] See Plut. *Adv. Col.* 1118d-e; Aët. 4. 3, 11, p. 388 Diels (hereafter D) (= Usener 315); Lucr. 3. 231-322. Sharples (1980) argues that Lucretius is talking about ordinary fire, air, and wind, not atoms that are fire*like* and so on. But our other sources give the more cautious view. Plutarch has *ek tinos thermou kai pneumatikou;* Aëtius has *ek poiou purōdous, ek poiou aērōdous, ek poiou pneumatikou.*

[50] Lucr. 3. 232-33.

[51] Lucretius translates it as *aura,* "breeze," or *ventus,* "wind." In Diogenes of Oenoanda new frag. 82 *pneuma* is ordinary wind, which is "cold and high" when there is hail.

[52] Lucr. 3. 288-322.

[53] Epicurus *Ep. Herod.* 63.

[54] *Adv. Col.* 1118e.

[55] Aët. 4. 3, 11, p. 388D (= Usener 315); cf. Lucr. 3. 237-42.

[56] Cf. Bailey (1928, 392), who sees a "thin disguise for the abandonment of the materialist position."

[57] This rules out theories that treat the fourth element alone as responsible for the soul's activity or that of its rational part (for a survey of theories on these lines, see Kerferd 1971, 84-87). One persistent version of this point is that the fourth nature is a transformation of Aristotle's "fifth element"; there is no reason to think this, and it is equally misguided to think of either as "wholly spiritual and non-material" (Bailey 1928, 392).

[58] 3. 258-87.

[59] 3. 285-87.

[60] As Diano (1974a) sees.

[61] 3. 232-32.

[62] Trans. Chilton; cf. new frags. 20, 94.

[63] School. in *Ep. Herod.* 66 (= Usener 311); Diogenes of Oenoanda frag. 37, col. 1.

[64] Schol. in *Ep. Herod.* 66 (= Usener 311); Lucr. 3. 95, 140-42.

[65] Lucr. 3. 359-69. Cicero refers to the "window" theory at *Tusc.* 1. 46.

[66] 3. 421-24.

[67] Schol. in *Ep. Herod.* 66 (= Usener 311); Lucr. 3. 140-42.

[68] Pap. 1012, cols. 29-30, pp. 38-39 de Falco (= Usener 313). See Croenert (1906, 117). De Falco thinks that some followers of Herophilus and Erasistratus may be meant, such as Demetrius of Apamea. Croenert identifies the doctors only as Empiricists.

[69] See part 2, chapter 2, section f.

[70] Diogenes of Oenoanda frag. 37, col. 1; Lucr. 3. 94-97.

[71] Lucr. 3. 147-60.

[72] Lucr. 3. 396-416.

[73] See section b of this chapter.

[74] Compare the distinction between wild and tame animals (in section a of this chapter).

[75] On this issue I am indebted to comments by Rob Cummins.

[76] 3. 136-37.

[77] Epicurus *Ep. Herod.* 63-66 contains three uses of forms of *to stegazon* for the body, and one of *ta periechonta*. Cf. 65: "When the whole assemblage is broken up the soul scatters." Lucr. 3. 425-44 is the passage in question; cf. 555. Cf. also Usener 337, where the soul is said to be in the body like wind (*pneuma*) in a wineskin (and thus to scatter at death).

[78] Lucr. 3. 323-32; cf. 337-49: "A body is never born by itself."

[79] Frag. 37, col. 1.

[80] 3. 331-36, 350-58.

[81] Diano (1974, 146ff.) suggests that this may be an inheritance from Democritus, who calls the body a *skēnos* (frags. A152, B37, B223 DK).

[82] This is particularly the case with his account of pleasure, where his crude and shocking slogans are quite misleading.

[83] D. L. 10. 137.

[84] D. L. 10. 22.

[85] *Kuria doxai* 2.

[86] Lucr. 3. 830-69, esp. 843-46.

[87] Epicurus *Ep. Men.* 124-25; Lucr. 3. 870-977.

[88] This idea, that one's happiness is "complete," embracing everything worth having, in a way that takes no account of the natural contours of a human life, is highly controversial. See Nagel (1979); Furley (1986); Mitsis (1988a, 1988b); Striker (1988); Rosenbaum (1990).

[89] Of course this would still leave imperfect Epicureans rationally wanting to live longer, so as to get nearer the goal of *ataraxia*. It is only the fully wise Epicurean who has no more to gain from another forty years than from another four minutes.

[90] 3. 425-829.

[91] He says that death is nothing to us because the (rational) soul's nature is mortal, and this just misstates the argument.

[92] See Asmis (1984, pt. 1).

[93] New frag. 2; frags. 34, 35.

[94] See Konstan (1973) for the claim that when Lucretius says that the terrors of hell are in our own lives, he means that hell is a projection onto the supposed afterlife of false beliefs about this life.

[95] Cf. the end of Philodemus *On Death*. See Gigante (1969a).

Works Cited

Annas, J., and Barnes, J. [1986] *The Modes of Scepticism,* Cambridge.

Annas, J. [1991] "Epicurean philosophy of mind." In *Ancient Philosophy of Mind,* ed. S. Everson, Cambridge.

Arrighetti, G. [1973] *Epicuro: Opere,* Turin.

Asmis, E. [1984] *Epicurus' Scientific Method.* Ithaca, NY.

Bailey, Cyril. [1928] *The Greek Atomists and Epicurus,* Oxford.

Burnyeat, M. [1976] "Protagoras and self-refutation in later Greek philosophy." *Philosophical Review* 75: 44-69.

Clay, D. [1983] *Lucretius and Epicurus,* Ithaca, NY.

Diano, C. [1946] *Epicuri ethica,* Florence.

Diano, C. [1974] *Scritti epicurei,* Florence.

Englert, W. [1988] *Epicurus on the Swerve and Free Action,* Atlanta.

Furley, D. J. [1967] *Two Studies in the Greek Atomists,* Princeton.

———. [1986] "Nothing to Us?" In *The Norms of Nature,* ed. M. Schofield and G. Striker, pp. 75-92, Cambridge and Paris.

Huby, P. [1969] "The Epicureans, animals, and free will." *Apeiron* 3: 17-19.

Gigante, M. [1969] *Ricerche Filodemee,* Naples.

———. [1981] *Scetticismo e epicureismo,* Naples.

Kerferd, G. [1971] "Epicurus' doctrine of the soul." *Phronesis* 116: 80-96.

Konstan, D. [1973] *Some Aspects of Epicurean Psychology,* Leiden.

Laks, A. [1981] "Un legerete de Democrite." *Cronache Ercolanesi* 11: 19-23.

Laursen, S. [1988] "Epicurus *On Nature* Book XXV." *Cronache Ercolanesi* 18: 7-18.

Long, A. A., and Sedley, D. N. [1987] *The Hellenistic Philosophers,* Cambridge.

Mitsis, P. [1988a] *Epicuruss Ethical Theory,* Ithaca, N.Y.

————. [1988b] "Epicurus on death and the duration of life." *Proceedings of the Boston Area Colloquium in Ancient Philosophy,* vol. 4, ed. J. J. Cleary, pp. 295-314.

Nagel, T. [1979] *Mortal Questions,* Cambridge.

Rosenbaum, S. [1990] "Epicurus on pleasure and the complete life." *The Monist* 73, no. 1 (January): 21-41.

Sedley, D. [1974] "The Structure of Epicurus' *On Nature."* *Cronache Ercolanesi* 4: 89-92.

————. [1983] "Epicurus' refutation of determinism." *SUZETESISi* 11-51, Naples.

————. [1989] "Epicurean anti-reductionism." In *Matter and Metaphysics,* ed. J. Barnes and M. Mignucci, pp. 295-327, Naples.

Sharples, R. [1980] "Lucretius' account of the composition of the soul." *Liverpool Classical Monthly* 5: 11-\7-20.

Striker, G. [1988] "Commentary on Mitsis." *Proceedings of the Boston Area Colloquium in Philosophy,* vol. 4, ed. J. J. Cleary, 315-20.

FURTHER READING

Asmis, Elizabeth. *Epicurus's Scientific Method.* Ithaca and London: Cornell University Press, 1984, 385 p.
Counters the view that "Epicurus did not have a coherent method of scientific inference" with an extended investigation of his principles of observation and resolution.

Brunschwig, Jacques. *Papers in Hellenistic Philosophy.* Trans. Janet Lloyd Cambridge, England: Cambridge University Press, 1994, 277 p.
Reprints two influential papers by an important professor of classical philosophy.

Clay, D. *Lucretius and Epicurus.* Ithaca and London: Cornell University Press, 1983.
In-depth study of the two major voices of Epicureanism, emphasizing Lucretius's inheritance from Epicurus.

Furley, D. J. *Two Studies in the Greek Atomists.* Princeton, N.J.: Princeton University Press, 1967, 256 p.
Delves into the details of Epicurus's atomical theories from the perspective of the physical sciences.

Konstan, David. *Some Aspects of Epicurean Psychology.* Leiden: E. J. Brill, 1973, 82 p.
Examines Epicurus's concept of human emotions—specifically fears and desires—to postulate the philosopher's notion of individual psychology and social organization.

Mitsis, J. *Epicurus' Ethical Theory.* Ithaca and London: Cornell University Press, 1988, 224 p.
Comprehensive examination of Epicurus's thought on ethics determines its overall coherence.

Nichols, James H., Jr. *Epicurean Political Philosophy.* Ithaca and London: Cornell University Press, 1972, 214 p.
Primarily concerned with Lucretius's *On the Nature of Things,* but through that argues for the political implications of Epicurus's thought.

Rist, J. M. *Epicurus: An Introduction.* Cambridge, England: Cambridge at the University Press, 1972, 185 p.
Provides a comprehensive view of Epicurus's philosophy, accessible to the novice but designed more for the reader familiar with classics.

Kojiki

712

Compilation of Japanese myths, history, and genealogy.

INTRODUCTION

The roots of the *Kojiki*—a collection of tales from ancient Japanese mythology and history—appear to reach back beyond human record. Known in English as "Record of Ancient Matters," the *Kojiki* may constitute "the start of Japanese prose literature," in the words of critic Masao Yaku. The *Kojiki* has no single author, since it is the product of individual efforts extended over almost a century. Early in the seventh century, the noble families of the Japanese empire kept their own mythologies and genealogical records, and many of the versions provided different, sometimes contradictory accounts of Japanese history. The earliest attempt—circa 620—to consolidate these histories came from an imperial desire to a create a single, consistent record that would give credence to the emperor's sovereignty. By 681, Emperor Temmu became the most zealous advocate of this work, assigning the project to Hiyeda no Are, an attendant at his court sometimes identified as male and sometimes as female who apparently possessed what is commonly referred to as a photographic memory. Whether she made a written version is unclear, but it is known that when Temmu died before the record could be completed, the project lapsed for twenty-five years. In 711, Empress Gemmio rejuvenated the effort, ordering the scholar Yasumaro to capture Are's memory in writing. This time, the work was finished in just four months.

Major Plots and Characters

Editors generally divide the *Kojiki* into three parts: the age of the gods, which is primarily mythical; the age of gods and men; and the age of men, which emphasizes the genealogies of noble families and has much to do with the history of the Japanese empire. Although liberally mixing mythological legend with dry genealogical record, the *Kojiki* is chronologically comprehensive, covering the epochs of Japanese culture from the earliest, legendary records to the beginning of the seventh century A.D.

Like the mythologies of many cultures, the *Kojiki* begins with creation. The first tales relate the inception of the universe and are soon followed by the creation of gods, who multiply quickly. Most students of the *Kojiki* feel that the significant material begins with the brother and sister deities Izanagi and Izanami, whose union produces the islands that make up Japan. They also people the world they have created with a family of gods related to such natural forces as fire, the moon, and the sun. The most prominent of these, whose actions dominate the first third of the *Kojiki,* are the Sun Goddess and her brother, Susano-o, or the "Impetuous Male Deity." These two, along with their sister, the Moon Goddess, inherit the universe from their father. Much of the first part of the *Kojiki* focuses on Susano-o's antics, particularly his conflicts with the Sun Goddess. Susano-o usually embodies the quintessential rebel, similar to characters in the mythologies of other cultures. The tales also closely follow his offspring, who apparently begin the empire's royal line.

The second and third sections of the record revolve more explicitly around the lineage of the royal family. They progress from fantastic tales of supernatural beings to stories of ancient emperors and empresses, including Jimmu, Sojin, the traditional Japanese hero Yamato-Take, and Jin-go, who conquered Korea. The scope of the work encompasses at least 17 monarchs and documents in detail the genealogies of centuries of noble families.

Major Themes

Scholars have generally discussed the *Kojiki* in terms of two central themes: the literary, with an emphasis on internal coherence, and the political, with an emphasis on the right of sovereignty. The two areas overlap to the extent that they focus on struggle, which all readers easily discern in the content of the *Kojiki*. Russian critic N. I. Conrad assigned distinct struggles to each of the sections of the *Kojiki,* boiling them down to the struggle for heaven, the struggle for earth, and the struggle for the empire on earth. Some literary discussions have reduced this even further, casting the entire work as one kind of struggle, such as the conflict between sun and storm or between sun and volcano. Political analyses treat the struggle in more concrete terms, taking a cue from the inception of the work with seventh-century emperors. These critics relate the content of the *Kojiki* directly to Emperor Temmu and Empress Gemmio's desire to create indisputable evidence of their right to rule, compelling the records of other noble families to conform.

Textual History

Unlike many early medieval texts, the complete *Kojiki* has remained intact to the present day. Diligently copied by Shinto priests, the tales survived in manuscript form through the Middle Ages. The earliest extant manuscript dates from 1371-72 and was followed by many later manuscripts. When much of Japanese literature went into print in the seventeenth century, the *Kojiki* was no exception. First printed in 1644, the record found a general readership and a significance that led to many more editions in the centuries that followed. By the nineteenth century, the editions were accompanied by many translations and volumes of criticism.

Critical Reception

Only eight years after its completion, the *Kojiki* was eclipsed by the *Nihon shoki,* or "Chronicles of Japan," and thus never achieved the status of an official history. While the *Nihon shoki* covers much the same territory, it displays the greater polish and consistency that scholars attribute to Chinese influence. The *Kojiki,* consequently, was comparatively neglected through the Middle Ages until it enjoyed a resurgence of interest in the seventeenth century that was probably spurred by the *kokugaku,* or "native learning" movement. Vital to this reevaluation was the work of Motoori Noringa, usually identified as the first great *Kojiki* scholar; he finished his extensive commentary, the *Kojiki-den,* in 1798, just three years before his death. By the nineteenth century, the *Kojiki*—often seen as more genuinely Japanese—rivalled the *Nihon shoki* in importance.

Previous to the eighteenth century, orthodox readings of the *Kojiki* insisted on literal interpretations of all its records, even the most fantastic supernatural events, much as some readers of the Bible insist on its facutality. Beginning in the eighteenth century, a more secular readership initiated a tradition of interpreting the *Kojiki* allegorically. Most twentieth-century criticism falls into one of two secular fields: cultural history or literary criticism. In the first instance, scholars read the *Kojiki* for some evidence of Japanese life in ancient times, combing the earlier sections in particular for evidence of Japan's early belief systems and daily life. This field also encompasses political analyses, which treat the *Kojiki* as part of an effort to consolidate imperial power, an idea first proposed by historian Tsuda Sokichi in 1913. The literary analyses often involve arguments about the work's consistency and internal coherence. While the *Kojiki* has generally been viewed as an awkward and inconsistent aggregation of tales, some recent scholars have insisted on its "harmony of style" and "symmetrical contours," in the words of Alexander Vannovsky.

PRINCIPAL ENGLISH TRANSLATIONS

Translation of "Kojiki" or "Records of Ancient Matters" (translated by Basil Hall Chamberlain) 1882
The Story of Ancient Japan or Tales from the Kojiki (translated by Yaichiro Isobe) 1929
Kojiki (translated by Donald L. Philippi) 1969

CRITICISM

Basil Hall Chamberlain (essay date 1882)

SOURCE: Basil Hall Chamberlain, in his introduction to *Translation of "Ko-Ji-Ki"; or, "Records of Ancient Matters,"* second edition, J. L. Thompson & Co., 1932, pp. i-lxxxi.

[*Chamberlain, a professor of Japanese and Philology at the Imperial University of Tokyo, was responsible for bringing many central works of classical Japanese literature into English. His translation of the* Kojiki, *first printed in 1882, has remained authoritative; excerpts from his original introduction appear below.*]

Of all the mass of Japanese literature, which lies before us as the result of nearly twelve centuries of bookmaking, the most important monument is the work entitled **Ko-ji-ki** or **Records of Ancient Matters,** which was completed in A.D. 712. It is the most important because it has preserved for us more faithfully than any other book the mythology, the manners, the language, and the traditional history of Ancient Japan. Indeed it is the earliest authentic connected literary product of that large division of the human race which has been variously denominated Turanian, Scythian and Altaïc, and it even precedes by at least a century the most ancient extant literary compositions of non-Aryan India. Soon after the date of its compilation, most of the salient features of distinctive Japanese nationality were buried under a superincumbent mass of Chinese culture, and it is to these **Records** and to a very small number of other ancient works, such as the poems of the "Collection of a Myriad Leaves" and the Shintō Rituals, that the investigator must look, if he would not at every step be misled into attributing originality to modern customs and ideas, which have simply been borrowed wholesale from the neighbouring continent.

It is of course not pretended that even these **Records** are untouched by Chinese influence: that influence is patent in the very characters with which the text is written. But the influence is less, and of another kind. If in the traditions preserved and in the customs alluded to we detect the Early Japanese in the act of borrowing from China and perhaps even from India, there is at least on our author's part no ostentatious decking out in Chinese trappings of what he believed to be original matter, after the fashion of the writers who immediately succeeded him. It is true that this abstinence on his part makes his compilation less pleasant to the ordinary native taste than that of subsequent historians, who put fine Chinese phrases into the mouths of emperors and heroes supposed to have lived before the time when intercourse with China began. But the European student, who reads all such books not as a pastime but in order to search for facts, will prefer the more genuine composition. It is also accorded the first place by the most learned of the native *literati*.

Of late years this paramount importance of the **Records of Ancient Matters** to investigators of Japanese subjects generally has become well known to European scholars; and even versions of a few passages are to be found scattered through the pages of their writings. Thus Mr. Aston has given us, in the Chrestomathy appended to his "Grammar of the Japanese Written Language," a couple of interesting extracts; Mr. Satow has illustrated by occasional extracts his elaborate papers on the Shintō Rituals printed in these "Transactions," and a remarkable essay by Mr. Kempermann published in the Fourth Number of the "Mittheilungen der Deutschen Gesellschaft für Natur und Völkerkunde Ostasiens," though containing no actual translations, bases on the accounts given in the **Records** some conjectures regarding the *origines* of Japanese civilization whith are fully substantiated by more minute research. All that has yet appeared in any European language does not, however, amount to one-twentieth part of the whole, and the most erroneous views of the style and scope of the book and its contents have found their way into popular works on Japan. It is hoped that the true nature of the book, and also the true nature of the traditions, customs, and ideas of the Early Japanese, will be made clearer by the present translation, the object of which is to give the entire work in a continuous English version, and thus to furnish the European student with a text to quote from, or at least to use as a guide in consulting the original. The only object aimed at has been a rigid and literal conformity with the Japanese text. Fortunately for this endeavour (though less fortunately for the student), one of the difficulties which often beset the translator of an Oriental classic is absent in the present case. There is no beauty of style, to preserve some trace of which he may be tempted to sacrifice a certain amount of accuracy. The **Records** sound queer and bald in Japanese, as will be noticed further on; and it is therefore right, even from a stylistic point of view, that they should sound bald and queer in English. The only portions of the text which, from obvious reasons, refuse to lend themselves to translation into English after this fashion are the indecent portions. But it has been thought that there could be no objection to rendering them into Latin,— Latin as rigidly literal as is the English of the greater part.

After these preliminary remarks, it will be most convenient to take the several points which a study of the **Records** and the turning of them into English suggest, and to consider the same one by one. These points are:

I.—Authenticity and Nature of the Text, together with Bibliographical Notes.
II.—Details concerning the Method of Translation.
III.—The *Nihon-Gi* or "Chronicles of Japan."
IV.—Manners and Customs of the Early Japanese.
V.—Religious and Political Ideas of the Early Japanese. Beginnings of the Japanese Nation, and Credibility of the National Traditions.

I. The Text and Its Authenticity, Together with Bibliographical Notes.

The latter portion of the Preface to the **Records of Ancient Matters** is the only documentary authority for the origin of the work. It likewise explains its scope. But though in so doing the author descends to a more matter-of-fact style than the high-sounding Chinese phrases and elaborate allusions with which he had set forth, still his meaning may be found to lack somewhat of clearness, and it will be as well to have the facts put into language more intelligible to the European student. This having already been done by Mr. Satow in his paper on the "Revival of Pure Shintô,"[2] it will be best simply to quote his words. They are as follows:

The Emperor Temmu, at what portion of his reign is not mentioned, lamenting that the records possessed by the chief families contained many errors, resolved to take steps to preserve the true traditions from oblivion. He therefore had the records carefully examined, compared, and weeded of their faults. There happened to be in his household a person of marvellous memory named Hiyeda no Are, who could repeat without mistake the contents of any document he had ever seen, and never forgot anything that he had heard. Temmu Tennô[3] took the pains to instruct this person in the genuine traditions and 'old language of former ages,' and to make him repeat them until he had the whole by heart. 'Before the undertaking was completed,' which probably means before it could be committed to writing, the Emperor died, and for twenty-five years Are's memory was the sole depository of what afterwards received the title of **Kojiki**[4] or *Furu-koto-bumi* as it is read by Motoori. At the end of this interval the Empress Gemmiō ordered Yasumaro to write it down from the mouth of Are, which accounts for the completion of the manuscript in so short a time as four months and a half. Are's age at this date is not stated, but as he was twenty-eight years of age some time in the reign of Temmu Tennô, it could not possibly have been more than sixty-eight, while taking into account the previous order of Temmu Tennô in 681 for the compilation of a history, and the statement that he was engaged on the composition of the Kojiki at the time of his death in 686, it would not be unreasonable to conclude that it belongs to about the last year of his reign, in which case Are was only fifty-three in 711.

The previous order of the Emperor Tem-mu mentioned in the above extract is usually supposed to have resulted in the compilation of a history which was early lost. But Hirata gives reasons for supposing that this and the project of the ***Records of Ancient Matters*** were identical. If this opinion be accepted, the ***Records,*** while the oldest *existing* Japanese book, are, not the third, but the second historical work of which mention has been preserved, one such having been compiled in the year 620, but lost in a fire in the year 645. It will thus be seen that it is rather hard to say whom we should designate as the author of the work. The Emperor Temmu, Hiyeda no Are, and Yasumaro may all three lay claim to that title. The question, however, is of no importance to us, and the share taken by Are may well have been exaggerated in the telling. What seems to remain as the residue of fact is that the plan of a purely national history originated with the Emperor Tem-mu and was finally carried out under his successor by Yasumaro, one of the Court Nobles.

Fuller evidence and confirmatory evidence from other sources as to the origin of our ***Records*** would doubtless be very acceptable. But the very small number of readers and writers at that early date, and the almost simultaneous compilation of a history (the "Chronicles of Japan") which was better calculated to hit the taste of the age, make the absence of such evidence almost unavoidable. In any case, and only noticing in passing the fact that Japan was never till quite recent years noted for such wholesale literary forgeries (for Motowori's condemnation of the "Chronicles of Old Matters of Former Ages" has been considered rash by later scholars),—it cannot be too much emphasized that in this instance authenticity is sufficiently proved by internal evidence. It is hard to believe that any forger living later than the eighth century of our era should have been so well able to discard the Chinese "padding" to the old traditions, which, after the acceptance by the Court of the "Chronicles of Japan," had come to be generally regarded as an integral portion of those very traditions; and it is more unlikely still that he should have invented a style so little calculated to bring his handiwork into repute. He would either have written in fair Chinese, like the mass of early Japanese prose writers (and his Preface shows that he could do so if he were so minded); or, if the tradition of there having been a history written in the native tongue had reached him, he would have made his composition unmistakably Japanese in form by arranging the char-

acters in the order demanded by Japanese syntax, and by the consistent use of characters employed phonetically to denote particles and terminations, after the fashion followed in the Rituals, and developed (apparently before the close of the ninth century) into what is technically known as the "Mixed Phonetic Style" (*Kana-mazhiri*), which has remained ever since as the most convenient vehicle for writing the language. As it is, his quasi-Chinese construction, which breaks down every now and then to be helped up again by a few Japanese words written phonetically, is surely the first clumsy attempt at combining two divergent elements. What however is simply incredible is that, if the supposed forger lived even only a hundred years later than A.D. 712, he should so well have imitated or divined the archaisms of that early period. For the eighth century of our era was a great turning point in the Japanese language, the Archaic Dialect being then replaced by the Classical; and as the Chinese language and literature were alone thenceforward considered worthy the student's attention, there was no means of keeping up an acquaintance with the diction of earlier reigns, neither do we find the poets of the time ever attempting to adorn their verse with obsolete phraseology. That was an affectation reserved for a later epoch, when the diffusion of books rendered it possible. The poets of the seventh, eighth, and ninth centuries apparently wrote as they spoke; and the test of language alone would almost allow of our arranging their compositions half century by half century, even without the dates which are given in many instances in the "Collection of a Myriad Leaves" and in the "Collection of Songs Ancient and Modern,"—the first two collections of poems published by imperial decree in the middle of the eighth, and at the commencement of the tenth, century respectively.

The above remarks are meant to apply more especially to the occasional Japanese words,—all of them Archaic,—which, as mentioned above, are used from time to time in the prose text of the ***Records*** to help out the author's meaning and to preserve names whose exact pronunciation he wished handed down. That he should have invented the Songs would be too monstrous a supposition for any one to entertain, even if we had not many of the same and other similar ones preserved in the pages of the "Chronicles of Japan," a work which was undoubtedly completed in A.D. 720. The history of the Japanese language is too well known to us, we can trace its development and decay in too many documents reaching from the eighth century to the present time, for it to be possible to entertain the notion that the latest of these Songs, which have been handed down with minute care in a syllabic transcription, is posterior to the first half of the eighth century, while the majority must be ascribed to an earlier, though uncertain, date. If we refer the greater number of them in their present form to the sixth century, and allow a further antiquity of one or two centuries to others more ancient in sentiment and in grammatical usage, we shall probably be making a moderate estimate. It is an estimate, moreover, which obtains confirmation from the fact that the first notice we have of the use of writing in Japan dates from early in the fifth century; for it is natural to suppose that the Songs believed to have been composed by the gods and heroes of antiquity should have been among the first things to be written down, while the reverence in which they were held would in some cases cause them to be transcribed exactly as tradition had bequeathed them, even if unintelligible or nearly so, while in others the same feeling would lead to the correction of what were supposed to be errors or inelegancies. Finally it may be well to observe that the authenticity of the **Records** has never been doubted, though, as has already been stated, some of the native commentators have not hesitated to charge with spuriousness another of their esteemed ancient histories. Now it is unlikely that, in the war which has been waged between the partisans of the **Records** and those of the "Chronicles," some flaw in the former's title to genuineness and to priority should not have been discovered and pointed out if it existed.

During the Middle Ages, when no native Japanese works were printed, and not many others excepting the Chinese Classics and Buddhist Scriptures, the **Records of Ancient Matters** remained in manuscript in the hands of the Shintō priesthood. They were first printed in the year 1644, at the time when, peace having been finally restored to the country and the taste for reading having become diffused, the great mass of the native literature first began to emerge from the manuscript state. This very rare edition (which was reprinted in fac-simile in 1798) is indispensable to any one who would make of the **Records** a special study. The next edition was by a Shintō priest, Deguchi Nobuyoshi, and appeared in 1687. It has marginal notes of no great value, and several emendations of the text. The first-mentioned of these two editions is commonly called the "Old Printed Edition," but has no title beyond that of the original work,—**Records of Ancient Matters**. The name of the other is "Records of Ancient Matters with Marginal Readings." . . . Each is in three volumes. They were succeeded in 1789-1822 by Motowori's great edition, entitled "Exposition of the Records of Ancient Matters." . . . This, which is perhaps the most admirable work of which Japanese erudition can boast, consists of forty-four large volumes, fifteen of which are devoted to the elucidation of the first volume of the original, seventeen to the second, ten to the third, and the rest to prolegomena, indexes, etc. To the ordinary student this Commentary will furnish all that he requires, and the charm of Motowori's style will be found to shed a glamour over the driest parts of the original work. The author's judgment only seems to fail him occasionally when confronted with the most difficult or corrupt passages, or with such as might be construed in a sense unfavourable to his predilections as an ardent Shintoist. He frequently

quotes the opinions of his master Mabuchi, whose own treatise on this subject is so rare that the present writer has never seen a copy of it, nor does the public library of Tōkiō possess one. Later and less important editions are the "Records of Ancient Matters with the Ancient Reading" . . . , a reprint by one of Motowori's pupils of the Chinese text and of his Master's *Kana* reading of it without his Commentary, and useful for reference, though the title is a misnomer, 1803; the "Records of Ancient Matters with Marginal Notes," by Murakami Tadanori, 1874; the "Records of Ancient Matters in the Syllabic Character," by Sakata no Kaneyasu, 1874, a misleading book, as it gives the modern *Kana* reading with its arbitrarily inserted Honorifics and other departures from the actual text, as the *ipsissima verba* of the original work; the "Records of Ancient Matters Revised," by Uyematsu Shigewoka, 1875. All these editions are in three volumes, and the "Records of Ancient Matters with the Ancient Reading" has also been reprinted in one volume on beautiful thin paper. Another in four volumes by Fujihara no Masaoki, 1871, entitled the "Records of Ancient Matters in the Divine Character," is a real curiosity of literature, though otherwise of no value. In it the editor has been at the pains of reproducing the whole work, according to its modern *Kana* reading, in that adaptation of the Korean alphabetic writing which some modern Japanese authors have supposed to be characters of peculiar age and sanctity, used by the ancient gods of their country and named "Divine Characters" accordingly.

Besides these actual editions of the **Records of Ancient Matters,** there is a considerable mass of literature bearing less directly on the same work, and all of which cannot be here enumerated. It may be sufficient to mention the "Correct Account of the Divine Age" . . . , by Motowori, 3 Vols. 1789, and a commentary thereon entitled *"Tokiha-Gusa"* . . . by Wosada Tominobu, from which the present translator has borrowed a few ideas; the "Sources of the Ancient Histories" . . . and its sequel entitled "Exposition of the Ancient Histories" . . . , by Hirata Atsutane, begun printing in 1819,— works which are specially admirable from a philological point of view, and in which the student will find the solution of not a few difficulties which even to Motowori had been insuperable; the *"Idzu no Chi-Waki"* . . . , by Tachibana no Moribe, begun printing in 1851, a useful commentary on the "Chronicles of Japan"; the *"Idzu no Koto-Waki"* . . . , by the same author, begun printing in 1847, an invaluable help to a comprehension of the Songs contained in both the **Records** and the "Chronicles"; the "Examination of Difficult Words" . . . , in 3 Vols., 1831, a sort of dictionary of specially perplexing terms and phrases, in which light is thrown on many a verbal crux and much originality of thought displayed; and the "Perpetual Commentary on the Chronicles of Japan" . . . , by Tanigaha Shihei, 1762, a painstaking work written in the Chinese language, 23 Vols. Neither must the

"*Kō Gan Shō*" . . . , a commentary on the Songs contained in the "Chronicles" and *Records* composed by the Buddhist priest Keichiū, who may be termed the father of the native school of criticism, be forgotten. It is true that most of Keichiū's judgments on doubtful points have been superseded by the more perfect erudition of later days; but some few of his interpretations may still be followed with advantage. The "*Kō Gan Shō,*" which was finished in the year 1691, has never been printed. It is from these and a few others and from the standard dictionaries and general books of reference, such as the "Japanese Words Classified and Explained" . . . the "Catalogue of Family Names" . . . and (coming down to more modern times) Arawi Hakuseki's "*Tōga*" . . . that the translator has derived most assistance. The majority of the useful quotations from the dictionaries, etc., having been incorporated by Motowori in his "Commentary," it has not often been necessary to mention them by name in the notes to the translation. At the same time the translator must express his conviction that, as the native authorities cannot possibly be dispensed with, so also must their assertions be carefully weighed and only accepted with discrimination by the critical European investigator. He must also thank Mr. Tachibana no Chimori, grandson of the eminent scholar Tachibana no Moribe, for kindly allowing him to make use of the manuscript of the unpublished portions of the "*Idzu no Chi-Waki*" and the "*Idzu no Koto-Waki,*" works indispensable to the comprehension of the more difficult portion of the text of the *Records*. To Mr. Satow he is indebted for the English and Latin equivalents of the Japanese botanical names, to Capt. Blakiston and Mr. Namiye Motokichi for similar assistance with regard to the zoological names.

Comparing what has been said above with what the author tells us in his Preface, the nature of the text, so far as language is concerned, will be easily understood. The Songs are written phonetically, syllable by syllable, in what is technically known as *Manyō-Gana, i.e.* entire Chinese characters used to represent sound and not sense. The rest of the text, which is in prose, is very poor Chinese, capable (owing to the ideographic nature of the Chinese written character), of being read off into Japanese. It is also not only full of "Japonisms," but irregularly interspersed with characters which turn the text into nonsense for a Chinaman, as they are used phonetically to represent certain Japanese words, for which the author could not find suitable Chinese equivalents. These phonetically written words prove, even apart from the notice in the Preface, that the text was never meant to be read as pure Chinese. The probability is that (sense being considered more important than sound) it was read partly in Chinese and partly in Japanese, according to a mode which has since been systematized and has become almost universal in this country even in the reading of genuine Chinese texts. The modern school of Japanese *literati,* who push their

hatred of everything foreign to the bounds of fanaticism, contend however that this, their most ancient and revered book, was from the first intended to be read exclusively into Japanese. Drawing from the other sources of our knowledge of the Archaic Dialect, Motowori has even hazarded a restoration of the Japanese reading of the entire prose text, in the whole of which not a single Chinese word is used, excepting for the titles of the two Chinese books (the "Confucian Analects" and the "Thousand Character Essay") which are said to have been brought over to Japan in the reign of the Emperor Ō-jin, and for the names of a Korean King and of three or four other Koreans and Chinese. Whatever may be their opinion on the question at issue, most European scholars, to whom the superior sanctity of the Japanese language is not an article of faith, will probably agree with Mr. Aston[7] in denying to this conjectural restoration the the credit of representing the genuine words into which Japanese eighth century students of history read off the text of the *Records*. . . .

III. The "Chronicles of Japan."

It will have been gathered from what has been already said, and it is indeed generally known, that the ***Records of Ancient Matters*** do not stand alone. To say nothing of the "Chronicles of Old Matters of Former Ages," whose genuineness is disputed. there is another undoubtedly authentic work with which no student of Japanese antiquity can dispense. It is entitled "*Nihon-Gi,*" i.e., "Chronicles of Japan," and is second only in value to the *Records,* which it has always excelled in popular favour. It was completed in A.D. 720, eight years after the ***Records of Ancient Matters*** had been presented to the Empress Gem-miyō.

The scope of the two histories is the same; but the language of the later one and its manner of treating the national traditions stand in notable contrast to the unpretending simplicity of the elder work. Not only is the style (excepting in the Songs, which had to be left as they were or sacrificed altogether) completely Chinese,—in fact to a great extent a cento of well-worn Chinese phrases,—but the subject-matter is touched up, re-arranged, and polished, so as to make the work resemble a Chinese history so far as that was possible. Chinese philosophical speculations and moral precepts are intermingled with the cruder traditions that had descended from Japanese antiquity. Thus the naturalistic Japanese account of the creation is ushered in by a few sentences which trace the origin of all things to *Yin* and *Yang* . . . the Passive and Active Essences of Chinese philosophy. The legendary Emperor Jim-mu is credited with speeches made up of quotations from the "*Yi Ching,*" the "*Li Chi,*" and other standard Chinese works. A few of the most childish of the national traditions are omitted, for instance the story of the "White Hare of Inaba," that of the gods obtaining counsel of a toad, and that of the hospitality which a speaking mouse extended to the deity Master-of-the-Great-Land. Sometimes the original tradition is simply softened down or explained away. A notable instance of this occurs in the account of the visit of the deity Izanagi16 to Hades, whither he goes in quest of his dead wife, and among other things has to scale the "Even Pass (or Hill) of Hades."17 In the tradition preserved in the ***Records*** and indeed even in the "Chronicles," this pass or hill is mentioned as a literal geographical fact. But the compiler of the latter work, whose object it was to appear and to make his forefathers appear, as reasonable as a learned Chinese, adds a gloss to the effect that "One account says that the Even Hill of Hades is no distinct place, but simply the moment when breathing ceases at the time of death;"—not a happy guess certainly, for this pass is mentioned in connection with Izanagi's return to the land of the living. In short we may say of this work what was said of the Septuagint,—that it *rationalizes*.

Perhaps it will be asked, how can it have come to pass that a book in which the national traditions are thus unmistakably tampered with, and which is moreover written in Chinese instead of in the native tongue, has enjoyed such a much greater share of popularity than the more genuine work?

The answer lies on the surface: the concessions made to Chinese notions went far towards satisfying minds trained on Chinese models, while at the same time the reader had his respect for the old native emperors increased, and was enabled to preserve some sort of belief in the native gods. People are rarely quite logical in such matters, particularly in an early stage of society; and difficulties are glossed over rather than insisted upon. The beginning of the world, for instance, or to use Japanese phraseology, the "separation of heaven and and earth" took place a long time ago; and perhaps, although there could of course be no philosophical doubt as to the cause of this event having been the interaction of the Passive and Active Essences, it might also somehow be true that Izanagi and Izanami (the "Male-Who-Invites" and the "Female-Who-Invites") were the progenitor and progenitrix of Japan. Who knows but what in them the formative principles may not have been embodied, represented, or figured forth after a fashion not quite determined, but none the less real? As a matter of fact, the two deities in question have often been spoken of in Japanese books under such designations as the "*Yin* Deity" and the "*Yang* Deity," and in his Chinese Preface the very compiler of these ***Records*** lends his sanction to the use of such phraseology, though, if we look closely at the part taken by the goddess in the legend narrated in Sect. IV, it would seem but imperfectly applicable. If again early sovereigns, such as the Empress Jin-gō, address their troops in sentences cribbed from the *"Shu Ching,"* or, like

the Emperor Kei-kō, describe the Ainos in terms that would only suit the pages of a Chinese topographer,—both these personages being supposed to have lived prior to the opening up of intercourse with the continent of Asia,—the anachronism was partly hidden by the fact of the work which thus recorded their doings being itself written in the Chinese language, where such phrases only sounded natural. In some instances, too, the Chinese usage had so completely superseded the native one as to cause the latter to have been almost forgotten excepting by the members of the Shintō priesthood. This happened in the case of the Chinese method of divination by means of a tortoise-shell, whose introduction caused the elder native custom of divination through the shoulder-blade of a deer to fall into desuetude. Whether indeed this native custom itself may not perhaps be traced back to still earlier continental influence is another question. So far as any documentary information reaches, divination through the shoulder-blade of a deer was the most ancient Japanese method of ascertaining the will of the gods. The use of the Chinese sexagenary cycle for counting years, months, and days is another instance of the imported usage having become so thoroughly incorporated with native habits of mind as to make the anachronism of employing it when speaking of a period confessedly anterior to the introduction of continental civilization pass unnoticed. As for the (to a modern European) grotesque notion of pretending to give the precise months and days of events supposed to have occurred a thousand years before the date assigned to the introduction of astronomical instruments, of observatories, and even of the art of writing, that is another of those inconsistencies which, while lying on the very surface, yet so easily escape the uncritical Oriental mind.19 Semi-civilized people tire of asking questions, and to question antiquity, which fills so great a place in their thoughts, is the last thing that would occur to any of their learned men, whose mental attitude is characteristically represented by Confucius when he calls himself "A transmitter and not a maker, believing in and loving the ancients."20 As regards the question of language, standard Chinese soon became easier to understand than Archaic Japanese, as the former alone was taught in the schools, and the native language changed rapidly during the century or two that followed the diffusion of the foreign tongue and civilization. We have only to call to mind the relative facility to most of ourselves of a Latin book and of one written in Early English. Of course, as soon as the principles of the Japanese *Renaissance* had taken hold of men's minds in the eighteenth century, the more genuine, more national work assumed its proper place in the estimation of students. But the uncouthness of the style according to modern ideas, and the greater amount of explanation of all sorts that is required in order to make the ***Records of Ancient Matters*** intelligible, must always prevent them from attaining to the popularity of the sister history. Thus, though published almost simultaneously, the tendencies of the two works were very different, and their fate has differed accordingly.

To the European student the chief value of the "Chronicles of Japan" lies in the fact that their author, in treating of the so-called "Divine Age," often gives a number of various forms of the same legend—under the heading of "One account says," suffixed in the form of a note to the main text. No phrase is more commonly met with in later treatises on Japanese history than this,—"One account in the 'Chronicles of Japan' says," and it will be met with occasionally in the Foot-notes to the present translation. There are likewise instances of the author of the "Chronicles" having preserved, either in the text or in "One account," traditions omitted by the compiler of the **Records** Such are, for instance, the quaint legend invented to explain the fact that the sun and moon do not shine simultaneously,[21] and the curious development of the legend of the expulsion of the deity *Susa-no-wo* ("Impetuous Male"), telling us of the hospitality which was refused to him by the other gods when he appeared before them to beg for shelter. Many of the Songs, too, in the "Chronicles" are different from those in the **Records,** and make a precious addition to our vocabulary of Archaic Japanese. The prose text, likewise, contains, in the shape of notes, numbers of readings by which the pronunciation of words written ideograpically, or the meaning of words written phonetically in the **Records** may be ascertained. Finally the "Chronicles" give us the annals of seventy-two years not comprised in the plan of the **Records** by carrying down to A.D. 700 the history which in the **Records** steps at the year 628. Although therefore it is a mistake to assert, as some have done, that the "Chronicles of Japan" must be placed at the head of all the Japanese historical works, their assistance can in no wise be dispensed with by the student of Japanese mythology and of the Japanese language.[22]

IV. Manners and Customs of the Early Japanese.

The Japanese of the mythical period, as pictured in the legends preserved by the compiler of the **Records of Ancient Matters**, were a race who had long emerged from the savage state, and had attained to a high level of barbaric skill. The Stone Age was forgotten by them—or nearly so,—and the evidence points to their never having passed through a genuine Bronze Age, though the knowledge of bronze was at a later period introduced from the neighbouring continent. They used iron for manufacturing spears, swords, and knives of various shapes, and likewise for the more peaceful purpose of making hooks wherewith to angle, or to fasten the doors of their huts. Their other warlike and hunting implements (besides traps and gins which appear to have been used equally for catching beasts and birds and for destroying human enemies) were bows

and arrows, spears and elbow-pads,—the latter seemingly of skin, while special allusion is made to the fact that the arrows were feathered. Perhaps clubs should be added to the list. Of the bows and arrows, swords and knives, there is perpetual mention; but nowhere do we hear of the tools with which they were manufactured, and there is the same remarkable silence regarding such widely spread domestic implements as the saw and the axe. We hear, however, of the pestle and mortar, of the fire-drill, of the wedge, of the sickle, and of the shuttle used in weaving.

Navigation seems to have been in a very elementary stage. Indeed the art of sailing was, as we know from the classical literature of the country, but little practised in Japan even so lafe as the middle of the tenth century of our era subsequent to the general diffusion of Chinese civilization, though rowing and punting are often mentioned by the early poets. In one passage of the **Records** and in another of the "Chronicles," mention is made of a "two-forked boat" used on inland pools or lakes; but, as a rule, in the earlier portions of those works, we read only of people going to sea or being sent down from heaven in water-proof baskets without oars, and reaching their destination not through any efforts of their own, but through supernatural interposition.[23]

To what we should call towns or villages very little reference is made anywhere in the **Records** or in that portion of the "Chronicles" which contains the account of the so-called "Divine Age." But from what we learn incidentally, it would seem that the scanty population was chiefly distributed in small hamlets and isolated dwellings along the coast and up the course of the larger streams. Of house-building there is frequent mention,—especially of the building of palaces or temples for sovereigns or gods,—the words "palace" and "temple" being (it should be mentioned) represented in Japanese by the same term. Sometimes, in describing the construction of such a sacred dwelling, the author of the **Records** abandoning his usual flat and monotonous style, soars away on poetic wings, as when, for instance, he tells how the monarch of Idzumo, on abdicating in favour of the Sun-Goddess's descendant, covenanted that the latter should "make stout his temple pillars on the nethermost rock-bottom, and make high the cross-beams to the plain of High Heaven."[24] It must not, however, be inferred from such language that these so-called palaces and temples were of very gorgeous and imposing aspect. The more exact notices to be culled from the ancient Shintō Rituals (which are but little posterior to the **Records** and in no wise contradict the inferences to be drawn from the latter) having been already summarized by Mr. Satow, it may be as well to quote that gentleman's words. He says:[25]

> The palace of the Japanese sovereign was a wooden hut, with its pillars planted in the ground, instead

of being erected upon broad flat stones as in modern buildings. The whole frame-work, consisting of posts, beams, rafters, door-posts and window-frames, was tied together with cords made by twisting the long fibrous stems of climbing plants, such as Pueraria Thunbergiana (*kuzu*) and Wistaria Sinensis (*fuji*). The floor must have been low down, so that the occupants of the building, as they squatted or lay on their mats, were exposed to the stealthy attacks of venomous snakes, which were probably far more numerous in the earliest ages when the country was for the most part uncultivated, than at the present day. . . . There seems some reason to think that the *yuka,* here translated floor, was originally nothing but a couch which ran round the sides of the hut, the rest of the space being simply a mud-floor, and that the size of the couch was gradually increased until it occupied the whole interior. The rafters projected upward beyond the ridge-pole, crossing each other as is seen in the roofs of modern Shin-tau temples, whether their architecture be in conformity with early traditions (in which case all the rafters are so crossed) or modified in accordance with more advanced principles of construction, and the crossed rafters retained only as ornaments at the two ends of the ridge. The roof was thatched, and perhaps had a gable at each end, with a hole to allow the smoke of the wood-fire to escape, so that it was possible for birds flying in and perching on the beams overhead, to defile the food, or the fire with which it was cooked.

To this description it need only be added that fences were in use, and that the wooden doors, sometimes fastened by means of hooks, resembled those with which we are familiar in Europe rather than the sliding, screen-like doors of modern Japan. The windows seem to have been mere holes. Rugs of skins and rush matting were occasionally brought in to sit 'upon, and we even hear once or twice of "silk rugs" being used for the same purpose by the noble and wealthy.

The habits of personal cleanliness which so pleasantly distinguish the modern Japanese from their neighbours, in continental Asia, though less fully developed than at present, would seem to have existed in the germ in early times, as we read more than once of bathing in rivers, and are told of bathing-women being specially attached to the person of a certain imperial infant. Lustrations, too, formed part of the religious practices of the race. Latrines are mentioned several times. They would appear to have been situated away from the houses and to have generally been placed over a running stream, whence doubtless the name for latrine in the Archaic Dialect,—*kaha-ya,* i.e. "river-house." A well-known Japanese classic of the tenth century, the "Yamato Tales,"[26] tells us indeed that "in older days the people dwelt in houses raised on platforms built out on the river Ikuta," and goes on to relate a story which presupposes such a method of architecture.[27] A passage in the account of the reign of the Emperor Jim-mu which occurs both in the **Records** and in the "Chronicles," and another in the reign of the Emperor Sui-nin occurring in the **Records** only, might be interpreted so as to support this statement.[28] But both are extremely obscure, and beyond the fact that people who habitually lived near the water *may* have built their houses after the aquatic fashion practised in different parts of the world by certain savage tribes both ancient and modern, the present writer is not aware of any authority for the assertion that they actually did so except the isolated passage in the "Yamato Tales," just quoted.

A peculiar sort of dwelling-place which the two old histories bring prominently under our notice, is the so-called "parturition-house,"—a one-roomed hut without windows which a woman was expected to build and retire into for the purpose of being delivered unseen.[29] It would also appear to be not unlikely that newly-married couples retired into a specially built hut for the purpose of consummating the marriage, and it is certain that for each sovereign a new palace was erected on his accession.

Castles are not distinctly spoken of till a period which, though still mythical in the opinion of the present writer, coincides according to the received chronology with the first century B.C. We then first meet with the curious term "rice-castle," whose precise signification is a matter of dispute among the native commentators, but which, on comparison with Chinese descriptions of the Early Japanese, should probably be understood to mean a kind of palisade serving the purpose of a redoubt, behind which the warriors could ensconce themselves.[30] If this conjecture be correct, we have here a good instance of a word, so to speak, moving upward with the march of civilization, the term, which formerly denoted something not much better than a fence, having later come to convey the idea of a stone castle.

To conclude the subject of dwelling-places, it should be stated that cave-dwellers are sometimes alluded to. The legend of the retirement of the Sun-Goddess into a cavern may possibly suggest to some the idea of an early period when such habitations were the normal abodes of the ancestors of the Japanese race.[31] But at the time when the national traditions assumed their present shape, such a state of things had certainly quite passed away, if it ever existed, and only barbarous Ainos and rough bands of robbers are credited with the construction of such primitive retreats. Natural caves (it may be well to state) are rare in Japan, and the caves that are alluded to were mostly artificial, as may be gathered from the context.

The food of the Early Japanese consisted of fish and of the flesh of the wild creatures which fell by the hunter's arrow or were taken in the trapper's snare—

an animal diet with which Buddhist prohibitions had not yet interfered, as they began to do in early historical times. Rice is the only cereal of which there is such mention made as to place it beyond a doubt that its cultivation dates back to time immemorial. Beans, millet, and barely are indeed named once, together with silkworms, in the account of the "Divine Age."[32] But the passage has every aspect of an interpolation in the legend, perhaps not dating back long before the time of the eighth century compiler. A few unimportant vegetables and fruits, of most of which there is but a single mention, will be found in the list of plants given below. The intoxicating liquor called *sake* was known in Japan during the mythical period,[33] and so were chopsticks for eating the food with. Cooking-pots and cups and dishes—the latter both of earthenware and of leaves of trees,—are also mentioned; but of the use of fire for warming purposes we hear nothing. Tables are named several times, but never in connection with food. They would seem to have been exclusively used for the purpose of presenting offerings on, and were probably quite small and low,—in fact rather trays than tables according to European ideas.

In the use of clothing and the specialization of garments the Early Japanese had reached a high level. We read in the most ancient legends of upper garments, skirts, trowsers, girdles, veils, and hats, while both sexes adorned themselves with necklaces, bracelets, and head-ornaments of stones considered precious,—in this respect offering a striking contrast to their descendants in modern times, of whose attire jewelry forms no part. The material of their clothes was hempen cloth and paper-mulberry bark, coloured by being rubbed with madder, and probably with woad and other tinctorial plants. All the garments, so far as we may judge, were woven, sewing being nowhere mentioned, and it being expressly stated by the Chinese commentator on the *"Shan Hai Ching,"* who wrote early in the fourth century, that the Japanese had no needles.[35] From the great place which the chase occupied in daily life we are led to suppose that skins also were used to make garments of. There is in the **Records** at least one passage which favours this supposition,[36] and the "Chronicles" in one place mention the straw rain-coat and broad-brimmed hat, which still form the Japanese peasant's effectual protection against the inclemencies of the weather. The tendrils of creeping plants served the purposes of string, and bound the warrior's sword round his waist. Combs are mentioned, and it is evident that much attention was devoted to the dressing of the hair. The men seem to have bound up their hair in two bunches, one on each side of the head, whilst the young boys tied theirs into a topknot, the unmarried girls let their locks hang down over their necks, and the married women dressed theirs after a fashion which apparently combined the two last-named methods. There is no mention in any of the old books of cutting the hair or beard except in token of disgrace; neither do we gather that the sexes, but for this matter of the head-dress, were distinguished by a diversity of apparel and ornamentation.

With regard to the precious stones mentioned above as having been used as ornaments for the head, neck, and arms, the texts themselves give us little or no information as to the identity of the stones meant to be referred to. Indeed it is plain (and the native commentators admit the fact) that a variety of Chinese characters properly denoting different sorts of jewels were used indiscriminately by the early Japanese writers to represent the single native word *tama,* which is the only one the language contains to denote any hard substance on which a special value is set, and which often refers chiefly to the rounded shape, so that it might in fact be translated by the word "bead" as fittingly as by the word "jewel." We know, however, from the specimens which have rewarded the labours of archaeological research in Japan that agate, crystal, glass, jade, serpentine, and steatite are the most usual materials, and curved and pierced cylindrical shapes (*maga-tama* and *kuda-tama*), the commonest forms.[37]

The horse (which was ridden, but not driven), the barn-door fowl, and the cormorant used for fishing, are the only domesticated creatures mentioned in the earlier traditions, with the doubtful exception of the silkworm, to which reference has already been made.[38] In the later portions of the **Records** and "Chronicles", dogs and cattle are alluded to; but sheep, swine, and even cats were apparently not yet introduced. Indeed sheep were scarcely to be seen in Japan until a few years ago, goats are still almost unknown, and swine and all poultry excepting the barn-door fowl are extremely uncommon.

The following enumeration of the animals and plants mentioned in the earlier portion[39] of the **Records** may be of interest. The Japanese equivalents, some few of which are obsolete, are put in parenthesis, together with the Chinese characters used to write them:

Mammals.

Bear, (*kuma . . .*).
Boar, (*wi . . .*).
Deer, (*shika . . .*).
Hare, (*usagi . . .*).
Horse, (*uma . . .* and *koma . . .*).
Mouse *or* Rat, (*nedzumi . . .*).
"Sea-ass" [Seal or Sea-lion?],
    (*michi . . .*).
Whale, (*kujira . . .*).

Birds.

Barndoor-fowl, (*kakei . . .*).
Cormorant, (*u . . .*).
Crow *or* Raven, (*karasu . . .*).

Dotterel *or* Plover *or* Sandpiper, (*chidori* . . .).
Heron *or* Egret, (*sagi* . . .).
Kingfisher, (*soni-dori* . . .).
Nuye, . . .).[40]
Pheasant, (*kigishi* . . .).
Snipe, (*shigi* . . .).
Swan, (*shiro-tori* . . .).
Wild-duck, (*kamo* . . .).
Wild-goose, (*kari* . . .).

REPTILES.

Crocodile, (*wani* . . .).[41]
Tortoise, (*kame* . . .).
Toad *or* Frog, (*taniguku,* written phonetically).
Serpent, (*worochi* . . .).
Snake [smaller than the preceding], (*hebi* . . .).

INSECTS.

Centipede, (*mukade* . . .).
Dragon-fly, (*akidzu* . . .).
Fly, (*hahi* . . .).
Louse, (*shirami* . . .).
Silkworm, (*kahiko* . . .).
Wasp *or* Bee, (*hachi* . . .).

FISHES, ETC.

Pagrus cardinalis [probably], (*aka-dahi* . . .) [or perhaps the *Pagrus cardinalis* (*tai* . . .) is intended].
Perch [*Percalabrax japonicus*], (*su-dzuki* . . .).
Bêche-de-mer [genus *Pentacta*], (*ko* . . .).
Medusa, (*kurage,* written phonetically).

SHELLS.

Area Suberenata [?], (*hirabu-kahi,* written phonetically).
Cockle [*Area Inflata*], (*kisa-gahi* . . .).
Turbinidá [a shell of the family], (*shitadami* . . .).

PLANTS.

Ampelopsis serianá folia [?], (*kagami* . . .).
Aphananthe aspera, (*muku,* written phonetically).
Aucuba japonica [probably], (*aha-gi,* written phonetically).
Bamboo, (*take* . . .).
Bamboo-grass [*Bambusa chino*],

(*sasa* . . .).
Barley [or wheat?], (*mugi* . . .).
Beans [two kinds, viz., *Soja glycine* and *Phaseolus radiatus*], (the general name is *mame* . . . that of the latter species in particular *adzuki* . . .).
Bulrush [*Typha japonica*], (*kama* . . .).
Bush-clover [*Lespedeza* of various species], (*hagi* . . .).
Camellia japonica, (*tsuba-ki* . . .).
Cassia [Chinese mythical; or perhaps the native *Cercidiphyllum japonica*], (*katsura,* variously written).
Chamácyparis obtusa, (*hi-no-ki* . . .).
Cleyera japonica [and another allied but undetermined species], (*saka-ki* . . .).
Clubmoss, (*hi-kage* . . .).
Cocculus thunbergi [probably], (*tsu-dzura* . . .).
Cryptomeria japonica, (*sugi* . . .).
Eulalia japonica, (*kaya* . . .).
Euonymus japonica, (*masa-ki* . . .).
Ginger [or perhaps the *Xanthoxylon* is intended], (*hazhikami* . . .).
Halochloa macrantha [but it is not certain that this is the sea-weed intended], (*kemo* . . .).
Holly [or rather the *Olea aquifolium,* which closely resembles holly], (*hihira-gi* . . .).
Knot-grass [*Polygonum tinctorium*], (*awi* . . .).
Lily, (*sawi* written phonetically, *yama-yuri-gusa* . . . , and *saki-kusa* . . .).
Madder, (*akane* . . .).
Millet [*Panicum italicum*], (*awa* . . .).
Moss, (*koke* . . .).
Oak [two species, one evergreen and one deciduous,—*Quercus myrsináfolia Q. dentata*], (*kashi* . . . , *kashiwa* . . .].
Peach, (*momo* . . .).
Photinia glabra [?], (*soba,* written phonetically).
Pine-tree, (*matsu* . . .).
Pueraria thunbergiana, (*kudzu* . . .).
Reed, (*ashi* . . .).
Rice, (*ine* . . .).
Sea-weed [or the original term may designate a particular species], (*me* . . .).
Sedge [*Scirpus maritimus*], (*suge* . . .).
Spindle-tree [*Euonymus radicans*], (*masaki no kadzura* . . .).
Vegetable Wax-tree [*Rhus succe-*

danca], (*hazhi* . . .).
Vine, (*yebi-kadzura* . . .).
Wild cherry [or birch?], (*hahaka* . . .).
Wild chive [or rather the *allium
odorum,* which closely resembles
it], (*ka-mira* . . .).
Winter-cherry [*Physalis alkekengi*],
(*aka-kagachi* written phoneti
cally, and also *hohodzuki* . . .).

The later portions of the work furnish in addition
the following:

ANIMALS.

Cow, (*ushi* . . .).
Dog, (*inu* . . .).
Crane [genus *Grus*], (*tadzu* . . .).
Dove *or* Pigeon, (*hato* . . .).
Grebe, (*niho-dori* . . .).
Lark, (*hibari* . . .).
Peregrine falcon, (*hayabusa* . . .).
Red-throated quail, (*udzura* . . .).
Tree-sparrow, (*suzume* . . .).
Wagtail [probably], (*mana-bashi-
ra,* written phonetically).
Wren, (*sazaki* . . .).
Dolphin, (*iruka* . . .).
Trout [*Plecoglossus altivelis*], (ayu . . .).
Tunny [a kind of, viz. *Thynnus
sibi*], (*shibi* . . .).
Crab, (*kani* . . .).
Horse-fly, (*amu* . . .).
Oyster, (*kaki* . . .).

PLANTS.

Alder [*Alnus maritima*], (*hari-no-ki* . . .).
Aralia, (*mi-tsuna-gashiha* . . .).
Brasenia peltata, (*nunaha* . . .).
Cabbage [*brassica*], (*awona* . . .).
Catalpa Kaempferi [but some say
the cherry is meant], (*adzusa* . . .).
Chestnut, (*kuri* . . .).
Dioscorea quinqueloba, (*tokoro-dzura* . . .).
Euonymus sieboldianus, (*mayumi* . . .).
Gourd, (*hisago* . . .).
Hedysarum esculentum, (*wogi* . . .).
Hydropyrum latifolium, (*komo* . . .).
Kadzura japonica, (*sana-kadzura* . . .).
Livistona sinensis, (*ajimasa* . . .).
Lotus [*nelumbium*], (*hachisu* . . .).
Musk-melon, (*hozochi* . . .).
Oak, [three species, *Quercus serrata*
(*kunugi* . . .), and *Q. glanduli-
fera* (*nara* . . .), both deciduous;
Q. gilva (*ichihi* . . .) ever-
green].
Orange, (*tachibana* . . .).

Podocarpus macrophylla, (*maki* . . .).
Radish [*Raphanus sativus*], (*oho-ne* . . .),
Sashibu (written phonetically), [not
identified].
Water caltrop [*Trapa bispinosa*],
(*hishi* . . .).
Wild garlic [*Allium nipponicum*],
(*nubiru* . . .).
Zelkowa keaki [probably], (*tsuki* . . .).

A few more are probably preserved in the names of places. Thus in Shinano, the name of a province, we seem to have the *shina* (*Tilia cordata*), and in Tadetsu the *tade* (*Polygonum japonicum*). But the identification in these cases is mostly uncertain. It must also be remembered that, as in the case of all non-scientific nomenclatures, several species, and occasionally even more than one genus, are included in a single Japanese term. Thus *chidori* (here always rendered "dotterel") is the name of any kind of sandpiper, plover or dotterel. *Kari* is a general name applied to geese, but not to all the species, and also to the great bustard. Again it should not be forgotten that there may have been, and probably were, in the application of some of these terms, differences of usage between the present day and eleven or twelve centuries ago. Absolute precision is therefore not attainable.[42]

Noticeable in the above lists is the abundant mention of plant-names in a work which is in no ways occupied with botany. Equally noticeable is the absence of some of those which are most common at the present day, such as the tea-plant and the plum-tree, while of the orange we are specially informed that it was introduced from abroad.[43] The difference between the various stones and metals seems, on the other hand, to have attracted very little attention from the Early Japanese. In later times the chief metals were named mostly according to their colour, as follows:

Yellow metal . . . (gold).
White metal . . . (silver).
Red metal . . . (copper).
Black metal . . . (iron).
Chinese (or Korean) . . . (bronze).

But in the ***Records*** the only metal of which it is implied that it was in use from time immemorial is iron, while "various treasures dazzling to the eye, from gold and silver downwards," are only referred to once as existing in the far-western land of Korea. Red clay is the sole kind of earth specially named.

The words relative to colour which occur are:

Black.
Blue (including Green).
Red.
Piebald (of horses).
White.

Yellow is not mentioned (except in the foreign Chinese phrase "the Yellow Stream," signifying Hades, and not to be counted in this context), neither are any of the numerous terms which in modern Japanese serve to distinguish delicate shades of colour. We hear of the "blue (or green), *i.e.* black[44] clouds" and also of the "blue (or green), sea;" but the "blue sky" is conspicuous by its absence here as in so many other early literatures, though strangely enough it does occur in the oldest written documents of the Chinese.

With regard to the subject of names for the different degrees of relationship,—a subject of sufficient interest to the student of sociology to warrant its being discussed at some length,—it may be stated that in modern Japanese parlance the categories according to which relationship is conceived of do not materially differ from those that are current in Europe. Thus we find father, grandfather, great-grandfather, uncle, nephew, stepfather, stepson, father-in-low, son-in-law, and the corresponding terms for females,—mother, grandmother, etc.,—as well as such vaguer designations as parents, ancestors, cousins, and kinsmen. The only striking difference is that brothers and sisters, instead of being considered as all mutually related in the same manner, are divided into two categories, viz.:

Ani . . . elder brother(s),
Otouto . . . younger brother(s),
Ane . . . elder sister(s),
Imouto . . . younger sister(s),

in exact accordance with Chinese usage.

Now in Archaic times there seems to have been a different and more complicated system, somewhat resembling that which still obtains among the natives of Korea, and which the introduction of Chinese ideas and especially the use of the Chinese written characters must have caused to be afterwards abandoned. There are indications of it in some of the phonetically written fragments of the **Records**. But they are not of themselves sufficient to furnish a satisfactory explanation, and the subject has puzzled the native *literati* themselves. Moreover the English language fails us at this point, and elder and younger brother, elder and younger sister are the only terms at the translator's command. It may therefore be as well to quote *in extenso* Motowori's elucidation of the Archaic usage to be found in Vol. XIII, pp. 63-4 of his "Exposition of the Records of Ancient Matters."[45] He says: "Anciently, when brothers and sisters were spoken of, the elder brother was called *se* or *ani* in contradistinction to the younger brothers and younger sisters, and the younger brother also was called *se* in contradistinction to the elder sister. The elder sister was called *ane* in contradistinction to the younger sister, and the younger brother also would use the word *ane* in speaking of his elder sister himself. The younger brother was called

oto in contradistinction to the elder brother, and the younger sister also was called *oto* in contradistinction to the elder sister. The younger sister was called *imo* in contradistinction to the elder brother, and the elder sister also was called *imo* in contradistinction to the younger brother. It was also the custom among brothers and sisters to use the words *iro-se* for *se,* *iro-ne* for *ane,* and *iro-do* for *oto,* and analogy forces us to conclude that *iro-mo* was used for *imo.*" (Motowori elsewhere explains *iro* as a term of endearment indentical with the word *iro,* "love;" but we may hesitate to accept this view.) It will be observed that the foundation of this system of nomenclature was a subordination of the younger to the elder-born modified by a subordination of the females to the males. In the East, especially in primitive times, it is not *"place aux dames,"* but *"place aux messieurs."*

Another important point to notice is that, though in a few passages of the **Records** we find a distinction drawn between the chief and the secondary wives,—perhaps nothing more than the favorite or better-born and the less well-born, are meant to be thus designated,—yet not only is this distinction not drawn throughout, but the wife is constantly spoken of as *imo, i.e.* "younger sister." In fact sister and wife were convertible terms and ideas; and what in a later stage of Japanese, as of Western, civilization is abhorred as incest was in Archaic Japanese times the common practice. We also hear of marriages with half-sisters, with stepmothers, and with aunts; and to wed two or three sisters at the same time was a recognized usage. Most such unions were naturally so contrary to Chinese ethical ideas, that one of the first traces of the influence of the latter in Japan was the stigmatizing of them as incest; and the conflict between the old native custom and the imported moral code is seen to have resulted in political troubles.[46] Marriage with sisters was naturally the first to disappear, and indeed it is only mentioned in the legends of the gods; but unions with half-sisters, aunts, etc., lasted on into the historic epoch. Of exogamy, such as obtains in China, there is no trace in any Japanese document, nor do any other artificial impediments seem to have stood in the way of the free choice of the Early Japanese man, who also (in some cases at least) received a dowry with his bride or brides.

. . . . .

If, taking as our guides the incidental notices which are scattered up and down the pages of the earlier portion of the **Records**, we endeavour to follow an Archaic Japanese through the chief events of his life from the cradle to the tomb, it will be necessary to begin by recalling what has already been alluded to as the "parturition-house" built by the mother, and in which, as we are specially told that it was made windowless, it would perhaps be contradictory to say that the infant first saw the light. Soon after birth a name was given to it,—given to it by the mother,—such name generally containing some appropriate personal reference. In the most ancient times each person (so far as we can judge) bore but one name, or rather one string of words compounded together into a sort of personal designation. But already at the dawn of the historical epoch we are met by the mention of surnames and of what, in the absence of a more fitting word, the translator has ventured to call "gentile names," bestowed by the sovereign as a recompense for some noteworthy deed.[47]

It may be gathered from our text that the idea of calling in the services of wet-nurses in certain exceptional cases had already suggested itself to the minds of the ruling class, whose infants were likewise sometimes attended by special bathing-women. To what we should call education, whether mental or physical, there is absolutely no reference made in the histories. All that can be inferred is that, when old enough to do so, the boys began to follow one of the callings of hunter or fisherman, while the girls staid at home weaving the garments of the family. There was also a great deal of fighting, generally of a treacherous kind, in the intervals of which the warriors occupied themselves in cultivating patches of ground. The very little which is to be gathered concerning the treatment of old people would seem to indicate that they were well cared for.

We are nowhere told of any wedding ceremonies except the giving of presents by the bride or her father, the probable reason being that no such ceremonies existed. Indeed late on into the Middle Ages cohabitation alone constituted matrimony,—cohabitation often secret at first, but afterwards acknowledged, when, instead of going round under cover of night to visit his mistress, the young man brought her back publicly to his parents' house. Mistress, wife, and concubine were thus terms which were not distinguished, and the woman could naturally be discarded at any moment. She indeed was expected to remain faithful to the man with whom she had had more than a passing intimacy, but no reciprocal obligation bound him to her. Thus the wife of one of the gods is made to address her husband in a poem which says:

"Thou . . . indeed, being a man, probably hast on the various island-headlands that thou seest, and on every beachheadland that thou lookest on, a wife like the young herbs. But I, alas! being a woman, have no man except thee; I have no spouse except thee," etc., etc.[48]

In this sombre picture the only graceful touch is the custom which lovers or spouses had of tying each other's girdles when about to part for a time,—a ceremony by which they implied that they would be constant to each other during the period of absence.[49] What became of the children in cases of conjugal separation does not clearly appear. In the only instance which is

related at length, we find the child left with the father; but this instance is not a normal one.[50] Adoption is not mentioned in the earliest traditions; so that when we meet with it later on we shall probably be justified in tracing its introduction to Chinese sources.

Of death-bed scenes and dying speeches we hear but little, and that little need not detain us. The burial rites are more important. The various ceremonies observed on such an occasion are indeed not explicitly detailed. But we gather thus much: that the hut tenanted by the deceased was abandoned,—an ancient custom to whose former existence the removal of the capital at the commencement of each new sovereign's reign long continued to bear witness,—and that the body was first deposited for some days in a "mourning-house," during which interval the survivors (though their tears and lamentations are also mentioned) held a carousal, feasting perhaps on the food which was specially prepared as an offering to the dead person. Afterwards, the corpse was interred, presumably in a wooden bier, as the introduction of stone tombs is specially noted by the historian as having taken place at the end of the reign of the Emperor Sui-nin, and was therefore believed by those who handed down the legendary history to have been a comparatively recent innovation, the date assigned to this monarch by the author of the "Chronicles" coinciding with the latter part of our first, and the first half of our second centuries. To a time not long anterior is attributed the abolition of a custom previously observed at the interments of royal personages. This custom was the burying alive of some of their retainers in the neighbourhood of the tomb. We know also, both from other early literary sources and from the finds which have recently rewarded the labours of archaeologists, that articles of clothing, ornaments, etc., were buried with the corpse. It is all the more curious that the ***Records*** should nowhere make any reference to such a custom, and is a proof (if any be needed) of the necessity of not relying exclusively on any single authority, however respectable, if the full and true picture of Japanese antiquity is to be restored. A few details as to the abolition of the custom of burying retainers alive round their master's tomb, and of the substitution for this cruel holocaust of images in clay will be found in Sect. LXIII, Note 23, and in Sect. LXXV, Note 4, of the following translation.[51] If the custom be one which is properly included under the heading of human sacrifices, it is the only form of such sacrifices of which the earliest recorded Japanese social state retained any trace. The absence of slavery is another honourable feature. On the other hand, the most cruel punishments were dealt out to enemies and wrongdoers. Their nails were extracted, the sinews of their knees were cut, they were buried up to the neck so that their eyes burst, etc. Death, too, was inflicted for the most trivial offences. Of branding, or rather tattooing, the face as a punishment there are one or two incidental mentions. But as no tattooing or other marking or painting of the body for any other purpose is ever alluded to, with the solitary exception in one passage of the painting of her eyebrows by a woman, it is possible that the penal use of tattooing may have been borrowed from the Chinese, to whom it was not unknown.

The shocking obscenity of word and act to which the **Records** bear witness is another ugly feature which must not quite be passed over in silence. It is true that decency, as we understand it, is a very modern product, and is not to be looked for in any society in the barbarous stage. At the same time, the whole range of literature might perhaps be ransacked in vain for a parallel to the naïve filthiness of the passage forming Sect. IV. of the following translation, or to the extraordinary topic which the hero Yamato-Take and his mistress Miyazu are made to select as the theme of poetical repartee.[52] One passage likewise would lead us to suppose that the most beastly crimes were commonly committed.[53]

To conclude this portion of the subject, it may be useful for the sake of comparison to call attention to a few arts and products with which the Early Japanese were *not* acquainted. Thus they had no tea, no fans, no porcelain, no lacquer,—none of the things, in fact, by which in later times they have been chiefly known. They did not yet use vehicles of any kind. They had no accurate method of computing time, no money, scarcely any knowledge of medicine. Neither, though they possessed some sort of music, and poems a few of which at least are not without merit,[54] do we hear anything of the art of drawing. But the most important art of which they were ignorant is that of writing. As some misapprehension has existed on this head, and scholars in Europe have been misled by the inventions of zealous champions of the Shintō religion into a belief in the so-called "Divine Characters," by them alleged to have been invented by the Japanese gods and to have been used by the Japanese people prior to the introduction of the Chinese ideographic writing, it must be stated precisely that all the traditions of the "Divine Age," and of the reigns of the earlier Emperors down to the third century of our era according to the received chronology, maintain a complete silence on the subject of writing, writing materials, and records of every kind. Books are nowhere mentioned till a period confessedly posterior to the opening up of intercourse with the Asiatic continent, and the first books whose names occur are the "Lun Yü" and the "Ch'ien Tzŭ Wên," which are said to have been brought over to Japan during the reign of the Emperor Ō-jin,—according to the same chronology in the year 284 after Christ. That even this statement is antedated, is shown by the fact that the "Ch'ien Tzŭ Wên" was not written till more than two centuries later,—a fact which is worthy the attention of those who have been disposed simply to take on trust the assertions of the Japanese historians.

It should likewise be mentioned that, as has already been pointed out by Mr. Aston, the Japanese terms *fumi* "written document," and *fude* "pen," are probably corruptions of foreign words. The present, indeed, is not the place to discuss the whole question of the so-called "Divine Characters," which Motowori, the most patriotic as well as the most learned of the Japanese *literati,* dismisses in a note to the Prolegomena of his "Exposition of the *Records of Ancient Matters*" with the remark that they "are a late forgery over which no words need be wasted." But as this mare's nest has been imported into the discussion of the Early Japanese social state, and as the point is one on which the absolute silence of the early traditions bears such clear testimony, it was impossible to pass it by without some brief allusion.

V. Religious and Political Ideas of the Early Japanese, Beginnings of the Japanese Nation, and Credibility of the National Records.

The religious beliefs of the modern upholders of Shintō
may be ascertained without much difficulty by a perusal of the works of the leaders of the movement which has endeavoured during the last century and a half to destroy the influence of Buddhism and of the Chinese philosophy, and which has latterly succeeded to some extent in supplanting those two foreign systems. But in Japan, as elsewhere, it has been impossible for men really to turn back a thousand years in religious thought and act; and when we try to discover the primitive opinions that were entertained by the Japanese people prior to the introduction of the Chinese culture, we are met by difficulties that at first seem insuperable. The documents are scanty, and the modern commentaries untrustworthy, for they are all written under the influence of a preconceived opinion. Moreover, the problem is apparently complicated by a mixture of races and mythologies, and by a filtering in of Chinese ideas previous to the compilation of documents of any sort, though these are considerations which have hitherto scarcely been taken into account by foreigners, and are designedly neglected and obscured by such narrowly patriotic native writers as Motowori and Hirata.

In the political field the difficulties are not less, but rather greater; for when once the Imperial House and the centralized Japanese polity, as we know it from the sixth or seventh century of our era downwards, became fully established, it was but too clearly in the interest of the powers that be to efface as far as possible the trace of different governmental arrangements which may have preceded them, and to cause it to be believed that, as things were then, so had they always been. The Emperor Tem-mu, with his anxiety to amend "the deviations from truth and the empty falsehoods" of the historical documents preserved by the various families, and the author of the "Chronicles of Japan" with his elaborate system of fictitious dates, recur to our minds, and we ask ourselves to what extent similar garblings of history,—sometimes intentional, sometimes unintentional,—may have gone on during earlier ages, when there was even less to check them than there was in the eighth century. If, therefore, the translator here gives expression to a few opinions founded chiefly on a careful study of the text of the *Records of Ancient Matters* helped out by a study of the "Chronicles of Japan," he would be understood to do so with great diffidence, especially with regard to his few (so to speak) constructive remarks. As to the destructive side of the criticism, there need be less hesitation; for the old histories bear evidence too conclusively against themselves for it to be possible for the earlier portions of them, at least, to stand the test of sober investigation. Before endeavouring to piece together the little that is found in the *Records* to illustrate the beliefs of Archaic Japanese times, it will be necessary, at the risk of dulness, to give a summary of the old traditions as they lie before us in their entirety, after which will be hazarded a few speculations on the subject of the earlier tribes which combined to form the Japanese people; for the four questions of religious beliefs, of political arrangements, of race, and of the credibility of documents, all hang closely together and, properly speaking, form but one highly complex problem.

Greatly condensed, the Early Japanese traditions amount to this: After an indefinitely long period, during which were born a number of abstract deities, who are differently enumerated in the *Records* and in the "Chronicles," two of these deities, a brother and sister named Izanagi and Izanami (*i.e.,* the "Male Who Invites" and the "Female Who Invites"), are united in marriage, and give birth to the various islands of the Japanese archipelago. When they have finished producing islands, they proceed to the production of a large number of gods and goddesses, many of whom correspond to what we should call personifications of the powers of nature, though personification is a word which, in its legitimate acceptation, is foreign to the Japanese mind. The birth of the Fire-God causes Izanami's death, and the most striking episode of the whole mythology then ensues, when her husband, Orpheus-like, visits her in the under-world to implore her to return to him. She would willingly do so, and bids him wait while she consults with the deities of the place. But he, impatient at her long tarrying, breaks off one of the end-teeth of the comb stuck in the left bunch of his hair, lights it and goes in, only to find her a hideous mass of corruption, in whose midst are seated the eight Gods of Thunder. This episode ends with the deification[58] of three peaches who had assisted him in his retreat before the armies of the under-world, and with bitter words exchanged between him and his wife, who herself pursues him as far as the "Even Pass of Hades."

Returning to Himuka in south-western Japan, Izanagi purifies himself by bathing in a stream, and, as he does so, fresh deities are born from each article of clothing that he throws down on the river-bank, and from each part of his person. One of these deities was the Sun-Goddess, who was born from his left eye, while the Moon-God sprang from his right eye, and the last born of all, Susa-no-Wo, whose name the translator renders by "the Impetuous Male," was born from his nose. Between these three children their father divides the inheritance of the universe.

At this point the story loses its unity. The Moon-God is no more heard of, and the traditions concerning the Sun-Goddess and those concerning the "Impetuous Male Deity" diverge in a manner which is productive of inconsistencies in the remainder of the mythology. The Sun-Goddess and the "Impetuous Male Deity" have a violent quarrel, and at last the latter breaks a hole in the roof of the hall in Heaven where his sister is sitting at work with the celestial weaving-maidens, and through it lets fall "a heavenly piebald horse which he had flayed with a backward flaying." The consequences of this act were so disastrous that the Sun-Goddess withdrew for a season into a cave, from which the rest of the eight hundred myriad (according to the "Chronicles" eighty myriad) deities with difficulty allured her. The "Impetuous Male Deity" was thereupon banished, and the Sun-Goddess remained mistress of the field. Yet, strange to say, she thenceforward retires into the background, and the most bulky section of the mythology consists of stories concerning the "Impetuous Male Deity" and his descendants, who are represented as the monarchs of Japan, or rather of the province of Idzumo. The "Impetuous Male Deity" himself, whom his father had charged with the dominion of the sea, never assumes that rule, but first has a curiously told amorous adventure and an encounter with an eight-forked serpent in Izumo, and afterwards reappears as the capricious and filthy deity of Hades, who however seems to retain some power over the land of the living, as he invests his descendant of the sixth generation with the sovereignty of Japan. Of this latter personage a whole cycle of stories is told, all centering in Idzumo. We learn of his conversations with a hare and with a mouse, of the prowess and cleverness which he displayed on the occasion of a visit to his ancestor in Hades, which is in this cycle of traditions a much less mysterious place than the Hades visited by Izanagi, of his amours, of his triumph over his eighty brethren, of his reconciliation with his jealous empress, and of his numerous descendants, many of whom have names that are particularly difficult of comprehension. We hear too in a tradition, which ends in a pointless manner, of a microscopic deity who comes across the sea to ask this monarch of Idzumo to share the sovereignty with him.

This last-mentioned legend repeats itself in the sequel. The Sun-Goddess, who on her second appearance is constantly represented as acting in concert with the "High August Producing Wondrous Deity,"—one of the abstractions mentioned at the commencement of the *Records,*—resolves to bestow the sovereignty of Japan on a child of whom it is doubtful whether he were hers or that of her brother the "Impetuous Male Deity." Three embassies are sent from Heaven to Idzumo to arrange matters, but it is only a fourth that is successful, the final ambassadors obtaining the submission of the monarch or deity of Idzumo, who surrenders his sovereignty and promises to serve the new dynasty (apparently in the under-world), if a palace or temple be built for him and he be appropriately worshipped. Thereupon the child of the deity whom the Sun-Goddess had originally wished to make sovereign of Japan, descends to earth,—not to Idzumo in the north-west, be it mentioned, as the logical sequence of the story would lead one to expect,—but to the peak of a mountain in the south-western island of Kiushiu.

Here follows a quaint tale accounting for the odd appearance of the bêche-de-mer, and another to account for the shortness of the lives of mortals, after which we are told of the birth under peculiar circumstances of the heaven-descended deity's three sons. Two of these, Ho-deri and Ho-wori, whose names may be Englished as "Fire-Shine" and "Fire-Subside," are the heroes of a very curious legend, which includes an elaborate account of a visit paid by the latter to the palace of the God of Ocean, and of a curse or spell which gained for him the victory over his elder brother, and enabled him to dwell peacefully in his palace at Takachiho for the space of five hundred and eighty years,—the first statement resembling a date which the *Records* contain. This personage's son married his own aunt, and was the father of four children, one of whom "treading on the crest of the waves, crossed over to the Eternal Land," while a second "went into the sea plain," and the two others moved eastward, fighting with the chiefs of Kibi and Yamato, having adventures with gods both with and without tails, being assisted by a miraculous sword and a gigantic crow, and naming the various places they passed through after incidents in their own career, as "the Impetuous Male" and other divine personages had done before them. One of these brothers was Kamu-Yamato-Ihare-Biko, who (the other having died before him) was first given the title of Jim-mu Ten-nō more than fourteen centuries after the date which in the "Chronicles" is assigned as that of his decease.

Henceforth Yamato, which had scarcely been mentioned before, and the provinces adjacent to it become the centre of the story, and Idzumo again emerges into importance. A very indecent love-tale forms a bridge which unites the two fragments of the mythology; and the "Great Deity of Miwa," who is identified with the deposed monarch of Idzumo, appears on the scene. Indeed during the rest of the story this "Great Deity of Miwa," and his colleague the "Small August Deity" (Sukuna-Mi-Kami[59]), the deity Izasa-Wake, the three Water-Gods of Sumi, and the "Great Deity of Kadzuraki," of whom there is so striking a mention in Sect. CLVIII, form, with the Sun-Goddess and with a certain divine sword preserved at the temple of Isonokami in Yamato, the only objects of worship specially named, the other gods and goddesses being no more heard of. This portion of the story is closed by an account of the troubles which inaugurated the reign of Jim-mu's successor, Sui-sei, and then occurs a blank of (according to the accepted chronology) five hundred years, during which absolutely nothing is told us excepting dreary genealogies, the place where each sovereign dwelt and where he was buried, and the age to which he lived,—this after the minute details which had previously been given concerning the successive gods or monarchs down to Sui-sei inclusive. It should likewise be noted that the average age of the first seventeen monarchs (counting Jim-mu Ten-nō as the first according to received ideas) is nearly 96 years if we follow the *Records* and over a hundred if we follow the accepted chronology which is based chiefly on the constantly divergent statements contained in the "Chronicles." The age of several of the monarchs exceeds 120 years.

The above-mentioned lapse of an almost blank period of five centuries brings us to the reign of the Emperor known to history by the name of Sū-jin, whose life of one hundred and sixty-eight years (one hundred and twenty according to the "Chronicles") is supposed to have immediately preceded the Christian era. In this reign the former monarch of Idzumo or god of Miwa again appears and produces a pestilence, of the manner of staying which Sū-jin is warned in a dream, while a curious but highly indecent episode tells us how a person called Oho-Tata-Ne-Ko was known to be a son of the deity in question, and was therefore appointed high priest of his temple. In the ensuing reign an elaborate legend, involving a variety of circumstances as miraculous as any in the earlier portion of the mythology, again centres in the necessity of pacifying the great god of Idzumo; and this, with details of internecine strife in the Imperial family, of the sovereign's amours, and of the importation of the orange from the "Eternal Land," brings us to the cycle of traditions of which Yamato-Take, a son of the Emperor Kei-kō, is the hero. This prince, after slaying one of his brothers in the privy, accomplishes the task of subduing both western and eastern Japan; and, notwithstanding certain details which are unsavoury to the European taste, his story, taken as a whole, is one of the most striking in the book. He performs marvels of valour, disguises himself as a woman to slay the brigands, is the possessor of a magic sword and fire-striker, has a devoted wife who stills the fury of the waves by sitting down upon their surface, has encounters with a deer and with a boar who are really gods in disguise, and finally dies on his way westward before he can reach his home in Yamato. His death is followed by a highly mythological account of the laying to rest of the white bird into which he ended by being transformed.

The succeeding reign is a blank, and the next after that transports us without a word of warning to quite another scene. The sovereign's home is now in Tsukushi, the south-western island of the Japanese archipelago, and four of the gods, through the medium of the sovereign's wife, who is known to history as the Empress Jin-gō, reveal the existence of the land of Korea, of which, however, this is not the first mention. The Emperor disbelieves the divine message, and is punished by death for his incredulity. But the Empress, after a special consultation between her prime minister and the gods, and the performance of various religious ceremonies, marshals her fleet, and, with the assistance of the fishes both great and small and of a miraculous wave, reaches Shiragi (one of the ancient divisions of Korea), and subdues it. She then returns to Japan, the legend ending with a curiously naïve tale of how she sat a-fishing one day on a shoal in the river Wo-gawa in Tsukushi with threads picked out of her skirt for lines.

The next section shows her going up by sea to Yamato,—another joint in the story, by means of which the Yamato cycle of legends and the Tsukushi cycle are brought into apparent unity. The "Chronicles of Japan" have even improved upon this by making Jin-gō's husband dwell in Yamato at the commencement of his reign and only remove to Tsukushi later, so that if the less elaborated **Records** had not been preserved, the two threads of the tradition would have been still more difficult to unravel. The Empress's army defeats the troops raised by the native kings or princes, who are represented as her step-sons; and from that time forward the story runs on in a single channel and always centres in Yamato. China likewise is now first mentioned, books are said to have been brought over from the mainland, and we hear of the gradual introduction of various useful arts. Even the annals of the reign of Ō-jin however, during which this civilizing impulse from abroad is said to have commenced, are not free from details as miraculous as any in the earlier portions of the book. Indeed Sects. CXIV-CXVI of the following translation, which form part of the narrative of his reign, are occupied with the recital of one of the most fanciful tales of the whole mythology. The monarch himself is said to have lived a hundred and thirty years, while his successor lived eighty-three (according to the "Chronicles" Ō-jin lived a hundred and ten and his successor Nin-toku reigned eighty-seven years). It is not till the next reign that the miraculous ceases, a fact which significantly coincides with the reign in which, according to a statement in the "Chronicles," "historiographers were first appointed to all the provinces to record words and events, and forward archives

from all directions." This brings us to the commencement of the fifth century of our era, just three centuries before the compilation of our histories, but only two centuries before the compilation of the first history of which mention has been preserved. From that time the story in the **Records,** though not well told, gives us some very curious pictures, and reads as if it were reliable. It is tolerably full for a few reigns, after which it again dwindles into mere genealogies, carrying us down to the commencement of the seventh century. The "Chronicles," on the contrary, give us full details down to A.D. 701, that is to within nineteen years of the date of their compilation.

The reader who has followed this summary, or who will take the trouble to read through the whole text for himself, will perceive that there is no break in the story,—at least no chronological break,—and no break between the fabulous and the real, unless indeed it be at the commencement of the fifth century of our era, *i.e.* more than a thousand years later than the date usually accepted as the commencement of genuine Japanese history. The only breaks are,—not chronological,—but topographical.

This fact of the continuity of the Japanese mythology and history has been fully recognized by the leading native commentators, whose opinions are those considered orthodox by modern Shintoists; and they draw from it the conclusion that everything in the standard national histories must be equally accepted as literal truth. All persons however cannot force their minds into the limits of such a belief; and early in the eighteenth century a celebrated writer and thinker, Arawi Hakuseki, published a work in which, while accepting the native mythology as an authentic chronicle of events, he did so with the reservation of proving to his own satisfaction that all the miraculous portions thereof were allegories, and the gods only men under another name. In this particular, the elasticity of the Japanese word for "deity," *kami,* which has already been noticed, stood the eastern Euhemerus in good stead. Some of his explanations are however extremely comical, and it is evident that such a system enables the person who uses it to prove whatever he has a mind to.[62] In the nineteenth century a diluted form of the same theory was adopted by Tachibana no Moribe, who, although endeavouring to remain an orthodox Shintoist, yet decided that some of the (so to speak) uselessly miraculous incidents need not be believed in as revealed truth. Such, for instance, are the story of the speaking mouse, and that of Izanagi's head-dress turning into a bunch of grapes. He accounts for many of these details by the supposition that they are what he calls *wosana-goto,* i.e. "child-like words," and thinks that they were invented for the sake of fixing the story in the minds of children, and are not binding on modern adults as articles of faith. He is also willing to allow that some passages show traces of Chinese influence, and he blames Motowori's uncompromising championship of every iota of the existing text of the **Records of Ancient Matters**. As belonging to this same school of what may perhaps be termed "rationalistic believers" in Japanese mythology, a contemporary Christian writer, Mr. Takahashi Gorō, must also be mentioned. Treading in the foot-steps of Arawi Hakuseki, but bringing to bear on the legends of his own country some knowledge of the mythology of other lands, he for instance explains the traditions of the Sun-Goddess and of the Eight-Forked Serpent of Yamada by postulating the existence of an ancient queen called Sun, whose brother, after having been banished from her realm for his improper behaviour, killed an enemy whose name was Serpent, etc., while such statements as that the microscopic deity who came over the waves to share the sovereignty of Idzumo would not tell his name, are explained by the assertion that, being a foreigner, he was unintelligible for some time until he had learnt the language. It is certainly strange that such theorists should not see that they are undermining with one hand that which they endeavour to prop up with the other, and that their own individual fancy is made by them the sole standard of historic truth. Yet Mr. Takahashi confidently asserts that "his explanations have nothing forced or fanciful" in them, and that "they cannot fail to solve the doubts even of the greatest of doubters."[63]

The general habit of the more sceptical Japanese of the present day,—*i.e.* of ninety-nine out of every hundred of the educated,—seems to be to reject, or at least to ignore, the history of the gods, while implicitly accepting the history of the emperors from Jim-mu downwards; and in so doing they have been followed with but little reserve by most Europeans,—almanacs, histories and cyclopædias all continuing to repeat on the antiquated authority of such writers as Kaempfer and Titsingh, that Japan possesses an authentic history covering more than two thousand years, while Siebold and Hoffman even go the length of discussing the *hour* of Jim-mu's accession in the year 660 B.C.! This is the attitude of mind now sanctioned by the governing class. Thus, in the historical compilations used as text-books in the schools, the stories of the gods,—that is to say the Japanese traditions down to Jim-mu exclusive,—are either passed over in silence or dismissed in a few sentences, while the annals of the human sovereigns,—that is to say the Japanese traditions from Jim-mu inclusive,—are treated precisely as if the events therein related had happened yesterday, and were as incontrovertibly historical as later statements for which there is contemporary evidence. The same plan is pursued elsewhere in official publications. Thus, to take but one example among many, the Imperial Commissioners to the Vienna Exhibition, in their "Notice sur l'Empire du Japon," tell us that "L'histoire de la dynastie impériale remonte très-haut. L'obscurité entoure ses débuts, vu l'absence de documents réguliers ou d'un calendrier parfait. Le premier Empereur de la dynastie

présente, dont il reste des annales dignes de confiance, est Jin-mou-ten-nô[64] qui organisa un soulèvement dans la province de Hiuga, marcha à l'Est avec ses compagnons, fonda sa capitale dans la vallée de Kashihara dans le Yamato, et monta sur le trône comme Empereur. C'est de cet Empereur que descend, per une succession régulière, la présente famille régnante du Japon. C'est de l'année de l'avènement de Jin-mou-ten-nô que date l'ère japonaise (Année 1-660 avant Jésus-Christ.")

As for the *ère Japonaise* mentioned by the commissioners, it may be pertinent to observe that it was only introduced by an edict dated 15th Dec., 1872,[65] that is to say just a fortnight before the publication of their report. *And this era, this accession, is confidently placed thirteen or fourteen centuries before the first history which records it was written, nine centuries before (at the earliest computation) the art of writing was introduced into the country, and on the sole authority of books teeming with miraculous legends!!* Does such a proceeding need any comment after once being formulated in precise terms, and can any unprejudiced person continue to accept the early Japanese chronology and the first thousand years of the so-called history of Japan?

. . . . .

Leaving this discussion, let us now see whether any information relative to the early religious and political state of the Japanese can be gleaned from the pages of the **Records** and of the "Chronicles." There are fragments of information,—fragments of two sorts,—some namely of clear import, others which are rather a matter for inference and for argument. Let us take the positive fragments first—the notices as to cosmological ideas, dreams, prayers, etc.

The first thing that strikes the student is that what, for want of a more appropriate name, we must call the religion of the Early Japanese, was not an organized religion. We can discover in it nothing corresponding to the body of dogma, the code of morals, and the sacred book authoritatively enforcing both, with which we are familiar in civilized religions, such as Buddhism, Christianity, and Islam. What we find is a bundle of miscellaneous superstitions rather than a co-ordinated system. Dreams evidently were credited with great importance, the future being supposed to be foretold in them, and the will of the gods made known. Sometimes even an actual object, such as a wonderful sword, was sent down in a dream, thus to our ideas mixing the material with the spiritual. The subject did not, however, present itself in that light to the Early Japanese, to whom there was evidently but one order of phenomena,—what we should call the natural order. Heaven, or rather the Sky, was an actual place,—not more ethereal than earth, nor thought of as the abode of the blessed after death—but simply a "high plain" situated above Japan and communicating with Japan by a bridge or ladder, and forming the residence of some of those powerful personages called *kami,*—a word which we must make shift to translate by "god" or "goddess," or "deity." An arrow shot from earth could reach Heaven, and make a hole in it. There was at least one mountain in Heaven, and one river with a broad stony bed like those with which the traveller in Japan becomes familiar, one or two caves, one or more wells, and animals, and trees. There is, however, some confusion as to the mountain,—the celebrated Mount Kagu,—for there is one of that name in the province of Yamato.

Some of the gods dwelt here on earth, or descended hither from Heaven, and had children by human women. Such, for instance, was the Emperor Jim-mu's great-grandfather. Some few gods had tails or were otherwise personally remarkable; and "savage deities" are often mentioned as inhabiting certain portions of Japan, both in the so-called "Divine Age" and during the reigns of the human emperors down to a time corresponding, according to the generally received chronology, with the first or second century of the Christian era. The human emperors themselves, moreover, were sometimes spoken of as deities, and even made personal use of that designation. The gods occasionally transformed themselves into animals, and at other times simple tangible objects were called gods,—or at least they were called *kami;* for the gulf separating the Japanese from the English term can never be too often recalled to mind. The word *kami,* as previously mentioned, properly signifies "superior," and it would be putting more into it than it really implies to say that the Early Japanese "deified,"—in our sense of the verb to "deify,"—the peaches which Izanagi used to pelt his assailants with, or any other natural objects whatsoever. It would, indeed, be to attribute to them a flight of imagination of which they were not capable, and a habit of personification not in accordance with the genius of their language. Some of the gods are mentioned collectively as "bad Deities like unto the flies in the fifth moon"; but there is nothing approaching a systematic division into good spirits and bad spirits. In fact the word "spirit" itself is not applicable at all to the gods of Archaic Japan. They were, like the gods of Greece, conceived of only as more powerful human beings. They were born, and some of them died, though here again there is inconsistency, as the death of some of them is mentioned in a manner leading one to suppose that they were conceived of as being then at an end, whereas in other cases such death seems simply to denote transference to Hades, or to what is called "the One Road," which is believed to be a synonym for Hades. Sometimes, again, a journey to Hades is undertaken by a god without any reference to his death. Nothing, indeed, could be less consistent than the various details.

Hades[66] itself is another instance of this inconsistency. In the legend of Oho-Kuni-Nushi (the "Master of the Great Land"),—one of the Idzumo cycle of legends,—Hades is described exactly as if it were part of the land of the living, or exactly as if it were Heaven, which indeed comes to the same thing. It has its trees, its houses, its family quarrels, etc., etc. In the legend of Izanagi, on the other hand, Hades means simply the abode of horrible putrefaction and of the vindictive dead, and is fitly described by the god himself who had ventured thither as "a hideous and polluted land." The only point in which the legends agree is in placing between the upper earth and Hades a barrier called the "Even Pass (or Hill) of Hades." The state of the dead in general is nowhere alluded to, nor are the dying ever made to refer to a future world, whether good or evil.

The objects of worship were of course the gods, or some of them. It has already been stated that during the later portions of the story, whose scene is laid almost exclusively on earth, the Sun-Goddess, the deity Izasa-Wake, the Divine Sword of Isono-kami, the Small August Deity (*Sukuna-Mi-Kami*), the "Great Gods" of Miwa and of Kadzuraki and the three Water-Deities of Sumi, alone are mentioned as having been specially worshipped. Of these the first and the last appear together, forming a sort of quaternion, while the other five appear singly and have no connection with each other. The deities of the mountains, the deities of the rivers, the deities of the sea, etc., are also mentioned in the aggregate, as are likewise the heavenly deities and the earthly deities; and the Empress Jin-gō is represented as conciliating them all previous to her departure for Korea by "putting into a gourd the ashes of a *maki* tree,[67] and likewise making a quantity of chopsticks and also of leaf-platters, and scattering them all on the waves."

This brings us to the subject of religious rites,—a subject on which we long for fuller information than the texts afford.[68] That the conciliatory offerings made to the gods were of a miscellaneous nature will be expected from the quotation just made. Nevertheless, a very natural method was in the main followed; for the people offered the things by which they themselves set most store, as we hear at a later period of the poet Tsurayuki, when in a storm at sea, flinging his mirror into the waves because he had but one. The Early Japanese made offerings of two kinds of cloth, one being hempen cloth and the other cloth manufactured from the bark of the paper-mulberry,—offerings very precious in their eyes, but which have in modern times been allowed to degenerate into useless strips of paper. They likewise offered shields, spears, and other things. Food was offered both to the gods and to the dead; indeed, the palace or tomb of the dead monarch and the temple of the god cannot always be distinguished from each other, and, as has already been mentioned, the Japanese use the same word *miya* for "palace" and for "temple." Etymologically signifying "august house," it is naturally susceptible of what are to us two distinct meanings.

With but one exception,[69] the **Records** do not give us the words of any prayers (or, as the Japanese term *norito* has elsewhere been translated, "rituals"). Conversations with the gods are indeed detailed, but no devotional utterances. Fortunately however a number of very ancient prayers have been preserved in other books, and translations of some of them by Mr. Satow will be found scattered through the volumes of the Transactions of this Society. They consist mostly of declarations of praise and statements of offerings made, either in return for favours received or conditionally on favours being granted. They are all in prose, and hymns do not seem to have been in use. Indeed of the hundred and eleven Songs preserved in the **Records,** not one has any religious reference.

The sacred rite of which most frequent mention is made is purification by water. Trial by hot water is also alluded to in both histories, but not till a time confessedly posterior to the commencement of intercourse with the mainland. We likewise hear of compacts occasionally entered into with a god, and somewhat resembling our European wager, oath, or curse. Priests are spoken of in a few passages, but without any details. We do not hear of their functions being in any way mediatorial, and the impression conveyed is that they did not exist in very early times as a separate class. When they did come into existence, the profession soon became hereditary, according to the general tendency in Japan towards the hereditability of offices and occupations.

Miscellaneous superstitions crop up in many places. Some of these were evidently obsolescent or unintelligible at the time when the legends crystallized into their present shape, and stories are told purporting to give their origin. Thus we learn either in the **Records** or in the "Chronicles," or in both works, why it is unlucky to use only one light, to break off the teeth of a comb at night-time, and to enter the house with straw hat and rain-coat on. The world-wide dread of going against the sun is connected with the Jim-mu legend, and recurs elsewhere.[70] We also hear of charms,—for instance, of the wondrous "Herb-Quelling Sabre" found by Susa-no-Wo (the "Impetuous Male Deity") inside a serpent's tail, and still preserved as one of the Imperial *regalia*. Other such charms were the "tide-flowing jewel" and "tide-ebbing jewel," that obtained for Jimmu's grandfather the victory over his elder brother, together with the fish-hook which figures so largely in the same legend.[71] Divination by means of the shoulder-blade of a stag was a favourite means of ascertaining the will of the gods. Sometimes also human beings seem to have been credited in a vague manner with the power of prophetic utterance. Earthenware pots were

buried at the point of his departure by an intending traveller. In a fight the initial arrow was regarded with superstitious awe. The great precautions with which the Empress Jin-gō is said to have set out on her expedition to Korea have already been alluded to, and indeed the commencement of any action or enterprise seems to have had special importance attributed to it.

To conclude this survey of the religious beliefs of the Early Japanese by referring, as was done in the case of the arts of life, to certain notable features which are conspicuous by their absence, attention may be called to the fact that there is no tradition of a deluge, no testimony to any effect produced on the imagination by the earthquakes from which the Japanese islanders suffer such constant alarms, no trace of star-worship, no notion of incarnation or of transmigration. This last remark goes to show that the Japanese mythology had assumed its present shape before the first echo of Buddhism reverberated on these shores. But the absence of any tradition of a deluge or inundation is still more remarkable, both because such catastrophes are likely to occur occasionally in all lands, and because the imagination of most nations seems to have been greatly impressed by their occurrence. Moreover what is specifically known to us as *the* Deluge has been lately claimed as an ancient Altaïc myth. Yet here we have the oldest of the *undoubtedly* Altaïc nations without any legend of the kind. As for the neglect of the stars, round whose names the imagination of other races has twined such fanciful conceits, it is as characteristic of Modern as of Archaic Japan. The Chinese designations of the constellations, and some few Chinese legends relating to them, have been borrowed in historic times; but no Japanese writer has ever thought of looking in the stars for "the poetry of heaven." Another detail worthy of mention is that the number seven, which in so many countries has been considered sacred, is here not prominent in any way, its place being taken by eight. Thus we have Eight Great Islands, an Eight-forked Serpent, a beard Eighty Handbreadths long, a God named "Eight-Thousand Spears," Eighty or Eight Hundred Myriads of Deities, etc., etc. The commentators think it necessary to tell us that all these eights and eighties need not be taken literally, as they simply mean a great number. The fact remains that the number eight had, for some unknown reason, a special significance attached to it; and as the documents which mention eight also mention nine and ten, besides higher numbers, and as in some test cases, such as that of the Eight Great Islands, each of the eight is separately enumerated, it is plain that when the Early Japanese said eight they meant eight, though they may doubtless have used that number in a vague manner, as we do a dozen, a hundred, and a thousand.

How glaringly different all this is from the fanciful accounts of Shintō that have been given by some recent popular writers calls for no comment. Thus one of them, whom another quotes as an authority,[72] tells us that Shintō "consists in the belief that the productive ethereal spirit being expanded through the whole universe, every part is in some degree impregnated with it, and therefore every part is in some measure the seat of the deity; whence local gods and goddesses are everywhere worshipped, and consequently multiplied without end. Like the ancient Romans and the Greeks, they acknowledge a Supreme Being, the first, the supreme, the intellectual, by which men have been reclaimed from rudeness and barbarism to elegance and refinement, and been taught through privileged men and women, not only to live with more comfort, but to die with better hopes."(!) Truly, when one peruses such utterly groundless assertions,—for that here quoted is but one among many,—one is tempted to believe that the nineteenth century must form part of the early mythopæc age.

With regard to the question of government, we learn little beyond such vague statements as that to so and-so was yielded by his eighty brethren the sovereignty of the land of Idzumo, or that Izanagi divided the dominion over all things between his three children, bestowing on one the "Plain of High Heaven," on another the Dominion of the Night, and on the third the "Sea-Plain." But we do not in the earlier legends see such sovereignty actually administered. The heavenly gods seem rather to have been conceived as forming a sort of commonwealth, who decided things by meeting together in council in the stony bed of the "River of Heaven," and taking the advice of the shrewdest of their number. Indeed the various divine assemblies, to which the story in the **Records** and "Chronicles" introduces us, remind us of nothing so much as of the village assemblies of primitive tribes in many parts of the world, where the cleverness of one and the general willingness to follow his suggestions fill the place of the more definite organization of later times.

Descending from heaven to earth, we find little during the so-called "Divine Age" but stories of isolated individuals and families; and it is not till the narrative of the wars of the earlier Emperors commences, that any kind of political organization comes into view. Then at once we hear of chieftains in every locality, who lead their men to battle, and are seemingly the sole depositories of power, each in his microscopic sphere. The legend of Jim-mu itself, however, is sufficient to show that autocracy, as we understand it, was not characteristic of the government of the Tsukushi tribes; for Jim-mu and his brother, until the latter's death, are represented as joint chieftains of their host. Similarly we find that the "Territorial Owners" of Yamato, and the "Rulers" of Idzumo, whom Jim-mu or his successors are said to have subjugated, are constantly spoken of in the Plural, as if to intimate that they exercised a divided sovereignty. During the whole of the so-called "Human Age" we meet, both in parts of the country

which were already subject to the Imperial rule and in others which were not yet annexed, with local magnates bearing these same titles of "Territorial Owners," "Rulers," "Chiefs," etc.; and the impression left on the mind is that in early historical times the sovereign's power was not exercised directly over all parts of Japan, but that in many cases the local chieftains continued to hold sway though owning some sort of allegiance to the emperor in Yamato, while in others the emperor was strong enough to depose these local rulers, and to put in their place his own kindred or retainers who however exercised unlimited authority in their own districts, and used the same titles as had been borne by the former native rulers,—that, in fact, the government was feudal rather than centralized. This characteristic of the political organization of Early Japan has not altogether escaped the attention of the native commentators. Indeed the great Shintō scholar Hirata not only recognizes the fact, but endeavours to prove that the system of centralization which obtained during the eighth, ninth, tenth, eleventh, and part of the twelfth centuries, and which has been revived in our own day, is nothing but an imitation of the Chinese bureaucratic system; and he asserts that an organized feudalism, similar to that which existed from the twelfth century down to the year 1867, was the sole really ancient and national Japanese form of government. The translator cannot follow Hirata to such lengths, as he sees no evidence in the early histories of the intricate organization of mediæval Japan. But that, beyond the immediate limits of the Imperial domain, the government *resembled* feudalism rather than centralization seems indisputable. It is also true that the seventh century witnessed a sudden move in the direction of bureaucratic organization, many of the titles which had up till that time denoted actual provincial chieftains being then either suppressed, or else allowed to sink into mere "gentile names." Another remark which is suggested by a careful perusal of the two ancient histories is that the Imperial succession was in early historical times very irregular. Strange gaps occur as late as the sixth century of our era; and even when it was one of the children who inherited his father's throne, that child was rarely the eldest son.

. . . . .

What now are we to gather from this analysis of the religious and political features revealed to us by a study of the books containing the Early Japanese traditions as to the still remoter history and tribal divisions of Japan, and as to the origin of the Japanese legends? Very little that is certain, perhaps; but, in the opinion of the present writer, two or three interesting probabilities.

In view of the multiplicity of gods and the complications of the so-called historical traditions, he thinks that it would be *à priori* difficult to believe that the development of Japanese civilization should have run on in a single stream broken only in the third century by the commencement of intercourse with the mainland of Asia. We are, however, not left to such a merely theoretical consideration. There are clear indications of there having been three centres of legendary cycles, three streams which mixed together to form the Japan which meets us at the dawn of authentic history in the fifth century of our era. One of these centres,—the most important in the mythology,—is Idzumo; the second is Yamato; the third is Tsukushi, called in modern times Kiushiu. Eastern and Northern Japan count for nothing; indeed, much of the North-East and North was, down to comparatively recent times, occupied by the barbarous Ainos or, as they are called by the Japanese Yemishi, Yebisu or Yezo. That the legends or traditions derived from the three parts of the country here mentioned accord but imperfectly together is an opinion which has already been alluded to, and upon which light may perhaps be thrown by a more thorough sifting of the myths and beliefs classified according to this three-fold system. The question of the ancient division of Japan into several independent states is, however, not completely a matter of opinion. For we have in the *"Shan Hai Ching"* a positive statement concerning a Northern and a Southern Yamato . . . , and the Chinese annals of both the Han dynasties tell us of the division of the country into a much larger number of kingdoms, of which, according to the annals of the later Han dynasty, Yamato . . . was the most powerful. A later official Chinese historian also tells us that *Jih-pên* (. . . our *Japan*) and Yamato had been two different states, and that *Jih-pên* was reported to have swallowed up Yamato. By *Jih-pên* the author evidently meant to speak of the island of Tsukushi or of part of it. That the Chinese were fairly well acquainted with Japan is shown by the fact of there being in the old Chinese literature more than one mention of "the country of the hairy people beyond the mountains in the East and North,"—that is of the Yemishi or Ainos. No Chinese book would seem to mention Idzumo as having formed a separate country; and this evidence must be allowed its full weight. It is possible, of course, that Idzumo may have been incorporated with Yamato before the conquest of the latter by the Tsukushi people, and in this case some of the inconsistencies of the history, may be traceable to a confusion of the traditions concerning the conquest of Idzumo by Yamato and of those concerning the conquest of Yamato by Tsukushi. Perhaps too (for so almost impossible a task is it to reconstruct history out of legend) there may not, after all, be sufficient warrant for believing in the former existence of Idzumo as a separate state, though it certainly seems hard to account otherwise for the peculiar place that Idzumo occupies in mythic story. In any case, and whatever light may hereafter be thrown on this very obscure question, it must be remembered that, so far

as clear native documentary evidence reaches, 400 A.D. is approximately the highest limit of reliable Japanese history, Beyond that date we are at once confronted with the miraculous; and if any facts relative to earlier Japan are to be extracted from the pages of the *Records* and "Chronicles," it must be by a process very different from that of simply reading and taking their assertions upon trust.

With regard to the origin, or rather to the significance, of the clearly fanciful portions of the Japanese legends, the question here mooted as to the probability of the Japanese mythology being a mixed one warns us to exercise more than usual caution in endeavouring to interpret it. In fact it bids us wait to interpret it until such time as further research shall have shown which legends belong together. For if they are of heterogeneous origin, it is hopeless to attempt to establish a genealogical tree of the gods, and the very phrase so often heard in discussions on this subject,—"the original religious beliefs of the Japanese,"—ceases to have any precise meaning; for different beliefs may have been equally ancient and original, but distinguished geographically by belonging to different parts of the country. Furthermore it may not be superfluous to call attention to the fact that the gods who are mentioned in the opening phrases of the histories as we now have them are not therefore necessarily the gods that were most anciently worshipped. Surely in religions, as in books, it is not often the preface that is written first. And yet this simple consideration has been constantly neglected, and, one after another, European writers having a tincture of knowledge of Japanese mythology, tell us of original Dualities, Trinities, and Supreme Deities, without so much as pausing to notice that the only two authorities in the matter,—viz., the *Records* and the "Chronicles,"—differ most gravely in the lists they furnish of primary gods. If the present writer ventured to throw out a suggestion where so many random assertions have been made, it would be to the effect that the various abstractions which figure at the commencement of the *Records* and of the "Chronicles" were probably later growths, and perhaps indeed mere inventions of individual priests. There is nothing either in the histories or in the Shintō Rituals to show that these gods, or some one or more of them, were in early days, as has been sometimes supposed, the objects of a purer worship which was afterwards obscured by the legends of Izanagi, Izanami, and their numerous descendants. On the contrary, with the exception of the deity Taka-Mi-Musu-Bi,[74] they are no sooner mentioned than they vanish into space.

Whether it is intrinsically likely that so rude a race as the Early Japanese, and a race so little given to metaphysical speculation as the Japanese at all times of their history, should have commenced by a highly abstract worship which they afterwards completely abandoned, is a question which may better be left to those whose general knowledge of early peoples and early religious beliefs entitles their decisions to respect. Their assistance, likewise, even after the resolution of the Japanese mythology into its several component parts, must be called in by the specialist to help in deciding how much of this mythology should be interpreted according to the "solar" method now so popular in England, how much should be accepted as history more or less perverted, how much should be regarded as embodying attempts at explaining facts in nature, and what residue may be rejected as simple fabrication of the priesthood in comparatively late times.[75] Those who are personally acquainted with the Japanese character will probably incline to enlarge the area of the three latter divisions more than would be prudent in the case of the highly imaginative Aryans, and to point out that, though some few Japanese legends or portions of legends can be traced to false etymologies invented to account for names of places, and are therefore true myths in the strictest acceptation of the term, yet the kindred process whereby personality is ascribed to inanimate objects,— a process which lies at the very root of Aryan mythology,—is altogether alien to the Japanese genius, and indeed to the Far-Eastern mind in general. Mythology thus originated has been aptly described as a "disease of language." But all persons are not liable to catch the same disease, neither presumably are all languages; and it is hard to see how a linguistic disease which consists in mistaking a metaphor for a reality can attack a tongue to which metaphor, even in its tamest shape, is an almost total stranger. Thus not only have Japanese Nouns no Genders and Japanese Verbs no Persons, but the names of inanimate objects cannot even be used as the subjects of Transitive Verbs. Nowhere for instance in Japanese, whether Archaic, Classical, or Modern, do we meet with such metaphorical,—mythological,—phrases as "the hot wind melts the ice," or "his conversation delights me," where the words "wind" and "conversation" are spoken of as if they were personal agents. No, the idea is invariably rendered in some other and impersonal way. Yet what a distance separates such statements, in which the ordinary European reader unacquainted with any Altaïc tongue would scarcely recognize the existence of any personification at all, from the bolder flights of Aryan metaphor! Indeed, though Altaïc Asia has produced very few wise men, the words of its languages closely correspond to the definition of words as "the wise man's counters;" for they are colourless and matter-of-fact, and rarely if ever carry him who speaks them above the level of sober reality. At the same time, it is patent that the sun plays *some* part in the Japanese mythology; and even the legend of Prince Yamato-Take, which has hitherto been generally accepted as historical or semi-historical, bears such close resemblance to legends in other countries which have been pronounced to be solar by great authorities that it may at least be worth while to subject it to investigation from that point of view.[76] The present writer has already expressed his conviction that this matter is not one for the specialist to decide alone. He would only, from the Japanese point of view, suggest very particular caution in the application to Japanese legend of a method of interpretation which has elsewhere been fruitful of great results.

A further particular which is deserving of notice is the almost certain fact of a recension of the various traditions at a comparatively late date. This is partly shown by the amount of geographical knowledge displayed in the enumeration of the various islands supposed to have been given birth to by Izanagi and Izanami (the "Male who Invites" and the "Female who Invites"),—an amount and an exactness of knowledge unattainable at a time prior to the union under one rule of all the provinces mentioned, and significantly not extending much beyond those provinces. Such a recension may likewise be inferred,—if the opinion of the manifold origin of the Japanese traditions be accepted,—from the fairly ingenious manner in which their component parts have generally been welded together. The way in which one or two legends,—for instance, that of the curious curse pronounced by the younger brother Howori on the elder Ho-deri—are repeated more than once exemplifies a less intelligent revision.[77] Under this heading may, perhaps, be included the legends of the conquest of Yamato by the Emperor Jim-mu and of the conquest of the same country by the Empress Jin-gō, which certainly bear a suspicious likeness to each other. Of the subjection of Korea by this last-named personage it should be observed that the Chinese and Korean histories, so far as they are known to us, make no mention, and indeed the dates, as more specifically given in the "Chronicles," clearly show the inconsistency of the whole story; for Jin-gō's husband, the Emperor Chiū-ai, is said to have been born in the 19th year of the reign of Sei-mu, *i.e.* in A.D. 149, while his father, Prince Yamato-Take, is said to have died in the 43rd year of Kei-kō, *i.e.* in A.D. 113, so that there is an interval of thirty-six years between the death of the father and the birth of the son![78]

One peculiarly interesting piece of information to be derived from a careful study of the **Records** and "Chronicles" (though it is one on which the patriotic Japanese commentators preserve complete silence) is that, at the very earliest period to which the twilight of legend stretches back, Chinese influence had already begun to make itself felt in these islands, communicating to the inhabitants both implements and ideas. This is surely a fact of very particular importance, lending, as it does, its weight to the mass of evidence which goes to prove that in almost all known cases culture has been introduced from abroad, and has not been spontaneously developed. The traces of Chinese influence are indeed not numerous, but they are unmistakable. Thus we find chopsticks mentioned both in the Idzumo and in the Kiushiu legendary cycle. The legend of the birth of the Sun-Goddess and Moon-God from Izanagi's eyes is a scarcely altered fragment of the Chinese myth of P'an Ku; the superstition that peaches had assisted Izanagi to repel the hosts of Hades can almost certainly be traced to a Chinese source, and the hand-maidens of the Japanese Sun-Goddess are mentioned under the exact title of the Spinning Damsel of Chinese myth . . . , while the River of Heaven . . . , which figures in the same legend, is equally Chinese,—for surely both names cannot be mere coincidences. A like remark applies to the name of the Deity of the Kitchen, and to the way in which that deity is mentioned.[79] The art of making an intoxicationg liquor is referred to in the very earliest Japanese legends. Are we to believe that its invention here was independent of its invention on the continent? In this instance moreover the old histories bear witness against themselves; for they mention this same liquor in terms showing that it was a curious rarity in what, according to the accepted chronology, corresponds to the century immediately preceding the Christian era, and again in the third century of that era. The whole story of the Sea-God's palace has a Chinese ring about it, and "cassia-tree" . . . mentioned in it is certainly Chinese, as are the crocodiles. That the so–called *maga-tama,* or "curved jewels," which figure so largely in the Japanese mythology, and with which the Early Japanese adorned themselves, were derived from China was already suspected by Mr. Henry von Siebold; and quite latterly Mr. Milne has thrown light on this subject from an altogether unexpected quarter. He has remarked, namely, that jade or the jade-like stone of which many of the *maga-tama* are made, is a mineral which has never yet been met with in Japan. We therefore know that *some* at least of the "curved jewels" or of the material for them came from the mainland, and the probability that the idea of curving these very oddly shaped ornaments was likewise imported thence gains in probability. The peculiar kind of arrow called *narikabura* . . . is another trace of Chinese influence in the material order, and a thorough search by a competent Chinese scholar would perhaps reveal others. But enough at least has been said to show the indisputable existence of that influence. From other sources we know that the more recent mythic fancy of Japan has shown itself as little impenetrable to such influence as have the manners and customs of the people. The only difference is that assimilation has of late proceeded with much greater rapidity.

In this, language is another guide; for, though the discoverable traces of Chinese influence are comparatively few in the Archaic Dialect, yet they are there. This is a subject which has as yet scarcely been touched. Two Japanese authors of an elder generation, Kahibara and Arawi Hakuseki, did indeed point out the existence of some such traces. But they drew no inference from

them, they did not set to work to discover new ones, and their indications, except in one or two obvious cases, have received little attention from later writers whether native or foreign. But when we compare such words as *kane; kume, kuni, saka, tana, uma,* and many others with the pronunciation now given, or with that which the phonetic laws of the language in its earlier stage would have caused to be given, to their Chinese equivalents . . . the idea forces way that such coincidences of sound and sense cannot all be purely accidental; and when moreover we find that the great majority of the words in question denote things or ideas that were almost certainly imported, we perceive that a more thorough sifting of Archaic Japanese (especially of botanical and zoological names and of the names of implements and manufactures) would probably be the best means of discovering at least the negative features of an antiquity remoter than all written documents, remoter even than the crystallization of the legends which those documents have preserved. In dealing with Korean words found in Archaic Japanese we tread on more delicate ground; for there we have a language which, unlike Chinese, stands to Japanese in the closest family relationship, making it plain that many coincidences of sound and sense should be ascribed to radical affinity rather than to later intercourse. At the same time it appears more probable that, for instance, such seemingly indigenous Japanese terms as *Hotoke,* "Buddha," and *tera,* "Buddhist temple," should have been in fact borrowed from the corresponding Korean words *Puchhö* and *chöl* than that both nations should have independently chosen homonyms to denote the same foreign ideas. Indeed, it will perhaps not be too bold to assume that in the case of *Hotoke,* "Buddha," we have before us a word whose journeyings consist of many stages, it having been first brought from India to China, then from China to Korea, and thirdly from Korea to Japan, where finally the ingenuity of philologists has discovered for it a Japanese etymology (*hito ke,* "human spirit") with which in reality it has nothing whatever to do.

These introductory remarks have already extended to such a length that a reference to the strikingly parallel case of borrowed customs and ideas which is presented by the Ainos in this same archipelago must be left undeveloped. In conclusion, it need only be remarked that a simple translation of one book, such as is here given, does not nearly exhaust the work which might be expended even on the elucidation of that single book, and much less can it fill the gap which still lies between us and a proper knowledge of Japanese antiquity. To do this, the co-operation of the archæologist must be obtained, while even in the field of the critical investigation of documents there is an immense deal still to be done. Not only must all the available Japanese sources be made to yield up the information which they contain, but the assistance of Chinese and Korean records must be called in. A large quantity of Chinese literature has already been ransacked for a similar purpose by Matsushita Ken-rin, a translation of part of whose very useful compilation entitled "An Exposition of the Foreign Notices of Japan" would be one of the greatest helps towards the desired knowledge. In fact there still remains to be done for Japanese antiquity from our standpoint what Hirata has done for it from the standpoint of a Japanese Shintoist. Except in some of Mr. Satow's papers published in these "Transactions," the subject has scarcely yet been studied in this spirit, and it is possible that the Japanese members of our Society may be somewhat alarmed at the idea of their national history being treated with so little reverence. Perhaps, however, the discovery of the interest of the field of study thus only waiting to be investigated may reconcile them to the view here propounded. In any case if the early history of Japan is not all true, no amount of make—believe can make it so. What we would like to do is to sift the true from the false. As an eminent writer on anthropology[80] has recently said, "Historical criticism, that is, judgment, is practised not for the purpose of disbelieving, but of believing, but of believing. Its object is not to find fault with the author, but to ascertain how much of what he says may be reasonably taken as true." Moreover, even in what is not to be accepted as historic fact there is often much that is valuable from other points of view. If, therefore, we lose a thousand years of so-called Japanese history, it must not be forgotten that Japanese mythology remains as the oldest existing product of the Altaïc mind.

Notes

[2] Published in Vol. iii, Pt. I, of these "Transactions." . . .

[3] *I.e.,* the Emperor Tem-mu.

[4] *I.e.,* "Records of Ancient Matters." The alternative reading, which is probably but an invention of Motowori's, gives the same meaning in pure Japanese (instead of Sinico-Japanese) sounds. . . .

[7] "Grammar of the Japanese Written Language," Second Edition, Appendix II., p. VI. . . .

[16] Rendered in the English translation by "the Male-Who-Invites."

[17] *Yomo tsu Hira-Saka.* . . .

[19] Details as to the adoption by the Japanese of the Chinese system of computing time will be found in the late Mr. Bramsen's "Japanese Chronological Tables," where that lamented scholar brands "the whole system of fictitious dates applied in the first histories of Japan," as "one of the greatest literary frauds ever perpetrated, from which we may infer how little trust can be placed in the early Japanese historical works." See

also Motowori's "Inquiry into the True Chronology," pp. 33-36, and his second work on the same subject entitled "Discussion of the Objections to the Inquiry into the True Chronology," p.p. 46 *et seq.*

[20] "Confucian Analects," Book VII. Chap. I. Dr. Legge's translation.

[21] It may perhaps be worth while to quote this legend in full. It is as follows:

> One account says that the Heaven-Shining Great Deity, being in Heaven, said: 'I hear that in the Central Land of Reed-Plains (*i.e.* Japan) there is a Food-Possessing Deity. Do thou, Thine Augustness Moon-Night-Possessor, go and see.' His Augustness the Moon-Night-Possessor, having received these orders, descended [to earth], and arrived at the place where the Food-Possessing Deity was. The Food-Possessing Deity forthwith, on turning her head towards the land, produced rice from her mouth; again, on turning to the sea, she also produced from her mouth things broad of fin and things narrow of fin; again, on turning to the mountains, she also produced from her mouth things rough of hair and things soft of hair. Having collected together all these things, she offered them [to the Moon-God] as a feast on a hundred tables. At this time His Augustness the Moon-Night-Possessor, being angry and colouring up, said: 'How filthy! how vulgar! What! shalt thou dare to feed me with things spat out from thy mouth?' [and with these words,] he drew his sabre and slew her. Afterwards he made his report [to the Sun-Goddess]. When he told her all the particulars, the Heaven-Shining Great Deity was very angry, and said: 'Thou art a wicked Deity, whom it is not right for me to see';—and forthwith she and His Augustness the Moon-Night-Possessor dwelt separately day and night.

The partly parallel legend given in these *Records* forms the subject of Sect. XVII of the Translation.

[22] Compare Mr. Satow's remarks on this subject in Vol. III, Pt. I, pp. 21-23 of these "Transactions."

[23] A curious scrap of the history of Japanese civilization is preserved in the word *kaji*, whose exclusive acceptation in the modern tongue is "rudder." In archaic Japanese it meant "oar," a signification which is now expressed by the term *ro*, which has been borrowed from the the Chinese. It is a matter of debate whether the ancient Japanese boats possessed such an appliance as a *rudder,* and the word *tagishi* or *taishi* has been credited with that meaning. The more likely opinion seems to be that both the thing and the word were specialized in later times, the early Japanese boatmen having made any oar do duty for a rudder when circumstances necessitated the use of one.

[24] See the end of Sect. XXXII.

[25] See Vol. IX, Pt. II, pp. 191-192, of these "Transactions."

[26] "*Yamato Mono-gatari.*"

[27] For a translation of this story see the present writer's "Classical Poetry of the Japanese," pp. 42-44.

[28] See sect. XLIV, Note 12 and Sect. LXXII, Note 29.

[29] Mr. Ernest Satow, who in 1878 visited the island of Hachijo, gives the following details concerning the observance down to modern times in that remote corner of the Japanese Empire of the custom mentioned in the text:

> In Hachijo women, when about to become mothers, were formerly driven out to the huts on the mountain-side, and according to the accounts of native writers, left to shift for themselves, the result not unfrequently being the death of the newborn infant, or if it survived the rude circumstances under which it first saw the light, the seeds of disease were sown which clung to it throughout its after life. The rule of non-intercourse was so strictly enforced, that the woman was not allowed to leave the hut even to visit her own parents at the point of death, and besides the injurious effects that this solitary confinement must have had on the wives themselves, their prolonged absence was a serious loss to households, where there were elder children and large establishments to be superintended. The rigour of the custom was so far relaxed in modern times, that the huts were no longer built on the hills, but were constructed inside the homestead. It was a subject of wonder to people from other parts of Japan that the senseless practice should still be kept up, and its abolition was often recommended, but the administration of the Shôguns was not animated by a reforming spirit, and it remained for the Government of the Mikado to exhort the islanders to abandon this and the previously mentioned custom. They are therefore no longer sanctioned by official authority and the force of social opinion against them is increasing, so that before long these relics of ancient ceremonial religion will in all probability have disappeared from the group of islands.

(Trans. of the Asiat. Soc. of Japan, Vol. VI, Pt. III, pp. 455-6.)

[30] See Sect. LXX, Note 6. The Japanese term is *ina-ki, ki* being an Archaic term for "castle."

[31] See Sect. XVI. Mention of cave-dwellers will also be found in Sects. XLVIII, and LXXX.

[32] See the latter part of Sect. XVII.

[33] See Sect. XVIII, Note 16. . . .

[35] See, however, the legend in Sect. LXV.

[36] See beginning of Sect. XXVII.

[37] For details on this subject and illustrations, see Mr. Henry von Siebold's "Notes on Japanese Archaeology," p. 15 and Table XI, and a paper by Professor Milne on the "Stone Age in Japan," read before the Anthropological Society of Great Britain on the 25th May, 1880, pp. 10 and 11.

[38] The tradition preserved in Sect. CXXIV, shows that in times almost, if not quite, historical (the 4th century of our era) the silkworm was a curious novelty, apparently imported from Korea. It is not only possible, but probable, that silken fabrics were occasionally imported into Japan from the mainland at an earlier period, which would account for the mention of "silk rugs" in Sects XL and LXXXIV.

[39] The (necessarily somewhat arbitrary) line between earlier and later times has been drawn at the epoch of the traditional conquest of Korea by the Empress Jingo at the commencement of the third century of our era, it being then, according to the received opinions, that the Japanese first came in contact with their continental neighbours, and began to borrow from them. (See however the concluding Section of this Introduction for a demonstration of the untrustworthiness of all the so-called history of Japan down to the commencement of the fifth century of the Christian era.)

[40] See Sect. XXIV, Note 4.

[41] Mr. Satow, in his translation of a passage of the *Records of Ancient Matters* forming part of a note to his third paper on the "Rituals" in Vol. IX, Pt. II of these "Transactions," renders *wani* by "shark." There is perhaps some want of clearness in the old historical books in the details concerning the creature in question, and its *fin* is mentioned in the "Chronicles." But the accounts point rather to an amphibious creature, conceived of as being somewhat similar to the serpent, than to a fish, and the Chinese descriptions quoted by the Japanese commentators unmistakably refer to the crocodile. The translator therefore sees no sufficient reason for abandoning the usually accepted interpretation of *wani* . . . as "crocodile." It should be noticed that the *wani* is never introduced into any but patently fabulous stories, and that the example of other nations, and indeed of Japan itself, shows that myth-makers have no objection to embellish their tales by the mention of wonders supposed to exist in foreign lands.

[42] Sect. CXXVIII preserves a very early ornithological observation in the shape of the Songs composed by the Emperor Nin-toku and his Minister Take-Uchi on the subject of a wild-goose laying eggs in Central Japan. These birds are not known to breed even so far south as the island of Yezo.

[43] See the legend in Sect. LXXIV.

[44] Mr. Satow suggests that *awo* ("blue" or "green") means properly any colour derived from the *awi* plant (*Polygonum tinctorium*).

[45] Only the foot-notes of the original are omitted, as not being essential.

[46] See the story of Prince Karu, which is probably historical, in Sects. CXLI *et seq.*

[47] The custom of using surnames was certainly borrowed from China, although the Japanese have not, like the Koreans, gone so far as to adopt the actual surnames in use in that country. The "gentile names" may have sprung up more naturally, though they too show traces of Chinese influence. Those most frequently met with are *Agata-nushi, Ason, Atahe, Kimi, Miyatsuko, Murazhi, Omi, Sukune,* and *Wake.* . . .

[48] See Sect. XXV, (the second Song in that Section).

[49] See Sect. LXXI, Note 12.

[50] See Sect. XLII.

[51] Representations of these clay images (*tsuchi-nin-giyō*) will be found in Table XII of Mr. Henry von Siebold's "Notes on Japanese Archaeology," and in Mr. Satow's paper on "Ancient Sepulchral Mounds in Kaudzuke" published in Vol. VII, Pt. III, pp. 313 *et seq.* of these "Transactions." . . .

[52] See Sect. LXXXVII.

[53] See Sect. XCVII.

[54] A translation,—especially a literal prose translation,—is not calculated to show off to best advantage the poetry of an alien race. But even subject to this drawback, the present writer would be surprised if it were not granted that poetic fire and grace are displayed in some of the Love-Songs (for instance the third Song in Sect. XXIV and both Songs in Sect. XXV), and a quaint pathos in certain others (for instance in Yamato-Take's address to his "elder brother the pine-tree," and in his Death-Songs contained in Sect. LXXXIX). . . .

[58] *Conf.* p. xix last paragraph for the modified sense in which alone the word "deification" can be used in speaking of the Early Japanese woship.

[59] In Sect. XXVII, where this deity is first mentioned, he is called *Sukuna-Biko-Na-no-Kami,* the "Little Prince the Renowned Deity." . . .

[62] As a specimen of the flexibility of his sytem, the reader to whom the Japanese language and Japanese legend are familiar is recommended to peruse pp. 13-24 of Vol. 1 of Arawi Hakuseki's *Ko Shi Tsū,* where an elaborate rationalistic interpretation is applied to the story of the amours of Izanagi and Izanami. It is amusing in its very gravity, and one finds it difficult to believe that the writer can have been in earnest when he penned it.

[63] Mr. Takahashi Goro's book here alluded to is his "Shinto Discussed Afresh."

[64] *I.e.* the Emperor Jim-mu,—*ten-nō* . . . being simply the Sinico-Japanese word for "emperor."

[65] 15th day of 11th moon of 5th year of Meiji.

[66] For the use of this word to represent the Japanese *Yomo* or *Yomi,* see Sect. IX, Note 1.

[67] *Podocarpus macrophylla.*

[68] The least meagre account will be found in Sects. XVI. and XXXII.

[69] To be found at the end of Sect. XXXII.

[70] In the Jim-mu legend we have the more usual form of the superstition, that, viz., which makes it unlucky to go from West to East, which is the contrary of the course pursued by the sun In Sect. CLIII, on the other hand, the Emperor Yū-riaku is found fault with for acting in precisely the reverse manner, viz., for going from East to West, *i.e.,* with his back to the sun. The idea is the same, though its practical application may thus diametrically differ, the fundamental objection being to going *against* the sun, in whatever manner the word *against,* or some kindred expression, may be interpreted.

[71] See Sects. XXXIX to XLI. For the "Herb-Quelling Sabre" see Sects. XVIII and LXXXII, *et seq.*

[72] General Le Gendre, quoted by Sir Edward Reed. . . .

[74] *I.e.* the High August Producing Wondrous Deity. He is the second divine personage whose birth is mentioned in the *Records* (see Sect. I Note 5). In the story of the creation given in the "Chronicles" he does not appear except in "One account."

[75] Sect. XXXVII is a good instance of the third of these categories. For an elaborate myth founded on the name of a place see Sect. LXV. Lesser instances occur in Sects. XLIV, LXV, and LXXIII.

[76] See Sects. LXXIX-XCI.

[77] See this legend as first given in Scets. XL and XLI. and afterwards in quite another context in Sect. CXVI.

The way in which "One account" of the "Chronicles of Japan" tells the story of the ravages committed on the fields of the Sun-Goddess by her brother, the "Impetuous Male Deity," might perhaps justify the opinion that that likewise is but the same tale in another form. The legend is evidently a very important one.

[78] The translator's attention was drawn to the inconsistency of these dates by Mr. Ernest Satow.

[79] See Sect. XXIX, Note 16.

[80] Dr. Tylor in his "Anthopology," Chap. XV.

Alexander Vannovsky (essay date 1960)

SOURCE: Alexander Vannovsky, in an introduction and "The Search for a Subject," in *Volcanoes and the Sun*, Bridgeway Press, 1960, pp. 11-29, 68-83.

[*Previous to 1960, scholars cast the central conflict of the* Kojiki *in terms of sun and storm; Vannovsky amended these to sun and volcano, noting both the significance of volcanoes in Japanese geology and culture and their absence as explicit references in the* Kojiki. *In the first part of the following excerpt, he relates the essential material of the mythological portion of the* Kojiki *focusing especially on the Susano-o tales. In the second part, Vannovsky examines that portion through the lens of his central thesis.*]

The original *Kojiki* is preceded by an introduction by the author, Oono Yasumaro, which clarifies the circumstances surrounding this literary movement and how he finally became its author.

The introduction relates that about the time of the reign of Emperor Temmu (673-686), several noble families possessed writings or chronicles of two kinds: one were called *teiki* or *senki*, meaning "Imperial annals," the others, *hondzi* or, "records about immemorial ancient things." The *hondzi* contained myths, folklore, legends, and songs, together with records about the origin of families from the heavenly or earthly gods.

The Emperor Temmu, noting that the *hondzi* contained many inaccuracies, also questioned the veracity of the "Imperial annals." He directed that all these ancient records be examined, errors be eliminated, and the truth transmitted to the coming generations.

Following the instructions of Temmu this work was entrusted to Hieda-no-Are-mitsu, a person whose biography is nebulous, but who, according to most scholars, was a lady-in-waiting with an immense erudition in reading of old writings and a phenomenal memory. Yasumaro, in his introduction says, "she was about 28 years of age, naturally endowed with intelligence, could remember everything she had ever read, and never forgot things she heard once."

The death of the Emperor Temmu in the year 686, terminated the work and it remained unfinished for 24 years. In 711 the Empress Gemmyo decided that the work should be continued and on September 18, 711, published an edict ordering the court official Oono Yasumaro, a celebrated sinologue and learned writer, to finish the work which Hieda-no-Are-mitsu had begun. After 4 months and 10 days the work was finished, and on January 28, 712 Yasumaro reverently offered the Empress three parts of the *Kojiki*.

The tale of the *Kojiki* begins with the moment of the creation of the universe, when there was not yet either heaven, nor earth, but existed only a certain intangible place called *Takama-no-hara*.

"At the beginning of the heaven and earth there appeared in the land of Takama-no-hara several gods whose names were: Ame-no-Minakanushi-no-kami (God Ruler of the Heavenly Center), then Takami-Musubi-no-kami, and Kammu-subi-no-kami."

Scholars agree that the names of the two latter gods point out the principle of generation, inherent in the first god, with divisions into male and female, or static and dynamic nature. "These three gods were formed as pillars. They appeared singly and then hid their images."

"Later, when the country was still new and resembled a floating drop of oil, something similar to a reed shoot blossomed, and gods emerged from it. The first two were Umashi-Ashi-Kabihikoji-no-kami and Ame-Tokotachi-no-kami. These gods, also pillars, appeared separately and then hid their images."

Following the gods mentioned above, there gradually appeared seven more generations of gods. The first two came singly, but the next five came each with a member of the opposite sex. The analysis of the names of these gods gives some idea of the gradual formation and hardening of the earth, the separation of heaven from the earth, and the appearance of the organic world.

The last of the previously mentioned generations of gods was the divine couple, God Izanagi and Goddess Izanami, who later formed the earth and created life thereon in accordance with the directive of the preceeding gods, "Organize and consolidate this floating (formless) land."

In order to fulfill this directive, the heavenly gods supplied Izanagi and Izanami with only the heavenly staff. The couple then descended to the Heavenly Floating Bridge, from which Izanagi lowered the Heavenly Staff into the depths of the sea. When he lifted the staff, drops of sea water fell from its tip, hardened, and formed an island, which was called Onokorojima, "the island which hardened by itself."

The heavenly couple then descended to this island, erected a palace 8 *ells* long, and joined in matrimony. This union led to the creation of eight great Japanese islands, numerous small islands, rivers, mountains, and life thereon, including the gods who were to rule over everything. The God of Fire, Hi-no-Kagutsuchi-no-kami was the last born for, upon his birth, he burned the productive organs of his mother and the Goddess Izanami died in agony.

Izanagi was grief stricken by the death of his beloved. In desperation, he threw himself at the feet of his dead wife and sobbing bitterly cried, "O my beloved wife! How can the new child replace thee in my heart—a splinter from a tree?"

The deceased goddess was buried in the hills of Hiba, on the boundary between Izumo and Hahaki.

The God Izanagi, filled with despair and hatred for the unfortunate baby who had caused the death of Izanami, decapitated Hi-no-Kagutsuchi-no-kami. The blood of the murdered son spread to the neighboring rocks, and from different members of his body, a whole row of gods were born. Amongst them was the Marital God Take-Mikazuchi, who plays an important part in the following tale.

"And the God Izanagi got an immense desire to see his wife, the Goddess Izanami, and he followed her to the land of Yomotsu-kuni—the land of shadows. When the goddess lifted the door of the underworld palace and came to him, Izanagi addressed her: 'My beloved wife! Come back to the land we created together, the creation is not yet finished.' The Goddess Izanami answered: 'What a pity thou didst not come earlier. I have already tasted the food prepared on the hearth of Yomotsu. But my husband, thy coming is precious to me and I will go back with thee. Only give me time to ask advice from the gods of the land of Yomotsu. While I am gone, pray, but do not look after me.'

With these words the goddess disappeared into the palace and did not return for a long time.

After waiting restlessly, Izanagi at last lost his patience. He took a comb from the left side of his hair, broke off the teeth, lighted it like a torch and threw it into the palace. The vision which appeared before his eyes was fearful—the body of Izanagi full of worms and matter and covered with thunder-rendering Demons.

Frightened by this spectacle, Izanagi took flight. The Goddess Izanami shouted after him, "Thou hath covered me with shame"—and sent the horrible witches

Shilome after him. Observing the pursuit, Izanagi took from his head a black band made from a grape vine—Kuromikazura—and threw it behind him. At once a wild vine sprung up which the witches began to devour. Izanagi fled, but the witches were soon after him once more. Izanagi then took the comb from the right side of his hair, broke out the teeth and scattered them after him. Shoots of bamboo soon sprung up, and while the witches were devouring these, the god continued his flight.

Izanami, angered at the witches' inability to overtake her husband, ordered the Thunder Demons and an additional army of 1,500 lesser demons from the land of Yomotsu to take up the chase. Izanagi was deftly brandishing his sword, but could not repel the pursuit. When Izanagi arrived at the foot of Mount Hirasaka, he saw a peach tree covered with fruit. The god plucked three peaches, and allowing the legion of pursuers to approach, threw the fruit at them. Finally the army from the land of Yomotsu turned in flight.

Izanami, enraged at the failure of her army, took up the pursuit herself. Izanagi, observing her approach, carried a huge rock—Chiba Iwa—to the foot of Hirasaka and thus blocked Izanami from ascending the mountain. Then the couple, separated by this rock, informed each other of the rupture of their marital union.

Izanami said, "My dearest husband! If thou actest in this way, I will kill the people of thy land by a thousand men per day."

Izanagi replied: "My dear wife! If you will act in this way, I will build lying-in chambers, a thousand five hundred a day."

And since then, every day one thousand men die, but one thousand five hundred are born without fail.

After this meeting with his wife, the God Izanagi hurried to the locality of Hagiwara, in the land of Hiuga, where he washed himself of the filth he had acquired in the land of Yomotsu. During his bathing in a small bay named Tachi-bana, a multitude of gods were born from the filth as it floated away. The last to be born were the great Goddess Amaterasu—as he washed his left eye, the Goddess Tsuki-yomi—as he washed his right eye, and the God Takehaya Susanoo—as he washed his nose.

Izanagi rejoiced upon seeing these three offspring and granted each of them a kingdom. The Goddess Amaterasu was entrusted to reign over the country of Takama-no-hara (land of heaven's light). The Goddess Tsuki-yomi was given the country of Yoru-no-osu-kuni (the land of the night). The God Susanoo was granted the country of Unabara (the marine element).

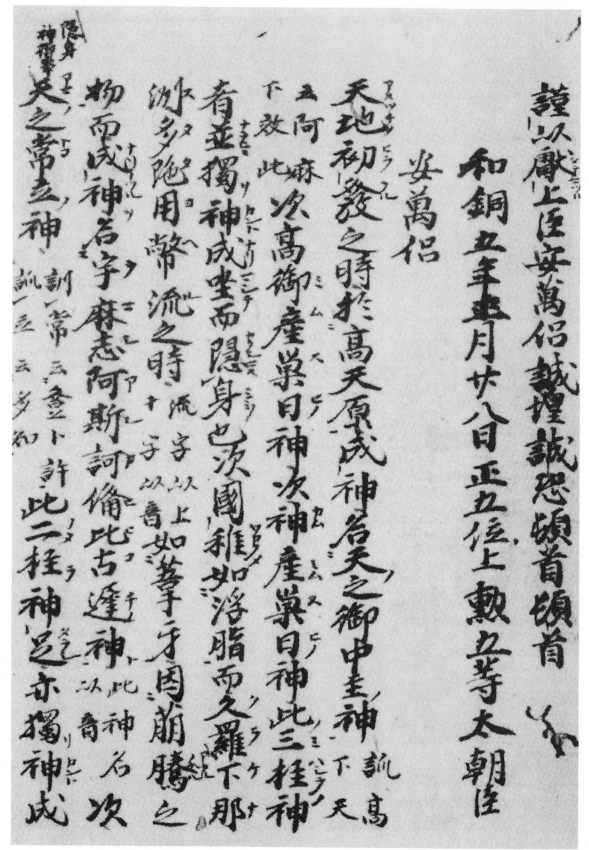

A handwritten copy from 1522 of the first page of Volume One of the Kojiki.

Amaterasu and Tsuki-yomi obediently carried out the will of their father. Only the God Susanoo rebelled. He did not want to rule the country Unabara. Susanoo began to cry and wail, stating that he wished to join his mother in the country of Neno-katasu-kuni. He bemoaned his fate so long and tearfully, that his beard grew 8 feet reaching his breast. His crying used up all the water in the rivers and seas and all the vegetation on the land dried up. Upon seeing this turmoil, the wicked gods began to move in great swarms and filled the land with their noise and confusion. Izanagi, angry at the disobedience of his son, exiled him from the country, forbidding him to dwell in heaven. Hence the God Susanoo, obliged to leave the country of his father, wished first to see his bright sister Amaterasu and, disobeying his father's directive, ascended to heaven. From his walking, all the mountains and rivers trembled and the earth shook.

The apparition of Susanoo near the frontier of the land Takama-no-hara quite upset his sister Amaterasu.

She suspected her brother had a wicked plan to take the country from her. Therefore, she met her brother in a man's garb with a bow and arrow in hand. Susanoo immediately recognized her and hastened to assure his sister that he had no bad intentions. He told her that he had come simply to say goodbye as their father had exiled him because he had cried in longing for the country of his mother. Amaterasu was still not convinced of her brother's good intentions. Susanoo, in order to prove his innocence, proposed to bring children into the world in a very original way. First the Goddess Amaterasu had to break her brother's sword into three parts, and wash them in the heavenly well. Putting the pieces into her mouth, she chewed them into powder, and when she exhaled, three girls were born. The God Susanoo did likewise with the hair ornaments and necklace of his sister and five boys were born.

The fact that Susanoo's sword had produced three innocent girls served as proof of the purity of his intentions. This filled him with self-conceit of such magnitude that in a display of pride he began to destroy. He filled the cultivation ditches in the rice fields with earth and made filthy his sister's palace. Still Amaterasu bore patiently the mischief of her brother, giving him the benefit of her doubt. This only irritated Susanoo the more and led him to still more violent action. When the goddess, with other women of the palace, were working in the spinning room, Susanoo broke the roof and threw at their feet a bloody skin, torn by him from a piebald horse. This frightened the women so much, that they pricked their hands on the weaving spindles and died from the wounds.

This wicked act of Susanoo saddened Amaterasu so greatly that she shut herself in the Heavenly Cave *Ama-no-Iwato*. Immediately the land of Takama-no-hara and the Land of the Luxurious Reeds were cloaked in an impenetrable darkness, having lost their source of light. It seemed that this darkness would be eternal. But worst of all, the wicked raised their voices from this darkness and misfortune occured throughout the land.

This threw the gods of Takama-no-hara into anguish. They assembled on the banks of the quiet Heavenly River, and decided the misery would not end unless Amaterasu could be convinced to return from the cave. Following the advice of the sage God Omoi-Kane, they decided to appeal to Amaterasu the next day. They placed an uprooted myrtle tree at the entrance of the cave, suspended on it jasper stones, a mirror, white pieces of cloth, and paper. The God Ame-no-Koyane-no-Mikoto began to read invocations loudly and at the same time the mighty God Tadzikara-no-kami hid himself at the entrance of the cave. They also placed an inverted barrel at the entrance, on which the Goddess Uzume began to execute a bacchic dance, accompanied by singing roosters. The comical gestures in her movements made the assemblage laugh so uproariously that the heavenly country shook. The laughter reached the ears of Amaterasu and interested her. She moved slightly the stone which closed the entrance to the cave and looked through the crack. The Goddess Uzume quickly put a mirror before the face of Amaterasu saying: "We rejoice and make merry because as you can see, we have a goddess better than you." When the goddess, completely amazed, emerged at the entrance, the mighty God Tadzikara-no-kami led her out by the hand. All the world was lit by her radiance, and Olympus was joyful.

Then the gods ruled that Susanoo, the cause of all the misery, should be punished. They plucked out his luxurious beard, pulled out his finger and toe nails, and then exiled him from the land of Takama-no-hara.

Further in the myth the place of action moves from the heavenly Takama-no-hara to earth and the land of Izumo.

The God Susanoo, so goes the story, after his exile from Takama-no-hara, descended to Tori-kami on Izumo, near the river of Hi-no-kawa. While standing by the river, he noticed a pair of chopsticks floating downstream. Realizing there must be people in that direction, he started upstream and came upon an old couple and a young girl. They were sitting on the ground crying bitterly.

When Susanoo asked who they were, the old man answered, "I am the son of Oyamatsumi, the god of this place. My name is Ashinozuchi, my wife's, Tenazuchi, and my daughter's, Kushinada-hime."

When Susanoo asked them why they were crying the old man related: "I had eight daughters, but every year, from the land of Koshi, the dreadful serpent Yamata-no-Orochi comes, and devours one daughter. Only this one child is left, and now is about the time when it will come. That is why we are crying."

Susanoo asked him to describe the serpent. The old man answered "Its eyes are as red as a ripe fruit. Its body is one, but it has eight heads and eight tails. Its skin is covered with moss and trees, and its body is so huge that it trails over eight hills and eight valleys. Blood constantly oozes from its body."

Having heard this story, Susanoo assured the old people that he would save them and their daughter from the serpent on the condition that they would offer the daughter in matrimony.

The old people agreed, whereupon Susanoo turned the girl into a comb, put it in his hair, ordered the old people to brew sake, and surround the area with a hedge. The hedge was to contain eight gates with a couch and a barrel of sake at each. These preparations were hardly finished when the serpent suddenly appeared from apparently nowhere. Sniffing the aroma of the sake, he emersed one head into each of the sake barrels and drank so greedily that he soon became quite drunk. He then dropped to the ground and fell soundly asleep.

Susanoo, who had been watching the serpent, quickly drew his magic sword and began to gash the serpent with such strength that even the river flowed full with blood. While Susanoo was cutting one of the serpent's tails, his sword struck something hard, causing his sword to dent. Interested, Susanoo cut open the tail and found another sword, which he offered later, as a curiosity, to his bright sister, the Goddess Amaterasu. *This sword, known as "Kusanagi-no-Tsurugi" is one of the most sacred relics passed from generation to generation down the line of Japanese Emperors.* This will be discussed later.

After killing the serpent, Susanoo married Kushinada-hime, the girl he saved, built himself a palace in a picturesque locale named Suga, and began to live happily and prosperously.

One of Susanoo's descendants, five generations removed, was the celebrated God Ookuni-nushi, who occupies a principal place in the myth. Many pages of the story are consumed by the descriptions of the amorous exploits of Ookuni-nushi, which we will not explore here due to lack of space. We must only say, that owing to his success in love, Ookuni-nushi alienated his 80 brothers and was obliged, in order to save his life, to flee the land of Neno-katasu-kuni, which the scholars consider to be the same as the land of shadows—Yomi.

The God Susanoo and his daughter Suseri-hime were residing in Yomi at the time of Ookuni-nushi's arrival. Ookuni-nushi and Suseri-hime fell in love at first sight and planned to marry at once. However, the cunning Susanoo, before he would give consent to the marriage, decided to test the courage and resourcefulness of his son-in-law to be. He first threw Ookuni-nushi into a pit of snakes. The next day, he locked him in a room filled with bees and centipedes. Both times Ookuni-nushi came out unhurt, owing to a miraculous talisman his beloved had given him. The third day, Susanoo shot an arrow into a field and sent Ookuni-nushi to look for it. While the search was in progress, Susanoo fired the grass in the field. Surrounded by fire from all sides, Ookuni-nushi was about to die when a mouse showed him a hole where he could escape the flames. Moreover, the mouse had already found the missing arrow and had been chewing its feathers when the fire began. Ookuni-nushi once again successfully completed his task without harm. Susanoo, not yet satisfied, subjected Ookuni-nushi to a new trial. He had to search for insects in Susanoo's hair which, to Ookuni-nushi's horror, proved to be full of poisonous centipedes.

That night, Ookuni-nushi decided he must attempt to escape. He patiently waited until Susanoo was asleep, then fastened separately each of Susanoo's hairs to a beam in the house. He next rolled a huge rock in front of the palace entrance, lifted his beloved onto his back, and before fleeing, took Susanoo's sword, bow and arrows, and musical *Koto*.

In his haste, Ookuni-nushi unfortunately entwined a string of the koto on a tree. There was a sound which shook the earth. Susanoo awoke and sprang up. Observing the fleeing pair, he took chase but could not overtake them. Stopping at the foot of Mount Yomotsu Hirasaka, where the rock Chibiki-Iwa had once barred Izanami's pursuit of Izanagi, Susanoo shouted loudly, "Hey there! Listen! Take my bow and arrows and sword. Carry them to thy brothers of the hills and rivers, and thou thyself (Ookuni-nushi) be 'Ruler of the Great Land.' Take my daughter as your wife, build thyself a palace at the foot of Mount Ugayama and live there with her, thou scoundrel!"

According to the bequest of his father-in-law, Ookuni-nushi became the ruler of the land and began life with his wife in a new palace. Their marital bliss was darkened only by the weakness of Ookuni-nushi toward the fair sex. Jealous protestations over the amorous adventures of Ookuni-nushi take no small place in the tales of the *Kojiki*. Many beautiful, lyric verses, which we must unfortunately omit, resulted from Suseri-hime's pleading.

When Ookuni-nushi was near the penninsula of Miono-Misaki, in the land of Mizuno, he saw a boat made from a nutshell coming toward him. A god, dressed in a cape of ant's skin, was occupying the boat. Ookuni-nushi asked his name, but the god did not answer. He asked his intimate friends but nobody knew who the strange god was or where he came from. The question was resolved by the toad Taniguku who happened to be present. She advised asking the garden scarecrow Kuebiko for information. He seemed to know everything in the world, although he had no feet and could not walk. When asked, Kuebiko at once gave answer. "This is the dwarf-God Sukunabiko, the son of the God Kammusubi."

Still uncertain they decided to ask the God Kammusubi himself and he confirmed, "Yes, it is really my son. He is the smallest among my sons and escaped my hands from between my fingers. Let Ookuni-nushi fraternize with him and together build this land."

Ookuni-nushi and Sukunabiko at once began to establish and fortify the country. But soon Ookuni-nushi lost his companion as Sukunabiko retired to Tokoyo-no-kuni, the Land of Eternity.

This loss saddened Ookuni-nushi and he repeated forlornly, "How can I fortify the land alone? With what god shall I organize it?"

Suddenly, the sea brightened from a wonderous light. A god swam to shore and told Ookuni-nushi, "If thou willst honor me I will organize the country with thee. Otherwise thy country will not form."

The astonished Ookuni-nushi asked, "How must I honor thee?"

"Worship me and pray in the eastern mountains of the land of Yamato which are hedged by green forests." This god, says the *Kojiki,* lives on all the mountains. This god, say the learned scholars of the *Kojiki,* is none other than the peaceful soul of Ookuni-nushi which was resting at the bottom of the sea and came to the surface at a difficult moment in his life.

Further, after the enumeration of the countless descendants of Ookuni-nushi, the narration of the *Kojiki* returns to heaven.

The Goddess Amaterasu allowed her son called Ameno-Oshio-mimi-no-mikoto, to descend from the heaven to earth and rule *The Land of Luxurious Reeds and Precious Rice-ears*. The God Ameno-Oshio-mimi-no-mikoto descended to the aerial Heavenly Bridge, looked down at what was earth, and returning to heaven informed his mother, "In the Land of Luxurious Reeds and Precious Rice-ears, complete disorder reigns."

Then, by order of the Gods Takami-Musubi and Amaterasu, a meeting of the council of gods was called on the banks of the "Quiet Heavenly River." First, a question was directed at the wise God Omoi-kane. "The Middle Land of the Plain of Reeds was bequeathed to Ameno-Oshio-mimi-no-mikoto to rule. But now in this land the earthly gods are rioting in great numbers. Who can we send to pacify them?"

The wise Omoi-kane meditated briefly, then answered, "Let us send Ameno-hohi."

The God Ameno-hohi was sent, but three years passed and no word of him was heard. It was finally learned that Ameno-hohi had gone to the land of Ookuni-nushi and did not wish to return to heaven.

Again the gods held council and the wise Omoi-kane advised, "Let us send Ame-Wakahiko, the son of the god Amatsu-kunitama."

The gods sent Ame-Wakahiko, armed with a bow and arrow. But he also fell short of the expectations of the heavenly gods. Descending to the earth, he married the daughter of Ookuni-nushi, Shitateru-hime. Deciding that it was much better to rule this country himself, he forget his heavenly mission, and sent no news for eight years.

The gods of Takama-no-hara then chose a third messenger—a pheasant, and sent him to find out why Ame-Wakahiko had not returned. But the faithless Ame-Wakahiko shot the pheasant with the same arrow the gods had given him. The arrow, after piercing the breast of the pheasant, soared to heaven and fell at the feet of the God Takami-musubi and the Goddess Amaterasu, who were sitting on the banks of the "Quiet Heavenly River." The God Takami-musubi picked up the arrow and noticed blood on its feathers. Looking more closely, he realized it was the same arrow that had been given to Ame-Wakahiko. Then addressing the council of heavenly gods, Takami-musubi said, "If Ame-Wakahiko did not disobey orders and killed with this arrow the riotous earthly gods, then let this arrow miss Ame-Wakahiko. But if his conscience is guilty, let Ame-Wakahiko perish by this arrow."

With these words, Takami-musubi threw the arrow through the hole it had made in the heaven. This proved fatal to Ame-Wakahiko as the arrow pierced his breast while he was resting on his couch.

For the third time the gods held council on the banks of the Quiet Heavenly River and decided this time to send two gods, Takemikazuchi and Ame-no-torifune.

Both gods descended near the shore of Inasa in the land of Izumo, dressed in a warlike fashion. They appeared sitting with crossed legs on the points of swords, which were immersed to the hilt in the crest of a wave. They addressed Ookuni-nushi categorically,

"We are sent here by orders of the Goddess Amaterasu. She bequeathed to her child the Middle Land of the Plain of the Reeds, which thou art governing. What dost thou intend to do?"

Ookuni-nushi avoided a direct answer and asked the gods that he allow his elder son, Yae-Kotoshiro-nushi to decide the matter. The eldest son at once obediently answered that the land must be given over to the heir of heaven. But the youngest son of Ookuni-nushi, the God Takeminakata, protested. He picked up a huge rock and demanded to test the strength of Takemikazuchi. The messenger god accepted the challenge and at the end of the struggle was defeated. The disobedient Takeminakata quickly thereafter became repentent, pleaded for pardon, and resolved that he would not act against the decision of his father and brother to transfer the land. Ookuni-nushi, seeing that his sons did not oppose the transfer, decided to retire, and gave the lands to the rule of the heavenly heir.

The Gods Takemikazuchi and Ameno-torifune, having successfully completed their mission, ascended to the heaven and reported that the Middle Land of the Plain of the Reeds had been pacified.

Then the Goddess Amaterasu ordered the Heir of the Sun, the Goddess Masaka-Akatsu-Kachi-Ameno-Mimi, to descend to earth and govern the Middle Land of the Plain of the Reeds.

The goddess answered, "While I was preparing to descend to the earth, I gave birth to a son named Ame-nigisi-Kuni-nigisi-Amatsu-Hidakahiko-Hono-Ninigi-no-mikoto. Let him descend to the earth." And so it was.

Then a historical bequest was given to the God Hiko-Hono-Ninigi by the council of gods. "We entrust you to govern the Land of Luxurious Reeds and Precious Rice-ears. According to the order you must descend at once from heaven to the earth."

Five of the eldest gods were designated to accompany Ninigi. They were, Ame-no-Koyane-no-mikoto, Futo-dama-no-mikoto, Ame-no-uzume-no-mikoto, Ishikiri-dome-no-mikoto, and Tamano-oya-no-mikoto. They were all considered to be scions of the noblest families.

In addition, three sacred relics were entrusted to the God Ninigi: the necklace Yasakani-no-magatama, the mirror Yata-no-kagami, and the sword *Kusanagi-no-Tsurugi*. When the Goddess Amaterasu entrusted the mirror, she said to her grandson, "Consider this mirror my soul and honor it as thou wouldst honor me."

Today, in Shinto temples throughout Japan, the mirror is honored as a symbol of the soul of the God-dess Amaterasu and is one of the principal features of the cult.

Ninigi, when Amaterasu had finished speaking, rose from his stone seat and with his entourage, majestically separated the clouds, descended to the Bridge of Heaven from where he finally arrived at the high mountain Takachiho, situated in southern Japan in the province of Tsukushi. They then proceeded to the penninsula Kasasa, which much pleased the God Ninigi. "This land is located opposite Kara (Korea). The sun shines in the morning as well as the evening. This land is very good."

Ninigi soon built a palace and took a wife, Konohana-Sukuya-hime, the daughter of the local deity Oyama-tsumi. This couple had three sons, Gideru-no-mikoto, Hosuseri-no-mikoto, and Hiko-Hohodemi-no-mikoto.

These gods are linked with a whole series of episodes and legends not concerned with the principal line of the narration.

The God Hiko-Hohodemi-no-mikoto had a son named Ugaya-fuki-aezu-no-mikoto, born prematurely when the roof of the chambers alloted to the lying-in women was not quite finished. Nonetheless, this god became known as the father of the first Emperor of Japan— Jimmu, with whose reign began the era of man. The mythological part of the *Kojiki* ends here.

. . . . .

The Soviet Professor N. I. Conrad [*Japanese Literature in Images and Sketches,* 1927] gives the following scheme of the mythology of the *Kojiki:*

1. The struggle for heaven (Amaterasu and Susanoo).

2. The struggle for earth (Ookuni-nushi and Takemi-kazuchi).

3. The struggle on earth (Jimmu and Naga-sunehiko).

We must add the struggle between the gods began first under the earth and only afterwards passed to the heaven. Moreover, we must notice that the gods do not only combat each other but also cooperate. Incidently, the last factor plays a prominent part in the development of the happenings in the myth. Generally, such purely external schemes are subject to a common fault— the lack of indication of the character of the conflicting and cooperating gods.

Therefore, we offer our own scheme where we take into account all these factors which include all the contents beginning with the appearance of the Gods Izanagi and Izanami and closing with the campaign of the Emperor Jimmu into interior of land of Yamato.

This scheme is broken into two parts. (1) Cooperation and conflict of the god of heaven with the goddess of the volcanoes during the process of the creation of the world, and (2) Cooperation and rivalry of the heavenly and the volcanic heirs in the process of the creation of the Japanese Empire.

To the first part of the scheme belongs the struggle under the earth and the second part comprises the struggle for the heaven and earth. Looking at this scheme in detail we find a full analogy between the birth of the universe and the creation of the Japanese Empire. To show this similarity we have divided the material for comparison into two columns:

1. As a result of the matrimony of the heavenly God Izanagi with the Goddess Izanami, goddess of volcanoes, the Japanese islands are born.

2. After the creation of the Japanese islands, a struggle develops out of which the heaven-god emerges victorious.

3. Having overpowered the goddess of the volcanoes, the god of heaven finishes the creation of the world.

1. As a result of a kind of matrimony between the sun goddess and the volcano God Susanoo, heavenly heirs are born, among them Ninigi, the heavenly ancestor of the first Emperor.

2. After the birth of the Emperor's ancestor, the parents quarrel and the Goddess of Heaven emerges victorious.

3. Having vanquished the volcano god Ookuni-nushi, the goddess of heaven completes the creations of the Japanese Empire.

We met with the same principal of cooperation and struggle during the whole length of the myth of the creation of the Empire. So the volcanic heir of Ookuni-nushi cooperates with the heavenly descendant, dwarfgod Sunabiko, and at the same time struggles with other heavenly heirs, which require from him the surrender of his Empire. After that the heavenly heir, the Emperor Jimmu, makes war on the wicked gods, who multiplied during the weeping and rioting of the volcanic God Susanoo and therefore had a connection with the volcanic elements. But here we must make a digression and talk about the marriage of the same Emperor with the daughter of the God Ookuni-nushi, who was born out of his arrow. We ask ourselves what the above mentioned god has accomplished to allow him to become a member of the Emperor's family? The commentator of the **Kojiki,** Professor Sugita, leaning on the *Nihongi,* compares the God Oomono-nushi to the God Ookuni-nushi, who built a temple to the above named god in Yamato. All this data forces one to think that Oomono-nushi and Ookuni-nushi are one and the same person. The conclusion one draws is that the Emperor married the daughter of volcano-god Ookuni-nushi. It means that the Emperor is not an exception among the other heavenly gods and like them, he struggles and cooperates with the the volcanic gods.

Moreover, during the expedition of the same Emperor into the depths of the country of Yamato there is an episode which reminds us of the struggle of the gods in the land of darkness. The Emperor Jimmu, after discussion with his elder brother Itsuse, decides to undertake an expedition to the land of Yamato where, evidently, the principal forces of the wicked gods were situated. During one outflanking movement, when the army was near the village of Kumano, there suddenly appeared something like a huge bear, which disappeared at once. As a result of this unexpected vision which the soldiers could not see clearly, the whole army and the Emperor himself fell unconscious on the ground. One has to suppose that they would never have returned to life if it had not been for the liberating sword of Amaterasu, which she sent through the earthly God Taka-Kurashi. And here an episode occurs which points to the accumulation of the wicked gods in this vicinity. All the wicked gods living in the hills around the village of Kumano, suddenly are found cut to pieces.

In connection with this narration arises the question, what kind of bear was this, the mere sight of which renders a whole army unconscious? The sentence which interests us is usually read like this: "And suddenly appeared a vision of a huge bear. . . ." An ancient scholar Norinaga supposes this is a mistake of the copyist who failed to use Chinese characters. In substituting these characters the result is: "And suddenly a huge bear came out of the mountains . . ." Chamberlain translates this controversial sentence according to the explanation of Norinaga, " . . . a large bear came out of the mountain and forthwith disappeared into it."

It appears from the works of Norinaga and Chamberlain that the tale is about an ordinary bear. But it is difficult to agree with them. Really, if it were an ordinary bear, how could it bring about the mowing down of a whole army? It is quite evident that we have before us not an ordinary beast, but some wicked being in the image of a bear. Yasumaru, in his introduction to the **Kojiki,** is of the same opinion. Briefly, we have before us some powerful and wicked god, because only such a being could produce such a frightening effect.

Professor Sugita supposes that the bear is a local god of Kumano, whose power depends on the oppressive feeling created by the wild and stern aspect of the adjacent mountains.[1] It must be noted that in the *Nihongi,* instead of a bear, a wicked God Nishi-kitobe appears. He halts the army of the heavenly heirs with his poisonous breath. Following this variation some scholars supplement the **Kojiki** and say that the bear affected the army merely by his destructive breath. The expression *ka-yu* supports also the opinion that here we have no ordinary bear. The expression *ka-yu* used in the original literally means the were-bear. And so if we take into account all these considerations we will come to the conclusion that one powerful wicked god, out of a number of them dwelling in the dark and wild region of Kumano, turned into a bear and poisoned the army of the Emperor Jimmu by his poisonous breathing.

But we know from the previous record that the wicked gods are connected with the volcanic elements and so we may say that behind the myth of the bear is hidden quite a realistic happening. The army of the heavenly descendants entered an area where they were poisoned by volcanic gas and evaporation emanating from the fissures of the earth. And when an especially dense and poisonous cloud of gas rose, taking the contours of a huge bear, the whole army swallowed so much of the poisonous gas that it lost consciousness.

In the collision of the army of the Emperor Jimmu with the monster, we find hidden the same volcanic motif that appears in the struggle of the gods in the land of Yomi. *As the God Izanagi, before the completion of the creation of the world, undergoes a bitter struggle with demons of the land of Yomi, so the Emperor Jimmu, before completing the foundation of the Empire is subject to an attack of the monster were-bear on the site of Kumano.* One would say that the **Kojiki** is built up symmetrically.

In conclusion, let us site one more example of cooperation and struggle of the heavenly and volcanic gods. We mean the episode with the unruly God Ame-wakahiko. Ajisuki is the son of Ookuni-nushi and therefore is a volcanic descendant. Ame-waka-hiko is a heavenly god, who took sides with the terrestrial gods and afterwards was pierced by his own returning arrow. The parents of the deceased god built a mausoleum and began a rite with the birds to resuscitate him. Just at this moment Ajisuki, like Susanoo when in heaven, lierally and without cause, begins to be noisy. He chases away the birds and destroys the grave itself, annihilating, therefore, the right of resuscitation. On the surface we see before us a simple riot, a debauché. It would be such in essence if the rite of resuscitation were not involved. This changes the whole meaning. The soul of the deceased stays near its grave and is somehow tied to it. It wants to return to the body and animate it, but the destruction of the mausoleum stands in its way, just as the rock Chibiki-iwa prevented the Goddess Izanami from returning to the earth. In this sense the behaviour of Ajisuki is not a simple violence, but the struggle of the volcanic god with the dead heavenly god. They were friends and had cooperated, but still the struggle motif came up, although after the death of the god Ame-waka-hiko. *In that way we encounter in different combinations the manifestations of the same principles of cooperation and struggle of the heavenly and volcanic gods.*

And so the Emperor like the universe emerges as the result of interaction and reciprocal actions of the gods expressing analogous cosmic origins. This unity of the creation of world and state causes us to suppose that ancient man looked at the latter as the crown of creation.

*The Empire grows out of the Cosmos as a plant from a seed, and so it is quite suitable to the country forming an organic whole. It is just this feeling of the complete fusion of the Empire with the cosmos of the country that, according to the **Kojiki**, creates the mysticism of the state and heavenly heirs.*

Here we can touch the question put by Professor Tsuda as to why a "violent man" was given the right to become the ancestor of the Emperors. In Susanoo, as we mentioned before, is laid down the character of a volcano, whose fate in nature is to riot. That is why, seeing in the violence in heaven not the result of wicked will but the natural demonstration of the power of a wildly violent nature, the myth does not pay any serious attention to the violence.

As soon as we agree with the widespread view that Susanoo is simply a violent man, behind whom no cosmic origin is hidden, his part in birth of the Emperor's ancestors and his behaviour in general, will acquire the character of a caprice of events. But Susanoo is the god of the volcanic element and in this circumstance is contained not only the key for the understanding of his character, but also for the understanding of the state of the heavenly descendants in general and of the mythology of the **Kojiki** in its whole.

*The Empire, according to the **Kojiki**, is not only a social-political institution but first of all an institution of nature, created by the gods, as nature itself. The Emperor, the people, and the country (in the sense of state and cosmos), constitute one unity, one family. This point of oneness is the most original and deep affirmation of the **Kojiki**. The Empire is an institution of nature and therefore naturally, owing to the inner connection the emperors receive the fullness of nature's gifts to their country.*

Japan is the Land of the Rising Sun and therefore the Emperors are the descendants of the sun. Japan is also a country of great volcanoes and therefore Susanoo, the god of volcanoes, is destined to be the ancestor of the Emperors. Japan in addition is the country of blue seas and therefore the genealogical tree of the Emperor contains a sea-branch in the person of the sea princess—the mother of the God Ugayafuki who is the father of the Emperor Jimmu.

We must look in the same manner at the sacred relics which the goddess hands over to her grandson Ninigi upon his departure to earth. A necklace which reminds one of the emerald chain of the Japanese islands is given a symbol that the Japanese Empire is an institution which like nature itself is eternal and invincible.

In this sense, it might be said that the words of Amaterasu—"the Empire will exist eternally, as long as heaven and earth exist"—are not poetic hyperbola but an exact expression of the world consciousness of the myth, which says that the *Empire and the country are one.*

An analogical comparison of the stones of the necklace and chain of islands is recorded in the ancient prayer to the ruler of the land of Izumo, which contains this behest to the Emperor. "With a unifying hand let him rule the Country of Eight Great Islands, just as these green stones are joined in a beautiful necklace . . ."[2]

A mirror is given. It is given as sign that the soul of the Empire is the heavenly soul of the sun, the soul of a goddess imprisoned in the mirror, and also as a sign that the power of the Emperor is a source of life for the people, as is the sun for the whole earth.

The idea that the Empire was created from interaction of the same principals that created the world, can be perceived in different *Norito* in which the heavenly gods are represented not only as pacifying the chaotic-minded gods but as elements of nature itself. So in the *Norito* for expelling gods which persecute by misfortunes, we read: "Then, following the orders of the Heavenly gods, a council was held again and two gods were sent to the earth. They dispersed all the unruly gods ands and pacified them, made silent the reverberating rocks and tree-stumps, and made silent the grasses to the last blade."[3]

The first part of the invocation of the pacifying of the unruly gods who created disorder on earth, is easy to understand. But how can we approach the second half, which tells of a kind of punitive expedition against the inanimate elements of nature? A belief which attributes to such elements a wicked will and a capacity to get out of the rut of established order, can be found in the ancient literature of other peoples too. The book of Enoch, penned by an unknown Jew who lived in Jerusalem about 200 B.C., tells the story of disobedient stars which appeared in the sky at a wrong time. God punished them by shutting them in a prison which resembled a huge precipice.

But the basic idea of the above mentioned *Norito*, as we said, conceals a volcanic motif. The disorder in nature is not a result of the ill will of its elements, but of the debauchery of volcanic elements acting not against, but in accordance with their own laws. The elements run loose beyond all measure in incessant earthquakes prevent the heavenly descendants from stepping down to the earth and beginning the creation and organization of the state. Therefore, first of all it is necessary to keep in check the elements, limiting their manifestations to acceptable forms.

It is with this aim that the punitive expedition, in the person of the heavenly gods Futsu-nishi and Taka-miko-zushi, is sent. We must add that for ancient man the picture of cosmic disorder was not a simple metaphor or poetic hyperbole, but the expression of forces which were quite real happenings. Listening to the tale of the *Norito* relating the subduing of the raging elements, the ancients admired their deeds, but rejoiced at the victory of the heavenly gods, which made life on earth possible.

Here it is opportune to remember the episode of the God Sarudabiko. This god appears at the crossing of the eight Heavenly Roads just at the time when the God Ninigi is ordered to descend to the earth. The appearance of some unknown god who began to shine in the lands of Takama no hara above and Ashiwara-nakatsu-kuni below creates alarm in heaven, as can be seen in the words of the Goddess Amaterasu to Usume: "Although you are a weak woman, you will not be frightened by the oncoming god, therefore go and ask him 'who is it blackening the path by which our son intends to descend from heaven to the earth.'"[4]

The "strange" god answered the question of Usume, saying he was Sarudabiko, the god of earth and he had come to meet the heavenly god whom he had heard was coming to the earth. He wished to lead him to earth and serve him there. The services of the God Sarudabiko are accepted benevolently and the Goddess Usume was ordered to accompany him after his decent to his land. Further the myth tells us that the God Sarudabiko was drowned in the sea when his hand came into contact with a shell which jammed his finger.

The God Sarudabiko is an earthly god. It is quite probable that he is connected with the volcanoes, because what other god could shine over sky and earth? His volcanic character is indicated by the alarm in the heaven. After Susanoo's riot, a volcanic god suddenly appearing in the sky was generally looked upon with suspicion. The question naturally arose as to whether this god came, as his brother of elements, to make a scandal and thus prevent the descent of the heavenly heirs to earth. The concern of the heavenly gods is well founded as the pacifying of the unruly volcanic gods had just recently been completed. The death of Sarudabiko in an element hostile to fire, also supports our supposition. If so, the myth of the God Sarudabiko acquires quite a special meaning.

The heavenly gods tamed the formidable volcanic element which by the orgies provoked chaos on the earth. The volcanoes quieted down and only the redness of the sky mirrored in the clouds remains. Not the fires of riot, but welcoming fires to light the way for the ruler of earth.

From this we see that the episode with the God Sarudabiko does not stand alone, but has an inner connection with all the previous events of the myth. *In the course of time the volcanic basis of the myth, lending a coherence to all its happenings, was forgotten and the* **Kojiki** *naturally began to appear not as an integral work which was cast out of the secret depths of a people's soul, but as a collection of pretentious myths and legends.*

To end the episode of the God Sarudabiko let us look at his appearance. Painters always depict him with a straight and long nose, resembling the handle of a tea pot and giving him a comical aspect. Sarudabiko's exterior really seems "strange" to the heavenly gods, but still it provokes not laughter, but alarm. Therefore, we think it not necessary to give Sarudabiko a comical aspect. Sarudabiko is a volcanic god . . . but we do not know how Japanese painters represent a volcanic god. We have images of blue and red *Oni* (dragons) at the exhibitions, but never a representation of the god of volcanoes. The descent of the heavenly heirs indicates the reconciliation of the earth with heaven, of the volcanoes with the sun. The external image of the God Sarudabiko not only reveals his volcanic character but also corresponds to the importance and solemnity of the moment.

Myths about heavenly origin of state power can be found among other peoples. A similar motif constitutes the contents of the Mongolian legend of Geshir-Pogdo. But the peculiarity of the Japanese myth consists in the just fact that the heavenly origin of the Emperors show not only their greatness but also the vital necessity of their power. In the sense of the myth and the *Norito* the Emperors appear as the heirs of the heavenly creator gods because they concluded the creation of the world, bringing order in the cosmos. Here we have before us the manifestation of the same method of creation by inter-action of the heavenly and volcanic origins by the organization and suppression of the volcanic chaos.

Thus we may say that according to the **Kojiki,** *the formation of the state, as the creation of the first men in the Bible, is the direct sequel and conclusion of the creation of the world.* In that sense the **Kojiki** is an organic work, revolving around only one subject. The unifying basis of the events of the myth is brought about not by one god, as is written in the first book of Genesis, but by the relations of the heavenly and volcanic gods, the result of which brought about the world and the state. The subject of the book of Genesis is the origin of the world and mankind, whereas the subject of the **Kojiki** is the origin of the world and the state. But if we advance the thesis that the **Kojiki** is an organic work, the events of which are connected internally with each other, we present an opinion in complete opposition to the scholars who maintain that the **Kojiki** is a collection of different myths and legends lacking internal connection. Thus Professor Takasu remarks: "The **Kojiki,** of course, is not constructed organically, it does not have a so-called 'line of narration,' but taking each part separately, we see that every one of them represents a quite finished legend or myth."[5]

Professor Doi says nearly the same, supposing that the myth about the creation of the world has no connection with the events in the **Kojiki,** but has been mechanically added later. Besides, the same scholar remarks that the basic materials of the **Kojiki** is for the most part, of foreign origin.[6]

There are really foreign myths in the **Kojiki**. Take for instance the legend of the sick hare. In this legend crocodiles (wani) appear which do not exist in Japan. Also the myth about the Gods Hoderi and Hiko, who could not divide their marine and mountainous fortunes, are similar to the legend of the last fish hook, which is widespread among the tribes of Indonesia. Such legends and myths form a multi-colored design which obscures the general line of narration in the **Kojiki.** Studying the principal events of the myth we can see all of them generating from the same principal—the principal of the creation of the world developed from a compulsory necessity. The god of heaven in the process of cooperation and struggle with the goddess of volcanoes, creates the world and the Japanese islands. The earth is created, but it bears traces of its volcanic birth, which appear in very strong earthquakes and eruptions. In such an order, or disorder, of affairs, it is difficult to exist on earth, and still more, to build a state on it. It is necessary to calm the volcanic manifestations, to confine them to firm limits, or, as says the *In Praise of the Ruler of the Land of Izumo*—"this land, let it be pacified and become a land of peace." Hence of necessity comes the intervention of the heavenly gods and their descendants into the affairs of the earth, as only they possess the gift for pacifying and organizing the volcanic elements. It is just this property of the heavenly gods which predestines the general order of creating the world and the state.

The Empire of the heavenly descendants is born out of volcanic chaos. The world is born out of the same chaos—this is doubtless the most striking and original characteristic of the Japanese myth.

But if the events of the myth develop out of the same origin, then what is the **Kojiki**—a collection of poetry? The **Kojiki** is a grandoise poem like an ancient building of a majestic style. An ivy, too luxuriously growing, masks its symmetrical contours and gives a wrong idea of its symmetrical contours and gives a wrong idea of its architecture. But as soon as we take away this twining cover, the harmony of the style will strike our eye.

Notes

[1] He told us that his own impression was, that it is probably the most sinister place in all the mountains of Japan.

[2] In praise of the ruler of the land of Izumo (*Izumo kuni no miyatsuko no kami Yogoto*)—translation by M. P. Grigorieff. Cited from the manuscript.

[3] *Norito* for expelling the gods, pursuing with misfortunes—M. P. Grigorieff, Tokyo, 1931.

[4] Translation by M. P. Grigorieff. We cite his manuscript.

[5] *Nihon Meisho Kaidan* (Popular exposition of the best known works of Japanese Literature), p. 12.

[6] Professor Doi, *Introduction to Japanese literature.*

Masao Yaku (essay date 1969)

SOURCE: Masao Yaku, "Love Songs" and "The Theme of the **Kojiki**," in *The* Kojiki *in the Life of Japan*, translated by G. W. Robinson, The Centre for East Asian Cultural Studies, 1969, pp. 82-121, 122-50.

[*In the following excerpt, the* Kojiki *is presented as a unified, literary work designed to provide a "basis and origin" for the Emperor's sovereignty. Combining literary and political analyses, Yaku contends that the "principle of conflict, fusion, and harmony" facilitates "an account of the creation of a state with centralized power brought about by the submission to the emperor of the chieftans and heads of clans at the base."*]

Were one to define the **Kojiki** in a single phrase, one would say that it gives an account of the origin of the rise and prosperity of our ancient Japanese state. Then, from another point of view, from the literary point of view, the work may be said to be made up of a number of heroic legends. And many of these legends are a sort of 'ballad tale' of which lyrics or ballads form the core.

But if we compare those tales in the **Kojiki** of which the core is lyric or ballad with the ballad tales of the Heian period, we find that while both share the essential character of the ballad tale in respect of the central importance in both of the hero's or heroine's song or songs, there seems to be some difference when it comes to such features as the character of the hero or heroine or the relative importance of song and prose narrative. Even so we can probably say that the literary form of the ballad tale from the Heian period on had its beginnings in the **Kojiki**. Moreover, the method adopted in the **Kojiki** to develop the single coherent theme that I have just described, by forming into a single whole a large number of short myths and legends may be regarded as exactly analogous to the narrative method of such later works as *Taketori Monogatari* [*The Tale of the Bamboo Cutter.* 2 books. An anonymous work written in the early Heian period.] *The Tale of Genji* and *Heike Monogatari*. The **Kojiki** may therefore be regarded as a forerunner of the Japanese literary form known as 'the long work made out of a series of short works.' Thus the **Kojiki**'s significance in point of literary form may be said to be unexpectedly profound. So that, if the *Manyoshu* can be described as the forerunner of Japanese poetry, we can certainly say that the **Kojiki** is the start of Japanese prose literature. It was a seed that has never ceased vigorously to put forth buds in the Japanese literature that developed in later periods. . . .

Myth, legend and actuality form a single chain, so that we may regard both myth and legend as expression of the attitude with which their transmitter apprehends the world. In point of time of formation, it is by no means inevitable that legend should follow on after the creation of myth. In so far as both are formed from actuality, one should perhaps regard simultaneity as the norm. Even so, individual, actual experience cannot be divorced from national historical consciousness, and I think that this connection between the two constitutes the essence of historical consciousness.

How, then, to apply this relationship to the **Kojiki**? . . . [The] first part of Naka-no-ōe's 'Song of the Three Mountains' is a tale of 'the Age of the Gods' and so corresponds to the **Kojiki**'s Volume One. About 'antiquity' the 'Song of the Three Mountains' does not particularize but, in saying, 'in antiquity just so too,' the poem simply carries on with the tradition of 'the Age of the Gods' and may thus be said to have omitted 'antiquity.' Corresponding to this we have that part of the **Kojiki**, from Volume Two on, which we call legendary. Whether this means both Volume Two and Volume Three or only Volume Two is a question, which does not admit of a simple answer. For the present I will leave it as meaning the legends in Volumes Two and Three. The theme of the 'Song of the Three Mountains,' 'We mortals too now seem to contend for our wives,' is, in that poem, that which had given the poet a sense of actuality, and as such, if transferred to the *Kojiki,* may be taken to correspond to the ideas of those who transmitted and compiled the myths and legends of the *Kojiki.*

. . . . .

The scope of the whole work is defined in Ō-no-Yasumaro's Preface to the *Kojiki* as 'from the beginning of heaven and earth up to the reign at Oharida,' and so the *Kojiki* does in fact start with the beginning of heaven and earth and end with the reign of the Empress Suiko. This is then divided into three volumes. In short, Volume One runs from Ame-no-minakanushi to Ugayafukiaezu, Volume Two from Jimmu to Ōjin and Volume Three from Nintoku to Suiko.

Volume One is a world of mythology which resulted from a process of searching back from the point of departure constituted by the Emperor Jimmu. Having first gone back to the emperor's birthplace in Himuka, they went right back further still and postulated the heavenly world, what they called the Plain of High Heaven. If we take the myths of Volume One to be an attempt to account for the emperor's rule over the whole country, then we may take Volume Two to be an attempt to provide a historical origin for the establishment of the great empire including the Korean conquests. While we may regard Volume One, with its mythological account of the activities of gods, to be a theoretical, once and for all, stereotyped explanation, Volume Two can be regarded as an account of the basis of that imperial rule, founded on considerations of historical development. In Volume One the gods act directly, in Volume Two they are shown as subserving the actions of the heroes. In Volume Two the gods are exhibited as helping or obstructing the heroes' activities, so that it is not they, but the heroes, who have the principal roles. Here perhaps lies the distinction between 'the Age of the Gods' and 'antiquity.'

In contrast to this, Volume Three consists entirely of stories of people, and, though gods do appear, they do so in their capacity as objects of worship and they themselves have no normative effect in the human sphere. We thus perceive that Volumes One, Two and Three have each its own character. Might we say that Volume One is the age of gods, Volume Two the age of gods and men together, and Volume Three the age of men?

In his Kadokawa Bunko edition of the *Kojiki,* Professor Takeda Yūkichi divides Volume One as follows:

    i. Izanagi and Izanami (the beginning of heaven and earth, the birth of the islands, the birth of the gods, the Land of Darkness, the purification).

    ii. The Great Goddess Amaterasu and Susanoö (the oath, the Rock Gate of Heaven).

    iii. Susanoö (cereal seeds, the eight-forked snake, genealogies).

    iv. The god Ōkuninushi (the hare and the crocodiles, the Cockle-shell Princess and the Clam Princess, the Remote Subterrancan Corner Land, the ballad story of the god of Eight-Thousand-Spears, genealogies, the god Sukunabikona, the god of Mount Mimoro, descendants of the god of Great Harvests).

    v. The Great Goddess Amaterasu and Ōkuninushi (Amewakahiko, the Cession of the Country).

    vi. Ninigi (the descent from heaven, Princess Sarume, Princess Konohanasakuya).

    vii. Prince Hikohohodemi (Sea Luck and Mountain Luck, Princess Toyotama).

    viii. Prince Ugayafukiaezu.

Such, then, is the outline of Volume One. To illustrate their relationships at various junctures, I use the attached diagram.

If we now look at the broad outline of Volume One arranged in this diagrammatic fashion, we are in a position to define the *Kojiki*'s schematization of the gods as follows: it is the story of negotiation, conflict and fusion between the gods of the Heavenly Grandson line (equally called the Amaterasu line or the Plain of High Heaven line) of which the apex is Takamimusubi, and the gods of the Izumo line, of which the apex is Kamumusubi. And the conclusion is the peaceful submission of the gods of the Izumo line to those of the Heavenly Grandson line. Ame-no-minakanushi may be regarded as the symbol of this fusion. The *Kojiki*'s opening passage provides the clue to this schematization of the gods. . . . And so what we may regard as the main theme of the *Kojiki* is this: 'In this world now too, not only the chieftain of Izumo, but all the chieftains and the clans should be obedient to the emperors directly descended from the Great Goddess Amaterasu.'

As I have said, the myths of Volume One may be defined as first providing an explanation of the origin of the Japanese nation and then demonstrating the basis for the sacred character of the imperial government. What, then, would be the themes of Volumes Two and Three? I think we may take it that the fact that Volume One breaks off with Ugayafukiaezu and Volume Two begins with Kamuyamato-iwarebiko is intended both to show, by placing the first emperor at the head of Volume Two, that Volume One should be regarded as his origin, and also to make a break between myth and legend. We may regard this division as intended to have some kind of significance. If this is the case it would also seem that starting Volume Two with the first emperor, Jimmu, and breaking it off with Ōjin, has some inherent reason over and above the threefold division required simply by the length of the work.

Now, the broad outline of Volume Two is this: it starts with Jimmu's pacification of Yamato and then goes on with Sujin's pacification of the eastern provinces and Koshi and Taniha, Suinin's despatch of Tajimamori to the Eternal Land, Yamatotakeru's unification of Honshu, and ends with the Empress Jingū's subjugation of Silla and Paekche in Korea. Such an outline principally takes account of territorial expansion, but there runs parallel what may be regarded as another very important element, the religious side of things. That is to say, we have the legends of Jimmu's marriage with the god Ōmononushi's daughter, Isukeyori, Sujin's worship of the god Ōmononushi, Suinin's worship of the great god of Izumo, Yamatotakeru's worship of Amaterasu, Jingū's worship of Amaterasu and the three deities of Suminoe, Ōjin's worship of Kehi, the god of food, and finally of Ame-no-hiboko and the goddess of Izushi. If we regard all this as running parallel to the theme of the expansion of the territory, we understand how that territorial expansion runs parallel to an expansion of relations with the gods of the territory.

In a general way, indeed, it is quite a natural development of mythological thought that the pacification of the territory should involve at the same time combining with, or, rather, pacifying the deities who preside over the territory. Pacification of the territory or worshipping the gods of the territory, it is the same thing. So we can see that the general outline of Volume Two is like this: it starts with the uniting of Jimmu with the god of Yamato, then it goes on by way of Sujin and Suinin's expansions and Yamatotakeru's unification of the whole country, to end up with Jingū's and Ōjin's Korean conquests, and the accompanying expansion involved in worshipping gods of a foreign kind. Thus Japan's maximum expansion, reached with the Korean conquests, is traced from the historical hypothesis of Jimmu's unification of Yamato; it may be a historical fact, but as it could also be a logical conjecture, I will leave it as a hypothesis for the time being. At this point we may ask what becomes in Volume Two of the relations between the imperial line gods and the Izumo line gods . . .

Jimmu's unification of Yamato in Volume Two of the *Kojiki* starts with his subjugation of the resister, Nagasunebiko, and his marriage with Isukeyori, daughter of the Izumo line. From Sujin on the expansion into the territories round Yamato runs parallel with worship of the Izumo line gods, while when we come to Yamato-takeru's pacification of the whole country, the

light of the Great Goddess Amaterasu spreads out to shine over all Ōyashima.

This interrelationship extends to Korea through Jingū's expedition to Silla. From the political point of view, we pass from the establishment of the Yamato court centred on the region of the three mountains of Asuka to the unification of the Ōyashima nation, and then to the extension overseas, and the establishment, as a consequence of the Korean expedition, of the powerful Far Eastern state, the state of the 'sovereign who rules over all under heaven.' On the religious side there is the corresponding ascendancy gained for the divine authority of Amaterasu over the great god of Izumo and numerous other local deities. In these circumstances, the particular prominence of Izumo should not perhaps be regarded as simply due to its being the name of an actual region rivalling Yamato in the cultural sphere; it may be that, as the alternative names of the gods Ōmononushi and Ōkuninushi suggest, Izumo bears a generalized significance symbolizing all the regions and localities ruled over by local gods or divine ancestors of the provincial chieftains, the *kuni-no-miyakko*. Thus Ōkuninushi is also a symbol of all local powerful clans or clan chieftains. We have thus a consistent single theme for Volumes One and Two which we may sum up thus: religiously, they provide an explanation of the basis and origin of Amaterasu's absolute character; politically, they explain the basis and origin of the imperial rule over a Far Eastern nation.

Volume Three starts with the Emperor Nintoku. Nintoku is called the 'Sage Sovereign.' His line, which broke off once with Seinei, went on through Woke and Ōke, i.e. the Emperors Ninken and Kenzō, and was once more broken off with Buretsu. At this juncture, we are told, the whole country was searched for a successor to the throne until finally a descendant from Ōjin in the fifth generation was found, the Emperor Keitai. Thus from Keitai to Suiko, the *Kojiki* consists almost solely of genealogical information about the dynasty, with virtually no other matter. So the contents of the greater part of Volume Three cover the reign of Nintoku down to that of Buretsu, last of Nintoku's line.

The start with the Sage Sovereign and the conclusion with the cruel prince, such as the *Nihon Shoki* depicts Buretsu as being, is on the stereotype of the rise and fall of kingdoms in ancient China, so one might say that the theme of Volume Three consists in the rise and fall of the Nintoku monarchy. By the connection of Keitai, the successor to this monarchy, to Ōjin, the succession is derived from the last emperor of the *Kojiki*'s Volume Two, so that Keitai, as the fifth generation descendant from Ōjin, symbolizes a revival of the epoch of Ōjin, after the interposition of the rise and fall of the Nintoku monarchy. In the light of this, it may be preferable not to regard the imperial clan's internal disputes about the throne in Volume Three as intended to emphasize the legitimacy of the throne; it may be more natural to regard all this as a reflection of historical fact, and there too we find treated without dissimulation the inevitable tragedy of human life. It would then follow that the ideals of the national life as a whole are to be sought in Volumes Two and One.

The expansion of the national territory to its greatest extent in Ōjin's reign, as described in Volume Two, is not treated in Volume Three. The contents of Volume Three are exclusively concerned with the internecine disputes of the imperial clan and the consolidation of the absolute power of the emperor. Japan's retreat from Korea, which started under Keitai, was the beginning of the long and bitter Korean question, later to become the central problem in Japanese policy. It is precisely for this reason that the desire in the period from Keitai on to revive the Ōjin period may be regarded as a natural tendency. . . .

If we thus arrange the development of this theme in the form of a pyramid, we can well understand what the *Kojiki* is saying.

The relation between Ame-no-minakanushi, Takamimusubi and Kamumusubi, at the apex of the triangle in the diagram, illustrates the basic principle of the theme of the myths and legends, while the myth of Izanagi and Izanami, which comes next, is an explanation of the origin of the earth and the birth of all living creatures. This myth at the same time illustrates, through the husband-wife relationship of the two deities, the principle of the conflict, fusion and harmony between the ancestors of the Yamato court and those of the chieftains of Izumo. Between the various gods and heroes who figure against one another further down the diagram, the main principle of division is between the line of the Plain of High Heaven or imperial ancestors on the one hand, and the line of the ancestors of the provincial chieftains, with special reference to those of Izumo, on the other; and this amounts to an attempt to explain the reason and basis for the submission of the ancestors of the provincial chieftains to those of the emperors. In short, we can probably regard it as an account of the creation of a state with centralized power brought about by the submission to the emperor of the chieftains and heads of clans at the base, in short a justification of the principles underlying the Taika Reform. [Political reform led by Prince Naka-no-ōe who destroyed the powerful Soga clan in 645.]

The reader will have understood now, from the foregoing diagram, the compilers' central intentions. One might call this a logical deduction of the compilers' intentions, based on analysis of the themes of the different volumes of the *Kojiki,* but there remains the question whether or not such intentions are congruous with those of the compilers that are considered historical facts. As I have said, there is no overt statement of the matter in the *Kojiki* itself. But we can draw conclusions by studying the *Nihon Shoki* and the Preface to the *Kojiki*.

Just who, then, were the compilers of the *Kojiki*? Difficult though it, of course, is to identify a particular person as the compiler, since the work was not spontaneously generated, we are obliged to some extent to point to some human agency. The *Nihon Shoki* and the Preface to the *Kojiki* justify us, I think, in taking as compilers those who were connected with the Emperor Temmu's compilation of the *Kojiki* as well as those responsible for the 'Chronicle of the Emperors' and the 'Chronicle of the Country' in Suiko's reign.

The first information we find with direct reference to the compilation of the *Kojiki* is the compilation of a record of the emperors and a record of the country, in the 28th year of the reign of the Empress Suiko (620). This was one of the things done by Prince Shōtoku, who is also regarded as responsible for establishing the twelve cap-ranks and for drawing up the Seventeen Articles, of which the third enjoins 'absolute submission to imperial commands.' The Prince strove with all his might to resolve the problems of the period I have just described, and it may be supposed that the spirit in which he strove provided one of the motives for national historiography.

About this record of the emperors and the record of the country, we have the entry for the fourth year of the reign of the Empress Kōgyoku (645), stating that Funano-Esaka, a scribe, hurriedly seized the burning record of the country and presented it to Naka-no-ōe. And so is related the destruction of this precious material by fire. However, in view of the statement that the record of the country was presented to Naka-no-ōe, it would hardly be a mere coincidence that Naka-no-ōe's, that is to say, the Emperor Tenchi's younger brother, the Emperor Temmu was responsible for having the *Kojiki* recited. The Taika Reform had already been carried through and a state had been created with centralized power and the emperor at its head. We may very well imagine the desire to account for the sacred character of the emperor and his authority over the whole country, which constituted that state's basis, by means of myths and legends. There can be no question that it was the purpose of the *Kojiki* to make plain, in the words of Temmu in its Preface, 'the fabric of the country, the grand foundation of the monarchy,' that is to say, the basic principle of the unified national life. Since this also means that the principal aims in compiling the *Kojiki* included the coordination of the traditions of the clans, one ought, of course, to touch on the historical development of the ideas involved, but as this is rather beyond my present scope, I am leaving the matter at that for the present.

If we assumed a considerable revision of the contents to have taken place after Temmu's time, we might also properly include as compilers of the *Kojiki* all those involved up to and including Ō-no-Yasumaro's definitive recension in the reign of the Empress Gemmei. However, since, according to Yasumaro's Preface, his work was confined, as is well known, to establishing the written text, there would seem no necessity to extend the time limit so far in point of contents. Moreover, we may also suppose that an oral prototype of the *Kojiki* had come into being by Suiko's time and that this was what had been orally transmitted down to the time of Temmu. However, taking into consideration such a fact as that whereas the *Kojiki* contains a large number of *tanka* or lyrics, there are no lyrics in the pre-Suiko part of the *Nihon Shoki* which can reliably be accepted as historical products of that period, it would seem reasonable to suppose that the *tanka* form, as a mode of individual lyrical expression, came into being round about the Suiko period; in which case, the *Kojiki* may well have been composed after Suiko. Moreover, since the myths and legends themselves contain matter which supposes some cultural advance, it is all the more difficult to accept a pre-Suiko date of composition. And even if one did go so far, one could hardly go back so far as the pre-Keitai period.

Reasoning along these lines, we may conclude that the composition of the *Kojiki* must, very broadly, have taken place during the period extending from the time of Keitai through that of Suiko up to the reign of Temmu. This period corresponds to that treated in the final part of Volume Three of the *Kojiki,* the period for which it records only the imperia genealogy and no other information. Thus the time of 'we mortals now,' i.e. the present time, in Naka-no-ōe's 'Song of the Three Mountains,' is that which is not recorded in the *Kojiki.* That is to say, the myths and legends were compiled for the purpose of finding a basis for the present, but the present itself was not directly handled. Accordingly, when we now read the *Kojiki,* we must extract from our reading of the myths and legends, in their background, the real preoccupations and feelings which constituted the thought of the compilers' period. This is what comprehension of the *Kojiki* should surely be.

This is not to say that the individual myths and legends were created by the *Kojiki*'s compilers. One can probably take it that the original forms of the myths and legends are almost all of ancient date, perhaps from about the Nintoku period. Nevertheless it is likely that such matters as giving shape to the general body of the mythology, the bringing together of the legends and their leading heroes, the casting of the myths and legends in literary form, all this would have been the work either of the compilers' or of the spirit of the age of the compilers. So we may take it that the main element for us to absorb from the *Kojiki* as a whole will be, in the first place, the compilers' intentions,

that is to say, the spirit of the Keitai-Suiko-Temmu period. Though we may well occupy ourselves with discovering the process by which particular myths were formed and the comparative importance of each in the whole, we must seize our primary understanding from the tendency of the whole of the *Kojiki,* from its narrative as a whole. Even if we are unable to produce proven accounts of the way in which particular myths took shape, we can, if we accept the simple significance of their presence in the *Kojiki*'s narrative, apprehend, not the social background to the creation of the myths in their original form, but the intentions of the *Kojiki*'s compilers. Resolution of the whole of the *Kojiki* into its component myths and legends, and investigation of their original forms and the process of their creation, may be a part of mythological or historical studies, but they do not amount to a direct apprehension of the *Kojiki.*

We will now consider what was the spirit of the age from the time of the Emperor Keitai to that of the Emperor Tenchi and what were the central problems for the ruling class of the period. The first item to consider here is the question of repulsing Silla's invasion of southern Korea and the restoration of Imna. The second is the question of the reception of Buddhism. The third is the establishment of a centralized bureacratic state with the emperor at its head.

The first of the above preoccupations ended, after a series of successes and failures in the collapse at the final battle of the Baekchon River. In respect of the second, Japan went the whole way and became a country of Budhist culture. The third achievement was made good by the Taika Reform. If we put these three together it would amount to saying that Japan's political and cultural independence had been achieved. By these means, the ancient barbarous nation had turned into a civilized state.

Such then, in outline, were the thoughts and preoccupations of the period which covered the compilation of the *Kojiki.*

I trust, then, that my readers agree that what the *Kojiki*'s myths and legends as a whole relate is on the whole consistent with the compilers' intentions, such as they may be made out to be from the *Nihon Shoki* and the *Kojiki*'s Preface and so on.

The period is somewhat early, but the *Sung Shu,* the History of the Liu Sung Dynasty, has preserved a 'memorial' addressed to the Emperor Shun-ti by the Emperor Yūryaku, in 478; and the text of this, in classical Chinese, shows a congruity between the political ideas and historical outlook of the Japanese court at that time and the intentions of the *Kojiki*'s compilers. The same reasoning, whereby 'the Age of the Gods' and 'antiquity' in Naka-no-ōe's Three Mountains expresses the author's sense of actuality of 'we mortals now,' serves to entitle the *Kojiki,* using myth and legend as material, to be regarded as a work of great narrative literature expressing the spirit of the Asuka and Hakuhō periods. The *Kojiki* is indeed the epic poem of the birth of Japanese culture.

The *Kojiki* has a Preface written by the great exponent of Chinese prose, Ō-no-Yasumaro, and this describes the origins of the compilation and the course of its composition. The Preface also deals with the division of the *Kojiki* into Volumes One, Two and Three and gives an outline of the myths and legends. The text being in Chinese, there are some points on which it is difficult to grasp the author's true intention, but it is the only clue we have to knowing how Ō-no-Yasumaro, one of the best scholars of the time, who left us the *Kojiki* and took part in the planning of the *Nihon Shoki,* took and interpreted the myths and legends of the *Kojiki.* One might say that what moves us so much is the thought of a sort of 'Discourse on the *Kojiki*' written by a scholar twelve hundred years ago. I propose now to extract and study just those parts of the Preface that give the outline.

I have given, first, a reading of the original Chinese text, based on Professor Takeda's and other comments, and I have then given my own translation with a certain amount of interpretative interpolation. I have written my version in colloquial style for the sake of intelligibility. I have also, for the sake of convenience, divided it into paragraphs, numbered to correspond with the translation. In this way the form of Ō-no-Yasumaro's outline, together with the thought that was its basis, may be understood. . . .

[1] I, Yasumaro, say: Now when chaos had begun to condense, but force and form were not yet manifest, and there were no names and no doing, who could know its shape? Then Heaven and Earth were separated for the first time, and the three gods performed the beginning of creation; the male and female principles then developed, and the two spirits became the ancestors of everything. So they entered the darkness and emerged into the light; and the sun and the moon appeared from the washing of his eyes; and when he floated on into the water of the sea, gods of heaven and gods of earth appeared from the ablution of his person.

[2] Therefore, in spite of the obscurity of the great origin, we may learn from the true doctrine about the time of the conception of the earth and the birth of the islands, and, in spite of the remoteness of the beginning, we may apprehend from the saintly ones of old the age of the genesis of the gods and the establishment of mankind.

[3] We know truly: a mirror was hung up, jewels were spat out, and then a hundred kings succeeded

one another; a blade was bitten, a serpent cut in pieces, and then a myriad gods flourished.

[4] After deliberations in the Tranquil River, the world was pacified; after discussions on the small beach, the land was purified.

[5] Then Ho-no-Ninigi-no-mikoto first descended on to the peak of Takachi, and the Emperor Kamuyamato proceeded to the island of Akitsu.

[6] A strange bear came out of a river; a heavenly sword was obtained at Takakura. Creatures with tails obstructed the road, and a great crow guided to Yoshino. Dancing in rows, they expelled the brigands, listening to songs, they overcame the enemy.

[7] Being instructed in a dream, he did reverence to the gods of heaven and earth, and was therefore called the Wise Monarch.

[8] Having seen the smoke from afar, he was benevolent to the black-haired people, and was therefore called the Sage Sovereign.

[9] Determining the frontiers and civilizing the country, he issued laws in Nearer Ōmi.

[10] Putting right the surnames and selecting the clan names, he held sway in Further Asuka.

[11] Though each differed in caution and in ardour, though all were unlike in accomplishments and character, yet there was none who did not by contemplating antiquity correct manners that had withered away, and by illumining the present repair laws that were approaching dissolution.

Wieslaw Kotański (essay date 1979)

SOURCE: Wieslaw Kotański, "The Belief in *Kotodama* and Some Earlier Misinterpretations of *Kojiki,*" in *European Studies on Japan,* edited by Ian Nish and Charles Dunn, Paul Norbury Publications, 1979, pp. 237-42.

[*In the following essay, Kotański discusses the significance of proper names in the* Kojiki, *charging that earlier translators had neglected to pay them sufficient attention.*]

While preparing the Polish translation of *Kojiki,* I have consulted some earlier European interpretations of that work, namely those of Chamberlain, Florenz and Philippi, and I have of course observed that they reveal no tendency to engage in translating the so-called proper names of the heroes of the *Kojiki,* or to include their contents in the course of the narrative. Such a tendency was certainly caused by their conviction that the contents of proper names, denoting natural and supernatural beings, in no way influences the narrative itself. The names contain, according to them, some information, e.g. about the functions of deities, but this seldom serves to enrich the narrative, and even more this is so with the names of human individuals. The said interpreters have tried only to elucidate the meaning of these names in footnotes or glossaries, considering their explanations as academic etymological studies. These attempts, containing in fact also many blanks and abortive attempts, have not led them to the conclusion that there is any necessity to treat the meaning of names in *Kojiki* in another way.

Now, however, the Polish translation of *Kojiki* will be quite different. It was found that all the names in *Kojiki* are rather a sort of substitute for proper names. Those substitutes can be in general divided into two groups, namely a set of some provisional denotations, mentioning mostly a title and residing place of the person, and a set of descriptive images, exposing some character features or some details from the lifetime of the given person. The first set may be regarded as of minor linguistic interest, being relatively easy to interpret, but the second of these sets proved to be a phenomenon, not only difficult to be linguistically analysed, but also entangled with the vital problems of the sociology of the old Japanese language. It is the reason why I have chosen it as my special object of study.

Let us first be concerned with sociological aspects of the question, because they have probably been the reason why up to now students of *Kojiki* could not grasp the peculiar character of these descriptive substitutes. It must above all be remembered that to use such descriptors instead of some real names, designating individuals without referring to their psychological or incidental characterization, must have had some concrete reason. It seems rather improbable that people in those times did not use personal names. We know even from the old literature many instances when the opportunity was taken of asking the name e.g. of a girl, as an equivalent of—say—a proposal to her. But the name used in the family circle, was mostly kept hidden from other people because to know the name of a being meant to grasp his soul and to be in a position to work through his name whatever one liked on his soul-substance. A name pronounced immediately conjures up the invisible spirit of the living or deceased person designated by that name. This was the basic principle of the belief in *Kotodama,* a kind of verbal taboo in ancient Japan, and a living custom in present day Japan too. In order not to evoke any unlucky consequences one must avoid using real names. They must be replaced by *azana,* i.e. 'misleading names' which are to avert any misfortunes, guilts and curses which might come to the person if

one used some real name (*tada-no-na*). Resorting to epithets which refer to various characteristic features of individuals was equivalent to preventing any magic misuse of the real names of rulers and gods.

The earlier students of *Kojiki* did not really perceive that peculiar aspect of those epithets and this was their most flagrant misinterpretation of the work. As it is possible to prove that the majority of these epithets carry anticipatory meaning, i.e. the meaning relating the given person with some events which could occur only towards the end of their lifetime, so it follows that in reality they could not serve the person before that event occurred. In searching for some causes of this misapprehension we come across not only sociological matters but also various linguistic difficulties. It may be that in order to conceal a name better tabooed or its bearer, the courtiers and priests of old Japan, who preserved various narratives of ancient events, deformed the epithets handed down to them by earlier generations, or else they no longer understood the morphemic and semantic structure of those epithets and had introduced into them some 'corrections' according to their own knowledge of verbal rules. One way or the other the present researcher of those epithets has to surmount many obstacles and it is my task now to formulate some principles, leading to a more safe method of their interpretation.

First of all, word formation rules of Archaic Japanese are, as a matter of fact, sufficiently recognized, but interpreters of *Kojiki* too scantily make use of them. They are acquinted relatively well with various types of umlaut, e.g.

kami-kamu, tsuki-tsuku, ma-me, kaza-kaze, ko-ki, yomo-yomi, shira-shiro, yami-yomi, shiro-shiru, no-nu, ata-atsu, kaga-kagu, se-so, kage-kago, kuni-kuna, shimu-sabu.

The exchange of consonants (omitting *nigori*) is of lesser importance and is often neglected by interpreters too. But more widespread and unfortunately not so much acknowledged are two other forms of transforming the composed word; we will call them provisionally bonding and overlapping. By bonding should be understood a transformation of the present form of a verb into a kind of bound form, serving mainly to generate compositions. There occur two such bound forms: one, ending in -a (e.g. *kana* from *kanu, yama* from *yamu* etc.) which appear in my conjectures about 70 times, the second one, ending in -o (e.g, *odo* from *ozu, shiko* from *shiku* etc.), which appear about 30 times.

In its turn overlapping is a kind of reduction, occuring between two catenated words, and appears in four varieties:

(a) Overlapping of vowels, e.g. *mitsu* from *mi-itsu* (pure and sacred), *nagahi* from *naga-hi* (long interval), totally about 90 cases.

(b) Overlapping of syllables, e.g. *ehito* from *oi-hito* (suiting man), *sanagi* from *sana-nagi* (appeasing of pudenda), totally about 30 cases.

(c) Informal overlapping of cognated syllables, e.g. *subiko* from *sube-biko* (ruling lad), altogether about 30 cases.

(d) Overlapping with different vowels, e.g. *homuya* from *home-uya* (glory and reverence), etc., altogether about 10 cases.

The semantics of the proper names under discussion present themselves far more dimly than their morphology. Some interpreters exhibit a lamentable tendency towards a stereotyped, monotonous and narrow-minded evaluation of morphemic meaning; they are not able to go beyond the limits of meaning assigned by a dictionary though it is notoriously certain that no dictionary can display all the shadows and intricacies of a word's meaning.

The most basic principles of an accurate semantic interpretation will be as follows:

—accordance of the contents of a composite name with the plot of the story or at least with structural features of the context

—ascertainment of a correct morphological and semantic interpretation of all constituents of the composition, in such a way that it will become a reasonable designation of the given person or deity in the target language.

Let us now give some more curious instances of convergence, kinship and multilateral function as reflected in the names of deities. These are examples of convergence:

IZANAGINŌKAMĬ and IZANAMINŌKAMĬ, analysed as *i-sane-nagi-no-kami, i-sane-nami-no-kami* 'spirit appeasing the precious pudenda', 'spirit agitating the precious pudenda'—together the couple advocating the sexual act (traditionally: *iza* derived from *izanu* 'to invite', *nagi* and *nami* are respectively masculine and feminine endings).

KANAYAMABIKO and KANAYAMABIME—children of the sick Izanami born while she vomits. *kane-yamu-hi-ko* or-*me* 'lad (or maiden) mighty to cause diseases of digestion' (trad.: 'metal mountain lad' or 'princess'—where is the connexion with vomiting?).

MITUPANŌME and WAKUMUSUBI—children of Izanami, born while she urinates. *mi-tsu-hane-no-me, waku-masu-hi* 'Female spurting water' and 'spirit bearing springs' (trad.: 'watergreens woman'; 'young or seething vital force'—evidently a deity of generation).

AMĔNŌKOYANE and PUTOTAMA—together embrace the domain of divine service (literally: plaintive singing and sacrifices). *ame-no-koyu-ne, futo-tamu* 'heavenly mourner or sorrower' and 'donor of ample offerings' (trad.: 'heavenly little roof' and 'solemn offerings presenter'—first interpretation out of place).

OPONAMUDI and SUKUNABIKONA—they together create and solidify the land. *ö-namu-chi, suku-nabi-ko-na* 'great force establishing order' and 'manikin establishing quickly order' (trad.: 'great revered one' and 'little lad deity'—why have the two no custodial function, particularly no creative mission?).

Next we will discuss groups of cognate deities, who similarly show great proximity of the intercessory functions exercised.

SUGANŌYATUMIMI and YASIMAZINUMI—grandfather who has influence on the education of his grandson. *suga-no-ya-tsu-imi-mi* 'spirit of harmlessness of the house of Suga'; *iya-ashi-maji/nai/-no-mi* 'spirit averting misfortune and evil' (trad.: 'Suga eight ears or rulers'; 'eight islands jinumi'—etymology not clear).

KÖNŌPANATIRUPIME and PUPANŌMÖDIKUNUSUNUKAMĬ—mother and her son. *ko-no-hana-chiru-hi-me* 'woman mighty to cause blossoms to fall'; *fu-hane-omo-ozu-ko-no-su-no-kami* 'spirit of nests on trees gravely careworn about denudation of the thicket' (trad.: 'blossoms of the trees falling princess'; the etymology of the second name not clear).

OKAMINŌKAMĬ,   PIKAPAPIME, PUKABUTINŌMIDUYAREPANANŌKAMĬ—randfather, mother and her son (his father is the 'spirit of nests . . . careworn about denudation of the thicket'). *okami-no-kami* 'dragon deity'; *hi-kae-hime* 'the maiden changing into ice'; *Fuka-muchi-no-mi-itsu-yare-hana-no-kami* 'deeply revered sacred and mighty spirit nipping flowers' (trad.: a dragon deity but etymology not clear; Hikawa Princess; 'deity sprinkle water on the flowers of Fukabuchi'—why Hikawa, why Fukabuchi?).

YASIMAMUDI,   TÖRIMIMI,   TÖRINIRUMI—grandfather, mother and her son. *iya-ashi-imu-muji* 'the noble undoing misfortunes and evils'; *tori-mi-mi* 'the spirit watching birds'; *tori-naru-mi* 'the spirit of learning from birds'. It is to be added that birds are carriers of misfortunes which should be carefully diagnosed (trad.: 'eight islands noble'; 'bird ear' or 'ruler of Tori'; 'bird sounding ocean', perhaps also combination of two place names Tori-Narumi, etymology not clear).

OKAMINOKAMI, PINARASIBIME, TAPIRIKISIMARUMI—grandfather, mother and her son. *okami-no-kami* 'dragon deity'; *hi-narashi-hi-me* 'the maiden mighty to tame the sun'; *ta-hihi-iri-iki-shimaru-mi* 'the spirit fettering alive with the affliction of hand trembling'—the affinity between the dragon, ruler of tempests and rainfalls with 'taming of the sun' and with producing of rheumatic diseases is quite clear (trad.: 'dragon deity' but the etymology of the other two names is unclear).

Many deities bear two, three or more names which in various aspects mutually complement their meanings.

ASINADAKANÖKAMI also named YAGAPAYEPIME—*ashi-no-take-no-kami* 'the spirit of the growth of reeds'; *ya-kae-hae-hi-me* 'the maiden causing luxuriant regeneration and vegetation' (trad.: 'reed nadaka deity': 'yakawa elder sibling princess' or 'many river inlets princess' or 'ever more flourishing princess').

KAMUATATUPIME also called KÖNÖPANANÖSAKIYABIME (or *sakuyabime*)—*kamu-ata-atsu-hime* 'the maiden subjecting to the divine heat'; *ko-no-hana-no-saki-kie-hime* 'the maiden causing blooming and withering of tree flowers' (trad.: 'divine Ata princess'; 'blossom of the trees blooming princess'—why should Ata princess be maiden of blooming?).

Among several categories of the deities' names the most interesting one is perhaps that which derives its occurrence from the circumstances of the birth of the deity or from happenings during his lifetime which are adduced in the text.

OPOKÖTÖOSIWO—the first deity born by the demiurges after they had finished bearing the land. *o-koto-oshi-o* 'the male forcing great undertakings'—apparently bound to support his parents in their doings (trad.: great male of the great undertaking).

KUMANOKUSUBI—who came into existence as the last offspring, testing the loyalty of the Raging Male who visits his sister. *kumu-no-kusu-hi* 'wondrous power of reconciliation' (trad.: 'wondrous Kumano deity').

INABANÖYAGAMIPIME—whom eighty deities wished to marry. Slight standard modification of reading *mi* as *mu*. *inaba-no-iya-agamu-hime*, 'extremely adored maiden from Inaba' (trad.: princess of Yagami in Inaba).

TAKEMINAKATANÖKAMI—who displays his strength and tries to test strength with heavenly deities. *take-mina-katsu-no-kami*, 'valiant spirit conquering everyone' (trad.: 'valiant Minakata deity' where Minakata related to Munakata—but without argumentation).

AMENÖZUME—who can face and overwhelm others. *ame-no-ozo-me*, 'heavenly clever woman' (trad.: 'heavenly formidable woman' or etymology not clear).

ITUSE—elder brother of the first emperor who serves the Sun Offspring in many battles, *itsu-se* 'a prodigious companion' (trad.: five rapids).

INAPINÖMIKÖTÖ—who entered the ocean. *inai-no-mikoto* 'the Lords which departed' (trad.: 'rice food lord').

Anticipatory types of names whose contents precede the events described therein and which occur from time to time among deities' names are far more frequent amongst the names of inhabitants of the earth.

TÖMINÖNAGASUMEBIKO—who opposed the entrance of the emperor into Yamato and killed the brother of the emperor. *tomi-no-nagasu-nebi-hiko* 'a cutting down mature lad from Tomi' (trad.: 'lad of Nagasune' or 'long shank lad').

TAGISIMIMI—who plots against his younger brothers in order to rule the kingdom. *ta-kishimi-mi* 'the spirit robbing hand' (trad.: 'Tagishi ruler').

KAMUYAWIMIMI—who ceded his birthright to his younger brother and served as a priest. *kamu-ya-i-mi-mi* 'venerable spirit staying in the house of god' (trad.: 'divine yai ruler').

SAPADIPIME—the empress who plots against her husband, flees from him and finally dies with her rebel brother. *sawa-haji-hime* 'the maiden greatly disgraced' (trad.: etymology not clear).

OPOTATANEKO—who worships in order to avert the divine wrath that the land be at ease. *o-tatane-ko* 'great man to rectify' (trad.: great tata ruler).

KUGAMIMINÖMIKASA—a rebel chieftain of Tamba. *kuga-mi-mino-mikasa* 'guardian (literally: straw-coat and hood) of lands and waters' (trad.: 'mikasa lord of Kuga').

KARABUKURÖ—an attendant who provoked the hunt during which a prince was killed and whose children were charged with care of the tomb of the slain prince. *karu-fuku-uro(uro)* 'worried to fan the hunt' (trad.: 'Korean bag' or 'Fukuro in Kara').

WODÖPIME—a maiden who seeing the approach of the emperor fled and hid on a hill. *o-ozu-hime* 'the maiden fearing men' (trad.: etymology not clear).

ARAKAPI—an *ömuraji* who was dispatched to kill a rebel. *ara-akai* 'returning the apostasy (or rebellion)' (trad.: etymology not clear or—according to Matsuoka—'visible deity' or 'god in human form'?). Designations of most rulers are difficult to analyse and to translate because they are artificially composed.

MIMATUPIKOKAWESINE—*mi-imu-tsu-hiko ha-e-ushi-ne* 'the sacrosanct off-spring of the sunbeamy smiling lord' (trad.: 'lord of the imperial lands—the rest is etymologically dubious').

WAKAYAMATŌNEKOPIKOOPOBIBI—*waka-yamato-ne-ikoi-hiko o-hibiki* 'young lad under whom Yamato enjoyed leisure ringing with great fame' (trad.: 'young root child lad great ruler').

Among the names probably referring to the circumstances our attention is drawn by a fairly large group which indicates a particular popularity of designations connected with the life of villages and with farming.

TADIMAMORŌSUKU—*tajima-moru-suku* 'one fond of riddling from Tajima' (trad.: etymology not clear).

TADIMAPIME—*tajima-hi-no* 'sifter from Tajima' (trad.: etymology not clear).

KIYOPIKO—certainly reading should be corrected into equivalent *sayapiko: saya-hihiko* 'lad riddling noisily' (trad.: 'pure lad').

SUGANŌMORŌWO (perhaps *Sugasimorowo*)—*Sugashi-moru-o* 'The man riddling clean' (trad.: 'Suga male' or etymology not clear).

I have analysed—on the occasion of preparing the Polish translation of *Kojiki*—all the designations of spirits and men quoted in that work. In this paper I can present only a small part of them. It is sure that not all the propositions of mine are sufficiently proved; some items must perhaps be reconsidered in order to seek other conclusions. But in general, the principles of analysis accepted by the author, seem to be rather promising, because they allow the replacement of many empty, unclear and unintelligible conjectures of earlier students.

Although the results presented in the paper, seem to be a critical revision of previous achievements, there is no doubt, that without predecessors whose works were very instructive and of great avail as a basis for criticism, there would be no present stage of studies, because the author who can see a way already paved is able to walk along it or to diverge from it. Previous pioneers could in their times walk only blindly and therefore they went often astray. Let then the author regard himself only as one who continues work which others, in more difficult conditions, have daringly begun.

Fuminobu Murakami (essay date 1988)

SOURCE: Fuminobu Murakami, "Incest and Rebirth in Kojiki," in *Monumenta Nipponica: Studies in Japanese Culture*, Vol. 43, No. 4, Winter, 1988, pp. 455-63.

[*In the excerpt that follows, Murakami grapples with the role of incest in the* Kojiki, *arguing that it is integral to the text's notion of eternal life.*]

In *Kojiki* . . . , Izanami . . . is referred to as an *imo* . . . , a term meaning both wife and younger sister in ancient Japanese, and scholars have generally considered this to mean that she was only the wife, and not the sister, of Izanagi. . . .[1] The first scholar to suggest an incestuous union between the two was Oka Masao . . . , who claimed that the tale of Izanagi and Izanami is based on a myth about an incestuous brother-sister union that is common in Southeast Asia, Central India, and other Asian regions.[2] According to this myth, long ago there was a great flood that exterminated all mankind with the exception of two people, a brother and sister, on a mountain. After performing a rite to abolish the incest taboo, they tried to produce children, but on their first attempt the woman gave birth to deformed offspring. But they succeeded in producing normal children on their second attempt and thus became the ancestors of present-day human beings.[3] Oka points out the similarity between this myth and the Izanagi-Izanami story, and claims that the latter closely parallels the Asian myth about the incestuous union between brother and sister.

Hattori Asake, on the other hand, finds three significant differences between the two versions: (1) the Izanagi-Izanami myth does not mention a flood; (2) there is no clear indication that Izanagi and Izanami are in fact brother and sister; and (3) the theme of the myth in *Kojiki* is the birth of lands, whereas that of the incestuous union between brother and sister is the birth of humans. Hattori concludes that Izanagi and Izanami are not brother and sister.[4]

Saigō Nobutsuna, however, has studied the use of the term *imo* in *Man'yōshū* . . . , and shows that when the word refers to a wife, it is used by only the husband to address his wife in person. He suggests that because *imo* is mentioned by the compiler only in the narrative part of *Kojiki,* the term must refer to a sister. In other words, Izanagi and Izanami are brother and sister, and therefore commit incest.[5] But Nishimiya Kazutami disagrees, arguing that the examples from *Man'yōshū* are not necessarily applicable to *Kojiki*.[6]

The purpose of the present article is not to resolve the above difference of opinion but to analyze the incest theme throughout *Kojiki,* assuming that the theme is in fact present in the work. It seems fair to make this assumption in view of the prevalence of the incest theme in various myths of different regions and in light of the relevant theories of Freud and Levi-Strauss.

Rebirth

Kojiki describes how three noble deities, Amaterasu-ō-mikami . . . , Tsuku-yomi-no-mikoto . . . , and Susa-no-o-no-mikoto . . . came into existence when Izanagi purified himself after Izanami was burned in the genitals and died while giving birth to the fire deity, Hi-no-kagu-tsuchi-no-kami. . . .[7] In the *Nihon Shoki* . . . version, however, the three deities are born as a result of Izanagi and Izanami's union as husband and wife before the latter's death.[8] Tsuda Sōkichi takes this latter version to be the true one,[9] and if this is indeed the case, we can accept the interpretation that the three noble deities were born before Izanami died. The story then continues in both *Nihon Shoki* and *Kojiki* with Izanagi's visit to the Yomi land, or underworld.[10]

As regards Izanagi's visit to the Yomi land, Matsumura Takeo points out that Izanagi's inspection of Izanami's corpse is related to the *mogari* . . . magico-religious funeral rite that is believed to have been performed in ancient Japan. When someone died, his family built a hut called a *mogari* near their house and laid the corpse there; they then went to inspect the corpse everyday until it turned putrid. This rite is believed to be a way of praying for the rebirth of the dead.[11] Although Izanami's rebirth is not mentioned in *Kojiki,* the story relates not only her death but also Izanagi's overwhelming desire for her return to life.

The above analysis suggests that Izanagi and Izanami committed incest and gave birth to the three noble deities, and that the rebirth of Izanami, after she had been burnt to death, was prayed for through the *mogari* magico-religious rite. The four elements—incest, sacred birth, death, and rebirth—are all present.

In the story of Amaterasu and Susa-no-o bearing offspring to test the sincerity of the latter's motives, the two give birth to the important deities, Ame-no-oshi-ho-mimi-no-mikoto . . . and Takiri-bime-no-mikoto. . . . Although Yokota Ken'ichi has denied the incestuous union between Amaterasu and Susa-no-o,[12] we presuppose it here again.

According to this story, Susa-no-o becomes violent after the birth of the offspring, makes a hole in the roof of the sacred weaving hall, and drops into it a dappled pony that he has cruelly skinned. At this, the weaving maiden becomes alarmed, strikes her genitals against the shuttle, and dies. As *Nihon Shoki* specifically mentions that Amaterasu herself is also injured in the same way,[13] Orikuchi Shinobu and Matsumura Takeo suppose that the deity who is wounded and dies in the original version of the story is Amaterasu herself.[14]

The *chinkonsai* . . . rite may well have been based on the myth of Amaterasu's secluding herself in the heavenly rock-cave, recorded immediately after the above story; certainly the rites in this tale are very similar to those of the *chinkonsai* ceremony. The *chinkonsai,* or *tama-shizume-matsuri,* that is, spirit pacification, was performed every winter. As the emperor was believed

to be the descendant of the sun-goddess Amaterasu, his soul was thought to become weaker as the weather became colder. He therefore performed the *chinkonsai* every winter to prevent his soul from leaving his body or to summon it back into his body. In *Kojiki,* therefore, Amaterasu, the divinity of both the sun and the emperor, dies and is reborn by entering and leaving the cave, as symbolized in the *chinkonsai.*

Thus we can suppose that, at a deeper level in the *Kojiki* version, the section from Amaterasu and Susa-no-o's bearing offspring to Amaterasu's hiding in the cave relates how Amaterasu and Susa-no-o produced the sacred deities, Oshi-ho-mimi and Takiri-bime, as a result of their incest, and then how Amaterasu died by being struck in the genitals and is brought back to life by the *chinkonsai.* But what do these repeated four themes of incest, sacred birth, death, and rebirth signify?

Yanagita Kunio has studied the rebirth of the ancestral soul, and describes a custom in Okinawa whereby the first son is named after his grandfather and the first daughter after her grandmother. He suggests, 'There might have been a time when the ancient Japanese people believed that the grandparents were reborn as their grandchildren.' He goes on to dismiss this theory by observing, 'A span of two generations is too short to allow the rebirth of the soul.'[15] That is, if the grandparents are still alive when their grandchildren are born, then the grandchildren's bodies come into existence too soon for their grandparents' souls to be reborn into them.

But an examination of the *daijōsai* . . . ceremony reveals a different perspective. The *daijōsai* is the rite marking the enthronement of a new emperor and is performed the day after the *chinkonsai.*[16] In the *daijōsai,* the new emperor performs a symbolic enactment of death and rebirth in order to free himself of his old soul and receive Amaterasu's soul. On the analogy of this rite, therefore, we may suppose that the ancient people may have believed that children's bodies could receive their grandparents' souls through the symbolic enactment of death and rebirth after the grandparents' deaths.

I personally consider that it was an ancient belief that the grandparents' souls could be reborn in their grandchildren's bodies. Orikuchi Shinobu supports this view, pointing out that *mima* in *sumemima* . . . , or emperor, has two meanings, body and grandchild. According to Orikuchi, the ancient Japanese recognized the emperor as a soul called *sumera-mikoto-no-mitama.* . . . Taking into account that the person whose body receives this soul in the *daijōsai* ceremony can become the next emperor, Orikuchi takes *mima* to mean body.[17] But let us examine the meaning of 'grandchild' that Orikuchi rejects. The *sumera-mikoto-no-mitama* is the ancestral soul of the emperor's family, and consequently Amaterasu's soul. Although Amaterasu's soul was believed to have been passed on to each new emperor's body, it is passed on from the grandparents' to the grandchildren's bodies in *Kojiki,* 1, as mentioned below. If this is the case, then we can readily accept both the Okinawan custom to name children after their grandparents, as noted by Yanagita, and also Orikuchi's etymological theory that *mima* means grandchild as well as body. Further, if we apply this supposition to the analysis of the incestuous unions described in *Kojiki,* it is plausible to suggest that the brother-sister union was believed to strengthen and purify the rebirth of the grandparents' souls in the grandchildren's bodies. A brother-sister union guaranteed the preservation of the parents' blood in the children's bodies. In short, Izanagi and Izanami, like Amaterasu and Susa-no-o, committed incest to allow their parents' souls to be reborn in their children. . . .

The above argument resolves several problems in *Kojiki.* Tsuda has asked why Amaterasu is called *kōsoshin* . . . , or the first ancestral deity of the imperial family, even though she had parents, and, conversely, why Izanagi and Izanami are not called *kōsoshin.* He answers that Izanagi and Izanami were necessary to produce Amaterasu, the ancestor of the imperial family, and Susa-no-o, the ancestor of the Izumo clan, elder sister and younger brother.[18] As is apparent, this reasoning is based on political considerations. But if Amaterasu is the deity in whom the soul of Izanagi and Izanami's mother is reborn as a result of their incest, she surely ought to be called *kōsoshin.* In other words, Amaterasu has two identities, (1) the daughter of Izanagi and Izanami, and (2) the mother of Izanagi and Izanami reborn through their incest. She should be seen as transforming herself successively from one identity to the other, rather than possessing the two identities or playing the two roles simultaneously. The occasion of the transformation was her death and rebirth in the heavenly cave. In this way, incest, sacred birth, death, and rebirth are now related to each other.

The second consideration is that Taka-mi-musubi-no-kami . . . , the deity who first appears in the Takama-no-hara in *Kojiki,* suddenly re-enters in the story of Ho-no-ninigi-no-mikoto's . . . descent from heaven. Before this story, *Kojiki* focuses on the genealogy from Taka-mi-musubi and Kami-musubi-no-kami . . . through Izanagi and Izanami to Amaterasu and Susa-no-o. It is therefore clearly not logical that in and after the story of Ho-no-ninigi's descent, Taka-mi-musubi suddenly reappears with Amaterasu as a ruler of the Takama-no-hara, as if they were husband and wife. Oka Masao points out that originally there may have been two different myths, one concerning Amaterasu and the other, Taka-mi-musubi. He suggests that Taka-mi-musubi's myth comes from Korea while that of

Amaterasu originates in Southeast Asia.[19] But the structure of *Kojiki* lends itself to another explanation, namely, that the apparent problem is also the result of Amaterasu's death and birth. Possessing her grandmother's soul by means of death and rebirth in the heavenly cave, Amaterasu returns to the same generation as Taka-mi-musubi.

The third point concerns the question why Ho-no-ninigi rather than his father, Oshi-ho-mimi, descends from heaven. By way of explanation, we should bear in mind that Ho-no-ninigi's mother is Toyo-aki-tsu-shi-hime-no-mikoto . . . , the daughter of Taka-mi-musubi. If, as mentioned above, Amaterasu receives her grandmother's soul in the heavenly rock-cave and returns to the same generation as Taka-mi-musubi, Toyo-aki-tsu-shi-hime must be Amaterasu's daughter as well as Taka-mi-musubi's. Then the incestuous relationship between Oshi-ho-mimi and Toyo-akitsu-shi-hime is obscured by their marriage. Thus Ho-no-ninigi is conceived through the incest between Oshi-ho-mimi and Toyo-aki-tsu-shi-hime, and as a result has the body in which Amaterasu's soul is to be housed. This would explain why Ho-no-ninigi, rather than Oshi-ho-mimi, descends from heaven. . . .

The structure of *Kojiki,* from the viewpoint of incest, sacred birth, death, and rebirth, now becomes clear. First, Izanagi and Izanami commit incest to bring about the rebirth of their parents, and give sacred birth to Amaterasu and Susa-no-o; Izanami then dies. Although there are prayers for her rebirth in the *mogari* funeral rite, her rebirth is not mentioned, probably because Izanami does not, according to *Kojiki,* have any grandparents. Second, Amaterasu and Susa-no-o, the sacred children of Izanagi and Izanami, commit incest and give birth to the sacred children, Oshi-ho-mimi and Takiri-bime, who may be regarded as the bodies housing the souls of Izanagi and Izanami. Amaterasu then dies and is simultaneously reborn in the heavenly cave with her grandmother's soul. Lastly, Ho-no-ninigi, conceived through the incest of Oshi-ho-mimi and Toyo-aki-tsu-shi-hime, descends from heaven possessing Amaterasu's soul.

Sacred Birth

The theme of incest is found not only in the myths of the Takama-no-hara sequence but also in those of the Izumo sequence, and it is instructive to study the deities Susa-no-o, Aji-shiki-taka-hikone . . . , and Taka-hime . . . , as well as Ho-muchi-wake-no-miko. . . . The father of Aji-shiki-taka-hikone and Taka-hime is Ō-kuni-nushi . . . , Susa-no-o's offspring, and their mother is Takiri-bime, the sacred daughter born to Susa-no-o and Amaterasu as a result of their incest. In other words, Susa-no-o, on the one hand, and Aji-shiki-taka-hikone and Taka-hime, on the other, are related as grandfather and grandchildren through the incestuous relationships in the Izumo sequence. As a result, Aji-shiki-taka-hikone possesses Susa-no-o's soul. . . .

In *Izumo Fudoki* . . . , Aji-shiki-taka-hikone is described as 'Aji-shiki-taka-hikone, the son of the great god Ōkuni-nushi, who could make only incomprehensible cries day and night until his beard grew eight hands long.'[20] Susa-no-o is similarly described in *Kojiki*, for he 'wept and howled [even] until his beard eight hands long extended down over his chest.'[21] Both Nakanishi Susumu and Takasaki Masahide assume that Aji-shiki-taka-hikone and Taka-hime are husband and wife as well as brother and sister, because of the pairing of their names Taka-hime and Taka-hiko (the abbreviation of Aji-shiki-taka-hikone) and for other reasons.[22]

There is yet another prince in *Kojiki* who is unable to speak until his beard grows eight hands long down over his chest. He is Ho-muchi-wake, a son of Emperor Suinin and Empress Sao-bime. . . . When Sao-biko . . . asks his younger sister, Empress Sao-bime, whom she loves more, her husband or her brother, she admits that she loves her brother more. Sao-biko then urges her to stab the emperor to death while he is sleeping. But she cannot bring herself to murder her emperor husband, and tells him about the plot. Sao-bime flees from the palace and joins her brother Sao-biko in a rice-stronghold to share his fate. There the prince Ho-muchi-wake is born.[23]

In this story the incestuous desire of Sao-biko and Sao-bime is so strong that they are prepared to risk their lives, and after the brother was killed, the sister apparently committed suicide to join him. So although *Kojiki* describes the prince Ho-muchi-wake as the son of Emperor Suinin and Empress Sao-bime, there exists the strong possibility that he is in fact the result of the incestuous union between Sao-biko and Sao-bime. . . .

Kojiki records that Ho-muchi-wake was unable to speak even when his beard extended eight hands down over his chest. Both Takasaki Masahide and Moriya Toshihiko suppose that this phenomenon of crying and howling (*nakiisachi* . . .) may have been an ancient magico-religious rite to summon down the deities or give rebirth to a dead person.[24] But what is common to all three cases cited above is that not only are they unable to speak but they are also the offspring of incestuous unions and are associated with the Izumo lineage. This suggests that the act of crying and howling is a rite not merely to summon down the deities but, more specifically, to receive the grandparents' souls by means of an incestuous union. It should be noted that although the Izumo sequence refers to the various incestuous relationships, it makes no mention of a sacred birth; on the contrary, deformed children are born. Thus, according to *Kojiki,* Takama-no-hara is the place where incestuous union results in sacred birth,

while Izumo is the place where the deformed children resulting from incestuous birth are exiled.

Death

The desire for incest in *Kojiki* reaches its climax with the love story of Kinashi-no-karu-no-hitsugi-no-miko . . . and his sister Karu-no-ō-iratsume . . . in Book 3. After the death of his father the emperor, Crown Prince Kinashi-no-karu was to have assumed the sun-lineage, but before he ascended the throne, he fell in love with and seduced his younger sister Karu-no-ō-iratsume. Betrayed by various officials, the prince is arrested by Emperor Ankō . . . , who has ascended the throne in his stead, and banished to the hot springs of Iyo. Unable to stop loving her brother, Princess Karu follows him into exile and there they kill themselves.[25] . . .

Although, as noted above, the incestuous unions in *Kojiki,* 1, are related to sacred birth, death, and rebirth, such unions in Books 2 and 3, involving Sao-biko and Sao-bime, Prince Karu and his sister, are connected with rebellion and suicide. The question arises whether this difference has any particular significance in the implications of incestuous union as recorded in *Kojiki*.

The difference is surely not due to any social development from inter-marriage to exogamy or to increased cultural sophistication. As seen above, the incestuous union of brother and sister brings about the rebirth of a grandparent's soul as a result of a sacred birth; to prohibit such a process, therefore, would make impossible the rebirth of the ancestral soul. If one recognizes oneself as a body in which one's ancestral soul is housed, one can obtain eternal life. In this sense, the ancient people do not die. But their soul is not their alone—it is something to be passed on perpetually from their ancestors through themselves to their offspring. To prohibit the rebirth of the ancestral soul would therefore mean rejecting eternal life. This sacrifice of eternal life gives rise to the concept of a human, a creature who lives and dies in this world, being distinct from a deity.

It is in the imperial line that eternal life, sacrificed elsewhere to make way for the concept of the human being, is preserved. In the *daijōsai* ceremony, the emperor appears in front of the people and receives his ancestral soul by symbolically enacting death and rebirth. This represents the ancient people's desire to preserve the notion of eternal life (which they had discarded for themselves) in the imperial line, destined to last forever.

Notes

[1] As long ago as 1896, the British scholar W. G. Aston referred to the two meanings of the term, but

added, 'It may be doubted whether this justifies any adverse inference as to the morals of the Japanese in early times.'

W. G. Aston, tr., *Nihongi: Chronicles of Japan from the Earliest Times to A.D. 697,* Allen & Unwin, London, 1956 reprint, p. 22, n. 7.

[2] In Ishida Eiichirō . . . *et al., Nihon Minzoku no Kigen,* . . . Heibonsha, 1958, pp. 45 & 232-33.

[3] Indonesian myths of brother-sister incest are collected in W. J. Perry, *The Megalithic Culture of Indonesia,* University of Manchester Press, 1918, Chapter 12.

[4] Hattori Asake . . . , *'Kuni Umi Shinwa no Kōzō'* . . . , in *Kōza Nihon no Shinwa* . . . , Yūseidō, 1976, 3, pp. 76-101.

[5] Saigō Nobutsuna . . . , *'Kinshinsōkan to Shinwa: Izanaki Izanami no Koto'* . . . , in *Kojiki Kenkyū* . . . , Miraisha, 1973, p. 78.

[6] Nishimiya Kazutami . . . , *'Saigō Nobutsuna-cho "Kojiki Chūshaku Dai Ikkan"'* . . . , in *Bungaku* . . . , 44:2 (1976), pp. 278-79.

[7] Kurano Kenji . . . & Takeda Yūkichi . . . , ed., *Kojiki* . . . (NKBT 1), Iwanami, 1958, pp. 60-61 & 70-71; Donald Philippi, tr., *Kojiki,* University of Tokyo Press, 1968, pp. 56-57 & 70.

[8] Sakamoto Tarō . . . *et al.,* ed., *Nihon Shoki* . . . (NKBT 67), Iwanami, 1967, 1, pp. 86-88; Aston, *Nihongi,* pp. 18-19.

[9] Tsuda Sōkichi . . . , *Nihon Koten no Kenkyū* . . . , Iwanami, 1948, 1, pp. 366-69.

[10] Sakamoto, *Nihon Shoki,* pp. 92-93; Aston, *Nihongi,* pp. 24-25. Kurano, *Kojiki,* pp. 62-65; Philippi, *Kojiki,* pp. 61-63.

Sugano Masao . . . takes the interpretation that Izanami's being burnt to death means that she is reborn with a stronger soul as a result of Izanagi's incantation and that they then give birth to the three noble deities. *Kojiki Setsuwa no Kenkyū* . . . , Ōfūsha, 1973, p. 78.

[11] Matsumura Takeo . . . , *Nihon Shinwa no Kenkyū* . . . , Baifūkan, 1954-1958, 2, pp. 445-48.

[12] Yokota Ken'ichi . . . , *'Ama-no-manai Ukei Shinwa Iden Kō* . . . , in *Nihon Shoki Kenkyū* . . . , Hanawa, 1970, 4, p. 339.

[13] Sakamoto, *Nihon Shoki,* pp. 112-13; Aston, *Nihongi,* p. 41.

[14] Orikuchi Shinobu . . . , *'Jōdai Sōgi no Seishin'* . . . , in *Orikuchi Shinobu Zenshū,* 20, Chūō Kōronsha, 1956, 20, pp. 353-54; Matsumura, 3, pp. 43-45.

[15] Yanagita Kunio . . . , *'Senzo no Hanashi'* . . . , in *Shimpen Yanagita Kunio Shū,* Chikuma, 1978, 5, p. 380.

[16] These two ceremonies are described in detail in *Engishiki* . . . , Chapters 7 & 8. Felicia Bock, tr., *Engi-Shiki: Procedures of the Engi Era,* Books 6-10, MN Monograph 46, 1972, pp. 31-56 & 93-94.

[17] Orikuchi, 20, pp. 356-57.

[18] Tsuda, 1, pp. 382-83.

[19] In *Nihon Minzoku,* 1, pp. 45-48.

[20] Akimoto Kichirō . . . , ed., *Fudoki* . . . (NKBT 2), Iwanami, 1958, p. 227; Michiko Yamaguchi Aoki, tr., *Izumo Fudoki,* MN Mongraph 44, 1971, p. 133.

[21] Kurano, *Kojiki,* pp. 72-73; Philippi, *Kojiki,* p. 72.

[22] Nakanishi Susumu . . . , *Kojiki o Yomu* . . . , Kadokawa, 1985-1986, 2, p. 30; Takasaki Masahide . . . , *Bungaku Izen* . . . , Ōfūsha, 1958, pp. 290 & 309-10.

[23] Kurano, *Kojiki,* pp. 186-87; Philippi, *Kojiki,* pp. 213-19.

[24] Takasaki, pp. 155-68; Moriya Toshihiko . . . , *Kiki Shinwa Ronkō* . . . , Yūzankaku, 1973, pp. 127-49.

[25] Kurano, *Kojiki,* pp. 292-99; Philippi, *Kojiki,* pp. 333-40.

FURTHER READING

Isobe, Yaichiro. *The Story of Ancient Japan or Tales from the Kojiki.* Tokyo: San Kaku Sha, 1929.
> Presents select tales from the *Kojiki* in simple and clear language, making the stories accessible to young readers.

Kawai, Hayao. "The Hollow Center in the Mythology of *Kojiki.*" *Review of Japanese Culture and Society* 1, No. 1 (October 1986): 72-77.
> Analyzes the concept of space defined by the *Kojiki* and argues that the concept is integral to Japanese culture in general.

Kidder, J. E., Jr. "The Protohistoric Period." In *Japan Before Buddhism.* New York: Frederick A. Praeger, 1959, pp. 131-207.

Relies on the *Kojiki,* as well as the *Nihon shoki,* to present a historical account of Japan in the centuries preceding the *Kojiki*'s composition.

Kotański, Wieslaw. "New Approach to Ancient Japanese Funeral Ceremonies as Depicted in the *Kojiki*." *Rocznik Orientalistyczny* 45, No. 1 (1986): 35-40.
Uses close study of passages in the *Kojiki* to reconstruct ancient Japanese beliefs regarding death.

Philippi, Donald L. An introduction to *Kojiki*. Princeton, N.J.: Princeton University Press, 1969, pp. 3-33.
Gathers together information pertaining to the *Kojiki* from modern scholarship, offering the reader "an introduction to the history, genealogy, social structure, mythology, language, and literature of early Japan."

Sakamoto, Taro. *The Six National Histories of Japan*. Translated by John S. Brownless. Vancouver: UBC Press, 1991, 232 p.
Considers the *Kojiki,* with a particular emphasis on compilation, in relation to the *Nihon shoki*.

Sansom, G. B. "Early Myths and Chronicles." In *Japan: A Short Cultural History*. Rev. Ed. New York: D. Appleton-Century Company Inc., 1943, pp. 22-45.
Discusses the *Kojiki* and the Nihon-shoki in terms of content and composition, placing them in the context of Japanese history.

Richard Rolle

c. 1300-1349

(Also known as Richard Rolle of Hampole) English author of biblical commentaries, devotional treatises, and religious lyrics.

INTRODUCTION

A medieval hermit and the author of many works on religious devotion, Rolle has been touted as an innovator both in his devotional and his literary styles. In the midst of an age typically described as authoritarian, Rolle maintained an unwavering individualism, remaining reclusive and unallied with any religious order. Traveling through Yorkshire, he preached his love of God to anyone in need and produced written works for spiritual guidance and celebration. Rolle wrote strikingly personal and emotive prose that was distinctly different from the the dominant scholastically-derived devotional literature and which relied on classical allusions and rhetoric. Rolle also broke fresh ground when he wrote prose in Middle English—the vernacular of the day—thus making his words accessible to a broader audience at a time when written English on lofty subjects defied convention. Rolle has since earned the title of "father" of English prose literature.

Biography

Historians place Rolle's birth at about 1300, in the town of Thornton in the North Riding of Yorkshire. His father, William Rolle, was a prosperous small landowner with a good reputation in the region; he may also have been a merchant. Richard received an education at home until his late teens, when he attended Oxford under the sponsorship of Thomas de Neville, who would later become Archdeacon of Durham. While Richard's interest did not mesh with the prevalent scholasticism of the environment, he made use of the opportunity to study theology and Holy Scripture. Dissatisfied with his experience there, Rolle left Oxford at age nineteen and returned to his father's home. Before long, however, he took his first dramatic steps to the eremitic life—the life of a hermit. According to a much-cited story, he asked his sister for two of her tunics, which she brought to him in a nearby wood. These he altered and donned so that they resembled a hermit's outfit, and when his sister called out that he had lost his mind, he ran off, never returning home.

Rolle found his first hermitage soon after in the home of John de Dalton, a local gentleman and friend of his father's. Impressed with the sincerity of Rolle's reli-

gious purpose, Dalton provided the young man with meals and a bare room, or cell, in which he could have solitude. Here Rolle began, as described in several of his major works, the process of a religious "conversion" or journey to union with God. It began with a stage of purification or penance, during which Rolle had to endure many temptations and other tests of his faith. According to H. R. Bramley the endeavor required Rolle to "subdue the flesh by watchings and fastings, praying with sobs and sighs, living in a little cottage, sleeping on a board, fixing his mind on heaven and desiring ever to be dissolved with Christ." The second stage comprised an 'illumination," during which the faithful perfects his love of God. The third stage, "sight"—which was the final stage before union—allowed Rolle to see into heaven. Union, which would constitute the purpose of his writings, came to Rolle after four years and three months of prayer and meditation, arriving first as a heat that he felt in his chest.

While the emotional experiences were for Rolle the most significant matter of his life and the substance on which his writings depended, in his worldly life he experienced changes and trials. He left Dalton's home after about four years. As he traveled through Yorkshire, he relied on offers of food and shelter in exchange for religious succor. His gifts of ministry and comfort won many of his listeners to the contemplative life, some even choosing to follow his eremitic example. He also won enemies, especially among the religious establishment, which saw his self-defined religious style as a challenge to its authority. At first angered by the criticism, Rolle eventually came to disdain it. By the middle of the fourteenth century he had moved from the north of Yorkshire to the south and settled in Hampole, offering spiritual guidance to an abbey of Cistercian nuns. When he died, probably from the plague, on September 29, 1349, the nuns buried him in their chapel yard and soon drew up an Office of his life and beliefs, anticipating his imminent canonization. Rolle's fame became widespread and powerful, drawing many pilgrims to his tomb, which by the 1380s was known for its miraculous effect on the sick and impaired. Rolle's reputation remained vigorous for at least another century, although he was never sainted by the church.

Major Works

Rolle produced a great many works both in Latin and English and various in kind. While his canon has gradually become solid and somewhat narrowed down, it began the twentieth century in a diffuse, almost unmanageable form. Many works attributed to him on the strength of his reputation have since been determined not to be his work. The primary Latin texts, mostly in prose, include the *Incendium Amoris (Fire of Love)*, *Emendatio Vitae (Mending of Life)*, and the *Melos Amoris*. The short list of his English canon usually spotlights *Ego Dormio, The Form of Living,* and *The Commandment*. The first three have been studied at great length for the in-depth and comprehensive accounts they provide of Rolle's spiritual autobiography which also necessarily reveals much of his religious doctrine. The *Fire of Love* not only includes his most complete spiritual autobiography, but also the most

complete explanation of his theory of contemplative life. *Melos Amoris* functions almost as a sequel to *Fire of Love,* focusing on the final stage in Rolle's spiritual journal—his complete union with God. The work is also, by virtue of this focus, predominantly a celebration of the love of God. *The Mending of Life* treats similar material at a simpler level, offering a kind of "beginner's guide" for followers interested in adopting a contemplative life. The works written in English reveal their purpose, to some degree, in the choice of language, since many lay people and most religious women would not have been able to read Latin. *Ego Dormio, The Form of Living,* and *The Commandment* are all epistles, written to one or many of Rolle's followers for their religious guidance.

Rolle also translated many of his own commentaries on scripture into English, again hoping to make them available to the less scholarly. His versions of the Song of Songs and the Psalter have become important works in his canon. Other minor works include the short treatises *On Grace, On Daily Work,* and *On Prayer,* written in English for religious instruction. Unlike the texts that celebrate the love of God, these works suggest Rolle's stricter side, stressing the dangers of any lapse in faith and purity. Among the works wrongly attributed to Rolle are *The Pricke of Conscience,* a long poem that once was central to most studies of his work, and *Instructions on the Active and Contemplative Life,* which has since been ascribed to Walter Hilton.

Textual History

Because Rolle's reputation remained strong for at least a century after his death, his writings have been preserved in abundance, with manuscripts available in libraries across Europe. While there were obvious variations in popularity—the ten extant manuscripts of *Melos Amoris* pale in comparison to the ninety of *Incendium Amoris*—all of Rolle's writings have fared relatively well. Availability was even expanded by early translations of his Latin works into English: *De Emendatio Vitae* and *Incendium Amoris* first appeared in English as early as the 1430s. By the time printing technology had burgeoned, however, Rolle's name had slipped into obscurity, leaving his works in manuscript form until the nineteenth century. A revival of interest in mysticism, however, prompted scholars to take up his manuscripts again, and the Early English Text Society included Rolle in their endeavor to bring early examples of written English into print. George Perry's edition of the English prose treatises appeared in 1866, and H. R. Bramley's edition of the English Psalter was published in 1884. Several more important editions appeared in the early twentieth century, despite which Frances Comper complained in 1928 that the relative neglect of Rolle's work was due to the general unavailability of his work in print. The strongest effort to correct this began in the 1980s, when the Institut fur Anglistik und Amerikanistik in Austria began its series on Elizabethan and Renaissance Studies, for which they produced scholarly editions of many of Rolle's major and minor works.

Critical Reception

Rolle was considered all but a saint for nearly a century and a half after his death; although canonization never came from the Vatican, many of his followers nonetheless thought of him as sainted. Among his fourteenth-century admirers were mystics whose reputations would eventually rival his own, including Walter Hilton and John Wycliffe. His written works commanded a large audience and much admiration throughout the period and throughout Europe. R. W. Chambers has suggested that Rolle was "probably the most widely read in England of all English writers" in both the fourteenth and fifteenth centuries. As the Renaissance progressed, however, Rolle was largely forgotten, especially among the literate classes.

When English and German scholars of the nineteenth century began to study the medieval mystics, they necessarily unearthed the wealth of Rolle's writings. Carl Horstman's late nineteenth-century study, in which he noted Rolle's stylistic weaknesses but lauded his depth and naturalness, set the tone for ensuing decades of scholarship. Despite renewed attention and interest, studies tended to focus on Rolle's biography and the quality of his mysticism, repeating the content of his work and Horstman's appraisal. In-depth analyses of his written work were still rare, even after R. W. Chambers declared him a progenitor of English prose literature. Rigorous scholarship has appeared to gain pace since the 1970s, when John Alford lamented its neglect and made his own contribution; since then, studies have tended to deal more directly with the structure and style of Rolle's texts instead of simply renewing his image as a modern or romantic spirit in a dark age.

PRINCIPAL WORKS

The Commandment (English epistle)
Contra Amatores Mundi (Against the Lovers of the World)
Ego Dormio (English epistle)
Emendatio Vitae (Mending of Life) (Latin prose treatise)
The Form of Living (English epistle)
Incendium Amoris (Fire of Love) (Latin prose treatise)
Melos Amoris (Latin prose treatise)

PRINCIPAL ENGLISH TRANSLATIONS

The Fire of Love, and the Mending of Life (translated by Richard Misyn) 1434-35
The Contra Amatores Mundi of Richard Rolle of Hampole (translated by Paul Theiner) 1968
The Fire of Love (translated by Clifton Wolters) 1972
The Fire of Love and the Mending of Life (translated by M. L. Mastro) 1981
Richard Rolle: The English Writings (translated by Rosamund S. Allen) 1988

CRITICISM

George G. Perry (essay date 1866)

SOURCE: George G. Perry, *English Prose Treatises of Richard Rolle de Sampole*, N. Trubner & Co., 1866.

[*Perry's 1866 edition of Rolle's treatises in English constituted the first time these manuscripts were made available since the Middle Ages. In the following excerpt, he touches on many issues central to Rolle scholarship, including Rolle's reputation, the authenticity of the manuscripts, and the matter and style of Rolle's English.*]

The treatises which follow, now for the first time printed, are taken from a miscellaneous collection of Poems, Tracts, Prayers, and Medical Receipts, made by Robert Thornton, archdeacon of Bedford, in the earlier half of the fifteenth century[1]. These religious tracts are especially valuable in two ways. First, as illustrating the teaching given to *the people*—the *unlered* or *lewed folke*—in the fourteenth and fifteenth centuries; next, as being genuine specimens of the old Northumbrian dialect—perhaps the finest form of the ancient English tongue. The publications of the E. E. T. S. have already furnished several excellent specimens of religious teaching for the unlettered, written *in verse;* an opportunity is now afforded for comparing these with the prose of about the same period on similar subjects. The present volume contains only those which are attributed to Richard Rolle, the hermit of Hampole; but another selection from the same MS., of religious treatises by other hands, is intended to follow. The date of those here printed may be assigned to the earlier part of the fourteenth century. The Hermit died in 1349, as is mentioned in several ancient MS. copies of treatises of his. Now, as an immense number of MS. works, both in English and Latin, are ascribed to Richard Rolle, and as there is good reason to suppose that very many thus attributed are not genuine, it is perhaps necessary to say a few words to explain why these English fragments are put forth as the true productions of Richard Rolle. The writer of the manuscript, Robert Thornton, was, if not actually connected with Richard Rolle's birthplace[2], at any rate a neighbour of it, and though a century later in date, must have without doubt heard much and known much about the famous Yorkshire Hermit. During Robert Thornton's lifetime the priory of Hampole was the favoured resort of pilgrims who came to the shrine of the Hermit; and an old authority informs us that his works were kept at the priory "in cheyn bondes," to preserve them from being tampered with[3]. Robert Thornton would therefore have every facility for obtaining genuine extracts from the Hermit's writings, and, as one proud of the fame of his fellow-countryman, would probably take care to transcribe him faithfully. Now, of the pieces here printed as Rolle's, Nos. 1, 2, 3, 4, 5, 6, 7 are given by name in Thornton's MS. to Richard Hermite. Nos. 8, 10 are without heading in the MS., but are assigned to Rolle on the ground of the internal evidence of style and matter[4]. No. 9, which has lost its earlier part, is the treatise *De Vitâ Activâ et Contemplativâ,* which exists also in the British Museum and in Cambridge University Library in another dialect, and is usually attributed to the Hermit. A difficulty as to the genuineness of the English of No. 1 may be thought to arise from the fact of its existing also in Latin. But it is clearly ascertained that Richard Rolle was in the habit of writing the same matter both in Latin and in English, and this in all probability is one of the instances of this practice. Thus he himself says in the *Pricke of Conscience,* which also exists in a Latin form:—

Tharfore this buk es on ynglysche drawen,
Of sere matters that er unknawen.
Til laude men that er unkunnund
That can na Latyn understand.

And in the Preface to the English *Exposition of the Psalms,* of which there is also a Latin version, it is said by a very early writer:—

But for the Psalms ben full darke in many a
place who wol take hede,
And the sentence is full merke—who so wol
rede.
It needeth exposicyon written wel with
cunning honde
To strive toward devocyon and hit the better
understonde.
Therfor a worthy holy man called Rychard
Hampole
Whom the Lord that all can lered lelely on his
scole,
Glo3ed the sauter that sues here in English
tong sykerly,
At a worthy recluse prayer call'd Dame
Marget Kirkby.
(From MS. in Bodleian Library—Laud. 286.)

Of the Treatise No. 1 there is at least one other copy (in Brit. Mus. Harl. 1022), and in this the spelling is somewhat more archaic than in the Lincoln MS., while the main peculiarities of the Northumbrian dialect remain the same. It would seem to follow from the substantial but not absolute identity of the two MSS. that the version here given cannot have been a translation made by R. Thornton from Hampole's Latin, but must have been the original composition of the Hermit, transcribed, with a few modifications of spelling and inflexion, by his countryman in the next century. It will further strengthen this view if we take into consideration that the quotations made by Thornton from the Hermit's works are not all in English,—which, if it had been the case, might rather suggest the inference that he himself had translated them from the Latin,—but are some of them in Latin, some in English. Probably, therefore, the extracts here printed are a genuine specimen of the true English style of the Yorkshire Hermit of the fourteenth century. It must, however, be remembered that they are no more than a specimen; and one of the chief objects which it is hoped will be served by this publication is the leading to further transcripts of genuine English works of Rolle's which may be found in our great libraries, and few of which have as yet been printed. In foreign collections of mediæval writers his name indeed figures as the writer of Latin treatises under the singular disguise of Pampolitanus; but neither Latin nor English of his has been published in this country, with the exception of a small collection of devotional writings printed by Wynkyn de Worde, and the poem of the *Pricke of Conscience,* published recently by the Philological Society. A cursory glance at the manuscript catalogues of our chief collections will at once reveal the fact that Richard Rolle of Hampole was one of the most prolific writers of his day; and the fact of the preservation of so large a mass of MSS., either his or attributed to him, testifies to the great estimation in which he was once held. Who then was this man who had in his time so much to do with controlling and influencing the opinions of his fellow-countrymen? Can we in any way realize and identify him? Can we discover any personality for the author of these numerous works, and in any way evoke him from the shadowy past as a living and acting man? Certainly Richard Rolle (usually called Hampole, from the priory where his death and burial took place) was an enigma and a puzzle to the various writers who have professed to give an account of the ancient authors of England. These gentlemen usually tread very faithfully in the track of one another; and it is amusing enough to follow the same mistake reappearing in a slightly different form in one grave folio after another through several centuries. Thus, if we look for Richard de Hampole in Pitz, Leland, Tanner, Wharton, Cave, or any other of the bibliographers, or, hoping for fresh information, hunt him up in more modern works, as in the "Archæologia" or in "Hunter's South Yorkshire," we find just the same account of the Hermit, equally baseless and conjectural. It has been attempted to construct a life for the saint without having any materials to make it out of, and the deficiency has been sought to be supplied by conjecturing what a hermit who wrote books would be likely to be, and then attributing this as the real account to the actual hermit. Thus, in the sketches alluded to, Richard Rolle is described as belonging to the Augustinian order, as a doctor of divinity[5], and as one who had seen much of the world, but who, disgusted with its emptiness and sinfulness, retired into solitude to pray and meditate. Hunter, in his laborious and accurate work, thus sketches the Hermit:—"Few persons, who have written so much, have left so little memorial of themselves. The place of his birth is unknown, the seat of his education, the scenes in which he passed the active part of his life, and the places in which he witnessed that luxury and extravagance which he so much deplores. It is only conjectured that he was born in this neighbourhood (Doncaster), and if that is admitted, we may conclude that he was educated in the Carmelite convent of Doncaster. But all that appears to be with certainty known respecting him is that some time about the beginning of the reign of Edward III. Richard withdrew himself from a world with whose manners he was disgusted, and devoted himself to a life of austerity and divine meditation in a cell not far from the monastery of Hampole. More might perhaps be recovered concerning him if we had the "Officium de Sancto Heremitâ," for he was admitted among the *sancti confessores* of the Church. This office, of which there was a copy in the Cotton Library, destroyed by the fire in which that library suffered so much, contained some particulars *de ipsius vitâ et miraculis*[6]."

We are glad to be able to contribute somewhat towards the more accurate delineation of Richard Rolle by supplying the deficiency here lamented. A copy of the "Officium et Legenda de Vitâ Ricardi Rolle" exists in the library of Lincoln Cathedral, being probably, since the destruction of the Cotton MS., the only copy remaining of this curious document. This is here printed in its entirety, so far as it can be deciphered[7], and the account of Richard Rolle which it furnishes will be seen to differ altogether from the conjectural sketches made of him by the bibliographers. It is not indeed contended that the "Legenda de Vita Ejus" is trustworthy in all its statements. We do not concede to our saint the miraculous powers claimed for him, nor do we treat as grave matter of fact his continual contests with devils. The life, however, such as it is, gives a personality to the Hermit, hitherto the most shadowy of existences, which will be found to accord very well with his admitted works. It supplies us with facts about his birthplace, his education, his early adoption of the eremite life, the way in which he practised that life,—not living solitary, but journeying from one place to another to instruct the people,—the scenes of his earlier labours, and his ultimate retirement to Hampole,

none of which facts were hit upon by the conjecturers. It shews us that he was neither an Augustinian friar, nor a doctor of divinity, nor in any degree of holy orders; that he was altogether an irregular sort of teacher, and in a great measure self-instructed; all which considerations must needs increase our wonder at the learning and power of his numerous writings.

To give any adequate account of these writings would occupy too much space for this place. Suffice it to say, that so far as the Editor has examined them he believes that the matter and manner of the Hermit's teaching are very well illustrated by the extracts here printed. Few, it is thought, can fail to be struck by the terse and vivid way in which, in the passages here given, the Hermit enforces his view of the truth, and the devout ardour which animates his words. The two stories about Shrift are especially remarkable, as giving a clear testimony against the *opus operatum* view of religion which is generally attributed to all mediaeval writers. Nor less striking is the strong way in which Rolle contends for the paramount importance of the duties of active over contemplative life in the case of those whose position gives them influence or power of assisting their fellows. This for his age and profession is highly creditable to the Hermit. Of course the contemplative life is in his view the higher state, but it is much to find an anchorite and an ecstatic allowing even any possibility of merit to the despised active life. And this we find Richard Rolle doing, not only in the treatise here printed, but also in divers other passages. For instance, in **The boke maad of Rycharde hampole heremyte to an ankeresse**[8] he thus writes:—"Thou shall understonde that ther ben in Holy Chyrche twey maner of lyves in the whyche cristen men schul bee saaf, that oon is clepyd actyf and that other contemplatyf. Without oon of these two may no man be saved. Actyf lyf lyeth in love and cheryte schewyd outward by goude bodili werkys, in fulfillynge of Godis commandmentis and of the seven dedis of mercy bodil and gostly to a manys euen cristen. This lyf langys to all wordly men which han rychesse and plenti of wordly goude. And also to alle other men that han goudis for to spend, lerned or lewid, temporal othere spiritual, and generally al wordly men ben bounden to fulfille it bi ther myght and ther kunnyng, ther reson and discrecion. 'If he moche have moche doo, if he a litell have litell or lasse do,' and if he nought have that he have thane a goude wille. There beth workys of actyf lyf othere gostly othere bodily." It will be observed that this passage is one of the numerous instances in which the English of Rolle has been re-written in a more southern dialect. Another quotation from the same treatise will further illustrate the practical and truly devout character of the Hermit's mind:—"Wyte thou wel a bodili turnyng to God without thyne hert folwyng is but a figure and a lykenesse of vertuce and of ne sothefastenesse. Whar-for a wreched man or woman is thylke that leeveth al the ynward kepynges of hym-self and chareth hym with-out forth only a fourme and a lykenesse of holynesse in habyte other clothyng in speche and in bodili werke, by-hooldyng other mennys dedys and demyng there defautys, wenyng hym-self to be ought whanne he is rigt nougt and so begylez hymself. Do thou not so but turne thyn harte with thy body principalli to God and shape thee withynne in His lykenesse by mekenesse and charite and other gostly vertues and thane art thou trewly turnyd to Hym." The man who could write this in an age of monkery and amidst the deifications of the principle of asceticism cannot be said to have been without some insight into the true divine life. Yet the wildest extravagances of mysticism are also to be found in plenty in the Hermit's writings. In the book *De Incendio Amoris*[9] he tells us that amidst the rigours of his ascetic devotions he became conscious of an actual physical heat and burning. At first he believed that this was due to some bodily cause, but he soon discovered that this was not so—that it was an inward spiritual power making itself felt on the body by its excessive strength. He experienced sensations of inconceivable pleasure, and was kindled to such a love of God that his whole being seemed to be dissolved in it; and the more he mortified the flesh by fast and vigil, the greater was his spiritual joy. He was often in ecstasies and absent from the body in spirit, and so great was his absorption in contemplation that his friends were able to take away the ragged dress which he wore and to put on him a more decent garment without attracting his attention. Under these circumstances we are not surprised to hear what he tells us in his book "**De Amore Dei,**" that many thought him mad; nor was it an unreasonable prudence on the part of Sir John de Dalton (his patron as he is represented in the *Life*) to require to be satisfied of his sanity before he extended to him his protection. Indeed, the thoughts and images that were present to the Hermit's mind were of so gloomy and awful a character that they might easily have overborne his reason. In his view the thought of death was ever to be present; and the death even of the righteous would be accompanied with such fearful terrors, the manifestation and sight of devils and the consciousness of their struggles for the departing spirit, that the mind quails at the contemplation. This is brought out with terrible vigour in his poem of *The Pricke of Conscience,* and in a short treatise of his called *The thre Arrows in the Dome,* which represents the terrors of the last day.[10] There was by no means a cheerful tone about the religion of the Hermit, yet at the same time he did not arrive at such an utter Manichean hatred of everything material as is to be found in some of his contemporaries. He was not one of those eremites satirized by the author of Piers Plowman, who

> Clothed them in copis to be knowe fro othire
> And made themselves eremites thare eise to have.

Yet, on the other hand, he was no Simeon Stylites, to court and practise bodily austerities simply for their own sakes. On the contrary, our Hermit was a travelling preacher, intensely devoted to the work of the instruction of his fellow-creatures. In the performance of this office we are told that he travelled about through the northern parts of Yorkshire, and his biographer thinks it necessary to apologize for his migratory habits lest he should be confounded with the crowd of careless and debauched hermits who went about collecting alms from the people. We are not informed in the Life at what period Richard Rolle left Richmondshire and its neighbourhood and went southward towards Doncaster. We are also left to conjecture what it was that drew him to Hampole, his ultimate dwelling and the place of his death and burial. At this place was a Cistercian nunnery, founded by William de Clairefai in the year 1170, for fourteen or fifteen nuns.[11] The *Life* tells us that on his death at this place his "gostly suster," Dame Margaret Kyrkby, the anchoress of Anderby, to whom he had addressed the treatise quoted above, being miraculously informed of the event, hastened to assist at his funeral at Hampole; and there can be no doubt that the Officium and Legenda and the account of the miracles which follow were drawn up by the pious care of the Hampole nuns, to whom the fame of Richard's sanctity was a source of great profit and honour. Crowds flocked to pray at the tomb of the saint, to whose intercession the greatest miracles were granted, while the nuns were careful to preserve authentic copies of their patron's works, which "yvel men of Lollardry" had, as they alleged, in many cases perverted to their own base purposes, feigning to "leude soles" that their noxious compositions were the works of Richard Hampole, and thus propping up their mischievous heresies by the support of his great and honoured name.[12]

Notes

[1] See Preface to *Morte Arthure,* E. E. T. S. 1865.

[2] Richard Rolle was born at Thornton in Yorkshire, probably Thornton-le-Street, Robert the archdeacon was born at East Newton, or Oswaldkirk, but his family may have been *of* the very place where the Hermit was born.

[3] MS. Bodl. (Laud. 286).

[4] When Sir F. Madden examined the Thornton MS. he assigned No. 8 to Richard Rolle.

[5] *Archæologia,* vol. xix. p. 319; Cave, Hist. Lit.; Pitz; Tanner; Wharton, A.-S. V.

[6] Hunter's *South Yorkshire,* i. 358.

[7] The first two or three pages of the MS. are extremely faded through the action of damp, and a part of one

leaf has been torn off. It will be observed that the plan of the service is to recite a short piece of the saint's history, and then to break off into hymns and psalms, thus giving the audience an opportunity of expressing the devout feelings which are supposed to be stirred up by the hearing of the perfect virtue of the Hermit. A long list of miracles follows the Officium, which are not printed here.

[8] MS. Bodleian (Laud. 602).

[9] The passage will be found printed in the Latin Life.

[10] Bodleian MSS. (Douce 13). This treatise, together with that called "The Rule of mannis bodi," has been cast into a longer one called "The Gostly Batell," usually attributed to Hampole, but not his genuine work. (MSS. Douce 322.)

[11] The last prioress was Isabella Arthington, who had been elected in 1518, and who surrendered the house on the 10th of November, 31 Henry VIII., upon which she had a pension of 10*l.* per annum. At the Dissolution the gross annual value of the Hampole Priory was 83*l.* 6*s.* 11*d.* (Lawton's Religious Houses of Yorkshire).

[12] See Rhyming Preface to R. de Hampole's *Exposition of the Psalms,* MS. Bodleian (Laud. 286).

H. R. Bramley (essay date 1884)

SOURCE: H. R. Bramley, in an introduction to *The Psalter or Psalms of David and Certain Canticles,* translated by Richard Rolle, Oxford at the Clarendon Press, 1884, pp. v-xvii.

[*In his introduction to Rolle's commentary on the Psalms, Bramley recounts Rolle's biography and summarizes his doctrine, relying mostly on the Office made shortly after his death by the nuns of Hampole. Bramley also expands on this text by collating Rolle's life with the larger political scene.*]

Richard Rolle, better known from the place of his death and burial as Hampole[1], was a famous preacher and highly venerated hermit in Yorkshire, during the former half of the fourteenth century.

The day of his death seems to be clearly fixed to September 29, 1349.

The day appropriated to his memory was January 20.

An office was drawn up for this Festival[2], probably under the direction of the nuns of Hampole, in anticipation of his Canonization: the Lessons of which furnish the fullest and most authentic record of his life

and acts. Additional particulars may be gleaned from some of his writings.

His father was William Rolle, a man apparently of respectable position; being the intimate friend of John de Dalton, the gentleman who afterwards became his son's patron.

Richard was born at Thornton, near Pickering: and was sent to Oxford by Thomas de Nevile, Archdeacon of Durham.

While he was at the University he applied himself, we are told, to the study of Theology and of the Holy Scriptures; rather than to the Natural Sciences, or to those subtilties of the Law[3], or arts of disputation, by which many sought to advance their fortunes at the peril of their souls.

At the age of nineteen, fearing that he might be entangled in the snares of sin, he left Oxford, and returned to his father's house.

Soon after this, as it would appear, he changed his habit, and assumed the profession of a hermit. The account given of this process is remarkably simple and graphic. He had a sister, whom he dearly loved. One day he begged of her two of her kirtles, a white one and a grey one: which, at his request, she carried, with the hood which their father wore in rainy weather, to a neighbouring wood. Her brother, having cut off the buttons of the white frock and the sleeves of the grey, stripped off his clothes and put on the white frock next his skin, and the grey one over it, thrusting his arms, with the white sleeves, which he had sewed up as well as he could, though the holes that were left in the grey frock: and thus, with his father's hood, completed, so far as he was able, the semblance of a Hermit. His sister, seeing him in this guise, raised the cry that he was mad: upon which, having kept her off with threatening gestures, he ran away from home.

He is next heard of at a church[4], where he arrived on the eve of the Assumption; and happened to take up his place for prayer on the spot usually occupied by a lady of the parish, the wife of John de Dalton already mentioned. Her servants would have turned him away; but she, seeing him at his devotions, would not allow him to be disturbed. Next morning he put on a surplice and sang in the choir at Mattins and Mass. After the Gospel, having obtained leave of the Priest, he went into the Pulpit, and so moved the hearts and touched the consciences of his hearers that they declared that they had never heard such a sermon in all their lives. The evening before, he had been recognized as the son of William Rolle by the young Daltons, who had seen him at Oxford. After his preaching their father asked him to dinner: and after he in his humility, and from a fear that he might be thwarted in his purpose, had made several attempts to escape, first by hiding himself in an outhouse, and afterwards by endeavouring to leave the table before the meal was ended, he took him aside, and having convinced himself of the purity of his intentions, and drawn from him the reluctant acknowledgment who he was, he invited him to remain in his house: and provided him with a proper habit, and suitable accommodation.

He has been said by Wharton[5], Tanner[6], and other writers, to have belonged to the Augustinian Friars. He probably imitated their dress: but he does not appear to have been a member of any order.

His devotion seems to have been spontaneous, and his rule of life unsanctioned by external authority. As the versicle to the first lesson in his office has it: '*Abbas amor dat morum formulam.*'

He has left an account of some of his early trials and struggles. In a small volume in his handwriting, found after his death, he relates what he regarded as a special temptation of the fiend; though there is nothing in the story which may not be explained from ordinary causes. It does indeed give an insight into the motive which lay deepest in his heart, which proved itself supreme even in his dreams. After relating the particulars of the illusion, he says, 'I perceyuede well þare was na womane bot þe deuell in schappe of womane. Tharefore I turnede me to Gode and w*ith* my mynde I said, "A Jh*esu* how pr*e*cyous es thi blude!" makand þe crosse w*ith* my fyngere in my breste, and als faste scho wexe wayke and sodanly all was awaye; and I thankked Gode þat delyuerd me, *and* sothely fra þat tym furthe I forced me for to luf Jh*esu*, and ay þe mare I profette in þe luf of Jh*esu* þe swette*er* I fand it[7].' There are but few names which can be put in competition with that of Richard Rolle in his claims to have inscribed upon the record of his life and labours, All for Jesus.

It appears incidentally in the same narrative that there was a fair young woman who loved him not a little 'in good love.' But as at the first he had regarded God more than his earthly father, so he continued to renounce all human affection: and laboured to subdue the flesh by watchings and fastings, praying with sobs and sighs, living in a little cottage, sleeping on a board, fixing his mind on heaven, and desiring ever to be dissolved and to be with Christ. This was at the beginning of his conversion. His prayers were answered beyond his expectations; and he attained to that 'soun & myrth of heuen' of which he speaks in his prologue to the Psalter, and in other passages[8].

His narrative of his progress in the contemplative life is as definite as it is singular. In his treatise **De incendio amoris,** quoted like the last-mentioned 'Tale' in the Office for his Commemoration, he relates his spiritual experience as follows. 'From the beginning of the alteration in my life and mind,' he says, 'to the opening of the heavenly door, so that with unveiled face the eye of the heart might behold those that are above, and see the way to seek the Beloved, and to sigh for Him, was a period of three years, all but three or four months. Then, the door remaining open, up to the time that the warmth of eternal love was truly felt in the heart, about a year passed away. I was sitting in a certain chapel, and being much delighted with the sweetness of prayer or meditation, suddenly I felt in me a strange and pleasant heat.'

For some time he was in doubt as to the nature of this heat, and often felt his breast, to see if it could arise from any outward cause. But he was convinced that it was purely a gift from his Maker: and so he was the more absorbed in heavenly love. 'And while this warmth, inexpressibly sweet, was sensibly kindling, so as to lead to the communication and perception of that celestial or spiritual sound which pertains to the song of everlasting praise, and to the sweetness of the invisible melody (inasmuch as it cannot be known or heard but by him who has received it, who must be cleansed and severed from this earth) there elapsed half a year, three months and some weeks. For as I was sitting in the same chapel, and singing the Psalms at night before supper[9] as well as I could, I heard a sort of chiming of voices overhead.' And so he was himself filled with this celestial music, and broke out before God into continual strains of melody, singing all that he had before been accustomed to say.

All this, however, was in secret, for he thought that if he divulged his privilege it might lead to vain-glory, and he might lose it. He regards it as a free gift from Christ; but one which will be accorded to those, and to those only, who so love and honour the blessed name of Jesus as never to let it go out of their recollection, except in sleep.

So from the beginning of the change in his mind to the attainment of the highest degree of the love of Christ, in which he was raised to uninterrupted joy, and in which he remained to the end of his days, was about four years and three months.

In its later stages the narrative of his life becomes more vague. For some unexplained reason, but not without good cause, as his biographer asserts with emphasis, he left the part of the North Riding where he had hitherto lived, and went into Richmondshire.

'I was wont,' he says, 'to seek for quiet; although to pass from one place to another, and even to leave their cells for a reasonable cause, and then, if it seem fit, to return to them again, is no bad thing for hermits. For some of the holy fathers did so.' But this seems to have given great occasion for fault-finding to those who were ill-disposed to him; and he found those the greatest backbiters whom he had before thought faithful friends[10]. 'But I did not,' he says, 'cease from what was useful to my soul for their words.'

All this time he seems to have travelled about, and to have laboured for the salvation of souls: turning great numbers to God by his exhortations, and assisting and comforting many by his advice and writings, and by the special efficacy which was granted to his prayers. His aid was particularly sought by recluses, by persons in need of ghostly comfort, and by those who suffered in mind or body from the attacks of evil spirits.

It is related that he was at one time molested in his cell by a troop of demons whom he had driven from the chamber of a dying lady; but by renewed prayers he was enabled to put them to flight a second time.

While he was in Richmondshire he was summoned to the aid of Margaret, a devout recluse at Anderby[11], whom he had before been accustomed to instruct in the love of God, and in the spiritual life, to whom he had a strong religious attachment. She was suffering from a severe seizure, in which she had lost her speech for thirteen days. During his visit she was suddenly relieved; and after the removal of a second violent attack, he promised her that so long as he lived she would never be tormented so again.

Some years afterwards the disorder returned, though without the loss of speech. Dame Margaret inferred that Richard was dead, and sending the same man who had before summoned him to her side from a distance of twelve miles to make enquiries at Hampole, where he had lately been leading a solitary life at a still greater distance from her, she found that he had departed this life shortly before the return of her complaint. She afterwards removed to Hampole, where he was interred in the Nuns' Church, and suffered no relapse.

This is probably the 'dame Merget kyrkby' for whom this ***English Translation and Commentary on the Psalter*** is said[12] to have been written. She is also supposed to be the 'Ankeresse,' his 'gostly syster,' to whom he addressed his *Instructions on the Active and Contemplative Life.* It may be noticed that in the passage from this work, printed in his English Prose Treatises, he twice recommends the use of 'the Sauter,' speaking of it as 'a sekyr standarde *that* will noghte faile: who so may cleue *the*rto he sall noghte erre[13].

There is nothing to shew when the hermit came to Hampole, or how long he remained there; nor is there any authentic record of his age. 'The English martyrologe,' published under Jesuit auspices in a second edition in 1640, which refers to a MS. in the English College at Douay, says that he 'reposed in our Lord,' 'full of sanctity of life, and venerable old age.'

Not long after his death his name began to be celebrated for miracles, principally of healing; and pilgrims came to Hampole, not only from York and other places in his native county, but even from Durham and Leicester.

Among the first of his miracles was the entire preservation from hurt of a man named Roger, a householder of Hampole, who was bringing two stones drawn by twelve oxen for the building of Richard's tomb. The oxen overturned the waggon beside the churchyard gate, and the stones fell on Roger, and held him fast by the foot. But he was unhurt.

Twenty-five other miracles are recorded in the Lessons appointed for the Sunday and other days within the Octave of his Commemoration. Two of them are dated, the years in which they occurred being A.D. 1381 and 1383. The catalogue includes the restoration of persons blind, deaf, dumb, mad, and apparently dead: and so coincides pretty closely with the terms of the Metrical Preface.

Hampole's writings were numerous, and shew him to have been a man of active mind and of considerable learning.

One of his short treatises was published at Paris in 1510[14], and again, with most of his Latin works, at Cologne, in 1536[15]. These, with the exception of the ***Commentaries on Scripture,*** were reprinted in the Bibliotheca Patrum Maxima[16] at Lyons in 1677.

Of his English works one was printed by Wynkyn de Worde, under the title ***Rycharde Rolle Hermyte of Hampull in his contemplacyons of the drede and loue of god*** with other dyuerse tytles as it sheweth in his table.' This ends, like the Paris edition of ***De emendations,*** with a prayer or address to a man's guardian angel[17]; but the matter of the two prayers is different.

The *Pricke of Conscience,* a poem extending to 9624 lines, was edited by Mr. Richard Morris, from MSS. in the Library of the British Museum, and published by the Philogical Society in 1863.

Some of his minor ***Prose Treatises*** were edited by the Rev. George G. Perry, from a MS. in Lincoln Cathedral Library, and published by the Early English Text Society in 1866. Besides these and the ***Psalter*** which follows, other works attributed to him, both in Latin and English, remain in MS. in various Libraries.

Dr. Waterland describes this ***Commentary*** as 'dry and insipid enough, after the mystical allegorical way current at that time[18]; and Mr. Lewis, the author of the 'Complete History of Translations of the Bible,' almost repeats his words[19]. But this account scarcely does justice to the author. It is clear from the copies extant that Hampole's **Psalter** was in high esteem and widely diffused in the century after it was written, and it has been warmly commended at various times since then by persons of very different ways of thinking.

Hampole's works are spoken of by the Dominican editor of the Cologne edition as *'viri citra omnem iactantiam et eruditi ac pii,'* while the author is characterized by another Dominican, Sixtus Senensis, in his *Bibliotheca Sancta,* as *'Vir sinceræ pietatis et eruditionis'.*

The learned Wesleyan, Dr. Adam Clarke, makes frequent reference to this **Commentary,** and gives copious extracts from it. 'The writer,' whom he supposes to have been a Scot, was, he says, 'not merely a commentator, but a truly religious man, who was well acquainted with the travail of the soul, and that faith in the Lord Jesus Christ which brings peace to the troubled heart[20].'

Dr. Littledale speaks of it as 'a terse mystical paraphrase, which often comes very little short in beauty and depth of Dionysius the Carthusian himself[21].'

The works of Richard Rolle exhibit the better and more spiritual side of one of the movements which led up to the Reformation.

In his **Comments on the Psalms and Canticles of the Old Testament** he sees Christ throughout. Christ's union with His Church, and His abiding in holy souls therein, are his perpetual theme. His Birth, His Passion, His Resurrection, His present and future reign over His saints, are brought in to shed light upon obscure passages, and are evidently the habitual subject of the writer's thoughts. The eternal separation between the righteous and the wicked is constantly in his mind.

At the same time he is free from the abnormal doctrines and political extravagances which vitiated the teaching of the Lollards.

Human merit is frequently denied, but never the necessity of holy living: indeed *fides formata,* 'trouth fowrmyd with luf,' is expressly said to be that through which men see God.[22]

The efficacy of the Sacraments and the functions of the priesthood are fully recognized. Wicked princes and worldly prelates and pastors are unhesitatingly condemned[23]; but no hint is given that their authority is impaired or their acts invalidated by their want of grace.

Though it is said of priests that many fail and few are holy, yet it is also asserted that 'oft sithe prestis opyns til other men the ʒate of heuen, gifand thaim the sacramentis; and thai for thaire ill life ere barrid out.'[24]

The clergy are the appointed leaders and teachers of the flock of Christ. 'That thou has mystire to kun (need to learn), thi prelate and thi preste ere haldyn to lere the[24a].' 'I bow in all thynge,' says the servant of the Lord, 'til the lare of halykirke, that is thi handmaydyn[25].'

God's bindings, by which now, as a leech, he binds up the breakings of our crooked hearts, are 'the sacramentis, in the whilke we hafe comforth til we perfytly be hale[25a].'

Baptism is frequently mentioned. It purges us of the filth of original sin: a christian man's heart was hallowed in baptism: it is life to them that keep it, death to them that keep it not: some turn away and keep not the covenant that they made with Christ in baptism, to renounce the devil and all his works. They are untrue sons that 'hald noght trouth till god that thai hight in baptem.' As God led Israel out of Egypt through the Red Sea, so he does his folk through baptism: and as 'he shot out pharao & his vertu' into the midst thereof, 'so he slees the vicis of his seruauntis in baptym or in penaunce[26].'

'Through trew shrift is a man made rightwis': 'for if we shrife vs clene with sorow of hert, we sall lepe out of the deuels chekis.' 'If .i. shrafe that the will of my heart was stird sumwhat fra stabilnes in temptacioun. thi mercy broght me agayn til my state. lo what shrift is worth[27].'

The Mass is not spoken of by that name, but in the Commentary on the 21st (22nd) Psalm, which is described at the beginning as 'the voice of crist in his passion,' the words, 'my vowes .i. sall þeld in syght of him dredand,' (my vows will I perform in the sight of them that fear him,) are thus interpreted: 'Lo, my vowis, that is, the sacrifice of my fleysse and blode that .i. offird til God, .i. sall ʒeld in syght of dredand him, that thai vndirstand that it is my verray body, and that thai sall be saued thrugh it.'

In later parts of the Commentary on the same Psalm the qualifications necessary for a profitable reception are insisted on. The poor, that is, 'meke men and despisers of this warld,' 'sall ete and sall be fild.' 'Pore men louys God, riche men thaim self:' they also 'resaiued the sacrament of cristis body: bot he says noght that thai ere fild as the pore; for thai folugh noght crist, bot thaire bely and the warld.' 'Thai sall fall: for thai take vnworthily the sacrament in the syght of God.' 'And forthi,' as he says in another place, 'thai ete thaire aghen dome[28].'

Here, as in some other passages, there is perhaps an exaggerated tendency to identify the poor of this world with the poor in spirit, and rich men with the worldly and ungodly; but it is said elsewhere of the Psalmist,

'He dampnes noght men *th*at has richesse, for *th*ai may wyn heuen with *th*ame: bot *tham* he dampnes *th*at settis *the* hert on *th*ame, for to halde *th*ame[29].'

The doctrine of predestination to life is clearly stated: 'The boke of life is the knawynge of god, in the whilke he has destaynd all goed men to be safe.' But 'noght all that sumtyme ere rightwis and dos wele dwellis in the boke of life, bot anly tha that endis in rightwisnes[30].'

The idea that a man's sins are the result of his destiny, which is said to be sometimes urged as an excuse, is denounced as 'wickidnes and defamynge of god[31].'

Wharton, in his Appendix to Cave's Historia Literaria, quotes Archbishop Ussher as saying that Hampole, in this ***Commentary***[31a], delivered his judgment on the necessity of vernacular translations of the Holy Scriptures: a statement which was probably borrowed from Foxe the 'Martyrologist'; who makes the same assertion in the Preface, addressed to Queen Elizabeth, which is prefixed to his edition of the Gospels in Saxon. But no such passage is to be found in the genuine text. He only alludes to the subject twice: once to the effect that no man should be so hardy as to translate or expound Holy Writ unless he feel in himself the Holy Ghost, who is the maker of it;[32] and in the other place he says that Holy Writ lay sleeping, while men understood it not.[32a]

There is a curious passage upon 'spectakils,'[33] which are said to make 'men to lose ther wit fra God,' directed against rope-dancers and similar performers; and 'new gises' and 'degyse atyre'[33a] are censured very much as they are in the *Pricke of Conscience*[34].

Other points in which the two works closely coincide are the account of the Judgment, in which occurs the doctrine frequently repeated in the Psalter, that all perfect men will take their seats with Christ, the domesman; and the description of Anti-Christ[35].

The notices of the Liturgical use of the Psalms are not very frequent. The sixth is noted as the first of the seven (penitential) Psalms[36], and also as 'songen in the office of dedmen'[36a], a remark which is made also on the twenty-second[36b], the forty-first[37], and the sixty-fourth[37a]; a reason being assigned in each case. The title Song of Degrees which is given to the fifteen Psalms beginning with the 119th (120th), is also mentioned and explained[38]. The use of Psalm 62 with Psalm 66 at 'lauds,' which in the second place is called 'matyns,' is noticed and accounted for[38a]. The 50th Psalm (51st) is said to be 'mast hauntid in halykirke[39].' The practice of concluding all Offices with the words *benedicamus domino,* and of children singing them, is commented on[39a], and so is the custom of striking the breast in confession[39b]. A superstitious value attributed by some to a particular verse of the Psalter is spoken of without comment[40].

The profane oaths which have left their mark on the English language to the present day are more than once denounced[41]; but on the whole the references to the actual life of the times are very scanty.

The description of a pestilence in the explanation of Ps. i. I[41a], may have been suggested by the Plague which is recorded by chroniclers as following upon the famine of the previous year in 1316. It can scarcely be due to any recollection of one of the more famous pestilences of that century: as the first of the three is not reckoned to have ended till the very day of Hampole's death.

Allusion is made to 'ill pryncys,' to 'oure pryncys now that ledis thaire life in filth of syn,' and to the strife which is poured out on them[42]; to the perplexities of the prelates, and to their being slain[43].

There can be little doubt that these expressions refer to the 'evil times' and character[44] of Edward II, to his wars with the nobles, to the entanglement of the bishops in the contending factions, and specially to the death of Walter de Stapledon, bishop of Exeter and Lord Treasurer, who having been left by the king as governor of the city of London was murdered in Cheapside, Oct. 14, 1326.

It might perhaps be conjectured from the absence of any clear allusion to the murder of the King, which took place Sept. 21, 1327, that the completion of this commentary is to be assigned to the period between those two events.

The ***Commentary*** does not profess to be original: 'In expounynge .i. fologh haly doctours[45].' But there are few authors cited by name. Besides writers or books of Scripture, references are made to 'saynt Austyne[46]', to 'the glose[47]', to Aquila[48]; to 'Raban and cassiodire[49]', on the significance of certain birds; to 'Remyge[50]', on the habits of the crow; and to 'strabʒ[51]', as to the different heavens which are below the heaven that angels are in. In one place[52] the Greek is appealed to, and the Latin is read and translated in accordance with the LXX, and against the sense of Hampole's Latin Commentary. But it does not follow that the author himself had any acquaintance with Greek. The passage is discussed in a similar manner by St. Augustine[53].

The phraseology of this translation is often very like that of the Prayer Book version of the Psalms, and one verse[54] is the same, with the exception of a single word and the transposition of two others. In Wycliffe's version of the passage the order of the words is further varied. But the whole verse is so simple that much stress cannot be laid upon these facts, as indicating the influence of Hampole's version upon our present translations, though it is very possible that it might be traced more definitely.

Notes

[1] A village about four miles from Doncaster on the road to Pontefract.

[2] Published by the Surtees Society as Appendix V to the second volume of the York Breviary (1883).

[3] This seems to be confirmed by his own words, in his Latin Commentary on Ps. i. 2, 'in lege ejus meditabitur die ac nocte.' 'Non ergo in physica vel in lege Justiniani meditatur: cum inter diem ac noctem medium non sit.'

[4] Possibly at Topcliffe near Thirsk, the parish of which include a township of the name of Dalton.

[5] Appendix to Cave's Hist. Lit. *s. a.* 1340

[6] Tanner's *Bibliotheca Britan. s. v.* Hampolus.

[7] Hampole's *English Prose Treatises,* E. E. T. S. 1866. P. 6.

[8] For instance in his *Commentary on Ps. xxvi.* 11, xxxii, 3, xxxix. 4, xli. 5.

[9] Or possibly in the night before the Thursday *in Cena Domini.*

[10] *De Incendio Amoris,* f. cxliij. v., Cologne Edition. Cp. Ps. ci. 9 (p. 353).

[11] ? Ainderby Steeple, near North Allerton.

[12] In the Metrical Preface (p. 1).

[13] P. 40.

[14] At the end of Speculum Spiritualium. 'Additur insuper opusculum Richardi hampole.'

[15] D. Richardi Pampolitani Anglosaxonis Eremitæ, viri in diuinis scripturis ac veteri illa solidaque Theologia eruditissimi, in Psalterium Davidicum, atque alia quædam sacræ scripturæ monumenta, compendiosa juxtaque pia Enarratio.

[16] Tom. xxvi, pp. 609 et seqq.

[17] Beginning, 'A good curteys aungell, ordeynd to my gouernale, I knowe well my feblenes and my vnconnynge.'

[18] *Works,* Oxford, 1823, vol. x, p. 293.

[19] *A Complete History of the several Translations of the Holy Bible,* &c., by John Lewis, A.M. Second Edition. London, 1739. p. 14.

[20] Dr. Adam Clarke's *Commentary on the Old Testament: Notes on Ps. xiii.* London. Butterworth and Son. 1825. Vol. iv. For an account of Dr. Clarke's MS. see p. xxiv.

[21] *Commentary on the Psalms* by Dr. Neale and Dr. Littledale. Vol. ii. Preface, p. ix. Third Edition. London, Masters. 1879.

[22] P. 82 (*Ps. xxi.* 29).

[23] Pp. 196 (*Ps. liv.* 10); 304, 305 (*Ps. lxxxii.* 11-14); 290, 291 (*Ps. lxxviii.* 1-4).

[24] Pp. 451 (*Ps. cxxxi.* 9); 276 (*Ps. lxxvi.* 20).

[24a] P. 514 (*Song of Moses* (ii.) 9).

[25] P. 405 (*Ps. cxv.* 6).

[25a] Pp. 483, 484 (*Ps. cxlvi.* 3).

[26] Pp. 185 (Ps. 1.6); 263 (*Ps. lxxiii.* 4); 279,287 (*Ps.* lxxvii. 16, 63); 517 (*Song of Moses* (ii.) 30); 458 (*Ps.* cxxxv. 14, 15).

[27] Pp. 310 (*Ps. lxxxiv.* 12); 241 (*Ps. lxviii.* 19); 340 (*Ps. xciii.* 18).

[28] Pp. 81,82 (*Ps. xxi.* 26, 31); 282 (*Ps. lxxvii.* 34). See also pp. 281 (*Ps. lxxvii.* 29); 300 (*Ps. lxxx.* 14, 15); 516 (*Song of Moses* (ii.) 21).

[29] *Ps.* lxi. 10 (N.).

[30] Pp. 243, 244 (*Ps. lxviii.* 33).

[31] P. 269 (*Ps. lxxiv.* 5). See also p. 470 (*Ps. cxl.* 4).

[31a] On *Ps. cxviii.* 43.

[32] P. 61 (*Ps. xvii.* 13).

[32a] P. 509 (*Prayer of Habakkuk,* 14).

[33] P. 147 (*Ps. xxxix.* 6, 7).

[33a] Pp. 99 (*Ps. xxvii.* 5); 485 (*Ps. cxlvi.* 11).

[34] Book ii, 1524-1572.

[35] Compare p.8 (*Ps. i.* 6) with the *Pricke of Conscience,* book v, 6017-6072; and pp. 35-39 (*Ps.* ix. 20-40) with the *Pricke of Conscience,* book v, 4102-4314.

[36] P. 21 (*Ps. vi.* 1).

[36a] P. 24 (*Ps. vi.* 10).

[36b] P. 85.

[37] P. 153.

[37a] P. 225.

[38] P. 437 (*Ps.* cxix. 1).

[38a] Pp. 218 (*Ps.* ixii. 1); 230 (*Ps.* ixvi. 6).

[39] P. 183 (*Ps.* l.1).

[39a] Pp. 214, 215 (*Ps.* lx. 8).

[39b] P. 216 (*Ps.* lxi. 8).

[40] P. 405 (*Ps.* cxv. 7).

[41] Pp. 266, 267 (*Ps.* lxxiii. 19, 23); 309 (*Ps.* lxxxiv. 7).

[41a] P.6.

[42] Pp. 323 (*Ps.* lxxxviii. 27); 370 (*Ps.* civ. 28); 385, 386 (*Ps.* cvi. 34, 40).

[43] Pp. 383, 384 (*Ps.* cvi. 26, 27); 325 (*Ps.* lxxxviii. 39).

[44] According to Stowe, 'he refused the company of his lordes and men of honoure, and hanted the company of villains and vile persons. He gaue hym self to ouermuch drinkyng,' and 'to the appetite and pleasure of the body:' 'so that shortly he becam to his lordes odible.' *A Summarie of ur Englysh Chronicles,* by John Stowe, 1566, ff. 110, 111.

[45] Prologue. p. 5.

[46] P. 5 (*Ps.* i. 1).

[47] Pp. 96 (*Ps.* xxvi. 11); 154 (*Ps.* xli. 5).

[48] P. 153 (*Ps.* xl. 14).

[49] P. 353 (*Ps.* ci. 7).

[50] P. 485 (*Ps.* cxlvi. 10).

[51] P. 488 (*Ps.* cxlviii. 4).

[52] P. 432 (*Ps.* cxviii. 147).

[53] Enarratio in *Ps.* cxviij; Sermo xxix. 3.

[54] *Ps.* xxxv. 10 (Prayer Book version xxxvi. 9), p. 129.

C. Horstman (essay date 1896)

SOURCE: C. Horstman, in an introduction to *Yorkshire Writers*, edited by C. Horstman, Swan Sonnenschein & Co., 1896, pp. v-xxxvi.

[*In the excerpted introduction that follows, Horstman provides a detailed rendition of Rolle's life and a comprehensive paraphrase of his works, organizing the paraphrase according to the tenets of Rolle's spiritual beliefs.*]

Richard Rolle, from the place of his death and burial surnamed Hampole, was born about, or shortly before, 1300[1], at Thornton (now Thornton Dale), a village 2 1/2 miles E. of Pickering, at the foot of the hills in the North Riding of Yorkshire. He died on the 29th of September 1349. His father was William Rolle[2], a man apparently of respectable position, being called an intimate friend of John de Dalton (iste armiger patrem suum veluti sibi familiarem grata affectione diligebat); he was perhaps a dependant of the Nevilles. Having received his primary education at home, he was at a more advanced age sent to Oxford by Thomas de Neville, afterwards (since 1334) archdeacon of Durham. Oxford, at that time, was in the zenith of its glory: only a few years had elapsed since the great Duns Scotus had given a new impulse to scholasticism and no fewer than 30,000 students had sat listening at the feet of the great master. R. Rolle cannot but have felt the influence of the great time, of the great men and the ardent young spirits then gathered there. His spirit, too, was kindled, but in another direction. Being a man of feeling rather than of discrimination, and endowed with strong religious instincts, he was not made to grapple with the subtle and barren questions of the schools. Indeed, he ever afterwards retained a strong dislike of the philosophers. His studies were chiefly given to Holy Scripture and theology, and no doubt he then and there became imbued with the doctrines of the mystics, St. Bernard, the Victorines, Bonaventura. So, conceiving that salvation was not to be obtained through dialectics and philosophy but through flight from the world, and fearing some imminent danger for his soul[3], he in his 19th year, when he can scarcely be supposed to have attained to classic composure[4] and to a sense of method and investigation, left the University and returned to his father's house, soon to adopt the profession of an hermit after the example of St. Guthlac. One day he procured from his sister two kirtles, a white one and a grey one, and a hood of his father's, cut off the buttoms of the white frock and the sleeves of the grey, donned the white one next his skin and the grey one over it, put on the hood, and so, in the semblance of an hermit, ran away from home, frightening off his sister who raised the cry that he was mad. On the eve of Assumption he appears at a church near John of Dalton's estate[5] ("probably at Topcliffe near Thirsk, the parish of which includes a township of the name of Dalton"), taking his seat on the spot where Lady Dalton is wont to pray. On her entering, her servants would have turned him away, but she, seeing him in his devotions, will not allow him to be disturbed. Her sons recognize him as the son of William Rolle, whom they had seen at Oxford. Next morning he—sine mandato cuiuscumque—puts on a surplice and sings in the choir at Matins and Mass; after the gospel he, having first obtained the benediction of the priest, ascends the pulpit and delivers a sermon, so moving the hearts of his hearers that all wept and declared they had never heard anything like it before. After mass John of Dalton invites him to dinner: he hides himself in an outhouse, from sheer humility, but is found and placed at table before the sons of the house. Silently he takes his meal, and, having eaten his fill, rises to withdraw, but is reminded that it is not the custom to leave before dinner is over. After dinner, the host takes him aside, asks him whether he is really the son of William Rolle, and, having satisfied himself as to the sincerity of his purpose, invites him to remain in the house, and provides him with the proper habit of an hermit, a solitary cell on his estate, and his daily sustenance.

Having so entered upon the career of an hermit, he tried to realize, and put to the test of his personal experience, the mystic ideal of contemplative life. He first went through the stage of "purificatio" or "purgatio", a time of penitence and repentance, of tears and sorrows, of fastings and watchings, of severe discipline, of ascetic exercises, so to withdraw the mind from the world and the self, from sin and carnal affection;—as long as any remorse is felt, the mind is not yet perfectly purified. Then through the stage of "illuminatio", in which the mind is kindled to perfect love of God, by meditation and prayer, by the remembrance of God's benefits to man as Creator, Redeemer, and Saviour, by meditations on the passion of Christ &c. After this preparation—which, as he carefully sums up, lasted 3 years minus 3-4 months, he at last got to the third stage, the "contemplatio" or "sight", when man "sees into heaven with his ghostly eye"; when "through the open door of heaven with unveiled face the eye of the heart 'contemplates' (sees) the heavenly spirits (superos)". In this stage he subsequently—the doors of heaven remaining open—experienced the 3 phases which he describes as calor, canor, dulcor. Nearly a year had passed in the stage of contemplatio, when, sitting one day in meditation in a certain church, he suddenly felt in him a strange and pleasant heat as of real, sensible fire, so that he often felt his breast to see if the heat was caused by some exterior cause; but finding that it arose from within and not from the flesh, and was a gift from his Maker, he was all liquefied in love, and the more so because with the cauma he felt a dulcor inexpressibly sweet. In this warmth he had continued for 9 months, when suddenly he felt the canor[6]. . . . This gift, so wonderful that, as he says,

"nec putavi tale quid etiam nec sanctissimum in hac vita accepisse", he calls a free gift of Christ (hoc arbitror nulli datum meritis, sed gratis, cui voluerit Christus), "accorded to those only who so specially love the name of Jesus that it never recedes from their minds"[7]. The dulcor—an ineffable sweetness, an anticipation of the joys of Heaven—accompanies both the calor and the canor. The stages once attained, remain henceforth; not "raptim" or "momentanee", but "jugiter" he feels the calor, canor, dulcor, though not always alike intensely, or all at the same time, sometimes the calor, sometimes the canor prevailing.

The whole process from his conversion to the attainment of the canor had lasted 4 years and 3 months.—(Thus far, we have the authority of the Vita).

So in his youth—the age most fitted for love—he has forsaken the wisdom, the love of the world and carnal love, and given himself entirely to divine love; enthralled by the sweet humanity of Christ, he has followed Him in voluntary poverty and lives in solitude, in divine contemplation. The beginning of his conversation had not been without temptations, especially of the flesh; but now he has overcome. Now his tears are dried, his sorrow is turned into joy. Fasting and watching are no longer required; nay a moderate fare is more conducive to contemplation than outrageous abstinence. He has attained to the highest stage of contemplation, to the highest degree of love, the degree represented by the Seraphin ("ardentes") in Heaven. He is now perfectus, justus, sanctus in his sense, and lays claim to saintship—for Saint is he who forsaking the world and the flesh, is all absorbed in the love of God (Istum virum jam justum, perfectum, et sanctum Christus dignatur ostendere, qui in vera caritate non cessat flagrare). Yea, by the gift of canor, so rarely, if ever, given to mortal man, he belongs to the few privilegiati.

Contemplative life necessarily requires quiet and rest, quiet of body and mind. The mind must be abstracted from visible things, be free from sinful thoughts, from carnal love, from envy, wrath and pride; be even-tempered in adversity and prosperity. The body must be in rest; "Tanto minus quis internis gaudiis rapitur, quanto externis rebus magis implicatur". Exterior works, fatigue of any kind, interrupt the canor (Fervorem felicem et cantum captatum fatigatio fugat, et fugere facit ministerium mechanicum vel cursus corporalis, **Mel.**). Even the psalmody of the congregation disturbs the holy strain. The true contemplative must be solitary, not conjoint (non conjunctus, in congregatione et tumultu positus) or "communis";—"solus suscipiet quod conjunctus carebit". He must be poor, unfettered by office or dignity; poor in spirit, unspoiled by worldly wisdom. His place is the solitude, the desert, where no discordant noise jars upon the ear listening to the divine melody. Lovers will not kiss in public but seek solitude, Christ is not found in the multitude but in the desert: "In solitudine Christus loquitur ad cor, tanquam verecundus amator qui amicam coram omnibus non amplectitur nec amicabiliter sed comiter tantum velut extraneam osculatur"; "Pax est in cella: nil exterius nisi bella". He must not rove about—instability proceeds from vice. The best thing he can do is to sit; not to run about (discurrere) on exterior work, but to sit; to sit still, inactive, to sit by day and night, all absorbed in his raptures. Indeed, exterior works, almsgiving, preaching &c., are not the proper domain of the contemplative, but belong to active life; his domain is "love-longing and still mourning"— . . . such is *his* work. He does not say his prayers: he sings (Jam non dicit orationes suas: sed in sublimitate mentis positus et amore raptus, mira suavitate supra se rapitur et Deo decantare spirituali organo in mirum modum sublevatur, **Cant.**). Yet, contemplative life is not "otium"; it is not attained without great efforts, not sustained without severe spiritual exercises. Indeed, contemplation is labour, though a sweet labour (Est utique contemplatio labor, sed dulcis, desiderabilis et suavis: laborantem laetificat, non gravat). It so emaciates and consumes the body that the contemplative is hardly fit for preaching and exterior work (Cum divinae caritatis dulcedo mentem absorbuerit, caro deficit et ulterius jam ad exteriores labores sustinendos fortis non erit). So the true contemplative is the solitarius, anachorita, eremita.

The degree of sanctity depends on the degree of love ("Þe diuersite of lufe makes þe diuersite of halynes and of mede"); the more ardent in love, the greater is the Saint: "Perfectior et excellentior, qui suavius ac jocundius in caritate ardet". The Seraphin are the highest angles because they are most ardent in love. Therefore contemplative life, as it is most given to love, is the saintliest, the highest life, and in dignity and merit exceeds all active life. St. Bernard had ranked contemplative life between the two kinds of active life—a lower and a higher; R. Rolle proclaims the superiority of contemplative life. . . . As the soul is more excellent than the body, so spiritual labour is more commendable than bodily labour; "Tanto quis aeterni amoris dulcedinem affluentius haurit, quanto solummodo divina et celestia cogitans, ad nullam exteriorem mundi occupationem se tradit". The contemplative, therefore, ranks before the prelate, the priest, and the monk. The prelate, the priest, are distracted by outward work, the duties of their office. The monk, the "obedientiarius sub abbate", is bound by obedience and not free. The monastic profession is commendable, if rightly observed; but it has not the monopoly of perfection. A layman, a man in the world, can attain to caritas (Tanta caritate nonnunquam aliquis inter homines conversatus erga Deum exuritur, quanta ille qui inter claustrales etiam optimus approbatur); then à fortiori the solitary who forsakes the world for the love of God. Anselm therefore errs in maintaining the superiority of conventual life under obedience. Christ certainly will prefer

him who loves nothing but Him; nothing but love is accepted by God, and He counts not so much the work as the will. The contemplative is God's special darling (specialissimus). "Talem suavitatem habet in mente qualem angeli in coelo, licet non tantam". He has true rest and freedom; he lives happy and dies secure (dulciter vivit, secure morietur); he will have a high place in Heaven and sit on the throne with God to judge the wicked. His privilege is such that he cannot err, because God would not allow it (inspiratus est a Spiritu sancto, non potest errare; etsi voluerit assensum praebere persuasioni aliorum, non permittitur a Deo, qui constringit ems ad suam voluntatem; agat quicquid libet, securus est, **Inc. Am.**); and though he may be subject to temptation while he lives in this world, his ardent love will burn out all sin (incendium amoris cuncta vitia destruit et omnium virtutum florem plantat; cum mortali peccato nunquam stat, etsi aliquando veniali, sed tamen tam ardens esse potest quod omnia venialia consumit.) The contemplative is truly a king, yea a fourfold king—"non unum tantum sed quatuor regna devicit: regnum mundi per paupertatem voluntariam, regnum carnis per temperantiam et prudentiam, regnum diaboli per humilem patientiam, regnum coeli per caritatem perfectam; regnum ejus non est de hoc mundo, quia gaudium non quaerit nisi de coelo" (**In Ps.** 20).

The hermit has no ministry, no place in the hierarchical body. R. Rolle himself belonged to no monastic institution, was not in holy orders, was neither priest nor monk, and consequently was not allowed to preach from the pulpit[8]; he was a mere layman. The hermit must give himself entirely up to contemplation, and to spiritual exercises as reading, prayer, meditation.[9] He may occasionally give spiritual advice, exhort to peace and charity; he may also write, if he feel inspired by the Spirit; but preaching is not his concern; indeed, contemplation makes him unfit for preaching. In the main, he is a free liver—in the better sense of the word—, subject to no control, to no rule but his own. "Abbas amor dat morum formulam" (*Off.*), "Soli Deo debet heremita obedientiam facere, quia ipse est abbas, prior, et praepositus claustri cordis sui" (*Reg. her.*). He has to submit to the statutes of the Church, to say the Hours, to hear Mass, to confess and to receive holy communion; he must also notify his life to the diocesan, or to the patron of the place if he be a prelate or priest of good life, and if they find in him something to correct, obey their counsels; or he may, with the consent of the bishop, have a wise old priest appointed in a neighbouring monastery or church to whom he may confess rarely and who may advise him in questions of conscience. But practically he is independent, his own master, and follows the dictates of his spirit. He claims exemption from the Congregation, which would tend to disturb the canor. He must be chaste, he must be poor, but obedience is not in his regulation. Indeed, the word "obedience" is distasteful to him—

Magis oportet Deo obedire quam hominibus. His approbation he has from God, not from men; his ruler is Love.

The soul of holy contemplation is Love—Cor vulneratum, liquefactum, crematum amore; love precedes and leads to it, and contemplation itself is perfect and highest love (contemplatio est caritas perfecta et summa). "Nisi Christum quis certe diligit, proculdubio in canore coelestis contemplationis non jubilat". Love is desire of the heart, ever thinking on that that it loves, and when it has that it loves then it joys (quia gaudium non creatur nisi ex amore) and nothing may make it sorry; a yearning between two, with lastingness of thought; a coupling together of the lover and the loved, sum of affections (I, p. 36); transformation of the affect into the thing beloved. Where is love? "in the heart and in the will of man, not in his hand or in his mouth, that is to say, not in his work; but in his soul". Love is a universal principle (universalitas mundialis creaturae diligere diligique cupit, et motiva cordis intentio quodammodo semper in amatum tendit, jugiter mens in illud quod summe amat progreditur, nec in ejus desiderio fatigatur); but it is the privilege of youth (abilis est haec aetas ad ardenter amandum)—what knows the child of love? and old age has spent it. No reasonable soul is, or can be, without love. Love, therefore, is the foot by which man goes either to Heaven or to Hell. A thing can be loved only "propter bonum quod est aut existens aut apparens". But love of woman, or of the world, is no real, no lasting good, but an illusion, a deceit, a sham. Therefore we damnably neglect our soul, if we fix our love on woman for lust; "dum oculi visus animum incendit, mox intrabit delectatio, et in corde concupiscentiam generat". "Omnis amor qui in Deum non intendit, iniquitas est, ac iniquos reddit suos possessores"; "Amarior absinthio huiusmodi amor algescit, et finis felle erit ferocior, quia fervor infinitus carnales consumet." Woman is the devil's deception. Carnal love leads to perdition. "Propter speciem mulieris multi perierunt, pulcritudo plurimos decepit, et concupiscentia corda etiam sapientum quandoque subvertit". Therefore flee women, "fugito feminas". . . . But divine love leads to Heaven. This love is true love, which deceives not. True love is chaste, holy; voluntary, selfless, impetuous, undying. It loves God for Himself, and all other things for God. It is meek, humble, suffers gladly tribulation; patient and stalworth as death—as death slays all, so love overcomes everything (amor vincit omnia); he that loves God perfectly, delights in persecution, joys if men reprove him, covets to be worthy to suffer torment (I, 40). It loves poverty, penance, and hard travail. It is shy and seeks solitude, to be alone with the beloved (non potest commisceri societatibus saecularium, qui solummodo delectatur in gaudiis angelorum). The first step is to keep the ten commaundments and eschew the deadly sins; the next is perfect love—when man forsakes his

kin, despises the world and follows Christ in poverty; the highest is contemplative love, "in which the soul is as burning fire, and as the nightingale that loves song and melody and fails for great love" (I, 52. 33); or, the degrees of love are defined as love insuperable, inseparable, singular (illum solum in solatium recipiens quem jugiter amare concupiscit). This love is attained only by the simple-minded, the pure-hearted, the poor—not by the proud, the rich, the philosophers and sophists. . . . Divine love is painful in the beginning, and attained only with greatest labour; but when possessed, it gives ineffable joy. It alone gives real joy. All carnal pleasures, all abundance of earthly possessions, are misery and abomination in comparison to the least drop of the sweetness infused by God into the loving soul; "Tantus est dulcor infusus in mentem Christum amantem, quod si omne mundi gaudium in uno loco fuerit adunatum, magis delectaretur in solitudinem currere, quam illud semel oculo aspicere"; "Tota terrena consolatio sibi videtur potius desolatio quam recreatio". It is a sweet burden. It makes us one with God, it couples Christ with the elected soul, reforms in us the image of the trinity, makes the creature similar to the Creator. It is death of sin, life of virtues. Without it, no man can please God; with it, no man sins. Who feels the sweetness of eternal love, cannot relapse to temporal love (Ut lac semel coagulatum nunquam iterum ad pristinum statum redire potest, sic qui vere aeterno amore inciditur, ad amorem temporalem nunquam relabitur). It gives wonderful delight and security. It gives true rest and freedom (quam nobilem libertatem omnes in aeternum ignorabunt qui nesciunt diligere suavitatem in Christo sentire). It secures salvation. And love only merits. . . . Not to us us anything to be imputed but to grace. . . . God works justification and sanctification through his grace: "Nisi Deus electos quos salvare decreverit, gratia praeveniret, inter filios hominum non inveniretur quem justificaret; ipse inspirat ut recte velit; subsequitur ut voluntatem perficere possit". Contemplation, also, is the work of grace: "Non in humana potestate est contemplationem accipere, nec labor alicuius quantumcumque extensus ipsam *meretur*: sed a bonitate divina tribuitur vere diligentibus se, qui utique supra humanam aestimationem Christum amare desideraverunt". Grace and will combined, work salvation (I, p. 306). Will, not works, is the essential thing, and will is love: "Sine bona voluntate nemo salvabitur; cum qua nec aliquis dampnabitur. Deus est finis bonae voluntatis. Caritas nunquam est nisi in bona voluntate, nec bona voluntas nisi in caritate". Works are but a *sign,* not a test or proof of love, or love itself: "Many speak good and do good, and love not God; are holy in men's sight, and in the sight of God the devil's sons and ravishing wolves; as hypocrites. Nothing that I do without, proves that I love God; for a wicked man might do as much penance, might wake and fast as much as I do—how may I then ween that I love, or hold myself better, for that that each man may do? Certes, my heart, whether it love or not, no one knows but God, for nought that they may see me do. Wherefore love is in will only, and not in work, save as a *sign* of lofe. For he that says he loves God and will not do in deed that in him is to schew love, tell him that he lies; love will not be idle: it is working some good evermore; if it cease of working, know that it cools and fades away" (I, p. 38).—So "dilectio est *quoddam maximum, quoddam optimum, quoddam carissimum;* quod nos intus et extra disponit, ad unum solum Deum amandum colligit, opera nostra componit et Deo placere facit; cum qua pauper dives est, sine qua dives pauper, immo nihil est". "Amor itaque omnia excellit, nemo nisi diligens ad Deum ducetur". "Pro caritate cuncti coronantur".

Only divine love gives true happiness and bliss. The mind which revels in the sweetness of this love, in the intoxication of holy contemplation, cannot but loathe the world and all the glory of the world (Ita fit quod praeter illa interna solatia nec aliquid amare aut cogitare quaerat; inde exteriora vilescunt, transitoria quaeque ac omnem mundi inanem gloriam nec appetere curat nec respicere). It has no taste for other love (Si mens aeterni amoris dulcedine perfunditur, non potest fieri quod ultra in carnali amore nequiter delectetur). Carnal love is beastly, horrid, bitter as absinth, leads to ruin, disease and death—the world is being diminished "de multis maculatis". The pleasures of the world are shallow; beauty, riches, honours, dignities, worldly wisdom, are absolutely vain. . . . "Al perisches and passes that we with eghe se; it wanes into wretchednes, the welth of this worlde" (s. p. 53). This earthly life is a vale of tears and woe, its pleasures and joys are illusory, being always accompanied by sin and suffering and evil, from which we can escape only by fixing our hopes upon the world to come. Man is foul from beginning to end: conceived and born in filth, at last "worms' cook". "Heu quam miser homo qui perdidit omnia pomo! Labimur et cadimus, praesto peccamini sumus: Vermibus dum morimur caro, spiritus igni donatur" (*Job*). Men are blinded by their vices (Excaecantur oculi saecularium tenebris vitiorum); all seek riches and carnal love; the rich and proud are honoured, the poor are despised, the saint is persecuted and exiled. The best thing is death which removes us hence and puts an end to our misery. So pessimistic world-sadness is the reverse side of divine love.

Such are the outlines of R. Rolle's system, if system may be called what lacks every philosophic or metaphysic ingredient. His system is not a metaphysic system, his God not a metaphysic God; he implicitly believes in the Bible and in the Fathers, and rigorously resists any attempt to introduce reason into the domain of faith or to construe the Trinity from a psychological basis[10]. His God is *Christ;*—"Totiens glorior, quotiens nominis tui, Jesu, recordor." His mysticism is "in amore Dei canere et jubilare quasi raptus super terrena, in se

deficere et *in Deum pergere*[10a]". His system is religious life, not theory. His "principle" is Love. In a time of utter depravity, of gross materialism, when immorality and cupidity pervaded all classes from the highest to the lowest; in juxtaposition to the reigning scholasticism, the vain efforts of the brain, he re-discovered, re-introduced the principle of Love, Cor, and proclaimed salvation through the heart. He contains the elements which constitute Christ, and came very nearly to the same results—but the greater light outshone the lesser; the work had been done before, had been done well, and that which crowned the work, the crucifixion, could not be overdone; every departure on the same line is necessarily drawn into the way of imitation. Still, his example may serve to explain the genesis of Christ. On the other side, by re-developing the original ideas of Christ which had been overlaid, and partly obscured, by an artificial, elaborate hierarchical system, he opened and started that revolution which commenced by restoring and re-asserting individual right and conscience, and ended in the Reformation, the breach of *obedience* to Rome by Luther. Many of the arguments of Wicliffe, Savonarola, and Luther are first found in R. Rolle. As a matter of fact, the renaissance of letters and the Reformation were preceded by the regeneration of the heart, and R. Rolle is the link between Bonaventura and the Reformers. In England, this regeneration met with the individual principle of the Saxon, and by it received that tincture of self-independence which negatived a given rule, a formal authority, *obedience*. Though perfectly correct in dogma, yet, by living a life after his own taste, in solitude, apart from a Congregation, without a head, with God only as his praepositus, with abbas amor ruling his life, a self-made saint, a "homo sui juris", a king in the realm of the Spirit, R. Rolle represents the extreme, excessive height of individualism on the side of feeling, as Scotus on the side of intellect. The novel ideal of the hermit, revived from more primitive times when a less elaborate organisation of the Church left more space for individual freedom; the unique position of the contemplative as above the religious orders and prelacy; the emphasis laid on the inner man, the heart, love, as against works; his unsparing criticism of the existing system,—all this was sure to give offence to the dominant classes, and might, if followed up in its consequences, lead to serious complications.—

Of R. Rolle's later life the Vita gives but scant information. We learn that he was wonderfully, and very usefully, busy in holy exhortations, by which he converted many to God, and in writing mellifluous treatises and books for the edification of others which in the hearts of the devout resound the sweetest melody; that from the abundance of his holy love he was wont to befriend recluses and such as needed spiritual consolation or suffered vexations from the malign operation of evil spirits in body or soul, and that God conferred on him the singular grace of relieving those that were so troubled. We learn that after a time he went to other parts—no doubt, by the will of Providence, that he, dwelling in many places, might be useful to many, and sometimes, also, to evade obstacles of contemplation; and that this frequent change of place gave occasion for fault-finding, although the holy Fathers of Egypt had done the same and the canons allow a change of place in certain cases (cum necessitas persecutionis loca eorum gravaverit; cum difficultas locorum fuerit; cum sancti malorum societate premantur). That so he went into Richmondshire, where for a time he had his cell 12 miles from his spiritual friend Margaret (Kirkby), a recluse near A(i)nderby; whom he used to instruct in the art of the love of God and in the ruling of life, and twice by his mere presence cured from a seizure, promising her the second time that she shoult not be seized again during his life-time. When—transactis postea quibusdam annorum curriculis—the same fit returned a third time, it was found that he had just died "apud domum sanctimonialium de Hampole, ubi illis diebus solitariam vitam egit". Thither the said recluse afterwards removed.

This meagre account of a life which must have been rich in incident and full of interest, can be largely supplemented from his works which abound in self-confessions, he being a very subjective writer. All the 4 years odd from his conversion to the attainment of the canor, he appears to have stayed with the Daltons, and there in his lonely cell, "remotus inter homines", provided with the necessaries of life by his kind friends, to have enjoyed that rest and quiet so indispensable to contemplation. "Comedi et bibi de his quae meliora videbantur." The solitude has taught him his "love" and the canorus jubilus, and he is happy. "Parentum seu amicorum subitis doloribus non concutitur nec illorum calamitate turbatur (contemplativus)"—he says, alluding perhaps to his own family. It was probably Lady Dalton ("domina quaedam in cuius manerio idem Ricardus cellam habuit longe a familia separatam ubi ipse solitarius sedere consuevit et contemplationi vacare"), at whose death he drove away a troop of horrible demons, as the Vita relates (Lect. 8); and we may suppose that it was this same lady ("matrona quaedam in mundo magna quae me una cum marito suo per annos nonnullos sustentaverat"), whose aspect in death produced in him that great horror described in "Contra amatores mundi", and which seems to re-echo in his awful descriptions of death. At the time of his conversion Lady Dalton had been an elderly matron, having grown-up sons at Oxford. Perhaps it was her death and her husband's that put an end to his residence there. When he left that place he was still young—"non inutile, he says, arbitrandum est si *in juventute mea* plura loca viderim, ut de melioribus statui meo convenientibus unum eligere possem." Hitherto he had enjoyed rest: henceforth his rest is broken. He becomes a wanderer upon earth.[11] "Quemadmodum Cayn[11a]" vagus et profugus super terram factus fuit pro

facinore fratricidii, ita et ego in hoc exilio incertae sedis fio; de loco ad locum transeo, donec omnipotens deus dignetur servum suum dirigere, ut deinceps jam non indigeam circumquaque transmigrare" (**Mel.**). The next period of his life is one of restlessness, conflict and fierce strife. He remained an hermit and adhered to contemplative life; but he had to live somehow. England was not Egypt, his time not St. Guthlac's; there were no longer lonely islands or waste places to occupy, the land had been parcelled out; to till the ground, to live by manual labour, did not agree with his delicate health and with his aspirations—he was dependent on men for his living. But, being no professional, neither priest in orders nor monk, he could offer little or no service—he had only ideas to give. He had to find friends who for God's sake could spare him a cell and his sustenance. And such friends he did find: we learn from his writings that he continued to live "cum divite domorum", dwelling on their estates and heartily joining in their meals. Who these friends were we know not—he never gives names of persons or places: but they must be sought amongst the gentry, the lords of manor, of the neighbourhood. However, not all friends were so kindly disposed, so constant, as the Daltons. He was of a sensitive, irritable nature, easily giving and taking offence, and yet exacting as to his dignity; his ways were strange, not in tune with the "world" ("non feci sicut ipsi fecerunt"), his theories new and incomprehensible to common intellect. He could not agree with men (cum hominibus concordare non potui); his friends soon became estranged (statim mutati fuerunt qui ministrare consueverunt), showed the cold shoulder; he suffered rebuff and ignominy. Slanderous tongues helped to embroil him with his patrons and to drive him "a domibus in quibus diligebar". Personal frictions hindered his contemplation. So he had no permanent home and changed his cell several times, living where he found a welcome, and leaving when friendships cooled; depending on the goodwill of men, on the seasons, on circumstances; staying a year or two at this manor, half a year at another, and changing from bad to worse.

Or, he left his cell for a while to return to it at convenience, in the meanwhile traversing the country. The reason is not far to seek: he began to appear in public. It is a remarkable fact that new systems of Love have generally implied a tendency to remodel the world, or rather that moral revolutions have proceeded from a deeper grasp of the principle of Love. Love and mercy are akin. Having found his system, he was naturally desirous to make it known, to propagate his ideas, to teach his love, to save others, to win souls. He appeared in the manor-houses of the neighbourhood, made friends with the lord, chatted with the women, knacked jokes with the girls, but all with that intent to preach his love, chastity and charity. . . . He appeared in the villages and mixed with the people; colloquially (as Socrates), not from the pulpit, inculcating love, loving-kindness, peace. He formed connections with clerics—one of his epistles (Cupienti mihi) is addressed to a young priest[12] whom he instructs in charity and invites to seek the solitude. He tried to revive anchoritical life. The "Regula heremitarum", which is undoubtedly his work, is a proof that at one time he contemplated to form a community of hermits under a rule. How far he succeeded in his missionary work it is difficult to judge: the Vita says that he converted many to God by his exhortations; I find no confirmation in his writings. He himself begs to be excused if, his health failing under the strain of contemplation, he, infirm and dead to the world, keeps within his cell, "non visitans villanos, fugiendo festis psallentiumque sonoro"; he maintains that "exterius ministerium" is not the sphere of the contemplative. In another work (Contra amatores mundi) he complains that his labour is lost, that "inter multos morans nec uni scio prodesse, et quae putabam lucrata timeo ne evanescant". As to his propaganda for anchoritical life, he complains that he can find no one willing to join him: "Heu mihi misero qualicunque solitario, ita fit in temporibus meis quod nec unum invenio qui mecum cupit currere ac sedendo et tacendo aeterni amoris delicias desiderare", "Vix unum invenio quem solitudinem amantem videbis", that no woman will last in his love: "Amor mulieris multivolae cito fluens evanet et nullicubi persistens innumeras mansiones affectat evagando; non miror si in amore mei non moretur aliqua, cum ab aeterno amore modico venti flatu in aliud redigatur." On the other side it would seem that the order of hermits, which before his time had become nearly extinct, was really revived by him, and that after a time his example was followed by many.[13] Piers Ploughman directs his satire against the hosts of begging hermits traversing the country. On the whole, his oral mission does not seem to have met with much success, or to have been long continued. Indeed, he had found a better and more congenial mode of conveying his ideas.

At that time he began to write. Love forces him to write. Love has given him wisdom and subtlety; the gift of canor, the power of lucid speech (lucide, liquide loquor). The old Fathers had written: so why should not he? why should a modern be less able? God is of no less bounty now than in the primitive times. If he is not allowed to preach, he will write, and preach in writing. "Non sum episcopus nec praelatus nec rector ecclesiarum, tamen solicitus sum pro ecclesia Dei, si possem aliquo bono modo quidquam facere aut scribere quo ecclesia Dei augmentum capiat in divina dilectione". He fears not, Love makes him bold.—His first attempts had been private, the outcome of the canor modulated into song: short rhapsodic effusions, ejaculation of love-longing, rhymes,—of course, in English—, made afterwards into songs to Christ and Mary. The Virgin he held in special veneration and to her he had dedicated his virginity; in her praise he wrote a Latin poem (Zelo tui langueo virgo speciosa,

in Ms. Rawl. C 397) in 39 4-lined stanzas, one of his earliest works—an imitation of Bonaventura's (or Peckham's) famous "Cantus philomenae", and in the same metre, but with frequent alliteration. But now he comes forward as a writer (proferor), and having once commenced, he wrote on, issuing work after work in quick succession. He writes with astounding facility, with an eloquence which brings out with ease whatever is in his mind, but he takes no trouble to revise or refine his writings. He writes to bring out his system, to win souls, to attack vice, to castigate society. Yes, he will not only edify, he will strike and sting (spinis pungendo principles perversos); he will not only show love, but hatred (Amorem et odium utrumque ostendi). He appears as a champion, enters the lists against the vices of the time—cupidity and concupiscense, throws down the gauntlet to the "saeculares miseri", the tyrants, the egotists, the hardhearted, the princes, the proud, the rich, the lovers of vanity, the pharisees and hypocrites—"Tutus non timeo tundere temptantes: *contra tyrannos thema tetendi*".— In embracing anchoritical life he had followed in the steps of St. Guthlac and other Northerners; his gift of canor reminds of Caedmon's miraculous gift of song— as a writer he took up the old traditions of the North: *he revived the alliterative verse*. I cannot discover any previous attempt in that direction, and do not hesitate to ascribe to him the revival of this verse which forms so prominent a part in the vernacular literature of the 14th century. He first employed it in Latin. The first work—or one of his first—with which he appeared before the public, "Of the glory and perfection of the Saints" i.e. hermits (in Ms. CCCO 193 titled **Melum contemplativorum**), is written in alliterative verse, mixed with alliterative prose. His next works are in prose: a "book on the life of hermits", quoted—with the preceding—in his "Job" and probably identical with the "Rule of hermits" in Ms. Mm. VI. 17; "Against the lovers of the world"; on God's judgment as against man's (Judica me Deus); an epistle to a young priest inculcating charity and contemplation (Cupienti mihi); postils on the first 2 verses of Canticum canticorum (Osculetur me osculo oris sui), and on the chapters of Job used as lessons for the dead. All these works are in Latin, at that time the common language of the learned. They all belong to this period and are written in his youth: in the "Melum" he calls himself juvenculus, puer, pusillus—it was written probably in 1326, when presumably he was 26 years old; in the other works he calls himself juvenis. They all bear the mark of youth in the strongly personal, subjective, combative, passionate, nervous, eruptive style, in the sweeping and uncompromising character of his assertions; the **Melum** betrays its primogeniture in a certain juvenile—shall I say frivolity? They are written in a time of conflict, when he had to make headway, to lay open, to maintain, and to defend his theories, and subjectivism will naturally appear when the "Ich" is not in concord with the time and has to assert itself.—All these works are written in praise of contemplation and divine love as against carnal love and the love of the world. His favourite form is the postil, i.e. he comments Holy Scripture—he is dependent on scriptural texts for the exposition of his views. In the "Melum" he thus chooses his texts indiscriminately, according to their bearing on contemplative life; in the postils on Canticum and Job he comments a couple or a series of texts. Those of his works in which he either abandons the support of texts (as Incendium amoris) or more regularly expounds whole books of the Bible verse by verse (as Psalter, Threni), must be assigned to a subsequent period—he certainly commenced his literary career as a—somewhat irregular—postillator; "de gloria et perfectione sanctorum praecellentium *postillas* proferam", "Positus in praesenti patiens pressuras pro pane perhenni, puto quod potero . . in publicum procedere probatus *postillator,* strictam scripturae masticans medullam, ut degam delicate dulcoribus divinis", so he says in the **Melum**. This is characteristic of his method. He propounds a biblical text: this text evokes a certain note or tune, a certain emotion, and on that he enlarges, so bringing out his views. His method is lyrical or musical, not deductive—a translation into words of the canor, the chiming in his breast; he is a poet, a lyric poet, not a philosopher, he writes from feeling. Guided by a biblical text as "Leitmotif", he brings out the sensations attending holy contemplation. In the **Melum** he so follows up the whole course of contemplative life from the first conversion to the attainment of caritas perfecta, and ends with the grand Finale: Doomsday, the glory of the saints, the pains of the damned; in the postils on Canticum he more particularly dwells on the dulcor. His plans are loose, invisible, introduced from without, the parts are exteriorly slung together like beads in a rosary, the sentences loosely connected, his style is strangely incoherent, there is no development, no progress: the progress is obstructed by variations and repetitions of the same theme, much in the wise of A.S. poetry; sometimes he repeats himself in different works in identical terms. His strength lies in his lyric fervour, in the truth of his feeling, in the depth of his inner life, as in graphic descriptiveness, in happy illustration from nature, life, his own experience; he strikes some of the deepest chords that ever have sounded in the human breast; he excels in terse sentences epigrammatically pointed and full of antithesis, which often convey truths far in advance of his time and of almost modern impress—indeed his style is largely made up of sentences, each the result of a spiritual experience, a momentary inspiration. He is strangely deficient in reasoning and all that pertains to reason and scientia acquisita: he is strong in point of feeling and scientia inspirata; he is all, entirely, and nothing but feeling. This, I think, explains the peculiarities of his strange style.—But he not only gives the sensations in the progress of contemplative life: he is also a preacher and teacher; his lyric effusions are mixed with admonitions and warnings, with polemic and satire. He appears as a reformer: he propounds his scheme of a higher and unworldly life, exhorts others to follow him, criticises the existing order of things, attacks the worldliness of the ruling classes. All these elements are combined in the **Melum,** his chief and most comprehensive work, while his other writings are more uniformly either exegetic and mystical, or exhortatory, or polemic, or written in self-defence; indeed, the polemic element may be said to prevail in his earlier writings in the same degree, as it recedes in his later. How he labours to win souls! O come, he says, ye youths and maidens, learn from me, a wonderful lover (amator mirabilis), how to love: forsake the impure love of one another and embrace eternal love! O maidens, do not hanker after men, do not adorn yourselves for men, to tempt them: lo Christ, lovely of shape before the sons of men, the King of Heaven, wants your beauty, woos your love—he loves maidens chaste and poor, he loves caritas, not libido (caritas est color quo pulcri paremus): he will adorn you with a wonderful crown, a worthy diadem, with shining garments; and her that now languishes in love for him, he will requite with everlasting sweetness. . . . — Be comforted o ye poor! you will be the rich in Heaven and sit with God on the throne to judge the wicked princes: . . . —He attacks the cupidi, carnales, directs his satire against all classes of society from the King down to the selfish poor, but mainly against the great, the proud, the rich, against all who love the world and the flesh, not God. . . . No less he censures the manifest abuses in the Church, insisting on inward religion, on caritas, as against "ministerium mechanicum", the formalism of the time; he censures the prevailing worldliness, exteriority, work-service, hypocrisy, the lack of true religious spirit. He declaims against the "ficti et falsi fideles, qui Deum se amare fingunt cum non diligunt"; against the priests who eagerly claim their tithes but neglect the cure of their parishioners . . . against the monks who are implicated in secular affairs, and in their presumption claim to possess the sole way to perfection; against the book-wise, the "doctores et philosophi et theologi, infinitis quaestionibus implicati, in omni scientia summi sed in amore Dei inferiores"; against the prelates, who bent on worldly pursuits, on secular business, on mammon, on carnal pleasures, and anxious to shine, to excel, indifferently perform the duties of their office and neglect to attend to the spiritual needs of their flocks, sending incompetent preachers and prohibiting the "missi a Deo", the poor hermits . . . If so the columns fall, how can the fabric stand: (Si columnae cadunt, quomodo stabit quod frondificatum est? Membra sequuntur caput; quia superiores insaniunt, etiam inferiores in vanitates et fantasias falsas deducuntur): So much the more it is necessary that the few elected should raise their voice against the prelates. . . . He so, leaning on his mission by God, challenges his own bishop: "Ecce juvenis, zelo animatus justitiae, insurgit contra senem, *heremita contra episcopum* et contra omnes taliter opinantes qui in quantumcumque exterioribus actibus supereminentia affirmant esse sanctitatis" (*Mel*).—Alas, the world is sadly deteriorated! . . . —Truly, the end of the world is near: "Et quidem in istis temporibus, in quibus deveniunt fines temporum, maxime superbi regnant, hypocritae praesident, homicidae dominantur, fornicatores sublevantur, avari divitias et dignitates adquirunt, iracundi et invidi praeponuntur".

From so appearing in public as a teacher and writer, his name soon began to be noised about. But in the same measure he found violent opposition: he was attacked by a host of enemies. His earlier works are full of bitter complaints against his detractors; he had to maintain his reputation, to defend his principles. His system ran counter to the common opinion of men, of the world that lives, and struck against the very root and foundation of society. He proclaimed chastity, divine love: but, mothers *will* marry their daughters although they know that the price is their virginity; girls *will* have their sweethearts and adorn themselves to please men, and will not cease to believe that they possess what men desire to know; young men are expected to be infatuated, illusioned—and disillusioned—it is the way to knowledge and to wisdom;— such is the course of the world. Matrimony is the natural law (lex) of man, though no community has ever formally proclaimed it such, leaving it to nature to enforce her ends. The sex is man's natural incumbency, his fate, his Cross, the tree on which he grows. The ways of sex are hideous indeed: but they are indispensable—the way to life leads through that gate, and nature herself has given beauty and illusion, love and curiosity, to unite the sexes for the creation of new life; chastity is the beau ideal, the essence of morality, indeed morality itself, but chiefly as the nursery, the mainspring of love, which is the foundation of human society. Love is life itself, and life was given to return love; it is primarily sexual, and divine love is but secondary love, love transferred in its ends. His system was transcendental idealism—flight from the "trieb", and, as such, as much above truth, as mere sensuality is beneath it, truth lying between the two, as between body and soul, between matter and spirit. His system was hostile to kind, and he who forsakes kind, is forsaken by kind, and liable to fall maybe as Joseph by the wife of Putiphar; the whole world becomes his enemy. He had raised the whirlwind: he became the "lapis offensionis, petra scandali", "scandalum Judaeis, gentibus autem stultitia."—He was a strange man: strange in his ways, strange in his words and teaching: people asked: Who is this man that so cometh forth? They did not understand him, or misunderstood him. They saw his gloominess, but not the joy he felt within; they saw him constantly absorbed, ecstatic, constantly talking of a love not of this world, and could not make him out. They called him a fool, mad, demented (stultus, insipiens, alienatus mente), nay wicked (iniquus), say-

ing he did irreverence to God and did not keep the statutes of the Church (dicentes irreverentiam Deo facere et statuta ecclesiae non observare), and did not run the right way to God (affirmant non recte currere ad coelestem mansionem). Others said: We give alms, feed the poor, clothe the naked and do all the works of mercy: how can those be equal to us who daily love quiet and do nothing of the kind? it is better to be in the world and do some good, than to sit idle in the solitude or in the cloister. His wanderings, his shifting from place to place, seemed at variance with the notions of an hermit, with the rest and quiet claimed by himself for the contemplative: people said he was no hermit (nonnulli cum heremiticam vitam considerant, me etiam heremitam non esse impudenter affirmare non formidant), but an hypocrite; some said he was a scamp (trutannus). His converse with the rich gave another occasion for slander: he who is so exhausted by absinence that he suffers excruciating head-aches, is said to be led away by the pleasures of the rich (dicunt derogantes: deliciis deducor quibus divites delectant, et indignus sum Deo), is accused of being a glutton and a wine-bibber, and they said of him as was said of Christ that he ate with sinners and publicans (Sancti saepius inter saeculares etiam solitarii sedebant: ideo tu dicis quod de Domino dicebatur: Quare cum peccatoribus et publicanis manducat magister vester? et iterum vocabant veritatem viventem quae angelos alit in sola visione, vini potatorem), that he was impure and ran after the girls (lubricum et lapsum me judicaverunt, putantes quod pro puellis persisterem cum pravis), that his "sittings" in holy contemplation were due to an overfull belly and to good wine, and his penance merely for the eyes of men (asserebant sophistice loquentes quod pro sumpto cibario sustinui sedere, et potibus deputantes quod Piissimus praestavit, ac populis ut placeam plerique publice praedicabant penitentiam me pati). These attacks he ascribes to envy, the envy of those who saw his goodly life and the wonders God worked in him, and found themselves deficient ("invidebant autem eo quod in magnis muneribus munitus mirabilis manebam, et seipsos mordebant morsibus malignis quia magnifica majestas me mirificavit in mente per musicum in melle melodis"; "Invidia uruntur quia lucide loquor"). But his worst enemies were those who called themselves followers and disciples of Christ, the professionals, the monks, the doctors, and especially the prelates; those that were encrusted in their traditional ways, in their self-conceit, their self-righteousness, and failed to comprehend the new gospel ("Odium et invidiam tantam non inveni nec habui sicut ab his qui dicebantur discipuli Jesu Christi"; "Hi qui praeferuntur (i. e. the prelates) maxime me odiunt"). They derided his self-assumed saintship— if he is a saint, where are the miracles which signalize the saint? They found fault with his quietism, his idle inactivity, his contemplation without works, his salvation by love, his independence without obedience. The generality of men are business-men and cannot understand the enthusiast: They jeered at his canor. The book-wise asked: Where has he learned and from what doctor? (Docti per acquisitam scientiam, non infusam, et inflati argumentationibus implicitis, dedignantur dicentes Ubi didicit iste et a doctore audivit?). They despised the layman who was not of their guild, scorned his inadequacy in things dialectic, questioned his qualification, thought it easy to beat him in disputation (nonnullos audivi me disputationibus velle vincere, quia apud opinionem hominum eos vivendo videbar superare), called him a rustic, an idiot (rusticus, idiota, insipiens). They maintained that he had no capacity to preach (Putant quod non potui pure praedicare nec sapere ut ceteri qui sancte subsistunt); they despise his words because he is poor, not a bishop, a prelate, or a rector (Quia pauper sum et non reputatus inter magistratus mundi, parvi penditis verba quae loquor vobis). They ridiculed his authorship—his teaching is to them a mystery (mysterium mitto modernis); they maintain that he errs in his interpretation of Holy Scripture (dicentes aut me in expositione errasse, aut sacra verba congruenter non tractasse, non acceptantes me quia *modernus* sum, *Job*)—to them he is a "homo novus", a modern. So—because he did not "run" as others in this world (quia non cucurri quemadmodum qui adhuc carnalitati inhaerent)—he was an object of universal hatred—*Horridum me habebant omnes insensati*. Those became his worst detractors whom before he had thought true friends (Eos pessimos detractores habui quos prius amicos fidos putavi). "Multi qui mecum loquebantur, similes fuerunt scorpionibus, quia capite blandiebantur adulantes, et cauda percutiebant detrahentes". They would fain have seen him fall into sin (Invidi undique obsistebant adversus me, qui si lapsus ligarer in lacum laetarentur); they tried to lure him into sin, so to catch him therein and make him belie his saintship. They contrived to drive him out of the houses where he was loved, and so did him great harm, as he was dependent on the benevolence of men. He has had so much annoyance from their defamations that in his "Cupienti mihi &c" he begs the dedicatee to use discretion in showing the book, lest he should incur new slander (vobis habenda est discretio non modica, ne dum circumquaque hunc libellum indesinenter ostenditis, juventutem meam invidorum dentibus acerbiter corrodendam exponatis).

How far this conflict went we are not informed. The annals of the time are silent with regard to him. His age treated him as a nonentity and gave him over to oblivion. Society simply took no notice of him. He himself will not disclose the names of his tormentors (Dirisiores et detractores non divulgavi ad dampnum, necnon et amavi eos qui me arguerunt et ostenderunt odia ut ab omnibus abominarer). Yet it seems that matters came to a crisis. It appears that he had one chief adversary—in his *Melum* he chiefly addresses one, who vainly curses . . . and I have no doubt that he refers to one and the same person. I mentioned

before that in one passage of the *Melum* he directly challenges his bishop, and it is very probable that his bishop was this one adversary. He also complains that the prelates prohibit the hermits from preaching and send unfit persons (prohibent praecipuos proferre sermonem, et alios admittunt qui a Deo non mittuntur; heremitas abiciunt), and that those in prelacy hate him most. In the register of Archbishop Melton (1317-42) I find the following memorandum: *1334 Aug. 5: An order forbidding any one to listen to the teaching of friar Henry de Staunton hermit* (Raine, Fasti Ebor. p. 421). Nothing more is known of this hermit, but we may readily suppose that he was a disciple or follower of R. Rolle. It is quite possible that some similar restriction, if not a severer censure, was issued against R. Rolle at an earlier date, and that he suffered some kind of check at the hands of his diocesan.

So, what with these conflicts, what with the loss of patrons and friends, and the increasing difficulty of living, what with his restlessness, his life in this period became more and more sad. In the two great passions of life, ambition and love, he is checkmated. He saw others rise to honours, and himself was nobody. He had a loving heart, was bound by no vow, was free to marry if he chose: yet he clung to chastity, a self-imposed burden. He was a fair young man, florid, not uncomely, and well worth a woman's love: all the greater was his temptation (elegans eligitur amplius amori, nam formosus in facie, qui fuerit facundus, oculos solicitat et taliter temptatur). Yet, absorbed in his holy love, he managed to escape carnal love and so to remain chaste—we have his positive testimony that he kept his chastity. But who can tell the struggles he had to go through as years came on, those years especially when the "trieb" is strongest, virility most potent, when every one succumbs—the height of generation, the years of Christ? The victory is gained, but at what price! By refusing himself to kind, he is refused by kind, his friends forsake him, his patrons repudiate him, no maiden will abide in the love he offers, he is overrun by enemies[14]. His life is that of the lonely man who, forsaken by all, is sent adrift, a prey to all. He tasted of that destitution in which man, stripped of all belongings, is reduced to the state of man simple, the son of man. He should so like to have an associate (sodalis in itinere; who would understand him, who could modulate his clamor (canor), so that it might become objective to him—but there is none. He has no home, no place where to rest his head. Despite his converse with the rich he is extremely poor, so poor that at times he has no water to drink, only rags to cover him, and suffers severely from frost and heat. . . . His health is delicate, his constitution is weakened by contemplation, he suffers from intolerable head-aches (Quippe sic carnem modo maceravi et caput contunditur dolore deducto, quod consistere non queo—ita gravatur—nisi corroberer cibario sanante); he has the presentiment of an early death (the *Melum* concludes with the remarkable words: Amorem et odium utrumque ostendi, et puer nunc propero ad finem felicem, nam paene perfudi gressus gravantes, ut calcans contagium in cantico consummer; caritatem carissimam cunctis commendo: amen). And what has come of his efforts, his vast projects? his plans have failed, his labour is lost, he is of no use to anybody. The world is too much for him; the very noises of the world are painful to him (penales sunt mihi vociferantes et crucior quasi per incommodum quando clamor clangentium me tangit). He languishes in still mourning, his youth is all consumed in yearning (prae amoris magnitudine assiduis horis ferme consumor), and there is no relief, the beloved tarries so long! He grieves over the sins of the time, the wickedness of man; that so many souls are lost that the king has redeemed (Dolui pro desolatione, nam multi merguntur mortifero in mari: quos Rex redimebat, vanos vidi et vacuos virtute); turpitude reigns supreme, the Saint has left the earth, the solitary are despised—and he can do nothing. So he suffers, his misery at times is extreme; his words sometimes betray utter desolation and sound like the outcry of the beast wounded to death. He wishes to die—it is better for him to die, as he is of no use. . . . He wishes to die because true love is gone and mean concupiscence only remains. . . . He can hardly await the end. . . . He longs for the day when the Saviour will come and do justice to the poor; when the truth will come out and he will be seen as he is, not as his detractors paint him. He joys that the end of the world is near: "Nam finis mundi appropiat, paene paratus est tubam caniturus, adest finis mundialis malitiae, terminus terrenae cupiditatis longe non moratur"; "Iam judex ut fulgur gladium suum acuit in quo ad judicium veniens peccatores ferit."—In this time of suffering he came to realise the sorrows of the "man of sorrows", the desolation of the "son of man". In this time he formed his pessimistic views of the miserableness of this earthly existence. In this time he conceived that deep sympathy with the suffering, the poor, the oppressed, which is one of his chief characteristics.

But all this misery and persecution is not able to overcome him: he bears up, stands firm, strikes home and hits hard. "Das Individuum richtet sich herrlich auf". He has found Jesus—he has found him in poverty, in affliction, in penance, in the desert. He joys in his poverty, he joys in his solitude, more than the king in all his riches: "Amplius gaudeo sedens in solitudine quam rex in cuius omnes terrenae divitiae veniunt potestate". He has found such joy that the tongue cannot express it; he is in so sweet a life that no misery, no wrong, no pain can make him sad, that he is as it were impassible in his mind. He allows no disparagement of his profession, and blesses the solitude that has taught him his love. . . . Perfect love kills pain: "Perfectus amor vincit penam, vincit minas, quia non sentit timorem creaturae"; tribulation and persecution will only enhance his merit and win him a higher re-

ward in Heaven. Temptations, "fantasmata noctis", have disappeared by the invocation of the name of Jesus; the flesh is overcome, he can live amongst women without feeling any emotion. . . . In his illnesses he is consoled and strengthened by the canor. . . . What does he care for grandeur or men's praise? . . . He prefers to be despised. . . . His tormentors cannot disturb him. . . . Against their defamations he flees to God, under the shadow of His wings, and appeals to Him who alone knows the heart and reins and does not judge by the exterior as man; He will reveal the truth in the last Judgment. He vindicates his character, the integrity of his life. He is no glutton, no wine-bibber, no parasite of the rich: he takes only what is necessary—"nullus enim sufficit seipsum portare nec etiam fortissimus per seipsum subsistit", and, aye, "inebrior ab ubertate domus Dei et torrente voluptatis suae potavit me" (Ps. 35). . . . Even in the repasts of the rich he hears the canor: "Inter delicias divitum saepe in me resonat melos coelicum et amoris canticum amoenum". He is not unchaste: "non fallit me femina nec pereo puellis, neque glorior in gula quae jugulat gentiles"; his addresses to women are only meant to teach them "ut amico mundano non maculentur nec langueant pro lubrico labentes in lacum, *horridum habentes humanum amorem,* osculis amplexibus non aveant immundis, caste et pie deinceps degentes"; if his words are not believed, let inquiries be made and the truth will appear: "Haec si non creditis, quaerite quid dixi, interrogare potestis qui me andierunt, si docui dampnabile, injuriam aut Deo, vel cogitavi corrumpere fragilem facturam", and he calls Christ to witness: "Christus quem cupio hoc contestetur et contra me consurgere faciat fideles, sed et ipse conquasset caput captivi et cunctos corroboret me premere procellis, si ab adolescentia ipsum non amavi(!)"; adding however: "Nimirum non nego plurima non prospera in me pervenisse ac temptamenta inter tales tolerasse, turbatus, tribulatus et turbidus primitus permansi", and concluding: "Tamen hoc teneo ut sistas securus: Fugito feminas qui Christum amare voluntarie vovisti, nam vitii venenum sic vincere vales, alioquin, nisi Auctor te altius assumpsit, in dira dulcedine decipieris" (*Mel.*). In another passage he affirms: "Ex quo ardebam aeterno amore, quievi a cupidine carnali", and praises God who has kept him chaste (In laude levabor gratias agendo, Conditorem complectens qui castum me custodit dum alii errabant juvenes a jure). He maintains his saintship: "Sanctus subsisto". Though it may seem strange that a man, however excellent, should call himself a saint when even St. Paul confesses himself a sinner, yet one must speak the truth when asked. . . . One can be a saint without miracles, and may not be a saint with miracles. . . . God is still wonderful in his saints, but in these latter days of the world miracles are not necessary, but example of elect work. . . . Oh the wretched who argue against the Saint, whom they ought to honour as intercessor and patron. . . . He maintains the superiority of contemplative over active life, of love over works, of hermit over monk. Anselm, in asserting that monks love God more than any secular because they "offer fruit and tree to God under an abbot", appears to flatter the monks rather than to speak the truth; "Ego Ricardus utique solitarius heremita vocatus, hoc quod novi assero: quoniam ille ardentius Deum diligit qui igne Spiritus sancti succensus a strepitu mundi et ab omni corporali sono quantum potest discedet; non monachi vel alii quicunque ad congregationem collecti summi sunt aut maxime Deum diligunt: sed solitarii contemplationi sublimati". No one can see another man's heart; no one, therefore, ought to judge himself worthier than another. . . . The monks say: "Propter obedientiam quam praepositis exhibemus, inter omnes ordines ecclesiae in meritis majores sumus": but those in congregation cannot realise in what sweetness of love he burns that is solitary, and those bent on exterior works are ignorant of the delights of eternal love; "Quia ignorant quam amoena et meritoria sit illa quam gustamus aeterna suavitas, non putant aliquem sanctiorem fieri posse qui exterioribus actibus non studeat mancipari". Therefore, ye monks &c, "illa quae contra conversationem vestrae vitae sunt scripta a sanctioribus, non debetis reprehendere, sed in quantum potestis humiliter imitari; nec dicatis: nos coram Deo maximum meritum habebimus; quia sic mentitores arrogantia totum amittitis". He maintains his literary position. His power is from God, his wisdom is infused, not acquired, he is taught by the interior doctor, the Holy Ghost, who inspires his lovers no less now than of old—he needs no further approbation. . . . God has predestined and emboldened him to preach, and he is full of the Spirit of God. . . . His enemies in their envy—quia lucide loquor—say that he is not fit to preach: but "Sciant simpliciter Auctorem amavi qui animum ardore Olympi implevit ut proferam praecipue sermones amoris, scripturam scrutans quae latet carnales"; "Hoc profero quod plures non possunt: nam lubricos latet luminis lucerna et nucleum nitentem nesciunt nudare nec pascere parvulos qui properant ad polum lacte laetitiae aut cibo salubri, cum seipsos substernunt stultitiae in stagno et student cum stolidis qui strangulantur". If his works are a mystery to them, it is because *they* do not understand the true meaning of Scripture: "Nimirum mysterium mitto modernis, etenim antiqui sublimia sciebant; archanum absconditum ab omnibus avaris vix unus hoc accipit dum est in hoc mundo. Claudit enim Conditor januam scripturae, ut lateant legentes quae liquide lucescunt; sed amicis hanc aperit ardenter qui amant, ut aliis ostenderent quod hi intellexerunt". If they sneer at his canor, it is because they have not got so high. . . . They read his words, but do not know the tune: "Mundi amatores scire possunt verba vel carmina nostrarum cantionum, non autem cantica nostrorum carminum; quia verba legunt, sed notam et tonum ac suavitatem odarum addiscere non possunt". If they despise him because he is poor

and nobody, let them know "quod nunquam Deus nec papae nec episcopo, nec alicui alii cuiuscunque status fuerit, singulari Virgine excepta, de gloria aeterni amoris in hac vita illam praerogativam tribuit quam vero solitario delegavit". They call him modern: "sed profecto qui bonos modernos reprobat, hesternos non laudat; non enim Deus est nunc minoris bonitatis quam fuit in primitiva ecclesia, qui adhuc electos suos ad amorem aeternitatis desiderandum praeparat et quos vult coelesti scientia sapientiaque divina inspirat". Many depreciate the moderns, as void of the spirit, but not all are so: "Hoc comperi quod virorum volumina moderne manentium minime cum multis magnificantur qui putant quod spiritus in istis non assistat quemadmodum affuit antiquos inspirans; et rationem reddere aliam non habent quam, quia ipsi vacuos se vident a flatu felice, etiam sic omnes esse suspicantur." And what are the arguments of the book-learned, compared to the inspirations of the living Spirit? how can they judge of what they have not got?. . . .

So he stands up firmly against his adversaries, and has an answer to all their accusations. So far from being overawed by their learning, he speaks with authority in his own person, leaning on his own experience as against book-knowledge (Ego Ricardus solitarius heremita dictus *hoc melius cognovi quia expertus sum;* or: hoc quod novi, assero), and triumphantly maintains his own views, his individual conviction.

These are the outlines of his live during this—his first—period. No more positive facts or dates can be gleaned from his writings, but in general his life was such as might be expected of a man who, raising a new religious ideal, meets with the hostility of the powers that be, is resisted by the inert mass of prejudice and tradition which always impede progress, and so becomes a martyr to his convictions. Indeed, though he manfully resisted and maintained his ground, he seems at last to have fallen a victim to his enemies. It may be presumed that his troubles at last reached such a climax that his life in the old neighbourhood became unbearable or impossible, and that this was the reason why he removed from thence and went into Richmondshire; but whether the immediate cause was his conflict with the authorities, or the persecution of his detractors, or the desertion of friends and patrons and the difficulty of his living, or whether all these points worked together, we have no means to ascertain.

From that time, however, a new period seems to begin. His life seems to enter into smoother waters. The storm is passed, the tension subsides; he recovers his equanimity and calms down. His works of this period are comparatively free from bitterness and from the excessive subjectivity of his earlier days, and show the serenity peculiar to those that have overcome. He is less personal, less combative, his language more moderate, his assertions are less sweeping and uncompromising.

There are traces to show that he wishes to appear more in line with the general practice of the Church; *f. i.,* if formerly he had said of the contemplative: "Iam non dicit orationes suas, sed in sublimitate mentis positus et amore raptus mira suavitate supra se rapitur et Deo decantare spirituali organo in mirum modum sublevatur"—words which might easily be misconstrued as implying that prayers in that stage were dispensable, we now read in his *Inc. Am.:* "Talis amator Christi non dicit orationes suas *more aliorum hominum etiam justorum,* quia in sublimitate mentis positus atque amore Christi raptus supra se suscipitur in mirabilem jocunditatem, et infuso in se sono divinitus quasi cum quodam neupna canens *preces modulatur*". In the *Incendium amoris* he gives his creed, which is rigidly orthodox, and he emphatically declines to admit reason in matters of faith. In substance, his views are the same as before, but he is more guarded, more conciliatory, in his utterance. The wild exuberance of his former works is sobered down; he is matured by experience and shows the even temper of the sage. His tone is even more pathetic than before, and sometimes seems to rise from an unfathomable depth. Before, he had meant to be a Saint: now, he *is* a Saint, stripped, at it seems, of all earthly concerns and passions.

His remove into Richmondshire seems to have taken place in the earlier half of the third decade of his age. He stayed there for a considerable time. Of his outward life we know nothing beyond the fact that he remained an hermit and for a time had his cell 12 miles from Margaret the recluse of Ainderby. But I am inclined to think that he now was a real hermit, no longer dependant on the goodwill of the great, and really lived retired in solitude, perhaps supported by voluntary contributions of friends. On the whole, however, he seems to have been comparatively at ease and to have had no difficulty about his daily bread. At least he was sufficiently at ease to concentrate his thought on comprehensive works. His literary activity continued with unabated or increased vigour. In his *Incendium Amoris* (an imitation of Bonaventura's Stimulus Amoris) he once more follows up the course of contemplative life from the first conversion to the final perfection—but now in prose, and without the guidance of biblical texts. In other works he is postillator, but now expounds more regularly and methodically whole books of the Bible verse by verse, a task which required a more settled mind, close study, and mature reflection. He so wrote commentaries on the Psalter and Cantica, and on Threni. Besides, he is now more bent upon questions of practical usefulness—so he wrote a direction for priests how to hear confession (in the Mss. combined with Cupienti mihi); expositions of the Creed, the Athanasian symbol, the Pater noster, for the instruction of laymen, &c. All these works are in Latin. But at the some time he now began more largely to write in English.

Foiled in his vast attempts at prostrating the tyrants and regenerating society, he now contents himself with a more moderate aim: he befriends recluses and nuns, and gives his spiritual advice to those that ask. One of his friends was "Margareta reclusa apud Anderby" (Vita), "Margareta anachorita, dilecta sua discipula" (*Form of living*), the Margret Kirkby mentioned in the Prologue (by a later poet) to his English commentary of the Psalms. She seems to have been his good angel, and perhaps helped to smooth down his ruffled spirits. This friendship *was* lasting—it lasted to their lives' end. He loved her "perfecta caritatis affectione", and "used to instruct her in the art of love of God, and to direct her in the ruling of life by his holy institution". He twice cured her, by his mere presence, from a seizure. What a pathetic picture is that given in the Life. She had been ill for 13 days, losing the power of speech and suffering such prickings and pains that she could nowhere find rest. A certain husbandman rides off to fetch R. Rolle. . . . Another friend was a sister in the nunnery of Yedingham (Little Mareis, or De parvo Marisco, in the East Riding—a nunnery founded in 1139 by Roger de Clere for 8 or 9 nuns of the Benedictine order), to whom he dedicated his Epistle *Ego dormio et cor meum vigilat*. Whether the Cecil to whom the *Form of living* is addressed in Ms. Rawl., was also a friend of his, cannot be made out. This relation to recluses was, no doubt, the main reason why he now began to employ the vernacular[15]. The time had long passed when—as in the Ancren Riwle—the ladies were expected to understand Latin: he had perforce to write in English if he wished to be understood; he translates even the few Latin quotations extant in his epistles, and these epistles are all addressed to ladies. So his first English prose works must be assigned to this period. In form, they are epistles, but written in a rythmical, half-poetic prose, interspersed with bits of poetry (ejaculations of love-longing). So the beautiful *Form of living* addressed (in most Mss) to Margaret (the same epistle in which he "instructs her in the ruling of life"), and the no less beautiful 2nd epistle (*Ego dormio &c*),—epistles which I do not hesitate to count amongst the pearls of Old English literature, and which are all the more valuable because they are the first really original productions and the first prose works of medieval English. To the same Margaret he dedicated his English prose *commentary on the Psalms and Canticles*[16] (ed. by Bramley), which is substantially a translation of his Latin *Psalter,* with this difference that, instead of expounding the verses *phrase by phrase* as in the Latin work, he leaves the verses entire and not broken up in phrases, each verse being headed by the Latin text with its English translation (which often agrees with the version given in the Northern Metrical Psalter).—To the same period must be ascribed most of his lyric poems, which form perhaps the best part of his productions—his genius being essentially lyric. Some of them are apparently written to ladies (*f. i.* I p 74. 83). I think I detect his hand in some stanzas inserted in the Vernon version of the old West-Midland song "Swete Ihesu now wil I synge" &c, which certainly bear the mark of his peculiar style (II p. 9 ff.); this—if my assumption be right—would not only prove his acquaintance with the earlier national literature, but directly connect the lyric of the North with that of the West (in Ms. Harl. 2255 &c)[17]. His first lyric attempts were, no doubt, short ejaculations of love-longing, effusions of the canor, and they seem to belong to his earliest works. These he now formed into songs, by combining them, or adding new stanzas on the same tune. Some of these combinations—those inserted in his epistles and written as prose in the Mss (I p 30. 34. 57. 60)—are very irregular in form, consisting of rhyme-tirades of an unequal number of verses, and stanzas mixed together, and somewhat resembling the old French or German laïs. Others are regular poems of even stanzas, but they too exhibit certain irregularities and may be dissolved into ejaculations. His favourite form is the 4-lined stanza (that employed in his Latin poem Zelo tui langueo), but besides he uses a great variety of forms: rhyming couples, rhyme couee, 6 and 8-lined stanzas, alliterative verses (I. 53), and makes freely use of inner rhyme and alliteration, sometimes showing considerable art[18]. He seems to have been in close touch with the popular poetry of his time, and even to have derived some of his themes from it (so I. 73. 373). His lyric poems comprise those extant in Ms. Dd v. 64 (under his name) and most of the poems of Ms. Thornton (though here his name is not given), and probably several of the minor poems of Ms. Vernon, especially some songs to Mary, who, as he expressly states, was next to Christ the object of his amorous effusions. In Ms. Dd they are called Cantica divini amoris, a title also used in John Hoveden's poems. They include addresses of Christ on the Cross to sinfull man, of the poet to Christ on the Cross, songs to Jesus, the Trinity, Mary, poems on mercy, on what is love, on the vanity of the world &c. The lyric fervour, the beauty, the melody of these lines have never been surpassed. He seems to have accumulated and issued his poems in batches, as they are often intermixed with prose sentences. Probably he also wrote some Latin hymns, perhaps those found in Ms. Thornton (I. p 381 and 410).—To the same period may also belong the Meditation on the Passion (I. 83 ff—devotions to be said in following the successive stages or stations of our Lord's Passion—and another meditation on the three arrows on Doomsday (I. 112: in the Mss., however, not given with his name); both written in rhythmical prose, the former intermixed with alliterative verses, the latter with occasional rhymes.

At last—presumably in the beginning of the fourties of his age—he removed to Hampole, and there stayed during the remainder of his life. The reason why he left Richmondshire for the South of Yorkshire, does not appear. One of his epistles (Þe commandment &c, I. 61) is written to "a certain nun of Hampole"—per-

haps it was this lady who invited him there or was instrumental in his coming. The place was a Cistercian nunnery, founded by William de Clarefai in 1170 for 14 or 15 nuns. He there continued his solitary life, having his cell near or in the grounds of the nunnery, and supported by the nuns, who seem to have employed him as their spiritual adviser. This time forms the 3[d] and last period of his life. More details cannot be gleaned of his life, as his later writings are singularly free from personal remarks. But he certainly continued to write in the same pace. Which of his works belong to this period it is difficult to make out in every instance; but I think we shall not be far wrong if we attribute to this time those works in which he appears least personal and subjective, most sobered, most practical; those in which he sums up, and in which he is most engrossed by the life to come. Of this kind is the **Emendatio peccatoris** (or 12 Capitula), which contains an abridged résumé of his doctrines; **De octo viridariis** (in Ms. Magd. Coll. 71, and here ascribed to R. Rolle) in which the verses of the Psalter containing the words misericordia, misericors, miserator, miserere, are connected and bound together in 8 viridaria or gardens of salutiferous herbs (these herbs being the auctoritates psalmorum de Dei misericordia); and his miscellaneous collections of epigrams, aphorisms, sentences, sayings from the Fathers &c., in Latin and English, likewise brought out in batches (as those in Ms. Baliol 224, Reg. 17 B XVII), and which form an important part of his works, he being one of the chief contributors to the stock of northern epigrams then forming (*see* I. p. 421). Of his English works, I ascribe to this period his well-known poem "Þe prick of conscience", which in the descriptions of old age, of death, of the day of judgment, of the pains of Hell and the joys of Heaven, shows the objects then predominant in his mind, and is the most matured of all his works.

But though, as in this poem, he describes the signs of old age, we nowhere in his works find him complaining of his own old age, and when death, so long anticipated, so impatiently desired and prayed for, overtook him at last, it found him still in the prime of manhood. He died, after several years' residence at Hampole, on the 29th of September 1349, probably of the pestilence[19] which in that year raged in the North, not sparing even the remotest and healthiest villages in the county of York (cf. Raine, Fasti Ebor. p. 444, Knyghton col. 2598, Stubbs 1732), and to which his enfeebled constitution could offer little resistance. He was buried at Hampole, and by the nuns regarded as a saint and their patron. Not long after his death his name began to be celebrated for miracles, especially of healing, and pilgrims flocked there not only from the neighbourhood, but from distant counties. The miracles related in the Officium, refer to events of the years 1381-3, and this most likely was the time when the nuns of Hampole, to whom the fame of his sanctity was a source of honour and profit, had his Officium[20] compiled, in view of his expected canonisation, which, however, never took place. His works were kept by the nuns in iron chains, to prevent their being further polluted by the Lollards, who had begun to interpolate his writings in their sense and to give out these interpolated writings as his, so covering their heresies with the authority of his name (*see* Prologue to Engl. Psalter).[21]

A well-preserved portrait of R. Rolle is extant in Ms. Faustina B VI (end of 14th cent.), in a northern poem on the trees of vices and virtues growing in the wilderness of life (falsely attributed to W. Hilton), illustrated by figures of hermits and nuns; he is represented sitting, with a book in his lap, in a white habit, J*hesus* is written in gold letters on his breast, angels above bear a scroll with the words Sanctus Sanctus Sanctus dominus deus sabaoth, pleni sunt celi et terra gloria tua; the picture is surrounded by the legend: A solitari here hermite life i lede, For J*hesu* loue so dere all flescli lufe i flede; Þat gastli comforthe clere Þat in my b*re*ste brede, Might me a thowsand zeere in heuenly strenghe haue stedd. Of the correctness of the likeness we have as little proof as in the case of the portraits of Wicliffe: but the features are certainly such as might be expected in a man of his character, and agree with the description he himself gives of his personal appearance as good-looking, florid, yet pale and emaciated.

R. Rolle was one of the most remarkable men of his time, yea of history. It is a strange, and not very creditable, fact that one of the greatest of Englishmen has hitherto been doomed to oblivion. In other cases the human beast first crucifies, and then glorifies or deifies, the nobler minds who, swayed by the Spirit, "do not live as others live", in quest of higher ideals by which to benefit the race; he, one of the noblest champions of humanity, a hero, a saint, a martyr in this cause, has never had his resurrection yet—a forgotten brave. And yet he has rendered greater service to his country, and to the world at large, than all the great names of his time. He re-discovered Love, the principle of Christ.[22] He re-installed feeling, the spring of life, which had been obliterated in the reign of scholasticism. He re-opened the inner eye of man, teaching contemplation in solitude, an unworldly life in abnegation, in chastity and charity—an ideal not unlike Christ's and Buddha's. He broke the hard crust that had gathered round the heart of Christianity by formalism and exteriority, and restored the free flow of spiritual life. He fought against the absorption of religion by the interested classes, and re-asserted the individual, individual right and conscience, against all tyranny, both seculer and ecclesiastic. He broke the way for the Reformers, and was the predecessor of Wicliffe and Luther, though to his credit it must be said that he himself never left, or meant to leave, the unity of the Church.[23] He was a great religious character, made of the stuff of which the builders of religions are made.

Of all the ideals of humanity—the hero, the sage, the poet, the king—the saint is perhaps the greatest, and that ideal he realised. Besides, he is one of the greatest English writers. He was the first to employ the vernacular. He is the true father of English literature. He revived the alliterative verse. He made the North the literary centre for half a century. He is the head and parent of the great mystic and religious writers of the 14th century—of W. Hilton, Wicliffe, Mirk &c, all of whom received their light from his light and followed in his steps. He shaped the thought of the next generations, and it is his influence when the typical Englishman even of the 15th century is described as a man seldom fatigued with hard labour, leading a life more spiritual and refined, indolent and contemplative, pre-eminent in urbanity but devoid of domestic affection (cf. Gairdner, Paston letters III. p. 1XIII).

His position as a mystic was mainly the result of the development of scholasticism. The exuberant, luxuriant growth of the brain in the system of Scotus called forth the re-action of the heart, and this reaction is embodied in R. Rolle, who as exclusively represents the side of feeling as Scotus that of reason and logical consequence, either lacking the corrective of the other element. Both are antagonists—but both are individualists, who subject the existing system to the test of their individual feeling and thought and, though supporting the dogma even to the exclusion of reason, yet, as individualists, break through that harmony, that "in Reihe und Glied"—catholicity wherein the individual as such disappears. R. Rolle, though following in the wake of Bonaventura, was not a mere repetition of Bonaventura, but, by bringing out his individuality, developed mysticism in the English spirit; his abhorrence of obedience and of a rule, his love of liberty and independence, his practical sense, his democratic tendencies are national features, which impart a new character to his system. But he is not only an Englishman: he is more especially a Northerner, and continues the traditions of the North. His "hermit"—the embodiment of his religious ideal—is a revival of an institution long familiar in the North. His almost morbid love of solitude and isolation, his boldness in defying prejudice, the uncouth, rugged side of his character are northern traits. It is this influence which made him revive the northern alliterative verse and vie with Caedmon in the gift of canor, with Bede as a commentator and epigrammatist. His chief charasteristic as a writer is originality—he is essentially a genius; everywhere he cuts out new ways, lays now foundations. Next, he is preeminently a lyric; whether he writes in prose or verse, he writes from feeling, from momentary inspiration. Besides, he is of a remarkable versatility and facility; he writes with equal ease in Latin and English, in verse and prose, and in all kinds of verse, frequently mixing prose and verse in the same work; he writes postils, commentaries, epistles, satires, polemic treatises, prayers and devotions, lyric and didactic poetry, epigrams. His defects lie on the side of method and discrimination; he is weak in argumentation, in developing and arranging his ideas. His sense of beauty is natural rather than acquired, and his mind is too restless to properly perfect his writings. His form is not sufficiently refined, and full of irregularities; his taste not unquestionable; his style frequently difficult, rambling, full of veiled allusions—much depends on the punctuation to make it intelligible; his Latin incorrect and not at all classic—it is the Latin of his time and, besides, full of solecisms and blunders of his own, it is not surprising that the learned of the guild should have looked down upon his rusticity. But all this cannot detract from his great qualities as a writer—the originality and depth of his thought, the truth and tenderness of his feeling; the vigour and eloquence of his prose, the grace and beauty of his verse, and everywhere we detect the marks of a great personality, a personality at once powerful, tender, and strange, the like of which was perhaps never seen again.

Notes

1 John Wilson in his "English Martyrologe" (1608 & 1640) has it that he died "full of sanctity and venerable old age", but this statement of a late writer is not borne out by any older authority. In the works of R. Rolle, who generally is very communicative about himself, I find no allusion to his old age. The large number of his works, however, proves that he must have attained a fair age. The Vita tells us that he was "exhibited" at Oxford by Thomas Neville. Now this Neville was not born before 1292—5. He may have taken R. Rolle with him while himself going to Oxford for his course, in which case Rolle might be of equal age; but more probably he sent him there after finishing his studies, in which case Rolle would be younger. In his earliest work, the Melum, in which he calls himself juvenculus, puer, pusillus, he prophesies a bad end for the King and Queen: "Reginas quae reprobe regebantur vermes rodent invisibiles; reges a regnis ruent quia sanguis sarcinatus sceleribus duces et divites inaniter decepit", alluding to the misgovernment of Edward II and his spouse. Now the Queen's infamous adultery with Mortimer, to which, it seems, allusion is made, commenced in 1325 and was known in England in 1326. In that year R. Rolle, if born in 1300, would be 26 years, an age which would allow him to call himself juvenculus and puer. So I fix 1300 as the most approximate date.

2 The name, probably Norman, is not found in northern registers of the time. . . .

3 It seems that he passed through an early love with all its bodily consequences. The lady was probably the same young woman who continued to haunt his imagination in the beginning of his conversation (cf. Off., Lect. VII). "Domine deus meus"—he confesses afterwards—"infantia mea stulta fuit, pueritia mea vana, adolescentia mea immunda: sed nunc inflammatum est cor meum amore sancto" (Inc. Am.); "Arripui iter agendum, habitum assumens prae omnibus abjectum; prorsus prospexi ad placitum potentis, sed *prius peccavi,* quod plane me penituit; et potius parabar purgare peccatum quod puer perpetravi, quam aliud addere" (*Mel.*).

4 He had a smattering of Greek, as proved by the many Greek words in his earlier writings (f. i. usya, sophia, cauma, euprepia, onoma, theoria, sophisma, carisma, trisagios), and of Hebrew, as proved by the interpretation of the Hebrew letters in his Postilla in Threnos.

5 The Daltons, extant in many branches, belonged to the inferior families (the gentry) of Yorkshire, who were originally dependents of the great families (the Percys, Nevilles), but had, as the feudal system grew weaker, acquired independence. The feudal system had been introduced in the North by Alan Rufus, a younger son of Eudo Duke of Bretagne, who after the defeat of Edwin, Earl of Mercia, had acquired the vast possessions of this earl and distributed large tracts of his possessions among his more favoured dependents, who in their turn rewarded their followers (the founders of the minor houses). Topcliffe was a dependency of the Percys. . . .

6 This canor is the perpetual theme in his writings. It is also called musica spiritualis, invisibilis melodia, canticum spirituale, sonus coelestis, iubilatio, canorus iubilus, canor iubilaeus, clamor, myrth and soun of heaven; and identified with contemplatio (contemplatio est iubilus divini amoris suscepto in mente sono coelicae melodiae vel cantico laudis aeternae) and perfecta caritas.

7 All this recalls what Bede says of Caedmon: Ipse non ab hominibus neque per hominem institutus canendi artem didicit, sed divinitus adiutus gratis canendi donum accepit. This canor—this divine melody chiming from above and resounding in his breast which henceforth is full of delightful harmony, so that his thought, his very prayers turn into songs to Jesus or Mary and that he now modulates what before he was used to say—what can it mean but the awakening of his poetical powers, which to him appear a miraculous gift imparted at the height of the ecstasis? We have here an instance how R. Rolle takes up the traditions of the North. . . .

8 It is erroneous to call R. Rolle a famous preacher. In the Melum he complains that the hermits are not allowed to preach. In "Cupienti mihi" he states: Sciatis quod de verbis praecedentium patrum illud extraxi et ad utilitatem legentium in quodam brevi compendio redegi, ut quod ego *nondum* in publico praedicando cogor dicere, saltem vobis ostendam scribendo qui necessitatem habetis praedicare ("nondum", he says,

as if possibly he may yet take holy orders later on, like Guthlac; but he never did).

[9] It is advisable that he should live by the work of his hands. . . .

[10] God and the Trinity is to him simply incomprehensible. . . .

[10a] "in Deum *pergere*" is *his* formula for the mystic process, as (the more pantheistic) "in Deum *redire*" that of the German mystics. . . .

[11] Of course, it was ultimately the "trieb" which, being unsatisfied, drove him about and made him ex-centric.

[11a] It is surprising to find the Cain-idea anticipated by R.R. . . .

[12] Perhaps one of the young Daltons who had studied with him at Oxford?

[13] The hermits in Rolle's sense have nothing to do with the order of the hermits or frairs of Knaresborough, founded by Robert Flower or Robert de Knaresborough who, when a monk in New Minister Abbey in Morpeth, resolved to lead a solitary life as an hermit and resorted to the rocks by the river Nid, where, being joined by others, he "instituted his companie in the sect of Friars of the order De Redemptione Captivorum, alias S. Trinitatis" (Dugdale Mon.); or with the Friars Eremites of the Order of St. Augustine, who were brought into England ab. 1250 and soon had 32 houses in England and Wales (they were one of the 4 begging orders, and some of the most celebrated learned men were of their number, as John Waldeby, Robert Waldeby, Capgrave). Piers Ploughman may allude to the latter. Of St. Robert of Knaresborough we have an Engl. metrical life ed. Roxb. Club 1824 by Thomas Drury, in Northern dialect. . . .

[14] His parents, also, seem to have been dead by this time. . . .

[15] Wharton, in his Appendix to Cave's Hist. lit. quotes Archb. Ussher as saying that R. Rolle, in his Commentary on the Psalms, pronounced the necessity of vernacular translations of Holy Scripture. This is a mistake. The error seems to have arisen from a remark to this effect in an exposition of the Pater noster in Ms. Bodl. 938, which may have been reputed a work of R. Rolle, but is of Lollard origin.

[16] This English commentary is undoubtedly genuine; it contains one poetic ejaculation: I wate na betere wele, than in my thoght to fele, the life of his lufynge; of al it is the best, Ihesu in hert to fest, and þerne nane othere thynge (Bramley p. 215), which proves R. Rolle's authorship.

[17] He also was acquainted with, though he did not approve of, the secular songs, the cantilenas carnales, of the day; so he says in the Melum: Nec lira letitiae quam lubrici laudabant mihi libebat, sed et cantum carnalium concito calcavi, *ad Christum convertens quod cantabatur,* Cantilenas quidem de feminis fecerunt—hoc reputavi rurusum ruinam.

[18] The North was for England the school of form; many new forms were here invented and introduced; I even find an attempt at an hexameter, in Ms. Ff 1. 14 (in a Latin treatise on the Hours &c.: "Dolenter refero"):

> Hi sunt qui psalmos corrumpunt nequiter almos:
> Ourelepers, forskyppers, bebbers, momelers quoque stutters. . . .

[19] In the same year, of the same disease, died Rob. Holcot, and Tho. Bradwardine.

[20] The Vita in the Officium is made up of traditions (transmitted probably by Margaret Kirkby) and extracts from R. Rolle's writings; the Miracula is a later work by another author (perhaps identical with the author of the Miracula S. Edmundi regis apud Wainflete, Ms. Bodl. 240).

[21] It is probably on account of his being identified with reformatory tendencies or Lollard heresies, that his canonization was not effected.

[22] He did not, however, come to equally realise the other principle of Christ, the Spirit ("Geist"), both—Love and Spirit—the evolution of the "Trieb" (the Absolute, the "Father"), which first proceeds into Love, and from Love into "Geist" (expressed in the biblical "cognovit eam").

[23] His difference from Wicliffe is briefly this: he is all *love,* Christ-like; Wicliffe all *hatred,* negation.

Geraldine E. Hodgson (essay date 1910)

SOURCE: Geraldine E. Hodgson, in an introduction to *The Form of Perfect Living and Other Prose Treatises,* Thomas Baker, 1910, pp. xi-xxxiv.

[*Below, Hodgson discusses Rolle's major works, summarizing their content and engaging the various controversies that had sprung up around them; she ultimately tends to defend Rolle's standing as a mystic.*]

Richard Rolle of Hampole is the earliest in time of our famous English Mystics. Born in or about 1300, he died in 1349, seven years after Mother Julian of Norwich was born. Walter Hilton died in 1392.

An exhaustive account of Rolle's life is given in Vol. ii. of Professor Horstman's Edition of his works, a book unfortunately out of print. The main facts are recorded in a brief "Life" appended to Fr. R. Hugh Benson's *A Book of the Love of JESUS*. Therefore, it will suffice to say here that Richard Rolle seems to have been born at Thornton, near Pickering, in Yorkshire, in or about 1300; that, finding the atmosphere of Oxford University uncongenial, he left it, and for some four years was supported, as a hermit, by the Dalton Family. By the end of that time, through prayer, contemplation and self-denial, he had attained the three stages of mystical life which he describes as *calor, dulcor, canor*; (heat, sweetness, melody.) The next period of his life was less easy. Having left the protection of the Daltons, and being without those means of subsistence which are within the reach of priest or monk, this hermit depended for his daily bread on other men's kindness. Not that he was a useless person: apart from the utility of a life of Prayer, he could point to counsel and exhortation given; to the existence of converts consequent upon his ministrations. To add to his difficulties, he preached a doctrine of high pure selflessness with which, the average man, in all times, seems to have no abundant sympathy: and to crown all he was endowed by nature with a sensitive temper. His remarkable gifts forced him into public notice; his cast of thought and his temperament were not calculated to win him ease or popularity. Professor Horstman is peculiarly severe to those among his enemies and detractors "who called themselves followers and disciples of Christ." The insertion here of this painful passage would introduce a jarring note; moreover, the raked embers of past controversy seldom tend to the spiritual improvement of the present. An interesting judgment by Professor Horstman on Rolle's place in mysticism is too long for quotation; but the following sentence may be taken as the pith of it:—"His position as a mystic was mainly the result of the development of scholasticism. The exuberant luxuriant growth of the brain in the system of Scotus called forth the reaction of the heart, and this reaction is embodied in Richard Rolle, who as exclusively represents the side of feeling as Scotus that of reason and logical consequence; either lacking the corrective of the other element."

It is consoling to know that Rolle's last years were passed in peace, in a cell, near a monastery of Cistercian nuns at Hampole, where the nuns supported him, while he acted as their spiritual adviser.

In the book mentioned above, Fr. Hugh Benson has translated some of Richard Rolle's Poems, and certain devotional Meditations. In this Volume, four of his Prose Treatises have been selected from the rest of his works, in the belief that they may supplement those parts of Rolle's writings with which, those who are interested in these phases of thought, are already familiar.

The first, *The Form of Perfect Living,* is a Rule of Life which he wrote for a nun of Anderby, Margaret Kirkby, of whom Professor Horstman writes: "She seems to have been his good angel, and perhaps helped to smooth down his ruffled spirits. This friendship was lasting—it lasted to their lives' ends."

This treatise was written of course to meet the requirements of the "religious" life. It has seemed expedient, because supplementary, then, to put next to it his work on *Our Daily Life,* which was meant for those who are "in the world"; and which may give pause to some who might otherwise criticise the first hastily, perhaps condemning it as unpractical, or even objectionable in a world where, after all, men must eat and drink and live, and where some, therefore must provide the necessary means. Most intensely practical is this second treatise, and perhaps nowhere more so than when it meets the needs of those who are inclined to split straws over the definition of the word "good." What *is* a good action?—such people love to inquire, and like "jesting Pilate," sometimes do not "stay for an answer." Richard Rolle has no manner of doubt about his reply. An action must be good in itself, *i.e.,* so he would tell us, pleasing to GOD in its own nature. But the matter by no means ends there for him. This good action must be performed,—and it is this which is, now palpably, now subtly, hard—*entirely* for the sake of goodness, without the slightest taint of self-seeking, of vanity, of secret satisfaction that we are not as other men are, not even as this Pharisee or this Publican.

Such a motive, inspiring each person's whole work, would surely go far to remove what is known as the Social Problem. It would make many a house the dwelling of peace, many a business-place an abode of honour. If we could get back to Richard Rolle's simplicity and to his unmovable faith, then, his goal, even the acquisition of perfect love, might seem to all of us less distressingly remote.

The present rendering has been taken from the longer and more elaborate of the two MSS. containing the Treatise. The shorter form of his work *On Grace* and the *Epistle* have been added in the hope that they may meet the need of all, contemplative or active as they may chance to be.

There is, among his voluminous writings, a curious and interesting *Revelation concerning Purgatory,* purporting to be a woman's dream about one, Margaret, a soul in Purgatory. Amidst much natural horror, not however exceeding that described by Dante, there are many quaint side-lights thrown upon our forefathers' ways of thought; as *e.g.,* when Margaret's soul is weighed in one scale, against the fiend, "and a great long worm with him," in the other; the worm of conscience, in fact. But the work has not been included in this volume, lest it should prove wholly unprofitable to a generation which if it be not readily disturbed by sin, is easily and quickly shocked by crude suggestions concerning its possible consequences and reward. They will find enough, perhaps, in the treatise **On Daily Work**.

If any one should think that there, and in one portion of the treatise **On Grace,** Rolle has dwelt harshly on considerations of fear, rather than on those of love, he must not make the mistake of concluding that these admonitions represent the whole of Catholic teaching on the point. Men's temperaments differ, and teachers, meeting these various tempers, differ in their modes of helping them. Side by side with Richard Rolle may be put the words of S. Francis Xavier, in what is perhaps the most beautiful of Christian hymns:—

> My GOD, I love Thee; not because
>   I hope for heaven thereby,
> Nor yet because who love Thee not
>   Are lost eternally.
>   . . . . .
> Not for the hope of gaining aught,
>   Not seeking a reward;
> But as Thyself hast loved me,
>   O ever-loving Lord!

Moreover, no reader of the Epistle **On Charity** can entertain any doubt as to whether our English Mystic understood the mystery of limitless love.

It is no doubt, easy to complain, as we read certain passages, that Richard Rolle's recommendations are neither new nor original: but if instead of dismissing them as familiar, we tried to put them into practice, we should perhaps have less leisure for idle criticism of others, and ourselves be less evil and tiresome people.

On the other hand, the accusation may be brought that he proposes an impossibly high aim. No doubt, in such a pitch of devotion as is suggested, *e.g.,* in ch. viii. of **The Form of Perfect Living,** some may think they find extravagance: but no doubt it was this same spirit which inspired SS. Peter and Paul, and the other Apostles; which built up the Early Church; which made Saints, Martyrs and Confessors; which suggested such apparently forlorn hopes as that of S. Augustine of Canterbury, when, to bring them the Gospel of JESUS Christ, he bearded the rough Men of Kent, and (according to Robert of Brunne) reaped, as his immediate reward, a string of fishtails hung on his habit, though later, the conversion of these sturdy pagans. It was doubtless, too, the spirit which inspired the best men and women in the English Church, before they began to confuse the spheres of Faith and Reason, and to disregard S. Hilary's warning about the difficulty of expressing in human language that which is truly "in-

comprehensible,"—incomprehensible in the old sense, as in the Athanasian Symbol, "Immensus Pater, immensus Filius, immensus Spiritus sanctus"; till, indeed, men forgot, for all practical purposes that infinity transcends the grasp of finite minds (in fact, as well as in placidly accepted and then immediately neglected theory); and can be apprehended only, and that imperfectly, by the best aspirations of a heart, set of fixed purpose on that high goal.

To the modern Englishman, immersed in business anxieties, imperial interests and domestic cares, the invitation repeated so often by Richard Rolle, to love GOD supremely, may seem incalculably unreal and remote, even though he might hesitate to confess it baldly. But what if the Englishman who so loved GOD, were also the greater Englishman? And what answer does history return to that plain question?

"Richard Rolle," Professor Horstman does not hesitate to write "was one of the most remarkable men of his time, yea, of history. It is a strange and not very creditable fact that one of the greatest of Englishmen has hitherto been doomed to oblivion. In other cases, the human beast first crucifies, and then glorifies or deifies the nobler minds, who swayed by the Spirit, do not live as others live, in quest of higher ideals by which to benefit the race; he, one of the noblest champions of humanity, a hero, a saint, a martyr in this cause has never had his resurrection yet—a forgotten brave. And yet, he has rendered greater service to his country, and to the world at large, than all the great names of his time. He rediscovered Love, the principle of Christ. He reinstalled feeling, the spring of life which had been obliterated in the reign of scholasticism. He re-opened the inner eye of man, teaching contemplation in solitude, an unworldly life in abnegation, in chastity, in charity . . . He broke the hard crust that had gathered round the heart of Christianity, by formalism and exteriority, and restored the free flow of spiritual life."

This passage, to those who feel that there has been no age since the Birth of Christ when the great principles of religious life have been wholly lost, and who remember that Richard Rolle lived in the age of Dante, may seem overstated. But it shews sufficiently at least, and for that reason is quoted here, what a great Englishman he was, and what a debt his unaware countrymen owe him; a debt which they could pay in the way most grateful to him, by listening to his words.

It may be remarked, by the way, that Rolle is not inclined to substitute individualism for the authority of the Church; a change which has been brought against some mystics. There is immense emphasis laid, all through his writings, on the importance of conduct. The penetrating analysis, in ch. vi, of **The Form of Perfect Living,** of the possible sins humanity can commit on its journey through the wilderness of this world, hardly leaves a corner of the heart unlighted; lets not one possible shift, twist or excuse of the human conscience go free. But it all has the Church as its immediate background; the Mystical *Body,* not the individual soul in isolation, is everywhere taken for granted. Man lives not to himself nor dies to himself, even though he be Richard Rolle the hermit, or Margaret Kirkby the recluse, that is the plain teaching of these plain-speaking pages. And all through them too is a tough common sense, and an unusually alert power of observation; and there is perhaps an element of that business capacity, which some of the Saints and Mystics have shewn, in his inclusion among "sins of deed" of "beginning a thing that is above our might"; for in that there is not only pride, but a kind of stupid incapacity surely.

It is quite possible that Rolle's tendency to repetition may tire any one who reads him "straight on," as the phrase is. But it is doubtful whether that be the best means of approach. If he be read in bits, he will prove far more effective: and his ability to hit the right nail on the head, and to hit it wonderfully hard, may occasionally bring his words home to our immediate circumstances with an appositeness that may be more than a coincidence.

In the past, the learned and ignorant alike have been guilty of the operation which may be described as cutting man up into parts: *i.e.,* they have been inclined to treat him now as if he were all intellect, then as if he were all feeling; while to the will a kind of intermediate part has generally been allotted, as if it were the handmaid instead of the master of the other two. And there is still, in some quarters, a tendency to relegate the will and the feelings to an inferior plane, if indeed they be allowed any place at all. In other quarters, the onslaught is made on intellect. Men are bidden to be humble, to become as little children; as if there were any humility in thinking incorrectly or not at all; as if the odd, though suppressed, assumption that children have no intellects had any ground in fact. It is surely a true apostrophe—

> GOD! Thou art mind! Unto the master-mind,
> Mind should be precious.

The Angelic Doctor himself paid a tribute to the importance and special difficulties of intellect, and also to the necessity of uniting it with will:—"the martyrs had greater merit in faith, not receding from the faith for persecutions; and likewise men of learning have greater merit of faith, not [Quoted by Fr. Joseph Rickaby, S.J., in *Scholasticism,* p. 121] receding from the faith for the reasons of philosophers or heretics alleged against it." Richard Rolle, following on the same lines as S. Thomas Aquinas, has nothing of this

spirit of division: the whole being is what he would fain see offered to GOD, whether it be so by Margaret Kirkby, or by those who are "in the world," for whom *Our Daily Work* was written. In the image of GOD was man made, and therefore GOD suffices for all the needs of man's nature: that, at least seems to be the underlying idea when Rolle writes:—"GOD is light and burning. Light clarifies our reason, burning kindles our will." May we not say here too?—"What GOD has joined together, that let not man put asunder."

Above all things, Rolle aims at a perfect balance, culminating in a harmony ruled by one power, and that the greatest in the world, Love. Real love, he asks; not the degraded things to which men give that great name, as to every passing gust of feeling, to every unworthy untamed emotion: but the divine quality, when to the "lastingness," which he requires, is also joined that which is the inner essence of Love, viz., sacrifice. "Love is a life," he writes, "joining together the loving and the loved." And then he remembers the other great gift to men, intellectual sincerity, which has inspired all "who follow Truth along her star-paved way"; and he gives to that its place and due: "Truth may be without love: but it cannot help without it." Even then, the whole tale is not complete; the way of the Saints is not "Primrosed and hung with shade." Love, with Rolle, is no easy sentimentality: it involves definite sacrifice in more directions than one; it demands thought, perseverance, supernatural strength, natural strenuousness; it is not a selfish enjoyment of a circumambient atmosphere wrapping humanity, without responsibility or effort of its own: "Love is a *Life.*"

"Love," he writes, "is a perfection of learning; virtue of prophecy; fruit of truth; help of sacraments; establishing of wit and knowledge; riches of pure men: life of dying men. So, how good love is. If we suffer to be slain; if we give all that we have (down) to a beggar's staff: if we know as much as men may know on earth, all this is naught but ordained sorrow and torment." Then, with that sound sense, which is not the least element in the sum of his attractiveness, he utters a subtle warning against that all too common sin, judging one another: "If thou wilt ask how good is he or she, ask how much he or she loves: and that no man can tell. For I hold it folly to judge a man's heart, that none knows save GOD."

After this it cannot be necessary to say that Rolle is a true mystic. "Many," so he tells us in this same chapter x., "Many speak and do good, and love not GOD." But that will not suffice his exacting demands. A man is not "good" until his interior disposition be all filled and taken up with pure love of GOD. And as he analyses the Christian Character, there is a pleasant blunt directness about this holy man:—"he that says he loves GOD and will not do what is in him to shew love, tell him that he lies."

It is possible that the alarming list of sins of the heart, in chapter vi., may give the heedless and even the heedful matter for grave thought, as each one finds himself ejaculating with spontaneous fear—"Who can tell how oft he offendeth? Cleanse thou me from my secret faults."

Surely no one need fear that the outcome of a study of Richard Rolle will be effeminacy. Not that that indeed is the special temptation of the English: a chill commonplace acquiescence in a convenient, if baseless, hope that somehow "things will come all right," is far more likely to lead them astray than any "burning yearning to GOD with a wonderful delight and certainty." Is not George Herbert's cry apposite still?

"O England, full of sin, but most of sloth!"

Nor can any one argue fairly that this absorption of the mystic is just selfish idleness. It is, so it seems, as we read Rolle's injunctions, of the nature of hard exacting toil. No doubt, there must be those who do the material work of the world; who gain, among other things, those "goods" which go to support the Mystics. But there will be no lack of such workers, through the inroads of religion; the broad ways of daily life are in no danger of contracting suddenly in to the path to the strait gate. Moreover, natural life itself is a poor thing unsupported by an unseen stream of spiritual refection. Here, as elsewhere in the ordered economy of things, two forms of life are found to be complementary. It is true, as Dr. Bigg once wrote:—"If Society is to be permeated by religion, there must be reservoirs of religion like those great storage places up among the hills which feed the pipes by which water is carried to every home in the city. We shall need a special class of students of GOD, men and women whose primary and absorbing interest it is to work out the spiritual life in all its purity and integrity" [*Wayside Sketches,* p. 135]. It is indeed the idlest of criticism that condemns such people as slothful or selfish.

There is one charm in our own Mystics which we may miss in S. John of the Cross or S. Teresa for example; viz., that with all their zeal, there is also an amazing reality and simplicity down at the bottom of it, which may seem to us not present in the rhapsodies of more southern lovers; though in all probability such seeming is purely racial. Nevertheless, we may be thankful if we find the antidote to our national prosaic ways in the sane zeal of others of our nation.

Lastly, as men read, they may be overcome perhaps by despair. This pure untainted selflessness of which Richard Rolle writes almost glibly, how can it be possible here and now? How can men and women, fixed in and condemned to the dusty ways of common life, unable as they are to leave the world even if they would, how can they so much as dream of such unat-

tainable heights? Is there no help for them in the often quoted lines of a later English Mystic?—

> Who aimeth at the sky
> Shoots higher much than he who means a tree.

For plain men and women, the key to the problem may lie in the question put by Robert Browning into the mouth of Innocent XII.:—

> Is this our ultimate stage, or starting place
> To try man's foot, if it will creep or climb,
> 'Mid obstacles in seeming, points that prove
> Advantage for who vaults from low to high,
> And makes the stumbling-block a stepping-stone?

Even though the goal be not reached, to have willed deliberately here the first step may prove to have been not wholly unavailing.

Dom David Knowles (essay date 1927)

SOURCE: Dom David Knowles, "Richard Rolle," in *The English Mystics,* Burns Oates & Washbourne Ltd., 1927, pp. 73-89.

[In the following excerpt, Knowles depicts Rolle as a kind of early Romantic poet—one whose art is spontaneous, natural, personal, and almost rebelliously individualistc.]

The four writers who have now to be considered are very different in mental outlook one from another, and may to some degree be taken as the representatives in English medieval religious life of four distinct types of spirituality. Richard Rolle, the first, is a poet, almost a romanticist; a troubadour of God, spiritual brother of St Francis, throwing off conventional habits, and of an essentially simplifying, outgoing mind. However orthodox he may remain he is always and before all an individualist.

Rolle has had the good fortune to attract a series of able scholars both in this country and in Germany within the last half-century, and in consequence he occupies an honourable, and perhaps disproportionately great, place in histories and manuals of English literature. This is due partly to the varied interest and style of his writings, and partly to the great influence he exercised over others, which appears in the many poems and treatises once ascribed to him; but it is due above all to the simplicity and enthusiasm of his outlook on life. What may be said of Chaucer and Dame Julian may be said pre-eminently of Rolle, that he is of the springtime of English literature, and the early sunlight and fresh dew rest upon his words. It is true also that Rolle had the imaginative mind of a poet, if not a musician, and song and melody are as surely characteristic of his writing as he found them characteristic of the working of grace. His words are always spontaneous and unreflecting; he "does but sing because he must," and such spontaneity, both of language and character, must always most powerfully attract in a world where so much is stale and affected and calculated and insincere.

Rolle wrote both in Latin and English, in verse and in prose. For students of English literature his English works and his verse are naturally most interesting, as are also his translations of parts of the Bible, especially the Psalms—a work in which he anticipated Wyclif, and has earned with some justice the title of father of English prose. Nevertheless, it is rather in his Latin prose treatises that he appears as a mystic, and it is with these that we are at present most concerned. Most of them were translated into English after Rolle's death by Richard Misyn.[1]

The story of Rolle's life has been told in almost identical words by all his editors, but it cannot be altogether omitted here. Its circumstances, in all their originality and picturesque details, which so nearly resemble the preconceived idea of a medieval hermit, have done much to concentrate attention upon him. The chief source for the external events of his conversation is the series of lessons drawn up for insertion in the office to be recited after his canonization.[2] According to this he was born near Pickering in Yorkshire (apparently about 1290), of well-to-do and perhaps gentle parents. It has been suggested that his father was in some way a dependent of the great family of Neville; certainly it was a Neville, sometime archdeacon at Durham, who paid for his education at Oxford. There the influence of the scholastic movement was at its height, but Rolle, unlike Hilton, and even unlike the author of the *Cloud,* found little to attract him in the intellectual atmosphere of the day, if we may believe some of his writings. Recently, however, the attractive suggestion has been put forward that he crossed to France and spent some time at the Sorbonne.[3] This, if correct, would help to explain Rolle's references to his worldly past, which, if his conversion took place immediately after his Oxford days (and in the Middle Ages the university career was begun and ended at a much earlier period of life than now) must be taken as the self-depreciatory exaggerations of a saint. As it is, till this point is settled, and till many other questions of authenticity and chronology in his writings have been decided, no adequate appreciation of his indebtedness to his education can be attempted, since in some writings there is little method and a scarcity of quotation, whereas in others many of the Fathers and ecclesiastical writers of the Middle Ages are quoted.

His decision to leave home and become a hermit was taken without consulting his parents. The lessons tell us that he took two of his sister's tunics, which she brought to him in a wood, and made of them a dress like a hermit's. He then left home, and was supported for a time by Sir John de Dalton, a friend of his father's and himself the father of two boys who had been fellow-students with Rolle at Oxford. It was in this period of his life that the growth in spirituality took place which he has himself described. After several years spent near the Daltons' home he moved from place to place in search of solitude, living for some time in Richmondshire, where he was the friend and counsellor of the ancress Margaret of Anderby, for whom some of his treatises were written. Finally he moved to Hampole, a small village near Doncaster, not far from the field of Towton, and almost in sight of the Great North Road and the London and North Eastern main line to York.[4] Here he lived as director of a convent of Cistercian nuns, here he died in 1349, perhaps of the Black Death, and here his remains were venerated by the nuns and by an increasing number of people as those of a saint. Many miracles attributed to his intercession were recorded, and it is supposed that only the unsettled state of the country and the rise of Lollardy, whose supporters claimed Rolle as one of themselves, cut short the regular process of his cause.

It will thus be seen that both in the knowledge we have of his life, and in the bulk and variety of his writings, Rolle has the advantage over all the English medieval mystics. Yet it cannot be said that his additions to our knowledge of the contemplative life, either in theory or practice, are so significant as those of Hilton or the *Cloud.* Dom Noetinger may be simplifying the matter too much when he says that Rolle hardly does more than reproduce in words the impressions he receives,[5] but the error, if any error there be, is not great. Rolle is throughout intensely personal. All the stages of the spiritual life are described in terms taken from his own experience, and this would seem to have been singularly simple in form. The most typical works of Rolle which are available to the general reader are the *Fire of Love* and the *Mending of Life.* From them we can form a fairly complete idea of the manner of his growth in holiness. Like all those who have been converted to a contemplative life, he looks upon the time spent before his conversion as passed in sin; perhaps we should do well not to regard this as a mere refinement of humility, especially if we bear in mind the possibility of some years spent in Paris. He says:

> Lord God, have mercy on me! My youth was fond; my childhood vain; my young age unclean. But now, Lord Jesu, my heart is inflamed with thy holy love and my reins are changed; and my soul also will not touch for bitterness what before was my food.[6]

After his conversion his growth in the mystical way was gradual. In an autobiographical passage he speaks of a sudden visitation that came to him for the first time, as it were a door opened.

> The high love of Christ standeth soothly in three things: in heat, in song, in sweetness. . . . Forsooth three years, except three or four months, were run from the beginning of the change of my life and of my mind, to the opening of the heavenly door; so that, the face being shown, the eyes of the heart might behold and see what way they might seek my love, and unto him continually desire. The door forsooth yet biding open, nearly a year passed until the time in which the heat of everlasting love was verily felt in my heart. I was sitting forsooth in a chapel, and whiles I was mickle delighted with sweetness of prayer or meditation, suddenly I felt within me a merry and unknown heat. But first I wavered, for a long time doubting what it could be. I was expert that it was not from a creature but from my Maker, because I found it grow hotter and more glad. Truly in this unhoped-for, sensible and sweet-smelling heat, half a year, three months and some weeks have run out, until the inshedding and receiving of this heavenly and ghostly sound. . . . Whiles truly I sat in this same chapel, and in the night before supper, as I could, I sang psalms, I beheld above me the noise as it were of readers, or rather singers. Whiles also I took heed, praying to heaven with my whole desire, suddenly, I wot not in what manner, I felt in me the noise of song, and received the most liking heavenly melody which dwelt with me in my mind. For my thought was forsooth changed to continual song of mirth . . . and in my prayers and psalm-saying I uttered the same sound, and henceforth, for plenteousness of inward sweetness, I burst out singing what before I said, but forsooth privily. . . . Wherefore from the beginning of my changed soul unto the high degree of Christ's love, the which, God granting, I was able to attain . . . I was four years and about three months.[7]

This passage, which has been quoted at some length because it is so typical of Rolle, shows clearly enough the peculiarities of his spiritual experience. Unlike most of the great mystics, he almost always describes it, not in terms of knowledge or ignorance, nor even in terms of love and union, but by the two words, "heat" and "song," taken directly from sense-perception. Indeed, so emphatic is his repetition of these words that we are driven to some sort of enquiry as to the nature of the experience he wished to describe. At first sight—and possibly enquiry will not remove this impression—he seems to stand out of the tradition of the great mystical Doctors, who teach with unanimity that sensible devotion of any kind is to be resisted, and that the permanent grace of contemplation is almost imperceptible, and sometimes least perceptible when most undoubtedly present. Rolle, in opposition to this, writes at times as if during his whole life this "heat" and "song" were at his call; and that his influence was to some extent mischievous, as tending to make would-be contem-

platives strive for some sensible realization of their prayer, is evident from the implied condemnation of Rolle in the *Cloud* and Hilton. Perhaps it is best to acknowledge that Rolle, owing to peculiarities of temperament, lies somewhat outside the normal course. Modern critics are inclined to assume that this "heat" and "song" were auto-suggestions. In the somewhat ponderous terms of modern psychology, "psycho-sensorial parallelisms are set up . . . in certain temperaments," and as a result there may be induced "sense-automatisms, which may vary from the slightest of suggestions to an intense hallucination."[8] In the passage just quoted Miss Underhill proceeds to bring under the heading of sense-automatisms cases of stigmatization and visions. As we have seen, it is not necessary to follow modern psychology to such lengths in all cases, nor should we ever, in regard to such cases as Rolle, be too ready to transfer to a great and sane religious genius theories which modern psychology has only verified in morbid and insignificant personalities. Nor need we assume that a soul touched by powerful grace need follow the ordinary rules of psychology.

Yet even if we assume the immediate cause of Rolle's heat or fire to have been purely natural, this need not reflect on the value of his testimony. It may be that the impalpable touch of the finger of God is thus translated into sense-perceptions. Rolle himself was surprised by his first experience of the heat, and though he is clear that there is nothing imaginary about it, his language suggests that it was in no sense an enlightenment of the intellect. He says:

> More have I marvelled than I showed when, forsooth, I first felt my heart wax warm, truly, and not in imagination, but as if it were burned with sensible fire. I was forsooth amazed as the burning in my soul burst up, and of an unwont solace; ofttimes, because of my ignorance of such healthful abundance, I have groped my breast seeking whether this burning were from any bodily cause outwardly. But when I knew that it was only kindled inwardly from a ghostly cause, and that this burning was nought of fleshly love or concupiscence, in this I conceived it was the gift of my Maker.[9]

However, we have to remember, in our attempts to rationalize Rolle's words, that he is committed to visions and diabolical visitations.[10]

Nevertheless, in spite of the recurrence of "heat" and "song," the chief impression gained from reading Rolle is not that of unusual experiences, but of the deeply loving and pure nature which was the basis and the result of his holy life. The love of God, not the knowledge of divinity, is the one thing needful.

"Alas, for shame!" he says, quoting St Augustine. "An old wife is more expert in God's love, and less in worldly pleasure, than the great divine whose study is vain."[11]

That he may have this love is his continual prayer.

> And yet I come not to as great love of God as mine elder fathers, the which have also done many other profitable things; wherefore I am full greatly ashamed in myself, and confused. Therefore, O Lord, make broad my heart that it may be more able to perceive thy love."[12]

For God alone can satisfy the soul.

> Man's soul is the taker of God only; anything less than God cannot fulfil it: wherefore earthly lovers never are fulfilled.[13]

This life but delays the moment when the lover shall meet his beloved.

> Thou, Lord Jesu, truly art my treasure, and all the desire of my heart; and because of thee I shall perfectly see thee, for then I shall have thee. And I spake thus to Death: O Death, where dwellest thou? Why comest thou so late to me, living but yet mortal? Why halsest[14] thou not him that desires thee? Who is enough to think thy sweetness, that art the end of sighing, the beginning of desire, the gate of unfailing yearning? Thou art the end of heaviness, the mark of labours, the beginning of fruits, the gate of joys. Behold I grow hot and desire after thee: if thou come I shall forthwith be safe. . . . I pray thee tarry not mickle; from me abide not long! . . . Now grant, my best Beloved, that I may cease; for death, that many dread, shall be to me as heavenly music.[15]

No one who reads Rolle and knows the circumstances of his life will accuse him of laxity or softness, but they will scarcely fail to be struck by his insistence—comparable to that of the great St Augustine—on the claims of the heart.

> I dare not say that all love is good, for that love that is more delighted in creatures than in the Maker of all things, and sets the lust of earthly beauty before ghostly fairness, is ill and to be hated; for it turns from eternal love and turns to temporal that cannot last. Yet peradventure it shall be the less punished; for it desires and joys more to love and to be loved than to defile or be defiled.[16]

> Therefore if our love be pure and perfect, whatever our heart loves it is God.[17]

> A soul can not be reasonable without love whiles it is in this life; wherefore the love thereof is the foot of the soul, by which, after this pilgrimage, it is borne to God or the fiend.[18]

Once or twice, also, he speaks almost with sadness of the lack of one to stand with him.

"But would to God thou hadst shown me a fellow in the way,"[19] he exclaims.

And again:

> I wot not soothly by what unhap it now befalls that scarcely or seldom is found a true friend . . . from God it truly is that amid the wretchedness of this exile we be comforted with the counsel and help of friends, until we come to him. Where we shall all be taught of God, and sit in eternal seats; and we shall be glad without end in him that we have loved, and in whom and by whom we have friends.[20]

And in another place, for once sounding the depths scanned by Dame Julian, he says:

> Wherefore when they [sinners] shall be deemed they shall see Christ sharp and intolerable to their eyes because in this life they never felt him sweet in their hearts. . . . Such truly as we now are to him, such a one shall he then appear to us; to a lover certain lovely and desirable, and to them that loved not, hateful and cruel. And yet this change is not on his part but on ours.[21]

But his natural inclination is to the sunshine.

> Therefore the life that can find love and truly know it in mind shall be turned from sorrow to joy unspoken, and is conversant in the service of melody. Song certain it shall love, and, singing in Jesu, shall be likened to a bird singing to the death. And peradventure in dying the solace of charitable song shall not want—if it happen to him to die and not go swiftly to his love. . . . There shall be halsing of love, and the sweetness of lovers shall be coupled in heart, and the joining of friends shall stand for ever. . . . Therefore let us love burningly, for if we love we shall sing in heavenly mirth to Christ with melody, whose love overcomes all things. Therefore let us live and also die in love.[22]

These last quotations have shown Rolle at his best, in the full stream of a deep and direct current of feeling that has rarely found purer expression and that overleaps all the barriers between the modern world and the Middle Ages. The book ends on the same passionate level.

> In the beginning truly of my conversion and singular purpose I thought I would be like the little bird that languishes for the love of his beloved, but is gladdened in his longing when he that it loves comes, and sings with joy, and in its song also languishes, but in sweetness and heat. It is said that the nightingale is given to song and melody all night, that she may please him to whom she is joined. How mickle more should I sing with greatest sweetness to Christ my Jesu, that is spouse of my soul through all this present life that is night in

regard to the clearness to come, so that I should languish in longing and die for love.[23]

The contemplative life, as Rolle saw it, or at least as he has recorded it, is singularly joyful. His fellow-countrymen of the fourteenth century, joyful and far from morbidity as they are, yet suggest a far more arduous and complex scheme of things. Yet even they, taking them as a body of feeling, may be set against too many modern mystics, whose days have been spent in darkness and sorrow and self-reproach. Even St Teresa, who is optimistic in spite of, or owing to, her desire for suffering, shows us a very different outlook on life, and the distrust and introspection of St John of the Cross, Father Baker, and a host of modern saints is too well known to need further indication. How far these apparent differences of view resolve themselves into different aspects of the same view seen by varying tempers of mind, how far either may err on the side of simplicity or complexity, how far, finally, the later and sadder outlook is a child of the sadder and less simple age that has followed upon the Renaissance, is a question too large for these pages. Here it is sufficient to quote a few words of Rolle which show that we may be wrong in assuming that with him was always the sunlight.

> And if it sometimes happen that sweet easiness be not to thee in praying or in good thinking, and that thou be not made high in mind by the song of holy contemplation, and thou canst not sing as thou wast wont: yet cease not to read or pray.[24]

As with almost all contemplatives whose life has been passed in men's eyes, Rolle was driven by outward attack and inward certainty alike to an apology for his form of life, and it is couched in a well-known and valid form of argument.

> Man is not holier or higher for the outward works that he does. Truly God that is the beholder of the heart rewards the will more than the deed. The deeds truly hang on the will, not the will on the deeds. For the more burningly that a man loves, in so mickle he ascends to a higher reward. . . . God forsooth has foreordained his chosen to fulfil divers services. It is not given truly to ilk man to execute or fulfil all offices, but ilk man has that that is most according to his state. . . . Yet there are many active better than some contemplative; but the best contemplative are higher than the best active.[25]

Only on one point does he seem to be opposed to the common teaching of the saints. In one place he asserts that the less holy are sometimes better fitted for the office of ruling souls,[26] but his exact meaning is not clear, as another passage contradicts what he has said before.

Contemplation is God's free gift:

But it is given soonest especially to those who have not lost that thing which is most pleasing to God, by their way of living, that is the flower of their youth.[27]

Rolle nowhere gives a set description of contemplative prayer, but in many places he describes the life of a soul in the state of perfection as a continuous prayer.

> We can forsooth, if we be true lovers of our Lord Jesu Christ, think upon him when we walk, and hold fast the song of his love whiles we sit in fellowship; and we may have mind of him at the board and also in tasting of meat and drink. . . . And if we labour with our hands, what lets us to lift our hearts to heaven and without ceasing to hold the thought of endless love? And so in all time of our life, being quick and not slow, nothing but sleep shall put our hearts from him.[28]

He agrees with Hilton (if it is not the latter who follows Rolle) in saying that illness, fatigue, or too great exertion make actual contemplative prayer impossible, and the contemplative should therefore be discreet.

> Therefore it behoves him that will sing in God's love, and in singing will rejoice and burn . . . not to live in too mickle abstinence.[29]

He also holds, with many of the great contemplative Doctors, that the perfect contemplative is without fear of falling.

> Nevertheless I trow that there is a degree of perfect love, the which whosoever attains he shall never afterwards lose. For truly it is one thing to be able to lose, and another alway to hold, what he will not leave although he can.[30]

Rolle has been called a free-lance in the religious life of his time, and there is much to justify such an opinion in the circumstances of his life—for he belonged to no religious order and was never a priest—and in his intensely personal outlook. At the risk of stressing what is obvious to all readers, it may be remarked that his originality did not extend to doctrine, and that there is nothing in his writings to suggest that he was in any way dissatisfied with the theological position or the ordinary religious practices of the Middle Ages. His temperament and outlook were unusual, but he was neither an innovator nor a reformer. The following passage shows alike his originality and his conservatism.

> Because in the kirk of God there are singers ordained in their degree, and set to praise God and to stir the people to devotion, some have come to me asking why I would not sing as other men when they have

ofttimes seen me in the solemn masses. They have stood up against me, because I fled the outward songs that are wont in the kirks, and the sweetness of the organ that is heard gladly by the people, only abiding among these either when the need of hearing mass—which elsewhere I could not hear—or the solemnity of the day asked it on account of the backbiting of the people. Truly I have desired to sit alone that I might take heed to Christ alone that had given to me ghostly song, in the which I might offer him praises and prayers. They that reproved me trowed not this . . . but I could not leave the grace of Christ and consent to fond men that knew me not within.[31]

Another curious characteristic of his contemplative prayer—to which a parallel may be found in Father Baker's *Confessions*—is his preference for a sitting position while engaged upon it.

And I have loved for to sit: for no penance, nor fantasy, nor that I wished men to talk of me, nor for no such thing: but only because I knew that I loved God more, and longer lasted within the comfort of love, than going, or standing, or kneeling. For sitting I am most at rest, and my heart most upward. But therefore, peradventure, it is not best that another should sit, as I did and will do to my death, save he were disposed in his soul as I was.[32]

It is not easy to form a judgement on Rolle's prose style. Apart from the question of authenticity, which puts several treatises under suspicion, and the large amount of modernization necessary to make him intelligible to the ordinary reader, there is the further difficulty that the greater part of his work, other than translation, is in Latin. Hence many of the extracts given above are specimens of Misyn's prose style, not of Rolle's. A few passages, however, too striking to be passed over, may be quoted from his English Corpus.

Alas! for shame, what can we, who are sinful and foul, say if we consider ourselves good, when they who are most clean and most love God consider themselves most sinful and most vile and most unworthy. . . . For, get who get may, this world is wide enough and good enough to win heaven in; and it is rich enough and pleasant enough and sinful enough to win hell with, flee who flee may. . . . Prayer freely beflowers our souls with flowers of sweetness, with the fairness and sweetness of the fruit falling into meek hearts, which is freely to behold the fairness of God, in all meek virtues, lighting with the beams of his brightness all clean consciences and all meek hearts.[33]

When thou hast gathered home thine heart and its wits, and hast destroyed the things that might hinder thee from praying, and won to that devotion which God sends to thee through his dear-worthy grace,

quickly rise from thy bed at the bell-ringing: and if no bell be there, let the cock be thy bell: if there be neither cock nor bell, let God's love wake thee, for that most pleases God. And zeal, rooted in love, wakens before both cock and bell, and has washed her face with sweet love-tears; and her soul within has joy in God with devotion, and liking, and bidding him good-morning.[34]

Rolle's sources have not as yet, I believe, been thoroughly explored by any editor, and for this again a canon of his writings is necessary. Thus, to take an example, in the **Daily Work** the Fathers of the Church and of the Desert are quoted plentifully, whereas in the **Fire of Love** the obvious quotations are very few. Nevertheless, certain influences can be discerned at work throughout Rolle. Richard of St Victor is traceable, as also are St Augustine, St Bernard, and St Gregory.

Like his followers in English religious life Rolle had a very deep devotion to the holy Name and to the Passion. Indeed, his meditation on the Passion, which has often been printed and quoted, though it is only a development of a theme found elsewhere—as in the *Ancren Riwle*—is perhaps the finest expression of that theme in English, and one of the best examples of Rolle's style. It is worth comparing this little treatise with the many similar meditations on the Passion which have been written since his day. Of the merely pictorial ones few, if any, are superior to his, for Rolle is always successful in avoiding false or strained sentiment, insignificant realism, and far-fetched symbolism.

The general reader will find Rolle at his best and most typical in the **Fire of Love** and **Mending of Life**. Of the minor works the little essay on Prayer is very attractive, as is also, in a different way, the **Meditation on the Passion**. The **Form of Perfect Living,** written for the nun Margaret Kirkby, is very like the **Mending of Life. Our Daily Work,** though interesting in many respects and spiritually valuable, has little mystical teaching, and, indeed, little of Rolle's genuine flavour. It is far more like the *Ancren Riwle,* to which it would seem to have been indebted.

Notes

[1] Misyn translated the *Mending of Life* and the *Fire of Love,* 1434-1435.

[2] See the *Fire of Love,* etc., ed. F. M. Comper, pp. xlv *ff.* The references in this chapter are to this edition.

[3] By that eminent authority on the English mystics, Dom Noetinger of Solesmes, in an article in the *Month,* January, 1926.

[4] For a description of Hampole as it is to-day, see R. H. Benson, *A Book of the Love of Jesus*, p. 226.

[5] *Scala Perfectionis,* ed. Noetinger, Preface, p. 14. "Lors même qu'il discute ou enseigne, il ne fait guère qu'extérioriser ses impressions."

[6] *Fire,* Book I, ch. xii.

[7] *Fire,* Book I, ch. xv. . . .

[8] *Fire,* Introduction, pp. xv-xvi.

[9] *Fire,* Prologue, p. II.

[10] *Minor Works,* ed. Hodgson, p. 53.

[11] *Fire,* Book I, ch. v.

[12] *Fire,* Book I, ch. ix.

[13] *Ibid.,* Book I, ch. xi.

[14] Halse=embrace.

[15] *Fire,* Book I, ch. xvi.

[16] *Fire,* Book I, ch. xvii.

[17] *Ibid.,* Book I, ch. xix.

[18] *Ibid.,* Book I, ch. xxiii.

[19] *Ibid.,* Book II, ch. v.

[20] *Ibid.,* Book II, ch. ix.

[21] *Fire,* Book II, ch. viii.

[22] *Ibid.,* Book II, ch. xi.

[23] *Fire,* Book II, ch. xii.

[24] *Ibid.,* Book I, ch. x.

[25] *Fire,* Book I, ch. xxi.

[26] *Ibid.*

[27] *Minor Works,* p. 151.

[28] *Fire,* Book II, ch. x.

[29] *Ibid.,* Book I, ch. xi.

[30] *Ibid.,* Book I, ch. xix.

[31] *Fire,* Book II, ch. i.

[32] *Form of Perfect Living,* ed. G. Hodgson, ch. x, p. 71.

[33] *Minor Works,* p. 153.

[34] *Form of Perfect Living,* etc., p. 116.

Hope Emily Allen (essay date 1927)

SOURCE: Hope Emily Allen, in an introduction to Writings Ascribed to Richard Rolle, D. C. Heath and Company, 1927, pp. 1-8.

[*Since her standard works of 1927 and 1931, Allen has been recognized as a leading Rolle scholar. In the following excerpts from the introduction to her 1927 volume, Allen discusses her efforts to establish a canon of Rolle's writings; she was the first to argue that* The Pricke of Conscience, *previously considered one of his major works, had been wrongly attributed to him. She also briefly characterizes his mysticism, defending its nonconformity and "wildness."*]

As is true of most of the great mystics, Rolle's life and writings show a striking consistency, and discussion of his biography and of his mystical doctrine are both necessary to give the impression of consistency and idiosyncrasy in his character which is carried away by any one who has read extensively in his works. The literary historian has generally not read Rolle's writings, and he has therefore lost the key to Rolle's canon. Rolle was much read during the later Middle Ages in England, and the lists of manuscripts in the present volume will show that the medieval scribes on the whole did not blunder in their ascriptions. The most serious errors that have found their place in literary history have arisen from the exaggerated attention given by modern writers to medieval mistakes that were sporadic. When the testimony of all the medieval scribes and authorities is seen in the subjoined lists, it will appear that they always give a strong consensus of opinion. The descriptions of the works will offer internal evidence in agreement with the external evidence. Richard Rolle of Hampole would have been a most individual writer in any age, and in the authority-loving Middle Ages his individualism was not easily mistaken. The study of his canon is simplified as a result, and it may be said that almost no uncertainties enter it. In the early part of the work the only conjectures may be said to be those concerned with the dating, a subject which really makes part of the narrative of Rolle's life.

Some aspects of Rolle's character and teaching lent themselves to use by the Lollards, and were abused by them, but these were minor elements; the gospel of mysticism, consistently expressed in his life and writings, is what makes his influence on literary history, when studied from the contemporary sources. Rolle's readers quoted him constantly, and usually his most characteristic passages. The sensational English poem, the *Prick of Conscience,* is never quoted with his name, and it will be seen that the medieval evidence for connecting it with his authorship is negligible. Such evidence as we find is probably due to the existence of an interpolated text coloured by Lollardy, to which, as to an interpolated text of his ***English Psalter,*** his name was probably attached as a safe-conduct. In the end, his influence seems to have become one of the main currents in what may be called 'the Counter-Reformation' directed against Lollardy during the fifteenth century. We shall see that in spite of some heterodox tendencies in his works his books were owned not only by lay persons of high position, but also by ecclesiastics of high rank (cathedral dignitaries especially) and by religious houses (for example, by Westminster and Reading Abbeys, and even by Rievaulx and Fountains, which we may imagine were hostile to Rolle in his lifetime). The popularity of Rolle's work at Syon and Shene Monasteries—the great royal foundations of the fifteenth century—is especially noteworthy, as will be later discussed in detail. It was natural that Carthusians (who were devoted to solitude) often owned his works, but there was a rift in Carthusian unity on the subject of Richard Hermit, for at least one prominent English Carthusian condemned his influence, saying that his writings 'made men judges of themselves'.

Probably at the time of the Reformation 'Richard Hermit's' influence was as great as, or greater than, that of any other medieval English writer of devotional works. The 'cult of the Holy Name of Jesus', in which his, though far from being the only, had probably been the decisive influence, had permeated general popular devotion. A 'Feast of the Holy Name of Jesus', with an office in nine lessons, had been established in the calendars of Sarum, York, &c., with such a pressure of popular devotion behind it that it was able to survive the great change, and to pass over into the calendar of the Church of England, where it still remains. Its persistence has real meaning, for it signifies a concentration of devotion on the Saviour, with the personal warmth more often in medieval times offered to His Mother, or to a saint. This was a characteristic of the later Middle Ages in England which doubtless made easy the simplification of devotion brought about when the cults of saints were swept away at the Reformation. Thus the Festival of the Holy Name of Jesus perpetuates a strain in Richard the hermit's influence which links him with English religious history up to modern times.

Rolle's influence was probably greatest at the time of the invention of printing, and some of his works were edited in the early days of the press. Strangely enough, all but one of the early editions of Rolle were printed on the Continent, where his writings were utilized in the Counter-Reformation of the sixteenth century. Several early English editions give spurious works with his name. Strangely enough, he was not used by the seventeenth-century English Benedictines, Father Baker[1] and Father Cressy, who used other fourteenth-century English mystics, and the continental editions gave the last signs of Rolle's living influence on religious history visible until the revival of interest in mysticism of the last few decades. Horstmann's volumes brought Richard into notice at a time when mysticism was again beginning to be popular among the readers of devotional literature, and Rolle's works have since appeared in modernized editions and been given their full significance in the history of mysticism. Horstmann's work, however, was neither complete nor systematic, and any one interested in the hermit was at a loss to find satisfactory information on his life and writings. So far as possible the raw material for the study of Rolle's life and work will be given in the present volume, and readers can verify all conclusions for themselves. . . .

In conclusion, something should be said as to the meaning in which the words 'mystic' and 'mysticism' are used in the following pages. It should be said at once that Rolle was the simplest possible type of mystic, and accordingly the term 'mysticism' is used in the present work in the broadest possible meaning. He was not given to philosophies nor to apocalypses, and his mysticism depended on the personal and emotional element in his religion. When described from his point of view, it may be defined as a Divine transmutation of his inner life. It was a relation with the Divinity which was not only an influence transforming his consciousness, but was also directly personal. To Rolle, the Divinity was 'Jesus', who was his friend. He held a highly spiritualized and emotionalized conception of friendship, and his friend out of friendly favour granted him, while in this life, a share in celestial experience. Thus Rolle's mysticism meant a concentration of the affections, and a resulting experience of celestial joy. In his own words (as given in two Latin works), contemplation was 'joy of the Divine love taken in the mind with the sound of the heavenly melody'. In an English work he calls it 'a wonderful joy of God's love'. 'That joy', he goes on, 'is in the soul, and for abundance of joy and sweetness it ascends into the mouth, so that the heart and the tongue accord in one, and body and soul rejoice, living in God.' Here we have indicated both the supernatural and the sensuous elements which generally go to make up the mystic's experience, and we have also the emphasis on joy which specially distinguishes Rolle and the mystics of his type. Other mystics in various ways emphasize knowledge, but with these he has very little kinship. His mysticism is not so much a revelation as a life, and that life is joy. . . .

Since, in the following pages, the establishment of Rolle's canon has been the main enterprise, his most extravagantly individual passages have naturally been chosen for quotation. As a result, it is the undisciplined strains in his character that have perhaps especially been brought to the attention: he has often appeared as a self-willed, bitter individualist, something very far from our conception of a Christian saint. This was the impression that he made in his own time on a few readers, as we shall see in the appendix, but it was not the general impression, for he seems to have been esteemed among a very wide circle. The truth is that in his youth sanctity and unregenerate bitterness were strangely mixed in Rolle, but from the first he gave flashes of rare mystical fervour, and of profound devoutness, and, by the end of his life, his works altogether express in a chastened and beautiful manner an idyllic romance, as it were, of the religious life. The later compositions, the four epistles (one in Latin, three in English), have perhaps not been quoted here sufficiently for their virtues to appear. They will probably rank among the classics of the devotional literature of England.

Though the fierceness of Rolle's early moods may disturb the impression of his holiness for some temperaments, this very wildness probably for some readers in the scholastic age had its own attraction of novelty and of vitality. We can use for the reader of Rolle what was recently written for the reader of Blake: 'The buzz of powerful words, the rocking motion of long rhythms, will keep him comatose and inflated in imagination.'[2] If only these moods had been expressed in English, even they might have given us something memorable. As it is, we have them in a bastard Latin, which bores and repels. By the time Rolle died, he had learned a delicate English style that makes us regret his loss the more. First, by his writing Latin, then by his death in mid career, we seem to have suffered one of the premature losses in English literature. In Rolle the later Middle Ages had an English prose-writer of great promise and of some achievement. On the whole he writes like a modern, but it is his peculiar charm that at times the Anglo-Saxon literary traditions break through, giving his prose cadences and ornaments archàic, but in his case, instinctive. Thus he gives the rare, perhaps unique, example of a style truly belonging to the Middle Age of English prose—something that inherits from the rich national literature before the Conquest as well as from the international traditions of writing brought over by the Normans (which now monopolize our literary expression). Fortunately Rolle's compositions sometimes expressed the vivacity of his temperament, and they sometimes therefore seem to give us the veritable utterances of a medieval Englishman, speaking with the human directness and intelligibility of a modern.

Notes

[1] Father Baker seems to have modernized the *Remedy Against Temptations* which was printed by Wynkyn de

Worde as Rolle's though it was not his (J. N. Sweeney, *Father Augustine Baker,* London, 1861, p. 92, and *infra,* p. 360).

[2] Alan Porter in *The Spectator,* June 26, 1926, p. 1086.

Frances M. M. Comper (essay date 1928)

SOURCE: Frances M. M. Comper, "Of the Union of the Soul with Christ: And How Perfect Love Stands in Heat and Song and Sweetness: And of the Three Degrees of This Love," in *The Life of Richard Rolle,* J. M. Dent & Sons Limited, 1928, pp. 98-124.

[*Aside from the Office composed soon after Rolle's death, Comper's biography was the first extended account of Rolle's life. In the following excerpt, she treats in detail the pinnacle of Rolle's union with God.*]

Richard nearly always speaks of mystical contemplation in terms of love. "To me it seems that contemplation is the joyful song of God's love taken into the mind with the sweetness of angels' praise." Correctly speaking love is the goal of mystical contemplation, but with Richard these two are inextricably involved, in spite of the fact that he writes a chapter on Love, and another on Contemplation, in **The Mending**. **The Fire of Love** is really a book of contemplation; his lyrics are songs of "love-longing," expressing his yearning after Union with God. Love is the keynote of all he writes, but when his feelings cannot be contained he breaks forth into lyrical rhapsodies as we often find in **The Fire,** but these are not in the actual form of verse as are the lyrics. To say, as M. Joly does, that "Le mysticisme, c'est l'amour de Dieu," or that the mystic is "one who has fallen in love with God," is, of course, inadequate as a definition, but is very true as a *description* of Richard's mysticism.

He is most akin with the Spanish mystics of a later date, and shares with them their dislike of abstractions and metaphysical subtleties. Owing but little to his immediate predecessors, he drew largely upon the Scriptures and the writings of the doctors of the early Church, as did the Spaniards.

This mystical love, although it is a personal love for the Beloved, is not selfish or merely emotional; it is supernatural. The will is its pivot, and the will must be purified and strengthened by suffering. All mystics are emphatic on this point. They teach it, if not by words, by their lives. Richard dwells but little upon pain because when he writes he has attained to the way of Union, and his book on contemplation, which he names so fittingly **The Fire of Love,** is not so much a guide for others as the expression of his own intimate experience of love.

Mgr. Farges in his latest work[1] has pointed out that the chief virtue of the Unitive Way is the Union of perfect Love, or "the blending of our life with God through our Lord Jesus Christ." It is this love which Richard never tires of describing under the terms of heat, sweetness and song. He tries by these figures to convey what in the language of psychology we should call the *projection* of the soul into God, and her *identification* with God through the humanity of Christ; so that henceforth God and the soul are one. "Love truly suffers not a loving soul to bide in itself, but ravishes it out to the Lover; so that the soul is more there where it loves, than where the body is, that by it lives and feels" (*The Mending,* p. 230). And in *The Fire* he says: "A better dwelling-place nor sweeter found I never, for it has made me and my love one, and made one out of two" (p. 187).

Some have tried to convey this sense of Union in terms of light and radiance, and have told us how they have felt themselves irradiated by a supernatural brilliance which seemed to bathe their whole being in a veil of light, so that they were clothed in light "as it were with a garment." But whether the experience comes by means of light or heat, it is the same Spirit who inspires our soul, "and lightens with celestial fire":

> Thy blessed unction from above
> Is comfort, life, and fire of love.

The experience must take a different form according to the temperature of the one who receives it. In every case with this sense of light or of heat there flows into the heart an overwhelming sweetness and joy. And it is a generating joy, which inspires, and does not rest in its own satisfaction. As Père Laberthonnière (from whom we have already quoted) expresses it:

> It is by loving that we get beyond ourselves, that we lift ourselves above our own temporal individuality. It is by loving that we find God and and other beings, that we rediscover ourselves. Nor do we find God and all the other beings and our true selves for any purpose other than to love again. And thus it is ever, without pause or ending. There is no end to love, for it is self-generating, it is eternally reborn from itself, eternally renewed and expanded. Love is at once light, heat and life.[2]

Love therefore to the mystic is no soft indulgence to lull the heart to rest, but a burning fire to inspire it to work out his salvation; a fire which is inflamed by the contemplation of the cross of Christ.

As Mgr. Farges says, the Union which was the object of Christ's prayer before His Passion is not that passive or mystical union in which the powers are suspended, but pure love which lives only for the glory of God; so that we try to unite our lives, as did Christ,

with God, "as far as the difference in nature and substance will allow a human being to do."

This Divine Union to which Richard attained finds perhaps its fullest expression in *The Fire* and in the lyrics, both of which were written not so much for the instruction and help of others as to ease his heart of this consuming love. But such intimate love of a personal Christ can only be had at the price of suffering and struggle. The soul must be purged by interior trials, by calumny and misunderstanding, and consequent loneliness. By such things it is detached from the exterior world which becomes of less and less importance, and as the love for self dwindles the love for God grows. The Carthusian motto "Stat crux dum volvitur orbis" is to the mystics a great reality. Their hearts are drawn upwards by aspiration and remain fixed upon the cross, while the world revolves as a globe below.

Richard speaks of love as a mystery, which most certainly it is, for the soul "would hie the quicklier to do God's will if she should perceive any hard thing she might offer for that cause."

Pain, hardness, suffering must be where love is, but it is turned to delight when borne for love's sake. Love is the true philosopher's stone by which the dross of pain is converted to the gold of endless joy in the Beloved, for this supernatural love eliminates pain.[3]

In his earlier book, the *Melum,* we find, as we should expect, the note of suffering more in evidence, but there is none of the agonising experiences of mental and spiritual torture which is so marked a feature in the life of St. Teresa, and which leave us aghast at the needless pain which they depict. Take for example this passage:

> I know not who could have invented such torture for one who felt bound to obey the counsel given her by her confessor, for she would have thought her soul was at stake had she disobeyed him.

and we know that here, as in many other such references, she is speaking of herself.

"Such torture" would have been impossible in Richard's case. Apart from the fact that, unlike Teresa, he was under no vow of religious obedience, his nature would have prohibited him from following direction which his conscience told him was mistaken. Love was alike his guide and his goal. He goes straight towards his Beloved by the urge of love. "Truly in the sweetness of high love the conscience shines."

Thus he is led by love to the source of all love. His outlook is objective rather than subjective. Although constantly harassed by temptations they seldom come to him under the veil of sanctity, as they so often seem to have done to the saintly women who have left their records behind them. We have no trace in Richard of any undue dependence upon direction. He speaks of the "shrift father," but always in connection with sin, never with direction. In our modern usage of the word "confession" when we mean "shrift," or the sacrament of penance, we have confused the issues. Richard himself became in later life "confessor" to the nuns at Hampole, but we have no certain evidence that he was a priest; for direction and absolution were then held always as two distinct things. Surely the most important virtues for a confessor are simplicity and all lack of scrupulosity, and in these Richard must have been accounted great, and perhaps we may hold this as not the least of the claims he has upon our sympathy to-day.

Though there is a gentler element in Richard than in St. John of the Cross, they are alike. St. John depicts mental agony in abundance, but as with Richard it is the suffering and thirst of the soul after God; it is not the cry of a soul tortured by the clumsy knife of an earthly surgeon, as with St. Theresa, but that of a Prometheus Bound, and his four books read like a great spiritual drama. There is no dramatic element in Richard yet he is nearer to St. John than to Teresa. Though there is little likelihood that the Spanish mystic ever read the writings of the Englishman who so long preceded him, yet the likeness to Richard in his description of love in *The Living Flame* is so striking as to be worth comparing.

First let us read what Richard says in his prologue to *The Fire:*

> More have I marvelled than I showed when, forsooth, I first felt my heart wax warm, truly, and not in imagination, but as if it were burned with sensible fire. I was forsooth amazed as the burning in my soul burst up, and of an unwont solace; ofttimes, because of my ignorance of such healthful abundance, I have groped[4] my breast seeking whether this burning were from any bodily cause outwardly. But when I knew that it was only kindled inwardly from a ghostly cause, and that this burning was nought of fleshly love or concupiscence, in this I conceived it was the gift of my Maker. Gladly therefore I am molten into the desire of greater love; and especially for the inflowing of this most sweet delight and ghostly sweetness; the which, with that ghostly flame, has pithily[5] comforted my mind.

If he had not known it he would have thought it impossible for any man to feel such an experience in this world:

> First truly before this comfortable heat, and sweetest in all devotion, was shed in me, I plainly trowed

such heat could happen to no man in this exile: for truly so it enflames the soul as if the element of fire were burning there. Nevertheless, as some say, there are some, burning in the love of Christ, because they see them despising this world, and with busyness given only to the service of God. But as it were if thy finger were put into fire it should be clad with sensible burning, so, as beforesaid, the soul set afire with love, truly feels most very[6] heat; but sometimes more and more intense, and sometimes less, as the frailty of the flesh suffers.

But none could suffer it for long:

> O who is there in mortal body that all this life may suffer this great heat in its high degree, or may bear for long its continual existence? Truly it behoves him fail for sweetness and greatness of desire after so high an outward love; and no marvel though many, passing out of this world, full greedily would catch it and yearn after it with full hot desire; so that unto this honey-sweet flame with wonderful gifts of mind he might yield his soul, and so be taken and forthwith enter the companies of them that sing praises to their Creator withouten end. (pp. 11-12.)

And now compare St. John of the Cross. He is speaking of the awakening of God in the soul, and the soul's consequent awakening to the realisation of God's presence within it:

> Then occurs the most delicate touch of the Beloved, which the soul feels at times, even when least expecting it, and which sets the heart on fire with love, as if a spark had fallen upon it and made it burn. Then the will in an instant, like one roused from sleep, burns with the fire of love for God, praises Him and gives Him thanks, worships and honours Him, and prays to Him in the sweetness of Love. (Cant. xxv. 5.)

And again in *The Living Flame,* paraphrasing the stanza:

> O sweet burn
> O delicious wound,
> O tender hand, O gentle touch
> Savouring of everlasting life
> And paying the whole debt,
> In destroying death thou hast changed it into life,

he comments:

> This is an infinite Fire of Love, so when God touches the soul somewhat sharply, the burning heat within it becomes so extreme as to surpass all the fires of the world. This is why the touch of God is said to "burn," for the fire there is more intense and more concentrated, and the effect of it surpasses that of all other fires . . . the burning of fire does not distress

(the soul) but gladdens it, does not weary but delights it and renders it glorious and rich. This is the reason why it is said to be *sweet.* (ii. 3-4.)

And this again recalls Richard:

When a soul is on fire with love . . . it will feel as if a seraph with a burning brand of love had struck it, and penetrated it, already on fire, as glowing coal, or rather as a flame, and burns it utterly. And then in that burn the flame rushes forth and surges vehemently, as in a glowing furnace or forge. . . . Then the soul feels that the wound it has received is delicious beyond all imaginatin. . . . It feels its love to glow, strengthen, and refine itself to such a degree as to seem to itself as if seas of fire were in it, filling it with love. . . . In this state of life, so perfect, the soul is as it were keeping a perpetual feast with the praises of God in its mouth, with a new song of joy and love. . . .[7] (ii. 10-11.)

The heat of love is, of course, a common simile with many mystical writers, more especially with St. Bernard; and sweetness is also often employed as descriptive of mystical states, but in his use of song and of music to express his union with God Richard is almost unique. With him the "inshedding and receiving of this heavenly and ghostly sound" followed his first experience of "the heat of everlasting love" which rested with him for about nine months.[8] It is possible that he may have borrowed this simile from Augustine who also uses it,[9] but that seems doubtful. It seems too spontaneous and too much a part of Richard's nature to be borrowed. It is a theme upon which he most constantly dwells, and he also speaks of contemplation as *musica spiritualis, invisibilis melodia, canticum spirituale, sonus coelestis, iubilatio, canorus iubilus, clamor;* and in his English works there are many references to this heavenly "myrth" and "melodie," and "soun of heaven"; and, as we have already seen, he identifies contemplation with this divine melody.

In chapter xiv. of **The Fire** he explains what he means by this *calor* or *fervor, canor* and *dulcor.* Yet, before we begin to read what may appear to be a definition, let us guard ourselves against thinking that any statement which Richard seems upon some sudden impulse to give is complete. We seize upon it with delight as upon a plank in a morass, only to find our hopes shattered; for he has turned aside to another thought, or breaks out into some rhapsody of love. He must be free of any such trammel as an exact and comprehensive definition, and to try to formulate one from anything he says is as difficult and impossible a task as it would be to imprison into musical notation the song of the nightingale; to which bird he compares himself:

In the beginning of my conversion . . . I thought I would be like the little bird that languishes for the love of his beloved, but is gladdened in his longing, when he that it loves comes, and sings with joy, and in its song also languishes, but in sweetness and heat. (p. 190.)

He seldom goes back upon what he has said, but he often modifies or enlarges upon it, so as to make his meaning obscure.

A modern French writer who has recently translated **The Mending of Life** describes Richard's style by this apt simile: "Nous dirions volontiers qu'il est clair par places, comme est claire l'eau de la petite rivière que les arbres surplombent et qui est tachée par le soleil de larges plages lumineuses."[10]

Dr. Horstman, who always thinks of Richard Rolle as a typical "Saxon," gives this interesting and true account of the workings of his mind:

The Saxon, kept from satisfaction, is in perpetual unrest, perpetually consumed by the *trieb* which he resists; a prey to confused feelings and conceits which throng upon him and rapidly succeed each other; of unbounded imagination; his mind is too full, too embarrassed to find expression, to sift, arrange, and lay clear its conceptions; too restless to follow and develop a particular object until it is properly brought out and perfected. His ideas, born in the immediate truth of his own sensation and experience, are right enough; he is an original thinker and has plenty of common sense; his difficulty lies in the forming.[11]

Therefore for our own enjoyment of Richard we had better steer as clear of definitions as he did, but such as he has given us I shall now try to set forth.

He tells us that "seeking in Scripture" he found "the high love of Christ soothly stands in three things: in heat, and song, and sweetness," and that

in these three that are tokens of most perfect love, the highest perfection of Christian religion without all doubt is found; and I have now, Jesu granting, received these three after the littleness of my capacity. Nevertheless I dare not make myself even to the saints that have shone in them, for they peradventure have received them more perfectly. Yet shall I be busy in virtue that I may more burningly love, more sweetly sing, and more plenteously feel the sweetness of love. (p. 66.)

And then he goes on to define these three:

Soothly, *heat* I call it when the mind is truly kindled in love everlasting; and the heart in the same manner, not hopingly but verily, is felt to burn. For the heart turned into fire gives the feeling of burning love.

Song I call it when in a soul the sweetness of everlasting praise is received with plenteous burning, and thought is turned into song; and the mind is changed[12] into full sweet sound.

These two are not gotten in idleness, but in high devotion; to the which the third is near, that is to say *sweetness* untrowed. For heat and song truly cause a marvellous sweetness in the soul; and also they may be caused by full great sweetness. (p. 67.)

And in his commentary on the Canticles he thus expresses how this gift of *song* acts upon him who receives it:

Now he does not say his prayers but, in a condition of mental exaltation and a rapture of love, he is carried away beyond himself with a marvellous sweetness and is enabled in a wonderful manner to sing to God with a spiritual instrument.

But for the enjoyment of these three gifts rest is essential. In many places he stresses this point, e.g. in the chapter from which we have cited (see p. 94).

And in *The Form* he asks:

In what state may men love God most? I answer in such state as it be that men are in most rest of body and soul, and least occupied with any needs or business of this world. For the thought of the love of Jesus Christ and of the joy that lasts aye seeks outward rest, so that it be not hindered by comers and goers, and occupation of worldly things; and it seeks within great silence from the annoyances of desires, and of vanities and of earthly thoughts. And especially all who love contemplative life, they seek rest in body and soul. For a great Doctor says: "They are God's throne who dwell still in one place, and are not running about but in sweetness of Christ's love are fixed."

He gives his own experience:

And I have loved for to sit, for no penance nor fantasy, nor that I wished men to talk of me, nor for no such thing, but only because I knew that I loved God more, and longer lasted within the comfort of love, than going, standing or kneeling. For sitting am I in most rest and my heart most upward.

It is curious how often he refers to "sitting," and yet he seems conscious that it is his own idiosyncrasy, for he adds: "But therefore, peradventure, it is not best that another should sit, as I did and will do till my death, save he were disposed in his soul as I was."[13]

From the passage which we have just cited *sweetness* seems to be always the concomitant of *heat* and *song;*

at once the cause and the effect, and can therefore hardly be thought of as existing apart, *per se.*

We shall find this note of song and melody in the joy of love in all Richard says or sings, beside it the progress of the soul is of minor importance. It is God rather than the soul which is the theme of all he writes; even when he speaks of actual sin it is from the objective point of view, and with no morbid dwelling upon or analysis of self. The more we read his works the more noticeable this seems, especially in comparison with contemporary continental writers, and with later English mystics. He appears to be one of the most objective mystical writers of whom we have knowledge.

Love, according to Richard, is possessed of *three degrees,* which correspond to those given us by Richard of St. Victor in *De gradibus caritatis;* to which the Victorine has added a *fourth,* viz. "Love Insatiable." Between the two Richards there is great similarity of thought, and to that we must return in the following chapter, on the sources upon which Rolle drew. We find these degrees described most clearly in **The Mending, The Form,** and more briefly in **The Commandment of Love to God**. These passages I shall now cite in full.

(I) *The Mending.*[14]

There are soothly three degrees of Christ's love, by one or another of which he that is chosen to love profits. The first is called, unable to be overcome; the second, unable to be parted; the third is called singular.[15]

Then truly is love *unovercomeable* when it can not be overcome by any other desire. When it casts away lettings, and slakes all temptations and fleshly desires; and when it patiently suffers all griefs for Christ, and is overcome by no flattery nor delight. All labour is light to a lover, nor can a man better overcome labour than by love.

Love truly is *undeparted* when the mind is kindled with great love, and cleaves to Christ with undeparted thought. Forsooth it suffers Him not to pass from the mind a minute, but as if he were bound in heart to Him it thinks and sighs after Him, and it cries to be holden with His love that He may loose him from the fetters of mortality, and may lead him to Him Whom only he desires to see. And most this name JESU he in so mickle worships and loves that It continually rests in his mind.

When therefore the love of Christ is set so mickle in the heart of God's lover and the world's despiser that it may not be overcome by other desire of love, it is called *high.* But when he holds undepartedly to

Christ, ever thinking of Christ, by no occasion forgetting Him, it is called *everlasting* and *undeparted*. And if this be high and everlasting, what love can be higher or more?

Yet there is the third degree that is called *singular*. It is one thing to be high, and another to be alone; as it is one thing to be ever presiding, and another to have to fellow. Truly we may have many fellows and yet have a place before all.

Truly if thou seekest or receivest any comfort other than of thy God, and if peradventure thou lovest the highest, yet it is not singular. Thou seest therefore to what the greatness of worthiness must increase, that when thou art high thou mayest be alone.

Therefore love ascends to the singular degree when it excludes all comfort but the one that is in Jesu; when nothing but Jesu may suffice it. The soul set in this degree loves Him alone; she yearns only for Christ, and Christ desires; only in His desire she abides, and after Him she sighs; in Him she burns; she rests in His warmth. Nothing is sweet to her, nothing she savours, except it be made sweet in Jesu; whose memory is as a song of music in a feast of wine. Whatever the self offers to her [besides] it or comes into mind, is straightway cast back and suddenly despised if it serve not His desire or accord not with His will. She suppresses all customs that she sees serve not to the love of Christ. Whatever she does seems unprofitable and intolerable unless it runs and leads to Christ, the End of her desire. When she can love Christ she trows she has all things that she wills to have, and withouten Him all things are abhorrent to her and wax foul. But because she trows to love Him endlessly she steadfastly abides, and wearies not in body nor heart but loves perseveringly and suffers all things gladly. And the more she thus lives in Him the more she is kindled in love, and the liker she is to Him.

No marvel loneliness accords with such a one that grants no fellow among men. For the more he is ravished inwardly by joys, the less is he occupied in outward things; nor is he let by heaviness or the cares[16] of this life. And now it seems as if the soul were unable to suffer pain, so that not being let by anguish, she ever joys in God.

(2) *The Form of Living*[17]

Three degrees of love I shall tell thee, for I would that thou mightest win to the highest. The first degree is called *Insuperable*. The second *Insuperable*. The third is *Singular*.

(1) Thy love is *Insuperable* when nothing that is contrary to God's love overcomes it, but it is stalwart against all temptations, and stable, whether thou beest in ease or in anguish, or in health or sickness;

so that men think that thou wouldest not, even to have all the world without end, make God angry at any time; and thou wert liefer if so it should be, to suffer all the pain and woe that might come to any creature, before thou wouldest do any the thing that should displease him. In this manner shall thy love be Insuperable, that nothing can bring it down, but it may aye spring on high. . . .

(2) *Inseparable* is thy love when all thine heart and thy thought and thy might is so wholly, so entirely and so perfectly fastened, set and established in Jesus Christ that thy thought comes never from Him, never departs from Him, sleeping excepted; and as soon as thou awakest thine heart is on Him; saying *Ave Maria* or *Gloria Tibi Domine* or *Pater Noster* or *Miserere mei Deus,* if thou hast been tempted in thy sleep; or thinking on His love and His praise as thou didst waking. When thou canst at no time forget Him, waking or sleeping, whatso thou dost or sayst, then is thy love *Inseparable*. . . .

(3) The third degree is highest and most wondrous to win. That is called *Singular,* for it has no peer. *Singular* love is when all comfort and solace is closed out of thine heart, but of Jesus Christ alone. Other joy it delights not in. For the sweetness of him that is in this degree is so comforting, and lasting in His love, so burning and gladdening, that he or she who is in this degree can as well feel the fire of love burning in their soul, as thou canst feel thy finger burn if thou puttest it in the fire. But that fire, if it be hot, is so delectable and so wonderful that I cannot tell it.

Then thy soul is Jesu loving: Jesu thinking: Jesu desiring: only in the desire of Him breathing: to Him singing: of Him burning: in Him resting. Then the song of loving and of love has come; then thy thought turns into song and into melody; then it behoves thee to sing the psalms which before thou saidst. Then thou must be long about few psalms; thou wilt think death sweeter than honey for then thou art full sicker[18] to see Him whom thou lovest. Then mayest thou boldly say: "I languish for love"; then mayest thou say: "I sleep and my heart wakes."

In the *first degree* men may say: "I languish for love," or "I long in love"; and in the *second degree* also; for languishing is when men fail for sickness, and they who are in these two degrees (fall) from all covetousness of this world, and from lust and liking of sinful life, and set their will and their heart to the love of God—therefore they may say "I languish for love"; and much more that are in the second degree than in the first.

But the soul that is in the *third degree* is all burning fire, and like the nightingale that loves song and melody, and falls (dies) for great love; so that the soul is only comforted in loving and praising of God, and till death come, is singing ghostly *to*

IHESU, and *in IHESU,* and *IHESU,* not bodily crying with the mouth—of that manner of singing I speak not, for both good and evil have that song.

And this manner of song have none unless they be in this *third degree* of love, to the which degree it is impossible to come but in a great multitude of love. Therefore if thou wilt wot what kind of joy that song has, I tell thee that no man wots, save he or she who feels it, who has it, and who loves God singing therewith. One thing I tell thee, it is of heaven and God gives it to whom He will, but not without great grace coming before. Who has it, he thinks all the song and all the minstrelsy of earth naught but sorrow and woe (compared) thereto. In sovereign rest are they that may get it. . . .

In the *first degree* are many; in the *second degree* are full few; but in the *third degree* are scarcely any; for ay the greater that the perfection is the fewer followers it has.

In the *first degree* men are likened to the stars; in the *second* to the moon; in the *third* to the sun. Therefore says S. Paul: "Others of the sun, others of the moon, others of the stars"; so it is of the lovers of God. In this *third degree,* if thou mayst win thereto, thou shalt know more joy than I have told thee yet.

And there follows, as a specimen of the songs of love, the lyric which is given on p. 224, "**When wilt thou come to comfort me?**" We notice that the song of the third degree of love is of heaven, and "God gives it *to whom He will, but not without great grace coming before,*" Richard has many a time shown that this grace is the result of painful discipline; but when the soul has attained to the third degree then it seems as if she *were unable to suffer pain.* All pain is now turned to joy by her love.

Is it surprising that to savour love like this the soul must cease from the love of this world?

O my soul, cease from the love of this world and melt in Christ's love, that always it may be sweet to thee to speak, read, write, and think of Him; to pray to Him and ever to praise Him. O God, my soul, to Thee devoted, desires to see Thee! She cries to Thee from afar. She burns in Thee and languishes in Thy love. O Love that fails not, Thou hast overcome me! O everlasting Sweetness and Fairness, Thou hast wounded my heart, and now overcome and wounded I fall. For joy scarcely I live, and nearly I die; for I may not suffer the sweetness of so great a Majesty in this flesh that shall rot.

All my heart truly, fastened in desire for JESU, is turned into heat of love, and it is swallowed into another joy and another form. Therefore O good Jesu have mercy upon a wretch. Show Thyself to me that longs; give medicine to me hurt. I feel myself not sick, but languishing in Thy love. He that loves Thee not altogether loses all; he that follows Thee not is mad. Meanwhile therefore be Thou my Joy, my Love, and Desire, until I may see Thee, O God of Gods, in Syon.

In *The Commandment of Love* he puts it more briefly:

And that thou mayst come to the sweetness of God's love I set here three degrees of love in the which thou be waxing.[19]

The first degree is called *Insuperable,* the tother *Inseparable,* the third *Singular.*

Thy love is *insuperable* when no thing may overcome it; that is neither weal nor woe, ease nor anguish, love of flesh nor liking of this world; but ay it lasteth in God though it were tempted greatly; and it hateth all sin, so that no thing may slake that love.

Thy love is *inseparable* when all thy thoughts and all thy wills are gathered together and fastened wholly in Jhesu Christ, so that thou may no time forget Him, but ay thou thinkest on Him; and therefore it is cleped inseparable for it may not be departed from thought of Jhesu Christ.

That love is *singular* when all thy delight is in Jhesu Christ, and in none other thing findest comfort or joy. In this degree is love stalwart as death, and hard as hell; for as death slays all living things in this world, so perfect love slays in a man's soul all fleshly desires and earthly covetousness. And as hell spareth not to dead men, but tormenteth all that come thereto, so a man that is in this degree of love, not only he forsaketh the wretched solace of this life, but also coveteth to suffer pain for God's love.[20]

In *The Fire* yet another definition is given of the *strength* of love:

Love forsooth has a diffusive, unitive and transformative strength.[21] In *Diffusion*[22] truly: for it spreads the beams of its goodness not only to friends and neighbours, but also to enemies and strangers. In *Union*[23] truly: for it makes lovers one in deed and will; and Christ and every holy soul it makes one. He truly that draws to God is one spirit, not in nature but in grace, and in onehood of will. Love has also a *Transforming*[24] strength, for it turns the loving into the loved, and ingrafts him. Wherefore the heart that truly receives the fire of the Holy Ghost is burned all wholly and turns as it were into fire; and it leads it into that form that is likest to God. Else had it not been said: *Ego dixi dii estis et filii Excelsi omnes;* that is to say: "I have said ye are gods, and are all the children of the high God."

Forsooth some men have so loved each other that they nearly trowed there were but one soul in them both. (pp. 80-1).

These three degrees of love, viz. insuperable, inseparable—or to use the English words: unovercomable, undeparted—and singular, and singular, are the same as the degrees which Mgr. Farges differentiates as belonging to the Unitive Way,[25] viz.:

(i.) Habitual forgetfulness of self in order to think only of the glory of God.

(ii.) Habitual pursuit of the greater glory of God.

(iii.) A constant state of indifference to anything else.

And he adds another:

(iv.) The choice between two things, which are equally pleasing to God, of that one which will be more crucifying to self.

This last degree is really included in what Richard calls *Singular* love; for in that degree the soul desireth to suffer pain for love of God; though he would hardly, being of an objective turn of mind, have stopped to weigh which of two things would be most crucifying to self. Indeed one questions whether his love of God was not of too wholesome a nature to imagine that what would be most crucifying and painful to self would, for that reason, be the more pleasing to Christ who was crucified for man; though Richard's love for God causes him to embrace pain which comes naturally, with a true delight, for through pain we grow in love. *Singular* love means simply that there is no delight for him save in Christ. All earthly comfort is as naught, "and now it seems as if the soul were unable to suffer pain," and death will seem "sweeter than honey."

In *The Form* (chap. x.) he gives seven *experiments* by which we may know if we have attained to Singular love. These are:

(i.) When all desire of earthly things is slaked in him.

(ii.) A burning yearning for heaven. For when men have felt aught of that savour, the more they have the more they covet; and he that nought has felt, nought he desires. Therefore when anyone is so much given till the love thereof, that he can find no joy in this life, he has token that he is in charity.

(iii.) If his tongue be changed, and he that was wont to speak of earthly things, now speaks of God and of the life that lasts ay.

(iv.) He gives himself entirely to God's business and not to earthly.

(v.) When the thing that is hard in itself, seems light for to do; the which love makes. For as Austin says: "Love it is which brings the thing that is far near-to-hand, and the impossible to the openly possible."

(vi.) Hardness of thought to suffer all anguish and noys that come; without this all the other suffices not. For whatso befalls him shall nought make a righteous man sorry. For he that is righteous he hates nought but sin, he loves nought but God and for God; he dreads nought but to wrath God.

(vii.) Delight in soul when he is in tribulation, and he makes praise to God in the anger (pain) that he suffers. And this shews well that he loves God, when no sorrow may bring him down. For many love God while they are in ease, and in adversity they grumble and fall into such mickle sorryness, that scarcely any may comfort them, and so slander they God striving and fighting against His judgements. And that is a caitiff praise that any wealth of the world makes; but that praise is of mickle price that no violence of sorrow can do away.[26]

This chapter of *The Form* should be read in full.[27] It begins thus:

Thou speakest so much of love tell me: What is love? and Where is love? And how shall I love God verily? And how may I know that I love Him? And in what state can I love Him most?

And he answers:

Thy first asking is: What is Love?

And I answer: Love is a burning yearning after God with a wonderful delight and certainty. God is light and burning; light clarifies our reason, burning kindles our desires, that we desire naught but Him. Love is a life, coupling together the loving and the loved. For Meekness makes us sweet to God; Purity joins us to God; Love makes us one with God. Love is the beauty of all virtues. Love is the thing through which God loves us and we God, and each one of us another. Love is the desire of the heart ay thinking til him that it loves; and when it has that it loves, then it joys and nothing can make it sorry. Love is yearning between two, with lastingness of thought. Love is a stirring of the soul for to love God for Himself, and all other things for God; the which love when it is ordained in God, it does away all inordinate love in anything that is not good. But all deadly sin is inordinate love for a thing that is naught; then love puts out all deadly sin. Love is a virtue which is the rightest affection of man's soul. Truth may be without love, but it cannot help without it. Love is perfection of letters, virtue of prophecy; fruit of truth, help of sacraments; stabiling of wit and knowledge; riches of poor men, life of dying men. See how good love is!

And his similes are remarkable, and remind us of the Sadhù Sundar Singh.

> We shall afforce us to clothe us in love, as iron or coal does in the fire; as the air does in the sun; as wool does in the dye. The coal so clothes itself in fire that it is fire. The air so clothes itself in the sun that it is light. And the wool so substantially takes the dye that it is like it. In this manner shall a true lover of Jesus Christ do: His heart shall so burn in love that it shall be turned into the fire of love, and be as it were all fire; and he shall so shine in virtues that no part of him shall be murky in vices.

The second asking is: Where is Love?

And I answer: Love is in the heart, and in the will of man; not in his hand nor in his mouth, that is to say, not in his work but in his soul. . . . when he forsakes the world only for God's love, and sets all his thought on God, and loves all men as himself. And all the good deeds that he may do, he does them with intent to please Jhesu Christ, and to come to the rest of heaven. Then he loves God; and that love is in his soul, and so his deeds shew without. . . . No thing that I do without proves that I love God; for a wicked man might do as much penance in body, as much waking and fasting as I do. How may I then ween that I love, or hold myself better for that that ilk man may do? Certes, whether my heart loves God or not wots none but God, for aught that they may see me do. Wherefore love is verily in will, not in work save as a sign of love. For he that says he loves God, and will not do in act what is in him to show love, tell him that he lies.

The third asking is: How shall I verily love God?

I answer: Verray love is to love Him with all thy might *stalwartly;* In all thy heart, *wisely;* In all thy soul, *devoutly and sweetly.*

Stalwartly can no man love Him, but he be stalwart. He is stalwart that is meek, for all ghostly strength comes of meekness. On whom rests the Holy Ghost? In a meek soul. . . . And he that loves God perfectly, it grieves him not what shame or anguish he suffers, but he has delight, and desires that he were worthy for to suffer torment and pain for Christ's love; and he has joy that men reprove him and speak ill of him.[28]

As a dead man, whatsoever men do or say, he answers nought; right so, whoso loves God perfectly, they are not stirred by any word that man may say.

For he or she cannot love that may not suffer pain and anger for their friend's love. For whoso loves, *they have no pain.* . . . In nothing may men sooner overcome the devil than in meekness, which he mickle hates. . . .

Also it behoves thee to *love God wisely;* and that thou canst not do but if thou be wise. Thou art wise when thou art poor and without covetousness of this world, and despisest thyself for the love of Ihesu Christ, and expendest all thy wit and all thy might in His service.

And here is another of Richard's similes which are not unlike those of the Sadhù:

> If thou saw a man have precious stones, that he might buy a kingdom with, if he gave them for an apple as a child will do, rightwisely might thou say that he was not wise, but a great fool. Just so, if we will, we have precious stones; poverty, and penance, and ghostly travail; with the which we may buy the kingdom of heaven.

> And if thou have *sorrow for thy sins,* and for thou art so long in exile, out of thy country, and forsakest the solace of this life; thou shalt have for this sorrow the joy of heaven. And if thou be in travail and punishest thy body reasonably and wisely . . . for the love of Ihesu Christ, for this travail thou shalt come to rest that lasts ay, and sit in a settle of joy with angels. But some are that love not wisely; like til children that love more an apple than a castle.

> And if thou wilt love Ihesu verily thou shalt also love *devoutly and sweetly. Sweet love* is when thy body is chaste and thy thought clean. *Devout love* is when thou offerest thy prayers and thy thoughts to God with ghostly joy, and burning heart, in the heat of the Holy Ghost, so that men think that thy soul is as it were drunken for delight and solace of the sweetness of Ihesu, and thy heart conceives so mickle of God's help, that thee thinks that thou mayest never be from Him departed. And then thou comest into such rest and peace in soul, and quiet, without thoughts of vanity or of vice, as if thou wert in silence and sleep, and set in Noe's ship, so that nothing may hinder thee from devotion and burning of sweet love. From (the time) thou hast gotten this love, all thy life, till death come, is joy and comfort; and thou art verily Christ's lover, and He rests in thee, whose stead is made in peace.

The fourth asking was: How thou might know that thou were in love and charity?

I answer: That no man wots on earth that they are in charity, save it be through any privilege or special grace that God has given to any man or woman, that all others may take ensample by. . . . A man wots not whether he be worthy hatred or love, but all is reserved uncertain till another world. Nevertheless, if any had grace that he might win to the third degree of love which is called *Singular,* he should know that he were in love. But in such manner is his knowing that he might never bear himself the higher, nor be in the less care to love God; but so much the more that he is sure of love, will he be busy to love Him and dread Him that has made him swilk (like this), and done that goodness to him. And he that is thus high, he will not hold himself worthier than the sinfullest man that walks on earth.

Then there follow the seven *experiments* by which to test whether we have this singular love, which we have cited; as also the answer to the question: *And in what state can I love Him most?*

The soul that has attained to this highest degree of love Richard likens to a "pipe of love." "The which soul knowing the *mystery of love,* with a great cry ascends to his love." Here indeed we have what he elsewhere speaks of as Love entering boldly into "the bedchamber of the Everlasting King,"[29] where is the espousal bed of Christ and the soul. That "settle of love" of which Richard so often sings in the lyrics:

> The settle of love is lift high,
> for in til heaven it ran. . . .
>
> The bed of bliss it goes full nigh,
> I tell thee as I can;
> Though us think the way be dregh,[30]
> love couples God and man.

This is the *mystery of the kingdom* which is the supreme quest of the mystic. Here alone, in Christ, can the soul find rest. "Nothing is sweet to her, nothing she savours, except it be made sweet in Ihesu, whose memory is as a song of music in a feast of wine." A truly haunting phrase and worthy to be placed beside the Canticles.

Nor do I know of anyone outside the writer of Solomon's Song who has more beautifully expressed this inexpressible love of the thirsting soul:

> O sweet Ihesu, I bind Thy love in me with a knot unable to be loosed, seeking the treasure that I desire, and longing I find, because I cease not to thirst for Thee. Therefore my sorrow vanishes as the wind, and my meed is ghostly song that no man sees. Mine inward nature is turned into sweet song, and I long to die for love. The greatness of the gifts delights me with light, and the tarrying of love punishes me with joy, whiles they come that receive me, and in receiving refresh.

> But those things want that my Beloved shall show to me, longing: they wound me, so that I languish,

and they heal not yet my languor fully, but rather increase it; for love growing, languor is also increased. (p. 165.)

And again:

> Alas what shall I do? How long shall I suffer delay? To whom shall I flee that I may happily enjoy that I desire? Needy am I and hungry, noyed and diseased, wounded and dis-coloured for the absence of my love; for love hurts me, and hope that is put back chastises my soul. Therefore the cry of the heart goes up, and amongst the heavenly citizens a songly thought runs desiring to be lifted up to the ear of the most High. And when it comes there it proffers its errand and says:

> O my love! O my honey! O my harp! O my psaltry and daily song! When shalt Thou help my heaviness? O my heart's rose, when shalt Thou come to me and take with Thee my spirit? Truly Thou seest that I am wounded to the quick with Thy fair beauty, and the longng relaxes not but grows more and more, and the penalties here present cast me down, and prick me to go to Thee, of whom only I trow I shall see solace and remedy. But who [meanwhile] shall sing me the end of my grief and the end of mine un-rest? And who shall show to me the greatness of my joy and the fulfilling of my song, that from this I might take comfort and sing with gladness, for I should know that the end of mine unhappiness and that joy were near? (p. 150.)

And here he actually breaks into verse; it is the only place in *The Fire* where he does so:

> O deus meus,
> O amor meus
> Illabere mihi,
> Tua caritate perforato,
> Tua pulcritudine vulnerato,
> Illabere, inquam,
> Et languentem.

which Misyn thus translates:

> O my God! O my Love! into me glide; with Thy charity thirled; with Thy beauty wounded:
> Slide down and comfort me, heavy;

and the original Latin continues in prose[31]:

> give medicine to me, wretched; show Thyself to Thy lover.
> Behold in Thee is all my desire, and all my heart seeks.
> After Thee my heart desires; after Thee my flesh thirsts.
> And Thou openest not to me but turnest Thy Face.
> Thou sparrest Thy door, and hidest Thyself; and at

the pains
of the innocent Thou laughest.

. . . Come into me, my Beloved! All that I had I gave for Thee, and that I should have, for Thee I have forsaken, that Thou in my soul mightest have a mansion for to comfort it. Never forsake Thou him that Thou feelest so sweetly glow with desire for Thee; so that with most burning desire I desire, to be ever within Thy halsing.[32] So grant me grace to love Thee, and in Thee to rest, that in Thy kingdom I may be worthy for to see Thee withouten end. . . . (p. 21.)

And again in *The Mending* he cries:

O sweet and true Joy, I pray Thee come! Come, O sweet and most desired! Come, my Love, that art all my comfort! Glide down into a soul longing for Thee and after Thee with sweet heat. Kindle with Thy heat the wholeness of my heart. With Thy light enlighten my inmost parts. Feed me with honeyed songs of love, as far I may receive them by my powers of body and soul. (p. 230.)

In the chapter (xi.) from which we have already quoted, he gives perhaps his most complete description of his burning love, of which he never tires of singing. In it he rises to an ecstasy, and cannot find words by which to express what this love is which seems to wound and tear his heart. Like the lark, he soars and sings; and every now and again, also like the lark, when singing, he drops down into fields of prose. The whole chapter should be read in order to understand this curious medley of prose and poetry; of common sense and rhapsody, which is one of his special characteristics. Here only the most striking passages can be quoted:

Charity truly is the noblest of virtues, the most excellent and sweetest, that joins the Beloved to the lover, and everlastingly couples Christ with the chosen soul. It re-forms in us the image of the high Trinity, and makes the creature most like to the Maker.

O gift of love, what is it worth before all other things, that challenges[33] the highest degree with the angels! Truly the more of love a man receives in this life, the greater and higher in heaven shall he be. O singular joy of everlasting love that ravishes all His to the heavens above all worldly things, binding them with the bands of virtue.

O dear charity, he is not wrought on earth that—whatever else he may have—has not thee. He truly that is busy to joy in thee, is forthwith lift above earthly things. Thou enterest boldly the bedchamber of the Everlasting King. Thou only art not ashamed to receive Christ. He it is that thou hast sought and loved. Christ is thine: hold Him, for He cannot but receive thee, whom only thou desirest to obey. For withouten thee plainly no work pleases Him.[34] Thou makest all things savoury. Thou art a heavenly seat; angels' fellowship; a marvellous holiness; a blissful sight; and life that lasts endlessly.

O holy charity, how sweet thou art and comfortable; that remakest that that was broken. The fallen thou restorest; the bond thou deliverest; man thou makest even with angels. Thou raisest up those sitting and resting, and the raised thou makest sweet.

And the following passage explains why every mystic finds it impossible to give any clear account of his progress in the experience of God's love:

Thus truly Christ's lover keeps no order in his loving nor covets no degree, because however fervent and joyful he be in the love of God in this life, yet he thinks to love God more and more. Yea, though he might live here evermore yet he should not trow at any time to stand still and not progress in love, but rather the longer he shall live the more he should burn in love. God truly is of infinite greatness, better than we can think; of un-reckoned sweetness; inconceivable of all natures wrought; and can never be comprehended by us as He is in Himself in eternity.

And he again breaks forth into a rhapsody of love:

O merry love, strong, ravishing, burning, wilful, stalwart, unslakened,[35] that brings all my soul to Thy service, and suffers it to think of nothing but Thee. Thou challengest for Thyself all that we live; all that we savour; all that we are.[36]

Thus therefore let Christ be the beginning of our love, whom we love for Himself. And so we love whatever is to be loved ordinately for Him that is the Well of love, and in whose hands we put all that we love and are loved by. Here soothly is perfect love shown; when all the intent of the mind, all the secret working of the heart, is lifted up into God's love, so that the strength and mirth of true love is so great that no worldly joy . . . is lawful or delights it.

And here we have the same selfless love as St. Francis Xavier expresses in his well-known hymn.

Although there were no torments for the wicked, nor no meed in heaven, should be trowed for chosen souls, yet shouldst thou never the sooner loose thee from thy Love. More tolerable it were to thee to suffer an untrowed grief than once to sin deadly. Therefore thou truly lovest God for Himself and for no other thing, nor thyself except for God; and thereof it follows that nothing but God is loved in thee. How else should God be all in ilk thing if there be any love of man in man?

And compare this passage from *The Fire*:

> For truly if we love God rightly we would sooner lose great meed in heaven than once sin venially; for most righteous is it to ask no meed of righteousness but the friendship of God, that is Himself. Therefore it is better ever to suffer tormentry than once, wilfully and knowingly, to be led from righteousness to wickedness. (p. 39.)

Then again he soars upward, singing thus of love:

> O clear charity, come into me, and take me into thee, and so present me before Thy Maker. Thou art savour well tasting; sweetness well smelling; and pleasant odour; a cleansing heat, and a comfort endlessly lasting. Thou makest men contemplative; heaven's gate thou openest; the mouths of accusers thou sparrest; thou makest God be seen, and thou hidest a multitude of sins. We praise thee; we preach thee; by the which we overcome the world; in whom we rejoice, and by whom we ascend the ladder of heaven. In thy sweetness glide into me: and I commend me and mine unto thee without end.

And in *The Fire* he gives us this prayer for love:

> Lord Ihesu, I ask Thee, give unto me movement in Thy love withouten measure; desire withouten limit; longing with outen order; burning withouten discretion. Truly the better the love of Thee is, the greedier it is; for neither by reason is it restrained, nor by dread thronged, nor by doom tempted. No man shall ever be more blest than he that for greatness of love can die. No creature truly can love too mickle. In all other things all that is too mickle turns to vice, but the more the strength of love surpasses, the more glorious it shall be. (p. 78.)

This perfect love embraces the love of our neighbour, for Richard, though carried away by excess of love, never forgets the earth from which he has taken flight, and constantly breaks off from his most impassioned utterances to give us some homely advice or warning. He is emphatic that all true love of God must include the love of man, since we dwell in God and God in us.

> Therefore [he says], if our love be pure and perfect, whatever our heart loves it is God. Truly if we love ourself, and all other creatures that are to be loved, only in God and for God, what other in us and in them love we but Him? For when our God truly is loved by us with a whole heart and all virtue, then, without doubt, our neighbour and all that is to be loved, is most rightly loved. If therefore we shed forth our heart before God and in the love of God being bound with Him, and holden with God, what more is there by which we can love any other thing? Truly in the love of God is the love of my neighbour. Therefore as he that loves God knows not but to love man, so he that truly knows to love Christ is proved to love nothing in himself but God. Also all that we are loved or love—all to God the Well of love we yield: because He commands that all the heart of man be given to Himself. All desires also, and all movings of the mind, He desires be fastened in Him. He forsooth that truly loves God feels nothing in his heart but God, and if he feel none other thing nought else has he; but whatso he has he loves for God, and he loves nought but that God wills he should love: wherefore nothing but God he loves and so all his love is God. (p. 87).

And he thus sums up all that he has said of heat and song and sweetness, in this account of a man who is perfectly turned to Christ:

> He despises all passing things, and he fastens himself immovably to the desire only of his Maker, as far as he is let by mortality, because of the corruption of the flesh. Then no marvel, manly using his might, first, the heaven as it were being opened, with the eye of his understanding he beholds the citizens of heaven; and afterward he feels sweetest heat as it were a burning fire. Then he is imbued with marvellous sweetness, and henceforth he is joyed by a songly noise.

> This therefore is perfect charity, which no man knows but he that receives it; and he that has received never leaves it: sweetly he lives, and sickerly shall he die. (p. 89.)

Naturally, and like all true mystics, he longs for death—that lowly door through which we must pass to reach the Hall of Everlasting Love.

> And I spake thus to death:

> O Death, where dwellest thou? Why comest thou so late to me, living but yet mortal? Why halsest thou not him that desires thee?

> Who is enough to think thy sweetness, that art the end of sighing, the beginning of desire, the gate of unfailing yearning? Thou art the end of heaviness, the mark of labours, the beginning of fruits, the gate of joys. Behold I grow hot and desire after thee: if thou come I shall forthwith be safe. Ravished, truly, because of love, I cannot fully love what I desire after, until I taste the joy that Thou shalt give to me.

> . . . . .

> Therefore truly I long after love the fairest of flowers, and I am inwardly burnt by the flame of fire. Would God I might go from the dwelling of

this exile. . . . Now, grant my best Beloved, that I may cease; for death, that many dread, shall be to me as *heavenly music.* Although I am sitting in wilderness yet I am now as it were set stable in Paradise, and there sweetly is sounding a loving song in the delights that my Love has given me. (p. 74-6.)

Here again we note the blending of the three: the burning of the flame; the heavenly music; and the sweet sound of the song of love.

Notes

[1] *Les Voies Ordinaires de la Vie Spirituelles* (trans. 1927; Burns, Oates & Washbourne). . . .

[2] Cf. *Life of Fogazzaro,* p. 290.

[3] We have a striking witness to this in the life of Sadhù Sundar Singh. Cf. *The Gospel of Sadhù Sundar Singh,* by Dr. Friedrich Heiler. See especially pp. 171 sqq. Abridged translation by Olive Wyon (Allen & Unwin, 1927).

[4] i.e. searched.

[5] To the core=Lat. *medullitus.*

[6] Real.

[7] Cf. *The Living Flame,* edited by Lewis and Zimmerman, pp. 33, 55 (Baker, 1912).

[8] See *The Fire,* chap. xv., as quoted on p. 83.

[9] "Abbot Butler says: The imagery of music to express the mystic experience occurs (so far as I know) only here in Augustine [i.e. *Enarration on Psalm xli.* 4], though it is employed by other mystics, as Richard Rolle"; and he cites the well-known passage from cap. xv. of the *Incendium.* Cf. *Western Mysticism,* p. 29. We shall refer to this later in speaking of Richard's debt to Augustine—see p. 134.

[10] See *Du Péché à l'Amour Divin, ou l'Amendement du Pécheur* (p. 41), par Léopold Denis, S.J. (Desclée, 30 rue Saint-Sulpice, Paris, 1927).

[11] Vol. i., p. v.

[12] Some MSS. read *immovatur* = tarries or dwells in.

[13] I quote from Dr. Geraldine Hodgson's edition of *The Form of Living,* etc., pp. 70-1 (Baker, 1910).

[14] Chap. xi., pp. 230 sqq.

[15] Cf. *The Form of Living,* where these degrees are called "*Insuperable, Inseparable,* and *Singular.*"

[16] i.e. charges.

[17] Chap. viii., pp. 46 sqq. In my quotations from Dr. Hodgson's edition of *The Form* I have allowed myself license occasionally to retain the word in the original, and in some places to punctuate differently; I have also inserted numbers—or used italics—when it seemed advisable for the sake of clearness.

[18] Dr. Hodgson translates *syker*=of sighs. I take it to be the northern form, *sicker*=sure.

[19] i.e. growing.

[20] I have modernised this from MS. Rawl. A. 384, printed by Horstman, vol. i., pp. 62 sqq.

[21] MS. C. "lufe forsoth has strength in spreding, in knytynge and turnynge."

[22] Spreading.

[23] Knitting.

[24] Turning.

[25] See *Ordinary Ways of the Spiritual Life,* p. 77.

[26] This is modernised from the version given in MS. Dd. 5.64, printed by Dr. Horstman, vol. i., pp. 43 sqq.

[27] Chap. x., p. 55.

[28] Cf. this from Douce MS. 322, Bodleian: "Through two things principally may a man know whether he be meek or no: Let his heart be not moved though his own will be contraried or againsaid, and when he is despused and falsely challenged and dislandered, yet his will stand unmovable from desiring of wrath, and his mouth be shut from unmeek answer." . . .

[29] Cf. *The Fire,* p. 233.

[30] i.e. long.

[31] "Consolare medicina tu miseri; ostende te amanti; ecce in te est omne desiderium meum, omne quod querit cor meum," etc. Dr. Horstman takes this absence of rhythm as one of the proofs of the later date of the *Incendium,* since the *Melum Contemplativorum,* a much earlier work, is constantly broken up into verse.

[32] i.e. embrace.

[33] i.e. claims.

[34] Cf. I Cor. xiii.

[35] Inextinguishable.

[36] Cf. Rom. xiv. 8.

T. W. Coleman (essay date 1938)

SOURCE: T. W. Coleman, "Richard Rolle," in *English Mystics of the Fourteenth Century*, The Epworth Press, 1938, pp. 64-83.

[*Below, Coleman describes Rolle not only as a true mystic, but also as a bridge from medieval to modern literature by virtue of the personal note in his devotional and literary styles.*]

History plays curious pranks. In the middle of the fourteenth century, Richard Rolle of Hampole was one of our most prolific writers, in verse and prose, on religious subjects. During his lifetime, and for some years after his death, alike in England and upon the Continent, his numerous works were eagerly sought and frequently copied. Unfortunately, after enjoying this blaze of popularity, he was banished to the night of neglect. Why he suffered this eclipse is a mystery. It may be that during the century of political disturbances and prolonged wars, through which this country passed soon after his decease, his name simply faded out of remembrance. Or, later still, his writings may have been swamped by the spate of literature released by the printing-press at the time of the Renaissance and the Reformation. Whatever the cause, the fact remains that the incomparable works of this saint and poet all but disappeared. At the dawn of the present century his name was hardly known outside a small circle of medieval scholars. In history books he was barely mentioned, and in anthologies seldom quoted. All this has recently changed. Owing to the present revival of interest in mysticism, diligent search has been made for the longlost manuscripts of this Yorkshire recluse, with gratifying results. His writings, to meet a widespread demand, are being reproduced in a variety of forms.

This newer knowledge is leading to a revised estimate of the Hermit. Expert authorities, after a critical examination of his works, and a careful endeavour to measure his influence upon the movements of his age, are of the opinion that he is a figure of some importance. He is fast becoming recognized as one of the main creative forces in the earlier development of our national literature and religion.

Undeniable claims for an original place of this kind can be advanced for Rolle. He was one of the earliest writers, after the Conquest, to express himself in the mothertongue. Scholars agree that his distinctive style of Middle English—terse, incisive, graphic—has exercised no small influence on the written form of our language. Some give him the title, Father of English prose. He was one of the first to translate parts of the Scriptures into the vernacular. Wycliffe made use of these renderings. Hence these two Yorkshiremen share the honour of being pioneers in the making of the English Bible. Rolle will always be of exceptional interest to students of our national religion—especially if they are lovers of the devout life—because he is one of the first of the English mystics whose writings we possess. How a figure of such dimensions could have fallen into comparative oblivion is a riddle of history.

This saintly hermit is certainly a most attractive personality. His candour and simplicity charm you. Without the faintest trace of self-consciousness, he opens to you the secret places of his soul. In his larger works, where the autobiographical element is most marked, his confessions at times are so intimate that you get the impression you are talking face to face with your closest friend. This frankness wins you.

In this, as in many other ways, he often reminds you of the Saint of Assisi. The parallel is irresistible. Richard, like Francis, was a born romanticist: his behaviour, private and public, was characterized by unexpected and daring elements, pregnant with delightful surprise—not the way of the prudent and discreet for him! Like Francis, too, he was a gay troubadour of the Spirit: when prose failed his ecstasy, he burst into lyric song; melody was his normal form of prayer. But not only did his soul wing its way to God on outbursts of praise, his life amongst men was also set to music: it was so sunny and carefree. Again like Francis, when he stepped out of the old world into the new, he symbolized the change by an act of stripping; off came his old clothes, and with a youth's ingenuity, he fashioned some new—an imitation of a hermit's habit. This curious costume was likewise intended to be a symbol—a badge of willing servitude: for still like the 'little poor man' of Assisi, he was going to serve his Lord in poverty, chastity, and obedience.

In addition to all this, as we turn the pages of Rolle's books, we soon learn that we are under the guidance of a scholar. We are first conscious of this because of the ease and culture of his style; but evidence is also there in his references to, and his ideas and phrases taken from, Fathers and Doctors of the Church like St. Augustine, St. Bernard, Richard of St. Victor, and St. Bonaventura.

For knowledge of the outward events of his life we are dependent upon the Lessons prepared for inclusion in the Office intended to be used after his canonization. This honour was never conferred, possibly because of the tension between the English Crown and the Papacy at that period; and also because, soon after his decease, his name became associated with Lollardy. The Lessons were drawn up shortly after his death—probably by the Cistercian nuns of Hampole, to whom he was spiritual adviser. While a strain of legend runs through the story, investigation has proved that the distinctly biographical parts are in the main trustworthy.

For the much more important facts of his inner life we turn to his own works. These, written in Latin and English, were many and varied. They range from the highest class of devotional writings in prose and poetry, through commentaries on the Scriptures and the Creeds, to practical treatises and popular tracts. For our purpose we shall chiefly consult two collections of his prose: *The Fire of Love and the Mending of Life,* translated from the Latin in 1434-5, by Richard Misyn, and modernized by Frances M. M. Comper; and *Selected Works of Richard Rolle,* transcribed by G. C. Heseltine, containing all his English writings, except his long translation and *commentary on the Psalter.*[1]

We learn from the Lessons that Richard was born at Thornton, near Pickering, in Yorkshire; no date is given, but other authorities give a choice of two, 1290 and 1300. His parents, judging from their social connexions, belonged to the well-to-do classes. No particulars are given anywhere about his early life; the only information available is the little to be gleaned from his writings. In one place he cries out:

> Lord God, have mercy on me! My youth was fond; my childhood vain; my young age unclean. But now Lord Jesu my heart is enflamed with Thy holy love and my reins are changed; and my soul will not touch for bitterness what before was my food: and my affections are now such that I hate nothing but sin.[2]

In his beautiful little treatise, **Of the Virtues of the Holy Name of Jesus,** he breaks forth:

> 'I went about, covetous of riches, and I found not Jesus. I ran in wantonness of the flesh, and I found not Jesus. I sat in companies of worldly mirth, and I found not Jesus. In all these I sought Jesus, but I found Him not. For He let me know by His grace that He is not found in the land of softly living. Therefore I turned another way, and I ran about in poverty, and I found Jesus, poorly born into the world, laid in a crib and lapped in cloths. I wandered in the suffering of weariness, and I found Jesus weary in the way, tormented with hunger, thirst and cold, filled with reproofs and blame. I sat by myself alone, fleeing the vanities of the world, and I found Jesus in the desert, fasting on the mountain, praying alone. I went the way of pain and penance, and I found Jesus bound, scourged, given gall to drink, nailed to the Cross, hanging on the Cross, and dying on the Cross.[3]

We must not accept too literally Richard's severe strictures upon his youth. He is regarding his past from the sun-lit heights of sanctity; from those shining summits his early days might well look dark and vain. When a young man, he was sent to Oxford by the help of Master Thomas de Neville, Archdeacon of Durham. Oxford, at that time one of the most famous seats of learning in Europe, was visited by scholars from all parts of the Continent; yet we can easily believe that the youthful Richard did not settle there with much enthusiasm. Although Scholasticism was past its prime, and its end was being hastened by William of Occam's persistent blows, it still retained the semblance of its age-long supremacy. Its method and spirit in its declining days would repel Richard; his warm heart and romantic nature would crave for something less bleak and arid. This makes it not improbable that he did, as some suggest, cross to France to complete his studies. For his residence at the Sorbonne evidence is not lacking. Be this as it may, at the age of nineteen he determined to be done with schools and universities, and even with home and friends; he was ready to take a fateful step. This should not surprise us. Adolescence is a time of instability and readjustment; more often than not it shapes the path of the future. Most young men, did we but realize it, in their pitiable confusion and craving for guidance, are 'not far from the Kingdom'.[4] Given Richard's ardent temperament, we may assume that during his growth into manhood, he would pass through times of mental stress and spiritual conflict, in which he would alternate between hope and fear, faith and doubt. The crisis—like most crises—would warm up gradually, simmering in the depths of his soul. Suddenly it sprang into consciousness. With him it would have the severity of an earthquake. He faced the upheaval manfully. He would flee from the embrace of the world to the arms of God. The story of the Lessons is here dramatic and absorbing:

> He said one day to his sister, "My beloved sister, thou hast two tunics which I greatly covet, one white and the other grey. Therefore I ask thee if thou wilt kindly give them to me, and bring them me tomorrow to the wood near by, together with my father's rain-hood. . . . " When he had received them he straightway cut off the sleeves from the grey tunic and the buttons from the white, and as best he could he fitted the sleeves to the white tunic, so that they might in some manner be suited to his purpose. Then he took off his own clothes, with which he was clad, and put on his sister's white tunic next his skin, but the grey, with the sleeves cut out, he put on over it, and put his arms through the holes which had been cut; and he covered his head with the rainhood aforesaid, so that thus in some measure, as far as was then in his power, he might present a certain likeness to a hermit. But when his sister saw this she was astounded and cried, "My brother is mad! My brother is mad!"[5]

Soon after, on the vigil of the Assumption, he entered a church to pray—possibly at Topcliffe, near Ripon. He occupied the place of a certain lady, the wife of a squire, John de Walton. Her servants wished to remove him, but she would not consent. At the close of the service, the lady's sons recognized Richard as a fellow-student at Oxford. On the day of the feast, without asking permission, he put on a surplice and sang matins and the office of mass with the others. Then, having secured the priest's blessing, he went into the pulpit and preached a sermon of such conviction and power that his hearers were brought to tears.

The squire was warmly attached to Richard's father as a friend, so he invited the young man to his home. After dinner he had an earnest talk with him in private. When the squire had convinced himself of Richard's serious purpose, he did a generous thing: he provided him not only with a habit suitable for a hermit, but also with food and lodging. The youth was now able to satisfy his heart's desire—to give himself to the full rigours of a recluse's life. He moved into a small cell, slept on a hard bench, and gave himself up to fasts, vigils, and frequent penitential acts.[6]

Richard was now firmly started on his life's adventure. He never looked back. With iron will he went forward in pursuit of his ideal—the achievement of sanctity. After living for some years in the vicinity of Sir John de Walton's home, and having attained a high degree of holiness, he had become a centre of interest and attraction. One day some visitors came and found him busily writing. They asked him for a word of exhortation. The good man spoke to them for two hours, yet he continued at the same time to write as quickly as before. On another occasion, he was so absorbed in prayer, that when a worn cloak was removed from him, stitched and replaced, he knew nothing about it. He had become so skilful in the use of his tongue and pen, that hearts were comforted by his words—especially his written ones:

> Yet wonderful and beyond measure useful was the work of this saintly man in holy exhortations, whereby he converted many to God, and in his sweet writings, both treatises and little books composed for the edification of his neighbours, which all sound like sweetest music in the hearts of the devout.[7]

By this time he was ready for wider fields of activity. He moved about from place to place, seeking by turns service and solitude. Wherever he went, many were blessed. He gave light to those in spiritual darkness, and relieved such as suffered mental or physical distress. His journeyings brought him to Richmondshire, where he became the friend and helper of Dame Margaret Kirkby, a recluse of Anderby. A mutually profitable fellowship sprang up between them. The ancress

seems thoroughly to have understood the hermit. On occasions when he was wounded by vicious tongues, Margaret was able to tranquillize his sensitive spirit. Some of his books were written for this fellow-seeker after the higher life.

His last move was to Hampole, near Doncaster. In between his times of devotions and writing, he gave his services to a convent of Cistercian nuns. Here he passed away in 1349. He appears to have been a victim of the Black Death. He gave his life in saving others: that is what we should have expected.

Richard's advance in the spiritual life is easy to trace because he describes its stages, in their nature and duration, with exactness. Reference has been made to his conversion. Though it had the violence of an earthquake, it did but herald the pilgrim's start; he now describes his progress on the way:

> And in process of time great profit in ghostly joy was given to me. Forsooth three years, except three or four months, were run from the beginning of the change of my life and mind, to the opening of the heavenly door; so that, the Face being shown, the eyes of the heart might behold and see by what way they might seek my Love, and unto Him continually desire. The door forsooth yet biding open, nearly a year passed until the time in which the heat of everlasting love was verily felt in my heart. I was sitting forsooth in a chapel, and whiles I was mickle delighted with sweetness of prayer or meditation, suddenly I felt within me a merry and unknown heat. But first I wavered, for a long time doubting what it could be. I was expert that it was not from a creature but from my Maker, because I found it grow hotter and more glad. Truly in this unhoped for, sensible, and sweet-smelling heat, half a year, three months and some weeks ran out, until the inshedding and receiving of this heavenly and ghostly sound; the which belongs to the songs of everlasting praise and the sweetness of the unseen melody . . .

> Whiles truly I sat in this same chapel, and in the night before supper, as I could, I sang psalms, I beheld above me the noise as it were of readers, or rather singers. Whiles also I took heed praying to heaven with my whole desire, suddenly I wot not in what manner, I felt in me the noise of song, and received the most liking heavenly melody which dwelt with me in my mind. For my thought was forsooth changed to continual song of mirth, and I had as it were praises in my meditation, and in my prayers and psalm saying I uttered the same sound, and henceforth, for plenteousness of inward sweetness, I burst out singing what before I said, but forsooth privily, because alone before my Maker. . . .

> Wherefore from the beginning of my changed soul unto the high degree of Christ's love, the which, God granting I was able to attain—in which degree

I might sing God's praise with joyful song—I was four years and about three months.[8]

That is a celebrated passage in the literature of English mysticism. We value it for its delightful simplicity of style and spirit, and for its illuminating description of the profound mystical changes which this dauntless seeker after the perfect life underwent. Students of mysticism point out how these changes correspond to the three stages of the mystic way: purgation, illumination, and union. It is highly probable that the Saint's advancement did reproduce these stages. Most readers, however, will prefer to interpret the passage as a poet's effort to express—as far as words will—his glad and progressive apprehension of Divine Reality.

It will be observed that Rolle describes his experiences in terms of *heat, song,* and *sweetness.* This he does consistently. He does not wish us to understand the words in a fanciful, or a merely figurative sense. For instance, when writing of *heat,* he assures us repeatedly that the term describes exactly what he feels 'truly, and not in imagination'. Lest any one should think he is suffering from illusions, he soberly writes in the Prologue of his book:

> I was forsooth amazed as the burning in my soul burst up, and of an unwont solace; ofttimes, because of my ignorance of such healthful abundance, I have groped my breast seeking whether this burning were from any bodily cause outwardly. But when I knew that it was only kindled inwardly from a ghostly cause, and that this burning was nought of fleshly love or concupiscence, in this I conceived it was the gift of my Maker.[9]

So far as we know, Rolle was the first and last of the mystics to use this trilogy of terms. Many mystics, to express their heart's feelings when kindled by Divine Love, have employed one or another of these words; and with them, each of the three words meant much the same thing—the terms were interchangeable. Rolle never actually defines the words, but he uses each one to represent a different phase of his spiritual experience. *Heat* stands for the conscious inflowing of heavenly love. *Song* for the pouring forth of his adoring soul in gratitude to the Beloved. *Sweetness,* the state of inward joy which results from this fellowship:

> Whence truly in these three that are tokens of the most perfect love, the highest perfection of Christian religion without all doubt is found; and I have now, Jesu granting, received these three after the littleness of my capacity. Nevertheless I dare not make myself even to the saints that have shone in them, for they peradventure have received them more perfectly. Yet I shall be busy in virtue that I may more burningly love, more sweetly sing, and more plenteously feel the sweetness of love. . . .[10]

What Rolle, with his keen sense of humour, would have said of some of our explanations of his ecstasies, might have been interesting to hear. Here is one by Miss Underhill: 'Those interior states or moods to which, by the natural method of comparison that governs all descriptive speech, the self gives such sense-names as these of "Heat, Sweetness, and Song", react in many mystics upon the bodily state. Psycho-sensorial parallelisms are set up. The well-known phenomenon of stigmatization, occurring in certain hypersensitive temperaments as the result of deep meditation upon the Passion of Christ, is perhaps the best clue by which we can come to understand how such a term as "the fire of love" has attained a double significance for mystical psychology.'[11]

Such descriptions of the machinery underlying the Saint's raptures should not be taken too seriously. A smile is a simple thing, and can be described in terms of mental and muscular movements; but how inadequate is the explanation. The essential element in a smile is personality; of this, psycho-physical accompaniments tell us nothing. So here. 'Psycho-sensorial parallelisms' is a phrase covering a network of mysteries. It says little of real enlightenment. Concerning the method of the Divine Spirit's operation upon our spirit it leaves us very much where we were. On this point, Dr. Thouless says, 'It is impossible to pretend that our knowledge of psychological laws is so complete that we can honestly say that it provides us with an explanation of the desires, thoughts, feelings, &c., of anybody'.[12]

Rolle freely admits the mystery, and at the same time regretfully confesses that words are useless to express the wonder of his experiences:

> The smallness of my mind certain knows not how to open that which as a blabberer, I am busy to show. Yet I am compelled to say somewhat, although it is unable to be spoken, that hearers or readers may study to follow it; finding that all love of the fairest and loveliest worldly thing in comparison to God's love, is sorrow and wretchedness.

> This delight, certain, which he has tasted in loving Jesu, passes all wit and feeling. Truly I can not tell a little point of this joy, for who can tell an untold heat? Who lay bare an infinite sweetness? Certain if I could speak of this joy unable to be told, it seems to me as if I should teem[13] the sea by drops, and spar[14] it all in a little hole of the earth.[15]

What are the conditions of this love? They are stated very simply:

> Truly affluence of this everlasting love comes not to me in idleness, nor might I feel this ghostly heat

while I was weary because of bodily travel, or truly immoderately occupied with worldly mirth, or else given without measure to disputation; but I have felt myself truly in such things wax cold, until, putting a-back all things in which I might outwardly be occupied, I have striven to be only in the sight of my Saviour and to dwell in full inward burning.[16]

Lest we think these conditions too simple, he states them again in a manner that would not be acceptable to many in his day:

Alas, for shame! An old wife is more expert in God's love, and less in worldly pleasure, than the great divine, whose study is vain. For why? For vanity he studies, that he may appear glorious and so be known, and may get rents and dignities: the which is worthy to be held a fool, and not wise.[17]

Of those who have merely book knowledge, and pride themselves upon their learning and skill, he is not a little scornful:

But those taught by knowledge gotten, not inshed, and puffed up with folded arguments, in this are disdainful: saying, Where learned he? Who read to him? For they trow not that the lovers of endless love might be taught by their inward master to speak better than they taught of men, that have studied at all times for vain honours.

Thou needest not covet greatly many books. Keep love in thine heart and work, and thou hast all that we may say or write. For the fullness of the law is charity; on that hangs all.[18]

In many places, Rolle, like most mystical writers, refers to the degrees of love. On such occasions he is emphasizing the fact that love is always growing; it never stops or stagnates; upwards and onwards it constantly climbs towards the Ideal. The fullest and finest exposition of some of the stages through which it passes is in the charming eighth chapter of *The Form of Living*.

Three degrees of love I shall tell thee, for I would that thou might win to the highest. The first degree is called *Insuperable,* the second *Inseparable,* and the third *Singular.*

Thy love is *Insuperable* when nothing that is contrary to God's love overcomes it, but it is stalwart against all temptations and stable whether thou be in ease or anguish, in health or sickness. So that thou thinkest that thou wouldest not, for all the world and to have it for ever, at any time make God wrath. . . .

Thy love is *Inseparable* when all thy heart and thy thought and thy might are so wholly, so entirely

and so perfectly fastened, set, and established in Jesus Christ, that thy thought goes never from Him, except sleeping. . . .

The third degree is highest and most wondrous to win. That is called *Singular,* for it has no peer. Singular love is when all comfort and solace are closed out of thy heart but that of Jesus Christ alone. It seeks no other joy. . . .[19]

He often warns those who would rise highest that they must work hardest:

The soul goes up into this height whiles, soaring by excess, it is taken up above itself, and heaven being open to the eye of the mind, it offers privy things to be beheld. But first truly it behoves to be exercised busily, and for not a few years, in praying and meditating, scarcely taking the needs of the body, so that it may be burning in fulfilling these; and, all feigning being cast out, it should not slacken day and night to seek and know God's love.[20]

He has no doubt about the superiority of the contemplative life over the active. He does not rush to this conclusion hastily; he carefully balances one against the other and then decides:

By some truly it is doubted which life is more meedful and better: contemplative or active. It seems to not a few that active is meedfuller because of the many deeds and preachings that it uses. But these err unknowingly, for they know not the virtue of contemplative. Yet there are many active better than some contemplative; but the best contemplative are higher than the best active.

Truly if any man might get both lives, that is to say contemplative and active, and keep and fulfil them, he were full great; that he might fulfil bodily service, and nevertheless feel the heavenly sound in himself, and be melted in singing into the joy of heavenly love. I wot not if ever any mortal man had this. To me it seems impossible that both should be together.[21]

At times, however, his references to those of active life are tinged with contempt; especially if once they were contemplatives:

This manner of man forsooth that is taken up to so high love, ought to be chosen neither to office nor outward prelacy; nor to be called to any secular errand. . . . Holy contemplatives are most rare and therefore most dear. . . . Those who will polish such, that is to say honour them with dignities, are busy to lessen their heat, and in a manner to make their fairness and their clearness dim; for truly if they get the honour of principality, they shall forsooth be made fouler and of less meed. Therefore they shall be left to take heed to their studies, that their clearness may increase.[22]

From passages such as these—and there are many sprinkled throughout his works—it is plain that the hermit had but little respect either for the Church dignitaries of his day, or for those who made the most pious professions: 'the religious'. Of some of these latter—monks and friars who had become degenerate and greedily preyed upon rich and poor alike—he writes in his *Commentaries* with biting scorn:

> Here we pray not to live a worldly life . . . ; nor to despoil the people and gather their goods into our castles, nor by the craft of flattery to please the world; but even to live the contrary life. . . . For by wandering in such ways men may well see whose children they are and for whom they make ready. For the king of all such children of pride, who is Antichrist, leads such religious and teaches them these deceits. Wherefore some men say that they are dead corpses gathered from their sepulchres, wrapped in the clothes of grief and driven by the devil to draw men. And thus they wear the badges of hypocrisy. It were less harmful to men of Christ's school to deal with a legion of the fiends of hell than with a little convent of such quick devils. For some they rob and some they make mad, and by feigned hypocrisy and the deceits of the devil they beguile more men than do other fiends. May the Lord deliver His folk from the perils of these false friars. . . .[23]

Of still another class, whose violent deeds and cruel deceptions were the terror and shame of that age, he writes with equal vehemence. No modern reformer could have commanded more fiery invective:

> But the mighty men and worldly rich that ever hungrily burn in getting possessions of others, and by their goods and riches grow in earthly greatness and worldly power—buying with little money what, after this passing substance, was of great value—or have received in the service of kings or great lords great gifts, without meed, that they might have delights and lusts with honours: let them hear not me but Saint Job: "Their days they led in pleasure, and to hell they fall in a point . . .".[24]

> Also here is forbidden trickery of weight or count, or of measure, or through usury, or violence or fear—as beadles or foresters do and ministers of the king—or through extortion, as lords do.[25]

No man could write or speak so trenchantly and hope to escape reprisals. Those attacked returned with no less spirit to the charge. They gave Richard a bad time. Repeatedly he cries out because of his 'enemies'. These complaints reveal to us one of the sorest troubles of his life: he was acutely sensitive. Any act or word of unkindness—especially from those he trusted—cut him to the quick. In many places he bitterly laments the unfaithfulness of certain friends—'scorpions', 'back-biters'—and deplores his consequent disappointment and loneliness.

Like all men of his class this hermit had a horror of lechery. To account for this it is not necessary to resort to the Freudian technique. Richard was as healthy-minded as any normal man. In expressing himself as he did, his intention was to maintain and enforce the traditional ideals of purity. Hence on many of his pages—particularly in *The Fire of Love*—you find passages such as this:

> Whiles a man weds not for pure love of God and virtue and chastity, but is busy to live in chastity and in array of all virtue, doubtless he gets to himself a great name in heaven; for as he ceases not to love God here, so in heaven he shall never cease from his praising. Wedlock soothly is good in itself; but when men constrain themselves under the band of matrimony for the fulfilling of their lust, they turn forsooth good into ill, and whereby they wean to profit, thereof they cease not to be worse.[26]

So he warns would-be contemplatives against the 'sweet words of fair women'. He is also impatient with the extreme freakishness of feminine fashions. We have heard similar denunciations in our own days; they remind us that while times change, things remain much the same:

> Next the women of our time are worthy of reproof that in such marvellous vanity have found new array for head and body, and have brought it in, so that they put beholders to dread and wonder. Not only against the sentence of the apostle in gold and dressing of the hair, in pride and wantonness, they go serving; but also against the honesty of man and nature ordained by God, they set broad horns upon their heads, and horrible greatness of wrought hair that grew not there, some of whom study to hide their foulness or increase their beauty and with painting of beguiling adultery they colour and whiten their faces.[27]

Lest any one should think, because of these fulminations, that Richard was the slave of an anti-feminine complex, it should be pointed out that several contemporary writers deplore the vanity, slackness, and infidelity of certain classes of women. These vices were attributed, in no small degree, to the interference of the friars in domestic relationships. This became a serious menace, and produced endless trouble. Of course, Richard knew the value of good women, and handsomely acknowledges his debt to them.[28] The deep and abiding friendship, wherein he found true solace of soul, between him and Margaret, shows his real attitude towards women; so, too, did his spiritual labours for the nuns at Hampole.

Some of Rolle's characteristics will commend—it may be endear—him, to many in our day. We cannot but admire his fine spirit of independence. It is specially creditable in those days, and undoubtedly had important historical consequences. It comes out in such a simple act as his sitting for devotions: though frequently reproved for this by 'fond men', he quietly went on his own way.[29]

We readily admit that a man of that temperament is not easy to control, or even to persuade; and doubtless he would be a thorn in the flesh of many, most of all, of those Church authorities who might try to curb him, and fasten him down to orthodox ways. The same spirit is seen in the following passage, where he is writing upon *The Creed of Athanasius:* here he distinctly reminds us of later Protestants:

> This psalm tells us much of the Trinity, but it is not necessary for every man here to know it, since a man may be saved if he believes in God and hopes that God will teach him afterwards what is necessary. . . . For our creed should be mixed with love and faith, so that faith may teach our reason how good God is. . . . So love and good living are necessary to a right faith. But God forbid that men believe that every man who will be saved must believe expressly every word that is said here, for few or none are in that state, either Greeks or Latins. And yet, even for us, English fails to express what little we believe. For faith is of truth, which is before our languages. And, as we say, God gives faith both to children and to men although they have not the power to learn faith of their brethren.[30]

His freedom of thought is also apparent in his attitude towards the ecclesiastical system of his times. While he recognizes that such practices as fasting, confession, penance, and regular attendance at mass are good as discipline and spiritual helps, he nowhere presses them as being necessary to salvation. His writings are markedly free from references to transubstantiation. He gives a more Protestant emphasis still when he says:

> The name of God is taken in vain in many ways. With heart, false Christian men take it in vain who receive the Sacrament without grace in the soul.[31]

On the other hand, he never tires of stressing the constant necessity of prayer, meditation upon the Scriptures, and 'the practice of the Presence of God'. Then, as he often gratefully acknowledges, his personal devotion to the Saviour is the centre of his spiritual life: a fact that comes out most clearly in his choice little work, *The Amending of Life*. All this may be summed

up by saying that Rolle stands for experimental religion as distinct from ecclesiastical, institutional, or sacramental. That is why I find it difficult to agree with Dom David Knowles when he says, 'His temperament and outlook were unusual, but he was neither an innovator, nor a reformer'.[32] I think he partook of both.

One is bound to refer to the vein of humour running through Richard's works: a dry broad humour—he was a Yorkshireman. On many a page you see the hermit's homely smile, especially when he is giving your folly or vanity a gentle rub. He often administers raps like this:

> How mayest thou for shame, who art but a servant, with many clothes and rich, follow thy Spouse and thy Lord, who went in a kirtle; and thou dost trail as much behind thee as all that He had on.[33]

His works abound in deep, pithy, paradoxical sayings, expressed in clear and incisive speech, which make an indelible impression on the mind. Here is a short catena on Love:

> What is love but the transforming of desire into the thing loved?

> Therefore if our love be pure and perfect, whatever our heart loves it is God.

> But, know it well, he himself knows not love that presumes to despise common nature in his brother; for he does wrong to his own condition that knows not his right in another.

> Such truly as we now are to Him, such a one shall He then appear to us; to a lover certain lovely and desirable, and to them that loved not, hateful and cruel.

> Hate thou no wretchedness on earth except that that thy pure love can cast over and disturb; for perfect love is strong as death, true love is hard as hell.[34]

Enough has now been said to suggest something of the true lineaments of this Saint. Richard Rolle was a great man—of that there can be no doubt. Look at the men whose work he foreshadowed, it may be, directly influenced: Langland, who voiced the sufferings and needs of the common people; Chaucer, often referred to as the creator of English literature; and Wycliffe, the precursor of the Reformation. From these men sprang prevailing movements, whose seeds were in the heart of Richard Rolle. But Richard's real greatness was in himself, in those essential qualities which mark him as a born mystic: his devotion to the spiritual life, his achievement of holiness, his joy of fellowship with the Beloved, and his care for the friendless, the afflicted, and the perplexed. These are the authentic unveilings of Richard's inner nature: they win our love, and find full expression in 'his sweet writings, both treatises and little books, which all sound like sweetest music in the hearts of the devout'.

Notes

[1] An exhaustive list of Rolle's works has been prepared by Miss Hope Emily Allen: *Writings ascribed to Richard Rolle, Hermit of Hampole*. For his poetry readers may consult *The Life and Lyrics of Richard Rolle*, by Frances M. M. Comper.

[2] *Fire of Love*, Bk. I, Ch. 12.

[3] *Selected Works*, p. 85.

[4] On this point Bede Frost has useful advice to spiritual directors: *Art of Mental Prayer*, pp. 225-6.

[5] *Fire of Love*, p. xlvi.

[6] *Fire of Love*, pp. xlviii and xlix.

[7] Ibid., p. xlix.

[8] *Fire of Love*, Book I, Ch. 15.

[9] Ibid., Prologue, p. 11.

[10] Ibid., Book I, Ch. 14.

[11] *Fire of Love*, Introduction, p. xv.

[12] *An Introduction to the Psychology of Religion*, p. 261.

[13] empty.

[14] bolt.

[15] *Fire of Love*, Book II, Chs. 10 and 4.

[16] Ibid., Prologue, pp. 12-13.

[17] Ibid., Book I, Ch. 5.

[18] *Fire of Love*, Book II, Ch. 3, and *Selected Works*, 'The Form of Living', Ch. 9.

[19] *Selected Works*, Ch. 8.

[20] *Fire of Love*, Book II, Ch. 2.

[21] Ibid., Book I, Ch. 21.

[22] Ibid., Book I, Ch. 14.

[23] *Selected Works*, 'Song of Zachary', p. 218.

[24] *Fire of Love*, Book I, Ch. 30.

[25] *Selected Works*, 'On the Ten Commandments', p. 77.

[26] *Fire of Love*, Book I, Ch. 24.

[27] *Fire of Love*, Book II, Ch. 9.

[28] Ibid., Book I, Ch. 12.

[29] Ibid., Book II, Ch. I.

[30] *Selected Works*, p. 225.

[31] Ibid., 'The Ten Commandments', p. 76.

[32] *The English Mystics*, pp. 86-7.

[33] *Selected Works*, 'The Commandment', p. 7.

[34] *The Fire of Love*, Book I, Chs. 17, 19, 25; Book II, Chs. 8, II.

Conrad Pepler (essay date 1958)

SOURCE: Conrad Pepler, "The Progress of Christian Life," in The English Religious Heritage, B. Herder Book Co., 1958, pp. 161-213.

[*In the excerpt below, Pepler places Rolle at the head of English mysticism. Reserving most of his attention for Rolle's English works, Pepler looks at Rolle's experiences and terminology in relation to broader conventions of medieval mysticism.*]

The New Light

Richard Rolle has been called 'The Father of English Mysticism' and it is to him we turn for the first introduction to mysticism in its strict sense among English writers. He was born some hundred years after the *Ancren Riwle* was written, and yet he is historically the first of the group of English mystics who experienced and wrote about the higher degrees of mystical prayer. Perhaps the greatest era of English sanctity had already passed when he was born in the last decade of the thirteenth century. There had been a succession of men and women from the time of Venerable Bede who had been led by the Spirit of God to transports of divine love and wisdom. But they had not been reflective in the way that the men of the fourteenth century were reflective so that the description of their lives does not enlighten later generations as to the nature of their prayer or their manner of reaching high degrees of contemplation. Rolle, amidst a profusion of Latin and English writings, did proclaim these hidden experiences, and his message was received with enthusiasm.

Geographically Rolle represents the most northerly point of the mystic path which seems to have run from Eckhart's Germany to the Low Countries, across the North Sea to East Anglia and so up to Yorkshire where Richard was born near Pickering just before 1300. Some have suggested that the trade route of the Yorkshire wool which crossed to the lower Germanies was responsible for opening the avenues of thought to the mystical teaching of Eckhart's disciples. This may well be so, for the spiritual seldom works entirely independently of the material, and it is not unlikely that Richard's father held some humble post in the important export business. Rolle himself ran away from Oxford to become a hermit before he was twenty, and there is no clear indication that he received at first any other influences for a mystical life than an incomplete ecclesiastical education with a reaction thereto, as well as a devout and poetical nature. But after spending some years as a hermit he completed his studies in Paris and there, apparently, first attained to real mystical heights of prayer. Of the period after that when he was back in Yorkshire Miss Hope Emily Allen has written: 'He then lived where he might have met anyone, from the king down, have had access to any book written, and learned of any movement stirring in the Church.'[1] And whatever may have been the influence on him, this situation in spite of his retired life gave him a wide audience in that part of the world. His experiences were dramatic and his language poetic and full of romantic metaphor so that he soon had disciples, both men and women, and was exercising sway over most of the spiritual writing of the period. It was inevitable that with such popularity the greater number should have mistaken his teaching and seized on the romance without understanding the meaning symbolised by the metaphor, so that after a while a Carthusian came to declare that he had known more men to be ruined by Rolle's writings than to have profited. The author of the *Cloud of Unknowing* takes these false followers to task as well: 'Oftimes the devil feigneth quiant sounds in their ears, quaint lights and shining in their eyes, and wonderful smells in their noses: and all is but a falsehood' (c. 57), and Walter Hilton has to caution his readers about such lights and 'feelings of comfortable heat and great sweetness' (*Scale,* p. 2, c. 29). Both these refer to a too literal understanding and copying of Rolle's special experiences. No one, however, has doubted the authenticity of Rolle's own mystical enlightenment and the accuracy of his interpretation thereof, and his effect stretched beyond the purely religious sphere of prayer and contemplation to that of English poetry.

It is his genuine mystical experience coupled with his emotional way of expressing that experience which suggests him as a model of the illuminative way. There is little emphasis on the hardships of purgation. An ascetic he undoubtedly was; but his writings in general speak of the joy of love rather than of the pains of penance; they certainly are not concerned very much with the purgative way. From the first he refers to himself as the 'sitter', because he had chosen that posture as the most conducive to contemplation as well as the most comfortable. Yet we could not easily class him among the higher ranks of those who have largely experienced the joy of perfect union in the unitive way. However diligently we may apply the interpretation of metaphor and analogy his constant insistence on the heat of love in his breast as being also a physical thing limits the scope of the love: he cannot have borne the full impact of the *Todo y Nada* of St John of the Cross.

We refer here, of course, more to his writings than to his own personal life. He was regarded by many after his death as a saint and an Office was composed for the celebration of his feast. He may therefore have reached the intimacies of union which mark the final stages of sanctification. But from what has come down to us of his own life he seems to have spent most of his years, which were untimely in their ending, in that somewhat uncertain and fluctuating time of the spiritual life called by many the Illuminative Way and by St Thomas the age of the *Proficient*—a term which conveys movement and development rather than a quiet rest. He seems to have passed to his comparatively quickly. In a celebrated chapter of the ***Incendium Amoris*** he describes how he came to the burning fire of love:

> Three years, except three or four months, were run from the beginning of the change of my life and of my mind, to the opening of the heavenly door: so that the Face being shown, the eyes of the heart might behold and see by what way they might seek my Love, and unto him continually desire. The door forsooth yet biding open, nearly a year passed until the time in which the heat of everlasting love was verily felt in my heart[2] (c. 15).

Certainly he regarded himself as having attained practically the highest degree in the spiritual life, for later in the same chapter he speaks of 'the high degree of Christ's love' which had been granted him, and concludes that the soul 'ascends not into another degree, but, as it were, confirmed in grace, as far as mortal man can, she rests'. That was his own opinion, but there is evidence to suggest that after he had received this special mystical gift he retained a good number of blemishes. Perhaps they were part of the bluff truculence of the Yorkshireman; he was somewhat resentful of opposition and inclined towards pride in his own graces. Apparently referring to his own special way of life he admonishes those who smile at it and regard it as uncanonical by asking: 'How do they dare to rebuke him whom rather they should honour as patron' (**Contra Amatores Mundi**). In his early writings he had challenged without sufficient humility—however right he may have been—the authorities of the Church and the spiritual state of many of the clergy. The effect of this lack of maturity led inevitably to persecution from diocesan officials as well as his own friends who had at first welcomed him hospitably. Yet gradually towards the end of his life his writings show a greater peace of mind and growing maturity which suggest that he is in fact reaching some further stage of union in love of God. It is mysterious that God's sudden mystical graces should leave the soul so much work to be done in adjusting her personal moral virtues to the situation. But it is a fact that many imperfections remain after these high passive graces have been bestowed. St Teresa herself was puzzled by this incongruity and put the difficulty, without resolving it, in her *LIFE*: 'How is it, when the Lord begins to grant a soul such sublime favours as that of bringing it to perfect contemplation, that it does not, as by rights it should, become perfect all at once? . . . How is it that it is only later, as time goes on, that the same Lord leaves it perfect in the virtues?' (c. 22, Peers, i, 143).

It is therefore later in life, after considerable change of domicile, passing hither and thither in the south and west of Yorkshire, that Richard finally settles down at Hampole in a quiet state of resignation. He is no longer concerned with what others think and say about him and his tendency to pride and arrogance is finally overcome. He is removed from the 'business of bodily things' partly by his greater retirement, but more through his greater interior peace. But his apostolic activities naturally increase, in the sense that he is constantly concerned with the spiritual upbringing of many devout religious and his fame as a man of wisdom and holiness begins to spread abroad and assist in a reviving of the Christian spirit. All this is characteristic of the age of the proficient with its early mystical experience and the consequent alignment of the normal life of the virtues with these special divine gifts. So that when death came, probably through assisting others during the Black Death in Yorkshire in 1349, Richard Rolle was really stabilised in the life of union and ready for its culmination in heaven.

In following the aim of this book to tap the spiritual literature in the English language before the Reformation, we should strictly leave out of consideration the greater part of Richard Rolle's writing which began in Latin. And this would in some ways be desirable because his English writings all belong to the later period when he was more surely rooted in the illuminative way. And they link up easily with the previous studies on the *Ancren Riwle* because he began to write in the vernacular for the sake of devout women who

were in fact leading the life outlined in that Rule. His first English work was probably **The English Psalter** written for an anchoress named Margaret Kirkeby who came from Hampole but after his death moved her cell further north to Anderby. Later, a year before his death, he wrote **The Form of Living** for the same anchoress. This is another instance of the influence of these holy women on the English literature of prayer and the devout life. The *Riwle* begins the tradition and Rolle continues it a century later writing several books and many spiritual lyrics for these his spiritual daughters. After his day the tradition was firmly rooted in English life. Rolle however was by no means tied to the English tongue and a great deal of his work was Latin, in particular the greatest of his works, the **Incendium Amoris** which was probably written at the beginning of the last period of his life. It would therefore be narrowminded to exclude from present consideration the treasures of his Latin pen which can happily elucidate and enlarge the thought behind his English works. We are in duty bound to consider all his works in so far as they apply to the way of the proficients, a policy which demands the neglect of some of Rolle's more elementary writings which will for that very reason repay a careful reading apart from this study. Moreover two of the most important Latin works are obtainable in a fifteenth-century translation by Richard Misyn whose language helps to link us directly with the pre-reformation times.

It is not easy to fix any chronology in his writings except in so far as the English are usually later than the Latin. So that we make no attempt here to follow Rolle's development as reflected in the series of his own books, letters and hymns. The method most suited to our purposes is to base ourselves on the English writings and expand their content by reference to the more celebrated of his Latin works.

. . . . .

'The Opening of the Heavenly Door'

The period of 'great business', described by Rolle in the **Incendium Amoris**[3] as the purgative way to 'sweetest rest' has passed and the obscurity of the night of the senses leads the soul on to this more secure life in Christ. The hermit was perfectly aware of the difficulties of the first period and the progress the devout man had to make to reach this sweetness. For some the progress is rapid and often accompanied by special graces from God.

> They that are sickerly ordained to holiness in the beginning of their turning for dread of God, forsake sins and worldly vanities: and then they set their flesh under strait penance, afterwards setting Christ's love before all other, and feeling a delight in

heavenly sweetness in devotion of mind they profit mickle. And so they pass from degree to degree and flourish with ghostly virtues; and so, made fair by grace, they come at last to the perfection that stands in heart, and word, and deed.[4]

He had himself passed through the normal stages in a matter of three or four years, and it is as well here to note in some detail the way in which God dealt with his own soul as described by his own pen. Each individual will reach this second length of the Christian life in a different way according to God's special designs and his own peculiar character; but the example set before us here will show how God works with those 'ordained to holiness'.

He had already been living some years as a hermit before he was given the opportunity to enter fully into this new way. God allowed him to be tempted in the solitude of his cell by a short and very sharp attack against his chastity. The temptation resembles in some ways that of St Thomas Aquinas in his prison, except that in Rolle's case the woman was a mere fantasy of someone he had loved previously to his adopting the hermit's life. The result of the triumph over this evil was something like that of St Thomas. The Gift of Fortitude had evidently been at work in his soul and the Spirit left within him as a consequence of the triumph a very sensible and intense devotion to the Holy Name. This may have been suggested by his Franciscan connections in Oxford, but it only came to life as a special source of grace at the moment of his victory.[5] The experience seems to have been almost as strong and lasting as Thomas's being girded by the angels.

It was after this that the heavenly door was opened to him. 'Three years except three or four months were run from the beginning of the change of my life and of my mind to the opening of the heavenly door' (*Incendium,* c. 15, p. 70). The effect of this strange opening of the door was to reveal in some new way the Face of God: and from that day for a year he had a time of peace tasting the sweetness of the Name and contemplating the Face through the door which remained open. This was a time of quieting of his boisterous nature and the increasing of his desire for God; 'so that, the Face being shown, the eyes of the heart might behold and see by what way they might seek my Love, and unto him continually desire'.

Then, the year completed, Rolle received the special grace by which he is peculiar among the mystics, the heat in his breast which was physical as well as spiritual. This came to him of a sudden while sitting in chapel at meditation, but it remained with him permanently. After nine or ten months more was added the experience of heavenly song which also remained:

Whiles truly I sat in this same chapel, and in the night before supper, as I could, I sang psalms, I beheld above me the noise as it were of readers, or rather singers. Whiles also I took heed praying to heaven, with my whole desire, suddenly, I wot not in what manner, I felt in me the noise of song (p. 71).

This was no external physical sound: his *thought* was changed into continual song and the burst forth in joyful melody before his Maker but not so that it could be heard by other ears. Indeed his description of his state might find a modern parallel in that of Sister Elizabeth of the Trinity who discovered her special vocation described in the name of *Laus Gloriae:* 'A "Praise of Glory" is a silent soul, a lyre beneath the Touch of the Holy Ghost, from which he can draw divine harmonies . . . In the heaven of glory, the blessed rest not day or night saying "Holy, Holy, Holy. . . . " In the heaven of her soul the "Praise of Glory" begins now the task which will be hers for all eternity. Her chant is uninterrupted . . . ' (quoted in *The Spiritual Doctrine of Sister Elizabeth,* p. 100). This passage of the modern Carmelite compares curiously with the account of heavenly song given by Rolle. The latter certainly had a peculiar mystical experience but it was fundamentally associated with the doctrine of grace as lived and understood by the former. Although Rolle describes what he felt and heard in terms of the senses it is evident that what he is trying to express is beyond such material things. He distinguishes later between two types of ravishing or rapture; the first takes the soul out of the senses so that 'he plainly feels nought in the flesh', which can happen to saint and sinner alike, and the second is 'the lifting of the mind into God by contemplation' which is the lot of the true lover (Bk. 2, ch. 7, pp. 161-2). This second type of rapture leaves the soul in possession of, and with dominion over, all faculties; this would make it possible to have some sensations such as physical heat and sound, which are associated with the really spiritual experience in the depth of the soul, without distraction or disturbance.

In trying to assess the nature and depth of this mystical experience we must turn to St Thomas on the subject of prophecy and visions, for the Angelic Doctor maintains that the pure manifestation of divine truth in contemplation without any emotional counterpart whatever is the highest experience which is in fact beyond prophecy. He will not admit that to have a counterpart in the imagination or external senses is anything but a lessening of the purity of this mystical intuition (II-II, 174, 2). This may be hard for the humanist to accept, but St Thomas will only agree that things of the senses in this context and in this life are for *use* only, for some practical purpose not for human perfection as such. Later, in heaven, there will be an outpouring from the mind transformed by vision into the lower powers and also into the body (II-II, 175, 4 and 1) for it is only after the resurrection that man can attain his full integrity. Consequently if there is a purpose in having imaginative or sensible expressions of the inner contemplation of truth he agrees that they should also be present, for the usefulness of the experience will be enhanced by the union of the two.

'When a particular supernatural truth has to be revealed by means of corporeal images, he that has both, namely the intellectual light and the imaginary vision, is more a prophet than he that has only one, because his prophecy is more perfect' (II-II, 174, 2 ad 1).

In this sense we might regard the double nature of Richard Rolle's experience as being granted to him as a teacher and master in the way of prayer. The sensations of heat and sound were given him not as part of his own perfection in the prayer of the illuminative way, but in order to lead others to it by the power of the experience. He himself insists that the inner ravishing of the spirit which may be likened to St Thomas's 'intellectual light' is the only thing of importance, confirming 'the shapeliness of the unseen life in the loving soul' and ravishing him 'to the height of contemplation and the accord of the angels' praise' (*Incendium,* I, c. 15, p. 73). In this he is in agreement with all the great saints who have reached the true heights of contemplation and his more external sensations are merely to be regarded as utilities, means of understanding what is meant by love and praise in their fullness.

In delaying on this outward aspect of Richard Rolle's initial experience we are not suggesting that he is a type to be followed in that particular respect. Every individual has his own grace conformable to his own personality. Grace is not a substance, not even a spiritual substance, poured out by God into rows and rows of souls like empty vases needing something to fill them. Certainly Christ merited by his death grace for all mankind and the Church preserves in her treasury these infinite merits to be conferred upon those chosen and fitted by God to receive them. But a too material conception of grace would lead us to expect the way to holiness to be exactly the same in every individual, as though having filled a hundred barrels one would expect all the taps to be turned on and pour out liquid in the same way. Grace is a habit which qualifies the soul so that each soul is possessed of it in its own individual nature, just as knowledge of the same subject will have its different emphasis and colouring in different men. And the more powerful the grace the more individual does it become; for two great theologians who have given their minds to the study of the same great dogmas on which they agree, will express themselves in far more different and variegated ways than two seminarians who have barely assimilated the elements of the science from text-books. For this reason the first stages of the spiritual life are more uni-

form in different people than the later stages. The purgative way is more easily traced in the lives of saints and sinners; but the illuminative and unitive ways become more and more 'peculiar' in their manifestations in each individual.

This fact of the 'diversity of Gifts' must be borne in mind when reading the life of any saint, but in particular in reading the personal and somewhat autobiographical writings of holy men and women on the spiritual life. The fundamental truth must be sought in the midst of the personal manifestations. The reader must never be diverted from an ever-growing directness towards God. It often happens that a person will model himself upon someone he has known or read about, someone who was evidently one of God's darlings; and despite frequent warnings he will find himself doing what he thinks his hero would have done in similar circumstances, praying as he imagines his hero prayed, seeking the same special graces as his hero received. But the hero of course was in direct communication with God so that it is impossible to copy him in truth without in a sense forgetting all about him and becoming more directly in touch with God. So the saints are given us as our models not so much to be copied, but in order that we may see how God worked with their special characteristics and learn more of the wonderful ways of divine grace in the individual soul. This is, as one would expect, Rolle's own teaching:

> Divers gifts truly are disposed to God's lovers: some are chosen to do; some to teach; some to love. Nevertheless all the holy covet one thing and run to one life, but by divers paths; for everyone chosen goes to the Kingdom of bliss by that way of virtue in the which he is most used. (*Incendium,* II, 6, p. 153.)

It is needful to delay on these matters here, at the outset of the illuminative way, because the diversities of God's ways become more manifest as we have explained, and many souls are given special assistance from God to confirm them in the right way. But it often happens that a devout Christian who has never had any kind of experience of this nature remains in this second period without knowing at all that he has reached it. One who has been faithful from the beginning, has had no violent reaction from the ways of God but has followed as diligently as might be the light that the he has received in faith, will have gone through the purifications permitted by the divine will in a true spirit of union with the Cross, and while regarding himself as still a humble beginner will in fact be enjoying the special union with Christ or even the prayer of quiet, which is one characteristic of the proficient soul. He must not be disquieted by finding none of the extraordinary graces he reads or hears about in the lives of others.

At the same time God often in the beginning of special periods of development will grant these extraordinary graces, not in any way as rewards for generous co-operation with his will, not as essential in any way to the Christian life, but precisely to encourage and lead the soul on to greater desires and greater heights of union. Visions, significant dreams, unmistakable 'co-incidences' or special feelings or comforts at prayer are not necessarily signs of sanctity, though they are often, as in the case of St Bernadette's visions, signs of God's election to sanctity. Someone at the beginning of this second period may hear a voice speaking to him from God, may see the figure on the crucifix move and incline towards him, may have a wonderful light to see all things in relation to God's love, may see a complete vision of heavenly joys or dream of some saint or of our Lord himself; these experiences if genuine are not the reality but only the sweet caresses of God the Lover showing his love and winning the soul. They are beginnings, enticements to enter. They are like the *Gloria* and the angels' appearance to the shepherds or the star appearing to the kings to introduce them to Christ the Lord. No store is to be set by them in themselves; they are almost trivial. At first they seem to be of breathtaking importance, but they are soon gone, merely sweet memories to keep the soul content in times of prolonged loneliness. If Richard's heat and song remained with him for long it was a great exception.

The parallel between this period of second conversion and illumination and that of the apostles from the Passion to the Ascension is clearly outlined by Père Garrigou-Lagrange in the *Three Ways of the Spiritual Life* (English edition, p. 31). Basing the parallel upon St Catherine's Dialogue he shows how our Lord appeared after the Resurrection to draw them into this new way, to console and to enlighten them. It was only the beginning of their life as apostles and the manifestations were tangible, but they did not last for more than forty days. And yet we can imagine the life time of complete preoccupation with God spent by the two disciples who went to Emmaus. 'And their eyes were opened, and they knew him.' It is unlikely that those eyes, the eyes of their spirit, were ever closed again; it is unlikely that they ever ceased from thinking of him and knowing him. Still the years rolled on after Pentecost and never again did he so manifest himself. Did they pine and fret at his absence? Their eyes had been opened and they knew; they knew his presence was in the soul, that it did not require the outward appearance, the walk to Emmaus, the sitting down to dinner, the breaking of bread. 'He vanished out of their sight.' He remained with them more intimately than ever before, and he never left them. They could say, as Richard Rolle echoed so many centuries later, that their hearts had been burning within them in his company. But the inner reality of that burning heart never disappeared though the feeling had gone when he vanished. So the good Christian who happens to have received some extraordinary grace at the beginning of this new way of enlightenment must not pine for its repetitions, must not look for it as necessary to his life. It was only the beginning. He may go many years without any more outward response from God. It is strange that this period is often marked more by an apparent deprivation of God than of any consolations or experiences.

As we, standing in darkness, see nothing, so in contemplation that invisibly lightens the soul. No seen light we see. Christ also makes darkness his resting place, and yet speaks to us in a pillar of a cloud. (*The Mending of Life,* c. 12, Misyn-Comper, p. 239).

. . . . .

Hesitations in the Face of Love

If we are right in supposing that when Richard Rolle describes the third and highest degree of love he is really considering the illuminative rather than the unitive way, we can fit him very neatly into a pattern of spiritual development. Thus we discover his own personal experiences of burning love and heavenly sound entering into his description of 'Singular Love' which is in his own eyes the most perfect state. The special but accessory favours which he had received from God at the beginning of this new way of life were the love in his breast which was so fervent as to convey even a physical sensation of heat and an interior sound of heavenly music. And these we find as part of the permament state of love which he calls 'Singular.'

> Singular love is when all comfort and solace are closed out of thy heart but that of Jesus Christ alone. It seeks no other joy. For the sweetness of him who is in this degree is so comforting and lasting in his love, so burning and gladdening that he or she that is in this degree may feel the fire of love burning in their souls . . . then the soul is Jesus-loving, Jesus-thinking, Jesus-desiring, only breathing in the desire for him, winging to him, burning for him, resting in him. Then the song of praise and love is come. . . . (*The Form of Living.*)[6]

But although this way of love seems to be very permanent and very comfortable 'so that the soul is so much comforted in the praise and love of God, and till death comes is singing spiritually to Jesus and in Jesus and of Jesus' (id.), nevertheless there are many sins which are still lurking in the soul even after the hardships of purification and which are still hindering the completion of the process of supernaturalising the whole man. There are times when the soul is given more special assurances as to the pureness of its love, but never can a man be satisfied or complacement about his state. He is always in danger, however many graces God may have poured upon him.

In this degree of love thou shalt overcome thine enemies, the world, the devil and the flesh. But nevertheless thou shalt always have fighting whilst thou livest: and till thou dost die it behoves thee to take care to stand so that thou fall not into delights, neither in evil thoughts, nor in evil words, nor in evil works (***Ego Dormio,*** Heseltine, p. 95).

And he says elsewhere that no man can completely slay 'engendered concupiscence' nor live so as never to sin in this life (***Fire of Love,*** Misyn, p. 158).

This is a salutary observation at all times and helps to explain how the really devout Christian is never the complacement one, and how the further advanced a man is on the way to perfection the more conscious he is of the danger of sin and of his own weakness. But it is a lesson which must be most urgently dinned into those who have passed through the initial stages of purification, have been given perhaps some of these 'experiences' which from time to time announce the beginning of a new phase, and are probably at the gateway to his singular way of love which St Thomas calls 'proficient'. For it is very easy to remain at the very gate and yet to miss the opportunity of pushing it open and stepping forward. If a man has progressed so far he will be tempted to feel that he is fairly 'safe', that the peace and virtue that have come to him are proud possessions, that any experience of God's presence he may have had was as though God has said, 'Well done thou good and faithful servant' and that he may definitely class himself among the elect. The result of these temptations if they are yielded to—and they are subtle and insidious temptations which easily deceive—is that progress ceases, and the man relapses into a pride or conceit which is very self-satisfied and which leads him to patronise others. The sign of this pride is a certain unteachableness in matters concerning the spiritual life; he holds on to his own opinions with a vehemence altogether out of proportion to their importance; he is unwilling to accept a contrary opinion even from his director or other authority. He feels so secure in the gifts that God has given him that he begins to act as so many heretics have acted, basing his certainty on an interior inspiration which he regards as of the Spirit, instead of on the outward judgment of authority.

The proud, truly, says Rolle, and those full of wrath seem to themselves so worthy that they can suffer nothing. . . . And that they have taken up they always defend, though it be false or untrue; and neither with authority nor reason will they be overcome, that they should not be seen to have said what were unaccording. And when they are untaught—and that they wot well—yet they will behave as if they were inspired in all things that belong to God. (***Fire of Love,*** Misyn, p. 43.)

There are surely many heretics who have begun well and have arrived at this second main stage of their life and then fallen into pride of intellect and confidence in their own 'spirit'.

By now the grosser sins have been overcome and even the more fleshly and sensual temptations will have ceased and the good Christian may have become so accustomed to that type of sin and temptation that the new forms catch him unawares; if he is not still conscious of the deep-rooted self-love which remains even through all that previous era of purification he will be easily led into conceit. Indeed the conceit of the 'pious' and the 'devout' is almost proverbial: they never recognise it in themselves, being too occupied with their experiences and interior states to be conscious of their overbearing attitude towards the rest of the world.

Wherefore they change the joy of incorruptible cleanness to wantoned beauty which shall not last. This soothly would they not do unless they were blinded with the fire of froward love, the which wastes (away) the burgeoning of virtue and nourishes the plants of all vice. Forsooth many are not set on womanly beauty nor like lechery, wherefore they trust themselves saved, as it were, with sickerness (security); and because of chastity only, which they bear outwardly, they ween they surpass all others as saints. . . . (id. p. 16).

Strangely in contrast with this sense of eminence and security there sometimes appears also an envy of others' spiritual well-being, an instinctive feeling of bitterness when a neighbour shows signs of holiness or of divine favours. This is a strange temptation in one who has been seeking the good and desiring to love God wholly, and often it is only a passing feeling which is quickly recognised for its ugly character. Nevertheless sometimes it does provide a very real obstacle to entering into this new way.

In contrast to 'the true soul' who casts out pride and wrath, Richard Rolle describes the envious man who raises ill reports about his neighbour, who feels downhearted when others are praised. 'But the soul the which is but a little kindled with heavenly contemplation cannot seek that vain glory of slipping (i.e. passing) praise. . . . For where any are that love God, they truly desire the profit of their fellows as of themselves' (id. p. 123).

Perhaps the most inevitable obstacle to a full entry into the illuminative way is the continual existence of weakness of character and of personal idiosyncrasies. For although the purifications have cleansed a good deal of the dross, a man's character has not been transformed or changed in any fundamental way in the first stage. He still lives and acts in a very human way and his own personal characteristics will still be present. The quick-tempered man will not give way to his temper wilfully, but he will remain irascible and easily riled. The sentimental man will find himself carried easily away by enthusiasm for passing things, such as the latest miracle or the sayings of some new ecstatic. Rolle himself does not show what would now be called psychological insight in this matter. He was not in danger of turning into himself; his spirituality was very objective so that he is mainly concerned with deliberate and outstanding sins on the one hand and the love of God on the other. But certain it is that these weaknesses appeared to him as the great stumbling block to progress (cf. *Fire of Love,* Misyn, p. 168).

The constant failure in one particular direction will often keep a man for long in the first stages of the spiritual life. It is only when he is willing to be plunged into the night of the senses that he releases himself from these imperfections and this very human mode of life. Especially, too, in the matter of the virtues, he must be ready to relinquish his habitual attitude towards them; he must not continue to exercise them as though he were only just beginning. He has to be generous and ready to be open-hearted and magnanimous for otherwise he will gauge his actions by what he is used to being instead of by what he is called to be. St Thomas, in speaking of the increase or lessening of charity, points out that it is of the nature of charity that it can itself never diminish without wholly being extinguished. If you love God, you cannot then proceed to love him less. Of itself the virtue brings a total love or none at all. And yet by a continuous lack of generosity the soul can be weakened and put in a state where what is contrary to charity may easily prevail. The reason is that venial sin itself is concerned with the things which lead to God rather than with God himself. Any sin that is directed against God himself would be serious and destroy charity which is concerned with him alone. Therefore venial sin is not directly against charity but only against the things that lead to charity; but venial sin does diminish charity indirectly by removing the means through which it usually works. Love of God will be shown in acts of obedience, consequently constant venial sins of disobedience will hamper the exercise of charity. In this way a man without falling into grave sin, which is not so likely at the end of the purgative way, will perhaps remain ungenerous and even careless in the matter of venial sins. He will hesitate to step any further forward.

Père Garrigou-Lagrange, writing of those who are shy of this new invitation of Christ, says: 'The proficient, who is content to behave as a beginner ceases to progress and becomes a "retarded soul". There is a considerable number of such souls and we do not take sufficient account of it. How many there are who set about developing their minds, extending their knowledge of their external activities . . . and yet take little trouble to grow in supernatural charity, which should have pride of place and inspire and enliven our whole life. . . . ' (*Perfection Chrétienne et Contemplation,* p. 230.) There will be many priests and those in charge of the spiritual welfare of Christians who will agree with this author with regard to the number who make a certain progress and then fall back into the uncertain state of the beginner because they are not ready to live really supernaturally but cling on to their old human ways.

Rolle for his part makes a continual plea for a complete turning to Christ. It would be a hopeless task to begin to quote him on this topic. He never ceases from urging his readers to hand themselves over completely to the love of Jesus. He is too principally concerned with contemplatives and even solitaries and he gives the impression that even many of these men and women hesitate on the edge of this new sea of love, not being prepared to plunge in. The third degree of love is contemplative love, which seeks solitude, and if his readers want to open their hearts to this love which is in God's gift alone, they must seek only Jesus with unstinted generosity.

> And therefore it behoves thee to forsake all worldly solace, that thy heart be bound to the love of no creature nor to any business on earth; that thou mayest be in silence, ever stable and stalwart, with thy heart in the love and fear of God. (*Ego Dormio,* Heseltine, p. 98.)

Always he is urging these solitaries to prepare their hearts for true love of Jesus.

Through the activities of spiritual exercises and the possibilities of mortification in the purgative way, the individual has learnt sufficiently how to subjugate his spirit to the human mode of Christian prayer and action. Now his spirit needs to be wholly surrendered to the Holy Spirit in order to live in the fullness of Christian life. It is therefore necessary to open the door which leads out into the darkness of the night of the senses. This new form of purification, which proceeds from God's own activities, is evidently necessary to overcome these tendencies to satisfaction and tardiness. This night of the senses is the first characteristic of the illuminative way and it follows the easy dalliance of the soul by God at the conclusion of the first stage.

The unsuspecting reader may at this stage throw up his hands in despair: what! more purifications, nights, darknesses, hardships, crosses: one would have thought that after the first stage of purification the Christian might be able to find some peace and joy somewhere. It would be an understandable mistake to regard these nights in terms of the hardships of the first stage of the spiritual life, for one who knows only that cross of striving to be virtuous and mortifying his passions and vices. But the 'purifications' to which the soul is now submitted are not to be compared with those that have gone before. It is almost a mistake to use the same word. That is why Richard Rolle is such an excellent guide to this new period, for he speaks always in terms of the love of Christ. And the dark night of the senses is first and foremost a new state of love. It is in fact a very positive thing. A recent writer thus distinguishes its principal characteristics: 'It is essentially a state of infused contemplation. . . . It is secondarily and as an accessory a state of suffering and purification' (*La Pratique de l'Oraison Mentale,* by Dom Belorgey, II, p. 25). This is a just distinction and it is important to realise that it is in itself a matter of a new kind of contemplation, rather than a new kind of mortification. It involves the latter, and certainly a good deal of pain is necessary to eradicate the pride and selfishness already alluded to. The nature of this contemplation frequently mentioned by Richard Rolle, theologically described by St John of the Cross, and placed in the centre of controversy in modern times will require a separate chapter. Here we will concentrate on the secondary aspects as they refer to the imperfections and temptations which beset the soul as it approaches this new life.

God leaves those who are making progress, says St John of the Cross, 'so completely in the dark that they know not whither to go with their sensible imagination and meditation: for they cannot advance a step in meditation . . . their inward sense being submerged in this night, and left with such dryness that not only do they experience no pleasure and consolation in the spiritual things . . . but they find insipidity and bitterness in the said things. . . . He (God) sets them down from his arms and teaches them to walk with their own feet, which they feel to be very strange for everything seems to be going wrong with them' (*Dark Night,* I, 8). And the Mystic Doctor proceeds to describe the signs which show this aridity to be the work of God rather than backsliding darkness.

The hermit of Hampole describes this state of dryness rather briefly when he is dealing with the length of time taken after the first conversion before a man can reach this true contemplation. He insists that it is in the gift of God above and is only 'gotten in great time and with great labour' (*Fire of Love,* Misyn, p. 134).

> Profiting little by little at the last they are made strong in spirit. Then afterward they have received sadness of manners, and so far as this present changeableness suffers have attained to stability of mind; for with great travails is some perfection gotten (id, p. 19).

But the insipidity of holy things which oppresses the soul at this time may account for his lack of apprecia-tion of the liturgy. For it is true that one who is really being called into this second way of love will strangely enough find all the things which had been at first such an inspiration become curiously meaningless. The mind can recognise their goodness, their utility, their theological soundness, but the spirit can make nothing of them. The splendours of the Christmas celebrations are assented to by the mind but the soul feels high and dry, wishing almost to run away from the great solemnities of Midnight Mass and the sweet holiness of the Crib—to run away into a corner alone. No wonder St John of the Cross says that everything seems to be going wrong.

> Because in the Kirk of God there are singers ordained in this degree and set to praise God and to stir the people to devotion, some have come to me asking why I would not sing as other men when they have oftimes seen me in solemn masses (*Fire of Love,* p. 132).

Of course for Rolle this difficulty arose mainly from the presence of the inward gift of song and the somewhat individualistic desire to be alone with this special experience, and yet it describes well the feeling of one who may have found great relish in the full solemnity of the liturgy and then suddenly finds it all withdrawn. He is naturally dismayed, and naturally also misunderstood by all those around who bide by the obvious teaching and encouragement of the Church. This is *the* way to praise God, join in the spirit of the liturgy, offer Mass with the people and sing happily in the services of the Church. Yes, replies the wondering soul, that is the way but it leaves me utterly cold. Rolle suffered much from the attacks of good-living people who noticed that he preferred low Masses and did not join in the singing even when he appeared at High Mass. And we may say in general that this is a period of misunderstandings and persecution from good people. It is particularly hard, for the poor individual is sufficiently perplexed by his own inward dryness; he cannot be sure where he is or what is happening to his spirit. Perhaps he is thrown aside after all, discarded by God because of his lack of generosity. And then authority steps in and tells him he is self-opinionated, proud and over-confident of his own views. His friends tell him he has ceased to be friendly and has removed himself to a distance, those who looked upon him as a budding saint tell him how disappointed they are in his apparent failure. His work seems not to prosper, his time of prayer is a torture. Indeed this is a night. Perhaps his critics are right; what use to continue in a life which has become almost meaningless?

> *Usquequo Domine obliviceris me in finem?*
> 'How long Lord forgettest thou me in the ending? How long away turn thou thy face from me?' The voice of holy men that covet and yearn the coming of Jesu Christ, that they might live with

him in joy. . . . His words may none say soothly but a perfect man or woman that has gathered together all the desires of their soul and with the nail of love fastened them in Jesu Christ, so that they think that one hour of the day were overlong to dwell from him, for them longs aye for him.[7]

The tempests and trials can only be overcome by the certainty of this longing which remains despite the apparent insipidity of spiritual things. *Accedia* brings a very different tastelessness, one which has no desire and no love for God. This is no acidity but aridity brought by God upon the soul to humble it, to increase its thirst for himself; to make it understand it can turn to no one but to him only, to him who has the power to heal and to perfect. Nothing now remains of much interest or desire save God alone. The things that were on the way to God, the acts of worship, the joy of companionship, the thrill of doing an act of mercy for his sake, these remain good and indeed very good, but they no longer retain much attraction in themselves. It is a Night of the Senses; the senses can find no joy in their natural object, in sights and sounds and feelings. This may be an unnatural state, against the nature of the senses, held back as it were by God from relishing what he had made them to relish, but it is needful for the birth in the soul of infused contemplation.

Ghostly gifts truly dress a devout soul to love burningly: to mediate sweetly; to contemplate highly; to pray devoutly; and praise worthily; to desire Jesu only, to wash the mind from filth of sin; to slaken fleshly desires; and to despise all earthly things; and to paint the wounds and Christ's cross in mind; and, with an unwearied desire, with desire to sigh for the sight of the most glorious clearness. (*Fire of Love,* Misyn, p. 112.)

. . . . .

Prayer from God

Anyone who has reached the period of spiritual life known as the Night of the Senses will find that prayer has so changed its character as to be almost a new kind of human activity. Hitherto the time devoted to actual prayers will have been divided up between liturgical practices and private meditations. He will have become accustomed, perhaps through the habits formed during many years, to set about these devotions in a methodical way, always bearing in mind the adage that the good Christian, while leaving all to God in his spirit, must act as though all depended on himself. He will have learned a manner of assisting at Mass; he will have recited the same number of *Paters* and *Aves,* acts of contrition and charity, while he kneels beside his bed morning and night; his rosary or 'stations' will be prominent in his regular horary; and finally his times of quiet at meditation will be organised by a method,

interspersed with 'acts' and sometimes be predominantly concerned with struggles against distractions and drowsiness. For these many years he may be said to have been trying to *acquire* prayer, to make it his own by his own efforts.

Now God begins to make the Christian's prayers into *his* (God's) own form of spiritual converse. The movement of the spiritual life comes from a divine rather than a human source. The soul finds that it can no longer acquire habits or states of prayer; it is almost forced to leave the initiative to God. The 'acquisitive' attitude gives place to the state of receptivity of God's actions; the infused virtues and above all infused contemplation require the soul to be passive rather than active in its way of prayer. We have already quoted the modern writer who has summed up the illuminative way as being essentially a state of infused contemplation, and we have noticed how Richard Rolle grew less comfortable in assisting at the liturgical functions of the Church. The effect of the new gifts God now gives the soul is to make it more than ever desirous of being alone and retiring from the activities, both internal and external, of its former life. For this middle state must necessarily incite a conflict between the active concerns of the earlier state and the quietude of the union to which the Christian is progressing. It is probable that now the communal liturgical prayers appeal less than at any other age of the spiritual life. Later the Christian strengthened by the power of infused contemplation and nourished by the spirit of quiet will return to these external forms of worship with a greater intensity and a wider capacity to share these spiritual goods with his fellow Christians. Thus Rolle visualises a time of union when all activities, even the most physical, are gathered into the life of uninterrupted prayer:

We can forsooth if we be true lovers of our Lord Jesu Christ think upon him when we walk, and hold fast the song of his loves whiles we sit in fellowship; and we may have mind of him at the board and also in the tasting of meat and drink. At every morsel of meat and draught of drink we ought to praise God. . . . And if we be in labour of our hands what lets us to lift our hearts to heaven without ceasing to hold the thought of endless love?[8]

This state of union has not been reached in the progressive with which we are concerned. Then the prayers of the Mass and the Office will be relished in a far deeper, more unified and affective manner. Now the Christian wants to be quiet and away from external preoccupations.

In this respect Rolle's language is borrowed from Jeremias who received the burning coal upon his lips. The soul should now be receptive of this infused love of God, coming down from its source in the bosom of the Father. This glowing ember must be allowed to rest in man's heart so that lying there it may soon set fire to that on which it rests.

> 'By the continuance of prayer the soul is burnt with the fire of God's love: our Lord truly says by his prophet . . . ' (Jer. 33, 29) 'Are not my words as burning fire?' The psalm (118, 140) also says . . . 'Thy speech is hugely burned' (Misyn, p. 91).

The insistence on acquiring virtues and the habit of prayer, the continued attachment to active forms of devotion, these stirrings which arise from the soul rather than from God only create a barrier to the divine gift; the burning ember is thrown out, not being allowed to rest where it might burn and begin a conflagration:

> There are many now that forthwith cast out the word of God from the mouth and heart, nor suffering it there to rest in them; and therefore they are not burnt with the heat of comfort but bide cold in sloth and negligence, even after innumerable prayers and meditations of scripture, because forsooth they neither pray nor meditate in mind (id.).

Certainly prayer has to remain active in character until such time as God himself chooses to turn its course aside into this new and heaven-sent way of receptivity. But it is easy to hold on to the innumerable prayers at the time when God is striving to effect the change. It is attachment to active prayer which prevents the burning love from descending into the heart.

When St Thomas is speaking of the attention due to vocal prayer he lists three ways in which the mind can be occupied with what the lips are saying—the first is to the actual recitation of the words of the prayer, the second to the meaning of the words. Both these represent an active form of participating in liturgical prayer as well as in recitation of private devotions. But it is the third way which is most fundamental and necessary to all prayer and that is rather by the intention of the will than by the attention of the mind; it may be present in the unlettered and stupid as well as in the most highly elevated soul whose every faculty is absorbed in God and forgetful of all else. The mind here is attentive not necessarily to the words but to the goal of prayer, namely God—*ad finem orationis, sc. ad Deum* (II-II, 83, 13). He goes on to say that prayer in this life can only be 'without ceasing' in so far as it proceeds from the desire of charity, that love which is a gift of God and which keeps every thought and action in contact with this very *finis orationis!* 'Prolixity in prayer', he says, 'does not consist in the asking for many things, but in this that the affection for the one thing to be desired is continued' (id. 14, c. ad 2). This the heart of prayer as outlined by St Thomas must be borne in mind in considering the illuminative way in general and infused contemplation

in particular. It shows that the prayer itself consists in an act of the will in loving God rather than in any act of any other virtue, even the virtue of religion. This act comes from an infused virtue, a gift from God which must necessarily reach the soul as a *perfect* gift as it does not in itself depend on the previous activities—the presence of the burning love of God does not of itself depend on the fact that the man has been making frequent and increasing acts of charity, but rather on the act of God placing that love in the soul, and God's action itself will have no blemish. And this means also that the feelings and emotions are not necessarily involved but that the will alone receives at least the principal virtue, the burning gift of love.

These considerations are important when we consider Rolle's language which so often conveys the atmosphere of intense emotional sweetness and delight; whereas the night of the senses has in fact isolated and to a certain extent destroyed these feelings and sensibilities. So that a passage such as the following must be read in the light of this fundamental reality of the *finis orationis,* the actual love of God springing from the will under the divine action.

> Truly the more I am lift from earthly thoughts the more I feel the sweetness desired. . . . I beseech he kiss me with the sweetness of his refreshing love, straitly halsing me by the kissing of his mouth so that I fail not.

> Ghostly gifts truly dress a devout soul to love burningly; to meditate sweetly; to contemplate highly; to pray devoutly; and praise worthily; to desire Jesu only, to wash the mind from filth of sin; to slaken fleshly desires; and to despise all earthly things; and to paint the wounds and Christ's cross in mind; and, with an unwearied desire, with desire to sigh for the sight of the most glorious clearness (Misyn, p. 112).

This is the genuine prayer springing from the infusion of love and remaining independent of the senses and emotions. He clearly states that meditation is turned into songs of joy (id. p. 68) and that the soul must continue to pray and meditate until such time as the 'heart is ravished in prayer to behold heavenly things' so that 'passing earthly things' it may be made perfect in Christ's love (id. p. 116). And there is one outstanding passage which we may be permitted to quote at some length as it brings us to the centre of the question of infused contemplation which is the principal characteristic of this stage in spiritual development, and gives a true understanding of this prayer which rests in the will in a more and more continuous act of love:

> The clearer certain the love of a lover is the nearer and the more present to him God is. And thereby he joys more clearly in God, and the more he feels of

his sweet goodness that is wont to *inshed itself to lovers and to glide into the hearts of the meek* with mirth beyond comparison. This forsooth is pure love: . . . The sharpness of his mind being cleansed, is altogether stabled into the one desire of everlastingness; and with *freeness of spirit* he continually beholds heavenly things—as he that is ravished by the beauty of any whom he beholding cannot but love.

But . . . ravishing is understood in two ways. One manner forsooth is when some man is ravished out of fleshly feeling. . . . [Rolle here describes the effects of the intensity of desire of God outlined by St Thomas at the end of II-II, 83, 13*c*.] Another manner of ravishing there is, that is the lifting of the mind into God by contemplation.[9]

Rolle continues to describe the effects of the *inshed* love leading to contemplation in relation to 'wisdom unwrought' and to the mind passing into 'stableness'; in other places too he refers to this stableness which comes from Jesus Christ after the Christian has prepared for it by meditation.[10] The change in prayer is thus described in terms of the coming of the Word into the heart to rescue it from 'the waverings of the mind' and to quieten it. It is the first prayer which may be said to be a direct act of God on the soul not also acquired by the exercise of the mind and will:

Which things are they that allure us to conform us to God's will? There are three. First, the example of creatures that is had by consideration: the goodliness of God that is gotten by mediation and prayer; and mirth of the heavenly kingdom *that is felt in a manner by contemplation.*[11]

There can be little doubt that the Yorkshire mystic in these passages is referring to what is now known as infused contemplation and which has been for some years the subject of dispute in comparing it with what is called acquired contemplation. We need not concern ourselves very closely with the modern discussion but it is interesting to note that the distinction between two types of contemplation, or contemplative prayer, had in Rolle's time been already of long standing, having been drawn by one who exercised an influence on fourteenth-century Oxford. This was Richard of St Victor, who had died late in the twelfth century but who had played a great part in the development of St Bonaventure's spiritual doctrine, and St Bonaventure has left his mark on Rolle.[12] Richard himself had made a threefold distinction of the 'quality of contemplation'; the expansion of the mind (*mentis dilatatio*) which does not overstep the limits of human ingenuity and application; the raising of the mind (*mentis sublevatio*) when a certain divine liveliness diffuses the understanding but without carrying it out of itself; the transformation of the mind (*mentis alienatio*) when the di-

vine activity goes quite beyond the powers of the understanding. He says that the first comes from human activity (and must therefore be an 'acquired' contemplation), the third from divine grace alone (and we should call it 'infused'), the second from a combination of the two activities. This second type of contemplation is difficult to analyse for he says that human effort is supported and elevated by grace; but it may well be the fruit of meditation and discursive prayer which leads the soul on to the abandonment of human forms and to this receptive attitude in which it may become subject to the divine influence.

This division, which is echoed by Rolle in the final quotation from the *Mending of Life* above, would seem to correspond with experience and psychological development. For as a rule a man will not undergo a sudden and complete change-over from human discursive activity to an equally complete passivity to the divine form of contemplation. There is a period in which the soul cannot meditate or occupy itself with its own considerations in prayer, but when the divine infusion is only perceived as a momentary actual grace bestowed at rare intervals. This is 'the space of life between' which has been described by a modern writer specifically as 'acquired contemplation', 'a contemplation in which a certain divine infusion comes to the assistance of the soul, so that it may hold itself in the presence of God by a gaze of living faith'.[13] It is an expression which is of some use in describing the period at the beginning of the night of the senses when 'active' prayer (liturgy or meditation) becomes increasingly difficult and a new type of aridity descends on the soul. The mind and heart together can practise a type of loving gaze on God which is made more practicable by the aridity—the dark night—sent by God. There is here a mixture of activity and passivity which St Teresa calls the prayer of recollection and Richard of St Victor *mentis sublevatio.*

The modern discussion is first of all a matter of names; for 'acquired contemplation' is a term not found among the great mystical writers. But secondly, and more seriously, some of those who use this terminology maintain that the normal route to perfection will lead only to this half-active, half-passive state in which the heart must be all the time maintaining its effort to gaze at the divine face. They aver that the fully infused contemplation is a mystical phenomenon lying off the beaten track and granted only as an exceptional grace to the chosen few who happen to be so favoured. It will be safer to return to the older terminology and the broader and more integrated view of the earlier teaching as expressed by Richard Rolle. For him, as for St Teresa and St John of the Cross, the word 'contemplation' is used for that perception of the divine 'Clearness' granted by God at first fitfully but eventually with that 'stableness' which gives the Christian a constant inner certainty of the presence of God and a constant outpouring of love. This state, which must characterise the illuminative way, according to Rolle is not a *gratia gratis data* but a stage in the normal development of the soul as its powers are gathered into a closer and closer unity and as God prepares it to be transfixed *wholly* by the fiery dart of his love. He speaks of it, for example, in the chapter on 'Clearness of Mind' in *The Mending of Life*. A man by spiritual reading, prayer and meditation can so cleanse his mind that he can 'have his mind busy to God' (St Teresa's loving gaze of affection)—'for in this degree all the thought is dressed to Christ; all the mind, although he *seems* to speak to others, is spread unto him'. And thus the soul prepared both by its own and by God's action is prepared for the next step when 'full oft a wonderful joy of God is given and heavenly song is inshed' (Misyn-Comper, p. 228).

The soul has been prepared by this cleansing for the activity of the Gifts of the Holy Ghost hitherto bound down by venial sins. The purgative way has gradually overcome the attachment to the slight sins and self-centredness which had prevented the Holy Spirit from working on the soul. The gifts of wisdom and under-standing, of counsel and fortitude, they are all there in the first infusion of grace, but the soul cannot be moved promptly and instinctively as it should by their power because it has tied itself to the earth as the Lilliputians tied Gulliver by the hundreds of tiny threads of venial sins. When, however, the soul has generously purified herself from these evil bonds then it is the normal development of the Gifts that the Holy Ghost should begin to work directly and instinctively upon the soul. This is infused contemplation, the essence of the illu-minative way and the normal experience of those who are growing in grace. Rolle sums it up beautifully in the last two chapters of *The Mending of Life*.

> O sweet and delectable *light* that is my Maker unmade; *enlighten* the face and sharpness of my inward eye with *clearness unmade,* that my mind, pithily cleansed from uncleanness and made marvellous with *gifts,* may swiftly flee into the high mirth of love; and *kindled with thy savour* I may sit and rest, joying in thee, Jesus. And gazing as it were ravished in heavenly sweetness, and *made stable* in the beholding of things unseen, never save by godly things shall I be gladdened (id. p. 229).

> To me it seems that contemplation is the joyful song of God's love taken into the mind with the sweetness of angel's praise. This is the jubilation which is the end of perfect prayer and high devotion in this life (id. p. 237).

Many people are naturally timid about this doctrine lest they fall into some kind of illuminism or quietism. They are reasonably hesitant about relinquishing their hold on their own activities. It is easy to be swept away on the tide of sloth into an ocean of delusion, moved hither and thither on the face of this awful deep by figments of their imagination—voices or visions, violent or vaunting devils, voluptuous angels or vainglorious vanities. Infused contemplation sug-gests by its very sound a launching out into the deep for which they are unprepared and which fills them with the dread of the unknown. Such people must comfort themselves with the assurance that these su-pernatural gifts, this infusion of divine powers (the virtues—and above all the virtue of charity) do not take place without the parallel preparation and co-operation of the man himself. If mystical states were all exceptional or extraordinary well might they fear, for there would be no relation between their own 'acquired' state and the sudden overpowering reality of the divine. But there is a correspondence between the two. The soul must be for ever vigilant and for ever increasing in humility in its surrender to the divine action. Rolle insists on this constant activity, as it were on the threshold of the soul:

> It must be taken to with all busyness that we wake in prayer, that is to say not to be lulled by vain thoughts that withdraw the mind and make it forget whither it is bound and always let, if they can, to overcome the effect of devotion; the which the mind of the pray-er would perceive if he prayed with wakefulness, busyness and desire. (*Fire of Love,* I, 22, p. 92.)

There is little danger of a false illuminism, untethered and fickle which cannot be driven in the shafts with reason and common sense, so long as the Christian is wholehearted in his penance and generous in his re-sponse to the day-to-day demands of the virtues. He will not abandon prudence, but he will discover that in response to his fidelity, wisdom and counsel will de-scend upon him and perfect his prudence. St John of the Cross may lead the way without being suspect.

> When the faculties had been perfectly annihilated and calmed, together with the passions, desires and affections of my soul, wherewith I had experienced and tasted God after a lowly manner, I went forth from my own human way and operation to the operation and way of God. That is to say, my understanding went forth from itself, turning from the human to the divine; for when it is united with God by means of this purgation its understanding no longer comes through its natural light and vigour, but through the divine Wisdom wherewith it has become united (*Dark Night* II, 4. Peers, I, 405).

. . . . .

The Prayer of Quiet

Young enthusiasts for the life of prayer cannot be too frequently reminded of the danger of applying directly to their own persons the doctrines they read about. As they grow older they often become so self-conscious or introspective that they cannot read the lives of saints or descriptions of mystic states without discovering parallels in their own interior lives. This is a weakness not confined to spiritual matters, for we remember the hero of *Three Men in a Boat* who began reading a medical handbook and soon decided that he had symptoms of *all* the diseases therein described except 'housemaid's knee'. This is typical of those who read spiritual or physical medicine. It is necessary to repeat the warning against this form of introspection before beginning to discuss in detail the more passive forms of prayer and the higher states of the spiritual life. Certainly in general all men are called to these passive ways of the spirit, but by no means all men, not even all who are interested, reach to these states. And of those who are raised to a more passive prayer it may be said that there are hardly two alike, so diverse is the direct action of God upon the soul. Readers, therefore, must be resolutely objective in their approach to the subject. For their own personal problems they should be more ready to refer to their director or confessor who often has a clearer insight into their state than they have themselves. The doctrine of the great mystics, like St John of the Cross or St Teresa, should be read in a wide, more comprehensive spirit by which the reader is led to see how wonderfully God works in the souls of the just, and thus to return indirectly to his own relationship with God. These pages, too, are a study of the doctrine of the English Mystics—a study, not a self-scrutiny. They should be read as the devout theologian reads books and articles about divine things—he is certainly involved personally in them in his life, but his study retains an abstractive character which only *after study* will have its reflex action on his own spiritual life.

The chief characteristic, then, of the illuminative way is a prayer which is caused by God rather than by the free will of man; and it is the consideration of this form of prayer which demands an objective approach, particularly if studied in relation to the very singular manner of Richard Rolle. He needs to be studied rather than copied as a model. Indeed Rolle himself makes this clear:

> For I do not say that thou or another that reads this shall do it all; for it is God's will to choose whom he will to do what is told here, or else another thing in another manner, as he gives men grace for their salvation. For various men take various graces of our Lord Jesus Christ: and all shall be set in the joy of heaven, that ends in charity. Whoever is in this degree has wisdom and discretion to love according to God's will.[14]

This degree in which God works as he wills brings an habitual mindfulness of God. The mind and will must necessarily be occupied with the general needs and activities of life; but even at such times when a person is busied about household duties or the requirements of a livelihood the habit of the presence of God remains. The habit may, and often is, deliberately brought into action by a conscious desire for and knowledge of God present in the soul and in all created things round about. But even when the *acts* of mind and will are concerned with other things God is present as a companion is present in a room with a friend who is concentrating all his faculties on some delicate work of his fingers or some deep mental problem. The friend 'knows' his companion is by his side but does not revert to it by an act of his mind; he is conscious in a passive way of companionship. So too God's companionship pervades the whole life of a man in this degree like an atmosphere. The man requires no words to speak with the divine companion; he hardly needs to make a deliberate act of his will; for all his will is permanently resting in God.

'Rest' is perhaps the key word to this type of prayer. It comes frequently in Rolle's account of the perfect form of life and prayer. It is the mark of 'spiritual circumcision' when all the attachments to this world have been cut off by the purgative way and the night of the senses, and the soul is set apart as the Jew of old from the Gentile.

> When a man feels himself in that degree, then is a man circumcised spiritually, when all other business and affections and thoughts are drawn away out of his soul, that he may *rest* in God's love without entanglement with other things. (*Of Delight in God,* Heseltine, p. 105.)

In one place Rolle admits that idleness destroys this heat of God's love which is otherwise habitual; and this we should expect since the greatest enemy to the prayer of rest or quiet is its material semblance the name of which is sloth. But he says also that weariness from travel or immoderate occupation also drives it away, and likewise being 'given without measure to disputation' (*Fire of Love,* Prologue: Misyn, p. 13). From this we may conclude that unnecessary or protracted journeyings and such-like activities which employ the mind and will too much with material things are enemies to the habit as well as to the act of this consciousness of God, are in other words contrary to the rest and quiet of which he speaks.

> And moreover sleep gainstands me as an enemy; for no time heavies me to lose save that in which, constrained, I yield to sleeping. Waking truly I am busy to warm my soul, thirled [pierced] as it were with cold, the which when settled [in the sense that dregs settle] in devotion, I know well is set on fire (id. p. 12).

Yet neither sleep nor any other activity except it be in some sense sinful and turning away however slight from God can break into this rest so as to disturb it seriously.

> Afterward truly strongly and well used in praying, and given to high rest in meditation . . . his affection goes up so that the entrance is opened, in the beholding of heavenly mysteries, to the eye of his mind. . . . Nevertheless (his soul) gladly suffers adversity that happens, for sweetly she rests in the joy of eternal love. And all these things that happen can not destroy that joyful song that she had received. . . . (id. bk. 2, c. 6, pp. 154-5).

The soul that rests in God in this way is evidently borne up by his presence as a swimmer resting from his exertions floats borne up by the deep of the ocean, immersed and yet supported without effort on his part. The resting in God seems to be closely allied to the prayer of quiet which might be called a speciality of St Teresa's. She describes it as the beginning of rest when the soul need not be continually at work. The will, she says, is occupied, has been made captive—'imprisoned by God, as one who well knows itself to be the captive of him whom it loves'. God begins to communicate himself to the soul in a new and unexpected way (cf. *Life*, chapter XIV).

As we have seen, this communication from God is the beginning of infused contemplation, and this contemplation lies at the heart of the prayer of quiet. A new kind of rhythm is set in motion in which the sudden manifestations of God ripple across the smooth surface of this restful certainty of God's presence. The soul is constantly mindful of God, and he in turn brings new treasures of grace to the soul when it is itself feeling powerless and unable to move of itself. The explanation of this state must be sought in the doctrine of the gifts, for it is now that the soul is sufficiently freed from entanglements of venial sin and worldly attachments for the Holy Spirit to be able to use his gifts. Rolle is as insistent as St Teresa that the world must by now be utterly given up, cut away by a ruthless severing of all earthly ties. This is the doctrine which often terrifies, but which is absolutely necessary as a prerequisite to the full working of the gifts.

St Teresa gives examples of how the Holy Spirit worked through his gifts when the prayer of quiet came upon her. Her feeble knowledge of Latin was suddenly illumined so that she could read the Psalter as though it were in Spanish, and further she could penetrate the meaning of the Spanish so that the Psalter began to reveal its mysteries without special study or mental argument. This was the gift of understanding which is the special feature of the illuminative way. Rolle shows that the other gifts are also at work, for example that of Fear of the Lord. This new state of love casts out all fear of any but God, and overcomes pain, so that the soul 'feels no dread of any creature' (*Fire of Love*, i, 26. p. 110). And so a gentle and undisturbing fear of anything which might in any way offend God or remove that sweet and now constant presence pervades the soul and keeps it clear from any new entanglements with the world. 'And he greatly dreads lest he be drawn into these things that the least grieve him' (id. ii, 6, p. 157).

This is a fear which springs wholly from love and is not the contrary passion which is cast out by love; it is a gift which the Spirit uses at the approach of evil or temptation to keep the soul free from worry or disturbance. A modern analogy might be found in the sensitive cell which is used as a burglar alarm; the slightest shadow cast over it reacts so as to set off the bells; in this way the household may rest untroubled by fears of being robbed unawares. So also the gift of fear helps to preserve the rest and quiet within the soul; it need not be anxious about being taken off its guard or falling unwittingly into evil.

But the principal gift, as we have said, is that of understanding which provides the illumination from which this stage gets its name. St Thomas, in his question on this gift, points out how the unaided intellect of man so often cannot pierce below the superficial appearances of things. We are prone to mistake accidentals for the essential reality beneath, words for their meaning, likenesses and figures for the truth they signify. We need a supernatural light to pierce through the words of the Bible, or to plunge into the divine reality which lies hidden behind all the sacramental manifestations of God's work. This gift, therefore, corresponds to the sixth beatitude—'Blessed are the clean of heart for they shall see God', not merely because man must be pure and purified before he can sense the divine truth in things but also in so far as the mind itself has to be freed from the bondage of vivid imaginations and purged of obfuscating errors. All this the gift of understanding does once the soul has been freed by various purifications from contamination with merely earthly things.[15] This new light which penetrates into the depths of reality like some new intellective way is a perfection of faith; it does not provide any new kind of knowledge; it is in fact a prompt and penetrating glance into the truths of faith, prompt to the sudden movement of the Spirit.

Rolle says in his prologue to the *Fire of Love* that he is writing not for the learned and scientific men who are in fact so concerned with the superficial things— the simple will 'pass temporal things' and reach this endless rest and all their knowledge contributes to their loving rightly (p. 13). There are in fact many parallels to St Thomas's teaching, referred to above, in Rolle's *Mending of Life,* particularly in the chapters where he writes of cleanness of mind and of contemplation. After writing of the mind's eye being taken up to behold heavenly things, yet still as in a shadow and in a mirror, he continues:

> Although truly the darkness of sin be gone from an holy soul, and murk things and unclean be passed, and the mind be purged and enlightened, yet whiles it bides in this mortal flesh that wonderful joy is not perfectly seen. Forsooth holy and contemplative men with a clear face behold God; that is either their wits are opened, for to understand holy writ. . . . As one might say all lettings betwixt their mind and God are put back. (*The Mending of Life,* Misyn, p. 239.)

Although the gift is a permanent possession of the soul's so that Rolle can write that the mind is 'enlightened with sweet mystery' and that God has 'opened to mine eyes the window of contemplation' (*Fire of Love,* ii, cc. 2 and 5, pp. 137, 151), yet it cannot be used actively like an additional faculty. It does not mean that a person at this stage of life can at will see the face of God within the external drapery of words, signs or material creation. The gift makes it possible for the mind to be moved instinctively, with immediate promptitude, to the inspiration of the Holy Spirit whenever the latter chooses to raise the veil leading more deeply into the mysteries. The way is illuminative because of these sudden flashes of understanding rather than from a permanently diffused brilliance. A man must still use logic, reasoning and argument to learn more about divine truths at other times than when the Spirit is in fact enlightening him. In other words the illuminative way with its gift of understanding does not spell illuminism; it does not mean that it creates an élite of inspired gnostics who have been raised to a new form of knowledge where theology would be out of place.

It is interesting to notice in respect of this illumination of the gift of understanding that Richard Rolle employs the simile of the sunbeam which was later a favourite with St John of the Cross. We may compare chapter 28 of the *Fire of Love* (Book i, p. 119) where he likens this enlightening fire of the Holy Spirit to a sunbeam with the following passage of St John of the Cross where he is treating of this same state of enlightenment: 'Let this suffice now to explain how meet it is that the soul should be occupied in this knowledge, so that it may turn aside from the way of spiritual meditation, and be sure that, although it seems to be doing nothing, it is well occupied. . . . It will also be realised . . . that if this light presents itself to the understanding in a more comprehensible and palpable manner, as the sun's ray presents itself to the eye when it is full of particles, the soul must not therefore consider it purer, brighter and more sublime'. (*Ascent,* ii, 14. Peers, 1, p. 126.) The Spanish mystic has perfected the simile and shows that although meditation and discursive reasoning in prayer may for the most part become impossible, yet the light vouchsafed does not bring an easy and palpable understanding, but is more like the sunbeam shining where there are no particles to make it manifest, shining more penetratingly, more purely, more 'darkly'. And yet it has not yet reached the purity of the light of wisdom. This the highest of all the gifts which proceeds more directly from the intensity of perfect love is characteristic of the way of union. Naturally this gift too has been released by the new freedom from wilful venial sins but it is not as yet the predominant gift. Rolle, however, looks forward to it when he speaks of the ravishings of love:

> They also are called ravished by love that are wholly and pefectly given to the desires of their Saviour, and worthily ascend to the height of contemplation. With wisdom unwrought are they enlightened, and are worthy to feel the beat of the undescried light, with whose fairness they are ravished (*Fire of Love,* ii, 7. p. 162).

Another sort of gift begins also to make its appearance at this time, namely a certain assurance from God that the person favoured by these graces will never fall away but will reach the fulfilment of his destiny in heaven. Before this time he will have had nothing more to judge his state from than the general hope shared by all who do what is asked of them and make use of the sacraments. But we often find in the mystics some more personal assurance than this general way of guessing that one is in a state of grace. Evidently it does not imply a Calvinistic idea of predestination and an experience of that special choice. It depends on the cooperative will of the man himself and on his perseverance. But Rolle says that once souls have been strengthened and enlightened in this way, they will be specially comforted. 'And if they at any time begin to err, through ignorance or frailty, he soon shows them the right way, and all that they have need of, he teaches them.' (*Form of Living,* 2, Heseltine, p. 20.) And he speaks elsewhere of knowing he is in a state of charity which he will never lose and of being confirmed in grace (cf. *Mending of Life,* c. 10, p. 228; *Fire of Love,* i, 15, p. 72). But he makes a more special claim on one occasion: 'He that has this joy, and in this life is thus gladdened, is inspired of the Holy Ghost: he cannot err, whatever he do it is lawful. No mortal man can give him counsel so good as that is that he has in himself of God Immortal' (*Fire of Love,* i, 11, p. 55).

He quotes in reference to this special gift the favourite text that 'the spiritual man judgeth all things'; but goes on to say that it would be presumption for anyone to think he had this gift, for even the highest contemplatives are not given it, and that it is granted but seldom and to few. He implies, however, that in some way the exceptional man to whom this gift is granted will know of the gift; he seems to suggest even that he, Rolle, had received some such assurance of inerrancy.

This is not a claim peculiar to Rolle and we shall find it later appearing in a rather dubious form in Mother Julian. Indeed, among those who have reached the stage of prayer of which we write an assurance of this kind, imagined or real, is not unknown at the present time. Yet if it be true it must be kept clear of any note of determinism and it must not interfere with the essential freedom of will and variety of knowledge and judgment in the individual. It may, however, be some kind of special experience in which a very few are privileged to share more deeply in the eternal knowledge of God. Rolle speaks of it here in connection with the gift of counsel; and it might be regarded as a divinely guaranteed prudential judgment.

Yet when such an assurance is given in reality it could only be granted to the one who would not in fact misuse it by turning it into a subject for conceit or presumption. The very fact that he misused such an assurance should prove at once that it was in fact only a subjective fancy and not an objective promise. Perhaps we could discover a parallel to this exceptional knowledge in the inevitability and yet freedom of choice involved in the workings of efficacious grace. In this way it might be some sort of conscious realisation of what is in fact a reality behind the scenes of every predestined soul. It is not impossible for God to make such a revelation; but it would not be, as the Calvinists would have it, an ordinary grace of God. The Church teaches explicitly that no one in this life can presume to claim to belong to the number of the elect. 'For, except by some special revelation, it is impossible to know whom God has chosen for himself.' This is the clear statement of the Council of Trent against the Calvinist position (cf. *Denzinger*, nn. 805 and 826). But the Council does allow for an occasional peculiar manifestation of God's choice, and it is probably to this that Richard Rolle and other mystics refer. But it is evidently a gift which of necessity must be ignored even by the very few to whom it is granted.

These are however special graces and do not form the usual furniture of the illuminative way. The Christian who is enlightened now by the gift of understanding will yet be often plunged in darkness and uncertainty. Aridity of a very deep and penetrating nature is still often the only outward aspect of his prayer. As the aridity had attacked his sensitive faculties in the night of the senses, so his 'enthusiasm' had died, and by now he has come to depend far more on the will of God working in the purity of his own will and mind. With this sensible dryness goes a bitter and burning desire and an intense love which is almost purely a thing of the will. And these last two features of the illuminative way are of course so characteristic of Richard Rolle that they will require another chapter for their treatment.

. . . . .

Love of the Word

We cannot take leave of Richard Rolle without listening to his principal message and the one which is the dominant theme of the illuminative way. His greatest work was on **The Fire of Love,** his most unique mystical experience was the burning of love in his breast, and his poetry which did more than anything else to spread his spirit among his contemporaries is concerned with the sweet love of Jesus, his spouse. Love is thought, with great desire of a fair Loving.[16]

The illumination as we have seen comes principally from the shining of the Gifts of the Holy Spirit in the beginning of infused contemplation. But this light cannot of course be separated from the Word whose function it is to enlighten the understanding. Indeed the activities of the second and third Persons of the Blessed Trinity in this respect cannot be separated; it is the one action of the *Verbum spirans amorem*.

> The mind truly disposed to cleanness, receives from God the thought of eternal love . . . [and it is necessary that this] mind be fully knit unto Christ, and it lasts in desires and thoughts of love—the which are certain and endless intent—and which thoughts, wherever he be, sitting or going, he meditates within himself without ceasing, desiring nothing but Christ's love. (**Fire of Love,** 25, Misyn-Comper, p. 107.)

This is typical of Rolle and of the period we are here considering. One of the sweetest joys now is to meet Jesus, the Word Incarnate, in this new and more intimate life of love.

On the side of the creature lover there has grown up through the various purifications and the 'cleansing' of his mind a desire far purer than when he first set out to serve the Lord. At first the yearning of the soul for God was occasioned principally by the knowledge of the *duty* of loving God above all things, then came the fuller understanding of the will of God as a personal love for the soul which in its turn responded more spontaneously in its longing; and now that the divine touch has been laid on her the soul begins to experience an almost bitter desire for the Beloved. Commenting on the opening verse of Psalm 12, Rolle says:

> The voice of holy men, who covet and yearn the coming of Jesus Christ, that they may live with him in joy, and complaining of delaying, says: 'Lord, how long forgettest thou me, in the ending,' which I covet to have and to hold, that is 'how long delayest thou me from the sight of Jesus Christ, who is the very ending of my intent?' 'And how long turnest thou thy face from me?' that is, 'When

wilt thou give me a perfect knowing of thee?' These words may none say truly save a perfect man or woman who has gathered together all the desires of her soul and with the nail of love fastened them in Jesus Christ. . . . (cf. H. E. Allen, *English Writings of Richard Rolle,* pp. 10-11).

The beginnings of love have stirred up a desire which in its turn feeds love and prepares the way for the divine love to descend more completely into the dwelling of his choice. 'For the longer we live the hotter we desire thee, and the more joy we feel in thy love, and painfully we hie to thee' (*Fire of Love,* 26, p. 110).

This desire regarded from the ascetic point of view arises from the renunciation of wordly, material desires and concupiscence. Rolle offers his book to those who 'all things forgetting and putting aback that are longing to this world, they love to be given only the desires of our Master' (*Prologue,* Misyn, p. 13); and in the eighth chapter of the first book he describes how they must fly all worldly attractions, and staunch the wounds of fleshly desires. He calls this 'highest poverty'; indeed it represents the cutting away of earthly ties and attachments; and in *The Form of Living* he gives as the first two signs of a man's being in charity that he has no covering of earthly things, and that he has a fervent longing for heaven so that he can find no joy in this life (cf. Heseltine, *Selected Works,* p. 46).

But this negative way of regarding the quenching of earthly lusts can only reveal a superficial aspect of the new-found joy in desiring. For it is not possible merely to destroy all human yearning. The heart is made to desire, and to destroy its every longing would be to destroy human life itself. Mere repression achieves ill results, as is manifest in a thousand ways in modern neurotic conditions. To insist that a man should not fix his heart on any creature without showing him an alternative object would dry up the spring of life. This in fact explains why some people who have forsaken the world by vow and state of life become withered in spirit, narrow in outlook, bitter in company. They have few desires and these are mostly of a negative character; they often become valetudinarians because they are conscious only of what they lack; being without joy in living they seek it in vain in physical health.

St Thomas teaches that poverty of itself is a negative state rather than a dynamic virtue, for it cuts away rather than fills up. One must cut the painter and push out into the deep in order to catch the big fish; but the cutting in itself is only the occasion of the catch—one does not haul in the fish with the stumpy end of the painter. Rolle follows the same teaching as the Angel of the Schools in this matter of the 'highest poverty'.

> Truly by itself poverty is no virtue but rather wretchedness; nor for itself praised, but because it

is the instrument of virtue and helps to get blessedness, and makes any eschew many occasions of sinning. And therefore it is to be praised and desired. It lets a man from being honoured, although he be virtuous; but rather it makes him despised and over-led, and cast out among lovers of the world. To suffer all which for Christ is highly needful (*The Mending of Life,* 3. Misyn-Comper, p. 205. Cf. *Form of Living,* 10. Heseltine, p. 42).

Our Lord himself takes the place of all these worldly desires. The positive fulfilment of desire in him is the only human way of assuaging all the variety of yearnings in the heart of man. It is as though all the rivulets of passing human wishes, the craving for little luxuries and human comforts, all flow into the one great stream of the burning desire for Christ himself. He is man and he is God, and he can fulfil all the passions of human nature by transforming them in some way into a part of divine love. So strong can this stream become as to convey the soul to the very threshold of death itself in a flood which is the exact contrary to the desire of self-destruction in suicide.

> 'Thou truly art my Treasure, and all the desire of my heart; and because of thee I shall perfectly see thee, for then I shall have thee.' And I spake thus to death: 'O Death, where dwellest thou? Why comest thou so late to me, living but yet mortal? Why halsest thou not him that desires thee? Who is enough to think [excogitare] thy sweetness, that art the end of sighing, the beginning of desire, the gate of unfailing yearning? Thou art the end of heaviness. . . . Behold I grow hot and desire after thee. . . . Behold I truly languish for love; I desire to die; for thee I burn; and yet truly not for thee but for my saviour Jesu.' (*Fire of Love,* 16. Misyn-Comper, pp. 74-5.)

Quia amore langueo. This is the theme not only of all Rolle's main work, but also of all the medieval spiritual literature; and it is a theme which is only realised in life by those who have entered into the new world of delights granted by infused contemplation.[17] Of course the sinner as soon as he had turned from his evil ways had received the gift of infused charity with the influx of grace; but charity in this life is a movement towards the beloved object. In heaven all will be at rest for desire will be fulfilled and love will reign perfect in its possession. But here it is always, or should be always, growing, moving towards its object. 'Lord Jesu, I ask thee, give me movement in thy love withouten measure', says Rolle, and a little later he defines the love of man on earth precisely in terms of this gradual reduction of the desire into the joy of possession: 'What is love but the transforming of desire into the thing loved?' (*Fire of Love,* Misyn, pp. 78 and 79.)

The whole of the way towards God, the entire extent of the progress of the spiritual life is, of course, simply a development in charity which gradually absorbs all the faculties of a human person, his intellect included, and brings them to cohesion point in God. At first charity lies almost hidden, like the foundations of a building, at the back of the active life of purification in which the moral virtues predominate. Charity is the form, the extrinsic form, of the patience and mercy, the humility and penance of the first steps in the spiritual life. Yet of necessity activity, service, prudential and 'moral' considerations hold sway. But as these virtues develop they become more and more rooted in love, and the extrinsic form itself begins to overshadow all others. At first a man will put up with trials because he knows that this is necessary, that God demands it, that it will cleanse his spirit and that patience is a human perfection. But there comes a time, if he has been growing up spiritually, when he will do all for the love of God; he will be patient because he loves our Lord and follows him by love step by step in the Passion.

This is, therefore, the point when the active life of the moral virtues gives place to the contemplative life of the theological virtues. This fact is borne out, as we shall see later, by Walter Hilton in his *Scale* up which the active only ascends to a point where he may have some fitful glimpses of the full transformation; but it is for Hilton the full re-forming of the soul in 'faith and feeling' where the contemplative really takes over. And this formation of the soul 'in faith and feeling' seems to correspond closely with the contemplative life of Rolle whose love of God seems to diffuse his whole being.

For Hilton the final stage of 're-forming in faith and feeling' would seem to be the state of union when love has transformed everything into God, but there is a lesser degree in which the *mens,* the supreme part of the soul, has not entirely been changed by the Gifts of the Spirit; so, as we should expect, contemplative life begins properly with the first regular influx of infused contemplation. And this is the period when the soul first really languishes for love.

The soul has approached closer than ever before to God, not, as St Thomas says following St Gregory, by physical paces but by steps of love. Rolle has himself set out briefly his measure of these steps of love. For instance in the *Mending of Life*: 'First therefore we are taught righteousness and corrected of ill by discipline; and after that we know what we should do, or what we should eschew. At the last we savour not fleshly things, but everlasting heavenly and godly' (Misyn, p. 209).

Or at great length in the eighth chapter of *The Form of Living* he sets out three degrees of love. The first he calls 'Insuperable', that is, that it is not conquered by temptation or adversity—'when nothing that is contrary to God's love overcomes it, but it is stalwart against all temptations and stable, whether thou be in ease or anguish'. Secondly, 'Inseparable' love comes 'when all thy heart and thy thought and thy might are so wholly, so entirely, and so perfectly fastened, set and established in Jesus Christ, that thy thought goes never from him'.

> The third degree is highest and most wondrous to win. That is called Singular for it has no peer. Singular love is when all comfort and solace are closed out of thy heart but that of Jesus Christ alone. It seeks no other joy. . . . Then thy soul is Jesus-loving, Jesus-thinking, Jesus-desiring, only breathing in the desire for him, singing to him, burning for him, resting in him (*The Form of Living,* Heseltine, pp. 35-7).

But it would seem that all these degrees of love are already within the contemplative mould of the illuminative way for he says that even in the first degree a man may say 'I languish for love'. And elsewhere, in the *Fire of Love,* he describes the 'heat', the 'song', and the 'sweetness' of this love which he himself experiences.

It is particularly noteworthy that our Lord, the Word Incarnate, plays the central part in this transformation in love. The Blessed Trinity of course lies as background of all thought and of all love, but at this point it is necessary to gather all the human forces into the power of love, and that it is achieved in the way God designed by sending his Son as our human brother. This delight in the manhood and Godhead of our Lord inspires all Rolle's lyrics and these more than any other of his writings influenced the religious thought of the anchorholds and contemplatives as well as the more pious section of the populace of Rolle's day. His vivid picture of the piteous bleeding of Christ in 'My king that was great' is paralleled closely by the whole of Mother Julian's *Revelations* which sprang from the same sort of concrete realisation of the pains of Christ:

> Naked is his white breast
> and red his bloody side;
> was his fair hue,
> his wounds deep and wide.

His hymns to the Holy Name, his songs of love, his more penitential lyrics like 'All vanities forsake', his hymn to the Creator, all are centred round the person of our Lord who dominates his poetic imagery as well as his love.[18] Theologically this movement springs from two important sources. First we find Rolle writing of the Son in relation to the Trinity as God, and in relation to ourselves as man.

> The Father, Life, getting the Son, Life, has given to him his whole substance. . . . Truly the everlasting Son of the Father is become Man in Time, born of

a maiden, that he might gainbuy man from the fiend's power. This is our Lord Jesus Christ: the which only be fastened in our minds the which for us only was tied on the cross. Nothing truly is so sweet as to love Christ. (**Fire of Love,** Misyn, p. 36.)

And he goes on to hint that we should not attempt to plumb too deeply with our minds the mystery of the Trinity, and to be content in this respect with the Son made man, hanging on the Cross. Secondly there is the doctrine of the mystical body which inspired in one way or another the majority of the English Mystics.

> Every mortal man ought to consider that he will never come to the heavenly Kingdom by the way of riches and fleshly liking and lust, since, forsooth, it is written of Christ . . . that Christ behoved to suffer and so enter his joy. If we be members of our Head, Jesu Christ, we shall follow him; and if we love Christ, it behoves us to go as he has gone (id. p. 84).

The member of the body is now not merely directed by the head but is in love with the head, conformed to it. His virtuous life is a life of Christ; he acts virtuously because he follows Christ who acts in this way; he accepts the will of the Father because he is in the Garden of Olives watching the seat of blood moistening the soil of the world. Life now is Christo-centric, to use an awkward but meaningful modern expression. Here may we find a meeting place for all the genuine writers on the spiritual life. St Augustine is as eloquent on the love of Christ as is St Bernard. *The Imitation* has been considered to be 'unmystical' in tone, and yet the seventh and eighth chapters of the second part have the same accent and tone as Rolle: 'If thou seek Jesu in all things, thou shalt find Jesu. . . . Among all therefore that are dear to thee, let Jesu be solely thy darling and thy special friend.' Or again in the *De Adhaerendo Deo,* attributed to St Albert and almost as formative of pre-reformation spirituality as *The Imitation,* we read: 'There is no other way by which we may be drawn away from outward and sensible things into ourselves and so into the divine secrets of Jesus Christ, than by the love of Christ, than by the desire of Christ's sweetness, so that we may feel, perceive and taste the nearness of Christ's divinity.'[19]

Rolle, in his descriptions of the transports of the love of Jesu, however, has not entered into the final union, which has been called beyond all others 'transforming'. He is not relying on feelings or sensible consolations, but he is still very imaginative in his conception of the meaning of union. He recognises its wholeness, and how this love of God embraces every aspect of a man's life bringing with it true integrity (cf. **Fire of Love,** Misyn, pp. 99-100). But there is still a certain distance, however brief, between the soul and God, a distance which those who have experienced the heights of love cross with further steps of love. To make this clear we may compare a passage of Richard Rolle with a similar one from the *Living Flame* of St John of the Cross. Thus Rolle writes:

> Therefore if our love be pure and perfect, whatever our heart loves it is God. Truly if we love ourselves, and all other creatures that are to be loved, only in God and for God, what other in us and in them love we but him? . . . He that truly knows to love Christ is proved to love nothing in himself but God. Also all that we are loved by and love—all to God the Well of love we yield . . . wherefore nothing but God he loves and so all his love is God (**Fire of Love,** i.c. 19, Misyn, p. 87).

This fine passage, which brings out a great deal of the nobility of Rolle and his attractiveness, yet suggests that there remains a sense of *otherness;* the soul still feels distinct from God though linked so closely in this deep activity of the will. St John of the Cross, however, in describing the final transformation of love, the most complete that can be attained in this life, would seem to draw out a new meaning in Rolle's words 'all his love is God'. We quote only a short passage from this tremendous description of the union of love:

> For the will of these two is one; and even as God is giving himself to the soul with free and gracious will, even so likewise the soul having a will that is the freer and the more generous in proportion as it has a greater degree of union with God, is giving God in God to God himself, and thus the gift of the soul to God is true and entire.

We shall find this further transformation of love more clearly indicated in the two greatest of English mystical writings, *The Cloud of Unknowing* and the *Revelations* of Mother Julian of Norwich. Richard Rolle is in many ways the leader of the mystical movement and often seems to have approximated to the highest forms of love. But these others, perhaps being more hidden and therefore less tempted by the snares of pride, seem to have drawn still closer to the end of all loving.

Notes

[1] *English Writings of Richard Rolle*. Introduction, p. 23.

[2] All quotations from the *Incendium Amoris* are taken from Richard Misyn's fifteenth-century translation edited by Miss F. M. M. Comper and published by Methuen.

[3] Chapter 18, Misyn's translation edited by Comper, pp. 83-4.

[4] *Incendium Amoris,* c. 28, p. 119.

[5] Cf. *Richard Rolle of Hampole,* edited by C. Horstman, vol. 1, p. 191.

[6] Quoted from *Selected Works of Richard Rolle,* by G. Heseltine (London, 1930), p. 37.

[7] The whole of this Commentary on Psalm 12 should be read in this context. I have here modernised the first paragraph from *English Writings of Richard Rolle,* H. E. Allen, p. 11. Cf. also *Fire of Love,* Misyn, p. 40.

[8] *The Fire of Love,* Bk. 2, c. 10. Misyn trans., Comper ed., p. 178. This compares closely with St Teresa's description of the Prayer of Union in her *Life,* c. 17 (Peers ed., I, 102).

[9] *The Fire of Love,* Bk. 2, c. 7. Misyn-Comper, p. 161-2. Italics are mine.

[10] Cf. *The Mending of Life,* cc. 7 and 8, same edition, pp. 220-1.

[11] Id. c. 4, p. 208. Italics mine.

[12] Cf. *'L'Oraison' Cahier de la Vie Spirituelle,* pp. 26 sqq. *L'Oraison dans l'Histoire,* by P. Philippe, O.P. The passage of Richard of St Victor here referred to is *Benjamin Major,* 5, 2. (P.L. 196, 170.)

[13] *St John of the Cross, Doctor of Divine Love,* by Father Gabriel of St Mary Magdalen (London, 1940), pp. 115-16.

[14] *Ego Dormio.* Heseltine, Selected Works of Richard Rolle, p. 97.

[15] Cf. *Summa Theologica,* II-II 8, art. 1 and 8.

[16] Cf. *The Life of Richard Rolle with his English Lyrics,* F. M. M. Comper, p. 248.

[17] It is useful to compare this medieval outpouring with the words of Dom Belorgey in the description of the joy of finding Jesus once more in the prayer of Quiet (*La Pratique de l'oraison mentale,* vol. 2, p. 72).

[18] For these lyrics cf. the volume already cited by F. M. M. Comper.

[19] *Of Cleaving to God.* Translated by Elizabeth Stopp (Blackfriars Publications).

E. J. Arnould (essay date 1960)

SOURCE: E. J. Arnould, "Richard Rolle of Hampole," in *The Month,* Vol. 23, No. 1, January, 1960, pp. 13-25.

[*In the essay below, Arnould seeks to synthesize the divergent portraits of Rolle that have dominated, one portraying him as wholly saintly, and the other as largely wild and temperamental. In his effort to draw a more complex picture of Rolle's character, Arnould examines the* De Emendatione Vitae, *the* Incendium Amoris; *and the* Melos Amoris.]

The fourteenth century was the heyday of English mysticism and is also famous for its hermits and anchorites. Richard Rolle, whose life-span covers the first half of the century, has a marked place among both hermits and mystics.[1] Professor R. W. Chambers has observed that "in English or in Latin Rolle was, during the latter half of the fourteenth century and the whole of the fifteenth, probably the most widely read in England of all English writers." His works came to be regarded by later generations as standards of orthodoxy—a fact attested not only by the numerous copies that found their way into the libraries of many religious houses on the Continent as well as in England, but also by the spurious ascription to him of popular books of common doctrine (such as the *Pricke of Conscience,* of which over one hundred copies have survived to this day); and, above all, by tributes paid to him well into the times of the Counter-Reformation, when he was still acclaimed as *Strenuus ac divinus catholicae fidei athleta Ricardus,* the valiant and godly champion of the catholic faith.

That Richard Rolle died in the odour of sanctity is attested by a Latin *Office* written in anticipation of his beatification, complete with the miraculous cures worked on his tomb in the precincts of Hampole monastery in Yorkshire. This *Office* is our main source of information on Richard's life. It depicts for us a young man of fiery temperament, who, after a few years at Oxford and at home, one day resolutely turned away from what he called his sinful youth, ruthlessly cut himself off from his worldly environment and thenceforth strove, amidst difficulties and temptations, towards union with God in solitary contemplation.

Such a summary portrait is amply confirmed and completed by Rolle's own writings—providing these are read in full and without bias. These two conditions, unfortunately, have not always been fulfilled even by competent and sympathetic scholars. As a result, a very inaccurate picture of Rolle has, until recent times, been offered to us. He came to be described, on the one hand, as a Doctor of Theology and a student of the Sorbonne, even a priest, and, on the other, as a rebel against Church authorities and a declared enemy of some religious houses. Fortunately, these inaccuracies and distortions have now been rectified, thanks to the careful editing of Rolle's main works. He appears to us in a truer light, as a dedicated young man with a sound theological training, steeped in the reading of the Bible, bent on achieving the perfection of union with God and, not unnaturally, anxious to draw disciples to his own way of life both by his example and his writings. No evidence can be found for suggesting that Rolle ever swerved from his allegiance to the Church. Throughout his life his motto remained: *I bow in alle thynge till the lare of Halykirke,* "I submit in everything to the teaching of Holy Church." Nor did his charity exclude even his detractors: "I have loved those who despised me. I did not call perdition upon those who derided or slandered me. I have always loved those who opposed me and denounced me as worthy of contempt." His exultation over God's gifts to him emanated not from pride but from the gratitude of a candid mind, the true mark of humility: *Non sic lingua nostra appetat humilitatem ut veritatem relinquat,* "let not our tongue thirst for humility to the extent of forsaking the truth."

Rolle was a prolific writer, and his works are far from presenting a uniform pattern. If we omit the delightful **Canticum Amoris,** a youthful outpouring of his love for the Mother of God[2] and fragments of doubtful authenticity, they may be classified into three groups, each of which corresponds to a particular stage or aspect of Rolle's spiritual career.

First we have the didactic writings, which belong to the traditional type of medieval devotional literature. They are nearly always commentaries of some Scriptural text or texts, and essentially compilations from previous authorities. Such are Rolle's Latin commentaries on the **Magnificat** or on **Psalm XX,** or on the first chapters of the **Apocalypse,** and two complete commentaries of the **Psalms,** one in Latin, one in English. These works, particularly the **English Psalter** (which is not, as has been asserted, a mere replica of Rolle's **Latin Psalter**), bear the stamp of our hermit's mind, and offer a good deal of corroborative evidence on his views and experiences.

Far more original and representative is a small group of treatises, which though they have the traditional ring, nevertheless contain many passages displaying the exclusive characteristics of his very personal style. The most important of these are the **Judica me Deus** (which takes its title from the 42nd Psalm), the **De Emendatione Vitae,** and the **Form of Living.**

The first part of the **Judica** reveals a youthful Rolle, the apprentice-hermit (*si heremita dicerer, cuius nomine indigne vocor,* "if I were called hermit, a name which I bear unworthily"), endeavouring to help a young priest-friend by compiling for him a manual of the chief duties of a parish priest, including a model sermon on the Last Judgment. The compilation is rather amateurish, and mainly derived from an almost contemporary Latin work known as *Pars Oculi* or *Oculus Sacerdotis.*

The **De Emendatione Vitae**[3] is of greater interest. Written for every Christian who aspires to a life of total dedication, it reflects Rolle's circumstances at this stage of his own spiritual progress. He describes his first steps in the way, from the contempt and renunciation of the world, through the practice of a regular and devout life and especially the meditation of Our Lord's Passion, up to the higher regions of love and contemplation. *Noli tardare,* "do not delay your conversion," begins Rolle. He describes conversion as "turning our minds towards Jesus and ceaselessly meditating on his counsels and commandments, with the resolve to follow and obey them." The obstacles (wealth, feminine charms, the grace and beauty of youth, that "threefold cord that is not easily broken") must be overcome through persistence. Contempt of wordly possessions is equally essential, for "attachment to worldly goods and the love of God are incompatible: the couch is so narrow that one of the bed-fellows must fall off." As a logical sequel, poverty becomes a necessary condition—poverty not only in fact, but in spirit, that is without regret, afterthought, or envy of others—humility of mind and heart.

> Learn from me, says Jesus, for I am meek and humble in heart. He does not say: Learn from me because I am poor. Poverty is not a virtue in itself, it is misery. It is not worthy of praise in itself, but only a means of perfection: it helps us to gain Heaven and spares us many occasions of sin. . . .

When these first obstacles have been removed, it is necessary to devise a rule of life for oneself. One must first eliminate what pollutes the soul, sins of thought, speech, and deed; next, seek what purifies it, contrition, confession, satisfaction, fasting, prayer, almsgiving; thirdly, safeguard the soul's purity—purity of thought by constant meditation, control of the senses, honest occupation such as reading, pious conversation, writing or other useful work; purity of speech, by reflecting before speaking, by avoiding idle talk, and showing a horror of untruth; purity of deed by temperance, avoidance of corrupting company, and meditation on death; fourthly, one must try to make one's will conform to the will of God, mainly by seeing His image in His creatures, by trying to live in familiarity with Him through prayer and meditation, and by thinking of the happiness of heaven. This happiness can be partially enjoyed in contemplation.

In this state of spiritual well-being, however, new obstacles must be expected and overcome—the tribulations which tempt us to look back towards worldly comforts. The remedy for this is the virtue of patience sustained by the thought of the rewards that await perseverance, and of the alternative facing us: material happiness in this world and eternal suffering in the next, or patient suffering on this earth and eternal bliss thereafter. In this serenity and firmness of purpose the soul is free to labour towards its goal: union with God. Prayer is the essential and consistent activity, one enriched by the reading of the Scriptures, one that grows easier by practice, until every action is itself a form of prayer. Its most important form is meditation—on the great mysteries of God's love, on the vanity of the world (a clear echo, this, of Pope Innocent III's classic work *De contemptu mundi*), and the mysteries of faith.

Finally, the soul reaches that "purity of heart that makes one see God and is accompanied by such joy and happiness that one feels these can never again be lost." Continuous enjoyment of this love is ensured by contemplation, the essential occupation of the soul dedicated to God. "The sweetness of contemplation is only acquired at the cost of immense efforts," but these efforts (later unnecessary, as Rolle himself emphasises in his later works) are soon munificently rewarded: "For, what is *grace,* if not the beginning of *glory*? And what is the perfection of glory, if not the consummation of grace, which holds in reserve for us a glorious eternity and an eternal glory?" Thus ends the *De Emendatione Vitae*.

The *Form of Perfect Living* is an adaptation of the *De Emendatione Vitae*. A classic of the Middle English devotional literature, it was written for a recluse named Margaret, probably the lady Margaret of whom the *Office* states that "Richard loved her with the perfect affection of Charity." Far from omitting the advice given to beginners in the *De Emendatione,* Rolle insists, here, too, on the main obstacles to conversion and the main snares of the Devil. He proclaims the greatness of the solitary life, but warns of its dangers (various temptations, excessive fondness of material ease, dreams and other illusions or delusions). He defines holiness: "Those alone are holy, whatever their status or position, who desire no earthly thing beyond their bare needs, who burn with the love of Jesus, and are bent on emjoying heavenly bliss." But he speaks at greater length than in the *De Emendatione* on the love of God, that same "insuperable, inseparable, singular" love, centred on the devotion to the Holy Name, one of Rolle's own favourite devotions in his youth. At some greater length, Rolle again defines this love: "a burning yearning for God, accompanied by a wonderful pleasure and sweetness, that makes us one with God." And, while clearly stating that "no man on earth can with certainty or without a special grace know whether he is in the state of perfect charity or not," Rolle enumerates seven signs by which one may feel confident of living in union with God.

Inevitably, the *Form of Perfect Living* ends with a chapter on the active and the contemplative modes of life, which is a concise summary of Rolle's views on the subject. Rolle is clearly biased in favour of the solitary life. We know that he was, at one time, en-

gaged in a heated controversy on this question with partisans of the "regular" life in some order or community. But his views are well supported by authorities such as St. Bernard and St. Thomas Aquinas. He also distinguishes at least two grades in the contemplative life: one, the more common, is essentially a life of prayer and meditation, the other is the mystic stage more akin to rapture or even ecstasy. The latter, Rolle points out, is a "gratuitous gift," and the indescribable joy it affords finds its expression in "inexpressible praise of God"—a remark aptly illustrated by his later and larger works, the *Incendium Amoris*[4] and the *Melos Amoris*.[5] These two works are his masterpieces. They reflect Rolle's maturity in the contemplative life. Both are eminently personal.

The *Incendium Amoris* remains the more accessible. Since it contains a comprehensive account of Rolle's mystical career, apart from its final stages, a brief summary of its scope and contents will not be amiss:

> The *Incendium Amoris* [writes Miss Deanesly] is a rambling biography, an explanation of "how Richard Hampole came to the Fire of Love". . . . The purpose of the book is described in the Prologue: "I have wondered more than I can tell," Rolle says, "when first I felt my heart grow warm and glow with no imaginary but with a real and, as it were, sensible flame. For I had not reckoned that such a warmth could happen to any man in this exile. . . . Therefore I offer this book to the sight, not of philosophers and wise men of this world, nor of great theologians wrapped in endless questionings, but of the simple and untaught, those who seek to love God rather than to know many things. For not by disputing, but by doing, is He known, and by loving. . . . Wherefore, because here I incite all to love, and I shall seek to explain the burning and supernatural feeling of love, let this book be allotted the title of Fire of Love."

> The book itself takes forty-two chapters to accomplish this end. In the Prologue, Rolle states his own desire to prove to others the joy of the life he has himself chosen. The next eleven chapters are devoted to considerations preliminary to the understanding of such a life; then come two chapters [XII and XV] where he passes from advice to autobiography and which contain most of the passages quoted in the *Office*. The remaining chapters are mainly a series of discourses strung together with no particular plan, on the various difficulties of the contemplative life, interspersed with prayers and meditations which are the Latin counterpart of Rolle's better known Middle English work. . . . The main idea of the book is simply: that the solitary finds Him whom he loves with a rapture and completeness no other life can afford. . . .

The *Melos Amoris* (wrongly called *Melum Contemplativorum* by Horstman and others after him) has been edited from all extant manuscripts: these are only ten in number, and, when we compare it with the ninety or so manuscripts of the *Incendium Amoris,* this number is significant. For the *Melos* is written in a curious kind of medieval Latin which accounts not only for the small number of manuscripts extant, but for the long-felt want of a complete printed text, as also for the absence of a translation. It is indeed doubtful whether such an extraordinary book can ever be satisfactorily translated. Certainly, no translation could hope to render the unique effect of the most lyrical and most alliterative Latin prose ever written. This style, highly artificial in appearance, yet quite spontaneous, has a charm of its own and is an instrument perfectly attuned for the expression of mystical experiences.

The *Melos* takes up where the *Incendium* left off: it carries us one stage further, and the emphasis is now on the climax of Rolle's mysticism: the melody. Having reached full enjoyment of union with God, Rolle is now less inclined to refer to the past or to preach a message. Although he still describes his endeavours, and the favours he has received, in order to encourage others, he is mostly concerned with the expression of joy and gratitude. Whatever the precise chronology of Rolle's works, there is no doubt that his *Melos Amoris* marks the climax in the spiritual elevation of the hermit. The apotheosis of Love which he describes there is, to him, a foretaste of the joys of heaven.

The last few pages of the book, on "the glory of the saints" as promulgated at the Last Judgment, are the fitting culmination of the many chapters he has devoted to "the perfection of the saints," as exemplified in his own spiritual pilgrimage. His conclusion is a farewell: "I now proceed towards a happy end—for I have nearly completed my arduous progress—in order that, trampling corruption under foot, I may find consummation in song." Either Rolle foresees the end of his earthly pilgrimage, or, more probably, having achieved the aim he had set himself, he now prepares to enjoy this highest gift, the *melos,* to the full.

From all these works of Rolle there emerges a fairly clear picture of his activities, of his experiences, and even of his temperament. For none of them, however traditional in character, is totally devoid of some autobiographical element. One gets the impression of a man with a sound university training—witness his expert handling of the Latin language both in verse and prose—particularly familiar with the Old and New Testaments, but bent on his own purpose (*singulare propositum*) and, in spite of his dependence on the traditional and Patristic literature, largely independent in the elaboration of his views on spiritual matters. This independence, however, entails no breach either of orthodoxy or charity. And it must be noted that on the few points of dogma to which he has occasion to refer, such as the question of predestination, the authority of the Scriptures, or the infallibility of the Church, his orthodoxy is unimpeachable. Again, when describing his own mystical experiences, he acknowledges these not as rewards for his endeavours, but as free gifts from God's bounty: nor does he claim credit for them, except, perhaps, in so far as he has striven to prepare for them. Even so, he does not present them as purely arbitrary privileges. It follows that his own case is not presented merely as an object of wonder and envy, but as an example containing a practical lesson even for beginners in the way of spiritual perfection.

Rolle's spiritual pilgrimage began with his "conversion." The *Office* gives a lively and somewhat melodramatic picture of a young man, freshly returned from Oxford, running away from home and friends, making for himself a crude hermit's outfit with one of his sister's dresses; and, a little later, boldly standing up in church, marching up to the pulpit—admittedly with the approval of the parish priest—and delivering an extempore sermon which those present declared to be the finest they had ever heard. Whatever the facts behind these highly-coloured scenes, Richard clearly came to a sudden resolve to flee the world of his youth and to devote his life to the pursuit of perfection. His first endeavours on that path show nothing exceptional. He meditates on the Passion of our Lord, one of the mysteries of divine love that had particularly struck him and contributed to his conversion. Then he turns to the worship of the name of Jesus, and, at the same time, his devotion to the holy Mother of God provides an outlet for the highly sensitive soul of the young hermit: a beautiful expression of this devotion is found in Rolle's *Canticum Amoris.*[6] He remained faithful to these devotions of his youth, but allusions to them are naturally less common in his later works, since they were eclipsed by the great mystical gifts on which the later works concentrate.

The young man's progress was not, however, without difficulties. Some of these were due largely to his impulsive, intransigent, and even eccentric temperament. He clashed with some of his patrons, like John Dalton, a friend of his father; he objected to interference from former gay companions; he had to face temptations of a sentimental, if not sensual, nature; loneliness sometimes seemed to him hardly bearable; and he suffered from temporary frustration in his yearning for perfect quiet, and in his desire to preach the ways of salvation to others. Hence his wanderings, "like Cain in flight after his crime," in search of the ideal hermitage; wanderings that were denounced by unfriendly tongues as a sign of restlessness—although Richard Rolle was certainly never the type of "Robert renne-aboute" pilloried by *Piers Plowman.* At last, he was able to settle down, probably in the vicinity of Hampole nunnery. In the solitude ultimately found, he continued to read and meditate, mostly the Sacred Books. Among these he recommends the

Prophets, the Gospels and the canonical Epistles, and he quotes freely from the *Apocalypse*. But his favourite seems to have been *The Song of Songs*. It is from this that he borrowed the phrase which recurs as a leit-motiv in most of his works: "Amore langueo." Characteristic of this time of reading and meditation are his "postils" or brief commentaries. He described himself as "*probatus postillator,* experienced writer of postils." Reading and meditation were his preparation for contemplation—*labor, sed dulcis, desiderabilis et suavis . . . bonus labor.* As usual Rolle speaks from experience, and it is from experience also that he describes the joy that rewards earlier efforts. It was surely in order to alleviate these efforts, and to ensure greater freedom from material conditions, that he came to adopt the sitting position at prayer, and insisted on this apparently trifling detail with a curious obstinacy in his English as well as his Latin works.

Gradually, almost imperceptibly, one can watch him pass from these early stages to higher spheres. Eventually the "door of heaven" opens before him, and he begins to be prepared for what would now be called the transforming union. He repeatedly describes these experiences, which are summed up in the three words: "*dulcor, calor, canor*" (later *melos*). Of these, only the last two are mystical gifts in the strict sense. "Sweetness" was felt by him as soon as the difficulties previously encountered had been overcome: it no doubt represents the sensation of relief and moral well-being normally experienced by a soul freshly detached from wordly bonds.

As for the "heat"—a phenomenon curiously parallel with Blaise Pascal's famous ecstasy—Rolle has given us an account of it with unusual precision, in the *Incendium Amoris*:

> Eventually, I made great progress in spiritual joy. From the beginning of my change of life and the transformation of my soul, three years, less three or four months, elapsed until the heavenly door opened before me, when the eye of my heart was able to behold the denizens of heaven and to discover the way to my Beloved and how I could go on sighing for Him. Since then, the heavenly door remaining open, barely one year passed until the time when I felt the heat of eternal love within my heart: I was sitting in a chapel and, enjoying the sweetness of prayer and meditation, I suddenly felt in myself an unusual and pleasant warmth. At first I wondered where this came from, but after a prolonged experience of it, I realised that it emanated not from a creature but from the Creator, for it became ever more ardent and more pleasant. This material and inexpressibly sweet warmth remained with me nine months and a few weeks, until the time when I received from above the gift of hearing the celestial melody. . . .

There is, however, a noticeable difference in his description of his experiences in the *Melos Amoris*. In the *Incendium Amoris,* Rolle says that the fire was succeeded by the "gift of hearing the celestial song." He is speaking here merely of "internal, or spiritual song" as opposed to the external and material, having been rebuked, so he tells us, for not taking part in public singing in church and having replied to this accusation at length. In the *Melos Amoris* the song becomes "melody," the main theme of the book, Rolle's last work. He describes it as the highest grade in the love of God; it drives away care, grief, and fear; spiritual joy turns to rapture when this supra-material harmony is heard. But only the soul in close union with the Beloved, and especially the solitary, can enjoy it fully. For the *melos* is incompatible not only with earthly songs, even those of the liturgy, but also with worldly contact of any kind. It is a foretaste of heavenly joys and, as such, defies accurate description.

Although these three gifts, *dulcor, calor, canor* (or *melos*), are the special reward of solitaries and contemplatives, they can be experienced by anybody, in any milieu. Even the *melos* can be enjoyed in the midst of various occupations, as was the case with Rolle. But one cannot expect to receive them as of right; and, admirable and desirable as they are, these exceptional gifts are not the sole or necessary signs of mystical union. What is more, they do not constitute the essence of perfection; and Rolle never refrains from giving more commonplace advice to beginners. He insists on remote preparation, on purity of mind and body, and on the other Christian virtues, humility, patience, self-denial—all necessary preliminaries before love can reign in the soul and transform it.

This way of preparation, too, is exemplified by Rolle's personal experience. And once he has reached the summit, he finds himself in a state of steadfastness, serenity, and confidence, which, in its highly lyrical expression, might easily, especially when taken out of context, be mistaken for overweening pride: God himself has been his teacher, and to God he appeals against all contradictors. Nothing will ever deprive him of the joy he derives from his permanent union with the Beloved or of his conviction that his salvation is assured. Such confidence, is, of course, the logical result of his profound conviction and his trust in God. It gives expression to feelings that cannot accurately be described, still less adequately explained. Intransigence is here a form of refusal to compromise with error or sin. Exhilaration in the description of God's gifts is a form of tribute to God's munificence. But Rolle's intransigence and his accents of triumph never degenerate into rebellion or vainglory. Indeed, in contrast to the eccentricities of his "conversion" as related in the *Office,* and despite the fierce tone he occasionally adopts in discussion, despite also the extravagance of his style, Rolle was never inclined to excess or violence. Just as his submission to the Church on any point of official doctrine was absolute at all times, so his attitude in practical matters of asceticism was always governed by common sense and reason. This may well explain his peculiar insistence on the advantages of the sitting position during prolonged contemplation. It also explains how he had occasion to refute malicious accusations of mixing with sinners (an accusation which, as he rightly pointed out, had been levelled at Jesus by the Pharisees) or of not practising severe fasting and maceration (to which he replied that mortification of the flesh should not be carried to the point of rendering mind and body unfit for prayer and meditation).

Again, no extraordinary supra-natural phenomenon marked Rolle's mysticism. He himself never claimed any special power over natural forces, even though the *Office* tells us that, through contact with him, Margaret, a recluse and his disciple, recovered her lost speech and her health. On the whole, Rolle remains profoundly human and, apart from the frequent lyrical outbursts found in his works, every one of these works contains useful advice. Unlike, for instance, Walter Hilton or the anonymous author of the *Cloud of Unknowing,* Rolle does not set out to teach. With the exception of the short works addressed to individuals—probably, in such cases, on request—he does not write treatises of the usual kind. Rather than a teacher, Rolle is a witness. His example, as he had hoped, presents a concrete case of man's elevation, through the normal stages of purgation and illumination, to constant union with God, and of the joy resulting from this intimate union. St. Teresa defined mysticism as "that which no skill or effort of ours, however much we labour, can attain to, though we should prepare ourselves for it, and that preparation must be of great service." This definition applies to Rolle perfectly and would have won his approval. Even the beginner can derive much benefit from following the holy hermit on his pilgrimage. To all, at one stage or another, Rolle is a guide as well as an example.

It is true that the average reader may sometimes find Rolle's style abstract or even abstruse. It is true also that a fair knowledge of Latin is required for a full appreciation of the verbal fireworks in the *Melos Amoris,* since, as we have already observed, a translation could hardly be more than a necessary evil. But Rolle's style is always appropriate to his mood of the moment; and, in several works of his, Latin or English, especially the latter, the thought is conveyed with great simplicity and clarity, while bearing always the personal mark of its author. The quality of Rolle's English writings can be judged from the fact that Rolle was selected by Professor R. W. Chambers as a master link in the continuous development from the Old English of King Alfred to the Elizabethan, English prose of St. Thomas More and his school. Richard Rolle's style, like his message, has lost nothing of its fresh-ness or its vigour. Both have won for him a permanent place of honour in the pageant of great English religious writers.

Notes

[1] The most convenient comprehensive account of the man, his times, and his works (in spite of a number of outdated passages) is still Miss Frances M. M. Comper's *The Life of Richard Rolle, together with an Edition of his Lyrics* (Dent, London, 1928).

The canon of Richard Rolle's works has been established by Miss Hope Emily Allen in *Writings ascribed to Richard Rolle of Hampole and Materials for his Biography* (P.M.L.A., New York, 1927).

[2] A. Wilmart, "Le Cantique d'Amour de Richard Rolle," *Revue d'Ascétique et de Mystique,* xxi (1940), pp. 143 sq.

The Oxford Book of Medieval Latin Verse, ed. by F. J. R. Raby (Clarendon Press (1959), p. 442).

[3] The best edition of the *De Emendatione Vitae* is by Léopold Denis, S.J., *Du Péché à l'amour Divin ou l'Amendement du Pécheur,* Editions de la Vie Spirituelle, Paris, Desclée et Cie, 1926. There is also an English translation by Frances M. M. Comper, *The Fire of Love and Mending of Life* (Methuen, 1914).

[4] Cf. Margaret Deanesly, *The Incendium Amoris of Richard Rolle of Hampole* (Manchester U.P., 1915). French annotated edition: Dom N. Noetinger, *Le Feu de l'Amour, le Modèle de la Vie Parfaite, le Pater, par Richard Rolle de Hampole* (Tours, 1928).

[5] E. J. Arnould, *The Melos Amoris of Richard Rolle of Hampole* (Blackwell, Oxford, 1957).

[6] A. Wilmart, "Le Cantique d'Amour de Richard Rolle," *Revue d' Ascétique et de Mystique,* xxi (1940), pp. 143 sq.

Rosemary Woolf (essay date 1968)

SOURCE: Rosemary Woolf, "The Lyrics of Richard Rolle and the Mystical School," in *The English Religious Lyric in the Middle Ages*, Oxford at the Clarendon Press, 1968, pp. 159-79.

[*In the excerpt that follows, Woolf considers Rolle in relation to the broader conventions and schools of mystical writing, focusing particularly on the tradition of the Passion meditation. Ultimately contradicting the pervasive image of Rolle as a "natural" writer, Woolf notes his innovative skill with literary form and places him at the beginning of "devotional-mystical writing in English."*]

All the poetry so far discussed is unmystical. It may vary in the degree of literary formality, but the emotion expressed in it has no affinities with the fervour and elevation of the mystics; in kind it is the emotion familiar to every man and woman. Even in such works as *Þe Wohunge of oure Laverd,* which was probably intended for the same kind of religious audience as the *Ancrene Wisse,* the emotion expressed is ordinary emotion highly intensified, rather than the quite different kind of love described by Richard Rolle and his followers. The poetical antecedents of Rolle's mystical poetry do not lie in vernacular literature, but they may be found in some of the great Anglo-Latin mystical poetry of the twelfth century, the *Philomena* of John of Howden and the *Dulcis Iesu memoria.* It is only from Rolle's time onwards that there is a continuous tradition of devotional-mystical writing in English— whether in prose or verse—and there can be no doubt that it was the work of Rolle and the outstanding authority of his name that restored the prestige of English as a medium for contemplative writing: evidence for this can be seen in the fact that vernacular works of Rolle were in due course to appear in the devotional *collectiones* of monks, who had hitherto copied for themselves only Latin treatises, the works of St. Bernard, St. Bonaventura, etc.[1]

Rolle's works fall roughly into two kinds. Firstly, those that are records of and reflections upon his own mystical experience.[2] These, according to established tradition, were written in Latin (his contemporary, Julian of Norwich, was unique in writing in English, even though a woman: the visions of women mystics on the Continent were usually set down in Latin, normally by means of a cleric who acted as their secretary). Secondly, the works intended for the instruction of women recluses. These, reviving the tradition begun by the *Ancrene Wisse,* were written in English.[3] The important distinction between the two is that, whilst the principle of the **Incendium amoris** and the **Melos amoris** is a faithful exposition of his own thought and experience, that of the **Ego dormio** and **The Form of Living** is a faithful adherence to the teaching appropriate to beginners in the spiritual life. Nevertheless Rolle's works of instruction were inevitably influenced by his thought as a contemplative, and the lyrics[4] too reflect this double current of the individualistic and the traditional.

In his own thought as a contemplative Rolle was scarcely concerned with meditation on the Passion; but, as an adviser to women in religious orders he taught meditation on the Passion according to the method that had become traditional.

Like the author of the *Cloud of Unknowing*[5] and Walter Hilton,[6] Rolle accepts meditation on the Passion as a grade in the Christian life. It is higher than the active life with the works of mercy and the basic assent of faith, but inferior to the life of mystical contemplation: in the thought of the writers on meditation it represents a midway stage on the ladder of the good life. It would seem that there is here the formulation of a theory designed to explain common practice. The harmonious scheme of St. Bernard, with its place for meditation on the Passion, cannot have convinced an exponent of the negative form of mysticism inherited from the Pseudo-Dionysius, and the fact, therefore, that the author of the *Cloud of Unknowing* praises it as yielding ' . . . moche good, moche helpe, moche profite, and moche grace'[7] shows both how strong was the tradition, and at the same time how it could be detached from the theological roots whence it had originally sprung. Even in the thought of Rolle, Passion meditation was less integral than in that of St. Bernard. It is clear from a comparison of the **Incendium amoris** with the English Epistles that Rolle considered Passion meditation to be a stage which the learner in contemplation made use of and then left behind: he therefore does not describe it in his own experience but recommends it to beginners. But to St. Bernard meditation on the Passion was, as it were, a gateway to contemplation of the Divinity, and was therefore never left behind, but constantly passed through on every mystical journey, and returned to for refreshment after the arduous experience of a more direct communion.

This difference between Rolle and St. Bernard, which may have been influenced by the popular practice of meditation on the Passion as an end in itself, is not, however, the only important one: the other is that Rolle and St. Bernard had quite different conceptions of love. St. Bernard's theory of love obviously had affinities with St. Augustine's, in that they both expound a love which has been called physical or natural, as against ecstatic, and both see no unbridgeable divide between true self-interest and the love of God. To St. Bernard, as we have already seen, love of oneself is an emotion which may be taught and guided to grow into the love of God: to St. Augustine the two were even closer, for God is the *summum bonum,* and the man who loves false objects is self-deceived concerning his own best interests, for, as the well-known quotation so perfectly expresses it, 'Thou has made us for Thyself, and our hearts are restless till they rest in Thee'. To the mystical school to which Rolle belongs, however, there can never be this tranquil relationship between love of God and man's natural desires, for love is violent, compelling, and unreasonable, and it does not make use of man's natural faculties, but possesses him by thwarting and overcoming them. A short passage from the translation of the *Philomena* on the *ecce sto* theme may be quoted as an illustration of the difference in tone:

> Kyng of love, strengest of alle,
> I here þe at my dore calle.

Þou fyndest it loke wiþ barres stronge,
But brek hem up, stond not to longe.[8]

Here man cannot open the door himself, and love must break in by violence. In the Passion meditations of Rolle it is this kind of love that is described, and therefore, whilst they make use of many traditional details, the tone and style are quite different from those of popular meditative poetry and, originally at least, they were probably intended for a religious, not a lay, audience.

Of this small group of mystical poems four are exclusively Passion meditations: 'My keyng þat water grette', from the *Ego dormio;* 'My trewest tresowre', one of the set of poems in MS. Dd. v. 64 attributed by the copyist to Rolle; and 'Ihesu þat hast me dere i-boght' and 'Crist makiþ to man a fair present', which both belong to the same 'school' of lyric writing, although there is no suggestion that either is by Rolle. The *Ego dormio* is a text written for an anchoress or nun: like Aelred, but unlike the author of the *Ancrene Wisse,* Rolle both advises meditation on the Passion and also provides a meditation. It may well be a sign of the strength of the previous lyric tradition that the meditation is in verse. Rolle advises the reader of his treatise 'Thynk oft on his passyon', and then follows the poem with the title *Meditacio de passione Christi.*[9] Like fifteenth-century Passion meditations, which we shall later be discussing, the poem does not confine itself to the Crucifixion, but traces the Passion sequence from the time of the scourging. For the Crucifixion itself Rolle borrows the description of the *Candet nudatum pectus,* but, despite such familiar details, the tone of the poem is quite unfamiliar. This is partly on account of the direct statements of mystical desire, 'Þi face when may I see', 'Al my desyre þou ert', or—with the image of burning, characteristic of Rolle's writing—'Kyndel me fire within'. But there is a change of tone, not only in the expressions of love and in the petitions associated with the Passion meditation, but also in the description of the Passion itself. In this Rolle exploits the device of paradox, whereby in a description of Christ's human suffering He is ostentatiously given a title referring to His divinity, as in 'And nayled on þe rode tre, þe bryght aungels brede', or in a much finer passage:

A wonder it es to se, wha sa understude,
How God of mageste was dyand on þe rude.[10]

In the ordinary Passion meditation this kind of splendour would have daunted the familiar tenderness which the writer wished to evoke, for only ecstatic love is the fitting response to it. The magnitude of the object is then matched by the intensity and excitement of the meditator's feeling. This type of paradox is often repeated in the mystical poetry, for example, the brief statement 'Lyf was slayne' and its immediate derivation is probably the *Philomena,* in which such paradoxes abound, and it is noteworthy that the English poems succeed in achieving the same dignity—though necessarily not the same succinctness—as the Latin. There is admittedly nothing in Rolle's poems which has the monumental and complex quality of Langland's 'The lorde of lyf and of liʒte tho leyed his eyen togideres',[11] which shows the imaginative range of a great poet. Nevertheless, in Rolle's work the potential magnificence of the form is never obscured by feebleness of expression.

In contrast to this poem, 'My trewest tresowre' is more nearly a meditation in the non-ecstatic style.[12] Though each stanza in it begins with a periphrasis for Christ, 'My well of my wele', 'My dere-worthly derlyng', 'My salve of my sare', they do not with dazzling directness refer to Christ's divinity, but have rather the tone of loving endearments, which accentuate the painfulness of the detailed description of the Passion sequence. Emotive adverbs and phrases, 'sa saryful in syght' or 'sa dolefully', with their reference to personal sorrow, lead up to the description of Christ as a knight, 'My fender of my fose', whose shield at the time of evensong is unlaced from His body. In general, the feeling of this poem is not unlike that of some of the Harley lyrics, but the absence of secular adornments, and the crowded and emotional descriptions, almost over-emphasized by alliteration, give a much stronger effect of urgency and distress.

'Ihesu þat hast me dere i-boght' is a poem deriving from the vernacular translation of the *Philomena* of John of Howden. This is a long Latin poem, of which the author himself composed a French version for Eleanor, wife of Henry III, to whom he was chaplain,[13] but which was not translated into English until about a hundred years later. In this very fine work, which is sustained throughout its length with an inexhaustible vigour and power of variation, a meditation on the Passion is given form by two images: firstly by the allegory that it was the force of love that compelled Christ at every stage, and secondly by the invocation to love to wound the heart of the meditator by writing upon it the details of the Passion. Neither of these ideas, however, is used in the short poem we are discussing. Although the theme of the compelling power of love is, as we shall see, a fairly common one in the mystical lyrics, the constructor of 'Ihesu þat hast me dere i-boght' has avoided it, and in the verses he has borrowed, in which love is implored to write on the meditator's heart, he has substituted for love the name Ihesu, as in the following:

Ihesu, write in my hert depe
how þat þou began to wepe
þo þy bak was to þe rode bent,
With rogget nayll þy handes rent.[14]

This poem is obviously a short popularization of the original. The translation of the *Philomena*, 2,254 lines in length, would clearly be too unwieldy for the normal type of meditation: whereas it survives only in one manuscript, 'Ihesu þat hast me dere i-boght' survives in a large number and remained popular into the fifteenth century. In some manuscripts it is preceded by a rubric prescribing it as a devotional exercise. There is no evidence that the compiler of the poem knew the Latin original: his method was to take and shorten a consecutive passage of Passion meditation, and then to append to this some of the striking protestations of love from various other parts of the poem. There is hardly a line that he has not transferred word for word from his source. Nevertheless, the effect of the poem is not one of patchwork. If the translation of the *Philomena* had not survived, it would have been impossible to detect the author's method of working. Indeed, the progress of thought in the poem develops with far greater logical steadiness than in many other lyrics. It is difficult, however, to praise the poem except in terms of selection and organization: for, whilst all of it is fine and many individual passages such as the following are moving,

> Whan I am lowe for þy love
> Þan am I moste at myn above,
> Fastynge is feest, murnynge is blis,
> For þy love povert is richesse.

this is the achievement of the translator of the *Philomena*, an excellent poet, whose work is nowadays unfortunately far too little known.

Though the author of 'Ihesu þat hast me dere i-boght' simplifies his poem by excluding from it the ideas of love writing upon the heart and of the compelling power of love, both of these are in fact found recurrently in the mystical lyrics, and respectively form the dominating themes of two poems, 'Ihesu, god sone' and 'My keyng þat water grette'. The image of love writing a meditation of the Passion on the heart of the meditator is a slightly conceited variation of the recurring mystical idea of the wound of love, the spiritual wound that Rolle so often prayed to be granted, particularly in his Passion meditations, 'In lufe þow wownde my thoght', or 'Wounde my hert with-in'. The text on which it was based, *amore langueo,* was one much quoted by the exponents of ecstatic love, such as Richard of St. Victor. Though this text could be taken to refer to the *languor* of love, 'I languysch for lufe', more often it was taken to refer to the wound of love, the Latin rendering of the Septuagint reading, *amore vulnerata sum,* being preferred to the Vulgate text[15]. The would of love was an experience often referred to by early medieval mystics, though it did not receive a full technical definition until the work of the Spanish

mystics in the fifteenth century: however, as Rousselot has so well pointed out, the use of this image is always a certain sign of the ecstatic view of love, and the violence of its effect.[16] In literary usage, however, it is possible to trace the associations of this image rather more precisely.

In origins it is, of course, not an invention of the mystical writers, but rather the classical idea of Cupid shooting with his bow (in contrast, for instance, to the Old Testament, where arrows are symbols of God's anger). The classical theme passed as a commonplace into Provençal and French poetry, either in the form of brief references—of which there is an imitation in one of the secular Harley lyrics[17]—or as an extended narrative description of the kind occurring in the *Roman de la rose*.[18] In the shape of classical allusion it appears in 'Ihesu Þat hast me dere i-boght':

> Lat now love his bow bende
> And love arowes to my hert send,
> Þat hit mow percen to þe roote,
> For suche woundes shold be my bote.[19]

The image is already in the Latin ('Telum arcus Amoris iaciat'),[20] but the English translation manipulates it a little to make the likeness to the love-shot of Cupid more explicit. Commonly, however, in Passion poetry the allusion to Cupid's wound of love is more undefined, for the wound is said to be inflicted, not by a bow and arrow, but by the spear that pierced Christ's side. The development of this idea can be traced in religious thought. In the Song of Songs there was a second reference to the wound of love, this time applied to the bridegroom, not the bride: 'Vulnerasti cor meum, soror mea . . . ' (iv. 9),[21] and inevitably this wound was associated both with that of *amore langueo* and with the wound in Christ's side, which, in that it touched His heart, was in itself a supreme symbol of Christ's love: the physical wound thus became an allegory of Christ's love for man. It was, however, possible to transfer this wound from Christ to man. The Pauline prayer to be crucified with Christ led quite easily to a full reversal, whereby the details of Christ's sufferings might be attributed to man as a symbol of his love for Christ. An example of this kind of reversal occurs in Gilbert of Hoyland's continuation St. Bernard's of *Sermons on the Song of Songs:* 'Talia in me utinam multiplicet [Christus] vulnera a planta pedis usque ad verticem, ut non sit in me sanitas. Mala enim sanitas, ubi vulnera vacant quae Christi pius infligit aspectus.'[22] This image could therefore be used very appropriately in Passion meditations as an expression of love for Christ in His Passion.

In a poem from the Cambridge Manuscript, 'Ihesu, god sone', the image is used very skilfully. The second stanza begins with a plea for the wound of love:

Ihesu, þe mayden sone, þat wyth þi blode me
  boght,
Thyrl my sawule wyth þispere, þat mykel luf
  in men hase wrought. [23]

This plea is repeated in the fourth stanza, 'Wounde my
hert with-in', and, with a variation in the fifth, 'Rote
it in my hert, þe memor of þi pyne'. It is answered in
the last section of the poem, in which there is a moving description of the Passion, made evocative by
emotive epithets. Unless this relationship is understood,
the last four stanzas may seem an ill-fitting appendage.
Here, in the way that we have described before, the
plea for ecstatic love is matched by an emotionally
heightened description of the Passion.

The other theme, that of the compelling power of
love, was also characteristic of writers on ecstatic
love. Their view of love, that it was by its nature
irresistibly violent, became transformed into an allegorical conceit, in which love was imagined to have
overcome Christ Himself. This idea was first fully
elaborated by Hugh of St. Victor in a short treatise
much read in the Middle Ages, the *De laude caritatis,*
of which it is the main theme:

> Sed fortassis facilius vincis Deum quam hominem,
> magis praevalere potes Deo quam homini, quia quo
> magis beatum, eo magis Deo est debitum a te
> superari. Hoc optime tu noveras, quae ut facilius
> vinceres, prius illum superabas; adhuc nos rebelles
> habuisti, quando illum tibi obedientem de sede
> paternae majestatis usque ad infirma nostrae
> mortalitatis suscipienda descendere coegisti.
> Adduxisti illum vinculis tuis alligatum, adduxisti
> illum sagittis tuis vulneratum. Amplius ut puderet
> hominem tibi resistere, cum te videret etiam in Deum
> triumphasse. Vulnerasti impassibilem, ligasti
> insuperabilem, traxisti incommutabilem, aeternum
> fecisti mortalem. [24]

It can be seen from this that the idea of Christ's submission to the omnipotent force of love is a brilliant
and paradoxical way of expressing the motive for
Christ's sufferings and their extent. Its natural context
is therefore a Passion meditation, and it is thus that it
is used in the English mystical lyrics. It occurred, for
instance, in the poem from the *Ego dormio* that we
have already discussed, 'My keyng þat water grette':

> A wonder it es to se, wha sa understude,
> How God of mageste was dyand on þe rude.
> Bot suth þan es it sayde þat lufe ledes þe
>   ryng;
> Þat hym sa law hase layde bot lufe it was na
>   thyng. [25]

The last two lines are to be found almost word for
word in the last chapter of the *Incendium amoris*:
'. . . sed verum dicitur quia amor preit in tripudio, et

coream ducit. Quod Christum ita demissum posuit,
nihil nisi amor fuit.'[26] The *O.E.D.* shows that by the
end of the fourteenth century the phrase 'to lead (or
rule) the ring' had acquired the meaning 'to be foremost', but the use of the expression in Latin suggests
that in Rolle's time awareness of the metaphor had
by no means been suppressed by common usage, and
that, with love as the subject, there is an allusion to
the God of love 'carolling', as he does in the *Roman
de la rose*.[27] The last line, with its statement that it
iwas nothing but love which laid Christ low, is a
clear, if slightly clumsy, expression of the domination of love.[28]

In 'My keyng þat water grette' the idea of the omnipotent force of love is a subordinate image in a Passion
meditation. It is in the very fine poem, 'Crist makiþ to
man a fair present', that a Passion meditation is organized entirely within the framework of this paradox.
This lyric, not by Rolle, though succeeding the *Form
of Living* in two of its three manuscripts, is more than
any other indebted to the tone and style of the
Philomena. In the opening stanza, as in a large section
of the *Philomena,* love is implored to explain the wild
incomprehensibility of its actions:

> O Love, love, what hast þou ment?
> Me þinkeþ þat love to wraþþe is went.[29]

The poem then shifts to a direct address to Christ, in
which is given a saddened description of what love has
done, 'þi loveliche hondis love haþ to-rent', and:

> Þi mylde boones love haþ to-drawe,
> Þe naylis þi feet han al to-gnawe;
> Þe lord of love love haþ now slawe—
> Whane love is strong it haþ no lawe.[30]

In this the violent irrationality of love is most powerfully expressed. In particular, the skilful syntactical
inversion in line 3 and the poised generalization of
line 4 show a style that has risen to the magnificence
and complexity of its subject. After three less effective stanzas, the poem returns to its initial theme of
the questioning of love, and it is in this passionate
questioning that it most clearly catches the tone of
the *Philomena*, 'O Love, love, what hast þou ment?',
'Love, love, where schalt þou wone?', 'Love, love,
whi doist þou so?'. These apostrophes may be compared in their vehemence with the opening of many
stanzas in the *Philomena,* such as 'Amor, audi: quis
est, quem crucias?' (274) or 'Amor, adhuc audi, quem
laceras' (312).[31] Likewise with the paradoxes of the
eighth stanza—

> Love haþ schewid his greet myʒt,
> For love haþ maad of day þe nyʒt;
> Love haþ slawe þe kyng of ryʒt,
> And love haþ endid þe strong fiʒt.

—it echoes the style of the innumerable paradoxes of the *Philomena*, 'Amatorem, Amor, cur proicis?' (271) or 'Vitam mori dum Amor imperat . . . ' (443).[32] The accomplishment of the English is, of course, by no means diminished by this comparison, and, fine though the English translation of the *Philomena* is, it might be thought that this short poem surpasses it in its catching of the impassioned tone of the Latin.

It is interesting to notice that the idea of Christ dominated by love did not remain restricted to the more sophisticated mystical poetry. In John of Grimestone's preaching-book the idea is effectively worked into the form of a complaint:

> Love me brouthte,
> And love me wrouthte,
> Man, to be þi fere.
> Love me fedde,
> And love me ledde,
> And love me lettet here.
> Love me slou,
> And love me drou,
> And love me leyde on bere.
> Love is my pes,
> For love i ches,
> Man to byȝen dere.
>
> Ne dred þe nouth,
> I have þe south,
> Boþen day and nith,
> to haven þe,
> Wel is me,
> I have þe wonnen in fith.[33]

The repetition of the word 'love' drives home the idea, though the verses lack the dignity of 'Crist makiþ to man'. The last verse, entirely mediocre in quality, inappropriately reduces the theme by confining it to the plea of a lover-knight. Two other short narrative verses in the same manuscript also make use of the idea: one a fairly perfunctory four lines, 'Love made crist in oure lady to lith',[34] and the other modelled upon it, but with *reuthe* instead of love as the compelling power:[35] this weakened substitution indicates how the original sublime and complex meaning had become lost in popular usage.

Besides the Passion poems there are also a small number of mystical poems that are mixed in content. They are held together by sustained intensity of tone rather than structure, and in them Passion meditation, praise of the beloved, and praise of Love itself are linked together: indeed, it is one of their characteristics that they are as much concerned with the idea of love itself as with the beloved. The two least interesting of these are from the Cambridge Manuscript, 'All vanitese forsake'[36] and 'Thy ioy be ilk a dele',[37] which could be called hortatory love songs, similar to the 'Love-Ron'

in their juxtaposition of the vanity of the world with the joy of loving Christ. But in contrast to the sweet reasonableness of the 'Love-Ron', the plea in these poems proceeds solely by appeals to the emotions. They contain many passages that are typical of the best style of Rolle's writing, but there is nothing in them that is not done consistently better in other poems.

Of these others the finest are 'Luf es lyf þat lastes ay' and the lyric with which the **Ego dormio** concludes, 'My sange es in syhting'. 'Luf es lyf' falls into two parts, which on both literary and textual grounds we may assume to have been originally distinct. The first part consists of a discussion of the nature of love, where discursive and sometimes homiletic comment is subordinated to a series of definitions, which produce, through taut parallelism, a strong emotional impact:

> Lufe es thought wyth grete desyre, of a fayre
>   lovyng;
> Lufe I lyken til a fyre, þat sloken may na
>   thyng;
> Lufe us clenses of oure syn, lufe us bote sall
>   bryng;
> Lufe þe keynges hert may wyn, lufe of ioy
>   may syng.
>
> Luf es a lyght byrthen, lufe gladdes ȝong and
>   alde,
> Lufe es with-owten pyne, als lofers hase me
>   talde,
> Lufe es a gastly wynne þat makes men bygge
>   and balde,
> Of luf sal he na thyng tyne, þat hit in hert
>   will halde.[38]

Behind verses such as these there lies a stylistic form common in French secular poetry, which may be illustrated by a famous example, that of the description of love in Reason's speech to the lover in Jean de Meung's continuation of *Le Roman de la rose:*

> Amour ce est pais haïneuse,
> Amour c'est haïne amoureuse;
> C'est leiautez la desleiaus,
> C'est la desleiautez leiaus
> C'est peeur toute asseuree,
> Esperaunce desesperee;
> C'est raison toute forsenanable,
> C'est forsenerie raisnable;
> C'est doux periz a sei neier;
> Griés fais legiers a paumeier;
> C'est Caribdis la perilleuse,
> Desagreable e gracieuse;
> C'est langueur toute santeïve,
> C'est santé toute maladive;
> C'est fain saoule en abondance;
> C'est couveiteuse soufisance.[39]

More immediately close to Rolle's work, however, are the English definitions of love preserved in MS. Digby 86:

> Love is þe softeste þing in herte mai slepe.
> Love is craft, love is goed wiþ kares to kepe.
> Love is les, love is lef, love is longinge.
> Love is fol, love is fast, love is frowringe.
> Love is sellich an þing, wose shal soþ singe.
> Love is wele, love is wo, love is gleddede
> Love is lif, love is deþ, love mai hous fede.[40]

The similarity of metre suggests that Rolle may have known the poem from which this quotation comes: certainly in style it could have formed a transition between the French manner and that of the mystical poetry. For the French style, with its many Latin analogues, insists primarily upon epigrammatic paradoxes: whereas the English is more concerned with the insistence upon the power of love, conveyed through the accumulation of definitions. In Rolle's poem there are no paradoxes ('Luf es a lyght byrthen' is a later variant, as the absence of internal rhyme shows),[41] and the substance of the poem is not in origin poetical, for it derives from the *Incendium amoris*.[42] But certainly it would not have been given this structural and stylistic form, had it not been for the precedents, remote perhaps, in French, and immediate in English literature.

In this poem there are altogether about twenty definitions of love: it is a fire, it is eternal, it is God's darling, it comforts, it purges of sin, etc. The ultimate sources are of various kinds: the symbol of fire, for instance, is characteristic of Rolle's mystical thought, whilst the idea that 'Lufe us reves þe nyght rest' suggests the conventions of secular poetry. There is, however, one definition in the poem which is particularly important, and which in a sense sums up all the rest. It is the line 'For luf es stalworth as þe dede, luf es hard as hell'. This is a translation of a text from the Song of Songs, 'Fortis est ut mors dilectio, dura ut infernus emulatio', which along with the other text, *amore langueo* (which we have already discussed), was frequently quoted by the great exponents of ecstatic love. In his *De iv gradibus violentae caritatis,* for instance, Richard of St. Victor uses this quotation in his analysis of the fourth (i.e. the highest) degree of love.[43] The *Glossa ordinaria* and other commentaries agreed in taking *aemulatio* to be synonymous with *amor,*[44] thus making it an imaginatively astounding definition of love. Rolle often quoted this text in his English epistles, and in 'Luf es lyf' it comes as a magnificent conclusion to a stanza, which in its first three lines was subdued and didactic in tone:

> For nou lufe þow, I rede, cryste, as I þe tell,
> And with aungels take þi stede—þat ioy loke
>   þou noght sell.

> In erth þow hate, I rede, all þat þi lufe may
>   fell;
> For luf es stalworth as þe dede, luf es hard as
>   hell.[45]

The second part of 'Luf es lyf' begins at line 69 with the opening, 'I sygh and sob bath day and nyght for ane sa fayre of hew': the manuscript evidence suggests that this may originally have been a separate poem,[46] and this is confirmed by the fact that the first line has the ring of an introduction. There follow four verses of love-song for the Christ-knight, 'þat swete chylde', in general theme resembling some of the Harley lyrics, but more passionate and inwardly orientated. Thereafter praise of Christ the lover is intermingled with ecstatic praise of love itself. In style and tone this part of 'Luf es lyf' resembles the love song (Rolle actually calls it 'A sang of lufe') which concludes the *Ego dormio,* 'My sange es in syhtyng'.[47] This is a pure love song, in that it contains no Passion meditation, nor any didactic warning. Its theme is 'Nou wax I pale and wan for luf of my lemman'. In its compactness, coherence, and sustained intensity, it is perhaps the finest of Rolle's lyrics.

Both 'Luf es lyf' and 'My sange es in syhtyng' include verses expressing the devotion to the Holy Name,[48] and for these to be fully appreciated it is an advantage to know something of the history of this devotion; and this in turn leads naturally into a discussion of the small group of poems in English which have this as their subject.

This devotion, which had its roots in the Old and New Testaments,[49] was to some extent formalized before the end of the patristic period. In Christian thought the Name of Jesus acquired both the sanctity attributed to the divine name in the Old Testament, and the power, deriving from an identity with Himself, which Christ attributes to it in the New Testament. Thus the Name, Jesus, was not thought to be an arbitrary means of identification, but to signify almost in a sacramental manner the Saviour to whom it refers: it was therefore endowed with a high sanctity and with an efficacy deriving from that which it signified. Much of this can be seen in the earliest extended reference, the poem of Paulinus of Nola, *De nomine Jesu,*[50] and in the much later passage from a sermon of Peter Chrysologus, in which the powers of Christ, the healing of the sick and the raising of the dead, are attributed to His Name.[51] In the twelfth century, however, in accordance with the new forms of spirituality, this idea acquired a fresh emphasis and its devotional implications were explored. The two most important texts of this period were the fifteenth of St. Bernard's *Sermons on the Song of Songs*[52] and the still well-known hymn, *Dulcis Iesu memoria,* long thought to be also by St. Bernard, but shown by Wilmart to be of Yorkshire Cistercian origin.[53] In both of these the Name is praised, not merely in objective Biblical terms, but also in terms of the religious experience of those who meditate upon it. It is honey in the mouth, melody in the ears, the comforter of the distressed, the hope of the penitent, the destroyer of vice, a light which heals and restores. Above all it is *dulcis,* a word repeated over and over again. In medieval spirituality, in fact, the devotion to the Holy Name becomes a form of devotion to Christ in His humanity, but, unlike that of the usual meditation, its practice does not involve a visual image. Its expression in literary terms demands a use of rhetoric and metaphor which will evoke a sensation of love without the help of the visualization of the object, and therefore the poetry on this subject, both Latin and English, is characterized by an incantatory repetition of the Name of Jesus—at the beginning of each stanza or even of each line—exotic and sensuous metaphors, often borrowed from the Song of Songs, by eloquent variations upon one idea, and by accumulation rather than by the steady development of a theme.

This devotion seems to have flourished especially in England. In the twelfth century there were written, not only the *Dulcis Iesu memoria,* which was to be repeatedly copied in manuscripts,[54] but also striking, though short, passages in other works, as in *Meditatio* ii of Anselm[55] (where the Name is lingered upon and praised as the refuge of the justly fearful), and in the *Philomena* of John of Howden.[56] The devotion also appeared early in vernacular poetry: the opening of the *Wohunge of oure Laverd*[57] echoes successfully the *Dulcis Iesu memoria,* and this Latin hymn was echoed again in two Anglo-Norman poems of the thirteenth century,[58] of which one forms part of the *Manuel des pechiez,* though Robert Manning did not include it in the *Handlyng Synne.* In these there first appears the typical English tendency to incorporate into poems on the Holy Name a passage of meditation on the Passion.

The two earliest English poems on the Holy Name are preserved in MS. Harley 2253. The less remarkable of these is that beginning 'Swete Ihesu, king of blisse', which seems to have begun as a short three-stanza poem (the text of MS. Digby 86),[59] and then to have become expanded into the text of the Harley manuscript.[60] The influence of the *Dulcis Iesu memorica* is seen in the opening of each of the fifteen stanzas with the words 'Swete Ihesu', and by turns of phrase in many individual lines, but, like a later poem in the Thornton Manuscript, 'Ihesu Criste, Saynte Marye sonne',[61] it is partly penitential. Whereas the Latin hymn is a poem of pure praise of Christ and His love, with one verse only set in the form of a prayer, the English in both its short and expanded forms is an expression of contrition and prayer for mercy. In other words, it develops one of the minor ideas of the hymn, that of Jesus as *spes penitentibus,* into the controlling idea of the work. It lacks entirely the sustained ecstatic expression which makes the *Dulcis Iesu memoria* so

exceptionally fine a poem. The second lyric, 'Ihesu, swete is þe love of þee', is much more striking, and in some ways anticipates by several decades the ecstatic style of Richard Rolle's poetry. After its first two verses, which are again closely dependent upon the Latin, it progresses independently, preserving the spirit, though not the thought and expression, of the original. One of its themes, for instance, is one we have already discussed, that of Christ overpowered by Love: 'Ihesu, þi love was us so fre / Þat it fro hevene brouʒte þee', an idea not found in the Latin. Again it has a kind of moving, simple directness, possible only in English:

Iheus my god, ihesu my kyng,
Þou axist me noon oþir þing,
But trewe love and herte ʒernyng,
And love teeris with swete mornyng.[62]

It is, perhaps, not so accomplished or so filled with fine emotional rhetoric as the slightly later poetry of the 'school' of Rolle, and it is occasionally feeble, as in the line 'I wole þee love and þat is riʒt': indeed, there is throughout a slight *naïveté* of expression, perhaps indicating the lack of literary precedent, but it is an agreeable early attempt at a poem of ecstatic love.

The devotion to the Holy Name did not receive its fullest expression in vernacular poetry until the work of the fourteenth-century mystics: it is a recurrent theme of the *Scale of Perfection* and a substantial element in the mystical thought of Rolle. Rolle in his **Comment on the Canticles** follows St. Bernard by turning the text, 'Oleum effusum nomen tuum', into a meditation on the Holy Name:

O nomen admirabile. O nomen delectabile. Hoc est nomen super omne nomen. Nomen altissimum, sine quo non operat quis salutem. Hoc est nomen suave et iocundum, humano cordi verum prebens solacium. Est autem Ihesus in mente mea cantus iubileus, in aure mea sonus celicus, in ore meo dulcor mellifluus. Unde non mirum si illud nomen diligam, quod michi in omni angustia prestat solamen. Nescio orare, nescio meditari nisi resonante nomine Ihesu. Non sapio gaudium quod non est Ihesu mixtum. Quocumque fuero, ubicumque sedero, quicquid egero, memoria nominis Ihesu a mente mea non recedit. Posui illud ut signaculum super cor meum, ut signaculum super brachium meum, quia fortis est ut mors dilectio.[63]

This exceptionally fine meditation, of which the above quotation is only a small part, was very popular: in a vernacular translation it circulated independently, and it also forms part of the didactic compilation, *The Pore Caitiff.*

The subject also recurs in Rolle's vernacular works, in the **Form of Living,** where he instructs that 'þis name Jhesu' should be rooted firmly in the heart,[64] and in

The Commandment, where he says: ' . . . forgete noght þis name Jhesu, bot thynk it in þi hert, nyght and day, as þi speciall and þi dere tresowre.'[65] Above all it is to be found in the fine lyric from 'My sange es in syntyng', where, as we have already seen, the theme of the Holy Name is combined with that of Christ the lover:

> Jhesu, þi lufe is fest, and me to lufe thynk
>   best.
> My hert, when may it brest to come to þe, my
>   rest?
> Jhesu, Jhesu, Jhesu, til þe it es þat I morne
> For my lyfe and my lyvyng. When may I
>   hethen torne?
>
> Jhesu, my dere and mi drewry, delyte ert þou
>   to syng.
> Jhesu, my myrth and melody, when will þow
>   com, my keyng?
> Jhesu, my hele and mi hony, my whart and
>   my comfortyng,
> Jhesu, I covayte for to dy when it es þi
>   payng.[66]

In some medieval verses the authors would seem to be the mechanical servants of rhetorical forms, but here Rolle manipulates them in order to attain a higher degree of passionate intensity. This craftsmanship must be stressed, since a modern reader might easily attribute the obvious poetic superiority merely to a greater degree of personal feeling. There is, of course, no doubt that Rolle is in one sense a romantic poet, in that it is his own experience, passionately apprehended, that is the subject-matter of his poetry. His experience itself, however, has been moulded by the traditional thought of the Church and the traditional literary forms for expressing it; but these literary forms he was able to use exceptionally, since, as his prose style demonstrates even more clearly, he had an ear sensitive to the rhythms of language.

The influence of Rolle can be seen in several later poems on the Holy Name: 'Swete Ihesu, now wol I synge',[67] a long poem, preserved in many later fourteenth- and early fifteenth-century manuscripts, shows in many places the marks of Rolle's thought. It is in part a combination of the two poems already described, but there are many additions. It contains, for instance, Rolle's ideas of fire ('Love-sparkes send þou me') and of melody ('Teche me, lord, þi luf-songe'), and other ideas we have already noticed, such as the wound of love. In it, too, can be seen the tendency, already mentioned, for the Name of Jesus to recall the Passion. In a long passage the chief stages of the Passion are enumerated in direct address, each verse beginning 'Ihesu':

> Ihesu swete, þou hynged on tre,
> Noght for þi gylte bot al for me;

> With synnes I gilte, so wo is me,
> Swete Ihesu, forgyf it me.[68]

The lack of logical arrangement inherent in the kind made such a digression possible, and enables the incoherence to appear, at least to some extent, deliberately contrived, and proper to the fervour and excited devotion of a lover.

The association of the Holy Name with expressions of penitence continued in poems of the late fourteenth century. One of these, 'Ihesu, þi name honourde myȝt be', is severely penitential in tone, but contains one verse that expresses touchingly the pure devotion to the Holy Name:

> Ihesu, my lufe and my lykynge,
>   for evere more blyste mot þou be.
> Mi lufely lorde, my dere darlynge,
>   ful were me [fayne] myght I þe se.
> Ihesu, my lorde, þou gar me synge
>   a lufely kynge is comen to me;
> My swete swetnes of alkyn thynge,
>   my hope and tryste is al in þe.[69]

The other poem from the Thornton Manuscript, 'Ihesu Criste, Saynte Marye sonne',[70] has been said to fall into two parts, one of penance, the other of devotion. But the transition from one to the other is not abrupt but gradual, so that it cannot be considered the combination of two originally distinct poems. In the second half there is the lingering upon the Name of Jesus, and the metaphorical variations of it, which always form the substance of this kind of poetry; and into it, too, there is incorporated, in weakened form, a verse from the lyric of the *Ego dormio:*

> Ihesu my Ioy and my lovynge,
> Ihesu my comforthe clere,
> Ihesu my godde, Ihesu my kynge,
> Ihesu with-owttene pere.
>
> . . . . .
>
> Ihesu my dere and my drewrye,
> Delyte þou arte to synge;
> Ihesu my myrthe and my melodye:
> In to thi lufe me brynge.[71]

Devotion to the Holy Name, even when blended with penitential themes or with meditation on the Passion, seems to have belonged chiefly to the contemplative, rather than to the active layman, or at least to the educated aspirant to contemplation, and not to those with little time for reflection. Nevertheless, like the idea of love's dominion over Christ, it also found expression in more popular poetry. An unpublished poem from John of Grimestone's preaching-book illustrates this:

> Ihesu God is becomen man,
> Ihesu mi love and my lemman.

Ihesu to Marie cam
Ihesu for to delivere man.
Ihesu of Marie was born,
Ihesu to saven þat was forlorn.
Ihesu for senne wep allas,
Ihesu for senne peined was.
Ihesu mi love stedefast,
Ihesu to rode was nailed fast.
Ihesu is herte let undo
Ihesu to bringen man him to,
Ihesu wit blode and water cler.
Ihesu wes man to bringen him ner.
Ihesu þe devel overcam,
Ihesu to blisse brouthte man.
Ihesu sal cumen to demen us,
Beseke we merci to swete Ihesus.
Ihesu of senne delivered us alle.
Ihesu þu bring us in to þin halle,
Ihesu to wonen wit þe in blisse,
Ihesu þeroffe þat we ne misse.[72]

To begin each line with the Name, Jesus, is a fairly common device of style in poems on the Holy Name. It occurs, for instance, in one of the verses we have just quoted from the Thornton poem, and in the fourteenth-century translation of the *Philomena* the substance of the passage on the Holy Name in the original is repeated, with the modification that nearly every line begins with the Name.[73] The use of anaphora in this simple Passion poem, however, is particularly striking, in that it is often unsyntactical, and its intrusion into the sentence effectively draws attention to its importance.

With the exception of the two poems from John of Grimestone's preaching-book discussed earlier, and some of the lesser poems on the Holy Name, the poems associated in this chapter form a quite distinct group, their distinctiveness being indicated by both manuscripts and style. They are preserved in manuscripts of contemplative works, and from their style it is clear that they could have no other useful place, for they could be of interest to the average person only in the modern period, when they can be read as literature: in the fourteenth century they clearly served as meditative adorations for the religious. In terms of style the audience is still important, for, despite the intensity of personal feeling, the design is still controlled by their needs. In homeliness and comprehensibility they are far nearer to the ordinary English Passion lyric than, for instance, to the poems of St. John of the Cross. It is perhaps this combination of homeliness with rapture that makes these poems so especially moving and aesthetically satisfying.

Notes

[1] For references to monastic collections, containing works in the vernacular, see W. A. Pantin, 'English Monks before the Suppression of the Monasteries', *Dublin Review,* cci (1937), 250-70.

[2] The most recent account of Rolle as a mystic is that of D. Knowles, *The English Mystical Tradition* (London, 1961), 48-66.

[3] Women would not normally know Latin (see the introduction to *The Chastising of God's Children,* ed. J. Bazire and E. Colledge, Oxford, 1957, 71).

[4] It is assumed in the following pages that the lyrics embodied in Rolle's prose works are by Rolle and that some of those in MS. C.U.L. Dd. v. 64 are there rightly ascribed to him. A fuller discussion of this is given in Appendix C.

[5] E.E.T.S. 218, 31-32, 47, and 54. The author distinguishes a kind of life that is partly that of Martha (with the works of mercy) and partly that of Mary (contemplation). The contemplation appropriate to the intermediate stage between the active and contemplative life is chiefly meditation on the Passion.

[6] *The Scale of Perfection,* ed. and trans. E. Underhill (London, 1948), 9, 79-81, and 358-60. Hilton recognizes meditation on the Passion as a grade of the contemplative life. For Hilton in general see Knowles, op. cit. 100-18, and Helen Gardner, 'Walter Hilton and the Mystical Tradition in England', *Essays and Studies,* xxii (1936), 103-27.

[7] E.E.T.S. 218, 39.

[8] E.E.T.S. 158, 22 (ll. 827-30). This is an exceptionally fine paraphrase translation of a twelfth-century Latin poem, the *Philomena* of John of Howden. The Latin text is edited by C. Blume (Leipzig, 1930). The value of the E.E.T.S. edition is diminished by the fact that the editor did not at that time recognize the English poem as a translation. Later, however, she made a comparison between the two: Charlotte d'Evelyn, 'Meditations on the Life and Passion of Christ', *Essays and Studies in Honor of Carleton Brown* (New York, 1940), 79-90.

[9] *English Writings of Richard Rolle,* ed. Hope Emily Allen (Oxford, 1931), 67-69.

[10] Ed. cit. 68.

[11] B Text xviii, 59, *Piers Plowman,* ed. Skeat, 524.

[12] Brown XIV, 79.

[13] L. W. Stone, 'Jean de Howden, poète anglo-normand du xiii siècle', *Romania,* lxix (1946-7), 496-519.

[14] Brown XIV, 91, p. 116.

[15] The Septuagint reading at Cant. ii. 5, was: ' . . . ὅτι τετρωμένη ἀγάπης ἀγώ'.

[16] P. Rousselot, *Pour l'histoire du problème de l'amour au moyen âge* (Münster, 1908). The analysis of ecstatic love, pp. 56-87, is very illuminating.

[17] Brown XIII, 86, 'Ant love is to myn herte gon wiþ one spere so kene.' There is already a confusion here between the secular and religious traditions, for the spear is of Christian origin.

[18] Ed. E. Langlois, S.A.T.F. ii. (Paris, 1920), 47-51.

[19] Brown XIV, 91, p. 118.

[20] Verse 620, ed. cit. 51. 'Let the bow of Love shoot forth an arrow.'

[21] 'Thou hast wounded my heart, my sister . . . '. The A. V. has 'ravished'.

[22] *P.L.* 184, 156. 'O that Christ would multiply such wounds in me, from the sole of my foot to the crown of my head, so that nothing in me would be healthy. For health is bad when the wounds are lacking that a devout gazing upon Christ inflicts.'

[23] Brown XIV, 83, p. 99. *Thyrl:* pierce.

[24] *P.L.* 176, 974-5. 'But perhaps it would be easier for you to conquer God than man, to prevail more strongly with God than with man, because the more blessed it is to be overcome the more God was bound to be so overcome. You knew this well and therefore, to have an easy victory, you conquered Him first; when in obedience to yourself you had made Him come down from the throne of His Father's glory to take on the weakness of our mortal state, you still had to deal with us, the rebels. You brought Him, bound with your chains and wounded by your arrows, so that man might be ashamed to resist you any longer when he saw that you had triumphed over God Himself. You wounded the Impassible, you bound the Invincible, you drew the Unchangeable, you made the Eternal mortal.'

[25] *English Works,* ed. Allen, 68.

[26] Ch. 42, ed. M. Deanesly (Manchester, 1915), 276. 'But it is truly said that love goes first in the dance and leads the ring. It was nothing but love that put Christ thus low.'

[27] Ed. cit. 51.

[28] F. M. Comper, *The Life and Lyrics of Richard Rolle* (London, 1928), 229, footnote 5, erroneously assumes the lines to mean that 'it was hate not love that nailed Christ upon the Cross'.

[29] Brown XIV, 90, p. 113.

[30] Ed. cit., p. 113.

[31] Ed. cit. 24 and 27. 'Hear me Love! Who is it whom you torment?'; 'Again, hear me Love! Whom are you wounding?'.

[32] Ed. cit. 24 and 36. 'Why, Love, do you thrust from you your lover?'; 'While Love commands Life to die . . . '.

[33] Brown XIV, 66.

[34] Ibid. p. 266.

[35] Inc. 'Reuthe made God on mayden to lithte', f. 119.

[36] *English Works,* 49-51.

[37] Brown XIV, 86.

[38] Brown XIV, 84, pp. 102 and 104. *Lovyng:* lover; *bote:* remedy; *gastly wynne:* joy for the spirit; *tyne:* lack.

[39] S.A.T.F. ii. 212-13. This passage with various other examples is referred to by P. Meyer, 'Mélanges de poésie anglo-normande, ix: Une définition de l'amour', *Romania,* iv (1875), 382-4.

[40] Brown XIII, 53, p. 108. *Craft:* strength (?); *les:* false; *frowringe:* comfort; *sellich:* wonderful.

[41] The reading in MS. Lambeth 853, 'a birþun fyne' (E.E.T.S. 24, 25), preserves the rhyme.

[42] Brown XIII, p. 209, and XIV, p. 270.

[43] Ives, *Épitre à Séverin sur la charité,* Richard de Saint Victor, *Les quatre degrés de la violente charité,* ed. and trans. G. Dumeige (Paris, 1955), 149. The *De iv gradibus violentae caritatis* contains one of the most important expositions of the theory of ecstatic love.

[44] *P.L.* 113, 1165.

[45] Brown XIV, p. 104. L. 3, 'I advise you to hate everything on earth that may destroy your love'.

[46] A text of the poem in southern dialect occurs in MS. Lambeth 853 (E.E.T.S. 24, 22-31) but with the poem, 'Ihesu god sone, lord of mageste' (Brown XIV, 83), inserted between II. 68-69. It is a fair inference that three originally distinct poems have here been conflated.

[47] *English Works,* 70-72.

[48] Brown XIV, p. 106; *English Works,* 71.

[49] F. M. Lemoine, 'Le Nom de Jésus dans l'ancient testament', and C. Spicq, 'Le Nom de Jésus dans le nouveau testament', *La vie spirituelle,* lxxxvi (1952), 5-18 and 19-37.

[50] *P.L.* 61, 740-2. This poem is referred to by A. Cabassut, 'La Dévotion au nom de Jésus dans l'église d'occident', *La vie spirituelle,* lxxxvi, 46-69, who provides a useful series of references to works on the subject of the Holy Name. See also M. Meertens, *De Godsvrucht in de Nederlanden,* i (Louvain, 1930), 103-11.

[51] *P.L.* 52, 586.

[52] *P.L.* 183, 843-8.

[53] A. Wilmart, *Le 'Jubilus' dit se saint Bernard* (Rome, 1944).

[54] Ibid. 17-24, 29-32.

[55] *P.L.* 158, 724-5. Cabassut, loc. cit. notes that this prayer was copied in many later books of hours.

[56] *A.H.* 1. 29-31.

[57] E.E.T.S. 241, 20.

[58] On these see H. E. Allen, "*The Mystical Lyrics of the Manuel des pechiez',* Romanic Review,* ix (1912), 154-93.

[59] Brown XIII, 50.

[60] *Harley Lyrics,* 51-52.

[61] F. A. Patterson, *The Middle English Penitential Lyric,* 53.

[62] Brown XIV, 89, p. 112 (from MS. Hunterian Mus. V. 8. 15). The Harley text, which is longer and in many of its readings inferior, is printed by Böddeker, *Altenglische Dichtungen,* 198-205.

[63] Wilmart, op. cit. 275. The title derives from Cant. i.2. Amongst the many Biblical texts that could be relevantly quoted by writers on the Holy Name this seems to have been the most popular. Ubertino of Casale, for instance, quotes it three times in his chapter on the Holy Name in the *Arbor vitae,* ii. 2 (edn. of Venice, 1485, fols. ii^v-vi). Rolle's *Oleum effusum* was later translated into the vernacular and survives in a number of manuscripts: it was also incorporated into *The Pore Caitiff.* The following is the translation of the above quotation from the text of MS. Harley 1022: 'A, þat wondurful name, A, þat delytabul name! Þis is þo name þat es above al names, name alþer-heghest, with-outen qwilk na man hopes hele. Þis

name es swete and Ioyful, gyfand sothfast comforth unto mans hert. Sothle þo name of Ihesu es in my mynde Ioyus sang, in my nere hevenly sounde, in my mouth hunyful swetnes. Qwarfor na wondur if I luf þat name þe qwylk gyfs comforth to me in al angwys. I can noght pray, I can noght have mynde, bot sownand þo name of Ihesu; I savour noght Ioy þat with Ihesu es noght mengyd. Qwar-so I be, qwar-so I sit, qwat-so I do, þo mynd of þo name of Ihesu departes noght fra my mynde. I have set it as a takenyng opon my hert, als takenyng apon myn arme: ffor "luf es strange as dede".' C. Horstman, *Yorkshire Writers,* i (London, 1895), 186-7.

[64] *English Writings,* 108.

[65] Ed. cit. 81.

[66] Ed. cit. 71. *Brest:* break; *drewry:* beloved; *whart:* health.

[67] *Yorkshire Writers,* ii. 9-24.

[68] Op. cit. 13.

[69] E.E.T.S. 15, 140. Brown XV, 144, prints this poem as a pendent to 'Ihū, Ihū, mercy I cry', which in both manuscripts precedes it. The *Index,* however, gives it a separate entry, and both Patterson, loc. cit. 54 and E.E.T.S. 15, 139-40, present it as an independent poem. The correctness of this is indicated by the style of the first line of this poem and by the finality of the last line of the preceding poem, 'Ihc, Amen, Maria, Amen'.

[70] *Yorkshire Writers,* i. 364-5; Patterson, op. cit. 53 and notes p. 190.

[71] Op. cit. 365. The second of these verses is a weakened version of two lines from the poem in the *Ego dormio,* quoted above, p. 176.

[72] f. 119^v.

[73] E.E.T.S. 158, 28-29, Latin text ed. Blume, 29-31.

Sister Mary Arthur Knowlton (essay date 1972)

SOURCE: Sister Mary Arthur Knowlton, "Rolle's Lyrics," in *The Influence of Richard Rolle and of Julian of Norwich on the Middle English Lyrics,* Mouton, 1973, pp. 49-70.

[*In the excerpt below, Knowlton sets out her basic reading of Rolle, noting the features that she considers definitive of his verse.*]

Lyric poetry, among the Greeks, meant poetry to be sung to the accompaniment of the lyre. Professor Frye suggests in the *Anatomy of Criticism* that the Greek word for lyric would be more meaningfully translated "poems to be chanted",[1] since the emphasis should be placed on the words, not on the music. The lyric is now generally found to be defined in some such terms as those used by M. L. Rosenthal and A. J. Smith in *Exploring Poetry,* namely, "a brief, unified expression of emotion in words as melodious as possible".[2] The best lyrics are necessarily brief since they express a single feeling at the moment of its greatest intensity. The emotion is ordinarily attached to some idea or object or experience which constitutes the subject or theme of the lyric.[3] John Drinkwater in his essay on the lyric exalts it as the highest kind of poetry:

> Poetry is the result of the intensest emotional activity attainable by man focussing itself upon some manifestation of life, and experiencing that manifestation completely. . . . The emotion of poetry expresses itself in rhythm and . . . the significance of the subject-matter is realised by the intellectual choice of the perfect word. We recognise in the finished art, which is the result of these conditions, the best words in the best order—poetry; and to put this essential poetry into different classes is impossible. But since it is most commonly found by itself in short poems which we call lyric, we may say that the characteristic of the lyric is that it is the product of the pure poetic energy unassociated with other energies, and that lyric and poetry are synonymous terms.[4]

Included in Rolle's English epistles are five lyrics, three in *Ego Dormio* and two in *The Form of Living.* Apart from these, we cannot be sure how many of the lyrics attributed to Rolle are certainly his. Our two principal sources are Cambridge MS. Dd. v. 64, III (late fourteenth century) and Longleat MS. 29 (fifteenth century). Neither manuscript is absolutely definite about the number of the lyrics found in them that are to be ascribed to Rolle. Miss Hope Emily Allen has examined all the lyrics in these manuscripts and from internal and external evidence has admitted six to the canon of Rolle's works, namely, *A Salutation to Jesus, A Song of Love-longing to Jesus, A Song of the Love of Jesus, The Nature of Love, Thy Joy be in the Love of Jesu,* and the prose lyric, *Gastly Gladnesse.*[5] Two others, *Exhortation* and *A Song of Mercy,* Miss Allen implies, may be accepted as Rolle's and she includes them in her edition of his *English Writings.* In this chapter I shall discuss Rolle's verse lyrics. His prose lyric, *Gastly Gladnesse,* I have treated with Rolle's prose works in Chapter I.

Rolle's lyrics present certain distinctive features. First, they all employ devotional religious themes. Love of God is the dominant theme, but the themes rarely appear singly in the lyrics; they are found interwoven with one another. For example, lyrics on divine love

usually include expressions of ardent confidence in the Holy Name. This is to be expected in view of Rolle's conviction, which is formulated in the *Incendium Amoris,* that no one will receive the highest gifts of love who does not honour and esteem the Holy Name of Jesus and keep it ever in his mind.[6] In examining the lyrics which are not incorporated in the prose works I shall try to indicate the main theme and the secondary themes treated, using the divisions of subject matter already employed in discussing the ideas in the prose works, namely, devotion to the Holy Name, divine love, the passion, penitence, mercy and death, and devotion to the Virgin Mary. In truth, with the exception of mercy and devotion to the Virgin Mary, the subject divisions I have listed resolve themselves in Rolle's lyrics into one subject, love in its three degrees. To the first degree of love, that in which a man "haldes þe ten commandments, and kepes hym fra þe seven dedely synnes",[7] belong lyrics treating the theme of penitence; to the second degree, that in which a man forsakes the world and follows Christ, "ay havand hym in mynde",[8] belong reflections on the passion, lyrics honouring the Holy Name and ones appealing for love; to the third degree, that in which the soul experiences a degree of vision and union with God, when "Jhesu es al þi desyre, al þi delyte, al þi joy, al þi solace, al þi comforth",[9] belong the poems of love-longing, of yearning for union with God, of desire for death as a means of union. The three lyrics of *Ego Dormio* which are incorporated into the structure of the piece as illustrations of the three degrees of love may best be studied from this point of view. The two lyrics found in *The Form of Living* serve the function of crystallizing Rolle's recommendations for those enjoying the two higher degrees of love; they, too, should be treated as organic parts of a whole. But Rolle's other lyrics do not generally keep the characteristic sentiments of the three degrees of love so sharply divided. Nor does his influence on the later lyric literature discernibly follow this pattern. Furthermore, since his major prose works, which play such a large part in this influence, are not as highly organized as is the *Ego Dormio,* it seems to me to be more profitable to adhere to the plan of looking at those lyrics which are not functional parts of the structure of his prose works from the point of view of subjects or themes treated.

The second distinctive feature of Rolle's lyrics concerns the emotions which animate them. They are those of joy, hope, confidence, compassion, and love-longing, never those of fear, gloom, or self-pity. The lyrics are the overflow of Rolle's love of God which reaches its culmination in the gift of "canor", the heavenly melody which belongs to the songs of everlasting praise,[10] turns his thoughts into song,[11] and transports his mind into singing the delights of eternal love, "rapitur mens ad canendum delicias amoris eterni".[12] His lyrics are, then, in general, ecstatic expressions of

the sweetness and joy that flooded his soul in his longing for God. Even the one lyric which is almost wholly
penitential in tone concludes with a reminder of the
joy that is to come and with a confident message of
hope for the one who loves Christ and hates sin.

Thirdly, Rolle's lyrics show great irregularity in structure and metre. Within single poems, stanza lengths, as
indicated by rhyme schemes, may vary from three to
six lines, as they do, for example, in the **"Cantus
Amoris"** of the *Ego Dormio*.[13] Rolle's commonest unit
in the lyrics is the four-line stanza; however, certain of
the lyrics do not admit of any divisions but run on for
the full length of the poem, as do the two lyrics incorporated into *The Form of Living*.[14] Identification of
his metre is just as elusive. Many of his lines are patterned on the four-stress line with medial pause and a
varying number of lightly accented syllables between
the stresses, the normal rhythm in Old English poetry
and the system used by Rolle in his Latin poem, the
Canticum Amoris. As Professor Frye has pointed out
in the *Anatomy of Criticism*,[15] it is this arrangement of
"a predominating stressed accent with a variable number of syllables between two stresses (usually four
stresses to a line, corresponding to 'common time' in
music)" which makes poetry musical.

Fourthly, elaborate rhyme schemes distinguish Rolle's
lyrics and assist in imparting to them their musical
quality. The system he most commonly uses is the
four-line rhyming stanza, but within a single poem he
may vary this to aabb, aaabbb, aabbcc, aabbb, as he
does in the **"Cantus Amoris"** of the *Ego Dormio*.[16]
Medial rhyme is generally present, employed in a variety of ways. His favourite method is the use of rhyming words immediately before the pause in each of the
four lines of a stanza, in addition to end rhymes, as for
example, in this stanza from *Thy Joy be in the Love
of Jesus:*

> Bot luf hym at þi myght, whils þu ert lyvand
>   here;
> And loke unto þi syght, þat nane be þe so
>   dere.
> Say to hym, bath day and nyght: 'When mai I
>   negh þe nere?
> Bring me to þi lyght, þi melodi to here.[17]

His scheme may vary from stanza to stanza within the
same poem, as in *A Song of Love-longing to Jesus*.[18]
In places alliteration seems to have been substituted in
lines where no medial rhyme appears, as in stanza
eleven of this poem:

> Blynded was his faire ene, his flesch blody
>   for bette.
> His lufsum lyf was layde ful low, and saryful
>   umbesette.
>
> (ll. 41-42)

Still another combination appears in the last stanza of
this poem. Internal rhyme is used within the first half-
line of each verse, and alliteration in the second half,
except in the last line of the stanza:

> Lyf was slayne, and rase agayne; in fairehede
>   may we fare;
> And dede es brought til litel or noght, and
>   kasten in endles kare.
> On hym, þat þe bought, hafe al þi thought,
>   and lede þe in his lare.
> Gyf al þi hert til Crist þi qwert, and lufe hym
>   evermare.
>
> (ll. 45-58)

There are examples, also, of lines in which the medial rhyme and the end rhyme are identical sounds.
Six lines at the beginning of the *"Meditacio de
passione Christi"* in *Ego Dormio*[19] have this elaborate rhyme scheme:

> My keyng, þat water grette and blode swette;
> Sythen ful sare bette, so þat hys blode hym
>   wette,
> When þair scowrges mette.
> Ful fast þai gan hym dyng and at þe pyler
>   swyng,
> And his fayre face defowlyng with spittyng.
>
> Þe thorne crownes þe keyng; ful sare es þat
>   prickyng.
> Alas! my joy and my swetyng es demed to
>   hung.
>
> (ll. 218-224)

Finally, there is noticeable in Rolle's lyrics a scarcity
of imagery. The ideas and emotions are expressed in
simple, vigorous language, carrying a straightforward
statement of his convictions and aspirations, intense
and effective in its very simplicity. The lyrics depend
for their beauty on the music of the lines and the
sincerity of the sentiments. There are, however, occasional examples of figurative writing, for example, in
A Song of Love-longing to Jesus,[20] Rolle uses the
concept of God piercing the soul with the spear of
love (l. 6); he asks that the memory of the passion
may be rooted in his heart (l. 17); he speaks of Christ
as the food of angels (l. 33), and of death and life
striving for mastery as Christ hung upon the cross (l.
43). He frequently uses the symbol of "light" for
heaven.[21] In *The Nature of Love*[22] he uses again the
figure of Christ wounding the soul with love, (l. 29),
and the idea of Christ as our "weddyd keyng", (l. 42).
The figure of Christ as king occurs in all but two of
the lyrics.[23] A rapid survey of three of the major prose
works reveals its use about four times in the
Incendium Amoris,[24] twice in the ***Emendatio Vitae,***[25]
and seventeen times in the ***Melos Amoris.***[26] This is
interesting in view of the fact that the "melos" is the

gift that inspires the lover to express "the delights of eternal love" in song,[27] and has, therefore, the closest connection with the lyrics. There is no doubt that Rolle uses it in the lyrics as a convenient word for rhyming with other "yng" words, seeming to preserve something of definiteness of the final syllable of the Old English "cyning", but the significance of its presence in the lyrics is deeper than that. In the lyrics, Rolle is, in almost every case, talking about his love of God and his longing for union with Him in the kingdom of heaven. It is eminently fitting, then, that he address his plea for this final grace to the king of that kingdom. This is precisely the association he is recalling in eight of the lyrics in which he uses the epithet. In *A Song of Mercy* he prays:

> God of al, Lorde and Keyng, I pray þe, Jhesu,
>   be my frende,
> Sa þat I may þi mercy syng in þi blys
>   withowten ende.[28]

In *A Song of Love-longing to Jesus,* the request is the same in substance:

> Jhesu, my God, Jhesu my keyng, forsake
>   noght my desyre.
>
>   . . . . .
>
> Þi wil es my ȝhernyng; of lufe þou kyndel þe
>   fyre,
> Þat I in swet lovyng with aungels take my
>   hyre.[29]

In *The Nature of Love,* the admonition at the end is directed towards the same consummation of love with the King in his kingdom:

> Take Jhesu in þi thynkyng, his lufe he will þe
>   send.
>
>   . . . . .
>
> And use þe in praiyng, þarin þou may be mend,
> Swa þat þow hafe þi keyng in joy withowten
>   endyng.[30]

In *Exhortation*[31] the concept is related, but the approach is different. The poet pictures the King of heaven coming in judgment on his enemies, while he himself hopes for a place in the kingdom.

A second association that Rolle establishes with the notion of kingship is that of a King crowned with thorns. In the lyric on the passion embedded in the *Ego Dormio,* the symbol is explicit, "þe thorne crownes þe keyng".[32]

The figure of the "fire of love" is another familiar one in the lyrics. In *A Song of Love-longing to Jesus* Rolle requests, "of lufe þou kyndel þe fyre";[33] and in *A Song*

of the Love of Jesus he asks to be made "byrnand" in the love of God.[34] He admonishes his readers in *Thy Joy be in the Love of Jesus* to forsake the joy of men and promises them that their hearts "sal bren with lufe þat never sal twynne".[35]

Structurally, the *Ego Dormio* and the *Form of Living* in their blend of prose and verse in various metres resemble Menippean Satire.[36] In the *Ego Dormio*[37] Rolle gives an exposition of the three degrees of love, and, following his description of each degree, he inserts a poem embodying the sentiments proper to that state. The first degree, essential for every man who wishes to save his soul, consists in the avoidance of sin, fidelity to the Church and to the service of God, and a determination to renounce any earthly pleasure rather than offend God. No man can come to heaven "bot if he lufe God and his neghbor" and avoid sin. Men, he says, think it sweet to sin, but the wages of sin are bitterness. At this point Rolle inserts an unrhymed, alliterative poem, ten lines in length, developing the theme of the transitoriness and false attractiveness of this world and its glittering shows:

> Alle perisches and passes þat we with eghe
>   see
> It wanes into wrechednes, þe welth of þis
>   worlde.
>
>   (104-105)

But while those who follow this "wretchedness" fall into hell, those who relinquish these deceitful pleasures for love of Christ are rewarded:

> Bot he may syng of solace, þat lufes Jhesu
>   Christe.
> Þe wretchesse fra wele falles into hell.
>
>   (112-113)

Rolle always has a positive attitude towards penance and renunciation of the world and sin. The threat of punishment for the sinner is recognized, but the motivation which he recommends, here and elsewhere, for purity of life is love, not fear.

When a man has proven himself in the first degree of love, he advances into the second. In this degree he forsakes the world and his kindred and follows Christ in poverty and the other virtues. Now he despises the world and covets the joy of heaven. In this stage Rolle recommends frequent prayer and constant recollection, especially thought of the passion and of the Holy Name of Jesus. "Gode thoghtes and hali prayers" (l. 160) shall make the soul burn in the love of Christ, and "lufe of þis nam Jhesu" (l. 183) will prepare the soul for the highest gifts of love which God may bestow upon it. The soul now "covaytes to be Goddes lufer". (l. 176) The second lyric embodied in the *Ego Dormio* repeats and elaborates these themes. It begins as a meditation on the passion: this stirs the poet, who now despises the world and covets the joy of heaven, to ask for the grace to become a lover of God.

The reflections on the passion concentrate on the physical sufferings of Christ. With realistic precision and compassion Rolle recalls the scourging, the defouling of Christ's "fayre face" with spittle, the painful crowning with thorns, the nailing of the hands and feet, and the piercing of the sacred side. He weaves into his text a variant of a four-line poem popular in the period, known as the *Candet Nudatum Pectus:*

> Naked es his whit breste, and rede es his
>   blody syde;
> Wan was his fayre hew, his wowndes depe
>   and wyde.
> In fyve stedes of his flesch þe blode gan
>   downe glyde
> Als stremes of þe strande; hys pyne es noght
>   to hyde.

(ll. 227-230)

Carleton Brown prints two versions of this poem from early fourteenth-century manuscripts. In his notes Professor Brown says this short lyric is a translation from a treatise ascribed in the Middle Ages to St. Augustine.[38] Miss Hope Emily Allen attributes the original to St. Anselm.[39] Migne prints it in the *Meditationes* of St. Augustine,[40] and also in the *Orationes* of St. Anselm.[41] In the "Admonitio" with which Migne prefaces the *Meditationes* of St. Augustine, he casts doubt on their authenticity. He cites Bernardus Vindingus' arguments from internal evidence of style, diction and inconsistency of statements in the *Meditationes* with the facts of Augustine's life, as sufficient proof to deny authorship to St. Augustine. He also points out that twenty-four of the forty chapters of the *Meditationes* have manuscript authority for the authorship of John, Abbot of Fécamp, who died in the year 1078. Migne is of the opinion that later copyists incorporated material from Abbot John's writings into St. Augustine's works, not that Abbot John stole from St. Augustine.[42]

Father Hugh Pope, who includes in his study of St. Augustine a list of his authentic works, believes that the *Meditationes,* though constantly spoken of as the genuine work of St. Augustine, are almost certainly to be attributed to John, the Abbot.[43]

It would seem that St. Augustine is not to be credited with the lines in question, usually referred to as the "Candet Nudatum Pectus", the first words of the Latin text. Since these lines do not appear in the twenty-four chapters of the *Meditationes* which are ascribed to Abbot John, they may belong to St. Anselm. But doubt has been attached to the genuineness of some of Anselm's *Meditationes* and *Orationes,* too, since the discovery of a late eleventh-century manuscript in which many are

combined with extracts from St. Augustine and the whole prefaced by a letter from Abbot John of Fécamp.[44] In any case Rolle's direct source was probably an English translation of the lines. S. Harrison Thomson, in his article, "The Date of the Early English Translation of the 'Candet Nudatum Pectus'", *Medium Aevum* IV (1935), 100-105, sums up the results of his investigations with a statement to the effect that there were two completely distinct translations of the passage in England before the end of the thirteenth century—one in four lines current in at least three recensions, the second in six lines in two recensions.

Let us return to the analysis of the lyric. Gratitude and compassion, surging in the poet's heart from reflection on the suffering of Christ, move him to desire love and he asks to be made God's lover. He no longer cares for this world; he seeks God alone and longs for the moment when he may see Him in everlasting joy and bliss. The gifts of heat and song, which belong to the highest degree of love, he earnestly requests in the sweet name of Jesus:

> Kyndel me fire within, . . .
>
> . . . . .
>
> Þou be my lufyng,
> Þat I lufe may syng.

(242, 255-256)

The change of address from "my keyng" in the section of the poem commemorating the passion to "Jhesu" in the part in which the poet asks for love, seems to indicate a growing intimacy of love which springs from reflection on the passion. There is still a great difference between the restrained use of the Holy Name here and the ecstatic repetition of it in the next lyric, which exemplifies the highest degree of love.

Rolle concludes the discussion of the second degree of love with the promise of exhilarating sweetness to the soul faithful to the ideals presented in his little poem. Then the privileged soul may, at God's good pleasure, enter into the third degree of love, that of the contemplative life, in which the "egh of þi hert mai loke intil heven" (ll. 261-262). In this state the soul feels surpassing "lufe, joy and swetnes" (l. 281), experiences the burning of love in the heart, and song and melody in the mind, and places all its desire and delight in Jesus. The heart must be set on God alone before this great grace will be bestowed. Now, Rolle says, he will write a song of love such as the lover of Christ will delight in. Then follows the **"Cantus Amoris"**, a song of yearning for the union of perfect love in heaven. The world means nothing to the lover now; there is not even mention of despising it; the whole attention is centred on the longing for death and the eternal vision and union of love into which the soul enters through death:

When wil þou come, Jhesu my joy,

(l. 318)

. . . . .

When wil þou me kall? me langes to þi hall,
To se þe þan al;

(ll. 327-328)

. . . . .

I sytt and syng of luf langyng þat in my
breste es bredde.
Jhesu, Jhesu, Jhesu, when war I to þe ledde?
Full wele I wate, þou sees my state; in lufe
my thought es stedde.
When I þe se, and dwels with þe, þan am I
fylde and fedde.

(ll. 333-336)

. . . . .

When wil þou rew on me, Jhesu, þat I myght
with þe be,
To lufe and lok on þe?

(ll. 358-359)

The intimacy of love which now floods the soul of the
lover pours itself out in repeated tender invocations to the
Holy Name. In the prose explanation preceding the lyric,
Rolle had written, "þan es Jhesu al þi desyre, al þi delyte,
al þi joy, al þi solace, al þi comforth" (ll. 285-286). In the
lyric he conveys perfectly this sense of complete fulfilment
and absorption in Jesus, his Beloved:

When wil þou come, Jhesu my joy,

(l. 318)

. . . . .

Jhesu my savyoure, Jhesu my comfortoure,

(l. 324)

. . . . .

Jhesu, Jhesu, Jhesu, when war I to þe ledde?

(l. 334)

. . . . .

Jhesu, Jhesu, Jhesu, til þe it es þat I morne.

(l. 339)

. . . . .

Jhesu, my dere and my drewry, delyte ert þou to syng.
Jhesu, my myrth and melody, when will þow
com, my keyng?
Jhesu, my hele and my hony, my whart and
my comfortyng,
Jhesu, I covayte for to dy when it es þi payng.

(ll. 341-344)

. . . . .

Jhesu, my lufe, my swetyng

(l. 350)

. . . . .

Jhesu, my hope, my hele, my joy ever ilk a
dele,

(l. 353)

The heat, sweetness and song, which Rolle promises
will be present in the heart and mind of the lover in the
third degree of love, are indicated in the lyric:

Al wa es fra me went, sen þat my hert es brent
In Criste luf sa swete . . .

(ll. 345-346)

. . . . .

Jhesu, my dere and my drewry, delyte ert þou
to syng.

(l. 341)

The song begun in this life will be continued in heaven
for ever:

And I þi lufe sal syng thorow syght of þi
schynyng
In heven withowten endyng.

(ll. 362-363)

With this exultant hope of an everlasting union of love
in heaven, he concludes the **"Cantus Amoris"** and the
Ego Dormio.

In the first part of the *Form of Living*[45] Rolle gives
instructions "how þou may dispose þi lyfe and rewle
it to Goddes will" (p. 102). But he is aware that his
disciple, Margaret de Kirkeby, desires "to here some
special poynt of þe luf of Jhesu Criste, and of
contemplatyf lyfe" (p. 103), and this he undertakes to
teach her. In a brief exposition he outlines the three
degrees of love discussed in *Ego Dormio*. Not all
men love God equally. All who keep his commandments certainly love Him; those who keep his counsels love Him more. But there is a higher love than
this in which a man feels "mykel joy and swetnes and
byrnyng in his lufe" (p. 103). A man to feel this love
must be "clene and fylled with his lufe"; he comes to
this love with "grete travayle in praier and thynkyng"
(p. 103). This is the work of the soul in the second
degree of love. To illustrate his meaning Rolle gives
Margaret an example of a prayer she may say in her
heart that will serve to focus her thoughts on God
while she is eating and at other times when she is not
engaged in formal prayer or conversation. There follows a short prayer written in verse, expressing love,
thanksgiving and petition. As in the lyric embodied
in the *Ego Dormio* as an exemplification of the second degree of love, reference to the passion is included. Christ is addressed as "keyng" three times in
this short poem and as "Jhesu" only once, an indication that the fulness of love is not yet reached. The

final petition of the prayer is a request for the gift Rolle attaches to the third degree of love—that of song:

> Þou gyf me grace to syng
> Þe sang of þi lovyng.
>
> (ll. 37-38)

Rolle goes on to assure Margaret that if she is faithful to prayer and meditation she will grow in the love of Jesus Christ in a short time.

A more detailed discussion of the three degrees of love follows, in this case given the labels, "insuperabel", "inseparabel" and "syngulere" (p. 104). Very few, he says, ever receive the third degree of love, for "God gyfes it til wham he wil, bot noght withouten grete grace comand before" (p. 106). If Margaret should be granted this great favour, she may sing to Jesus Christ in her heart this song of love which he is composing for her. She may sing it when she is longing for "hys comyng" and her own "gangyng" forth to union with him (p. 107). A twelve-line lyric of ardent love and longing for union and the vision of heaven follows. The ideas of the *Ego Dormio* lyric of love-longing are repeated here; some of the lines are almost identical; the sweetness of love and the burning of love are mentioned but song is not nor is the Holy Name. The omission of reference to the gift of song may be accounted for by the prefacing instruction that makes the whole poem a song to be sung in the heart: "And ymang other affeccions and sanges þou may in þi langyng syng þis in þi hert til þi Lord Jhesu" (p. 107). The absence of direct address to the Holy Name is unusual but interesting here in view of the comment Rolle had made on this devotion a few sentences before the composition of the lyric. He says: "Bot þe sawle þat es in þe thyrd degre . . . es anely comforted in loving and lufyng of God and til þe dede com es syngand gastly til Jhesu, and in Jhesu, and Jhesu, noght bodily cryand wyth mouth" (p. 106). It is sufficient that the name be in the heart. Immediately following the lyric is a chapter on devotion to the Holy Name in which Rolle points out its wonderful effects on the soul. "þis name Jhesu", he says, "fest it swa fas tin þi hert, þat it come never out of þi thought" (p. 108).

Rolle has written one lyric dedicated to the Holy Name, *A Salutation to Jesus*.[46] Reverence, confidence, faith and love inspire the invocations to Jhesu, my creatowre (l. 1), Jhesu, mi saveowre (1. 2), Jhesu, helpe and sokowre (l. 3), Jhesu, þe blyssed flowre of þi moder virgyne (l. 4), Jhesu, leder to lyght (l. 5), Jhesu, Lorde of Mageste (l. 13), joy þat lastes ay (l. 14) and all delyte to se (l. 14). A brief sentiment of penitence (l. 12), desire to be God's lover (l. 15), longing to come to Him (l. 16), yearning to see God in heaven (l. 7), and to share in His bliss (l. 9), compassion with the sufferings of Christ (ll. 17-20) are themes woven in with the main subject of devotion to the Holy Name.

Four of Rolle's lyrics are composed with love as the dominant theme. *A Song of the Love of Jesus*[47] is a sustained exposition of what love is. It covers recommendations and petitions for all three degrees of love. In it are repeated many phrases from the *Form of Living* and from the *Incendium Amoris*. In the *Form of Living,* Rolle asks the question, "What is lufe?" and he answers it:

> Luf es a byrnand ʒernyng in God, with a wonderfull delyte and sykernes. God es lyght and byrnyng . . . Lufe es a lyf, copuland togedyr þe lufand and þe lufed . . . Lufe es desyre of þe hert, ay thynkand til þat þat it lufes; and when it hase þat it lufes, þan it joyes, and na thyng may make it sary . . . Verray lufe clenses þe saule . . . for luf es stalworth als þe dede, . . . and hard als hell. . . .[48]

In the lyric these ideas appear in wording that is only slightly different:

> Luf es lyf þat lastes ay, . . .
>
> (l. 1)
>
> . . . . .
>
> Þe nyght it tournes intil þe day, . . .
>
> (l. 3)
>
> . . . . .
>
> Lufe es thoght with grete desyre, of a fayre lovyng,
> Lufe I lyken til a fyre, . . .
> Lufe us clenses of oure syn, . . .
> Lufe þe keynges hert may wyn, lufe of joy may syng.
>
> (ll. 5-8)
>
> . . . . .
>
> . . . luf copuls God and manne.
>
> (l. 12)
>
> . . . . .
>
> Take til þe al myne entent, þat þow be my ʒhernyng.
>
> (l. 22)
>
> . . . . .
>
> Fra kare it tornes þat kyend, and lendes in myrth and glew.
>
> (l. 44)
>
> . . . . .
>
> For luf es stalworth as þe dede, luf es hard as hell.
>
> (l. 48)

Miss H. E. Allen has pointed out in *Writings Ascribed to Richard Rolle* (p. 299) that the first sixty lines of this poem are a close translation of scattered sentences from chapters forty and forty-one of the *Incendium Amoris*. Indeed, the similarity is very striking both in scattered phrases and in whole blocks, especially from chapter forty-one. The stanza in the lyric which reads:

> If I lufe any erthly thyng þat payes to my wyll,
> And settes my joy and my lykyng when it
>   may come me tyll,
> I mai drede of partyng, þat wyll be hate and yll;
> For al my welth es bot wepyng, when pyne
>   mi saule sal spyll.
>
> (ll. 29-32)

is almost a literal translation of a passage in the *Incendium Amoris:*

> Si enim amavero aliquam creaturam mundi huius, que mee voluntati per omnia placeret, et posuero gaudium meum et finem solacii mei ac desiderii, quando ad me ipsa eveniret, timere potero de separacione ardente et amara, quoniam omnis felicitas quam habeo in huiusmodi amore, in fine non est nisi fletus et anxietas quando iam prope est, quod pena amarissime animam cruciabit.[49]

Lines forty-nine to sixty of the poem translate another block from the *Incendium Amoris:*

> Luf es a lyght byrthen, lufe gladdens ȝong
>   and alde;
>
>   . . . . .
>
> Luf es a gastly wynne, þat makes men bygge
>   and balde.
>
>   . . . . .
>
> Luf es þe swettest thyng þat man in erth hase tane;
>
>   . . . . .
>
> Luf es Goddes derlyng; lufe byndes blode and
>   bane.
>
>   . . . . .
>
> For me and my lufyng, lufe makes bath be ane.
> Bot fleschly lufe sal fare as dose þe flowre in May,
> And, lastand be na mare þan ane houre of a day;
> And sythen syghe ful sare þar lust, þar pryde,
>   þar play,
> When þai er casten in kare til pyne þat lastes ay.

In the *Incendium Amoris* we read the following sentences which cover exactly these ideas:

> Amor enim est levis sarcina, . . . que iuvenes cum senibus letificat, . . . Amor est vinum spirituale inebrians mentes electorum, et faciens provectos et viriles, ut venenosam mundi delectacionem obliviscantur, et nec cogitare current, immo de hac vehementer dedignentur; . . . Amor igitur res dulcissima est et utilissima quam unquam accepit creatura racionalis. Est enim Deo amor acceptissimus et dilectissimus, qui ligat non solum nexibus

> sapiencie et suavitatis Deoque coniungit, sed eciam carnem et sanguinem constringit. . . . Verumtamen carnalis dileccio prosperabitur et peribit quemadmodum flos agri in estate, et non erit amplius exultans et existens quam si non nisi per diem unum perduraret, . . . Superbia eorum, et ludus in falsa pulchritudine, in putredinem et turpitudinem detrudetur, quoniam iam precipitati sunt in tormentum, quod cum eis erit in eternum.[50]

"Calor", "canor" and "dulcor" are prominent in the poem. Heat is mentioned more than once: "Lufe I lyken to a fyre" (l. 6); "Lufe es hatter þen þe cole" (l. 13); "þe flawme of lufe" (l. 14). Song is spoken of as the usual accompaniment of love:

> If þat my sawle had herd and hent þe sang of
>   þi lovyng. (l. 24)
>
>   . . . . .
>
> If þou wil lufe, þan may þou syng til Cryst in
>   melody.
>
> (l. 67)

Sweetness and joy flow into the soul with love:

> In myrth he lyfes, nyght and day, þat lufes
>   þat swete chylde;
>
>   . . . . .
>
> Þar es na tonge in erth may tell of lufe þe
>   swetnesse.
> Þat stedfastly in lufe kan dwell, his joy es endlesse.
>
> (ll. 89-90)

The doctrine of the indwelling of God in the soul is one that has little prominence in Rolle's writings. It appears here in much the same words as it is stated in the *Ego Dormio:*

> If þou luf in all þi thoght, and hate þe fylth of syn,
> And gyf hym þi sawle, þat it boght, þat he þe
>   dwell within.
>
> (ll. 37-38)

In the *Ego Dormio* he writes: "For he wil with þe dwelle, if þou lufe hym."[51] Julian of Norwich in her *Revelations of Divine Love* gives this doctrine of the indwelling of God in man's soul an important place in her teaching on divine love. It is simply a difference of point of view. Rolle usually writes of man's love for God and his yearnings for union with Him; Julian commonly writes of God's love for man, and she feels filled with gratitude at this wonderful manifestation of it. Neither one excludes the point of view of the other; but the emphasis is different.

References to the spirit of penitence (ll. 37, 57-66), to the passion (ll. 80, 85-88), and to the Holy Name supplement the main theme. In the last stanza the confident devotion to the Holy Name, the ardent love-longing and yearning for the eternal vision of heaven, and the hopeful spirit of joy are summed up in a great overflow of sincere and tender feeling:

> Jhesu es lufe þat lastes ay, till hym es owre langyng.
> Jhesu þe nyght turnes to þe day, þe dawyng intil spryng.
> Jhesu, thynk on us now and ay, for þe we halde oure keyng.
> Jhesu, gyf us grace, as þou wel may, to luf þe withowten endyng.
>
> (ll. 93-96)

A Song of Love-longing to Jesus has some lines identical with and some similar to those in the *Ego Dormio* lyrics. It is a strange medley of the aspirations that belong to all three degrees of love. As the poem opens, it would seem to reveal the state of soul of one in the early stages of love. The poet is asking for the courage and determination to seek God only and for the grace of detachment from the world in order that God may be his love. He begs for the virtue of meekness and protests his hatred of pride and anger, the two vices which Rolle most often repudiates.[52] He makes his request for the grace of purity of soul, which belongs to the first degree of love, "And make me clene of syn, þat I may come þe tylle." (l. 16); for recollection, which belongs to the second degree of love, "þat I þi lufe may wyn, of grace my thoght þou fylle. (l. 15); and for the sweetness and fire that belong to the third degree of love:

> Me langes, lede me to þi lyght, and festen in þe al my thoght.
> In þi swetnes fyll my hert . . . (ll. 7-8)
>
> . . . . .
>
> . . . of lufe þou kyndel þe fyre,
> Þat I in swet lovyng with aungels take my hyre.
>
> (ll. 11-12)

Three stanzas of love-longing in the centre of the poem are taken, with some re-arrangement and slight changes, from the "Cantus amoris" of the *Ego Dormio*. These are followed by lines on the passion made up of phrases drawn from the "Meditacio de passione Christi" in the *Ego Dormio*.

The first thirty-two lines of this poem are requests or reflections made in the first person; the next ten lines refer to the passion of Christ and are written in the third person singular; the next four lines are impersonal except for one first person plural pronoun and corresponding adjective; the last two lines are addressed to a second person.

It seems hardly credible that Rolle, after making such a careful distinction between the second and third degrees of love in the *Ego Dormio* lyrics, would mix lines from the two poems in such a disorderly manner in this lyric. The shifting of point of view also gives it a very patchwork quality. Even though it is ascribed to Rolle in Longleat MS. 29,[53] one wonders if it may not be the work of one of his imitators who did not see the significance of what he was doing in the *Ego Dormio*.

The two lyrics, *Thy Joy be in the Love of Jesus*[54] and *The Nature of Love,*[55] are addressed to beginners in the life of love. The first of these, *Thy Joy be in the Love of Jesus,* is an urgent exhortation to such a novice to give his love to God. Rolle points out the difficult preliminary steps to be taken by the earnest soul, and the joys that may be hoped for:

> Þou kepe his byddyngs ten; hald þe fra dedely synne;
> Forsake þe joy of men, þat þou his lufe may wynne.
> Þi hert of hym sal bren with lufe þat never sal twynne.
> Langyng he will þe len heven to won withinne.
>
> (ll. 17-20)

Recollection and meditation on the passion, recommendations belonging to the second degree of love are briefly mentioned:

> In Cryst þou cast þi thoght, þou hate all wreth and pryde,
> And thynk how he þe boght with woundes depe and wyde. (ll. 5-6)
>
> . . . . .
>
> Þou thynk on hys mekenes, how pore he was borne.
> Behald, his blody flesch es prikked with thorne.
>
> (ll. 21-22)

The soul that is steadfast in love, longing, and praying, "Bryng me to þi lyght, þi melodi to here" (l. 32), is promised joy, sweetness and the fire of love:

> Joy in þi brest es bredde, when þou ert hym lufand.
> Þi sawle þan hase he fedde, in swete lufe brennand.
>
> (ll. 35-36)

There is reference in this lyric to the predilection for a sitting position:

> With joy þou take his trace, and seke to sytt hym nere.
>
> (l. 14)

This lyric lacks the intensely personal and ecstatic character of the lyrics in which Rolle pours out his love-longing and his tender devotion to the Holy Name. The Holy Name is not mentioned once. The reason may be that Rolle is concentrating here on the first degree of love, even though he includes some instructions proper to the second degree; and devotion to the Holy Name does not belong to the first degree. The other possible explanation is that he was following his own explicit statement in the *Form of Living* that it was sufficient that the name of Jesus be in the heart and mind; it need not be cried aloud.[56]

The exhortations of *The Nature of Love* are also addressed to those not far advanced in the life of love. The recommendations are suitable to persons in the first and second degrees who are desirous of being lovers of God:

All vanitese forsake, if þou his lufe will fele.
(l. 1)

. . . . .

Of synne þe bitternes, þou fle ay fast þerfra.
Þis worldes wikkednes, let it noght with þe ga.
(ll. 5-6)

. . . . .

Þe world, cast it behynd, and say: 'Jhesu, my swete,
Fast in þi lufe me bynd, and gyf me grace to grete,
To lufe þe over al thyng; . . .
(ll. 25-27)

The more positive aspects of recollection, prayer and devotion to the Holy Name, exercises belonging to the second degree of love, are urged in the last stanza:

Take Jhesu in þi thynkyng, his lufe he will þe send.
Þi lufe and þi lykyng, in hym þou lat it lend.
And use þe in praiyng, þarin þou may be mend,
Swa þat þow hafe þi keyng in joy withowten endyng.
(ll. 57-60)

The rewards of a life of love are re-phrased from lines 327-329 of the **"Cantus Amoris"** of *Ego Dormio.* In that lyric they are a personal outpouring of love-longing:

When wil þou me kall? me langes to þi hall,
To se þe þan al; þi luf, lat it not fal.
My hert payntes þe pall þat steds us in stal.[57]

Here they are a sober argument to persuade the reader of the advantage of choosing God for his love:

His lufe es lyf of all þat wele lyvand may be.
Þou sted hym in þi stal, lat hym noght fra þe fle.

Ful sone he wil þe call (þi setell es made for þe),
And have þe in his hall, ever his face to se.
(ll. 45-58)

In spite of the serious, penitential tone of this lyric, there are a few lines expressive of the joy of loving God. Rolle is never gloomy in his love of God. Even penance, undertaken for the love of God, is a joyful thing, and the rewards of fidelity are happiness in this life and union in the next:

For joy þi hert burd brest, to have swylk a swetyng. (l. 43)

. . . . .

When þe dede neghes negh, and þou sall hethen wende,
Þou sal hym se wyth hegh, and come till Cryste þi frende.
(ll. 39-40)

One lyric ascribed to Rolle in Longleat MS. 29[58] is wholly penitential in tone. It is the **Exhortation,**[59] beginning "All synnes sal þou hate thorow castyng of skylle." Following a warning that "Dede dynges al sa sare, þat nane may defende; . . . For þi of synn make þe bare, þou knawes not þi ende." (ll. 10, 12), the poet passes on to a description of the Day of Judgment. The little poem draws to a close with the expression of hope and joy which we always find in Rolle's attitude towards penance. The Judgment must be feared by those who are not God's friends; but for his faithful ones who have loved God and hated sin here, it is a day of triumph. They will go forth with joy to take their long-awaited places within the kingdom of heaven:

Þat day owre joy sal begyn, þat here suffers pyne;
Owre flesch wytt of mykel wyn and bryght as sonn schyne.
Owre setels heven ar within, me lyst sytt in myne.
Lufe Criste and hate syn, and sa purches þe þune.
(ll. 21-24)

The authorship of *A Song of Mercy* is not certain. Miss Allen prints it in the *English Writings of Richard Rolle*[60] as one of those from the Cambridge MS. Dd. v. 64 which "seem certainly to be covered by the colophon there ascribing lyrics to Rolle",[61] but in her earlier volume, *Writings Ascribed to Richard Rolle,* she had written that "the poem needs more external evidence to make Rolle's authorship certain".[62] The poem is written in praise of mercy, and is informed by a spirit of confidence in that attribute of God in his dealings with men. In life and at the hour of death, mercy is, for Rolle, his guiding beacon, his source of trust, his help, his salvation. The word "mercy" is repeated over and over in the poem; it is used nineteen times in the twenty-four lines; it is the pivot about which the reflections turn as the various depths of its beauty reveal themselves to the contemplating mind. Mercy is "curtayse and kynde" (1. 2), that is, it treats its object with respect and consideration and charity; mercy is powerful in lifting one from the bonds of evil, "fra al mischeves he mai me rayse" (1. 2); mercy guides one's final faltering steps in this life and saves him from the fiend, "lede me at þe last, when I owt of þis world sal wende; . . . þat þou save me fra þe fende" (II. 5-6); mercy is true and dependable and always ready to respond to man's appeal, "it fayles noght" (1. 8); mercy is the comfort and nourishment of the soul, "þat es my solace and my fode" (1. 12); mercy is most worthy of esteem because, through mercy, man's salvation was accomplished, "for thorogh mercy was I boght" (1. 10); mercy transcends and comprehends the wretchedness of men, "Mercy es sa hegh a poynt, þar may na syn it suppryse" (1. 19); mercy embraces both our particular needs and our general condition; it is source and ground of all our confidence, "Mercy es bath al and some; þarin I trayst and after pray" (1. 24).

The appeal for mercy from the creature to the Sovereign Being, "þou graunte mercy" (1. 12); the request to be conducted to the presence of the Beloved in the royal tower; the desire to gaze upon the beauty of the Loved One, "And bring me til þe rial toure, whare I mai se mi God sa bryght" (1. 16); these concepts establish a contact with the courtly love tradition, but at the same time transcend it in the recognition of the futility of the artificial convention when placed in juxtaposition with the reality of God's power to extend true mercy, "þou graunte mercy, þat mercy may" (1. 12).

Rolle's characteristic desire to turn into song the enthusiastic conviction welling up in his heart is expressed here in a manner which foreshadows the eternizing conceit of later poetry, "God of al, Lorde and Keyng, I pray þe, Jhesu, be my frende, / Sa þat I may þi mercy syng in þi blys withowten ende" (II. 17-18).

The richness of Rolle's poem is deepened by the addition of legal associations to the theological and literary relationships already pointed out. In the final stanza the poet prays that God's mercy may be at hand to preserve his soul when he comes before his Judge at the last great court of Judgment:

> Lord, lat it noght be aloynt, when þou sal sett þi gret assyse.
> With þy mercy my sawle anoynt, when I sal come to þi jugise.
> Til þe Juge sal I come, bot I wate noght my day.
>
> (II. 21-23)

These lines bring forward an interesting question. About the year 1366 Chaucer translated Guillaume de Deguilleville's poem, *Pèlerinage de l'Ame,* composed in 1330 or 1331.[63] Lines 55-56 of that poem read:

> Las! mes quant la grant assise
> Sera, se n'y es assise[64]

Chaucer translates these in the poem he calls *A B C* as follows:

> But mercy, lady, at the grete assyse,
> Whan we shul come bifore the hye Iustyse!
>
> (II. 36-37)

The likeness in thought and wording in lines 21-22 of Rolle's *Song of Mercy* (quoted above) and in lines 36-37 of Chaucer's *A B C* raises the question of the possible influence of Rolle's poem on Chaucer. The similarity may be purely accidental, but it is striking and may indicate an impression left on Chaucer's mind by an earlier reading of Rolle's poem.

Rolle has written no lyrics in English on the Virgin Mary. He has, however, composed in her honour, in Latin, one long poem, the *Canticum Amoris*. The poem has definite lyrical qualities. The metre is musical—the four stress line with a variable number of unstressed syllables between the stresses. The poem is filled with praises of Our Lady and with the poet's love which breaks out in joyful song:

> Letum carmen concino, pondus portans spei,
> Et amore langueo resplendentis rei.
> Celo est serenior inquisita mei;
> Omnibus amancior, sum electus ei.
>
> (Stanza 31)[65]

Rolle's lyrics have beauty in their melody and intensity. They celebrate the loftiest emotion possible—that of love of God—in simple, sincere words. The medium of verse seems, however, not to have been the most congenial mode of expression for his gift of "canor". The passages of lyrical intensity in his prose seem to me to reveal the deepest emotions of his soul more completely than do his few lyrics.

Notes

[1] Frye, *Anatomy of Criticism,* [1957] 273.

[2] Rosenthal and Smith, *Exploring Poetry,* [1955] 119.

[3] Black, ed., *Elizabethan and Seventeenth-Century Lyrics,* [1938] 5, 9, 10.

[4] Drinkwater, [1922] *The Lyric,* 85-86.

[5] Allen, *Writings Ascribed to Richard Rolle,* [1927] 294-302.

[6] Ed. Deanesly, [1915] 190.

[7] *English Writings of Richard Rolle*, ed. Allen, 63. Quotation from *Ego Dormio*.

[8] *English Writings of Richard Rolle*, ed. Allen, 64, 67.

[9] *English Writings of Richard Rolle*, ed. Allen, 69-70.

[10] *Incendium Amoris*, ed. Deanesly, 188.

[11] *Incendium Amoris*, ed. Deanesly, 185.

[12] *Incendium Amoris*, ed. Deanesly, 174.

[13] *English Writings of Richard Rolle*, ed. Allen, 70-72.

[14] *English Writings of Richard Rolle*, ed. Allen, 104, 107.

[15] Frye, *Anatomy of Criticism*, 255.

[16] *English Writings of Richard Rolle*, ed. Allen, 70-72.

[17] *English Writings of Richard Rolle*, ed. Allen, 53.

[18] *English Writings of Richard Rolle*, ed. Allen, 41-43.

[19] *English Writings of Richard Rolle*, ed. Allen, 67.

[20] *English Writings of Richard Rolle*, ed. Allen, 41-43.

[21] Dom Cuthbert Butler in *Western Mysticism* [1923] (page 110) points out that "light" was a favourite symbol of St. Gregory's for the contemplative life. Rolle uses it as the symbol for heaven in *A Salutation to Jesus (English Writings of Richard Rolle*, ed. Allen, 48-49, lines 5, 28); *Thy Joy be in the Love of Jesus (ibid.,* 53, line 32); *Ego Dormio (ibid.,* 70, line 316.)

[22] *English Writings of Richard Rolle*, ed. Allen, 49-51.

[23] The first poem incorporated in *Ego Dormio (ibid.,* 64), and the "Cantus amoris" of the *Form of Living (ibid.,* 107).

[24] Ed. Deanesly, 268, 269, 276, 278.

[25] Ed. M. de LaBigne, 616.

[26] Ed. Arnould, 58, 73, 74, 89, 94, 112, 133, 136, 137, 138, 140, 142, 149, 156, 157, 160. If, as Miss Allen conjectures, in *Writings Ascribed to Richard Rolle,* 129, the *Melos Amoris* was written in 1326-1327, Rolle had good reason to be conscious of the symbol of kingship. Speaking of the period before the deposition and execution of Edward II, Miss Allen writes (*Writings Ascribed,* 128): "The Scotch wars brought king, court, and parliament as well as army to Yorkshire during these years."

[27] *Incendium Amoris,* ed. Deanesly, 174.

[28] *English Writings of Richard Rolle,* ed. Allen, 40, lines 17-18.

[29] *English Writings of Richard Rolle,* ed. Allen, 41, lines 9, 11-12.

[30] *English Writings of Richard Rolle,* ed. Allen, 51, lines 57, 59-60.

[31] *English Writings of Richard Rolle,* ed. Allen, 39, lines 15-16, 21-24.

[32] *English Writings of Richard Rolle,* ed. Allen, 67, line 6.

[33] *English Writings of Richard Rolle,* ed. Allen, 41, line 11. This request is made in almost identical words in *Ego Dormio (ibid.,* 68, line 242, "Kyndel me fire within.")

[34] *English Writings of Richard Rolle,* ed. Allen, 44, line 26.

[35] *English Writings of Richard Rolle,* ed. Allen, 53, line 19.

[36] J. Wight Duff writes the following account of Menippean Satire in *A Literary History of Rome,* [1909] 334-335: "From Quintilian we learn that Varro was the author of an older type of satire than that of Lucilius—one composed in many sorts of metre and in prose as well. These are the *Saturae Menippeae.* They were so entitled by Varro as being based on the Cynic dialogues of Menippus, the philosopher of Gadara in the third century, whose spirit and figure are so amusing in his imitator Lucian. Varro's aim was comparable to Addison's in the *Spectator*—to introduce academic thought to the average reader. Realizing the need of gilding the philosophic pill for the unlearned, and bent on overcoming the national repugnance to speculation, he seasoned esoteric truth and logical discussion with jocularity in his treatment of contemporary society. The outcome was a mass of 150 books, as motley in theme as in form. The tradition of this medley passed through Seneca's *Apocolocyntosis* and Petronius's *Satyricon* into the pedantic fantasia of Martianus Capella, *De Nuptiis Philologiae et Mercurii.* Through that educational manual, once a standard, it influenced medieval compositions of the "chante fable" order. Boethius also represents the tradition when he diversifies the prose of his *De Consolatione Philosophiae* with poems on varied metres—like so many lyric interludes amidst his tragic sorrows."

In *Roman Satire,* [1936] Professor Duff adds the information that Menippean Satire was revived in France at the end of the sixteenth century (p. 84).

[37] The references to the *Ego Dormio* are from *English Writings of Richard Rolle,* ed. Allen, 61-72.

[38] Brown ed., *Religious Lyrics of the XIVth Century,* rev. G. V. Smithers, 241.

[39] Allen, *Writings Ascribed to Richard Rolle,* 290.

[40] J. P. Migne, ed., *Patrologiae Cursus Completus,* Vol. XL, 906.

[41] Migne, ed., *Patrologiae Cursus Completus,* Vol. CLVIII, 861.

[42] Migne, ed., *Patrologiae Cursus Completus,* Vol. XL, 898-902.

[43] Pope, *St. Augustine of Hippo,* 382-383. Eligius Dekkers lists the *Meditations* under spurious works of St. Augustine. *Clavis Patrum Latinorum* (1961).

[44] H. E. Allen, "Mystical Lyrics of the *Manuel des Pechiez*", *Romanic Review,* 9 (1918), 183-184, note 65.

[45] References to the *Form of Living* are from *English Writings of Richard Rolle,* ed. Allen, 85-119.

[46] *English Writings of Richard Rolle,* ed. Allen, 48-49.

[47] *English Writings of Richard Rolle,* ed. 43-47.

[48] *English Writings of Richard Rolle,* ed. Allen, 108-111.

[49] Ed. Deanesly, 272-273.

[50] Ed. Deanesly, 274-275.

[51] *English Writings of Richard Rolle,* ed. Allen, 61.

[52] *Cf. A Salutation to Jesus (ibid.,* 78, line 12); also *Thy Joy be in the Love of Jesus (ibid.,* 52, line 5).

[53] Allen, *Writings Ascribed to Richard Rolle,* 299.

[54] *English Writing of Richard Rolle,* ed. Allen, 52-53.

[55] *English Writings of Richard Rolle,* ed. Allen, 49-51.

[56] *English Writings of Richard Rolle,* ed., Allen, 106.

[57] *English Writings of Richard Rolle,* ed. Allen, 71.

[58] Allen, *Writings Ascribed to Richard Rolle,* 297.

[59] *English Writings of Richard Rolle,* ed. Allen, 39.

[60] *English Writings of Richard Rolle,* ed. Allen, 40-41.

[61] *English Writings of Richard Rolle,* ed. Allen, 37.

[62] Allen, *Writings Ascribed to Richard Rolle,* 298.

[63] Chaucer, *Complete Works,* ed. W. Skeat, [1926] I, 59.

[64] Chaucer. *Complete Works,* ed. W. Skeat, I, 261.

[65] Ed. André Wilmart, *Revue d' Ascétique et de Mystique,* 21 (1940), 143-148. For a translation of the *Canticum Amoris* see Appendix A. Text, Appendix B.

John A. Alford (essay date 1973)

SOURCE: John A. Alford, "Biblical *Imitatio* in the Writings of Richard Rolle," in *ELH,* Vol. 40, No. 1, Spring, 1973, pp. 1-23.

[*In the following essay, Alford makes an effort to correct what he sees to be the paucity of true literary studies of Rolle. In his analysis, Alford examines the relationship of Rolle's works to the biblical imitatio—a rhetorical tradition based on study of the Holy Scripture.*]

Though R. W. Chambers was not the first to appreciate Richard Rolle's prose style, his famous essay on the continuity of English prose had much to do with the subsequent direction of Rolle criticism—if it is accurate to speak of "direction" where there has been so little movement. "Rolle's date, his style and his popularity," said Chambers, "give him a supreme place in the history of English prose. In English or in Latin he was, during the latter half of the Fourteenth Century and the whole of the Fifteenth, probably the most widely read in England of all English writers."[1] Criticism of Rolle's vernacular style has hardly gone beyond the concerns expressed in this quotation. Chambers was not interested in making a detailed analysis of Rolle's style (nor, given the purpose of his essay, should he have been): he simply described some of its salient characteristics and tried to assess its place in the development of English prose. Much subsequent criticism has been content to do the same thing—to provide description ("forceful," "uneven," etc.), supported by appropriately chosen examples, and to remind us of Rolle's "place" in literary tradition. (Frequently the writer will cite the above quotation from Chambers, in lieu of any real evidence, as proof of Rolle's influence on the course of English prose; or he may offer as an impressive "fact" the well-worn assertion by Rolle's nineteenth-century editor, Carl Horstmann, that the hermit was the first master of

English prose—with hardly a protest, I might add, from students of the *Ancren Riwle*.)

The influence of Chambers' essay is, of course, only part of the reason for the poverty of Rolle criticism—not every writer mentioned in his essay has fared poorly ever since! Superficial treatment of Rolle's prose has undoubtedly been encouraged by the general nature of the works in which comment on the subject must be sought—literary histories, editions, studies in mysticism. Incredible though it may seem, in the forty years since Chambers' essay not so much as an article given to an analysis of Rolle's style, whether English or Latin, has seen publication.[2] One might conclude that in spite of the high esteem in which it has been held, Rolle's style has not proved very interesting for modern readers. And yet I think this conclusion would be wrong. Paradoxically his English style has been, at least as far as modern criticism is concerned, a casualty of its own success. What it shares with modern English has impressed us so favorably, and particularly the writers of textbooks on the history of English, that we value it less for itself than for what it predicts, or embodies, of subsequent history. In short, we do not *see* it. Its affinities with modern English have blinded us to its distinctively medieval qualities; for however striking these affinities may be—and I am not minimizing their importance—Rolle's style nevertheless grew out of very different soil and was produced by methods of writing which hardly any of us would think of using.

These peculiarly medieval methods of composition are my primary concern in the following pages. I want to show what they reflect both of the general tradition of biblical *imitatio* and of the individual literary experience of Richard Rolle. As for biblical *imitatio,* very little has been said either about the method or about Rolle's use of it.[3] Where scholarship has tried to place Rolle in a rhetorical tradition, it has usually preferred to emphasize his knowledge of the classics, for which the evidence is scant, rather than appeal to his knowledge of the Scriptures, for which the evidence is overwhelming. As for Rolle's literary experience, this is too little considered in its totality. When he turned to write in the vernacular, did he forget the habits of composition acquired through writing Latin, did his extensive work on biblical commentaries not intrude in some way, did his constant meditation on Scripture have no part in shaping his expression?

I have divided the discussion into five parts, in which I consider, in order: (1) the essential nature of biblical *imitatio,* (2) Rolle's knowledge of the Bible, (3) his use of the biblical commentary as an intermediary between the Vulgate text and his own Latin writing, (4) commentary-form in his English writing, (5) a few consequences of this method of composition for the study of his prose style.

I

During much of the Middle Ages, there were two distinct kinds of literary imitation, one based on the curricular authors, or *auctores,* and the other on Holy Scripture. Imitation of the *auctores* was never very thoroughgoing—concentrating almost exclusively on rhetorical figures—and was limited by a superficial view of the relation between style and content. This view was dominant throughout the Middle Ages and seems to have been little affected by the so-called battle of the *artes* and *auctores* in the late twelfth century. Geoffrey of Vinsauf, presumably a representative of the *artes,*[4] makes the usual rhetorical distinction in his *Poetria Nova* between *res* and *verba,* the poem as intellectual construct and the poem as verbal construct, a distinction everywhere implied by his favorite metaphor—clothing. "When due order has arranged the material in the hidden chamber of the mind," he says, "let poetic art come forward to clothe the matter with words."[5] Aside from matters of propriety—e.g., "let rich meaning be honoured by rich diction, lest a noble lady blush in pauper's rags"—Geoffrey is not much interested in the relation between words and things. Words are like clothes, some plain and some elegant, to be changed as the occasion requires; they are not an inevitable or even natural extension of the work's meaning. The most famous apologist for study of the *auctores,* John of Salisbury, seems to have agreed with this view:

> The grammarian should also point out metaplasms, schematisms, and oratorical tropes, as well as various other forms of expression that may be present. He should further suggest the various possible ways of saying things, and impress them on the memory of his listeners by repeated reminders. Let him "shake out" the authors, and, without exciting ridicule, despoil them of their feathers, which (crow fashion) they have borrowed from the several branches of learning in order to bedeck their words and make them more colorful. One will more fully perceive and more lucidly explain the charming elegance of the authors in proportion to the breadth and thoroughness of his knowledge of various disciplines. The authors by *diacrisis,* which we may translate as "vivid representation" or "graphic imagery," when they would take the crude materials of history, arguments, narratives, and other topics, would so copiously embellish them by the various branches of knowledge, in such charming style, with such pleasing ornament, that their finished masterpiece would seem to image all the arts.[6]

So long as the relation between content and language or imagery was seen in this way, as accidental and at best factitious, imitation of the "authors" could never be more than superficial. The entire corpus of classical literature becomes, from a rhetorical point of view, mainly a gigantic Bartlett's, a source of apt quotations and imagery, a quarry for the writer searching for rhetorical gems with which to adorn his own work. The proof for this statement lies not merely in the opinion of John of Salisbury but also in his practice and in the practice of countless other writers as well until the Renaissance gave to the word *imitatio* a new meaning.[7]

When one turns to imitation of the Bible, however, he finds an entirely different situation. Medieval man never regarded the Bible as a textbook of rhetorical tricks, and there is, consequently, a unity of language and content in biblical *imitatio* which is utterly lacking in its secular counterpart. This fact can be demonstrated by a simple test (part of which is provided later by my analysis of Rolle's prose): go through an example of medieval imitation of the *auctores,* remove the phrases modeled on the classical sources and also the allusions and borrowed imagery, the rhetorical "feathers" as John calls them, and you will still have an argument left, however diminished. But do the same with a work modeled upon the Bible, remove the scriptural reminiscences, and you will have almost nothing left. Isn't this exactly what one might have expected? How could the medieval writer speak of God, of Judgment and Redemption except in the idiom of the Bible? Christian thought and language are inseparable, and the most natural language for expressing Christian ideas is biblical language, the language which gave Christian thought its birth and which continues to nourish it. On this matter St. Augustine, the chief if not the earliest apologist for biblical rhetoric, is explicit: "He who wishes to speak not only wisely but also eloquently, since he can be of more worth if he can do both, should more eagerly engage in reading or hearing the works of the eloquent and in imitating them in practice than in setting himself to learn from the masters of the art of rhetoric." Do the Scriptures qualify as "works of the eloquent?" "This question is most easily solved for me," says Augustine, "and for those who think like me. For where I understand these authors, not only can nothing seem to me more wise than they are, but also nothing can seem more eloquent. And I venture to say that all who understand rightly what they say understand at the same time that it should not have been said in any other way."[8] Because the words of Scripture are never merely ornamental—"feathers" or apparel to delight the eye and ear—but rather the reflection of the soul of wisdom itself, anyone desiring to speak with eloquence is enjoined to follow them, and eloquence will come behind, says Augustine, like "an inseparable servant who was not called." The vitality of this rhetorical tradition is not to be sought in the textbooks which repeat Augustine's precepts but rather in the writings which embody them. And these writings are, for the most part, monastic, for it was in the monasteries that all the activities most conducive to biblical *imitatio*—constant read-

ing, meditation, and memorization—took place.[9] It was through these activities that the true practitioners of biblical *imitatio* were produced, those for whom the language of the Bible became so familiar that it was their own language as well, the language of impulse. In his study of St. Bernard and the Bible, P. Dumontier asks, "What is the language of Bernard?" "Mais n'est-ce pas du latin? non, c'est de la Bible, ce qui n'est point pour éclaircir l'affaire: de la Bible, non pas citée, mais parlée."[10]

The chief difference between imitation of the *auctores* and imitation of the Bible, as I have just described it, stems ultimately from medieval man's view of the past, from his sense of what historical events truly made up his heritage. He did not generally feel that he was continuing classical traditions and, unlike the Renaissance scholar, made little effort to assimilate classical ways of thinking. Thus his imitation of classical literature was bound to be superficial, however much he may have admired its felicities of style. But the Bible was a different matter, and medieval man felt himself a part of its world when he didn't that of classical antiquity. He was, in fact, a character in the biblical story, himself a part of the sacred history which had been written but not yet fulfilled. This sense of identification with the ideas and expression of the Bible is the one thing which all writers who follow the Sacred Bard may be said to have in common. Specific *methods* of imitation, however, differ considerably from one writer to another. This is hardly surprising. Each writer brings to his work his own judgment of which stylistic details deserve imitation, his own individual purposes. Moreover, even if all other things were equal, the writer who imitates the Psalms is not going to produce the same style as one who imitates the Pauline epistles—the Bible is not one book but many, each having a distinctive character of its own. For these reasons it is not possible to be more specific about the nature of biblical *imitatio* than I have been already; we must examine the practice of an individual writer.

II

Like all writers in the tradition of biblical *imitatio,* Richard Rolle occupied a large part of his time in meditating upon and memorizing Holy Scripture. The *Officium de Sancto Ricardo,* written in anticipation of his canonization, notes his love of the Bible: "Desideravit plenius et perficudius imbui theologicis sacrae Scripturae doctrinis, quam phisicis aut secularis scientie disciplinis."[11] Rolle not only meditated upon Scripture himself, but he urged his disciples to do the same and even facilitated their task by translating the Psalms into English—all of which has prompted some scholars to refer to him as a forerunner of Wyclif and the Lollards. Rolle's interest in Scripture is not incidental to his mysticism: both are intimately related, growing out of an intense desire for a personal and immediate experience of God. Together they form the way. "God leris his chosen," says Rolle, "thurgh bokis and inspiracioun."[12] Each nourishes the other. Correct interpretation of Scripture can only be accomplished with the aid of divine inspiration, as we learn in Rolle's gloss on Psalm 17:13: "Her may we see that nan sould be swa hardy to translate or expound haly writ. bot if he felid the haly gast in him, that is makere of haly writ. for soen sall he erre that is noght led with him." Obviously Rolle considered himself inspired, and we may suspect that he saw his commentaries in part as testimony to his special gift. Elsewhere he is quite explicit about the benefits of Bible-reading: "If thou desire to come to the love of God, and be kindled in thy desire for heavenly joys, and be brought to the despising of earthly things, be not negligent in meditating and reading holy scripture; and most in those places where it teaches manners, and to eschew the deceits of the fiend, and where it speaks of God's love, and of contemplative life."[13] Indeed, the lower half of the contemplative life "es meditacion of haly wrytyng, þat es Goddes wordes."[14] This close connection between mysticism and Bible reading is suggested by Evelyn Underhill's observation that "Bible reading, sometimes considered peculiarly characteristic of English piety, is historically the child of mysticism."[15]

Although the prevalence of biblical quotations in Rolle's work has been noted by many critics—indeed, these could hardly be missed—the full extent of his enormous debt to Scripture has escaped most readers simply because he was able to adapt the language of Scripture so perfectly and naturally to his own expression. As one of his most recent editors puts it, "Only a familiarity equal to that of Rolle with the text of the Vulgate can enable one to realize fully how steeped the hermit was in the Biblical text."[16] Assuming that very few of us enjoy such a familiarity, I intend to exemplify by two means the nature of biblical influence in Rolle's expression, first by taking a single text and following it through its various transformations in a number of Rolle's works, and then by taking whole passages in Latin and English and identifying the scriptural reminiscences.

A central concept in Rolle's thought is the triad of *dulcor, calor,* and *canor,* three ascending levels of the mystical experience. Such triads are typical of Rolle: he habitually reduces thought to verbal formulas, in which each word, highly charged with new meaning, attracts verbally related scriptural texts. *Canor,* for example, his term for the secret and ineffable experience of the contemplative at the highest level, is constantly described by Rolle in the words of Apoc. 2:17: "Vincenti dabo manna absconditum, et dabo illi calculum candidum, et in calculo nomen novum scriptum, quod nemo scit, nisi qui accipit" (Douay version: "To him that overcometh, I will give the hid-

den manna, and will give him a white counter, and in the counter, a new name written, which no man knoweth, but he that receiveth it"). In his *Contra Amatores Mundi,*[17] Rolle says that the gift of interior song cannot be communicated because "vero nemo hominum hoc donum novit, nisi qui accepit" (IV. 119). In the same work, Apoc. 2:17 underlies the wording of an earlier reference to song: "Mirabar quippe quod aliquis mortalium aliquando ad tantam melodiam caperetur, sed iam vere scivi per experimentum quod vera est dileccio apud deum. Alii autem, qui illud donum nesciunt, nec illud ideo ab aliis percipi putant" (II. 82-85). And in the *Melos Amoris,* we find "Nam supra humanam estimacionem est quod exigit, et ideo aperte non audet ostendere loquens mortalium more; ymno tam excelsum est quod accipit, quod nemo preter habentem novit quatinus usque in canoram conscendens jubilacionem" (p. 174). Glossing Psalm 26:11 ("cantabo & psalmum dicam domino"), Rolle comments, "All the clerkis in erth may noght ymagyn it, ne wit what it is, bot he that has it. and in that .i. sall synge in dilatabilte of contemplacyon." And in his *Form of Living*: "Forþi, if þou will wytt whatkyn joy þat sang has, I say þe þat na man wate, bot he or scho þat feles it, þat has it, and þat loves God, syngand þarwyth" (p. 106). In noting Rolle's debt to Apoc. 2:17 for his description of *canor,* however, we have not exhausted his use of the verse by any means; the text can apply to any of the special gifts (the *manna absconditum*) enjoyed by the contemplative. Of love, for example, Rolle says, "Quam impetuosus, quam violens, sit vis amoris, nemo novit nisi qui amavit" (*Melos,* p. 9). And of wisdom, "bot that all men wate noght, bot whaim he shewis it til."[18] Rolle's use of Apoc. 2:17 is characteristic. He rarely quotes it directly—which is one reason his editors have not noted the debt—but rather echoes the wording and phrasing as the new context requires.[19]

Not only are Rolle's favorite concepts tied to particular biblical texts, but even his most personal experiences are filtered through the medium of Scripture. When he tries to describe the fear which came over him at the death of a woman-friend, he does so in the words of Job 4:5, Exodus 15:15, and Psalm 54:6-7 (*Contra Amatores,* VI. 1-18). When he tries to answer the charges of his enemies, those "detractores Deo odibiles" of Romans 1:30, he does so again in the words of Scripture (*Contra Amatores,* V. 75 sqq.). Hope Emily Allen has noted that in his commentary on Job, "it is often hard to draw the line between what is autobiography and what is interpretation of the texts. We may suspect, however, that the young hermit often describes the situation of his forlorn and tormented hero in terms that he feels are suitable to his own state."[20] Because of Rolle's tendency to describe his personal condition in terms of biblical language and personalities—an extremely common phenomenon among medieval writers—we should be doubly cautious in approaching his autobiographical comments. It must be remembered, for example, that in all his talk about backbiters and slanderers, he is following a conventional complaint of the Psalmist. This is not to say that his enemies were not real, but the value and intensity of their reality for Rolle came from his life in the Bible, the world in which, in a very real sense, he lived and moved and had his being. He seems to have felt that persecution was a sign of his own election—an idea from which he must have drawn considerable strength—and he keeps returning to the fact that biblical heroes had their enemies. For Rolle, as for countless of his predecessors, Scripture was a mirror in which he beheld all truth, past and present, social and individual. The longer he looked into it, the more his own identity merged with the reflection, until he was himself Job, and David, and Paul.

III

Rolle's use of Scripture had its effect not only on the content of his writing but also on the form. He frequently models his sentence structure on certain favorite biblical texts, a practice which must have been greatly reinforced by his experience with biblical commentaries. I am going to suggest, in fact, that some of the structural aspects of his style—in particular, his methods of transition and amplification—owe more to the tradition of biblical commentaries than to school rhetoric. That Rolle's work on his commentaries might have influenced his prose style has not been considered, not, at least, beyond perfunctory admissions of the possibility. Yet, given their number and their personal importance for Rolle, it is difficult to imagine otherwise, Moreover, Rolle would probably have felt the modern division of his work into genres, such as commentaries, treatises, and epistles, to be artificial. His works are a whole, closely related by similarities of tone, purpose, and frequently of style. We could open Rolle's commentaries anywhere and see the same structural methods which characterize his prose sentences, but I have chosen for its succinctness the following example from his gloss on Psalm 63:

> 1. *Exaudi deus oracionem meam cum deprecor: a timore inimici eripe animam meam.* "Here god my prayer, when J pray: fra the dredde of ennemy take out my sawle." The voice of christe in his passion, that preyes not that he nought dye, but that his lovers drede not them that nought may doe but slay the bodye: "& for ever iche manne dredes inne the dede."

> 2. *Protexisti me a conventu malignancium: & a multitudine operancium iniquitatem.* "Thou hilde me fra the convent of ill willand: & fra the multitude of workeand wickednesse." That is, thou hilde me fra the getheringe of ill men, and fra tha that wirkid to sla me.

> 3. *Quia exacuerunt ut gladium linguas suas: intenderunt arcum rem amaram, ut sagittent in occultis immaculatum.* "for thai sharpid as swerd thaire tunges: thai bent boghe bittere thyngis, that thai shote in hidils the unfilde." Thai sharpid, as swerd, *apertly criand his ded,* thaire tungis, *with the whilke thai sloghe crist.* thai bent bowe. *that is tresons,* that was bitter thynge, *thof thaire wordis ware swete:* that thai shote in hidils, *as thai wend,* the unfilid. *forthi thai may not be excused.*

There is nothing at all unusual in this. Rolle is commenting in the traditional manner and, in fact—as Middendorf demonstrated almost a hundred years ago—he follows Peter Lombard's commentary on the Psalms rather closely. Rolle's method is simply to explain each verse in turn, usually in one or more of three ways:

(1) by *association* with another scriptural text, related usually by verbal concordance. For example, in verse 1, the prayer "fra the dredde of ennemy take out my sawle" associates verbally with Christ's words in Matt. 10:28, "And do not be afraid of those who kill the body but cannot kill the soul." Hence the gloss that Christ is praying here in Psalms "that his lovers drede not them that nought may doe but slay the bodye."

(2) by *substitution* of an equivalent word or phrase which may clarify the meaning: "Thou hilde me fra the covent of ill willand. . . . That is, thou hilde me fra the getheringe of ill men."

(3) by *amplification* of the text. This may be achieved in several ways, but the most common—the insertion of explanatory matter—is illustrated by verse 3 (I have italicized the interpolations). Another kind of amplification can be seen in verse 1, the insertion of a statement denying the alternative (not *that,* but *this*): "The voice of christe in his passion, htat preyes *not that he nought dye,* but that his lovers drede not them that nought may doe but sla the bodye." Such definition by contrast, the rhetorical principle of *oppositio,* is very popular in the commentary tradition and is a major element of Rolle's style.

These principles of commentary writing were carried over by Rolle into his prose writing where they served as principles of composition. Sometimes the general form of the commentary is hardly disguised, as in his *Melos Amoris,* the structure of which has been characterized by Gabriel Liegey as "postill-form": "Ordinarily a postill on the text forms the chapter or several chapters, and these postills, strung together loosely at times, form the *Melos.*"[21] The influence of the commentary is not confined to such larger aspects of structure, however, nor is it confined to the *Melos* (where it is simply more visible, owing to the unusual frequency of direct scriptural quotations); it extends to almost every paragraph of Rolle's works, both Latin and English. Close analysis of the following excerpts from his Latin *Incendium Amoris* and his English *Commandment* will reveal the typical commentary-like structure of his writing: a network of submerged biblical texts, joined by association and transformed by substitution and amplification. In the first chapter of the *Incendium,* Rolle characterizes the lovers of the world in contrast to the lovers of God:

> Assimulantur siquidem suo amato, quia conformantur concupiscencie seculari, et retinentes veterem hominem, vanitate visibilis vite pro fervore felici perfruuntur. Mutant igitur gloriam incorruptibilis charitatis in lasciviam momentanee pulchritudinis. Hoc utique non agerent nisi excecarentur perversi amoris igne, qui cuncta devastat germina virtutum, et augmentum iugerit omnium viciorum. Porro plerique in formam femineam non figuntur, neque luxuriam lambunt, unde se salvari quasi cum securitate estimant, et propter solam castitatem quam exterius exhiberent, se velut sanctos inter alios eminere vident; sed nequiter et inaniter sic suspiciantur, quando cupiditatem que radix est peccatorum non extirpant. Et quidem, ut scriptum est, nihil iniquius quam amare pecuniam, quia dum cor alicuius occupat amor rei temporalis, nullam penitus devocionem habere permittit. Dileccio namque mundi et Dei nunquam simul in eodem animo existunt; sed cuius amor forcior est reliquum expellit, ut manifeste appareat quis sit mundi amator, et quis Christi imitator. Erumpit enim in ostencione operis fervor amoris. Siquidem sicut se habent amatores Christi erga mundum et carnem, sic amatores mundi se habent erga Deum et animum suum.[22]

What gives coherence to this passage is the opposition of *caritas* and *cupiditas* (or *concupiscencia*), a major structural device in other works by Rolle (most obviously, as the title shows, in his *Liber de amore dei contra amatores mundi*). Around this theme are grouped the several biblical texts which make up the passage as a whole. The first sentence notes that the lovers of this world are conformed to the concupiscence of this world ("conformantur concupiscencie seculari")—in direct opposition to Paul's exhortation, "Be ye not conformed to this world" ("Et nolite conformari huic saeculo"), Romans 12:2; they retain the old man ("retinentes veterem hominem")—although Paul said to "Put off . . . the old man, which is corrupt according to the deceitful lusts" ("Deponere vos . . . veterem hominem, qui corrumpitur secundum desideria errois"), Eph. 4:22; they enjoy the vanities of the visible world ("vanitate visibilis vite") before the love of eternal bliss ("pro fervore felici"), an echo perhaps of Col. 1:15-16; where Paul speaks of Christ as "the image of the invisible God . . . for in him were created all things in the heavens and on the earth, things visible and things invisible" ("qui est imago Dei invisibilis . . . quoniam in ipso condita sunt universa in caelis et in terra, visibilia et invisibilia"), an echo, I would suggest, not

only because it repeats the word *visibilis* and maintains the principle of opposition established by the two previous texts, but also because it shares with those texts a special relationship: all three are joined in their biblical contexts with the metaphor of the Church as the body of Christ, an especially appropriate metaphor here which might well have served Rolle as a foil against which to consider the lovers of this world. But more on this later. The structure of opposition is continued in Rolle's next sentence, "mutant igitur gloriam incorruptibilis charitatis in lasciviam momentanee pulchritudinis," an obvious paraphrase of Romans 1:23, "Et mutaverunt gloriam incorruptibilis Dei in similitudinem imagis corruptibilis hominis." (The verbal correspondences with the previous texts should be noted: the phrase "imaginis corruptibilis hominis" recalls Rolle's reference to the "veterem hominem qui corrumpitur" and at the same time contrasts with the "imago Dei invisibilis.")

So far, then, Rolle has used four scriptural texts in the construction of two sentences, and in both he proceeds as if he were writing a biblical commentary. One text is associated with another, verbally or thematically, and all are modified by substitution and amplification *in such a way as to reinforce the central theme of earthly love versus love of God.* For example, Paul's exhortation "Et nolite conformari huic saeculo" becomes by amplification "conformantur *concupiscencie* seculari"; the contrast between things visible and invisible becomes by substitution "vanitate visibilis vite *pro fervore felici* perfruuntur"; the first half of Romans 1:23, "Et mutaverunt gloriam incorruptibilis Dei," becomes by substitution "mutant igitur gloriam incorruptibilis *charitatis*" (for "Deus charitas est," I John 4:18), and the second half of the same text, "in similitudinem imaginis corruptibilis hominis," becomes by radical substitution "*in lasciviam* momentanee pulchritudinis."

Of the four texts identified thus far, three are indisputably the models for Rolle's first two sentences. The influence of the fourth (Col. 1:15-16) is problematic. And yet it will seem less so once we appreciate the associative power of metaphor in Rolle's writing. Because of his extreme familiarity with Scripture, any given biblical verse must have existed in Rolle's mind as part of a context, and not (as for those of us brought up on a new verse each Sunday) as an apt saying or isolated piece of biblical wisdom. As I have noted, Romans 12:2, Eph. 4:22, and Col. 1:15-16 are all related in their biblical contexts with the metaphor of the Church as the body of Christ, and although it is not inevitable, neither is it coincidental that Rolle should have thought about these particular verses together as he wrote about the lovers of God and the lovers of the world, that is, about those within the Church or body of Christ and those without. Perhaps there is no very satisfactory way to prove the influence of the metaphor here, but we can appeal to similar examples as some evidence that Rolle worked in this fashion. Aside from the body of Christ, what other figure of comparison might occur to a medieval writer engaged in distinguishing the lovers of God from the lovers of this world? Certainly and foremost, the parable of the wise and foolish virgins—those who will be present at the marriage of Christ to his bride the Church and those who will be left on the outside. According to exegetical tradition the five foolish virgins represent those who, because they keep their bodies from sin, appear holy in the sight of other men, "who look upon the outward appearance," but because their love is not directed towards God, "who looketh upon the heart," they will not enter into the bliss of heaven. John Wyclif's interpretation of the parable is the traditional one (however unorthodox he may have been in other respects) and may be quoted here:

> Þis rewme of hevene is þis Chirche: þes ten virginis ben þei þat ben spiritual, as ben prestis, and religious, and many oþer in þe Chirche; for as þe soule shulde quykene þe bodi, so þes shulden quykene þe actyve part. But þes ten virginis be partid in two, in fyve foolis and fyve wise. Alle þei ben virgyns herfore, for þei ben chast of bodi, and kepen hem from outward synnes þat mai be knowun to siȝte of men. . . . Þis oile is riȝt devocioun, þat alle þes virgyns shulden have. Þes vesselis of þe virginis ben þe poweris of her soulis; for riȝt as a vessel holdiþ oile, so þe power of þe soule shulde holde riȝt devocioun in alle þe workes þat man doiþ. . . . Þes lampis ben goode workes in kynde, þat boþ þes partis of virgins done; but ȝes lampis brennen not ne shynen bifore God, but þif þei have riȝt devocioun in þe workes þat þei done.[23]

Although Rolle does not refer explicitly to the parable, it clearly underlies the remainder of our passage. True, the lovers of this world are not without fire, but it is the fire of cupidity or perverse love ("perversi amoris igne") rather than the fire of charity ("incendium amoris"). Like the foolish virgins many think that they will enter heaven because of the chastity which they exhibit outwardly ("propter solam castitatem quam exterius exhiberent"). But their chastity is worthless so long as *cupiditas* rather than *caritas* occupies the heart: "sed nequiter et inaniter sic suspiciantur, quando cupiditatem que radix est peccatorum non extirpant." Here, use of the word *cupiditas* has led Rolle to the classic text on the subject, I Tim. 6:10 ("Radix enim omnium malorum est cupiditas"), and the *radix* metaphor, in turn, probably influenced his choice of the main verb, *extirpant. Cupiditas* hardly permits one to have *devocionem* (a key word also in Wyclif's exposition of the parable), for love of God and love of the world cannot exist in the same soul ("dileccio namque mundi et Dei nunquam simul in eodem animo existunt")—a rough paraphrase of Christ's words in Matt. 6:24, "Nemo potest duobus dominis servire: aut

enim unum odio habebit, et alterum diliget, aut unum sustinebit, et alterum contemnet. Non potestis Deo servire et mammonae" (cf. James 4:4). Continuing the imagery of the parable, Rolle notes that true charity—like the oil of "right devotion"—flares forth in works that are seen, "erumpit enim in ostencione operis fervor amoris."[24]

To summarize my analysis of the passage: the major structural device is the opposition between *caritas* and *cupiditas,* or lovers of God and lovers of the world; two images (the body of Christ and the parable of the virgins) underlie this theme and give rise to a number of scriptural associations—in fact, more than half of the lines are echoes or paraphrases of specific texts (Romans 12: 12, Eph. 4:22, Col. 1:15-16, Romans 1:23, I Tim. 6:10, and Matt. 4:24—not to mention the reminiscences of the parable itself, Matt. 25:1-13, and the commentaries on it). This method of composition, based on his knowledge of Scripture and his experience with biblical commentaries, is fairly typical of Rolle throughout the rest of the **Incendium** and in his other Latin writings as well.[25]

IV

When we turn to Rolle's English writings, we find much the same method of composition, though now we face a new obstacle: translation has obscured a large number of debts to the Vulgate text which in Rolle's Latin writings would have been obvious. The sources are fairly clear, however, in the following example; it comes from the **Commandment,** an epistle written to an unidentified nun and usually dated late in Rolle's life:

> Skyful prayer es, til cristen mans sawle, to seke and aske nyght and day þe lufe of Jhesu Criste, þat it may lufe hym verraly, feland comfort and delyte in hym, owtkastyng worldes thoughtes and il bysynes. And sykir be þou, if þou covayte his lufe trewly and lastandly, swa þat na lufe of þi flesche, ne angers of þe worlde, ne speche, ne hatreden of men draw þe agayne and caste þe nought in bisynes of bodily thyng; þou sal have his lufe, and fynde and fele þat it es delitabeler in an owre þan al þe welthe þat we here se may til domesday. And if þou fayle and fall for temptacions, or for angers, or for over mykel lufe of þi frendes, it es na wonder if he halde fra þe thyng þat þow covaytes noght trewly. He says þat "he lufes þam þat lufes hym, and þai þat arely wakes til hym sal fynde him." Þow ert arely wakand oftsythe, why þan fyndes þou hym noght? Certes, if þou seke hym ryght, þou sall fynde hym. Bot ay whiles þou sekes erthly joy, if þou wake never sa arely, Criste may þou noght fynde. For he es noght funden in þair lande þat lyves in fleschly lustes. Hys moder, when he was willed fra hyr, scho soght hym gretand arely and late ymang his kynredyn and hirs; bot scho fand hym noght, for al hyr sekyng, til at þe laste scho

come intil þe tempyl, and þare scho fand hym syttand ymange þe maysters, herand and answerand. Swa behoves þe do, if þou wil fynd hym: seke hym inwardly, in trouth and hope and charite of haly kyrk, castand owt al syn, hatand it in al þi hert: for þat haldes hym fra þe, and lettes þe, þat þou may noght fynd hym.[26]

Here, as in the excerpt from the *Incendium,* Rolle organizes his writing by means of the opposition of the two loves. This time, however, the discussion receives its impetus not from unexpressed imagery but from a pair of words, *seek* and *find,* whose very commonness in Scripture guarantees a cluster of verbally related texts. Among the numerous possibilities Cant. 3:1-2 seems to have exerted the chief influence (like other mystics Rolle had a special fondness for Canticles—he wrote a commentary on the book, and after the Psalms he quotes it more frequently than any other book of the Bible). The text reads: "In my bed by night I sought him whom my soul loveth: I sought him and found him not. I will rise, and will go about the city: in the streets and the broad ways I will seek him whom my soul loveth: I sought him, and I found him not." The theme of Canticles—the soul in search of Christ—is also the theme of our excerpt from the *Commandment.* Rolle's first sentence notes, "Skyful prayer es, til cristen mans sawle, to seke and aske nyght and day þe lufe of Jhesu Criste." In his next sentence Rolle imitates the structure of one of those classic biblical texts which, like I Cor. 13, always find their way into a discussion of love: "And sykir be þou, if þou covayte his life trewly and lastandly, swa þat na lufe of þi flesche, ne angers of þe worlde, ne speche, ne hatreden of men draw þe agayne and caste þe nought in bisynes of bodily thyng; þou sal have his lufe." The series of correlative conjunctions in this context points unmistakably to Romans 8:38-39, "For I am sure that neither death, nor life, nor angels, nor principalities, nor things present, nor things to come, nor powers, nor height, nor depth, nor any other creature will be able to separate us from the love of God, which is in Christ Jesus our Lord." For abstractions such as life and death, heights and depths, Rolle substitutes concrete phenomena (such as "angers of þe worlde") which are not only closer to his immediate theme but, if we may believe his autobiographical asides, closer to his own experience as well. Nor does the influence of Romans 8 end here, inasmuch as this sentence determined the structure of the next one: "And if þou fayle and fall for temptacions, or for angers, or for over mykel lufe of þi frendes, it es na wonder if he halde fra þe thyng þat þow covaytes noght trewly." This is simply a rewording, by means of rhetorical *oppositio,* of the previous sentence—even the order of obstacles is carefully preserved. Then quoting Prov. 8:17 almost directly, Rolle says, "He lufes þam þat lufes hym, and þai þat arely wakes til hym sal fynde him." However, in its biblical context this verse does not refer to Christ; it is wisdom

which says, "I love them that love me; and those that seek me early shall find me." What is noteworthy here is not Rolle's substitution of Christ for wisdom—this is supported by exegetical tradition—but the fact that he continued, as he wrote, to be influenced by the identification. The word "wisdom" (like the metaphor of the body of Christ in an earlier example—unexpressed) led Rolle a few sentences further to Job 28:12-13 ("Where is wisdom to be found, and where is the place of understanding? Man knoweth not the price thereof, *neither is it found in the land of them that live in delights*"). Rolle's paraphrase of the last part of the text is very close: "For he es noght funden in þair lande þat lyves in fleschly lustes." The bridge between these two texts on wisdom is mostly a reworking of what has already been said and consists of a few sentences drawing again upon Cant. 3:1-2 and Prov. 8:17. However, in writing "Certes, if þou seke hym ryght, þou sall fynde hym," Rolle may also have been amplifying upon Christ's words in Luke 11:9, "Seek, and you shall find," which was taken by medieval exegetes to be a conditional promise. The *Glossa ordinaria* comments on Christ's words by quoting Psalm 144:18, "Prope est Dominus omnibus invocantibus eum in veritate." To "seke hym ryght," therefore, is to seek him in truth, or as Rolle puts it, to "seke hym inwardly, in trouth and hope and charite of haly kyrk."[27] As support for this view, Luke 2:44-46 is interpreted by Rolle as a parable of the soul's search for Christ: Mary sought her son "gretand arely and late ymang his kynredyn and hirs; bot scho fand hym noght, for al hyr sekyng, til at þe laste scho come intil þe tempyl, and þare scho fand hym syttand ymange þe maysters, herand and answerand." This is a fairly close paraphrase of the scriptural text, with only a few modifications: Joseph, who searched with Mary for their son, is necessarily omitted as supernumerary in Rolle's application of the story to the individual soul, and the phrases "arely and late" and "for al hyr sekyng," repeating key words from previous texts, are added to enhance the general coherence. The final participle phrase is a direct translation from the Latin: "sedentem in medio doctorum, audientem illos, et interrogantem eos."

In short, then, hardly a line of this passage from the *Commandment* is untouched by scriptural influence of some sort, and the method of composition is very similar to what we have already seen in a typical example from Rolle's Latin writings. Again, Rolle takes a basic opposition and develops it in terms of appropriate scriptural texts, modifying them by amplification and substitution, and joining them all by means of verbal association, in particular by means of the words "seek" and "find."

V

By concentrating on what is the dominant method of composition in both his Latin and English writings, I have perhaps given the impression that Rolle's style is more or less uniform throughout his works. Nothing could be further from the truth, as anyone could see in an instant by comparing, say, the *Incendium Amoris* and the heavily alliterative *Melos Amoris*. I would assume, however, that those of us interested in a more detailed study of what is distinctive about any one of Rolle's several styles would wish to start from the knowledge of what is common to them all. Rolle's method of composition has immense ramifications for his style, whatever the work in question. Take, for example, the large amount of verbal repetition which characterizes much of his writing. What can we say about the fact that in the above excerpt from the *Commandment* the word "seek" occurs six times—not to mention synonyms like "covayte"—and "find," ten times? Frances Comper says, "We have always to bear in mind that Richard suffered from what I have called an untidy mind. . . . [His] writings are apt to be confused, full of repetitions and often redundant."[28] Since the only evidence for Rolle's "untidy mind" is his writing, Comper's opinion begs the question and is based on the dubious assumption that expression always mirrors the state of mind which produced it. Though it barely misses the same pitfall, G. C. Heseltine's explanation is a little more acceptable: "His repetition, seemingly excessive, is due to his unceasing attempts to express what he knows he has never expressed adequately."[29] Of course, we can never know if Rolle thought his expression adequate or not. In short, neither opinion is subject to proof. However, in light of what has just been demonstrated, we can say with some assurance that much of Rolle's verbal repetition grows out of the earliest stages of composition and is not merely a rhetorical veneer, something added for the sake of emphasis or coherence (though, of course, it sometimes serves this function too); it is a natural by-product of scriptural association (and serves, incidentally, as a key to the biblical texts just below the surface of the work). In the above passage the words "seek" and "find" are the most visible manifestations of these texts and, in fact, the chief means by which they were originally brought together.

If verbal repetition in Rolle's style cannot be studied apart from his use of the Bible, neither can the supposed influence of Latin upon his English prose. The relation between his Latin and English writings, as I have tried to show, is primarily one of method, and efforts to link the two in other ways, such as by vocabulary and word-order, have not been notably successful. William Matthews, for example, suggests that Rolle's English prose style was influenced by habits formed in writing Latin. He compares two passages from Rolle on the same subject (the three degrees of love), one taken from Rolle's *Form of Living* and the other taken from a fifteenth-century translation of Rolle's *Emendatio Vitae*. His conclusion: "Rolle's original English version has been expanded by rhetori-

cal devices, but the sentence patterns and their rhythms, the vocabulary, and the composition of the whole are much the same as in the independent translation from his Latin. Manifestly, his Latin composition determined the form of his English discussion."[30] Even aside from some rather serious objections to the methodology which underlies Matthews' conclusion—and chiefly to his arguing from an English translation of Rolle's *Emendatio* rather than from the original Latin version itself, fairly accessible in LaBigne's edition—we must remain unconvinced that "manifestly, his Latin composition determined the form of his English discussion." The similarities are not nearly so striking as Matthews suggests (e.g., there is nothing particularly Latinate about Rolle's English here), and what similarities there are can be explained in other ways than by direct influence. For example, speaking of Rolle's Latin and English Psalters, Hope Emily Allen says, "whole passages are sometimes repeated, and repetitions of phrases, sentences, and subjects are the very stuff of all of Rolle's writings, and perhaps the inevitable effects of a life like his dedicated to concentration on a few topics."[31] Matthews' comparison of two passages on the three grades of love is a particularly unhappy choice, for this is a central idea in Rolle's mysticism, one to which he returns again and again. As often as he expressed himself on the subject of the three loves—or the three levels of contemplation (*dulcor, calor, canor*)—he was bound to fall into a certain amount of repetition. We have all experienced this phenomenon in our own writing; we know the tyranny which expression can hold over our favorite concepts, how we habitually explain these concepts in the same words and often in the same order. In the case of Rolle, this natural tendency was intensified by his deliberate association of ideas with specific scriptural texts, a practice we examined earlier in some detail. Just as he imitates the vocabulary and structure of Apoc. 2:17 whenever he refers to the state of *canor*, so he always describes the three stages of love—insuperable, inseparable, and singular—in the language, respectively, of Romans 8:35-39, Luke 10:27, and Cant. 8:6-7. For example, love is inseparable according to the *Commandment* "when al þi thoghtes and þi willes er gederd togeder and festend haly in Jhesu Criste" (*English Writings*, p. 74), or according to the *Form of Living* "when al þi hert and þi thoght and þi myght es swa haly, swa enterely and swa perfytely festend, sett, and stabeld in Jhesu Cryste" (*English Writings*, p. 105). The scriptural debt is evident, especially in the second example, which is a rather mechanical amplification of Luke 10:27, "Thou shalt love the Lord thy God with thy whole heart, and with thy whole soul, and with thy whole strength." Given the fact that Rolle describes each of the three grades of love in terms of a particular scriptural text and the fact that the triad itself demands a consistent order of treatment, it is not so remarkable that in the two passages chosen by Matthews for comparison "the sentence patterns and their rhythms, the vocabulary and the composition of the whole are much the same." Undoubtedly, many of the similarities of style between Rolle's Latin and English writings are the result not of one's borrowing from the other but of the common debt which both owe to the Bible and to Rolle's special brand of *imitatio.*

These matters—Rolle's verbal repetition and the influence of his Latin upon his English—are not the only ones requiring further study in the light of biblical *imitatio.* His characteristic use of participles (which owes a great deal to St. Paul), his special store of translation words ("genges" for *gentes,* "covent" for *coventus,* and so forth), his stylistic debt to the Victorines (and to Richard, in particular)—these are a few more things that merit investigation against the background I have been describing. Perhaps some day we shall see the kind of full-length study which Rolle's style deserves. To iterate E. J. F. Arnould's hope: "Varied opinions on Rolle's style have been advanced. Most are highly subjective and based on impressions derived from an incomplete or a cursory reading of some, rarely all, of his works. An adequate study of this style would be a brilliant contribution to mediaeval stylistics."[32] Indeed it would be, and not because Rolle is so unusual—"the first master of English prose" or what have you—but because he is in many ways so typical of numerous other medieval writers who composed with one ear to the Bible, their Sacred Muse.

Notes

[1] "The Continuity of English Prose from Alfred to More and His School," in *Harpsfield's Life of More,* ed. E. V. Hitchcock, EETS, 186 (1932), p. ci.

[2] Only two full-length studies of Rolle's style have appeared within this century: J. P. Schneider, *The Prose Style of Richard Rolle of Hampole, with especial reference to its Euphuistic tendencies* (Baltimore, 1906), and A. Olmes, "Sprache und Stil der englischen Mystik des Mittelalters, unter besonderer Berücksichtigung des Richard Rolle von Hampole," *Studien zur englischen Philologie,* 76 (1933), 1-100. Neither assigns much importance to the Bible as an influence on Rolle's style, though Schneider does consider it briefly as an encouragement to euphuism.

[3] There is no study of biblical *imitatio* as such, though scholars have long recognized the debt of medieval writers to the style of the Vulgate; e.g., Jean Leclercq, *The Love of Learning and the Desire for God,* trans. Catharine Misrahi (New York, 1961), esp. pp. 91-96; or R. W. Southern, *The Making of the Middle Ages* (New Haven, 1953, rpt. 1963), pp. 211-18. I am in the process of writing a general history of biblical *imitatio* in the Middle Ages. Besides Rolle, other fourteenth-century English writers in the tradition include William Langland (see my unpublished dissertation, "*Piers Plowman* and the Tradition of Biblical *Imitatio,*" University of North Carolina, 1969) and John Gower (see Paul Beichner, "Gower's Use of *Aurora* in *Vox Clamantis,*" *Speculum,* 30 [1955], 582-95).

[4] However, see Ernst Lewalter, "'Auctores' und 'artes,' zu einer neuen Auffassung von der mittelalterlichen Poetik," *Rom. Forschungen, 52* (1938), 318-23.

[5] Trans. Margaret Nims (Toronto, 1967), p. 17.

[6] *Metalogicon,* trans. Daniel McGarry (Berkeley, 1955), pp. 66-67.

[7] See R. R. Bolgar, *The Classical Heritage* (Cambridge, 1954; rpt. New York, 1964), pp. 199-200.

[8] *On Christian Doctrine,* trans. D. W. Robertson, Jr. (New York, 1958), p. 122.

[9] See Leclercq, pp. 91-96.

[10] *St. Bernard et la Bible* (Paris, 1953), p. 17.

[11] *English Prose Treatises of Richard Rolle de Hampole,* ed. G. G. Perry, EETS, 20 (1866), p. xvii.

[12] *The Psalter, or Psalms of David and Certain Canticles,* ed. H. R. Bramley (Oxford, 1884), p. 250. Subsequent quotations from Rolle's Psalter are from this edition.

[13] *The Fire of Love* and *The Mending of Life,* trans. Richard Misyn and done into Modern English by Frances Comper (London, 1914), p. 225.

[14] *English Writings of Richard Rolle,* ed. Hope Emily Allen (Oxford, 1931; rpt. 1963), p. 118.

[15] *The Mystics of the Church* (London, 1925), p. 114.

[16] E. J. F. Arnould, ed., *The Melos Amoris of Richard Rolle of Hampole* (Oxford, 1957), p. lx.

[17] Ed. Paul Theiner, University of California English Studies, No. 33 (Berkeley, 1968).

[18] Gloss on Psalm 50:7. Add to these examples the following from Rolle's commentary on Canticles (not having seen the manuscript, I cannot ascertain the context): "Forsitan non credis verum esse quod dico, ideo experire modicum et invenies me veracem, quia nemo illud novit nisi qui accipit"—Hope Emily Allen, *Writings Ascribed to Richard Rolle,* Monograph Series of the Modern Language Association of America, Vol. III (New York, 1927), p. 71.

[19] This same practice may be seen in another of his favorite triads; see below, p. 22.

[20] *Writings Ascribed to Richard Rolle,* p. 141.

[21] "Richard Rolle's *Carmen Prosaicum,* an edition and commentary," *Mediaeval Studies,* 19 (1957), 23.

[22] Ed. Margaret Deanesly, Publications of the University of Manchester Historical Series, No. 26 (1915), p. 149. Misyn's translation is as follows:

They sicker are made like to that love because they are conformed to wanton concupiscence; and holding to old manners of wickedness, they love the vanity of this life before holy love. Wherefore they change the joy of incorruptible clearness [sic] to wantoned beauty that shall not last. This soothly would they not do unless they were blinded with the fire of forward love, the which wastes the burgeoning of virtue and nourishes the plants of all vice. Forsooth many are not set on womanly beauty nor like lechery, wherefore they trust themselves saved, as it were with sickerness; and because of chastity only, which they bear outwardly, they ween they surpass all others as saints. But wickedly they thus suppose and all in vain, when covetousness, the root of sins, is not drawn out. And truly, as it is written, nothing is worse than to love money. For whiles the love of temporal things occupies the heart of any man, it altogether suffers him to have no devotion. Truly the love of God and of this world may never be together in one soul, but whichever love is stronger puts out the other that thus it may openly be known who is this world's lover and who Christ's follower. For the heat of love breaks out in works which are seen. Certainly as Christ's lovers behave themselves towards the world and the flesh, so lovers of the world behave themselves towards God and their own souls. (*The Fire of Love,* pp. 16-17)

[23] *Select English Works of John Wyclif,* ed. Thomas Arnold (Oxford, 1869-1871), I, 289-91.

[24] The way in which Rolle echoes the parable of the virgins, without ever mentioning it explicitly, is by no means unique in medieval literature; William Langland does the same thing. See Ben Smith, Jr., *Traditional Imagery of Charity in Piers Plowman* (The Hague, 1966), pp. 38-39.

[25] See, for example, the *Contra Amatores Mundi,* V.197-243. These lines are organized around the opposition of *light* and *dark,* a motif introduced by the text "per speculum et in enigmate videmus" (I Cor. 13:12). Or see the *Melos,* chap. lvi, especially paragraphs four and five which may be viewed as representative of two stages in the development of biblical *imitatio.* The structure of paragraph four, an exposition of certain verses from Psalm 149, is nothing more or less than commentary form. Paragraph five, however, is bound less by a particular text than

by particular words, namely *gloria* and *congregare,* both of which continue motifs established by the scriptural text at the beginning of the chapter. The more important texts which make up the paragraph are, in order, I Cor. 15:41-42, Psalm 149:9, Romans 12:9, Luke 1:52, Matt. 5:3, Psalm 46:10. Finally, see the *Melos,* chap. lii, lines 22-35: the significant word here is *fides,* and the texts are Heb. 11:33, I Peter 2:5 (cf. Romans 12:1), I Cor. 12:31, I Cor. 13:2, Romans 1:17, James 2:17, Luke 10:27.

[26] *English Writings,* pp. 76-77.

[27] Of course "trouth" here may also mean "faith" (cf. I Cor. 13:13).

[28] *The Life of Richard Rolle* (London, 1929), p. 126.

[29] *Selected Works of Richard Rolle* (London, 1930), p. xxvii.

[30] *Later Medieval English Prose* (London, 1962), p. 24.

[31] *Writings Ascribed to Richard Rolle,* p. 177.

[32] *Melos,* p. lxi.

Nicholas Watson (essay date 1991)

SOURCE: Nicholas Watson, "The Structure of Rolle's Thought," in *Richard Rolle and the Invention of Authority,* Cambridge University Press, 1991, pp. 54-72.

[*In the following excerpt from his book-length study, Watson sets out the basis for his analysis, focusing on the function of* canor *in Rolle's work and thought. Considering Rolle in relation to larger mystical traditions, Watson finds him distinctive by virtue of "an idiosyncrasy not of thought but of focus."*]

[Here I will examine] the major themes of [Rolle's] writing, through which he articulates his audacious argument as to the status of the solitary mystic in the Church, and points to ways in which these, too, are idiosyncratic. In theory I am here concerned merely with a broad exposition of ideas and make no assessment of the purpose they are made to serve. Yet in practice the assessment tends to make itself. Since the structure of Rolle's thought is explicitly built around a particular view of his own status, even this introductory account of his exposition of the perfect life cannot avoid conveying that he is deeply concerned with the matter. Thus, in spite of itself, this survey anticipates the findings of my overall argument by pointing to the conclusion that Rolle's writing is not primarily didactic at all, but apologetic in its fundamental orientation.

There would be small point in building a discussion of Rolle's thought around his teachings on the central doctrines of Christianity, as if he were a theologian. He has little to say about Creation and Fall, Redemption and the Trinity, and what he does say is conventional and closely based on a source. His only systematic theological works are *Super Orationem Dominicam, Super Symbolum Apostolorum* and *Super Symbolum S. Athanasii*: derivative verse-by-verse expositions of major doctrinal texts, which indicate (as was perhaps intended) no more than that their author is wholly orthodox. Elsewhere he usually assumes that the nature of true belief is self-evident. *Incendium Amoris,* caps. 5-7, one of a very few formal doctrinal expositions in his works, is exceptional in putting his Trinitarian orthodoxy ostentatiously on show; but here again his account is wholly conventional, and his main point is that the Trinity is a mystery on which it is unwise to ponder: 'Let us not examine too closely things we cannot understand in this life' (163.28-29: 'Non nimis investigemus ea que in via comprehendere non possumus'). Regarding doctrinal deliberation as speculative rather than devotional, he seems to have heeded his own warning against it—that 'the harder teachings should be left to academics and learned men with long experience of sacred doctrine' (*Emendatio Vitae,* f. 139v. 15-17: 'Difficiliores vero sententiae disputantibus et ingeniosis viris longo tempore in sancta doctrina exercitatis relinquant'). When he requires doctrinal information himself, he relies on general guides: the *Gloss Ordinaria* for biblical glosses and Hugh of Strasbourg's *Compendium Theologicae Veritatis* for much of the rest. With the help of these and perhaps a small number of other works, he is always adequately informed, even about detailed theological points; but he is seldom concerned to be informative.

Nor does Rolle have much to say about the major Christian doctrines from a devotional point of view. He wrote a good deal about Christ, including lyrics, Passion meditations, and a scattering of devotional passages, one of which acquired fame as the *Enconium Nominis Ihesu,* gaining him a medieval reputation as the foremost exponent of the popular devotion to the Holy Name of Jesus.[1] Malcolm Moyes ([*Richard Rolles Expositio Super Novem Lectiones Mortuorum,*] 1988, chapter 2) has shown that, as a Yorkshire writer, Rolle was heir to a local tradition of Cistercian and Cistercian-inspired spiritual writing, in which affective devotion to Christ played a major part; he can, indeed, himself be regarded as an exponent of this love-centred spirituality, which derives not only from Bernard but from Aelred of Rievaulx, the poet John of Hoveden, and the anonymous author of the hymn *Dulcis Ihesu Memoria . . .* Rolle was certainly influenced by the affective, celebratory attitude of these writers towards Christ, and could neither have lived nor written as he did without them. Yet it would be a mistake to regard him as mainly a Christocentric writer. His debts to Cistercian spiri-

tuality are those of mood and imagery more than of Christology. His Passion lyrics and meditations were written to fulfil a relatively lowly function in the lives of spiritual beginners, while his more sophisticated English and Latin works make fairly few references to the Passion (although see *Melos Amoris,* caps. 29-32), except to say that meditation thereon belongs to the early stages of the spiritual life (see *Emendatio Vitae,* cap. 8). It is true that he associates devotion to the Holy Name with more advanced spiritual states; but his invocations of Jesus are almost devoid of theological content, and their structural importance, as we shall see, is in their connection with his experience of *dulcor*. Christology has none of the complexity and interest in Rolle's thought that it has, for example, in that of Julian of Norwich.

Similar things can be said about the importance of penitential themes in Rolle's writing. While he made notable contributions to the literature of penitence (as Moyes 1988, chapter 3 forcefully points out), especially in *Super Threnos Ieremiae* and *Super Lectiones Mortuorum,* his exercises in this mode seldom impinge upon the usual foci of his writing. He knew several of the classic expositions of the *de contemptu mundi* theme, such as Innocent III's *De Miseria Condicionis Humane,* the *Speculum Peccatoris* and the pseudo-Bernardine *Meditationes Piissimae.* But his interest in this theme is limited to a small number of works and passages in works, mostly written towards the end of his career, and all concerned with the early stages of the spiritual life. Thus in *Emendatio Vitae,* references to the *de contemptu mundi* theme are confined to the description of conversion in the first two chapters; in the epistle *Ego Dormio,* the penitential lyric 'Al perisshethe and passeth þat we with eigh see' (84-91) illustrates the lowest stage of the spiritual life. In Rolle's view, advanced contemplatives, whose careers form by far the most important subject of his writing, have moved beyond the need to articulate self-abnegatory contempt for the world, just as they have moved beyond the need to focus intensively on the humanity and Passion of Christ.

All in all, Rolle tends to take the main themes of Christian theology and religiosity for granted to such an extent that his writing often gives the impression of being disconnected from the mainstream of Christian thought. Reading him, it frequently seems that we have strayed into an esoteric world in which the principal landmarks are structures distinctive to Rolle himself. It is true that much of this air of eccentricity turns out to be the product of an idiosyncrasy not of thought but of focus, and that (as we saw in the introduction) a certain number of apparent oddities are in fact endemic to a literary tradition in which he is working, of writings extolling and analysing 'violent' love. Yet even when he mirrors pre-existing structures of thought most closely, the literalistic way in which he applies them to his own situation, and his concentration on a few issues to the exclusion of others, makes them assume a new and puzzling aspect.

The only moment of salvation history (and the only corner of Christian doctrine) with which Rolle's thought is almost invariably involved is the Judgement. Almost all his works are concerned with the division of souls that takes place at the end of the world. *Judica Me* contains two accounts of the Day of Judgement; *Super Apocalypsim* and *Super Threnos* are concerned with apocalyptic events prophetically foretold; both Psalter commentaries are incessantly concerned with the division of humanity into the good and the bad; almost half the chapters of *Incendium Amoris* end by anticipating the joys of the elect or the sorrows of the reprobate; the climax of *Melos Amoris* is its account of the coming *gloria sanctorum* and the horrors of damnation. Rolle's imagination is as dominated by the concept of future judgement as if he was after all the author of the *Prick of Conscience*.

His presentation of the Judgement is not, though, as crude as this remark suggests. He is not concerned with the more pictorial kinds of apocalyptic—with its descriptions of the vale of Jehoshaphat and the physical location and structure of hell—and he does not deal in the inflationary *topoi* meant merely to scare the reader into virtue: the Fourteen Torments, the Thousand Tongues of Steel (*Prick of Conscience* 6446). For Rolle the Judgement is rather a moment of moral revelation, when the true nature of the good and the wicked will be made known, and a transcendent order will triumph over the corrupt earthly one; it is a moment of reversal for the wicked and vindication for the elect, but of realization, in different senses, for both. The elect can now experience fully what before they only anticipated:

> *Exultabunt itaque sancti in gloria* pre dotibus anime, que sunt: cognicio, amor et fruicio Creatoris. *Letabuntur in cubilibus suis* [Psalm 149.5] pre dotibus corporis glorificati, que sunt: claritas, impassibilitas, agilitas, subtilitas. (*Melos Amoris* 181.18-21)[2]

> [*The saints will exult in glory* for their spiritual endowments, which are knowledge, love, and enjoyment of the Creator. *They will rejoice in their beds* for the endowments of their glorified bodies, which are clarity, immunity to suffering, agility, keenness.]

The damned have to recognize their earthly blindness to their condition:

> Videntes namque reprobi se iusto Dei iudicio ab electorum gloria perhenni excommunicacione sequestratos, inexcogitabili tristicia contabescent . . . Tunc dicent illi miseri in inferno collocati: '*Ve nobis*

quia peccavimus [Lamentations 5.16]; obtenebrati erant oculi nostri ut mala nostra videre non poteramus'. (*Judica Me* 8.19-21, 9.12-14)

> [For the reprobate will be consumed with unthinkable sadness when they see themselves cut off in eternal excommunication from the glory of the elect by God's just judgement. Then those wretches gathered in hell will say, '*Woe to us, for we sinned;* our eyes were blinded so we could not see our evil'.]

Cut off from the sight of God, they are still granted a kind of insight.[3]

For Rolle, then, one of the most important things about the Judgement will be that the wicked will have to admit that they were wrong and that the elect were right. Hell, as well as heaven, will witness the vindication of the elect. A group of the elect (the *pauperes*), however, will be summoned to the Judgement not to be judged but to judge: 'O ineffabilis gloria pauperum, o inestimabilis laus sanctorum, qui a consiliis et iudiciis deiecti sunt, et cum Christo congregati in eius iudicio sedentes iudicabunt' (*Melos Amoris* 180.36-181.2: 'O unutterable glory of the poor, O inestimable renown of the saints, who were cast out from courts and councils and now will judge, gathered together with Christ, sitting in his court!').[4] After the Judgement the elect will rejoice in the suffering of the damned: 'Et in ultimo iudicio cum viderit mundanum miserum terre quam dilexerat derelictum, non solum non compacietur, sed etiam de morte mali letabitur. Unde Propheta: *Videbunt iusti et super eum ridebunt* [Psalm 51.8]'[5] (*Judica Me* 6.19-22: 'And at the Last Judgement, when he sees the wordly wretch bereaved of the earth that he loved, not only will he have no compassion, but he will even rejoice at the death of the wicked—as the prophet says: *The just will look on and laugh at him*'). The scorn that the elect will feel for the damned is a saintly equivalent of the contempt that the reprobate feel for the elect now; they will laugh ('ridebunt') because the reprobate derided ('deridebant'): 'Et [reprobi] electos Dei habebunt accusantes, quos bene vivere videbant, nec opera eorum neque exhortaciones imitabantur, sed eos deridebant et despexerant' (*Judica Me* 7.15-17: 'And the reprobate will have God's elect for accusers, whom they saw living virtuously, and followed neither their works nor their exhortations but derided and despised them'). Like Lazarus, the elect are paupers here but will be blessed in the next life; like Dives, the reprobate are rich here, 'tiranni, perversi divites, pauperum oppressores, iniqui principes' (*Super Psalmum Vicesimum* 22.25-23.1)—and will be judged worthy of damnation.

The positions of elect and reprobate after the Judgement will thus be the exact reverse of their current positions except that they will be immovable. The elect have bought an eternal reward by giving up the temporal world and its pleasures; the reprobate have bargained away eternity to gain the fleeting riches of the temporal: 'Proinde pensemus dum adhuc peccare possimus, prospera mundi fugere, adversa libenter tollerare. Mala namque mens cum gaudet deperit, et seipsam quasi blando veneno, dum in creatura iocunditatem querit, occidit' (*Incendium Amoris* 156.9-12: 'Accordingly, while we are still able to sin, let us decide to flee the world's prosperity and to sustain its adversities willingly. For the evil soul perishes while it rejoices, and kills itself, as with sweet poison, while it searches for pleasure in created things').

As notes 2-5 show, there is nothing of itself unusual in this depiction of the Judgement. What is unusual, at least in so concentrated a form, is the way that these ideas become for Rolle the building-blocks of a narrowly antithetical and symmetrical model of Christian moral history as a whole. For Judgement does not only occupy a crucial place as a future event in his works; the coming division of souls suffuses his thinking about this life to such an extent that it often seems that it has already occurred, and elect and reprobate know their places in advance. Both the title and the content of the **Liber de Amore Dei contra Amatores Mundi** suggests this predestinarian view: 'Habent igitur celestis amor et secularis sectatores suos; sed inter se continue decertant, quis illorum amatum suum amplius diligat, cum alter ad Christum alter ad mundum tanto ambitu suspirat' (3.27-30: 'So both worldly and heavenly love have their followers; but they continually contend with one another as to which of them loves his beloved more, the one sighing after Christ, the other after the world, with such great eagerness"). This depiction of spiritual warfare is deliberately fanciful in imagining the lovers of God and of the world in conscious competition. But while Rolle normally assumes the wicked to be culpably ignorant of their spiritual state, he almost always speaks of *electi* and *reprobi,* and the patterns of behaviour which distinguish each group, as though it is clear who fits into which category. He denies having any knowledge of or interest in the predestined fate of individuals, and denounces those who judge others (*Judica Me* 1); but he still satirizes the wicked as though their obduracy was established, their damnation assured. Just as their eyes are to be forcibly opened on the Day of Wrath, so in this life they are irrecoverably blinded (a favourite image) by their foolishness: 'Excecantur utique oculi secularium tenebris viciorum; sed et sapiencia mundi per quam magnos se esse putant nimirum stultos efficit et a vere sapiencie lumine in obscura ducit' (*Contra Amatores Mundi* 3.41-44: 'You see, worldly eyes are blinded by the darkness of sin. But the world's wisdom, through which they think themselves great, also certainly makes them fools, and leads them from the light of true wisdom into the dark'). The division of souls at the Judgement thus has its counterpart for Rolle in a schematic opposition between the good and the evil in this life. The wicked, though rick and powerful, are already reprobate and can do no right; the good, though poor and despised, are already elect and can, in effect, do no wrong. Instead of viewing the world tropologically, as a vale of soul-making (in the way a pastoral writer like Walter Hilton generally does), Rolle habitually sees it anagogically, as though through the foreseeing eyes of God himself, and in the form in which the Judgement is to fix it forever.

Yet when Rolle speaks of *electi* and *reprobi* he is not generally concerned with the whole of humanity, but with two smaller groups, one good, one evil:

> Unde notandum est quod quatuor erunt ordines in iudicio: duo electorum et duo reproborum. Primus ordo electorum erit apostolorum et sequencium eos, scilicet, perfectorum, qui omnia pro Christo perfecte reliquerant et in viam paupertatis Christum secuti sunt. Et isti iudicabunt alios, unde Job ait, *Non salvat impios, et pauperibus iudicium tribuit* [Job 36.6]. Quoniam et hic a tirannis et malis hominibus incaute iudicamur et contempnimur, ibi a nobis tiranni et alii mali discrete iudicabuntur. Secundus ordo electorum erit beatorum Christianorum, qui fidem et dileccionem Christi tenuerunt et opera misericordie ex iuste acquisitis diligenter fecerunt . . . Tertius ordo erit falsorum Christianorum, qui fidem Christi habuerunt et illam bonis operibus non impleverunt. Et istis improperabitur quia non pascebant esurientes, nec potabant sicientes . . . Quartus ordo erit illorum qui fidem Christi non habuerunt. (*Judica Me* 74.5-75.4)

> [Concerning which it is to be noted that there will be four groups in the Judgement, two elect and two reprobate. The first group of elect will be of apostles and their followers, that is the perfect, who left everything perfectly for Christ, and followed Christ in the way of poverty. These will judge others, as Job says: *He does not save the impious, and entrusts judgement to the poor.* For since we are judged and despised foolishly here by tyrannical and wicked people, so there tyrants and the other wicked will be judged discerningly by us. The second group of elect will be of blessed Christians, who held to the faith and to the love of Christ, and who dutifully performed the works of mercy with goods justly acquired. The third group will be of false Christians, who had the Christian faith and did not implement it by good works. These will be reproved for not feeding the hungry, not giving drink to the thirsty. The fourth group will be of those who did not have Christian faith.]

This distinction between groups of saved and damned is common in medieval theology;[6] but in many of his works Rolle uses it in his own way by applying it directly to his picture of the world *before* the Judgement. *Electi, pauperes* and *perfecti* are thus distinguished from ordinary Christians (the *pusilli fideles* or *mediocriter boni*)[7] in his accounts of this life; and this distinction regularly corresponds to one he draws between contemplatives or hermits and Christians in active life. The former group are the main concern of almost all his works and (we shall see) are treated as members of an elite club: different criteria apply to them than to ordinary Christians; different rewards will be allotted to them. In dealing with the evil, Rolle always writes of the first of the groups of reprobate:

> Reprobi vero, omnino inaniter se habent erga Deum. Audiunt enim verbum Dei cum anxietate, orant sine affeccione, cogitant sine dulcedine. Intrant ecclesiam, implent parietes, tundant pectora, emittunt suspiria, sed ficta plane, quia ad oculos hominum, non ad aures Dei perveniunt. (*Incendium Amoris* 149.34-150.3)

> [But the reprobate conduct themselves with utter futility towards God. For they hear the word of God restlessly, pray without desire, think without sweetness. They go into church, fill it from wall to wall, beat their breasts, gasp out sighs—but all quite falsely, since they reach the eyes of people, not the ears of God.]

For most of the occasions on which he uses the words, *reprobi* refers only to false Christians (not also to pagans), and *electi* to those (especially solitaries) who have attained the summits of perfection (not also to the *mediocriter boni*); indeed much of his writing scarcely acknowledges the existence of anyone who fits into neither category.

Thus in Rolle's account of this world there is for the most part no middle ground on which the evil could repent and reform or the good suffer a fall from grace. Not that he believed that there was no such middle ground: it is clear from his few attempts to write for the *mediocriter boni* (as in most of *Judica Me* and in *Super Lectiones Mortuorum*) that in theory he saw the life of ordinary Christians as a continual and uncertain struggle with sin. But he has little interest in and small ability to write about this struggle; indeed, for all his theoretical knowledge of its existence he often seems to forget about it. His portrayal of evil is so undifferentiated that even when he tries to analyse the process of damnation in the manner of a pastoral writer (as in *Incendium Amoris,* cap. 23), the result shares the harshness and externality of satire. Instead of being analyses of a problem that afflicts everybody, his portrayals of sin seem to anticipate the joy he will have in triumphing over the reprobate at the Judgement, by triumphing over them on earth. Far from inviting them to be converted, his treatments of the wicked consist mainly of reproofs, the objects of which are satirical types whose lot is already determined: corrupt clergy, rulers, lovers of the world, who play

out their role of persecuting the elect, while the latter contend with them by going on, heedless of tribulation, to their enormous heavenly reward.

The one spiritual process which Rolle does write about is that whereby the *perfecti* achieve their high state. If the reprobate are homogeneous stereotypes in his works, the *electi* are described with great particularity as those whose regeneration has taken place according to a specific model. The way in which this model is applied varies according to the context in which it appears, but nowhere does it diverge substantially from his accounts of his own spiritual experiences. One corollary of this fact is that in spite of the significance of the theme of regeneration in his works, the focus of interest, even in his depictions of the elect, is never the psychological intricacies or moral difficulties of spiritual advance; his own experience of such complexities was evidently so slight that he is naive and indifferent in dealing with them. His interest is rather in the structure of advance and the interpretation of that structure—and 'interpretation' here equals 'elevation'. If Rolle's treatment of the reprobate is concerned more with the *topoi* of blame than with analysis, in discussing the elect he is always somehow concerned with their praise; indeed, those whose progress towards holiness follows the pattern he describes come to be accorded the highest spiritual status. In order to grasp the logic of his position we must look at his version of the ascent to God from its beginning: an enterprise that involves examining the affective and autobiographical accounts found in works like *Incendium Amoris,* in the context of the more structured and distanced pastoral discussions found, pre-eminently, in *Emendatio Vitae*.

The elect are those who set their hearts to love Christ, not the world:

> Noverint universi in hoc erumpnoso exilii habitaculo immorantes, neminem posse amore eternitatis imbui, neque suavitate celica deliniri, nisi ad Deum vere conventantur. Converti quippe ad ipsum oportet, et ab omnibus rebus visibilibus in mente penitus averti, priusquam poterit divini amoris dulcedinem saltem ad modicum experiri. Hec quidem conversio fit per ordinatum amorem, ut diligat diligenda, vel non diligenda non diligat. (*Incendium Amoris* 148.1-7)

> [Everyone lingering in this wretched place of exile should know that they cannot be imbued with the love of eternity nor be anointed with heavenly sweetness unless they are truly converted to God. For a person must be converted to him and totally turned away from everything visible in his mind before he can experience even a little of the sweetness of divine love. This conversion occurs through ordered love, so that what should be loved is loved, while what ought not to be loved is not loved.]

For Rolle, the process of spiritual advance begins not with moral doubt or confusion, but with conversion and the ordering of the affections, so that the will is put in tune with the self-evident moral structure of the world, and so that the individual can say, in the words of the Song of Songs (2.4), *'Ordinavit in me charitatem'*. The opening four chapters of *Emendatio Vitae,* a work which self-consciously mirrors Rolle's model of spiritual ascent in its own structure, are thus respectively entitled *De Conversio, De Contemptu Mundi, De Paupertate* and *De Institutione Vitae,* the first urging readers to this turning to God, the next three indicating what it is they are to turn from and how the converted life, in its broad outlines, should be organized. Conversion is, of course, initiated by God: 'For if God, in his grace, did not go before those elect whom he has determined to save, he would not find anyone among the sons of men whom he might justify' (*Super Psalmum Vicesimum* 7.13-15: 'Nisi enim Deus electos quos salvare decrevit gratia preveniret, inter filios hominum non inveniretur quem iustificaret').[8] Yet it is also a process which begins at a definitive moment and requires vigorous human activity. Rolle's own spiritual ascent began with his flight into the wilderness, an act of headstrong determination in which he literally turned away from the world. *Emendatio Vitae* exhorts the reader in more abstract terms to do the same thing, citing the brevity of human life, the uncertainty of the hour of death, and other *de contemptu mundi* motifs (f. 130r.). One of the Passion meditations is an aid for readers who wish to convert their affections from the world to Christ in the more positive and forcible way popularized by the *Stimulus Amoris;* by dwelling on the details of Christ's death, and on their own incapacity to respond to that death as emotionally as they should, the readers of these works are meant to wrench their wills away from wordliness and into a proper attitude of faith and feeling:

> Now is þe malice of my hert, þat is so wikked,
> more þan is þy passioun, þat is þy precious deth,
> þat wroght such wondres and manyfold more, and
> þe mynd þerof stirreth nat my hert? Bot, swet lord,
> a drop of þy blode droped vpon my soul in mynd
> of þy passioun may suple and soft my soule in þy
> grace, þat is so hard. I wot wel, swet Ihesu, þat my
> hert is nat worþy þat þou sholdest come þerto and
> þerin aly3t. I ask hit nat of þe dignite of þy sepulcre.
> Bot, swete Ihesus, þou ly3ted in to helle to visite
> þer and ryghtyn; and in þat manere I ask þy comynge
> in to my soule. (*Meditation B,* 507-16)

Here it is Christ who is begged to induce a response in the work's readers, but their own wills (sustained by the affective force of Rolle's prose) are nonetheless assumed to be very much active participants.

Conversion is turning from the world to Christ. It is also a movement from an existence centred on the body to one focussed inwardly: a convert 'has almost let go external perception, is wholly gathered within, is wholly lifted up into Christ' (*Emendatio Vitae,* f. 135v. I: 'Pene exteriores sensus amittit, totus intus colligitur, totus in Christum elevatur'). Such language is commonplace in itself, but Rolle's application of it is typically extreme. The outside world is given almost no place in his writing. For spiritual and economic reasons, most contemplatives recognize a need to maintain a balance between inner activities and various kinds of structured engagement in the world. Thus *Ancrene Wisse* divides its injunctions for the solitary life into 'outer' and 'inner' rules, including in the latter liturgical prayer, food, clothing and day-to-day conduct; in this it follows Aelred's *De Institutis Inclusarum,* as do many other late-medieval Rules (see Ayto and Barratt 1984, p. xli). Aelred's own ultimate source is the *Benedictine Rule,* which of course places much emphasis on the liturgy, and also directs monks to manual work as a way of avoiding idleness; thus cap. 48 (*De Opere Manuum Cotidiano*) opens 'Otiositas inimica est animae'—'Idleness is the enemy of the soul'. In obedience to the injunction to manual work, even the Carthusians, who considered themselves an eremitic order of especial rigour, copied books as a physical labour which was meant to balance the strenuous inner life expected of them.[9] Rolle, however, does not prescribe such a balance. He is anxious to avoid the charge of idleness (e.g. 'Non ergo contemplatores celestis iubili ociosi sunt', *Super Canticum Canticorum* 6.9-10), but the labour he enjoins is rather the 'labor . . . dulcis, desiderabilis et suavis' of contemplation (6.22-23) than bodily labour, which he thinks of small value ('Parum enim prodest corporalis exercitacio', 6.15)—and the term *contemplatio,* here as always in his work, refers to private not liturgical prayer.[10] His own anchoritic rule, *The Form of Living,* is almost entirely concerned with the inner life, and gives no help as to how a recluse is to pray, structure her day or keep herself in food. Where he does write of the matters comprised in the outer rule it is to urge their unimportance. Although he first experienced *canor* while engaged in a communal recitation of the psalms (*Incendium Amoris,* cap. 15), he ceased to regard even the liturgy as relevant to him (cap. 31). Similarly, as we saw in Chapter 1, asceticism has little value for him, and he recommends conformity with others as a guide to eating habits (*Emendatio Vitae,* f. 137r. 7). He does not envisage a life in which food and shelter is a problem; his own life was economically dependent on patrons, and he did not regard himself as obliged to do anything to support himself. For Rolle, the living of an inwardly gathered life entails a rejection of the concerns of the outer life so total as to require that contemplatives be accorded a wholly special status.[11]

The movement from a sensual outwardly directed existence to an inner and spiritual one has, of course, its difficulties. *Super Canticum Canticorum* contains a famous anecdote of one of Rolle's temptations, in which a devil appears to him as a beautiful woman, but is scared off by his praising the blood of Christ (47.26-48.16). In *Emendatio Vitae* he writes more generally of the 'triple cord' that binds men (*sic*) to the earth: riches, female flattery and youthful beauty (f. 135r. 44-45). But this obviously personal list (compare *Incendium Amoris* 166.22-167.14), like his other accounts of temptations encountered by converts, is of interest mainly for what it omits. Unlike more practical spiritual guides, Rolle dwells almost exclusively on problems caused by the blandishments of world or flesh, and says little about inner dryness, sins of pride and envy, and other spiritual trials.[12] On the few occasions when he alludes to a range of sins and temptations, such as in the last part of *Judica A* (10-15), cap. 4 of *Emendatio Vitae,* and a passage of *The Form of Living* (332-484), his writing is often mechanical. The last of these works merely lists categories of sins and their remedies, borrowing its material directly from the *Compendium Theologicae Veritatis* (as Ogilvie-Thomson's notes show), without regard for relevance; it is unlikely that any of its intended readers can have needed injunctions against drunkenness, gifts to harlots or usury. Moreover, Rolle's discussions of temptations seldom invoke the commonplaces which regard them as instruments of growth, and so give them a positive role in the structure of spiritual ascent; even his accounts of the early stages of this ascent treat temptation merely as a nuisance to be dealt with as quickly as possible. Lacking an appreciation (and probably much experience) of spiritual struggle, Rolle has little sense that sin is hard for contemplatives to deal with. He often uses the formula 'At the beginning we are sharply stung, but at the middle and end we are delighted by heavenly sweetness' (*Judica Me* 16.2-3: 'In inicio graviter pungimur, sed in medio et in fine celesti suavitate delectamur'); yet he has little use for the idea that the elect, at any stages of their careers, encounter internal obstacles serious enough to threaten them.

The most serious obstacle contemplatives encounter is not a temptation at all but the external trial of persecution. All the elect must expect to suffer opprobrium, scandal-mongering and detraction (*Judica Me* 10.21-22); whoever wishes to rejoice with Christ must first be a partner with him in tribulation (11.2-3). Where *Ancrene Wisse,* like most works in the tradition of penitential spirituality, regards suffering as something which any would-be follower of Christ must deliberately seek (see part VI), Rolle assumes it will be brought about mostly by the external agency of the enemies of the elect. Moreover, he usually identifies it not with bodily pain or temptation but with verbal abuse. Even caps. 5-6 of *Emendatio Vitae* (*De Tribulatione Patienter Sustinenda* and *De Patientia*), which generalize the theme of tribulation in order to appeal to a broad readership, frequently betray the assumption that

it is equivalent to persecution. Yet while he often refers to his own enemies, he does not tell elect readers what persecution to expect for themselves, nor how to deal with it. For the most part, his interest in the theme is that it shows those who suffer persecution to be the chosen of God, linking them with the early Christian witnesses and martyrs:

> *Palam facere,* dico, *ea que oportet fieri cito* [Revelation 1.1] . . . Animat nos sanctus Iohannes quasi inevitabilia ostendens adversa calumpniarum, improperiorum et magnarum tribulacionum, non solum ab extraneis sed eciam a falsis fratribus, quorum persecucio eo est magis periculosa, quo occulta . . . Hos perverse mentis ideo permittit Deus longe lateque discurrere, et malivolas linguas ac venenosas relaxare, ut paciencia electorum exerceatur et gloriosius coronentur . . . (*Super Apocalypsim,* 120.17-32)

> [*To make known,* I say, *those things which must soon come to pass.* St John encourages us by showing as virtually inevitable the suffering of calumnies, reproaches, and great tribulations, not only from outsiders but also from false brothers, whose persecution is the more dangerous in that it is secret. For God allows these perverseminded people to rush about hither and thither and give free rein to their malevolent and poisonous tongues, so the patience of the elect may be tested, and they may be crowned the more gloriously.]

It is true that this emphasis on persecution is typical of eremitic writing from the *Vitae Patrum* on, so that even *Ancrene Wisse* (especially the opening pages of part III) is somewhat improbably preoccupied with the opprobrium the anchoresses must suffer (see also William of St Thierry's *Epistola Aurea* III-VI). But Rolle's handling of this traditional theme is still notable for the narrowness of its focus and the repetitiveness of its treatment.

If Rolle is not very helpful, as a pastoral writer, in his depictions of the difficulties new converts must expect to have to face, he is hardly more so in his positive instructions. Almost the only tool for directing the mind to God he describes in any detail in the generalized Benedictine triad of spiritual exercises, *lectio, meditatio* and *oratio:*

> Tria vera exercicia cognoscere debemus quibus succendimur in amore Dei, videlicet, sacra leccio, oracio, meditacio. Leccio amantem . . . nobis insinuat. Oracio ad amorem Christi nos inflammat. Meditacio in amoris dulcedinem nobis continuacionem subministrat. (*Judica Me* 17.1-5)

> [We should recognize three exercises by which we are set alight in the love of God, namely holy reading, prayer, meditation. Reading introduces us to the beloved. Prayer inflames us in the love of

Christ. Meditation affords us a continuation in the sweetness of love.]

In the same vein as **Judica Me, Emendatio Vitae** recommends contemplatives to move between these three exercises at will, in order to inspire love in themselves (f. 139v. 35-38): a use of the triad that recalls the prologue to Anselm's *Orationes sive Meditationes,* where the reader is encouraged to let her or his thoughts move from reading, to meditation, to prayer, as seems best.[13] **Emendatio Vitae** gives a chapter to each of the three. *Oratio* has pride of place (cap. 7), but the term covers so wide a range (from recitation of the office to the moments before the experience of *canor*) as to render the chapter's advice on the subject of only general relevance. One of the most striking indications of Rolle's indifference to the mundane details of the spiritual life is this lack of clarity about the forms and occasions of prayer. *Canor* is a heightening of a kind of verbal prayer; Rolle's works are full of elaborate and impassioned prayers; yet the most specific advice he gives about prayer is that one should sit, not kneel, to do it. *Lectio* (cap. 9) has special importance for Rolle: reading the affective parts of the Scriptures kindles love ('accendunt nos ad amandum', f. 139v. 19) and teaches us to avoid sin. His biblical commentaries were presumably intended to assist in this process, and indicate how important he thought it to be; but his treatment of the exercise, here and elsewhere, is brief. *Meditatio* receives a fuller treatment than either *lectio* or *oratio* (cap. 8), because Rolle is anxious to warn readers against treating it as more than a means to an end. The practical tone of this chapter derives from its negativity: meditation is easy to practise to excess; it makes no difference what subject is chosen for meditation, since the exercise is of only temporary use. Such advice is conventional (visual meditation was often seen as a mere prologue to contemplation), but gives few indications as to how the exercise is to be performed. Like the other stages of the spiritual life discussed so far, prayer, reading and meditation are mainly significant for Rolle because they lead to something else.[14]

What this 'something else' is the last three chapters of **Emendatio Vitae** sketch in different ways. Cap. 10 (*De Puritate Mentis*) describes the goal of the conversion of the will as inner purity; once this is achieved, love is 'ordered' in the way the opening of **Incendium Amoris** says it must be. Total purity is not possible in this life, because venial sin cannot quite be destroyed. But affective prayer, reading and meditation can destroy the effects of venial sins as soon as they occur, by burning them up in the heat of charity (see Chapter 5, n. 22): 'Quamvis enim aliunde peccet venialiter cito tamen propter suam integram intentionem ad Deum directam deletur; fervor namque charitatis in ipso existens, omnem rubiginem peccatorum consumit' (**Emendatio Vitae,** f. 139v. 42-44: 'For while he may

sin venially sometimes, his sin is at once annihilated, because his whole will is turned to God; for the fire of love dwelling in him consumes every speck of sin'). Cap. 11 (*De Amore*) then gives an account of the *fervor caritatis,* which draws on many of Rolle's earlier writings (see Excursus 1, item 2.1-6), as well as on Richard of St Victor's *De Quattuor Gradibus Violentae Caritatis* (see pp. 216-218), and in a general sense on Bernard. Had Rolle's account of the spiritual life stopped at this point, there would still be relatively little to distinguish him from any of the writers of luxuriant prose in celebration of passionate love whom I discussed in the introduction (pp. 18-22). However, it does not stop. As cap. 12 of **Emendatio Vitae** (*De Contemplatio*) implies and many of his other works make very clear, for Rolle 'violent' love cannot constitute the fulfilment of a contemplative's aspirations until it expresses itself in four specific mystical experiences: Sight into Heaven, *fervor, dulcor* and the climax of the perfect life, *canor*. With the adumbration of these experiences, he passes beyond the traditional language of affective spirituality on to ground which is increasingly his own, and where his own life is by far his most significant source. Indeed, writing of *fervor* and *canor* near the end of **Incendium Amoris,** Rolle admits that he is himself unable to suggest parallels for them: 'Ob hoc utique evenit huiusmodi amatori quod nequaquam in aliquorum doctorum scriptis inveni aut reperi expressum' (237.21-23: 'Then indeed there happens to this kind of lover something I never discovered in any of the writings of the learned nor heard expounded').[15] Here, accordingly, we must explore in a little more detail.

The final chapter of **Emendatio Vitae** gives a somewhat allusive rendering of Rolle's mystical thought. For a fuller account we must turn to **Incendium Amoris,** which, as well as containing the most famous narrative of his experiences (in cap. 15), provides several shorter third-person summaries:

> Cum ergo homo ad Christum perfecte conversus cuncta transitoria despexerit, et se in solo conditoris desiderio immobiliter ut mortalibus pro corrupcione carnis permittitur fixerit: tunc nimirum vires viriliter exercens primo quasi aperto celo supernos cives oculo intellectuali conspicit, et postea calorem suavissimum, quasi ignem ardentem, sentit. Deinde mira suavitate imbuitur, et deinceps in canore iubilo gloriatur. Hec est ergo perfecta caritas, quam *nemo novit nisi qui accipit* [Relevation 2.17], et qui accipit nunquam amittit, dulciter vivit, secure morietur. (*Incendium Amoris* 202.26-35)

> [So when someone perfectly turned to Christ despises all transitory things and unmovingly attaches himself solely in desire for the Creator (so far as fleshly corruption renders this possible for mortals), then truly, exercising his strength manfully, first with intellectual vision he sees the celestial

citizens, as though heaven had been opened; then he feels a very sweet heat like fire burning; next he is imbued with wonderful sweetness; and thereafter he glories in joyful song. This then is perfect charity, *which nobody knows unless he receives it;* and he who receives it never lays it down. Sweetly he lives; confidently he will die.]

The images used to describe the four experiences are derived from all five senses: sight (Sight into Heaven), touch (*fervor*), smell or taste (*dulcor*), sound (*canor*). They occur in this order (to be understood as an ascending scale) in most of Rolle's works, and in pastoral as well as autobiographical contexts. *Ego Dormio* tells a nun that she will have these same experiences:

> At þe begynnynge, when þou comest thereto, þi goostly egh is taken vp in to þe light of heuyn, and þare enlumyned in grace and kyndlet of þe fyre of Cristes loue, so þat þou shal feel verraily þe brennynge of loue in þi herte, euermore lyftynge þi thoght to God and fillynge þe ful of ioy and swetnesse, so myche þat no sekenesse ne shame ne anguys ne penaunce may gref þe, bot al þi lif shal turne in to ioy. And þan for heynesse of þi hert, þi praiers turneth in to ioyful songe and þi þoghtes to melodi. (*Ego Dormio* 225-233)

The images may shift their meaning in different contexts, but the structure of Rolle's account, once formulated, is rigid. In his view it constitutes the definitive form in which the elect, while in this life, rejoice in God.

The first experience, Sight into Heaven, is notable as a sign of blessings to come, but is otherwise of obscure significance. It seems to be a temporary state which is made insignificant by the experiences that succeed it—perhaps because it lacks their affective force. *Incendium Amoris* says this about it:

> Ab inicio namque alteracionis vite mee et mentis usque ad apercionem hoscii celestis, ut revelata facie oculus cordis superos contemplaretur, et videret qua via amatum suum quereret, et ad ipsum iugiter anhelaret, effluxerunt tres anni, exceptis tribus vel quattuor mensibus. Manente siquidem hoscio aperto usque ad tempus in quo in corde realiter senciebatur calor eterni amoris, annus unus pene transivit. (*Incendium Amoris* 188.24-189-6)

[From the beginning of the transformation of my life and mind up until the opening of the heavenly gates—so that the heart's eye could contemplate the supernal with face unveiled, and could see by what way it should seek its beloved and continually desire him—three years less three or four months went by. Nearly a <further> year passed (the heavenly gates staying open) before the time when the heat of eternal love was really felt in the heart.]

Sight is here contrasted with the feeling of love that accompanies *fervor;* its low status is made clear by its presentation as 'seeing the way' rather than as part of that way. But while Rolle's accounts of the ascent to God seldom do more than mention it, he has at least two reasons for retaining it in his exemplary model. One is that he experienced something which he thought of as a sight into heaven, and considered that this fact alone made it important. The other is that without invoking such an experience it would be difficult for him to draw on the visual imagery of contemplation employed by the Fathers: Gregory's description of God as an 'incircumscriptum lumen' (see, e.g., **Super Canticum Canticorum** 1.7-8), or the pseudo-Dionysian image of 'ascent' to God. Such metaphors would be hard for any mystical writer to dispense with, and are important for Rolle as indications that he is describing a genuine and spiritual experience with authoritative precedents, for all his insistence on literal heat and a spiritually audible song.

The source of the image of 'Sight into Heaven' is Revelation 4.1. The comment on this passage in **Super Apocalypsim** implies a good deal about the place of the experience in the overall structure of Rolle's thought:

> *Et ecce ostium aperto in celo.* Cum obscuritas scripturarum in Ecclesia ostenditur, quasi ostium in celo aperitur. Vel sic: dum devota mens perfecte nititur ut a sordibus purgetur, dumque continua meditacione et oracione se sursum erigit . . . subito insolita lux apparet et mentem attonitam rapit, sicque ut contemplativus efficiatur cum oculis cordis iam mundatus ad celestia contemplanda suscipitur, ostium in celo aperitur, non corpori sed spiritui, et deinde dona melliflua descendunt et archana patefiunt. (156.13-21)

[*And behold, a door open in heaven.* When the darkness of the Scriptures is set forth by the Church, it is as though a door into heaven is opened. Or thus: when the devout soul strives perfectly to be purged from uncleannesses, and when it lifts itself upward by continual meditation and prayer, an unusual light suddenly appears and snatches away the amazed mind. And so, in order that he may become a contemplative, and with his heart's eye now cleansed, he is caught up to the sight of heavenly things, a door is opened in heaven (not corporeally but spiritually) and from it descend mellifluous gifts, and secrets are thrown open.]

Here Rolle gives two interpretations of the same verse, the first derived from his source, a commentary by pseudo-Anselm of Laon, the second his own.[16] The juxtaposition of these readings suggests that he saw this experience as a culmination of *lectio,* in which he suddenly understood the spiritual sense of the Scriptures, without as yet having the affective experience of the divine which *fervor* was to provide. **Emendatio**

Vitae describes *lectio* as an intellectual exercise ('Ad lectio pertinet ratio et inquisitio veritatis', f. 141r. 23-24), from which affective meditation and prayer can arise; **Super Apocalypsim** here suggests a reciprocal process in which meditation and prayer lead back to *lectio* at a higher level, where 'secrets are thrown open'.

Rolle's next two experiences can be dealt with quickly. The one to which he gave the name *fervor* was the culmination of a long period of prayer and meditation, in which his soul was suddenly granted the gift of response to and feeling for God, and kindled in love. This sensation evoked *dulcor,* a mixture of longing and fulfilment summed up by the Bride's cry *'Let him kiss me with the kiss of his mouth'* (Song of Songs 1.1). The prologue to **Incendium Amoris** (quoted on pp. 113-115) conveys vividly the excitement these feelings create, and the way they transcend all the contemplative's earlier spiritual exercises. Indeed, *fervor* and *dulcor* stand in the same relation to *meditatio* and *oratio* as Sight into Heaven does to *lectio.* Cap. 15 of **Incendium Amoris** says that Rolle first experienced them while delighting in the sweetness of meditation or prayer (189.7-8: 'Dum suavitate oracionis vel meditacionis multum delectarer'). Cap. 7 (*De Oratione*) of **Emendatio Vitae** likewise says that 'We truly pray when our soul is inflamed by the fire of the Holy Spirit' (f. 138v. 38-40: 'Tunc enim veraciter oramus cum . . . animus noster igne Spiritus Sancti inflammatur'), and later adds that true prayer leads to 'ineffabilis dulcor' (46). Cap. 8 (*De Meditatione*) makes the same claims for the higher forms of meditation, in which love is fervent and sweet (f. 139r. 36: 'Qui utique amor fervor et dulcor est'). More dramatically, at their height both experiences are seen as raising those who undergo them to exalted spiritual conditions. As **Incendium Amoris** says, contemplatives who burn in love are like the burning Seraphim who contemplate God, and after death will take their seat with them (cap. 3):[17]

> Amor namque inhabitat cor solitarii . . . Fervet hinc funditus et languet lumini, cum sic sinceriter sapit celescia; et canit mellite sine mesticia, clamorem efferens dilecto nobili sicut seraphycum [*see* Isaiah 6.3], quia conformitur in mente amorosa; dicitur, 'En amans ardeo anhelans avide!' Sic igne uritur inestimabili amantis anima . . . Sanctus quidem solitarius quia pro Salvatore sedere sustinuit in solitudine, sedem accipiet in celestibus auream et excellentem inter ordines angelorum. (**Incendium Amoris** 184.5-11, 14-16)

> [For love inhabits the heart of the solitary. On this account he burns from his very centre, and languishes for the light, when he thus truly tastes the celestial, and he sings honeyedly without heaviness like the Seraphim, uttering a cry to his noble beloved, which is fashioned in an amorous mind; <and> it says, 'Ah! avidly panting, loving I burn!' So the soul of the lover is consumed in an unthinkable fire. Indeed, since the holy solitary suffered to sit in solitude for his Saviour, he will receive in the heavens a golden and excellent seat among the ranks of the angels.]

Dulcor does not become the basis of any claim so specific as this, but the opening of **Super Canticum Canticorum** suggests, echoing the third of Bernard's *Sermones super Cantica Canticorum,* that only one who has truly experienced the sweetness of heavenly communion with God will dare to ask for the 'kiss of the mouth'. The imagery of *dulcor,* like that of *fervor,* also gives Rolle an automatic link with other exponents of affective mysticism, and ties his experience closely, if implicitly, to that of the Bride in the Song of Songs, of the psalmist (mystically interpreted), or of the contemplative who ascends through the four grades of violent love described by Richard of St Victor.

Yet while *fervor* and *dulcor* are of lasting importance in all of Rolle's writings, even these experiences are significant mainly on account of the culmination to which they point: to the gift of *canor,* the highest earthly goal of the contemplative. Cap. 15 of **Incendium Amoris** tells us that Rolle received *fervor* and *dulcor* while he was praying and meditating in a chapel. The same chapel was the setting for his reception of *canor* nine months later:

> Dum enim in eadem capella sederem, et in nocte ante cenam psalmos prout potui decantarem, quasi tinnitum psallencium vel pocius canencium supra me ascultavi. Cumque celestibus eciam orando toto desiderio intenderem, nescio quomodo mox in me concentum canorum sensi, et delectabilissimam armoniam celicus excepi, mecum manentem in mente. Nam cogitacio mea continuo in carmen canorum commutabatur, et quasi odas habui meditando, et eciam oracionibus ipsis et psalmodia eundem sonum edidi. Deinceps usque ad canendum que prius dixeram, pre affluencia suavitatis interne prorupi, occulte quidem, quia tantummodo coram Conditore meo. Non cognitus eram ab hiis qui me cernebant, ne si scivissent me supra modum honorassent, et sic perdidissem partem floris pulcherrime, et decidissem in desolacionem. (**Incendium Amoris** 189.19-190.6)

> [While I was sitting in the same chapel and saying the night-psalms before supper as best I could, I heard as it were a ringing of psalmody, or rather of singing, above me. And when I was stretched out in prayer and with all my desire towards heavenly things, I do not know how but I soon felt a symphony of song within myself and caught up from heaven the most delicious harmony, which remained with me in my mind. For my thought was forthwith

changed into a tuneful song; and I had as it were melodies in my meditation, and I also gave out the same song in my prayers and psalmody. Finally, because of the abundance of the internal sweetness, I burst forth into singing what before I had spoken— but silently, because only before my Maker. I was not noticed by those who observed me, in case they should have recognized me and honored me immoderately—and so I would have lost part of the loveliest flower and descended into desolation.]

Canor is superficially similar to *fervor,* although affecting a different spiritual sense. Like *fervor* it develops out of the exercises practised by contemplatives during their time of self-preparation, rising out of *cogitacio* (which stands in here for *lectio*) and *meditatio,* but especially out of *oratio* (in this case, the saying of the night-psalms). As **Emendatio Vitae** implies, *oratio* is the exercise that, above all, leads to contemplative experience: 'Ad orationem pertinet laus, hymnus, speculatio, excessus, admiratio; et sic in oratione vita contemplativa consistit vel meditatio' (f. 141r. 19-21: 'To [the exercise of] prayer pertain praise, hymnody, contemplation, rapture, wonder; and thus the contemplative life consists in prayer or meditation'). Moreover, the heavenly source of Rolle's *canor* is itself a 'psallencium', while if *canor* has any non-experiential source, it is to be found in the psalms, with their adjurations to sing, in the general concept of the liturgy, and perhaps in the specific practice of the singing of the *jubilus,* the wordless musical elaborations on the last syllable of the *Alleluia,* at High Mass (Womack 1961, chapter 1). Again like *fervor, canor* is a gift from above that at first seems to involve merely an intensification of the recipient's spiritual life, a new dimension of richness. Yet in Rolle's developed account it is of far more importance than this. Whereas *fervor* and *dulcor* are little more than gifts that refresh the pilgrim *in via, canor* emerges as in effect the goal of the journey, arrival at the Heavenly City: a final transformation of the soul. In this chapter, I can describe the elaborate structure that Rolle erects around his experience of *canor* only in a preliminary way.

Cap. 15 of **Incendium Amoris** tells us that Rolle was initially silent about his gift of *canor;* in cap. 31 (quoted on pp. 136-137), he describes his first attempt to articulate the significance of the gift, after being goaded by people critical of his way of life, and especially of his refusal to sing in the choir at Mass. His reply to these critics becomes an important theme of his writings. *Canor,* he argues, is incompatible with earthly song and noise. He is a solitary because only in quiet can be experience *canor.* On the other hand, those who criticize him—Christians in the world or in religious communities—are scarely able to experience or even understand it, since they live amidst noise. It is difficult to tell how literal this argument is meant to be, although in caps. 31-33 of **Incendium Amoris** it is presented in crudely physical terms; the fact that **Emendatio Vitae,** cap. 10 speaks of *canor* as arising

directly from a purified mind (f. 140v. 45-52) suggests equations between earthly sound and worldly sin on the one hand and solitude and purity of thought on the other, and may imply that we are dealing here with a sustained metaphor. Yet **Contra Amatores Mundi** also says:

> Omnis melodia mundialis, omnisque corporalis musica instrumentis organicis machinata, quantumcumque activis seu secularibus viris negociis implicatis placuerint, contemplativis vero desiderabilia non erunt. Immo fugiunt corporalem audire sonitum, quia in se contemplativi viri iam sonum susceperunt celestem. Activi vero in exterioribus gaudent canticis, nos contemplacione divina succensi *in sono epulantis* [Psalm 41.5] terrena transvolamus . . . Alioquin iam desinimus canere, atque ab illa invisibilis gaudii affluencia cessare, ut dum ab illis corporaliter perstrepentibus non fugimus, veraciter [discamus] quia nemo unquam in amore Dei gaudere potuit, qui prius vana istius mundi solacia non dereliquit. (**Contra Amatores Mundi** 4.102-117)

> [All mundane melody, all corporal music contrived by instruments and organs, however much they may satisfy active people and seculars bound up in business, will certainly not be desirable things for holy contemplatives. Indeed they flee from hearing corporeal sound because contemplative people have already received celestial sound in themselves. Actives rejoice in external songs; but we, set alight by divine contemplation, transcend the terrestrial *With the sound of feasting.* Otherwise we fall away from song and lose the richness of that invisible melody; so that while we do not flee from those bodily pandemoniums, we truly learn that nobody can ever rejoice in the love of God unless he first relinquishes the vain solaces of this world.]

It follows from this depiction of *canor* that solitaries like Rolle are more or less beyond the criticism of all those who have not experienced it, since they cannot know the significance of what they are missing. It also follows that those who experience *canor* will wish to take as little part in communal events as possible, including the liturgical worship of the Church, since their inner music will be interrupted; this is why Rolle says he did not want to sing in the choir, and is his most individual reason for insisting on the superiority of the solitary life to all other ways of serving God—that quiet can only be found in solitude. Unlike *fervor* and *dulcor, canor* thus radically distinguishes those who receive it from the rest of humanity.

Yet if *canor* is important enough for its recipient to be justified in shunning all but nominal participation in the Church's worship, and if it is impossible to criticize those who have it, the gift must have enormous intrinsic significance. This significance Rolle defines by means of a daring antithesis. Although the *perfecti* no longer profitably participate in the worship of the earthly Church, their practice of *canor* is also an act of participation—in the worship of the heavenly Church. In singing spiritual songs, the perfect are joining, while still on earth, with the chorus of the saved and the angels in heaven; they are enjoying a part of their heavenly reward in advance:

> Est enim angelica suavitas quam in animam accipit et eadem oda, etsi non eisdem verbis laudes Deo resonabitur. Qualis angelorum, talis est iscius concentus, etsi non tantus, nec tam perspicuus, propter carnem corruptibilem que adhuc aggravat amantem. Qui hoc experitur eciam angelica cantica expertus est, cum sit eiusdem speciei in via et in patria. (*Incendium Amoris* 237.4-10)

> [So it is an angelic sweetness that he takes into his soul, and angelic song, even if he will not resound the praises of God in the same words. For this harmony is like that of the angels, although neither so great nor so clear, because of the corruptible flesh which still weighs down the lover. He who has experienced this <harmony> has also experienced angelic song, since this is of the same sort both on the road and in the Fatherland.]

The transformation brought about in the elect soul by the gift of *canor* is thus fundamental. In effect, the mature contemplative is already *in patria*—already a member of the Church Triumphant, who participates in the felicity to which all the saved will eventually be called, and who is almost disengaged from the world's sin. Indeed, Rolle's contemplatives, while they are still on earth, participate not merely in the common joys of heaven but in the higher forms of ecstasy. Their place on earth is lowest of all, but their place in heaven will be (and already implicitly is) the highest, with the Seraphim who burn in contemplation of God. These *perfectissimi* experience frustration at the barriers their flesh imposes between them and God, and long to die, for their conversion from this world to the next is already so complete that they have nothing to fear, and much to relish, in the prospect of the Judgement— where it will be they who will judge sinful humanity with Christ and his apostles. *Canor,* in short, is the highest gift attainable in this life and an expression of the highest degree of holiness: *Incendium Amoris* calls it (with *fervor* and *dulcor*) 'summa perfeccio christiane religionis' (185.16-17), while in *Melos Amoris* (cap. 1) its existence in today's world is taken as proof that sanctity is still not dead. The gift of *canor* brings the earthly careers of the elect to a joyful standstill, for they can subsequently have nothing further to look forward to and little to fear in this life; the ordering of their affections is already complete.

Canor is the keystone of the simple, even in its way logical, structure that is Rolle's thought, the basis of his high view of the status of the earthly elect, the source of his idiosyncrasy as a mystical writer. Other late medieval writers, from Bernard and Richard of St Victor to Ruusbroec and the Rhineland mystics, express from time to time the view that something approaching complete perfection is possible in this life; works like Ruusbroec's *Spiritual Espousals,* and indeed the *De Quattuor Gradibus Violentae Caritatis,* present as ambitious and extreme a view of the holiness attainable by the contemplative as anything we might find in *Incendium Amoris.* However, we would have to look far—and to writers Rolle could not have known, such as Marguerite Porete, or Hadewijch—to find other structures built so high from such slight and tendentious foundations of personal experience; even in mystical literature it is remarkable for an individual's experience to be the overt basis of so ambitious a position. Richard of St Victor may be allowed the last word, for the peroration of his great work on violent love, which speaks of the boldness love engenders in the soul, applies strikingly well to Rolle—who not only experienced such love, but told the world that he had, and spent a lifetime trying to prove that the form of his experience was definitive: 'Ecce in quantam pie presumptionis audaciam consummatio caritatis solet mentem hominis erigere, ecce quomodo facit hominem ultra hominem presumere!' (177.1-5)—'See in what boldness of pious presumption the consummation of charity elevates the human mind! See how it makes a human presume beyond the human!'

Notes

[1] Allen, pp. 66-68 lists Latin and English MSS of the *Enconium* (the fourth section of *Super Canticum Canticorum*); the texts found in two of the latter are printed in Horstmann 1895—1896, vol. 1, pp. 186-191. There is a compilation of passages from Rolle's work concerned with Jesus in the fifteenth-century MS Kk. vi. 20, ff. 11r.-26v., called *Orationes Excerpte de Diversis Tractatibus quos Composuit Beatus Richardus Heremita ad Honorem Nominis Ihesu* (edited by Esposito 1982); see Moyes 1988, vol. 1, pp. 83-86.

[2] Here Rolle may be following *Compendium Theologicae Veritatis* VII, caps. 26-28, which, however, lists the *dotes animae* as *cognitio, dilectio, comprehensio;* the *dotes corporis* are the same as in Rolle's list. For other lists of the attributes of the saved compare Aquinas's *Summa Theologica* III, q. 95, arts. 1, 5, *Prick of Conscience* 7813ff., and *Speculum Ecclesie,* sections 87-88. *Judica Me* 69.4-6 provides its own, shorter list.

[3] Aquinas's *Summa Theologica* III, qq. 97-98, similarly makes much of the remorse felt by the damned (q. 97, art. 2), of their belated repentance for sin (q. 98, art. 2), and of the torment they experience seeing the blessed in joy, or, after the Judgement (when such

sight is lost—see *Compendium Theologicae Veritatis* VII, cap. 22), remembering that sight (q. 98, art. 9).

4 The description of those elect who will judge others at the Judgement as *pauperes* is standard: Aquinas's *Summa Theologica* III, q. 89, art. 2, argues that Matthew 19.28, which gives the apostles a hand in the Judgement, applies to all the *pauperes. Compendium Theologicae Veritatis* also writes of a group of the elect who will judge others and not be judged themselves (VII, cap. 19).

5 See also *Super Canticum Canticorum* 11.24-12.4. Saintly rejoicing in the damnation of the evil is not mentioned in *Compendium Theologicae Veritatis,* but is part of a usual picture of the Judgement: see, e.g., *Summa Theologica* III, q. 94, arts. 1-3, and Innocent III's *De Miseria Condicionis Humane* 3.4.

6 Rolle is probably following either *Compendium Theologicae Veritatis* VII, cap. 19 ('Ordines quatuor erunt in judicio . . . ') or Lombard's gloss on Psalm 1.6 (which Rolle translates directly in *English Psalter* 8).

7 *Judica Me* 1.10 uses both phrases, the second of which can also be found in, e.g., Lombard's *Sententiae* IV, dist. xlv, 5 (entitled *Quibus Suffragiis Iuvabuntur Mediocriter Boni qui in Fine Reperientur*).

8 Rolle here alludes formally to the doctrine of prevenient grace, which states that even humanity's desire for grace is the product of grace; see, e.g., Lombard's *Sententiae* II, dist. xxvi, where much of the terminology of this passage of *Super Psalmum Vicesimum* can be found.

9 See cap. 36 of Guigo II's *Liber de Exercitio Cellae,* entitled *De Opere Manuum* (PL 153, cols. 880-883), where Benedict's injunction against idleness is used to introduce the subject of writing as manual work (col. 883).

10 Rolle alludes here to 1 Timothy, 4.8—*'Nam corporalis exercitatio ad modicum utilis est, pietas autem ad omnia utilis est'*—misquoting a verse which is commonly used by monastic writers to counter too great an emphasis on outer works; see, e.g., Bernard's *Sermones super Cantica Canticorum* 33.10. By citing this verse in support of its argument that contemplatives avoid *otiositas* not by working with the hands but by engaging in the sweet labour of contemplation, Rolle is reinterpreting the Benedictine concept of *labor.*

11 Womack [*The jubilus theme in the later writings of Richard Rolle,* Dissertation, Duke University,] 1961, pp. 104-111 rightly discusses Rolle's attitude to food and drink in terms of the monastic concept of *discretio,* citing in particular a discourse by Abbot Moses in Cassian's *Collationes* (11, PL 49, cols. 523-558, especially 549ff.). Rolle could have found discussions of

conformity and discretion similar to his own in the *Meditationes Vitae Christi,* cap. 44, a study of poverty which draws heavily on Bernard and on William of St Thierry's *Epistola Aurea.* What is distinctive about his treatment is his emphasis on avoiding over-abstinence and corresponding lack of interest in the danger of over-indulgence; see, e.g., *The Form of Living* 45-86, in which three lines are given to the former, nearly forty to the latter.

12 Contrast, e.g., Hilton's *Scale of Perfection,* with its intricate treatments of the variety of problems afflicting contemplatives (e.g. 1, caps. 36-40).

13 'Orationes sive meditationes quae subscriptae sunt, quoniam ad excitandum mentem ad Dei amorem vel timorem, seu ad suimet discussionem editae sunt, non sunt legendae in tumultu, sed in quiete . . . Nec debet intendere lector ut quamlibet earum totam perlegat, sed quantum sentit sibi Deo adiuvante valere ad accendendum affectum orandi, vel quantum illum delectat' (3.2-4, 5-8). Directly or indirectly this passage lies behind Rolle's devotional and private (i.e. nonliturgical) use of the triad *lectio, meditatio, oratio.*

14 Contrast the elaborate treatment of prayer and meditation in Book 1 of *The Scale of Perfection,* caps. 24-36.

15 Compare *Contra Amatores Mundi* 4.120-122: 'Pauci ergo sunt vel nulli quid illud [canor] referunt, quia forsitan illud nescierunt, si autem habuerint sed et aliis predicare nec verbo nec exemplo voluerunt.'

16 Pseudo-Anselm's gloss on this verse runs: '*Et ecce ostium apertum in coelo,* scilicet, clausura Scripturarum quae est via ad vitam, vel obscuritas coelestium mysteriorum, vel in his qui coelum sunt' (PL 162, col. 1517).

17 *Compendium Theologicae Veritatis* 11, cap. 14 describes the Seraphim as distinguished by their fervent love: 'Proprium est Seraphim ardere et alios ad incendium divini amoris promovere.' For the analogy between the Seraphim and contemplatives see Bernard's *Sermones super Cantica Canticorum* 19.5.

FURTHER READING

Bibliography

Lagoria, Valerie Marie and Ritamary Bradley. *The 14th-Century English Mystics: A Comprehensive Annotated Bibliography.* New York and London: Garland Publishing, 1981, 197 pp.

Provides a thorough overview of Rolle's work and Rolle scholarship, divided into easily navigated sections.

Criticism

Alford, John A. "Richard Rolle and Related Works." In *Middle English Prose: A Critical Guide to Major Authors and Genres*. Ed. A. S. G. Edwards. New Brunswick, N.J.: Rutgers University Press, 1984, pp. 35-60.

Provides a thorough and concise synopsis of Rolle's life and works, as well as a summary of the critical heritage; bibliography arranged by Rolle's works included.

Allen, Rosamund S. In an introduction to *Richard Rolle: The English Writings*. Mahwah, N.J.: Paulist Press, 1988, pp. 9-63.

Comments on some of the harsher qualities in Rolle's mysticism.

Chambers, R. W. "The Continuity of English Prose From Alfred to More and His School." In *The Life and Death of Sir Thomas More, Knight, Sometimes Lord High Chancellor of England*. London: Oxford University Press, 1932, pp. xlv-clxxiv.

Makes an often-cited argument that Rolle deserves "a supreme place in the history of English prose."

Downside Review 93 (1975): 193-200; 101, No. 343 (April 1983): 108-39; 104, No. 356 (July 1986): 165-213.

The journal has printed a series of important articles on Rolle; the ones cited here are, respectively, Margaret Jennings, "Richard Rolle and the Three Degrees of Love"; J. P. H. Clark, "Richard Rolle: A Theological Re-Assessment"; J. P. H. Clark, "Richard Rolle as Biblical Commentator."

Fourteenth-Century Mystics Quarterly 7, No. 1 (March 1981): 20-31; 10, No. 1 (March 1984): 9-16; 10, No. 4 (December 1984): 171-74.

The journal has printed a series of important articles on Rolle; the ones cited here are, respectively, Mary Teresa Brady, "The Seynt and His Boke: Rolle's *Emendatio Vitae* and *The Pore Caitif*"; Ellen Caldwell, "The Rhetorics of Enthusiasm and of Restraint in *The Form of Living* and *The Cloud of Unknowing*"; Robert Boenig, "The God-as-Mother Theme in Richard Rolle's Biblical Commentaries."

Glasscoe, Marion, ed. *The Medieval Mystical Tradition in England: Papers Read at Dartington Hall, July 1984*. Cambridge, England: D. S. Brewer, 1984.

Contains several close and rigorous studies of Rolle's written works; Rolle scholars included are R. Allen, R. Copeland, and M. Moyes.

Hodgson, Geraldine E. *The Sanity of Mysticism: A Study of Richard Rolle*. London: Faith Press, 1926, 227 pp.

Assesses Rolle's status as a mystic in the European tradition; appendices provide excerpts from some of Rolle's minor writings.

Knowles, David. "Richard Rolle." In *The English Mystical Tradition*. New York: Harper and Brothers, 1961, pp. 48-66.

Reviews the current image of and scholarship on Rolle, generally lauding its "clearer," "firmer," and "less romantic light."

Mystics Quarterly 13, No. 1 (March 1987): 12-18; 14, No. 4 (December 1988): 177-85; 15, No. 3 (September 1989): 117-24; 16, No. 1 (March 1990): 27-33.

The journal has printed a series of important articles on Rolle; the ones cited here are, respectively, Rosamund S. Allen, "Tactile and Kinaesthetic Imagery in Richard Rolle's Works"; Laquita M. Higgs, "Richard Rolle and his Concern for 'Even Christians'"; Ann Astell, "Feminine Figurae in the Writings of Richard Rolle: A Register of Growth"; Robert Boenig, "Contemplations of the Dread and Love of God, Richard Rolle, and Aelred of Rievaulx."

Renevey, Denis. "Encoding and Decoding: Metaphorical Discourse of Love in Richard Rolle's Commentary on the First Verses of the Song of Songs." *The Medieval Translator* 123, No. 4 (1994): pp. 200-217.

Uses Rolle's commentary on the Song of Songs to discuss the impact of biblical translation and interpretation on Rolle's writings and mysticism.

Riehle, Wolfgang. *The Middle English Mystics*. Trans. Bernard Standring. London and Boston: Routledge and Kegan Paul, 1981, 244 pp.

Examines the paradox of mystical writing, specifically "the problem of having to express the union with the divine in a language that proves to be inadequate because it is limited to earthly things."

Sitwell, Gerard Sitwell. "Richard Rolle." In *Spiritual Writers of the Middle Ages*. New York: Hawthorn Books, 1961, pp. 88-91.

Emphasizes Rolle's weaknesses and limitations and casts his written works as too often defensive.

Smedick, Lois K. "Parallelism and Pointing in Rolle's Rhythmical Style." *Medieval Studies* 41 (1979): 404-67.

Uses a close study of *The Form of Living* to build arguments both about the character of Rolle's style and about medieval use of punctuation.

Wolters, Clifton, ed. and trans. *The Fire of Love*. London: Penguin Books, 1972, 192 pp.

Wolters' translation of *The Fire of Love* into modern English also includes an introduction that makes Rolle easily available to the novice.

Additional coverage of Rolle's life and career is contained in the following source published by Gale Research: *Dictionary of Literary Biography*, Vol. 146.

CLASSICAL AND MEDIEVAL LITERATURE CRITICISM

INDEXES

Literary Criticism Series
Cumulative Author Index

Literary Criticism Series
Cumulative Topic Index

CMLC Cumulative Nationality Index

CMLC Cumulative Title Index

CMLC Cumulative Critic Index

How to Use This Index

The main references

> Calvino, Italo
> 1923-1985.....CLC 5, 8, 11, 22, 33, 39,
> 73; SSC 3

list all author entries in the following Gale Literary Criticism series:

BLC = *Black Literature Criticism*
CLC = *Contemporary Literary Criticism*
CLR = *Children's Literature Review*
CMLC = *Classical and Medieval Literature Criticism*
DA = *DISCovering Authors*
DAB = *DISCovering Authors: British*
DAC = *DISCovering Authors: Canadian*
DAM = *DISCovering Authors Modules*
    DRAM: *Dramatists module*
    MST: *Most-studied authors module*
    MULT: *Multicultural authors module*
    NOV: *Novelists module*
    POET: *Poets module*
    POP: *Popular/genre writers module*

DC = *Drama Criticism*
HLC = *Hispanic Literature Criticism*
LC = *Literature Criticism from 1400 to 1800*
NCLC = *Nineteenth-Century Literature Criticism*
PC = *Poetry Criticism*
SSC = *Short Story Criticism*
TCLC = *Twentieth-Century Literary Criticism*
WLC = *World Literature Criticism, 1500 to the Present*

The cross-references

> See also CANR 23; CA 85-88;
> obituary CA 116

list all author entries in the following Gale biographical and literary sources:

AAYA = *Authors & Artists for Young Adults*
AITN = *Authors in the News*
BEST = *Bestsellers*
BW = *Black Writers*
CA = *Contemporary Authors*
CAAS = *Contemporary Authors Autobiography Series*
CABS = *Contemporary Authors Bibliographical Series*
CANR = *Contemporary Authors New Revision Series*
CAP = *Contemporary Authors Permanent Series*
CDALB = *Concise Dictionary of American Literary Biography*
CDBLB = *Concise Dictionary of British Literary Biography*

DLB = *Dictionary of Literary Biography*
DLBD = *Dictionary of Literary Biography Documentary Series*
DLBY = *Dictionary of Literary Biography Yearbook*
HW = *Hispanic Writers*
JRDA = *Junior DISCovering Authors*
MAICYA = *Major Authors and Illustrators for Children and Young Adults*
MTCW = *Major 20th-Century Writers*
NNAL = *Native North American Literature*
SAAS = *Something about the Author Autobiography Series*
SATA = *Something about the Author*
YABC = *Yesterday's Authors of Books for Children*

Literary Criticism Series
Cumulative Author Index

Abasiyanik, Sait Faik 1906-1954
See Sait Faik
See also CA 123

Abbey, Edward 1927-1989 ...... CLC 36, 59
See also CA 45-48; 128; CANR 2, 41

Abbott, Lee K(ittredge) 1947- ...... CLC 48
See also CA 124; CANR 51; DLB 130

Abe, Kobo
1924-1993 .... CLC 8, 22, 53, 81;
DAM NOV
See also CA 65-68; 140; CANR 24; MTCW

Abelard, Peter c. 1079-c. 1142 ... CMLC 11
See also DLB 115

Abell, Kjeld 1901-1961............ CLC 15
See also CA 111

Abish, Walter 1931-.............. CLC 22
See also CA 101; CANR 37; DLB 130

Abrahams, Peter (Henry) 1919- ..... CLC 4
See also BW 1; CA 57-60; CANR 26;
DLB 117; MTCW

Abrams, M(eyer) H(oward) 1912-... CLC 24
See also CA 57-60; CANR 13, 33; DLB 67

Abse, Dannie
1923- ... CLC 7, 29; DAB; DAM POET
See also CA 53-56; CAAS 1; CANR 4, 46;
DLB 27

Achebe, (Albert) Chinua(lumogu)
1930- ..... CLC 1, 3, 5, 7, 11, 26, 51, 75;
BLC; DA; DAB; DAC; DAM MST,
MULT, NOV; WLC
See also AAYA 15; BW 2; CA 1-4R;
CANR 6, 26, 47; CLR 20; DLB 117;
MAICYA; MTCW; SATA 40;
SATA-Brief 38

Acker, Kathy 1948- .... CLC 45
See also CA 117; 122; CANR 55

Ackroyd, Peter 1949-.......... CLC 34, 52
See also CA 123; 127; CANR 51; DLB 155;
INT 127

Acorn, Milton 1923-........ CLC 15; DAC
See also CA 103; DLB 53; INT 103

Adamov, Arthur
1908-1970 .... CLC 4, 25; DAM DRAM
See also CA 17-18; 25-28R; CAP 2; MTCW

Adams, Alice (Boyd)
1926- .... CLC 6, 13, 46; SSC 24
See also CA 81-84; CANR 26, 53;
DLBY 86; INT CANR-26; MTCW

Adams, Andy 1859-1935......... TCLC 56
See also YABC 1

Adams, Douglas (Noel)
1952- .... CLC 27, 60; DAM POP
See also AAYA 4; BEST 89:3; CA 106;
CANR 34; DLBY 83; JRDA

Adams, Francis 1862-1893....... NCLC 33

Adams, Henry (Brooks)
1838-1918 ..... TCLC 4, 52; DA; DAB;
DAC; DAM MST
See also CA 104; 133; DLB 12, 47

Adams, Richard (George)
1920- .... CLC 4, 5, 18; DAM NOV
See also AAYA 16; AITN 1, 2; CA 49-52;
CANR 3, 35; CLR 20; JRDA; MAICYA;
MTCW; SATA 7, 69

Adamson, Joy(-Friederike Victoria)
1910-1980 .... CLC 17
See also CA 69-72; 93-96; CANR 22;
MTCW; SATA 11; SATA-Obit 22

Adcock, Fleur 1934-.............. CLC 41
See also CA 25-28R; CAAS 23; CANR 11,
34; DLB 40

Addams, Charles (Samuel)
1912-1988 .... CLC 30
See also CA 61-64; 126; CANR 12

Addison, Joseph 1672-1719 .... LC 18
See also CDBLB 1660-1789; DLB 101

Adler, Alfred (F.) 1870-1937 ..... TCLC 61
See also CA 119

Adler, C(arole) S(chwerdtfeger)
1932- .... CLC 35
See also AAYA 4; CA 89-92; CANR 19,
40; JRDA; MAICYA; SAAS 15;
SATA 26, 63

Adler, Renata 1938-............ CLC 8, 31
See also CA 49-52; CANR 5, 22, 52;
MTCW

Ady, Endre 1877-1919 .... TCLC 11
See also CA 107

Aeschylus
525B.C.-456B.C. .... CMLC 11; DA;
DAB; DAC; DAM DRAM, MST

Afton, Effie
See Harper, Frances Ellen Watkins

Agapida, Fray Antonio
See Irving, Washington

Agee, James (Rufus)
1909-1955 .... TCLC 1, 19; DAM NOV
See also AITN 1; CA 108; 148;
CDALB 1941-1968; DLB 2, 26, 152

Aghill, Gordon
See Silverberg, Robert

Agnon, S(hmuel) Y(osef Halevi)
1888-1970 .... CLC 4, 8, 14
See also CA 17-18; 25-28R; CAP 2; MTCW

Agrippa von Nettesheim, Henry Cornelius
1486-1535 .... LC 27

Aherne, Owen
See Cassill, R(onald) V(erlin)

Ai 1947-.................. CLC 4, 14, 69
See also CA 85-88; CAAS 13; DLB 120

Aickman, Robert (Fordyce)
1914-1981 .... CLC 57
See also CA 5-8R; CANR 3

Aiken, Conrad (Potter)
1889-1973 .... CLC 1, 3, 5, 10, 52;
DAM NOV, POET; SSC 9
See also CA 5-8R; 45-48; CANR 4;
CDALB 1929-1941; DLB 9, 45, 102;
MTCW; SATA 3, 30

Aiken, Joan (Delano) 1924-........ CLC 35
See also AAYA 1; CA 9-12R; CANR 4, 23,
34; CLR 1, 19; DLB 161; JRDA;
MAICYA; MTCW; SAAS 1; SATA 2,
30, 73

Ainsworth, William Harrison
1805-1882 .... NCLC 13
See also DLB 21; SATA 24

Aitmatov, Chingiz (Torekulovich)
1928- .... CLC 71
See also CA 103; CANR 38; MTCW;
SATA 56

Akers, Floyd
See Baum, L(yman) Frank

Akhmadulina, Bella Akhatovna
1937- .... CLC 53; DAM POET
See also CA 65-68

Akhmatova, Anna
1888-1966 .... CLC 11, 25, 64;
DAM POET; PC 2
See also CA 19-20; 25-28R; CANR 35;
CAP 1; MTCW

Aksakov, Sergei Timofeyvich
1791-1859 .... NCLC 2

Aksenov, Vassily
See Aksyonov, Vassily (Pavlovich)

Aksyonov, Vassily (Pavlovich)
1932- .... CLC 22, 37
See also CA 53-56; CANR 12, 48

Akutagawa, Ryunosuke
1892-1927 .... TCLC 16
See also CA 117; 154

Alain 1868-1951 .... TCLC 41

Alain-Fournier.................... TCLC 6
See also Fournier, Henri Alban
See also DLB 65

Alarcon, Pedro Antonio de
1833-1891 .... NCLC 1

Alas (y Urena), Leopoldo (Enrique Garcia)
1852-1901 .... TCLC 29
See also CA 113; 131; HW

Albee, Edward (Franklin III)
1928- ...... CLC 1, 2, 3, 5, 9, 11, 13, 25,
53, 86; DA; DAB; DAC; DAM DRAM,
MST; WLC
See also AITN 1; CA 5-8R; CABS 3;
CANR 8, 54; CDALB 1941-1968; DLB 7;
INT CANR-8; MTCW

Alberti, Rafael 1902- .... CLC 7
See also CA 85-88; DLB 108

Albert the Great 1200(?)-1280.... CMLC 16
See also DLB 115

Alcala-Galiano, Juan Valera y
  See Valera y Alcala-Galiano, Juan

Alcott, Amos Bronson   1799-1888 .. **NCLC 1**
  See also DLB 1

Alcott, Louisa May
    1832-1888 ..... **NCLC 6, 58; DA; DAB;**
            DAC; DAM MST, NOV; WLC
  See also CDALB 1865-1917; CLR 1, 38;
    DLB 1, 42, 79; DLBD 14; JRDA;
    MAICYA; YABC 1

Aldanov, M. A.
  See Aldanov, Mark (Alexandrovich)

Aldanov, Mark (Alexandrovich)
    1886(?)-1957 .... **TCLC 23**
  See also CA 118

Aldington, Richard   1892-1962...... **CLC 49**
  See also CA 85-88; CANR 45; DLB 20, 36,
    100, 149

Aldiss, Brian W(ilson)
    1925- ...... **CLC 5, 14, 40; DAM NOV**
  See also CA 5-8R; CAAS 2; CANR 5, 28;
    DLB 14; MTCW; SATA 34

Alegria, Claribel
    1924- .... **CLC 75; DAM MULT**
  See also CA 131; CAAS 15; DLB 145; HW

Alegria, Fernando   1918-........... **CLC 57**
  See also CA 9-12R; CANR 5, 32; HW

Aleichem, Sholom .... **TCLC 1, 35**
  See also Rabinovitch, Sholem

Aleixandre, Vicente
    1898-1984 .... **CLC 9, 36; DAM POET;**
                              PC 15
  See also CA 85-88; 114; CANR 26;
    DLB 108; HW; MTCW

Alepoudelis, Odysseus
  See Elytis, Odysseus

Aleshkovsky, Joseph   1929-
  See Aleshkovsky, Yuz
  See also CA 121; 128

Aleshkovsky, Yuz .... **CLC 44**
  See also Aleshkovsky, Joseph

Alexander, Lloyd (Chudley)   1924- .. **CLC 35**
  See also AAYA 1; CA 1-4R; CANR 1, 24,
    38, 55; CLR 1, 5; DLB 52; JRDA;
    MAICYA; MTCW; SAAS 19; SATA 3,
    49, 81

Alexie, Sherman (Joseph, Jr.)
    1966- .... **CLC 96; DAM MULT**
  See also CA 138; NNAL

Alfau, Felipe   1902-.............. **CLC 66**
  See also CA 137

Alger, Horatio, Jr.   1832-1899 ..... **NCLC 8**
  See also DLB 42; SATA 16

Algren, Nelson   1909-1981 .... **CLC 4, 10, 33**
  See also CA 13-16R; 103; CANR 20;
    CDALB 1941-1968; DLB 9; DLBY 81,
    82; MTCW

Ali, Ahmed   1910-................ **CLC 69**
  See also CA 25-28R; CANR 15, 34

Alighieri, Dante   1265-1321 .... **CMLC 3, 18**

Allan, John B.
  See Westlake, Donald E(dwin)

Allen, Edward   1948-............. **CLC 59**

Allen, Paula Gunn
    1939- .... **CLC 84; DAM MULT**
  See also CA 112; 143; NNAL

Allen, Roland
  See Ayckbourn, Alan

Allen, Sarah A.
  See Hopkins, Pauline Elizabeth

Allen, Woody
    1935- .... **CLC 16, 52; DAM POP**
  See also AAYA 10; CA 33-36R; CANR 27,
    38; DLB 44; MTCW

Allende, Isabel
    1942- .... **CLC 39, 57, 97; DAM MULT,**
                              NOV; HLC
  See also AAYA 18; CA 125; 130;
    CANR 51; DLB 145; HW; INT 130;
    MTCW

Alleyn, Ellen
  See Rossetti, Christina (Georgina)

Allingham, Margery (Louise)
    1904-1966 .... **CLC 19**
  See also CA 5-8R; 25-28R; CANR 4;
    DLB 77; MTCW

Allingham, William   1824-1889 ... **NCLC 25**
  See also DLB 35

Allison, Dorothy E.   1949- .... **CLC 78**
  See also CA 140

Allston, Washington   1779-1843.... **NCLC 2**
  See also DLB 1

Almedingen, E. M. .... **CLC 12**
  See also Almedingen, Martha Edith von
  See also SATA 3

Almedingen, Martha Edith von   1898-1971
  See Almedingen, E. M.
  See also CA 1-4R; CANR 1

Almqvist, Carl Jonas Love
    1793-1866 .... **NCLC 42**

Alonso, Damaso   1898-1990 .... **CLC 14**
  See also CA 110; 131; 130; DLB 108; HW

Alov
  See Gogol, Nikolai (Vasilyevich)

Alta   1942-...................... **CLC 19**
  See also CA 57-60

Alter, Robert B(ernard)   1935-...... **CLC 34**
  See also CA 49-52; CANR 1, 47

Alther, Lisa   1944-.............. **CLC 7, 41**
  See also CA 65-68; CANR 12, 30, 51;
    MTCW

Altman, Robert   1925-............. **CLC 16**
  See also CA 73-76; CANR 43

Alvarez, A(lfred)   1929-.......... **CLC 5, 13**
  See also CA 1-4R; CANR 3, 33; DLB 14,
    40

Alvarez, Alejandro Rodriguez   1903-1965
  See Casona, Alejandro
  See also CA 131; 93-96; HW

Alvarez, Julia   1950-.............. **CLC 93**
  See also CA 147

Alvaro, Corrado   1896-1956 .... **TCLC 60**

Amado, Jorge
    1912- .... **CLC 13, 40; DAM MULT,**
                              NOV; HLC
  See also CA 77-80; CANR 35; DLB 113;
    MTCW

Ambler, Eric   1909-........... **CLC 4, 6, 9**
  See also CA 9-12R; CANR 7, 38; DLB 77;
    MTCW

Amichai, Yehuda   1924- ...... **CLC 9, 22, 57**
  See also CA 85-88; CANR 46; MTCW

Amiel, Henri Frederic   1821-1881 .. **NCLC 4**

Amis, Kingsley (William)
    1922-1995 ..... **CLC 1, 2, 3, 5, 8, 13, 40,**
          44; DA; DAB; DAC; DAM MST, NOV
  See also AITN 2; CA 9-12R; 150; CANR 8,
    28, 54; CDBLB 1945-1960; DLB 15, 27,
    100, 139; INT CANR-8; MTCW

Amis, Martin (Louis)
    1949-.................... **CLC 4, 9, 38, 62**
  See also BEST 90:3; CA 65-68; CANR 8,
    27, 54; DLB 14; INT CANR-27

Ammons, A(rchie) R(andolph)
    1926-......... **CLC 2, 3, 5, 8, 9, 25, 57;**
                         DAM POET; PC 16
  See also AITN 1; CA 9-12R; CANR 6, 36,
    51; DLB 5, 165; MTCW

Amo, Tauraatua i
  See Adams, Henry (Brooks)

Anand, Mulk Raj
    1905- .... **CLC 23, 93; DAM NOV**
  See also CA 65-68; CANR 32; MTCW

Anatol
  See Schnitzler, Arthur

Anaya, Rudolfo A(lfonso)
    1937- .... **CLC 23; DAM MULT, NOV;**
                              HLC
  See also CA 45-48; CAAS 4; CANR 1, 32,
    51; DLB 82; HW 1; MTCW

Andersen, Hans Christian
    1805-1875 .... **NCLC 7; DA; DAB;**
          DAC; DAM MST, POP; SSC 6; WLC
  See also CLR 6; MAICYA; YABC 1

Anderson, C. Farley
  See Mencken, H(enry) L(ouis); Nathan,
    George Jean

Anderson, Jessica (Margaret) Queale
    .... **CLC 37**
  See also CA 9-12R; CANR 4

Anderson, Jon (Victor)
    1940-............. **CLC 9; DAM POET**
  See also CA 25-28R; CANR 20

Anderson, Lindsay (Gordon)
    1923-1994 .... **CLC 20**
  See also CA 125; 128; 146

Anderson, Maxwell
    1888-1959 ...... **TCLC 2; DAM DRAM**
  See also CA 105; 152; DLB 7

Anderson, Poul (William)   1926- .... **CLC 15**
  See also AAYA 5; CA 1-4R; CAAS 2;
    CANR 2, 15, 34; DLB 8; INT CANR-15;
    MTCW; SATA 90; SATA-Brief 39

Anderson, Robert (Woodruff)
    1917- .... **CLC 23; DAM DRAM**
  See also AITN 1; CA 21-24R; CANR 32;
    DLB 7

Anderson, Sherwood
    1876-1941 .... **TCLC 1, 10, 24; DA;**
      DAB; DAC; DAM MST, NOV; SSC 1;
                              WLC
  See also CA 104; 121; CDALB 1917-1929;
    DLB 4, 9, 86; DLBD 1; MTCW

Andier, Pierre
See Desnos, Robert

Andouard
See Giraudoux, (Hippolyte) Jean

Andrade, Carlos Drummond de ...... **CLC 18**
See also Drummond de Andrade, Carlos

Andrade, Mario de 1893-1945..... **TCLC 43**

Andreae, Johann V(alentin)
1586-1654 .... **LC 32**
See also DLB 164

Andreas-Salome, Lou 1861-1937... **TCLC 56**
See also DLB 66

Andrewes, Lancelot 1555-1626 .... **LC 5**
See also DLB 151, 172

Andrews, Cicily Fairfield
See West, Rebecca

Andrews, Elton V.
See Pohl, Frederik

Andreyev, Leonid (Nikolaevich)
1871-1919 .... **TCLC 3**
See also CA 104

Andric, Ivo 1892-1975 .... **CLC 8**
See also CA 81-84; 57-60; CANR 43;
DLB 147; MTCW

Angelique, Pierre
See Bataille, Georges

Angell, Roger 1920- .... **CLC 26**
See also CA 57-60; CANR 13, 44; DLB 171

Angelou, Maya
1928- .... **CLC 12, 35, 64, 77; BLC; DA;
DAB; DAC; DAM MST, MULT, POET,
POP**
See also AAYA 7; BW 2; CA 65-68;
CANR 19, 42; DLB 38; MTCW;
SATA 49

Annensky, Innokenty Fyodorovich
1856-1909 .... **TCLC 14**
See also CA 110; 155

Annunzio, Gabriele d'
See D'Annunzio, Gabriele

Anon, Charles Robert
See Pessoa, Fernando (Antonio Nogueira)

Anouilh, Jean (Marie Lucien Pierre)
1910-1987 ...... **CLC 1, 3, 8, 13, 40, 50;
DAM DRAM**
See also CA 17-20R; 123; CANR 32;
MTCW

Anthony, Florence
See Ai

Anthony, John
See Ciardi, John (Anthony)

Anthony, Peter
See Shaffer, Anthony (Joshua); Shaffer,
Peter (Levin)

Anthony, Piers 1934-.. **CLC 35; DAM POP**
See also AAYA 11; CA 21-24R; CANR 28;
DLB 8; MTCW; SAAS 22; SATA 84

Antoine, Marc
See Proust, (Valentin-Louis-George-Eugene-)
Marcel

Antoninus, Brother
See Everson, William (Oliver)

Antonioni, Michelangelo 1912-..... **CLC 20**
See also CA 73-76; CANR 45

Antschel, Paul 1920-1970
See Celan, Paul
See also CA 85-88; CANR 33; MTCW

Anwar, Chairil 1922-1949 .... **TCLC 22**
See also CA 121

Apollinaire, Guillaume
1880-1918 .... **TCLC 3, 8, 51;
DAM POET; PC 7**
See also Kostrowitzki, Wilhelm Apollinaris
de
See also CA 152

Appelfeld, Aharon 1932- ...... **CLC 23, 47**
See also CA 112; 133

Apple, Max (Isaac) 1941-....... **CLC 9, 33**
See also CA 81-84; CANR 19, 54; DLB 130

Appleman, Philip (Dean) 1926-..... **CLC 51**
See also CA 13-16R; CAAS 18; CANR 6,
29

Appleton, Lawrence
See Lovecraft, H(oward) P(hillips)

Apteryx
See Eliot, T(homas) S(tearns)

Apuleius, (Lucius Madaurensis)
125(?)-175(?) .... **CMLC 1**

Aquin, Hubert 1929-1977......... **CLC 15**
See also CA 105; DLB 53

Aragon, Louis
1897-1982 ..... **CLC 3, 22; DAM NOV,
POET**
See also CA 69-72; 108; CANR 28;
DLB 72; MTCW

Arany, Janos 1817-1882........ **NCLC 34**

Arbuthnot, John 1667-1735.......... **LC 1**
See also DLB 101

Archer, Herbert Winslow
See Mencken, H(enry) L(ouis)

Archer, Jeffrey (Howard)
1940- .... **CLC 28; DAM POP**
See also AAYA 16; BEST 89:3; CA 77-80;
CANR 22, 52; INT CANR-22

Archer, Jules 1915- .... **CLC 12**
See also CA 9-12R; CANR 6; SAAS 5;
SATA 4, 85

Archer, Lee
See Ellison, Harlan (Jay)

Arden, John
1930- ..... **CLC 6, 13, 15; DAM DRAM**
See also CA 13-16R; CAAS 4; CANR 31;
DLB 13; MTCW

Arenas, Reinaldo
1943-1990 ...... **CLC 41; DAM MULT;
HLC**
See also CA 124; 128; 133; DLB 145; HW

Arendt, Hannah 1906-1975 ..... **CLC 66, 98**
See also CA 17-20R; 61-64; CANR 26;
MTCW

Aretino, Pietro 1492-1556 .... **LC 12**

Arghezi, Tudor.................... **CLC 80**
See also Theodorescu, Ion N.

Arguedas, Jose Maria
1911-1969 .... **CLC 10, 18**
See also CA 89-92; DLB 113; HW

Argueta, Manlio 1936-............ **CLC 31**
See also CA 131; DLB 145; HW

Ariosto, Ludovico 1474-1533........ **LC 6**

Aristides
See Epstein, Joseph

Aristophanes
450B.C.-385B.C. .... **CMLC 4; DA;
DAB; DAC; DAM DRAM, MST; DC 2**

Arlt, Roberto (Godofredo Christophersen)
1900-1942 ..... **TCLC 29; DAM MULT;
HLC**
See also CA 123; 131; HW

Armah, Ayi Kwei
1939- .... **CLC 5, 33; BLC;
DAM MULT, POET**
See also BW 1; CA 61-64; CANR 21;
DLB 117; MTCW

Armatrading, Joan 1950-.......... **CLC 17**
See also CA 114

Arnette, Robert
See Silverberg, Robert

**Arnim, Achim von (Ludwig Joachim von
Arnim)** 1781-1831 .... **NCLC 5**
See also DLB 90

Arnim, Bettina von 1785-1859.... **NCLC 38**
See also DLB 90

Arnold, Matthew
1822-1888 ..... **NCLC 6, 29; DA; DAB;
DAC; DAM MST, POET; PC 5; WLC**
See also CDBLB 1832-1890; DLB 32, 57

Arnold, Thomas 1795-1842 ...... **NCLC 18**
See also DLB 55

Arnow, Harriette (Louisa) Simpson
1908-1986 .... **CLC 2, 7, 18**
See also CA 9-12R; 118; CANR 14; DLB 6;
MTCW; SATA 42; SATA-Obit 47

Arp, Hans
See Arp, Jean

Arp, Jean 1887-1966............... **CLC 5**
See also CA 81-84; 25-28R; CANR 42

Arrabal
See Arrabal, Fernando

Arrabal, Fernando 1932- ... **CLC 2, 9, 18, 58**
See also CA 9-12R; CANR 15

Arrick, Fran..................... **CLC 30**
See also Gaberman, Judie Angell

Artaud, Antonin (Marie Joseph)
1896-1948 ... **TCLC 3, 36; DAM DRAM**
See also CA 104; 149

Arthur, Ruth M(abel) 1905-1979.... **CLC 12**
See also CA 9-12R; 85-88; CANR 4;
SATA 7, 26

Artsybashev, Mikhail (Petrovich)
1878-1927 .... **TCLC 31**

Arundel, Honor (Morfydd)
1919-1973 .... **CLC 17**
See also CA 21-22; 41-44R; CAP 2;
CLR 35; SATA 4; SATA-Obit 24

Arzner, Dorothy 1897-1979....... **CLC 98**

Asch, Sholem 1880-1957 .... **TCLC 3**
See also CA 105

Ash, Shalom
See Asch, Sholem

Ashbery, John (Lawrence)
1927- ...... **CLC 2, 3, 4, 6, 9, 13, 15, 25, 41, 77; DAM POET**
See also CA 5-8R; CANR 9, 37; DLB 5, 165; DLBY 81; INT CANR-9; MTCW

Ashdown, Clifford
See Freeman, R(ichard) Austin

Ashe, Gordon
See Creasey, John

Ashton-Warner, Sylvia (Constance)
1908-1984 .... **CLC 19**
See also CA 69-72; 112; CANR 29; MTCW

Asimov, Isaac
1920-1992 ...... **CLC 1, 3, 9, 19, 26, 76, 92; DAM POP**
See also AAYA 13; BEST 90:2; CA 1-4R; 137; CANR 2, 19, 36; CLR 12; DLB 8; DLBY 92; INT CANR-19; JRDA; MAICYA; MTCW; SATA 1, 26, 74

Assis, Joaquim Maria Machado de
See Machado de Assis, Joaquim Maria

Astley, Thea (Beatrice May)
1925- .... **CLC 41**
See also CA 65-68; CANR 11, 43

Aston, James
See White, T(erence) H(anbury)

Asturias, Miguel Angel
1899-1974 .... **CLC 3, 8, 13; DAM MULT, NOV; HLC**
See also CA 25-28; 49-52; CANR 32; CAP 2; DLB 113; HW; MTCW

Atares, Carlos Saura
See Saura (Atares), Carlos

Atheling, William
See Pound, Ezra (Weston Loomis)

Atheling, William, Jr.
See Blish, James (Benjamin)

Atherton, Gertrude (Franklin Horn)
1857-1948 .... **TCLC 2**
See also CA 104; 155; DLB 9, 78

Atherton, Lucius
See Masters, Edgar Lee

Atkins, Jack
See Harris, Mark

Attaway, William (Alexander)
1911-1986 .... **CLC 92; BLC; DAM MULT**
See also BW 2; CA 143; DLB 76

Atticus
See Fleming, Ian (Lancaster)

Atwood, Margaret (Eleanor)
1939- ..... **CLC 2, 3, 4, 8, 13, 15, 25, 44, 84; DA; DAB; DAC; DAM MST, NOV, POET; PC 8; SSC 2; WLC**
See also AAYA 12; BEST 89:2; CA 49-52; CANR 3, 24, 33; DLB 53; INT CANR-24; MTCW; SATA 50

Aubigny, Pierre d'
See Mencken, H(enry) L(ouis)

Aubin, Penelope 1685-1731(?) .... **LC 9**
See also DLB 39

Auchincloss, Louis (Stanton)
1917- .... **CLC 4, 6, 9, 18, 45; DAM NOV; SSC 22**
See also CA 1-4R; CANR 6, 29, 55; DLB 2; DLBY 80; INT CANR-29; MTCW

Auden, W(ystan) H(ugh)
1907-1973 ..... **CLC 1, 2, 3, 4, 6, 9, 11, 14, 43; DA; DAB; DAC; DAM DRAM, MST, POET; PC 1; WLC**
See also AAYA 18; CA 9-12R; 45-48; CANR 5; CDBLB 1914-1945; DLB 10, 20; MTCW

Audiberti, Jacques
1900-1965 ...... **CLC 38; DAM DRAM**
See also CA 25-28R

Audubon, John James
1785-1851 .... **NCLC 47**

Auel, Jean M(arie)
1936- .... **CLC 31; DAM POP**
See also AAYA 7; BEST 90:4; CA 103; CANR 21; INT CANR-21; SATA 91

Auerbach, Erich 1892-1957 ...... **TCLC 43**
See also CA 118; 155

Augier, Emile 1820-1889 .... **NCLC 31**

August, John
See De Voto, Bernard (Augustine)

Augustine, St. 354-430 ...... **CMLC 6; DAB**

Aurelius
See Bourne, Randolph S(illiman)

Aurobindo, Sri 1872-1950 .... **TCLC 63**

Austen, Jane
1775-1817 ..... **NCLC 1, 13, 19, 33, 51; DA; DAB; DAC; DAM MST, NOV; WLC**
See also AAYA 19; CDBLB 1789-1832; DLB 116

Auster, Paul 1947- .... **CLC 47**
See also CA 69-72; CANR 23, 52

Austin, Frank
See Faust, Frederick (Schiller)

Austin, Mary (Hunter)
1868-1934 .... **TCLC 25**
See also CA 109; DLB 9, 78

Autran Dourado, Waldomiro
See Dourado, (Waldomiro Freitas) Autran

Averroes 1126-1198 .... **CMLC 7**
See also DLB 115

Avicenna 980-1037 .... **CMLC 16**
See also DLB 115

Avison, Margaret
1918- .... **CLC 2, 4, 97; DAC; DAM POET**
See also CA 17-20R; DLB 53; MTCW

Axton, David
See Koontz, Dean R(ay)

Ayckbourn, Alan
1939- ...... **CLC 5, 8, 18, 33, 74; DAB; DAM DRAM**
See also CA 21-24R; CANR 31; DLB 13; MTCW

Aydy, Catherine
See Tennant, Emma (Christina)

Ayme, Marcel (Andre) 1902-1967 ... **CLC 11**
See also CA 89-92; CLR 25; DLB 72; SATA 91

Ayrton, Michael 1921-1975 .... **CLC 7**
See also CA 5-8R; 61-64; CANR 9, 21

Azorin .... **CLC 11**
See also Martinez Ruiz, Jose

Azuela, Mariano
1873-1952 ..... **TCLC 3; DAM MULT; HLC**
See also CA 104; 131; HW; MTCW

Baastad, Babbis Friis
See Friis-Baastad, Babbis Ellinor

Bab
See Gilbert, W(illiam) S(chwenck)

Babbis, Eleanor
See Friis-Baastad, Babbis Ellinor

Babel, Isaac
See Babel, Isaak (Emmanuilovich)

Babel, Isaak (Emmanuilovich)
1894-1941(?) ...... **TCLC 2, 13; SSC 16**
See also CA 104; 155

Babits, Mihaly 1883-1941 .... **TCLC 14**
See also CA 114

Babur 1483-1530 .... **LC 18**

Bacchelli, Riccardo 1891-1985 ..... **CLC 19**
See also CA 29-32R; 117

Bach, Richard (David)
1936- ...... **CLC 14; DAM NOV, POP**
See also AITN 1; BEST 89:2; CA 9-12R; CANR 18; MTCW; SATA 13

Bachman, Richard
See King, Stephen (Edwin)

Bachmann, Ingeborg 1926-1973 ..... **CLC 69**
See also CA 93-96; 45-48; DLB 85

Bacon, Francis 1561-1626 .... **LC 18, 32**
See also CDBLB Before 1660; DLB 151

Bacon, Roger 1214(?)-1292 ...... **CMLC 14**
See also DLB 115

Bacovia, George .... **TCLC 24**
See also Vasiliu, Gheorghe

Badanes, Jerome 1937- .... **CLC 59**

Bagehot, Walter 1826-1877 ...... **NCLC 10**
See also DLB 55

Bagnold, Enid
1889-1981 ...... **CLC 25; DAM DRAM**
See also CA 5-8R; 103; CANR 5, 40; DLB 13, 160; MAICYA; SATA 1, 25

Bagritsky, Eduard 1895-1934 ..... **TCLC 60**

Bagrjana, Elisaveta
See Belcheva, Elisaveta

Bagryana, Elisaveta .... **CLC 10**
See also Belcheva, Elisaveta
See also DLB 147

Bailey, Paul 1937- .... **CLC 45**
See also CA 21-24R; CANR 16; DLB 14

Baillie, Joanna 1762-1851 .... **NCLC 2**
See also DLB 93

Bainbridge, Beryl (Margaret)
1933- .... **CLC 4, 5, 8, 10, 14, 18, 22, 62; DAM NOV**
See also CA 21-24R; CANR 24, 55; DLB 14; MTCW

Baker, Elliott 1922- .... **CLC 8**
See also CA 45-48; CANR 2

Baker, Jean H. .... **TCLC 3, 10**
See also Russell, George William

Baker, Nicholson
1957- .... **CLC 61; DAM POP**
See also CA 135

Baker, Ray Stannard 1870-1946 . . . **TCLC 47**
See also CA 118

Baker, Russell (Wayne) 1925- . . . . . . **CLC 31**
See also BEST 89:4; CA 57-60; CANR 11, 41; MTCW

Bakhtin, M.
See Bakhtin, Mikhail Mikhailovich

Bakhtin, M. M.
See Bakhtin, Mikhail Mikhailovich

Bakhtin, Mikhail
See Bakhtin, Mikhail Mikhailovich

Bakhtin, Mikhail Mikhailovich
1895-1975 . . . . **CLC 83**
See also CA 128; 113

Bakshi, Ralph 1938(?)- . . . . **CLC 26**
See also CA 112; 138

Bakunin, Mikhail (Alexandrovich)
1814-1876 . . . . **NCLC 25, 58**

Baldwin, James (Arthur)
1924-1987 . . . . . . **CLC 1, 2, 3, 4, 5, 8, 13, 15, 17, 42, 50, 67, 90; BLC; DA; DAB; DAC; DAM MST, MULT, NOV, POP; DC 1; SSC 10; WLC**
See also AAYA 4; BW 1; CA 1-4R; 124; CABS 1; CANR 3, 24; CDALB 1941-1968; DLB 2, 7, 33; DLBY 87; MTCW; SATA 9; SATA-Obit 54

Ballard, J(ames) G(raham)
1930- . . . . **CLC 3, 6, 14, 36; DAM NOV, POP; SSC 1**
See also AAYA 3; CA 5-8R; CANR 15, 39; DLB 14; MTCW

Balmont, Konstantin (Dmitriyevich)
1867-1943 . . . . **TCLC 11**
See also CA 109; 155

Balzac, Honore de
1799-1850 . . . . **NCLC 5, 35, 53; DA; DAB; DAC; DAM MST, NOV; SSC 5; WLC**

See also DLB 119

Bambara, Toni Cade
1939-1995 . . . . . . **CLC 19, 88; BLC; DA; DAC; DAM MST, MULT**
See also AAYA 5; BW 2; CA 29-32R; 150; CANR 24, 49; DLB 38; MTCW

Bamdad, A.
See Shamlu, Ahmad

Banat, D. R.
See Bradbury, Ray (Douglas)

Bancroft, Laura
See Baum, L(yman) Frank

Banim, John 1798-1842 . . . . **NCLC 13**
See also DLB 116, 158, 159

Banim, Michael 1796-1874 . . . . . . **NCLC 13**
See also DLB 158, 159

Banjo, The
See Paterson, A(ndrew) B(arton)

Banks, Iain
See Banks, Iain M(enzies)

Banks, Iain M(enzies) 1954- . . . . **CLC 34**
See also CA 123; 128; INT 128

Banks, Lynne Reid . . . . **CLC 23**
See also Reid Banks, Lynne
See also AAYA 6

Banks, Russell 1940- . . . . **CLC 37, 72**
See also CA 65-68; CAAS 15; CANR 19, 52; DLB 130

Banville, John 1945- . . . . **CLC 46**
See also CA 117; 128; DLB 14; INT 128

Banville, Theodore (Faullain) de
1832-1891 . . . . **NCLC 9**

Baraka, Amiri
1934- . . . . **CLC 1, 2, 3, 5, 10, 14, 33; BLC; DA; DAC; DAM MST, MULT, POET, POP; DC 6; PC 4**
See also Jones, LeRoi
See also BW 2; CA 21-24R; CABS 3; CANR 27, 38; CDALB 1941-1968; DLB 5, 7, 16, 38; DLBD 8; MTCW

Barbauld, Anna Laetitia
1743-1825 . . . . **NCLC 50**
See also DLB 107, 109, 142, 158

Barbellion, W. N. P. . . . . **TCLC 24**
See also Cummings, Bruce F(rederick)

Barbera, Jack (Vincent) 1945- . . . . . . **CLC 44**
See also CA 110; CANR 45

Barbey d'Aurevilly, Jules Amedee
1808-1889 . . . . **NCLC 1; SSC 17**
See also DLB 119

Barbusse, Henri 1873-1935 . . . . **TCLC 5**
See also CA 105; 154; DLB 65

Barclay, Bill
See Moorcock, Michael (John)

Barclay, William Ewert
See Moorcock, Michael (John)

Barea, Arturo 1897-1957 . . . . **TCLC 14**
See also CA 111

Barfoot, Joan 1946- . . . . **CLC 18**
See also CA 105

Baring, Maurice 1874-1945 . . . . **TCLC 8**
See also CA 105; DLB 34

Barker, Clive 1952- . . . **CLC 52; DAM POP**
See also AAYA 10; BEST 90:3; CA 121; 129; INT 129; MTCW

Barker, George Granville
1913-1991 . . . . . **CLC 8, 48; DAM POET**
See also CA 9-12R; 135; CANR 7, 38; DLB 20; MTCW

Barker, Harley Granville
See Granville-Barker, Harley
See also DLB 10

Barker, Howard 1946- . . . . **CLC 37**
See also CA 102; DLB 13

Barker, Pat(ricia) 1943- . . . . **CLC 32, 94**
See also CA 117; 122; CANR 50; INT 122

Barlow, Joel 1754-1812 . . . . **NCLC 23**
See also DLB 37

Barnard, Mary (Ethel) 1909- . . . . **CLC 48**
See also CA 21-22; CAP 2

Barnes, Djuna
1892-1982 . . . **CLC 3, 4, 8, 11, 29; SSC 3**
See also CA 9-12R; 107; CANR 16, 55; DLB 4, 9, 45; MTCW

Barnes, Julian (Patrick)
1946- . . . . **CLC 42; DAB**
See also CA 102; CANR 19, 54; DLBY 93

Barnes, Peter 1931- . . . . **CLC 5, 56**
See also CA 65-68; CAAS 12; CANR 33, 34; DLB 13; MTCW

Baroja (y Nessi), Pio
1872-1956 . . . . **TCLC 8; HLC**
See also CA 104

Baron, David
See Pinter, Harold

Baron Corvo
See Rolfe, Frederick (William Serafino Austin Lewis Mary)

Barondess, Sue K(aufman)
1926-1977 . . . . **CLC 8**
See also Kaufman, Sue
See also CA 1-4R; 69-72; CANR 1

Baron de Teive
See Pessoa, Fernando (Antonio Nogueira)

Barres, Maurice 1862-1923 . . . . **TCLC 47**
See also DLB 123

Barreto, Afonso Henrique de Lima
See Lima Barreto, Afonso Henrique de

Barrett, (Roger) Syd 1946- . . . . **CLC 35**

Barrett, William (Christopher)
1913-1992 . . . . **CLC 27**
See also CA 13-16R; 139; CANR 11; INT CANR-11

Barrie, J(ames) M(atthew)
1860-1937 . . . . **TCLC 2; DAB; DAM DRAM**
See also CA 104; 136; CDBLB 1890-1914; CLR 16; DLB 10, 141, 156; MAICYA; YABC 1

Barrington, Michael
See Moorcock, Michael (John)

Barrol, Grady
See Bograd, Larry

Barry, Mike
See Malzberg, Barry N(athaniel)

Barry, Philip 1896-1949 . . . . **TCLC 11**
See also CA 109; DLB 7

Bart, Andre Schwarz
See Schwarz-Bart, Andre

Barth, John (Simmons)
1930- . . . . . . **CLC 1, 2, 3, 5, 7, 9, 10, 14, 27, 51, 89; DAM NOV; SSC 10**
See also AITN 1, 2; CA 1-4R; CABS 1; CANR 5, 23, 49; DLB 2; MTCW

Barthelme, Donald
1931-1989 . . . . . . **CLC 1, 2, 3, 5, 6, 8, 13, 23, 46, 59; DAM NOV; SSC 2**
See also CA 21-24R; 129; CANR 20; DLB 2; DLBY 80, 89; MTCW; SATA 7; SATA-Obit 62

Barthelme, Frederick 1943- . . . . **CLC 36**
See also CA 114; 122; DLBY 85; INT 122

Barthes, Roland (Gerard)
1915-1980 . . . . **CLC 24, 83**
See also CA 130; 97-100; MTCW

Barzun, Jacques (Martin) 1907- . . . . **CLC 51**
See also CA 61-64; CANR 22

Bashevis, Isaac
See Singer, Isaac Bashevis

Bashkirtseff, Marie 1859-1884 . . . **NCLC 27**

Basho
See Matsuo Basho

Bass, Kingsley B., Jr.
See Bullins, Ed

Bass, Rick 1958- . . . . **CLC 79**
See also CA 126; CANR 53

Bassani, Giorgio 1916- . . . . **CLC 9**
See also CA 65-68; CANR 33; DLB 128;
MTCW

Bastos, Augusto (Antonio) Roa
See Roa Bastos, Augusto (Antonio)

Bataille, Georges 1897-1962 . . . . **CLC 29**
See also CA 101; 89-92

Bates, H(erbert) E(rnest)
1905-1974 . . . . **CLC 46; DAB;**
DAM POP; SSC 10
See also CA 93-96; 45-48; CANR 34;
DLB 162; MTCW

Bauchart
See Camus, Albert

Baudelaire, Charles
1821-1867 . . . . **NCLC 6, 29, 55; DA;**
DAB; DAC; DAM MST, POET; PC 1;
SSC 18; WLC

Baudrillard, Jean 1929- . . . . **CLC 60**

Baum, L(yman) Frank 1856-1919 . . . **TCLC 7**
See also CA 108; 133; CLR 15; DLB 22;
JRDA; MAICYA; MTCW; SATA 18

Baum, Louis F.
See Baum, L(yman) Frank

Baumbach, Jonathan 1933- . . . . . . **CLC 6, 23**
See also CA 13-16R; CAAS 5; CANR 12;
DLBY 80; INT CANR-12; MTCW

Bausch, Richard (Carl) 1945- . . . . . . **CLC 51**
See also CA 101; CAAS 14; CANR 43;
DLB 130

Baxter, Charles
1947- . . . . **CLC 45, 78; DAM POP**
See also CA 57-60; CANR 40; DLB 130

Baxter, George Owen
See Faust, Frederick (Schiller)

Baxter, James K(eir) 1926-1972 . . . . **CLC 14**
See also CA 77-80

Baxter, John
See Hunt, E(verette) Howard, (Jr.)

Bayer, Sylvia
See Glassco, John

Baynton, Barbara 1857-1929 . . . . . . **TCLC 57**

Beagle, Peter S(oyer) 1939- . . . . **CLC 7**
See also CA 9-12R; CANR 4, 51;
DLBY 80; INT CANR-4; SATA 60

Bean, Normal
See Burroughs, Edgar Rice

Beard, Charles A(ustin)
1874-1948 . . . . **TCLC 15**
See also CA 115; DLB 17; SATA 18

Beardsley, Aubrey 1872-1898 . . . . . **NCLC 6**

Beattie, Ann
1947- . . . . **CLC 8, 13, 18, 40, 63;**
DAM NOV, POP; SSC 11
See also BEST 90:2; CA 81-84; CANR 53;
DLBY 82; MTCW

Beattie, James 1735-1803 . . . . **NCLC 25**
See also DLB 109

Beauchamp, Kathleen Mansfield 1888-1923
See Mansfield, Katherine
See also CA 104; 134; DA; DAC;
DAM MST

Beaumarchais, Pierre-Augustin Caron de
1732-1799 . . . . **DC 4**
See also DAM DRAM

Beaumont, Francis
1584(?)-1616 . . . . **LC 33; DC 6**
See also CDBLB Before 1660; DLB 58, 121

Beauvoir, Simone (Lucie Ernestine Marie
Bertrand) de
1908-1986 . . . . **CLC 1, 2, 4, 8, 14, 31, 44,**
50, 71; DA; DAB; DAC; DAM MST,
NOV; WLC
See also CA 9-12R; 118; CANR 28;
DLB 72; DLBY 86; MTCW

Becker, Carl 1873-1945 . . . . **TCLC 63:**
See also DLB 17

Becker, Jurek 1937- . . . . **CLC 7, 19**
See also CA 85-88; DLB 75

Becker, Walter 1950- . . . . **CLC 26**

Beckett, Samuel (Barclay)
1906-1989 . . . . . **CLC 1, 2, 3, 4, 6, 9, 10,**
11, 14, 18, 29, 57, 59, 83; DA; DAB;
DAC; DAM DRAM, MST, NOV;
SSC 16; WLC
See also CA 5-8R; 130; CANR 33;
CDBLB 1945-1960; DLB 13, 15;
DLBY 90; MTCW

Beckford, William 1760-1844 . . . . **NCLC 16**
See also DLB 39

Beckman, Gunnel 1910- . . . . **CLC 26**
See also CA 33-36R; CANR 15; CLR 25;
MAICYA; SAAS 9; SATA 6

Becque, Henri 1837-1899 . . . . **NCLC 3**

Beddoes, Thomas Lovell
1803-1849 . . . . **NCLC 3**
See also DLB 96

Bede c. 673-735 . . . . **CMLC 20**
See also DLB 146

Bedford, Donald F.
See Fearing, Kenneth (Flexner)

Beecher, Catharine Esther
1800-1878 . . . . **NCLC 30**
See also DLB 1

Beecher, John 1904-1980 . . . . **CLC 6**
See also AITN 1; CA 5-8R; 105; CANR 8

Beer, Johann 1655-1700 . . . . **LC 5**
See also DLB 168

Beer, Patricia 1924- . . . . **CLC 58**
See also CA 61-64; CANR 13, 46; DLB 40

Beerbohm, Max
See Beerbohm, (Henry) Max(imilian)

Beerbohm, (Henry) Max(imilian)
1872-1956 . . . . **TCLC 1, 24**
See also CA 104; 154; DLB 34, 100

Beer-Hofmann, Richard
1866-1945 . . . . **TCLC 60**
See also DLB 81

Begiebing, Robert J(ohn) 1946- . . . . . **CLC 70**
See also CA 122; CANR 40

Behan, Brendan
1923-1964 . . . . **CLC 1, 8, 11, 15, 79;**
DAM DRAM
See also CA 73-76; CANR 33;
CDBLB 1945-1960; DLB 13; MTCW

Behn, Aphra
1640(?)-1689 . . . . . . **LC 1, 30; DA; DAB;**
DAC; DAM DRAM, MST, NOV,
POET; DC 4; PC 13; WLC
See also DLB 39, 80, 131

Behrman, S(amuel) N(athaniel)
1893-1973 . . . . **CLC 40**
See also CA 13-16; 45-48; CAP 1; DLB 7,
44

Belasco, David 1853-1931 . . . . **TCLC 3**
See also CA 104; DLB 7

Belcheva, Elisaveta 1893- . . . . **CLC 10**
See also Bagryana, Elisaveta

Beldone, Phil "Cheech"
See Ellison, Harlan (Jay)

Beleno
See Azuela, Mariano

Belinski, Vissarion Grigoryevich
1811-1848 . . . . **NCLC 5**

Belitt, Ben 1911- . . . . **CLC 22**
See also CA 13-16R; CAAS 4; CANR 7;
DLB 5

Bell, Gertrude 1868-1926 . . . . **TCLC 67**
See also DLB 174

Bell, James Madison
1826-1902 . . . . **TCLC 43; BLC;**
DAM MULT
See also BW 1; CA 122; 124; DLB 50

Bell, Madison Smartt 1957- . . . . **CLC 41**
See also CA 111; CANR 28, 54

Bell, Marvin (Hartley)
1937- . . . . **CLC 8, 31; DAM POET**
See also CA 21-24R; CAAS 14; DLB 5;
MTCW

Bell, W. L. D.
See Mencken, H(enry) L(ouis)

Bellamy, Atwood C.
See Mencken, H(enry) L(ouis)

Bellamy, Edward 1850-1898 . . . . . . **NCLC 4**
See also DLB 12

Bellin, Edward J.
See Kuttner, Henry

Belloc, (Joseph) Hilaire (Pierre Sebastien
Rene Swanton)
1870-1953 . . . **TCLC 7, 18; DAM POET**
See also CA 106; 152; DLB 19, 100, 141,
174; YABC 1

Belloc, Joseph Peter Rene Hilaire
See Belloc, (Joseph) Hilaire (Pierre Sebastien
Rene Swanton)

Belloc, Joseph Pierre Hilaire
See Belloc, (Joseph) Hilaire (Pierre Sebastien
Rene Swanton)

Belloc, M. A.
See Lowndes, Marie Adelaide (Belloc)

Bellow, Saul
1915- . . . . . . **CLC 1, 2, 3, 6, 8, 10, 13, 15,**
25, 33, 34, 63, 79; DA; DAB; DAC;
DAM MST, NOV, POP; SSC 14; WLC
See also AITN 2; BEST 89:3; CA 5-8R;
CABS 1; CANR 29, 53;
CDALB 1941-1968; DLB 2, 28; DLBD 3;
DLBY 82; MTCW

Belser, Reimond Karel Maria de 1929-
See Ruyslinck, Ward
See also CA 152

Bely, Andrey . . . . **TCLC 7; PC 11**
See also Bugayev, Boris Nikolayevich

Benary, Margot
See Benary-Isbert, Margot

Benary-Isbert, Margot 1889-1979 . . . **CLC 12**
See also CA 5-8R; 89-92; CANR 4;
CLR 12; MAICYA; SATA 2;
SATA-Obit 21

Benavente (y Martinez), Jacinto
1866-1954 . . . . . **TCLC 3; DAM DRAM,**
MULT
See also CA 106; 131; HW; MTCW

Benchley, Peter (Bradford)
1940- . . . . . **CLC 4, 8; DAM NOV, POP**
See also AAYA 14; AITN 2; CA 17-20R;
CANR 12, 35; MTCW; SATA 3, 89

Benchley, Robert (Charles)
1889-1945 . . . . **TCLC 1, 55**
See also CA 105; 153; DLB 11

Benda, Julien 1867-1956 . . . . **TCLC 60**
See also CA 120; 154

Benedict, Ruth 1887-1948 . . . . **TCLC 60**

Benedikt, Michael 1935- . . . . **CLC 4, 14**
See also CA 13-16R; CANR 7; DLB 5

Benet, Juan 1927- . . . . **CLC 28**
See also CA 143

Benet, Stephen Vincent
1898-1943 . . . . . . **TCLC 7; DAM POET;**
SSC 10
See also CA 104; 152; DLB 4, 48, 102;
YABC 1

Benet, William Rose
1886-1950 . . . . . . **TCLC 28; DAM POET**
See also CA 118; 152; DLB 45

Benford, Gregory (Albert) 1941- . . . . **CLC 52**
See also CA 69-72; CANR 12, 24, 49;
DLBY 82

Bengtsson, Frans (Gunnar)
1894-1954 . . . . **TCLC 48**

Benjamin, David
See Slavitt, David R(ytman)

Benjamin, Lois
See Gould, Lois

Benjamin, Walter 1892-1940 . . . . . . **TCLC 39**

Benn, Gottfried 1886-1956 . . . . **TCLC 3**
See also CA 106; 153; DLB 56

Bennett, Alan
1934- . . . **CLC 45, 77; DAB; DAM MST**
See also CA 103; CANR 35, 55; MTCW

Bennett, (Enoch) Arnold
1867-1931 . . . . **TCLC 5, 20**
See also CA 106; 155; CDBLB 1890-1914;
DLB 10, 34, 98, 135

Bennett, Elizabeth
See Mitchell, Margaret (Munnerlyn)

Bennett, George Harold 1930-
See Bennett, Hal
See also BW 1; CA 97-100

Bennett, Hal . . . . **CLC 5**
See also Bennett, George Harold
See also DLB 33

Bennett, Jay 1912- . . . . **CLC 35**
See also AAYA 10; CA 69-72; CANR 11,
42; JRDA; SAAS 4; SATA 41, 87;
SATA-Brief 27

Bennett, Louise (Simone)
1919- . . . . . **CLC 28; BLC; DAM MULT**
See also BW 2; CA 151; DLB 117

Benson, E(dward) F(rederic)
1867-1940 . . . . **TCLC 27**
See also CA 114; DLB 135, 153

Benson, Jackson J. 1930- . . . . **CLC 34**
See also CA 25-28R; DLB 111

Benson, Sally 1900-1972 . . . . **CLC 17**
See also CA 19-20; 37-40R; CAP 1;
SATA 1, 35; SATA-Obit 27

Benson, Stella 1892-1933 . . . . **TCLC 17**
See also CA 117; 155; DLB 36, 162

Bentham, Jeremy 1748-1832 . . . . . **NCLC 38**
See also DLB 107, 158

Bentley, E(dmund) C(lerihew)
1875-1956 . . . . **TCLC 12**
See also CA 108; DLB 70

Bentley, Eric (Russell) 1916- . . . . . . **CLC 24**
See also CA 5-8R; CANR 6; INT CANR-6

Beranger, Pierre Jean de
1780-1857 . . . . **NCLC 34**

Berdyaev, Nicolas
See Berdyaev, Nikolai (Aleksandrovich)

Berdyaev, Nikolai (Aleksandrovich)
1874-1948 . . . . **TCLC 67**
See also CA 120

Berendt, John (Lawrence) 1939- . . . . **CLC 86**
See also CA 146

Berger, Colonel
See Malraux, (Georges-)Andre

Berger, John (Peter) 1926- . . . . . . **CLC 2, 19**
See also CA 81-84; CANR 51; DLB 14

Berger, Melvin H. 1927- . . . . **CLC 12**
See also CA 5-8R; CANR 4; CLR 32;
SAAS 2; SATA 5, 88

Berger, Thomas (Louis)
1924- . . . . **CLC 3, 5, 8, 11, 18, 38;**
DAM NOV
See also CA 1-4R; CANR 5, 28, 51; DLB 2;
DLBY 80; INT CANR-28; MTCW

Bergman, (Ernst) Ingmar
1918- . . . . **CLC 16, 72**
See also CA 81-84; CANR 33

Bergson, Henri 1859-1941 . . . . **TCLC 32**

Bergstein, Eleanor 1938- . . . . **CLC 4**
See also CA 53-56; CANR 5

Berkoff, Steven 1937- . . . . **CLC 56**
See also CA 104

Bermant, Chaim (Icyk) 1929- . . . . . . **CLC 40**
See also CA 57-60; CANR 6, 31

Bern, Victoria
See Fisher, M(ary) F(rances) K(ennedy)

Bernanos, (Paul Louis) Georges
1888-1948 . . . . **TCLC 3**
See also CA 104; 130; DLB 72

Bernard, April 1956- . . . . **CLC 59**
See also CA 131

Berne, Victoria
See Fisher, M(ary) F(rances) K(ennedy)

Bernhard, Thomas
1931-1989 . . . . **CLC 3, 32, 61**
See also CA 85-88; 127; CANR 32;
DLB 85, 124; MTCW

Berriault, Gina 1926- . . . . **CLC 54**
See also CA 116; 129; DLB 130

Berrigan, Daniel 1921- . . . . **CLC 4**
See also CA 33-36R; CAAS 1; CANR 11,
43; DLB 5

Berrigan, Edmund Joseph Michael, Jr.
1934-1983
See Berrigan, Ted
See also CA 61-64; 110; CANR 14

Berrigan, Ted . . . . **CLC 37**
See also Berrigan, Edmund Joseph Michael,
Jr.
See also DLB 5, 169

Berry, Charles Edward Anderson 1931-
See Berry, Chuck
See also CA 115

Berry, Chuck . . . . **CLC 17**
See also Berry, Charles Edward Anderson

Berry, Jonas
See Ashbery, John (Lawrence)

Berry, Wendell (Erdman)
1934- . . . . **CLC 4, 6, 8, 27, 46;**
DAM POET
See also AITN 1; CA 73-76; CANR 50;
DLB 5, 6

Berryman, John
1914-1972 . . . . . . **CLC 1, 2, 3, 4, 6, 8, 10,**
13, 25, 62; DAM POET
See also CA 13-16; 33-36R; CABS 2;
CANR 35; CAP 1; CDALB 1941-1968;
DLB 48; MTCW

Bertolucci, Bernardo 1940- . . . . **CLC 16**
See also CA 106

Bertrand, Aloysius 1807-1841 . . . . **NCLC 31**

Bertran de Born c. 1140-1215 . . . . . **CMLC 5**

Besant, Annie (Wood) 1847-1933 . . . **TCLC 9**
See also CA 105

Bessie, Alvah 1904-1985 . . . . **CLC 23**
See also CA 5-8R; 116; CANR 2; DLB 26

Bethlen, T. D.
See Silverberg, Robert

Beti, Mongo . . . . **CLC 27; BLC; DAM MULT**
See also Biyidi, Alexandre

Betjeman, John
1906-1984 . . . . **CLC 2, 6, 10, 34, 43;**
DAB; DAM MST, POET
See also CA 9-12R; 112; CANR 33;
CDBLB 1945-1960; DLB 20; DLBY 84;
MTCW

Bettelheim, Bruno 1903-1990 . . . . . . **CLC 79**
See also CA 81-84; 131; CANR 23; MTCW

Betti, Ugo 1892-1953 . . . . **TCLC 5**
See also CA 104; 155

Betts, Doris (Waugh) 1932- . . . . **CLC 3, 6, 28**
See also CA 13-16R; CANR 9; DLBY 82;
INT CANR-9

Bevan, Alistair
See Roberts, Keith (John Kingston)

Bialik, Chaim Nachman
1873-1934 . . . . **TCLC 25**

Bickerstaff, Isaac
See Swift, Jonathan

Bidart, Frank 1939- . . . . **CLC 33**
See also CA 140

Bienek, Horst 1930- . . . . **CLC 7, 11**
See also CA 73-76; DLB 75

Bierce, Ambrose (Gwinett)
1842-1914(?) . . . . . . **TCLC 1, 7, 44; DA;**
DAC; DAM MST; SSC 9; WLC
See also CA 104; 139; CDALB 1865-1917;
DLB 11, 12, 23, 71, 74

Biggers, Earl Derr 1884-1933 . . . . . **TCLC 65**
See also CA 108; 153

Billings, Josh
See Shaw, Henry Wheeler

Billington, (Lady) Rachel (Mary)
1942- . . . . **CLC 43**
See also AITN 2; CA 33-36R; CANR 44

Binyon, T(imothy) J(ohn) 1936- . . . . **CLC 34**
See also CA 111; CANR 28

Bioy Casares, Adolfo
1914- . . . . **CLC 4, 8, 13, 88;**
DAM MULT; HLC; SSC 17
See also CA 29-32R; CANR 19, 43;
DLB 113; HW; MTCW

Bird, Cordwainer
See Ellison, Harlan (Jay)

Bird, Robert Montgomery
1806-1854 . . . . **NCLC 1**

Birney, (Alfred) Earle
1904- . . . . **CLC 1, 4, 6, 11; DAC;**
DAM MST, POET
See also CA 1-4R; CANR 5, 20; DLB 88;
MTCW

Bishop, Elizabeth
1911-1979 . . . . . . **CLC 1, 4, 9, 13, 15, 32;**
DA; DAC; DAM MST, POET; PC 3
See also CA 5-8R; 89-92; CABS 2;
CANR 26; CDALB 1968-1988; DLB 5,
169; MTCW; SATA-Obit 24

Bishop, John 1935- . . . . **CLC 10**
See also CA 105

Bissett, Bill 1939- . . . . **CLC 18; PC 14**
See also CA 69-72; CAAS 19; CANR 15;
DLB 53; MTCW

Bitov, Andrei (Georgievich) 1937- . . . **CLC 57**
See also CA 142

Biyidi, Alexandre 1932-
See Beti, Mongo
See also BW 1; CA 114; 124; MTCW

Bjarme, Brynjolf
See Ibsen, Henrik (Johan)

Bjornson, Bjornstjerne (Martinius)
1832-1910 . . . . **TCLC 7, 37**
See also CA 104

Black, Robert
See Holdstock, Robert P.

Blackburn, Paul 1926-1971 . . . . . . **CLC 9, 43**
See also CA 81-84; 33-36R; CANR 34;
DLB 16; DLBY 81

Black Elk
1863-1950 . . . . . **TCLC 33; DAM MULT**
See also CA 144; NNAL

Black Hobart
See Sanders, (James) Ed(ward)

Blacklin, Malcolm
See Chambers, Aidan

Blackmore, R(ichard) D(oddridge)
1825-1900 . . . . **TCLC 27**
See also CA 120; DLB 18

Blackmur, R(ichard) P(almer)
1904-1965 . . . . **CLC 2, 24**
See also CA 11-12; 25-28R; CAP 1; DLB 63

Black Tarantula
See Acker, Kathy

Blackwood, Algernon (Henry)
1869-1951 . . . . **TCLC 5**
See also CA 105; 150; DLB 153, 156

Blackwood, Caroline 1931-1996 . . . **CLC 6, 9**
See also CA 85-88; 151; CANR 32;
DLB 14; MTCW

Blade, Alexander
See Hamilton, Edmond; Silverberg, Robert

Blaga, Lucian 1895-1961 . . . . **CLC 75**

Blair, Eric (Arthur) 1903-1950
See Orwell, George
See also CA 104; 132; DA; DAB; DAC;
DAM MST, NOV; MTCW; SATA 29

Blais, Marie-Claire
1939- . . . . **CLC 2, 4, 6, 13, 22; DAC;**
DAM MST
See also CA 21-24R; CAAS 4; CANR 38;
DLB 53; MTCW

Blaise, Clark 1940- . . . . **CLC 29**
See also AITN 2; CA 53-56; CAAS 3;
CANR 5; DLB 53

Blake, Nicholas
See Day Lewis, C(ecil)
See also DLB 77

Blake, William
1757-1827 . . . . **NCLC 13, 37, 57; DA;**
DAB; DAC; DAM MST, POET; PC 12;
WLC
See also CDBLB 1789-1832; DLB 93, 163;
MAICYA; SATA 30

Blake, William J(ames) 1894-1969 . . . **PC 12**
See also CA 5-8R; 25-28R

Blasco Ibanez, Vicente
1867-1928 . . . . **TCLC 12; DAM NOV**
See also CA 110; 131; HW; MTCW

Blatty, William Peter
1928- . . . . **CLC 2; DAM POP**
See also CA 5-8R; CANR 9

Bleeck, Oliver
See Thomas, Ross (Elmore)

Blessing, Lee 1949- . . . . **CLC 54**

Blish, James (Benjamin)
1921-1975 . . . . **CLC 14**
See also CA 1-4R; 57-60; CANR 3; DLB 8;
MTCW; SATA 66

Bliss, Reginald
See Wells, H(erbert) G(eorge)

Blixen, Karen (Christentze Dinesen)
1885-1962
See Dinesen, Isak
See also CA 25-28; CANR 22, 50; CAP 2;
MTCW; SATA 44

Bloch, Robert (Albert) 1917-1994 . . . **CLC 33**
See also CA 5-8R; 146; CAAS 20; CANR 5;
DLB 44; INT CANR-5; SATA 12;
SATA-Obit 82

Blok, Alexander (Alexandrovich)
1880-1921 . . . . **TCLC 5**
See also CA 104

Blom, Jan
See Breytenbach, Breyten

Bloom, Harold 1930- . . . . **CLC 24**
See also CA 13-16R; CANR 39; DLB 67

Bloomfield, Aurelius
See Bourne, Randolph S(illiman)

Blount, Roy (Alton), Jr. 1941- . . . . . **CLC 38**
See also CA 53-56; CANR 10, 28;
INT CANR-28; MTCW

Bloy, Leon 1846-1917 . . . . **TCLC 22**
See also CA 121; DLB 123

Blume, Judy (Sussman)
1938- . . . **CLC 12, 30; DAM NOV, POP**
See also AAYA 3; CA 29-32R; CANR 13,
37; CLR 2, 15; DLB 52; JRDA;
MAICYA; MTCW; SATA 2, 31, 79

Blunden, Edmund (Charles)
1896-1974 . . . . **CLC 2, 56**
See also CA 17-18; 45-48; CANR 54;
CAP 2; DLB 20, 100, 155; MTCW

Bly, Robert (Elwood)
1926- . . . . **CLC 1, 2, 5, 10, 15, 38;**
DAM POET
See also CA 5-8R; CANR 41; DLB 5;
MTCW

Boas, Franz 1858-1942 . . . . **TCLC 56**
See also CA 115

Bobette
See Simenon, Georges (Jacques Christian)

Boccaccio, Giovanni
1313-1375 . . . . **CMLC 13; SSC 10**

Bochco, Steven 1943- . . . . **CLC 35**
See also AAYA 11; CA 124; 138

Bodenheim, Maxwell 1892-1954 . . . **TCLC 44**
See also CA 110; DLB 9, 45

Bodker, Cecil 1927- . . . . **CLC 21**
See also CA 73-76; CANR 13, 44; CLR 23;
MAICYA; SATA 14

Boell, Heinrich (Theodor)
1917-1985 . . . . **CLC 2, 3, 6, 9, 11, 15, 27,**
32, 72; DA; DAB; DAC; DAM MST,
NOV; SSC 23; WLC
See also CA 21-24R; 116; CANR 24;
DLB 69; DLBY 85; MTCW

Boerne, Alfred
See Doeblin, Alfred

Boethius 480(?)-524(?) . . . . **CMLC 15**
See also DLB 115

Bogan, Louise
1897-1970 . . . . **CLC 4, 39, 46, 93;**
DAM POET; PC 12
See also CA 73-76; 25-28R; CANR 33;
DLB 45, 169; MTCW

Bogarde, Dirk . . . . **CLC 19**
See also Van Den Bogarde, Derek Jules
Gaspard Ulric Niven
See also DLB 14

Bogosian, Eric 1953- .... **CLC 45**
See also CA 138

Bograd, Larry 1953-.............. **CLC 35**
See also CA 93-96; SAAS 21; SATA 33, 89

Boiardo, Matteo Maria 1441-1494 .... **LC 6**

Boileau-Despreaux, Nicolas
1636-1711 .... **LC 3**

Bojer, Johan 1872-1959 .... **TCLC 64**

Boland, Eavan (Aisling)
1944- .... **CLC 40, 67; DAM POET**
See also CA 143; DLB 40

Bolt, Lee
See Faust, Frederick (Schiller)

Bolt, Robert (Oxton)
1924-1995 ..... **CLC 14; DAM DRAM**
See also CA 17-20R; 147; CANR 35;
DLB 13; MTCW

Bombet, Louis-Alexandre-Cesar
See Stendhal

Bomkauf
See Kaufman, Bob (Garnell)

Bonaventura .... **NCLC 35**
See also DLB 90

Bond, Edward
1934- ... **CLC 4, 6, 13, 23; DAM DRAM**
See also CA 25-28R; CANR 38; DLB 13;
MTCW

Bonham, Frank 1914-1989 .... **CLC 12**
See also AAYA 1; CA 9-12R; CANR 4, 36;
JRDA; MAICYA; SAAS 3; SATA 1, 49;
SATA-Obit 62

Bonnefoy, Yves
1923- ...... **CLC 9, 15, 58; DAM MST,
POET**
See also CA 85-88; CANR 33; MTCW

Bontemps, Arna(ud Wendell)
1902-1973 .... **CLC 1, 18; BLC;
DAM MULT, NOV, POET**
See also BW 1; CA 1-4R; 41-44R; CANR 4,
35; CLR 6; DLB 48, 51; JRDA;
MAICYA; MTCW; SATA 2, 44;
SATA-Obit 24

Booth, Martin 1944-.............. **CLC 13**
See also CA 93-96; CAAS 2

Booth, Philip 1925-.............. **CLC 23**
See also CA 5-8R; CANR 5; DLBY 82

Booth, Wayne C(layson) 1921- ..... **CLC 24**
See also CA 1-4R; CAAS 5; CANR 3, 43;
DLB 67

Borchert, Wolfgang 1921-1947 ..... **TCLC 5**
See also CA 104; DLB 69, 124

Borel, Petrus 1809-1859 .... **NCLC 41**

Borges, Jorge Luis
1899-1986 ... **CLC 1, 2, 3, 4, 6, 8, 9, 10,
13, 19, 44, 48, 83; DA; DAB; DAC;
DAM MST, MULT; HLC; SSC 4; WLC**
See also AAYA 19; CA 21-24R; CANR 19,
33; DLB 113; DLBY 86; HW; MTCW

Borowski, Tadeusz 1922-1951 ...... **TCLC 9**
See also CA 106; 154

Borrow, George (Henry)
1803-1881 .... **NCLC 9**
See also DLB 21, 55, 166

Bosman, Herman Charles
1905-1951 .... **TCLC 49**

Bosschere, Jean de 1878(?)-1953... **TCLC 19**
See also CA 115

Boswell, James
1740-1795 ...... **LC 4; DA; DAB; DAC;
DAM MST; WLC**
See also CDBLB 1660-1789; DLB 104, 142

Bottoms, David 1949-............. **CLC 53**
See also CA 105; CANR 22; DLB 120;
DLBY 83

Boucicault, Dion 1820-1890 ...... **NCLC 41**

Boucolon, Maryse 1937(?)-
See Conde, Maryse
See also CA 110; CANR 30, 53

Bourget, Paul (Charles Joseph)
1852-1935 .... **TCLC 12**
See also CA 107; DLB 123

Bourjaily, Vance (Nye) 1922- .... **CLC 8, 62**
See also CA 1-4R; CAAS 1; CANR 2;
DLB 2, 143

Bourne, Randolph S(illiman)
1886-1918 .... **TCLC 16**
See also CA 117; 155; DLB 63

Bova, Ben(jamin William) 1932- .... **CLC 45**
See also AAYA 16; CA 5-8R; CAAS 18;
CANR 11; CLR 3; DLBY 81;
INT CANR-11; MAICYA; MTCW;
SATA 6, 68

Bowen, Elizabeth (Dorothea Cole)
1899-1973 ...... **CLC 1, 3, 6, 11, 15, 22;
DAM NOV; SSC 3**
See also CA 17-18; 41-44R; CANR 35;
CAP 2; CDBLB 1945-1960; DLB 15, 162;
MTCW

Bowering, George 1935-........ **CLC 15, 47**
See also CA 21-24R; CAAS 16; CANR 10;
DLB 53

Bowering, Marilyn R(uthe) 1949- ... **CLC 32**
See also CA 101; CANR 49

Bowers, Edgar 1924- .... **CLC 9**
See also CA 5-8R; CANR 24; DLB 5

Bowie, David .... **CLC 17**
See also Jones, David Robert

Bowles, Jane (Sydney)
1917-1973 .... **CLC 3, 68**
See also CA 19-20; 41-44R; CAP 2

Bowles, Paul (Frederick)
1910- .... **CLC 1, 2, 19, 53; SSC 3**
See also CA 1-4R; CAAS 1; CANR 1, 19,
50; DLB 5, 6; MTCW

Box, Edgar
See Vidal, Gore

Boyd, Nancy
See Millay, Edna St. Vincent

Boyd, William 1952-........ **CLC 28, 53, 70**
See also CA 114; 120; CANR 51

Boyle, Kay
1902-1992 ..... **CLC 1, 5, 19, 58; SSC 5**
See also CA 13-16R; 140; CAAS 1;
CANR 29; DLB 4, 9, 48, 86; DLBY 93;
MTCW

Boyle, Mark
See Kienzle, William X(avier)

Boyle, Patrick 1905-1982 .... **CLC 19**
See also CA 127

Boyle, T. C. 1948-
See Boyle, T(homas) Coraghessan

Boyle, T(homas) Coraghessan
1948- ..... **CLC 36, 55, 90; DAM POP;
SSC 16**
See also BEST 90:4; CA 120; CANR 44;
DLBY 86

Boz
See Dickens, Charles (John Huffam)

Brackenridge, Hugh Henry
1748-1816 .... **NCLC 7**
See also DLB 11, 37

Bradbury, Edward P.
See Moorcock, Michael (John)

Bradbury, Malcolm (Stanley)
1932- .... **CLC 32, 61; DAM NOV**
See also CA 1-4R; CANR 1, 33; DLB 14;
MTCW

Bradbury, Ray (Douglas)
1920- ..... **CLC 1, 3, 10, 15, 42, 98; DA;
DAB; DAC; DAM MST, NOV, POP;
WLC**
See also AAYA 15; AITN 1, 2; CA 1-4R;
CANR 2, 30; CDALB 1968-1988; DLB 2,
8; INT CANR-30; MTCW; SATA 11, 64

Bradford, Gamaliel 1863-1932 ..... **TCLC 36**
See also DLB 17

Bradley, David (Henry, Jr.)
1950- ..... **CLC 23; BLC; DAM MULT**
See also BW 1; CA 104; CANR 26; DLB 33

Bradley, John Ed(mund, Jr.)
1958- .... **CLC 55**
See also CA 139

Bradley, Marion Zimmer
1930- .... **CLC 30; DAM POP**
See also AAYA 9; CA 57-60; CAAS 10;
CANR 7, 31, 51; DLB 8; MTCW;
SATA 90

Bradstreet, Anne
1612(?)-1672 ...... **LC 4, 30; DA; DAC;
DAM MST, POET; PC 10**
See also CDALB 1640-1865; DLB 24

Brady, Joan 1939- .... **CLC 86**
See also CA 141

Bragg, Melvyn 1939-.............. **CLC 10**
See also BEST 89:3; CA 57-60; CANR 10,
48; DLB 14

Braine, John (Gerard)
1922-1986 .... **CLC 1, 3, 41**
See also CA 1-4R; 120; CANR 1, 33;
CDBLB 1945-1960; DLB 15; DLBY 86;
MTCW

Brammer, William 1930(?)-1978 .... **CLC 31**
See also CA 77-80

Brancati, Vitaliano 1907-1954 ..... **TCLC 12**
See also CA 109

Brancato, Robin F(idler) 1936- ..... **CLC 35**
See also AAYA 9; CA 69-72; CANR 11,
45; CLR 32; JRDA; SAAS 9; SATA 23

Brand, Max
See Faust, Frederick (Schiller)

Brand, Millen 1906-1980 .... **CLC 7**
See also CA 21-24R; 97-100

Branden, Barbara .... **CLC 44**
See also CA 148

Brandes, Georg (Morris Cohen)
1842-1927 . . . . **TCLC 10**
See also CA 105

Brandys, Kazimierz 1916- . . . . **CLC 62**

Branley, Franklyn M(ansfield)
1915- . . . . **CLC 21**
See also CA 33-36R; CANR 14, 39;
CLR 13; MAICYA; SAAS 16; SATA 4,
68

Brathwaite, Edward Kamau
1930- . . . . **CLC 11; DAM POET**
See also BW 2; CA 25-28R; CANR 11, 26,
47; DLB 125

Brautigan, Richard (Gary)
1935-1984 . . . . **CLC 1, 3, 5, 9, 12, 34, 42;
DAM NOV**
See also CA 53-56; 113; CANR 34; DLB 2,
5; DLBY 80, 84; MTCW; SATA 56

Brave Bird, Mary 1953-
See Crow Dog, Mary (Ellen)
See also NNAL

Braverman, Kate 1950- . . . . **CLC 67**
See also CA 89-92

Brecht, Bertolt
1898-1956 . . . . . . **TCLC 1, 6, 13, 35; DA;
DAB; DAC; DAM DRAM, MST; DC 3;
WLC**
See also CA 104; 133; DLB 56, 124; MTCW

Brecht, Eugen Berthold Friedrich
See Brecht, Bertolt

Bremer, Fredrika 1801-1865 . . . . . **NCLC 11**

Brennan, Christopher John
1870-1932 . . . . **TCLC 17**
See also CA 117

Brennan, Maeve 1917- . . . . **CLC 5**
See also CA 81-84

Brentano, Clemens (Maria)
1778-1842 . . . . **NCLC 1**
See also DLB 90

Brent of Bin Bin
See Franklin, (Stella Maraia Sarah) Miles

Brenton, Howard 1942- . . . . **CLC 31**
See also CA 69-72; CANR 33; DLB 13;
MTCW

Breslin, James 1930-
See Breslin, Jimmy
See also CA 73-76; CANR 31; DAM NOV;
MTCW

Breslin, Jimmy . . . . **CLC 4, 43**
See also Breslin, James
See also AITN 1

Bresson, Robert 1901- . . . . **CLC 16**
See also CA 110; CANR 49

Breton, Andre
1896-1966 . . . . . **CLC 2, 9, 15, 54; PC 15**
See also CA 19-20; 25-28R; CANR 40;
CAP 2; DLB 65; MTCW

Breytenbach, Breyten
1939(?)- . . . . . . **CLC 23, 37; DAM POET**
See also CA 113; 129

Bridgers, Sue Ellen 1942- . . . . **CLC 26**
See also AAYA 8; CA 65-68; CANR 11,
36; CLR 18; DLB 52; JRDA; MAICYA;
SAAS 1; SATA 22, 90

Bridges, Robert (Seymour)
1844-1930 . . . . . . **TCLC 1; DAM POET**
See also CA 104; 152; CDBLB 1890-1914;
DLB 19, 98

Bridie, James . . . . **TCLC 3**
See also Mavor, Osborne Henry
See also DLB 10

Brin, David 1950- . . . . **CLC 34**
See also CA 102; CANR 24;
INT CANR-24; SATA 65

Brink, Andre (Philippus)
1935- . . . . **CLC 18, 36**
See also CA 104; CANR 39; INT 103;
MTCW

Brinsmead, H(esba) F(ay) 1922- . . . . **CLC 21**
See also CA 21-24R; CANR 10; MAICYA;
SAAS 5; SATA 18, 78

Brittain, Vera (Mary)
1893(?)-1970 . . . . **CLC 23**
See also CA 13-16; 25-28R; CAP 1; MTCW

Broch, Hermann 1886-1951 . . . . **TCLC 20**
See also CA 117; DLB 85, 124

Brock, Rose
See Hansen, Joseph

Brodkey, Harold (Roy) 1930-1996 . . **CLC 56**
See also CA 111; 151; DLB 130

Brodsky, Iosif Alexandrovich 1940-1996
See Brodsky, Joseph
See also AITN 1; CA 41-44R; 151;
CANR 37; DAM POET; MTCW

Brodsky, Joseph . . **CLC 4, 6, 13, 36, 50; PC 9**
See also Brodsky, Iosif Alexandrovich

Brodsky, Michael Mark 1948- . . . . . **CLC 19**
See also CA 102; CANR 18, 41

Bromell, Henry 1947- . . . . **CLC 5**
See also CA 53-56; CANR 9

Bromfield, Louis (Brucker)
1896-1956 . . . . **TCLC 11**
See also CA 107; 155; DLB 4, 9, 86

Broner, E(sther) M(asserman)
1930- . . . . **CLC 19**
See also CA 17-20R; CANR 8, 25; DLB 28

Bronk, William 1918- . . . . **CLC 10**
See also CA 89-92; CANR 23; DLB 165

Bronstein, Lev Davidovich
See Trotsky, Leon

Bronte, Anne 1820-1849 . . . . **NCLC 4**
See also DLB 21

Bronte, Charlotte
1816-1855 . . . . . **NCLC 3, 8, 33, 58; DA;
DAB; DAC; DAM MST, NOV; WLC**
See also AAYA 17; CDBLB 1832-1890;
DLB 21, 159

Bronte, Emily (Jane)
1818-1848 . . . . **NCLC 16, 35; DA; DAB;
DAC; DAM MST, NOV, POET; PC 8;
WLC**
See also AAYA 17; CDBLB 1832-1890;
DLB 21, 32

Brooke, Frances 1724-1789 . . . . **LC 6**
See also DLB 39, 99

Brooke, Henry 1703(?)-1783 . . . . **LC 1**
See also DLB 39

Brooke, Rupert (Chawner)
1887-1915 . . . . . . **TCLC 2, 7; DA; DAB;
DAC; DAM MST, POET; WLC**
See also CA 104; 132; CDBLB 1914-1945;
DLB 19; MTCW

Brooke-Haven, P.
See Wodehouse, P(elham) G(renville)

Brooke-Rose, Christine 1926- . . . . . . **CLC 40**
See also CA 13-16R; DLB 14

Brookner, Anita
1928- . . . . **CLC 32, 34, 51; DAB;
DAM POP**
See also CA 114; 120; CANR 37; DLBY 87;
MTCW

Brooks, Cleanth 1906-1994 . . . . . **CLC 24, 86**
See also CA 17-20R; 145; CANR 33, 35;
DLB 63; DLBY 94; INT CANR-35;
MTCW

Brooks, George
See Baum, L(yman) Frank

Brooks, Gwendolyn
1917- . . . . . . **CLC 1, 2, 4, 5, 15, 49; BLC;
DA; DAC; DAM MST, MULT, POET;
PC 7; WLC**
See also AITN 1; BW 2; CA 1-4R;
CANR 1, 27, 52; CDALB 1941-1968;
CLR 27; DLB 5, 76, 165; MTCW;
SATA 6

Brooks, Mel . . . . **CLC 12**
See also Kaminsky, Melvin
See also AAYA 13; DLB 26

Brooks, Peter 1938- . . . . **CLC 34**
See also CA 45-48; CANR 1

Brooks, Van Wyck 1886-1963 . . . . . . **CLC 29**
See also CA 1-4R; CANR 6; DLB 45, 63,
103

Brophy, Brigid (Antonia)
1929-1995 . . . . **CLC 6, 11, 29**
See also CA 5-8R; 149; CAAS 4; CANR 25,
53; DLB 14; MTCW

Brosman, Catharine Savage 1934- . . . . **CLC 9**
See also CA 61-64; CANR 21, 46

Brother Antoninus
See Everson, William (Oliver)

Broughton, T(homas) Alan 1936- . . . **CLC 19**
See also CA 45-48; CANR 2, 23, 48

Broumas, Olga 1949- . . . . **CLC 10, 73**
See also CA 85-88; CANR 20

Brown, Charles Brockden
1771-1810 . . . . **NCLC 22**
See also CDALB 1640-1865; DLB 37, 59,
73

Brown, Christy 1932-1981 . . . . **CLC 63**
See also CA 105; 104; DLB 14

Brown, Claude
1937- . . . . . **CLC 30; BLC; DAM MULT**
See also AAYA 7; BW 1; CA 73-76

Brown, Dee (Alexander)
1908- . . . . **CLC 18, 47; DAM POP**
See also CA 13-16R; CAAS 6; CANR 11,
45; DLBY 80; MTCW; SATA 5

Brown, George
See Wertmueller, Lina

Brown, George Douglas
1869-1902 . . . . **TCLC 28**

Brown, George Mackay
1921-1996 . . . . **CLC 5, 48**
See also CA 21-24R; 151; CAAS 6;
CANR 12, 37; DLB 14, 27, 139; MTCW;
SATA 35

Brown, (William) Larry 1951- . . . . . . **CLC 73**
See also CA 130; 134; INT 133

Brown, Moses
See Barrett, William (Christopher)

Brown, Rita Mae
1944- . . . . . **CLC 18, 43, 79; DAM NOV,**
POP
See also CA 45-48; CANR 2, 11, 35;
INT CANR-11; MTCW

Brown, Roderick (Langmere) Haig-
See Haig-Brown, Roderick (Langmere)

Brown, Rosellen 1939- . . . . **CLC 32**
See also CA 77-80; CAAS 10; CANR 14, 44

Brown, Sterling Allen
1901-1989 . . . . **CLC 1, 23, 59; BLC;**
DAM MULT, POET
See also BW 1; CA 85-88; 127; CANR 26;
DLB 48, 51, 63; MTCW

Brown, Will
See Ainsworth, William Harrison

Brown, William Wells
1813-1884 . . . . **NCLC 2; BLC;**
DAM MULT; DC 1
See also DLB 3, 50

Browne, (Clyde) Jackson 1948(?)- . . . **CLC 21**
See also CA 120

Browning, Elizabeth Barrett
1806-1861 . . . . . **NCLC 1, 16; DA; DAB;**
DAC; DAM MST, POET; PC 6; WLC
See also CDBLB 1832-1890; DLB 32

Browning, Robert
1812-1889 . . . . **NCLC 19; DA; DAB;**
DAC; DAM MST, POET; PC 2
See also CDBLB 1832-1890; DLB 32, 163;
YABC 1

Browning, Tod 1882-1962 . . . . **CLC 16**
See also CA 141; 117

Brownson, Orestes (Augustus)
1803-1876 . . . . **NCLC 50**

Bruccoli, Matthew J(oseph) 1931- . . **CLC 34**
See also CA 9-12R; CANR 7; DLB 103

Bruce, Lenny . . . . **CLC 21**
See also Schneider, Leonard Alfred

Bruin, John
See Brutus, Dennis

Brulard, Henri
See Stendhal

Brulls, Christian
See Simenon, Georges (Jacques Christian)

Brunner, John (Kilian Houston)
1934-1995 . . . . . . **CLC 8, 10; DAM POP**
See also CA 1-4R; 149; CAAS 8; CANR 2,
37; MTCW

Bruno, Giordano 1548-1600 . . . . **LC 27**

Brutus, Dennis
1924- . . . . . **CLC 43; BLC; DAM MULT,**
POET
See also BW 2; CA 49-52; CAAS 14;
CANR 2, 27, 42; DLB 117

Bryan, C(ourtlandt) D(ixon) B(arnes)
1936- . . . . **CLC 29**
See also CA 73-76; CANR 13;
INT CANR-13

Bryan, Michael
See Moore, Brian

Bryant, William Cullen
1794-1878 . . . . . **NCLC 6, 46; DA; DAB;**
DAC; DAM MST, POET
See also CDALB 1640-1865; DLB 3, 43, 59

Bryusov, Valery Yakovlevich
1873-1924 . . . . **TCLC 10**
See also CA 107; 155

Buchan, John
1875-1940 . . . . **TCLC 41; DAB;**
DAM POP
See also CA 108; 145; DLB 34, 70, 156;
YABC 2

Buchanan, George 1506-1582 . . . . **LC 4**

Buchheim, Lothar-Guenther 1918- . . . **CLC 6**
See also CA 85-88

Buchner, (Karl) Georg
1813-1837 . . . . **NCLC 26**

Buchwald, Art(hur) 1925- . . . . **CLC 33**
See also AITN 1; CA 5-8R; CANR 21;
MTCW; SATA 10

Buck, Pearl S(ydenstricker)
1892-1973 . . . . **CLC 7, 11, 18; DA; DAB;**
DAC; DAM MST, NOV
See also AITN 1; CA 1-4R; 41-44R;
CANR 1, 34; DLB 9, 102; MTCW;
SATA 1, 25

Buckler, Ernest
1908-1984 . . **CLC 13; DAC; DAM MST**
See also CA 11-12; 114; CAP 1; DLB 68;
SATA 47

Buckley, Vincent (Thomas)
1925-1988 . . . . **CLC 57**
See also CA 101

Buckley, William F(rank), Jr.
1925- . . . . **CLC 7, 18, 37; DAM POP**
See also AITN 1; CA 1-4R; CANR 1, 24,
53; DLB 137; DLBY 80; INT CANR-24;
MTCW

Buechner, (Carl) Frederick
1926- . . . . . . **CLC 2, 4, 6, 9; DAM NOV**
See also CA 13-16R; CANR 11, 39;
DLBY 80; INT CANR-11; MTCW

Buell, John (Edward) 1927- . . . . **CLC 10**
See also CA 1-4R; DLB 53

Buero Vallejo, Antonio 1916- . . . **CLC 15, 46**
See also CA 106; CANR 24, 49; HW;
MTCW

Bufalino, Gesualdo 1920(?)- . . . . **CLC 74**

Bugayev, Boris Nikolayevich 1880-1934
See Bely, Andrey
See also CA 104

Bukowski, Charles
1920-1994 . . . . **CLC 2, 5, 9, 41, 82;**
DAM NOV, POET
See also CA 17-20R; 144; CANR 40;
DLB 5, 130, 169; MTCW

Bulgakov, Mikhail (Afanas'evich)
1891-1940 . . . . **TCLC 2, 16;**
DAM DRAM, NOV; SSC 18
See also CA 105; 152

Bulgya, Alexander Alexandrovich
1901-1956 . . . . **TCLC 53**
See also Fadeyev, Alexander
See also CA 117

Bullins, Ed
1935- . . . . **CLC 1, 5, 7; BLC;**
DAM DRAM, MULT; DC 6
See also BW 2; CA 49-52; CAAS 16;
CANR 24, 46; DLB 7, 38; MTCW

Bulwer-Lytton, Edward (George Earle Lytton)
1803-1873 . . . . **NCLC 1, 45**
See also DLB 21

Bunin, Ivan Alexeyevich
1870-1953 . . . . **TCLC 6; SSC 5**
See also CA 104

Bunting, Basil
1900-1985 . . . . **CLC 10, 39, 47;**
DAM POET
See also CA 53-56; 115; CANR 7; DLB 20

Bunuel, Luis
1900-1983 . . . . **CLC 16, 80;**
DAM MULT; HLC
See also CA 101; 110; CANR 32; HW

Bunyan, John
1628-1688 . . . . . . **LC 4; DA; DAB; DAC;**
DAM MST; WLC
See also CDBLB 1660-1789; DLB 39

Burckhardt, Jacob (Christoph)
1818-1897 . . . . **NCLC 49**

Burford, Eleanor
See Hibbert, Eleanor Alice Burford

Burgess, Anthony
. **CLC 1, 2, 4, 5, 8, 10, 13, 15, 22, 40, 62,**
81, 94; DAB
See also Wilson, John (Anthony) Burgess
See also AITN 1; CDBLB 1960 to Present;
DLB 14

Burke, Edmund
1729(?)-1797 . . . . . . **LC 7, 36; DA; DAB;**
DAC; DAM MST; WLC
See also DLB 104

Burke, Kenneth (Duva)
1897-1993 . . . . **CLC 2, 24**
See also CA 5-8R; 143; CANR 39; DLB 45,
63; MTCW

Burke, Leda
See Garnett, David

Burke, Ralph
See Silverberg, Robert

Burke, Thomas 1886-1945 . . . . **TCLC 63**
See also CA 113; 155

Burney, Fanny 1752-1840 . . . . **NCLC 12, 54**
See also DLB 39

Burns, Robert 1759-1796 . . . . **PC 6**
See also CDBLB 1789-1832; DA; DAB;
DAC; DAM MST, POET; DLB 109;
WLC

Burns, Tex
See L'Amour, Louis (Dearborn)

Burnshaw, Stanley 1906- . . . . . **CLC 3, 13, 44**
See also CA 9-12R; DLB 48

Burr, Anne 1937- . . . . **CLC 6**
See also CA 25-28R

Burroughs, Edgar Rice
1875-1950 .... **TCLC 2, 32; DAM NOV**
See also AAYA 11; CA 104; 132; DLB 8;
MTCW; SATA 41

Burroughs, William S(eward)
1914- .... **CLC 1, 2, 5, 15, 22, 42, 75;**
DA; DAB; DAC; DAM MST, NOV,
POP; WLC
See also AITN 2; CA 9-12R; CANR 20, 52;
DLB 2, 8, 16, 152; DLBY 81; MTCW

Burton, Richard F. 1821-1890 .... **NCLC 42**
See also DLB 55

Busch, Frederick 1941- ... **CLC 7, 10, 18, 47**
See also CA 33-36R; CAAS 1; CANR 45;
DLB 6

Bush, Ronald 1946- .... **CLC 34**
See also CA 136

Bustos, F(rancisco)
See Borges, Jorge Luis

Bustos Domecq, H(onorio)
See Bioy Casares, Adolfo; Borges, Jorge
Luis

Butler, Octavia E(stelle)
1947- ..... **CLC 38; DAM MULT, POP**
See also AAYA 18; BW 2; CA 73-76;
CANR 12, 24, 38; DLB 33; MTCW;
SATA 84

Butler, Robert Olen (Jr.)
1945- .... **CLC 81; DAM POP**
See also CA 112; DLB 173; INT 112

Butler, Samuel 1612-1680 .... **LC 16**
See also DLB 101, 126

Butler, Samuel
1835-1902 ...... **TCLC 1, 33; DA; DAB;**
DAC; DAM MST, NOV; WLC
See also CA 143; CDBLB 1890-1914;
DLB 18, 57, 174

Butler, Walter C.
See Faust, Frederick (Schiller)

Butor, Michel (Marie Francois)
1926- .... **CLC 1, 3, 8, 11, 15**
See also CA 9-12R; CANR 33; DLB 83;
MTCW

Buzo, Alexander (John) 1944- ...... **CLC 61**
See also CA 97-100; CANR 17, 39

Buzzati, Dino 1906-1972 .... **CLC 36**
See also CA 33-36R

Byars, Betsy (Cromer) 1928- .... **CLC 35**
See also AAYA 19; CA 33-36R; CANR 18,
36; CLR 1, 16; DLB 52; INT CANR-18;
JRDA; MAICYA; MTCW; SAAS 1;
SATA 4, 46, 80

Byatt, A(ntonia) S(usan Drabble)
1936- ... **CLC 19, 65; DAM NOV, POP**
See also CA 13-16R; CANR 13, 33, 50;
DLB 14; MTCW

Byrne, David 1952- .... **CLC 26**
See also CA 127

Byrne, John Keyes 1926-
See Leonard, Hugh
See also CA 102; INT 102

Byron, George Gordon (Noel)
1788-1824 ..... **NCLC 2, 12; DA; DAB;**
DAC; DAM MST, POET; PC 16; WLC
See also CDBLB 1789-1832; DLB 96, 110

Byron, Robert 1905-1941 .... **TCLC 67**

C. 3. 3.
See Wilde, Oscar (Fingal O'Flahertie Wills)

Caballero, Fernan 1796-1877..... **NCLC 10**

Cabell, Branch
See Cabell, James Branch

Cabell, James Branch 1879-1958 ... **TCLC 6**
See also CA 105; 152; DLB 9, 78

Cable, George Washington
1844-1925 .... **TCLC 4; SSC 4**
See also CA 104; 155; DLB 12, 74;
DLBD 13

Cabral de Melo Neto, Joao
1920- .... **CLC 76; DAM MULT**
See also CA 151

Cabrera Infante, G(uillermo)
1929- ..... **CLC 5, 25, 45; DAM MULT;**
HLC
See also CA 85-88; CANR 29; DLB 113;
HW; MTCW

Cade, Toni
See Bambara, Toni Cade

Cadmus and Harmonia
See Buchan, John

Caedmon fl. 658-680............. **CMLC 7**
See also DLB 146

Caeiro, Alberto
See Pessoa, Fernando (Antonio Nogueira)

Cage, John (Milton, Jr.) 1912- ..... **CLC 41**
See also CA 13-16R; CANR 9;
INT CANR-9

Cain, G.
See Cabrera Infante, G(uillermo)

Cain, Guillermo
See Cabrera Infante, G(uillermo)

Cain, James M(allahan)
1892-1977 .... **CLC 3, 11, 28**
See also AITN 1; CA 17-20R; 73-76;
CANR 8, 34; MTCW

Caine, Mark
See Raphael, Frederic (Michael)

Calasso, Roberto 1941- .... **CLC 81**
See also CA 143

Calderon de la Barca, Pedro
1600-1681 .... **LC 23; DC 3**

Caldwell, Erskine (Preston)
1903-1987 .... **CLC 1, 8, 14, 50, 60;**
DAM NOV; SSC 19
See also AITN 1; CA 1-4R; 121; CAAS 1;
CANR 2, 33; DLB 9, 86; MTCW

Caldwell, (Janet Miriam) Taylor (Holland)
1900-1985 .... **CLC 2, 28, 39;**
DAM NOV, POP
See also CA 5-8R; 116; CANR 5

Calhoun, John Caldwell
1782-1850 .... **NCLC 15**
See also DLB 3

Calisher, Hortense
1911- ..... **CLC 2, 4, 8, 38; DAM NOV;**
SSC 15
See also CA 1-4R; CANR 1, 22; DLB 2;
INT CANR-22; MTCW

Callaghan, Morley Edward
1903-1990 ..... **CLC 3, 14, 41, 65; DAC;**
DAM MST
See also CA 9-12R; 132; CANR 33;
DLB 68; MTCW

Callimachus
c. 305B.C.-c. 240B.C........ **CMLC 18**

Calvin, John 1509-1564 .... **LC 37**

Calvino, Italo
1923-1985 ..... **CLC 5, 8, 11, 22, 33, 39,**
73; DAM NOV; SSC 3
See also CA 85-88; 116; CANR 23; MTCW

Cameron, Carey 1952- .... **CLC 59**
See also CA 135

Cameron, Peter 1959-............. **CLC 44**
See also CA 125; CANR 50

Campana, Dino 1885-1932........ **TCLC 20**
See also CA 117; DLB 114

Campanella, Tommaso 1568-1639 .... **LC 32**

Campbell, John W(ood, Jr.)
1910-1971 .... **CLC 32**
See also CA 21-22; 29-32R; CANR 34;
CAP 2; DLB 8; MTCW

Campbell, Joseph 1904-1987 .... **CLC 69**
See also AAYA 3; BEST 89:2; CA 1-4R;
124; CANR 3, 28; MTCW

Campbell, Maria 1940-....... **CLC 85; DAC**
See also CA 102; CANR 54; NNAL

Campbell, (John) Ramsey
1946- .... **CLC 42; SSC 19**
See also CA 57-60; CANR 7; INT CANR-7

Campbell, (Ignatius) Roy (Dunnachie)
1901-1957 .... **TCLC 5**
See also CA 104; 155; DLB 20

Campbell, Thomas 1777-1844 .... **NCLC 19**
See also DLB 93; 144

Campbell, Wilfred .... **TCLC 9**
See also Campbell, William

Campbell, William 1858(?)-1918
See Campbell, Wilfred
See also CA 106; DLB 92

Campion, Jane .... **CLC 95**
See also CA 138

Campos, Alvaro de
See Pessoa, Fernando (Antonio Nogueira)

Camus, Albert
1913-1960 .... **CLC 1, 2, 4, 9, 11, 14, 32,**
63, 69; DA; DAB; DAC; DAM DRAM,
MST, NOV; DC 2; SSC 9; WLC
See also CA 89-92; DLB 72; MTCW

Canby, Vincent 1924-............ **CLC 13**
See also CA 81-84

Cancale
See Desnos, Robert

Canetti, Elias
1905-1994 .... **CLC 3, 14, 25, 75, 86**
See also CA 21-24R; 146; CANR 23;
DLB 85, 124; MTCW

Canin, Ethan 1960-.............. **CLC 55**
See also CA 131; 135

Cannon, Curt
See Hunter, Evan

Cape, Judith
See Page, P(atricia) K(athleen)

Capek, Karel
  1890-1938 ...... **TCLC 6, 37; DA; DAB;**
    DAC; DAM DRAM, MST, NOV; DC 1;
                                      WLC
  See also CA 104; 140

Capote, Truman
  1924-1984 ...... **CLC 1, 3, 8, 13, 19, 34,**
    38, 58; DA; DAB; DAC; DAM MST,
    NOV, POP; SSC 2; WLC
  See also CA 5-8R; 113; CANR 18;
    CDALB 1941-1968; DLB 2; DLBY 80,
    84; MTCW; SATA 91

Capra, Frank 1897-1991.......... **CLC 16**
  See also CA 61-64; 135

Caputo, Philip 1941-.............. **CLC 32**
  See also CA 73-76; CANR 40

Card, Orson Scott
  1951- ...... **CLC 44, 47, 50; DAM POP**
  See also AAYA 11; CA 102; CANR 27, 47;
    INT CANR-27; MTCW; SATA 83

Cardenal, Ernesto
  1925- .... **CLC 31; DAM MULT,**
                                  POET; HLC
  See also CA 49-52; CANR 2, 32; HW;
    MTCW

Cardozo, Benjamin N(athan)
  1870-1938 .... **TCLC 65**
  See also CA 117

Carducci, Giosue 1835-1907....... **TCLC 32**

Carew, Thomas 1595(?)-1640....... **LC 13**
  See also DLB 126

Carey, Ernestine Gilbreth 1908-.... **CLC 17**
  See also CA 5-8R; SATA 2

Carey, Peter 1943-......... **CLC 40, 55, 96**
  See also CA 123; 127; CANR 53; INT 127;
    MTCW

Carleton, William 1794-1869...... **NCLC 3**
  See also DLB 159

Carlisle, Henry (Coffin) 1926-...... **CLC 33**
  See also CA 13-16R; CANR 15

Carlsen, Chris
  See Holdstock, Robert P.

Carlson, Ron(ald F.) 1947-......... **CLC 54**
  See also CA 105; CANR 27

Carlyle, Thomas
  1795-1881 ...... **NCLC 22; DA; DAB;**
                          DAC; DAM MST
  See also CDBLB 1789-1832; DLB 55; 144

Carman, (William) Bliss
  1861-1929 .... **TCLC 7; DAC**
  See also CA 104; 152; DLB 92

Carnegie, Dale 1888-1955 .... **TCLC 53**

Carossa, Hans 1878-1956......... **TCLC 48**
  See also DLB 66

Carpenter, Don(ald Richard)
  1931-1995 .... **CLC 41**
  See also CA 45-48; 149; CANR 1

Carpentier (y Valmont), Alejo
  1904-1980 .... **CLC 8, 11, 38;**
                          DAM MULT; HLC
  See also CA 65-68; 97-100; CANR 11;
    DLB 113; HW

Carr, Caleb 1955(?)-.............. **CLC 86**
  See also CA 147

Carr, Emily 1871-1945.......... **TCLC 32**
  See also DLB 68

Carr, John Dickson 1906-1977 ...... **CLC 3**
  See also CA 49-52; 69-72; CANR 3, 33;
    MTCW

Carr, Philippa
  See Hibbert, Eleanor Alice Burford

Carr, Virginia Spencer 1929-....... **CLC 34**
  See also CA 61-64; DLB 111

Carrere, Emmanuel 1957- .... **CLC 89**

Carrier, Roch
  1937- ... **CLC 13, 78; DAC; DAM MST**
  See also CA 130; DLB 53

Carroll, James P. 1943(?)-......... **CLC 38**
  See also CA 81-84

Carroll, Jim 1951- .... **CLC 35**
  See also AAYA 17; CA 45-48; CANR 42

Carroll, Lewis .... **NCLC 2, 53; WLC**
  See also Dodgson, Charles Lutwidge
  See also CDBLB 1832-1890; CLR 2, 18;
    DLB 18, 163; JRDA

Carroll, Paul Vincent 1900-1968.... **CLC 10**
  See also CA 9-12R; 25-28R; DLB 10

Carruth, Hayden
  1921- ...... **CLC 4, 7, 10, 18, 84; PC 10**
  See also CA 9-12R; CANR 4, 38; DLB 5,
    165; INT CANR-4; MTCW; SATA 47

Carson, Rachel Louise
  1907-1964 .... **CLC 71; DAM POP**
  See also CA 77-80; CANR 35; MTCW;
    SATA 23

Carter, Angela (Olive)
  1940-1992 ...... **CLC 5, 41, 76; SSC 13**
  See also CA 53-56; 136; CANR 12, 36;
    DLB 14; MTCW; SATA 66;
    SATA-Obit 70

Carter, Nick
  See Smith, Martin Cruz

Carver, Raymond
  1938-1988 .... **CLC 22, 36, 53, 55;**
                          DAM NOV; SSC 8
  See also CA 33-36R; 126; CANR 17, 34;
    DLB 130; DLBY 84, 88; MTCW

Cary, Elizabeth, Lady Falkland
  1585-1639 .... **LC 30**

Cary, (Arthur) Joyce (Lunel)
  1888-1957 .... **TCLC 1, 29**
  See also CA 104; CDBLB 1914-1945;
    DLB 15, 100

Casanova de Seingalt, Giovanni Jacopo
  1725-1798 .... **LC 13**

Casares, Adolfo Bioy
  See Bioy Casares, Adolfo

Casely-Hayford, J(oseph) E(phraim)
  1866-1930 .... **TCLC 24; BLC;**
                              DAM MULT
  See also BW 2; CA 123; 152

Casey, John (Dudley) 1939-........ **CLC 59**
  See also BEST 90:2; CA 69-72; CANR 23

Casey, Michael 1947-.............. **CLC 2**
  See also CA 65-68; DLB 5

Casey, Patrick
  See Thurman, Wallace (Henry)

Casey, Warren (Peter) 1935-1988 ... **CLC 12**
  See also CA 101; 127; INT 101

Casona, Alejandro .... **CLC 49**
  See also Alvarez, Alejandro Rodriguez

Cassavetes, John 1929-1989....... **CLC 20**
  See also CA 85-88; 127

Cassill, R(onald) V(erlin) 1919-... **CLC 4, 23**
  See also CA 9-12R; CAAS 1; CANR 7, 45;
    DLB 6

Cassirer, Ernst 1874-1945 .... **TCLC 61**

Cassity, (Allen) Turner 1929- .... **CLC 6, 42**
  See also CA 17-20R; CAAS 8; CANR 11;
    DLB 105

Castaneda, Carlos 1931(?)-........ **CLC 12**
  See also CA 25-28R; CANR 32; HW;
    MTCW

Castedo, Elena 1937- .... **CLC 65**
  See also CA 132

Castedo-Ellerman, Elena
  See Castedo, Elena

Castellanos, Rosario
  1925-1974 ...... **CLC 66; DAM MULT;**
                                      HLC
  See also CA 131; 53-56; DLB 113; HW

Castelvetro, Lodovico 1505-1571..... **LC 12**

Castiglione, Baldassare 1478-1529 ... **LC 12**

Castle, Robert
  See Hamilton, Edmond

Castro, Guillen de 1569-1631........ **LC 19**

Castro, Rosalia de
  1837-1885 ...... **NCLC 3; DAM MULT**

Cather, Willa
  See Cather, Willa Sibert

Cather, Willa Sibert
  1873-1947 .... **TCLC 1, 11, 31; DA;**
    DAB; DAC; DAM MST, NOV; SSC 2;
                                      WLC
  See also CA 104; 128; CDALB 1865-1917;
    DLB 9, 54, 78; DLBD 1; MTCW;
    SATA 30

Catton, (Charles) Bruce
  1899-1978 .... **CLC 35**
  See also AITN 1; CA 5-8R; 81-84;
    CANR 7; DLB 17; SATA 2;
    SATA-Obit 24

Catullus c. 84B.C.-c. 54B.C. ..... **CMLC 18**

Cauldwell, Frank
  See King, Francis (Henry)

Caunitz, William J. 1933-1996 ..... **CLC 34**
  See also BEST 89:3; CA 125; 130; 152;
    INT 130

Causley, Charles (Stanley) 1917-..... **CLC 7**
  See also CA 9-12R; CANR 5, 35; CLR 30;
    DLB 27; MTCW; SATA 3, 66

Caute, David 1936-.... **CLC 29; DAM NOV**
  See also CA 1-4R; CAAS 4; CANR 1, 33;
    DLB 14

Cavafy, C(onstantine) P(eter)
  1863-1933 .... **TCLC 2, 7; DAM POET**
  See also Kavafis, Konstantinos Petrou
  See also CA 148

Cavallo, Evelyn
  See Spark, Muriel (Sarah)

Cavanna, Betty . . . . **CLC 12**
See also Harrison, Elizabeth Cavanna
See also JRDA; MAICYA; SAAS 4;
SATA 1, 30

Cavendish, Margaret Lucas
1623-1673 . . . . **LC 30**
See also DLB 131

Caxton, William 1421(?)-1491(?) . . . . . **LC 17**
See also DLB 170

Cayrol, Jean 1911- . . . . **CLC 11**
See also CA 89-92; DLB 83

Cela, Camilo Jose
1916- . . . . . **CLC 4, 13, 59; DAM MULT;**
HLC
See also BEST 90:2; CA 21-24R; CAAS 10;
CANR 21, 32; DLBY 89; HW; MTCW

Celan, Paul . . . . . **CLC 10, 19, 53, 82; PC 10**
See also Antschel, Paul
See also DLB 69

Celine, Louis-Ferdinand
. . . . **CLC 1, 3, 4, 7, 9, 15, 47**
See also Destouches, Louis-Ferdinand
See also DLB 72

Cellini, Benvenuto 1500-1571 . . . . **LC 7**

Cendrars, Blaise . . . . **CLC 18**
See also Sauser-Hall, Frederic

Cernuda (y Bidon), Luis
1902-1963 . . . . . . **CLC 54; DAM POET**
See also CA 131; 89-92; DLB 134; HW

Cervantes (Saavedra), Miguel de
1547-1616 . . . . **LC 6, 23; DA; DAB;**
DAC; DAM MST, NOV; SSC 12; WLC

Cesaire, Aime (Fernand)
1913- . . . . **CLC 19, 32; BLC;**
DAM MULT, POET
See also BW 2; CA 65-68; CANR 24, 43;
MTCW

Chabon, Michael 1963- . . . . **CLC 55**
See also CA 139

Chabrol, Claude 1930- . . . . **CLC 16**
See also CA 110

Challans, Mary 1905-1983
See Renault, Mary
See also CA 81-84; 111; SATA 23;
SATA-Obit 36

Challis, George
See Faust, Frederick (Schiller)

Chambers, Aidan 1934- . . . . **CLC 35**
See also CA 25-28R; CANR 12, 31; JRDA;
MAICYA; SAAS 12; SATA 1, 69

Chambers, James 1948-
See Cliff, Jimmy
See also CA 124

Chambers, Jessie
See Lawrence, D(avid) H(erbert Richards)

Chambers, Robert W. 1865-1933 . . . **TCLC 41**

Chandler, Raymond (Thornton)
1888-1959 . . . . **TCLC 1, 7; SSC 23**
See also CA 104; 129; CDALB 1929-1941;
DLBD 6; MTCW

Chang, Jung 1952- . . . . **CLC 71**
See also CA 142

Channing, William Ellery
1780-1842 . . . . **NCLC 17**
See also DLB 1, 59

Chaplin, Charles Spencer
1889-1977 . . . . **CLC 16**
See also Chaplin, Charlie
See also CA 81-84; 73-76

Chaplin, Charlie
See Chaplin, Charles Spencer
See also DLB 44

Chapman, George
1559(?)-1634 . . . . . **LC 22; DAM DRAM**
See also DLB 62, 121

Chapman, Graham 1941-1989 . . . . . . **CLC 21**
See also Monty Python
See also CA 116; 129; CANR 35

Chapman, John Jay 1862-1933 . . . . . **TCLC 7**
See also CA 104

Chapman, Lee
See Bradley, Marion Zimmer

Chapman, Walker
See Silverberg, Robert

Chappell, Fred (Davis) 1936- . . . . **CLC 40, 78**
See also CA 5-8R; CAAS 4; CANR 8, 33;
DLB 6, 105

Char, Rene(-Emile)
1907-1988 . . . . **CLC 9, 11, 14, 55;**
DAM POET
See also CA 13-16R; 124; CANR 32;
MTCW

Charby, Jay
See Ellison, Harlan (Jay)

Chardin, Pierre Teilhard de
See Teilhard de Chardin, (Marie Joseph)
Pierre

Charles I 1600-1649 . . . . **LC 13**

Charyn, Jerome 1937- . . . . **CLC 5, 8, 18**
See also CA 5-8R; CAAS 1; CANR 7;
DLBY 83; MTCW

Chase, Mary (Coyle) 1907-1981 . . . . . . **DC 1**
See also CA 77-80; 105; SATA 17;
SATA-Obit 29

Chase, Mary Ellen 1887-1973 . . . . **CLC 2**
See also CA 13-16; 41-44R; CAP 1;
SATA 10

Chase, Nicholas
See Hyde, Anthony

Chateaubriand, Francois Rene de
1768-1848 . . . . **NCLC 3**
See also DLB 119

Chatterje, Sarat Chandra 1876-1936(?)
See Chatterji, Saratchandra
See also CA 109

Chatterji, Bankim Chandra
1838-1894 . . . . **NCLC 19**

Chatterji, Saratchandra . . . . **TCLC 13**
See also Chatterje, Sarat Chandra

Chatterton, Thomas
1752-1770 . . . . **LC 3; DAM POET**
See also DLB 109

Chatwin, (Charles) Bruce
1940-1989 . . **CLC 28, 57, 59; DAM POP**
See also AAYA 4; BEST 90:1; CA 85-88;
127

Chaucer, Daniel
See Ford, Ford Madox

Chaucer, Geoffrey
1340(?)-1400 . . . . **LC 17; DA; DAB;**
DAC; DAM MST, POET
See also CDBLB Before 1660; DLB 146

Chaviaras, Strates 1935-
See Haviaras, Stratis
See also CA 105

Chayefsky, Paddy . . . . **CLC 23**
See also Chayefsky, Sidney
See also DLB 7, 44; DLBY 81

Chayefsky, Sidney 1923-1981
See Chayefsky, Paddy
See also CA 9-12R; 104; CANR 18;
DAM DRAM

Chedid, Andree 1920- . . . . **CLC 47**
See also CA 145

Cheever, John
1912-1982 . . . . . . **CLC 3, 7, 8, 11, 15, 25,**
64; DA; DAB; DAC; DAM MST, NOV,
POP; SSC 1; WLC
See also CA 5-8R; 106; CABS 1; CANR 5,
27; CDALB 1941-1968; DLB 2, 102;
DLBY 80, 82; INT CANR-5; MTCW

Cheever, Susan 1943- . . . . **CLC 18, 48**
See also CA 103; CANR 27, 51; DLBY 82;
INT CANR-27

Chekhonte, Antosha
See Chekhov, Anton (Pavlovich)

Chekhov, Anton (Pavlovich)
1860-1904 . . . . . **TCLC 3, 10, 31, 55; DA;**
DAB; DAC; DAM DRAM, MST; SSC 2;
WLC
See also CA 104; 124; SATA 90

Chernyshevsky, Nikolay Gavrilovich
1828-1889 . . . . **NCLC 1**

Cherry, Carolyn Janice 1942-
See Cherryh, C. J.
See also CA 65-68; CANR 10

Cherryh, C. J. . . . . **CLC 35**
See also Cherry, Carolyn Janice
See also DLBY 80

Chesnutt, Charles W(addell)
1858-1932 . . . . **TCLC 5, 39; BLC;**
DAM MULT; SSC 7
See also BW 1; CA 106; 125; DLB 12, 50,
78; MTCW

Chester, Alfred 1929(?)-1971 . . . . **CLC 49**
See also CA 33-36R; DLB 130

Chesterton, G(ilbert) K(eith)
1874-1936 . . . . **TCLC 1, 6, 64;**
DAM NOV, POET; SSC 1
See also CA 104; 132; CDBLB 1914-1945;
DLB 10, 19, 34, 70, 98, 149; MTCW;
SATA 27

Chiang Pin-chin 1904-1986
See Ding Ling
See also CA 118

Ch'ien Chung-shu 1910- . . . . **CLC 22**
See also CA 130; MTCW

Child, L. Maria
See Child, Lydia Maria

Child, Lydia Maria 1802-1880 . . . . **NCLC 6**
See also DLB 1, 74; SATA 67

Child, Mrs.
See Child, Lydia Maria

Child, Philip   1898-1978 . . . .   **CLC 19, 68**
    See also CA 13-14; CAP 1; SATA 47

Childers, (Robert) Erskine
        1870-1922 . . . .   **TCLC 65**
    See also CA 113; 153; DLB 70

Childress, Alice
        1920-1994 . . . .   **CLC 12, 15, 86, 96; BLC;
            DAM DRAM, MULT, NOV; DC 4**
    See also AAYA 8; BW 2; CA 45-48; 146;
        CANR 3, 27, 50; CLR 14; DLB 7, 38;
        JRDA; MAICYA; MTCW; SATA 7, 48,
        81

Chislett, (Margaret) Anne   1943- . . . .   **CLC 34**
    See also CA 151

Chitty, Thomas Willes   1926- . . . .   **CLC 11**
    See also Hinde, Thomas
    See also CA 5-8R

Chivers, Thomas Holley
        1809-1858 . . . .   **NCLC 49**
    See also DLB 3

Chomette, Rene Lucien   1898-1981
    See Clair, Rene
    See also CA 103

Chopin, Kate
        . . . .   **TCLC 5, 14; DA; DAB; SSC 8**
    See also Chopin, Katherine
    See also CDALB 1865-1917; DLB 12, 78

Chopin, Katherine   1851-1904
    See Chopin, Kate
    See also CA 104; 122; DAC; DAM MST,
        NOV

Chretien de Troyes
        c. 12th cent. - . . . .   **CMLC 10**

Christie
    See Ichikawa, Kon

Christie, Agatha (Mary Clarissa)
        1890-1976 . . . . . .   **CLC 1, 6, 8, 12, 39, 48;
            DAB; DAC; DAM NOV**
    See also AAYA 9; AITN 1, 2; CA 17-20R;
        61-64; CANR 10, 37; CDBLB 1914-1945;
        DLB 13, 77; MTCW; SATA 36

Christie, (Ann) Philippa
    See Pearce, Philippa
    See also CA 5-8R; CANR 4

Christine de Pizan   1365(?)-1431(?) . . . .   **LC 9**

Chubb, Elmer
    See Masters, Edgar Lee

Chulkov, Mikhail Dmitrievich
        1743-1792 . . . .   **LC 2**
    See also DLB 150

Churchill, Caryl   1938- . . .   **CLC 31, 55; DC 5**
    See also CA 102; CANR 22, 46; DLB 13;
        MTCW

Churchill, Charles   1731-1764 . . . .   **LC 3**
    See also DLB 109

Chute, Carolyn   1947- . . . .   **CLC 39**
    See also CA 123

Ciardi, John (Anthony)
        1916-1986 . . . .   **CLC 10, 40, 44;
            DAM POET**
    See also CA 5-8R; 118; CAAS 2; CANR 5,
        33; CLR 19; DLB 5; DLBY 86;
        INT CANR-5; MAICYA; MTCW;
        SATA 1, 65; SATA-Obit 46

Cicero, Marcus Tullius
        106B.C.-43B.C. . . . .   **CMLC 3**

Cimino, Michael   1943- . . . .   **CLC 16**
    See also CA 105

Cioran, E(mil) M.   1911-1995 . . . . . .   **CLC 64**
    See also CA 25-28R; 149

Cisneros, Sandra
        1954- . . . . .   **CLC 69; DAM MULT; HLC**
    See also AAYA 9; CA 131; DLB 122, 152;
        HW

Cixous, Helene   1937- . . . .   **CLC 92**
    See also CA 126; CANR 55; DLB 83;
        MTCW

Clair, Rene . . . .   **CLC 20**
    See also Chomette, Rene Lucien

Clampitt, Amy   1920-1994 . . .   **CLC 32; PC 17**
    See also CA 110; 146; CANR 29; DLB 105

Clancy, Thomas L., Jr.   1947-
    See Clancy, Tom
    See also CA 125; 131; INT 131; MTCW

Clancy, Tom . . . . .   **CLC 45; DAM NOV, POP**
    See also Clancy, Thomas L., Jr.
    See also AAYA 9; BEST 89:1, 90:1

Clare, John
        1793-1864 . . . .   **NCLC 9; DAB;
            DAM POET**
    See also DLB 55, 96

Clarin
    See Alas (y Urena), Leopoldo (Enrique
        Garcia)

Clark, Al C.
    See Goines, Donald

Clark, (Robert) Brian   1932- . . . .   **CLC 29**
    See also CA 41-44R

Clark, Curt
    See Westlake, Donald E(dwin)

Clark, Eleanor   1913-1996 . . . .   **CLC 5, 19**
    See also CA 9-12R; 151; CANR 41; DLB 6

Clark, J. P.
    See Clark, John Pepper
    See also DLB 117

Clark, John Pepper
        1935- . . . .   **CLC 38; BLC; DAM DRAM,
            MULT; DC 5**
    See also Clark, J. P.
    See also BW 1; CA 65-68; CANR 16

Clark, M. R.
    See Clark, Mavis Thorpe

Clark, Mavis Thorpe   1909- . . . .   **CLC 12**
    See also CA 57-60; CANR 8, 37; CLR 30;
        MAICYA; SAAS 5; SATA 8, 74

Clark, Walter Van Tilburg
        1909-1971 . . . .   **CLC 28**
    See also CA 9-12R; 33-36R; DLB 9;
        SATA 8

Clarke, Arthur C(harles)
        1917- . . . .   **CLC 1, 4, 13, 18, 35;
            DAM POP; SSC 3**
    See also AAYA 4; CA 1-4R; CANR 2, 28,
        55; JRDA; MAICYA; MTCW; SATA 13,
        70

Clarke, Austin
        1896-1974 . . . . . .   **CLC 6, 9; DAM POET**
    See also CA 29-32; 49-52; CAP 2; DLB 10,
        20

Clarke, Austin C(hesterfield)
        1934- . . . .   **CLC 8, 53; BLC; DAC;
            DAM MULT**
    See also BW 1; CA 25-28R; CAAS 16;
        CANR 14, 32; DLB 53, 125

Clarke, Gillian   1937- . . . .   **CLC 61**
    See also CA 106; DLB 40

Clarke, Marcus (Andrew Hislop)
        1846-1881 . . . .   **NCLC 19**

Clarke, Shirley   1925- . . . .   **CLC 16**

Clash, The
    See Headon, (Nicky) Topper; Jones, Mick;
        Simonon, Paul; Strummer, Joe

Claudel, Paul (Louis Charles Marie)
        1868-1955 . . . .   **TCLC 2, 10**
    See also CA 104

Clavell, James (duMaresq)
        1925-1994 . . . .   **CLC 6, 25, 87;
            DAM NOV, POP**
    See also CA 25-28R; 146; CANR 26, 48;
        MTCW

Cleaver, (Leroy) Eldridge
        1935- . . . . .   **CLC 30; BLC; DAM MULT**
    See also BW 1; CA 21-24R; CANR 16

Cleese, John (Marwood)   1939- . . . . .   **CLC 21**
    See also Monty Python
    See also CA 112; 116; CANR 35; MTCW

Cleishbotham, Jebediah
    See Scott, Walter

Cleland, John   1710-1789 . . . .   **LC 2**
    See also DLB 39

Clemens, Samuel Langhorne   1835-1910
    See Twain, Mark
    See also CA 104; 135; CDALB 1865-1917;
        DA; DAB; DAC; DAM MST, NOV;
        DLB 11, 12, 23, 64, 74; JRDA;
        MAICYA; YABC 2

Cleophil
    See Congreve, William

Clerihew, E.
    See Bentley, E(dmund) C(lerihew)

Clerk, N. W.
    See Lewis, C(live) S(taples)

Cliff, Jimmy . . . .   **CLC 21**
    See also Chambers, James

Clifton, (Thelma) Lucille
        1936- . . . .   **CLC 19, 66; BLC;
            DAM MULT, POET; PC 17**
    See also BW 2; CA 49-52; CANR 2, 24, 42;
        CLR 5; DLB 5, 41; MAICYA; MTCW;
        SATA 20, 69

Clinton, Dirk
    See Silverberg, Robert

Clough, Arthur Hugh   1819-1861 . .   **NCLC 27**
    See also DLB 32

Clutha, Janet Paterson Frame   1924-
    See Frame, Janet
    See also CA 1-4R; CANR 2, 36; MTCW

Clyne, Terence
    See Blatty, William Peter

Cobalt, Martin
    See Mayne, William (James Carter)

Cobbett, William   1763-1835 . . . . .   **NCLC 49**
    See also DLB 43, 107, 158

Coburn, D(onald) L(ee) 1938- . . . . . . **CLC 10**
See also CA 89-92

Cocteau, Jean (Maurice Eugene Clement)
1889-1963 . . . . **CLC 1, 8, 15, 16, 43; DA;
DAB; DAC; DAM DRAM, MST, NOV;
WLC**
See also CA 25-28; CANR 40; CAP 2;
DLB 65; MTCW

Codrescu, Andrei
1946- . . . . **CLC 46; DAM POET**
See also CA 33-36R; CAAS 19; CANR 13,
34, 53

Coe, Max
See Bourne, Randolph S(illiman)

Coe, Tucker
See Westlake, Donald E(dwin)

Coetzee, J(ohn) M(ichael)
1940- . . . . . . **CLC 23, 33, 66; DAM NOV**
See also CA 77-80; CANR 41, 54; MTCW

Coffey, Brian
See Koontz, Dean R(ay)

Cohan, George M. 1878-1942 . . . . . **TCLC 60**

Cohen, Arthur A(llen)
1928-1986 . . . . **CLC 7, 31**
See also CA 1-4R; 120; CANR 1, 17, 42;
DLB 28

Cohen, Leonard (Norman)
1934- . . . . **CLC 3, 38; DAC; DAM MST**
See also CA 21-24R; CANR 14; DLB 53;
MTCW

Cohen, Matt 1942- . . . . **CLC 19; DAC**
See also CA 61-64; CAAS 18; CANR 40;
DLB 53

Cohen-Solal, Annie 19(?)- . . . . **CLC 50**

Colegate, Isabel 1931- . . . . **CLC 36**
See also CA 17-20R; CANR 8, 22; DLB 14;
INT CANR-22; MTCW

Coleman, Emmett
See Reed, Ishmael

Coleridge, Samuel Taylor
1772-1834 . . . . . **NCLC 9, 54; DA; DAB;
DAC; DAM MST, POET; PC 11; WLC**
See also CDBLB 1789-1832; DLB 93, 107

Coleridge, Sara 1802-1852 . . . . . . **NCLC 31**

Coles, Don 1928- . . . . **CLC 46**
See also CA 115; CANR 38

Colette, (Sidonie-Gabrielle)
1873-1954 . . . . **TCLC 1, 5, 16;
DAM NOV; SSC 10**
See also CA 104; 131; DLB 65; MTCW

Collett, (Jacobine) Camilla (Wergeland)
1813-1895 . . . . **NCLC 22**

Collier, Christopher 1930- . . . . **CLC 30**
See also AAYA 13; CA 33-36R; CANR 13,
33; JRDA; MAICYA; SATA 16, 70

Collier, James L(incoln)
1928- . . . . **CLC 30; DAM POP**
See also AAYA 13; CA 9-12R; CANR 4,
33; CLR 3; JRDA; MAICYA; SAAS 21;
SATA 8, 70

Collier, Jeremy 1650-1726 . . . . **LC 6**

Collier, John 1901-1980 . . . . **SSC 19**
See also CA 65-68; 97-100; CANR 10;
DLB 77

Collingwood, R(obin) G(eorge)
1889(?)-1943 . . . . **TCLC 67**
See also CA 117; 155

Collins, Hunt
See Hunter, Evan

Collins, Linda 1931- . . . . **CLC 44**
See also CA 125

Collins, (William) Wilkie
1824-1889 . . . . **NCLC 1, 18**
See also CDBLB 1832-1890; DLB 18, 70,
159

Collins, William
1721-1759 . . . . **LC 4; DAM POET**
See also DLB 109

Collodi, Carlo 1826-1890 . . . . **NCLC 54**
See also Lorenzini, Carlo
See also CLR 5

Colman, George
See Glassco, John

Colt, Winchester Remington
See Hubbard, L(afayette) Ron(ald)

Colter, Cyrus 1910- . . . . **CLC 58**
See also BW 1; CA 65-68; CANR 10;
DLB 33

Colton, James
See Hansen, Joseph

Colum, Padraic 1881-1972 . . . . **CLC 28**
See also CA 73-76; 33-36R; CANR 35;
CLR 36; MAICYA; MTCW; SATA 15

Colvin, James
See Moorcock, Michael (John)

Colwin, Laurie (E.)
1944-1992 . . . . **CLC 5, 13, 23, 84**
See also CA 89-92; 139; CANR 20, 46;
DLBY 80; MTCW

Comfort, Alex(ander)
1920- . . . . **CLC 7; DAM POP**
See also CA 1-4R; CANR 1, 45

Comfort, Montgomery
See Campbell, (John) Ramsey

Compton-Burnett, I(vy)
1884(?)-1969 . . . . . . **CLC 1, 3, 10, 15, 34;
DAM NOV**
See also CA 1-4R; 25-28R; CANR 4;
DLB 36; MTCW

Comstock, Anthony 1844-1915 . . . . **TCLC 13**
See also CA 110

Comte, Auguste 1798-1857 . . . . **NCLC 54**

Conan Doyle, Arthur
See Doyle, Arthur Conan

Conde, Maryse
1937- . . . . . . **CLC 52, 92; DAM MULT**
See also Boucolon, Maryse
See also BW 2

Condillac, Etienne Bonnot de
1714-1780 . . . . **LC 26**

Condon, Richard (Thomas)
1915-1996 . . . . **CLC 4, 6, 8, 10, 45;
DAM NOV**
See also BEST 90:3; CA 1-4R; 151;
CAAS 1; CANR 2, 23; INT CANR-23;
MTCW

Confucius
551B.C.-479B.C. . . . . **CMLC 19; DA;
DAB; DAC; DAM MST**

Congreve, William
1670-1729 . . . . **LC 5, 21; DA; DAB;
DAC; DAM DRAM, MST, POET;
DC 2; WLC**
See also CDBLB 1660-1789; DLB 39, 84

Connell, Evan S(helby), Jr.
1924- . . . . **CLC 4, 6, 45; DAM NOV**
See also AAYA 7; CA 1-4R; CAAS 2;
CANR 2, 39; DLB 2; DLBY 81; MTCW

Connelly, Marc(us Cook)
1890-1980 . . . . **CLC 7**
See also CA 85-88; 102; CANR 30; DLB 7;
DLBY 80; SATA-Obit 25

Connor, Ralph . . . . **TCLC 31**
See also Gordon, Charles William
See also DLB 92

Conrad, Joseph
1857-1924 . . . . **TCLC 1, 6, 13, 25, 43, 57;
DA; DAB; DAC; DAM MST, NOV;
SSC 9; WLC**
See also CA 104; 131; CDBLB 1890-1914;
DLB 10, 34, 98, 156; MTCW; SATA 27

Conrad, Robert Arnold
See Hart, Moss

Conroy, Donald Pat(rick)
1945- . . . **CLC 30, 74; DAM NOV, POP**
See also AAYA 8; AITN 1; CA 85-88;
CANR 24, 53; DLB 6; MTCW

Constant (de Rebecque), (Henri) Benjamin
1767-1830 . . . . **NCLC 6**
See also DLB 119

Conybeare, Charles Augustus
See Eliot, T(homas) S(tearns)

Cook, Michael 1933- . . . . **CLC 58**
See also CA 93-96; DLB 53

Cook, Robin 1940- . . . . **CLC 14; DAM POP**
See also BEST 90:2; CA 108; 111;
CANR 41; INT 111

Cook, Roy
See Silverberg, Robert

Cooke, Elizabeth 1948- . . . . **CLC 55**
See also CA 129

Cooke, John Esten 1830-1886 . . . . . **NCLC 5**
See also DLB 3

Cooke, John Estes
See Baum, L(yman) Frank

Cooke, M. E.
See Creasey, John

Cooke, Margaret
See Creasey, John

Cook-Lynn, Elizabeth
1930- . . . . **CLC 93; DAM MULT**
See also CA 133; NNAL

Cooney, Ray . . . . **CLC 62**

Cooper, Douglas 1960- . . . . **CLC 86**

Cooper, Henry St. John
See Creasey, John

Cooper, J(oan) California
. . . . **CLC 56; DAM MULT**
See also AAYA 12; BW 1; CA 125;
CANR 55

Cooper, James Fenimore
1789-1851 . . . . **NCLC 1, 27, 54**
See also CDALB 1640-1865; DLB 3;
SATA 19

Coover, Robert (Lowell)
  1932- .... **CLC 3, 7, 15, 32, 46, 87;**
                      DAM NOV; SSC 15
  See also CA 45-48; CANR 3, 37; DLB 2;
  DLBY 81; MTCW

Copeland, Stewart (Armstrong)
  1952- .... **CLC 26**

Coppard, A(lfred) E(dgar)
  1878-1957 .... **TCLC 5; SSC 21**
  See also CA 114; DLB 162; YABC 1

Coppee, Francois 1842-1908 ..... **TCLC 25**

Coppola, Francis Ford 1939-....... **CLC 16**
  See also CA 77-80; CANR 40; DLB 44

Corbiere, Tristan 1845-1875 ..... **NCLC 43**

Corcoran, Barbara 1911-.......... **CLC 17**
  See also AAYA 14; CA 21-24R; CAAS 2;
  CANR 11, 28, 48; DLB 52; JRDA;
  SAAS 20; SATA 3, 77

Cordelier, Maurice
  See Giraudoux, (Hippolyte) Jean

Corelli, Marie 1855-1924........ **TCLC 51**
  See also Mackay, Mary
  See also DLB 34, 156

Corman, Cid .... **CLC 9**
  See also Corman, Sidney
  See also CAAS 2; DLB 5

Corman, Sidney 1924-
  See Corman, Cid
  See also CA 85-88; CANR 44; DAM POET

Cormier, Robert (Edmund)
  1925- .... **CLC 12, 30; DA; DAB; DAC;**
                      DAM MST, NOV
  See also AAYA 3, 19; CA 1-4R; CANR 5,
  23; CDALB 1968-1988; CLR 12; DLB 52;
  INT CANR-23; JRDA; MAICYA;
  MTCW; SATA 10, 45, 83

Corn, Alfred (DeWitt III) 1943-.... **CLC 33**
  See also CA 104; CAAS 25; CANR 44;
  DLB 120; DLBY 80

Corneille, Pierre
  1606-1684 .... **LC 28; DAB; DAM MST**

Cornwell, David (John Moore)
  1931- .... **CLC 9, 15; DAM POP**
  See also le Carre, John
  See also CA 5-8R; CANR 13, 33; MTCW

Corso, (Nunzio) Gregory 1930-... **CLC 1, 11**
  See also CA 5-8R; CANR 41; DLB 5, 16;
  MTCW

Cortazar, Julio
  1914-1984 ...... **CLC 2, 3, 5, 10, 13, 15,**
              33, 34, 92; DAM MULT, NOV; HLC;
                      SSC 7
  See also CA 21-24R; CANR 12, 32;
  DLB 113; HW; MTCW

CORTES, HERNAN 1484-1547..... **LC 31**

Corwin, Cecil
  See Kornbluth, C(yril) M.

Cosic, Dobrica 1921-............. **CLC 14**
  See also CA 122; 138

Costain, Thomas B(ertram)
  1885-1965 .... **CLC 30**
  See also CA 5-8R; 25-28R; DLB 9

Costantini, Humberto
  1924(?)-1987 .... **CLC 49**
  See also CA 131; 122; HW

Costello, Elvis 1955-............. **CLC 21**

Cotter, Joseph Seamon Sr.
  1861-1949 .... **TCLC 28; BLC;**
                      DAM MULT
  See also BW 1; CA 124; DLB 50

Couch, Arthur Thomas Quiller
  See Quiller-Couch, Arthur Thomas

Coulton, James
  See Hansen, Joseph

Couperus, Louis (Marie Anne)
  1863-1923 .... **TCLC 15**
  See also CA 115

Coupland, Douglas
  1961- .... **CLC 85; DAC; DAM POP**
  See also CA 142

Court, Wesli
  See Turco, Lewis (Putnam)

Courtenay, Bryce 1933-........... **CLC 59**
  See also CA 138

Courtney, Robert
  See Ellison, Harlan (Jay)

Cousteau, Jacques-Yves 1910-...... **CLC 30**
  See also CA 65-68; CANR 15; MTCW;
  SATA 38

Coward, Noel (Peirce)
  1899-1973 .... **CLC 1, 9, 29, 51;**
                      DAM DRAM
  See also AITN 1; CA 17-18; 41-44R;
  CANR 35; CAP 2; CDBLB 1914-1945;
  DLB 10; MTCW

Cowley, Malcolm 1898-1989 .... **CLC 39**
  See also CA 5-8R; 128; CANR 3, 55;
  DLB 4, 48; DLBY 81, 89; MTCW

Cowper, William
  1731-1800 ...... **NCLC 8; DAM POET**
  See also DLB 104, 109

Cox, William Trevor
  1928- .... **CLC 9, 14, 71; DAM NOV**
  See also Trevor, William
  See also CA 9-12R; CANR 4, 37, 55;
  DLB 14; INT CANR-37; MTCW

Coyne, P. J.
  See Masters, Hilary

Cozzens, James Gould
  1903-1978 .... **CLC 1, 4, 11, 92**
  See also CA 9-12R; 81-84; CANR 19;
  CDALB 1941-1968; DLB 9; DLBD 2;
  DLBY 84; MTCW

Crabbe, George 1754-1832....... **NCLC 26**
  See also DLB 93

Craddock, Charles Egbert
  See Murfree, Mary Noailles

Craig, A. A.
  See Anderson, Poul (William)

Craik, Dinah Maria (Mulock)
  1826-1887 .... **NCLC 38**
  See also DLB 35, 163; MAICYA; SATA 34

Cram, Ralph Adams 1863-1942.... **TCLC 45**

Crane, (Harold) Hart
  1899-1932 .... **TCLC 2, 5; DA; DAB;**
              DAC; DAM MST, POET; PC 3; WLC
  See also CA 104; 127; CDALB 1917-1929;
  DLB 4, 48; MTCW

Crane, R(onald) S(almon)
  1886-1967 .... **CLC 27**
  See also CA 85-88; DLB 63

Crane, Stephen (Townley)
  1871-1900 ...... **TCLC 11, 17, 32; DA;**
              DAB; DAC; DAM MST, NOV, POET;
                      SSC 7; WLC
  See also CA 109; 140; CDALB 1865-1917;
  DLB 12, 54, 78; YABC 2

Crase, Douglas 1944-............. **CLC 58**
  See also CA 106

Crashaw, Richard 1612(?)-1649...... **LC 24**
  See also DLB 126

Craven, Margaret
  1901-1980 .... **CLC 17; DAC**
  See also CA 103

Crawford, F(rancis) Marion
  1854-1909 .... **TCLC 10**
  See also CA 107; DLB 71

Crawford, Isabella Valancy
  1850-1887 .... **NCLC 12**
  See also DLB 92

Crayon, Geoffrey
  See Irving, Washington

Creasey, John 1908-1973.......... **CLC 11**
  See also CA 5-8R; 41-44R; CANR 8;
  DLB 77; MTCW

Crebillon, Claude Prosper Jolyot de (fils)
  1707-1777 .... **LC 28**

Credo
  See Creasey, John

Creeley, Robert (White)
  1926- ..... **CLC 1, 2, 4, 8, 11, 15, 36, 78;**
                      DAM POET
  See also CA 1-4R; CAAS 10; CANR 23, 43;
  DLB 5, 16, 169; MTCW

Crews, Harry (Eugene)
  1935- .... **CLC 6, 23, 49**
  See also AITN 1; CA 25-28R; CANR 20;
  DLB 6, 143; MTCW

Crichton, (John) Michael
  1942- .... **CLC 2, 6, 54, 90; DAM NOV,**
                      POP
  See also AAYA 10; AITN 2; CA 25-28R;
  CANR 13, 40, 54; DLBY 81;
  INT CANR-13; JRDA; MTCW; SATA 9,
  88

Crispin, Edmund .... **CLC 22**
  See also Montgomery, (Robert) Bruce
  See also DLB 87

Cristofer, Michael
  1945(?)-........ **CLC 28; DAM DRAM**
  See also CA 110; 152; DLB 7

Croce, Benedetto 1866-1952 ...... **TCLC 37**
  See also CA 120; 155

Crockett, David 1786-1836 .... **NCLC 8**
  See also DLB 3, 11

Crockett, Davy
  See Crockett, David

Crofts, Freeman Wills
  1879-1957 .... **TCLC 55**
  See also CA 115; DLB 77

Croker, John Wilson 1780-1857 .. **NCLC 10**
  See also DLB 110

Crommelynck, Fernand 1885-1970 . . **CLC 75**
See also CA 89-92

Cronin, A(rchibald) J(oseph)
1896-1981 . . . . **CLC 32**
See also CA 1-4R; 102; CANR 5; SATA 47;
SATA-Obit 25

Cross, Amanda
See Heilbrun, Carolyn G(old)

Crothers, Rachel 1878(?)-1958. . . . . **TCLC 19**
See also CA 113; DLB 7

Croves, Hal
See Traven, B.

Crow Dog, Mary (Ellen) (?)-. . . . . . . **CLC 93**
See also Brave Bird, Mary
See also CA 154

Crowfield, Christopher
See Stowe, Harriet (Elizabeth) Beecher

Crowley, Aleister. . . . . **TCLC 7**
See also Crowley, Edward Alexander

Crowley, Edward Alexander 1875-1947
See Crowley, Aleister
See also CA 104

Crowley, John 1942-. . . . . **CLC 57**
See also CA 61-64; CANR 43; DLBY 82;
SATA 65

Crud
See Crumb, R(obert)

Crumarums
See Crumb, R(obert)

Crumb, R(obert) 1943-. . . . . **CLC 17**
See also CA 106

Crumbum
See Crumb, R(obert)

Crumski
See Crumb, R(obert)

Crum the Bum
See Crumb, R(obert)

Crunk
See Crumb, R(obert)

Crustt
See Crumb, R(obert)

Cryer, Gretchen (Kiger) 1935-. . . . . . **CLC 21**
See also CA 114; 123

Csath, Geza 1887-1919. . . . . **TCLC 13**
See also CA 111

Cudlip, David 1933-. . . . . **CLC 34**

Cullen, Countee
1903-1946 . . . . . . **TCLC 4, 37; BLC; DA;**
DAC; DAM MST, MULT, POET
See also BW 1; CA 108; 124;
CDALB 1917-1929; DLB 4, 48, 51;
MTCW; SATA 18

Cum, R.
See Crumb, R(obert)

Cummings, Bruce F(rederick) 1889-1919
See Barbellion, W. N. P.
See also CA 123

Cummings, E(dward) E(stlin)
1894-1962 . . . . . . **CLC 1, 3, 8, 12, 15, 68;**
DA; DAB; DAC; DAM MST, POET;
PC 5; WLC 2
See also CA 73-76; CANR 31;
CDALB 1929-1941; DLB 4, 48; MTCW

Cunha, Euclides (Rodrigues Pimenta) da
1866-1909 . . . . **TCLC 24**
See also CA 123

Cunningham, E. V.
See Fast, Howard (Melvin)

Cunningham, J(ames) V(incent)
1911-1985 . . . . **CLC 3, 31**
See also CA 1-4R; 115; CANR 1; DLB 5

Cunningham, Julia (Woolfolk)
1916-. . . . . **CLC 12**
See also CA 9-12R; CANR 4, 19, 36;
JRDA; MAICYA; SAAS 2; SATA 1, 26

Cunningham, Michael 1952-. . . . . . . **CLC 34**
See also CA 136

Cunninghame Graham, R(obert) B(ontine)
1852-1936 . . . . **TCLC 19**
See also Graham, R(obert) B(ontine)
Cunninghame
See also CA 119; DLB 98

Currie, Ellen 19(?)-. . . . . **CLC 44**

Curtin, Philip
See Lowndes, Marie Adelaide (Belloc)

Curtis, Price
See Ellison, Harlan (Jay)

Cutrate, Joe
See Spiegelman, Art

Czaczkes, Shmuel Yosef
See Agnon, S(hmuel) Y(osef Halevi)

Dabrowska, Maria (Szumska)
1889-1965 . . . . **CLC 15**
See also CA 106

Dabydeen, David 1955-. . . . . **CLC 34**
See also BW 1; CA 125

Dacey, Philip 1939-. . . . . **CLC 51**
See also CA 37-40R; CAAS 17; CANR 14,
32; DLB 105

Dagerman, Stig (Halvard)
1923-1954 . . . . **TCLC 17**
See also CA 117; 155

Dahl, Roald
1916-1990 . . . . . . **CLC 1, 6, 18, 79; DAB;**
DAC; DAM MST, NOV, POP
See also AAYA 15; CA 1-4R; 133;
CANR 6, 32, 37; CLR 1, 7, 41; DLB 139;
JRDA; MAICYA; MTCW; SATA 1, 26,
73; SATA-Obit 65

Dahlberg, Edward 1900-1977. . . **CLC 1, 7, 14**
See also CA 9-12R; 69-72; CANR 31;
DLB 48; MTCW

Dale, Colin. **TCLC 18**
See also Lawrence, T(homas) E(dward)

Dale, George E.
See Asimov, Isaac

Daly, Elizabeth 1878-1967. . . . . **CLC 52**
See also CA 23-24; 25-28R; CAP 2

Daly, Maureen 1921-. . . . . **CLC 17**
See also AAYA 5; CANR 37; JRDA;
MAICYA; SAAS 1; SATA 2

Damas, Leon-Gontran 1912-1978 . . . **CLC 84**
See also BW 1; CA 125; 73-76

Dana, Richard Henry Sr.
1787-1879 . . . . **NCLC 53**

Daniel, Samuel 1562(?)-1619. . . . . . . **LC 24**
See also DLB 62

Daniels, Brett
See Adler, Renata

Dannay, Frederic
1905-1982 . . . . **CLC 11; DAM POP**
See also Queen, Ellery
See also CA 1-4R; 107; CANR 1, 39;
DLB 137; MTCW

D'Annunzio, Gabriele
1863-1938 . . . . **TCLC 6, 40**
See also CA 104; 155

Danois, N. le
See Gourmont, Remy (-Marie-Charles) de

d'Antibes, Germain
See Simenon, Georges (Jacques Christian)

Danticat, Edwidge 1969-. . . . . **CLC 94**
See also CA 152

Danvers, Dennis 1947-. . . . . **CLC 70**

Danziger, Paula 1944-. . . . . **CLC 21**
See also AAYA 4; CA 112; 115; CANR 37;
CLR 20; JRDA; MAICYA; SATA 36,
63; SATA-Brief 30

Da Ponte, Lorenzo 1749-1838. . . . **NCLC 50**

Dario, Ruben
1867-1916 . . . . . **TCLC 4; DAM MULT;**
HLC; PC 15
See also CA 131; HW; MTCW

Darley, George 1795-1846. . . . . **NCLC 2**
See also DLB 96

Darwin, Charles 1809-1882 . . . . . . **NCLC 57**
See also DLB 57, 166

Daryush, Elizabeth 1887-1977. . . . **CLC 6, 19**
See also CA 49-52; CANR 3; DLB 20

Dashwood, Edmee Elizabeth Monica de la
Pasture 1890-1943
See Delafield, E. M.
See also CA 119; 154

Daudet, (Louis Marie) Alphonse
1840-1897 . . . . **NCLC 1**
See also DLB 123

Daumal, Rene 1908-1944. . . . . **TCLC 14**
See also CA 114

Davenport, Guy (Mattison, Jr.)
1927-. . . . . **CLC 6, 14, 38; SSC 16**
See also CA 33-36R; CANR 23; DLB 130

Davidson, Avram 1923-
See Queen, Ellery
See also CA 101; CANR 26; DLB 8

Davidson, Donald (Grady)
1893-1968 . . . . **CLC 2, 13, 19**
See also CA 5-8R; 25-28R; CANR 4;
DLB 45

Davidson, Hugh
See Hamilton, Edmond

Davidson, John 1857-1909. . . . . **TCLC 24**
See also CA 118; DLB 19

Davidson, Sara 1943-. . . . . **CLC 9**
See also CA 81-84; CANR 44

Davie, Donald (Alfred)
1922-1995 . . . . **CLC 5, 8, 10, 31**
See also CA 1-4R; 149; CAAS 3; CANR 1,
44; DLB 27; MTCW

Davies, Ray(mond Douglas) 1944-. . **CLC 21**
See also CA 116; 146

Author Index

Davies, Rhys 1903-1978 . . . . **CLC 23**
See also CA 9-12R; 81-84; CANR 4;
DLB 139

Davies, (William) Robertson
1913-1995 . . . . . **CLC 2, 7, 13, 25, 42, 75,
91; DA; DAB; DAC; DAM MST, NOV,
POP; WLC**
See also BEST 89:2; CA 33-36R; 150;
CANR 17, 42; DLB 68; INT CANR-17;
MTCW

Davies, W(illiam) H(enry)
1871-1940 . . . . **TCLC 5**
See also CA 104; DLB 19, 174

Davies, Walter C.
See Kornbluth, C(yril) M.

Davis, Angela (Yvonne)
1944- . . . . **CLC 77; DAM MULT**
See also BW 2; CA 57-60; CANR 10

Davis, B. Lynch
See Bioy Casares, Adolfo; Borges, Jorge
Luis

Davis, Gordon
See Hunt, E(verette) Howard, (Jr.)

Davis, Harold Lenoir 1896-1960 . . . . **CLC 49**
See also CA 89-92; DLB 9

Davis, Rebecca (Blaine) Harding
1831-1910 . . . . **TCLC 6**
See also CA 104; DLB 74

Davis, Richard Harding
1864-1916 . . . . **TCLC 24**
See also CA 114; DLB 12, 23, 78, 79;
DLBD 13

Davison, Frank Dalby 1893-1970 . . . **CLC 15**
See also CA 116

Davison, Lawrence H.
See Lawrence, D(avid) H(erbert Richards)

Davison, Peter (Hubert) 1928- . . . . . **CLC 28**
See also CA 9-12R; CAAS 4; CANR 3, 43;
DLB 5

Davys, Mary 1674-1732 . . . . **LC 1**
See also DLB 39

Dawson, Fielding 1930- . . . . **CLC 6**
See also CA 85-88; DLB 130

Dawson, Peter
See Faust, Frederick (Schiller)

Day, Clarence (Shepard, Jr.)
1874-1935 . . . . **TCLC 25**
See also CA 108; DLB 11

Day, Thomas 1748-1789 . . . . **LC 1**
See also DLB 39; YABC 1

Day Lewis, C(ecil)
1904-1972 . . . . **CLC 1, 6, 10;
DAM POET; PC 11**
See also Blake, Nicholas
See also CA 13-16; 33-36R; CANR 34;
CAP 1; DLB 15, 20; MTCW

Dazai, Osamu . . . . **TCLC 11**
See also Tsushima, Shuji

de Andrade, Carlos Drummond
See Drummond de Andrade, Carlos

Deane, Norman
See Creasey, John

**de Beauvoir, Simone (Lucie Ernestine Marie
Bertrand)**
See Beauvoir, Simone (Lucie Ernestine
Marie Bertrand) de

de Brissac, Malcolm
See Dickinson, Peter (Malcolm)

de Chardin, Pierre Teilhard
See Teilhard de Chardin, (Marie Joseph)
Pierre

Dee, John 1527-1608 . . . . **LC 20**

Deer, Sandra 1940- . . . . **CLC 45**

De Ferrari, Gabriella 1941- . . . . **CLC 65**
See also CA 146

Defoe, Daniel
1660(?)-1731 . . . . **LC 1; DA; DAB; DAC;
DAM MST, NOV; WLC**
See also CDBLB 1660-1789; DLB 39, 95,
101; JRDA; MAICYA; SATA 22

de Gourmont, Remy(-Marie-Charles)
See Gourmont, Remy (-Marie-Charles) de

de Hartog, Jan 1914- . . . . **CLC 19**
See also CA 1-4R; CANR 1

de Hostos, E. M.
See Hostos (y Bonilla), Eugenio Maria de

de Hostos, Eugenio M.
See Hostos (y Bonilla), Eugenio Maria de

Deighton, Len . . . . **CLC 4, 7, 22, 46**
See also Deighton, Leonard Cyril
See also AAYA 6; BEST 89:2;
CDBLB 1960 to Present; DLB 87

Deighton, Leonard Cyril 1929-
See Deighton, Len
See also CA 9-12R; CANR 19, 33;
DAM NOV, POP; MTCW

Dekker, Thomas
1572(?)-1632 . . . . . **LC 22; DAM DRAM**
See also CDBLB Before 1660; DLB 62, 172

Delafield, E. M. 1890-1943 . . . . **TCLC 61**
See also Dashwood, Edmee Elizabeth
Monica de la Pasture
See also DLB 34

de la Mare, Walter (John)
1873-1956 . . . . **TCLC 4, 53; DAB; DAC;
DAM MST, POET; SSC 14; WLC**
See also CDBLB 1914-1945; CLR 23;
DLB 162; SATA 16

Delaney, Franey
See O'Hara, John (Henry)

Delaney, Shelagh
1939- . . . . **CLC 29; DAM DRAM**
See also CA 17-20R; CANR 30;
CDBLB 1960 to Present; DLB 13;
MTCW

Delany, Mary (Granville Pendarves)
1700-1788 . . . . **LC 12**

Delany, Samuel R(ay, Jr.)
1942- . . . . **CLC 8, 14, 38; BLC;
DAM MULT**
See also BW 2; CA 81-84; CANR 27, 43;
DLB 8, 33; MTCW

De La Ramee, (Marie) Louise 1839-1908
See Ouida
See also SATA 20

de la Roche, Mazo 1879-1961 . . . . . . **CLC 14**
See also CA 85-88; CANR 30; DLB 68;
SATA 64

Delbanco, Nicholas (Franklin)
1942- . . . . **CLC 6, 13**
See also CA 17-20R; CAAS 2; CANR 29,
55; DLB 6

del Castillo, Michel 1933- . . . . **CLC 38**
See also CA 109

Deledda, Grazia (Cosima)
1875(?)-1936 . . . . **TCLC 23**
See also CA 123

Delibes, Miguel . . . . **CLC 8, 18**
See also Delibes Setien, Miguel

Delibes Setien, Miguel 1920-
See Delibes, Miguel
See also CA 45-48; CANR 1, 32; HW;
MTCW

DeLillo, Don
1936- . . . . . **CLC 8, 10, 13, 27, 39, 54, 76;
DAM NOV, POP**
See also BEST 89:1; CA 81-84; CANR 21;
DLB 6, 173; MTCW

de Lisser, H. G.
See De Lisser, H(erbert) G(eorge)
See also DLB 117

De Lisser, H(erbert) G(eorge)
1878-1944 . . . . **TCLC 12**
See also de Lisser, H. G.
See also BW 2; CA 109; 152

Deloria, Vine (Victor), Jr.
1933- . . . . **CLC 21; DAM MULT**
See also CA 53-56; CANR 5, 20, 48;
MTCW; NNAL; SATA 21

Del Vecchio, John M(ichael)
1947- . . . . **CLC 29**
See also CA 110; DLBD 9

de Man, Paul (Adolph Michel)
1919-1983 . . . . **CLC 55**
See also CA 128; 111; DLB 67; MTCW

De Marinis, Rick 1934- . . . . **CLC 54**
See also CA 57-60; CAAS 24; CANR 9, 25,
50

Dembry, R. Emmet
See Murfree, Mary Noailles

Demby, William
1922- . . . . . **CLC 53; BLC; DAM MULT**
See also BW 1; CA 81-84; DLB 33

Demijohn, Thom
See Disch, Thomas M(ichael)

de Montherlant, Henry (Milon)
See Montherlant, Henry (Milon) de

Demosthenes 384B.C.-322B.C. . . . . **CMLC 13**

de Natale, Francine
See Malzberg, Barry N(athaniel)

Denby, Edwin (Orr) 1903-1983 . . . . . **CLC 48**
See also CA 138; 110

Denis, Julio
See Cortazar, Julio

Denmark, Harrison
See Zelazny, Roger (Joseph)

Dennis, John 1658-1734 . . . . **LC 11**
See also DLB 101

Dennis, Nigel (Forbes) 1912-1989 . . . . **CLC 8**
See also CA 25-28R; 129; DLB 13, 15;
MTCW

De Palma, Brian (Russell) 1940- . . . . **CLC 20**
See also CA 109

De Quincey, Thomas 1785-1859 . . . **NCLC 4**
See also CDBLB 1789-1832; DLB 110; 144

Deren, Eleanora 1908(?)-1961
See Deren, Maya
See also CA 111

Deren, Maya . . . . **CLC 16**
See also Deren, Eleanora

Derleth, August (William)
1909-1971 . . . . **CLC 31**
See also CA 1-4R; 29-32R; CANR 4;
DLB 9; SATA 5

Der Nister 1884-1950 . . . . **TCLC 56**

de Routisie, Albert
See Aragon, Louis

Derrida, Jacques 1930- . . . . **CLC 24, 87**
See also CA 124; 127

Derry Down Derry
See Lear, Edward

Dersonnes, Jacques
See Simenon, Georges (Jacques Christian)

Desai, Anita
1937- . . . . **CLC 19, 37, 97; DAB;
DAM NOV**
See also CA 81-84; CANR 33, 53; MTCW;
SATA 63

de Saint-Luc, Jean
See Glassco, John

de Saint Roman, Arnaud
See Aragon, Louis

Descartes, Rene 1596-1650 . . . . . . **LC 20, 35**

De Sica, Vittorio 1901(?)-1974 . . . . . **CLC 20**
See also CA 117

Desnos, Robert 1900-1945 . . . . **TCLC 22**
See also CA 121; 151

Destouches, Louis-Ferdinand
1894-1961 . . . . **CLC 9, 15**
See also Celine, Louis-Ferdinand
See also CA 85-88; CANR 28; MTCW

de Tolignac, Gaston
See Griffith, D(avid Lewelyn) W(ark)

Deutsch, Babette 1895-1982 . . . . **CLC 18**
See also CA 1-4R; 108; CANR 4; DLB 45;
SATA 1; SATA-Obit 33

Devenant, William 1606-1649 . . . . **LC 13**

Devkota, Laxmiprasad
1909-1959 . . . . **TCLC 23**
See also CA 123

De Voto, Bernard (Augustine)
1897-1955 . . . . **TCLC 29**
See also CA 113; DLB 9

De Vries, Peter
1910-1993 . . . . **CLC 1, 2, 3, 7, 10, 28, 46;
DAM NOV**
See also CA 17-20R; 142; CANR 41;
DLB 6; DLBY 82; MTCW

Dexter, John
See Bradley, Marion Zimmer

Dexter, Martin
See Faust, Frederick (Schiller)

Dexter, Pete
1943- . . . . **CLC 34, 55; DAM POP**
See also BEST 89:2; CA 127; 131; INT 131;
MTCW

Diamano, Silmang
See Senghor, Leopold Sedar

Diamond, Neil 1941- . . . . **CLC 30**
See also CA 108

Diaz del Castillo, Bernal 1496-1584 . . **LC 31**

di Bassetto, Corno
See Shaw, George Bernard

Dick, Philip K(indred)
1928-1982 . . . . **CLC 10, 30, 72;
DAM NOV, POP**
See also CA 49-52; 106; CANR 2, 16;
DLB 8; MTCW

Dickens, Charles (John Huffam)
1812-1870 . . . . . . **NCLC 3, 8, 18, 26, 37,
50; DA; DAB; DAC; DAM MST, NOV;
SSC 17; WLC**
See also CDBLB 1832-1890; DLB 21, 55,
70, 159, 166; JRDA; MAICYA; SATA 15

Dickey, James (Lafayette)
1923- . . . . **CLC 1, 2, 4, 7, 10, 15, 47;
DAM NOV, POET, POP**
See also AITN 1, 2; CA 9-12R; CABS 2;
CANR 10, 48; CDALB 1968-1988;
DLB 5; DLBD 7; DLBY 82, 93;
INT CANR-10; MTCW

Dickey, William 1928-1994 . . . . . . **CLC 3, 28**
See also CA 9-12R; 145; CANR 24; DLB 5

Dickinson, Charles 1951- . . . . **CLC 49**
See also CA 128

Dickinson, Emily (Elizabeth)
1830-1886 . . . . **NCLC 21; DA; DAB;
DAC; DAM MST, POET; PC 1; WLC**
See also CDALB 1865-1917; DLB 1;
SATA 29

Dickinson, Peter (Malcolm)
1927- . . . . **CLC 12, 35**
See also AAYA 9; CA 41-44R; CANR 31;
CLR 29; DLB 87, 161; JRDA; MAICYA;
SATA 5, 62

Dickson, Carr
See Carr, John Dickson

Dickson, Carter
See Carr, John Dickson

Diderot, Denis 1713-1784 . . . . **LC 26**

Didion, Joan
1934- . . **CLC 1, 3, 8, 14, 32; DAM NOV**
See also AITN 1; CA 5-8R; CANR 14, 52;
CDALB 1968-1988; DLB 2, 173;
DLBY 81, 86; MTCW

Dietrich, Robert
See Hunt, E(verette) Howard, (Jr.)

Dillard, Annie
1945- . . . . **CLC 9, 60; DAM NOV**
See also AAYA 6; CA 49-52; CANR 3, 43;
DLBY 80; MTCW; SATA 10

Dillard, R(ichard) H(enry) W(ilde)
1937- . . . . **CLC 5**
See also CA 21-24R; CAAS 7; CANR 10;
DLB 5

Dillon, Eilis 1920-1994 . . . . **CLC 17**
See also CA 9-12R; 147; CAAS 3; CANR 4,
38; CLR 26; MAICYA; SATA 2, 74;
SATA-Obit 83

Dimont, Penelope
See Mortimer, Penelope (Ruth)

Dinesen, Isak . . . . **CLC 10, 29, 95; SSC 7**
See also Blixen, Karen (Christentze
Dinesen)

Ding Ling . . . . **CLC 68**
See also Chiang Pin-chin

Disch, Thomas M(ichael) 1940- . . . **CLC 7, 36**
See also AAYA 17; CA 21-24R; CAAS 4;
CANR 17, 36, 54; CLR 18; DLB 8;
MAICYA; MTCW; SAAS 15; SATA 54

Disch, Tom
See Disch, Thomas M(ichael)

d'Isly, Georges
See Simenon, Georges (Jacques Christian)

Disraeli, Benjamin 1804-1881 . . **NCLC 2, 39**
See also DLB 21, 55

Ditcum, Steve
See Crumb, R(obert)

Dixon, Paige
See Corcoran, Barbara

Dixon, Stephen 1936- . . . . . **CLC 52; SSC 16**
See also CA 89-92; CANR 17, 40, 54;
DLB 130

Dobell, Sydney Thompson
1824-1874 . . . . **NCLC 43**
See also DLB 32

Doblin, Alfred . . . . **TCLC 13**
See also Doeblin, Alfred

Dobrolyubov, Nikolai Alexandrovich
1836-1861 . . . . **NCLC 5**

Dobyns, Stephen 1941- . . . . **CLC 37**
See also CA 45-48; CANR 2, 18

Doctorow, E(dgar) L(aurence)
1931- . . . . . **CLC 6, 11, 15, 18, 37, 44, 65;
DAM NOV, POP**
See also AITN 2; BEST 89:3; CA 45-48;
CANR 2, 33, 51; CDALB 1968-1988;
DLB 2, 28, 173; DLBY 80; MTCW

Dodgson, Charles Lutwidge 1832-1898
See Carroll, Lewis
See also CLR 2; DA; DAB; DAC;
DAM MST, NOV, POET; MAICYA;
YABC 2

Dodson, Owen (Vincent)
1914-1983 . . . . **CLC 79; BLC;
DAM MULT**
See also BW 1; CA 65-68; 110; CANR 24;
DLB 76

Doeblin, Alfred 1878-1957 . . . . **TCLC 13**
See also Doblin, Alfred
See also CA 110; 141; DLB 66

Doerr, Harriet 1910- . . . . **CLC 34**
See also CA 117; 122; CANR 47; INT 122

Domecq, H(onorio) Bustos
See Bioy Casares, Adolfo; Borges, Jorge
Luis

Domini, Rey
See Lorde, Audre (Geraldine)

Dominique
See Proust, (Valentin-Louis-George-Eugene-) Marcel

Don, A
See Stephen, Leslie

Donaldson, Stephen R.
1947- . . . . CLC 46; DAM POP
See also CA 89-92; CANR 13, 55; INT CANR-13

Donleavy, J(ames) P(atrick)
1926- . . . . CLC 1, 4, 6, 10, 45
See also AITN 2; CA 9-12R; CANR 24, 49; DLB 6, 173; INT CANR-24; MTCW

Donne, John
1572-1631 . . . . LC 10, 24; DA; DAB; DAC; DAM MST, POET; PC 1
See also CDBLB Before 1660; DLB 121, 151

Donnell, David 1939(?)- . . . . CLC 34

Donoghue, P. S.
See Hunt, E(verette) Howard, (Jr.)

Donoso (Yanez), Jose
1924-1996 . . . . CLC 4, 8, 11, 32; DAM MULT; HLC
See also CA 81-84; 155; CANR 32; DLB 113; HW; MTCW

Donovan, John 1928-1992 . . . . CLC 35
See also CA 97-100; 137; CLR 3; MAICYA; SATA 72; SATA-Brief 29

Don Roberto
See Cunninghame Graham, R(obert) B(ontine)

Doolittle, Hilda
1886-1961 . . . . . CLC 3, 8, 14, 31, 34, 73; DA; DAC; DAM MST, POET; PC 5; WLC
See also H. D.
See also CA 97-100; CANR 35; DLB 4, 45; MTCW

Dorfman, Ariel
1942- . . . . CLC 48, 77; DAM MULT; HLC
See also CA 124; 130; HW; INT 130

Dorn, Edward (Merton) 1929-. . . CLC 10, 18
See also CA 93-96; CANR 42; DLB 5; INT 93-96

Dorsan, Luc
See Simenon, Georges (Jacques Christian)

Dorsange, Jean
See Simenon, Georges (Jacques Christian)

Dos Passos, John (Roderigo)
1896-1970 . . . . . . CLC 1, 4, 8, 11, 15, 25, 34, 82; DA; DAB; DAC; DAM MST, NOV; WLC
See also CA 1-4R; 29-32R; CANR 3; CDALB 1929-1941; DLB 4, 9; DLBD 1; MTCW

Dossage, Jean
See Simenon, Georges (Jacques Christian)

Dostoevsky, Fedor Mikhailovich
1821-1881 . . . . . . NCLC 2, 7, 21, 33, 43; DA; DAB; DAC; DAM MST, NOV; SSC 2; WLC

Doughty, Charles M(ontagu)
1843-1926 . . . . TCLC 27
See also CA 115; DLB 19, 57, 174

Douglas, Ellen . . . . CLC 73
See also Haxton, Josephine Ayres; Williamson, Ellen Douglas

Douglas, Gavin 1475(?)-1522 . . . . LC 20

Douglas, Keith 1920-1944 . . . . TCLC 40
See also DLB 27

Douglas, Leonard
See Bradbury, Ray (Douglas)

Douglas, Michael
See Crichton, (John) Michael

Douglas, Norman 1868-1952 . . . . . . TCLC 68

Douglass, Frederick
1817(?)-1895 . . . . NCLC 7, 55; BLC; DA; DAC; DAM MST, MULT; WLC
See also CDALB 1640-1865; DLB 1, 43, 50, 79; SATA 29

Dourado, (Waldomiro Freitas) Autran
1926- . . . . CLC 23, 60
See also CA 25-28R; CANR 34

Dourado, Waldomiro Autran
See Dourado, (Waldomiro Freitas) Autran

Dove, Rita (Frances)
1952- . . . . CLC 50, 81; DAM MULT, POET; PC 6
See also BW 2; CA 109; CAAS 19; CANR 27, 42; DLB 120

Dowell, Coleman 1925-1985. . . . . . . CLC 60
See also CA 25-28R; 117; CANR 10; DLB 130

Dowson, Ernest (Christopher)
1867-1900 . . . . TCLC 4
See also CA 105; 150; DLB 19, 135

Doyle, A. Conan
See Doyle, Arthur Conan

Doyle, Arthur Conan
1859-1930 . . . . TCLC 7; DA; DAB; DAC; DAM MST, NOV; SSC 12; WLC
See also AAYA 14; CA 104; 122; CDBLB 1890-1914; DLB 18, 70, 156; MTCW; SATA 24

Doyle, Conan
See Doyle, Arthur Conan

Doyle, John
See Graves, Robert (von Ranke)

Doyle, Roddy 1958(?)- . . . . CLC 81
See also AAYA 14; CA 143

Doyle, Sir A. Conan
See Doyle, Arthur Conan

Doyle, Sir Arthur Conan
See Doyle, Arthur Conan

Dr. A
See Asimov, Isaac; Silverstein, Alvin

Drabble, Margaret
1939- . . . . CLC 2, 3, 5, 8, 10, 22, 53; DAB; DAC; DAM MST, NOV, POP
See also CA 13-16R; CANR 18, 35; CDBLB 1960 to Present; DLB 14, 155; MTCW; SATA 48

Drapier, M. B.
See Swift, Jonathan

Drayham, James
See Mencken, H(enry) L(ouis)

Drayton, Michael 1563-1631. . . . . LC 8

Dreadstone, Carl
See Campbell, (John) Ramsey

Dreiser, Theodore (Herman Albert)
1871-1945 . . . . . . TCLC 10, 18, 35; DA; DAC; DAM MST, NOV; WLC
See also CA 106; 132; CDALB 1865-1917; DLB 9, 12, 102, 137; DLBD 1; MTCW

Drexler, Rosalyn 1926- . . . . CLC 2, 6
See also CA 81-84

Dreyer, Carl Theodor 1889-1968. . . . CLC 16
See also CA 116

Drieu la Rochelle, Pierre(-Eugene)
1893-1945 . . . . TCLC 21
See also CA 117; DLB 72

Drinkwater, John 1882-1937 . . . . . . TCLC 57
See also CA 109; 149; DLB 10, 19, 149

Drop Shot
See Cable, George Washington

Droste-Hulshoff, Annette Freiin von
1797-1848 . . . . NCLC 3
See also DLB 133

Drummond, Walter
See Silverberg, Robert

Drummond, William Henry
1854-1907 . . . . TCLC 25
See also DLB 92

Drummond de Andrade, Carlos
1902-1987 . . . . CLC 18
See also Andrade, Carlos Drummond de
See also CA 132; 123

Drury, Allen (Stuart) 1918-. . . . . CLC 37
See also CA 57-60; CANR 18, 52; INT CANR-18

Dryden, John
1631-1700 . . . . LC 3, 21; DA; DAB; DAC; DAM DRAM, MST, POET; DC 3; WLC
See also CDBLB 1660-1789; DLB 80, 101, 131

Duberman, Martin 1930-. . . . . CLC 8
See also CA 1-4R; CANR 2

Dubie, Norman (Evans) 1945-. . . . . . CLC 36
See also CA 69-72; CANR 12; DLB 120

Du Bois, W(illiam) E(dward) B(urghardt)
1868-1963 . . . . CLC 1, 2, 13, 64, 96; BLC; DA; DAC; DAM MST, MULT, NOV; WLC
See also BW 1; CA 85-88; CANR 34; CDALB 1865-1917; DLB 47, 50, 91; MTCW; SATA 42

Dubus, Andre
1936- . . . . CLC 13, 36, 97; SSC 15
See also CA 21-24R; CANR 17; DLB 130; INT CANR-17

Duca Minimo
See D'Annunzio, Gabriele

Ducharme, Rejean 1941- . . . . CLC 74
See also DLB 60

Duclos, Charles Pinot 1704-1772 . . . . . LC 1

Dudek, Louis 1918- . . . . CLC 11, 19
See also CA 45-48; CAAS 14; CANR 1; DLB 88

Duerrenmatt, Friedrich
 1921-1990 ...... **CLC 1, 4, 8, 11, 15, 43;**
 DAM DRAM
 See also CA 17-20R; CANR 33; DLB 69,
 124; MTCW

Duffy, Bruce (?)-................ **CLC 50**

Duffy, Maureen 1933- .... **CLC 37**
 See also CA 25-28R; CANR 33; DLB 14;
 MTCW

Dugan, Alan 1923- .... **CLC 2, 6**
 See also CA 81-84; DLB 5

du Gard, Roger Martin
 See Martin du Gard, Roger

Duhamel, Georges 1884-1966 .... **CLC 8**
 See also CA 81-84; 25-28R; CANR 35;
 DLB 65; MTCW

Dujardin, Edouard (Emile Louis)
 1861-1949 .... **TCLC 13**
 See also CA 109; DLB 123

Dumas, Alexandre (Davy de la Pailleterie)
 1802-1870 .... **NCLC 11; DA; DAB;**
 DAC; DAM MST, NOV; WLC
 See also DLB 119; SATA 18

Dumas, Alexandre
 1824-1895 .... **NCLC 9; DC 1**

Dumas, Claudine
 See Malzberg, Barry N(athaniel)

Dumas, Henry L. 1934-1968 ..... **CLC 6, 62**
 See also BW 1; CA 85-88; DLB 41

du Maurier, Daphne
 1907-1989 .... **CLC 6, 11, 59; DAB;**
 DAC; DAM MST, POP; SSC 18
 See also CA 5-8R; 128; CANR 6, 55;
 MTCW; SATA 27; SATA-Obit 60

Dunbar, Paul Laurence
 1872-1906 ...... **TCLC 2, 12; BLC; DA;**
 DAC; DAM MST, MULT, POET; PC 5;
 SSC 8; WLC
 See also BW 1; CA 104; 124;
 CDALB 1865-1917; DLB 50, 54, 78;
 SATA 34

Dunbar, William 1460(?)-1530(?) .... **LC 20**
 See also DLB 132, 146

Duncan, Dora Angela
 See Duncan, Isadora

Duncan, Isadora 1877(?)-1927..... **TCLC 68**
 See also CA 118; 149

Duncan, Lois 1934-............... **CLC 26**
 See also AAYA 4; CA 1-4R; CANR 2, 23,
 36; CLR 29; JRDA; MAICYA; SAAS 2;
 SATA 1, 36, 75

Duncan, Robert (Edward)
 1919-1988 .... **CLC 1, 2, 4, 7, 15, 41, 55;**
 DAM POET; PC 2
 See also CA 9-12R; 124; CANR 28; DLB 5,
 16; MTCW

Duncan, Sara Jeannette
 1861-1922 .... **TCLC 60**
 See also DLB 92

Dunlap, William 1766-1839 .... **NCLC 2**
 See also DLB 30, 37, 59

Dunn, Douglas (Eaglesham)
 1942-..................... **CLC 6, 40**
 See also CA 45-48; CANR 2, 33; DLB 40;
 MTCW

Dunn, Katherine (Karen) 1945-..... **CLC 71**
 See also CA 33-36R

Dunn, Stephen 1939- .... **CLC 36**
 See also CA 33-36R; CANR 12, 48, 53;
 DLB 105

Dunne, Finley Peter 1867-1936.... **TCLC 28**
 See also CA 108; DLB 11, 23

Dunne, John Gregory 1932-....... **CLC 28**
 See also CA 25-28R; CANR 14, 50;
 DLBY 80

Dunsany, Edward John Moreton Drax
 Plunkett 1878-1957
 See Dunsany, Lord
 See also CA 104; 148; DLB 10

Dunsany, Lord................. TCLC 2, 59
 See also Dunsany, Edward John Moreton
 Drax Plunkett
 See also DLB 77, 153, 156

du Perry, Jean
 See Simenon, Georges (Jacques Christian)

Durang, Christopher (Ferdinand)
 1949-.................... **CLC 27, 38**
 See also CA 105; CANR 50

Duras, Marguerite
 1914-1996 .. **CLC 3, 6, 11, 20, 34, 40, 68**
 See also CA 25-28R; 151; CANR 50;
 DLB 83; MTCW

Durban, (Rosa) Pam 1947-......... **CLC 39**
 See also CA 123

Durcan, Paul
 1944- .... **CLC 43, 70; DAM POET**
 See also CA 134

Durkheim, Emile 1858-1917 ...... **TCLC 55**

Durrell, Lawrence (George)
 1912-1990 .... **CLC 1, 4, 6, 8, 13, 27, 41;**
 DAM NOV
 See also CA 9-12R; 132; CANR 40;
 CDBLB 1945-1960; DLB 15, 27;
 DLBY 90; MTCW

Durrenmatt, Friedrich
 See Duerrenmatt, Friedrich

Dutt, Toru 1856-1877........... **NCLC 29**

Dwight, Timothy 1752-1817...... **NCLC 13**
 See also DLB 37

Dworkin, Andrea 1946- .... **CLC 43**
 See also CA 77-80; CAAS 21; CANR 16,
 39; INT CANR-16; MTCW

Dwyer, Deanna
 See Koontz, Dean R(ay)

Dwyer, K. R.
 See Koontz, Dean R(ay)

Dylan, Bob 1941-...... **CLC 3, 4, 6, 12, 77**
 See also CA 41-44R; DLB 16

Eagleton, Terence (Francis) 1943-
 See Eagleton, Terry
 See also CA 57-60; CANR 7, 23; MTCW

Eagleton, Terry .... CLC 63
 See also Eagleton, Terence (Francis)

Early, Jack
 See Scoppettone, Sandra

East, Michael
 See West, Morris L(anglo)

Eastaway, Edward
 See Thomas, (Philip) Edward

Eastlake, William (Derry) 1917-..... **CLC 8**
 See also CA 5-8R; CAAS 1; CANR 5;
 DLB 6; INT CANR-5

Eastman, Charles A(lexander)
 1858-1939 ..... **TCLC 55; DAM MULT**
 See also NNAL; YABC 1

Eberhart, Richard (Ghormley)
 1904- .. **CLC 3, 11, 19, 56; DAM POET**
 See also CA 1-4R; CANR 2;
 CDALB 1941-1968; DLB 48; MTCW

Eberstadt, Fernanda 1960-........ **CLC 39**
 See also CA 136

Echegaray (y Eizaguirre), Jose (Maria Waldo)
 1832-1916 .... **TCLC 4**
 See also CA 104; CANR 32; HW; MTCW

Echeverria, (Jose) Esteban (Antonino)
 1805-1851 .... **NCLC 18**

Echo
 See Proust, (Valentin-Louis-George-Eugene-)
 Marcel

Eckert, Allan W. 1931- .... **CLC 17**
 See also AAYA 18; CA 13-16R; CANR 14,
 45; INT CANR-14; SAAS 21; SATA 29,
 91; SATA-Brief 27

Eckhart, Meister 1260(?)-1328(?) .. **CMLC 9**
 See also DLB 115

Eckmar, F. R.
 See de Hartog, Jan

Eco, Umberto
 1932- ... **CLC 28, 60; DAM NOV, POP**
 See also BEST 90:1; CA 77-80; CANR 12,
 33, 55; MTCW

Eddison, E(ric) R(ucker)
 1882-1945 .... **TCLC 15**
 See also CA 109; 154

Edel, (Joseph) Leon 1907-...... **CLC 29, 34**
 See also CA 1-4R; CANR 1, 22; DLB 103;
 INT CANR-22

Eden, Emily 1797-1869 .... **NCLC 10**

Edgar, David
 1948- .... **CLC 42; DAM DRAM**
 See also CA 57-60; CANR 12; DLB 13;
 MTCW

Edgerton, Clyde (Carlyle) 1944- .... **CLC 39**
 See also AAYA 17; CA 118; 134; INT 134

Edgeworth, Maria 1768-1849... **NCLC 1, 51**
 See also DLB 116, 159, 163; SATA 21

Edmonds, Paul
 See Kuttner, Henry

Edmonds, Walter D(umaux) 1903- .. **CLC 35**
 See also CA 5-8R; CANR 2; DLB 9;
 MAICYA; SAAS 4; SATA 1, 27

Edmondson, Wallace
 See Ellison, Harlan (Jay)

Edson, Russell .... CLC 13
 See also CA 33-36R

Edwards, Bronwen Elizabeth
 See Rose, Wendy

Edwards, G(erald) B(asil)
 1899-1976 .... **CLC 25**
 See also CA 110

Edwards, Gus 1939-.............. **CLC 43**
 See also CA 108; INT 108

Edwards, Jonathan
 1703-1758 . . . . LC 7; DA; DAC;
                                           DAM MST
 See also DLB 24

Efron, Marina Ivanovna Tsvetaeva
 See Tsvetaeva (Efron), Marina (Ivanovna)

Ehle, John (Marsden, Jr.) 1925- . . . . CLC 27
 See also CA 9-12R

Ehrenbourg, Ilya (Grigoryevich)
 See Ehrenburg, Ilya (Grigoryevich)

Ehrenburg, Ilya (Grigoryevich)
 1891-1967 . . . . CLC 18, 34, 62
 See also CA 102; 25-28R

Ehrenburg, Ilyo (Grigoryevich)
 See Ehrenburg, Ilya (Grigoryevich)

Eich, Guenter 1907-1972 . . . . CLC 15
 See also CA 111; 93-96; DLB 69, 124

Eichendorff, Joseph Freiherr von
 1788-1857 . . . . NCLC 8
 See also DLB 90

Eigner, Larry. . . . . CLC 9
 See also Eigner, Laurence (Joel)
 See also CAAS 23; DLB 5

Eigner, Laurence (Joel) 1927-1996
 See Eigner, Larry
 See also CA 9-12R; 151; CANR 6

Einstein, Albert 1879-1955 . . . . . . TCLC 65
 See also CA 121; 133; MTCW

Eiseley, Loren Corey 1907-1977 . . . . . CLC 7
 See also AAYA 5; CA 1-4R; 73-76;
   CANR 6

Eisenstadt, Jill 1963- . . . . CLC 50
 See also CA 140

Eisenstein, Sergei (Mikhailovich)
 1898-1948 . . . . TCLC 57
 See also CA 114; 149

Eisner, Simon
 See Kornbluth, C(yril) M.

Ekeloef, (Bengt) Gunnar
 1907-1968 . . . . CLC 27; DAM POET
 See also CA 123; 25-28R

Ekelof, (Bengt) Gunnar
 See Ekeloef, (Bengt) Gunnar

Ekwensi, C. O. D.
 See Ekwensi, Cyprian (Odiatu Duaka)

Ekwensi, Cyprian (Odiatu Duaka)
 1921- . . . . . . CLC 4; BLC; DAM MULT
 See also BW 2; CA 29-32R; CANR 18, 42;
   DLB 117; MTCW; SATA 66

Elaine. . . . . TCLC 18
 See also Leverson, Ada

El Crummo
 See Crumb, R(obert)

Elia
 See Lamb, Charles

Eliade, Mircea 1907-1986 . . . . CLC 19
 See also CA 65-68; 119; CANR 30; MTCW

Eliot, A. D.
 See Jewett, (Theodora) Sarah Orne

Eliot, Alice
 See Jewett, (Theodora) Sarah Orne

Eliot, Dan
 See Silverberg, Robert

Eliot, George
 1819-1880 . . . . . NCLC 4, 13, 23, 41, 49;
   DA; DAB; DAC; DAM MST, NOV;
                                              WLC
 See also CDBLB 1832-1890; DLB 21, 35, 55

Eliot, John 1604-1690 . . . . LC 5
 See also DLB 24

Eliot, T(homas) S(tearns)
 1888-1965 . . . . . CLC 1, 2, 3, 6, 9, 10, 13,
   15, 24, 34, 41, 55, 57; DA; DAB; DAC;
   DAM DRAM, MST, POET; PC 5;
                                             WLC 2
 See also CA 5-8R; 25-28R; CANR 41;
   CDALB 1929-1941; DLB 7, 10, 45, 63;
   DLBY 88; MTCW

Elizabeth 1866-1941. . . . . TCLC 41

Elkin, Stanley L(awrence)
 1930-1995 . . . . . . CLC 4, 6, 9, 14, 27, 51,
   91; DAM NOV, POP; SSC 12
 See also CA 9-12R; 148; CANR 8, 46;
   DLB 2, 28; DLBY 80; INT CANR-8;
   MTCW

Elledge, Scott. . . . . CLC 34

Elliot, Don
 See Silverberg, Robert

Elliott, Don
 See Silverberg, Robert

Elliott, George P(aul) 1918-1980. . . . . CLC 2
 See also CA 1-4R; 97-100; CANR 2

Elliott, Janice 1931- . . . . CLC 47
 See also CA 13-16R; CANR 8, 29; DLB 14

Elliott, Sumner Locke 1917-1991 . . . CLC 38
 See also CA 5-8R; 134; CANR 2, 21

Elliott, William
 See Bradbury, Ray (Douglas)

Ellis, A. E.. . . . . CLC 7

Ellis, Alice Thomas. . . . . CLC 40
 See also Haycraft, Anna

Ellis, Bret Easton
 1964- . . . . CLC 39, 71; DAM POP
 See also AAYA 2; CA 118; 123; CANR 51;
   INT 123

Ellis, (Henry) Havelock
 1859-1939 . . . . TCLC 14
 See also CA 109

Ellis, Landon
 See Ellison, Harlan (Jay)

Ellis, Trey 1962-. . . . . CLC 55
 See also CA 146

Ellison, Harlan (Jay)
 1934- . . . . . . CLC 1, 13, 42; DAM POP;
                                             SSC 14
 See also CA 5-8R; CANR 5, 46; DLB 8;
   INT CANR-5; MTCW

Ellison, Ralph (Waldo)
 1914-1994 . . . . CLC 1, 3, 11, 54, 86;
   BLC; DA; DAB; DAC; DAM MST,
   MULT, NOV; WLC
 See also AAYA 19; BW 1; CA 9-12R; 145;
   CANR 24, 53; CDALB 1941-1968;
   DLB 2, 76; DLBY 94; MTCW

Ellmann, Lucy (Elizabeth) 1956-. . . . CLC 61
 See also CA 128

Ellmann, Richard (David)
 1918-1987 . . . . CLC 50
 See also BEST 89:2; CA 1-4R; 122;
   CANR 2, 28; DLB 103; DLBY 87;
   MTCW

Elman, Richard 1934-. . . . . CLC 19
 See also CA 17-20R; CAAS 3; CANR 47

Elron
 See Hubbard, L(afayette) Ron(ald)

Eluard, Paul. . . . . TCLC 7, 41
 See also Grindel, Eugene

Elyot, Sir Thomas 1490(?)-1546 . . . . . LC 11

Elytis, Odysseus
 1911-1996 . . . . CLC 15, 49; DAM POET
 See also CA 102; 151; MTCW

Emecheta, (Florence Onye) Buchi
 1944- . . CLC 14, 48; BLC; DAM MULT
 See also BW 2; CA 81-84; CANR 27;
   DLB 117; MTCW; SATA 66

Emerson, Ralph Waldo
 1803-1882 . . . . . NCLC 1, 38; DA; DAB;
   DAC; DAM MST, POET; WLC
 See also CDALB 1640-1865; DLB 1, 59, 73

Eminescu, Mihail 1850-1889 . . . . . NCLC 33

Empson, William
 1906-1984 . . . . CLC 3, 8, 19, 33, 34
 See also CA 17-20R; 112; CANR 31;
   DLB 20; MTCW

Enchi Fumiko (Ueda) 1905-1986. . . . CLC 31
 See also CA 129; 121

Ende, Michael (Andreas Helmuth)
 1929-1995 . . . . CLC 31
 See also CA 118; 124; 149; CANR 36;
   CLR 14; DLB 75; MAICYA; SATA 61;
   SATA-Brief 42; SATA-Obit 86

Endo, Shusaku
 1923-1996 . . . . CLC 7, 14, 19, 54;
                                         DAM NOV
 See also CA 29-32R; 153; CANR 21, 54;
   MTCW

Engel, Marian 1933-1985. . . . . CLC 36
 See also CA 25-28R; CANR 12; DLB 53;
   INT CANR-12

Engelhardt, Frederick
 See Hubbard, L(afayette) Ron(ald)

Enright, D(ennis) J(oseph)
 1920- . . . . CLC 4, 8, 31
 See also CA 1-4R; CANR 1, 42; DLB 27;
   SATA 25

Enzensberger, Hans Magnus
 1929- . . . . CLC 43
 See also CA 116; 119

Ephron, Nora 1941-. . . . . CLC 17, 31
 See also AITN 2; CA 65-68; CANR 12, 39

Epsilon
 See Betjeman, John

Epstein, Daniel Mark 1948- . . . . CLC 7
 See also CA 49-52; CANR 2, 53

Epstein, Jacob 1956- . . . . CLC 19
 See also CA 114

Epstein, Joseph 1937-. . . . . CLC 39
 See also CA 112; 119; CANR 50

Epstein, Leslie 1938- . . . . CLC 27
 See also CA 73-76; CAAS 12; CANR 23

Equiano, Olaudah
1745(?)-1797 . . . . **LC 16; BLC;**
DAM MULT
See also DLB 37, 50

Erasmus, Desiderius 1469(?)-1536. . . . **LC 16**

Erdman, Paul E(mil) 1932- . . . . **CLC 25**
See also AITN 1; CA 61-64; CANR 13, 43

Erdrich, Louise
1954- . . . . . . **CLC 39, 54; DAM MULT,**
NOV, POP
See also AAYA 10; BEST 89:1; CA 114;
CANR 41; DLB 152; MTCW; NNAL

Erenburg, Ilya (Grigoryevich)
See Ehrenburg, Ilya (Grigoryevich)

Erickson, Stephen Michael 1950-
See Erickson, Steve
See also CA 129

Erickson, Steve . . . . **CLC 64**
See also Erickson, Stephen Michael

Ericson, Walter
See Fast, Howard (Melvin)

Eriksson, Buntel
See Bergman, (Ernst) Ingmar

Ernaux, Annie 1940- . . . . **CLC 88**
See also CA 147

Eschenbach, Wolfram von
See Wolfram von Eschenbach

Eseki, Bruno
See Mphahlele, Ezekiel

Esenin, Sergei (Alexandrovich)
1895-1925 . . . . **TCLC 4**
See also CA 104

Eshleman, Clayton 1935- . . . . **CLC 7**
See also CA 33-36R; CAAS 6; DLB 5

Espriella, Don Manuel Alvarez
See Southey, Robert

Espriu, Salvador 1913-1985 . . . . **CLC 9**
See also CA 154; 115; DLB 134

Espronceda, Jose de 1808-1842 . . . **NCLC 39**

Esse, James
See Stephens, James

Esterbrook, Tom
See Hubbard, L(afayette) Ron(ald)

Estleman, Loren D.
1952- . . . . . . **CLC 48; DAM NOV, POP**
See also CA 85-88; CANR 27;
INT CANR-27; MTCW

Eugenides, Jeffrey 1960(?)- . . . . **CLC 81**
See also CA 144

Euripides c. 485B.C.-406B.C. . . . . **DC 4**
See also DA; DAB; DAC; DAM DRAM,
MST

Evan, Evin
See Faust, Frederick (Schiller)

Evans, Evan
See Faust, Frederick (Schiller)

Evans, Marian
See Eliot, George

Evans, Mary Ann
See Eliot, George

Evarts, Esther
See Benson, Sally

Everett, Percival L. 1956- . . . . **CLC 57**
See also BW 2; CA 129

Everson, R(onald) G(ilmour)
1903- . . . . **CLC 27**
See also CA 17-20R; DLB 88

Everson, William (Oliver)
1912-1994 . . . . **CLC 1, 5, 14**
See also CA 9-12R; 145; CANR 20; DLB 5,
16; MTCW

Evtushenko, Evgenii Aleksandrovich
See Yevtushenko, Yevgeny (Alexandrovich)

Ewart, Gavin (Buchanan)
1916-1995 . . . . **CLC 13, 46**
See also CA 89-92; 150; CANR 17, 46;
DLB 40; MTCW

Ewers, Hanns Heinz 1871-1943 . . . **TCLC 12**
See also CA 109; 149

Ewing, Frederick R.
See Sturgeon, Theodore (Hamilton)

Exley, Frederick (Earl)
1929-1992 . . . . **CLC 6, 11**
See also AITN 2; CA 81-84; 138; DLB 143;
DLBY 81

Eynhardt, Guillermo
See Quiroga, Horacio (Sylvestre)

Ezekiel, Nissim 1924- . . . . **CLC 61**
See also CA 61-64

Ezekiel, Tish O'Dowd 1943- . . . . **CLC 34**
See also CA 129

Fadeyev, A.
See Bulgya, Alexander Alexandrovich

Fadeyev, Alexander . . . . **TCLC 53**
See also Bulgya, Alexander Alexandrovich

Fagen, Donald 1948- . . . . **CLC 26**

Fainzilberg, Ilya Arnoldovich 1897-1937
See Ilf, Ilya
See also CA 120

Fair, Ronald L. 1932- . . . . **CLC 18**
See also BW 1; CA 69-72; CANR 25;
DLB 33

Fairbairns, Zoe (Ann) 1948- . . . . **CLC 32**
See also CA 103; CANR 21

Falco, Gian
See Papini, Giovanni

Falconer, James
See Kirkup, James

Falconer, Kenneth
See Kornbluth, C(yril) M.

Falkland, Samuel
See Heijermans, Herman

Fallaci, Oriana 1930- . . . . **CLC 11**
See also CA 77-80; CANR 15; MTCW

Faludy, George 1913- . . . . **CLC 42**
See also CA 21-24R

Faludy, Gyoergy
See Faludy, George

Fanon, Frantz
1925-1961 . . . . **CLC 74; BLC;**
DAM MULT
See also BW 1; CA 116; 89-92

Fanshawe, Ann 1625-1680 . . . . **LC 11**

Fante, John (Thomas) 1911-1983 . . . **CLC 60**
See also CA 69-72; 109; CANR 23;
DLB 130; DLBY 83

Farah, Nuruddin
1945- . . . . . **CLC 53; BLC; DAM MULT**
See also BW 2; CA 106; DLB 125

Fargue, Leon-Paul 1876(?)-1947 . . . **TCLC 11**
See also CA 109

Farigoule, Louis
See Romains, Jules

Farina, Richard 1936(?)-1966 . . . . **CLC 9**
See also CA 81-84; 25-28R

Farley, Walter (Lorimer)
1915-1989 . . . . **CLC 17**
See also CA 17-20R; CANR 8, 29; DLB 22;
JRDA; MAICYA; SATA 2, 43

Farmer, Philip Jose 1918- . . . . **CLC 1, 19**
See also CA 1-4R; CANR 4, 35; DLB 8;
MTCW

Farquhar, George
1677-1707 . . . . **LC 21; DAM DRAM**
See also DLB 84

Farrell, J(ames) G(ordon)
1935-1979 . . . . **CLC 6**
See also CA 73-76; 89-92; CANR 36;
DLB 14; MTCW

Farrell, James T(homas)
1904-1979 . . . . **CLC 1, 4, 8, 11, 66**
See also CA 5-8R; 89-92; CANR 9; DLB 4,
9, 86; DLBD 2; MTCW

Farren, Richard J.
See Betjeman, John

Farren, Richard M.
See Betjeman, John

Fassbinder, Rainer Werner
1946-1982 . . . . **CLC 20**
See also CA 93-96; 106; CANR 31

Fast, Howard (Melvin)
1914- . . . . **CLC 23; DAM NOV**
See also AAYA 16; CA 1-4R; CAAS 18;
CANR 1, 33, 54; DLB 9; INT CANR-33;
SATA 7

Faulcon, Robert
See Holdstock, Robert P.

Faulkner, William (Cuthbert)
1897-1962 . . . . . **CLC 1, 3, 6, 8, 9, 11, 14,**
18, 28, 52, 68; DA; DAB; DAC;
DAM MST, NOV; SSC 1; WLC
See also AAYA 7; CA 81-84; CANR 33;
CDALB 1929-1941; DLB 9, 11, 44, 102;
DLBD 2; DLBY 86; MTCW

Fauset, Jessie Redmon
1884(?)-1961 . . . . **CLC 19, 54; BLC;**
DAM MULT
See also BW 1; CA 109; DLB 51

Faust, Frederick (Schiller)
1892-1944(?) . . . . . **TCLC 49; DAM POP**
See also CA 108; 152

Faust, Irvin 1924- . . . . **CLC 8**
See also CA 33-36R; CANR 28; DLB 2, 28;
DLBY 80

Fawkes, Guy
See Benchley, Robert (Charles)

Fearing, Kenneth (Flexner)
1902-1961 . . . . **CLC 51**
See also CA 93-96; DLB 9

Fecamps, Elise
See Creasey, John

Federman, Raymond 1928- ...... **CLC 6, 47**
See also CA 17-20R; CAAS 8; CANR 10,
43; DLBY 80

Federspiel, J(uerg) F. 1931-........ **CLC 42**
See also CA 146

Feiffer, Jules (Ralph)
1929- ...... **CLC 2, 8, 64; DAM DRAM**
See also AAYA 3; CA 17-20R; CANR 30;
DLB 7, 44; INT CANR-30; MTCW;
SATA 8, 61

Feige, Hermann Albert Otto Maximilian
See Traven, B.

Feinberg, David B. 1956-1994...... **CLC 59**
See also CA 135; 147

Feinstein, Elaine 1930-............ **CLC 36**
See also CA 69-72; CAAS 1; CANR 31;
DLB 14, 40; MTCW

Feldman, Irving (Mordecai) 1928-.... **CLC 7**
See also CA 1-4R; CANR 1; DLB 169

Fellini, Federico 1920-1993..... **CLC 16, 85**
See also CA 65-68; 143; CANR 33

Felsen, Henry Gregor 1916- .... **CLC 17**
See also CA 1-4R; CANR 1; SAAS 2;
SATA 1

Fenton, James Martin 1949-....... **CLC 32**
See also CA 102; DLB 40

Ferber, Edna 1887-1968........ **CLC 18, 93**
See also AITN 1; CA 5-8R; 25-28R; DLB 9,
28, 86; MTCW; SATA 7

Ferguson, Helen
See Kavan, Anna

Ferguson, Samuel 1810-1886..... **NCLC 33**
See also DLB 32

Fergusson, Robert 1750-1774 .... **LC 29**
See also DLB 109

Ferling, Lawrence
See Ferlinghetti, Lawrence (Monsanto)

Ferlinghetti, Lawrence (Monsanto)
1919(?)-............. **CLC 2, 6, 10, 27;
DAM POET; PC 1**
See also CA 5-8R; CANR 3, 41;
CDALB 1941-1968; DLB 5, 16; MTCW

Fernandez, Vicente Garcia Huidobro
See Huidobro Fernandez, Vicente Garcia

Ferrer, Gabriel (Francisco Victor) Miro
See Miro (Ferrer), Gabriel (Francisco
Victor)

Ferrier, Susan (Edmonstone)
1782-1854 .... **NCLC 8**
See also DLB 116

Ferrigno, Robert 1948(?)-.......... **CLC 65**
See also CA 140

Ferron, Jacques 1921-1985 ... **CLC 94; DAC**
See also CA 117; 129; DLB 60

Feuchtwanger, Lion 1884-1958..... **TCLC 3**
See also CA 104; DLB 66

Feuillet, Octave 1821-1890 ...... **NCLC 45**

Feydeau, Georges (Leon Jules Marie)
1862-1921 ..... **TCLC 22; DAM DRAM**
See also CA 113; 152

Ficino, Marsilio 1433-1499 .... **LC 12**

Fiedeler, Hans
See Doeblin, Alfred

Fiedler, Leslie A(aron)
1917- .... **CLC 4, 13, 24**
See also CA 9-12R; CANR 7; DLB 28, 67;
MTCW

Field, Andrew 1938-.............. **CLC 44**
See also CA 97-100; CANR 25

Field, Eugene 1850-1895 .... **NCLC 3**
See also DLB 23, 42, 140; DLBD 13;
MAICYA; SATA 16

Field, Gans T.
See Wellman, Manly Wade

Field, Michael .... **TCLC 43**

Field, Peter
See Hobson, Laura Z(ametkin)

Fielding, Henry
1707-1754 ...... **LC 1; DA; DAB; DAC;
DAM DRAM, MST, NOV; WLC**
See also CDBLB 1660-1789; DLB 39, 84,
101

Fielding, Sarah 1710-1768 .... **LC 1**
See also DLB 39

Fierstein, Harvey (Forbes)
1954- ..... **CLC 33; DAM DRAM, POP**
See also CA 123; 129

Figes, Eva 1932-.................. **CLC 31**
See also CA 53-56; CANR 4, 44; DLB 14

Finch, Robert (Duer Claydon)
1900- .... **CLC 18**
See also CA 57-60; CANR 9, 24, 49;
DLB 88

Findley, Timothy
1930- ...... **CLC 27; DAC; DAM MST**
See also CA 25-28R; CANR 12, 42;
DLB 53

Fink, William
See Mencken, H(enry) L(ouis)

Firbank, Louis 1942-
See Reed, Lou
See also CA 117

Firbank, (Arthur Annesley) Ronald
1886-1926 .... **TCLC 1**
See also CA 104; DLB 36

Fisher, M(ary) F(rances) K(ennedy)
1908-1992 .... **CLC 76, 87**
See also CA 77-80; 138; CANR 44

Fisher, Roy 1930-................ **CLC 25**
See also CA 81-84; CAAS 10; CANR 16;
DLB 40

Fisher, Rudolph
1897-1934 .... **TCLC 11; BLC;
DAM MULT**
See also BW 1; CA 107; 124; DLB 51, 102

Fisher, Vardis (Alvero) 1895-1968.... **CLC 7**
See also CA 5-8R; 25-28R; DLB 9

Fiske, Tarleton
See Bloch, Robert (Albert)

Fitch, Clarke
See Sinclair, Upton (Beall)

Fitch, John IV
See Cormier, Robert (Edmund)

Fitzgerald, Captain Hugh
See Baum, L(yman) Frank

FitzGerald, Edward 1809-1883 .... **NCLC 9**
See also DLB 32

Fitzgerald, F(rancis) Scott (Key)
1896-1940 .... **TCLC 1, 6, 14, 28, 55;
DA; DAB; DAC; DAM MST, NOV;
SSC 6; WLC**
See also AITN 1; CA 110; 123;
CDALB 1917-1929; DLB 4, 9, 86;
DLBD 1; DLBY 81; MTCW

Fitzgerald, Penelope 1916-... **CLC 19, 51, 61**
See also CA 85-88; CAAS 10; DLB 14

Fitzgerald, Robert (Stuart)
1910-1985 .... **CLC 39**
See also CA 1-4R; 114; CANR 1; DLBY 80

FitzGerald, Robert D(avid)
1902-1987 .... **CLC 19**
See also CA 17-20R

Fitzgerald, Zelda (Sayre)
1900-1948 .... **TCLC 52**
See also CA 117; 126; DLBY 84

Flanagan, Thomas (James Bonner)
1923- .... **CLC 25, 52**
See also CA 108; CANR 55; DLBY 80;
INT 108; MTCW

Flaubert, Gustave
1821-1880 .... **NCLC 2, 10, 19; DA;
DAB; DAC; DAM MST, NOV; SSC 11;
WLC**
See also DLB 119

Flecker, Herman Elroy
See Flecker, (Herman) James Elroy

Flecker, (Herman) James Elroy
1884-1915 .... **TCLC 43**
See also CA 109; 150; DLB 10, 19

Fleming, Ian (Lancaster)
1908-1964 ...... **CLC 3, 30; DAM POP**
See also CA 5-8R; CDBLB 1945-1960;
DLB 87; MTCW; SATA 9

Fleming, Thomas (James) 1927- .... **CLC 37**
See also CA 5-8R; CANR 10;
INT CANR-10; SATA 8

Fletcher, John 1579-1625...... **LC 33; DC 6**
See also CDBLB Before 1660; DLB 58

Fletcher, John Gould 1886-1950 ... **TCLC 35**
See also CA 107; DLB 4, 45

Fleur, Paul
See Pohl, Frederik

Flooglebuckle, Al
See Spiegelman, Art

Flying Officer X
See Bates, H(erbert) E(rnest)

Fo, Dario 1926-..... **CLC 32; DAM DRAM**
See also CA 116; 128; MTCW

Fogarty, Jonathan Titulescu Esq.
See Farrell, James T(homas)

Folke, Will
See Bloch, Robert (Albert)

Follett, Ken(neth Martin)
1949- ...... **CLC 18; DAM NOV, POP**
See also AAYA 6; BEST 89:4; CA 81-84;
CANR 13, 33, 54; DLB 87; DLBY 81;
INT CANR-33; MTCW

Fontane, Theodor 1819-1898..... **NCLC 26**
See also DLB 129

Foote, Horton
1916- ...... **CLC 51, 91; DAM DRAM**
See also CA 73-76; CANR 34, 51; DLB 26;
INT CANR-34

Foote, Shelby
1916- ...... **CLC 75; DAM NOV, POP**
See also CA 5-8R; CANR 3, 45; DLB 2, 17

Forbes, Esther 1891-1967......... **CLC 12**
See also AAYA 17; CA 13-14; 25-28R;
CAP 1; CLR 27; DLB 22; JRDA;
MAICYA; SATA 2

Forche, Carolyn (Louise)
1950- .... **CLC 25, 83, 86; DAM POET;**
PC 10
See also CA 109; 117; CANR 50; DLB 5;
INT 117

Ford, Elbur
See Hibbert, Eleanor Alice Burford

Ford, Ford Madox
1873-1939 .... **TCLC 1, 15, 39, 57;**
DAM NOV
See also CA 104; 132; CDBLB 1914-1945;
DLB 162; MTCW

Ford, John 1895-1973............ **CLC 16**
See also CA 45-48

Ford, Richard 1944-.............. **CLC 46**
See also CA 69-72; CANR 11, 47

Ford, Webster
See Masters, Edgar Lee

Foreman, Richard 1937-........... **CLC 50**
See also CA 65-68; CANR 32

Forester, C(ecil) S(cott)
1899-1966 .... **CLC 35**
See also CA 73-76; 25-28R; SATA 13

Forez
See Mauriac, Francois (Charles)

Forman, James Douglas 1932-...... **CLC 21**
See also AAYA 17; CA 9-12R; CANR 4,
19, 42; JRDA; MAICYA; SATA 8, 70

Fornes, Maria Irene 1930-...... **CLC 39, 61**
See also CA 25-28R; CANR 28; DLB 7;
HW; INT CANR-28; MTCW

Forrest, Leon 1937- .... **CLC 4**
See also BW 2; CA 89-92; CAAS 7;
CANR 25, 52; DLB 33

Forster, E(dward) M(organ)
1879-1970 .... **CLC 1, 2, 3, 4, 9, 10, 13,**
15, 22, 45, 77; DA; DAB; DAC;
DAM MST, NOV; WLC
See also AAYA 2; CA 13-14; 25-28R;
CANR 45; CAP 1; CDBLB 1914-1945;
DLB 34, 98, 162; DLBD 10; MTCW;
SATA 57

Forster, John 1812-1876 .... **NCLC 11**
See also DLB 144

Forsyth, Frederick
1938- .. **CLC 2, 5, 36; DAM NOV, POP**
See also BEST 89:4; CA 85-88; CANR 38;
DLB 87; MTCW

Forten, Charlotte L. .... **TCLC 16; BLC**
See also Grimke, Charlotte L(ottie) Forten
See also DLB 50

Foscolo, Ugo 1778-1827......... **NCLC 8**

Fosse, Bob .... **CLC 20**
See also Fosse, Robert Louis

Fosse, Robert Louis 1927-1987
See Fosse, Bob
See also CA 110; 123

Foster, Stephen Collins
1826-1864 .... **NCLC 26**

Foucault, Michel
1926-1984 .... **CLC 31, 34, 69**
See also CA 105; 113; CANR 34; MTCW

Fouque, Friedrich (Heinrich Karl) de la Motte
1777-1843 .... **NCLC 2**
See also DLB 90

Fourier, Charles 1772-1837 ...... **NCLC 51**

Fournier, Henri Alban 1886-1914
See Alain-Fournier
See also CA 104

Fournier, Pierre 1916-........... **CLC 11**
See also Gascar, Pierre
See also CA 89-92; CANR 16, 40

Fowles, John
1926- ...... **CLC 1, 2, 3, 4, 6, 9, 10, 15,**
33, 87; DAB; DAC; DAM MST
See also CA 5-8R; CANR 25; CDBLB 1960
to Present; DLB 14, 139; MTCW;
SATA 22

Fox, Paula 1923-................ **CLC 2, 8**
See also AAYA 3; CA 73-76; CANR 20,
36; CLR 1, 44; DLB 52; JRDA;
MAICYA; MTCW; SATA 17, 60

Fox, William Price (Jr.) 1926- ..... **CLC 22**
See also CA 17-20R; CAAS 19; CANR 11;
DLB 2; DLBY 81

Foxe, John 1516(?)-1587 .... **LC 14**

Frame, Janet
1924- .... **CLC 2, 3, 6, 22, 66, 96**
See also Clutha, Janet Paterson Frame

France, Anatole .... **TCLC 9**
See also Thibault, Jacques Anatole Francois
See also DLB 123

Francis, Claude 19(?)- .... **CLC 50**

Francis, Dick
1920- .... **CLC 2, 22, 42; DAM POP**
See also AAYA 5; BEST 89:3; CA 5-8R;
CANR 9, 42; CDBLB 1960 to Present;
DLB 87; INT CANR-9; MTCW

Francis, Robert (Churchill)
1901-1987 .... **CLC 15**
See also CA 1-4R; 123; CANR 1

Frank, Anne(lies Marie)
1929-1945 .... **TCLC 17; DA; DAB;**
DAC; DAM MST; WLC
See also AAYA 12; CA 113; 133; MTCW;
SATA 87; SATA-Brief 42

Frank, Elizabeth 1945-............ **CLC 39**
See also CA 121; 126; INT 126

Frankl, Viktor E(mil) 1905-........ **CLC 93**
See also CA 65-68

Franklin, Benjamin
See Hasek, Jaroslav (Matej Frantisek)

Franklin, Benjamin
1706-1790 ..... **LC 25; DA; DAB; DAC;**
DAM MST
See also CDALB 1640-1865; DLB 24, 43,
73

Franklin, (Stella Maraia Sarah) Miles
1879-1954 .... **TCLC 7**
See also CA 104

Fraser, (Lady) Antonia (Pakenham)
1932-........................ **CLC 32**
See also CA 85-88; CANR 44; MTCW;
SATA-Brief 32

Fraser, George MacDonald 1925-.... **CLC 7**
See also CA 45-48; CANR 2, 48

Fraser, Sylvia 1935-.............. **CLC 64**
See also CA 45-48; CANR 1, 16

Frayn, Michael
1933- .... **CLC 3, 7, 31, 47;**
DAM DRAM, NOV
See also CA 5-8R; CANR 30; DLB 13, 14;
MTCW

Fraze, Candida (Merrill) 1945-..... **CLC 50**
See also CA 126

Frazer, J(ames) G(eorge)
1854-1941 .... **TCLC 32**
See also CA 118

Frazer, Robert Caine
See Creasey, John

Frazer, Sir James George
See Frazer, J(ames) G(eorge)

Frazier, Ian 1951-............... **CLC 46**
See also CA 130; CANR 54

Frederic, Harold 1856-1898...... **NCLC 10**
See also DLB 12, 23; DLBD 13

Frederick, John
See Faust, Frederick (Schiller)

Frederick the Great 1712-1786 ...... **LC 14**

Fredro, Aleksander 1793-1876..... **NCLC 8**

Freeling, Nicolas 1927- .... **CLC 38**
See also CA 49-52; CAAS 12; CANR 1, 17,
50; DLB 87

Freeman, Douglas Southall
1886-1953 .... **TCLC 11**
See also CA 109; DLB 17

Freeman, Judith 1946-............ **CLC 55**
See also CA 148

Freeman, Mary Eleanor Wilkins
1852-1930 .... **TCLC 9; SSC 1**
See also CA 106; DLB 12, 78

Freeman, R(ichard) Austin
1862-1943 .... **TCLC 21**
See also CA 113; DLB 70

French, Albert 1943- .... **CLC 86**

French, Marilyn
1929-................ **CLC 10, 18, 60;**
DAM DRAM, NOV, POP
See also CA 69-72; CANR 3, 31;
INT CANR-31; MTCW

French, Paul
See Asimov, Isaac

Freneau, Philip Morin 1752-1832.. **NCLC 1**
See also DLB 37, 43

Freud, Sigmund 1856-1939 .... **TCLC 52**
See also CA 115; 133; MTCW

Friedan, Betty (Naomi) 1921-...... **CLC 74**
See also CA 65-68; CANR 18, 45; MTCW

Friedlander, Saul 1932-........... **CLC 90**
See also CA 117; 130

Friedman, B(ernard) H(arper)
1926- .... CLC 7
See also CA 1-4R; CANR 3, 48

Friedman, Bruce Jay 1930- .... CLC 3, 5, 56
See also CA 9-12R; CANR 25, 52; DLB 2, 28; INT CANR-25

Friel, Brian 1929- .... CLC 5, 42, 59
See also CA 21-24R; CANR 33; DLB 13; MTCW

Friis-Baastad, Babbis Ellinor
1921-1970 .... CLC 12
See also CA 17-20R; 134; SATA 7

Frisch, Max (Rudolf)
1911-1991 ..... CLC 3, 9, 14, 18, 32, 44; DAM DRAM, NOV
See also CA 85-88; 134; CANR 32; DLB 69, 124; MTCW

Fromentin, Eugene (Samuel Auguste)
1820-1876 .... NCLC 10
See also DLB 123

Frost, Frederick
See Faust, Frederick (Schiller)

Frost, Robert (Lee)
1874-1963 .... CLC 1, 3, 4, 9, 10, 13, 15, 26, 34, 44; DA; DAB; DAC; DAM MST, POET; PC 1; WLC
See also CA 89-92; CANR 33; CDALB 1917-1929; DLB 54; DLBD 7; MTCW; SATA 14

Froude, James Anthony
1818-1894 .... NCLC 43
See also DLB 18, 57, 144

Froy, Herald
See Waterhouse, Keith (Spencer)

Fry, Christopher
1907- ..... CLC 2, 10, 14; DAM DRAM
See also CA 17-20R; CAAS 23; CANR 9, 30; DLB 13; MTCW; SATA 66

Frye, (Herman) Northrop
1912-1991 .... CLC 24, 70
See also CA 5-8R; 133; CANR 8, 37; DLB 67, 68; MTCW

Fuchs, Daniel 1909-1993 .... CLC 8, 22
See also CA 81-84; 142; CAAS 5; CANR 40; DLB 9, 26, 28; DLBY 93

Fuchs, Daniel 1934- .... CLC 34
See also CA 37-40R; CANR 14, 48

Fuentes, Carlos
1928- ...... CLC 3, 8, 10, 13, 22, 41, 60; DA; DAB; DAC; DAM MST, MULT, NOV; HLC; SSC 24; WLC
See also AAYA 4; AITN 2; CA 69-72; CANR 10, 32; DLB 113; HW; MTCW

Fuentes, Gregorio Lopez y
See Lopez y Fuentes, Gregorio

Fugard, (Harold) Athol
1932- .... CLC 5, 9, 14, 25, 40, 80; DAM DRAM; DC 3
See also AAYA 17; CA 85-88; CANR 32, 54; MTCW

Fugard, Sheila 1932- .... CLC 48
See also CA 125

Fuller, Charles (H., Jr.)
1939- .... CLC 25; BLC; DAM DRAM, MULT; DC 1
See also BW 2; CA 108; 112; DLB 38; INT 112; MTCW

Fuller, John (Leopold) 1937- .... CLC 62
See also CA 21-24R; CANR 9, 44; DLB 40

Fuller, Margaret .... NCLC 5, 50
See also Ossoli, Sarah Margaret (Fuller marchesa d')

Fuller, Roy (Broadbent)
1912-1991 .... CLC 4, 28
See also CA 5-8R; 135; CAAS 10; CANR 53; DLB 15, 20; SATA 87

Fulton, Alice 1952- .... CLC 52
See also CA 116

Furphy, Joseph 1843-1912 .... TCLC 25

Fussell, Paul 1924- .... CLC 74
See also BEST 90:1; CA 17-20R; CANR 8, 21, 35; INT CANR-21; MTCW

Futabatei, Shimei 1864-1909 ..... TCLC 44

Futrelle, Jacques 1875-1912 ...... TCLC 19
See also CA 113; 155

Gaboriau, Emile 1835-1873 ...... NCLC 14

Gadda, Carlo Emilio 1893-1973 .... CLC 11
See also CA 89-92

Gaddis, William
1922- ..... CLC 1, 3, 6, 8, 10, 19, 43, 86
See also CA 17-20R; CANR 21, 48; DLB 2; MTCW

Gage, Walter
See Inge, William (Motter)

Gaines, Ernest J(ames)
1933- .... CLC 3, 11, 18, 86; BLC; DAM MULT
See also AAYA 18; AITN 1; BW 2; CA 9-12R; CANR 6, 24, 42; CDALB 1968-1988; DLB 2, 33, 152; DLBY 80; MTCW; SATA 86

Gaitskill, Mary 1954- .... CLC 69
See also CA 128

Galdos, Benito Perez
See Perez Galdos, Benito

Gale, Zona
1874-1938 ...... TCLC 7; DAM DRAM
See also CA 105; 153; DLB 9, 78

Galeano, Eduardo (Hughes) 1940- ... CLC 72
See also CA 29-32R; CANR 13, 32; HW

Galiano, Juan Valera y Alcala
See Valera y Alcala-Galiano, Juan

Gallagher, Tess
1943- .. CLC 18, 63; DAM POET; PC 9
See also CA 106; DLB 120

Gallant, Mavis
1922- .... CLC 7, 18, 38; DAC; DAM MST; SSC 5
See also CA 69-72; CANR 29; DLB 53; MTCW

Gallant, Roy A(rthur) 1924- .... CLC 17
See also CA 5-8R; CANR 4, 29, 54; CLR 30; MAICYA; SATA 4, 68

Gallico, Paul (William) 1897-1976 ... CLC 2
See also AITN 1; CA 5-8R; 69-72; CANR 23; DLB 9, 171; MAICYA; SATA 13

Gallo, Max Louis 1932- .... CLC 95
See also CA 85-88

Gallois, Lucien
See Desnos, Robert

Gallup, Ralph
See Whitemore, Hugh (John)

Galsworthy, John
1867-1933 ...... TCLC 1, 45; DA; DAB; DAC; DAM DRAM, MST, NOV; SSC 22; WLC 2
See also CA 104; 141; CDBLB 1890-1914; DLB 10, 34, 98, 162

Galt, John 1779-1839 .... NCLC 1
See also DLB 99, 116, 159

Galvin, James 1951- .... CLC 38
See also CA 108; CANR 26

Gamboa, Federico 1864-1939 ...... TCLC 36

Gandhi, M. K.
See Gandhi, Mohandas Karamchand

Gandhi, Mahatma
See Gandhi, Mohandas Karamchand

Gandhi, Mohandas Karamchand
1869-1948 ..... TCLC 59; DAM MULT
See also CA 121; 132; MTCW

Gann, Ernest Kellogg 1910-1991.... CLC 23
See also AITN 1; CA 1-4R; 136; CANR 1

Garcia, Cristina 1958- .... CLC 76
See also CA 141

Garcia Lorca, Federico
1898-1936 ... TCLC 1, 7, 49; DA; DAB; DAC; DAM DRAM, MST, MULT, POET; DC 2; HLC; PC 3; WLC
See also CA 104; 131; DLB 108; HW; MTCW

Garcia Marquez, Gabriel (Jose)
1928- .... CLC 2, 3, 8, 10, 15, 27, 47, 55, 68; DA; DAB; DAC; DAM MST, MULT, NOV, POP; HLC; SSC 8; WLC
See also AAYA 3; BEST 89:1, 90:4; CA 33-36R; CANR 10, 28, 50; DLB 113; HW; MTCW

Gard, Janice
See Latham, Jean Lee

Gard, Roger Martin du
See Martin du Gard, Roger

Gardam, Jane 1928- .... CLC 43
See also CA 49-52; CANR 2, 18, 33, 54; CLR 12; DLB 14, 161; MAICYA; MTCW; SAAS 9; SATA 39, 76; SATA-Brief 28

Gardner, Herb(ert) 1934- .... CLC 44
See also CA 149

Gardner, John (Champlin), Jr.
1933-1982 ..... CLC 2, 3, 5, 7, 8, 10, 18, 28, 34; DAM NOV, POP; SSC 7
See also AITN 1; CA 65-68; 107; CANR 33; DLB 2; DLBY 82; MTCW; SATA 40; SATA-Obit 31

Gardner, John (Edmund)
1926- .... CLC 30; DAM POP
See also CA 103; CANR 15; MTCW

Gardner, Miriam
See Bradley, Marion Zimmer

Gardner, Noel
See Kuttner, Henry

Gardons, S. S.
See Snodgrass, W(illiam) D(e Witt)

Garfield, Leon 1921-1996......... **CLC 12**
See also AAYA 8; CA 17-20R; 152;
CANR 38, 41; CLR 21; DLB 161; JRDA;
MAICYA; SATA 1, 32, 76;
SATA-Obit 90

Garland, (Hannibal) Hamlin
1860-1940 .... **TCLC 3; SSC 18**
See also CA 104; DLB 12, 71, 78

Garneau, (Hector de) Saint-Denys
1912-1943 .... **TCLC 13**
See also CA 111; DLB 88

Garner, Alan
1934- .... **CLC 17; DAB; DAM POP**
See also AAYA 18; CA 73-76; CANR 15;
CLR 20; DLB 161; MAICYA; MTCW;
SATA 18, 69

Garner, Hugh 1913-1979 .... **CLC 13**
See also CA 69-72; CANR 31; DLB 68

Garnett, David 1892-1981 .... **CLC 3**
See also CA 5-8R; 103; CANR 17; DLB 34

Garos, Stephanie
See Katz, Steve

Garrett, George (Palmer)
1929- .... **CLC 3, 11, 51**
See also CA 1-4R; CAAS 5; CANR 1, 42;
DLB 2, 5, 130, 152; DLBY 83

Garrick, David
1717-1779 .... **LC 15; DAM DRAM**
See also DLB 84

Garrigue, Jean 1914-1972 .... **CLC 2, 8**
See also CA 5-8R; 37-40R; CANR 20

Garrison, Frederick
See Sinclair, Upton (Beall)

Garth, Will
See Hamilton, Edmond; Kuttner, Henry

Garvey, Marcus (Moziah, Jr.)
1887-1940 .... **TCLC 41; BLC;
DAM MULT**
See also BW 1; CA 120; 124

Gary, Romain .... **CLC 25**
See also Kacew, Romain
See also DLB 83

Gascar, Pierre .... **CLC 11**
See also Fournier, Pierre

Gascoyne, David (Emery) 1916- .... **CLC 45**
See also CA 65-68; CANR 10, 28, 54;
DLB 20; MTCW

Gaskell, Elizabeth Cleghorn
1810-1865 .. **NCLC 5; DAB; DAM MST**
See also CDBLB 1832-1890; DLB 21, 144,
159

Gass, William H(oward)
1924- ... **CLC 1, 2, 8, 11, 15, 39; SSC 12**
See also CA 17-20R; CANR 30; DLB 2;
MTCW

Gasset, Jose Ortega y
See Ortega y Gasset, Jose

Gates, Henry Louis, Jr.
1950- .... **CLC 65; DAM MULT**
See also BW 2; CA 109; CANR 25, 53;
DLB 67

Gautier, Theophile
1811-1872 .... **NCLC 1, 59;
DAM POET; SSC 20**
See also DLB 119

Gawsworth, John
See Bates, H(erbert) E(rnest)

Gay, Oliver
See Gogarty, Oliver St. John

Gaye, Marvin (Penze) 1939-1984 ... **CLC 26**
See also CA 112

Gebler, Carlo (Ernest) 1954-....... **CLC 39**
See also CA 119; 133

Gee, Maggie (Mary) 1948-........ **CLC 57**
See also CA 130

Gee, Maurice (Gough) 1931-...... **CLC 29**
See also CA 97-100; SATA 46

Gelbart, Larry (Simon) 1923- ... **CLC 21, 61**
See also CA 73-76; CANR 45

Gelber, Jack 1932-........ **CLC 1, 6, 14, 79**
See also CA 1-4R; CANR 2; DLB 7

Gellhorn, Martha (Ellis) 1908- .. **CLC 14, 60**
See also CA 77-80; CANR 44; DLBY 82

Genet, Jean
1910-1986 ...... **CLC 1, 2, 5, 10, 14, 44,
46; DAM DRAM**
See also CA 13-16R; CANR 18; DLB 72;
DLBY 86; MTCW

Gent, Peter 1942-................ **CLC 29**
See also AITN 1; CA 89-92; DLBY 82

Gentlewoman in New England, A
See Bradstreet, Anne

Gentlewoman in Those Parts, A
See Bradstreet, Anne

George, Jean Craighead 1919-...... **CLC 35**
See also AAYA 8; CA 5-8R; CANR 25;
CLR 1; DLB 52; JRDA; MAICYA;
SATA 2, 68

George, Stefan (Anton)
1868-1933 .... **TCLC 2, 14**
See also CA 104

Georges, Georges Martin
See Simenon, Georges (Jacques Christian)

Gerhardi, William Alexander
See Gerhardie, William Alexander

Gerhardie, William Alexander
1895-1977 .... **CLC 5**
See also CA 25-28R; 73-76; CANR 18;
DLB 36

Gerstler, Amy 1956-.............. **CLC 70**
See also CA 146

Gertler, T. .... **CLC 34**
See also CA 116; 121; INT 121

gfgg .... **CLC XvXzc**

Ghalib............................ **NCLC 39**
See also Ghalib, Hsadullah Khan

Ghalib, Hsadullah Khan 1797-1869
See Ghalib
See also DAM POET

Ghelderode, Michel de
1898-1962 .... **CLC 6, 11; DAM DRAM**
See also CA 85-88; CANR 40

Ghiselin, Brewster 1903- .... **CLC 23**
See also CA 13-16R; CAAS 10; CANR 13

Ghose, Zulfikar 1935-............ **CLC 42**
See also CA 65-68

Ghosh, Amitav 1956-............ **CLC 44**
See also CA 147

Giacosa, Giuseppe 1847-1906 ...... **TCLC 7**
See also CA 104

Gibb, Lee
See Waterhouse, Keith (Spencer)

Gibbon, Lewis Grassic .... **TCLC 4**
See also Mitchell, James Leslie

Gibbons, Kaye
1960- .... **CLC 50, 88; DAM POP**
See also CA 151

Gibran, Kahlil
1883-1931 .... **TCLC 1, 9; DAM POET,
POP; PC 9**
See also CA 104; 150

Gibran, Khalil
See Gibran, Kahlil

Gibson, William
1914- .... **CLC 23; DA; DAB; DAC;
DAM DRAM, MST**
See also CA 9-12R; CANR 9, 42; DLB 7;
SATA 66

Gibson, William (Ford)
1948- .... **CLC 39, 63; DAM POP**
See also AAYA 12; CA 126; 133; CANR 52

Gide, Andre (Paul Guillaume)
1869-1951 .... **TCLC 5, 12, 36; DA;
DAB; DAC; DAM MST, NOV; SSC 13;
WLC**
See also CA 104; 124; DLB 65; MTCW

Gifford, Barry (Colby) 1946-....... **CLC 34**
See also CA 65-68; CANR 9, 30, 40

Gilbert, W(illiam) S(chwenck)
1836-1911 ..... **TCLC 3; DAM DRAM,
POET**
See also CA 104; SATA 36

Gilbreth, Frank B., Jr. 1911-....... **CLC 17**
See also CA 9-12R; SATA 2

Gilchrist, Ellen
1935- .... **CLC 34, 48; DAM POP;
SSC 14**
See also CA 113; 116; CANR 41; DLB 130;
MTCW

Giles, Molly 1942-.............. **CLC 39**
See also CA 126

Gill, Patrick
See Creasey, John

Gilliam, Terry (Vance) 1940-....... **CLC 21**
See also Monty Python
See also AAYA 19; CA 108; 113;
CANR 35; INT 113

Gillian, Jerry
See Gilliam, Terry (Vance)

Gilliatt, Penelope (Ann Douglass)
1932-1993 .... **CLC 2, 10, 13, 53**
See also AITN 2; CA 13-16R; 141;
CANR 49; DLB 14

Gilman, Charlotte (Anna) Perkins (Stetson)
1860-1935 .... **TCLC 9, 37; SSC 13**
See also CA 106; 150

Gilmour, David 1949-............. **CLC 35**
See also CA 138; 147

Gilpin, William 1724-1804 .... **NCLC 30**

Gilray, J. D.
See Mencken, H(enry) L(ouis)

Gilroy, Frank D(aniel) 1925-........ **CLC 2**
See also CA 81-84; CANR 32; DLB 7

Ginsberg, Allen
1926-...... **CLC 1, 2, 3, 4, 6, 13, 36, 69;**
DA; DAB; DAC; DAM MST, POET;
PC 4; WLC 3
See also AITN 1; CA 1-4R; CANR 2, 41;
CDALB 1941-1968; DLB 5, 16, 169;
MTCW

Ginzburg, Natalia
1916-1991 .... **CLC 5, 11, 54, 70**
See also CA 85-88; 135; CANR 33; MTCW

Giono, Jean 1895-1970......... **CLC 4, 11**
See also CA 45-48; 29-32R; CANR 2, 35;
DLB 72; MTCW

Giovanni, Nikki
1943-...... **CLC 2, 4, 19, 64; BLC; DA;**
DAB; DAC; DAM MST, MULT, POET
See also AITN 1; BW 2; CA 29-32R;
CAAS 6; CANR 18, 41; CLR 6; DLB 5,
41; INT CANR-18; MAICYA; MTCW;
SATA 24

Giovene, Andrea 1904-............ **CLC 7**
See also CA 85-88

Gippius, Zinaida (Nikolayevna) 1869-1945
See Hippius, Zinaida
See also CA 106

Giraudoux, (Hippolyte) Jean
1882-1944 .... **TCLC 2, 7; DAM DRAM**
See also CA 104; DLB 65

Gironella, Jose Maria 1917-........ **CLC 11**
See also CA 101

Gissing, George (Robert)
1857-1903 .... **TCLC 3, 24, 47**
See also CA 105; DLB 18, 135

Giurlani, Aldo
See Palazzeschi, Aldo

Gladkov, Fyodor (Vasilyevich)
1883-1958 .... **TCLC 27**

Glanville, Brian (Lester) 1931-...... **CLC 6**
See also CA 5-8R; CAAS 9; CANR 3;
DLB 15, 139; SATA 42

Glasgow, Ellen (Anderson Gholson)
1873(?)-1945 .... **TCLC 2, 7**
See also CA 104; DLB 9, 12

Glaspell, Susan 1882(?)-1948...... **TCLC 55**
See also CA 110; 154; DLB 7, 9, 78;
YABC 2

Glassco, John 1909-1981 .... **CLC 9**
See also CA 13-16R; 102; CANR 15;
DLB 68

Glasscock, Amnesia
See Steinbeck, John (Ernst)

Glasser, Ronald J. 1940(?)-........ **CLC 37**

Glassman, Joyce
See Johnson, Joyce

Glendinning, Victoria 1937-........ **CLC 50**
See also CA 120; 127; DLB 155

Glissant, Edouard
1928-....... **CLC 10, 68; DAM MULT**
See also CA 153

Gloag, Julian 1930- .... **CLC 40**
See also AITN 1; CA 65-68; CANR 10

Glowacki, Aleksander
See Prus, Boleslaw

Gluck, Louise (Elisabeth)
1943-............. **CLC 7, 22, 44, 81;**
DAM POET; PC 16
See also CA 33-36R; CANR 40; DLB 5

Gobineau, Joseph Arthur (Comte) de
1816-1882 .... **NCLC 17**
See also DLB 123

Godard, Jean-Luc 1930-.......... **CLC 20**
See also CA 93-96

Godden, (Margaret) Rumer 1907-... **CLC 53**
See also AAYA 6; CA 5-8R; CANR 4, 27,
36, 55; CLR 20; DLB 161; MAICYA;
SAAS 12; SATA 3, 36

Godoy Alcayaga, Lucila 1889-1957
See Mistral, Gabriela
See also BW 2; CA 104; 131; DAM MULT;
HW; MTCW

Godwin, Gail (Kathleen)
1937-........... **CLC 5, 8, 22, 31, 69;**
DAM POP
See also CA 29-32R; CANR 15, 43; DLB 6;
INT CANR-15; MTCW

Godwin, William 1756-1836...... **NCLC 14**
See also CDBLB 1789-1832; DLB 39, 104,
142, 158, 163

Goebbels, Josef
See Goebbels, (Paul) Joseph

Goebbels, (Paul) Joseph
1897-1945 .... **TCLC 68**
See also CA 115; 148

Goebbels, Joseph Paul
See Goebbels, (Paul) Joseph

Goethe, Johann Wolfgang von
1749-1832 .... **NCLC 4, 22, 34; DA;**
DAB; DAC; DAM DRAM, MST,
POET; PC 5; WLC 3
See also DLB 94

Gogarty, Oliver St. John
1878-1957 .... **TCLC 15**
See also CA 109; 150; DLB 15, 19

Gogol, Nikolai (Vasilyevich)
1809-1852 .... **NCLC 5, 15, 31; DA;**
DAB; DAC; DAM DRAM, MST; DC 1;
SSC 4; WLC

Goines, Donald
1937(?)-1974 .... **CLC 80; BLC;**
DAM MULT, POP
See also AITN 1; BW 1; CA 124; 114;
DLB 33

Gold, Herbert 1924-....... **CLC 4, 7, 14, 42**
See also CA 9-12R; CANR 17, 45; DLB 2;
DLBY 81

Goldbarth, Albert 1948-........ **CLC 5, 38**
See also CA 53-56; CANR 6, 40; DLB 120

Goldberg, Anatol 1910-1982 .... **CLC 34**
See also CA 131; 117

Goldemberg, Isaac 1945-.......... **CLC 52**
See also CA 69-72; CAAS 12; CANR 11,
32; HW

Golding, William (Gerald)
1911-1993 .... **CLC 1, 2, 3, 8, 10, 17, 27,**
58, 81; DA; DAB; DAC; DAM MST,
NOV; WLC
See also AAYA 5; CA 5-8R; 141;
CANR 13, 33, 54; CDBLB 1945-1960;
DLB 15, 100; MTCW

Goldman, Emma 1869-1940...... **TCLC 13**
See also CA 110; 150

Goldman, Francisco 1955-......... **CLC 76**

Goldman, William (W.) 1931-.... **CLC 1, 48**
See also CA 9-12R; CANR 29; DLB 44

Goldmann, Lucien 1913-1970 ...... **CLC 24**
See also CA 25-28; CAP 2

Goldoni, Carlo
1707-1793 .... **LC 4; DAM DRAM**

Goldsberry, Steven 1949-......... **CLC 34**
See also CA 131

Goldsmith, Oliver
1728-1774 ...... **LC 2; DA; DAB; DAC;**
DAM DRAM, MST, NOV, POET;
WLC
See also CDBLB 1660-1789; DLB 39, 89,
104, 109, 142; SATA 26

Goldsmith, Peter
See Priestley, J(ohn) B(oynton)

Gombrowicz, Witold
1904-1969 .... **CLC 4, 7, 11, 49;**
DAM DRAM
See also CA 19-20; 25-28R; CAP 2

Gomez de la Serna, Ramon
1888-1963 .... **CLC 9**
See also CA 153; 116; HW

Goncharov, Ivan Alexandrovich
1812-1891 .... **NCLC 1**

Goncourt, Edmond (Louis Antoine Huot) de
1822-1896 .... **NCLC 7**
See also DLB 123

Goncourt, Jules (Alfred Huot) de
1830-1870 .... **NCLC 7**
See also DLB 123

Gontier, Fernande 19(?)- .... **CLC 50**

Goodman, Paul 1911-1972.... **CLC 1, 2, 4, 7**
See also CA 19-20; 37-40R; CANR 34;
CAP 2; DLB 130; MTCW

Gordimer, Nadine
1923- .... **CLC 3, 5, 7, 10, 18, 33, 51, 70;**
DA; DAB; DAC; DAM MST, NOV;
SSC 17
See also CA 5-8R; CANR 3, 28;
INT CANR-28; MTCW

Gordon, Adam Lindsay
1833-1870 .... **NCLC 21**

Gordon, Caroline
1895-1981 ... **CLC 6, 13, 29, 83; SSC 15**
See also CA 11-12; 103; CANR 36; CAP 1;
DLB 4, 9, 102; DLBY 81; MTCW

Gordon, Charles William 1860-1937
See Connor, Ralph
See also CA 109

Gordon, Mary (Catherine)
1949-.................... **CLC 13, 22**
See also CA 102; CANR 44; DLB 6;
DLBY 81; INT 102; MTCW

Gordon, Sol 1923-.............. **CLC 26**
See also CA 53-56; CANR 4; SATA 11

Gordone, Charles
1925-1995 ..... **CLC 1, 4; DAM DRAM**
See also BW 1; CA 93-96; 150; CANR 55;
DLB 7; INT 93-96; MTCW

Gorenko, Anna Andreevna
See Akhmatova, Anna

Gorky, Maxim........ **TCLC 8; DAB; WLC**
See also Peshkov, Alexei Maximovich

Goryan, Sirak
See Saroyan, William

Gosse, Edmund (William)
1849-1928 .... **TCLC 28**
See also CA 117; DLB 57, 144

Gotlieb, Phyllis Fay (Bloom)
1926-...................... **CLC 18**
See also CA 13-16R; CANR 7; DLB 88

Gottesman, S. D.
See Kornbluth, C(yril) M.; Pohl, Frederik

Gottfried von Strassburg
fl. c. 1210-................. **CMLC 10**
See also DLB 138

Gould, Lois .... **CLC 4, 10**
See also CA 77-80; CANR 29; MTCW

Gourmont, Remy (-Marie-Charles) de
1858-1915 .... **TCLC 17**
See also CA 109; 150

Govier, Katherine 1948-........... **CLC 51**
See also CA 101; CANR 18, 40

Goyen, (Charles) William
1915-1983 .... **CLC 5, 8, 14, 40**
See also AITN 2; CA 5-8R; 110; CANR 6;
DLB 2; DLBY 83; INT CANR-6

Goytisolo, Juan
1931- ..... **CLC 5, 10, 23; DAM MULT;**
HLC
See also CA 85-88; CANR 32; HW; MTCW

Gozzano, Guido 1883-1916 .... **PC 10**
See also CA 154; DLB 114

Gozzi, (Conte) Carlo 1720-1806 .. **NCLC 23**

Grabbe, Christian Dietrich
1801-1836 .... **NCLC 2**
See also DLB 133

Grace, Patricia 1937-............. **CLC 56**

Gracian y Morales, Baltasar
1601-1658 .... **LC 15**

Gracq, Julien................ **CLC 11, 48**
See also Poirier, Louis
See also DLB 83

Grade, Chaim 1910-1982 .... **CLC 10**
See also CA 93-96; 107

Graduate of Oxford, A
See Ruskin, John

Graham, John
See Phillips, David Graham

Graham, Jorie 1951-............. **CLC 48**
See also CA 111; DLB 120

Graham, R(obert) B(ontine) Cunninghame
See Cunninghame Graham, R(obert)
B(ontine)
See also DLB 98, 135, 174

Graham, Robert
See Haldeman, Joe (William)

Graham, Tom
See Lewis, (Harry) Sinclair

Graham, W(illiam) S(ydney)
1918-1986 .... **CLC 29**
See also CA 73-76; 118; DLB 20

Graham, Winston (Mawdsley)
1910-...................... **CLC 23**
See also CA 49-52; CANR 2, 22, 45;
DLB 77

Grahame, Kenneth
1859-1932 .... **TCLC 64; DAB**
See also CA 108; 136; CLR 5; DLB 34, 141;
MAICYA; YABC 1

Grant, Skeeter
See Spiegelman, Art

Granville-Barker, Harley
1877-1946 ...... **TCLC 2; DAM DRAM**
See also Barker, Harley Granville
See also CA 104

Grass, Guenter (Wilhelm)
1927- ..... **CLC 1, 2, 4, 6, 11, 15, 22, 32,**
49, 88; DA; DAB; DAC; DAM MST,
NOV; WLC
See also CA 13-16R; CANR 20; DLB 75,
124; MTCW

Gratton, Thomas
See Hulme, T(homas) E(rnest)

Grau, Shirley Ann
1929- .... **CLC 4, 9; SSC 15**
See also CA 89-92; CANR 22; DLB 2;
INT CANR-22; MTCW

Gravel, Fern
See Hall, James Norman

Graver, Elizabeth 1964-........... **CLC 70**
See also CA 135

Graves, Richard Perceval 1945- .... **CLC 44**
See also CA 65-68; CANR 9, 26, 51

Graves, Robert (von Ranke)
1895-1985 ...... **CLC 1, 2, 6, 11, 39, 44,**
45; DAB; DAC; DAM MST, POET;
PC 6
See also CA 5-8R; 117; CANR 5, 36;
CDBLB 1914-1945; DLB 20, 100;
DLBY 85; MTCW; SATA 45

Graves, Valerie
See Bradley, Marion Zimmer

Gray, Alasdair (James) 1934- ...... **CLC 41**
See also CA 126; CANR 47; INT 126;
MTCW

Gray, Amlin 1946- .... **CLC 29**
See also CA 138

Gray, Francine du Plessix
1930- .... **CLC 22; DAM NOV**
See also BEST 90:3; CA 61-64; CAAS 2;
CANR 11, 33; INT CANR-11; MTCW

Gray, John (Henry) 1866-1934 .... **TCLC 19**
See also CA 119

Gray, Simon (James Holliday)
1936-................... **CLC 9, 14, 36**
See also AITN 1; CA 21-24R; CAAS 3;
CANR 32; DLB 13; MTCW

Gray, Spalding 1941-.. **CLC 49; DAM POP**
See also CA 128

Gray, Thomas
1716-1771 ...... **LC 4; DA; DAB; DAC;**
DAM MST; PC 2; WLC
See also CDBLB 1660-1789; DLB 109

Grayson, David
See Baker, Ray Stannard

Grayson, Richard (A.) 1951-....... **CLC 38**
See also CA 85-88; CANR 14, 31

Greeley, Andrew M(oran)
1928- .... **CLC 28; DAM POP**
See also CA 5-8R; CAAS 7; CANR 7, 43;
MTCW

Green, Anna Katharine
1846-1935 .... **TCLC 63**
See also CA 112

Green, Brian
See Card, Orson Scott

Green, Hannah
See Greenberg, Joanne (Goldenberg)

Green, Hannah .... **CLC 3**
See also CA 73-76

Green, Henry 1905-1973 ..... **CLC 2, 13, 97**
See also Yorke, Henry Vincent
See also DLB 15

Green, Julian (Hartridge) 1900-
See Green, Julien
See also CA 21-24R; CANR 33; DLB 4, 72;
MTCW

Green, Julien................ **CLC 3, 11, 77**
See also Green, Julian (Hartridge)

Green, Paul (Eliot)
1894-1981 ...... **CLC 25; DAM DRAM**
See also AITN 1; CA 5-8R; 103; CANR 3;
DLB 7, 9; DLBY 81

Greenberg, Ivan 1908-1973
See Rahv, Philip
See also CA 85-88

Greenberg, Joanne (Goldenberg)
1932-...................... **CLC 7, 30**
See also AAYA 12; CA 5-8R; CANR 14,
32; SATA 25

Greenberg, Richard 1959(?)- .... **CLC 57**
See also CA 138

Greene, Bette 1934-............. **CLC 30**
See also AAYA 7; CA 53-56; CANR 4;
CLR 2; JRDA; MAICYA; SAAS 16;
SATA 8

Greene, Gael .... **CLC 8**
See also CA 13-16R; CANR 10

Greene, Graham
1904-1991 .... **CLC 1, 3, 6, 9, 14, 18, 27,**
37, 70, 72; DA; DAB; DAC; DAM MST,
NOV; WLC
See also AITN 2; CA 13-16R; 133;
CANR 35; CDBLB 1945-1960; DLB 13,
15, 77, 100, 162; DLBY 91; MTCW;
SATA 20

Greer, Richard
See Silverberg, Robert

Gregor, Arthur 1923-............. **CLC 9**
See also CA 25-28R; CAAS 10; CANR 11;
SATA 36

Gregor, Lee
See Pohl, Frederik

Gregory, Isabella Augusta (Persse)
 1852-1932 . . . . **TCLC 1**
 See also CA 104; DLB 10

Gregory, J. Dennis
 See Williams, John A(lfred)

Grendon, Stephen
 See Derleth, August (William)

Grenville, Kate 1950- . . . . **CLC 61**
 See also CA 118; CANR 53

Grenville, Pelham
 See Wodehouse, P(elham) G(renville)

Greve, Felix Paul (Berthold Friedrich)
 1879-1948
 See Grove, Frederick Philip
 See also CA 104; 141; DAC; DAM MST

Grey, Zane
 1872-1939 . . . . **TCLC 6; DAM POP**
 See also CA 104; 132; DLB 9; MTCW

Grieg, (Johan) Nordahl (Brun)
 1902-1943 . . . . **TCLC 10**
 See also CA 107

Grieve, C(hristopher) M(urray)
 1892-1978 . . . . **CLC 11, 19; DAM POET**
 See also MacDiarmid, Hugh; Pteleon
 See also CA 5-8R; 85-88; CANR 33;
 MTCW

Griffin, Gerald 1803-1840 . . . . **NCLC 7**
 See also DLB 159

Griffin, John Howard 1920-1980 . . . . **CLC 68**
 See also AITN 1; CA 1-4R; 101; CANR 2

Griffin, Peter 1942- . . . . **CLC 39**
 See also CA 136

Griffith, D(avid Lewelyn) W(ark)
 1875(?)-1948 . . . . **TCLC 68**
 See also CA 119; 150

Griffith, Lawrence
 See Griffith, D(avid Lewelyn) W(ark)

Griffiths, Trevor 1935- . . . . **CLC 13, 52**
 See also CA 97-100; CANR 45; DLB 13

Grigson, Geoffrey (Edward Harvey)
 1905-1985 . . . . **CLC 7, 39**
 See also CA 25-28R; 118; CANR 20, 33;
 DLB 27; MTCW

Grillparzer, Franz 1791-1872 . . . . . . **NCLC 1**
 See also DLB 133

Grimble, Reverend Charles James
 See Eliot, T(homas) S(tearns)

Grimke, Charlotte L(ottie) Forten
 1837(?)-1914
 See Forten, Charlotte L.
 See also BW 1; CA 117; 124; DAM MULT,
 POET

Grimm, Jacob Ludwig Karl
 1785-1863 . . . . **NCLC 3**
 See also DLB 90; MAICYA; SATA 22

Grimm, Wilhelm Karl 1786-1859 . . **NCLC 3**
 See also DLB 90; MAICYA; SATA 22

Grimmelshausen, Johann Jakob Christoffel
 von 1621-1676 . . . . **LC 6**
 See also DLB 168

Grindel, Eugene 1895-1952
 See Eluard, Paul
 See also CA 104

Grisham, John 1955- . . **CLC 84; DAM POP**
 See also AAYA 14; CA 138; CANR 47

Grossman, David 1954- . . . . **CLC 67**
 See also CA 138

Grossman, Vasily (Semenovich)
 1905-1964 . . . . **CLC 41**
 See also CA 124; 130; MTCW

Grove, Frederick Philip . . . . **TCLC 4**
 See also Greve, Felix Paul (Berthold
 Friedrich)
 See also DLB 92

Grubb
 See Crumb, R(obert)

Grumbach, Doris (Isaac)
 1918- . . . . **CLC 13, 22, 64**
 See also CA 5-8R; CAAS 2; CANR 9, 42;
 INT CANR-9

Grundtvig, Nicolai Frederik Severin
 1783-1872 . . . . **NCLC 1**

Grunge
 See Crumb, R(obert)

Grunwald, Lisa 1959- . . . . **CLC 44**
 See also CA 120

Guare, John
 1938- . . . . **CLC 8, 14, 29, 67;
 DAM DRAM**
 See also CA 73-76; CANR 21; DLB 7;
 MTCW

Gudjonsson, Halldor Kiljan 1902-
 See Laxness, Halldor
 See also CA 103

Guenter, Erich
 See Eich, Guenter

Guest, Barbara 1920- . . . . **CLC 34**
 See also CA 25-28R; CANR 11, 44; DLB 5

Guest, Judith (Ann)
 1936- . . . . **CLC 8, 30; DAM NOV, POP**
 See also AAYA 7; CA 77-80; CANR 15;
 INT CANR-15; MTCW

Guevara, Che . . . . **CLC 87; HLC**
 See also Guevara (Serna), Ernesto

Guevara (Serna), Ernesto 1928-1967
 See Guevara, Che
 See also CA 127; 111; DAM MULT; HW

Guild, Nicholas M. 1944- . . . . **CLC 33**
 See also CA 93-96

Guillemin, Jacques
 See Sartre, Jean-Paul

Guillen, Jorge
 1893-1984 . . . . . . **CLC 11; DAM MULT,
 POET**
 See also CA 89-92; 112; DLB 108; HW

Guillen, Nicolas (Cristobal)
 1902-1989 . . . . **CLC 48, 79; BLC;
 DAM MST, MULT, POET; HLC**
 See also BW 2; CA 116; 125; 129; HW

Guillevic, (Eugene) 1907- . . . . **CLC 33**
 See also CA 93-96

Guillois
 See Desnos, Robert

Guillois, Valentin
 See Desnos, Robert

Guiney, Louise Imogen
 1861-1920 . . . . **TCLC 41**
 See also DLB 54

Guiraldes, Ricardo (Guillermo)
 1886-1927 . . . . **TCLC 39**
 See also CA 131; HW; MTCW

Gumilev, Nikolai Stephanovich
 1886-1921 . . . . **TCLC 60**

Gunesekera, Romesh . . . . **CLC 91**

Gunn, Bill . . . . **CLC 5**
 See also Gunn, William Harrison
 See also DLB 38

Gunn, Thom(son William)
 1929- . . . . **CLC 3, 6, 18, 32, 81;
 DAM POET**
 See also CA 17-20R; CANR 9, 33;
 CDBLB 1960 to Present; DLB 27;
 INT CANR-33; MTCW

Gunn, William Harrison 1934(?)-1989
 See Gunn, Bill
 See also AITN 1; BW 1; CA 13-16R; 128;
 CANR 12, 25

Gunnars, Kristjana 1948- . . . . **CLC 69**
 See also CA 113; DLB 60

Gurganus, Allan
 1947- . . . . **CLC 70; DAM POP**
 See also BEST 90:1; CA 135

Gurney, A(lbert) R(amsdell), Jr.
 1930- . . . . **CLC 32, 50, 54; DAM DRAM**
 See also CA 77-80; CANR 32

Gurney, Ivor (Bertie) 1890-1937 . . . **TCLC 33**

Gurney, Peter
 See Gurney, A(lbert) R(amsdell), Jr.

Guro, Elena 1877-1913 . . . . **TCLC 56**

Gustafson, Ralph (Barker) 1909- . . . . **CLC 36**
 See also CA 21-24R; CANR 8, 45; DLB 88

Gut, Gom
 See Simenon, Georges (Jacques Christian)

Guterson, David 1956- . . . . **CLC 91**
 See also CA 132

Guthrie, A(lfred) B(ertram), Jr.
 1901-1991 . . . . **CLC 23**
 See also CA 57-60; 134; CANR 24; DLB 6;
 SATA 62; SATA-Obit 67

Guthrie, Isobel
 See Grieve, C(hristopher) M(urray)

Guthrie, Woodrow Wilson 1912-1967
 See Guthrie, Woody
 See also CA 113; 93-96

Guthrie, Woody . . . . **CLC 35**
 See also Guthrie, Woodrow Wilson

Guy, Rosa (Cuthbert) 1928- . . . . **CLC 26**
 See also AAYA 4; BW 2; CA 17-20R;
 CANR 14, 34; CLR 13; DLB 33; JRDA;
 MAICYA; SATA 14, 62

Gwendolyn
 See Bennett, (Enoch) Arnold

H. D. . . . . **CLC 3, 8, 14, 31, 34, 73; PC 5**
 See also Doolittle, Hilda

H. de V.
 See Buchan, John

Haavikko, Paavo Juhani
 1931- . . . . **CLC 18, 34**
 See also CA 106

Habbema, Koos
 See Heijermans, Herman

Hacker, Marilyn
   1942- . . . . CLC **5, 9, 23, 72, 91;**
                                        DAM POET
   See also CA 77-80; DLB 120

Haggard, H(enry) Rider
   1856-1925 . . . . TCLC **11**
   See also CA 108; 148; DLB 70, 156, 174;
   SATA 16

Hagiosy, L.
   See Larbaud, Valery (Nicolas)

Hagiwara Sakutaro 1886-1942 . . . . TCLC **60**

Haig, Fenil
   See Ford, Ford Madox

Haig-Brown, Roderick (Langmere)
   1908-1976 . . . . CLC **21**
   See also CA 5-8R; 69-72; CANR 4, 38;
   CLR 31; DLB 88; MAICYA; SATA 12

Hailey, Arthur
   1920- . . . . CLC **5; DAM NOV, POP**
   See also AITN 2; BEST 90:3; CA 1-4R;
   CANR 2, 36; DLB 88; DLBY 82; MTCW

Hailey, Elizabeth Forsythe 1938- . . . CLC **40**
   See also CA 93-96; CAAS 1; CANR 15, 48;
   INT CANR-15

Haines, John (Meade) 1924- . . . . CLC **58**
   See also CA 17-20R; CANR 13, 34; DLB 5

Hakluyt, Richard 1552-1616 . . . . LC **31**

Haldeman, Joe (William) 1943- . . . . . CLC **61**
   See also CA 53-56; CAAS 25; CANR 6;
   DLB 8; INT CANR-6

Haley, Alex(ander Murray Palmer)
   1921-1992 . . . . CLC **8, 12, 76; BLC; DA;**
      DAB; DAC; DAM MST, MULT, POP
   See also BW 2; CA 77-80; 136; DLB 38;
   MTCW

Haliburton, Thomas Chandler
   1796-1865 . . . . NCLC **15**
   See also DLB 11, 99

Hall, Donald (Andrew, Jr.)
   1928- . . CLC **1, 13, 37, 59; DAM POET**
   See also CA 5-8R; CAAS 7; CANR 2, 44;
   DLB 5; SATA 23

Hall, Frederic Sauser
   See Sauser-Hall, Frederic

Hall, James
   See Kuttner, Henry

Hall, James Norman 1887-1951 . . . TCLC **23**
   See also CA 123; SATA 21

Hall, (Marguerite) Radclyffe
   1886-1943 . . . . TCLC **12**
   See also CA 110; 150

Hall, Rodney 1935- . . . . CLC **51**
   See also CA 109

Halleck, Fitz-Greene 1790-1867 . . NCLC **47**
   See also DLB 3

Halliday, Michael
   See Creasey, John

Halpern, Daniel 1945- . . . . CLC **14**
   See also CA 33-36R

Hamburger, Michael (Peter Leopold)
   1924- . . . . CLC **5, 14**
   See also CA 5-8R; CAAS 4; CANR 2, 47;
   DLB 27

Hamill, Pete 1935- . . . . CLC **10**
   See also CA 25-28R; CANR 18

Hamilton, Alexander
   1755(?)-1804 . . . . NCLC **49**
   See also DLB 37

Hamilton, Clive
   See Lewis, C(live) S(taples)

Hamilton, Edmond 1904-1977 . . . . . . CLC **1**
   See also CA 1-4R; CANR 3; DLB 8

Hamilton, Eugene (Jacob) Lee
   See Lee-Hamilton, Eugene (Jacob)

Hamilton, Franklin
   See Silverberg, Robert

Hamilton, Gail
   See Corcoran, Barbara

Hamilton, Mollie
   See Kaye, M(ary) M(argaret)

Hamilton, (Anthony Walter) Patrick
   1904-1962 . . . . CLC **51**
   See also CA 113; DLB 10

Hamilton, Virginia
   1936- . . . . CLC **26; DAM MULT**
   See also AAYA 2; BW 2; CA 25-28R;
   CANR 20, 37; CLR 1, 11, 40; DLB 33,
   52; INT CANR-20; JRDA; MAICYA;
   MTCW; SATA 4, 56, 79

Hammett, (Samuel) Dashiell
   1894-1961 . . . . CLC **3, 5, 10, 19, 47;**
                                              SSC 17
   See also AITN 1; CA 81-84; CANR 42;
   CDALB 1929-1941; DLBD 6; MTCW

Hammon, Jupiter
   1711(?)-1800(?) . . . . NCLC **5; BLC;**
                        DAM MULT, POET; PC 16
   See also DLB 31, 50

Hammond, Keith
   See Kuttner, Henry

Hamner, Earl (Henry), Jr. 1923- . . . CLC **12**
   See also AITN 2; CA 73-76; DLB 6

Hampton, Christopher (James)
   1946- . . . . CLC **4**
   See also CA 25-28R; DLB 13; MTCW

Hamsun, Knut . . . . TCLC **2, 14, 49**
   See also Pedersen, Knut

Handke, Peter
   1942- . . . . CLC **5, 8, 10, 15, 38;**
                                       DAM DRAM, NOV
   See also CA 77-80; CANR 33; DLB 85,
   124; MTCW

Hanley, James 1901-1985 . . . CLC **3, 5, 8, 13**
   See also CA 73-76; 117; CANR 36; MTCW

Hannah, Barry 1942- . . . . CLC **23, 38, 90**
   See also CA 108; 110; CANR 43; DLB 6;
   INT 110; MTCW

Hannon, Ezra
   See Hunter, Evan

Hansberry, Lorraine (Vivian)
   1930-1965 . . . . . . CLC **17, 62; BLC; DA;**
            DAB; DAC; DAM DRAM, MST,
                                 MULT; DC 2
   See also BW 1; CA 109; 25-28R; CABS 3;
   CDALB 1941-1968; DLB 7, 38; MTCW

Hansen, Joseph 1923- . . . . CLC **38**
   See also CA 29-32R; CAAS 17; CANR 16,
   44; INT CANR-16

Hansen, Martin A. 1909-1955 . . . . . TCLC **32**

Hanson, Kenneth O(stlin) 1922- . . . . CLC **13**
   See also CA 53-56; CANR 7

Hardwick, Elizabeth
   1916- . . . . CLC **13; DAM NOV**
   See also CA 5-8R; CANR 3, 32; DLB 6;
   MTCW

Hardy, Thomas
   1840-1928 . . . . . TCLC **4, 10, 18, 32, 48,**
      53; DA; DAB; DAC; DAM MST, NOV,
                           POET; PC 8; SSC 2; WLC
   See also CA 104; 123; CDBLB 1890-1914;
   DLB 18, 19, 135; MTCW

Hare, David 1947- . . . . CLC **29, 58**
   See also CA 97-100; CANR 39; DLB 13;
   MTCW

Harford, Henry
   See Hudson, W(illiam) H(enry)

Hargrave, Leonie
   See Disch, Thomas M(ichael)

Harjo, Joy 1951- . . . CLC **83; DAM MULT**
   See also CA 114; CANR 35; DLB 120;
   NNAL

Harlan, Louis R(udolph) 1922- . . . . . CLC **34**
   See also CA 21-24R; CANR 25, 55

Harling, Robert 1951(?)- . . . . CLC **53**
   See also CA 147

Harmon, William (Ruth) 1938- . . . . . CLC **38**
   See also CA 33-36R; CANR 14, 32, 35;
   SATA 65

Harper, F. E. W.
   See Harper, Frances Ellen Watkins

Harper, Frances E. W.
   See Harper, Frances Ellen Watkins

Harper, Frances E. Watkins
   See Harper, Frances Ellen Watkins

Harper, Frances Ellen
   See Harper, Frances Ellen Watkins

Harper, Frances Ellen Watkins
   1825-1911 . . . . TCLC **14; BLC;**
                                  DAM MULT, POET
   See also BW 1; CA 111; 125; DLB 50

Harper, Michael S(teven) 1938- . . CLC **7, 22**
   See also BW 1; CA 33-36R; CANR 24;
   DLB 41

Harper, Mrs. F. E. W.
   See Harper, Frances Ellen Watkins

Harris, Christie (Lucy) Irwin
   1907- . . . . CLC **12**
   See also CA 5-8R; CANR 6; DLB 88;
   JRDA; MAICYA; SAAS 10; SATA 6, 74

Harris, Frank 1856-1931 . . . . TCLC **24**
   See also CA 109; 150; DLB 156

Harris, George Washington
   1814-1869 . . . . NCLC **23**
   See also DLB 3, 11

Harris, Joel Chandler
   1848-1908 . . . . TCLC **2; SSC 19**
   See also CA 104; 137; DLB 11, 23, 42, 78,
   91; MAICYA; YABC 1

Harris, John (Wyndham Parkes Lucas)
   Beynon 1903-1969
   See Wyndham, John
   See also CA 102; 89-92

Harris, MacDonald . . . . CLC **9**
   See also Heiney, Donald (William)

Harris, Mark 1922- . . . . **CLC 19**
See also CA 5-8R; CAAS 3; CANR 2, 55;
DLB 2; DLBY 80

Harris, (Theodore) Wilson 1921- . . . . **CLC 25**
See also BW 2; CA 65-68; CAAS 16;
CANR 11, 27; DLB 117; MTCW

Harrison, Elizabeth Cavanna 1909-
See Cavanna, Betty
See also CA 9-12R; CANR 6, 27

Harrison, Harry (Max) 1925- . . . . . . **CLC 42**
See also CA 1-4R; CANR 5, 21; DLB 8;
SATA 4

Harrison, James (Thomas)
1937- . . . . . . **CLC 6, 14, 33, 66; SSC 19**
See also CA 13-16R; CANR 8, 51;
DLBY 82; INT CANR-8

Harrison, Jim
See Harrison, James (Thomas)

Harrison, Kathryn 1961- . . . . **CLC 70**
See also CA 144

Harrison, Tony 1937- . . . . **CLC 43**
See also CA 65-68; CANR 44; DLB 40;
MTCW

Harriss, Will(ard Irvin) 1922- . . . . . . **CLC 34**
See also CA 111

Harson, Sley
See Ellison, Harlan (Jay)

Hart, Ellis
See Ellison, Harlan (Jay)

Hart, Josephine
1942(?)- . . . . **CLC 70; DAM POP**
See also CA 138

Hart, Moss
1904-1961 . . . . . . **CLC 66; DAM DRAM**
See also CA 109; 89-92; DLB 7

Harte, (Francis) Bret(t)
1836(?)-1902 . . . . **TCLC 1, 25; DA; DAC;
DAM MST; SSC 8; WLC**
See also CA 104; 140; CDALB 1865-1917;
DLB 12, 64, 74, 79; SATA 26

Hartley, L(eslie) P(oles)
1895-1972 . . . . **CLC 2, 22**
See also CA 45-48; 37-40R; CANR 33;
DLB 15, 139; MTCW

Hartman, Geoffrey H. 1929- . . . . **CLC 27**
See also CA 117; 125; DLB 67

Hartmann von Aue
c. 1160-c. 1205 . . . . **CMLC 15**
See also DLB 138

Hartmann von Aue 1170-1210 . . . . **CMLC 15**

Haruf, Kent 1943- . . . . **CLC 34**
See also CA 149

Harwood, Ronald
1934- . . . . **CLC 32; DAM DRAM, MST**
See also CA 1-4R; CANR 4, 55; DLB 13

Hasek, Jaroslav (Matej Frantisek)
1883-1923 . . . . **TCLC 4**
See also CA 104; 129; MTCW

Hass, Robert 1941- . . . . . **CLC 18, 39; PC 16**
See also CA 111; CANR 30, 50; DLB 105

Hastings, Hudson
See Kuttner, Henry

Hastings, Selina . . . . **CLC 44**

Hatteras, Amelia
See Mencken, H(enry) L(ouis)

Hatteras, Owen . . . . **TCLC 18**
See also Mencken, H(enry) L(ouis); Nathan,
George Jean

Hauptmann, Gerhart (Johann Robert)
1862-1946 . . . . . . **TCLC 4; DAM DRAM**
See also CA 104; 153; DLB 66, 118

Havel, Vaclav
1936- . . . . **CLC 25, 58, 65;
DAM DRAM; DC 6**
See also CA 104; CANR 36; MTCW

Haviaras, Stratis . . . . **CLC 33**
See also Chaviaras, Strates

Hawes, Stephen 1475(?)-1523(?) . . . . . **LC 17**

Hawkes, John (Clendennin Burne, Jr.)
1925- . . . . . . **CLC 1, 2, 3, 4, 7, 9, 14, 15,
27, 49**
See also CA 1-4R; CANR 2, 47; DLB 2, 7;
DLBY 80; MTCW

Hawking, S. W.
See Hawking, Stephen W(illiam)

Hawking, Stephen W(illiam)
1942- . . . . **CLC 63**
See also AAYA 13; BEST 89:1; CA 126;
129; CANR 48

Hawthorne, Julian 1846-1934 . . . . . **TCLC 25**

Hawthorne, Nathaniel
1804-1864 . . . . **NCLC 39; DA; DAB;
DAC; DAM MST, NOV; SSC 3; WLC**
See also AAYA 18; CDALB 1640-1865;
DLB 1, 74; YABC 2

Haxton, Josephine Ayres 1921-
See Douglas, Ellen
See also CA 115; CANR 41

Hayaseca y Eizaguirre, Jorge
See Echegaray (y Eizaguirre), Jose (Maria
Waldo)

Hayashi Fumiko 1904-1951 . . . . . . **TCLC 27**

Haycraft, Anna
See Ellis, Alice Thomas
See also CA 122

Hayden, Robert E(arl)
1913-1980 . . . . . . **CLC 5, 9, 14, 37; BLC;
DA; DAC; DAM MST, MULT, POET;
PC 6**
See also BW 1; CA 69-72; 97-100; CABS 2;
CANR 24; CDALB 1941-1968; DLB 5,
76; MTCW; SATA 19; SATA-Obit 26

Hayford, J(oseph) E(phraim) Casely
See Casely-Hayford, J(oseph) E(phraim)

Hayman, Ronald 1932- . . . . **CLC 44**
See also CA 25-28R; CANR 18, 50;
DLB 155

Haywood, Eliza (Fowler)
1693(?)-1756 . . . . **LC 1**

Hazlitt, William 1778-1830 . . . . . . **NCLC 29**
See also DLB 110, 158

Hazzard, Shirley 1931- . . . . **CLC 18**
See also CA 9-12R; CANR 4; DLBY 82;
MTCW

Head, Bessie
1937-1986 . . . . **CLC 25, 67; BLC;
DAM MULT**
See also BW 2; CA 29-32R; 119; CANR 25;
DLB 117; MTCW

Headon, (Nicky) Topper 1956(?)- . . . **CLC 30**

Heaney, Seamus (Justin)
1939- . . . . . . **CLC 5, 7, 14, 25, 37, 74, 91;
DAB; DAM POET**
See also CA 85-88; CANR 25, 48;
CDBLB 1960 to Present; DLB 40;
DLBY 95; MTCW

Hearn, (Patricio) Lafcadio (Tessima Carlos)
1850-1904 . . . . **TCLC 9**
See also CA 105; DLB 12, 78

Hearne, Vicki 1946- . . . . **CLC 56**
See also CA 139

Hearon, Shelby 1931- . . . . **CLC 63**
See also AITN 2; CA 25-28R; CANR 18,
48

Heat-Moon, William Least . . . . **CLC 29**
See also Trogdon, William (Lewis)
See also AAYA 9

Hebbel, Friedrich
1813-1863 . . . . **NCLC 43; DAM DRAM**
See also DLB 129

Hebert, Anne
1916- . . . . **CLC 4, 13, 29; DAC;
DAM MST, POET**
See also CA 85-88; DLB 68; MTCW

Hecht, Anthony (Evan)
1923- . . . . . . **CLC 8, 13, 19; DAM POET**
See also CA 9-12R; CANR 6; DLB 5, 169

Hecht, Ben 1894-1964 . . . . **CLC 8**
See also CA 85-88; DLB 7, 9, 25, 26, 28, 86

Hedayat, Sadeq 1903-1951 . . . . **TCLC 21**
See also CA 120

Hegel, Georg Wilhelm Friedrich
1770-1831 . . . . **NCLC 46**
See also DLB 90

Heidegger, Martin 1889-1976 . . . . . . **CLC 24**
See also CA 81-84; 65-68; CANR 34;
MTCW

Heidenstam, (Carl Gustaf) Verner von
1859-1940 . . . . **TCLC 5**
See also CA 104

Heifner, Jack 1946- . . . . **CLC 11**
See also CA 105; CANR 47

Heijermans, Herman 1864-1924 . . . **TCLC 24**
See also CA 123

Heilbrun, Carolyn G(old) 1926- . . . . . **CLC 25**
See also CA 45-48; CANR 1, 28

Heine, Heinrich 1797-1856 . . . . **NCLC 4, 54**
See also DLB 90

Heinemann, Larry (Curtiss) 1944- . . **CLC 50**
See also CA 110; CAAS 21; CANR 31;
DLBD 9; INT CANR-31

Heiney, Donald (William) 1921-1993
See Harris, MacDonald
See also CA 1-4R; 142; CANR 3

Heinlein, Robert A(nson)
1907-1988 . . . . . . **CLC 1, 3, 8, 14, 26, 55;
DAM POP**
See also AAYA 17; CA 1-4R; 125;
CANR 1, 20, 53; DLB 8; JRDA;
MAICYA; MTCW; SATA 9, 69;
SATA-Obit 56

Helforth, John
See Doolittle, Hilda

Hellenhofferu, Vojtech Kapristian z
See Hasek, Jaroslav (Matej Frantisek)

Heller, Joseph
1923- . . . . CLC 1, 3, 5, 8, 11, 36, 63; DA;
DAB; DAC; DAM MST, NOV, POP;
WLC
See also AITN 1; CA 5-8R; CABS 1;
CANR 8, 42; DLB 2, 28; DLBY 80;
INT CANR-8; MTCW

Hellman, Lillian (Florence)
1906-1984 . . . . . . **CLC 2, 4, 8, 14, 18, 34,
44, 52; DAM DRAM; DC 1**
See also AITN 1, 2; CA 13-16R; 112;
CANR 33; DLB 7; DLBY 84; MTCW

Helprin, Mark
1947- . . . . CLC 7, 10, 22, 32;
DAM NOV, POP
See also CA 81-84; CANR 47; DLBY 85;
MTCW

Helvetius, Claude-Adrien
1715-1771 . . . . LC 26

Helyar, Jane Penelope Josephine 1933-
See Poole, Josephine
See also CA 21-24R; CANR 10, 26;
SATA 82

Hemans, Felicia 1793-1835 . . . . . . NCLC 29
See also DLB 96

Hemingway, Ernest (Miller)
1899-1961 . . . . CLC 1, 3, 6, 8, 10, 13, 19,
30, 34, 39, 41, 44, 50, 61, 80; DA; DAB;
DAC; DAM MST, NOV; SSC 1; WLC
See also AAYA 19; CA 77-80; CANR 34;
CDALB 1917-1929; DLB 4, 9, 102;
DLBD 1; DLBY 81, 87; MTCW

Hempel, Amy 1951- . . . . CLC 39
See also CA 118; 137

Henderson, F. C.
See Mencken, H(enry) L(ouis)

Henderson, Sylvia
See Ashton-Warner, Sylvia (Constance)

Henley, Beth . . . . CLC 23; DC 6
See also Henley, Elizabeth Becker
See also CABS 3; DLBY 86

Henley, Elizabeth Becker 1952-
See Henley, Beth
See also CA 107; CANR 32; DAM DRAM,
MST; MTCW

Henley, William Ernest
1849-1903 . . . . TCLC 8
See also CA 105; DLB 19

Hennissart, Martha
See Lathen, Emma
See also CA 85-88

Henry, O. . . . . TCLC 1, 19; SSC 5; WLC
See also Porter, William Sydney

Henry, Patrick 1736-1799 . . . . LC 25

Henryson, Robert 1430(?)-1506(?). . . . LC 20
See also DLB 146

Henry VIII 1491-1547 . . . . LC 10

Henschke, Alfred
See Klabund

Hentoff, Nat(han Irving) 1925- . . . . . CLC 26
See also AAYA 4; CA 1-4R; CAAS 6;
CANR 5, 25; CLR 1; INT CANR-25;
JRDA; MAICYA; SATA 42, 69;
SATA-Brief 27

Heppenstall, (John) Rayner
1911-1981 . . . . CLC 10
See also CA 1-4R; 103; CANR 29

Herbert, Frank (Patrick)
1920-1986 . . . . . . CLC 12, 23, 35, 44, 85;
DAM POP
See also CA 53-56; 118; CANR 5, 43;
DLB 8; INT CANR-5; MTCW; SATA 9,
37; SATA-Obit 47

Herbert, George
1593-1633 . . . . LC 24; DAB;
DAM POET; PC 4
See also CDBLB Before 1660; DLB 126

Herbert, Zbigniew
1924- . . . . CLC 9, 43; DAM POET
See also CA 89-92; CANR 36; MTCW

Herbst, Josephine (Frey)
1897-1969 . . . . CLC 34
See also CA 5-8R; 25-28R; DLB 9

Hergesheimer, Joseph
1880-1954 . . . . TCLC 11
See also CA 109; DLB 102, 9

Herlihy, James Leo 1927-1993 . . . . . . CLC 6
See also CA 1-4R; 143; CANR 2

Hermogenes fl. c. 175- . . . . CMLC 6

Hernandez, Jose 1834-1886 . . . . . . NCLC 17

Herodotus c. 484B.C.-429B.C. . . . . CMLC 17

Herrick, Robert
1591-1674 . . . . . LC 13; DA; DAB; DAC;
DAM MST, POP; PC 9
See also DLB 126

Herring, Guilles
See Somerville, Edith

Herriot, James
1916-1995 . . . . CLC 12; DAM POP
See also Wight, James Alfred
See also AAYA 1; CA 148; CANR 40;
SATA 86

Herrmann, Dorothy 1941- . . . . CLC 44
See also CA 107

Herrmann, Taffy
See Herrmann, Dorothy

Hersey, John (Richard)
1914-1993 . . . . CLC 1, 2, 7, 9, 40, 81, 97;
DAM POP
See also CA 17-20R; 140; CANR 33;
DLB 6; MTCW; SATA 25;
SATA-Obit 76

Herzen, Aleksandr Ivanovich
1812-1870 . . . . NCLC 10

Herzl, Theodor 1860-1904 . . . . TCLC 36

Herzog, Werner 1942- . . . . CLC 16
See also CA 89-92

Hesiod c. 8th cent. B.C.- . . . . CMLC 5

Hesse, Hermann
1877-1962 . . . . CLC 1, 2, 3, 6, 11, 17, 25,
69; DA; DAB; DAC; DAM MST, NOV;
SSC 9; WLC
See also CA 17-18; CAP 2; DLB 66;
MTCW; SATA 50

Hewes, Cady
See De Voto, Bernard (Augustine)

Heyen, William 1940- . . . . CLC 13, 18
See also CA 33-36R; CAAS 9; DLB 5

Heyerdahl, Thor 1914- . . . . CLC 26
See also CA 5-8R; CANR 5, 22; MTCW;
SATA 2, 52

Heym, Georg (Theodor Franz Arthur)
1887-1912 . . . . TCLC 9
See also CA 106

Heym, Stefan 1913- . . . . CLC 41
See also CA 9-12R; CANR 4; DLB 69

Heyse, Paul (Johann Ludwig von)
1830-1914 . . . . TCLC 8
See also CA 104; DLB 129

Heyward, (Edwin) DuBose
1885-1940 . . . . TCLC 59
See also CA 108; DLB 7, 9, 45; SATA 21

Hibbert, Eleanor Alice Burford
1906-1993 . . . . CLC 7; DAM POP
See also BEST 90:4; CA 17-20R; 140;
CANR 9, 28; SATA 2; SATA-Obit 74

Hichens, Robert S. 1864-1950 . . . . . TCLC 64
See also DLB 153

Higgins, George V(incent)
1939- . . . . CLC 4, 7, 10, 18
See also CA 77-80; CAAS 5; CANR 17, 51;
DLB 2; DLBY 81; INT CANR-17;
MTCW

Higginson, Thomas Wentworth
1823-1911 . . . . TCLC 36
See also DLB 1, 64

Highet, Helen
See MacInnes, Helen (Clark)

Highsmith, (Mary) Patricia
1921-1995 . . . . CLC 2, 4, 14, 42;
DAM NOV, POP
See also CA 1-4R; 147; CANR 1, 20, 48;
MTCW

Highwater, Jamake (Mamake)
1942(?)- . . . . CLC 12
See also AAYA 7; CA 65-68; CAAS 7;
CANR 10, 34; CLR 17; DLB 52;
DLBY 85; JRDA; MAICYA; SATA 32,
69; SATA-Brief 30

Highway, Tomson
1951- . . . . . CLC 92; DAC; DAM MULT
See also CA 151; NNAL

Higuchi, Ichiyo 1872-1896 . . . . NCLC 49

Hijuelos, Oscar
1951- . . . . CLC 65; DAM MULT, POP;
HLC
See also BEST 90:1; CA 123; CANR 50;
DLB 145; HW

Hikmet, Nazim 1902(?)-1963 . . . . . . CLC 40
See also CA 141; 93-96

Hildegard von Bingen
1098-1179 . . . . CMLC 20
See also DLB 148

Hildesheimer, Wolfgang
    1916-1991 .... **CLC 49**
    See also CA 101; 135; DLB 69, 124

Hill, Geoffrey (William)
    1932- ... **CLC 5, 8, 18, 45; DAM POET**
    See also CA 81-84; CANR 21;
        CDBLB 1960 to Present; DLB 40;
        MTCW

Hill, George Roy 1921- .... **CLC 26**
    See also CA 110; 122

Hill, John
    See Koontz, Dean R(ay)

Hill, Susan (Elizabeth)
    1942- .. **CLC 4; DAB; DAM MST, NOV**
    See also CA 33-36R; CANR 29; DLB 14,
        139; MTCW

Hillerman, Tony
    1925- .... **CLC 62; DAM POP**
    See also AAYA 6; BEST 89:1; CA 29-32R;
        CANR 21, 42; SATA 6

Hillesum, Etty 1914-1943 .... **TCLC 49**
    See also CA 137

Hilliard, Noel (Harvey) 1929- ..... **CLC 15**
    See also CA 9-12R; CANR 7

Hillis, Rick 1956- .... **CLC 66**
    See also CA 134

Hilton, James 1900-1954 .... **TCLC 21**
    See also CA 108; DLB 34, 77; SATA 34

Himes, Chester (Bomar)
    1909-1984 .... **CLC 2, 4, 7, 18, 58; BLC;
                                    DAM MULT**
    See also BW 2; CA 25-28R; 114; CANR 22;
        DLB 2, 76, 143; MTCW

Hinde, Thomas .... **CLC 6, 11**
    See also Chitty, Thomas Willes

Hindin, Nathan
    See Bloch, Robert (Albert)

Hine, (William) Daryl 1936- .... **CLC 15**
    See also CA 1-4R; CAAS 15; CANR 1, 20;
        DLB 60

Hinkson, Katharine Tynan
    See Tynan, Katharine

Hinton, S(usan) E(loise)
    1950- .... **CLC 30; DA; DAB; DAC;
                                    DAM MST, NOV**
    See also AAYA 2; CA 81-84; CANR 32;
        CLR 3, 23; JRDA; MAICYA; MTCW;
        SATA 19, 58

Hippius, Zinaida .... **TCLC 9**
    See also Gippius, Zinaida (Nikolayevna)

Hiraoka, Kimitake 1925-1970
    See Mishima, Yukio
    See also CA 97-100; 29-32R; DAM DRAM;
        MTCW

Hirsch, E(ric) D(onald), Jr. 1928-... **CLC 79**
    See also CA 25-28R; CANR 27, 51;
        DLB 67; INT CANR-27; MTCW

Hirsch, Edward 1950- .... **CLC 31, 50**
    See also CA 104; CANR 20, 42; DLB 120

Hitchcock, Alfred (Joseph)
    1899-1980 .... **CLC 16**
    See also CA 97-100; SATA 27;
        SATA-Obit 24

Hitler, Adolf 1889-1945 .... **TCLC 53**
    See also CA 117; 147

Hoagland, Edward 1932- .... **CLC 28**
    See also CA 1-4R; CANR 2, 31; DLB 6;
        SATA 51

Hoban, Russell (Conwell)
    1925- .... **CLC 7, 25; DAM NOV**
    See also CA 5-8R; CANR 23, 37; CLR 3;
        DLB 52; MAICYA; MTCW; SATA 1,
        40, 78

Hobbes, Thomas 1588-1679 .... **LC 36**
    See also DLB 151

Hobbs, Perry
    See Blackmur, R(ichard) P(almer)

Hobson, Laura Z(ametkin)
    1900-1986 .... **CLC 7, 25**
    See also CA 17-20R; 118; CANR 55;
        DLB 28; SATA 52

Hochhuth, Rolf
    1931- ..... **CLC 4, 11, 18; DAM DRAM**
    See also CA 5-8R; CANR 33; DLB 124;
        MTCW

Hochman, Sandra 1936- .... **CLC 3, 8**
    See also CA 5-8R; DLB 5

Hochwaelder, Fritz
    1911-1986 ...... **CLC 36; DAM DRAM**
    See also CA 29-32R; 120; CANR 42;
        MTCW

Hochwalder, Fritz
    See Hochwaelder, Fritz

Hocking, Mary (Eunice) 1921- ..... **CLC 13**
    See also CA 101; CANR 18, 40

Hodgins, Jack 1938- .... **CLC 23**
    See also CA 93-96; DLB 60

Hodgson, William Hope
    1877(?)-1918 .... **TCLC 13**
    See also CA 111; DLB 70, 153, 156

Hoeg, Peter 1957- .... **CLC 95**
    See also CA 151

Hoffman, Alice
    1952- .... **CLC 51; DAM NOV**
    See also CA 77-80; CANR 34; MTCW

Hoffman, Daniel (Gerard)
    1923- .... **CLC 6, 13, 23**
    See also CA 1-4R; CANR 4; DLB 5

Hoffman, Stanley 1944- .... **CLC 5**
    See also CA 77-80

Hoffman, William M(oses) 1939- ... **CLC 40**
    See also CA 57-60; CANR 11

Hoffmann, E(rnst) T(heodor) A(madeus)
    1776-1822 .... **NCLC 2; SSC 13**
    See also DLB 90; SATA 27

Hofmann, Gert 1931- .... **CLC 54**
    See also CA 128

Hofmannsthal, Hugo von
    1874-1929 .... **TCLC 11; DAM DRAM;
                                    DC 4**
    See also CA 106; 153; DLB 81, 118

Hogan, Linda
    1947- .... **CLC 73; DAM MULT**
    See also CA 120; CANR 45; NNAL

Hogarth, Charles
    See Creasey, John

Hogarth, Emmett
    See Polonsky, Abraham (Lincoln)

Hogg, James 1770-1835 .... **NCLC 4**
    See also DLB 93, 116, 159

Holbach, Paul Henri Thiry Baron
    1723-1789 .... **LC 14**

Holberg, Ludvig 1684-1754 .... **LC 6**

Holden, Ursula 1921- .... **CLC 18**
    See also CA 101; CAAS 8; CANR 22

Holderlin, (Johann Christian) Friedrich
    1770-1843 .... **NCLC 16; PC 4**

Holdstock, Robert
    See Holdstock, Robert P.

Holdstock, Robert P. 1948-........ **CLC 39**
    See also CA 131

Holland, Isabelle 1920- .... **CLC 21**
    See also AAYA 11; CA 21-24R; CANR 10,
        25, 47; JRDA; MAICYA; SATA 8, 70

Holland, Marcus
    See Caldwell, (Janet Miriam) Taylor
        (Holland)

Hollander, John 1929- ...... **CLC 2, 5, 8, 14**
    See also CA 1-4R; CANR 1, 52; DLB 5;
        SATA 13

Hollander, Paul
    See Silverberg, Robert

Holleran, Andrew 1943(?)-......... **CLC 38**
    See also CA 144

Hollinghurst, Alan 1954-....... **CLC 55, 91**
    See also CA 114

Hollis, Jim
    See Summers, Hollis (Spurgeon, Jr.)

Holly, Buddy 1936-1959 .... **TCLC 65**

Holmes, John
    See Souster, (Holmes) Raymond

Holmes, John Clellon 1926-1988.... **CLC 56**
    See also CA 9-12R; 125; CANR 4; DLB 16

Holmes, Oliver Wendell
    1809-1894 .... **NCLC 14**
    See also CDALB 1640-1865; DLB 1;
        SATA 34

Holmes, Raymond
    See Souster, (Holmes) Raymond

Holt, Victoria
    See Hibbert, Eleanor Alice Burford

Holub, Miroslav 1923-............. **CLC 4**
    See also CA 21-24R; CANR 10

Homer
    c. 8th cent. B.C.-..... **CMLC 1, 16; DA;
                                    DAB; DAC; DAM MST, POET**

Honig, Edwin 1919-............... **CLC 33**
    See also CA 5-8R; CAAS 8; CANR 4, 45;
        DLB 5

Hood, Hugh (John Blagdon)
    1928- .... **CLC 15, 28**
    See also CA 49-52; CAAS 17; CANR 1, 33;
        DLB 53

Hood, Thomas 1799-1845........ **NCLC 16**
    See also DLB 96

Hooker, (Peter) Jeremy 1941-...... **CLC 43**
    See also CA 77-80; CANR 22; DLB 40

hooks, bell .... **CLC 94**
    See also Watkins, Gloria

Hope, A(lec) D(erwent) 1907-.... **CLC 3, 51**
    See also CA 21-24R; CANR 33; MTCW

Hope, Brian
    See Creasey, John

Hope, Christopher (David Tully)
1944- . . . . CLC 52
See also CA 106; CANR 47; SATA 62

Hopkins, Gerard Manley
1844-1889 . . . . NCLC 17; DA; DAB;
DAC; DAM MST, POET; PC 15; WLC
See also CDBLB 1890-1914; DLB 35, 57

Hopkins, John (Richard) 1931- . . . . . . CLC 4
See also CA 85-88

Hopkins, Pauline Elizabeth
1859-1930 . . . . TCLC 28; BLC;
DAM MULT
See also BW 2; CA 141; DLB 50

Hopkinson, Francis 1737-1791 . . . . . . LC 25
See also DLB 31

Hopley-Woolrich, Cornell George 1903-1968
See Woolrich, Cornell
See also CA 13-14; CAP 1

Horatio
See Proust, (Valentin-Louis-George-Eugene-)
Marcel

Horgan, Paul (George Vincent O'Shaughnessy)
1903-1995 . . . . . . CLC 9, 53; DAM NOV
See also CA 13-16R; 147; CANR 9, 35;
DLB 102; DLBY 85; INT CANR-9;
MTCW; SATA 13; SATA-Obit 84

Horn, Peter
See Kuttner, Henry

Hornem, Horace Esq.
See Byron, George Gordon (Noel)

Hornung, E(rnest) W(illiam)
1866-1921 . . . . TCLC 59
See also CA 108; DLB 70

Horovitz, Israel (Arthur)
1939- . . . . CLC 56; DAM DRAM
See also CA 33-36R; CANR 46; DLB 7

Horvath, Odon von
See Horvath, Oedoen von
See also DLB 85, 124

Horvath, Oedoen von 1901-1938 . . . TCLC 45
See also Horvath, Odon von
See also CA 118

Horwitz, Julius 1920-1986 . . . . CLC 14
See also CA 9-12R; 119; CANR 12

Hospital, Janette Turner 1942- . . . . . CLC 42
See also CA 108; CANR 48

Hostos, E. M. de
See Hostos (y Bonilla), Eugenio Maria de

Hostos, Eugenio M. de
See Hostos (y Bonilla), Eugenio Maria de

Hostos, Eugenio Maria
See Hostos (y Bonilla), Eugenio Maria de

Hostos (y Bonilla), Eugenio Maria de
1839-1903 . . . . TCLC 24
See also CA 123; 131; HW

Houdini
See Lovecraft, H(oward) P(hillips)

Hougan, Carolyn 1943- . . . . CLC 34
See also CA 139

Household, Geoffrey (Edward West)
1900-1988 . . . . CLC 11
See also CA 77-80; 126; DLB 87; SATA 14;
SATA-Obit 59

Housman, A(lfred) E(dward)
1859-1936 . . . . . TCLC 1, 10; DA; DAB;
DAC; DAM MST, POET; PC 2
See also CA 104; 125; DLB 19; MTCW

Housman, Laurence 1865-1959 . . . . . TCLC 7
See also CA 106; 155; DLB 10; SATA 25

Howard, Elizabeth Jane 1923- . . . CLC 7, 29
See also CA 5-8R; CANR 8

Howard, Maureen 1930- . . . . . CLC 5, 14, 46
See also CA 53-56; CANR 31; DLBY 83;
INT CANR-31; MTCW

Howard, Richard 1929- . . . . . . CLC 7, 10, 47
See also AITN 1; CA 85-88; CANR 25;
DLB 5; INT CANR-25

Howard, Robert Ervin 1906-1936 . . . TCLC 8
See also CA 105

Howard, Warren F.
See Pohl, Frederik

Howe, Fanny 1940- . . . . CLC 47
See also CA 117; SATA-Brief 52

Howe, Irving 1920-1993 . . . . CLC 85
See also CA 9-12R; 141; CANR 21, 50;
DLB 67; MTCW

Howe, Julia Ward 1819-1910 . . . . . TCLC 21
See also CA 117; DLB 1

Howe, Susan 1937- . . . . CLC 72
See also DLB 120

Howe, Tina 1937- . . . . CLC 48
See also CA 109

Howell, James 1594(?)-1666 . . . . LC 13
See also DLB 151

Howells, W. D.
See Howells, William Dean

Howells, William D.
See Howells, William Dean

Howells, William Dean
1837-1920 . . . . TCLC 7, 17, 41
See also CA 104; 134; CDALB 1865-1917;
DLB 12, 64, 74, 79

Howes, Barbara 1914-1996 . . . . CLC 15
See also CA 9-12R; 151; CAAS 3;
CANR 53; SATA 5

Hrabal, Bohumil 1914- . . . . CLC 13, 67
See also CA 106; CAAS 12

Hsun, Lu
See Lu Hsun

Hubbard, L(afayette) Ron(ald)
1911-1986 . . . . CLC 43; DAM POP
See also CA 77-80; 118; CANR 52

Huch, Ricarda (Octavia)
1864-1947 . . . . TCLC 13
See also CA 111; DLB 66

Huddle, David 1942- . . . . CLC 49
See also CA 57-60; CAAS 20; DLB 130

Hudson, Jeffrey
See Crichton, (John) Michael

Hudson, W(illiam) H(enry)
1841-1922 . . . . TCLC 29
See also CA 115; DLB 98, 153, 174;
SATA 35

Hueffer, Ford Madox
See Ford, Ford Madox

Hughart, Barry 1934- . . . . CLC 39
See also CA 137

Hughes, Colin
See Creasey, John

Hughes, David (John) 1930- . . . . . . CLC 48
See also CA 116; 129; DLB 14

Hughes, Edward James
See Hughes, Ted
See also DAM MST, POET

Hughes, (James) Langston
1902-1967 . . . . . CLC 1, 5, 10, 15, 35, 44;
BLC; DA; DAB; DAC; DAM DRAM,
MST, MULT, POET; DC 3; PC 1;
SSC 6; WLC
See also AAYA 12; BW 1; CA 1-4R;
25-28R; CANR 1, 34; CDALB 1929-1941;
CLR 17; DLB 4, 7, 48, 51, 86; JRDA;
MAICYA; MTCW; SATA 4, 33

Hughes, Richard (Arthur Warren)
1900-1976 . . . . . . CLC 1, 11; DAM NOV
See also CA 5-8R; 65-68; CANR 4;
DLB 15, 161; MTCW; SATA 8;
SATA-Obit 25

Hughes, Ted
1930- . . . . CLC 2, 4, 9, 14, 37; DAB;
DAC; PC 7
See also Hughes, Edward James
See also CA 1-4R; CANR 1, 33; CLR 3;
DLB 40, 161; MAICYA; MTCW;
SATA 49; SATA-Brief 27

Hugo, Richard F(ranklin)
1923-1982 . . . . CLC 6, 18, 32;
DAM POET
See also CA 49-52; 108; CANR 3; DLB 5

Hugo, Victor (Marie)
1802-1885 . . . . NCLC 3, 10, 21; DA;
DAB; DAC; DAM DRAM, MST, NOV,
POET; PC 17; WLC
See also DLB 119; SATA 47

Huidobro, Vicente
See Huidobro Fernandez, Vicente Garcia

Huidobro Fernandez, Vicente Garcia
1893-1948 . . . . TCLC 31
See also CA 131; HW

Hulme, Keri 1947- . . . . CLC 39
See also CA 125; INT 125

Hulme, T(homas) E(rnest)
1883-1917 . . . . TCLC 21
See also CA 117; DLB 19

Hume, David 1711-1776 . . . . LC 7
See also DLB 104

Humphrey, William 1924- . . . . CLC 45
See also CA 77-80; DLB 6

Humphreys, Emyr Owen 1919- . . . . . CLC 47
See also CA 5-8R; CANR 3, 24; DLB 15

Humphreys, Josephine 1945- . . . . CLC 34, 57
See also CA 121; 127; INT 127

Huneker, James Gibbons
1857-1921 . . . . TCLC 65
See also DLB 71

Hungerford, Pixie
See Brinsmead, H(esba) F(ay)

Hunt, E(verette) Howard, (Jr.)
1918- . . . . CLC 3
See also AITN 1; CA 45-48; CANR 2, 47

Hunt, Kyle
See Creasey, John

Hunt, (James Henry) Leigh
1784-1859 . . . . . . **NCLC 1; DAM POET**

Hunt, Marsha 1946- . . . . **CLC 70**
See also BW 2; CA 143

Hunt, Violet 1866-1942 . . . . **TCLC 53**
See also DLB 162

Hunter, E. Waldo
See Sturgeon, Theodore (Hamilton)

Hunter, Evan
1926- . . . . **CLC 11, 31; DAM POP**
See also CA 5-8R; CANR 5, 38; DLBY 82;
INT CANR-5; MTCW; SATA 25

Hunter, Kristin (Eggleston) 1931- . . . **CLC 35**
See also AITN 1; BW 1; CA 13-16R;
CANR 13; CLR 3; DLB 33;
INT CANR-13; MAICYA; SAAS 10;
SATA 12

Hunter, Mollie 1922- . . . . **CLC 21**
See also McIlwraith, Maureen Mollie
Hunter
See also AAYA 13; CANR 37; CLR 25;
DLB 161; JRDA; MAICYA; SAAS 7;
SATA 54

Hunter, Robert (?)-1734 . . . . **LC 7**

Hurston, Zora Neale
1903-1960 . . . . **CLC 7, 30, 61; BLC; DA;
DAC; DAM MST, MULT, NOV; SSC 4**
See also AAYA 15; BW 1; CA 85-88;
DLB 51, 86; MTCW

Huston, John (Marcellus)
1906-1987 . . . . **CLC 20**
See also CA 73-76; 123; CANR 34; DLB 26

Hustvedt, Siri 1955- . . . . **CLC 76**
See also CA 137

Hutten, Ulrich von 1488-1523 . . . . . . **LC 16**

Huxley, Aldous (Leonard)
1894-1963 . . . . . **CLC 1, 3, 4, 5, 8, 11, 18,
35, 79; DA; DAB; DAC; DAM MST,
NOV; WLC**
See also AAYA 11; CA 85-88; CANR 44;
CDBLB 1914-1945; DLB 36, 100, 162;
MTCW; SATA 63

Huysmans, Charles Marie Georges
1848-1907
See Huysmans, Joris-Karl
See also CA 104

Huysmans, Joris-Karl . . . . **TCLC 7**
See also Huysmans, Charles Marie Georges
See also DLB 123

Hwang, David Henry
1957- . . . . **CLC 55; DAM DRAM; DC 4**
See also CA 127; 132; INT 132

Hyde, Anthony 1946- . . . . **CLC 42**
See also CA 136

Hyde, Margaret O(ldroyd) 1917- . . . **CLC 21**
See also CA 1-4R; CANR 1, 36; CLR 23;
JRDA; MAICYA; SAAS 8; SATA 1, 42,
76

Hynes, James 1956(?)- . . . . **CLC 65**

Ian, Janis 1951- . . . . **CLC 21**
See also CA 105

Ibanez, Vicente Blasco
See Blasco Ibanez, Vicente

Ibarguengoitia, Jorge 1928-1983 . . . . **CLC 37**
See also CA 124; 113; HW

Ibsen, Henrik (Johan)
1828-1906 . . . . . . **TCLC 2, 8, 16, 37, 52;
DA; DAB; DAC; DAM DRAM, MST;
DC 2; WLC**
See also CA 104; 141

Ibuse Masuji 1898-1993 . . . . **CLC 22**
See also CA 127; 141

Ichikawa, Kon 1915- . . . . **CLC 20**
See also CA 121

Idle, Eric 1943- . . . . **CLC 21**
See also Monty Python
See also CA 116; CANR 35

Ignatow, David 1914- . . . . . . **CLC 4, 7, 14, 40**
See also CA 9-12R; CAAS 3; CANR 31;
DLB 5

Ihimaera, Witi 1944- . . . . **CLC 46**
See also CA 77-80

Ilf, Ilya . . . . **TCLC 21**
See also Fainzilberg, Ilya Arnoldovich

Illyes, Gyula 1902-1983 . . . . **PC 16**
See also CA 114; 109

Immermann, Karl (Lebrecht)
1796-1840 . . . . **NCLC 4, 49**
See also DLB 133

Inclan, Ramon (Maria) del Valle
See Valle-Inclan, Ramon (Maria) del

Infante, G(uillermo) Cabrera
See Cabrera Infante, G(uillermo)

Ingalls, Rachel (Holmes) 1940- . . . . . **CLC 42**
See also CA 123; 127

Ingamells, Rex 1913-1955 . . . . **TCLC 35**

Inge, William (Motter)
1913-1973 . . **CLC 1, 8, 19; DAM DRAM**
See also CA 9-12R; CDALB 1941-1968;
DLB 7; MTCW

Ingelow, Jean 1820-1897 . . . . **NCLC 39**
See also DLB 35, 163; SATA 33

Ingram, Willis J.
See Harris, Mark

Innaurato, Albert (F.) 1948(?)- . . **CLC 21, 60**
See also CA 115; 122; INT 122

Innes, Michael
See Stewart, J(ohn) I(nnes) M(ackintosh)

Ionesco, Eugene
1909-1994 . . . . **CLC 1, 4, 6, 9, 11, 15, 41,
86; DA; DAB; DAC; DAM DRAM,
MST; WLC**
See also CA 9-12R; 144; CANR 55;
MTCW; SATA 7; SATA-Obit 79

Iqbal, Muhammad 1873-1938 . . . . . **TCLC 28**

Ireland, Patrick
See O'Doherty, Brian

Iron, Ralph
See Schreiner, Olive (Emilie Albertina)

Irving, John (Winslow)
1942- . . . . . **CLC 13, 23, 38; DAM NOV,
POP**
See also AAYA 8; BEST 89:3; CA 25-28R;
CANR 28; DLB 6; DLBY 82; MTCW

Irving, Washington
1783-1859 . . . . . **NCLC 2, 19; DA; DAB;
DAM MST; SSC 2; WLC**
See also CDALB 1640-1865; DLB 3, 11, 30,
59, 73, 74; YABC 2

Irwin, P. K.
See Page, P(atricia) K(athleen)

Isaacs, Susan 1943- . . . **CLC 32; DAM POP**
See also BEST 89:1; CA 89-92; CANR 20,
41; INT CANR-20; MTCW

Isherwood, Christopher (William Bradshaw)
1904-1986 . . . . **CLC 1, 9, 11, 14, 44;
DAM DRAM, NOV**
See also CA 13-16R; 117; CANR 35;
DLB 15; DLBY 86; MTCW

Ishiguro, Kazuo
1954- . . . . **CLC 27, 56, 59; DAM NOV**
See also BEST 90:2; CA 120; CANR 49;
MTCW

Ishikawa, Hakuhin
See Ishikawa, Takuboku

Ishikawa, Takuboku
1886(?)-1912 . . . . **TCLC 15;
DAM POET; PC 10**
See also CA 113; 153

Iskander, Fazil 1929- . . . . **CLC 47**
See also CA 102

Isler, Alan . . . . **CLC 91**

Ivan IV 1530-1584 . . . . **LC 17**

Ivanov, Vyacheslav Ivanovich
1866-1949 . . . . **TCLC 33**
See also CA 122

Ivask, Ivar Vidrik 1927-1992 . . . . **CLC 14**
See also CA 37-40R; 139; CANR 24

Ives, Morgan
See Bradley, Marion Zimmer

J. R. S.
See Gogarty, Oliver St. John

Jabran, Kahlil
See Gibran, Kahlil

Jabran, Khalil
See Gibran, Kahlil

Jackson, Daniel
See Wingrove, David (John)

Jackson, Jesse 1908-1983 . . . . **CLC 12**
See also BW 1; CA 25-28R; 109; CANR 27;
CLR 28; MAICYA; SATA 2, 29;
SATA-Obit 48

Jackson, Laura (Riding) 1901-1991
See Riding, Laura
See also CA 65-68; 135; CANR 28; DLB 48

Jackson, Sam
See Trumbo, Dalton

Jackson, Sara
See Wingrove, David (John)

Jackson, Shirley
1919-1965 . . . . **CLC 11, 60, 87; DA;
DAC; DAM MST; SSC 9; WLC**
See also AAYA 9; CA 1-4R; 25-28R;
CANR 4, 52; CDALB 1941-1968; DLB 6;
SATA 2

Jacob, (Cyprien-)Max 1876-1944 . . . **TCLC 6**
See also CA 104

Jacobs, Jim 1942- . . . . **CLC 12**
See also CA 97-100; INT 97-100

Jacobs, W(illiam) W(ymark)
1863-1943 . . . . **TCLC 22**
See also CA 121; DLB 135

Jacobsen, Jens Peter 1847-1885 . . **NCLC 34**

Jacobsen, Josephine 1908-........ **CLC 48**
See also CA 33-36R; CAAS 18; CANR 23,
48

Jacobson, Dan 1929- .... **CLC 4, 14**
See also CA 1-4R; CANR 2, 25; DLB 14;
MTCW

Jacqueline
See Carpentier (y Valmont), Alejo

Jagger, Mick 1944-.............. **CLC 17**

Jakes, John (William)
1932- ...... **CLC 29; DAM NOV, POP**
See also BEST 89:4; CA 57-60; CANR 10,
43; DLBY 83; INT CANR-10; MTCW;
SATA 62

James, Andrew
See Kirkup, James

James, C(yril) L(ionel) R(obert)
1901-1989 .... **CLC 33**
See also BW 2; CA 117; 125; 128; DLB 125;
MTCW

James, Daniel (Lewis) 1911-1988
See Santiago, Danny
See also CA 125

James, Dynely
See Mayne, William (James Carter)

James, Henry Sr. 1811-1882..... **NCLC 53**

James, Henry
1843-1916 ...... **TCLC 2, 11, 24, 40, 47,
64; DA; DAB; DAC; DAM MST, NOV;
SSC 8; WLC**
See also CA 104; 132; CDALB 1865-1917;
DLB 12, 71, 74; DLBD 13; MTCW

James, M. R.
See James, Montague (Rhodes)
See also DLB 156

James, Montague (Rhodes)
1862-1936 .... **TCLC 6; SSC 16**
See also CA 104

James, P. D. .... **CLC 18, 46**
See also White, Phyllis Dorothy James
See also BEST 90:2; CDBLB 1960 to
Present; DLB 87

James, Philip
See Moorcock, Michael (John)

James, William 1842-1910..... **TCLC 15, 32**
See also CA 109

James I 1394-1437 .... **LC 20**

Jameson, Anna 1794-1860....... **NCLC 43**
See also DLB 99, 166

Jami, Nur al-Din 'Abd al-Rahman
1414-1492 .... **LC 9**

Jandl, Ernst 1925- .... **CLC 34**

Janowitz, Tama
1957- .... **CLC 43; DAM POP**
See also CA 106; CANR 52

Japrisot, Sebastien 1931-......... **CLC 90**

Jarrell, Randall
1914-1965 ...... **CLC 1, 2, 6, 9, 13, 49;
DAM POET**
See also CA 5-8R; 25-28R; CABS 2;
CANR 6, 34; CDALB 1941-1968; CLR 6;
DLB 48, 52; MAICYA; MTCW; SATA 7

Jarry, Alfred
1873-1907 .... **TCLC 2, 14;
DAM DRAM; SSC 20**
See also CA 104; 153

Jarvis, E. K.
See Bloch, Robert (Albert); Ellison, Harlan
(Jay); Silverberg, Robert

Jeake, Samuel, Jr.
See Aiken, Conrad (Potter)

Jean Paul 1763-1825 .... **NCLC 7**

Jefferies, (John) Richard
1848-1887 .... **NCLC 47**
See also DLB 98, 141; SATA 16

Jeffers, (John) Robinson
1887-1962 .... **CLC 2, 3, 11, 15, 54; DA;
DAC; DAM MST, POET; PC 17; WLC**
See also CA 85-88; CANR 35;
CDALB 1917-1929; DLB 45; MTCW

Jefferson, Janet
See Mencken, H(enry) L(ouis)

Jefferson, Thomas 1743-1826 .... **NCLC 11**
See also CDALB 1640-1865; DLB 31

Jeffrey, Francis 1773-1850....... **NCLC 33**
See also DLB 107

Jelakowitch, Ivan
See Heijermans, Herman

Jellicoe, (Patricia) Ann 1927-...... **CLC 27**
See also CA 85-88; DLB 13

Jen, Gish .... **CLC 70**
See also Jen, Lillian

Jen, Lillian 1956(?)-
See Jen, Gish
See also CA 135

Jenkins, (John) Robin 1912-....... **CLC 52**
See also CA 1-4R; CANR 1; DLB 14

Jennings, Elizabeth (Joan)
1926- .... **CLC 5, 14**
See also CA 61-64; CAAS 5; CANR 8, 39;
DLB 27; MTCW; SATA 66

Jennings, Waylon 1937-.......... **CLC 21**

Jensen, Johannes V. 1873-1950.... **TCLC 41**

Jensen, Laura (Linnea) 1948- ...... **CLC 37**
See also CA 103

Jerome, Jerome K(lapka)
1859-1927 .... **TCLC 23**
See also CA 119; DLB 10, 34, 135

Jerrold, Douglas William
1803-1857 .... **NCLC 2**
See also DLB 158, 159

Jewett, (Theodora) Sarah Orne
1849-1909 .... **TCLC 1, 22; SSC 6**
See also CA 108; 127; DLB 12, 74;
SATA 15

Jewsbury, Geraldine (Endsor)
1812-1880 .... **NCLC 22**
See also DLB 21

Jhabvala, Ruth Prawer
1927- .... **CLC 4, 8, 29, 94; DAB;
DAM NOV**
See also CA 1-4R; CANR 2, 29, 51;
DLB 139; INT CANR-29; MTCW

Jibran, Kahlil
See Gibran, Kahlil

Jibran, Khalil
See Gibran, Kahlil

Jiles, Paulette 1943-.......... **CLC 13, 58**
See also CA 101

Jimenez (Mantecon), Juan Ramon
1881-1958 ..... **TCLC 4; DAM MULT,
POET; HLC; PC 7**
See also CA 104; 131; DLB 134; HW;
MTCW

Jimenez, Ramon
See Jimenez (Mantecon), Juan Ramon

Jimenez Mantecon, Juan
See Jimenez (Mantecon), Juan Ramon

Joel, Billy .... **CLC 26**
See also Joel, William Martin

Joel, William Martin 1949-
See Joel, Billy
See also CA 108

John of the Cross, St. 1542-1591 .... **LC 18**

Johnson, B(ryan) S(tanley William)
1933-1973 .... **CLC 6, 9**
See also CA 9-12R; 53-56; CANR 9;
DLB 14, 40

Johnson, Benj. F. of Boo
See Riley, James Whitcomb

Johnson, Benjamin F. of Boo
See Riley, James Whitcomb

Johnson, Charles (Richard)
1948- .... **CLC 7, 51, 65; BLC;
DAM MULT**
See also BW 2; CA 116; CAAS 18;
CANR 42; DLB 33

Johnson, Denis 1949-............. **CLC 52**
See also CA 117; 121; DLB 120

Johnson, Diane 1934-........ **CLC 5, 13, 48**
See also CA 41-44R; CANR 17, 40;
DLBY 80; INT CANR-17; MTCW

Johnson, Eyvind (Olof Verner)
1900-1976 .... **CLC 14**
See also CA 73-76; 69-72; CANR 34

Johnson, J. R.
See James, C(yril) L(ionel) R(obert)

Johnson, James Weldon
1871-1938 .... **TCLC 3, 19; BLC;
DAM MULT, POET**
See also BW 1; CA 104; 125;
CDALB 1917-1929; CLR 32; DLB 51;
MTCW; SATA 31

Johnson, Joyce 1935-............. **CLC 58**
See also CA 125; 129

Johnson, Lionel (Pigot)
1867-1902 .... **TCLC 19**
See also CA 117; DLB 19

Johnson, Mel
See Malzberg, Barry N(athaniel)

Johnson, Pamela Hansford
1912-1981 .... **CLC 1, 7, 27**
See also CA 1-4R; 104; CANR 2, 28;
DLB 15; MTCW

Johnson, Samuel
1709-1784 ..... **LC 15; DA; DAB; DAC;
DAM MST; WLC**
See also CDBLB 1660-1789; DLB 39, 95,
104, 142

Johnson, Uwe
1934-1984 .... **CLC 5, 10, 15, 40**
See also CA 1-4R; 112; CANR 1, 39;
DLB 75; MTCW

Johnston, George (Benson) 1913-... **CLC 51**
See also CA 1-4R; CANR 5, 20; DLB 88

Johnston, Jennifer 1930-.......... **CLC 7**
See also CA 85-88; DLB 14

Jolley, (Monica) Elizabeth
1923-.............. **CLC 46; SSC 19**
See also CA 127; CAAS 13

Jones, Arthur Llewellyn 1863-1947
See Machen, Arthur
See also CA 104

Jones, D(ouglas) G(ordon) 1929-.... **CLC 10**
See also CA 29-32R; CANR 13; DLB 53

Jones, David (Michael)
1895-1974 .... **CLC 2, 4, 7, 13, 42**
See also CA 9-12R; 53-56; CANR 28;
CDBLB 1945-1960; DLB 20, 100; MTCW

Jones, David Robert 1947-
See Bowie, David
See also CA 103

Jones, Diana Wynne 1934- .... **CLC 26**
See also AAYA 12; CA 49-52; CANR 4,
26; CLR 23; DLB 161; JRDA; MAICYA;
SAAS 7; SATA 9, 70

Jones, Edward P. 1950-.......... **CLC 76**
See also BW 2; CA 142

Jones, Gayl
1949- .... **CLC 6, 9; BLC; DAM MULT**
See also BW 2; CA 77-80; CANR 27;
DLB 33; MTCW

Jones, James 1921-1977.... **CLC 1, 3, 10, 39**
See also AITN 1, 2; CA 1-4R; 69-72;
CANR 6; DLB 2, 143; MTCW

Jones, John J.
See Lovecraft, H(oward) P(hillips)

Jones, LeRoi .... **CLC 1, 2, 3, 5, 10, 14**
See also Baraka, Amiri

Jones, Louis B. .... **CLC 65**
See also CA 141

Jones, Madison (Percy, Jr.) 1925- ... **CLC 4**
See also CA 13-16R; CAAS 11; CANR 7,
54; DLB 152

Jones, Mervyn 1922-.......... **CLC 10, 52**
See also CA 45-48; CAAS 5; CANR 1;
MTCW

Jones, Mick 1956(?)-.............. **CLC 30**

Jones, Nettie (Pearl) 1941- .... **CLC 34**
See also BW 2; CA 137; CAAS 20

Jones, Preston 1936-1979 .... **CLC 10**
See also CA 73-76; 89-92; DLB 7

Jones, Robert F(rancis) 1934-....... **CLC 7**
See also CA 49-52; CANR 2

Jones, Rod 1953-................ **CLC 50**
See also CA 128

Jones, Terence Graham Parry
1942-..................... **CLC 21**
See also Jones, Terry; Monty Python
See also CA 112; 116; CANR 35; INT 116

Jones, Terry
See Jones, Terence Graham Parry
See also SATA 67; SATA-Brief 51

Jones, Thom 1945(?)-............. **CLC 81**

Jong, Erica
1942-............ **CLC 4, 6, 8, 18, 83;**
DAM NOV, POP
See also AITN 1; BEST 90:2; CA 73-76;
CANR 26, 52; DLB 2, 5, 28, 152;
INT CANR-26; MTCW

Jonson, Ben(jamin)
1572(?)-1637 ...... **LC 6, 33; DA; DAB;**
DAC; DAM DRAM, MST, POET;
DC 4; PC 17; WLC
See also CDBLB Before 1660; DLB 62, 121

Jordan, June
1936- ..... **CLC 5, 11, 23; DAM MULT,**
POET
See also AAYA 2; BW 2; CA 33-36R;
CANR 25; CLR 10; DLB 38; MAICYA;
MTCW; SATA 4

Jordan, Pat(rick M.) 1941- .... **CLC 37**
See also CA 33-36R

Jorgensen, Ivar
See Ellison, Harlan (Jay)

Jorgenson, Ivar
See Silverberg, Robert

Josephus, Flavius c. 37-100 ..... **CMLC 13**

Josipovici, Gabriel 1940-........ **CLC 6, 43**
See also CA 37-40R; CAAS 8; CANR 47;
DLB 14

Joubert, Joseph 1754-1824 .... **NCLC 9**

Jouve, Pierre Jean 1887-1976...... **CLC 47**
See also CA 65-68

Joyce, James (Augustine Aloysius)
1882-1941 .... **TCLC 3, 8, 16, 35, 52;**
DA; DAB; DAC; DAM MST, NOV,
POET; SSC 3; WLC
See also CA 104; 126; CDBLB 1914-1945;
DLB 10, 19, 36, 162; MTCW

Jozsef, Attila 1905-1937......... **TCLC 22**
See also CA 116

Juana Ines de la Cruz 1651(?)-1695 ... **LC 5**

Judd, Cyril
See Kornbluth, C(yril) M.; Pohl, Frederik

Julian of Norwich 1342(?)-1416(?) .... **LC 6**
See also DLB 146

Juniper, Alex
See Hospital, Janette Turner

Junius
See Luxemburg, Rosa

Just, Ward (Swift) 1935-........ **CLC 4, 27**
See also CA 25-28R; CANR 32;
INT CANR-32

Justice, Donald (Rodney)
1925- .... **CLC 6, 19; DAM POET**
See also CA 5-8R; CANR 26, 54;
DLBY 83; INT CANR-26

Juvenal c. 55-c. 127 .... **CMLC 8**

Juvenis
See Bourne, Randolph S(illiman)

Kacew, Romain 1914-1980
See Gary, Romain
See also CA 108; 102

Kadare, Ismail 1936- .... **CLC 52**

Kadohata, Cynthia................. **CLC 59**
See also CA 140

Kafka, Franz
1883-1924 .... **TCLC 2, 6, 13, 29, 47, 53;**
DA; DAB; DAC; DAM MST, NOV;
SSC 5; WLC
See also CA 105; 126; DLB 81; MTCW

Kahanovitsch, Pinkhes
See Der Nister

Kahn, Roger 1927-............... **CLC 30**
See also CA 25-28R; CANR 44; DLB 171;
SATA 37

Kain, Saul
See Sassoon, Siegfried (Lorraine)

Kaiser, Georg 1878-1945 .... **TCLC 9**
See also CA 106; DLB 124

Kaletski, Alexander 1946-......... **CLC 39**
See also CA 118; 143

Kalidasa fl. c. 400- .... **CMLC 9**

Kallman, Chester (Simon)
1921-1975 .... **CLC 2**
See also CA 45-48; 53-56; CANR 3

Kaminsky, Melvin 1926-
See Brooks, Mel
See also CA 65-68; CANR 16

Kaminsky, Stuart M(elvin) 1934-... **CLC 59**
See also CA 73-76; CANR 29, 53

Kane, Francis
See Robbins, Harold

Kane, Paul
See Simon, Paul (Frederick)

Kane, Wilson
See Bloch, Robert (Albert)

Kanin, Garson 1912-.............. **CLC 22**
See also AITN 1; CA 5-8R; CANR 7;
DLB 7

Kaniuk, Yoram 1930-............. **CLC 19**
See also CA 134

Kant, Immanuel 1724-1804 ...... **NCLC 27**
See also DLB 94

Kantor, MacKinlay 1904-1977 ...... **CLC 7**
See also CA 61-64; 73-76; DLB 9, 102

Kaplan, David Michael 1946- ...... **CLC 50**

Kaplan, James 1951- .... **CLC 59**
See also CA 135

Karageorge, Michael
See Anderson, Poul (William)

Karamzin, Nikolai Mikhailovich
1766-1826 .... **NCLC 3**
See also DLB 150

Karapanou, Margarita 1946-....... **CLC 13**
See also CA 101

Karinthy, Frigyes 1887-1938...... **TCLC 47**

Karl, Frederick R(obert) 1927-..... **CLC 34**
See also CA 5-8R; CANR 3, 44

Kastel, Warren
See Silverberg, Robert

Kataev, Evgeny Petrovich 1903-1942
See Petrov, Evgeny
See also CA 120

Kataphusin
See Ruskin, John

Katz, Steve 1935-................ **CLC 47**
See also CA 25-28R; CAAS 14; CANR 12;
DLBY 83

Kauffman, Janet 1945-............ **CLC 42**
See also CA 117; CANR 43; DLBY 86

Kaufman, Bob (Garnell)
1925-1986 .... **CLC 49**
See also BW 1; CA 41-44R; 118; CANR 22;
DLB 16, 41

Kaufman, George S.
1889-1961 ...... **CLC 38; DAM DRAM**
See also CA 108; 93-96; DLB 7; INT 108

Kaufman, Sue .... **CLC 3, 8**
See also Barondess, Sue K(aufman)

Kavafis, Konstantinos Petrou 1863-1933
See Cavafy, C(onstantine) P(eter)
See also CA 104

Kavan, Anna 1901-1968...... **CLC 5, 13, 82**
See also CA 5-8R; CANR 6; MTCW

Kavanagh, Dan
See Barnes, Julian (Patrick)

Kavanagh, Patrick (Joseph)
1904-1967 .... **CLC 22**
See also CA 123; 25-28R; DLB 15, 20;
MTCW

Kawabata, Yasunari
1899-1972 .... **CLC 2, 5, 9, 18;
DAM MULT; SSC 17**
See also CA 93-96; 33-36R

Kaye, M(ary) M(argaret) 1909-..... **CLC 28**
See also CA 89-92; CANR 24; MTCW;
SATA 62

Kaye, Mollie
See Kaye, M(ary) M(argaret)

Kaye-Smith, Sheila 1887-1956..... **TCLC 20**
See also CA 118; DLB 36

Kaymor, Patrice Maguilene
See Senghor, Leopold Sedar

Kazan, Elia 1909-........... **CLC 6, 16, 63**
See also CA 21-24R; CANR 32

Kazantzakis, Nikos
1883(?)-1957 .... **TCLC 2, 5, 33**
See also CA 105; 132; MTCW

Kazin, Alfred 1915- .... **CLC 34, 38**
See also CA 1-4R; CAAS 7; CANR 1, 45;
DLB 67

Keane, Mary Nesta (Skrine) 1904-1996
See Keane, Molly
See also CA 108; 114; 151

Keane, Molly..................... **CLC 31**
See also Keane, Mary Nesta (Skrine)
See also INT 114

Keates, Jonathan 19(?)-........... **CLC 34**

Keaton, Buster 1895-1966 .... **CLC 20**

Keats, John
1795-1821 .... **NCLC 8; DA; DAB;
DAC; DAM MST, POET; PC 1; WLC**
See also CDBLB 1789-1832; DLB 96, 110

Keene, Donald 1922- .... **CLC 34**
See also CA 1-4R; CANR 5

Keillor, Garrison................. **CLC 40**
See also Keillor, Gary (Edward)
See also AAYA 2; BEST 89:3; DLBY 87;
SATA 58

Keillor, Gary (Edward) 1942-
See Keillor, Garrison
See also CA 111; 117; CANR 36;
DAM POP; MTCW

Keith, Michael
See Hubbard, L(afayette) Ron(ald)

Keller, Gottfried 1819-1890...... **NCLC 2**
See also DLB 129

Kellerman, Jonathan
1949- .... **CLC 44; DAM POP**
See also BEST 90:1; CA 106; CANR 29, 51;
INT CANR-29

Kelley, William Melvin 1937-...... **CLC 22**
See also BW 1; CA 77-80; CANR 27;
DLB 33

Kellogg, Marjorie 1922-........... **CLC 2**
See also CA 81-84

Kellow, Kathleen
See Hibbert, Eleanor Alice Burford

Kelly, M(ilton) T(erry) 1947-....... **CLC 55**
See also CA 97-100; CAAS 22; CANR 19,
43

Kelman, James 1946-......... **CLC 58, 86**
See also CA 148

Kemal, Yashar 1923- .... **CLC 14, 29**
See also CA 89-92; CANR 44

Kemble, Fanny 1809-1893 .... **NCLC 18**
See also DLB 32

Kemelman, Harry 1908-1996........ **CLC 2**
See also AITN 1; CA 9-12R; 155; CANR 6;
DLB 28

Kempe, Margery 1373(?)-1440(?) ..... **LC 6**
See also DLB 146

Kempis, Thomas a 1380-1471 .... **LC 11**

Kendall, Henry 1839-1882....... **NCLC 12**

Keneally, Thomas (Michael)
1935- ...... **CLC 5, 8, 10, 14, 19, 27, 43;
DAM NOV**
See also CA 85-88; CANR 10, 50; MTCW

Kennedy, Adrienne (Lita)
1931- ..... **CLC 66; BLC; DAM MULT;
DC 5**
See also BW 2; CA 103; CAAS 20; CABS 3;
CANR 26, 53; DLB 38

Kennedy, John Pendleton
1795-1870 .... **NCLC 2**
See also DLB 3

Kennedy, Joseph Charles 1929-
See Kennedy, X. J.
See also CA 1-4R; CANR 4, 30, 40;
SATA 14, 86

Kennedy, William
1928- ... **CLC 6, 28, 34, 53; DAM NOV**
See also AAYA 1; CA 85-88; CANR 14,
31; DLB 143; DLBY 85; INT CANR-31;
MTCW; SATA 57

Kennedy, X. J................... **CLC 8, 42**
See also Kennedy, Joseph Charles
See also CAAS 9; CLR 27; DLB 5;
SAAS 22

Kenny, Maurice (Francis)
1929- .... **CLC 87; DAM MULT**
See also CA 144; CAAS 22; NNAL

Kent, Kelvin
See Kuttner, Henry

Kenton, Maxwell
See Southern, Terry

Kenyon, Robert O.
See Kuttner, Henry

Kerouac, Jack ..... **CLC 1, 2, 3, 5, 14, 29, 61**
See also Kerouac, Jean-Louis Lebris de
See also CDALB 1941-1968; DLB 2, 16;
DLBD 3; DLBY 95

Kerouac, Jean-Louis Lebris de 1922-1969
See Kerouac, Jack
See also AITN 1; CA 5-8R; 25-28R;
CANR 26, 54; DA; DAB; DAC;
DAM MST, NOV, POET, POP; MTCW;
WLC

Kerr, Jean 1923-................. **CLC 22**
See also CA 5-8R; CANR 7; INT CANR-7

Kerr, M. E. .... **CLC 12, 35**
See also Meaker, Marijane (Agnes)
See also AAYA 2; CLR 29; SAAS 1

Kerr, Robert .... **CLC 55**

Kerrigan, (Thomas) Anthony
1918- .... **CLC 4, 6**
See also CA 49-52; CAAS 11; CANR 4

Kerry, Lois
See Duncan, Lois

Kesey, Ken (Elton)
1935- ...... **CLC 1, 3, 6, 11, 46, 64; DA;
DAB; DAC; DAM MST, NOV, POP;
WLC**
See also CA 1-4R; CANR 22, 38;
CDALB 1968-1988; DLB 2, 16; MTCW;
SATA 66

Kesselring, Joseph (Otto)
1902-1967 ..... **CLC 45; DAM DRAM,
MST**
See also CA 150

Kessler, Jascha (Frederick) 1929-.... **CLC 4**
See also CA 17-20R; CANR 8, 48

Kettelkamp, Larry (Dale) 1933- .... **CLC 12**
See also CA 29-32R; CANR 16; SAAS 3;
SATA 2

Key, Ellen 1849-1926........... **TCLC 65**

Keyber, Conny
See Fielding, Henry

Keyes, Daniel
1927- .... **CLC 80; DA; DAC;
DAM MST, NOV**
See also CA 17-20R; CANR 10, 26, 54;
SATA 37

Keynes, John Maynard
1883-1946 .... **TCLC 64**
See also CA 114; DLBD 10

Khanshendel, Chiron
See Rose, Wendy

Khayyam, Omar
1048-1131 .... **CMLC 11; DAM POET;
PC 8**

Kherdian, David 1931-........... **CLC 6, 9**
See also CA 21-24R; CAAS 2; CANR 39;
CLR 24; JRDA; MAICYA; SATA 16, 74

Khlebnikov, Velimir .... **TCLC 20**
See also Khlebnikov, Viktor Vladimirovich

Khlebnikov, Viktor Vladimirovich 1885-1922
See Khlebnikov, Velimir
See also CA 117

Khodasevich, Vladislav (Felitsianovich)
1886-1939 .... **TCLC 15**
See also CA 115

Kielland, Alexander Lange
1849-1906 . . . . **TCLC 5**
See also CA 104

Kiely, Benedict 1919- . . . . **CLC 23, 43**
See also CA 1-4R; CANR 2; DLB 15

Kienzle, William X(avier)
1928- . . . . **CLC 25; DAM POP**
See also CA 93-96; CAAS 1; CANR 9, 31;
INT CANR-31; MTCW

Kierkegaard, Soren 1813-1855. . . . **NCLC 34**

Killens, John Oliver 1916-1987 . . . . . **CLC 10**
See also BW 2; CA 77-80; 123; CAAS 2;
CANR 26; DLB 33

Killigrew, Anne 1660-1685 . . . . **LC 4**
See also DLB 131

Kim
See Simenon, Georges (Jacques Christian)

Kincaid, Jamaica
1949- . . . . **CLC 43, 68; BLC;
DAM MULT, NOV**
See also AAYA 13; BW 2; CA 125;
CANR 47; DLB 157

King, Francis (Henry)
1923- . . . . **CLC 8, 53; DAM NOV**
See also CA 1-4R; CANR 1, 33; DLB 15,
139; MTCW

King, Martin Luther, Jr.
1929-1968 . . . . **CLC 83; BLC; DA; DAB;
DAC; DAM MST, MULT**
See also BW 2; CA 25-28; CANR 27, 44;
CAP 2; MTCW; SATA 14

King, Stephen (Edwin)
1947- . . . . **CLC 12, 26, 37, 61;
DAM NOV, POP; SSC 17**
See also AAYA 1, 17; BEST 90:1;
CA 61-64; CANR 1, 30, 52; DLB 143;
DLBY 80; JRDA; MTCW; SATA 9, 55

King, Steve
See King, Stephen (Edwin)

King, Thomas
1943- . . . . . **CLC 89; DAC; DAM MULT**
See also CA 144; NNAL

Kingman, Lee . . . . **CLC 17**
See also Natti, (Mary) Lee
See also SAAS 3; SATA 1, 67

Kingsley, Charles 1819-1875 . . . . . **NCLC 35**
See also DLB 21, 32, 163; YABC 2

Kingsley, Sidney 1906-1995 . . . . **CLC 44**
See also CA 85-88; 147; DLB 7

Kingsolver, Barbara
1955- . . . . **CLC 55, 81; DAM POP**
See also AAYA 15; CA 129; 134; INT 134

Kingston, Maxine (Ting Ting) Hong
1940- . . . . **CLC 12, 19, 58; DAM MULT,
NOV**
See also AAYA 8; CA 69-72; CANR 13,
38; DLB 173; DLBY 80; INT CANR-13;
MTCW; SATA 53

Kinnell, Galway
1927- . . . . **CLC 1, 2, 3, 5, 13, 29**
See also CA 9-12R; CANR 10, 34; DLB 5;
DLBY 87; INT CANR-34; MTCW

Kinsella, Thomas 1928- . . . . **CLC 4, 19**
See also CA 17-20R; CANR 15; DLB 27;
MTCW

Kinsella, W(illiam) P(atrick)
1935- . . . . **CLC 27, 43; DAC;
DAM NOV, POP**
See also AAYA 7; CA 97-100; CAAS 7;
CANR 21, 35; INT CANR-21; MTCW

Kipling, (Joseph) Rudyard
1865-1936 . . . . . . **TCLC 8, 17; DA; DAB;
DAC; DAM MST, POET; PC 3; SSC 5;
WLC**
See also CA 105; 120; CANR 33;
CDBLB 1890-1914; CLR 39; DLB 19, 34,
141, 156; MAICYA; MTCW; YABC 2

Kirkup, James 1918- . . . . **CLC 1**
See also CA 1-4R; CAAS 4; CANR 2;
DLB 27; SATA 12

Kirkwood, James 1930(?)-1989 . . . . . . **CLC 9**
See also AITN 2; CA 1-4R; 128; CANR 6,
40

Kirshner, Sidney
See Kingsley, Sidney

Kis, Danilo 1935-1989 . . . . **CLC 57**
See also CA 109; 118; 129; MTCW

Kivi, Aleksis 1834-1872 . . . . **NCLC 30**

Kizer, Carolyn (Ashley)
1925- . . . . . **CLC 15, 39, 80; DAM POET**
See also CA 65-68; CAAS 5; CANR 24;
DLB 5, 169

Klabund 1890-1928 . . . . **TCLC 44**
See also DLB 66

Klappert, Peter 1942- . . . . **CLC 57**
See also CA 33-36R; DLB 5

Klein, A(braham) M(oses)
1909-1972 . . . . **CLC 19; DAB; DAC;
DAM MST**
See also CA 101; 37-40R; DLB 68

Klein, Norma 1938-1989 . . . . **CLC 30**
See also AAYA 2; CA 41-44R; 128;
CANR 15, 37; CLR 2, 19;
INT CANR-15; JRDA; MAICYA;
SAAS 1; SATA 7, 57

Klein, T(heodore) E(ibon) D(onald)
1947- . . . . **CLC 34**
See also CA 119; CANR 44

Kleist, Heinrich von
1777-1811 . . . . **NCLC 2, 37;
DAM DRAM; SSC 22**
See also DLB 90

Klima, Ivan 1931- . . . . . **CLC 56; DAM NOV**
See also CA 25-28R; CANR 17, 50

Klimentov, Andrei Platonovich 1899-1951
See Platonov, Andrei
See also CA 108

Klinger, Friedrich Maximilian von
1752-1831 . . . . **NCLC 1**
See also DLB 94

Klopstock, Friedrich Gottlieb
1724-1803 . . . . **NCLC 11**
See also DLB 97

Knebel, Fletcher 1911-1993 . . . . **CLC 14**
See also AITN 1; CA 1-4R; 140; CAAS 3;
CANR 1, 36; SATA 36; SATA-Obit 75

Knickerbocker, Diedrich
See Irving, Washington

Knight, Etheridge
1931-1991 . . . . **CLC 40; BLC;
DAM POET; PC 14**
See also BW 1; CA 21-24R; 133; CANR 23;
DLB 41

Knight, Sarah Kemble 1666-1727 . . . . . **LC 7**
See also DLB 24

Knister, Raymond 1899-1932 . . . . . . **TCLC 56**
See also DLB 68

Knowles, John
1926- . . . . . . **CLC 1, 4, 10, 26; DA; DAC;
DAM MST, NOV**
See also AAYA 10; CA 17-20R; CANR 40;
CDALB 1968-1988; DLB 6; MTCW;
SATA 8, 89

Knox, Calvin M.
See Silverberg, Robert

Knox, John c. 1505-1572 . . . . **LC 37**
See also DLB 132

Knye, Cassandra
See Disch, Thomas M(ichael)

Koch, C(hristopher) J(ohn) 1932- . . . **CLC 42**
See also CA 127

Koch, Christopher
See Koch, C(hristopher) J(ohn)

Koch, Kenneth
1925- . . . . **CLC 5, 8, 44; DAM POET**
See also CA 1-4R; CANR 6, 36; DLB 5;
INT CANR-36; SATA 65

Kochanowski, Jan 1530-1584 . . . . **LC 10**

Kock, Charles Paul de
1794-1871 . . . . **NCLC 16**

Koda Shigeyuki 1867-1947
See Rohan, Koda
See also CA 121

Koestler, Arthur
1905-1983 . . . . **CLC 1, 3, 6, 8, 15, 33**
See also CA 1-4R; 109; CANR 1, 33;
CDBLB 1945-1960; DLBY 83; MTCW

Kogawa, Joy Nozomi
1935- . . . . . . **CLC 78; DAC; DAM MST,
MULT**
See also CA 101; CANR 19

Kohout, Pavel 1928- . . . . **CLC 13**
See also CA 45-48; CANR 3

Koizumi, Yakumo
See Hearn, (Patricio) Lafcadio (Tessima
Carlos)

Kolmar, Gertrud 1894-1943 . . . . **TCLC 40**

Komunyakaa, Yusef 1947- . . . . . . **CLC 86, 94**
See also CA 147; DLB 120

Konrad, George
See Konrad, Gyoergy

Konrad, Gyoergy 1933- . . . . . . **CLC 4, 10, 73**
See also CA 85-88

Konwicki, Tadeusz 1926- . . . . . **CLC 8, 28, 54**
See also CA 101; CAAS 9; CANR 39;
MTCW

Koontz, Dean R(ay)
1945- . . . . . . **CLC 78; DAM NOV, POP**
See also AAYA 9; BEST 89:3, 90:2;
CA 108; CANR 19, 36, 52; MTCW

Kopit, Arthur (Lee)
1937- ..... **CLC 1, 18, 33; DAM DRAM**
See also AITN 1; CA 81-84; CABS 3;
DLB 7; MTCW

Kops, Bernard 1926-.............. **CLC 4**
See also CA 5-8R; DLB 13

Kornbluth, C(yril) M. 1923-1958.... **TCLC 8**
See also CA 105; DLB 8

Korolenko, V. G.
See Korolenko, Vladimir Galaktionovich

Korolenko, Vladimir
See Korolenko, Vladimir Galaktionovich

Korolenko, Vladimir G.
See Korolenko, Vladimir Galaktionovich

Korolenko, Vladimir Galaktionovich
1853-1921 .... **TCLC 22**
See also CA 121

Korzybski, Alfred (Habdank Skarbek)
1879-1950 .... **TCLC 61**
See also CA 123

Kosinski, Jerzy (Nikodem)
1933-1991 .... **CLC 1, 2, 3, 6, 10, 15, 53,
70; DAM NOV**
See also CA 17-20R; 134; CANR 9, 46;
DLB 2; DLBY 82; MTCW

Kostelanetz, Richard (Cory) 1940- .. **CLC 28**
See also CA 13-16R; CAAS 8; CANR 38

Kostrowitzki, Wilhelm Apollinaris de
1880-1918
See Apollinaire, Guillaume
See also CA 104

Kotlowitz, Robert 1924-............ **CLC 4**
See also CA 33-36R; CANR 36

Kotzebue, August (Friedrich Ferdinand) von
1761-1819 .... **NCLC 25**
See also DLB 94

Kotzwinkle, William 1938- ... **CLC 5, 14, 35**
See also CA 45-48; CANR 3, 44; CLR 6;
DLB 173; MAICYA; SATA 24, 70

Kozol, Jonathan 1936-............ **CLC 17**
See also CA 61-64; CANR 16, 45

Kozoll, Michael 1940(?)- .... **CLC 35**

Kramer, Kathryn 19(?)- .... **CLC 34**

Kramer, Larry 1935- .. **CLC 42; DAM POP**
See also CA 124; 126

Krasicki, Ignacy 1735-1801 .... **NCLC 8**

Krasinski, Zygmunt 1812-1859 .... **NCLC 4**

Kraus, Karl 1874-1936........... **TCLC 5**
See also CA 104; DLB 118

Kreve (Mickevicius), Vincas
1882-1954 .... **TCLC 27**

Kristeva, Julia 1941- .... **CLC 77**
See also CA 154

Kristofferson, Kris 1936-.......... **CLC 26**
See also CA 104

Krizanc, John 1956-.............. **CLC 57**

Krleza, Miroslav 1893-1981........ **CLC 8**
See also CA 97-100; 105; CANR 50;
DLB 147

Kroetsch, Robert
1927-............ **CLC 5, 23, 57; DAC;
DAM POET**
See also CA 17-20R; CANR 8, 38; DLB 53;
MTCW

Kroetz, Franz
See Kroetz, Franz Xaver

Kroetz, Franz Xaver 1946- .... **CLC 41**
See also CA 130

Kroker, Arthur 1945-............. **CLC 77**

Kropotkin, Peter (Aleksieevich)
1842-1921 .... **TCLC 36**
See also CA 119

Krotkov, Yuri 1917-.............. **CLC 19**
See also CA 102

Krumb
See Crumb, R(obert)

Krumgold, Joseph (Quincy)
1908-1980 .... **CLC 12**
See also CA 9-12R; 101; CANR 7;
MAICYA; SATA 1, 48; SATA-Obit 23

Krumwitz
See Crumb, R(obert)

Krutch, Joseph Wood 1893-1970.... **CLC 24**
See also CA 1-4R; 25-28R; CANR 4;
DLB 63

Krutzch, Gus
See Eliot, T(homas) S(tearns)

Krylov, Ivan Andreevich
1768(?)-1844 .... **NCLC 1**
See also DLB 150

Kubin, Alfred (Leopold Isidor)
1877-1959 .... **TCLC 23**
See also CA 112; 149; DLB 81

Kubrick, Stanley 1928-............ **CLC 16**
See also CA 81-84; CANR 33; DLB 26

Kumin, Maxine (Winokur)
1925- ..... **CLC 5, 13, 28; DAM POET;
PC 15**
See also AITN 2; CA 1-4R; CAAS 8;
CANR 1, 21; DLB 5; MTCW; SATA 12

Kundera, Milan
1929-........... **CLC 4, 9, 19, 32, 68;
DAM NOV; SSC 24**
See also AAYA 2; CA 85-88; CANR 19,
52; MTCW

Kunene, Mazisi (Raymond) 1930-... **CLC 85**
See also BW 1; CA 125; DLB 117

Kunitz, Stanley (Jasspon)
1905-.................. **CLC 6, 11, 14**
See also CA 41-44R; CANR 26; DLB 48;
INT CANR-26; MTCW

Kunze, Reiner 1933-.............. **CLC 10**
See also CA 93-96; DLB 75

Kuprin, Aleksandr Ivanovich
1870-1938 .... **TCLC 5**
See also CA 104

Kureishi, Hanif 1954(?)-.......... **CLC 64**
See also CA 139

Kurosawa, Akira
1910- .... **CLC 16; DAM MULT**
See also AAYA 11; CA 101; CANR 46

Kushner, Tony
1957(?)- .... **CLC 81; DAM DRAM**
See also CA 144

Kuttner, Henry 1915-1958....... **TCLC 10**
See also CA 107; DLB 8

Kuzma, Greg 1944-............... **CLC 7**
See also CA 33-36R

Kuzmin, Mikhail 1872(?)-1936 .... **TCLC 40**

Kyd, Thomas
1558-1594 ...... **LC 22; DAM DRAM;
DC 3**
See also DLB 62

Kyprianos, Iossif
See Samarakis, Antonis

La Bruyere, Jean de 1645-1696...... **LC 17**

Lacan, Jacques (Marie Emile)
1901-1981 .... **CLC 75**
See also CA 121; 104

**Laclos, Pierre Ambroise Francois Choderlos
de** 1741-1803 .... **NCLC 4**

La Colere, Francois
See Aragon, Louis

Lacolere, Francois
See Aragon, Louis

La Deshabilleuse
See Simenon, Georges (Jacques Christian)

Lady Gregory
See Gregory, Isabella Augusta (Persse)

Lady of Quality, A
See Bagnold, Enid

**La Fayette, Marie (Madelaine Pioche de la
Vergne Comtes** 1634-1693....... **LC 2**

Lafayette, Rene
See Hubbard, L(afayette) Ron(ald)

Laforgue, Jules
1860-1887 .... **NCLC 5, 53; PC 14;
SSC 20**

Lagerkvist, Paer (Fabian)
1891-1974 .... **CLC 7, 10, 13, 54;
DAM DRAM, NOV**
See also Lagerkvist, Par
See also CA 85-88; 49-52; MTCW

Lagerkvist, Par .... **SSC 12**
See also Lagerkvist, Paer (Fabian)

Lagerloef, Selma (Ottiliana Lovisa)
1858-1940 .... **TCLC 4, 36**
See also Lagerlof, Selma (Ottiliana Lovisa)
See also CA 108; SATA 15

Lagerlof, Selma (Ottiliana Lovisa)
See Lagerloef, Selma (Ottiliana Lovisa)
See also CLR 7; SATA 15

La Guma, (Justin) Alex(ander)
1925-1985 .... **CLC 19; DAM NOV**
See also BW 1; CA 49-52; 118; CANR 25;
DLB 117; MTCW

Laidlaw, A. K.
See Grieve, C(hristopher) M(urray)

Lainez, Manuel Mujica
See Mujica Lainez, Manuel
See also HW

Laing, R(onald) D(avid)
1927-1989 .... **CLC 95**
See also CA 107; 129; CANR 34; MTCW

Lamartine, Alphonse (Marie Louis Prat) de
1790-1869 ..... **NCLC 11; DAM POET;
PC 16**

Lamb, Charles
1775-1834 .... **NCLC 10; DA; DAB;
DAC; DAM MST; WLC**
See also CDBLB 1789-1832; DLB 93, 107,
163; SATA 17**

Lamb, Lady Caroline 1785-1828 . . **NCLC 38**
 See also DLB 116

Lamming, George (William)
 1927- . . . . **CLC 2, 4, 66; BLC;**
             DAM MULT
 See also BW 2; CA 85-88; CANR 26;
  DLB 125; MTCW

L'Amour, Louis (Dearborn)
 1908-1988 . . . . **CLC 25, 55; DAM NOV,**
                POP
 See also AAYA 16; AITN 2; BEST 89:2;
  CA 1-4R; 125; CANR 3, 25, 40;
  DLBY 80; MTCW

Lampedusa, Giuseppe (Tomasi) di . . . **TCLC 13**
 See also Tomasi di Lampedusa, Giuseppe

Lampman, Archibald 1861-1899 . . **NCLC 25**
 See also DLB 92

Lancaster, Bruce 1896-1963 . . . . **CLC 36**
 See also CA 9-10; CAP 1; SATA 9

Landau, Mark Alexandrovich
 See Aldanov, Mark (Alexandrovich)

Landau-Aldanov, Mark Alexandrovich
 See Aldanov, Mark (Alexandrovich)

Landis, Jerry
 See Simon, Paul (Frederick)

Landis, John 1950- . . . . **CLC 26**
 See also CA 112; 122

Landolfi, Tommaso 1908-1979 . . . **CLC 11, 49**
 See also CA 127; 117

Landon, Letitia Elizabeth
 1802-1838 . . . . **NCLC 15**
 See also DLB 96

Landor, Walter Savage
 1775-1864 . . . . **NCLC 14**
 See also DLB 93, 107

Landwirth, Heinz 1927-
 See Lind, Jakov
 See also CA 9-12R; CANR 7

Lane, Patrick
 1939- . . . . **CLC 25; DAM POET**
 See also CA 97-100; CANR 54; DLB 53;
  INT 97-100

Lang, Andrew 1844-1912 . . . . **TCLC 16**
 See also CA 114; 137; DLB 98, 141;
  MAICYA; SATA 16

Lang, Fritz 1890-1976 . . . . **CLC 20**
 See also CA 77-80; 69-72; CANR 30

Lange, John
 See Crichton, (John) Michael

Langer, Elinor 1939- . . . . **CLC 34**
 See also CA 121

Langland, William
 1330(?)-1400(?) . . . . . . **LC 19; DA; DAB;**
         DAC; DAM MST, POET
 See also DLB 146

Langstaff, Launcelot
 See Irving, Washington

Lanier, Sidney
 1842-1881 . . . . . . **NCLC 6; DAM POET**
 See also DLB 64; DLBD 13; MAICYA;
  SATA 18

Lanyer, Aemilia 1569-1645 . . . . . . **LC 10, 30**
 See also DLB 121

Lao Tzu . . . . **CMLC 7**

Lapine, James (Elliot) 1949- . . . . **CLC 39**
 See also CA 123; 130; CANR 54; INT 130

Larbaud, Valery (Nicolas)
 1881-1957 . . . . **TCLC 9**
 See also CA 106; 152

Lardner, Ring
 See Lardner, Ring(gold) W(ilmer)

Lardner, Ring W., Jr.
 See Lardner, Ring(gold) W(ilmer)

Lardner, Ring(gold) W(ilmer)
 1885-1933 . . . . **TCLC 2, 14**
 See also CA 104; 131; CDALB 1917-1929;
  DLB 11, 25, 86; MTCW

Laredo, Betty
 See Codrescu, Andrei

Larkin, Maia
 See Wojciechowska, Maia (Teresa)

Larkin, Philip (Arthur)
 1922-1985 . . . . **CLC 3, 5, 8, 9, 13, 18, 33,**
      39, 64; DAB; DAM MST, POET
 See also CA 5-8R; 117; CANR 24;
  CDBLB 1960 to Present; DLB 27;
  MTCW

Larra (y Sanchez de Castro), Mariano Jose de
 1809-1837 . . . . **NCLC 17**

Larsen, Eric 1941- . . . . **CLC 55**
 See also CA 132

Larsen, Nella
 1891-1964 . . . . **CLC 37; BLC;**
             DAM MULT
 See also BW 1; CA 125; DLB 51

Larson, Charles R(aymond) 1938- . . . **CLC 31**
 See also CA 53-56; CANR 4

Las Casas, Bartolome de 1474-1566 . . **LC 31**

Lasker-Schueler, Else 1869-1945 . . **TCLC 57**
 See also DLB 66, 124

Latham, Jean Lee 1902- . . . . **CLC 12**
 See also AITN 1; CA 5-8R; CANR 7;
  MAICYA; SATA 2, 68

Latham, Mavis
 See Clark, Mavis Thorpe

Lathen, Emma . . . . **CLC 2**
 See also Hennissart, Martha; Latsis, Mary
  J(ane)

Lathrop, Francis
 See Leiber, Fritz (Reuter, Jr.)

Latsis, Mary J(ane)
 See Lathen, Emma
 See also CA 85-88

Lattimore, Richmond (Alexander)
 1906-1984 . . . . **CLC 3**
 See also CA 1-4R; 112; CANR 1

Laughlin, James 1914- . . . . **CLC 49**
 See also CA 21-24R; CAAS 22; CANR 9,
  47; DLB 48

Laurence, (Jean) Margaret (Wemyss)
 1926-1987 . . . . **CLC 3, 6, 13, 50, 62;**
           DAC; DAM MST; SSC 7
 See also CA 5-8R; 121; CANR 33; DLB 53;
  MTCW; SATA-Obit 50

Laurent, Antoine 1952- . . . . **CLC 50**

Lauscher, Hermann
 See Hesse, Hermann

Lautreamont, Comte de
 1846-1870 . . . . **NCLC 12; SSC 14**

Laverty, Donald
 See Blish, James (Benjamin)

Lavin, Mary 1912-1996 . . **CLC 4, 18; SSC 4**
 See also CA 9-12R; 151; CANR 33;
  DLB 15; MTCW

Lavond, Paul Dennis
 See Kornbluth, C(yril) M.; Pohl, Frederik

Lawler, Raymond Evenor 1922- . . . . **CLC 58**
 See also CA 103

Lawrence, D(avid) H(erbert Richards)
 1885-1930 . . . . **TCLC 2, 9, 16, 33, 48, 61;**
      DA; DAB; DAC; DAM MST, NOV,
          POET; SSC 4, 19; WLC
 See also CA 104; 121; CDBLB 1914-1945;
  DLB 10, 19, 36, 98, 162; MTCW

Lawrence, T(homas) E(dward)
 1888-1935 . . . . **TCLC 18**
 See also Dale, Colin
 See also CA 115

Lawrence of Arabia
 See Lawrence, T(homas) E(dward)

Lawson, Henry (Archibald Hertzberg)
 1867-1922 . . . . **TCLC 27; SSC 18**
 See also CA 120

Lawton, Dennis
 See Faust, Frederick (Schiller)

Laxness, Halldor . . . . **CLC 25**
 See also Gudjonsson, Halldor Kiljan

Layamon fl. c. 1200- . . . . **CMLC 10**
 See also DLB 146

Laye, Camara
 1928-1980 . . . . **CLC 4, 38; BLC;**
             DAM MULT
 See also BW 1; CA 85-88; 97-100;
  CANR 25; MTCW

Layton, Irving (Peter)
 1912- . . . . **CLC 2, 15; DAC; DAM MST,**
                POET
 See also CA 1-4R; CANR 2, 33, 43;
  DLB 88; MTCW

Lazarus, Emma 1849-1887 . . . . **NCLC 8**

Lazarus, Felix
 See Cable, George Washington

Lazarus, Henry
 See Slavitt, David R(ytman)

Lea, Joan
 See Neufeld, John (Arthur)

Leacock, Stephen (Butler)
 1869-1944 . . **TCLC 2; DAC; DAM MST**
 See also CA 104; 141; DLB 92

Lear, Edward 1812-1888 . . . . **NCLC 3**
 See also CLR 1; DLB 32, 163, 166;
  MAICYA; SATA 18

Lear, Norman (Milton) 1922- . . . . . . **CLC 12**
 See also CA 73-76

Leavis, F(rank) R(aymond)
 1895-1978 . . . . **CLC 24**
 See also CA 21-24R; 77-80; CANR 44;
  MTCW

Leavitt, David 1961- . . . **CLC 34; DAM POP**
 See also CA 116; 122; CANR 50; DLB 130;
  INT 122

Leblanc, Maurice (Marie Emile)
1864-1941 .... **TCLC 49**
See also CA 110

Lebowitz, Fran(ces Ann)
1951(?)- .... **CLC 11, 36**
See also CA 81-84; CANR 14;
INT CANR-14; MTCW

Lebrecht, Peter
See Tieck, (Johann) Ludwig

le Carre, John .... **CLC 3, 5, 9, 15, 28**
See Cornwell, David (John Moore)
See also BEST 89:4; CDBLB 1960 to
Present; DLB 87

Le Clezio, J(ean) M(arie) G(ustave)
1940- .... **CLC 31**
See also CA 116; 128; DLB 83

Leconte de Lisle, Charles-Marie-Rene
1818-1894 .... **NCLC 29**

Le Coq, Monsieur
See Simenon, Georges (Jacques Christian)

Leduc, Violette 1907-1972 .... **CLC 22**
See also CA 13-14; 33-36R; CAP 1

Ledwidge, Francis 1887(?)-1917 ... **TCLC 23**
See also CA 123; DLB 20

Lee, Andrea
1953- ..... **CLC 36; BLC; DAM MULT**
See also BW 1; CA 125

Lee, Andrew
See Auchincloss, Louis (Stanton)

Lee, Chang-rae 1965- .... **CLC 91**
See also CA 148

Lee, Don L. .... **CLC 2**
See also Madhubuti, Haki R.

Lee, George W(ashington)
1894-1976 .... **CLC 52; BLC;**
DAM MULT
See also BW 1; CA 125; DLB 51

Lee, (Nelle) Harper
1926- .... **CLC 12, 60; DA; DAB; DAC;**
DAM MST, NOV; WLC
See also AAYA 13; CA 13-16R; CANR 51;
CDALB 1941-1968; DLB 6; MTCW;
SATA 11

Lee, Helen Elaine 1959(?)- .... **CLC 86**
See also CA 148

Lee, Julian
See Latham, Jean Lee

Lee, Larry
See Lee, Lawrence

Lee, Laurie
1914- .... **CLC 90; DAB; DAM POP**
See also CA 77-80; CANR 33; DLB 27;
MTCW

Lee, Lawrence 1941-1990 .... **CLC 34**
See also CA 131; CANR 43

Lee, Manfred B(ennington)
1905-1971 .... **CLC 11**
See also Queen, Ellery
See also CA 1-4R; 29-32R; CANR 2;
DLB 137

Lee, Stan 1922- .... **CLC 17**
See also AAYA 5; CA 108; 111; INT 111

Lee, Tanith 1947- .... **CLC 46**
See also AAYA 15; CA 37-40R; CANR 53;
SATA 8, 88

Lee, Vernon .... **TCLC 5**
See also Paget, Violet
See also DLB 57, 153, 156, 174

Lee, William
See Burroughs, William S(eward)

Lee, Willy
See Burroughs, William S(eward)

Lee-Hamilton, Eugene (Jacob)
1845-1907 .... **TCLC 22**
See also CA 117

Leet, Judith 1935- .... **CLC 11**

Le Fanu, Joseph Sheridan
1814-1873 .... **NCLC 9, 58; DAM POP;**
SSC 14
See also DLB 21, 70, 159

Leffland, Ella 1931- .... **CLC 19**
See also CA 29-32R; CANR 35; DLBY 84;
INT CANR-35; SATA 65

Leger, Alexis
See Leger, (Marie-Rene Auguste) Alexis
Saint-Leger

Leger, (Marie-Rene Auguste) Alexis
Saint-Leger
1887-1975 ...... **CLC 11; DAM POET**
See also Perse, St.-John
See also CA 13-16R; 61-64; CANR 43;
MTCW

Leger, Saintleger
See Leger, (Marie-Rene Auguste) Alexis
Saint-Leger

Le Guin, Ursula K(roeber)
1929- ...... **CLC 8, 13, 22, 45, 71; DAB;**
DAC; DAM MST, POP; SSC 12
See also AAYA 9; AITN 1; CA 21-24R;
CANR 9, 32, 52; CDALB 1968-1988;
CLR 3, 28; DLB 8, 52; INT CANR-32;
JRDA; MAICYA; MTCW; SATA 4, 52

Lehmann, Rosamond (Nina)
1901-1990 .... **CLC 5**
See also CA 77-80; 131; CANR 8; DLB 15

Leiber, Fritz (Reuter, Jr.)
1910-1992 .... **CLC 25**
See also CA 45-48; 139; CANR 2, 40;
DLB 8; MTCW; SATA 45;
SATA-Obit 73

Leibniz, Gottfried Wilhelm von
1646-1716 .... **LC 35**
See also DLB 168

Leimbach, Martha 1963-
See Leimbach, Marti
See also CA 130

Leimbach, Marti .... **CLC 65**
See also Leimbach, Martha

Leino, Eino .... **TCLC 24**
See also Loennbohm, Armas Eino Leopold

Leiris, Michel (Julien) 1901-1990 ... **CLC 61**
See also CA 119; 128; 132

Leithauser, Brad 1953- .... **CLC 27**
See also CA 107; CANR 27; DLB 120

Lelchuk, Alan 1938- .... **CLC 5**
See also CA 45-48; CAAS 20; CANR 1

Lem, Stanislaw 1921- .... **CLC 8, 15, 40**
See also CA 105; CAAS 1; CANR 32;
MTCW

Lemann, Nancy 1956- .... **CLC 39**
See also CA 118; 136

Lemonnier, (Antoine Louis) Camille
1844-1913 .... **TCLC 22**
See also CA 121

Lenau, Nikolaus 1802-1850 ...... **NCLC 16**

L'Engle, Madeleine (Camp Franklin)
1918- .... **CLC 12; DAM POP**
See also AAYA 1; AITN 2; CA 1-4R;
CANR 3, 21, 39; CLR 1, 14; DLB 52;
JRDA; MAICYA; MTCW; SAAS 15;
SATA 1, 27, 75

Lengyel, Jozsef 1896-1975 .... **CLC 7**
See also CA 85-88; 57-60

Lenin 1870-1924
See Lenin, V. I.
See also CA 121

Lenin, V. I. .... **TCLC 67**
See also Lenin

Lennon, John (Ono)
1940-1980 .... **CLC 12, 35**
See also CA 102

Lennox, Charlotte Ramsay
1729(?)-1804 .... **NCLC 23**
See also DLB 39

Lentricchia, Frank (Jr.) 1940- ..... **CLC 34**
See also CA 25-28R; CANR 19

Lenz, Siegfried 1926- .... **CLC 27**
See also CA 89-92; DLB 75

Leonard, Elmore (John, Jr.)
1925- ...... **CLC 28, 34, 71; DAM POP**
See also AITN 1; BEST 89:1, 90:4;
CA 81-84; CANR 12, 28, 53; DLB 173;
INT CANR-28; MTCW

Leonard, Hugh .... **CLC 19**
See also Byrne, John Keyes
See also DLB 13

Leonov, Leonid (Maximovich)
1899-1994 .... **CLC 92; DAM NOV**
See also CA 129; MTCW

Leopardi, (Conte) Giacomo
1798-1837 .... **NCLC 22**

Le Reveler
See Artaud, Antonin (Marie Joseph)

Lerman, Eleanor 1952- .... **CLC 9**
See also CA 85-88

Lerman, Rhoda 1936- .... **CLC 56**
See also CA 49-52

Lermontov, Mikhail Yuryevich
1814-1841 .... **NCLC 47**

Leroux, Gaston 1868-1927 .... **TCLC 25**
See also CA 108; 136; SATA 65

Lesage, Alain-Rene 1668-1747 ...... **LC 28**

Leskov, Nikolai (Semyonovich)
1831-1895 .... **NCLC 25**

Lessing, Doris (May)
1919- ..... **CLC 1, 2, 3, 6, 10, 15, 22, 40,**
94; DA; DAB; DAC; DAM MST, NOV;
SSC 6
See also CA 9-12R; CAAS 14; CANR 33,
54; CDBLB 1960 to Present; DLB 15,
139; DLBY 85; MTCW

Lessing, Gotthold Ephraim
1729-1781 .... **LC 8**
See also DLB 97

Lester, Richard 1932-............ **CLC 20**

Lever, Charles (James)
1806-1872 .... **NCLC 23**
See also DLB 21

Leverson, Ada 1865(?)-1936(?) .... **TCLC 18**
See also Elaine
See also CA 117; DLB 153

Levertov, Denise
1923- ...... **CLC 1, 2, 3, 5, 8, 15, 28, 66;**
DAM POET; PC 11
See also CA 1-4R; CAAS 19; CANR 3, 29,
50; DLB 5, 165; INT CANR-29; MTCW

Levi, Jonathan.................... **CLC 76**

Levi, Peter (Chad Tigar) 1931-..... **CLC 41**
See also CA 5-8R; CANR 34; DLB 40

Levi, Primo
1919-1987 .... **CLC 37, 50; SSC 12**
See also CA 13-16R; 122; CANR 12, 33;
MTCW

Levin, Ira 1929- .... **CLC 3, 6; DAM POP**
See also CA 21-24R; CANR 17, 44;
MTCW; SATA 66

Levin, Meyer
1905-1981 .... **CLC 7; DAM POP**
See also AITN 1; CA 9-12R; 104;
CANR 15; DLB 9, 28; DLBY 81;
SATA 21; SATA-Obit 27

Levine, Norman 1924-............ **CLC 54**
See also CA 73-76; CAAS 23; CANR 14;
DLB 88

Levine, Philip
1928-........... **CLC 2, 4, 5, 9, 14, 33;**
DAM POET
See also CA 9-12R; CANR 9, 37, 52;
DLB 5

Levinson, Deirdre 1931-........... **CLC 49**
See also CA 73-76

Levi-Strauss, Claude 1908- .... **CLC 38**
See also CA 1-4R; CANR 6, 32; MTCW

Levitin, Sonia (Wolff) 1934- .... **CLC 17**
See also AAYA 13; CA 29-32R; CANR 14,
32; JRDA; MAICYA; SAAS 2; SATA 4,
68

Levon, O. U.
See Kesey, Ken (Elton)

Levy, Amy 1861-1889.......... **NCLC 59**
See also DLB 156

Lewes, George Henry
1817-1878 .... **NCLC 25**
See also DLB 55, 144

Lewis, Alun 1915-1944............ **TCLC 3**
See also CA 104; DLB 20, 162

Lewis, C. Day
See Day Lewis, C(ecil)

Lewis, C(live) S(taples)
1898-1963 ..... **CLC 1, 3, 6, 14, 27; DA;**
DAB; DAC; DAM MST, NOV, POP;
WLC
See also AAYA 3; CA 81-84; CANR 33;
CDBLB 1945-1960; CLR 3, 27; DLB 15,
100, 160; JRDA; MAICYA; MTCW;
SATA 13

Lewis, Janet 1899-.............. **CLC 41**
See also Winters, Janet Lewis
See also CA 9-12R; CANR 29; CAP 1;
DLBY 87

Lewis, Matthew Gregory
1775-1818 .... **NCLC 11**
See also DLB 39, 158

Lewis, (Harry) Sinclair
1885-1951 ..... **TCLC 4, 13, 23, 39; DA;**
DAB; DAC; DAM MST, NOV; WLC
See also CA 104; 133; CDALB 1917-1929;
DLB 9, 102; DLBD 1; MTCW

Lewis, (Percy) Wyndham
1884(?)-1957 .... **TCLC 2, 9**
See also CA 104; DLB 15

Lewisohn, Ludwig 1883-1955...... **TCLC 19**
See also CA 107; DLB 4, 9, 28, 102

Leyner, Mark 1956-.............. **CLC 92**
See also CA 110; CANR 28, 53

Lezama Lima, Jose
1910-1976 .... **CLC 4, 10; DAM MULT**
See also CA 77-80; DLB 113; HW

L'Heureux, John (Clarke) 1934-.... **CLC 52**
See also CA 13-16R; CANR 23, 45

Liddell, C. H.
See Kuttner, Henry

Lie, Jonas (Lauritz Idemil)
1833-1908(?) .... **TCLC 5**
See also CA 115

Lieber, Joel 1937-1971............. **CLC 6**
See also CA 73-76; 29-32R

Lieber, Stanley Martin
See Lee, Stan

Lieberman, Laurence (James)
1935-..................... **CLC 4, 36**
See also CA 17-20R; CANR 8, 36

Lieksman, Anders
See Haavikko, Paavo Juhani

Li Fei-kan 1904-
See Pa Chin
See also CA 105

Lifton, Robert Jay 1926-.......... **CLC 67**
See also CA 17-20R; CANR 27;
INT CANR-27; SATA 66

Lightfoot, Gordon 1938-.......... **CLC 26**
See also CA 109

Lightman, Alan P. 1948-.......... **CLC 81**
See also CA 141

Ligotti, Thomas (Robert)
1953-.............. **CLC 44; SSC 16**
See also CA 123; CANR 49

Li Ho 791-817.................... **PC 13**

Liliencron, (Friedrich Adolf Axel) Detlev von
1844-1909 .... **TCLC 18**
See also CA 117

Lilly, William 1602-1681.......... **LC 27**

Lima, Jose Lezama
See Lezama Lima, Jose

Lima Barreto, Afonso Henrique de
1881-1922 .... **TCLC 23**
See also CA 117

Limonov, Edward 1944-.......... **CLC 67**
See also CA 137

Lin, Frank
See Atherton, Gertrude (Franklin Horn)

Lincoln, Abraham 1809-1865..... **NCLC 18**

Lind, Jakov .... **CLC 1, 2, 4, 27, 82**
See also Landwirth, Heinz
See also CAAS 4

Lindbergh, Anne (Spencer) Morrow
1906-............ **CLC 82; DAM NOV**
See also CA 17-20R; CANR 16; MTCW;
SATA 33

Lindsay, David 1878-1945........ **TCLC 15**
See also CA 113

Lindsay, (Nicholas) Vachel
1879-1931 .... **TCLC 17; DA; DAC;**
DAM MST, POET; WLC
See also CA 114; 135; CDALB 1865-1917;
DLB 54; SATA 40

Linke-Poot
See Doeblin, Alfred

Linney, Romulus 1930-........... **CLC 51**
See also CA 1-4R; CANR 40, 44

Linton, Eliza Lynn 1822-1898.... **NCLC 41**
See also DLB 18

Li Po 701-763................. **CMLC 2**

Lipsius, Justus 1547-1606 .... **LC 16**

Lipsyte, Robert (Michael)
1938-............. **CLC 21; DA; DAC;**
DAM MST, NOV
See also AAYA 7; CA 17-20R; CANR 8;
CLR 23; JRDA; MAICYA; SATA 5, 68

Lish, Gordon (Jay) 1934-.. **CLC 45; SSC 18**
See also CA 113; 117; DLB 130; INT 117

Lispector, Clarice 1925-1977....... **CLC 43**
See also CA 139; 116; DLB 113

Littell, Robert 1935(?)- .... **CLC 42**
See also CA 109; 112

Little, Malcolm 1925-1965
See Malcolm X
See also BW 1; CA 125; 111; DA; DAB;
DAC; DAM MST, MULT; MTCW

Littlewit, Humphrey Gent.
See Lovecraft, H(oward) P(hillips)

Litwos
See Sienkiewicz, Henryk (Adam Alexander
Pius)

Liu E 1857-1909............... **TCLC 15**
See also CA 115

Lively, Penelope (Margaret)
1933-......... **CLC 32, 50; DAM NOV**
See also CA 41-44R; CANR 29; CLR 7;
DLB 14, 161; JRDA; MAICYA; MTCW;
SATA 7, 60

Livesay, Dorothy (Kathleen)
1909-............ **CLC 4, 15, 79; DAC;**
DAM MST, POET
See also AITN 2; CA 25-28R; CAAS 8;
CANR 36; DLB 68; MTCW

Livy c. 59B.C.-c. 17............ **CMLC 11**

Lizardi, Jose Joaquin Fernandez de
1776-1827 .... **NCLC 30**

Llewellyn, Richard
See Llewellyn Lloyd, Richard Dafydd
Vivian
See also DLB 15

Llewellyn Lloyd, Richard Dafydd Vivian
    1906-1983 . . . . **CLC 7, 80**
    See also Llewellyn, Richard
    See also CA 53-56; 111; CANR 7;
    SATA 11; SATA-Obit 37

Llosa, (Jorge) Mario (Pedro) Vargas
    See Vargas Llosa, (Jorge) Mario (Pedro)

Lloyd Webber, Andrew   1948-
    See Webber, Andrew Lloyd
    See also AAYA 1; CA 116; 149;
    DAM DRAM; SATA 56

Llull, Ramon   c. 1235-c. 1316 . . . . . **CMLC 12**

Locke, Alain (Le Roy)
    1886-1954 . . . . **TCLC 43**
    See also BW 1; CA 106; 124; DLB 51

Locke, John   1632-1704 . . . . **LC 7, 35**
    See also DLB 101

Locke-Elliott, Sumner
    See Elliott, Sumner Locke

Lockhart, John Gibson
    1794-1854 . . . . **NCLC 6**
    See also DLB 110, 116, 144

Lodge, David (John)
    1935- . . . . **CLC 36; DAM POP**
    See also BEST 90:1; CA 17-20R; CANR 19,
    53; DLB 14; INT CANR-19; MTCW

Loennbohm, Armas Eino Leopold   1878-1926
    See Leino, Eino
    See also CA 123

Loewinsohn, Ron(ald William)
    1937- . . . . **CLC 52**
    See also CA 25-28R

Logan, Jake
    See Smith, Martin Cruz

Logan, John (Burton)   1923-1987 . . . . . **CLC 5**
    See also CA 77-80; 124; CANR 45; DLB 5

Lo Kuan-chung   1330(?)-1400(?) . . . . . . **LC 12**

Lombard, Nap
    See Johnson, Pamela Hansford

London, Jack . . **TCLC 9, 15, 39; SSC 4; WLC**
    See also London, John Griffith
    See also AAYA 13; AITN 2;
    CDALB 1865-1917; DLB 8, 12, 78;
    SATA 18

London, John Griffith   1876-1916
    See London, Jack
    See also CA 110; 119; DA; DAB; DAC;
    DAM MST, NOV; JRDA; MAICYA;
    MTCW

Long, Emmett
    See Leonard, Elmore (John, Jr.)

Longbaugh, Harry
    See Goldman, William (W.)

Longfellow, Henry Wadsworth
    1807-1882 . . . . . **NCLC 2, 45; DA; DAB;**
                      DAC; DAM MST, POET
    See also CDALB 1640-1865; DLB 1, 59;
    SATA 19

Longley, Michael   1939- . . . . **CLC 29**
    See also CA 102; DLB 40

Longus   fl. c. 2nd cent. - . . . . **CMLC 7**

Longway, A. Hugh
    See Lang, Andrew

Lonnrot, Elias   1802-1884 . . . . **NCLC 53**

Lopate, Phillip   1943- . . . . **CLC 29**
    See also CA 97-100; DLBY 80; INT 97-100

Lopez Portillo (y Pacheco), Jose
    1920- . . . . **CLC 46**
    See also CA 129; HW

Lopez y Fuentes, Gregorio
    1897(?)-1966 . . . . **CLC 32**
    See also CA 131; HW

Lorca, Federico Garcia
    See Garcia Lorca, Federico

Lord, Bette Bao   1938- . . . . **CLC 23**
    See also BEST 90:3; CA 107; CANR 41;
    INT 107; SATA 58

Lord Auch
    See Bataille, Georges

Lord Byron
    See Byron, George Gordon (Noel)

Lorde, Audre (Geraldine)
    1934-1992 . . . . **CLC 18, 71; BLC;**
                      DAM MULT, POET; PC 12
    See also BW 1; CA 25-28R; 142; CANR 16,
    26, 46; DLB 41; MTCW

Lord Jeffrey
    See Jeffrey, Francis

Lorenzini, Carlo   1826-1890
    See Collodi, Carlo
    See also MAICYA; SATA 29

Lorenzo, Heberto Padilla
    See Padilla (Lorenzo), Heberto

Loris
    See Hofmannsthal, Hugo von

Loti, Pierre . . . . **TCLC 11**
    See also Viaud, (Louis Marie) Julien
    See also DLB 123

Louie, David Wong   1954- . . . . **CLC 70**
    See also CA 139

Louis, Father M.
    See Merton, Thomas

Lovecraft, H(oward) P(hillips)
    1890-1937 . . . . **TCLC 4, 22; DAM POP;**
                                       SSC 3
    See also AAYA 14; CA 104; 133; MTCW

Lovelace, Earl   1935- . . . . **CLC 51**
    See also BW 2; CA 77-80; CANR 41;
    DLB 125; MTCW

Lovelace, Richard   1618-1657 . . . . **LC 24**
    See also DLB 131

Lowell, Amy
    1874-1925 . . . . **TCLC 1, 8; DAM POET;**
                                      PC 13
    See also CA 104; 151; DLB 54, 140

Lowell, James Russell   1819-1891 . . **NCLC 2**
    See also CDALB 1640-1865; DLB 1, 11, 64,
    79

Lowell, Robert (Traill Spence, Jr.)
    1917-1977 . . . **CLC 1, 2, 3, 4, 5, 8, 9, 11,**
    15, 37; DA; DAB; DAC; DAM MST,
                              NOV; PC 3; WLC
    See also CA 9-12R; 73-76; CABS 2;
    CANR 26; DLB 5, 169; MTCW

Lowndes, Marie Adelaide (Belloc)
    1868-1947 . . . . **TCLC 12**
    See also CA 107; DLB 70

Lowry, (Clarence) Malcolm
    1909-1957 . . . . **TCLC 6, 40**
    See also CA 105; 131; CDBLB 1945-1960;
    DLB 15; MTCW

Lowry, Mina Gertrude   1882-1966
    See Loy, Mina
    See also CA 113

Loxsmith, John
    See Brunner, John (Kilian Houston)

Loy, Mina . . . . **CLC 28; DAM POET; PC 16**
    See also Lowry, Mina Gertrude
    See also DLB 4, 54

Loyson-Bridet
    See Schwob, (Mayer Andre) Marcel

Lucas, Craig   1951- . . . . **CLC 64**
    See also CA 137

Lucas, George   1944- . . . . **CLC 16**
    See also AAYA 1; CA 77-80; CANR 30;
    SATA 56

Lucas, Hans
    See Godard, Jean-Luc

Lucas, Victoria
    See Plath, Sylvia

Ludlam, Charles   1943-1987 . . . . . **CLC 46, 50**
    See also CA 85-88; 122

Ludlum, Robert
    1927- . . . **CLC 22, 43; DAM NOV, POP**
    See also AAYA 10; BEST 89:1, 90:3;
    CA 33-36R; CANR 25, 41; DLBY 82;
    MTCW

Ludwig, Ken . . . . **CLC 60**

Ludwig, Otto   1813-1865 . . . . **NCLC 4**
    See also DLB 129

Lugones, Leopoldo   1874-1938 . . . . . **TCLC 15**
    See also CA 116; 131; HW

Lu Hsun   1881-1936 . . . . . . **TCLC 3; SSC 20**
    See also Shu-Jen, Chou

Lukacs, George . . . . **CLC 24**
    See also Lukacs, Gyorgy (Szegeny von)

Lukacs, Gyorgy (Szegeny von)   1885-1971
    See Lukacs, George
    See also CA 101; 29-32R

Luke, Peter (Ambrose Cyprian)
    1919-1995 . . . . **CLC 38**
    See also CA 81-84; 147; DLB 13

Lunar, Dennis
    See Mungo, Raymond

Lurie, Alison   1926- . . . . **CLC 4, 5, 18, 39**
    See also CA 1-4R; CANR 2, 17, 50; DLB 2;
    MTCW; SATA 46

Lustig, Arnost   1926- . . . . **CLC 56**
    See also AAYA 3; CA 69-72; CANR 47;
    SATA 56

Luther, Martin   1483-1546 . . . . **LC 9, 37**

Luxemburg, Rosa   1870(?)-1919 . . . . **TCLC 63**
    See also CA 118

Luzi, Mario   1914- . . . . **CLC 13**
    See also CA 61-64; CANR 9; DLB 128

L'Ymagier
    See Gourmont, Remy (-Marie-Charles) de

Lynch, B. Suarez
    See Bioy Casares, Adolfo; Borges, Jorge
    Luis

Lynch, David (K.) 1946-.......... **CLC 66**
See also CA 124; 129

Lynch, James
See Andreyev, Leonid (Nikolaevich)

Lynch Davis, B.
See Bioy Casares, Adolfo; Borges, Jorge
Luis

Lyndsay, Sir David 1490-1555 ...... **LC 20**

Lynn, Kenneth S(chuyler) 1923-.... **CLC 50**
See also CA 1-4R; CANR 3, 27

Lynx
See West, Rebecca

Lyons, Marcus
See Blish, James (Benjamin)

Lyre, Pinchbeck
See Sassoon, Siegfried (Lorraine)

Lytle, Andrew (Nelson) 1902-1995 .. **CLC 22**
See also CA 9-12R; 150; DLB 6; DLBY 95

Lyttelton, George 1709-1773........ **LC 10**

Maas, Peter 1929- .... **CLC 29**
See also CA 93-96; INT 93-96

Macaulay, Rose 1881-1958 ..... **TCLC 7, 44**
See also CA 104; DLB 36

Macaulay, Thomas Babington
1800-1859 .... **NCLC 42**
See also CDBLB 1832-1890; DLB 32, 55

MacBeth, George (Mann)
1932-1992 .... **CLC 2, 5, 9**
See also CA 25-28R; 136; DLB 40; MTCW;
SATA 4; SATA-Obit 70

MacCaig, Norman (Alexander)
1910- ..... **CLC 36; DAB; DAM POET**
See also CA 9-12R; CANR 3, 34; DLB 27

MacCarthy, (Sir Charles Otto) Desmond
1877-1952 .... **TCLC 36**

MacDiarmid, Hugh
.... **CLC 2, 4, 11, 19, 63; PC 9**
See also Grieve, C(hristopher) M(urray)
See also CDBLB 1945-1960; DLB 20

MacDonald, Anson
See Heinlein, Robert A(nson)

Macdonald, Cynthia 1928-...... **CLC 13, 19**
See also CA 49-52; CANR 4, 44; DLB 105

MacDonald, George 1824-1905 ..... **TCLC 9**
See also CA 106; 137; DLB 18, 163;
MAICYA; SATA 33

Macdonald, John
See Millar, Kenneth

MacDonald, John D(ann)
1916-1986 .... **CLC 3, 27, 44;**
DAM NOV, POP
See also CA 1-4R; 121; CANR 1, 19;
DLB 8; DLBY 86; MTCW

Macdonald, John Ross
See Millar, Kenneth

Macdonald, Ross..... CLC 1, 2, 3, 14, 34, 41
See also Millar, Kenneth
See also DLBD 6

MacDougal, John
See Blish, James (Benjamin)

MacEwen, Gwendolyn (Margaret)
1941-1987 .... **CLC 13, 55**
See also CA 9-12R; 124; CANR 7, 22;
DLB 53; SATA 50; SATA-Obit 55

Macha, Karel Hynek 1810-1846 .. **NCLC 46**

Machado (y Ruiz), Antonio
1875-1939 .... **TCLC 3**
See also CA 104; DLB 108

Machado de Assis, Joaquim Maria
1839-1908 ..... **TCLC 10; BLC; SSC 24**
See also CA 107; 153

Machen, Arthur.......... TCLC 4; SSC 20
See also Jones, Arthur Llewellyn
See also DLB 36, 156

Machiavelli, Niccolo
1469-1527 .... **LC 8, 36; DA; DAB;**
DAC; DAM MST

MacInnes, Colin 1914-1976...... **CLC 4, 23**
See also CA 69-72; 65-68; CANR 21;
DLB 14; MTCW

MacInnes, Helen (Clark)
1907-1985 ..... **CLC 27, 39; DAM POP**
See also CA 1-4R; 117; CANR 1, 28;
DLB 87; MTCW; SATA 22;
SATA-Obit 44

Mackay, Mary 1855-1924
See Corelli, Marie
See also CA 118

Mackenzie, Compton (Edward Montague)
1883-1972 .... **CLC 18**
See also CA 21-22; 37-40R; CAP 2;
DLB 34, 100

Mackenzie, Henry 1745-1831 .... **NCLC 41**
See also DLB 39

Mackintosh, Elizabeth 1896(?)-1952
See Tey, Josephine
See also CA 110

MacLaren, James
See Grieve, C(hristopher) M(urray)

Mac Laverty, Bernard 1942-....... **CLC 31**
See also CA 116; 118; CANR 43; INT 118

MacLean, Alistair (Stuart)
1922-1987 .... **CLC 3, 13, 50, 63;**
DAM POP
See also CA 57-60; 121; CANR 28; MTCW;
SATA 23; SATA-Obit 50

Maclean, Norman (Fitzroy)
1902-1990 .... **CLC 78; DAM POP;**
SSC 13
See also CA 102; 132; CANR 49

MacLeish, Archibald
1892-1982 .... **CLC 3, 8, 14, 68;**
DAM POET
See also CA 9-12R; 106; CANR 33; DLB 4,
7, 45; DLBY 82; MTCW

MacLennan, (John) Hugh
1907-1990 .... **CLC 2, 14, 92; DAC;**
DAM MST
See also CA 5-8R; 142; CANR 33; DLB 68;
MTCW

MacLeod, Alistair
1936- ...... **CLC 56; DAC; DAM MST**
See also CA 123; DLB 60

MacNeice, (Frederick) Louis
1907-1963 ...... **CLC 1, 4, 10, 53; DAB;**
DAM POET
See also CA 85-88; DLB 10, 20; MTCW

MacNeill, Dand
See Fraser, George MacDonald

Macpherson, James 1736-1796 ...... **LC 29**
See also DLB 109

Macpherson, (Jean) Jay 1931-...... **CLC 14**
See also CA 5-8R; DLB 53

MacShane, Frank 1927-.......... **CLC 39**
See also CA 9-12R; CANR 3, 33; DLB 111

Macumber, Mari
See Sandoz, Mari(e Susette)

Madach, Imre 1823-1864........ **NCLC 19**

Madden, (Jerry) David 1933- .... **CLC 5, 15**
See also CA 1-4R; CAAS 3; CANR 4, 45;
DLB 6; MTCW

Maddern, Al(an)
See Ellison, Harlan (Jay)

Madhubuti, Haki R.
1942- .... **CLC 6, 73; BLC;**
DAM MULT, POET; PC 5
See also Lee, Don L.
See also BW 2; CA 73-76; CANR 24, 51;
DLB 5, 41; DLBD 8

Maepenn, Hugh
See Kuttner, Henry

Maepenn, K. H.
See Kuttner, Henry

Maeterlinck, Maurice
1862-1949 ...... **TCLC 3; DAM DRAM**
See also CA 104; 136; SATA 66

Maginn, William 1794-1842....... **NCLC 8**
See also DLB 110, 159

Mahapatra, Jayanta
1928- .... **CLC 33; DAM MULT**
See also CA 73-76; CAAS 9; CANR 15, 33

Mahfouz, Naguib (Abdel Aziz Al-Sabilgi)
1911(?)-
See Mahfuz, Najib
See also BEST 89:2; CA 128; CANR 55;
DAM NOV; MTCW

Mahfuz, Najib................. CLC 52, 55
See also Mahfouz, Naguib (Abdel Aziz
Al-Sabilgi)
See also DLBY 88

Mahon, Derek 1941-.............. **CLC 27**
See also CA 113; 128; DLB 40

Mailer, Norman
1923- ...... **CLC 1, 2, 3, 4, 5, 8, 11, 14,**
28, 39, 74; DA; DAB; DAC; DAM MST,
NOV, POP
See also AITN 2; CA 9-12R; CABS 1;
CANR 28; CDALB 1968-1988; DLB 2,
16, 28; DLBD 3; DLBY 80, 83; MTCW

Maillet, Antonine 1929-...... **CLC 54; DAC**
See also CA 115; 120; CANR 46; DLB 60;
INT 120

Mais, Roger 1905-1955 .... **TCLC 8**
See also BW 1; CA 105; 124; DLB 125;
MTCW

Maistre, Joseph de 1753-1821 .... **NCLC 37**

Maitland, Frederic 1850-1906 ..... **TCLC 65**

Maitland, Sara (Louise) 1950-...... **CLC 49**
See also CA 69-72; CANR 13

Major, Clarence
1936- .... **CLC 3, 19, 48; BLC;**
DAM MULT
See also BW 2; CA 21-24R; CAAS 6;
CANR 13, 25, 53; DLB 33

Major, Kevin (Gerald)
  1949- . . . . CLC 26; DAC
  See also AAYA 16; CA 97-100; CANR 21,
    38; CLR 11; DLB 60; INT CANR-21;
    JRDA; MAICYA; SATA 32, 82

Maki, James
  See Ozu, Yasujiro

Malabaila, Damiano
  See Levi, Primo

Malamud, Bernard
  1914-1986 . . . . . . CLC 1, 2, 3, 5, 8, 9, 11,
    18, 27, 44, 78, 85; DA; DAB; DAC;
    DAM MST, NOV, POP; SSC 15; WLC
  See also AAYA 16; CA 5-8R; 118; CABS 1;
    CANR 28; CDALB 1941-1968; DLB 2,
    28, 152; DLBY 80, 86; MTCW

Malaparte, Curzio 1898-1957 . . . . . TCLC 52

Malcolm, Dan
  See Silverberg, Robert

Malcolm X . . . . CLC 82; BLC
  See also Little, Malcolm

Malherbe, Francois de 1555-1628 . . . . . LC 5

Mallarme, Stephane
  1842-1898 . . . . NCLC 4, 41;
    DAM POET; PC 4

Mallet-Joris, Francoise 1930- . . . . . . CLC 11
  See also CA 65-68; CANR 17; DLB 83

Malley, Ern
  See McAuley, James Phillip

Mallowan, Agatha Christie
  See Christie, Agatha (Mary Clarissa)

Maloff, Saul 1922- . . . . CLC 5
  See also CA 33-36R

Malone, Louis
  See MacNeice, (Frederick) Louis

Malone, Michael (Christopher)
  1942- . . . . CLC 43
  See also CA 77-80; CANR 14, 32

Malory, (Sir) Thomas
  1410(?)-1471(?) . . . . . . LC 11; DA; DAB;
    DAC; DAM MST
  See also CDBLB Before 1660; DLB 146;
    SATA 59; SATA-Brief 33

Malouf, (George Joseph) David
  1934- . . . . CLC 28, 86
  See also CA 124; CANR 50

Malraux, (Georges-)Andre
  1901-1976 . . . . . . CLC 1, 4, 9, 13, 15, 57;
    DAM NOV
  See also CA 21-22; 69-72; CANR 34;
    CAP 2; DLB 72; MTCW

Malzberg, Barry N(athaniel) 1939- . . . CLC 7
  See also CA 61-64; CAAS 4; CANR 16;
    DLB 8

Mamet, David (Alan)
  1947- . . . . CLC 9, 15, 34, 46, 91;
    DAM DRAM; DC 4
  See also AAYA 3; CA 81-84; CABS 3;
    CANR 15, 41; DLB 7; MTCW

Mamoulian, Rouben (Zachary)
  1897-1987 . . . . CLC 16
  See also CA 25-28R; 124

Mandelstam, Osip (Emilievich)
  1891(?)-1938(?) . . . . . . TCLC 2, 6; PC 14
  See also CA 104; 150

Mander, (Mary) Jane 1877-1949. . . TCLC 31

Mandeville, John fl. 1350- . . . . . . CMLC 19
  See also DLB 146

Mandiargues, Andre Pieyre de . . . . . . CLC 41
  See also Pieyre de Mandiargues, Andre
  See also DLB 83

Mandrake, Ethel Belle
  See Thurman, Wallace (Henry)

Mangan, James Clarence
  1803-1849 . . . . NCLC 27

Maniere, J.-E.
  See Giraudoux, (Hippolyte) Jean

Manley, (Mary) Delariviere
  1672(?)-1724 . . . . LC 1
  See also DLB 39, 80

Mann, Abel
  See Creasey, John

Mann, (Luiz) Heinrich 1871-1950. . . TCLC 9
  See also CA 106; DLB 66

Mann, (Paul) Thomas
  1875-1955 . . . . TCLC 2, 8, 14, 21, 35, 44,
    60; DA; DAB; DAC; DAM MST, NOV;
    SSC 5; WLC
  See also CA 104; 128; DLB 66; MTCW

Mannheim, Karl 1893-1947 . . . . . . TCLC 65

Manning, David
  See Faust, Frederick (Schiller)

Manning, Frederic 1887(?)-1935 . . . TCLC 25
  See also CA 124

Manning, Olivia 1915-1980 . . . . . . CLC 5, 19
  See also CA 5-8R; 101; CANR 29; MTCW

Mano, D. Keith 1942- . . . . CLC 2, 10
  See also CA 25-28R; CAAS 6; CANR 26;
    DLB 6

Mansfield, Katherine
  . . TCLC 2, 8, 39; DAB; SSC 9, 23; WLC
  See also Beauchamp, Kathleen Mansfield
  See also DLB 162

Manso, Peter 1940- . . . . CLC 39
  See also CA 29-32R; CANR 44

Mantecon, Juan Jimenez
  See Jimenez (Mantecon), Juan Ramon

Manton, Peter
  See Creasey, John

Man Without a Spleen, A
  See Chekhov, Anton (Pavlovich)

Manzoni, Alessandro 1785-1873 . . NCLC 29

Mapu, Abraham (ben Jekutiel)
  1808-1867 . . . . NCLC 18

Mara, Sally
  See Queneau, Raymond

Marat, Jean Paul 1743-1793 . . . . LC 10

Marcel, Gabriel Honore
  1889-1973 . . . . CLC 15
  See also CA 102; 45-48; MTCW

Marchbanks, Samuel
  See Davies, (William) Robertson

Marchi, Giacomo
  See Bassani, Giorgio

Margulies, Donald . . . . CLC 76

Marie de France c. 12th cent. - . . . . CMLC 8

Marie de l'Incarnation 1599-1672 . . . . LC 10

Marier, Captain Victor
  See Griffith, D(avid Lewelyn) W(ark)

Mariner, Scott
  See Pohl, Frederik

Marinetti, Filippo Tommaso
  1876-1944 . . . . TCLC 10
  See also CA 107; DLB 114

Marivaux, Pierre Carlet de Chamblain de
  1688-1763 . . . . LC 4

Markandaya, Kamala . . . . CLC 8, 38
  See also Taylor, Kamala (Purnaiya)

Markfield, Wallace 1926- . . . . CLC 8
  See also CA 69-72; CAAS 3; DLB 2, 28

Markham, Edwin 1852-1940 . . . . . TCLC 47
  See also DLB 54

Markham, Robert
  See Amis, Kingsley (William)

Marks, J
  See Highwater, Jamake (Mamake)

Marks-Highwater, J
  See Highwater, Jamake (Mamake)

Markson, David M(errill) 1927- . . . . CLC 67
  See also CA 49-52; CANR 1

Marley, Bob . . . . CLC 17
  See also Marley, Robert Nesta

Marley, Robert Nesta 1945-1981
  See Marley, Bob
  See also CA 107; 103

Marlowe, Christopher
  1564-1593 . . . . . LC 22; DA; DAB; DAC;
    DAM DRAM, MST; DC 1; WLC
  See also CDBLB Before 1660; DLB 62

Marlowe, Stephen 1928-
  See Queen, Ellery
  See also CA 13-16R; CANR 6, 55

Marmontel, Jean-Francois
  1723-1799 . . . . LC 2

Marquand, John P(hillips)
  1893-1960 . . . . CLC 2, 10
  See also CA 85-88; DLB 9, 102

Marques, Rene
  1919-1979 . . . . . . CLC 96; DAM MULT;
    HLC
  See also CA 97-100; 85-88; DLB 113; HW

Marquez, Gabriel (Jose) Garcia
  See Garcia Marquez, Gabriel (Jose)

Marquis, Don(ald Robert Perry)
  1878-1937 . . . . TCLC 7
  See also CA 104; DLB 11, 25

Marric, J. J.
  See Creasey, John

Marrow, Bernard
  See Moore, Brian

Marryat, Frederick 1792-1848 . . . . NCLC 3
  See also DLB 21, 163

Marsden, James
  See Creasey, John

Marsh, (Edith) Ngaio
  1899-1982 . . . . . . CLC 7, 53; DAM POP
  See also CA 9-12R; CANR 6; DLB 77;
    MTCW

Marshall, Garry 1934- . . . . CLC 17
  See also AAYA 3; CA 111; SATA 60

Marshall, Paule
1929- . . . . **CLC 27, 72; BLC;**
DAM MULT; SSC 3
See also BW 2; CA 77-80; CANR 25;
DLB 157; MTCW

Marsten, Richard
See Hunter, Evan

Marston, John
1576-1634 . . . . **LC 33; DAM DRAM**
See also DLB 58, 172

Martha, Henry
See Harris, Mark

Martial   c. 40-c. 104 . . . . **PC 10**

Martin, Ken
See Hubbard, L(afayette) Ron(ald)

Martin, Richard
See Creasey, John

Martin, Steve   1945- . . . . **CLC 30**
See also CA 97-100; CANR 30; MTCW

Martin, Valerie   1948- . . . . **CLC 89**
See also BEST 90:2; CA 85-88; CANR 49

Martin, Violet Florence
1862-1915 . . . . **TCLC 51**

Martin, Webber
See Silverberg, Robert

Martindale, Patrick Victor
See White, Patrick (Victor Martindale)

Martin du Gard, Roger
1881-1958 . . . . **TCLC 24**
See also CA 118; DLB 65

Martineau, Harriet   1802-1876. . . . **NCLC 26**
See also DLB 21, 55, 159, 163, 166;
YABC 2

Martines, Julia
See O'Faolain, Julia

Martinez, Jacinto Benavente y
See Benavente (y Martinez), Jacinto

Martinez Ruiz, Jose   1873-1967
See Azorin; Ruiz, Jose Martinez
See also CA 93-96; HW

Martinez Sierra, Gregorio
1881-1947 . . . . **TCLC 6**
See also CA 115

Martinez Sierra, Maria (de la O'LeJarraga)
1874-1974 . . . . **TCLC 6**
See also CA 115

Martinsen, Martin
See Follett, Ken(neth Martin)

Martinson, Harry (Edmund)
1904-1978 . . . . **CLC 14**
See also CA 77-80; CANR 34

Marut, Ret
See Traven, B.

Marut, Robert
See Traven, B.

Marvell, Andrew
1621-1678 . . . . . . **LC 4; DA; DAB; DAC;**
DAM MST, POET; PC 10; WLC
See also CDBLB 1660-1789; DLB 131

Marx, Karl (Heinrich)
1818-1883 . . . . **NCLC 17**
See also DLB 129

Masaoka Shiki. . . . . **TCLC 18**
See also Masaoka Tsunenori

Masaoka Tsunenori   1867-1902
See Masaoka Shiki
See also CA 117

Masefield, John (Edward)
1878-1967 . . . . **CLC 11, 47; DAM POET**
See also CA 19-20; 25-28R; CANR 33;
CAP 2; CDBLB 1890-1914; DLB 10, 19,
153, 160; MTCW; SATA 19

Maso, Carole   19(?)- . . . . **CLC 44**

Mason, Bobbie Ann
1940- . . . . **CLC 28, 43, 82; SSC 4**
See also AAYA 5; CA 53-56; CANR 11,
31; DLB 173; DLBY 87; INT CANR-31;
MTCW

Mason, Ernst
See Pohl, Frederik

Mason, Lee W.
See Malzberg, Barry N(athaniel)

Mason, Nick   1945- . . . . **CLC 35**

Mason, Tally
See Derleth, August (William)

Mass, William
See Gibson, William

Masters, Edgar Lee
1868-1950 . . . . . . **TCLC 2, 25; DA; DAC;**
DAM MST, POET; PC 1
See also CA 104; 133; CDALB 1865-1917;
DLB 54; MTCW

Masters, Hilary   1928- . . . . **CLC 48**
See also CA 25-28R; CANR 13, 47

Mastrosimone, William   19(?)- . . . . . . **CLC 36**

Mathe, Albert
See Camus, Albert

Matheson, Richard Burton   1926- . . . **CLC 37**
See also CA 97-100; DLB 8, 44; INT 97-100

Mathews, Harry   1930- . . . . **CLC 6, 52**
See also CA 21-24R; CAAS 6; CANR 18,
40

Mathews, John Joseph
1894-1979 . . . . . . **CLC 84; DAM MULT**
See also CA 19-20; 142; CANR 45; CAP 2;
NNAL

Mathias, Roland (Glyn)   1915- . . . . . . **CLC 45**
See also CA 97-100; CANR 19, 41; DLB 27

Matsuo Basho   1644-1694. . . . . **PC 3**
See also DAM POET

Mattheson, Rodney
See Creasey, John

Matthews, Greg   1949- . . . . **CLC 45**
See also CA 135

Matthews, William   1942- . . . . **CLC 40**
See also CA 29-32R; CAAS 18; CANR 12;
DLB 5

Matthias, John (Edward)   1941- . . . . . . **CLC 9**
See also CA 33-36R

Matthiessen, Peter
1927- . . . . **CLC 5, 7, 11, 32, 64;**
DAM NOV
See also AAYA 6; BEST 90:4; CA 9-12R;
CANR 21, 50; DLB 6, 173; MTCW;
SATA 27

Maturin, Charles Robert
1780(?)-1824 . . . . **NCLC 6**

Matute (Ausejo), Ana Maria
1925- . . . . **CLC 11**
See also CA 89-92; MTCW

Maugham, W. S.
See Maugham, W(illiam) Somerset

Maugham, W(illiam) Somerset
1874-1965 . . . . **CLC 1, 11, 15, 67, 93;**
DA; DAB; DAC; DAM DRAM, MST,
NOV; SSC 8; WLC
See also CA 5-8R; 25-28R; CANR 40;
CDBLB 1914-1945; DLB 10, 36, 77, 100,
162; MTCW; SATA 54

Maugham, William Somerset
See Maugham, W(illiam) Somerset

Maupassant, (Henri Rene Albert) Guy de
1850-1893 . . . . . **NCLC 1, 42; DA; DAB;**
DAC; DAM MST; SSC 1; WLC
See also DLB 123

Maupin, Armistead
1944- . . . . **CLC 95; DAM POP**
See also CA 125; 130; INT 130

Maurhut, Richard
See Traven, B.

Mauriac, Claude   1914-1996. . . . . **CLC 9**
See also CA 89-92; 152; DLB 83

Mauriac, Francois (Charles)
1885-1970 . . . . **CLC 4, 9, 56; SSC 24**
See also CA 25-28; CAP 2; DLB 65;
MTCW

Mavor, Osborne Henry   1888-1951
See Bridie, James
See also CA 104

Maxwell, William (Keepers, Jr.)
1908- . . . . **CLC 19**
See also CA 93-96; CANR 54; DLBY 80;
INT 93-96

May, Elaine   1932- . . . . **CLC 16**
See also CA 124; 142; DLB 44

Mayakovski, Vladimir (Vladimirovich)
1893-1930 . . . . **TCLC 4, 18**
See also CA 104

Mayhew, Henry   1812-1887 . . . . . . **NCLC 31**
See also DLB 18, 55

Mayle, Peter   1939(?)- . . . . **CLC 89**
See also CA 139

Maynard, Joyce   1953- . . . . **CLC 23**
See also CA 111; 129

Mayne, William (James Carter)
1928- . . . . **CLC 12**
See also CA 9-12R; CANR 37; CLR 25;
JRDA; MAICYA; SAAS 11; SATA 6, 68

Mayo, Jim
See L'Amour, Louis (Dearborn)

Maysles, Albert   1926- . . . . **CLC 16**
See also CA 29-32R

Maysles, David   1932- . . . . **CLC 16**

Mazer, Norma Fox   1931- . . . . **CLC 26**
See also AAYA 5; CA 69-72; CANR 12,
32; CLR 23; JRDA; MAICYA; SAAS 1;
SATA 24, 67

Mazzini, Guiseppe   1805-1872 . . . . **NCLC 34**

McAuley, James Phillip
1917-1976 . . . . **CLC 45**
See also CA 97-100

McBain, Ed
See Hunter, Evan

McBrien, William Augustine
1930- .... **CLC 44**
See also CA 107

McCaffrey, Anne (Inez)
1926- ...... **CLC 17; DAM NOV, POP**
See also AAYA 6; AITN 2; BEST 89:2;
CA 25-28R; CANR 15, 35, 55; DLB 8;
JRDA; MAICYA; MTCW; SAAS 11;
SATA 8, 70

McCall, Nathan 1955(?)- .... **CLC 86**
See also CA 146

McCann, Arthur
See Campbell, John W(ood, Jr.)

McCann, Edson
See Pohl, Frederik

McCarthy, Charles, Jr. 1933-
See McCarthy, Cormac
See also CANR 42; DAM POP

McCarthy, Cormac 1933- ..... **CLC 4, 57, 59**
See also McCarthy, Charles, Jr.
See also DLB 6, 143

McCarthy, Mary (Therese)
1912-1989 ...... **CLC 1, 3, 5, 14, 24, 39,**
59; SSC 24
See also CA 5-8R; 129; CANR 16, 50;
DLB 2; DLBY 81; INT CANR-16;
MTCW

McCartney, (James) Paul
1942- .... **CLC 12, 35**
See also CA 146

McCauley, Stephen (D.) 1955- ..... **CLC 50**
See also CA 141

McClure, Michael (Thomas)
1932- .... **CLC 6, 10**
See also CA 21-24R; CANR 17, 46;
DLB 16

McCorkle, Jill (Collins) 1958- ..... **CLC 51**
See also CA 121; DLBY 87

McCourt, James 1941- .... **CLC 5**
See also CA 57-60

McCoy, Horace (Stanley)
1897-1955 .... **TCLC 28**
See also CA 108; 155; DLB 9

McCrae, John 1872-1918 .... **TCLC 12**
See also CA 109; DLB 92

McCreigh, James
See Pohl, Frederik

McCullers, (Lula) Carson (Smith)
1917-1967 .... **CLC 1, 4, 10, 12, 48; DA;**
DAB; DAC; DAM MST, NOV; SSC 24;
WLC
See also CA 5-8R; 25-28R; CABS 1, 3;
CANR 18; CDALB 1941-1968; DLB 2, 7,
173; MTCW; SATA 27

McCulloch, John Tyler
See Burroughs, Edgar Rice

McCullough, Colleen
1938(?)- .... **CLC 27; DAM NOV, POP**
See also CA 81-84; CANR 17, 46; MTCW

McDermott, Alice 1953- .... **CLC 90**
See also CA 109; CANR 40

McElroy, Joseph 1930- .... **CLC 5, 47**
See also CA 17-20R

McEwan, Ian (Russell)
1948- .... **CLC 13, 66; DAM NOV**
See also BEST 90:4; CA 61-64; CANR 14,
41; DLB 14; MTCW

McFadden, David 1940- .... **CLC 48**
See also CA 104; DLB 60; INT 104

McFarland, Dennis 1950- .... **CLC 65**

McGahern, John
1934- .... **CLC 5, 9, 48; SSC 17**
See also CA 17-20R; CANR 29; DLB 14;
MTCW

McGinley, Patrick (Anthony)
1937- .... **CLC 41**
See also CA 120; 127; INT 127

McGinley, Phyllis 1905-1978 ...... **CLC 14**
See also CA 9-12R; 77-80; CANR 19;
DLB 11, 48; SATA 2, 44; SATA-Obit 24

McGinniss, Joe 1942- .... **CLC 32**
See also AITN 2; BEST 89:2; CA 25-28R;
CANR 26; INT CANR-26

McGivern, Maureen Daly
See Daly, Maureen

McGrath, Patrick 1950- .... **CLC 55**
See also CA 136

McGrath, Thomas (Matthew)
1916-1990 .... **CLC 28, 59; DAM POET**
See also CA 9-12R; 132; CANR 6, 33;
MTCW; SATA 41; SATA-Obit 66

McGuane, Thomas (Francis III)
1939- .... **CLC 3, 7, 18, 45**
See also AITN 2; CA 49-52; CANR 5, 24,
49; DLB 2; DLBY 80; INT CANR-24;
MTCW

McGuckian, Medbh
1950- .... **CLC 48; DAM POET**
See also CA 143; DLB 40

McHale, Tom 1942(?)-1982 .... **CLC 3, 5**
See also AITN 1; CA 77-80; 106

McIlvanney, William 1936- .... **CLC 42**
See also CA 25-28R; DLB 14

McIlwraith, Maureen Mollie Hunter
See Hunter, Mollie
See also SATA 2

McInerney, Jay
1955- .... **CLC 34; DAM POP**
See also AAYA 18; CA 116; 123;
CANR 45; INT 123

McIntyre, Vonda N(eel) 1948- ..... **CLC 18**
See also CA 81-84; CANR 17, 34; MTCW

McKay, Claude
.... **TCLC 7, 41; BLC; DAB; PC 2**
See also McKay, Festus Claudius
See also DLB 4, 45, 51, 117

McKay, Festus Claudius 1889-1948
See McKay, Claude
See also BW 1; CA 104; 124; DA; DAC;
DAM MST, MULT, NOV, POET;
MTCW; WLC

McKuen, Rod 1933- .... **CLC 1, 3**
See also AITN 1; CA 41-44R; CANR 40

McLoughlin, R. B.
See Mencken, H(enry) L(ouis)

McLuhan, (Herbert) Marshall
1911-1980 .... **CLC 37, 83**
See also CA 9-12R; 102; CANR 12, 34;
DLB 88; INT CANR-12; MTCW

McMillan, Terry (L.)
1951- .... **CLC 50, 61; DAM MULT,**
NOV, POP
See also BW 2; CA 140

McMurtry, Larry (Jeff)
1936- .... **CLC 2, 3, 7, 11, 27, 44;**
DAM NOV, POP
See also AAYA 15; AITN 2; BEST 89:2;
CA 5-8R; CANR 19, 43;
CDALB 1968-1988; DLB 2, 143;
DLBY 80, 87; MTCW

McNally, T. M. 1961- .... **CLC 82**

McNally, Terrence
1939- ... **CLC 4, 7, 41, 91; DAM DRAM**
See also CA 45-48; CANR 2; DLB 7

McNamer, Deirdre 1950- .... **CLC 70**

McNeile, Herman Cyril 1888-1937
See Sapper
See also DLB 77

McNickle, (William) D'Arcy
1904-1977 ...... **CLC 89; DAM MULT**
See also CA 9-12R; 85-88; CANR 5, 45;
NNAL; SATA-Obit 22

McPhee, John (Angus) 1931- ...... **CLC 36**
See also BEST 90:1; CA 65-68; CANR 20,
46; MTCW

McPherson, James Alan
1943- .... **CLC 19, 77**
See also BW 1; CA 25-28R; CAAS 17;
CANR 24; DLB 38; MTCW

McPherson, William (Alexander)
1933- .... **CLC 34**
See also CA 69-72; CANR 28;
INT CANR-28

Mead, Margaret 1901-1978 .... **CLC 37**
See also AITN 1; CA 1-4R; 81-84;
CANR 4; MTCW; SATA-Obit 20

Meaker, Marijane (Agnes) 1927-
See Kerr, M. E.
See also CA 107; CANR 37; INT 107;
JRDA; MAICYA; MTCW; SATA 20, 61

Medoff, Mark (Howard)
1940- .... **CLC 6, 23; DAM DRAM**
See also AITN 1; CA 53-56; CANR 5;
DLB 7; INT CANR-5

Medvedev, P. N.
See Bakhtin, Mikhail Mikhailovich

Meged, Aharon
See Megged, Aharon

Meged, Aron
See Megged, Aharon

Megged, Aharon 1920- .... **CLC 9**
See also CA 49-52; CAAS 13; CANR 1

Mehta, Ved (Parkash) 1934- .... **CLC 37**
See also CA 1-4R; CANR 2, 23; MTCW

Melanter
See Blackmore, R(ichard) D(oddridge)

Melikow, Loris
See Hofmannsthal, Hugo von

Melmoth, Sebastian
See Wilde, Oscar (Fingal O'Flahertie Wills)

Meltzer, Milton 1915- . . . . **CLC 26**
See also AAYA 8; CA 13-16R; CANR 38;
CLR 13; DLB 61; JRDA; MAICYA;
SAAS 1; SATA 1, 50, 80

Melville, Herman
1819-1891 . . . . . **NCLC 3, 12, 29, 45, 49;**
DA; DAB; DAC; DAM MST, NOV;
SSC 1, 17; WLC
See also CDALB 1640-1865; DLB 3, 74;
SATA 59

Menander
c. 342B.C.-c. 292B.C. . . . . **CMLC 9;**
DAM DRAM; DC 3

Mencken, H(enry) L(ouis)
1880-1956 . . . . **TCLC 13**
See also CA 105; 125; CDALB 1917-1929;
DLB 11, 29, 63, 137; MTCW

Mercer, David
1928-1980 . . . . . . **CLC 5; DAM DRAM**
See also CA 9-12R; 102; CANR 23;
DLB 13; MTCW

Merchant, Paul
See Ellison, Harlan (Jay)

Meredith, George
1828-1909 . . **TCLC 17, 43; DAM POET**
See also CA 117; 153; CDBLB 1832-1890;
DLB 18, 35, 57, 159

Meredith, William (Morris)
1919- . . **CLC 4, 13, 22, 55; DAM POET**
See also CA 9-12R; CAAS 14; CANR 6, 40;
DLB 5

Merezhkovsky, Dmitry Sergeyevich
1865-1941 . . . . **TCLC 29**

Merimee, Prosper
1803-1870 . . . . **NCLC 6; SSC 7**
See also DLB 119

Merkin, Daphne 1954- . . . . **CLC 44**
See also CA 123

Merlin, Arthur
See Blish, James (Benjamin)

Merrill, James (Ingram)
1926-1995 . . . . **CLC 2, 3, 6, 8, 13, 18, 34,**
91; DAM POET
See also CA 13-16R; 147; CANR 10, 49;
DLB 5, 165; DLBY 85; INT CANR-10;
MTCW

Merriman, Alex
See Silverberg, Robert

Merritt, E. B.
See Waddington, Miriam

Merton, Thomas
1915-1968 . . **CLC 1, 3, 11, 34, 83; PC 10**
See also CA 5-8R; 25-28R; CANR 22, 53;
DLB 48; DLBY 81; MTCW

Merwin, W(illiam) S(tanley)
1927- . . . . . . **CLC 1, 2, 3, 5, 8, 13, 18, 45,**
88; DAM POET
See also CA 13-16R; CANR 15, 51; DLB 5,
169; INT CANR-15; MTCW

Metcalf, John 1938- . . . . **CLC 37**
See also CA 113; DLB 60

Metcalf, Suzanne
See Baum, L(yman) Frank

Mew, Charlotte (Mary)
1870-1928 . . . . **TCLC 8**
See also CA 105; DLB 19, 135

Mewshaw, Michael 1943- . . . . **CLC 9**
See also CA 53-56; CANR 7, 47; DLBY 80

Meyer, June
See Jordan, June

Meyer, Lynn
See Slavitt, David R(ytman)

Meyer-Meyrink, Gustav 1868-1932
See Meyrink, Gustav
See also CA 117

Meyers, Jeffrey 1939- . . . . **CLC 39**
See also CA 73-76; CANR 54; DLB 111

Meynell, Alice (Christina Gertrude Thompson)
1847-1922 . . . . **TCLC 6**
See also CA 104; DLB 19, 98

Meyrink, Gustav . . . . **TCLC 21**
See also Meyer-Meyrink, Gustav
See also DLB 81

Michaels, Leonard
1933- . . . . **CLC 6, 25; SSC 16**
See also CA 61-64; CANR 21; DLB 130;
MTCW

Michaux, Henri 1899-1984 . . . . . . **CLC 8, 19**
See also CA 85-88; 114

Michelangelo 1475-1564 . . . . **LC 12**

Michelet, Jules 1798-1874 . . . . **NCLC 31**

Michener, James A(lbert)
1907(?)- . . . . **CLC 1, 5, 11, 29, 60;**
DAM NOV, POP
See also AITN 1; BEST 90:1; CA 5-8R;
CANR 21, 45; DLB 6; MTCW

Mickiewicz, Adam 1798-1855 . . . . . **NCLC 3**

Middleton, Christopher 1926- . . . . . . **CLC 13**
See also CA 13-16R; CANR 29, 54;
DLB 40

Middleton, Richard (Barham)
1882-1911 . . . . **TCLC 56**
See also DLB 156

Middleton, Stanley 1919- . . . . **CLC 7, 38**
See also CA 25-28R; CAAS 23; CANR 21,
46; DLB 14

Middleton, Thomas
1580-1627 . . . . . . **LC 33; DAM DRAM,**
MST; DC 5
See also DLB 58

Migueis, Jose Rodrigues 1901- . . . . . **CLC 10**

Mikszath, Kalman 1847-1910 . . . . . **TCLC 31**

Miles, Josephine (Louise)
1911-1985 . . . . **CLC 1, 2, 14, 34, 39;**
DAM POET
See also CA 1-4R; 116; CANR 2, 55;
DLB 48

Militant
See Sandburg, Carl (August)

Mill, John Stuart 1806-1873 . . **NCLC 11, 58**
See also CDBLB 1832-1890; DLB 55

Millar, Kenneth
1915-1983 . . . . **CLC 14; DAM POP**
See also Macdonald, Ross
See also CA 9-12R; 110; CANR 16; DLB 2;
DLBD 6; DLBY 83; MTCW

Millay, E. Vincent
See Millay, Edna St. Vincent

Millay, Edna St. Vincent
1892-1950 . . . . . . **TCLC 4, 49; DA; DAB;**
DAC; DAM MST, POET; PC 6
See also CA 104; 130; CDALB 1917-1929;
DLB 45; MTCW

Miller, Arthur
1915- . . . . **CLC 1, 2, 6, 10, 15, 26, 47, 78;**
DA; DAB; DAC; DAM DRAM, MST;
DC 1; WLC
See also AAYA 15; AITN 1; CA 1-4R;
CABS 3; CANR 2, 30, 54;
CDALB 1941-1968; DLB 7; MTCW

Miller, Henry (Valentine)
1891-1980 . . . . **CLC 1, 2, 4, 9, 14, 43, 84;**
DA; DAB; DAC; DAM MST, NOV;
WLC
See also CA 9-12R; 97-100; CANR 33;
CDALB 1929-1941; DLB 4, 9; DLBY 80;
MTCW

Miller, Jason 1939(?)- . . . . **CLC 2**
See also AITN 1; CA 73-76; DLB 7

Miller, Sue 1943- . . . . . **CLC 44; DAM POP**
See also BEST 90:3; CA 139; DLB 143

Miller, Walter M(ichael, Jr.)
1923- . . . . **CLC 4, 30**
See also CA 85-88; DLB 8

Millett, Kate 1934- . . . . **CLC 67**
See also AITN 1; CA 73-76; CANR 32, 53;
MTCW

Millhauser, Steven 1943- . . . . **CLC 21, 54**
See also CA 110; 111; DLB 2; INT 111

Millin, Sarah Gertrude 1889-1968 . . **CLC 49**
See also CA 102; 93-96

Milne, A(lan) A(lexander)
1882-1956 . . . . **TCLC 6; DAB; DAC;**
DAM MST
See also CA 104; 133; CLR 1, 26; DLB 10,
77, 100, 160; MAICYA; MTCW;
YABC 1

Milner, Ron(ald)
1938- . . . . . **CLC 56; BLC; DAM MULT**
See also AITN 1; BW 1; CA 73-76;
CANR 24; DLB 38; MTCW

Milosz, Czeslaw
1911- . . . . **CLC 5, 11, 22, 31, 56, 82;**
DAM MST, POET; PC 8
See also CA 81-84; CANR 23, 51; MTCW

Milton, John
1608-1674 . . . . . . **LC 9; DA; DAB; DAC;**
DAM MST, POET; WLC
See also CDBLB 1660-1789; DLB 131, 151

Min, Anchee 1957- . . . . **CLC 86**
See also CA 146

Minehaha, Cornelius
See Wedekind, (Benjamin) Frank(lin)

Miner, Valerie 1947- . . . . **CLC 40**
See also CA 97-100

Minimo, Duca
See D'Annunzio, Gabriele

Minot, Susan 1956- . . . . **CLC 44**
See also CA 134

Minus, Ed 1938- . . . . **CLC 39**

Miranda, Javier
See Bioy Casares, Adolfo

Mirbeau, Octave 1848-1917 . . . . **TCLC 55**
See also DLB 123

Miro (Ferrer), Gabriel (Francisco Victor)
1879-1930 .... **TCLC 5**
See also CA 104

Mishima, Yukio
...... **CLC 2, 4, 6, 9, 27; DC 1; SSC 4**
See also Hiraoka, Kimitake

Mistral, Frederic 1830-1914 ...... **TCLC 51**
See also CA 122

Mistral, Gabriela........... **TCLC 2; HLC**
See also Godoy Alcayaga, Lucila

Mistry, Rohinton 1952- ...... **CLC 71; DAC**
See also CA 141

Mitchell, Clyde
See Ellison, Harlan (Jay); Silverberg, Robert

Mitchell, James Leslie 1901-1935
See Gibbon, Lewis Grassic
See also CA 104; DLB 15

Mitchell, Joni 1943- .... **CLC 12**
See also CA 112

Mitchell, Joseph (Quincy)
1908-1996 .... **CLC 98**
See also CA 77-80; 152

Mitchell, Margaret (Munnerlyn)
1900-1949 ...... **TCLC 11; DAM NOV,
POP**
See also CA 109; 125; CANR 55; DLB 9;
MTCW

Mitchell, Peggy
See Mitchell, Margaret (Munnerlyn)

Mitchell, S(ilas) Weir 1829-1914 .. **TCLC 36**

Mitchell, W(illiam) O(rmond)
1914- ...... **CLC 25; DAC; DAM MST**
See also CA 77-80; CANR 15, 43; DLB 88

Mitford, Mary Russell 1787-1855.. **NCLC 4**
See also DLB 110, 116

Mitford, Nancy 1904-1973........ **CLC 44**
See also CA 9-12R

Miyamoto, Yuriko 1899-1951 ..... **TCLC 37**

Mo, Timothy (Peter) 1950(?)- ...... **CLC 46**
See also CA 117; MTCW

Modarressi, Taghi (M.) 1931- ...... **CLC 44**
See also CA 121; 134; INT 134

Modiano, Patrick (Jean) 1945- ..... **CLC 18**
See also CA 85-88; CANR 17, 40; DLB 83

Moerck, Paal
See Roelvaag, O(le) E(dvart)

Mofolo, Thomas (Mokopu)
1875(?)-1948 .... **TCLC 22; BLC;
DAM MULT**
See also CA 121; 153

Mohr, Nicholasa
1935- ..... **CLC 12; DAM MULT; HLC**
See also AAYA 8; CA 49-52; CANR 1, 32;
CLR 22; DLB 145; HW; JRDA; SAAS 8;
SATA 8

Mojtabai, A(nn) G(race)
1938- .... **CLC 5, 9, 15, 29**
See also CA 85-88

Moliere
1622-1673 ..... **LC 28; DA; DAB; DAC;
DAM DRAM, MST; WLC**

Molin, Charles
See Mayne, William (James Carter)

Molnar, Ferenc
1878-1952 ..... **TCLC 20; DAM DRAM**
See also CA 109; 153

Momaday, N(avarre) Scott
1934- ..... **CLC 2, 19, 85, 95; DA; DAB;
DAC; DAM MST, MULT, NOV, POP**
See also AAYA 11; CA 25-28R; CANR 14,
34; DLB 143; INT CANR-14; MTCW;
NNAL; SATA 48; SATA-Brief 30

Monette, Paul 1945-1995......... **CLC 82**
See also CA 139; 147

Monroe, Harriet 1860-1936...... **TCLC 12**
See also CA 109; DLB 54, 91

Monroe, Lyle
See Heinlein, Robert A(nson)

Montagu, Elizabeth 1917- .... **NCLC 7**
See also CA 9-12R

Montagu, Mary (Pierrepont) Wortley
1689-1762 .... **LC 9; PC 16**
See also DLB 95, 101

Montagu, W. H.
See Coleridge, Samuel Taylor

Montague, John (Patrick)
1929- .... **CLC 13, 46**
See also CA 9-12R; CANR 9; DLB 40;
MTCW

Montaigne, Michel (Eyquem) de
1533-1592 ...... **LC 8; DA; DAB; DAC;
DAM MST; WLC**

Montale, Eugenio
1896-1981 .... **CLC 7, 9, 18; PC 13**
See also CA 17-20R; 104; CANR 30;
DLB 114; MTCW

Montesquieu, Charles-Louis de Secondat
1689-1755 .... **LC 7**

Montgomery, (Robert) Bruce 1921-1978
See Crispin, Edmund
See also CA 104

Montgomery, L(ucy) M(aud)
1874-1942 .... **TCLC 51; DAC;
DAM MST**
See also AAYA 12; CA 108; 137; CLR 8;
DLB 92; DLBD 14; JRDA; MAICYA;
YABC 1

Montgomery, Marion H., Jr. 1925-.. **CLC 7**
See also AITN 1; CA 1-4R; CANR 3, 48;
DLB 6

Montgomery, Max
See Davenport, Guy (Mattison, Jr.)

Montherlant, Henry (Milon) de
1896-1972 .... **CLC 8, 19; DAM DRAM**
See also CA 85-88; 37-40R; DLB 72;
MTCW

Monty Python
See Chapman, Graham; Cleese, John
(Marwood); Gilliam, Terry (Vance); Idle,
Eric; Jones, Terence Graham Parry; Palin,
Michael (Edward)
See also AAYA 7

Moodie, Susanna (Strickland)
1803-1885 .... **NCLC 14**
See also DLB 99

Mooney, Edward 1951-
See Mooney, Ted
See also CA 130

Mooney, Ted .... **CLC 25**
See also Mooney, Edward

Moorcock, Michael (John)
1939- .... **CLC 5, 27, 58**
See also CA 45-48; CAAS 5; CANR 2, 17,
38; DLB 14; MTCW

Moore, Brian
1921- ...... **CLC 1, 3, 5, 7, 8, 19, 32, 90;
DAB; DAC; DAM MST**
See also CA 1-4R; CANR 1, 25, 42; MTCW

Moore, Edward
See Muir, Edwin

Moore, George Augustus
1852-1933 .... **TCLC 7; SSC 19**
See also CA 104; DLB 10, 18, 57, 135

Moore, Lorrie .... **CLC 39, 45, 68**
See also Moore, Marie Lorena

Moore, Marianne (Craig)
1887-1972 ..... **CLC 1, 2, 4, 8, 10, 13, 19,
47; DA; DAB; DAC; DAM MST, POET;
PC 4**
See also CA 1-4R; 33-36R; CANR 3;
CDALB 1929-1941; DLB 45; DLBD 7;
MTCW; SATA 20

Moore, Marie Lorena 1957-
See Moore, Lorrie
See also CA 116; CANR 39

Moore, Thomas 1779-1852....... **NCLC 6**
See also DLB 96, 144

Morand, Paul 1888-1976 .. **CLC 41; SSC 22**
See also CA 69-72; DLB 65

Morante, Elsa 1918-1985........ **CLC 8, 47**
See also CA 85-88; 117; CANR 35; MTCW

Moravia, Alberto....... **CLC 2, 7, 11, 27, 46**
See also Pincherle, Alberto

More, Hannah 1745-1833 .... **NCLC 27**
See also DLB 107, 109, 116, 158

More, Henry 1614-1687............. **LC 9**
See also DLB 126

More, Sir Thomas 1478-1535 .... **LC 10, 32**

Moreas, Jean.................... **TCLC 18**
See also Papadiamantopoulos, Johannes

Morgan, Berry 1919- .... **CLC 6**
See also CA 49-52; DLB 6

Morgan, Claire
See Highsmith, (Mary) Patricia

Morgan, Edwin (George) 1920-..... **CLC 31**
See also CA 5-8R; CANR 3, 43; DLB 27

Morgan, (George) Frederick
1922- .... **CLC 23**
See also CA 17-20R; CANR 21

Morgan, Harriet
See Mencken, H(enry) L(ouis)

Morgan, Jane
See Cooper, James Fenimore

Morgan, Janet 1945- .... **CLC 39**
See also CA 65-68

Morgan, Lady 1776(?)-1859...... **NCLC 29**
See also DLB 116, 158

Morgan, Robin 1941- .... **CLC 2**
See also CA 69-72; CANR 29; MTCW;
SATA 80

Morgan, Scott
See Kuttner, Henry

Morgan, Seth 1949(?)-1990 . . . . **CLC 65**
See also CA 132

Morgenstern, Christian
1871-1914 . . . . **TCLC 8**
See also CA 105

Morgenstern, S.
See Goldman, William (W.)

Moricz, Zsigmond 1879-1942 . . . . . **TCLC 33**

Morike, Eduard (Friedrich)
1804-1875 . . . . **NCLC 10**
See also DLB 133

Mori Ogai . . . . **TCLC 14**
See also Mori Rintaro

Mori Rintaro 1862-1922
See Mori Ogai
See also CA 110

Moritz, Karl Philipp 1756-1793 . . . . . . **LC 2**
See also DLB 94

Morland, Peter Henry
See Faust, Frederick (Schiller)

Morren, Theophil
See Hofmannsthal, Hugo von

Morris, Bill 1952- . . . . **CLC 76**

Morris, Julian
See West, Morris L(anglo)

Morris, Steveland Judkins 1950(?)-
See Wonder, Stevie
See also CA 111

Morris, William 1834-1896 . . . . **NCLC 4**
See also CDBLB 1832-1890; DLB 18, 35,
57, 156

Morris, Wright 1910- . . . **CLC 1, 3, 7, 18, 37**
See also CA 9-12R; CANR 21; DLB 2;
DLBY 81; MTCW

Morrison, Chloe Anthony Wofford
See Morrison, Toni

Morrison, James Douglas 1943-1971
See Morrison, Jim
See also CA 73-76; CANR 40

Morrison, Jim . . . . **CLC 17**
See also Morrison, James Douglas

Morrison, Toni
1931- . . . . **CLC 4, 10, 22, 55, 81, 87;**
BLC; DA; DAB; DAC; DAM MST,
MULT, NOV, POP
See also AAYA 1; BW 2; CA 29-32R;
CANR 27, 42; CDALB 1968-1988;
DLB 6, 33, 143; DLBY 81; MTCW;
SATA 57

Morrison, Van 1945- . . . . **CLC 21**
See also CA 116

Mortimer, John (Clifford)
1923- . . . . . . **CLC 28, 43; DAM DRAM,**
POP
See also CA 13-16R; CANR 21;
CDBLB 1960 to Present; DLB 13;
INT CANR-21; MTCW

Mortimer, Penelope (Ruth) 1918- . . . . **CLC 5**
See also CA 57-60; CANR 45

Morton, Anthony
See Creasey, John

Mosher, Howard Frank 1943- . . . . . . **CLC 62**
See also CA 139

Mosley, Nicholas 1923- . . . . **CLC 43, 70**
See also CA 69-72; CANR 41; DLB 14

Mosley, Walter
1952- . . . . . **CLC 97; DAM MULT, POP**
See also AAYA 17; BW 2; CA 142

Moss, Howard
1922-1987 . . . . **CLC 7, 14, 45, 50;**
DAM POET
See also CA 1-4R; 123; CANR 1, 44;
DLB 5

Mossgiel, Rab
See Burns, Robert

Motion, Andrew (Peter) 1952- . . . . . . **CLC 47**
See also CA 146; DLB 40

Motley, Willard (Francis)
1909-1965 . . . . **CLC 18**
See also BW 1; CA 117; 106; DLB 76, 143

Motoori, Norinaga 1730-1801 . . . . **NCLC 45**

Mott, Michael (Charles Alston)
1930- . . . . **CLC 15, 34**
See also CA 5-8R; CAAS 7; CANR 7, 29

Mountain Wolf Woman
1884-1960 . . . . **CLC 92**
See also CA 144; NNAL

Moure, Erin 1955- . . . . **CLC 88**
See also CA 113; DLB 60

Mowat, Farley (McGill)
1921- . . . . . . **CLC 26; DAC; DAM MST**
See also AAYA 1; CA 1-4R; CANR 4, 24,
42; CLR 20; DLB 68; INT CANR-24;
JRDA; MAICYA; MTCW; SATA 3, 55

Moyers, Bill 1934- . . . . **CLC 74**
See also AITN 2; CA 61-64; CANR 31, 52

Mphahlele, Es'kia
See Mphahlele, Ezekiel
See also DLB 125

Mphahlele, Ezekiel
1919- . . . . . **CLC 25; BLC; DAM MULT**
See also Mphahlele, Es'kia
See also BW 2; CA 81-84; CANR 26

Mqhayi, S(amuel) E(dward) K(rune Loliwe)
1875-1945 . . . . **TCLC 25; BLC;**
DAM MULT
See also CA 153

Mrozek, Slawomir 1930- . . . . **CLC 3, 13**
See also CA 13-16R; CAAS 10; CANR 29;
MTCW

Mrs. Belloc-Lowndes
See Lowndes, Marie Adelaide (Belloc)

Mtwa, Percy (?)- . . . . **CLC 47**

Mueller, Lisel 1924- . . . . **CLC 13, 51**
See also CA 93-96; DLB 105

Muir, Edwin 1887-1959 . . . . **TCLC 2**
See also CA 104; DLB 20, 100

Muir, John 1838-1914 . . . . **TCLC 28**

Mujica Lainez, Manuel
1910-1984 . . . . **CLC 31**
See also Lainez, Manuel Mujica
See also CA 81-84; 112; CANR 32; HW

Mukherjee, Bharati
1940- . . . . **CLC 53; DAM NOV**
See also BEST 89:2; CA 107; CANR 45;
DLB 60; MTCW

Muldoon, Paul
1951- . . . . **CLC 32, 72; DAM POET**
See also CA 113; 129; CANR 52; DLB 40;
INT 129

Mulisch, Harry 1927- . . . . **CLC 42**
See also CA 9-12R; CANR 6, 26

Mull, Martin 1943- . . . . **CLC 17**
See also CA 105

Mulock, Dinah Maria
See Craik, Dinah Maria (Mulock)

Munford, Robert 1737(?)-1783 . . . . **LC 5**
See also DLB 31

Mungo, Raymond 1946- . . . . **CLC 72**
See also CA 49-52; CANR 2

Munro, Alice
1931- . . . . . . **CLC 6, 10, 19, 50, 95; DAC;**
DAM MST, NOV; SSC 3
See also AITN 2; CA 33-36R; CANR 33,
53; DLB 53; MTCW; SATA 29

Munro, H(ector) H(ugh) 1870-1916
See Saki
See also CA 104; 130; CDBLB 1890-1914;
DA; DAB; DAC; DAM MST, NOV;
DLB 34, 162; MTCW; WLC

Murasaki, Lady . . . . **CMLC 1**

Murdoch, (Jean) Iris
1919- . . . . **CLC 1, 2, 3, 4, 6, 8, 11, 15,**
22, 31, 51; DAB; DAC; DAM MST,
NOV
See also CA 13-16R; CANR 8, 43;
CDBLB 1960 to Present; DLB 14;
INT CANR-8; MTCW

Murfree, Mary Noailles
1850-1922 . . . . **SSC 22**
See also CA 122; DLB 12, 74

Murnau, Friedrich Wilhelm
See Plumpe, Friedrich Wilhelm

Murphy, Richard 1927- . . . . **CLC 41**
See also CA 29-32R; DLB 40

Murphy, Sylvia 1937- . . . . **CLC 34**
See also CA 121

Murphy, Thomas (Bernard) 1935- . . . **CLC 51**
See also CA 101

Murray, Albert L. 1916- . . . . **CLC 73**
See also BW 2; CA 49-52; CANR 26, 52;
DLB 38

Murray, Les(lie) A(llan)
1938- . . . . **CLC 40; DAM POET**
See also CA 21-24R; CANR 11, 27

Murry, J. Middleton
See Murry, John Middleton

Murry, John Middleton
1889-1957 . . . . **TCLC 16**
See also CA 118; DLB 149

Musgrave, Susan 1951- . . . . **CLC 13, 54**
See also CA 69-72; CANR 45

Musil, Robert (Edler von)
1880-1942 . . . . **TCLC 12, 68; SSC 18**
See also CA 109; CANR 55; DLB 81, 124

Muske, Carol 1945- . . . . **CLC 90**
See also Muske-Dukes, Carol (Anne)

Muske-Dukes, Carol (Anne) 1945-
See Muske, Carol
See also CA 65-68; CANR 32

Musset, (Louis Charles) Alfred de
1810-1857 . . . . NCLC 7

My Brother's Brother
See Chekhov, Anton (Pavlovich)

Myers, L. H. 1881-1944. . . . . TCLC 59
See also DLB 15

Myers, Walter Dean
1937- . . . . . CLC 35; BLC; DAM MULT,
NOV
See also AAYA 4; BW 2; CA 33-36R;
CANR 20, 42; CLR 4, 16, 35; DLB 33;
INT CANR-20; JRDA; MAICYA;
SAAS 2; SATA 41, 71; SATA-Brief 27

Myers, Walter M.
See Myers, Walter Dean

Myles, Symon
See Follett, Ken(neth Martin)

Nabokov, Vladimir (Vladimirovich)
1899-1977 . . . . . CLC 1, 2, 3, 6, 8, 11, 15,
23, 44, 46, 64; DA; DAB; DAC;
DAM MST, NOV; SSC 11; WLC
See also CA 5-8R; 69-72; CANR 20;
CDALB 1941-1968; DLB 2; DLBD 3;
DLBY 80, 91; MTCW

Nagai Kafu. . . . . TCLC 51
See also Nagai Sokichi

Nagai Sokichi 1879-1959
See Nagai Kafu
See also CA 117

Nagy, Laszlo 1925-1978. . . . . CLC 7
See also CA 129; 112

Naipaul, Shiva(dhar Srinivasa)
1945-1985 . . . . . CLC 32, 39; DAM NOV
See also CA 110; 112; 116; CANR 33;
DLB 157; DLBY 85; MTCW

Naipaul, V(idiadhar) S(urajprasad)
1932- . . . . CLC 4, 7, 9, 13, 18, 37; DAB;
DAC; DAM MST, NOV
See also CA 1-4R; CANR 1, 33, 51;
CDBLB 1960 to Present; DLB 125;
DLBY 85; MTCW

Nakos, Lilika 1899(?)- . . . . CLC 29

Narayan, R(asipuram) K(rishnaswami)
1906- . . . . CLC 7, 28, 47; DAM NOV
See also CA 81-84; CANR 33; MTCW;
SATA 62

Nash, (Frediric) Ogden
1902-1971 . . . . . . CLC 23; DAM POET
See also CA 13-14; 29-32R; CANR 34;
CAP 1; DLB 11; MAICYA; MTCW;
SATA 2, 46

Nathan, Daniel
See Dannay, Frederic

Nathan, George Jean 1882-1958. . . TCLC 18
See also Hatteras, Owen
See also CA 114; DLB 137

Natsume, Kinnosuke 1867-1916
See Natsume, Soseki
See also CA 104

Natsume, Soseki . . . . TCLC 2, 10
See also Natsume, Kinnosuke

Natti, (Mary) Lee 1919-
See Kingman, Lee
See also CA 5-8R; CANR 2

Naylor, Gloria
1950- . . . . . CLC 28, 52; BLC; DA; DAC;
DAM MST, MULT, NOV, POP
See also AAYA 6; BW 2; CA 107;
CANR 27, 51; DLB 173; MTCW

Neihardt, John Gneisenau
1881-1973 . . . . CLC 32
See also CA 13-14; CAP 1; DLB 9, 54

Nekrasov, Nikolai Alekseevich
1821-1878 . . . . NCLC 11

Nelligan, Emile 1879-1941. . . . . . . TCLC 14
See also CA 114; DLB 92

Nelson, Willie 1933- . . . . CLC 17
See also CA 107

Nemerov, Howard (Stanley)
1920-1991 . . . . CLC 2, 6, 9, 36;
DAM POET
See also CA 1-4R; 134; CABS 2; CANR 1,
27, 53; DLB 5, 6; DLBY 83;
INT CANR-27; MTCW

Neruda, Pablo
1904-1973 . . . . . CLC 1, 2, 5, 7, 9, 28, 62;
DA; DAB; DAC; DAM MST, MULT,
POET; HLC; PC 4; WLC
See also CA 19-20; 45-48; CAP 2; HW;
MTCW

Nerval, Gerard de
1808-1855 . . . . . NCLC 1; PC 13; SSC 18

Nervo, (Jose) Amado (Ruiz de)
1870-1919 . . . . TCLC 11
See also CA 109; 131; HW

Nessi, Pio Baroja y
See Baroja (y Nessi), Pio

Nestroy, Johann 1801-1862 . . . . . . NCLC 42
See also DLB 133

Neufeld, John (Arthur) 1938- . . . . . . CLC 17
See also AAYA 11; CA 25-28R; CANR 11,
37; MAICYA; SAAS 3; SATA 6, 81

Neville, Emily Cheney 1919- . . . . CLC 12
See also CA 5-8R; CANR 3, 37; JRDA;
MAICYA; SAAS 2; SATA 1

Newbound, Bernard Slade 1930-
See Slade, Bernard
See also CA 81-84; CANR 49;
DAM DRAM

Newby, P(ercy) H(oward)
1918- . . . . CLC 2, 13; DAM NOV
See also CA 5-8R; CANR 32; DLB 15;
MTCW

Newlove, Donald 1928- . . . . CLC 6
See also CA 29-32R; CANR 25

Newlove, John (Herbert) 1938- . . . . . CLC 14
See also CA 21-24R; CANR 9, 25

Newman, Charles 1938- . . . . CLC 2, 8
See also CA 21-24R

Newman, Edwin (Harold) 1919- . . . . CLC 14
See also AITN 1; CA 69-72; CANR 5

Newman, John Henry
1801-1890 . . . . NCLC 38
See also DLB 18, 32, 55

Newton, Suzanne 1936- . . . . CLC 35
See also CA 41-44R; CANR 14; JRDA;
SATA 5, 77

Nexo, Martin Andersen
1869-1954 . . . . TCLC 43

Nezval, Vitezslav 1900-1958 . . . . . . TCLC 44
See also CA 123

Ng, Fae Myenne 1957(?)- . . . . CLC 81
See also CA 146

Ngema, Mbongeni 1955- . . . . CLC 57
See also BW 2; CA 143

Ngugi, James T(hiong'o). . . . . CLC 3, 7, 13
See also Ngugi wa Thiong'o

Ngugi wa Thiong'o
1938- . . . . . CLC 36; BLC; DAM MULT,
NOV
See also Ngugi, James T(hiong'o)
See also BW 2; CA 81-84; CANR 27;
DLB 125; MTCW

Nichol, B(arrie) P(hillip)
1944-1988 . . . . CLC 18
See also CA 53-56; DLB 53; SATA 66

Nichols, John (Treadwell) 1940- . . . . CLC 38
See also CA 9-12R; CAAS 2; CANR 6;
DLBY 82

Nichols, Leigh
See Koontz, Dean R(ay)

Nichols, Peter (Richard)
1927- . . . . CLC 5, 36, 65
See also CA 104; CANR 33; DLB 13;
MTCW

Nicolas, F. R. E.
See Freeling, Nicolas

Niedecker, Lorine
1903-1970 . . . . CLC 10, 42; DAM POET
See also CA 25-28; CAP 2; DLB 48

Nietzsche, Friedrich (Wilhelm)
1844-1900 . . . . TCLC 10, 18, 55
See also CA 107; 121; DLB 129

Nievo, Ippolito 1831-1861 . . . . NCLC 22

Nightingale, Anne Redmon 1943-
See Redmon, Anne
See also CA 103

Nik. T. O.
See Annensky, Innokenty Fyodorovich

Nin, Anais
1903-1977 . . . . . . CLC 1, 4, 8, 11, 14, 60;
DAM NOV, POP; SSC 10
See also AITN 2; CA 13-16R; 69-72;
CANR 22, 53; DLB 2, 4, 152; MTCW

Nishiwaki, Junzaburo 1894-1982 . . . . PC 15
See also CA 107

Nissenson, Hugh 1933- . . . . CLC 4, 9
See also CA 17-20R; CANR 27; DLB 28

Niven, Larry . . . . CLC 8
See also Niven, Laurence Van Cott
See also DLB 8

Niven, Laurence Van Cott 1938-
See Niven, Larry
See also CA 21-24R; CAAS 12; CANR 14,
44; DAM POP; MTCW

Nixon, Agnes Eckhardt 1927- . . . . . . CLC 21
See also CA 110

Nizan, Paul 1905-1940 . . . . TCLC 40
See also DLB 72

Nkosi, Lewis
1936- . . . . . CLC 45; BLC; DAM MULT
See also BW 1; CA 65-68; CANR 27;
DLB 157

Nodier, (Jean) Charles (Emmanuel)
1780-1844 .... **NCLC 19**
See also DLB 119

Nolan, Christopher 1965- .... **CLC 58**
See also CA 111

Noon, Jeff 1957- .... **CLC 91**
See also CA 148

Norden, Charles
See Durrell, Lawrence (George)

Nordhoff, Charles (Bernard)
1887-1947 .... **TCLC 23**
See also CA 108; DLB 9; SATA 23

Norfolk, Lawrence 1963- .... **CLC 76**
See also CA 144

Norman, Marsha
1947- .... **CLC 28; DAM DRAM**
See also CA 105; CABS 3; CANR 41;
DLBY 84

Norris, Benjamin Franklin, Jr.
1870-1902 .... **TCLC 24**
See also Norris, Frank
See also CA 110

Norris, Frank
See Norris, Benjamin Franklin, Jr.
See also CDALB 1865-1917; DLB 12, 71

Norris, Leslie 1921- .... **CLC 14**
See also CA 11-12; CANR 14; CAP 1;
DLB 27

North, Andrew
See Norton, Andre

North, Anthony
See Koontz, Dean R(ay)

North, Captain George
See Stevenson, Robert Louis (Balfour)

North, Milou
See Erdrich, Louise

Northrup, B. A.
See Hubbard, L(afayette) Ron(ald)

North Staffs
See Hulme, T(homas) E(rnest)

Norton, Alice Mary
See Norton, Andre
See also MAICYA; SATA 1, 43

Norton, Andre 1912- .... **CLC 12**
See also Norton, Alice Mary
See also AAYA 14; CA 1-4R; CANR 2, 31;
DLB 8, 52; JRDA; MTCW; SATA 91

Norton, Caroline 1808-1877 ...... **NCLC 47**
See also DLB 21, 159

Norway, Nevil Shute 1899-1960
See Shute, Nevil
See also CA 102; 93-96

Norwid, Cyprian Kamil
1821-1883 .... **NCLC 17**

Nosille, Nabrah
See Ellison, Harlan (Jay)

Nossack, Hans Erich 1901-1978 ..... **CLC 6**
See also CA 93-96; 85-88; DLB 69

Nostradamus 1503-1566 .... **LC 27**

Nosu, Chuji
See Ozu, Yasujiro

Notenburg, Eleanora (Genrikhovna) von
See Guro, Elena

Nova, Craig 1945- .... **CLC 7, 31**
See also CA 45-48; CANR 2, 53

Novak, Joseph
See Kosinski, Jerzy (Nikodem)

Novalis 1772-1801 .... **NCLC 13**
See also DLB 90

Nowlan, Alden (Albert)
1933-1983 .. **CLC 15; DAC; DAM MST**
See also CA 9-12R; CANR 5; DLB 53

Noyes, Alfred 1880-1958 .... **TCLC 7**
See also CA 104; DLB 20

Nunn, Kem 19(?)- .... **CLC 34**

Nye, Robert
1939- .... **CLC 13, 42; DAM NOV**
See also CA 33-36R; CANR 29; DLB 14;
MTCW; SATA 6

Nyro, Laura 1947- .... **CLC 17**

Oates, Joyce Carol
1938- ...... **CLC 1, 2, 3, 6, 9. 11, 15, 19,
33, 52; DA; DAB; DAC; DAM MST,
NOV, POP; SSC 6; WLC**
See also AAYA 15; AITN 1; BEST 89:2;
CA 5-8R; CANR 25, 45;
CDALB 1968-1988; DLB 2, 5, 130;
DLBY 81; INT CANR-25; MTCW

O'Brien, Darcy 1939- .... **CLC 11**
See also CA 21-24R; CANR 8

O'Brien, E. G.
See Clarke, Arthur C(harles)

O'Brien, Edna
1936- .... **CLC 3, 5, 8, 13, 36, 65;
DAM NOV; SSC 10**
See also CA 1-4R; CANR 6, 41;
CDBLB 1960 to Present; DLB 14;
MTCW

O'Brien, Fitz-James 1828-1862 ... **NCLC 21**
See also DLB 74

O'Brien, Flann .... **CLC 1, 4, 5, 7, 10, 47**
See also O Nuallain, Brian

O'Brien, Richard 1942- .... **CLC 17**
See also CA 124

O'Brien, Tim
1946- .... **CLC 7, 19, 40; DAM POP**
See also AAYA 16; CA 85-88; CANR 40;
DLB 152; DLBD 9; DLBY 80

Obstfelder, Sigbjoern 1866-1900 ... **TCLC 23**
See also CA 123

O'Casey, Sean
1880-1964 ...... **CLC 1, 5, 9, 11, 15, 88;
DAB; DAC; DAM DRAM, MST**
See also CA 89-92; CDBLB 1914-1945;
DLB 10; MTCW

O'Cathasaigh, Sean
See O'Casey, Sean

Ochs, Phil 1940-1976 .... **CLC 17**
See also CA 65-68

O'Connor, Edwin (Greene)
1918-1968 .... **CLC 14**
See also CA 93-96; 25-28R

O'Connor, (Mary) Flannery
1925-1964 .... **CLC 1, 2, 3, 6, 10, 13, 15,
21, 66; DA; DAB; DAC; DAM MST,
NOV; SSC 1, 23; WLC**
See also AAYA 7; CA 1-4R; CANR 3, 41;
CDALB 1941-1968; DLB 2, 152;
DLBD 12; DLBY 80; MTCW

O'Connor, Frank .... **CLC 23; SSC 5**
See also O'Donovan, Michael John
See also DLB 162

O'Dell, Scott 1898-1989 .... **CLC 30**
See also AAYA 3; CA 61-64; 129;
CANR 12, 30; CLR 1, 16; DLB 52;
JRDA; MAICYA; SATA 12, 60

Odets, Clifford
1906-1963 .... **CLC 2, 28, 98;
DAM DRAM; DC 6**
See also CA 85-88; DLB 7, 26; MTCW

O'Doherty, Brian 1934- .... **CLC 76**
See also CA 105

O'Donnell, K. M.
See Malzberg, Barry N(athaniel)

O'Donnell, Lawrence
See Kuttner, Henry

O'Donovan, Michael John
1903-1966 .... **CLC 14**
See also O'Connor, Frank
See also CA 93-96

Oe, Kenzaburo
1935- ..... **CLC 10, 36, 86; DAM NOV;
SSC 20**
See also CA 97-100; CANR 36, 50;
DLBY 94; MTCW

O'Faolain, Julia 1932- .... **CLC 6, 19, 47**
See also CA 81-84; CAAS 2; CANR 12;
DLB 14; MTCW

O'Faolain, Sean
1900-1991 .... **CLC 1, 7, 14, 32, 70;
SSC 13**
See also CA 61-64; 134; CANR 12;
DLB 15, 162; MTCW

O'Flaherty, Liam
1896-1984 .... **CLC 5, 34; SSC 6**
See also CA 101; 113; CANR 35; DLB 36,
162; DLBY 84; MTCW

Ogilvy, Gavin
See Barrie, J(ames) M(atthew)

O'Grady, Standish James
1846-1928 .... **TCLC 5**
See also CA 104

O'Grady, Timothy 1951- .... **CLC 59**
See also CA 138

O'Hara, Frank
1926-1966 .... **CLC 2, 5, 13, 78;
DAM POET**
See also CA 9-12R; 25-28R; CANR 33;
DLB 5, 16; MTCW

O'Hara, John (Henry)
1905-1970 .... **CLC 1, 2, 3, 6, 11, 42;
DAM NOV; SSC 15**
See also CA 5-8R; 25-28R; CANR 31;
CDALB 1929-1941; DLB 9, 86; DLBD 2;
MTCW

O Hehir, Diana 1922- .... **CLC 41**
See also CA 93-96

Okigbo, Christopher (Ifenayichukwu)
1932-1967 . . . . CLC **25, 84; BLC;**
DAM MULT, POET; PC 7
See also BW 1; CA 77-80; DLB 125;
MTCW

Okri, Ben 1959- . . . . CLC **87**
See also BW 2; CA 130; 138; DLB 157;
INT 138

Olds, Sharon
1942- . . . . . CLC **32, 39, 85; DAM POET**
See also CA 101; CANR 18, 41; DLB 120

Oldstyle, Jonathan
See Irving, Washington

Olesha, Yuri (Karlovich)
1899-1960 . . . . CLC **8**
See also CA 85-88

Oliphant, Laurence
1829(?)-1888 . . . . NCLC **47**
See also DLB 18, 166

Oliphant, Margaret (Oliphant Wilson)
1828-1897 . . . . NCLC **11**
See also DLB 18, 159

Oliver, Mary 1935- . . . . CLC **19, 34, 98**
See also CA 21-24R; CANR 9, 43; DLB 5

Olivier, Laurence (Kerr)
1907-1989 . . . . CLC **20**
See also CA 111; 150; 129

Olsen, Tillie
1913- . . . . . CLC **4, 13; DA; DAB; DAC;**
DAM MST; SSC 11
See also CA 1-4R; CANR 1, 43; DLB 28;
DLBY 80; MTCW

Olson, Charles (John)
1910-1970 . . . . . CLC **1, 2, 5, 6, 9, 11, 29;**
DAM POET
See also CA 13-16; 25-28R; CABS 2;
CANR 35; CAP 1; DLB 5, 16; MTCW

Olson, Toby 1937- . . . . CLC **28**
See also CA 65-68; CANR 9, 31

Olyesha, Yuri
See Olesha, Yuri (Karlovich)

Ondaatje, (Philip) Michael
1943- . . . . CLC **14, 29, 51, 76; DAB;**
DAC; DAM MST
See also CA 77-80; CANR 42; DLB 60

Oneal, Elizabeth 1934-
See Oneal, Zibby
See also CA 106; CANR 28; MAICYA;
SATA 30, 82

Oneal, Zibby . . . . CLC **30**
See also Oneal, Elizabeth
See also AAYA 5; CLR 13; JRDA

O'Neill, Eugene (Gladstone)
1888-1953 . . . . . . TCLC **1, 6, 27, 49; DA;**
DAB; DAC; DAM DRAM, MST; WLC
See also AITN 1; CA 110; 132;
CDALB 1929-1941; DLB 7; MTCW

Onetti, Juan Carlos
1909-1994 . . . . CLC **7, 10; DAM MULT,**
NOV; SSC 23
See also CA 85-88; 145; CANR 32;
DLB 113; HW; MTCW

O Nuallain, Brian 1911-1966
See O'Brien, Flann
See also CA 21-22; 25-28R; CAP 2

Oppen, George 1908-1984 . . . . CLC **7, 13, 34**
See also CA 13-16R; 113; CANR 8; DLB 5,
165

Oppenheim, E(dward) Phillips
1866-1946 . . . . TCLC **45**
See also CA 111; DLB 70

Origen c. 185-c. 254 . . . . CMLC **19**

Orlovitz, Gil 1918-1973 . . . . CLC **22**
See also CA 77-80; 45-48; DLB 2, 5

Orris
See Ingelow, Jean

Ortega y Gasset, Jose
1883-1955 . . . . . TCLC **9; DAM MULT;**
HLC
See also CA 106; 130; HW; MTCW

Ortese, Anna Maria 1914- . . . . CLC **89**

Ortiz, Simon J(oseph)
1941- . . . . CLC **45; DAM MULT,**
POET; PC 17
See also CA 134; DLB 120; NNAL

Orton, Joe . . . . CLC **4, 13, 43; DC 3**
See also Orton, John Kingsley
See also CDBLB 1960 to Present; DLB 13

Orton, John Kingsley 1933-1967
See Orton, Joe
See also CA 85-88; CANR 35;
DAM DRAM; MTCW

Orwell, George
. . . . TCLC **2, 6, 15, 31, 51; DAB; WLC**
See also Blair, Eric (Arthur)
See also CDBLB 1945-1960; DLB 15, 98

Osborne, David
See Silverberg, Robert

Osborne, George
See Silverberg, Robert

Osborne, John (James)
1929-1994 . . . . . CLC **1, 2, 5, 11, 45; DA;**
DAB; DAC; DAM DRAM, MST; WLC
See also CA 13-16R; 147; CANR 21;
CDBLB 1945-1960; DLB 13; MTCW

Osborne, Lawrence 1958- . . . . CLC **50**

Oshima, Nagisa 1932- . . . . CLC **20**
See also CA 116; 121

Oskison, John Milton
1874-1947 . . . . . TCLC **35; DAM MULT**
See also CA 144; NNAL

Ossoli, Sarah Margaret (Fuller marchesa d')
1810-1850
See Fuller, Margaret
See also SATA 25

Ostrovsky, Alexander
1823-1886 . . . . NCLC **30, 57**

Otero, Blas de 1916-1979 . . . . CLC **11**
See also CA 89-92; DLB 134

Otto, Whitney 1955- . . . . CLC **70**
See also CA 140

Ouida . . . . TCLC **43**
See also De La Ramee, (Marie) Louise
See also DLB 18, 156

Ousmane, Sembene 1923- . . . . CLC **66; BLC**
See also BW 1; CA 117; 125; MTCW

Ovid
43B.C.-18(?) . . . CMLC **7; DAM POET;**
PC 2

Owen, Hugh
See Faust, Frederick (Schiller)

Owen, Wilfred (Edward Salter)
1893-1918 . . . . . . TCLC **5, 27; DA; DAB;**
DAC; DAM MST, POET; WLC
See also CA 104; 141; CDBLB 1914-1945;
DLB 20

Owens, Rochelle 1936- . . . . CLC **8**
See also CA 17-20R; CAAS 2; CANR 39

Oz, Amos
1939- . . . . CLC **5, 8, 11, 27, 33, 54;**
DAM NOV
See also CA 53-56; CANR 27, 47; MTCW

Ozick, Cynthia
1928- . . . . CLC **3, 7, 28, 62; DAM NOV,**
POP; SSC 15
See also BEST 90:1; CA 17-20R; CANR 23;
DLB 28, 152; DLBY 82; INT CANR-23;
MTCW

Ozu, Yasujiro 1903-1963 . . . . CLC **16**
See also CA 112

Pacheco, C.
See Pessoa, Fernando (Antonio Nogueira)

Pa Chin . . . . CLC **18**
See also Li Fei-kan

Pack, Robert 1929- . . . . CLC **13**
See also CA 1-4R; CANR 3, 44; DLB 5

Padgett, Lewis
See Kuttner, Henry

Padilla (Lorenzo), Heberto 1932- . . . CLC **38**
See also AITN 1; CA 123; 131; HW

Page, Jimmy 1944- . . . . CLC **12**

Page, Louise 1955- . . . . CLC **40**
See also CA 140

Page, P(atricia) K(athleen)
1916- . . . . CLC **7, 18; DAC; DAM MST;**
PC 12
See also CA 53-56; CANR 4, 22; DLB 68;
MTCW

Page, Thomas Nelson 1853-1922 . . . . SSC **23**
See also CA 118; DLB 12, 78; DLBD 13

Paget, Violet 1856-1935
See Lee, Vernon
See also CA 104

Paget-Lowe, Henry
See Lovecraft, H(oward) P(hillips)

Paglia, Camille (Anna) 1947- . . . . CLC **68**
See also CA 140

Paige, Richard
See Koontz, Dean R(ay)

Pakenham, Antonia
See Fraser, (Lady) Antonia (Pakenham)

Palamas, Kostes 1859-1943 . . . . TCLC **5**
See also CA 105

Palazzeschi, Aldo 1885-1974 . . . . CLC **11**
See also CA 89-92; 53-56; DLB 114

Paley, Grace
1922- . . . . CLC **4, 6, 37; DAM POP;**
SSC 8
See also CA 25-28R; CANR 13, 46;
DLB 28; INT CANR-13; MTCW

Palin, Michael (Edward) 1943- . . . . . CLC **21**
See also Monty Python
See also CA 107; CANR 35; SATA 67

Palliser, Charles 1947-........... **CLC 65**
See also CA 136

Palma, Ricardo 1833-1919....... **TCLC 29**

Pancake, Breece Dexter 1952-1979
See Pancake, Breece D'J
See also CA 123; 109

Pancake, Breece D'J............. **CLC 29**
See also Pancake, Breece Dexter
See also DLB 130

Panko, Rudy
See Gogol, Nikolai (Vasilyevich)

Papadiamantis, Alexandros
1851-1911 .... **TCLC 29**

Papadiamantopoulos, Johannes 1856-1910
See Moreas, Jean
See also CA 117

Papini, Giovanni 1881-1956...... **TCLC 22**
See also CA 121

Paracelsus 1493-1541............. **LC 14**

Parasol, Peter
See Stevens, Wallace

Parfenie, Maria
See Codrescu, Andrei

Parini, Jay (Lee) 1948- .... **CLC 54**
See also CA 97-100; CAAS 16; CANR 32

Park, Jordan
See Kornbluth, C(yril) M.; Pohl, Frederik

Parker, Bert
See Ellison, Harlan (Jay)

Parker, Dorothy (Rothschild)
1893-1967 .... **CLC 15, 68;**
DAM POET; SSC 2
See also CA 19-20; 25-28R; CAP 2;
DLB 11, 45, 86; MTCW

Parker, Robert B(rown)
1932- ...... **CLC 27; DAM NOV, POP**
See also BEST 89:4; CA 49-52; CANR 1,
26, 52; INT CANR-26; MTCW

Parkin, Frank 1940-.............. **CLC 43**
See also CA 147

Parkman, Francis, Jr.
1823-1893 .... **NCLC 12**
See also DLB 1, 30

Parks, Gordon (Alexander Buchanan)
1912- ... **CLC 1, 16; BLC; DAM MULT**
See also AITN 2; BW 2; CA 41-44R;
CANR 26; DLB 33; SATA 8

Parnell, Thomas 1679-1718......... **LC 3**
See also DLB 94

Parra, Nicanor
1914- ...... **CLC 2; DAM MULT; HLC**
See also CA 85-88; CANR 32; HW; MTCW

Parrish, Mary Frances
See Fisher, M(ary) F(rances) K(ennedy)

Parson
See Coleridge, Samuel Taylor

Parson Lot
See Kingsley, Charles

Partridge, Anthony
See Oppenheim, E(dward) Phillips

Pascal, Blaise 1623-1662 .... **LC 35**

Pascoli, Giovanni 1855-1912 ...... **TCLC 45**

Pasolini, Pier Paolo
1922-1975 .... **CLC 20, 37; PC 17**
See also CA 93-96; 61-64; DLB 128;
MTCW

Pasquini
See Silone, Ignazio

Pastan, Linda (Olenik)
1932- .... **CLC 27; DAM POET**
See also CA 61-64; CANR 18, 40; DLB 5

Pasternak, Boris (Leonidovich)
1890-1960 ...... **CLC 7, 10, 18, 63; DA;**
DAB; DAC; DAM MST, NOV, POET;
PC 6; WLC
See also CA 127; 116; MTCW

Patchen, Kenneth
1911-1972 ... **CLC 1, 2, 18; DAM POET**
See also CA 1-4R; 33-36R; CANR 3, 35;
DLB 16, 48; MTCW

Pater, Walter (Horatio)
1839-1894 .... **NCLC 7**
See also CDBLB 1832-1890; DLB 57, 156

Paterson, A(ndrew) B(arton)
1864-1941 .... **TCLC 32**
See also CA 155

Paterson, Katherine (Womeldorf)
1932- .... **CLC 12, 30**
See also AAYA 1; CA 21-24R; CANR 28;
CLR 7; DLB 52; JRDA; MAICYA;
MTCW; SATA 13, 53

Patmore, Coventry Kersey Dighton
1823-1896 .... **NCLC 9**
See also DLB 35, 98

Paton, Alan (Stewart)
1903-1988 ...... **CLC 4, 10, 25, 55; DA;**
DAB; DAC; DAM MST, NOV; WLC
See also CA 13-16; 125; CANR 22; CAP 1;
MTCW; SATA 11; SATA-Obit 56

Paton Walsh, Gillian 1937-
See Walsh, Jill Paton
See also CANR 38; JRDA; MAICYA;
SAAS 3; SATA 4, 72

Paulding, James Kirke 1778-1860.. **NCLC 2**
See also DLB 3, 59, 74

Paulin, Thomas Neilson 1949-
See Paulin, Tom
See also CA 123; 128

Paulin, Tom..................... **CLC 37**
See also Paulin, Thomas Neilson
See also DLB 40

Paustovsky, Konstantin (Georgievich)
1892-1968 .... **CLC 40**
See also CA 93-96; 25-28R

Pavese, Cesare
1908-1950 ..... **TCLC 3; PC 13; SSC 19**
See also CA 104; DLB 128

Pavic, Milorad 1929-............. **CLC 60**
See also CA 136

Payne, Alan
See Jakes, John (William)

Paz, Gil
See Lugones, Leopoldo

Paz, Octavio
1914- ...... **CLC 3, 4, 6, 10, 19, 51, 65;**
DA; DAB; DAC; DAM MST, MULT,
POET; HLC; PC 1; WLC
See also CA 73-76; CANR 32; DLBY 90;
HW; MTCW

p'Bitek, Okot
1931-1982 .... **CLC 96; BLC;**
DAM MULT
See also BW 2; CA 124; 107; DLB 125;
MTCW

Peacock, Molly 1947-............. **CLC 60**
See also CA 103; CAAS 21; CANR 52;
DLB 120

Peacock, Thomas Love
1785-1866 .... **NCLC 22**
See also DLB 96, 116

Peake, Mervyn 1911-1968....... **CLC 7, 54**
See also CA 5-8R; 25-28R; CANR 3;
DLB 15, 160; MTCW; SATA 23

Pearce, Philippa .... **CLC 21**
See Christie, (Ann) Philippa
See also CLR 9; DLB 161; MAICYA;
SATA 1, 67

Pearl, Eric
See Elman, Richard

Pearson, T(homas) R(eid) 1956- .... **CLC 39**
See also CA 120; 130; INT 130

Peck, Dale 1967- .... **CLC 81**
See also CA 146

Peck, John 1941- .... **CLC 3**
See also CA 49-52; CANR 3

Peck, Richard (Wayne) 1934-...... **CLC 21**
See also AAYA 1; CA 85-88; CANR 19,
38; CLR 15; INT CANR-19; JRDA;
MAICYA; SAAS 2; SATA 18, 55

Peck, Robert Newton
1928- .. **CLC 17; DA; DAC; DAM MST**
See also AAYA 3; CA 81-84; CANR 31;
JRDA; MAICYA; SAAS 1; SATA 21, 62

Peckinpah, (David) Sam(uel)
1925-1984 .... **CLC 20**
See also CA 109; 114

Pedersen, Knut 1859-1952
See Hamsun, Knut
See also CA 104; 119; MTCW

Peeslake, Gaffer
See Durrell, Lawrence (George)

Peguy, Charles Pierre
1873-1914 .... **TCLC 10**
See also CA 107

Pena, Ramon del Valle y
See Valle-Inclan, Ramon (Maria) del

Pendennis, Arthur Esquir
See Thackeray, William Makepeace

Penn, William 1644-1718.......... **LC 25**
See also DLB 24

Pepys, Samuel
1633-1703 ..... **LC 11; DA; DAB; DAC;**
DAM MST; WLC
See also CDBLB 1660-1789; DLB 101

Percy, Walker
1916-1990 .... **CLC 2, 3, 6, 8, 14, 18, 47,**
65; DAM NOV, POP
See also CA 1-4R; 131; CANR 1, 23;
DLB 2; DLBY 80, 90; MTCW

Perec, Georges 1936-1982 . . . . **CLC 56**
See also CA 141; DLB 83

Pereda (y Sanchez de Porrua), Jose Maria de
1833-1906 . . . . **TCLC 16**
See also CA 117

Pereda y Porrua, Jose Maria de
See Pereda (y Sanchez de Porrua), Jose
Maria de

Peregoy, George Weems
See Mencken, H(enry) L(ouis)

Perelman, S(idney) J(oseph)
1904-1979 . . . . . **CLC 3, 5, 9, 15, 23, 44,
49; DAM DRAM**
See also AITN 1, 2; CA 73-76; 89-92;
CANR 18; DLB 11, 44; MTCW

Peret, Benjamin 1899-1959 . . . . . . **TCLC 20**
See also CA 117

Peretz, Isaac Loeb 1851(?)-1915 . . . **TCLC 16**
See also CA 109

Peretz, Yitzkhok Leibush
See Peretz, Isaac Loeb

Perez Galdos, Benito 1843-1920 . . . **TCLC 27**
See also CA 125; 153; HW

Perrault, Charles 1628-1703 . . . . **LC 2**
See also MAICYA; SATA 25

Perry, Brighton
See Sherwood, Robert E(mmet)

Perse, St.-John . . . . **CLC 4, 11, 46**
See also Leger, (Marie-Rene Auguste) Alexis
Saint-Leger

Perutz, Leo 1882-1957 . . . . **TCLC 60**
See also DLB 81

Peseenz, Tulio F.
See Lopez y Fuentes, Gregorio

Pesetsky, Bette 1932- . . . . **CLC 28**
See also CA 133; DLB 130

Peshkov, Alexei Maximovich 1868-1936
See Gorky, Maxim
See also CA 105; 141; DA; DAC;
DAM DRAM, MST, NOV

Pessoa, Fernando (Antonio Nogueira)
1888-1935 . . . . . . **TCLC 27; HLC**
See also CA 125

Peterkin, Julia Mood 1880-1961 . . . . **CLC 31**
See also CA 102; DLB 9

Peters, Joan K. 1945- . . . . **CLC 39**

Peters, Robert L(ouis) 1924- . . . . **CLC 7**
See also CA 13-16R; CAAS 8; DLB 105

Petofi, Sandor 1823-1849 . . . . **NCLC 21**

Petrakis, Harry Mark 1923- . . . . **CLC 3**
See also CA 9-12R; CANR 4, 30

Petrarch
1304-1374 . . . . **CMLC 20; DAM POET;
PC 8**

Petrov, Evgeny . . . . **TCLC 21**
See also Kataev, Evgeny Petrovich

Petry, Ann (Lane) 1908- . . . . . . **CLC 1, 7, 18**
See also BW 1; CA 5-8R; CAAS 6;
CANR 4, 46; CLR 12; DLB 76; JRDA;
MAICYA; MTCW; SATA 5

Petursson, Halligrimur 1614-1674 . . . . **LC 8**

Philips, Katherine 1632-1664 . . . . **LC 30**
See also DLB 131

Philipson, Morris H. 1926- . . . . **CLC 53**
See also CA 1-4R; CANR 4

Phillips, Caryl
1958- . . . . **CLC 96; DAM MULT**
See also BW 2; CA 141; DLB 157

Phillips, David Graham
1867-1911 . . . . **TCLC 44**
See also CA 108; DLB 9, 12

Phillips, Jack
See Sandburg, Carl (August)

Phillips, Jayne Anne
1952- . . . . **CLC 15, 33; SSC 16**
See also CA 101; CANR 24, 50; DLBY 80;
INT CANR-24; MTCW

Phillips, Richard
See Dick, Philip K(indred)

Phillips, Robert (Schaeffer) 1938- . . . **CLC 28**
See also CA 17-20R; CAAS 13; CANR 8;
DLB 105

Phillips, Ward
See Lovecraft, H(oward) P(hillips)

Piccolo, Lucio 1901-1969 . . . . **CLC 13**
See also CA 97-100; DLB 114

Pickthall, Marjorie L(owry) C(hristie)
1883-1922 . . . . **TCLC 21**
See also CA 107; DLB 92

Pico della Mirandola, Giovanni
1463-1494 . . . . **LC 15**

Piercy, Marge
1936- . . . . **CLC 3, 6, 14, 18, 27, 62**
See also CA 21-24R; CAAS 1; CANR 13,
43; DLB 120; MTCW

Piers, Robert
See Anthony, Piers

Pieyre de Mandiargues, Andre 1909-1991
See Mandiargues, Andre Pieyre de
See also CA 103; 136; CANR 22

Pilnyak, Boris . . . . **TCLC 23**
See also Vogau, Boris Andreyevich

Pincherle, Alberto
1907-1990 . . . . . **CLC 11, 18; DAM NOV**
See also Moravia, Alberto
See also CA 25-28R; 132; CANR 33;
MTCW

Pinckney, Darryl 1953- . . . . **CLC 76**
See also BW 2; CA 143

Pindar 518B.C.-446B.C. . . . . **CMLC 12**

Pineda, Cecile 1942- . . . . **CLC 39**
See also CA 118

Pinero, Arthur Wing
1855-1934 . . . . . **TCLC 32; DAM DRAM**
See also CA 110; 153; DLB 10

Pinero, Miguel (Antonio Gomez)
1946-1988 . . . . **CLC 4, 55**
See also CA 61-64; 125; CANR 29; HW

Pinget, Robert 1919- . . . . **CLC 7, 13, 37**
See also CA 85-88; DLB 83

Pink Floyd
See Barrett, (Roger) Syd; Gilmour, David;
Mason, Nick; Waters, Roger; Wright,
Rick

Pinkney, Edward 1802-1828 . . . . . **NCLC 31**

Pinkwater, Daniel Manus 1941- . . . . **CLC 35**
See also Pinkwater, Manus
See also AAYA 1; CA 29-32R; CANR 12,
38; CLR 4; JRDA; MAICYA; SAAS 3;
SATA 46, 76

Pinkwater, Manus
See Pinkwater, Daniel Manus
See also SATA 8

Pinsky, Robert
1940- . . **CLC 9, 19, 38, 94; DAM POET**
See also CA 29-32R; CAAS 4; DLBY 82

Pinta, Harold
See Pinter, Harold

Pinter, Harold
1930- . . . . . **CLC 1, 3, 6, 9, 11, 15, 27, 58,
73; DA; DAB; DAC; DAM DRAM,
MST; WLC**
See also CA 5-8R; CANR 33; CDBLB 1960
to Present; DLB 13; MTCW

Piozzi, Hester Lynch (Thrale)
1741-1821 . . . . **NCLC 57**
See also DLB 104, 142

Pirandello, Luigi
1867-1936 . . . . . . **TCLC 4, 29; DA; DAB;
DAC; DAM DRAM, MST; DC 5;
SSC 22; WLC**
See also CA 104; 153

Pirsig, Robert M(aynard)
1928- . . . . **CLC 4, 6, 73; DAM POP**
See also CA 53-56; CANR 42; MTCW;
SATA 39

Pisarev, Dmitry Ivanovich
1840-1868 . . . . **NCLC 25**

Pix, Mary (Griffith) 1666-1709 . . . . . . **LC 8**
See also DLB 80

Pixerecourt, Guilbert de
1773-1844 . . . . **NCLC 39**

Plaidy, Jean
See Hibbert, Eleanor Alice Burford

Planche, James Robinson
1796-1880 . . . . **NCLC 42**

Plant, Robert 1948- . . . . **CLC 12**

Plante, David (Robert)
1940- . . . . **CLC 7, 23, 38; DAM NOV**
See also CA 37-40R; CANR 12, 36;
DLBY 83; INT CANR-12; MTCW

Plath, Sylvia
1932-1963 . . . . . **CLC 1, 2, 3, 5, 9, 11, 14,
17, 50, 51, 62; DA; DAB; DAC;
DAM MST, POET; PC 1; WLC**
See also AAYA 13; CA 19-20; CANR 34;
CAP 2; CDALB 1941-1968; DLB 5, 6,
152; MTCW

Plato
428(?)B.C.-348(?)B.C. . . . . . **CMLC 8; DA;
DAB; DAC; DAM MST**

Platonov, Andrei . . . . **TCLC 14**
See also Klimentov, Andrei Platonovich

Platt, Kin 1911- . . . . **CLC 26**
See also AAYA 11; CA 17-20R; CANR 11;
JRDA; SAAS 17; SATA 21, 86

Plautus c. 251B.C.-184B.C. . . . . **DC 6**

Plick et Plock
See Simenon, Georges (Jacques Christian)

Plimpton, George (Ames) 1927-..... **CLC 36**
See also AITN 1; CA 21-24R; CANR 32;
MTCW; SATA 10

Plomer, William Charles Franklin
1903-1973 .... **CLC 4, 8**
See also CA 21-22; CANR 34; CAP 2;
DLB 20, 162; MTCW; SATA 24

Plowman, Piers
See Kavanagh, Patrick (Joseph)

Plum, J.
See Wodehouse, P(elham) G(renville)

Plumly, Stanley (Ross) 1939- ...... **CLC 33**
See also CA 108; 110; DLB 5; INT 110

Plumpe, Friedrich Wilhelm
1888-1931 .... **TCLC 53**
See also CA 112

Poe, Edgar Allan
1809-1849 .... **NCLC 1, 16, 55; DA;**
DAB; DAC; DAM MST, POET; PC 1;
SSC 1, 22; WLC
See also AAYA 14; CDALB 1640-1865;
DLB 3, 59, 73, 74; SATA 23

Poet of Titchfield Street, The
See Pound, Ezra (Weston Loomis)

Pohl, Frederik 1919- .... **CLC 18**
See also CA 61-64; CAAS 1; CANR 11, 37;
DLB 8; INT CANR-11; MTCW;
SATA 24

Poirier, Louis 1910-
See Gracq, Julien
See also CA 122; 126

Poitier, Sidney 1927- .... **CLC 26**
See also BW 1; CA 117

Polanski, Roman 1933- .... **CLC 16**
See also CA 77-80

Poliakoff, Stephen 1952- .... **CLC 38**
See also CA 106; DLB 13

Police, The
See Copeland, Stewart (Armstrong);
Summers, Andrew James; Sumner,
Gordon Matthew

Polidori, John William
1795-1821 .... **NCLC 51**
See also DLB 116

Pollitt, Katha 1949- .... **CLC 28**
See also CA 120; 122; MTCW

Pollock, (Mary) Sharon
1936- .... **CLC 50; DAC; DAM DRAM,**
MST
See also CA 141; DLB 60

Polo, Marco 1254-1324 .... **CMLC 15**

Polonsky, Abraham (Lincoln)
1910- .... **CLC 92**
See also CA 104; DLB 26; INT 104

Polybius c. 200B.C.-c. 118B.C. .... **CMLC 17**

Pomerance, Bernard
1940- .... **CLC 13; DAM DRAM**
See also CA 101; CANR 49

Ponge, Francis (Jean Gaston Alfred)
1899-1988 ..... **CLC 6, 18; DAM POET**
See also CA 85-88; 126; CANR 40

Pontoppidan, Henrik 1857-1943 ... **TCLC 29**

Poole, Josephine .... **CLC 17**
See also Helyar, Jane Penelope Josephine
See also SAAS 2; SATA 5

Popa, Vasko 1922-1991 .... **CLC 19**
See also CA 112; 148

Pope, Alexander
1688-1744 ...... **LC 3; DA; DAB; DAC;**
DAM MST, POET; WLC
See also CDBLB 1660-1789; DLB 95, 101

Porter, Connie (Rose) 1959(?)- ..... **CLC 70**
See also BW 2; CA 142; SATA 81

Porter, Gene(va Grace) Stratton
1863(?)-1924 .... **TCLC 21**
See also CA 112

Porter, Katherine Anne
1890-1980 ...... **CLC 1, 3, 7, 10, 13, 15,**
27; DA; DAB; DAC; DAM MST, NOV;
SSC 4
See also AITN 2; CA 1-4R; 101; CANR 1;
DLB 4, 9, 102; DLBD 12; DLBY 80;
MTCW; SATA 39; SATA-Obit 23

Porter, Peter (Neville Frederick)
1929- .... **CLC 5, 13, 33**
See also CA 85-88; DLB 40

Porter, William Sydney 1862-1910
See Henry, O.
See also CA 104; 131; CDALB 1865-1917;
DA; DAB; DAC; DAM MST; DLB 12,
78, 79; MTCW; YABC 2

Portillo (y Pacheco), Jose Lopez
See Lopez Portillo (y Pacheco), Jose

Post, Melville Davisson
1869-1930 .... **TCLC 39**
See also CA 110

Potok, Chaim
1929- .... **CLC 2, 7, 14, 26; DAM NOV**
See also AAYA 15; AITN 1, 2; CA 17-20R;
CANR 19, 35; DLB 28, 152;
INT CANR-19; MTCW; SATA 33

Potter, Beatrice
See Webb, (Martha) Beatrice (Potter)
See also MAICYA

Potter, Dennis (Christopher George)
1935-1994 .... **CLC 58, 86**
See also CA 107; 145; CANR 33; MTCW

Pound, Ezra (Weston Loomis)
1885-1972 ...... **CLC 1, 2, 3, 4, 5, 7, 10,**
13, 18, 34, 48, 50; DA; DAB; DAC;
DAM MST, POET; PC 4; WLC
See also CA 5-8R; 37-40R; CANR 40;
CDALB 1917-1929; DLB 4, 45, 63;
MTCW

Povod, Reinaldo 1959-1994 .... **CLC 44**
See also CA 136; 146

Powell, Adam Clayton, Jr.
1908-1972 .... **CLC 89; BLC;**
DAM MULT
See also BW 1; CA 102; 33-36R

Powell, Anthony (Dymoke)
1905- .... **CLC 1, 3, 7, 9, 10, 31**
See also CA 1-4R; CANR 1, 32;
CDBLB 1945-1960; DLB 15; MTCW

Powell, Dawn 1897-1965 .... **CLC 66**
See also CA 5-8R

Powell, Padgett 1952-............. **CLC 34**
See also CA 126

Power, Susan .... **CLC 91**

Powers, J(ames) F(arl)
1917- .... **CLC 1, 4, 8, 57; SSC 4**
See also CA 1-4R; CANR 2; DLB 130;
MTCW

Powers, John J(ames) 1945-
See Powers, John R.
See also CA 69-72

Powers, John R. .... **CLC 66**
See also Powers, John J(ames)

Powers, Richard (S.) 1957- .... **CLC 93**
See also CA 148

Pownall, David 1938-............. **CLC 10**
See also CA 89-92; CAAS 18; CANR 49;
DLB 14

Powys, John Cowper
1872-1963 .... **CLC 7, 9, 15, 46**
See also CA 85-88; DLB 15; MTCW

Powys, T(heodore) F(rancis)
1875-1953 .... **TCLC 9**
See also CA 106; DLB 36, 162

Prager, Emily 1952-.............. **CLC 56**

Pratt, E(dwin) J(ohn)
1883(?)-1964 .... **CLC 19; DAC;**
DAM POET
See also CA 141; 93-96; DLB 92

Premchand.................... **TCLC 21**
See also Srivastava, Dhanpat Rai

Preussler, Otfried 1923-.......... **CLC 17**
See also CA 77-80; SATA 24

Prevert, Jacques (Henri Marie)
1900-1977 .... **CLC 15**
See also CA 77-80; 69-72; CANR 29;
MTCW; SATA-Obit 30

Prevost, Abbe (Antoine Francois)
1697-1763 .... **LC 1**

Price, (Edward) Reynolds
1933- .... **CLC 3, 6, 13, 43, 50, 63;**
DAM NOV; SSC 22
See also CA 1-4R; CANR 1, 37; DLB 2;
INT CANR-37

Price, Richard 1949- .... **CLC 6, 12**
See also CA 49-52; CANR 3; DLBY 81

Prichard, Katharine Susannah
1883-1969 .... **CLC 46**
See also CA 11-12; CANR 33; CAP 1;
MTCW; SATA 66

Priestley, J(ohn) B(oynton)
1894-1984 .... **CLC 2, 5, 9, 34;**
DAM DRAM, NOV
See also CA 9-12R; 113; CANR 33;
CDBLB 1914-1945; DLB 10, 34, 77, 100,
139; DLBY 84; MTCW

Prince 1958(?)- .... **CLC 35**

Prince, F(rank) T(empleton) 1912- .. **CLC 22**
See also CA 101; CANR 43; DLB 20

Prince Kropotkin
See Kropotkin, Peter (Aleksieevich)

Prior, Matthew 1664-1721 .... **LC 4**
See also DLB 95

Pritchard, William H(arrison)
1932- .... **CLC 34**
See also CA 65-68; CANR 23; DLB 111

Pritchett, V(ictor) S(awdon)
1900- .... CLC 5, 13, 15, 41;
DAM NOV; SSC 14
See also CA 61-64; CANR 31; DLB 15,
139; MTCW

Private 19022
See Manning, Frederic

Probst, Mark 1925- .... CLC 59
See also CA 130

Prokosch, Frederic 1908-1989.... CLC 4, 48
See also CA 73-76; 128; DLB 48

Prophet, The
See Dreiser, Theodore (Herman Albert)

Prose, Francine 1947-............. CLC 45
See also CA 109; 112; CANR 46

Proudhon
See Cunha, Euclides (Rodrigues Pimenta) da

Proulx, E. Annie 1935- .... CLC 81

Proust, (Valentin-Louis-George-Eugene-)
Marcel
1871-1922 .... TCLC 7, 13, 33; DA;
DAB; DAC; DAM MST, NOV; WLC
See also CA 104; 120; DLB 65; MTCW

Prowler, Harley
See Masters, Edgar Lee

Prus, Boleslaw 1845-1912 .... TCLC 48

Pryor, Richard (Franklin Lenox Thomas)
1940- .... CLC 26
See also CA 122

Przybyszewski, Stanislaw
1868-1927 .... TCLC 36
See also DLB 66

Pteleon
See Grieve, C(hristopher) M(urray)
See also DAM POET

Puckett, Lute
See Masters, Edgar Lee

Puig, Manuel
1932-1990 .... CLC 3, 5, 10, 28, 65;
DAM MULT; HLC
See also CA 45-48; CANR 2, 32; DLB 113;
HW; MTCW

Purdy, Al(fred Wellington)
1918- .... CLC 3, 6, 14, 50; DAC;
DAM MST, POET
See also CA 81-84; CAAS 17; CANR 42;
DLB 88

Purdy, James (Amos)
1923- .... CLC 2, 4, 10, 28, 52
See also CA 33-36R; CAAS 1; CANR 19,
51; DLB 2; INT CANR-19; MTCW

Pure, Simon
See Swinnerton, Frank Arthur

Pushkin, Alexander (Sergeyevich)
1799-1837 ..... NCLC 3, 27; DA; DAB;
DAC; DAM DRAM, MST, POET;
PC 10; WLC
See also SATA 61

P'u Sung-ling 1640-1715 .... LC 3

Putnam, Arthur Lee
See Alger, Horatio, Jr.

Puzo, Mario
1920- ..... CLC 1, 2, 6, 36; DAM NOV,
POP
See also CA 65-68; CANR 4, 42; DLB 6;
MTCW

Pygge, Edward
See Barnes, Julian (Patrick)

Pym, Barbara (Mary Crampton)
1913-1980 .... CLC 13, 19, 37
See also CA 13-14; 97-100; CANR 13, 34;
CAP 1; DLB 14; DLBY 87; MTCW

Pynchon, Thomas (Ruggles, Jr.)
1937- ..... CLC 2, 3, 6, 9, 11, 18, 33, 62,
72; DA; DAB; DAC; DAM MST, NOV,
POP; SSC 14; WLC
See also BEST 90:2; CA 17-20R; CANR 22,
46; DLB 2, 173; MTCW

Qian Zhongshu
See Ch'ien Chung-shu

Qroll
See Dagerman, Stig (Halvard)

Quarrington, Paul (Lewis) 1953-.... CLC 65
See also CA 129

Quasimodo, Salvatore 1901-1968 ... CLC 10
See also CA 13-16; 25-28R; CAP 1;
DLB 114; MTCW

Quay, Stephen 1947- .... CLC 95

Quay, The Brothers
See Quay, Stephen; Quay, Timothy

Quay, Timothy 1947-............. CLC 95

Queen, Ellery................... CLC 3, 11
See also Dannay, Frederic; Davidson,
Avram; Lee, Manfred B(ennington);
Marlowe, Stephen; Sturgeon, Theodore
(Hamilton); Vance, John Holbrook

Queen, Ellery, Jr.
See Dannay, Frederic; Lee, Manfred
B(ennington)

Queneau, Raymond
1903-1976 .... CLC 2, 5, 10, 42
See also CA 77-80; 69-72; CANR 32;
DLB 72; MTCW

Quevedo, Francisco de 1580-1645.... LC 23

Quiller-Couch, Arthur Thomas
1863-1944 .... TCLC 53
See also CA 118; DLB 135, 153

Quin, Ann (Marie) 1936-1973 .... CLC 6
See also CA 9-12R; 45-48; DLB 14

Quinn, Martin
See Smith, Martin Cruz

Quinn, Peter 1947-............... CLC 91

Quinn, Simon
See Smith, Martin Cruz

Quiroga, Horacio (Sylvestre)
1878-1937 ..... TCLC 20; DAM MULT;
HLC
See also CA 117; 131; HW; MTCW

Quoirez, Francoise 1935-........... CLC 9
See also Sagan, Francoise
See also CA 49-52; CANR 6, 39; MTCW

Raabe, Wilhelm 1831-1910 .... TCLC 45
See also DLB 129

Rabe, David (William)
1940- ...... CLC 4, 8, 33; DAM DRAM
See also CA 85-88; CABS 3; DLB 7

Rabelais, Francois
1483-1553 ...... LC 5; DA; DAB; DAC;
DAM MST; WLC

Rabinovitch, Sholem 1859-1916
See Aleichem, Sholom
See also CA 104

Rachilde 1860-1953 .... TCLC 67
See also DLB 123

Racine, Jean
1639-1699 .... LC 28; DAB; DAM MST

Radcliffe, Ann (Ward)
1764-1823 .... NCLC 6, 55
See also DLB 39

Radiguet, Raymond 1903-1923 .... TCLC 29
See also DLB 65

Radnoti, Miklos 1909-1944 .... TCLC 16
See also CA 118

Rado, James 1939-............... CLC 17
See also CA 105

Radvanyi, Netty 1900-1983
See Seghers, Anna
See also CA 85-88; 110

Rae, Ben
See Griffiths, Trevor

Raeburn, John (Hay) 1941-........ CLC 34
See also CA 57-60

Ragni, Gerome 1942-1991 .... CLC 17
See also CA 105; 134

Rahv, Philip 1908-1973 .... CLC 24
See also Greenberg, Ivan
See also DLB 137

Raine, Craig 1944-............... CLC 32
See also CA 108; CANR 29, 51; DLB 40

Raine, Kathleen (Jessie) 1908- ... CLC 7, 45
See also CA 85-88; CANR 46; DLB 20;
MTCW

Rainis, Janis 1865-1929.......... TCLC 29

Rakosi, Carl..................... CLC 47
See also Rawley, Callman
See also CAAS 5

Raleigh, Richard
See Lovecraft, H(oward) P(hillips)

Raleigh, Sir Walter 1554(?)-1618 .... LC 31
See also CDBLB Before 1660; DLB 172

Rallentando, H. P.
See Sayers, Dorothy L(eigh)

Ramal, Walter
See de la Mare, Walter (John)

Ramon, Juan
See Jimenez (Mantecon), Juan Ramon

Ramos, Graciliano 1892-1953 ..... TCLC 32

Rampersad, Arnold 1941-......... CLC 44
See also BW 2; CA 127; 133; DLB 111;
INT 133

Rampling, Anne
See Rice, Anne

Ramsay, Allan 1684(?)-1758 .... LC 29
See also DLB 95

Ramuz, Charles-Ferdinand
1878-1947 .... TCLC 33

Rand, Ayn
1905-1982 . . . . . **CLC 3, 30, 44, 79; DA;
DAC; DAM MST, NOV, POP; WLC**
See also AAYA 10; CA 13-16R; 105;
CANR 27; MTCW

Randall, Dudley (Felker)
1914- . . . . . . **CLC 1; BLC; DAM MULT**
See also BW 1; CA 25-28R; CANR 23;
DLB 41

Randall, Robert
See Silverberg, Robert

Ranger, Ken
See Creasey, John

Ransom, John Crowe
1888-1974 . . . . **CLC 2, 4, 5, 11, 24;
DAM POET**
See also CA 5-8R; 49-52; CANR 6, 34;
DLB 45, 63; MTCW

Rao, Raja 1909- . . . **CLC 25, 56; DAM NOV**
See also CA 73-76; CANR 51; MTCW

Raphael, Frederic (Michael)
1931- . . . . **CLC 2, 14**
See also CA 1-4R; CANR 1; DLB 14

Ratcliffe, James P.
See Mencken, H(enry) L(ouis)

Rathbone, Julian 1935- . . . . **CLC 41**
See also CA 101; CANR 34

Rattigan, Terence (Mervyn)
1911-1977 . . . . **CLC 7; DAM DRAM**
See also CA 85-88; 73-76;
CDBLB 1945-1960; DLB 13; MTCW

Ratushinskaya, Irina 1954- . . . . **CLC 54**
See also CA 129

Raven, Simon (Arthur Noel)
1927- . . . . **CLC 14**
See also CA 81-84

Rawley, Callman 1903-
See Rakosi, Carl
See also CA 21-24R; CANR 12, 32

Rawlings, Marjorie Kinnan
1896-1953 . . . . **TCLC 4**
See also CA 104; 137; DLB 9, 22, 102;
JRDA; MAICYA; YABC 1

Ray, Satyajit
1921-1992 . . . **CLC 16, 76; DAM MULT**
See also CA 114; 137

Read, Herbert Edward 1893-1968. . . . **CLC 4**
See also CA 85-88; 25-28R; DLB 20, 149

Read, Piers Paul 1941- . . . . . . **CLC 4, 10, 25**
See also CA 21-24R; CANR 38; DLB 14;
SATA 21

Reade, Charles 1814-1884 . . . . **NCLC 2**
See also DLB 21

Reade, Hamish
See Gray, Simon (James Holliday)

Reading, Peter 1946- . . . . **CLC 47**
See also CA 103; CANR 46; DLB 40

Reaney, James
1926- . . . . . . **CLC 13; DAC; DAM MST**
See also CA 41-44R; CAAS 15; CANR 42;
DLB 68; SATA 43

Rebreanu, Liviu 1885-1944 . . . . **TCLC 28**

Rechy, John (Francisco)
1934- . . . . **CLC 1, 7, 14, 18;
DAM MULT; HLC**
See also CA 5-8R; CAAS 4; CANR 6, 32;
DLB 122; DLBY 82; HW; INT CANR-6

Redcam, Tom 1870-1933 . . . . **TCLC 25**

Reddin, Keith . . . . **CLC 67**

Redgrove, Peter (William)
1932- . . . . **CLC 6, 41**
See also CA 1-4R; CANR 3, 39; DLB 40

Redmon, Anne . . . . **CLC 22**
See also Nightingale, Anne Redmon
See also DLBY 86

Reed, Eliot
See Ambler, Eric

Reed, Ishmael
1938- . . . . **CLC 2, 3, 5, 6, 13, 32, 60;
BLC; DAM MULT**
See also BW 2; CA 21-24R; CANR 25, 48;
DLB 2, 5, 33, 169; DLBD 8; MTCW

Reed, John (Silas) 1887-1920 . . . . . . **TCLC 9**
See also CA 106

Reed, Lou . . . . **CLC 21**
See also Firbank, Louis

Reeve, Clara 1729-1807 . . . . **NCLC 19**
See also DLB 39

Reich, Wilhelm 1897-1957 . . . . **TCLC 57**

Reid, Christopher (John) 1949- . . . . . **CLC 33**
See also CA 140; DLB 40

Reid, Desmond
See Moorcock, Michael (John)

Reid Banks, Lynne 1929-
See Banks, Lynne Reid
See also CA 1-4R; CANR 6, 22, 38;
CLR 24; JRDA; MAICYA; SATA 22, 75

Reilly, William K.
See Creasey, John

Reiner, Max
See Caldwell, (Janet Miriam) Taylor
(Holland)

Reis, Ricardo
See Pessoa, Fernando (Antonio Nogueira)

Remarque, Erich Maria
1898-1970 . . . . **CLC 21; DA; DAB; DAC;
DAM MST, NOV**
See also CA 77-80; 29-32R; DLB 56;
MTCW

Remizov, A.
See Remizov, Aleksei (Mikhailovich)

Remizov, A. M.
See Remizov, Aleksei (Mikhailovich)

Remizov, Aleksei (Mikhailovich)
1877-1957 . . . . **TCLC 27**
See also CA 125; 133

Renan, Joseph Ernest
1823-1892 . . . . **NCLC 26**

Renard, Jules 1864-1910 . . . . **TCLC 17**
See also CA 117

Renault, Mary . . . . **CLC 3, 11, 17**
See also Challans, Mary
See also DLBY 83

Rendell, Ruth (Barbara)
1930- . . . . **CLC 28, 48; DAM POP**
See also Vine, Barbara
See also CA 109; CANR 32, 52; DLB 87;
INT CANR-32; MTCW

Renoir, Jean 1894-1979 . . . . **CLC 20**
See also CA 129; 85-88

Resnais, Alain 1922- . . . . **CLC 16**

Reverdy, Pierre 1889-1960 . . . . **CLC 53**
See also CA 97-100; 89-92

Rexroth, Kenneth
1905-1982 . . . . . . **CLC 1, 2, 6, 11, 22, 49;
DAM POET**
See also CA 5-8R; 107; CANR 14, 34;
CDALB 1941-1968; DLB 16, 48, 165;
DLBY 82; INT CANR-14; MTCW

Reyes, Alfonso 1889-1959 . . . . **TCLC 33**
See also CA 131; HW

Reyes y Basoalto, Ricardo Eliecer Neftali
See Neruda, Pablo

Reymont, Wladyslaw (Stanislaw)
1868(?)-1925 . . . . **TCLC 5**
See also CA 104

Reynolds, Jonathan 1942- . . . . **CLC 6, 38**
See also CA 65-68; CANR 28

Reynolds, Joshua 1723-1792 . . . . **LC 15**
See also DLB 104

Reynolds, Michael Shane 1937- . . . . **CLC 44**
See also CA 65-68; CANR 9

Reznikoff, Charles 1894-1976 . . . . **CLC 9**
See also CA 33-36; 61-64; CAP 2; DLB 28,
45

Rezzori (d'Arezzo), Gregor von
1914- . . . . **CLC 25**
See also CA 122; 136

Rhine, Richard
See Silverstein, Alvin

Rhodes, Eugene Manlove
1869-1934 . . . . **TCLC 53**

R'hoone
See Balzac, Honore de

Rhys, Jean
1890(?)-1979 . . . . **CLC 2, 4, 6, 14, 19, 51;
DAM NOV; SSC 21**
See also CA 25-28R; 85-88; CANR 35;
CDBLB 1945-1960; DLB 36, 117, 162;
MTCW

Ribeiro, Darcy 1922- . . . . **CLC 34**
See also CA 33-36R

Ribeiro, Joao Ubaldo (Osorio Pimentel)
1941- . . . . **CLC 10, 67**
See also CA 81-84

Ribman, Ronald (Burt) 1932- . . . . **CLC 7**
See also CA 21-24R; CANR 46

Ricci, Nino 1959- . . . . **CLC 70**
See also CA 137

Rice, Anne 1941- . . . . . **CLC 41; DAM POP**
See also AAYA 9; BEST 89:2; CA 65-68;
CANR 12, 36, 53

Rice, Elmer (Leopold)
1892-1967 . . . . **CLC 7, 49; DAM DRAM**
See also CA 21-22; 25-28R; CAP 2; DLB 4,
7; MTCW

Rice, Tim(othy Miles Bindon)
1944- .... CLC 21
See also CA 103; CANR 46

Rich, Adrienne (Cecile)
1929- .... CLC 3, 6, 7, 11, 18, 36, 73, 76;
DAM POET; PC 5
See also CA 9-12R; CANR 20, 53; DLB 5,
67; MTCW

Rich, Barbara
See Graves, Robert (von Ranke)

Rich, Robert
See Trumbo, Dalton

Richard, Keith.................... CLC 17
See also Richards, Keith

Richards, David Adams
1950- .... CLC 59; DAC
See also CA 93-96; DLB 53

Richards, I(vor) A(rmstrong)
1893-1979 .... CLC 14, 24
See also CA 41-44R; 89-92; CANR 34;
DLB 27

Richards, Keith 1943-
See Richard, Keith
See also CA 107

Richardson, Anne
See Roiphe, Anne (Richardson)

Richardson, Dorothy Miller
1873-1957 .... TCLC 3
See also CA 104; DLB 36

Richardson, Ethel Florence (Lindesay)
1870-1946
See Richardson, Henry Handel
See also CA 105

Richardson, Henry Handel......... TCLC 4
See also Richardson, Ethel Florence
(Lindesay)

Richardson, John
1796-1852 .... NCLC 55; DAC
See also DLB 99

Richardson, Samuel
1689-1761 ...... LC 1; DA; DAB; DAC;
DAM MST, NOV; WLC
See also CDBLB 1660-1789; DLB 39

Richler, Mordecai
1931- .... CLC 3, 5, 9, 13, 18, 46, 70;
DAC; DAM MST, NOV
See also AITN 1; CA 65-68; CANR 31;
CLR 17; DLB 53; MAICYA; MTCW;
SATA 44; SATA-Brief 27

Richter, Conrad (Michael)
1890-1968 .... CLC 30
See also CA 5-8R; 25-28R; CANR 23;
DLB 9; MTCW; SATA 3

Ricostranza, Tom
See Ellis, Trey

Riddell, J. H. 1832-1906 .... TCLC 40

Riding, Laura.................... CLC 3, 7
See also Jackson, Laura (Riding)

Riefenstahl, Berta Helene Amalia 1902-
See Riefenstahl, Leni
See also CA 108

Riefenstahl, Leni................. CLC 16
See also Riefenstahl, Berta Helene Amalia

Riffe, Ernest
See Bergman, (Ernst) Ingmar

Riggs, (Rolla) Lynn
1899-1954 ..... TCLC 56; DAM MULT
See also CA 144; NNAL

Riley, James Whitcomb
1849-1916 ...... TCLC 51; DAM POET
See also CA 118; 137; MAICYA; SATA 17

Riley, Tex
See Creasey, John

Rilke, Rainer Maria
1875-1926 .... TCLC 1, 6, 19;
DAM POET; PC 2
See also CA 104; 132; DLB 81; MTCW

Rimbaud, (Jean Nicolas) Arthur
1854-1891 ..... NCLC 4, 35; DA; DAB;
DAC; DAM MST, POET; PC 3; WLC

Rinehart, Mary Roberts
1876-1958 .... TCLC 52
See also CA 108

Ringmaster, The
See Mencken, H(enry) L(ouis)

Ringwood, Gwen(dolyn Margaret) Pharis
1910-1984 .... CLC 48
See also CA 148; 112; DLB 88

Rio, Michel 19(?)-................ CLC 43

Ritsos, Giannes
See Ritsos, Yannis

Ritsos, Yannis 1909-1990..... CLC 6, 13, 31
See also CA 77-80; 133; CANR 39; MTCW

Ritter, Erika 1948(?)-............ CLC 52

Rivera, Jose Eustasio 1889-1928... TCLC 35
See also HW

Rivers, Conrad Kent 1933-1968...... CLC 1
See also BW 1; CA 85-88; DLB 41

Rivers, Elfrida
See Bradley, Marion Zimmer

Riverside, John
See Heinlein, Robert A(nson)

Rizal, Jose 1861-1896.......... NCLC 27

Roa Bastos, Augusto (Antonio)
1917- ..... CLC 45; DAM MULT; HLC
See also CA 131; DLB 113; HW

Robbe-Grillet, Alain
1922- ...... CLC 1, 2, 4, 6, 8, 10, 14, 43
See also CA 9-12R; CANR 33; DLB 83;
MTCW

Robbins, Harold
1916- .... CLC 5; DAM NOV
See also CA 73-76; CANR 26, 54; MTCW

Robbins, Thomas Eugene 1936-
See Robbins, Tom
See also CA 81-84; CANR 29; DAM NOV,
POP; MTCW

Robbins, Tom.................... CLC 9, 32, 64
See also Robbins, Thomas Eugene
See also BEST 90:3; DLBY 80

Robbins, Trina 1938- .... CLC 21
See also CA 128

Roberts, Charles G(eorge) D(ouglas)
1860-1943 .... TCLC 8
See also CA 105; CLR 33; DLB 92;
SATA 88; SATA-Brief 29

Roberts, Elizabeth Madox
1886-1941 .... TCLC 68
See also CA 111; DLB 9, 54, 102;
SATA 33; SATA-Brief 27

Roberts, Kate 1891-1985 .... CLC 15
See also CA 107; 116

Roberts, Keith (John Kingston)
1935- .... CLC 14
See also CA 25-28R; CANR 46

Roberts, Kenneth (Lewis)
1885-1957 .... TCLC 23
See also CA 109; DLB 9

Roberts, Michele (B.) 1949-........ CLC 48
See also CA 115

Robertson, Ellis
See Ellison, Harlan (Jay); Silverberg, Robert

Robertson, Thomas William
1829-1871 .... NCLC 35; DAM DRAM

Robinson, Edwin Arlington
1869-1935 .... TCLC 5; DA; DAC;
DAM MST, POET; PC 1
See also CA 104; 133; CDALB 1865-1917;
DLB 54; MTCW

Robinson, Henry Crabb
1775-1867 .... NCLC 15
See also DLB 107

Robinson, Jill 1936-............. CLC 10
See also CA 102; INT 102

Robinson, Kim Stanley 1952- ...... CLC 34
See also CA 126

Robinson, Lloyd
See Silverberg, Robert

Robinson, Marilynne 1944-........ CLC 25
See also CA 116

Robinson, Smokey................. CLC 21
See also Robinson, William, Jr.

Robinson, William, Jr. 1940-
See Robinson, Smokey
See also CA 116

Robison, Mary 1949-.......... CLC 42, 98
See also CA 113; 116; DLB 130; INT 116

Rod, Edouard 1857-1910 .... TCLC 52

Roddenberry, Eugene Wesley 1921-1991
See Roddenberry, Gene
See also CA 110; 135; CANR 37; SATA 45;
SATA-Obit 69

Roddenberry, Gene .... CLC 17
See also Roddenberry, Eugene Wesley
See also AAYA 5; SATA-Obit 69

Rodgers, Mary 1931-............. CLC 12
See also CA 49-52; CANR 8, 55; CLR 20;
INT CANR-8; JRDA; MAICYA;
SATA 8

Rodgers, W(illiam) R(obert)
1909-1969 .... CLC 7
See also CA 85-88; DLB 20

Rodman, Eric
See Silverberg, Robert

Rodman, Howard 1920(?)-1985 ..... CLC 65
See also CA 118

Rodman, Maia
See Wojciechowska, Maia (Teresa)

Rodriguez, Claudio 1934-......... CLC 10
See also DLB 134

Roelvaag, O(le) E(dvart)
1876-1931 .... **TCLC 17**
See also CA 117; DLB 9

Roethke, Theodore (Huebner)
1908-1963 ...... **CLC 1, 3, 8, 11, 19, 46;**
DAM POET; PC 15
See also CA 81-84; CABS 2;
CDALB 1941-1968; DLB 5; MTCW

Rogers, Thomas Hunton 1927- ..... **CLC 57**
See also CA 89-92; INT 89-92

Rogers, Will(iam Penn Adair)
1879-1935 ...... **TCLC 8; DAM MULT**
See also CA 105; 144; DLB 11; NNAL

Rogin, Gilbert 1929- .... **CLC 18**
See also CA 65-68; CANR 15

Rohan, Koda .... **TCLC 22**
See also Koda Shigeyuki

Rohmer, Eric .... **CLC 16**
See also Scherer, Jean-Marie Maurice

Rohmer, Sax .... **TCLC 28**
See also Ward, Arthur Henry Sarsfield
See also DLB 70

Roiphe, Anne (Richardson)
1935- .... **CLC 3, 9**
See also CA 89-92; CANR 45; DLBY 80;
INT 89-92

Rojas, Fernando de 1465-1541 ...... **LC 23**

Rolfe, Frederick (William Serafino Austin
Lewis Mary) 1860-1913..... **TCLC 12**
See also CA 107; DLB 34, 156

Rolland, Romain 1866-1944 ...... **TCLC 23**
See also CA 118; DLB 65

Rolle, Richard c. 1300-c. 1349 ... **CMLC 21**
See also DLB 146

Rolvaag, O(le) E(dvart)
See Roelvaag, O(le) E(dvart)

Romain Arnaud, Saint
See Aragon, Louis

Romains, Jules 1885-1972 .... **CLC 7**
See also CA 85-88; CANR 34; DLB 65;
MTCW

Romero, Jose Ruben 1890-1952 ... **TCLC 14**
See also CA 114; 131; HW

Ronsard, Pierre de
1524-1585 .... **LC 6; PC 11**

Rooke, Leon
1934- .... **CLC 25, 34; DAM POP**
See also CA 25-28R; CANR 23, 53

Roper, William 1498-1578......... **LC 10**

Roquelaure, A. N.
See Rice, Anne

Rosa, Joao Guimaraes 1908-1967 ... **CLC 23**
See also CA 89-92; DLB 113

Rose, Wendy
1948- .... **CLC 85; DAM MULT; PC 13**
See also CA 53-56; CANR 5, 51; NNAL;
SATA 12

Rosen, Richard (Dean) 1949- .... **CLC 39**
See also CA 77-80; INT CANR-30

Rosenberg, Isaac 1890-1918....... **TCLC 12**
See also CA 107; DLB 20

Rosenblatt, Joe .... **CLC 15**
See also Rosenblatt, Joseph

Rosenblatt, Joseph 1933-
See Rosenblatt, Joe
See also CA 89-92; INT 89-92

Rosenfeld, Samuel 1896-1963
See Tzara, Tristan
See also CA 89-92

Rosenstock, Sami
See Tzara, Tristan

Rosenstock, Samuel
See Tzara, Tristan

Rosenthal, M(acha) L(ouis)
1917-1996 .... **CLC 28**
See also CA 1-4R; 152; CAAS 6; CANR 4,
51; DLB 5; SATA 59

Ross, Barnaby
See Dannay, Frederic

Ross, Bernard L.
See Follett, Ken(neth Martin)

Ross, J. H.
See Lawrence, T(homas) E(dward)

Ross, Martin
See Martin, Violet Florence
See also DLB 135

Ross, (James) Sinclair
1908- ...... **CLC 13; DAC; DAM MST;**
SSC 24
See also CA 73-76; DLB 88

Rossetti, Christina (Georgina)
1830-1894 ..... **NCLC 2, 50; DA; DAB;**
DAC; DAM MST, POET; PC 7; WLC
See also DLB 35, 163; MAICYA; SATA 20

Rossetti, Dante Gabriel
1828-1882 .... **NCLC 4; DA; DAB;**
DAC; DAM MST, POET; WLC
See also CDBLB 1832-1890; DLB 35

Rossner, Judith (Perelman)
1935- .... **CLC 6, 9, 29**
See also AITN 2; BEST 90:3; CA 17-20R;
CANR 18, 51; DLB 6; INT CANR-18;
MTCW

Rostand, Edmond (Eugene Alexis)
1868-1918 ...... **TCLC 6, 37; DA; DAB;**
DAC; DAM DRAM, MST
See also CA 104; 126; MTCW

Roth, Henry 1906-1995 ...... **CLC 2, 6, 11**
See also CA 11-12; 149; CANR 38; CAP 1;
DLB 28; MTCW

Roth, Joseph 1894-1939......... **TCLC 33**
See also DLB 85

Roth, Philip (Milton)
1933- ...... **CLC 1, 2, 3, 4, 6, 9, 15, 22,**
31, 47, 66, 86; DA; DAB; DAC;
DAM MST, NOV, POP; WLC
See also BEST 90:3; CA 1-4R; CANR 1, 22,
36, 55; CDALB 1968-1988; DLB 2, 28,
173; DLBY 82; MTCW

Rothenberg, Jerome 1931- .... **CLC 6, 57**
See also CA 45-48; CANR 1; DLB 5

Roumain, Jacques (Jean Baptiste)
1907-1944 .... **TCLC 19; BLC;**
DAM MULT
See also BW 1; CA 117; 125

Rourke, Constance (Mayfield)
1885-1941 .... **TCLC 12**
See also CA 107; YABC 1

Rousseau, Jean-Baptiste 1671-1741 ... **LC 9**

Rousseau, Jean-Jacques
1712-1778 ...... **LC 14, 36; DA; DAB;**
DAC; DAM MST; WLC

Roussel, Raymond 1877-1933 ..... **TCLC 20**
See also CA 117

Rovit, Earl (Herbert) 1927-......... **CLC 7**
See also CA 5-8R; CANR 12

Rowe, Nicholas 1674-1718.......... **LC 8**
See also DLB 84

Rowley, Ames Dorrance
See Lovecraft, H(oward) P(hillips)

Rowson, Susanna Haswell
1762(?)-1824 .... **NCLC 5**
See also DLB 37

Roy, Gabrielle
1909-1983 .... **CLC 10, 14; DAB; DAC;**
DAM MST
See also CA 53-56; 110; CANR 5; DLB 68;
MTCW

Rozewicz, Tadeusz
1921- .... **CLC 9, 23; DAM POET**
See also CA 108; CANR 36; MTCW

Ruark, Gibbons 1941- .... **CLC 3**
See also CA 33-36R; CAAS 23; CANR 14,
31; DLB 120

Rubens, Bernice (Ruth) 1923-... **CLC 19, 31**
See also CA 25-28R; CANR 33; DLB 14;
MTCW

Rubin, Harold
See Robbins, Harold

Rudkin, (James) David 1936- ...... **CLC 14**
See also CA 89-92; DLB 13

Rudnik, Raphael 1933-............. **CLC 7**
See also CA 29-32R

Ruffian, M.
See Hasek, Jaroslav (Matej Frantisek)

Ruiz, Jose Martinez .... **CLC 11**
See also Martinez Ruiz, Jose

Rukeyser, Muriel
1913-1980 .... **CLC 6, 10, 15, 27;**
DAM POET; PC 12
See also CA 5-8R; 93-96; CANR 26;
DLB 48; MTCW; SATA-Obit 22

Rule, Jane (Vance) 1931-.......... **CLC 27**
See also CA 25-28R; CAAS 18; CANR 12;
DLB 60

Rulfo, Juan
1918-1986 .... **CLC 8, 80; DAM MULT;**
HLC
See also CA 85-88; 118; CANR 26;
DLB 113; HW; MTCW

Rumi, Jalal al-Din 1297-1373 .... **CMLC 20**

Runeberg, Johan 1804-1877...... **NCLC 41**

Runyon, (Alfred) Damon
1884(?)-1946 .... **TCLC 10**
See also CA 107; DLB 11, 86, 171

Rush, Norman 1933-............. **CLC 44**
See also CA 121; 126; INT 126

Rushdie, (Ahmed) Salman
1947- ..... **CLC 23, 31, 55; DAB; DAC;**
DAM MST, NOV, POP
See also BEST 89:3; CA 108; 111;
CANR 33; INT 111; MTCW

Rushforth, Peter (Scott) 1945- ..... **CLC 19**
See also CA 101

Ruskin, John 1819-1900.........**TCLC 63**
See also CA 114; 129; CDBLB 1832-1890;
DLB 55, 163; SATA 24

Russ, Joanna 1937-..............**CLC 15**
See also CA 25-28R; CANR 11, 31; DLB 8;
MTCW

Russell, George William 1867-1935
See Baker, Jean H.
See also CA 104; 153; CDBLB 1890-1914;
DAM POET

Russell, (Henry) Ken(neth Alfred)
1927-........................**CLC 16**
See also CA 105

Russell, Willy 1947-..............**CLC 60**

Rutherford, Mark ....**TCLC 25**
See also White, William Hale
See also DLB 18

Ruyslinck, Ward 1929-...........**CLC 14**
See also Belser, Reimond Karel Maria de

Ryan, Cornelius (John) 1920-1974 ...**CLC 7**
See also CA 69-72; 53-56; CANR 38

Ryan, Michael 1946-..............**CLC 65**
See also CA 49-52; DLBY 82

Rybakov, Anatoli (Naumovich)
1911-...................**CLC 23, 53**
See also CA 126; 135; SATA 79

Ryder, Jonathan
See Ludlum, Robert

Ryga, George
1932-1987 ..**CLC 14; DAC; DAM MST**
See also CA 101; 124; CANR 43; DLB 60

S. S.
See Sassoon, Siegfried (Lorraine)

Saba, Umberto 1883-1957 ....**TCLC 33**
See also CA 144; DLB 114

Sabatini, Rafael 1875-1950 ....**TCLC 47**

Sabato, Ernesto (R.)
1911-.......**CLC 10, 23; DAM MULT;**
                                    HLC
See also CA 97-100; CANR 32; DLB 145;
HW; MTCW

Sacastru, Martin
See Bioy Casares, Adolfo

Sacher-Masoch, Leopold von
1836(?)-1895 ....**NCLC 31**

Sachs, Marilyn (Stickle) 1927-.....**CLC 35**
See also AAYA 2; CA 17-20R; CANR 13,
47; CLR 2; JRDA; MAICYA; SAAS 2;
SATA 3, 68

Sachs, Nelly 1891-1970 ....**CLC 14, 98**
See also CA 17-18; 25-28R; CAP 2

Sackler, Howard (Oliver)
1929-1982 ....**CLC 14**
See also CA 61-64; 108; CANR 30; DLB 7

Sacks, Oliver (Wolf) 1933- ....**CLC 67**
See also CA 53-56; CANR 28, 50;
INT CANR-28; MTCW

Sade, Donatien Alphonse Francois Comte
1740-1814 ....**NCLC 47**

Sadoff, Ira 1945-..................**CLC 9**
See also CA 53-56; CANR 5, 21; DLB 120

Saetone
See Camus, Albert

Safire, William 1929-.............**CLC 10**
See also CA 17-20R; CANR 31, 54

Sagan, Carl (Edward) 1934-1996....**CLC 30**
See also AAYA 2; CA 25-28R; 155;
CANR 11, 36; MTCW; SATA 58

Sagan, Francoise ....**CLC 3, 6, 9, 17, 36**
See also Quoirez, Francoise
See also DLB 83

Sahgal, Nayantara (Pandit) 1927-...**CLC 41**
See also CA 9-12R; CANR 11

Saint, H(arry) F. 1941- ....**CLC 50**
See also CA 127

St. Aubin de Teran, Lisa 1953-
See Teran, Lisa St. Aubin de
See also CA 118; 126; INT 126

Sainte-Beuve, Charles Augustin
1804-1869 ....**NCLC 5**

Saint-Exupery, Antoine (Jean Baptiste Marie
Roger) de
1900-1944 ....**TCLC 2, 56; DAM NOV;**
                                       WLC
See also CA 108; 132; CLR 10; DLB 72;
MAICYA; MTCW; SATA 20

St. John, David
See Hunt, E(verette) Howard, (Jr.)

Saint-John Perse
See Leger, (Marie-Rene Auguste) Alexis
Saint-Leger

Saintsbury, George (Edward Bateman)
1845-1933 ....**TCLC 31**
See also DLB 57, 149

Sait Faik ....**TCLC 23**
See also Abasiyanik, Sait Faik

Saki ....**TCLC 3; SSC 12**
See also Munro, H(ector) H(ugh)

Sala, George Augustus ....**NCLC 46**

Salama, Hannu 1936-.............**CLC 18**

Salamanca, J(ack) R(ichard)
1922-....................**CLC 4, 15**
See also CA 25-28R

Sale, J. Kirkpatrick
See Sale, Kirkpatrick

Sale, Kirkpatrick 1937-...........**CLC 68**
See also CA 13-16R; CANR 10

Salinas, Luis Omar
1937-.....**CLC 90; DAM MULT; HLC**
See also CA 131; DLB 82; HW

Salinas (y Serrano), Pedro
1891(?)-1951 ....**TCLC 17**
See also CA 117; DLB 134

Salinger, J(erome) D(avid)
1919-......**CLC 1, 3, 8, 12, 55, 56; DA;**
DAB; DAC; DAM MST, NOV, POP;
                                      SSC 2; WLC
See also AAYA 2; CA 5-8R; CANR 39;
CDALB 1941-1968; CLR 18; DLB 2, 102,
173; MAICYA; MTCW; SATA 67

Salisbury, John
See Caute, David

Salter, James 1925- ....**CLC 7, 52, 59**
See also CA 73-76; DLB 130

Saltus, Edgar (Everton)
1855-1921 ....**TCLC 8**
See also CA 105

Saltykov, Mikhail Evgrafovich
1826-1889 ....**NCLC 16**

Samarakis, Antonis 1919- ....**CLC 5**
See also CA 25-28R; CAAS 16; CANR 36

Sanchez, Florencio 1875-1910.....**TCLC 37**
See also CA 153; HW

Sanchez, Luis Rafael 1936-........**CLC 23**
See also CA 128; DLB 145; HW

Sanchez, Sonia
1934-......**CLC 5; BLC; DAM MULT;**
                                       PC 9
See also BW 2; CA 33-36R; CANR 24, 49;
CLR 18; DLB 41; DLBD 8; MAICYA;
MTCW; SATA 22

Sand, George
1804-1876 ....**NCLC 2, 42, 57; DA;**
DAB; DAC; DAM MST, NOV; WLC
See also DLB 119

Sandburg, Carl (August)
1878-1967 ....**CLC 1, 4, 10, 15, 35; DA;**
DAB; DAC; DAM MST, POET; PC 2;
                                             WLC
See also CA 5-8R; 25-28R; CANR 35;
CDALB 1865-1917; DLB 17, 54;
MAICYA; MTCW; SATA 8

Sandburg, Charles
See Sandburg, Carl (August)

Sandburg, Charles A.
See Sandburg, Carl (August)

Sanders, (James) Ed(ward) 1939- ...**CLC 53**
See also CA 13-16R; CAAS 21; CANR 13,
44; DLB 16

Sanders, Lawrence
1920-............**CLC 41; DAM POP**
See also BEST 89:4; CA 81-84; CANR 33;
MTCW

Sanders, Noah
See Blount, Roy (Alton), Jr.

Sanders, Winston P.
See Anderson, Poul (William)

Sandoz, Mari(e Susette)
1896-1966 ....**CLC 28**
See also CA 1-4R; 25-28R; CANR 17;
DLB 9; MTCW; SATA 5

Saner, Reg(inald Anthony) 1931- ....**CLC 9**
See also CA 65-68

Sannazaro, Jacopo 1456(?)-1530......**LC 8**

Sansom, William
1912-1976 ......**CLC 2, 6; DAM NOV;**
                                        SSC 21
See also CA 5-8R; 65-68; CANR 42;
DLB 139; MTCW

Santayana, George 1863-1952.....**TCLC 40**
See also CA 115; DLB 54, 71; DLBD 13

Santiago, Danny ....**CLC 33**
See also James, Daniel (Lewis)
See also DLB 122

Santmyer, Helen Hoover
1895-1986 ....**CLC 33**
See also CA 1-4R; 118; CANR 15, 33;
DLBY 84; MTCW

Santos, Bienvenido N(uqui)
1911-1996 ......**CLC 22; DAM MULT**
See also CA 101; 151; CANR 19, 46

Sapper .... **TCLC 44**
See also McNeile, Herman Cyril

Sappho
fl. 6th cent. B.C.- .... **CMLC 3;
DAM POET; PC 5**

Sarduy, Severo 1937-1993 ...... **CLC 6, 97**
See also CA 89-92; 142; DLB 113; HW

Sargeson, Frank 1903-1982 .... **CLC 31**
See also CA 25-28R; 106; CANR 38

Sarmiento, Felix Ruben Garcia
See Dario, Ruben

Saroyan, William
1908-1981 ..... **CLC 1, 8, 10, 29, 34, 56;
DA; DAB; DAC; DAM DRAM, MST,
NOV; SSC 21; WLC**
See also CA 5-8R; 103; CANR 30; DLB 7,
9, 86; DLBY 81; MTCW; SATA 23;
SATA-Obit 24

Sarraute, Nathalie
1900- .... **CLC 1, 2, 4, 8, 10, 31, 80**
See also CA 9-12R; CANR 23; DLB 83;
MTCW

Sarton, (Eleanor) May
1912-1995 .... **CLC 4, 14, 49, 91;
DAM POET**
See also CA 1-4R; 149; CANR 1, 34, 55;
DLB 48; DLBY 81; INT CANR-34;
MTCW; SATA 36; SATA-Obit 86

Sartre, Jean-Paul
1905-1980 .... **CLC 1, 4, 7, 9, 13, 18, 24,
44, 50, 52; DA; DAB; DAC;
DAM DRAM, MST, NOV; DC 3; WLC**
See also CA 9-12R; 97-100; CANR 21;
DLB 72; MTCW

Sassoon, Siegfried (Lorraine)
1886-1967 .... **CLC 36; DAB;
DAM MST, NOV, POET; PC 12**
See also CA 104; 25-28R; CANR 36;
DLB 20; MTCW

Satterfield, Charles
See Pohl, Frederik

Saul, John (W. III)
1942- .... **CLC 46; DAM NOV, POP**
See also AAYA 10; BEST 90:4; CA 81-84;
CANR 16, 40

Saunders, Caleb
See Heinlein, Robert A(nson)

Saura (Atares), Carlos 1932- .... **CLC 20**
See also CA 114; 131; HW

Sauser-Hall, Frederic 1887-1961.... **CLC 18**
See also Cendrars, Blaise
See also CA 102; 93-96; CANR 36; MTCW

Saussure, Ferdinand de
1857-1913 .... **TCLC 49**

Savage, Catharine
See Brosman, Catharine Savage

Savage, Thomas 1915- .... **CLC 40**
See also CA 126; 132; CAAS 15; INT 132

Savan, Glenn 19(?)- .... **CLC 50**

Sayers, Dorothy L(eigh)
1893-1957 ..... **TCLC 2, 15; DAM POP**
See also CA 104; 119; CDBLB 1914-1945;
DLB 10, 36, 77, 100; MTCW

Sayers, Valerie 1952- .... **CLC 50**
See also CA 134

Sayles, John (Thomas)
1950- .... **CLC 7, 10, 14**
See also CA 57-60; CANR 41; DLB 44

Scammell, Michael .... **CLC 34**

Scannell, Vernon 1922- .... **CLC 49**
See also CA 5-8R; CANR 8, 24; DLB 27;
SATA 59

Scarlett, Susan
See Streatfeild, (Mary) Noel

Schaeffer, Susan Fromberg
1941- .... **CLC 6, 11, 22**
See also CA 49-52; CANR 18; DLB 28;
MTCW; SATA 22

Schary, Jill
See Robinson, Jill

Schell, Jonathan 1943- .... **CLC 35**
See also CA 73-76; CANR 12

Schelling, Friedrich Wilhelm Joseph von
1775-1854 .... **NCLC 30**
See also DLB 90

Schendel, Arthur van 1874-1946 ... **TCLC 56**

Scherer, Jean-Marie Maurice 1920-
See Rohmer, Eric
See also CA 110

Schevill, James (Erwin) 1920- ...... **CLC 7**
See also CA 5-8R; CAAS 12

Schiller, Friedrich
1759-1805 .... **NCLC 39; DAM DRAM**
See also DLB 94

Schisgal, Murray (Joseph) 1926- ..... **CLC 6**
See also CA 21-24R; CANR 48

Schlee, Ann 1934- .... **CLC 35**
See also CA 101; CANR 29; SATA 44;
SATA-Brief 36

Schlegel, August Wilhelm von
1767-1845 .... **NCLC 15**
See also DLB 94

Schlegel, Friedrich 1772-1829 .... **NCLC 45**
See also DLB 90

Schlegel, Johann Elias (von)
1719(?)-1749 .... **LC 5**

Schlesinger, Arthur M(eier), Jr.
1917- .... **CLC 84**
See also AITN 1; CA 1-4R; CANR 1, 28;
DLB 17; INT CANR-28; MTCW;
SATA 61

Schmidt, Arno (Otto) 1914-1979.... **CLC 56**
See also CA 128; 109; DLB 69

Schmitz, Aron Hector 1861-1928
See Svevo, Italo
See also CA 104; 122; MTCW

Schnackenberg, Gjertrud 1953- ..... **CLC 40**
See also CA 116; DLB 120

Schneider, Leonard Alfred 1925-1966
See Bruce, Lenny
See also CA 89-92

Schnitzler, Arthur
1862-1931 .... **TCLC 4; SSC 15**
See also CA 104; DLB 81, 118

Schopenhauer, Arthur
1788-1860 .... **NCLC 51**
See also DLB 90

Schor, Sandra (M.) 1932(?)-1990 ... **CLC 65**
See also CA 132

Schorer, Mark 1908-1977 .... **CLC 9**
See also CA 5-8R; 73-76; CANR 7;
DLB 103

Schrader, Paul (Joseph) 1946-...... **CLC 26**
See also CA 37-40R; CANR 41; DLB 44

Schreiner, Olive (Emilie Albertina)
1855-1920 .... **TCLC 9**
See also CA 105; DLB 18, 156

Schulberg, Budd (Wilson)
1914- .... **CLC 7, 48**
See also CA 25-28R; CANR 19; DLB 6, 26,
28; DLBY 81

Schulz, Bruno
1892-1942 .... **TCLC 5, 51; SSC 13**
See also CA 115; 123

Schulz, Charles M(onroe) 1922- .... **CLC 12**
See also CA 9-12R; CANR 6;
INT CANR-6; SATA 10

Schumacher, E(rnst) F(riedrich)
1911-1977 .... **CLC 80**
See also CA 81-84; 73-76; CANR 34

Schuyler, James Marcus
1923-1991 ..... **CLC 5, 23; DAM POET**
See also CA 101; 134; DLB 5, 169; INT 101

Schwartz, Delmore (David)
1913-1966 ... **CLC 2, 4, 10, 45, 87; PC 8**
See also CA 17-18; 25-28R; CANR 35;
CAP 2; DLB 28, 48; MTCW

Schwartz, Ernst
See Ozu, Yasujiro

Schwartz, John Burnham 1965- .... **CLC 59**
See also CA 132

Schwartz, Lynne Sharon 1939- ..... **CLC 31**
See also CA 103; CANR 44

Schwartz, Muriel A.
See Eliot, T(homas) S(tearns)

Schwarz-Bart, Andre 1928-....... **CLC 2, 4**
See also CA 89-92

Schwarz-Bart, Simone 1938-........ **CLC 7**
See also BW 2; CA 97-100

Schwob, (Mayer Andre) Marcel
1867-1905 .... **TCLC 20**
See also CA 117; DLB 123

Sciascia, Leonardo
1921-1989 .... **CLC 8, 9, 41**
See also CA 85-88; 130; CANR 35; MTCW

Scoppettone, Sandra 1936-........ **CLC 26**
See also AAYA 11; CA 5-8R; CANR 41;
SATA 9

Scorsese, Martin 1942- .... **CLC 20, 89**
See also CA 110; 114; CANR 46

Scotland, Jay
See Jakes, John (William)

Scott, Duncan Campbell
1862-1947 .... **TCLC 6; DAC**
See also CA 104; 153; DLB 92

Scott, Evelyn 1893-1963........... **CLC 43**
See also CA 104; 112; DLB 9, 48

Scott, F(rancis) R(eginald)
1899-1985 .... **CLC 22**
See also CA 101; 114; DLB 88; INT 101

Scott, Frank
See Scott, F(rancis) R(eginald)

Author Index

Scott, Joanna 1960- . . . . **CLC 50**
See also CA 126; CANR 53

Scott, Paul (Mark) 1920-1978. . . . **CLC 9, 60**
See also CA 81-84; 77-80; CANR 33;
DLB 14; MTCW

Scott, Walter
1771-1832 . . . . **NCLC 15; DA; DAB;
DAC; DAM MST, NOV, POET; PC 13;
WLC**
See also CDBLB 1789-1832; DLB 93, 107,
116, 144, 159; YABC 2

Scribe, (Augustin) Eugene
1791-1861 . . . . **NCLC 16; DAM DRAM;
DC 5**

Scrum, R.
See Crumb, R(obert)

Scudery, Madeleine de 1607-1701 . . . . . **LC 2**

Scum
See Crumb, R(obert)

Scumbag, Little Bobby
See Crumb, R(obert)

Seabrook, John
See Hubbard, L(afayette) Ron(ald)

Sealy, I. Allan 1951- . . . . **CLC 55**

Search, Alexander
See Pessoa, Fernando (Antonio Nogueira)

Sebastian, Lee
See Silverberg, Robert

Sebastian Owl
See Thompson, Hunter S(tockton)

Sebestyen, Ouida 1924- . . . . **CLC 30**
See also AAYA 8; CA 107; CANR 40;
CLR 17; JRDA; MAICYA; SAAS 10;
SATA 39

Secundus, H. Scriblerus
See Fielding, Henry

Sedges, John
See Buck, Pearl S(ydenstricker)

Sedgwick, Catharine Maria
1789-1867 . . . . **NCLC 19**
See also DLB 1, 74

Seelye, John 1931- . . . . **CLC 7**

Seferiades, Giorgos Stylianou 1900-1971
See Seferis, George
See also CA 5-8R; 33-36R; CANR 5, 36;
MTCW

Seferis, George . . . . **CLC 5, 11**
See also Seferiades, Giorgos Stylianou

Segal, Erich (Wolf)
1937- . . . . **CLC 3, 10; DAM POP**
See also BEST 89:1; CA 25-28R; CANR 20,
36; DLBY 86; INT CANR-20; MTCW

Seger, Bob 1945- . . . . **CLC 35**

Seghers, Anna . . . . **CLC 7**
See also Radvanyi, Netty
See also DLB 69

Seidel, Frederick (Lewis) 1936- . . . . . **CLC 18**
See also CA 13-16R; CANR 8; DLBY 84

Seifert, Jaroslav
1901-1986 . . . . **CLC 34, 44, 93**
See also CA 127; MTCW

Sei Shonagon c. 966-1017(?) . . . . . . **CMLC 6**

Selby, Hubert, Jr.
1928- . . . . **CLC 1, 2, 4, 8; SSC 20**
See also CA 13-16R; CANR 33; DLB 2

Selzer, Richard 1928- . . . . **CLC 74**
See also CA 65-68; CANR 14

Sembene, Ousmane
See Ousmane, Sembene

Senancour, Etienne Pivert de
1770-1846 . . . . **NCLC 16**
See also DLB 119

Sender, Ramon (Jose)
1902-1982 . . **CLC 8; DAM MULT; HLC**
See also CA 5-8R; 105; CANR 8; HW;
MTCW

Seneca, Lucius Annaeus
4B.C.-65. . . . . . . **CMLC 6; DAM DRAM;
DC 5**

Senghor, Leopold Sedar
1906- . . . . . **CLC 54; BLC; DAM MULT,
POET**
See also BW 2; CA 116; 125; CANR 47;
MTCW

Serling, (Edward) Rod(man)
1924-1975 . . . . **CLC 30**
See also AAYA 14; AITN 1; CA 65-68;
57-60; DLB 26

Serna, Ramon Gomez de la
See Gomez de la Serna, Ramon

Serpieres
See Guillevic, (Eugene)

Service, Robert
See Service, Robert W(illiam)
See also DAB; DLB 92

Service, Robert W(illiam)
1874(?)-1958 . . . . . . **TCLC 15; DA; DAC;
DAM MST, POET; WLC**
See Service, Robert
See also CA 115; 140; SATA 20

Seth, Vikram
1952- . . . . **CLC 43, 90; DAM MULT**
See also CA 121; 127; CANR 50; DLB 120;
INT 127

Seton, Cynthia Propper
1926-1982 . . . . **CLC 27**
See also CA 5-8R; 108; CANR 7

Seton, Ernest (Evan) Thompson
1860-1946 . . . . **TCLC 31**
See also CA 109; DLB 92; DLBD 13;
JRDA; SATA 18

Seton-Thompson, Ernest
See Seton, Ernest (Evan) Thompson

Settle, Mary Lee 1918- . . . . **CLC 19, 61**
See also CA 89-92; CAAS 1; CANR 44;
DLB 6; INT 89-92

Seuphor, Michel
See Arp, Jean

**Sevigne, Marie (de Rabutin-Chantal) Marquise
de** 1626-1696 . . . . **LC 11**

Sexton, Anne (Harvey)
1928-1974 . . . . **CLC 2, 4, 6, 8, 10, 15, 53;
DA; DAB; DAC; DAM MST, POET;
PC 2; WLC**
See also CA 1-4R; 53-56; CABS 2;
CANR 3, 36; CDALB 1941-1968; DLB 5,
169; MTCW; SATA 10

Shaara, Michael (Joseph, Jr.)
1929-1988 . . . . **CLC 15; DAM POP**
See also AITN 1; CA 102; 125; CANR 52;
DLBY 83

Shackleton, C. C.
See Aldiss, Brian W(ilson)

Shacochis, Bob . . . . **CLC 39**
See also Shacochis, Robert G.

Shacochis, Robert G. 1951-
See Shacochis, Bob
See also CA 119; 124; INT 124

Shaffer, Anthony (Joshua)
1926- . . . . **CLC 19; DAM DRAM**
See also CA 110; 116; DLB 13

Shaffer, Peter (Levin)
1926- . . . . . . **CLC 5, 14, 18, 37, 60; DAB;
DAM DRAM, MST**
See also CA 25-28R; CANR 25, 47;
CDBLB 1960 to Present; DLB 13;
MTCW

Shakey, Bernard
See Young, Neil

Shalamov, Varlam (Tikhonovich)
1907(?)-1982 . . . . **CLC 18**
See also CA 129; 105

Shamlu, Ahmad 1925- . . . . **CLC 10**

Shammas, Anton 1951- . . . . **CLC 55**

Shange, Ntozake
1948- . . . . **CLC 8, 25, 38, 74; BLC;
DAM DRAM, MULT; DC 3**
See also AAYA 9; BW 2; CA 85-88;
CABS 3; CANR 27, 48; DLB 38; MTCW

Shanley, John Patrick 1950- . . . . **CLC 75**
See also CA 128; 133

Shapcott, Thomas W(illiam) 1935- . . **CLC 38**
See also CA 69-72; CANR 49

Shapiro, Jane . . . . **CLC 76**

Shapiro, Karl (Jay) 1913- . . **CLC 4, 8, 15, 53**
See also CA 1-4R; CAAS 6; CANR 1, 36;
DLB 48; MTCW

Sharp, William 1855-1905 . . . . **TCLC 39**
See also DLB 156

Sharpe, Thomas Ridley 1928-
See Sharpe, Tom
See also CA 114; 122; INT 122

Sharpe, Tom . . . . **CLC 36**
See also Sharpe, Thomas Ridley
See also DLB 14

Shaw, Bernard . . . . **TCLC 45**
See also Shaw, George Bernard
See also BW 1

Shaw, G. Bernard
See Shaw, George Bernard

Shaw, George Bernard
1856-1950 . . . **TCLC 3, 9, 21; DA; DAB;
DAC; DAM DRAM, MST; WLC**
See also Shaw, Bernard
See also CA 104; 128; CDBLB 1914-1945;
DLB 10, 57; MTCW

Shaw, Henry Wheeler
1818-1885 . . . . **NCLC 15**
See also DLB 11

Shaw, Irwin
1913-1984 . . . . CLC 7, 23, 34;
DAM DRAM, POP
See also AITN 1; CA 13-16R; 112;
CANR 21; CDALB 1941-1968; DLB 6,
102; DLBY 84; MTCW

Shaw, Robert 1927-1978 . . . . CLC 5
See also AITN 1; CA 1-4R; 81-84;
CANR 4; DLB 13, 14

Shaw, T. E.
See Lawrence, T(homas) E(dward)

Shawn, Wallace 1943- . . . . CLC 41
See also CA 112

Shea, Lisa 1953- . . . . CLC 86
See also CA 147

Sheed, Wilfrid (John Joseph)
1930- . . . . CLC 2, 4, 10, 53
See also CA 65-68; CANR 30; DLB 6;
MTCW

Sheldon, Alice Hastings Bradley
1915(?)-1987
See Tiptree, James, Jr.
See also CA 108; 122; CANR 34; INT 108;
MTCW

Sheldon, John
See Bloch, Robert (Albert)

Shelley, Mary Wollstonecraft (Godwin)
1797-1851 . . . . NCLC 14, 59; DA; DAB;
DAC; DAM MST, NOV; WLC
See also CDBLB 1789-1832; DLB 110, 116,
159; SATA 29

Shelley, Percy Bysshe
1792-1822 . . . . . . NCLC 18; DA; DAB;
DAC; DAM MST, POET; PC 14; WLC
See also CDBLB 1789-1832; DLB 96, 110,
158

Shepard, Jim 1956- . . . . CLC 36
See also CA 137; SATA 90

Shepard, Lucius 1947- . . . . CLC 34
See also CA 128; 141

Shepard, Sam
1943- . . . . CLC 4, 6, 17, 34, 41, 44;
DAM DRAM; DC 5
See also AAYA 1; CA 69-72; CABS 3;
CANR 22; DLB 7; MTCW

Shepherd, Michael
See Ludlum, Robert

Sherburne, Zoa (Morin) 1912- . . . . . CLC 30
See also AAYA 13; CA 1-4R; CANR 3, 37;
MAICYA; SAAS 18; SATA 3

Sheridan, Frances 1724-1766 . . . . LC 7
See also DLB 39, 84

Sheridan, Richard Brinsley
1751-1816 . . . . NCLC 5; DA; DAB;
DAC; DAM DRAM, MST; DC 1; WLC
See also CDBLB 1660-1789; DLB 89

Sherman, Jonathan Marc . . . . CLC 55

Sherman, Martin 1941(?)- . . . . CLC 19
See also CA 116; 123

Sherwin, Judith Johnson 1936- . . . CLC 7, 15
See also CA 25-28R; CANR 34

Sherwood, Frances 1940- . . . . CLC 81
See also CA 146

Sherwood, Robert E(mmet)
1896-1955 . . . . . TCLC 3; DAM DRAM
See also CA 104; 153; DLB 7, 26

Shestov, Lev 1866-1938 . . . . TCLC 56

Shevchenko, Taras 1814-1861 . . . . NCLC 54

Shiel, M(atthew) P(hipps)
1865-1947 . . . . TCLC 8
See also CA 106; DLB 153

Shields, Carol 1935- . . . . CLC 91; DAC
See also CA 81-84; CANR 51

Shields, David 1956- . . . . CLC 97
See also CA 124; CANR 48

Shiga, Naoya 1883-1971 . . . CLC 33; SSC 23
See also CA 101; 33-36R

Shilts, Randy 1951-1994 . . . . CLC 85
See also AAYA 19; CA 115; 127; 144;
CANR 45; INT 127

Shimazaki, Haruki 1872-1943
See Shimazaki Toson
See also CA 105; 134

Shimazaki Toson . . . . TCLC 5
See also Shimazaki, Haruki

Sholokhov, Mikhail (Aleksandrovich)
1905-1984 . . . . CLC 7, 15
See also CA 101; 112; MTCW;
SATA-Obit 36

Shone, Patric
See Hanley, James

Shreve, Susan Richards 1939- . . . . . . CLC 23
See also CA 49-52; CAAS 5; CANR 5, 38;
MAICYA; SATA 46; SATA-Brief 41

Shue, Larry
1946-1985 . . . . . . CLC 52; DAM DRAM
See also CA 145; 117

Shu-Jen, Chou 1881-1936
See Lu Hsun
See also CA 104

Shulman, Alix Kates 1932- . . . . . . CLC 2, 10
See also CA 29-32R; CANR 43; SATA 7

Shuster, Joe 1914- . . . . CLC 21

Shute, Nevil . . . . CLC 30
See also Norway, Nevil Shute

Shuttle, Penelope (Diane) 1947- . . . . . CLC 7
See also CA 93-96; CANR 39; DLB 14, 40

Sidney, Mary 1561-1621 . . . . LC 19

Sidney, Sir Philip
1554-1586 . . . . . LC 19; DA; DAB; DAC;
DAM MST, POET
See also CDBLB Before 1660; DLB 167

Siegel, Jerome 1914-1996 . . . . CLC 21
See also CA 116; 151

Siegel, Jerry
See Siegel, Jerome

Sienkiewicz, Henryk (Adam Alexander Pius)
1846-1916 . . . . TCLC 3
See also CA 104; 134

Sierra, Gregorio Martinez
See Martinez Sierra, Gregorio

Sierra, Maria (de la O'LeJarraga) Martinez
See Martinez Sierra, Maria (de la
O'LeJarraga)

Sigal, Clancy 1926- . . . . CLC 7
See also CA 1-4R

Sigourney, Lydia Howard (Huntley)
1791-1865 . . . . NCLC 21
See also DLB 1, 42, 73

Siguenza y Gongora, Carlos de
1645-1700 . . . . LC 8

Sigurjonsson, Johann 1880-1919 . . . TCLC 27

Sikelianos, Angelos 1884-1951 . . . . TCLC 39

Silkin, Jon 1930- . . . . CLC 2, 6, 43
See also CA 5-8R; CAAS 5; DLB 27

Silko, Leslie (Marmon)
1948- . . . . CLC 23, 74; DA; DAC;
DAM MST, MULT, POP
See also AAYA 14; CA 115; 122;
CANR 45; DLB 143; NNAL

Sillanpaa, Frans Eemil 1888-1964 . . . CLC 19
See also CA 129; 93-96; MTCW

Sillitoe, Alan
1928- . . . . CLC 1, 3, 6, 10, 19, 57
See also AITN 1; CA 9-12R; CAAS 2;
CANR 8, 26, 55; CDBLB 1960 to
Present; DLB 14, 139; MTCW; SATA 61

Silone, Ignazio 1900-1978 . . . . CLC 4
See also CA 25-28; 81-84; CANR 34;
CAP 2; MTCW

Silver, Joan Micklin 1935- . . . . CLC 20
See also CA 114; 121; INT 121

Silver, Nicholas
See Faust, Frederick (Schiller)

Silverberg, Robert
1935- . . . . CLC 7; DAM POP
See also CA 1-4R; CAAS 3; CANR 1, 20,
36; DLB 8; INT CANR-20; MAICYA;
MTCW; SATA 13, 91

Silverstein, Alvin 1933- . . . . CLC 17
See also CA 49-52; CANR 2; CLR 25;
JRDA; MAICYA; SATA 8, 69

Silverstein, Virginia B(arbara Opshelor)
1937- . . . . CLC 17
See also CA 49-52; CANR 2; CLR 25;
JRDA; MAICYA; SATA 8, 69

Sim, Georges
See Simenon, Georges (Jacques Christian)

Simak, Clifford D(onald)
1904-1988 . . . . CLC 1, 55
See also CA 1-4R; 125; CANR 1, 35;
DLB 8; MTCW; SATA-Obit 56

Simenon, Georges (Jacques Christian)
1903-1989 . . . . CLC 1, 2, 3, 8, 18, 47;
DAM POP
See also CA 85-88; 129; CANR 35;
DLB 72; DLBY 89; MTCW

Simic, Charles
1938- . . . . CLC 6, 9, 22, 49, 68;
DAM POET
See also CA 29-32R; CAAS 4; CANR 12,
33, 52; DLB 105

Simmel, Georg 1858-1918 . . . . TCLC 64

Simmons, Charles (Paul) 1924- . . . . . CLC 57
See also CA 89-92; INT 89-92

Simmons, Dan 1948- . . . CLC 44; DAM POP
See also AAYA 16; CA 138; CANR 53

Simmons, James (Stewart Alexander)
1933- . . . . CLC 43
See also CA 105; CAAS 21; DLB 40

Simms, William Gilmore
1806-1870 . . . . **NCLC 3**
See also DLB 3, 30, 59, 73

Simon, Carly 1945- . . . . **CLC 26**
See also CA 105

Simon, Claude
1913- . . . . **CLC 4, 9, 15, 39; DAM NOV**
See also CA 89-92; CANR 33; DLB 83;
MTCW

Simon, (Marvin) Neil
1927- . . . . **CLC 6, 11, 31, 39, 70;**
DAM DRAM
See also AITN 1; CA 21-24R; CANR 26,
54; DLB 7; MTCW

Simon, Paul (Frederick) 1941(?)- . . . **CLC 17**
See also CA 116; 153

Simonon, Paul 1956(?)- . . . . **CLC 30**

Simpson, Harriette
See Arnow, Harriette (Louisa) Simpson

Simpson, Louis (Aston Marantz)
1923- . . . . **CLC 4, 7, 9, 32; DAM POET**
See also CA 1-4R; CAAS 4; CANR 1;
DLB 5; MTCW

Simpson, Mona (Elizabeth) 1957- . . . **CLC 44**
See also CA 122; 135

Simpson, N(orman) F(rederick)
1919- . . . . **CLC 29**
See also CA 13-16R; DLB 13

Sinclair, Andrew (Annandale)
1935- . . . . **CLC 2, 14**
See also CA 9-12R; CAAS 5; CANR 14, 38;
DLB 14; MTCW

Sinclair, Emil
See Hesse, Hermann

Sinclair, Iain 1943- . . . . **CLC 76**
See also CA 132

Sinclair, Iain MacGregor
See Sinclair, Iain

Sinclair, Irene
See Griffith, D(avid Lewelyn) W(ark)

Sinclair, Mary Amelia St. Clair 1865(?)-1946
See Sinclair, May
See also CA 104

Sinclair, May . . . . **TCLC 3, 11**
See also Sinclair, Mary Amelia St. Clair
See also DLB 36, 135

Sinclair, Roy
See Griffith, D(avid Lewelyn) W(ark)

Sinclair, Upton (Beall)
1878-1968 . . . . . . **CLC 1, 11, 15, 63; DA;**
DAB; DAC; DAM MST, NOV; WLC
See also CA 5-8R; 25-28R; CANR 7;
CDALB 1929-1941; DLB 9;
INT CANR-7; MTCW; SATA 9

Singer, Isaac
See Singer, Isaac Bashevis

Singer, Isaac Bashevis
1904-1991 . . . . **CLC 1, 3, 6, 9, 11, 15, 23,**
38, 69; DA; DAB; DAC; DAM MST,
NOV; SSC 3; WLC
See also AITN 1, 2; CA 1-4R; 134;
CANR 1, 39; CDALB 1941-1968; CLR 1;
DLB 6, 28, 52; DLBY 91; JRDA;
MAICYA; MTCW; SATA 3, 27;
SATA-Obit 68

Singer, Israel Joshua 1893-1944 . . . **TCLC 33**

Singh, Khushwant 1915- . . . . **CLC 11**
See also CA 9-12R; CAAS 9; CANR 6

Sinjohn, John
See Galsworthy, John

Sinyavsky, Andrei (Donatevich)
1925- . . . . **CLC 8**
See also CA 85-88

Sirin, V.
See Nabokov, Vladimir (Vladimirovich)

Sissman, L(ouis) E(dward)
1928-1976 . . . . **CLC 9, 18**
See also CA 21-24R; 65-68; CANR 13;
DLB 5

Sisson, C(harles) H(ubert) 1914- . . . . . **CLC 8**
See also CA 1-4R; CAAS 3; CANR 3, 48;
DLB 27

Sitwell, Dame Edith
1887-1964 . . . . **CLC 2, 9, 67;**
DAM POET; PC 3
See also CA 9-12R; CANR 35;
CDBLB 1945-1960; DLB 20; MTCW

Sjoewall, Maj 1935- . . . . **CLC 7**
See also CA 65-68

Sjowall, Maj
See Sjoewall, Maj

Skelton, Robin 1925- . . . . **CLC 13**
See also AITN 2; CA 5-8R; CAAS 5;
CANR 28; DLB 27, 53

Skolimowski, Jerzy 1938- . . . . **CLC 20**
See also CA 128

Skram, Amalie (Bertha)
1847-1905 . . . . **TCLC 25**

Skvorecky, Josef (Vaclav)
1924- . . . . **CLC 15, 39, 69; DAC;**
DAM NOV
See also CA 61-64; CAAS 1; CANR 10, 34;
MTCW

Slade, Bernard . . . . **CLC 11, 46**
See also Newbound, Bernard Slade
See also CAAS 9; DLB 53

Slaughter, Carolyn 1946- . . . . **CLC 56**
See also CA 85-88

Slaughter, Frank G(ill) 1908- . . . . . . **CLC 29**
See also AITN 2; CA 5-8R; CANR 5;
INT CANR-5

Slavitt, David R(ytman) 1935- . . . . **CLC 5, 14**
See also CA 21-24R; CAAS 3; CANR 41;
DLB 5, 6

Slesinger, Tess 1905-1945 . . . . **TCLC 10**
See also CA 107; DLB 102

Slessor, Kenneth 1901-1971 . . . . **CLC 14**
See also CA 102; 89-92

Slowacki, Juliusz 1809-1849 . . . . . **NCLC 15**

Smart, Christopher
1722-1771 . . . **LC 3; DAM POET; PC 13**
See also DLB 109

Smart, Elizabeth 1913-1986 . . . . **CLC 54**
See also CA 81-84; 118; DLB 88

Smiley, Jane (Graves)
1949- . . . . **CLC 53, 76; DAM POP**
See also CA 104; CANR 30, 50;
INT CANR-30

Smith, A(rthur) J(ames) M(arshall)
1902-1980 . . . . **CLC 15; DAC**
See also CA 1-4R; 102; CANR 4; DLB 88

Smith, Adam 1723-1790 . . . . **LC 36**
See also DLB 104

Smith, Alexander 1829-1867 . . . . . **NCLC 59**
See also DLB 32, 55

Smith, Anna Deavere 1950- . . . . **CLC 86**
See also CA 133

Smith, Betty (Wehner) 1896-1972 . . . **CLC 19**
See also CA 5-8R; 33-36R; DLBY 82;
SATA 6

Smith, Charlotte (Turner)
1749-1806 . . . . **NCLC 23**
See also DLB 39, 109

Smith, Clark Ashton 1893-1961 . . . . **CLC 43**
See also CA 143

Smith, Dave . . . . **CLC 22, 42**
See also Smith, David (Jeddie)
See also CAAS 7; DLB 5

Smith, David (Jeddie) 1942-
See Smith, Dave
See also CA 49-52; CANR 1; DAM POET

Smith, Florence Margaret 1902-1971
See Smith, Stevie
See also CA 17-18; 29-32R; CANR 35;
CAP 2; DAM POET; MTCW

Smith, Iain Crichton 1928- . . . . **CLC 64**
See also CA 21-24R; DLB 40, 139

Smith, John 1580(?)-1631 . . . . **LC 9**

Smith, Johnston
See Crane, Stephen (Townley)

Smith, Joseph, Jr. 1805-1844 . . . . **NCLC 53**

Smith, Lee 1944- . . . . **CLC 25, 73**
See also CA 114; 119; CANR 46; DLB 143;
DLBY 83; INT 119

Smith, Martin
See Smith, Martin Cruz

Smith, Martin Cruz
1942- . . . . . **CLC 25; DAM MULT, POP**
See also BEST 89:4; CA 85-88; CANR 6,
23, 43; INT CANR-23; NNAL

Smith, Mary-Ann Tirone 1944- . . . . . **CLC 39**
See also CA 118; 136

Smith, Patti 1946- . . . . **CLC 12**
See also CA 93-96

Smith, Pauline (Urmson)
1882-1959 . . . . **TCLC 25**

Smith, Rosamond
See Oates, Joyce Carol

Smith, Sheila Kaye
See Kaye-Smith, Sheila

Smith, Stevie . . . . **CLC 3, 8, 25, 44; PC 12**
See also Smith, Florence Margaret
See also DLB 20

Smith, Wilbur (Addison) 1933- . . . . . **CLC 33**
See also CA 13-16R; CANR 7, 46; MTCW

Smith, William Jay 1918- . . . . **CLC 6**
See also CA 5-8R; CANR 44; DLB 5;
MAICYA; SAAS 22; SATA 2, 68

Smith, Woodrow Wilson
See Kuttner, Henry

Smolenskin, Peretz 1842-1885 . . . . **NCLC 30**

Smollett, Tobias (George) 1721-1771 . . **LC 2**
See also CDBLB 1660-1789; DLB 39, 104

Snodgrass, W(illiam) D(e Witt)
1926- . . . . **CLC 2, 6, 10, 18, 68;**
DAM POET
See also CA 1-4R; CANR 6, 36; DLB 5;
MTCW

Snow, C(harles) P(ercy)
1905-1980 . . . . . . **CLC 1, 4, 6, 9, 13, 19;**
DAM NOV
See also CA 5-8R; 101; CANR 28;
CDBLB 1945-1960; DLB 15, 77; MTCW

Snow, Frances Compton
See Adams, Henry (Brooks)

Snyder, Gary (Sherman)
1930- . . **CLC 1, 2, 5, 9, 32; DAM POET**
See also CA 17-20R; CANR 30; DLB 5, 16,
165

Snyder, Zilpha Keatley 1927- . . . . . . **CLC 17**
See also AAYA 15; CA 9-12R; CANR 38;
CLR 31; JRDA; MAICYA; SAAS 2;
SATA 1, 28, 75

Soares, Bernardo
See Pessoa, Fernando (Antonio Nogueira)

Sobh, A.
See Shamlu, Ahmad

Sobol, Joshua . . . . **CLC 60**

Soderberg, Hjalmar 1869-1941 . . . . **TCLC 39**

Sodergran, Edith (Irene)
See Soedergran, Edith (Irene)

Soedergran, Edith (Irene)
1892-1923 . . . . **TCLC 31**

Softly, Edgar
See Lovecraft, H(oward) P(hillips)

Softly, Edward
See Lovecraft, H(oward) P(hillips)

Sokolov, Raymond 1941- . . . . **CLC 7**
See also CA 85-88

Solo, Jay
See Ellison, Harlan (Jay)

Sologub, Fyodor . . . . **TCLC 9**
See also Teternikov, Fyodor Kuzmich

Solomons, Ikey Esquir
See Thackeray, William Makepeace

Solomos, Dionysios 1798-1857 . . . **NCLC 15**

Solwoska, Mara
See French, Marilyn

Solzhenitsyn, Aleksandr I(sayevich)
1918- . . . . . . **CLC 1, 2, 4, 7, 9, 10, 18, 26,**
34, 78; DA; DAB; DAC; DAM MST,
NOV; WLC
See also AITN 1; CA 69-72; CANR 40;
MTCW

Somers, Jane
See Lessing, Doris (May)

Somerville, Edith 1858-1949 . . . . . **TCLC 51**
See also DLB 135

Somerville & Ross
See Martin, Violet Florence; Somerville,
Edith

Sommer, Scott 1951- . . . . **CLC 25**
See also CA 106

Sondheim, Stephen (Joshua)
1930- . . . . **CLC 30, 39; DAM DRAM**
See also AAYA 11; CA 103; CANR 47

Sontag, Susan
1933- . . . . **CLC 1, 2, 10, 13, 31;**
DAM POP
See also CA 17-20R; CANR 25, 51; DLB 2,
67; MTCW

Sophocles
496(?)B.C.-406(?)B.C. . . . . . **CMLC 2; DA;**
DAB; DAC; DAM DRAM, MST; DC 1

Sordello 1189-1269 . . . . **CMLC 15**

Sorel, Julia
See Drexler, Rosalyn

Sorrentino, Gilbert
1929- . . . . **CLC 3, 7, 14, 22, 40**
See also CA 77-80; CANR 14, 33; DLB 5,
173; DLBY 80; INT CANR-14

Soto, Gary
1952- . . . . **CLC 32, 80; DAM MULT;**
HLC
See also AAYA 10; CA 119; 125;
CANR 50; CLR 38; DLB 82; HW;
INT 125; JRDA; SATA 80

Soupault, Philippe 1897-1990 . . . . . . **CLC 68**
See also CA 116; 147; 131

Souster, (Holmes) Raymond
1921- . . . **CLC 5, 14; DAC; DAM POET**
See also CA 13-16R; CAAS 14; CANR 13,
29, 53; DLB 88; SATA 63

Southern, Terry 1924(?)-1995 . . . . **CLC 7**
See also CA 1-4R; 150; CANR 1, 55;
DLB 2

Southey, Robert 1774-1843 . . . . **NCLC 8**
See also DLB 93, 107, 142; SATA 54

Southworth, Emma Dorothy Eliza Nevitte
1819-1899 . . . . **NCLC 26**

Souza, Ernest
See Scott, Evelyn

Soyinka, Wole
1934- . . . . **CLC 3, 5, 14, 36, 44; BLC;**
DA; DAB; DAC; DAM DRAM, MST,
MULT; DC 2; WLC
See also BW 2; CA 13-16R; CANR 27, 39;
DLB 125; MTCW

Spackman, W(illiam) M(ode)
1905-1990 . . . . **CLC 46**
See also CA 81-84; 132

Spacks, Barry (Bernard) 1931- . . . . . **CLC 14**
See also CA 154; CANR 33; DLB 105

Spanidou, Irini 1946- . . . . **CLC 44**

Spark, Muriel (Sarah)
1918- . . . . . **CLC 2, 3, 5, 8, 13, 18, 40, 94;**
DAB; DAC; DAM MST, NOV; SSC 10
See also CA 5-8R; CANR 12, 36;
CDBLB 1945-1960; DLB 15, 139;
INT CANR-12; MTCW

Spaulding, Douglas
See Bradbury, Ray (Douglas)

Spaulding, Leonard
See Bradbury, Ray (Douglas)

Spence, J. A. D.
See Eliot, T(homas) S(tearns)

Spencer, Elizabeth 1921- . . . . **CLC 22**
See also CA 13-16R; CANR 32; DLB 6;
MTCW; SATA 14

Spencer, Leonard G.
See Silverberg, Robert

Spencer, Scott 1945- . . . . **CLC 30**
See also CA 113; CANR 51; DLBY 86

Spender, Stephen (Harold)
1909-1995 . . . . . . **CLC 1, 2, 5, 10, 41, 91;**
DAM POET
See also CA 9-12R; 149; CANR 31, 54;
CDBLB 1945-1960; DLB 20; MTCW

Spengler, Oswald (Arnold Gottfried)
1880-1936 . . . . **TCLC 25**
See also CA 118

Spenser, Edmund
1552(?)-1599 . . . . **LC 5; DA; DAB; DAC;**
DAM MST, POET; PC 8; WLC
See also CDBLB Before 1660; DLB 167

Spicer, Jack
1925-1965 . . . . **CLC 8, 18, 72;**
DAM POET
See also CA 85-88; DLB 5, 16

Spiegelman, Art 1948- . . . . **CLC 76**
See also AAYA 10; CA 125; CANR 41, 55

Spielberg, Peter 1929- . . . . **CLC 6**
See also CA 5-8R; CANR 4, 48; DLBY 81

Spielberg, Steven 1947- . . . . **CLC 20**
See also AAYA 8; CA 77-80; CANR 32;
SATA 32

Spillane, Frank Morrison 1918-
See Spillane, Mickey
See also CA 25-28R; CANR 28; MTCW;
SATA 66

Spillane, Mickey . . . . **CLC 3, 13**
See also Spillane, Frank Morrison

Spinoza, Benedictus de 1632-1677 . . . . **LC 9**

Spinrad, Norman (Richard) 1940- . . . **CLC 46**
See also CA 37-40R; CAAS 19; CANR 20;
DLB 8; INT CANR-20

Spitteler, Carl (Friedrich Georg)
1845-1924 . . . . **TCLC 12**
See also CA 109; DLB 129

Spivack, Kathleen (Romola Drucker)
1938- . . . . **CLC 6**
See also CA 49-52

Spoto, Donald 1941- . . . . **CLC 39**
See also CA 65-68; CANR 11

Springsteen, Bruce (F.) 1949- . . . . . . **CLC 17**
See also CA 111

Spurling, Hilary 1940- . . . . **CLC 34**
See also CA 104; CANR 25, 52

Spyker, John Howland
See Elman, Richard

Squires, (James) Radcliffe
1917-1993 . . . . **CLC 51**
See also CA 1-4R; 140; CANR 6, 21

Srivastava, Dhanpat Rai 1880(?)-1936
See Premchand
See also CA 118

Stacy, Donald
See Pohl, Frederik

Stael, Germaine de
See Stael-Holstein, Anne Louise Germaine
Necker Baronn
See also DLB 119

Stael-Holstein, Anne Louise Germaine Necker
Baronn 1766-1817 . . . . NCLC 3
See also Stael, Germaine de

Stafford, Jean 1915-1979 . . . CLC 4, 7, 19, 68
See also CA 1-4R; 85-88; CANR 3; DLB 2,
173; MTCW; SATA-Obit 22

Stafford, William (Edgar)
1914-1993 . . . CLC 4, 7, 29; DAM POET
See also CA 5-8R; 142; CAAS 3; CANR 5,
22; DLB 5; INT CANR-22

Staines, Trevor
See Brunner, John (Kilian Houston)

Stairs, Gordon
See Austin, Mary (Hunter)

Stannard, Martin 1947- . . . . CLC 44
See also CA 142; DLB 155

Stanton, Maura 1946- . . . . CLC 9
See also CA 89-92; CANR 15; DLB 120

Stanton, Schuyler
See Baum, L(yman) Frank

Stapledon, (William) Olaf
1886-1950 . . . . TCLC 22
See also CA 111; DLB 15

Starbuck, George (Edwin)
1931-1996 . . . . CLC 53; DAM POET
See also CA 21-24R; 153; CANR 23

Stark, Richard
See Westlake, Donald E(dwin)

Staunton, Schuyler
See Baum, L(yman) Frank

Stead, Christina (Ellen)
1902-1983 . . . . CLC 2, 5, 8, 32, 80
See also CA 13-16R; 109; CANR 33, 40;
MTCW

Stead, William Thomas
1849-1912 . . . . TCLC 48

Steele, Richard 1672-1729 . . . . LC 18
See also CDBLB 1660-1789; DLB 84, 101

Steele, Timothy (Reid) 1948- . . . . . . CLC 45
See also CA 93-96; CANR 16, 50; DLB 120

Steffens, (Joseph) Lincoln
1866-1936 . . . . TCLC 20
See also CA 117

Stegner, Wallace (Earle)
1909-1993 . . . CLC 9, 49, 81; DAM NOV
See also AITN 1; BEST 90:3; CA 1-4R;
141; CAAS 9; CANR 1, 21, 46; DLB 9;
DLBY 93; MTCW

Stein, Gertrude
1874-1946 . . . . . . TCLC 1, 6, 28, 48; DA;
DAB; DAC; DAM MST, NOV, POET;
WLC
See also CA 104; 132; CDALB 1917-1929;
DLB 4, 54, 86; MTCW

Steinbeck, John (Ernst)
1902-1968 . . . . . . CLC 1, 5, 9, 13, 21, 34,
45, 75; DA; DAB; DAC; DAM DRAM,
MST, NOV; SSC 11; WLC
See also AAYA 12; CA 1-4R; 25-28R;
CANR 1, 35; CDALB 1929-1941; DLB 7,
9; DLBD 2; MTCW; SATA 9

Steinem, Gloria 1934- . . . . CLC 63
See also CA 53-56; CANR 28, 51; MTCW

Steiner, George
1929- . . . . CLC 24; DAM NOV
See also CA 73-76; CANR 31; DLB 67;
MTCW; SATA 62

Steiner, K. Leslie
See Delany, Samuel R(ay, Jr.)

Steiner, Rudolf 1861-1925 . . . . TCLC 13
See also CA 107

Stendhal
1783-1842 . . . . NCLC 23, 46; DA; DAB;
DAC; DAM MST, NOV; WLC
See also DLB 119

Stephen, Leslie 1832-1904 . . . . TCLC 23
See also CA 123; DLB 57, 144

Stephen, Sir Leslie
See Stephen, Leslie

Stephen, Virginia
See Woolf, (Adeline) Virginia

Stephens, James 1882(?)-1950 . . . . . . TCLC 4
See also CA 104; DLB 19, 153, 162

Stephens, Reed
See Donaldson, Stephen R.

Steptoe, Lydia
See Barnes, Djuna

Sterchi, Beat 1949- . . . . CLC 65

Sterling, Brett
See Bradbury, Ray (Douglas); Hamilton,
Edmond

Sterling, Bruce 1954- . . . . CLC 72
See also CA 119; CANR 44

Sterling, George 1869-1926 . . . . TCLC 20
See also CA 117; DLB 54

Stern, Gerald 1925- . . . . CLC 40
See also CA 81-84; CANR 28; DLB 105

Stern, Richard (Gustave) 1928- . . . CLC 4, 39
See also CA 1-4R; CANR 1, 25, 52;
DLBY 87; INT CANR-25

Sternberg, Josef von 1894-1969 . . . . . CLC 20
See also CA 81-84

Sterne, Laurence
1713-1768 . . . . . . LC 2; DA; DAB; DAC;
DAM MST, NOV; WLC
See also CDBLB 1660-1789; DLB 39

Sternheim, (William Adolf) Carl
1878-1942 . . . . TCLC 8
See also CA 105; DLB 56, 118

Stevens, Mark 1951- . . . . CLC 34
See also CA 122

Stevens, Wallace
1879-1955 . . . . TCLC 3, 12, 45; DA;
DAB; DAC; DAM MST, POET; PC 6;
WLC
See also CA 104; 124; CDALB 1929-1941;
DLB 54; MTCW

Stevenson, Anne (Katharine)
1933- . . . . CLC 7, 33
See also CA 17-20R; CAAS 9; CANR 9, 33;
DLB 40; MTCW

Stevenson, Robert Louis (Balfour)
1850-1894 . . . . . NCLC 5, 14; DA; DAB;
DAC; DAM MST, NOV; SSC 11; WLC
See also CDBLB 1890-1914; CLR 10, 11;
DLB 18, 57, 141, 156, 174; DLBD 13;
JRDA; MAICYA; YABC 2

Stewart, J(ohn) I(nnes) M(ackintosh)
1906-1994 . . . . CLC 7, 14, 32
See also CA 85-88; 147; CAAS 3;
CANR 47; MTCW

Stewart, Mary (Florence Elinor)
1916- . . . . CLC 7, 35; DAB
See also CA 1-4R; CANR 1; SATA 12

Stewart, Mary Rainbow
See Stewart, Mary (Florence Elinor)

Stifle, June
See Campbell, Maria

Stifter, Adalbert 1805-1868 . . . . . . NCLC 41
See also DLB 133

Still, James 1906- . . . . CLC 49
See also CA 65-68; CAAS 17; CANR 10,
26; DLB 9; SATA 29

Sting
See Sumner, Gordon Matthew

Stirling, Arthur
See Sinclair, Upton (Beall)

Stitt, Milan 1941- . . . . CLC 29
See also CA 69-72

Stockton, Francis Richard 1834-1902
See Stockton, Frank R.
See also CA 108; 137; MAICYA; SATA 44

Stockton, Frank R. . . . . TCLC 47
See also Stockton, Francis Richard
See also DLB 42, 74; DLBD 13;
SATA-Brief 32

Stoddard, Charles
See Kuttner, Henry

Stoker, Abraham 1847-1912
See Stoker, Bram
See also CA 105; DA; DAC; DAM MST,
NOV; SATA 29

Stoker, Bram
1847-1912 . . . . TCLC 8; DAB; WLC
See also Stoker, Abraham
See also CA 150; CDBLB 1890-1914;
DLB 36, 70

Stolz, Mary (Slattery) 1920- . . . . CLC 12
See also AAYA 8; AITN 1; CA 5-8R;
CANR 13, 41; JRDA; MAICYA;
SAAS 3; SATA 10, 71

Stone, Irving
1903-1989 . . . . CLC 7; DAM POP
See also AITN 1; CA 1-4R; 129; CAAS 3;
CANR 1, 23; INT CANR-23; MTCW;
SATA 3; SATA-Obit 64

Stone, Oliver (William) 1946- . . . . . . CLC 73
See also AAYA 15; CA 110; CANR 55

Stone, Robert (Anthony)
1937- . . . . CLC 5, 23, 42
See also CA 85-88; CANR 23; DLB 152;
INT CANR-23; MTCW

Stone, Zachary
See Follett, Ken(neth Martin)

Stoppard, Tom
1937- ...... **CLC 1, 3, 4, 5, 8, 15, 29, 34, 63, 91; DA; DAB; DAC; DAM DRAM, MST; DC 6; WLC**
See also CA 81-84; CANR 39; CDBLB 1960 to Present; DLB 13; DLBY 85; MTCW

Storey, David (Malcolm)
1933- ..... **CLC 2, 4, 5, 8; DAM DRAM**
See also CA 81-84; CANR 36; DLB 13, 14; MTCW

Storm, Hyemeyohsts
1935- .... **CLC 3; DAM MULT**
See also CA 81-84; CANR 45; NNAL

Storm, (Hans) Theodor (Woldsen)
1817-1888 .... **NCLC 1**

Storni, Alfonsina
1892-1938 ..... **TCLC 5; DAM MULT; HLC**
See also CA 104; 131; HW

Stout, Rex (Todhunter) 1886-1975 ... **CLC 3**
See also AITN 2; CA 61-64

Stow, (Julian) Randolph 1935- .. **CLC 23, 48**
See also CA 13-16R; CANR 33; MTCW

Stowe, Harriet (Elizabeth) Beecher
1811-1896 ..... **NCLC 3, 50; DA; DAB; DAC; DAM MST, NOV; WLC**
See also CDALB 1865-1917; DLB 1, 12, 42, 74; JRDA; MAICYA; YABC 1

Strachey, (Giles) Lytton
1880-1932 .... **TCLC 12**
See also CA 110; DLB 149; DLBD 10

Strand, Mark
1934- .. **CLC 6, 18, 41, 71; DAM POET**
See also CA 21-24R; CANR 40; DLB 5; SATA 41

Straub, Peter (Francis)
1943- .... **CLC 28; DAM POP**
See also BEST 89:1; CA 85-88; CANR 28; DLBY 84; MTCW

Strauss, Botho 1944- .... **CLC 22**
See also DLB 124

Streatfeild, (Mary) Noel
1895(?)-1986 .... **CLC 21**
See also CA 81-84; 120; CANR 31; CLR 17; DLB 160; MAICYA; SATA 20; SATA-Obit 48

Stribling, T(homas) S(igismund)
1881-1965 .... **CLC 23**
See also CA 107; DLB 9

Strindberg, (Johan) August
1849-1912 ...... **TCLC 1, 8, 21, 47; DA; DAB; DAC; DAM DRAM, MST; WLC**
See also CA 104; 135

Stringer, Arthur 1874-1950 .... **TCLC 37**
See also DLB 92

Stringer, David
See Roberts, Keith (John Kingston)

Strugatskii, Arkadii (Natanovich)
1925-1991 .... **CLC 27**
See also CA 106; 135

Strugatskii, Boris (Natanovich)
1933- .... **CLC 27**
See also CA 106

Strummer, Joe 1953(?)- .... **CLC 30**

Stuart, Don A.
See Campbell, John W(ood, Jr.)

Stuart, Ian
See MacLean, Alistair (Stuart)

Stuart, Jesse (Hilton)
1906-1984 .... **CLC 1, 8, 11, 14, 34**
See also CA 5-8R; 112; CANR 31; DLB 9, 48, 102; DLBY 84; SATA 2; SATA-Obit 36

Sturgeon, Theodore (Hamilton)
1918-1985 .... **CLC 22, 39**
See also Queen, Ellery
See also CA 81-84; 116; CANR 32; DLB 8; DLBY 85; MTCW

Sturges, Preston 1898-1959 ...... **TCLC 48**
See also CA 114; 149; DLB 26

Styron, William
1925- .... **CLC 1, 3, 5, 11, 15, 60; DAM NOV, POP**
See also BEST 90:4; CA 5-8R; CANR 6, 33; CDALB 1968-1988; DLB 2, 143; DLBY 80; INT CANR-6; MTCW

Suarez Lynch, B.
See Bioy Casares, Adolfo; Borges, Jorge Luis

Su Chien 1884-1918
See Su Man-shu
See also CA 123

Suckow, Ruth 1892-1960 .... **SSC 18**
See also CA 113; DLB 9, 102

Sudermann, Hermann 1857-1928 .. **TCLC 15**
See also CA 107; DLB 118

Sue, Eugene 1804-1857 .... **NCLC 1**
See also DLB 119

Sueskind, Patrick 1949- .... **CLC 44**
See also Suskind, Patrick

Sukenick, Ronald 1932- ..... **CLC 3, 4, 6, 48**
See also CA 25-28R; CAAS 8; CANR 32; DLB 173; DLBY 81

Suknaski, Andrew 1942- .... **CLC 19**
See also CA 101; DLB 53

Sullivan, Vernon
See Vian, Boris

Sully Prudhomme 1839-1907 ...... **TCLC 31**

Su Man-shu .... **TCLC 24**
See also Su Chien

Summerforest, Ivy B.
See Kirkup, James

Summers, Andrew James 1942- ..... **CLC 26**

Summers, Andy
See Summers, Andrew James

Summers, Hollis (Spurgeon, Jr.)
1916- .... **CLC 10**
See also CA 5-8R; CANR 3; DLB 6

Summers, (Alphonsus Joseph-Mary Augustus) Montague 1880-1948 .... **TCLC 16**
See also CA 118

Sumner, Gordon Matthew 1951- .... **CLC 26**

Surtees, Robert Smith
1803-1864 .... **NCLC 14**
See also DLB 21

Susann, Jacqueline 1921-1974 ...... **CLC 3**
See also AITN 1; CA 65-68; 53-56; MTCW

Su Shih 1036-1101 .... **CMLC 15**

Suskind, Patrick
See Sueskind, Patrick
See also CA 145

Sutcliff, Rosemary
1920-1992 .... **CLC 26; DAB; DAC; DAM MST, POP**
See also AAYA 10; CA 5-8R; 139; CANR 37; CLR 1, 37; JRDA; MAICYA; SATA 6, 44, 78; SATA-Obit 73

Sutro, Alfred 1863-1933 .... **TCLC 6**
See also CA 105; DLB 10

Sutton, Henry
See Slavitt, David R(ytman)

Svevo, Italo .... **TCLC 2, 35**
See also Schmitz, Aron Hector

Swados, Elizabeth (A.) 1951- .... **CLC 12**
See also CA 97-100; CANR 49; INT 97-100

Swados, Harvey 1920-1972 .... **CLC 5**
See also CA 5-8R; 37-40R; CANR 6; DLB 2

Swan, Gladys 1934- .... **CLC 69**
See also CA 101; CANR 17, 39

Swarthout, Glendon (Fred)
1918-1992 .... **CLC 35**
See also CA 1-4R; 139; CANR 1, 47; SATA 26

Sweet, Sarah C.
See Jewett, (Theodora) Sarah Orne

Swenson, May
1919-1989 .... **CLC 4, 14, 61; DA; DAB; DAC; DAM MST, POET; PC 14**
See also CA 5-8R; 130; CANR 36; DLB 5; MTCW; SATA 15

Swift, Augustus
See Lovecraft, H(oward) P(hillips)

Swift, Graham (Colin) 1949- .... **CLC 41, 88**
See also CA 117; 122; CANR 46

Swift, Jonathan
1667-1745 ...... **LC 1; DA; DAB; DAC; DAM MST, NOV, POET; PC 9; WLC**
See also CDBLB 1660-1789; DLB 39, 95, 101; SATA 19

Swinburne, Algernon Charles
1837-1909 ...... **TCLC 8, 36; DA; DAB; DAC; DAM MST, POET; WLC**
See also CA 105; 140; CDBLB 1832-1890; DLB 35, 57

Swinfen, Ann .... **CLC 34**

Swinnerton, Frank Arthur
1884-1982 .... **CLC 31**
See also CA 108; DLB 34

Swithen, John
See King, Stephen (Edwin)

Sylvia
See Ashton-Warner, Sylvia (Constance)

Symmes, Robert Edward
See Duncan, Robert (Edward)

Symonds, John Addington
1840-1893 .... **NCLC 34**
See also DLB 57, 144

Symons, Arthur 1865-1945 .... **TCLC 11**
See also CA 107; DLB 19, 57, 149

Symons, Julian (Gustave)
1912-1994 . . . . **CLC 2, 14, 32**
See also CA 49-52; 147; CAAS 3; CANR 3,
33; DLB 87, 155; DLBY 92; MTCW

Synge, (Edmund) J(ohn) M(illington)
1871-1909 . . . . **TCLC 6, 37;**
DAM DRAM; DC 2
See also CA 104; 141; CDBLB 1890-1914;
DLB 10, 19

Syruc, J.
See Milosz, Czeslaw

Szirtes, George 1948- . . . . **CLC 46**
See also CA 109; CANR 27

T. O., Nik
See Annensky, Innokenty Fyodorovich

Tabori, George 1914- . . . . **CLC 19**
See also CA 49-52; CANR 4

Tagore, Rabindranath
1861-1941 . . . . **TCLC 3, 53;**
DAM DRAM, POET; PC 8
See also CA 104; 120; MTCW

Taine, Hippolyte Adolphe
1828-1893 . . . . **NCLC 15**

Talese, Gay 1932- . . . . **CLC 37**
See also AITN 1; CA 1-4R; CANR 9;
INT CANR-9; MTCW

Tallent, Elizabeth (Ann) 1954- . . . . . **CLC 45**
See also CA 117; DLB 130

Tally, Ted 1952- . . . . **CLC 42**
See also CA 120; 124; INT 124

Tamayo y Baus, Manuel
1829-1898 . . . . **NCLC 1**

Tammsaare, A(nton) H(ansen)
1878-1940 . . . . **TCLC 27**

Tan, Amy (Ruth)
1952- . . . . **CLC 59; DAM MULT, NOV,**
POP
See also AAYA 9; BEST 89:3; CA 136;
CANR 54; DLB 173; SATA 75

Tandem, Felix
See Spitteler, Carl (Friedrich Georg)

Tanizaki, Jun'ichiro
1886-1965 . . . . . . **CLC 8, 14, 28; SSC 21**
See also CA 93-96; 25-28R

Tanner, William
See Amis, Kingsley (William)

Tao Lao
See Storni, Alfonsina

Tarassoff, Lev
See Troyat, Henri

Tarbell, Ida M(inerva)
1857-1944 . . . . **TCLC 40**
See also CA 122; DLB 47

Tarkington, (Newton) Booth
1869-1946 . . . . **TCLC 9**
See also CA 110; 143; DLB 9, 102;
SATA 17

Tarkovsky, Andrei (Arsenyevich)
1932-1986 . . . . **CLC 75**
See also CA 127

Tartt, Donna 1964(?)- . . . . **CLC 76**
See also CA 142

Tasso, Torquato 1544-1595 . . . . **LC 5**

Tate, (John Orley) Allen
1899-1979 . . . . **CLC 2, 4, 6, 9, 11, 14, 24**
See also CA 5-8R; 85-88; CANR 32;
DLB 4, 45, 63; MTCW

Tate, Ellalice
See Hibbert, Eleanor Alice Burford

Tate, James (Vincent) 1943- . . . **CLC 2, 6, 25**
See also CA 21-24R; CANR 29; DLB 5,
169

Tavel, Ronald 1940- . . . . **CLC 6**
See also CA 21-24R; CANR 33

Taylor, C(ecil) P(hilip) 1929-1981 . . . **CLC 27**
See also CA 25-28R; 105; CANR 47

Taylor, Edward
1642(?)-1729 . . . . **LC 11; DA; DAB;**
DAC; DAM MST, POET
See also DLB 24

Taylor, Eleanor Ross 1920- . . . . **CLC 5**
See also CA 81-84

Taylor, Elizabeth 1912-1975 . . . **CLC 2, 4, 29**
See also CA 13-16R; CANR 9; DLB 139;
MTCW; SATA 13

Taylor, Henry (Splawn) 1942- . . . . . . **CLC 44**
See also CA 33-36R; CAAS 7; CANR 31;
DLB 5

Taylor, Kamala (Purnaiya) 1924-
See Markandaya, Kamala
See also CA 77-80

Taylor, Mildred D. . . . . **CLC 21**
See also AAYA 10; BW 1; CA 85-88;
CANR 25; CLR 9; DLB 52; JRDA;
MAICYA; SAAS 5; SATA 15, 70

Taylor, Peter (Hillsman)
1917-1994 . . . . . **CLC 1, 4, 18, 37, 44, 50,**
71; SSC 10
See also CA 13-16R; 147; CANR 9, 50;
DLBY 81, 94; INT CANR-9; MTCW

Taylor, Robert Lewis 1912- . . . . **CLC 14**
See also CA 1-4R; CANR 3; SATA 10

Tchekhov, Anton
See Chekhov, Anton (Pavlovich)

Teasdale, Sara 1884-1933 . . . . **TCLC 4**
See also CA 104; DLB 45; SATA 32

Tegner, Esaias 1782-1846 . . . . **NCLC 2**

Teilhard de Chardin, (Marie Joseph) Pierre
1881-1955 . . . . **TCLC 9**
See also CA 105

Temple, Ann
See Mortimer, Penelope (Ruth)

Tennant, Emma (Christina)
1937- . . . . **CLC 13, 52**
See also CA 65-68; CAAS 9; CANR 10, 38;
DLB 14

Tenneshaw, S. M.
See Silverberg, Robert

Tennyson, Alfred
1809-1892 . . . . **NCLC 30; DA; DAB;**
DAC; DAM MST, POET; PC 6; WLC
See also CDBLB 1832-1890; DLB 32

Teran, Lisa St. Aubin de . . . . **CLC 36**
See also St. Aubin de Teran, Lisa

Terence 195(?)B.C.-159B.C. . . . . **CMLC 14**

Teresa de Jesus, St. 1515-1582 . . . . . . **LC 18**

Terkel, Louis 1912-
See Terkel, Studs
See also CA 57-60; CANR 18, 45; MTCW

Terkel, Studs . . . . **CLC 38**
See also Terkel, Louis
See also AITN 1

Terry, C. V.
See Slaughter, Frank G(ill)

Terry, Megan 1932- . . . . **CLC 19**
See also CA 77-80; CABS 3; CANR 43;
DLB 7

Tertz, Abram
See Sinyavsky, Andrei (Donatevich)

Tesich, Steve 1943(?)-1996 . . . . . . **CLC 40, 69**
See also CA 105; 152; DLBY 83

Teternikov, Fyodor Kuzmich 1863-1927
See Sologub, Fyodor
See also CA 104

Tevis, Walter 1928-1984 . . . . **CLC 42**
See also CA 113

Tey, Josephine . . . . **TCLC 14**
See also Mackintosh, Elizabeth
See also DLB 77

Thackeray, William Makepeace
1811-1863 . . . . **NCLC 5, 14, 22, 43; DA;**
DAB; DAC; DAM MST, NOV; WLC
See also CDBLB 1832-1890; DLB 21, 55,
159, 163; SATA 23

Thakura, Ravindranatha
See Tagore, Rabindranath

Tharoor, Shashi 1956- . . . . **CLC 70**
See also CA 141

Thelwell, Michael Miles 1939- . . . . . **CLC 22**
See also BW 2; CA 101

Theobald, Lewis, Jr.
See Lovecraft, H(oward) P(hillips)

Theodorescu, Ion N. 1880-1967
See Arghezi, Tudor
See also CA 116

Theriault, Yves
1915-1983 . . **CLC 79; DAC; DAM MST**
See also CA 102; DLB 88

Theroux, Alexander (Louis)
1939- . . . . **CLC 2, 25**
See also CA 85-88; CANR 20

Theroux, Paul (Edward)
1941- . . . . **CLC 5, 8, 11, 15, 28, 46;**
DAM POP
See also BEST 89:4; CA 33-36R; CANR 20,
45; DLB 2; MTCW; SATA 44

Thesen, Sharon 1946- . . . . **CLC 56**

Thevenin, Denis
See Duhamel, Georges

Thibault, Jacques Anatole Francois
1844-1924
See France, Anatole
See also CA 106; 127; DAM NOV; MTCW

Thiele, Colin (Milton) 1920- . . . . **CLC 17**
See also CA 29-32R; CANR 12, 28, 53;
CLR 27; MAICYA; SAAS 2; SATA 14,
72

Thomas, Audrey (Callahan)
1935- . . . . **CLC 7, 13, 37; SSC 20**
See also AITN 2; CA 21-24R; CAAS 19;
CANR 36; DLB 60; MTCW

Thomas, D(onald) M(ichael)
1935- . . . . **CLC 13, 22, 31**
See also CA 61-64; CAAS 11; CANR 17,
45; CDBLB 1960 to Present; DLB 40;
INT CANR-17; MTCW

Thomas, Dylan (Marlais)
1914-1953 . . . **TCLC 1, 8, 45; DA; DAB;
DAC; DAM DRAM, MST, POET;
PC 2; SSC 3; WLC**
See also CA 104; 120; CDBLB 1945-1960;
DLB 13, 20, 139; MTCW; SATA 60

Thomas, (Philip) Edward
1878-1917 . . . . . . **TCLC 10; DAM POET**
See also CA 106; 153; DLB 19

Thomas, Joyce Carol 1938- . . . . **CLC 35**
See also AAYA 12; BW 2; CA 113; 116;
CANR 48; CLR 19; DLB 33; INT 116;
JRDA; MAICYA; MTCW; SAAS 7;
SATA 40, 78

Thomas, Lewis 1913-1993 . . . . **CLC 35**
See also CA 85-88; 143; CANR 38; MTCW

Thomas, Paul
See Mann, (Paul) Thomas

Thomas, Piri 1928- . . . . **CLC 17**
See also CA 73-76; HW

Thomas, R(onald) S(tuart)
1913- . . . . **CLC 6, 13, 48; DAB;
DAM POET**
See also CA 89-92; CAAS 4; CANR 30;
CDBLB 1960 to Present; DLB 27;
MTCW

Thomas, Ross (Elmore) 1926-1995 . . **CLC 39**
See also CA 33-36R; 150; CANR 22

Thompson, Francis Clegg
See Mencken, H(enry) L(ouis)

Thompson, Francis Joseph
1859-1907 . . . . **TCLC 4**
See also CA 104; CDBLB 1890-1914;
DLB 19

Thompson, Hunter S(tockton)
1939- . . . . **CLC 9, 17, 40; DAM POP**
See also BEST 89:1; CA 17-20R; CANR 23,
46; MTCW

Thompson, James Myers
See Thompson, Jim (Myers)

Thompson, Jim (Myers)
1906-1977(?) . . . . **CLC 69**
See also CA 140

Thompson, Judith . . . . **CLC 39**

Thomson, James
1700-1748 . . . . . **LC 16, 29; DAM POET**
See also DLB 95

Thomson, James
1834-1882 . . . . . **NCLC 18; DAM POET**
See also DLB 35

Thoreau, Henry David
1817-1862 . . . . . **NCLC 7, 21; DA; DAB;
DAC; DAM MST; WLC**
See also CDALB 1640-1865; DLB 1

Thornton, Hall
See Silverberg, Robert

Thucydides c. 455B.C.-399B.C. . . . . **CMLC 17**

Thurber, James (Grover)
1894-1961 . . . . **CLC 5, 11, 25; DA; DAB;
DAC; DAM DRAM, MST, NOV; SSC 1**
See also CA 73-76; CANR 17, 39;
CDALB 1929-1941; DLB 4, 11, 22, 102;
MAICYA; MTCW; SATA 13

Thurman, Wallace (Henry)
1902-1934 . . . . **TCLC 6; BLC;
DAM MULT**
See also BW 1; CA 104; 124; DLB 51

Ticheburn, Cheviot
See Ainsworth, William Harrison

Tieck, (Johann) Ludwig
1773-1853 . . . . **NCLC 5, 46**
See also DLB 90

Tiger, Derry
See Ellison, Harlan (Jay)

Tilghman, Christopher 1948(?)- . . . . . **CLC 65**

Tillinghast, Richard (Williford)
1940- . . . . **CLC 29**
See also CA 29-32R; CAAS 23; CANR 26,
51

Timrod, Henry 1828-1867 . . . . **NCLC 25**
See also DLB 3

Tindall, Gillian 1938- . . . . **CLC 7**
See also CA 21-24R; CANR 11

Tiptree, James, Jr. . . . . **CLC 48, 50**
See also Sheldon, Alice Hastings Bradley
See also DLB 8

Titmarsh, Michael Angelo
See Thackeray, William Makepeace

**Tocqueville, Alexis (Charles Henri Maurice
Clerel Comte)** 1805-1859 . . . . . **NCLC 7**

Tolkien, J(ohn) R(onald) R(euel)
1892-1973 . . . . **CLC 1, 2, 3, 8, 12, 38;
DA; DAB; DAC; DAM MST, NOV,
POP; WLC**
See also AAYA 10; AITN 1; CA 17-18;
45-48; CANR 36; CAP 2;
CDBLB 1914-1945; DLB 15, 160; JRDA;
MAICYA; MTCW; SATA 2, 32;
SATA-Obit 24

Toller, Ernst 1893-1939 . . . . **TCLC 10**
See also CA 107; DLB 124

Tolson, M. B.
See Tolson, Melvin B(eaunorus)

Tolson, Melvin B(eaunorus)
1898(?)-1966 . . . . **CLC 36; BLC;
DAM MULT, POET**
See also BW 1; CA 124; 89-92; DLB 48, 76

Tolstoi, Aleksei Nikolaevich
See Tolstoy, Alexey Nikolaevich

Tolstoy, Alexey Nikolaevich
1882-1945 . . . . **TCLC 18**
See also CA 107

Tolstoy, Count Leo
See Tolstoy, Leo (Nikolaevich)

Tolstoy, Leo (Nikolaevich)
1828-1910 . . . . . . **TCLC 4, 11, 17, 28, 44;
DA; DAB; DAC; DAM MST, NOV;
SSC 9; WLC**
See also CA 104; 123; SATA 26

Tomasi di Lampedusa, Giuseppe 1896-1957
See Lampedusa, Giuseppe (Tomasi) di
See also CA 111

Tomlin, Lily . . . . **CLC 17**
See also Tomlin, Mary Jean

Tomlin, Mary Jean 1939(?)-
See Tomlin, Lily
See also CA 117

Tomlinson, (Alfred) Charles
1927- . . . . **CLC 2, 4, 6, 13, 45;
DAM POET; PC 17**
See also CA 5-8R; CANR 33; DLB 40

Tonson, Jacob
See Bennett, (Enoch) Arnold

Toole, John Kennedy
1937-1969 . . . . **CLC 19, 64**
See also CA 104; DLBY 81

Toomer, Jean
1894-1967 . . . . . . **CLC 1, 4, 13, 22; BLC;
DAM MULT; PC 7; SSC 1**
See also BW 1; CA 85-88;
CDALB 1917-1929; DLB 45, 51; MTCW

Torley, Luke
See Blish, James (Benjamin)

Tornimparte, Alessandra
See Ginzburg, Natalia

Torre, Raoul della
See Mencken, H(enry) L(ouis)

Torrey, E(dwin) Fuller 1937- . . . . **CLC 34**
See also CA 119

Torsvan, Ben Traven
See Traven, B.

Torsvan, Benno Traven
See Traven, B.

Torsvan, Berick Traven
See Traven, B.

Torsvan, Berwick Traven
See Traven, B.

Torsvan, Bruno Traven
See Traven, B.

Torsvan, Traven
See Traven, B.

Tournier, Michel (Edouard)
1924- . . . . **CLC 6, 23, 36, 95**
See also CA 49-52; CANR 3, 36; DLB 83;
MTCW; SATA 23

Tournimparte, Alessandra
See Ginzburg, Natalia

Towers, Ivar
See Kornbluth, C(yril) M.

Towne, Robert (Burton) 1936(?)- . . . . **CLC 87**
See also CA 108; DLB 44

Townsend, Sue 1946- . . **CLC 61; DAB; DAC**
See also CA 119; 127; INT 127; MTCW;
SATA 55; SATA-Brief 48

Townshend, Peter (Dennis Blandford)
1945- . . . . **CLC 17, 42**
See also CA 107

Tozzi, Federigo 1883-1920 . . . . **TCLC 31**

Traill, Catharine Parr
1802-1899 . . . . **NCLC 31**
See also DLB 99

Trakl, Georg 1887-1914 . . . . **TCLC 5**
See also CA 104

Transtroemer, Tomas (Goesta)
1931- . . . . **CLC 52, 65; DAM POET**
See also CA 117; 129; CAAS 17

Transtromer, Tomas Gosta
  See Transtroemer, Tomas (Goesta)

Traven, B. (?)-1969 . . . . **CLC 8, 11**
  See also CA 19-20; 25-28R; CAP 2; DLB 9,
  56; MTCW

Treitel, Jonathan 1959- . . . . **CLC 70**

Tremain, Rose 1943- . . . . **CLC 42**
  See also CA 97-100; CANR 44; DLB 14

Tremblay, Michel
  1942- . . . . . . **CLC 29; DAC; DAM MST**
  See also CA 116; 128; DLB 60; MTCW

Trevanian . . . . **CLC 29**
  See also Whitaker, Rod(ney)

Trevor, Glen
  See Hilton, James

Trevor, William
  1928- . . . . . **CLC 7, 9, 14, 25, 71; SSC 21**
  See also Cox, William Trevor
  See also DLB 14, 139

Trifonov, Yuri (Valentinovich)
  1925-1981 . . . . **CLC 45**
  See also CA 126; 103; MTCW

Trilling, Lionel 1905-1975 . . . . **CLC 9, 11, 24**
  See also CA 9-12R; 61-64; CANR 10;
  DLB 28, 63; INT CANR-10; MTCW

Trimball, W. H.
  See Mencken, H(enry) L(ouis)

Tristan
  See Gomez de la Serna, Ramon

Tristram
  See Housman, A(lfred) E(dward)

Trogdon, William (Lewis) 1939-
  See Heat-Moon, William Least
  See also CA 115; 119; CANR 47; INT 119

Trollope, Anthony
  1815-1882 . . . . . **NCLC 6, 33; DA; DAB;**
                        DAC; DAM MST, NOV; WLC
  See also CDBLB 1832-1890; DLB 21, 57,
  159; SATA 22

Trollope, Frances 1779-1863 . . . . . **NCLC 30**
  See also DLB 21, 166

Trotsky, Leon 1879-1940 . . . . **TCLC 22**
  See also CA 118

Trotter (Cockburn), Catharine
  1679-1749 . . . . **LC 8**
  See also DLB 84

Trout, Kilgore
  See Farmer, Philip Jose

Trow, George W. S. 1943- . . . . **CLC 52**
  See also CA 126

Troyat, Henri 1911- . . . . **CLC 23**
  See also CA 45-48; CANR 2, 33; MTCW

Trudeau, G(arretson) B(eekman) 1948-
  See Trudeau, Garry B.
  See also CA 81-84; CANR 31; SATA 35

Trudeau, Garry B. . . . . **CLC 12**
  See also Trudeau, G(arretson) B(eekman)
  See also AAYA 10; AITN 2

Truffaut, Francois 1932-1984 . . . . . . **CLC 20**
  See also CA 81-84; 113; CANR 34

Trumbo, Dalton 1905-1976 . . . . **CLC 19**
  See also CA 21-24R; 69-72; CANR 10;
  DLB 26

Trumbull, John 1750-1831 . . . . . . **NCLC 30**
  See also DLB 31

Trundlett, Helen B.
  See Eliot, T(homas) S(tearns)

Tryon, Thomas
  1926-1991 . . . . . . **CLC 3, 11; DAM POP**
  See also AITN 1; CA 29-32R; 135;
  CANR 32; MTCW

Tryon, Tom
  See Tryon, Thomas

Ts'ao Hsueh-ch'in 1715(?)-1763 . . . . **LC 1**

Tsushima, Shuji 1909-1948
  See Dazai, Osamu
  See also CA 107

Tsvetaeva (Efron), Marina (Ivanovna)
  1892-1941 . . . . **TCLC 7, 35; PC 14**
  See also CA 104; 128; MTCW

Tuck, Lily 1938- . . . . **CLC 70**
  See also CA 139

Tu Fu 712-770 . . . . **PC 9**
  See also DAM MULT

Tunis, John R(oberts) 1889-1975 . . . **CLC 12**
  See also CA 61-64; DLB 22, 171; JRDA;
  MAICYA; SATA 37; SATA-Brief 30

Tuohy, Frank . . . . **CLC 37**
  See also Tuohy, John Francis
  See also DLB 14, 139

Tuohy, John Francis 1925-
  See Tuohy, Frank
  See also CA 5-8R; CANR 3, 47

Turco, Lewis (Putnam) 1934- . . . **CLC 11, 63**
  See also CA 13-16R; CAAS 22; CANR 24,
  51; DLBY 84

Turgenev, Ivan
  1818-1883 . . . . **NCLC 21; DA; DAB;**
                 DAC; DAM MST, NOV; SSC 7; WLC

Turgot, Anne-Robert-Jacques
  1727-1781 . . . . **LC 26**

Turner, Frederick 1943- . . . . **CLC 48**
  See also CA 73-76; CAAS 10; CANR 12,
  30; DLB 40

Tutu, Desmond M(pilo)
  1931- . . . . . **CLC 80; BLC; DAM MULT**
  See also BW 1; CA 125

Tutuola, Amos
  1920- . . . . **CLC 5, 14, 29; BLC;**
                                      DAM MULT
  See also BW 2; CA 9-12R; CANR 27;
  DLB 125; MTCW

Twain, Mark
  . . . . . **TCLC 6, 12, 19, 36, 48, 59; SSC 6;**
                                                    WLC
  See also Clemens, Samuel Langhorne
  See also DLB 11, 12, 23, 64, 74

Tyler, Anne
  1941- . . . . **CLC 7, 11, 18, 28, 44, 59;**
                                      DAM NOV, POP
  See also AAYA 18; BEST 89:1; CA 9-12R;
  CANR 11, 33, 53; DLB 6, 143; DLBY 82;
  MTCW; SATA 7, 90

Tyler, Royall 1757-1826 . . . . **NCLC 3**
  See also DLB 37

Tynan, Katharine 1861-1931 . . . . **TCLC 3**
  See also CA 104; DLB 153

Tyutchev, Fyodor 1803-1873 . . . . . **NCLC 34**

Tzara, Tristan
  1896-1963 . . . . **CLC 47; DAM POET**
  See also Rosenfeld, Samuel; Rosenstock,
  Sami; Rosenstock, Samuel
  See also CA 153

Uhry, Alfred
  1936- . . . . . **CLC 55; DAM DRAM, POP**
  See also CA 127; 133; INT 133

Ulf, Haerved
  See Strindberg, (Johan) August

Ulf, Harved
  See Strindberg, (Johan) August

Ulibarri, Sabine R(eyes)
  1919- . . . . **CLC 83; DAM MULT**
  See also CA 131; DLB 82; HW

Unamuno (y Jugo), Miguel de
  1864-1936 . . . **TCLC 2, 9; DAM MULT,**
                                 NOV; HLC; SSC 11
  See also CA 104; 131; DLB 108; HW;
  MTCW

Undercliffe, Errol
  See Campbell, (John) Ramsey

Underwood, Miles
  See Glassco, John

Undset, Sigrid
  1882-1949 . . . . **TCLC 3; DA; DAB;**
                       DAC; DAM MST, NOV; WLC
  See also CA 104; 129; MTCW

Ungaretti, Giuseppe
  1888-1970 . . . . **CLC 7, 11, 15**
  See also CA 19-20; 25-28R; CAP 2;
  DLB 114

Unger, Douglas 1952- . . . . **CLC 34**
  See also CA 130

Unsworth, Barry (Forster) 1930- . . . . **CLC 76**
  See also CA 25-28R; CANR 30, 54

Updike, John (Hoyer)
  1932- . . . . . . **CLC 1, 2, 3, 5, 7, 9, 13, 15,**
                  23, 34, 43, 70; DA; DAB; DAC;
                  DAM MST, NOV, POET, POP;
                                              SSC 13; WLC
  See also CA 1-4R; CABS 1; CANR 4, 33,
  51; CDALB 1968-1988; DLB 2, 5, 143;
  DLBD 3; DLBY 80, 82; MTCW

Upshaw, Margaret Mitchell
  See Mitchell, Margaret (Munnerlyn)

Upton, Mark
  See Sanders, Lawrence

Urdang, Constance (Henriette)
  1922- . . . . **CLC 47**
  See also CA 21-24R; CANR 9, 24

Uriel, Henry
  See Faust, Frederick (Schiller)

Uris, Leon (Marcus)
  1924- . . . . **CLC 7, 32; DAM NOV, POP**
  See also AITN 1, 2; BEST 89:2; CA 1-4R;
  CANR 1, 40; MTCW; SATA 49

Urmuz
  See Codrescu, Andrei

Urquhart, Jane 1949- . . . . **CLC 90; DAC**
  See also CA 113; CANR 32

Ustinov, Peter (Alexander) 1921- . . . . **CLC 1**
  See also AITN 1; CA 13-16R; CANR 25,
  51; DLB 13

Vaculik, Ludvik 1926- . . . . **CLC 7**
See also CA 53-56

Valdez, Luis (Miguel)
1940- . . . . . **CLC 84; DAM MULT; HLC**
See also CA 101; CANR 32; DLB 122; HW

Valenzuela, Luisa
1938- . . . **CLC 31; DAM MULT; SSC 14**
See also CA 101; CANR 32; DLB 113; HW

Valera y Alcala-Galiano, Juan
1824-1905 . . . . **TCLC 10**
See also CA 106

Valery, (Ambroise) Paul (Toussaint Jules)
1871-1945 . . . . **TCLC 4, 15;**
        DAM POET; PC 9
See also CA 104; 122; MTCW

Valle-Inclan, Ramon (Maria) del
1866-1936 . . . . . **TCLC 5; DAM MULT;**
        HLC
See also CA 106; 153; DLB 134

Vallejo, Antonio Buero
See Buero Vallejo, Antonio

Vallejo, Cesar (Abraham)
1892-1938 . . . . **TCLC 3, 56;**
        DAM MULT; HLC
See also CA 105; 153; HW

Vallette, Marguerite Eymery
See Rachilde

Valle Y Pena, Ramon del
See Valle-Inclan, Ramon (Maria) del

Van Ash, Cay 1918- . . . . **CLC 34**

Vanbrugh, Sir John
1664-1726 . . . . **LC 21; DAM DRAM**
See also DLB 80

Van Campen, Karl
See Campbell, John W(ood, Jr.)

Vance, Gerald
See Silverberg, Robert

Vance, Jack . . . . **CLC 35**
See also Vance, John Holbrook
See also DLB 8

Vance, John Holbrook 1916-
See Queen, Ellery; Vance, Jack
See also CA 29-32R; CANR 17; MTCW

**Van Den Bogarde, Derek Jules Gaspard Ulric
Niven** 1921-
See Bogarde, Dirk
See also CA 77-80

Vandenburgh, Jane . . . . **CLC 59**

Vanderhaeghe, Guy 1951- . . . . **CLC 41**
See also CA 113

van der Post, Laurens (Jan)
1906-1996 . . . . **CLC 5**
See also CA 5-8R; 155; CANR 35

van de Wetering, Janwillem 1931- . . **CLC 47**
See also CA 49-52; CANR 4

Van Dine, S. S. . . . . **TCLC 23**
See also Wright, Willard Huntington

Van Doren, Carl (Clinton)
1885-1950 . . . . **TCLC 18**
See also CA 111

Van Doren, Mark 1894-1972 . . . . . **CLC 6, 10**
See also CA 1-4R; 37-40R; CANR 3;
DLB 45; MTCW

Van Druten, John (William)
1901-1957 . . . . **TCLC 2**
See also CA 104; DLB 10

Van Duyn, Mona (Jane)
1921- . . . . . . **CLC 3, 7, 63; DAM POET**
See also CA 9-12R; CANR 7, 38; DLB 5

Van Dyne, Edith
See Baum, L(yman) Frank

van Itallie, Jean-Claude 1936- . . . . **CLC 3**
See also CA 45-48; CAAS 2; CANR 1, 48;
DLB 7

van Ostaijen, Paul 1896-1928 . . . . . **TCLC 33**

Van Peebles, Melvin
1932- . . . . **CLC 2, 20; DAM MULT**
See also BW 2; CA 85-88; CANR 27

Vansittart, Peter 1920- . . . . **CLC 42**
See also CA 1-4R; CANR 3, 49

Van Vechten, Carl 1880-1964 . . . . . . **CLC 33**
See also CA 89-92; DLB 4, 9, 51

Van Vogt, A(lfred) E(lton) 1912- . . . . . **CLC 1**
See also CA 21-24R; CANR 28; DLB 8;
SATA 14

Varda, Agnes 1928- . . . . **CLC 16**
See also CA 116; 122

Vargas Llosa, (Jorge) Mario (Pedro)
1936- . . . . **CLC 3, 6, 9, 10, 15, 31, 42, 85;**
  DA; DAB; DAC; DAM MST, MULT,
        NOV; HLC
See also CA 73-76; CANR 18, 32, 42;
DLB 145; HW; MTCW

Vasiliu, Gheorghe 1881-1957
See Bacovia, George
See also CA 123

Vassa, Gustavus
See Equiano, Olaudah

Vassilikos, Vassilis 1933- . . . . **CLC 4, 8**
See also CA 81-84

Vaughan, Henry 1621-1695 . . . . **LC 27**
See also DLB 131

Vaughn, Stephanie . . . . **CLC 62**

Vazov, Ivan (Minchov)
1850-1921 . . . . **TCLC 25**
See also CA 121; DLB 147

Veblen, Thorstein (Bunde)
1857-1929 . . . . **TCLC 31**
See also CA 115

Vega, Lope de 1562-1635 . . . . **LC 23**

Venison, Alfred
See Pound, Ezra (Weston Loomis)

Verdi, Marie de
See Mencken, H(enry) L(ouis)

Verdu, Matilde
See Cela, Camilo Jose

Verga, Giovanni (Carmelo)
1840-1922 . . . . **TCLC 3; SSC 21**
See also CA 104; 123

Vergil
70B.C.-19B.C. . . . . . **CMLC 9; DA; DAB;**
  DAC; DAM MST, POET; PC 12

Verhaeren, Emile (Adolphe Gustave)
1855-1916 . . . . **TCLC 12**
See also CA 109

Verlaine, Paul (Marie)
1844-1896 . . . . **NCLC 2, 51;**
        DAM POET; PC 2

Verne, Jules (Gabriel)
1828-1905 . . . . **TCLC 6, 52**
See also AAYA 16; CA 110; 131; DLB 123;
JRDA; MAICYA; SATA 21

Very, Jones 1813-1880 . . . . **NCLC 9**
See also DLB 1

Vesaas, Tarjei 1897-1970 . . . . **CLC 48**
See also CA 29-32R

Vialis, Gaston
See Simenon, Georges (Jacques Christian)

Vian, Boris 1920-1959 . . . . **TCLC 9**
See also CA 106; DLB 72

Viaud, (Louis Marie) Julien 1850-1923
See Loti, Pierre
See also CA 107

Vicar, Henry
See Felsen, Henry Gregor

Vicker, Angus
See Felsen, Henry Gregor

Vidal, Gore
1925- . . . . . **CLC 2, 4, 6, 8, 10, 22, 33, 72;**
        DAM NOV, POP
See also AITN 1; BEST 90:2; CA 5-8R;
CANR 13, 45; DLB 6, 152;
INT CANR-13; MTCW

Viereck, Peter (Robert Edwin)
1916- . . . . **CLC 4**
See also CA 1-4R; CANR 1, 47; DLB 5

Vigny, Alfred (Victor) de
1797-1863 . . . . . . **NCLC 7; DAM POET**
See also DLB 119

Vilakazi, Benedict Wallet
1906-1947 . . . . **TCLC 37**

**Villiers de l'Isle Adam, Jean Marie Mathias
Philippe Auguste Comte**
1838-1889 . . . . **NCLC 3; SSC 14**
See also DLB 123

Villon, Francois 1431-1463(?) . . . . **PC 13**

Vinci, Leonardo da 1452-1519 . . . . **LC 12**

Vine, Barbara . . . . **CLC 50**
See also Rendell, Ruth (Barbara)
See also BEST 90:4

Vinge, Joan D(ennison)
1948- . . . . **CLC 30; SSC 24**
See also CA 93-96; SATA 36

Violis, G.
See Simenon, Georges (Jacques Christian)

Visconti, Luchino 1906-1976 . . . . **CLC 16**
See also CA 81-84; 65-68; CANR 39

Vittorini, Elio 1908-1966 . . . . . **CLC 6, 9, 14**
See also CA 133; 25-28R

Vizinczey, Stephen 1933- . . . . **CLC 40**
See also CA 128; INT 128

Vliet, R(ussell) G(ordon)
1929-1984 . . . . **CLC 22**
See also CA 37-40R; 112; CANR 18

Vogau, Boris Andreyevich 1894-1937(?)
See Pilnyak, Boris
See also CA 123

Vogel, Paula A(nne) 1951- . . . . **CLC 76**
See also CA 108

Voight, Ellen Bryant 1943- . . . . CLC 54
See also CA 69-72; CANR 11, 29, 55;
DLB 120

Voigt, Cynthia 1942- . . . . CLC 30
See also AAYA 3; CA 106; CANR 18, 37,
40; CLR 13; INT CANR-18; JRDA;
MAICYA; SATA 48, 79; SATA-Brief 33

Voinovich, Vladimir (Nikolaevich)
1932- . . . . CLC 10, 49
See also CA 81-84; CAAS 12; CANR 33;
MTCW

Vollmann, William T.
1959- . . . . . . CLC 89; DAM NOV, POP
See also CA 134

Voloshinov, V. N.
See Bakhtin, Mikhail Mikhailovich

Voltaire
1694-1778 . . . . . LC 14; DA; DAB; DAC;
DAM DRAM, MST; SSC 12; WLC

von Daeniken, Erich 1935- . . . . CLC 30
See also AITN 1; CA 37-40R; CANR 17,
44

von Daniken, Erich
See von Daeniken, Erich

von Heidenstam, (Carl Gustaf) Verner
See Heidenstam, (Carl Gustaf) Verner von

von Heyse, Paul (Johann Ludwig)
See Heyse, Paul (Johann Ludwig von)

von Hofmannsthal, Hugo
See Hofmannsthal, Hugo von

von Horvath, Odon
See Horvath, Oedoen von

von Horvath, Oedoen
See Horvath, Oedoen von

von Liliencron, (Friedrich Adolf Axel) Detlev
See Liliencron, (Friedrich Adolf Axel)
Detlev von

Vonnegut, Kurt, Jr.
1922- . . . . . . CLC 1, 2, 3, 4, 5, 8, 12, 22,
40, 60; DA; DAB; DAC; DAM MST,
NOV, POP; SSC 8; WLC
See also AAYA 6; AITN 1; BEST 90:4;
CA 1-4R; CANR 1, 25, 49;
CDALB 1968-1988; DLB 2, 8, 152;
DLBD 3; DLBY 80; MTCW

Von Rachen, Kurt
See Hubbard, L(afayette) Ron(ald)

von Rezzori (d'Arezzo), Gregor
See Rezzori (d'Arezzo), Gregor von

von Sternberg, Josef
See Sternberg, Josef von

Vorster, Gordon 1924- . . . . CLC 34
See also CA 133

Vosce, Trudie
See Ozick, Cynthia

Voznesensky, Andrei (Andreievich)
1933- . . . . . . CLC 1, 15, 57; DAM POET
See also CA 89-92; CANR 37; MTCW

Waddington, Miriam 1917- . . . . CLC 28
See also CA 21-24R; CANR 12, 30;
DLB 68

Wagman, Fredrica 1937- . . . . CLC 7
See also CA 97-100; INT 97-100

Wagner, Richard 1813-1883. . . . . . . NCLC 9
See also DLB 129

Wagner-Martin, Linda 1936- . . . . CLC 50

Wagoner, David (Russell)
1926- . . . . CLC 3, 5, 15
See also CA 1-4R; CAAS 3; CANR 2;
DLB 5; SATA 14

Wah, Fred(erick James) 1939-. . . . . . CLC 44
See also CA 107; 141; DLB 60

Wahloo, Per 1926-1975 . . . . CLC 7
See also CA 61-64

Wahloo, Peter
See Wahloo, Per

Wain, John (Barrington)
1925-1994 . . . . CLC 2, 11, 15, 46
See also CA 5-8R; 145; CAAS 4; CANR 23,
54; CDBLB 1960 to Present; DLB 15, 27,
139, 155; MTCW

Wajda, Andrzej 1926-. . . . . CLC 16
See also CA 102

Wakefield, Dan 1932-. . . . . CLC 7
See also CA 21-24R; CAAS 7

Wakoski, Diane
1937- . . . . CLC 2, 4, 7, 9, 11, 40;
DAM POET; PC 15
See also CA 13-16R; CAAS 1; CANR 9;
DLB 5; INT CANR-9

Wakoski-Sherbell, Diane
See Wakoski, Diane

Walcott, Derek (Alton)
1930- . . . . CLC 2, 4, 9, 14, 25, 42, 67, 76;
BLC; DAB; DAC; DAM MST, MULT,
POET
See also BW 2; CA 89-92; CANR 26, 47;
DLB 117; DLBY 81; MTCW

Waldman, Anne 1945- . . . . CLC 7
See also CA 37-40R; CAAS 17; CANR 34;
DLB 16

Waldo, E. Hunter
See Sturgeon, Theodore (Hamilton)

Waldo, Edward Hamilton
See Sturgeon, Theodore (Hamilton)

Walker, Alice (Malsenior)
1944- . . . . CLC 5, 6, 9, 19, 27, 46, 58;
BLC; DA; DAB; DAC; DAM MST,
MULT, NOV, POET, POP; SSC 5
See also AAYA 3; BEST 89:4; BW 2;
CA 37-40R; CANR 9, 27, 49;
CDALB 1968-1988; DLB 6, 33, 143;
INT CANR-27; MTCW; SATA 31

Walker, David Harry 1911-1992. . . . CLC 14
See also CA 1-4R; 137; CANR 1; SATA 8;
SATA-Obit 71

Walker, Edward Joseph 1934-
See Walker, Ted
See also CA 21-24R; CANR 12, 28, 53

Walker, George F.
1947- . . . . CLC 44, 61; DAB; DAC;
DAM MST
See also CA 103; CANR 21, 43; DLB 60

Walker, Joseph A.
1935- . . . . CLC 19; DAM DRAM, MST
See also BW 1; CA 89-92; CANR 26;
DLB 38

Walker, Margaret (Abigail)
1915- . . . . CLC 1, 6; BLC; DAM MULT
See also BW 2; CA 73-76; CANR 26, 54;
DLB 76, 152; MTCW

Walker, Ted. . . . . CLC 13
See also Walker, Edward Joseph
See also DLB 40

Wallace, David Foster 1962-. . . . . . . CLC 50
See also CA 132

Wallace, Dexter
See Masters, Edgar Lee

Wallace, (Richard Horatio) Edgar
1875-1932 . . . . TCLC 57
See also CA 115; DLB 70

Wallace, Irving
1916-1990 . . . . . CLC 7, 13; DAM NOV,
POP
See also AITN 1; CA 1-4R; 132; CAAS 1;
CANR 1, 27; INT CANR-27; MTCW

Wallant, Edward Lewis
1926-1962 . . . . CLC 5, 10
See also CA 1-4R; CANR 22; DLB 2, 28,
143; MTCW

Walley, Byron
See Card, Orson Scott

Walpole, Horace 1717-1797. . . . . LC 2
See also DLB 39, 104

Walpole, Hugh (Seymour)
1884-1941 . . . . TCLC 5
See also CA 104; DLB 34

Walser, Martin 1927-. . . . . CLC 27
See also CA 57-60; CANR 8, 46; DLB 75,
124

Walser, Robert
1878-1956 . . . . TCLC 18; SSC 20
See also CA 118; DLB 66

Walsh, Jill Paton. . . . . CLC 35
See also Paton Walsh, Gillian
See also AAYA 11; CLR 2; DLB 161;
SAAS 3

Walter, Villiam Christian
See Andersen, Hans Christian

Wambaugh, Joseph (Aloysius, Jr.)
1937- . . . . CLC 3, 18; DAM NOV, POP
See also AITN 1; BEST 89:3; CA 33-36R;
CANR 42; DLB 6; DLBY 83; MTCW

Ward, Arthur Henry Sarsfield 1883-1959
See Rohmer, Sax
See also CA 108

Ward, Douglas Turner 1930-. . . . . . . CLC 19
See also BW 1; CA 81-84; CANR 27;
DLB 7, 38

Ward, Mary Augusta
See Ward, Mrs. Humphry

Ward, Mrs. Humphry
1851-1920 . . . . TCLC 55
See also DLB 18

Ward, Peter
See Faust, Frederick (Schiller)

Warhol, Andy 1928(?)-1987. . . . . CLC 20
See also AAYA 12; BEST 89:4; CA 89-92;
121; CANR 34

Warner, Francis (Robert le Plastrier)
1937- . . . . CLC 14
See also CA 53-56; CANR 11

Warner, Marina 1946-. . . . . CLC 59
See also CA 65-68; CANR 21, 55

Warner, Rex (Ernest) 1905-1986. . . . CLC 45
See also CA 89-92; 119; DLB 15

Warner, Susan (Bogert)
  1819-1885 . . . . NCLC 31
  See also DLB 3, 42

Warner, Sylvia (Constance) Ashton
  See Ashton-Warner, Sylvia (Constance)

Warner, Sylvia Townsend
  1893-1978 . . . . CLC 7, 19; SSC 23
  See also CA 61-64; 77-80; CANR 16;
  DLB 34, 139; MTCW

Warren, Mercy Otis 1728-1814. . . NCLC 13
  See also DLB 31

Warren, Robert Penn
  1905-1989 . . . . CLC 1, 4, 6, 8, 10, 13, 18,
  39, 53, 59; DA; DAB; DAC; DAM MST,
  NOV, POET; SSC 4; WLC
  See also AITN 1; CA 13-16R; 129;
  CANR 10, 47; CDALB 1968-1988;
  DLB 2, 48, 152; DLBY 80, 89;
  INT CANR-10; MTCW; SATA 46;
  SATA-Obit 63

Warshofsky, Isaac
  See Singer, Isaac Bashevis

Warton, Thomas
  1728-1790 . . . . LC 15; DAM POET
  See also DLB 104, 109

Waruk, Kona
  See Harris, (Theodore) Wilson

Warung, Price 1855-1911. . . . . . . TCLC 45

Warwick, Jarvis
  See Garner, Hugh

Washington, Alex
  See Harris, Mark

Washington, Booker T(aliaferro)
  1856-1915 . . . . TCLC 10; BLC;
  DAM MULT
  See also BW 1; CA 114; 125; SATA 28

Washington, George 1732-1799. . . . . LC 25
  See also DLB 31

Wassermann, (Karl) Jakob
  1873-1934 . . . . TCLC 6
  See also CA 104; DLB 66

Wasserstein, Wendy
  1950- . . . . CLC 32, 59, 90;
  DAM DRAM; DC 4
  See also CA 121; 129; CABS 3; CANR 53;
  INT 129

Waterhouse, Keith (Spencer)
  1929- . . . . CLC 47
  See also CA 5-8R; CANR 38; DLB 13, 15;
  MTCW

Waters, Frank (Joseph)
  1902-1995 . . . . CLC 88
  See also CA 5-8R; 149; CAAS 13; CANR 3,
  18; DLBY 86

Waters, Roger 1944-. . . . . CLC 35

Watkins, Frances Ellen
  See Harper, Frances Ellen Watkins

Watkins, Gerrold
  See Malzberg, Barry N(athaniel)

Watkins, Gloria 1955(?)-
  See hooks, bell
  See also BW 2; CA 143

Watkins, Paul 1964-. . . . . CLC 55
  See also CA 132

Watkins, Vernon Phillips
  1906-1967 . . . . CLC 43
  See also CA 9-10; 25-28R; CAP 1; DLB 20

Watson, Irving S.
  See Mencken, H(enry) L(ouis)

Watson, John H.
  See Farmer, Philip Jose

Watson, Richard F.
  See Silverberg, Robert

Waugh, Auberon (Alexander) 1939-. . CLC 7
  See also CA 45-48; CANR 6, 22; DLB 14

Waugh, Evelyn (Arthur St. John)
  1903-1966 . . . . . . CLC 1, 3, 8, 13, 19, 27,
  44; DA; DAB; DAC; DAM MST, NOV,
  POP; WLC
  See also CA 85-88; 25-28R; CANR 22;
  CDBLB 1914-1945; DLB 15, 162; MTCW

Waugh, Harriet 1944- . . . . CLC 6
  See also CA 85-88; CANR 22

Ways, C. R.
  See Blount, Roy (Alton), Jr.

Waystaff, Simon
  See Swift, Jonathan

Webb, (Martha) Beatrice (Potter)
  1858-1943 . . . . TCLC 22
  See also Potter, Beatrice
  See also CA 117

Webb, Charles (Richard) 1939-. . . . . CLC 7
  See also CA 25-28R

Webb, James H(enry), Jr. 1946-. . . . CLC 22
  See also CA 81-84

Webb, Mary (Gladys Meredith)
  1881-1927 . . . . TCLC 24
  See also CA 123; DLB 34

Webb, Mrs. Sidney
  See Webb, (Martha) Beatrice (Potter)

Webb, Phyllis 1927-. . . . . CLC 18
  See also CA 104; CANR 23; DLB 53

Webb, Sidney (James)
  1859-1947 . . . . TCLC 22
  See also CA 117

Webber, Andrew Lloyd. . . . . CLC 21
  See also Lloyd Webber, Andrew

Weber, Lenora Mattingly
  1895-1971 . . . . CLC 12
  See also CA 19-20; 29-32R; CAP 1;
  SATA 2; SATA-Obit 26

Webster, John
  1579(?)-1634(?) . . . . . LC 33; DA; DAB;
  DAC; DAM DRAM, MST; DC 2; WLC
  See also CDBLB Before 1660; DLB 58

Webster, Noah 1758-1843 . . . . . . NCLC 30

Wedekind, (Benjamin) Frank(lin)
  1864-1918 . . . . . . TCLC 7; DAM DRAM
  See also CA 104; 153; DLB 118

Weidman, Jerome 1913-. . . . . CLC 7
  See also AITN 2; CA 1-4R; CANR 1;
  DLB 28

Weil, Simone (Adolphine)
  1909-1943 . . . . TCLC 23
  See also CA 117

Weinstein, Nathan
  See West, Nathanael

Weinstein, Nathan von Wallenstein
  See West, Nathanael

Weir, Peter (Lindsay) 1944-. . . . . . CLC 20
  See also CA 113; 123

Weiss, Peter (Ulrich)
  1916-1982 . . . . CLC 3, 15, 51;
  DAM DRAM
  See also CA 45-48; 106; CANR 3; DLB 69,
  124

Weiss, Theodore (Russell)
  1916- . . . . CLC 3, 8, 14
  See also CA 9-12R; CAAS 2; CANR 46;
  DLB 5

Welch, (Maurice) Denton
  1915-1948 . . . . TCLC 22
  See also CA 121; 148

Welch, James
  1940- . . . . . CLC 6, 14, 52; DAM MULT,
  POP
  See also CA 85-88; CANR 42; NNAL

Weldon, Fay
  1933- . . . . CLC 6, 9, 11, 19, 36, 59;
  DAM POP
  See also CA 21-24R; CANR 16, 46;
  CDBLB 1960 to Present; DLB 14;
  INT CANR-16; MTCW

Wellek, Rene 1903-1995. . . . . CLC 28
  See also CA 5-8R; 150; CAAS 7; CANR 8;
  DLB 63; INT CANR-8

Weller, Michael 1942-. . . . . CLC 10, 53
  See also CA 85-88

Weller, Paul 1958-. . . . . CLC 26

Wellershoff, Dieter 1925-. . . . . CLC 46
  See also CA 89-92; CANR 16, 37

Welles, (George) Orson
  1915-1985 . . . . CLC 20, 80
  See also CA 93-96; 117

Wellman, Mac 1945-. . . . . CLC 65

Wellman, Manly Wade 1903-1986. . CLC 49
  See also CA 1-4R; 118; CANR 6, 16, 44;
  SATA 6; SATA-Obit 47

Wells, Carolyn 1869(?)-1942 . . . . . TCLC 35
  See also CA 113; DLB 11

Wells, H(erbert) G(eorge)
  1866-1946 . . . . TCLC 6, 12, 19; DA;
  DAB; DAC; DAM MST, NOV; SSC 6;
  WLC
  See also AAYA 18; CA 110; 121;
  CDBLB 1914-1945; DLB 34, 70, 156;
  MTCW; SATA 20

Wells, Rosemary 1943-. . . . . CLC 12
  See also AAYA 13; CA 85-88; CANR 48;
  CLR 16; MAICYA; SAAS 1; SATA 18,
  69

Welty, Eudora
  1909- . . . . . . CLC 1, 2, 5, 14, 22, 33; DA;
  DAB; DAC; DAM MST, NOV; SSC 1;
  WLC
  See also CA 9-12R; CABS 1; CANR 32;
  CDALB 1941-1968; DLB 2, 102, 143;
  DLBD 12; DLBY 87; MTCW

Wen I-to 1899-1946 . . . . TCLC 28

Wentworth, Robert
  See Hamilton, Edmond

Werfel, Franz (V.) 1890-1945 . . . . . . TCLC 8
  See also CA 104; DLB 81, 124

Wergeland, Henrik Arnold
        1808-1845 .... NCLC 5

Wersba, Barbara   1932-........... CLC 30
        See also AAYA 2; CA 29-32R; CANR 16,
        38; CLR 3; DLB 52; JRDA; MAICYA;
        SAAS 2; SATA 1, 58

Wertmueller, Lina   1928- .... CLC 16
        See also CA 97-100; CANR 39

Wescott, Glenway   1901-1987....... CLC 13
        See also CA 13-16R; 121; CANR 23;
        DLB 4, 9, 102

Wesker, Arnold
        1932- .... CLC 3, 5, 42; DAB;
                                        DAM DRAM
        See also CA 1-4R; CAAS 7; CANR 1, 33;
        CDBLB 1960 to Present; DLB 13;
        MTCW

Wesley, Richard (Errol)   1945-....... CLC 7
        See also BW 1; CA 57-60; CANR 27;
        DLB 38

Wessel, Johan Herman   1742-1785 .... LC 7

West, Anthony (Panther)
        1914-1987 .... CLC 50
        See also CA 45-48; 124; CANR 3, 19;
        DLB 15

West, C. P.
        See Wodehouse, P(elham) G(renville)

West, (Mary) Jessamyn
        1902-1984 .... CLC 7, 17
        See also CA 9-12R; 112; CANR 27; DLB 6;
        DLBY 84; MTCW; SATA-Obit 37

West, Morris L(anglo)   1916-..... CLC 6, 33
        See also CA 5-8R; CANR 24, 49; MTCW

West, Nathanael
        1903-1940 ..... TCLC 1, 14, 44; SSC 16
        See also CA 104; 125; CDALB 1929-1941;
        DLB 4, 9, 28; MTCW

West, Owen
        See Koontz, Dean R(ay)

West, Paul   1930- .... CLC 7, 14, 96
        See also CA 13-16R; CAAS 7; CANR 22,
        53; DLB 14; INT CANR-22

West, Rebecca   1892-1983 .. CLC 7, 9, 31, 50
        See also CA 5-8R; 109; CANR 19; DLB 36;
        DLBY 83; MTCW

Westall, Robert (Atkinson)
        1929-1993 .... CLC 17
        See also AAYA 12; CA 69-72; 141;
        CANR 18; CLR 13; JRDA; MAICYA;
        SAAS 2; SATA 23, 69; SATA-Obit 75

Westlake, Donald E(dwin)
        1933- .... CLC 7, 33; DAM POP
        See also CA 17-20R; CAAS 13; CANR 16,
        44; INT CANR-16

Westmacott, Mary
        See Christie, Agatha (Mary Clarissa)

Weston, Allen
        See Norton, Andre

Wetcheek, J. L.
        See Feuchtwanger, Lion

Wetering, Janwillem van de
        See van de Wetering, Janwillem

Wetherell, Elizabeth
        See Warner, Susan (Bogert)

Whale, James   1889-1957 .... TCLC 63

Whalen, Philip   1923-........... CLC 6, 29
        See also CA 9-12R; CANR 5, 39; DLB 16

Wharton, Edith (Newbold Jones)
        1862-1937 ...... TCLC 3, 9, 27, 53; DA;
        DAB; DAC; DAM MST, NOV; SSC 6;
                                        WLC
        See also CA 104; 132; CDALB 1865-1917;
        DLB 4, 9, 12, 78; DLBD 13; MTCW

Wharton, James
        See Mencken, H(enry) L(ouis)

Wharton, William (a pseudonym)
        .... CLC 18, 37
        See also CA 93-96; DLBY 80; INT 93-96

Wheatley (Peters), Phillis
        1754(?)-1784 .... LC 3; BLC; DA; DAC;
        DAM MST, MULT, POET; PC 3; WLC
        See also CDALB 1640-1865; DLB 31, 50

Wheelock, John Hall   1886-1978.... CLC 14
        See also CA 13-16R; 77-80; CANR 14;
        DLB 45

White, E(lwyn) B(rooks)
        1899-1985 .. CLC 10, 34, 39; DAM POP
        See also AITN 2; CA 13-16R; 116;
        CANR 16, 37; CLR 1, 21; DLB 11, 22;
        MAICYA; MTCW; SATA 2, 29;
        SATA-Obit 44

White, Edmund (Valentine III)
        1940- .... CLC 27; DAM POP
        See also AAYA 7; CA 45-48; CANR 3, 19,
        36; MTCW

White, Patrick (Victor Martindale)
        1912-1990 .. CLC 3, 4, 5, 7, 9, 18, 65, 69
        See also CA 81-84; 132; CANR 43; MTCW

White, Phyllis Dorothy James   1920-
        See James, P. D.
        See also CA 21-24R; CANR 17, 43;
        DAM POP; MTCW

White, T(erence) H(anbury)
        1906-1964 .... CLC 30
        See also CA 73-76; CANR 37; DLB 160;
        JRDA; MAICYA; SATA 12

White, Terence de Vere
        1912-1994 .... CLC 49
        See also CA 49-52; 145; CANR 3

White, Walter F(rancis)
        1893-1955 .... TCLC 15
        See also White, Walter
        See also BW 1; CA 115; 124; DLB 51

White, William Hale   1831-1913
        See Rutherford, Mark
        See also CA 121

Whitehead, E(dward) A(nthony)
        1933- .... CLC 5
        See also CA 65-68

Whitemore, Hugh (John)   1936-..... CLC 37
        See also CA 132; INT 132

Whitman, Sarah Helen (Power)
        1803-1878 .... NCLC 19
        See also DLB 1

Whitman, Walt(er)
        1819-1892 ..... NCLC 4, 31; DA; DAB;
        DAC; DAM MST, POET; PC 3; WLC
        See also CDALB 1640-1865; DLB 3, 64;
        SATA 20

Whitney, Phyllis A(yame)
        1903- .... CLC 42; DAM POP
        See also AITN 2; BEST 90:3; CA 1-4R;
        CANR 3, 25, 38; JRDA; MAICYA;
        SATA 1, 30

Whittemore, (Edward) Reed (Jr.)
        1919- .... CLC 4
        See also CA 9-12R; CAAS 8; CANR 4;
        DLB 5

Whittier, John Greenleaf
        1807-1892 .... NCLC 8, 59
        See also DLB 1

Whittlebot, Hernia
        See Coward, Noel (Peirce)

Wicker, Thomas Grey   1926-
        See Wicker, Tom
        See also CA 65-68; CANR 21, 46

Wicker, Tom .... CLC 7
        See also Wicker, Thomas Grey

Wideman, John Edgar
        1941- .... CLC 5, 34, 36, 67; BLC;
                                        DAM MULT
        See also BW 2; CA 85-88; CANR 14, 42;
        DLB 33, 143

Wiebe, Rudy (Henry)
        1934- .... CLC 6, 11, 14; DAC;
                                        DAM MST
        See also CA 37-40R; CANR 42; DLB 60

Wieland, Christoph Martin
        1733-1813 .... NCLC 17
        See also DLB 97

Wiene, Robert   1881-1938........ TCLC 56

Wieners, John   1934-.............. CLC 7
        See also CA 13-16R; DLB 16

Wiesel, Elie(zer)
        1928- ...... CLC 3, 5, 11, 37; DA; DAB;
                                DAC; DAM MST, NOV
        See also AAYA 7; AITN 1; CA 5-8R;
        CAAS 4; CANR 8, 40; DLB 83;
        DLBY 87; INT CANR-8; MTCW;
        SATA 56

Wiggins, Marianne   1947-.......... CLC 57
        See also BEST 89:3; CA 130

Wight, James Alfred   1916-
        See Herriot, James
        See also CA 77-80; SATA 55;
        SATA-Brief 44

Wilbur, Richard (Purdy)
        1921- ... CLC 3, 6, 9, 14, 53; DA; DAB;
                                DAC; DAM MST, POET
        See also CA 1-4R; CABS 2; CANR 2, 29;
        DLB 5, 169; INT CANR-29; MTCW;
        SATA 9

Wild, Peter   1940-................ CLC 14
        See also CA 37-40R; DLB 5

Wilde, Oscar (Fingal O'Flahertie Wills)
        1854(?)-1900 .... TCLC 1, 8, 23, 41; DA;
        DAB; DAC; DAM DRAM, MST, NOV;
                                        SSC 11; WLC
        See also CA 104; 119; CDBLB 1890-1914;
        DLB 10, 19, 34, 57, 141, 156; SATA 24

Wilder, Billy .... CLC 20
        See also Wilder, Samuel
        See also DLB 26

Wilder, Samuel 1906-
See Wilder, Billy
See also CA 89-92

Wilder, Thornton (Niven)
1897-1975 ...... **CLC 1, 5, 6, 10, 15, 35,**
82; DA; DAB; DAC; DAM DRAM,
MST, NOV; DC 1; WLC
See also AITN 2; CA 13-16R; 61-64;
CANR 40; DLB 4, 7, 9; MTCW

Wilding, Michael 1942- .... **CLC 73**
See also CA 104; CANR 24, 49

Wiley, Richard 1944- .... **CLC 44**
See also CA 121; 129

Wilhelm, Kate .... **CLC 7**
See also Wilhelm, Katie Gertrude
See also CAAS 5; DLB 8; INT CANR-17

Wilhelm, Katie Gertrude 1928-
See Wilhelm, Kate
See also CA 37-40R; CANR 17, 36; MTCW

Wilkins, Mary
See Freeman, Mary Eleanor Wilkins

Willard, Nancy 1936- .... **CLC 7, 37**
See also CA 89-92; CANR 10, 39; CLR 5;
DLB 5, 52; MAICYA; MTCW;
SATA 37, 71; SATA-Brief 30

Williams, C(harles) K(enneth)
1936- .... **CLC 33, 56; DAM POET**
See also CA 37-40R; DLB 5

Williams, Charles
See Collier, James L(incoln)

Williams, Charles (Walter Stansby)
1886-1945 .... **TCLC 1, 11**
See also CA 104; DLB 100, 153

Williams, (George) Emlyn
1905-1987 ...... **CLC 15; DAM DRAM**
See also CA 104; 123; CANR 36; DLB 10,
77; MTCW

Williams, Hugo 1942- .... **CLC 42**
See also CA 17-20R; CANR 45; DLB 40

Williams, J. Walker
See Wodehouse, P(elham) G(renville)

Williams, John A(lfred)
1925- ... **CLC 5, 13; BLC; DAM MULT**
See also BW 2; CA 53-56; CAAS 3;
CANR 6, 26, 51; DLB 2, 33;
INT CANR-6

Williams, Jonathan (Chamberlain)
1929- .... **CLC 13**
See also CA 9-12R; CAAS 12; CANR 8;
DLB 5

Williams, Joy 1944- .... **CLC 31**
See also CA 41-44R; CANR 22, 48

Williams, Norman 1952- .... **CLC 39**
See also CA 118

Williams, Sherley Anne
1944- ..... **CLC 89; BLC; DAM MULT,**
POET
See also BW 2; CA 73-76; CANR 25;
DLB 41; INT CANR-25; SATA 78

Williams, Shirley
See Williams, Sherley Anne

Williams, Tennessee
1911-1983 ..... **CLC 1, 2, 5, 7, 8, 11, 15,**
19, 30, 39, 45, 71; DA; DAB; DAC;
DAM DRAM, MST; DC 4; WLC
See also AITN 1, 2; CA 5-8R; 108;
CABS 3; CANR 31; CDALB 1941-1968;
DLB 7; DLBD 4; DLBY 83; MTCW

Williams, Thomas (Alonzo)
1926-1990 .... **CLC 14**
See also CA 1-4R; 132; CANR 2

Williams, William C.
See Williams, William Carlos

Williams, William Carlos
1883-1963 .... **CLC 1, 2, 5, 9, 13, 22, 42,**
67; DA; DAB; DAC; DAM MST, POET;
PC 7
See also CA 89-92; CANR 34;
CDALB 1917-1929; DLB 4, 16, 54, 86;
MTCW

Williamson, David (Keith) 1942- .... **CLC 56**
See also CA 103; CANR 41

Williamson, Ellen Douglas 1905-1984
See Douglas, Ellen
See also CA 17-20R; 114; CANR 39

Williamson, Jack .... **CLC 29**
See also Williamson, John Stewart
See also CAAS 8; DLB 8

Williamson, John Stewart 1908-
See Williamson, Jack
See also CA 17-20R; CANR 23

Willie, Frederick
See Lovecraft, H(oward) P(hillips)

Willingham, Calder (Baynard, Jr.)
1922-1995 .... **CLC 5, 51**
See also CA 5-8R; 147; CANR 3; DLB 2,
44; MTCW

Willis, Charles
See Clarke, Arthur C(harles)

Willy
See Colette, (Sidonie-Gabrielle)

Willy, Colette
See Colette, (Sidonie-Gabrielle)

Wilson, A(ndrew) N(orman) 1950- .. **CLC 33**
See also CA 112; 122; DLB 14, 155

Wilson, Angus (Frank Johnstone)
1913-1991 .. **CLC 2, 3, 5, 25, 34; SSC 21**
See also CA 5-8R; 134; CANR 21; DLB 15,
139, 155; MTCW

Wilson, August
1945- .... **CLC 39, 50, 63; BLC; DA;**
DAB; DAC; DAM DRAM, MST,
MULT; DC 2
See also AAYA 16; BW 2; CA 115; 122;
CANR 42, 54; MTCW

Wilson, Brian 1942- .... **CLC 12**

Wilson, Colin 1931- .... **CLC 3, 14**
See also CA 1-4R; CAAS 5; CANR 1, 22,
33; DLB 14; MTCW

Wilson, Dirk
See Pohl, Frederik

Wilson, Edmund
1895-1972 .... **CLC 1, 2, 3, 8, 24**
See also CA 1-4R; 37-40R; CANR 1, 46;
DLB 63; MTCW

Wilson, Ethel Davis (Bryant)
1888(?)-1980 .... **CLC 13; DAC;**
DAM POET
See also CA 102; DLB 68; MTCW

Wilson, John 1785-1854 .... **NCLC 5**

Wilson, John (Anthony) Burgess 1917-1993
See Burgess, Anthony
See also CA 1-4R; 143; CANR 2, 46; DAC;
DAM NOV; MTCW

Wilson, Lanford
1937- ..... **CLC 7, 14, 36; DAM DRAM**
See also CA 17-20R; CABS 3; CANR 45;
DLB 7

Wilson, Robert M. 1944- .... **CLC 7, 9**
See also CA 49-52; CANR 2, 41; MTCW

Wilson, Robert McLiam 1964- ..... **CLC 59**
See also CA 132

Wilson, Sloan 1920- .... **CLC 32**
See also CA 1-4R; CANR 1, 44

Wilson, Snoo 1948- .... **CLC 33**
See also CA 69-72

Wilson, William S(mith) 1932- ..... **CLC 49**
See also CA 81-84

Winchilsea, Anne (Kingsmill) Finch Counte
1661-1720 .... **LC 3**

Windham, Basil
See Wodehouse, P(elham) G(renville)

Wingrove, David (John) 1954- ...... **CLC 68**
See also CA 133

Winters, Janet Lewis .... **CLC 41**
See also Lewis, Janet
See also DLBY 87

Winters, (Arthur) Yvor
1900-1968 .... **CLC 4, 8, 32**
See also CA 11-12; 25-28R; CAP 1;
DLB 48; MTCW

Winterson, Jeanette
1959- .... **CLC 64; DAM POP**
See also CA 136

Winthrop, John 1588-1649 .... **LC 31**
See also DLB 24, 30

Wiseman, Frederick 1930- .... **CLC 20**

Wister, Owen 1860-1938 .... **TCLC 21**
See also CA 108; DLB 9, 78; SATA 62

Witkacy
See Witkiewicz, Stanislaw Ignacy

Witkiewicz, Stanislaw Ignacy
1885-1939 .... **TCLC 8**
See also CA 105

Wittgenstein, Ludwig (Josef Johann)
1889-1951 .... **TCLC 59**
See also CA 113

Wittig, Monique 1935(?)- .... **CLC 22**
See also CA 116; 135; DLB 83

Wittlin, Jozef 1896-1976 .... **CLC 25**
See also CA 49-52; 65-68; CANR 3

Wodehouse, P(elham) G(renville)
1881-1975 ... **CLC 1, 2, 5, 10, 22; DAB;**
DAC; DAM NOV; SSC 2
See also AITN 2; CA 45-48; 57-60;
CANR 3, 33; CDBLB 1914-1945;
DLB 34, 162; MTCW; SATA 22

Woiwode, L.
See Woiwode, Larry (Alfred)

Woiwode, Larry (Alfred) 1941-... **CLC 6, 10**
See also CA 73-76; CANR 16; DLB 6;
INT CANR-16

Wojciechowska, Maia (Teresa)
1927- .... **CLC 26**
See also AAYA 8; CA 9-12R; CANR 4, 41;
CLR 1; JRDA; MAICYA; SAAS 1;
SATA 1, 28, 83

Wolf, Christa 1929- .... **CLC 14, 29, 58**
See also CA 85-88; CANR 45; DLB 75;
MTCW

Wolfe, Gene (Rodman)
1931- .... **CLC 25; DAM POP**
See also CA 57-60; CAAS 9; CANR 6, 32;
DLB 8

Wolfe, George C. 1954- .... **CLC 49**
See also CA 149

Wolfe, Thomas (Clayton)
1900-1938 ..... **TCLC 4, 13, 29, 61; DA;
DAB; DAC; DAM MST, NOV; WLC**
See also CA 104; 132; CDALB 1929-1941;
DLB 9, 102; DLBD 2; DLBY 85; MTCW

Wolfe, Thomas Kennerly, Jr. 1931-
See Wolfe, Tom
See also CA 13-16R; CANR 9, 33;
DAM POP; INT CANR-9; MTCW

Wolfe, Tom .... **CLC 1, 2, 9, 15, 35, 51**
See also Wolfe, Thomas Kennerly, Jr.
See also AAYA 8; AITN 2; BEST 89:1;
DLB 152

Wolff, Geoffrey (Ansell) 1937- ..... **CLC 41**
See also CA 29-32R; CANR 29, 43

Wolff, Sonia
See Levitin, Sonia (Wolff)

Wolff, Tobias (Jonathan Ansell)
1945- .... **CLC 39, 64**
See also AAYA 16; BEST 90:2; CA 114;
117; CAAS 22; CANR 54; DLB 130;
INT 117

Wolfram von Eschenbach
c. 1170-c. 1220 .... **CMLC 5**
See also DLB 138

Wolitzer, Hilma 1930- .... **CLC 17**
See also CA 65-68; CANR 18, 40;
INT CANR-18; SATA 31

Wollstonecraft, Mary 1759-1797...... **LC 5**
See also CDBLB 1789-1832; DLB 39, 104,
158

Wonder, Stevie .... **CLC 12**
See also Morris, Steveland Judkins

Wong, Jade Snow 1922-........... **CLC 17**
See also CA 109

Woodcott, Keith
See Brunner, John (Kilian Houston)

Woodruff, Robert W.
See Mencken, H(enry) L(ouis)

Woolf, (Adeline) Virginia
1882-1941 .... **TCLC 1, 5, 20, 43, 56;
DA; DAB; DAC; DAM MST, NOV;
SSC 7; WLC**
See also CA 104; 130; CDBLB 1914-1945;
DLB 36, 100, 162; DLBD 10; MTCW

Woollcott, Alexander (Humphreys)
1887-1943 .... **TCLC 5**
See also CA 105; DLB 29

Woolrich, Cornell 1903-1968....... **CLC 77**
See also Hopley-Woolrich, Cornell George

Wordsworth, Dorothy
1771-1855 .... **NCLC 25**
See also DLB 107

Wordsworth, William
1770-1850 .... **NCLC 12, 38; DA; DAB;
DAC; DAM MST, POET; PC 4; WLC**
See also CDBLB 1789-1832; DLB 93, 107

Wouk, Herman
1915-... **CLC 1, 9, 38; DAM NOV, POP**
See also CA 5-8R; CANR 6, 33; DLBY 82;
INT CANR-6; MTCW

Wright, Charles (Penzel, Jr.)
1935- .... **CLC 6, 13, 28**
See also CA 29-32R; CAAS 7; CANR 23,
36; DLB 165; DLBY 82; MTCW

Wright, Charles Stevenson
1932- .... **CLC 49; BLC 3;
DAM MULT, POET**
See also BW 1; CA 9-12R; CANR 26;
DLB 33

Wright, Jack R.
See Harris, Mark

Wright, James (Arlington)
1927-1980 .... **CLC 3, 5, 10, 28;
DAM POET**
See also AITN 2; CA 49-52; 97-100;
CANR 4, 34; DLB 5, 169; MTCW

Wright, Judith (Arandell)
1915- .... **CLC 11, 53; PC 14**
See also CA 13-16R; CANR 31; MTCW;
SATA 14

Wright, L(aurali) R. 1939-........ **CLC 44**
See also CA 138

Wright, Richard (Nathaniel)
1908-1960 .... **CLC 1, 3, 4, 9, 14, 21, 48,
74; BLC; DA; DAB; DAC; DAM MST,
MULT, NOV; SSC 2; WLC**
See also AAYA 5; BW 1; CA 108;
CDALB 1929-1941; DLB 76, 102;
DLBD 2; MTCW

Wright, Richard B(ruce) 1937-...... **CLC 6**
See also CA 85-88; DLB 53

Wright, Rick 1945-............... **CLC 35**

Wright, Rowland
See Wells, Carolyn

Wright, Stephen Caldwell 1946-.... **CLC 33**
See also BW 2

Wright, Willard Huntington 1888-1939
See Van Dine, S. S.
See also CA 115

Wright, William 1930-........... **CLC 44**
See also CA 53-56; CANR 7, 23

Wroth, LadyMary 1587-1653(?) ..... **LC 30**
See also DLB 121

Wu Ch'eng-en 1500(?)-1582(?)........ **LC 7**

Wu Ching-tzu 1701-1754 .... **LC 2**

Wurlitzer, Rudolph 1938(?)-... **CLC 2, 4, 15**
See also CA 85-88; DLB 173

Wycherley, William
1641-1715 ..... **LC 8, 21; DAM DRAM**
See also CDBLB 1660-1789; DLB 80

Wylie, Elinor (Morton Hoyt)
1885-1928 .... **TCLC 8**
See also CA 105; DLB 9, 45

Wylie, Philip (Gordon) 1902-1971... **CLC 43**
See also CA 21-22; 33-36R; CAP 2; DLB 9

Wyndham, John .... **CLC 19**
See also Harris, John (Wyndham Parkes
Lucas) Beynon

Wyss, Johann David Von
1743-1818 .... **NCLC 10**
See also JRDA; MAICYA; SATA 29;
SATA-Brief 27

Xenophon
c. 430B.C.-c. 354B.C......... **CMLC 17**

Yakumo Koizumi
See Hearn, (Patricio) Lafcadio (Tessima
Carlos)

Yanez, Jose Donoso
See Donoso (Yanez), Jose

Yanovsky, Basile S.
See Yanovsky, V(assily) S(emenovich)

Yanovsky, V(assily) S(emenovich)
1906-1989 .... **CLC 2, 18**
See also CA 97-100; 129

Yates, Richard 1926-1992 ..... **CLC 7, 8, 23**
See also CA 5-8R; 139; CANR 10, 43;
DLB 2; DLBY 81, 92; INT CANR-10

Yeats, W. B.
See Yeats, William Butler

Yeats, William Butler
1865-1939 ..... **TCLC 1, 11, 18, 31; DA;
DAB; DAC; DAM DRAM, MST,
POET; WLC**
See also CA 104; 127; CANR 45;
CDBLB 1890-1914; DLB 10, 19, 98, 156;
MTCW

Yehoshua, A(braham) B.
1936- .... **CLC 13, 31**
See also CA 33-36R; CANR 43

Yep, Laurence Michael 1948-...... **CLC 35**
See also AAYA 5; CA 49-52; CANR 1, 46;
CLR 3, 17; DLB 52; JRDA; MAICYA;
SATA 7, 69

Yerby, Frank G(arvin)
1916-1991 .... **CLC 1, 7, 22; BLC;
DAM MULT**
See also BW 1; CA 9-12R; 136; CANR 16,
52; DLB 76; INT CANR-16; MTCW

Yesenin, Sergei Alexandrovich
See Esenin, Sergei (Alexandrovich)

Yevtushenko, Yevgeny (Alexandrovich)
1933- .... **CLC 1, 3, 13, 26, 51;
DAM POET**
See also CA 81-84; CANR 33, 54; MTCW

Yezierska, Anzia 1885(?)-1970 ..... **CLC 46**
See also CA 126; 89-92; DLB 28; MTCW

Yglesias, Helen 1915-........... **CLC 7, 22**
See also CA 37-40R; CAAS 20; CANR 15;
INT CANR-15; MTCW

Yokomitsu Riichi 1898-1947 ...... **TCLC 47**

Yonge, Charlotte (Mary)
1823-1901 .... **TCLC 48**
See also CA 109; DLB 18, 163; SATA 17

York, Jeremy
See Creasey, John

York, Simon
  See Heinlein, Robert A(nson)

Yorke, Henry Vincent   1905-1974 . . . **CLC 13**
  See also Green, Henry
  See also CA 85-88; 49-52

Yosano Akiko   1878-1942 . . **TCLC 59; PC 11**

Yoshimoto, Banana . . . . **CLC 84**
  See also Yoshimoto, Mahoko

Yoshimoto, Mahoko   1964-
  See Yoshimoto, Banana
  See also CA 144

Young, Al(bert James)
  1939- . . . . . **CLC 19; BLC; DAM MULT**
  See also BW 2; CA 29-32R; CANR 26;
    DLB 33

Young, Andrew (John)   1885-1971 . . . . **CLC 5**
  See also CA 5-8R; CANR 7, 29

Young, Collier
  See Bloch, Robert (Albert)

Young, Edward   1683-1765 . . . . **LC 3**
  See also DLB 95

Young, Marguerite (Vivian)
  1909-1995 . . . . **CLC 82**
  See also CA 13-16; 150; CAP 1

Young, Neil   1945- . . . . **CLC 17**
  See also CA 110

Young Bear, Ray A.
  1950- . . . . **CLC 94; DAM MULT**
  See also CA 146; NNAL

Yourcenar, Marguerite
  1903-1987 . . . . **CLC 19, 38, 50, 87;**
                                          DAM NOV
  See also CA 69-72; CANR 23; DLB 72;
    DLBY 88; MTCW

Yurick, Sol   1925- . . . . **CLC 6**
  See also CA 13-16R; CANR 25

Zabolotskii, Nikolai Alekseevich
  1903-1958 . . . . **TCLC 52**
  See also CA 116

Zamiatin, Yevgenii
  See Zamyatin, Evgeny Ivanovich

Zamora, Bernice (B. Ortiz)
  1938- . . . . . **CLC 89; DAM MULT; HLC**
  See also CA 151; DLB 82; HW

Zamyatin, Evgeny Ivanovich
  1884-1937 . . . . **TCLC 8, 37**
  See also CA 105

Zangwill, Israel   1864-1926 . . . . **TCLC 16**
  See also CA 109; DLB 10, 135

Zappa, Francis Vincent, Jr.   1940-1993
  See Zappa, Frank
  See also CA 108; 143

Zappa, Frank . . . . **CLC 17**
  See also Zappa, Francis Vincent, Jr.

Zaturenska, Marya   1902-1982 . . . . **CLC 6, 11**
  See also CA 13-16R; 105; CANR 22

Zelazny, Roger (Joseph)
  1937-1995 . . . . **CLC 21**
  See also AAYA 7; CA 21-24R; 148;
    CANR 26; DLB 8; MTCW; SATA 57;
    SATA-Brief 39

Zhdanov, Andrei A(lexandrovich)
  1896-1948 . . . . **TCLC 18**
  See also CA 117

Zhukovsky, Vasily   1783-1852 . . . . **NCLC 35**

Ziegenhagen, Eric . . . . **CLC 55**

Zimmer, Jill Schary
  See Robinson, Jill

Zimmerman, Robert
  See Dylan, Bob

Zindel, Paul
  1936- . . . . . **CLC 6, 26; DA; DAB; DAC;**
                    DAM DRAM, MST, NOV; DC 5
  See also AAYA 2; CA 73-76; CANR 31;
    CLR 3; DLB 7, 52; JRDA; MAICYA;
    MTCW; SATA 16, 58

Zinov'Ev, A. A.
  See Zinoviev, Alexander (Aleksandrovich)

Zinoviev, Alexander (Aleksandrovich)
  1922- . . . . **CLC 19**
  See also CA 116; 133; CAAS 10

Zoilus
  See Lovecraft, H(oward) P(hillips)

Zola, Emile (Edouard Charles Antoine)
  1840-1902 . . . . . . **TCLC 1, 6, 21, 41; DA;**
            DAB; DAC; DAM MST, NOV; WLC
  See also CA 104; 138; DLB 123

Zoline, Pamela   1941- . . . . **CLC 62**

Zorrilla y Moral, Jose   1817-1893 . . **NCLC 6**

Zoshchenko, Mikhail (Mikhailovich)
  1895-1958 . . . . **TCLC 15; SSC 15**
  See also CA 115

Zuckmayer, Carl   1896-1977 . . . . **CLC 18**
  See also CA 69-72; DLB 56, 124

Zuk, Georges
  See Skelton, Robin

Zukofsky, Louis
  1904-1978 . . . . **CLC 1, 2, 4, 7, 11, 18;**
                                    DAM POET; PC 11
  See also CA 9-12R; 77-80; CANR 39;
    DLB 5, 165; MTCW

Zweig, Paul   1935-1984 . . . . **CLC 34, 42**
  See also CA 85-88; 113

Zweig, Stefan   1881-1942 . . . . **TCLC 17**
  See also CA 112; DLB 81, 118

Zwingli, Huldreich   1484-1531 . . . . **LC 37**

Literary Criticism Series
Cumulative Topic Index

This index lists all topic entries in Gale's *Classical and Medieval Literature Criticism, Contemporary Literary Criticism, Literature Criticism from 1400 to 1800, Nineteenth-Century Literature Criticism,* and *Twentieth-Century Literary Criticism.*

Age of Johnson LC 15: 1-87
   Johnson's London, 3-15
   aesthetics of neoclassicism, 15-36
   "age of prose and reason," 36-45
   clubmen and bluestockings, 45-56
   printing technology, 56-62
   periodicals: "a map of busy life," 62-74
   transition, 74-86

AIDS in Literature CLC 81: 365-416

American Abolitionism NCLC 44: 1-73
   overviews, 2-26
   abolitionist ideals, 26-46
   the literature of abolitionism, 46-72

American Black Humor Fiction TCLC 54: 1-85
   characteristics of black humor, 2-13
   origins and development, 13-38
   black humor distinguished from related literary trends, 38-60
   black humor and society, 60-75
   black humor reconsidered, 75-83

American Civil War in Literature NCLC 32: 1-109
   overviews, 2-20
   regional perspectives, 20-54
   fiction popular during the war, 54-79
   the historical novel, 79-108

American Frontier in Literature NCLC 28: 1-103
   definitions, 2-12
   development, 12-17
   nonfiction writing about the frontier, 17-30
   frontier fiction, 30-45
   frontier protagonists, 45-66
   portrayals of Native Americans, 66-86
   feminist readings, 86-98

twentieth-century reaction against frontier literature, 98-100

American Humor Writing NCLC 52: 1-59
   overviews, 2-12
   the Old Southwest, 12-42
   broader impacts, 42-5
   women humorists, 45-58

American Popular Song, Golden Age of TCLC 42: 1-49
   background and major figures, 2-34
   the lyrics of popular songs, 34-47

American Proletarian Literature TCLC 54: 86-175
   overviews, 87-95
   American proletarian literature and the American Communist Party, 95-111
   ideology and literary merit, 111-7
   novels, 117-36
   Gastonia, 136-48
   drama, 148-54
   journalism, 154-9
   proletarian literature in the United States, 159-74

American Romanticism NCLC 44: 74-138
   overviews, 74-84
   sociopolitical influences, 84-104
   Romanticism and the American frontier, 104-15
   thematic concerns, 115-37

American Western Literature TCLC 46: 1-100
   definition and development of American Western literature, 2-7
   characteristics of the Western novel, 8-23
   Westerns as history and fiction, 23-34

critical reception of American Western literature, 34-41
   the Western hero, 41-73
   women in Western fiction, 73-91
   later Western fiction, 91-9

Art and Literature TCLC 54: 176-248
   overviews, 176-93
   definitions, 193-219
   influence of visual arts on literature, 219-31
   spatial form in literature, 231-47

Arthurian Literature CMLC 10: 1-127
   historical context and literary beginnings, 2-27
   development of the legend through Malory, 27-64
   development of the legend from Malory to the Victorian Age, 65-81
   themes and motifs, 81-95
   principal characters, 95-125

Arthurian Revival NCLC 36: 1-77
   overviews, 2-12
   Tennyson and his influence, 12-43
   other leading figures, 43-73
   the Arthurian legend in the visual arts, 73-6

Australian Literature TCLC 50: 1-94
   origins and development, 2-21
   characteristics of Australian literature, 21-33
   historical and critical perspectives, 33-41
   poetry, 41-58
   fiction, 58-76
   drama, 76-82
   Aboriginal literature, 82-91

Beat Generation, Literature of the TCLC 42: 50-102

overviews, 51-9
the Beat generation as a social phenomenon, 59-62
development, 62-5
Beat literature, 66-96
influence, 97-100

The Bell Curve Controversy CLC 91: 281-
330

Bildungsroman in Nineteenth-Century
Literature NCLC 20: 92-168
  surveys, 93-113
  in Germany, 113-40
  in England, 140-56
  female *Bildungsroman,* 156-67

Bloomsbury Group TCLC 34: 1-73
  history and major figures, 2-13
  definitions, 13-7
  influences, 17-27
  thought, 27-40
  prose, 40-52
  and literary criticism, 52-4
  political ideals, 54-61
  response to, 61-71

Bly, Robert, *Iron John: A Book about Men
and Men's Work* CLC 70: 414-62

The Book of J CLC 65: 289-311

Businessman in American Literature
TCLC 26: 1-48
  portrayal of the businessman, 1-32
  themes and techniques in business
    fiction, 32-47

Celtic Twilight
See Irish Literary Renaissance

Children's Literature, Nineteenth-
Century NCLC 52: 60-135
  overviews, 61-72
  moral tales, 72-89
  fairy tales and fantasy, 90-119
  making men/making women, 119-34

Civic Critics, Russian NCLC 20: 402-46
  principal figures and background, 402-9
  and Russian Nihilism, 410-6

aesthetic and critical views, 416-45

Colonial America: The Intellectual
Background LC 25: 1-98
  overviews, 2-17
  philosophy and politics, 17-31
  early religious influences in Colonial
    America, 31-60
  consequences of the Revolution, 60-78
  religious influences in post-revolution-
    ary America, 78-87
  colonial literary genres, 87-97

Colonialism in Victorian English
Literature NCLC 56: 1-77
  overviews, 2-34
  colonialism and gender, 34-51
  monsters and the occult, 51-76

Columbus, Christopher, Books on the
Quincentennial of His Arrival in the
New World CLC 70: 329-60

Comic Books TCLC 66: 1-139
  historical and critical perspectives, 2-48
  superheroes, 48-67
  underground comix, 67-88
  comic books and society, 88-122
  adult comics and graphic novels, 122-36

Connecticut Wits NCLC 48: 1-95
  general overviews, 2-40
  major works, 40-76
  intellectual context, 76-95

Crime in Literature TCLC 54: 249-307
  evolution of the criminal figure in
    literature, 250-61
  crime and society, 261-77
  literary perspectives on crime and
    punishment, 277-88
  writings by criminals, 288-306

Czechoslovakian Literature of the
Twentieth Century TCLC 42: 103-96
  through World War II, 104-35
  de-Stalinization, the Prague Spring, and
    contemporary literature, 135-72
  Slovak literature, 172-85
  Czech science fiction, 185-93

Dadaism TCLC 46: 101-71

background and major figures, 102-16
definitions, 116-26
manifestos and commentary by
  Dadaists, 126-40
theater and film, 140-58
nature and characteristics of Dadaist
  writing, 158-70

Darwinism and Literature NCLC 32:
110-206
  background, 110-31
  direct responses to Darwin, 131-71
  collateral effects of Darwinism, 171-205

de Man, Paul, Wartime Journalism of
CLC 55: 382-424

Detective Fiction, Nineteenth-Century
NCLC 36: 78-148
  origins of the genre, 79-100
  history of nineteenth-century detective
    fiction, 101-33
  significance of nineteenth-century
    detective fiction, 133-46

Detective Fiction, Twentieth-Century
TCLC 38: 1-96
  genesis and history of the detective
    story, 3-22
  defining detective fiction, 22-32
  evolution and varieties, 32-77
  the appeal of detective fiction, 77-90

Disease and Literature TCLC 66: 140-
283
  overviews, 141-65
  disease in nineteenth-century literature,
    165-81
  tuberculosis and literature, 181-94
  women and disease in literature, 194-221
  plague literature, 221-53
  AIDS in literature, 253-82

The Double in Nineteenth-Century
Literature NCLC 40: 1-95
  genesis and development of the theme,
    2-15
  the double and Romanticism, 16-27
  sociological views, 27-52
  psychological interpretations, 52-87
  philosophical considerations, 87-95

Dramatic Realism NCLC 44: 139-202

overviews, 140-50
origins and definitions, 150-66
impact and influence, 166-93
realist drama and tragedy, 193-201

Electronic "Books": Hypertext and Hyperfiction CLC 86: 367-404
books vs. CD-ROMS, 367-76
hypertext and hyperfiction, 376-95
implications for publishing, libraries, and the public, 395-403

Eliot, T. S., Centenary of Birth CLC 55: 345-75

Elizabethan Drama LC 22: 140-240
origins and influences, 142-67
characteristics and conventions, 167-83
theatrical production, 184-200
histories, 200-12
comedy, 213-20
tragedy, 220-30

The Encyclopedists LC 26: 172-253
overviews, 173-210
intellectual background, 210-32
views on esthetics, 232-41
views on women, 241-52

English Caroline Literature LC 13: 221-307
background, 222-41
evolution and varieties, 241-62
the Cavalier mode, 262-75
court and society, 275-91
politics and religion, 291-306

English Decadent Literature of the 1890s NCLC 28: 104-200
fin de siècle: the Decadent period, 105-19
definitions, 120-37
major figures: "the tragic generation," 137-50
French literature and English literary Decadence, 150-7
themes, 157-61
poetry, 161-82
periodicals, 182-96

English Essay, Rise of the LC 18: 238-308
definitions and origins, 236-54

influence on the essay, 254-69
historical background, 269-78
the essay in the seventeenth century, 279-93
the essay in the eighteenth century, 293-307

English Mystery Cycle Dramas LC 34: 1-88
overviews, 1-27
the nature of dramatic performances, 27-42
the medieval worldview and the mystery cycles, 43-67
the doctrine of repentance and the mystery cycles, 67-76
the fall from grace in the mystery cycles, 76-88

English Romantic Poetry NCLC 28: 201-327
overviews and reputation, 202-37
major subjects and themes, 237-67
forms of Romantic poetry, 267-78
politics, society, and Romantic poetry, 278-99
philosophy, religion, and Romantic poetry, 299-324

Espionage Literature TCLC 50: 95-159
overviews, 96-113
espionage fiction/formula fiction, 113-26
spies in fact and fiction, 126-38
the female spy, 138-44
social and psychological perspectives, 144-58

European Romanticism NCLC 36: 149-284
definitions, 149-77
origins of the movement, 177-82
Romantic theory, 182-200
themes and techniques, 200-23
Romanticism in Germany, 223-39
Romanticism in France, 240-61
Romanticism in Italy, 261-4
Romanticism in Spain, 264-8
impact and legacy, 268-82

Existentialism and Literature TCLC 42: 197-268
overviews and definitions, 198-209
history and influences, 209-19
Existentialism critiqued and defended, 220-35

philosophical and religious perspectives, 235-41
Existentialist fiction and drama, 241-67

Familiar Essay NCLC 48: 96-211
definitions and origins, 97-130
overview of the genre, 130-43
elements of form and style, 143-59
elements of content, 159-73
the Cockneys: Hazlitt, Lamb, and Hunt, 173-91
status of the genre, 191-210

Feminism in the 1990s: Commentary on Works by Naomi Wolf, Susan Faludi, and Camille Paglia CLC 76: 377-415

Feminist Criticism in 1990 CLC 65: 312-60

Fifteenth-Century English Literature LC 17: 248-334
background, 249-72
poetry, 272-315
drama, 315-23
prose, 323-33

Film and Literature TCLC 38: 97-226
overviews, 97-119
film and theater, 119-34
film and the novel, 134-45
the art of the screenplay, 145-66
genre literature/genre film, 167-79
the writer and the film industry, 179-90
authors on film adaptations of their works, 190-200
fiction into film: comparative essays, 200-23

French Drama in the Age of Louis XIV LC 28: 94-185
overview, 95-127
tragedy, 127-46
comedy, 146-66
tragicomedy, 166-84

French Enlightenment LC 14: 81-145
the question of definition, 82-9
Le siècle des lumières, 89-94
women and the salons, 94-105
censorship, 105-15
the philosophy of reason, 115-31
influence and legacy, 131-44

French Realism NCLC 52: 136-216
　　origins and definitions, 137-70
　　issues and influence, 170-98
　　realism and representation, 198-215

French Revolution and English Literature NCLC 40: 96-195
　　history and theory, 96-123
　　romantic poetry, 123-50
　　the novel, 150-81
　　drama, 181-92
　　children's literature, 192-5

Futurism, Italian TCLC 42: 269-354
　　principles and formative influences, 271-9
　　manifestos, 279-88
　　literature, 288-303
　　theater, 303-19
　　art, 320-30
　　music, 330-6
　　architecture, 336-9
　　and politics, 339-46
　　reputation and significance, 346-51

Gaelic Revival
See **Irish Literary Renaissance**

Gates, Henry Louis, Jr., and African-American Literary Criticism CLC 65: 361-405

Gay and Lesbian Literature CLC 76: 416-39

German Exile Literature TCLC 30: 1-58
　　the writer and the Nazi state, 1-10
　　definition of, 10-4
　　life in exile, 14-32
　　surveys, 32-50
　　Austrian literature in exile, 50-2
　　German publishing in the United States, 52-7

German Expressionism TCLC 34: 74-160
　　history and major figures, 76-85
　　aesthetic theories, 85-109
　　drama, 109-26
　　poetry, 126-38
　　film, 138-42
　　painting, 142-7
　　music, 147-53
　　and politics, 153-8

***Glasnost* and Contemporary Soviet Literature** CLC 59: 355-97

Gothic Novel NCLC 28: 328-402
　　development and major works, 328-34
　　definitions, 334-50
　　themes and techniques, 350-78
　　in America, 378-85
　　in Scotland, 385-91
　　influence and legacy, 391-400

Graphic Narratives CLC 86: 405-32
　　history and overviews, 406-21
　　the "Classics Illustrated" series, 421-2
　　reviews of recent works, 422-32

Greek Historiography CMLC 17: 1-49

Harlem Renaissance TCLC 26: 49-125
　　principal issues and figures, 50-67
　　the literature and its audience, 67-74
　　theme and technique in poetry, fiction, and drama, 74-115
　　and American society, 115-21
　　achievement and influence, 121-2

Havel, Václav, Playwright and President CLC 65: 406-63

Historical Fiction, Nineteenth-Century NCLC 48: 212-307
　　definitions and characteristics, 213-36
　　Victorian historical fiction, 236-65
　　American historical fiction, 265-88
　　realism in historical fiction, 288-306

Holocaust and the Atomic Bomb: Fifty Years Later CLC 91: 331-82
　　the Holocaust remembered, 333-52
　　Anne Frank revisited, 352-62
　　the atomic bomb and American memory, 362-81

Holocaust Denial Literature TCLC 58: 1-110
　　overviews, 1-30
　　Robert Faurisson and Noam Chomsky, 30-52
　　Holocaust denial literature in America, 52-71
　　library access to Holocaust denial literature, 72-5

　　the authenticity of Anne Frank's diary, 76-90
　　David Irving and the "normalization" of Hitler, 90-109

Holocaust, Literature of the TCLC 42: 355-450
　　historical overview, 357-61
　　critical overview, 361-70
　　diaries and memoirs, 370-95
　　novels and short stories, 395-425
　　poetry, 425-41
　　drama, 441-8

Homosexuality in Nineteenth-Century Literature NCLC 56: 78-182
　　defining homosexuality, 80-111
　　Greek love, 111-44
　　trial and danger, 144-81

Hungarian Literature of the Twentieth Century TCLC 26: 126-88
　　surveys of, 126-47
　　Nyugat and early twentieth-century literature, 147-56
　　mid-century literature, 156-68
　　and politics, 168-78
　　since the 1956 revolt, 178-87

Indian Literature in English TCLC 54: 308-406
　　overview, 309-13
　　origins and major figures, 313-25
　　the Indo-English novel, 325-55
　　Indo-English poetry, 355-67
　　Indo-English drama, 367-72
　　critical perspectives on Indo-English literature, 372-80
　　modern Indo-English literature, 380-9
　　Indo-English authors on their work, 389-404

Industrial Revolution in Literature, The NCLC 56: 183-273
　　historical and cultural perspectives, 184-201
　　contemporary reactions to the machine, 201-21
　　themes and symbols in literature, 221-73

Irish Literary Renaissance TCLC 46: 172-287
　　overview, 173-83
　　development and major figures, 184-202

influence of Irish folklore and mythology, 202-22
Irish poetry, 222-34
Irish drama and the Abbey Theatre, 234-56
Irish fiction, 256-86

Irish Nationalism and Literature NCLC 44: 203-73
the Celtic element in literature, 203-19
anti-Irish sentiment and the Celtic response, 219-34
literary ideals in Ireland, 234-45
literary expressions, 245-73

Italian Futurism
See **Futurism, Italian**

Italian Humanism LC 12: 205-77
origins and early development, 206-18
revival of classical letters, 218-23
humanism and other philosophies, 224-39
humanisms and humanists, 239-46
the plastic arts, 246-57
achievement and significance, 258-76

Jacobean Drama LC 33: 1-37
the Jacobean worldview: an era of transition, 2-14
the moral vision of Jacobean drama, 14-22
Jacobean tragedy, 22-3
the Jacobean masque, 23-36

Jewish-American Fiction TCLC 62: 1-181
overviews, 2-24
major figures, 24-48
Jewish writers and American life, 48-78
Jewish characters in American fiction, 78-108
themes in Jewish-American fiction, 108-43
Jewish-American women writers, 143-59
the Holocaust and Jewish-American fiction, 159-81

Knickerbocker Group, The NCLC 56: 274-341
overviews, 276-314
Knickerbocker periodicals, 314-26
writers and artists, 326-40

Lake Poets, The NCLC 52: 217-304
characteristics of the Lake Poets and their works, 218-27
literary influences and collaborations, 227-66
defining and developing Romantic ideals, 266-84
embracing Conservatism, 284-303

Larkin, Philip, Controversy CLC 81: 417-64

Latin American Literature, Twentieth-Century TCLC 58: 111-98
historical and critical perspectives, 112-36
the novel, 136-45
the short story, 145-9
drama, 149-60
poetry, 160-7
the writer and society, 167-86
Native Americans in Latin American literature, 186-97

Madness in Twentieth-Century Literature TCLC 50: 160-225
overviews, 161-71
madness and the creative process, 171-86
suicide, 186-91
madness in American literature, 191-207
madness in German literature, 207-13
madness and feminist artists, 213-24

Metaphysical Poets LC 24: 356-439
early definitions, 358-67
surveys and overviews, 367-92
cultural and social influences, 392-406
stylistic and thematic variations, 407-38

Modern Essay, The TCLC 58: 199-273
overview, 200-7
the essay in the early twentieth century, 207-19
characteristics of the modern essay, 219-32
modern essayists, 232-45
the essay as a literary genre, 245-73

Modern Japanese Literature TCLC 66: 284-389
poetry, 285-305
drama, 305-29
fiction, 329-61
western influences, 361-87

Muckraking Movement in American Journalism TCLC 34: 161-242
development, principles, and major figures, 162-70
publications, 170-9
social and political ideas, 179-86
targets, 186-208
fiction, 208-19
decline, 219-29
impact and accomplishments, 229-40

Multiculturalism in Literature and Education CLC 70: 361-413

Music and Modern Literature TCLC 62: 182-329
overviews, 182-211
musical form/literary form, 211-32
music in literature, 232-50
the influence of music on literature, 250-73
literature and popular music, 273-303
jazz and poetry, 303-28

Native American Literature CLC 76: 440-76

Natural School, Russian NCLC 24: 205-40
history and characteristics, 205-25
contemporary criticism, 225-40

Naturalism NCLC 36: 285-382
definitions and theories, 286-305
critical debates on Naturalism, 305-16
Naturalism in theater, 316-32
European Naturalism, 332-61
American Naturalism, 361-72
the legacy of Naturalism, 372-81

Negritude TCLC 50: 226-361
origins and evolution, 227-56
definitions, 256-91
Negritude in literature, 291-343
Negritude reconsidered, 343-58

New Criticism TCLC 34: 243-318
development and ideas, 244-70
debate and defense, 270-99
influence and legacy, 299-315

The New World in Renaissance Literature LC 31: 1-51

Topic Index

overview, 1-18
utopia vs. terror, 18-31
explorers and Native Americans, 31-51

New York Intellectuals and *Partisan Review* TCLC 30: 117-98
development and major figures, 118-28
influence of Judaism, 128-39
Partisan Review, 139-57
literary philosophy and practice, 157-75
political philosophy, 175-87
achievement and significance, 187-97

The New Yorker TCLC 58: 274-357
overviews, 274-95
major figures, 295-304
New Yorker style, 304-33
fiction, journalism, and humor at *The New Yorker,* 333-48
the new *New Yorker,* 348-56

Newgate Novel NCLC 24: 166-204
development of Newgate literature, 166-73
Newgate Calendar, 173-7
Newgate fiction, 177-95
Newgate drama, 195-204

Nigerian Literature of the Twentieth Century TCLC 30: 199-265
surveys of, 199-227
English language and African life, 227-45
politics and the Nigerian writer, 245-54
Nigerian writers and society, 255-62

Northern Humanism LC 16: 281-356
background, 282-305
precursor of the Reformation, 305-14
the Brethren of the Common Life, the Devotio Moderna, and education, 314-40
the impact of printing, 340-56

Novel of Manners, The NCLC 56: 342-96
social and political order, 343-53
domestic order, 353-73
depictions of gender, 373-83
the American novel of manners, 383-95

Nuclear Literature: Writings and Criticism in the Nuclear Age TCLC 46: 288-390
overviews, 290-301

fiction, 301-35
poetry, 335-8
nuclear war in Russo-Japanese literature, 338-55
nuclear war and women writers, 355-67
the nuclear referent and literary criticism, 367-88

Occultism in Modern Literature TCLC 50: 362-406
influence of occultism on literature, 363-72
occultism, literature, and society, 372-87
fiction, 387-96
drama, 396-405

Opium and the Nineteenth-Century Literary Imagination NCLC 20: 250-301
original sources, 250-62
historical background, 262-71
and literary society, 271-9
and literary creativity, 279-300

Periodicals, Nineteenth-Century British NCLC 24: 100-65
overviews, 100-30
in the Romantic Age, 130-41
in the Victorian era, 142-54
and the reviewer, 154-64

Plath, Sylvia, and the Nature of Biography CLC 86: 433-62
the nature of biography, 433-52
reviews of *The Silent Woman,* 452-61

Political Theory from the 15th to the 18th Century LC 36: 1-55
overview, 1-26
Natural Law, 26-42
Empiricism, 42-55

Polish Romanticism NCLC 52: 305-71
overviews, 306-26
major figures, 326-40
Polish Romantic drama, 340-62
influences, 362-71

Pre-Raphaelite Movement NCLC 20: 302-401
overview, 302-4
genesis, 304-12
Germ and *Oxford and Cambridge Magazine,* 312-20
Robert Buchanan and the "Fleshly School of Poetry," 320-31

satires and parodies, 331-4
surveys, 334-51
aesthetics, 351-75
sister arts of poetry and painting, 375-94
influence, 394-9

Protestant Reformation, Literature of the LC 37: 1-83
overviews, 1-49
humanism and scholasticism, 49-69
the reformation and literature, 69-82

Psychoanalysis and Literature TCLC 38: 227-338
overviews, 227-46
Freud on literature, 246-51
psychoanalytic views of the literary process, 251-61
psychoanalytic theories of response to literature, 261-88
psychoanalysis and literary criticism, 288-312
psychoanalysis as literature/literature as psychoanalysis, 313-34

Rap Music CLC 76: 477-50

Renaissance Natural Philosophy LC 27: 201-87
cosmology, 201-28
astrology, 228-54
magic, 254-86

Restoration Drama LC 21: 184-275
general overviews, 185-230
Jeremy Collier stage controversy, 230-9
other critical interpretations, 240-75

Revising the Literary Canon CLC 81: 465-509

Robin Hood, Legend of LC 19: 205-58
origins and development of the Robin Hood legend, 206-20
representations of Robin Hood, 220-44
Robin Hood as hero, 244-56

Rushdie, Salman, *Satanic Verses* Controversy CLC 55 214-63; 59: 404-56

Russian Nihilism NCLC 28: 403-47

definitions and overviews, 404-17
women and Nihilism, 417-27
literature as reform: the Civic Critics,
    427-33
Nihilism and the Russian novel:
    Turgenev and Dostoevsky, 433-47

Russian Thaw TCLC 26: 189-247
    literary history of the period, 190-206
    theoretical debate of socialist realism,
        206-11
    Novy Mir, 211-7
    Literary Moscow, 217-24
    Pasternak, *Zhivago,* and the Nobel
        Prize, 224-7
    poetry of liberation, 228-31
    Brodsky trial and the end of the Thaw,
        231-6
    achievement and influence, 236-46

Salinger, J. D., Controversy Surrounding
In Search of J. D. Salinger CLC 55: 325-44

Science Fiction, Nineteenth-Century
NCLC 24: 241-306
    background, 242-50
    definitions of the genre, 251-6
    representative works and writers, 256-75
    themes and conventions, 276-305

Scottish Chaucerians LC 20: 363-412

Scottish Poetry, Eighteenth-Century LC
29: 95-167
    overviews, 96-114
    the Scottish Augustans, 114-28
    the Scots Vernacular Revival, 132-63
    Scottish poetry after Burns, 163-6

Sherlock Holmes Centenary TCLC 26:
248-310
    Doyle's life and the composition of the
        Holmes stories, 248-59
    life and character of Holmes, 259-78
    method, 278-9
    Holmes and the Victorian world, 279-92
    Sherlockian scholarship, 292-301
    Doyle and the development of the
        detective story, 301-7
    Holmes's continuing popularity, 307-9

Slave Narratives, American NCLC 20: 1-
91

background, 2-9
overviews, 9-24
contemporary responses, 24-7
language, theme, and technique, 27-70
historical authenticity, 70-5
antecedents, 75-83
role in development of Black American
    literature, 83-8

Spanish Civil War Literature TCLC 26:
311-85
    topics in, 312-33
    British and American literature, 333-59
    French literature, 359-62
    Spanish literature, 362-73
    German literature, 373-5
    political idealism and war literature, 375-
        83

Spanish Golden Age Literature LC 23:
262-332
    overviews, 263-81
    verse drama, 281-304
    prose fiction, 304-19
    lyric poetry, 319-31

Spasmodic School of Poetry NCLC 24:
307-52
    history and major figures, 307-21
    the Spasmodics on poetry, 321-7
    Firmilian and critical disfavor, 327-39
    theme and technique, 339-47
    influence, 347-51

Steinbeck, John, Fiftieth Anniversary of
The Grapes of Wrath CLC 59: 311-54

Sturm und Drang NCLC 40: 196-276
    definitions, 197-238
    poetry and poetics, 238-58
    drama, 258-75

**Supernatural Fiction in the Nineteenth
Century** NCLC 32: 207-87
    major figures and influences, 208-35
    the Victorian ghost story, 236-54
    the influence of science and occultism,
        254-66
    supernatural fiction and society, 266-86

Supernatural Fiction, Modern TCLC 30:
59-116
    evolution and varieties, 60-74

"decline" of the ghost story, 74-86
as a literary genre, 86-92
technique, 92-101
nature and appeal, 101-15

Surrealism TCLC 30: 334-406
    history and formative influences, 335-43
    manifestos, 343-54
    philosophic, aesthetic, and political
        principles, 354-75
    poetry, 375-81
    novel, 381-6
    drama, 386-92
    film, 392-8
    painting and sculpture, 398-403
    achievement, 403-5

Symbolism, Russian TCLC 30: 266-333
    doctrines and major figures, 267-92
    theories, 293-8
    and French Symbolism, 298-310
    themes in poetry, 310-4
    theater, 314-20
    and the fine arts, 320-32

Symbolist Movement, French NCLC 20:
169-249
    background and characteristics, 170-86
    principles, 186-91
    attacked and defended, 191-7
    influences and predecessors, 197-211
    and Decadence, 211-6
    theater, 216-26
    prose, 226-33
    decline and influence, 233-47

Theater of the Absurd TCLC 38: 339-415
    "The Theater of the Absurd," 340-7
    major plays and playwrights, 347-58
    and the concept of the absurd, 358-86
    theatrical techniques, 386-94
    predecessors of, 394-402
    influence of, 402-13

Tin Pan Alley
See American Popular Song, Golden Age of

Transcendentalism, American NCLC 24:
1-99
    overviews, 3-23
    contemporary documents, 23-41
    theological aspects of, 42-52
    and social issues, 52-74
    literature of, 74-96

Topic Index

Travel Writing in the Nineteenth Century NCLC 44: 274-392
the European grand tour, 275-303
the Orient, 303-47
North America, 347-91

Travel Writing in the Twentieth Century TCLC 30: 407-56
conventions and traditions, 407-27
and fiction writing, 427-43
comparative essays on travel writers, 443-54

Ulysses **and the Process of Textual Reconstruction** TCLC 26: 386-416
evaluations of the new *Ulysses,* 386-94
editorial principles and procedures, 394-401
theoretical issues, 401-16

Utopian Literature, Nineteenth-Century NCLC 24: 353-473
definitions, 354-74
overviews, 374-88
theory, 388-408
communities, 409-26
fiction, 426-53
women and fiction, 454-71

Utopian Literature, Renaissance LC-32: 1-63
overviews, 2-25
classical background, 25-33
utopia and the social contract, 33-9
origins in mythology, 39-48
utopia and the Renaissance country house, 48-52
influence of millenarianism, 52-62

Vampire in Literature TCLC 46: 391-454
origins and evolution, 392-412
social and psychological perspectives, 413-44
vampire fiction and science fiction, 445-53

Victorian Autobiography NCLC 40: 277-363
development and major characteristics, 278-88
themes and techniques, 289-313
the autobiographical tendency in Victorian prose and poetry, 313-47
Victorian women's autobiographies, 347-62

Victorian Novel NCLC 32: 288-454
development and major characteristics, 290-310
themes and techniques, 310-58
social criticism in the Victorian novel, 359-97
urban and rural life in the Victorian novel, 397-406
women in the Victorian novel, 406-25
Mudie's Circulating Library, 425-34
the late-Victorian novel, 434-51

Vietnam War in Literature and Film CLC 91: 383-437
overview, 384-8
prose, 388-412
film and drama, 412-24
poetry, 424-35

Vorticism TCLC 62: 330-426
Wyndham Lewis and Vorticism, 330-8
characteristics and principles of Vorticism, 338-65
Lewis and Pound, 365-82
Vorticist writing, 382-416
Vorticist painting, 416-26

Women's Diaries, Nineteenth-Century NCLC 48: 308-54
overview, 308-13
diary as history, 314-25
sociology of diaries, 325-34
diaries as psychological scholarship, 334-43
diary as autobiography, 343-8
diary as literature, 348-53

Women Writers, Seventeenth-Century LC 30: 2-58
overview, 2-15
women and education, 15-9
women and autobiography, 19-31
women's diaries, 31-9
early feminists, 39-58

World War I Literature TCLC 34: 392-486
overview, 393-403
English, 403-27
German, 427-50
American, 450-66
French, 466-74
and modern history, 474-82

Yellow Journalism NCLC 36: 383-456
overviews, 384-96
major figures, 396-413

Young Playwrights Festival
1988—CLC 55: 376-81
1989—CLC 59: 398-403
1990—CLC 65: 444-8

CMLC Cumulative Nationality Index

ARABIC
Alf Layla wa-Layla (The Arabian Nights) **2**
Averroes **7**
Avicenna **16**

BABYLONIAN
Epic of Gilgamesh **3**

CATALAN
Llull, Ramon **12**

CHINESE
Confucius **19**
Lao Tzu **7**
Li Po **2**
Su Shih **15**

ENGLISH
The Alliterative *Morte Arthure* **10**
Anglo-Saxon Chronicle **4**
Bacon, Roger **14**
Bede **20**
Beowulf **1**
Caedmon **7**
The Dream of the Rood **14**
Layamon **10**
Pearl **19**
Rolle, Richard **21**
Sir Gawain and the Green Knight **2**

FINNISH
Kalevala **6**

FRENCH
Abelard, Peter **11**
La chanson de Roland (The Song of Roland) **1**
Chretien de Troyes **10**

Marie de France **8**
Ordo Representacionis Ade (Mystery of Adam) **4**
Le Roman de la Rose (The Romance of the Rose) **8**

GERMAN
Albert the Great **16**
Gottfried von Strassburg **10**
Hartmann von Aue **15**
Hildegard von Bingen **20**
Meister Eckhart **9**
Das Nibelungenlied **12**
Wolfram von Eschenbach **5**

GREEK
Aeschylus **11**
Aristophanes **4**
Callimachus **18**
Demosthenes **13**
Epicurus **21**
Hermogenes **6**
Herodotus **17**
Hesiod **5**
Iliad (Homer) **1**
Longus **7**
Menander **9**
Odyssey (Homer) **16**
Origen **19**
Pindar **12**
Plato **8**
Polybius **17**
Sappho **3**
Sophocles **2**
Thucydides **17**
Xenophon **17**

HEBREW
The Book of Job **14**
Josephus, Flavius **13**

Song of Songs **18**
Tehillim (The Book of Psalms) **4**

ICELANDIC
Hrafnkels saga Freysgoda (Hrafnkel's Saga) **2**
Njals saga **13**

INDIAN
Bhagavad Gita **12**
Kalidasa **9**
Mahabharata **5**

ITALIAN
Boccaccio, Giovanni **13**
Inferno (Dante) **3**
Petrarch **20**
Polo, Marco **15**
Sordello **15**
Vita Nuova (Dante) **18**

JAPANESE
Kojiki **21**
Lady Murasaki (*Genji monogatori* [*The Tale of Genji*]) **1**
Sei Shonagon **6**

PERSIAN
Khayyam, Omar **11**
Rumi, Jalal al-Din **20**

PROVENCAL
Betran de Born **5**

ROMAN
Aeneid (Vergil) **9**
Apuleius **1**
Augustine, St. **6**
Boethius **15**

Cato, Marcus Porcius **21**
Catullus **18**
Cicero, Marcus Tullius **3**
Juvenal **8**
Livy **11**
Ovid **7**
Seneca, Lucius Annaeus **6**
Terence **14**

RUSSIAN
Slovo o polku Igoreve (*The Igor Tale*) **1**

SPANISH
Poema de mio Cid (*Poem of the Cid*) **4**
Razón de amor **16**

TURKISH
Kitab-i-dedem Qorkut (*Book of Dede Korkut*) **8**

WELSH
Mabinogion **9**

CMLC Cumulative Title Index

Ab urbe condita libri (Livy) **11**:310-86
"Abdallah-the-Hunter" **2**:63
"Abdallah-the-Mariner" **2**:42, 63
Abhijñana-sakuntala (Kalidasa) **9**:82, 86-7, 89-97, 100-02, 108-13, 127, 130-34, 136-39
"Aboulhusn ed Duraj and the Leper" **2**:40
About Gods (Cicero)
   See *De natura deorum*
"Abu Kasem's Slippers" **2**:32-5
Academics (Cicero) **3**:193,202
The Academics; or, A History and Defense of the Beliefs of the New Academy (Cicero)
   See *Academics*
Acharnae (Aristophanes) **4**:44, 62, 69, 76, 87, 94, 97-99, 105-06, 108-10, 113, 123-28, 131-33, 135, 137, 142-43, 149, 151-52, 157, 159-60, 162-63, 165-66
The Acharnians (Aristophanes)
   See *Acharnae*
Acontius (Callimachus) 18: 7-9, 42, 43
Ad Atticum (Cicero) **3**:186-87, 200
Ad Brutum (Cicero) **3**:200
Ad familiares (Cicero) **3**:200
Ad filium (Cato) **21**:28, 39, 46, 48-9
Ad helviam matrem de consolatione (Seneca) **6**:382, 410
Ad Leptinem (Demosthenes)
   See *Against Leptines*
Ad Marciam (Seneca) **6**:382
Ad P. Lentulum (Cicero) **3**:186
Ad Polybium de consolatione (Seneca) **6**:382
Ad Q. fratrem (Cicero) **3**:200
Ad Simplicium (Augustine) **6**:9
Adam
   See *Ordo Representacionis Ade*
Adelphi (Terence) **14**:301, 303-04, 306-07, 309, 313-14, 316, 320-21, 332-37, 339-40, 347-49, 352, 357-60, 362-66, 368, 370-71, 374-77, 381, 383-85, 387, 394, 397
Adelphoi (Menander) **9**:270
The Aeneid (Vergil) **9**:294-447
Africa (Petrarch) **20**:212, 214, 226, 235-39, 245, 251, 260, 308, 326-27, 333
"After Being Separated for a Long Time" (Li Po) **2**:132
Against Androtion (Demosthenes) **13**:148-9, 156, 163-4, 169, 171, 184
Against Aphobus (Demosthenes) **13**:163, 184
Against Apion (Josephus)
   See *Contra Apionem*
Against Aristocrates (Demosthenes) **13**:148, 156-8, 164, 169, 189
Against Aristogiton (Demosthenes) **13**:149
Against Callicles (Demosthenes) **13**:168
Against Catilina (Cicero)
   See *In Catilinam*
Against Conon (Demosthenes) **13**:144
Against Eratosthenes (Demosthenes) **13**:179
Against Leptines (Demosthenes) **13**:137, 148-51, 156, 163-4, 169-71, 197
Against Medias (Demosthenes)
   See *Against Midias*
Against Midias (Demosthenes) **13**:140, 149, 165, 169
Against Neaera (Demosthenes) **13**:169
Against Onetor (Demosthenes) **13**:163, 168, 184
Against Praxiphanes (Callimachus) 18: 36-7, 48
Against Superstitions (Seneca) **6**:330, 342
Against the Academicians (Augustine)
   See *Contra academicos*
Against the Gentiles (Josephus)
   See *Contra Apionem*
Against the Greeks (Josephus)
   See *Contra Apionem*
Against the Megarians (Epicurus) **21**:165
Against the Physicists (Epicurus) **21**:165
Against Theophrastus (Epicurus) **21**:71, 165
Against Timocrates (Demosthenes) **13**:146-8, 156, 163-4, 169
Agamemnon (Aeschylus) **11**:85-6, 101-02, 104-05, 107-08, 110-11, 113, 116-20, 126, 128, 132-34, 136, 138-42, 148, 150-55, 158, 162-63, 165, 167, 171, 175-76, 179-82, 184-85, 187, 190-91, 194-97, 200-07, 217, 220-22
Agamemnon (Seneca) **6**:339, 343, 363, 366-69, 377-81, 389, 407, 409, 414, 417, 431-32, 440, 442, 447
Agesilaus (Xenophon) **17**:329, 330, 331, 339, 340, 349, 350, 352, 353, 354, 355, 359, 362, 374
Ahwal al-Nafs (Avicenna) **16**:166
"Ailas e que'm miey huelh" (Sordello) **15**:367
Aitia (Callimachus) 18: 6-9, 11, 18, 22-4, 30, 32, 34-8, 42, 44, 48-50, 53, 62-4, 68
Aitnaiai (Aeschylus) **11**:217
Akharnes (Aristophanes)
   See *Acharnae*
"Al poco giorno e al gan cerchio d'ombra" (Petrarch) **20**:283
Alcibiades (Plato)
   See *Alcibiades I*
Alcibiades Major (Plato)
   See *Alcibiades I*
Alcibiades I (Plato) **8**:218, 305-06, 311, 356
Alcibiades II (Plato) **8**:250, 305, 311
Alf Layla wa-Layla **2**:1-73
"Ali and the Kurd Sharper" **2**:40

"Ali Baba and the Forty Thieves" 2:1-2, 23, 45, 49

"Alî Shâr" 2:43

"Ali Sher and Zumurrud" 2:114

"Ali the Son of Bakkar and Shems-en-Nahar" 2:14

al-Isharat wa al-Tanbihat (Avicenna) 169, 171

Alku Kalevala
   See *Kalevala*

"Alladin and the Wonderful Lamp" 2:1-2, 8, 21, 23-24, 72

Allegoria mitologica (Boccaccio) 13:63-4

"Alliterative*Morte Arthure*"
   See *Morte Arthure "Alliterative"*

al-Tacliqat (Avicenna) 16:167

Ameto (Boccaccio) 13:9, 18, 23, 27-8, 30, 32-3, 44-5, 48, 61

"Amor, tu vedi ben che quesra donna" (Petrarch) 20:283

Amores (Ovid) 7:292-93, 295-97, 299, 305, 323, 326, 329, 336, 343, 346-49, 353, 355-56, 376-79, 388, 390, 393, 396, 398, 413, 417, 419-21, 423, 426-27, 436, 441, 444

Amorosa visione (Boccaccio) 13:18, 27-8, 32-3, 68, 72, 87

Anabasis (Xenophon) 17:322, 324, 326, 327, 328, 330, 339, 340, 341, 342, 348, 349, 354, 357 358, 359, 360, 361, 362, 364, 365, 366, 372, 374

Analects (Confucius)
   See *Lun Yu*

Analysis of the Analects (Su Shih) 15:407

Ancient History of the Jews (Josephus)
   See *Antiquitates Judaicae*

Andria (Terence) 14:302-08, 311-13, 315-17, 331, 333-35, 337-41, 344-45, 347-49, 352, 355-356, 358, 363-65, 369-70, 383-85, 389-90, 392-93

Androtion (Demosthenes)
   See *Against Androtion*

Anger (Menander)
   See *Orge*

Anglo-Saxon Chronicle 4:1-33

Animals (Albert the Great)
   See *De animalibus*

"Answering a Layman's Question" (Li Po) 2:140

Antigone (Sophocles) 2:289, 296, 299-301, 303-04, 306-09, 311, 314-15, 318-20, 324-25, 327, 331, 334-35, 338-40, 342-43, 345, 349-55, 360, 366, 368, 377-78, 380-83, 393-97, 417-19, 423, 426-28

Antiquitates Judaicae (Josephus) 13:199-207, 211-3, 215-8, 220, 224, 226-35, 239, 242, 247-51, 256-65, 268-71, 286, 291-2, 294-7, 299-300, 302, 305, 308-9, 311-3, 315-20

Antiquities of the Jews (Josephus)
   See *Antiquitates Judaicae*

"Aphrodite Ode" (Sappho)
   See "Ode to Aphrodite"

Apion Answered (Josephus)
   See *Contra Apionem*

Apionem (Josephus)
   See *Contra Apionem*

Apocalypse (Rolle) 21:351

Apocolocyntosis Divi Claudii (Seneca) 6:244, 374, 382-84

Apologia (Plato) 8:250, 260, 277, 306, 357

Apologia sive oratoria de magia (Apuleius) 1:7-8, 10, 12-13, 20, 23, 26, 33-4

Apologia Socratis (Xenophon)
   See *Apology*

Apology (Apuleius)
   See *Apologia sive oratoria de magia*

Apology (Plato)
   See *Apologia*

Apology (Xenophon) 17:342, 343, 369-71

Apology of Origen (Origen) 19:188-89, 199

Apomnemoneumata (Xenophon)
   See *Memorabilia*

Apophthegmata (Cato) 21:22, 41, 54

Apotheosis of Arsinoe (Callimachus)
   See *Deification of Arsinoe*

"The Apples of Paradise" 2:40

The Arabian Nights
   See *Alf Layla wa-Layla*

The Arabian Nights' Entertainments
   See *Alf Layla wa-Layla*

The Arbitrants (Menander)
   See *Epitrepontes*

The Arbitration (Menander)
   See *Epitrepontes*

Arbor scientiae (Llull) 12:108-11, 115, 125

El arbre de filosofia d'amor (Llull)
   See *The Tree of the Philosophy of Love*

Arbre de Sciencia (Llull)
   See *Arbor scientiae*

Archias (Cicero) 3:198-99, 210

Argo (Aeschylus) 11:124

Arithmetic (Boethius)
   See *De Arithmetica*

Der arme Heinrich (Hartmann von Aue) 15:148-54, 164, 191, 194, 205-07, 209, 220, 224, 241-44, 244-49

"*Arrius and His Aitches*" (Catullus)
   See "*Poem 84*"

Ars Amandi (Ovid)
   See *Ars amatoria*

Ars amatoria (Ovid) 7:281-83, 292-98, 304-06, 309-10, 326, 329, 331, 342-47, 349, 353, 377-79, 386-87, 396-98, 401-02, 404, 412-13, 416-19, 421-23, 426, 430, 435-43, 446

Ars brevis (Llull) 12:106-07, 109, 133

Ars demonstrativa (Llull) 12:105-06, 110, 117, 134

Ars generalis (Llull) 12:104, 107-08

Ars generalis ultima (Llull) 12:114-16, 128

Ars inventiva (Llull) 12:97, 109, 114-15, 120, 128, 132

Ars magna (Llull) 12:93-4, 104, 111, 132

Art of Contemplation (Llull) 12:125, 129

Art of Finding Truth (Llull)
   See *Ars inventiva*

Art of Love (Ovid)
   See *Ars amatoria*

Art of Rhetoric (Hermogenes) 6:186

"The Ash Tree" (Marie de France)
   See "Le Fraisne"

Asinus aureus (Apuleius) 1:6-9, 11-12, 14-18, 20, 22-23, 26, 32, 37-38, 46-50

Aspis (Menander) 9:253-58, 260-61, 263, 265, 267-70, 276-77

Assembly of Women (Aristophanes)
   See *Ekklesiazousai*

"At Kuo Hsiang-cheng's When I was Drunk I Painted" (Su Shih) 15:402

Athamas (Aeschylus) 11:122

Atomic Films (Epicurus) 21:73

Atoms and Space (Epicurus) 21:73

"Atretan deu ben chantar finamen" (Sordello) 15:362-63, 368

"*Attis*" (Catullus)
   See "*Poem 63*"

"*Atys*" (Catullus)
   See "*Poem 63*"

"Augustinus" (Petrarch) 20:286-87

Authorized Doctrines (Epicurus)
   See *Principal Doctrines*

"Autumn Banks Song" (Li Po) 2:161, 164

The Babylonians (Aristophanes) 4:99, 126, 159, 163, 165

Bad Temper (Menander)
   See *Orge*

"Baghach Khan Son of Dirse Khan" 8:104

"Bamsi Beyrek of the Grey Horse"
   See "Bamsi-Beyrek"

"Bamsi-Beyrek" 8: 98, 103, 108-09

The Banqueters (Aristophanes) 4:37, 100, 163

"The Barber's Sixth Brother" 2:21

Batrakhoi (Aristophanes) 4:44-5, 61-3, 69. 79. 86-90, 94. 98. 102. 105-6. 110-11. 120-21. 123-24, 127, 129-30, 133, 135, 137-38, 140, 145-46. 148, 150, 154, 156, 159, 161-63, 165

"The Battle of Brunanburh" 4:4, 7, 9, 13-15, 17-19, 27-30

"The Battle of Maldon" 4:2-9, 11-15, 25-7, 29-31

"Battle to the South of the City" (Li Po) 2:132

"Beginning of Autumn: A Poem to Send to Tzu-yu" (Su Shih) 15:414

"Bel m'es ab motz legiers a far" (Sordello) 15:361-62

Bellum Judaicum (Josephus) 13:201-5, 209, 211-20, 222, 224, 229-30, 232-5, 239, 241-56, 263-73, 275-301, 303-8, 310-2, 314-5, 317-20

"Bending Bamboos of Yun-tang Valley" (Su Shih) 15:382, 386

Benedictus (Eckhart)
   See *Book of Divine Consolation*

Beowulf 1:53-159

"Berenice's Lock of Hair" (Catullus)
   See "*Poem 66*"

Bhagavad Gita 12:1-90

Bhagavadgita 5:187, 196-99, 216-19, 223, 226, 228, 235-38, 242-43, 246, 248, 250, 269, 272, 275

Bhagavat Gita
   See *Bhagavadgita*

Bharata
   See *Mahabharata*

Bidayat al-mujtahid (Averroes) 7:37, 41, 43

Big Epitome (Epicurus) 21:154

The Birds (Aristophanes)
   See *Ornithes*

The Birth of Kumara (Kalidasa)
   See *Kumarasambhava*

The Birth of the Prince (Kalidasa)
   See *Kumarasambhava*

The Birth of the War-God (Kalidasa)
   See *Kumarasambhava*

"Bisclavret" (Marie de France) 8:114, 121-23, 131, 134, 147-48, 154, 158, 161-66, 171, 181

"Bitterness on the Stairs of Jade" (Li Po) 2:144, 160

Black Sea Letters (Ovid)
   See *Epistulae ex Ponto*

"The Blacksmith Who Could Handle Fire" 2:40

Blanquerna (Llull) 12:93-5, 97, 106-07, 112,

122-24, 126, 129, 133

The boke maad of Rycharde hampole hetemyte to an ankeresse (Rolle) **21**:274

Bone-Collectors (Aeschylus) **11**:124

Book of Changes (Confucius)
See *I Ching*

Book of Chaos (Llull) **12**:129

Book of Contemplation of God (Llull) **12**:95-8, 100-03, 109, 113-14, 120-23, 125-28, 132

Book of Dede Korkut
See *Kitabi-i Dedem Qorkut*

Book of Divine Consolation (Eckhart) **9**:35-6, 40, 42, 56-7, 70-6

Book of Divine Works (Hildegard von Bingen)
See *Liber divinorum Operum*

Book of Doctrine for Boys (Llull) **12**:97

Book of Godly Comfort (Eckhart)
See *Book of Divine Consolation*

Book of Grandfather Qorkut
See *Kitabi-i Dedem Qorkut*

Book of History (Confucius)
See *Shu Ching*

The Book of Job **14**:117-214

The Book of Korkut
See *Kitabi-i Dedem Qorkut*

Book of Life's Merits (Hildegard von Bingen)
See *Liber vitae meritorum*

The Book of Marco Polo (Polo)
See *The Travels of Marco Polo the Venetian*

Book of Minerals (Albert the Great)
See *Liber mineralium*

Book of Music (Confucius)
See *Yueh*

The Book of My Grandfather Korkut
See *Kitabi-i Dedem Qorkut*

Book of Odes (Confucius)
See *Shih Ching*

Book of Poetry (Confucius)
See *Shih Ching*

The Book of Psalms
See *Tehillim*

The Book of Purgatory (Marie de France)
See *L'Espurgatoire Saint Patrice*

Book of Rites (Confucius)
See *Li Chi*

Book of Simple Medicine (Hildegard von Bingen) **20**:167

Book of Songs (Confucius)
See *Shih Ching*

Book of Tao (Lao Tzu)
See *Tao te Ching*

Book of the Ascent and Descent of the Mind (Llull)
See *Liber de ascensu et descensu intellectus*

Book of the Beasts (Llull) **12**:133-34

The Book of the Five Wise Men (Llull) **12**:125

Book of the Friend and the Beloved (Llull)
See *Book of the Lover and the Beloved*

Book of the Gentile and the Three Wise Men (Llull) **12**:113, 118, 125-26

Book of the Lover and the Beloved (Llull) **12**:93-4, 101, 122-23, 125-29, 131-33

Book of the Order of Chivalry (Llull)
See *Libre del orde de cavalleria*

Book of the Principles and Grades of Medicine (Llull)
See *Liber principiorum medicinae*

Book of the Tartar and the Christian (Llull) **12**:125

The Book of the Thousand Nights and One Night
See *Alf Layla wa-Layla*

Book of Wonders (Llull) **12**:134

The Bookes of the Golden Asse (Apuleius)
See *Asinus aureus*

Brennu-Njáls Saga
See *Njáls saga*

Brief Art of Finding Truth (Llull)
See *Ars brevis*

"Bring in the Wine" (Li Po) **2**:159

Brothers (Menander)
See *Adelphoi*

The Brothers (Terence)
See *Adelphi*

"Brunanburh"
See "The Battle of Brunanburh"

Brut (Layamon) **10**:311-21, 326-29, 333, 335-38, 341, 343-50, 353, 355-60, 362, 364, 370-71

Brutus (Cicero)
See *De claris oratoribus*

Brutus: On Famous Orators (Cicero)
See *De claris oratoribus*

Brutus; or the illustrious Orators (Cicero)
See *De claris oratoribus*

Bucolicum carmen (Petrarch) **20**:327

"Buying Rice" (Su Shih) **15**:416

"By the Passes" (Li Po) **2**:160

"Byrhtnoth's Death"
See "The Battle of Maldon"

Cabiri (Aeschylus) **11**:124

Caccia di Diana (Boccaccio) **13**:62-3, 65, 67-74, 94-102

"Camaralzaman and Badoura" **2**:36, 42-3, 50

Canon (Avicenna) **16**:171-80

The Canon (Epicurus) **21**:73, 119, 130, 153-54, 165

Canonice (Epicurus) **21**:130

Cant de Ramon (Llull) **12**:122

Cantar de mio Cid
See *Poema de mio Cid*

Canticum amoris (Rolle) **21**:353, 368, 376

"Cantus amoris" (Rolle) **21**:368, 370-71, 374-75

"Canzone IV" (Petrarch) **20**:257

Canzoniere (Petrarch) **20**:205, 215-17, 226, 236-37, 239-53, 257, 269, 271-84, 293-97, 299-303, 305, 307, 311-12, 314-20, 323, 327-28, 331-35

Carmen bucolicum (Petrarch) **20**:237

Carmen de moribus (Cato) **21**:22, 28, 40, 46-50, 54-5

Catechism (Epicurus) **21**:124, 126-27

Catilinarians (Cicero)
See *In Catilinam*

Cato maior (Cicero)
See *De senectute*

Cato the Elder: On Old Age (Cicero)
See *De senectute*

"Catullus's Yacht" (Catullus)
See "Poem 4"

Causae et Curae (Hildegard von Bingen) **20**:154, 158, 182-83

Cent Noms de Déu (Llull)
See *Hundred Names of God*

Cerberus (Pindar)
See *Descent of Heracles into the Underworld*

"Le Chaitivel" (Marie de France) **8**:120-21, 130-31, 133-34, 138, 143-44, 147, 151-52, 156, 162, 164-65, 169-70, 182, 186-89

La Chanson de Roland **1**:160-267

Charioteer (Menander) **9**:214

"Charite and Tlepolemus" (Apuleius) **1**:40

Charmides (Plato) **8**:255, 263-65, 286, 306, 310, 314, 349, 356

Charrette (Chretien de Troyes)
See *Lancelot*

Cheat Him Twice (Menander)
See *Dis Exapaton*

Le Chevalier à l'épée (Chretien de Troyes) **10**:232

Le Chevalier au Lion (Chretien de Troyes)
See *Yvain*

Le Chevalier de la Charrette (Chretien de Troyes)
See *Lancelot*

"Chevrefoil" (Marie de France) **8**:116, 120-21, 130-31, 133-34, 137, 139, 147-48, 150, 158-59, 161, 163-65, 170, 179, 182-84, 189

"Chiare fresche e dolci acque" (Petrarch) **20**:300

"Chievrefueil" (Marie de France)
See "Chevrefoil"

Choephori (Aeschylus)
See *Libation Bearers*

Choephoroe (Aeschylus)
See *Libation Bearers*

"Christ and Satan" (Caedmon) **7**:84, 91-3, 102-03

Christian Theology (Abelard) **11**:9, 10, 11, 12, 14, 16, 17, 21, 26, 51-3, 64, 65

Chronicle
See *Anglo-Saxon Chronicle*

ch'uch'iu (Confucius)
See *Ch'un Ch'iu*

Ch'un Ch'iu (Confucius) **19**:29, 31, 35, 38, 42, 46, 50, 84-85

Cimone (Boccaccio) **13**:28

Circe (Aeschylus) **11**:124

"The City Mouse and the Country Mouse" (Marie de France) **8**:190

"City of Brass" **2**:2, 23-4, 40, 51-3

"The City of Irem" **2**:40

Classic of History (Confucius)
See *Shu Ching*

Classic of Poetry (Confucius)
See *Shih Ching*

Cligés (Chretien de Troyes) **10**:133, 138-44, 147, 149, 159-61, 163-64, 166-69, 171-75, 178-79, 183, 190-95, 198, 204-05, 207-08, 210, 215, 218, 222-25, 229-30, 232-39

Clitophon (Plato) **8**:218, 305, 311

The Cloud-Messenger (Kalidasa)
See *Meghaduta*

The Clouds (Aristophanes)
See *Nephelai*

Collatio laureationis (Petrarch) **20**:326

Collations (Eckhart)
See *Rede der Unterscheidungen*

Coma Berenices (Callimachus)
See *Lock of Berenice*

Comedia delle ninfe fiorentine (Boccaccio) **13**:63-5, 97

The Commandment of Love to God (Rolle) **21**:314, 316, 363, 383-86

Commentaries (Bede) **20**:61

Commentaries on Isaiah (Origen) **19**:188

Commentaries on Scripture (Rolle) **21**:278, 328

Commentaries on the Sentences (Albert the Great)

See *Commentary on the Book of the Sentences*

Commentarii (Xenophon)
  See *Memorabilia*

Commentarius quo medetu filio, servis, familiaribus (Cato) **21**:21

Commentary on Aristotle's De Generatione et de Coruptione (Averroes) **7**:30

Commentary on Aristotle's Nichomachean Ethics (Averroes) **7**:43

Commentary on Artistotle's Meteorology (Albert the Great) **16**:97

Commentary on Genesis (Origen) **19**:186, 201, 246

Commentary on III de Anima (Averroes) **7**:24

Commentary on Plato's Republic (Averroes) **7**:30, 38, 40-3

Commentary on St. John (Origen) **19**:186-88, 209, 247, 257, 260, 262-63

Commentary on St Luke (Albert the Great) **16**:29

Commentary on the Book of the Sentences (Albert the Great) **16**:6-7, 14, 16, 26, 31, 44, 66, 68, 76, 86, 93-4

Commentary on the Divine Names (Albert the Great) **16**:28-9

Commentary on the Gospel according to Matthew (Origen) **19**:187, 240, 246

Commentary on the Psalms (Origen) **19**:202

Commentary on the Psalms and Canticles of the Old Testament (Rolle) **21**:273, 279, 284, 294, 362

Commentary on the Sentences of Peter Lombard (Albert the Great)
  See *Commentary on the Book of the Sentences*

Commentary on the Song of Songs (Origen) **19**:210, 212, 240, 255-62

The Commonplace Book of Sei Shonagon (Sei Shonagon)
  See *Makura no soshi*

Communia Mathematica (Bacon) **14**:15, 46, 80

Communium Naturalium (Bacon) **14**:15, 48, 80, 100, 104-05

Compendium artis demonstrativae (Llull)
  See *Ars demonstrativa*

Compendium of Philosophy (Bacon)
  See *Compendium Studii Philosophiae*

Compendium of the Logic of al-ghazzali (Llull) **12**:113-14, 116, 126, 128, 132

Compendium of the Study of Philosophy (Bacon)
  See *Compendium Studii Philosophiae*

Compendium Studii Philosophiae (Bacon) **14**:8-9, 28-31, 36-37, 42, 45, 50, 68-69, 100-01, 105

Compendium Studii Theologiae (Bacon) **14**:9, 15, 22, 25, 42, 45, 50, 64

Compotus naturalium (Bacon) **14**:63

Concerning Contempt for the World (Petrarch) **20**:221

Concerning Famous Women (Boccaccio)
  See *De claris mulieribus*

Concerning the Antiquities of the Jews (Josephus)
  See *Antiquitates Judaicae*

Concerning the Capture (Josephus)
  See *Bellum Judaicum*

Concerning the Jewish War (Josephus)
  See *Bellum Judaicum*

Confessions (Augustine) **6**:4, 8, 14, 16, 19, 21-4, 29, 34, 41, 44, 46, 52-6, 60, 63-9, 72, 78, 84, 92, 96-8, 100-04, 110-13, 116-20, 122, 126-29, 131-33, 136-38, 140-42, 146, 149

Connection by Marriage (Menander)
  See *Samia*

Consolatio (Boethius)
  See *De consolatione philosophiae*

Consolation (Cicero)
  See *Consolationes*

The Consolation of Philosophy (Boethius)
  See *De consolatione philosophiae*

Consolationes (Cicero) **3**:227

Constitution of Sparta (Xenophon) **17**:326, 334, 341, 348, 349

Conte de la Charrette (Chretien de Troyes)
  See *Lancelot*

Conte du Graal (Chretien de Troyes)
  See *Perceval*

Contes del Graal (Chretien de Troyes)
  See *Perceval*

Contest for the Arms (Aeschylus) **11**:125

Contra academicos (Augustine) **6**:5, 46, 65, 68, 90

Contra amatores mundi (Rolle) **21**:332, 381, 398

Contra Apionem (Josephus) **13**:207-8, 211-2, 214, 219-20, 225-39, 247, 250, 253, 256, 259-60, 262-3, 268, 270, 272, 279, 281, 296, 301-2, 306-8, 312-3, 315, 317-20

Contra Celsum (Origen) **19**:211, 217, 225-27, 249

Contra epistolum Manichaei (Augustine) **6**:9

Contra Eutychen et Nestorium (Boethius) **15**:86, 125-6, 128, 130, 132-3, 135-6, 138

"Conversation in the Mountains" (Li Po) **2**:144

A Conversation of Origen with Heracleides (Origen) **19**:233

Corbaccio (Boccaccio) **13**:9, 37, 67, 70-1, 73-4, 88-94

Counsels on Discernment (Eckhart) **9**:69

Cratylus (Plato) **8**:306, 336, 361

Critias (Plato) **8**:232, 259, 261, 306, 311

Crito (Plato) **8**:282

"Crossing at Seven Li Shallows" (Su Shih) **15**:396-97

"The Crow Instructing His Child" (Marie de France) **8**:194

Crown Speech (Demosthenes)
  See *On the Crown*

Cupid and Psyche (Apuleius) **1**:22, 26, 40-2

Cynegeticus (Xenophon) **17**:350, 375

Cyropaedia (Xenophon) **17**:318-22, 323, 326, 327, 329-31, 335, 337, 340, 341, 343, 348, 349, 350, 351-52, 361-68, 372, 375, 376-85

Daitaleis (Aristophanes) **4**:62

Danaids (Aeschylus) **11**:88, 119, 158, 160, 167, 179, 183, 192

Danesh Namesh (Avicenna) **16**:150

"Daniel" (Caedmon) **7**:84, 87, 89-90

Daphnephorica (Pindar) **12**:321

Daphnis (Longus)
  See *Daphnis and Chloe*

Daphnis and Chloe (Longus) **7**;214-76

Daughters of Danäus (Aeschylus)
  See *Danaids*

Daughters of Phorcus (Aeschylus) **11**:124

De agricultura (Cato) **21**:17, 26-30, 39, 41-50, 54-7

De Alchimia (Albert the Great)
  See *Libellus de Alchimia*

De amicitia (Cicero) **3**:193, 195, 202

De anima (Albert the Great) **16**:7, 61, 106, 109, 113, 115

De anima (Avicenna) **16**:176

De animalibus (Albert the Great) **16**:18, 21, 35-7, 61, 64, 82-3, 103, 107, 110

De Arithmetica (Boethius) **15**:63, 69, 86

De arte metrica (Bede) **20**:42, 93, 120

De beneficiis (Seneca) **6**:344, 348, 374, 381-83

De bono (Albert the Great) **16**:44-7, 49-50, 53-4, 65-7, 69, 71-2, 74-7, 79-81

De brevitate vitae (Seneca) **6**:344, 382

De caelo et mundo (Albert the Great) **16**:7, 18, 22, 61

De casibus virorum illustrium (Boccaccio) **13**:33, 38, 45-7, 52, 66

De catechizandis rudibus (Augustine) **6**:93

De causis elementorum (Albert the Great)
  See *De causis et proprietatibus elementorum et planetarum*

De causis et procreatione un'iversi (Albert the Great) **16**:7

De causis et proprietatibus elementorum et planetarum (Albert the Great) **16**:7, 9, 56, 61, 83, 99

De Celestibus (Bacon)
  See *De Coelestibus*

De civitate Dei (Augustine) **6**:4, 10-11, 21-22, 29, 43, 54, 57-8, 60, 66-8, 83, 90-1, 105-08, 122-23, 142

De civitate Dei (Petrarch) **20**:288

De claris mulieribus (Boccaccio) **13**:33, 38, 45-7, 52, 55-8, 66, 97-8

De claris oratoribus (Cicero) **3**:193, 201-02, 206-09, 218, 259, 261, 263, 288

De clementia (Seneca) **6**:344, 374, 381-82, 397, 399, 401-02, 408

De clementia I (Seneca) **6**:399

De clementia II (Seneca) **6**:399

De Coelestibus (Bacon) **14**:47

De consolatione philosophiae (Boethius) **3**, 4, 9, 10-15, 15-23, 24, 31, 33, 37-43, 43-47, 47-53, 53-58, 58-69, 69-79, 87, 88, 88-97, 97-124, 125-26, 128-32, 134-45

De constantia (Seneca) **6**:382

De consulatu suo (Cicero) **3**:198

De contemptu mundi (Petrarch) **20**:213

De Corona (Cicero) **3**:267

De correptione et gratia (Augustine) **6**:9-10, 89

De Coruna (Demosthenes)
  See *On the Crown*

De dialectica (Augustine) **6**:133-36, 138

De diversis quaestionibus (Augustine) **6**:90

De divinatione (Cicero) **3**:216, 243, 248

De doctrina Christiana (Augustine) **6**:69, 81-2, 85, 92-4, 111, 113, 126, 133-36, 138

De domo (Cicero) **3**:269

De dono perseverantiae (Augustine) **6**:10

De Eucharistico Sacramento (Albert the Great) **16**:42

De Falsa Legatione (Demosthenes)
  See *On the Misconduct of the Embassy*

De Fastis (Ovid)
  See *Fasti*

De fide catholica (Boethius) **15**:9, 24, 3, 43, 52, 57, 62, 67

De finibus (Cicero) **3**:193, 202, 260, 288

De genealogiis deorum (Boccaccio)
  See *Genealogia deorum gentilium*

De generatione et corruptione (Albert the Great) **16**:7, 61

De genesi ad litteram (Augustine) **6**:9, 137, 139

De Genesi ad litteram imperfectum (Augustine) **6**:137

De Genesi adversus Manichaeos (Augustine) **6**:137

De gratia et libero arbitrio (Augustine) **6**:89, 118, 122

De ideis (Hermogenes)
See *On Types of Style*

De ignorantia (Petrarch) **20**:258, 286-90

De immortalitate animae (Augustine) **6**:68

De incendio amoris (Rolle)
See *Incendium amoris*

De Institutione Musica (Boethius)
See *In topica Ciceronis*

De intellectu et intelligibili (Albert the Great) **16**:61, 112, 116, 118

De interpretatione (Abelard) **11**:63

De inventione (Cicero) **3**:182, 193, 201, 206, 216, 218-19, 244, 258-60, 263

De inventione (Hermogenes)
See *On Invention*

De ira (Seneca) **6**:344, 347, 382, 385, 411, 424, 436-37

De iuventute et senectute (Albert the Great) **16**:90

De lege agraria (Cicero) **3**:268

De legibus (Cicero) **3**:177, 194, 201, 211, 214-15, 221, 249-51, 256-57, 276-77, 296-98

De libero arbitrio voluntatis (Augustine) **6**:5, 9-10, 68, 102, 117-18, 149

De magistro (Augustine) **6**:126, 133-36, 138

De memoria et reminiscentia (Albert the Great) **16**:61, 110

De meteoris (Albert the Great) **16**:7, 36, 55, 61

De methodo vehementiae (Hermogenes)
See *On the Method of Deinotes*

De metrica arte (Bede)
See *De arte metrica*

De Mineralibus (Albert the Great) **16**:18, 35, 61

De montibus (Boccaccio) **13**:33, 38, 52

De morte et vita (Albert the Great) **16**:61

De motibus animalium (Albert the Great) **16**:61

De Multiplicatione Specierum (Bacon)
See *Tractatus de Mulitiplicatione Specierum*

De mundo (Apuleius) **1**:12, 24

De musica (Augustine) **6**:33, 68, 73, 133-34

De Musica (Boethius)
See *In topica Ciceronis*

De natura deorum (Cicero) **3**:182, 202, 243, 248, 255-56, 268, 278, 279, 287

De natura et gratia (Augustine) **6**:9-10

De natura et origine animae (Albert the Great) **16**:112

De natura locorum (Albert the Great) **16**:7, 22, 61

De notitia caelestium (Bacon) **14**:62

De nutrimento et nutribili (Albert the Great) **16**:61

De octo viridariis (Rolle) **21**:295

De officiis (Cicero) **3**:192-93, 196, 202-03, 214, 221, 228-29, 242, 245, 254-57, 288-89, 296-98

De Optimo (Cicero)
See *De optimo genere oratorum*

De optimo genere dicendi (Cicero) **3**:188, 193, 199, 201, 217-18, 259-63, 288

De optimo genere oratorum (Cicero) **3**:201, 261

De oratore (Cicero) **3**:186, 193, 200-01, 207-11, 217-18, 227, 246, 258-59, 261, 263, 270, 288

De oratore ad filium (Cato) **21**:21

De ordine (Augustine) **6**:5, 102

De originibus (Cato) **21**:20

De orthographia (Bede) **20**:42

De otio (Seneca) **6**:382

De otio religiosorum (Petrarch) **20**:213, 263

De Plantis (Albert the Great) **16**:18

De Platone et eius dogmate (Apuleius) **1**:24

De praedestinatione sanctorum (Augustine) **6**:89

De Principiis (Origen) **19**:186, 199, 201, 203, 205, 209, 225, 227, 235-36, 246, 248, 258, 261, 263, 265

De principiis motus processivi (Albert the Great) **16**:61

De providentia (Seneca) **6**:374, 381

De provinciis consularibus (Cicero) **3**:215, 271

De quantitate animae (Augustine) **6**:68

De re militari (Cato) **21**:40, 47-8

De re rustica (Cato)
See *De agricultura*

De Rebus Metallicis (Albert the Great) **16**:18

De remediis utriusque fortunae (Petrarch) **20**:213-14, 261-62, 290-91, 308, 312, 326

De republica (Cicero) **3**:177-78, 194, 200-01, 211-12, 214, 221, 225-26, 232, 244, 249-51, 254, 256-57, 285, 288, 296-98

De rerum generatione ex elementis (Bacon) **14**:62

De Resurrectione (Albert the Great) **16**:118, 125

De Sacrificio Missae (Albert the Great) **16**:42

De schematibus et tropis sacrae scripturae (Bede) **20**:42,93

De scientia experimentali (Bacon) **14**:5, 80

De Scientia Perspectiva (Bacon) **14**:20, 47

De secreto conflictu curarum mearum (Petrarch) **20**:318

De senectute (Cicero) **3**:193, 195, 202, 204, 227, 231, 288

De sensu et sensato (Albert the Great) **16**:61, 106, 110

De sinderesi (Albert the Great) **16**:49

De somno et vigilia (Albert the Great) **16**:7, 61, 110

De Spiritu et Anima (Albert the Great) **16**:128

De spiritu et respiratione (Albert the Great) **16**:61

De statibus (Hermogenes)
See *On Stases*

De tabernaculo (Bede) **20**:89

De temporibus (Bede) **20**:34, 43-4, 49, 66, 75, 78, 121

De temporibus meis (Cicero) **3**:198

De temporum ratione (Bede) **20**:34, 49, 66, 75, 78, 91, 93, 120-21

De termino Paschali (Bacon) **14**:63

De topicis differentiis (Boethius) **15**:7, 27, 29, 88, 129, 131, 136

De tranquillitate animi (Seneca) **6**:344, 382, 393

De Trinitate (Augustine) **6**:21, 27, 62, 68, 70, 77, 85-7, 90-1, 116, 119-21, 138-40

De trinitate (Boethius) **15**:31-2, 43, 56, 59, 79, 86, 95, 125-30, 136, 141

de Unitate et Trinitate Divina (Abelard)
See *Theologia 'Summi boni'*

De utilitate grammaticae (Bacon) **14**:46, 64

De utilitate mathematicae (Bacon) **14**:5

De vegetabilibus (Albert the Great) **16**:20, 36-7, 61, 64

De vera religione (Augustine) **6**:68

De viris illustribus (Petrarch) **20**:237, 256, 260

De vita activa contemplativa (Rolle) **21**:273

De vita beata (Seneca) **6**:382, 412

De vita solitaria (Petrarch) **20**:213, 259-60, 287, 290

De vulgari eloquentia (Boccaccio) **13**:65

"The Death of Edward the Confessor" **4**:13

"The Death of Enkidu" **3**:336

"The Death of Gilgamesh" **3**:333, 336-37, 349

Decameron (Boccaccio) **13**:3-28, 30-8, 42-3, 45, 47-52, 55-7, 59-65, 67, 71-2, 74-5, 82-4, 86, 88-91, 94, 114-8, 122-31

Decisive Treatise (Averroes)
See *Fasl al-maqal*

Dede Korkut
See *Kitabi-i Dedem Qorkut*

Dede Korkut nameh
See *Kitabi-i Dedem Qorkut*

"The Defence of Walled Towns" (Sordello) **15**:330, 344

Defense (Plato)
See *Apologia*

Defense (Xenophon)
See *Apology*

Deification of Arsinoe (Callimachus) **18**: 34, 39, 60

Descent of Heracles into the Underworld (Pindar) **12**:321

Descent of the Gods (Hesiod)
See *Theogony*

Desconort (Llull) **12**:108, 120, 122

Destructio destructionis philosophorum (Averroes)
See *Tahafut al-tahafut*

Destructio Destructionum (Averroes)
See *Tahafut al-tahafut*

Destruction of the Destruction (Averroes)
See *Tahafut al-tahafut*

"Deus Amanz" (Marie de France)
See "Les Dous Amanz"

"The Devout Prince" **2**:40

Dialectica (Abelard) **11**:62, 64, 66

Dialogi (Seneca) **6**:374, 381-82, 410, 413

Dialogue between a Christian and a Jew (Abelard)
See *Dialogue between a Philosopher, a Jew and A Christian*

Dialogue between a Philosopher, a Jew and A Christian (Abelard) **11**:4, 11, 21, 24, 51-53, 67

Dialogue of the Philosopher with a Jew and a Christian (Abelard)
See *Dialogue between a Philosopher, a Jew and A Christian*

Dialogue of Trismegistus (Apuleius) **1**:17

Dialogues (Seneca)
See *Dialogi*

Dialogues on the Supreme Good, the End of All Moral Action (Cicero)
See *De finibus*

Diana's Hunt (Boccaccio)
See *Caccia di Diana*

Dictyluci (Aeschylus)
See *Net-Draggers*

"Dido" (Ovid) **7**:312

"Dirge for Blacatz" (Sordello)
See "Planher vuelh en Blacatz"

Dis Exapaton (Menander) **9**:258, 270

"Discourse on Dragon and Tiger (Lead and

Mercury)" (Su Shih) **15**:400

"Discourse on Literature" (Su Shih) **15**:420

Disputation (Llull) **12**:119

Dithyrambs (Pindar) **12**:320, 355

Divine Song
  See *Bhagavad Gita*

Divisions (Boethius) **15**:27, 29-30

The Divisions of Oratory (Cicero)
  See *Partiones oratoriae*

Diwan-i shams-i tabrizi (Rumi) **20**:352-53, 371-72

Doctrina pueril (Llull) **12**:104-05, 107, 121

"The Doe and Her Fawn" (Marie de France) **8**:193-94

"Dompna meillz qu om pot pensar" (Sordello) **15**:361

"Donna mi vene" (Petrarch) **20**:273

"Una donna piu bella" (Petrarch) **20**:241

A Double Deceit (Menander)
  See *Dis Exapaton*

The Dour Man (Menander)
  See *Dyskolos*

"Les Dous Amanz" (Marie de France) **8**:116-17, 121, 131, 133-34, 136-39, 147, 153-54, 156, 162-65, 181, 187

"A Draught of Sesamum" (Su Shih) **15**:383, 391

Dream (Cicero)
  See *Somnium Scipionis*

Dream of Scipio (Cicero)
  See *Somnium Scipionis*

The Dream of the Rood **14**:215-294

"Dreams of the Sky-land" (Li Po) **2**:134

"Drinking Alone by Moonlight" (Li Po) **2**:132, 143, 163

Drunkenness (Menander) **9**:248

"A Dung-Beetle" (Marie de France)
  See "A Wolf and a Dung-Beetle"

Duties (Cicero)
  See *De officiis*

The Dynasty of Raghu (Kalidasa)
  See *Raghuvamsa*

Dyskolos (Menander) **9**:231-33, 235-41, 243-52, 257, 260-65, 269-70, 272-77, 279-84, 286-87

"The Ebony Horse" **2**:51

Ecclesiazusae (Aristophanes)
  See *Ekklesiazousai*

"Ecloga I" (Petrarch) **20**:263

The Education of Cyrus (Xenophon)
  See *Cyropaedia*

Ego dormio (Rolle) **21**:294, 336-37, 356-57, 359-61, 363, 367-69, 371-75, 389, 396

Ego dormio et cor meum vigilat (Rolle)
  See *Ego dormio*

Egyptians (Aeschylus) **11**:88, 160, 179

Eight Questions (Bede) **20**:121

"Eight Sights of Feng-hsiang" (Su Shih) **15**:410

Eighth Isthmian (Pindar)
  See *Isthmian 8*

Eighth Olympian (Pindar)
  See *Olympian 8*

"Eighty some paces" (Su Shih) **15**:398

Eirene (Aristophanes) **4**:44-5, 60-2, 78, 87, 93, 108-09, 124-26, 132-33, 138, 142-44, 148-49, 153-54, 160, 162-63. 165-68

Ekklesiazousai (Aristophanes) **4**:44, 60-62, 65, 68, 78, 87, 94, 110, 124-26, 128-29, 147, 149-50, 152, 155-56, 161-62, 166, 168-77, 179-80

Elegia di Constanza (Boccaccio) **13**:62-4, 73

Elegia di madonna Fiammetta (Boccaccio)
  See *Fiammetta*

Elegies (Ovid)
  See *Tristia*

Elegies of Gloom (Ovid)
  See *Tristia*

Elektra (Sophocles) **2**:289, 293, 300, 314-15, 319-22, 324, 326-27, 331, 335, 338-40, 347, 349, 351, 353-54, 357-58, 368, 380, 384-85, 395-96, 417-18, 421

Elementary Exercises (Hermogenes)
  See *Progymnasmata*

Eleusinians (Aeschylus) **11**:192

Eleventh Nemean (Pindar)
  See *Nemean 11*

Eleventh Olympian (Pindar)
  See *Olympian 11*

Eleventh Pythian (Pindar)
  See *Pythian 11*

"Eliduc" (Marie de France) **8**:114, 118, 121, 129-30, 133, 135, 140, 144-45, 147-49, 152, 158, 160-61, 164-66, 170, 182

Embassy (Demosthenes)
  See *On the Misconduct of the Embassy*

Emendatio peccatoris (Rolle) **21**:295

Emendatio vitae (Rolle) **21**:278, 303, 307, 310-11, 313-14, 320, 329, 335, 341-42, 344-45, 347-48, 351-52, 369, 386, 389, 392-95, 397-98

"An Emperor and his Ape" (Marie de France) **8**:175

"Emril Son of Beyril" **8**:105

Enarration on Psalm 90 (Augustine) **6**:111

Enarration on Psalm 136 (Augustine) **6**:116

Enarrationes in psalmos (Augustine) **6**:83

Enchiridion ad laurentium (Augustine) **6**:9, 21, 68

Encomia (Pindar) **12**:320-21, 357, 363-64

Encomion on Sosibius (Callimachus) **18**: 43

Encomium (Pindar)
  See *Encomia*

Encomium nominis Ihesu (Rolle) **21**:389

Ends (Epicurus) **21**:124

English Translation and Commentary on the Psalter (Rolle) **21**:278-80, 284, 294, 309, 332, 351

Enid (Chretien de Troyes)
  See *Erec et Enide*

Ensegnamen d'Onor (Sordello) **15**:331-32, 354, 256, 270, 376-76

Epic of Gilgamesh **3**:301-75

Epicleros (Menander) **9**:203

Epigrams (Callimachus) **18**: 18, 25, 32, 34-8, 48

Epinicia (Pindar) **12**:320-22

Epinomis (Plato) **8**:248, 305-06, 311

"Episode of Nala"
  See *Nalopakhyana*

Epistle (Rolle) **21**:299

Epistle ad P. Lentulum (Cicero)
  See *Ad P. Lentulum*

Epistle XLVII (Seneca) **6**:384

Epistles (Ovid)
  See *Heroides*

Epistles (Plato) **8**:305, 311

Epistles (Seneca)
  See *Epistulae morales*

Epistola de secretis operibus naturae (Bacon) **14**:64

Epistola fratris Rogerii Baconis de secretis operibus naturae et de nullitate magiae

(Bacon) **14**:44

Epistolae familiares (Petrarch) **20**:237, 266-68, 288-90, 294, 296-97, 303-05, 308, 314, 318, 320, 326, 331, 333

Epistolæ Heroidum (Ovid)
  See *Heroides*

Epistolae rerum familiarium (Petrarch) **20**:256-57, 261

Epistolae seniles (Petrarch) **20**:266, 296, 323, 326, 331

Epistole metrice (Petrarch) **20**:327, 333

Epistulae ex Ponto (Ovid) **7**:323, 343, 344, 347, 378, 398, 423, 426

Epistulae morales (Seneca) **6**:347, 352-53, 374-75, 381-83, 410-11, 417

"Epithalamium of Peleus and Thetis" (Catullus)
  See "Poem 64"

Epitrepontes (Menander) **9**:203, 207-09, 211-13, 215-18, 223-24, 227, 230, 232, 238-44, 246-47, 249-52, 260, 269-71, 278, 281

Eptiaphios (Demosthenes) **13**:166

"Equitan" (Marie de France) **8**:114, 121, 123, 131-32, 134, 136, 143, 147, 149-50, 157, 159, 162-65, 171, 175, 182

"Er encontra'l temps de mai" (Sordello) **15**:363

Erec (Hartmann von Aue) **15**:158, 164-65, 176, 183, 185, 188-96, 196-202, 207-13, 218-23, 228-41, 244

Erec and Enid (Chretien de Troyes)
  See *Erec et Enide*

Erec et Enide (Chretien de Troyes) **10**:132-33, 139, 141-43, 146-48, 159-61, 163, 165-67, 169, 171-73, 178, 183-89, 191-93, 195, 197, 200-01, 204-10, 218-19, 223-26, 229-39

Erga (Hesiod)
  See *Works and Days*

Erotic Adventures (Ovid)
  See *Amores*

Esope (Marie de France)
  See *The Fables*

Esposizioni (Boccaccio) **13**:62, 67

Espurgatoire (Marie de France)
  See *L'Espurgatoire Saint Patrice*

L'Espurgatoire Saint Patrice (Marie de France) **8**:114-15, 128, 146, 159-61, 173-77

Ethica seu Scito te ipsum (Abelard)
  See *Scito Te Ipsum*

Ethics (Abelard)
  See *Scito Te Ipsum*

Eumenides (Aeschylus) **11**:85-7, 92, 96, 100, 102, 105, 107, 114, 116-17, 119, 132, 134-35, 137-38, 140, 143, 150, 152-53, 155-57, 162, 165-66, 172, 178-79, 180-85, 191-92, 194, 197-98, 204-05, 207, 216, 218, 222, 225

Eunich (Terence)
  See *Eunuchus*

Eunuchus (Terence) **14**:299, 303-08, 311-15, 317-18, 321, 330-33, 335, 337, 340, 342-43, 345-49, 352-54, 357-58, 364-66, 369-71, 383-84, 387

Euthydemus (Plato) **8**:218, 250, 265-66, 306, 314, 357, 361

Euthyphro (Plato)
  See *Euthyphron*

Euthyphron (Plato) **8**:263, 286, 306

Evast and Blanquerna (Llull)
  See *Blanquerna*

Ex Ponto (Ovid)
  See *Epistulae ex Ponto*

Exemplaria Adamantii (Origen) **19**:192

"Exhortation" (Rolle) **21**:367, 369, 375

"Exile's Letter" (Li Po) **2**:140

"Exodus" (Caedmon) **7**:83-4, 87, 89-90, 93, 104

Expositio epistolae ad Galatas (Augustine) **6**:10

Expositio in Epist. ad Romanos (Abelard) **11**:10, 12, 53

An Exposition of the Methods of Argument Concerning the Doctrine of the Faith and a Determination of Doubts and Misleading Innovations Brought into the Faith (Averroes)
See *Kitab al-kashf 'an manahij al-adilla fi 'aqa'id al-milla,wa ta'rif ma waqa'a fiha bi-hasb at-ta'wil min ash-shibah al-muzigha wal-bida 'al-mudilla*

Exposition of the Psalms (Rolle)
See *Commentary on the Psalms and Canticles of the Old Testament*

Expositions on the Gospel according to John (Origen)
See *Commentary on St. John*

Exxlesisastical History of the English People (Bede)
See *Historia ecclesiastica gentis Anglorum*

The Fables (Marie de France) **8**:115, 128, 146, 160-61, 171-75, 179

"Fall of Angels" (Caedmon)
See "Lament of the Fallen Angels"

Fang Chi (Confucius) **19**:20

Fasl (Averroes)
See *Fasl al-maqal*

Fasl al-maqal (Averroes) **7**:39, 41-4, 69-72

Fasti (Ovid) **7**:284, 286, 292-93, 323-27, 330, 335, 343-46, 362-65, 377, 389, 401-03, 413-19, 424-35, 444

Felix (Llull) **12**:105-07, 109, 123, 125, 133-34

Felix or The Book of Marvels (Llull)
See *Felix*

"The Ferryman and the Hermit" **2**:40

Fiammetta (Boccaccio) **13**:7, 29-30, 32-3, 63, 67, 88, 97

Fifth Isthmian (Pindar)
See *Isthmian 5*

Fifth Nemean (Pindar)
See *Nemean 5*

"Fighting to the South of the City" (Li Po) **2**:132

Fihi ma fihi (Rumi) **20**:371

Filocolo (Boccaccio) **13**:23, 32-3, 44-5, 61-5, 102-3, 105, 112, 114-22

Filocopo (Boccaccio) **13**:9, 26-8, 30

Filostrato (Boccaccio) **13**:9, 29, 32-3, 62-3, 65, 87-8, 102-3, 106, 110, 112

Fire of Love (Rolle)
See *Incendium amoris*

First Isthmian (Pindar)
See *Isthmian 1*

First Nemean (Pindar)
See *Nemean 1*

First Olympian (Pindar)
See *Olympian 1*

First Olynthiac (Demosthenes)
See *Olynthiac I*

First Philippic (Cicero)
See *Philippics*

First Philippic (Demosthenes)
See *Philippic I*

First Pythian (Pindar)
See *Pythian 1*

"The Fisherman and the Genie" **2**:45, 53-5, 68

The Fisherman's Art (Ovid)
See *Halieutica*

The Flatterer (Menander)
See *Kolax*

Florida (Apuleius)
See *Floridium*

Floridium (Apuleius) **1**:7, 12, 23-4

"Following the Rhymes of Chiang Hui shi" (Su Shih) **15**:414, 416

For Cluentius (Cicero)
See *Pro Cluentio*

For Marcus Caelius (Cicero)
See *Pro Caelio*

For Megalopolis (Demosthenes) **13**:137, 148, 156-7, 159, 164, 197

For Phormio (Demosthenes) **13**:184

For Quinctius (Cicero)
See *Pro Quinctio*

For the Liberty of the Rhodians (Demosthenes)
See *For the Rhodians*

For the Megalopolitans (Demosthenes)
See *For Megalopolis*

For the Rhodians (Demosthenes) **13**:137, 148, 156-7, 159, 164, 171

The Form of Living (Rolle) **21**:294, 299-300, 307, 314-15, 317, 327, 332, 335, 345, 347-48, 351-52, 356, 359, 362, 367-69, 371-72, 375, 381, 386, 393-94

The Form of Perfect Living (Rolle)
See *The Form of Living*

The Four Branches of the Mabinogi
See *Pedeir Keinc y Mabinogi*

"The Four Sorrows" (Marie de France)
See "Le Chaitivel"

Fourteenth Olympian (Pindar)
See *Olympian 14*

Fourth Philippic (Demosthenes)
See *Philippic IV*

Fourth Pythian (Pindar)
See *Pythian 4*

"The Fox and the Bear" (Marie de France) **8**:190

"Le Fraisne" (Marie de France) **8**:114, 116, 121, 131, 133-34, 136, 138, 140, 147, 152-53, 159-60, 162-63, 165-66, 181

Free Choice of the Will (Augustine)
See *De libero arbitrio voluntatis*

Free Will (Augustine)
See *De libero arbitrio voluntatis*

"Fresne" (Marie de France)
See "Le Fraisne"

The Friars (Aristophanes) **4**:100

The Frogs (Aristophanes)
See *Batrakhoi*

Furens (Seneca)
See *Hercules furens*

Furies (Aeschylus)
See *Eumenides*

Furious Hercules (Seneca)
See *Hercules furens*

Galatia (Callimachus) **18**: 34

"Ganem, Son to Abou Ayoub, and Known by the Surname of Love's Slave" **2**:14, 36, 38

Gastly Gladnesse (Rolle) **21**:367

Gauvain (Chretien de Troyes)
See *Perceval*

Genealogia deorum gentilium (Boccaccio) **13**:33, 38, 41, 43-4, 52-4, 62, 66, 96, 98, 103

Genealogies of the Gentile Gods (Boccaccio)
See *Genealogia deorum gentilium*

Genealogies of the Pagan Gods (Boccaccio)
See *Genealogia deorum gentilium*

Genealogy of the Gods (Boccaccio)
See *Genealogia deorum gentilium*

"Genesis" (Caedmon) **7**:78-9, 82-9, 91-4, 104

"Genesis A" (Caedmon) **7**:84-90

"Genesis B" (Caedmon) **7**:85-6, 91, 93

Genesis of the Gods (Hesiod)
See *Theogony*

Genji Monogatari (Murasaki) **1**:413-76

Georgos (Menander) **9**:250

Gertadés (Aristophanes) **4**:102, 105

Gerusalemme liberata (Petrarch) **20**:214

Gilgamesh
See *Epic of Gilgamesh*

"Gilgamesh and the Agga of Kish" **3**:336

"Gilgamesh and the Bull of Heaven" **3**:337, 349

"Gilgamesh and the Huluppu Tree" **3**:326, 337, 349, 362

"Gilgamesh and the Land of the Living" **3**:325, 332-33, 336-37, 349

"Gilgamesh, Enkidu and the Nether World"
See "Gilgamesh and the Huluppu Tree"

Gilgamesh Epic
See *Epic of Gilgamesh*

Gilgamish
See *Epic of Gilgamesh*

"Giovene donna" (Petrarch) **20**:299, 305

The Girl from Andros (Terence)
See *Andria*

The Girl from Samos (Menander)
See *Samia*

The Girl Who Gets Her Hair Cut Short (Menander)
See *Perikeiromene*

The Girl with Shorn Hair (Menander)
See *Perikeiromene*

Gita
See *Bhagavadgita*

Gita
See *Bhagavad Gita*

Glaucus Potnieus (Aeschylus) **11**:159, 179

"Goat's Leaf" (Marie de France)
See "Chevrefoil"

The Golden Ass (Apuleius)
See *Asinus aureus*

Gorgias (Plato) **8**:217, 233, 235, 239, 247-48, 255, 264, 266-68, 270, 274, 283, 285-87, 306, 322

Great Epic
See *Mahabharata*

Gregorius (Hartmann von Aue) **15**:164, 171-75, 175-83, 194, 207, 213-18, 218

Grumpy (Menander)
See *Dyskolos*

"Guigemar" (Marie de France)
See "Lay of Guigemar"

"Guildeluec and Gualadun" (Marie de France)
See "Eliduc"

Guillaume d'Angleterre (Chretien de Troyes) **10**:137, 139, 142-43, 183, 218, 225, 232

"Guingamor" (Marie de France) **8**:122-23, 126-28, 131

"Gulnare of the Sea" **2**:14, 23

"Hair of Berenice" (Catullus)
See "Poem 66"

Halieticon/On Fishing (Ovid)
See *Halieutica*

Halieutica (Ovid) **7**:328-29

Title Index

"Hard Roads to Shu" (Li Po) **2**:131-32, 145, 158, 166

"Hardships of Travel" (Li Po) **2**:139

The Harpist (Menander) **9**:288

"Harrowing of Hell" (Caedmon) **7**:79, 91-2

Hated (Menander)
See *Misoumenos*

"The Hawk and the Owl" (Marie de France) **8**:192, 194

Hazar Afsana
See *Alf Layla wa-Layla*

He Clips Her Hair (Menander)
See *Perikeiromene*

Healing (Avicenna)
See *Kitab al-Shifa*

Heautontimoreumenos (Terence) **14**:299, 302-04, 306-07, 309, 311, 313-14, 316-18, 332-35, 337-38, 345, 347, 349, 352, 358-59, 363-66, 381, 383-84, 386-87

Heautontimorumenus (Menander) **9**:243, 269

Hecale (Callimachus) **18**: 9, 18, 35, 38-42, 50, 52-3, 60-2

Hecyra (Terence) **14**:299, 301-08, 311-13, 317-20, 325, 329, 332-36, 340, 342-44, 347-49, 352-53, 356-58, 364-65, 368, 383-84, 386, 389, 398

Heliades (Aeschylus) **11**:211

Hell (Dante)
See *Inferno*

Hellenica (Xenophon) **17**:328, 329, 330, 339, 342, 344, 346, 347, 348, 349, 350, 352, 359, 368, 371-76, 378

"Heng-chiang Lyrics" (Li Po) **2**:161

Hercules furens (Seneca) **6**:340, 342-43, 363, 366, 369-70, 372-73, 379-81, 402-03, 405, 413, 415-17, 422-23, 431-32, 440-41, 446

Hercules oetaeus (Seneca) **6**:342-44, 363, 366, 370, 377, 379, 381, 414, 417-18, 423, 431-32, 446

Hercules on Oeta (Seneca)
See *Hercules oetaeus*

Hero (Menander) **9**:207, 211, 217, 246, 252

Heroides (Ovid) **7**:291-93, 296-97, 299-301, 303, 310-13, 316-19, 321, 329-36, 343-44, 346-47, 355, 376-83, 388, 417, 419-20, 425, 444

Heroines (Ovid)
See *Heroides*

Hexapla (Origen) **19**:184, 191-93

Hiero (Xenophon) **17**:327, 331-36, 365, 374, 375

Hikayet-i Oguzname-i Kazan Beg ve Gayri
See *Kitabi-i Dedem Qorkut*

Hiketides (Aeschylus)
See *Suppliants*

Hipparchus (Plato) **8**:305, 311

Hippeis (Aristophanes) **4**:38, 43, 46, 60, 62-3, 65, 74, 94, 98-9, 101, 114-15, 126-28, 132, 143, 146, 148, 152, 162-63, 167

Hippias maior (Plato) **8**:270, 305-06

Hippias Major (Plato)
See *Hippias maior*

Hippias Minor (Plato) **8**:306

Historia abbetum (Bede) **20**:29, 38, 49, 57, 72-3, 75, 85, 89

Historia Calamitatum (Abelard) **11**:24, 28, 32, 33, 40, 45, 48, 51, 52, 55, 57-59, 61, 63-66

Historia ecclesiastica gentis Anglorum (Bede) **20**:4, 6, 10-11, 14, 18-19, 26-32, 34-5, 38-40, 46-57, 61-3, 67-86, 89, 92-3, 98-101, 103, 106, 117, 119, 121-22

Historical Records (Confucius)
See *Shih Chi*

Histories (Polybius) **17**:148-207

History (Herodotus) **17**:49-147

History of My Troubles (Abelard)
See *Historia Calamitatum*

The History of Rome from Its Foundation (Livy)
See *Ab urbe condita libri*

History of the Abbots (Bede)
See *Historia abbetum*

History of the House of Aragon (Sordello)
See *Los progres e avansaments dei Res d'Aragon*

History of the Jewish War (Josephus)
See *Bellum Judaicum*

History of the Peloponnesian War (Thucydides) **17**:208-315

History of the War (Thucydides)
See *History of the Peloponnesian War*

Homilies (Bede) **20**:3, 7-8

Homily on Exodus (Origen) **19**:260

"Homily on the Ending of the Four Thousand" (Bede) **20**:8

"Homily on the Eve of the Resurrection" (Bede) **20**:5

Homily on the Song of Songs (Origen) **19**:255-56, 258, 262, 268

"The Honeysuckle" (Marie de France)
See "Chevrefoil"

Hortensius (Cicero) **3**:178, 242, 288

"How Basat Killed Goggle-eye" **8**:103, 108-09

"How Prince Urez Son of Prince Kazan was Taken Prisoner" **8**:103

"How Salur Kazan's House was Pillaged"
See "The Plunder of the Home of Salur-Kazan"

"How the Outer Oghuz Rebelled Against the Inner Oghuz and How Beyrek Died" **8**:103

Hrafnkatla
See *Hrafnkel's saga Freysgodi*

Hrafnkel's Saga
See *Hrafnkel's saga Freysgodi*

Hrafnkel's saga Freysgodi **2**:74-129

"Hsiang-yang Song" (Li Po) **2**:161

Hundred Names of God (Llull) **12**:122, 125

"Hundred Pace Rapids" (Su Shih) **15**:410

"Hymn" (Caedmon) **7**:84-5, 93-7, 100-01, 103-13

Hymn (Pindar) **12**:355-56

Hymn I (Callimachus) **18**: 3-6, 23, 28-31, 34, 39

Hymn II (Callimachus) **18**: 11, 28-31, 33-8, 40, 44, 52

Hymn III (Callimachus) **18**: 10-11, 24, 28-9, 33, 39, 42-3, 50-1, 56-8

Hymn IV (Callimachus) **18**: 10-11, 24, 28-32, 34, 39, 51, 58-9

"Hymn to Aphrodite" (Sappho)
See "Ode to Aphrodite"

Hymn to Apollo (Callimachus)
See *Hymn II*

Hymn to Artemis (Callimachus)
See *Hymn III*

Hymn to Athena Bath of Pallas (Callimachus)
See *Hymn V*

Hymn to Delos (Callimachus)
See *Hymn IV*

Hymn to Demeter (Callimachus)
See *Hymn VI*

"Hymn to the Virgin" (Petrarch) **20**:217

Hymn to Zeus (Callimachus)
See *Hymn I*

Hymn to Zeus (Pindar) **12**:276-78, 320

Hymn V (Callimachus) **18**: 9, 11, 30-2, 35-6, 38-9, 52

Hymn VI (Callimachus) **18**: 11-15, 28-9, 31-2, 34-6, 38-9, 52, 58

Hymns (Callimachus) **18**: 28, 38, 50, 53, 62

Hymns to the Gods (Pindar) **12**:320

Hypobolimaeus (Menander) **9**:203

Hyporcemata (Pindar) **12**:320-21, 355-57, 364

Hyporcheme (Pindar)
See *Hyporcemata*

Hyppolytus (Seneca) **6**:340, 342, 363, 373

Hypsipyle (Aeschylus) **11**:124

I Ching (Confucius) **19**:16, 38, 48, 50, 68, 71

"I have left my post in Hsu-chou" (Su Shih) **15**:412

"I shâk El-Mausili with the Merchant" **2**:43

"I' vo pensando" (Petrarch) **20**:273, 301

I. 3 (Pindar)
See *Isthmian 3*

I. 4 (Pindar)
See *Isthmian 4*

Iambi (Callimachus) **18**: 9, 24, 34-8, 42, 49, 53, 55-6, 58

Ibis (Callimachus) **18**: 11, 37, 62-4

Ibis (Ovid) **7**:327-28, 444

Ichneutai (Sophocles) **2**:289, 338, 388, 408

I-king (Confucius)
See *I Ching*

Iliad (Homer) **1**:268-412

Iliads (Homer)
See *Iliad*

Ilias (Homer)
See *Iliad*

In Catilinam (Cicero) **3**:193, 196, 198, 268, 270

In Collation (Eckhart)
See *Rede der Unterscheidungen*

In enigmatibus (Bacon) **14**:62

In Pisonem (Cicero) **3**:269, 284

"In Quest of the Tao in An-Ling, I Met Kai Huan Who Fashioned for Me a Register of the Realized Ones; (This Poem) Left Behind As a Present When About to Depart" (Li Po) **2**:175

In topica Ciceronis (Boethius) **15**:7, 26, 54-5, 62, 74, 95

In Vatinium (Cicero) **3**:223

Incendium amoris (Rolle) **21**:275, 284, 294, 303, 307, 310-13, 316, 319, 321, 328, 331-34, 336-39, 342-49, 352-54, 356, 359, 361, 367-68, 372-73, 383-86, 389-99

Inferno (Dante) **3**:1-169

'Ingredientibus' (Abelard)
See *Logica 'Ingredientibus'*

The Innocent Mother-in-Law (Terence)
See *Hecyra*

"Inscription for Six one Spring" (Su Shih) **15**:399

"Inscription for the Lotus Clepsydra at Hsu-chou" (Su Shih) **15**:399,409

Instruction in Honor (Sordello)
See *Ensegnamen d'Onor*

The Intellect (Albert the Great)
See *De intellectu et intelligibili*

Introductio (Abelard) **11**:10

An Introduction to Categorical Syllogisms

(Boethius) **15**:27, 29

Invecativae contra medicum (Petrarch) **20**:263, 266, 288-89

Invectiva in quedam ignarum dialectices (Abelard) **11**:67

Invectivae against the One Who Criticized Italy (Petrarch) **20**:258

Invective against the Doctor of Medicine (Petrarch)
See *Invecativae contra medicum*

Invective on His Own Ignorance and That of Many Other (Petrarch)
See *De ignorantia*

"Io son ventu al punto de la rota" (Petrarch) **20**:283

Ion (Plato) **8**:305-06, 331

Iphigenia (Aeschylus) **11**:125

Isharat wa al-Tanbihat (Avicenna) **16**:150

Isth. 9 (Pindar)
See *Isthmian 9*

Isthm. VII (Pindar)
See *Isthmian 7*

Isthmian Odes (Pindar) **12**:321, 353, 357

Isthmian 1 (Pindar) **12**:271, 319, 344, 352, 355-56, 365-66, 369, 378, 383-84

Isthmian 2 (Pindar) **12**:312-13, 319, 352-53, 362-63, 383

Isthmian 3 (Pindar) **12**:295, 306, 313, 356, 365-66

Isthmian 4 (Pindar) **12**:288, 295, 301, 312, 353, 356, 365, 367, 371, 376, 378, 380, 383

Isthmian 5 (Pindar) **12**:273, 278, 288, 306-07, 310, 323, 337, 357-58, 370, 378

Isthmian 6 (Pindar) **12**:319, 325-26, 354, 357-58, 366, 370, 377-79, 382-83

Isthmian 7 (Pindar) **12**:263, 270, 306-07, 326, 356, 362, 365-67, 383

Isthmian 8 (Pindar) **12**:271-73, 319, 325, 355-58, 382-83

Isthmian 9 (Pindar) **12**:357

"Italia mia" (Petrarch) **20**:239, 241, 245, 280

Iwein (Hartmann von Aue) **15**:154-63, 164-71, 176, 183-96, 202-06, 233, 244-45

Ixion (Broughton) **11**:122

"Jaefer and the Old Bedouin" **2**:40

"Jaudar" **2**:42

Jaya
See *Mahabharata*

Jeu d'Adam
See *Ordo Representacionis Ade*

Jewish Antiquities (Josephus)
See *Antiquitates Judaicae*

Jewish War (Josephus)
See *Bellum Judaicum*

Job
See *The Book of Job*

Judica (Rolle) **21**:394

Judica me Deus (Rolle) **21**:351, 390-92, 394-95

"Kafour the Eunuch" **2**:40

Kalevala **6**:206-88

Kalewala
See *Kalevala*

"Kan Turali Son of Kanli Koja" **8**:103, 108-09

Kedeia (Menander)
See *Samia*

"Khalifeh the Fisherman" **2**:14, 40

Kindly Ones (Aeschylus)
See *Eumenides*

King Mark and Iseut the Fair (Chretien de

Troyes) **10**:139, 218

King Oedipus (Sophocles)
See *Oedipous Tyrannos*

Kitab al-kashf 'an manahij al-adilla (Averroes)
See *Kitab al-kashf 'an manahij al-adilla fi 'aqa'id al-milla,wa ta'rif ma waqa'a fiha bi-hasb at-ta'wil min ash-shibah al-muzigha wal-bida 'al-mudilla*

Kitab al-kashf 'an manahij al-adilla fi 'aqa'id al-milla,wa ta'rif ma waqa'a fiha bi-hasb at-ta'wil min ash-shibah al-muzigha wal-bida 'al-mudilla (Averroes) **7**:37-43, 45, 69-70

Kitab al-Najat (Avicenna) **16**:147, 150, 162

Kitab al-Shifa (Avicenna) **16**:136-37, 147, 150, 157-58, 162-64

Kitabi Qorqut
See *Kitabi-i Dedem Qorkut*

Kitabi-i Dedem Qorkut **8**:95-110

"The Kite and the Jay" (Marie de France) **8**:194

The Knight of the Cart (Chretien de Troyes)
See *Lancelot*

The Knight with the Lion (Chretien de Troyes)
See *Yvain*

The Knight with the Sword (Chretien de Troyes)
See *Le Chevalier à l'épée*

The Knights (Aristophanes)
See *Hippeis*

Know the Ways of God (Hildegard von Bingen)
See *Scivias*

Know Thyself (Abelard)
See *Scito Te Ipsum*

Kojiki **21**:217-68

Kolax (Menander) **9**:213, 269

Kulliyyat (Averroes) **7**:66

Kumarasambhava (Kalidasa) **9**:82-6, 89-90, 95-6, 102, 107, 114-15, 118-19, 125, 128-29

Laberinto d'amore (Boccaccio) **13**:16

Lacedaemoniorum respublica (Xenophon)
See *Constitution of Sparta*

Laches (Plato) **8**:263-65, 286, 306, 356

Ladies Lunching Together (Menander)
See *Synaristosai*

The Lady of Andros (Terence)
See *Andria*

"The Lady of the Highest Prime" **2**:174

Laelius (Cicero)
See *De amicitia*

Laelius: On Friendship (Cicero)
See *De amicitia*

"Lai des Deuz Amanz" (Marie de France)
See "Les Dous Amanz"

Lais (Marie de France) 114-15, 130, 141, 146, 150, 157-62, 167, 172-73, 175, 177, 179-81, 184-85, 187-89, 195

Laïus (Aeschylus) **11**:122, 124, 159, 174

"The Lamb and the Goat" (Marie de France) **8**:192

"Lament for Blacas" (Sordello)
See "Planher vuelh en Blacatz"

"Lament for Lord Blacatz" (Sordello)
See "Planher vuelh en Blacatz"

"Lament of the Fallen Angels" (Caedmon) **7**;91, 93

Lancelot (Chretien de Troyes) **10**:133-39, 141-44, 147-49, 157, 159-63, 165-67, 169, 171-74, 176, 178-81, 183, 189-90, 195-98, 200, 208-10, 214-16, 218, 222-26, 228-30, 232-40

"Lanval" (Marie de France) **8**:122-23, 125, 127-28, 130-31, 133, 140-47, 149, 154, 156, 158,

161-64, 166, 169-70

"Laostic" (Marie de France)
See "Laüstic"

Lao-tzu: hck (Lao Tzu)
See *Tao te Ching*

Latin Psalter (Rolle) **21**:351

"Laüstic" (Marie de France) **8**:114, 120, 129, 131-34, 136-39, 144-45, 147-48, 153, 158-59, 161-66, 170, 181, 188

The Law (Cicero)
See *De legibus*

Laws (Cicero)
See *De legibus*

Laws (Plato) **8**:207, 217-18, 147, 249-50, 258-59, 261-62, 265-68, 279, 282-83, 305-06, 311, 318, 325, 328, 345-46, 362-64

"Lay le Freyne" (Marie de France)
See "Le Fraisne"

"Lay of Guigemar" (Marie de France) **8**:114-17, 122-23, 125, 127-28, 130-31, 133-35, 140, 145-49, 152-53, 161-67, 170, 172, 177-79, 181, 184, 188-89

Lay of the Nibelungen
See *Book of Chaos*

Lay of the Nibelungs
See *Book of Chaos*

Lays (Marie de France)
See *Lais*

Leading Doctrines (Epicurus)
See *Principal Doctrines*

Leges (Plato)
See *Laws*

Leptinea (Demosthenes)
See *Against Leptines*

Leptines (Demosthenes)
See *Against Leptines*

Lesbian Pastorals (Longus)
See *Daphnis and Chloe*

The Lesbian Pastorals of Daphnis and Chloe (Longus)
See *Daphnis and Chloe*

Lesser Hippias (Plato)
See *Hippias Minor*

Lesson of Honour (Sordello)
See *Ensegnamen d'Onor*

"Letter in Answer to Hsieh Min-shihn" (Su Shih) **15**:420

Letter on the Secret Works of Art and the Nullity of Magic (Bacon)
See *Epistola fratris Rogerii Baconis de secretis operibus naturae et de nullitate magiae*

Letter to Egbert (Bede) **20**:69-71, 92

"Letter to Han Ching-chou" (Li Po) **2**:169-73

Letter to Herodotus (Epicurus) **21**:73, 130-31, 165, 167-68, 170-75, 179-81, 188, 205, 207

Letter to Menoeceus (Epicurus) **21**:147-48, 161, 165, 176, 178, 182, 184-87

"Letter to Posterity" (Petrarch) **20**:237-40, 242, 246

Letter to Pythocles (Epicurus) **21**:118, 121, 164-65, 167, 169

"Letter to the Chief Administrator of Anchou, P'ei" (Li Po) **2**:170

"Letter Written on Behalf of Longevity Mountain in Answer to the Proclamation of Meng Shao-fu" (Li Po) **2**:172

Letters (Epicurus) **21**:73

Letters (Ovid)

Title Index

See *Heroides*
Letters (Seneca)
  See *Epistulae morales*
Letters from the Black Sea (Ovid)
  See *Epistulae ex Ponto*
Letters of Hloise and Abelard (Abelard) **11**:55-6
Letters of the Heroines (Ovid)
  See *Heroides*
Letters to Atticus (Cicero)
  See *Ad Atticum*
Letters to Friends (Cicero)
  See *Ad familiares*
Letters to Lucilius (Seneca)
  See *Epistulae morales*
"Letting the Intellect Go and Experiencing Pure Ignorance" (Eckhart) **9**:24
Li (Confucius)
  See *Li Chi*
Li Chi (Confucius) **19**:11, 20-21, 26-28, 35-36, 38, 40, 46, 69
Libation Bearers (Aeschylus) **11**:85, 87-8, 102, 104-05, 107, 116, 118-19, 131, 138, 140, 151, 153-54, 159, 162-64, 181, 184-85, 191, 193-95, 202, 205-07, 211, 217, 223
Libation-Pourers (Aeschylus)
  See *Libation Bearers*
Libellus de Alchimia (Albert the Great) **16**:65
Liber contemplationis (Llull) **12**:104
Liber de amore Dei contra amatores mundi (Rolle) **21**:275, 391
Liber de ascensu et descensu intellectus (Llull) **12**:107. 111
Liber de lumine (Llull) **12**:110
Liber de retardatione accidentium senectutis (Bacon) **14**:64
Liber de sancta virginitate (Augustine) **6**:38
Liber divinorum Operum (Hildegard von Bingen) **20**:132-33, 135-39, 145, 152-55, 161-63, 174-75, 180
Liber epigrammatum (Bede) **20**:121
Liber Hymnorum (Abelard) **11**:45
Liber mineralium (Albert the Great) **16**:55, 62-4, 97, 100-02
Liber Positionum (Eckhart) **9**:56
Liber praedicationis contra Iudaeos (Llull) **12**:117
Liber principiorum medicinae (Llull) **12**:107
Liber vitae meritorum (Hildegard von Bingen) **20**:132-33, 152-53, 161-62, 175
Liberum arbitrium voluntatis (Augustine)
  See *De libero arbitrio voluntatis*
Libre d'amic e Amat (Llull)
  See *Book of the Lover and the Beloved*
Libre de meravelles (Llull)
  See *Felix*
Libre del orde de cavalleria (Llull) **12**:104, 107
Libri quoestionum epistolicarum (Cato) **21**:22
Life (Josephus)
  See *Vita*
Life of Dante (Boccaccio)
  See *Vita di Dante*
Life of St. Cuthbert (Bede)
  See *Vita sancti Cuthberti*
Liki (Confucius)
  See *Li Chi*
Little Epitome (Epicurus) **21**:75, 154
Lives of the Abbots (Bede)
  See *Historia abbetum*
The Living Flame (Rolle) **21**:312

Le Livre de l'Espurgatorie (Marie de France)
  See *L'Espurgatoire Saint Patrice*
Le Livre de Marco Polo (Polo)
  See *The Travels of Marco Polo the Venetian*
Lock of Berenice (Callimachus) **18**: 15-17, 30, 35, 43, 59, 61, 63-4
Locri (Menander) **9**:203
Logica 'Ingredientibus' (Abelard) **11**:63, 64, 66
Logica 'Nostrorum' (Abelard) **11**:62, 64, 66
Logical Treatises (Albert the Great) **16**:4
"The Lonely Wife" (Li Po) **2**:132
Long Commentary on the Metaphysics (Averroes)
  See *Tafsir ma ba'd al-tabi'ah*
Longer Work (Bacon)
  See *Opus Majus*
Lord's Song
  See *Bhagavadgita*
The Lord's Song
  See *Bhagavad Gita*
Love-Poems (Ovid)
  See *Amores*
"The Lovers of the Benou Udreh" **2**:40
"A Lu Mountain Song for the Palace Censor Empty-Boat Lu" (Li Po) **2**:152, 164
Lun Yu (Confucius) **19**:10-11, 17-23, 26, 28-33, 35-36, 38-42, 48-50, 68-69, 72-76, 78-85, 88-89, 95-101
Lykourgeia (Aeschylus) **11**:192
Lysis (Plato) **8**:254, 264-66, 306, 314
Lysistrata (Aristophanes) **4**:44, 60-2, 65, 68, 88, 93-94, 107-10, 113, 123-26, 133, 142, 144-45, 151, 153-56, 160, 163, 166, 169-75
The Mabinogion
  See *Pedeir Keinc y Mabinogi*
Mad Hercules (Seneca)
  See *Hercules furens*
"The Mad Lover" **2**:40
"The Magic Horse" **2**:49
Magnificat (Rolle) **21**:351
Mahabharata **5**:177-287
The Maid of Andros (Terence)
  See *Andria*
Makura no soshi (Sei Shonagon) **6**:291-96, 299-309, 311-26
Makura Zoshi (Sei Shonagon)
  See *Makura no soshi*
Malavika and Agnimitra (Kalidasa)
  See *Malavikagnimitra*
Malavikagnimitra (Kalidasa) **9**:82, 85, 90, 96-7, 99-102, 126, 128, 131-33, 137-38
"Maldon"
  See "The Battle of Maldon"
The Man from Sikyon (Menander)
  See *Sikyonios*
"The Man of Yemen and His Six Slave Girls" **2**:40
The Man She Hated (Menander)
  See *Misoumenos*
"The Man Who Never Laughed Again" **2**:40
The Man Who Punished Himself (Menander)
  See *Heautontimorumenus*
Manahij (Averroes)
  See *Kitab al-kashf 'an manahij al-adilla fi 'aqa'id al-milla,wa ta'rif ma waqa'a fiha bi-hasb at-ta'wil min ash-shibah al-muzigha wal-bida 'al-mudilla*
Mandeville's Travels (Mandeville) **19**:107-80
Manilian (Cicero)
  See *Pro Lege Manilia*

Marco Polo (Polo)
  See *The Travels of Marco Polo the Venetian*
Marco Polo's Travels (Polo)
  See *The Travels of Marco Polo the Venetian*
Mariale (Albert the Great) **16**:42
Marius (Cicero) **3**:198
Marriage of Arsinoe (Callimachus) **18**: 34
Martyrology (Bede) **20**:61
Masnavi (Rumi)
  See *Mathnawi*
Masters of the Frying Pan (Aristophanes) **4**:167
Mathnavi (Rumi)
  See *Mathnawi*
Mathnawi (Rumi) **20**:338-40, 342, 352-54, 356, 365-67, 371, 373-74, 376-83, 385-88
Medea (Ovid) **7**:312 **7**:286, 297, 336, 346-47, 376, 420, 425, 444-45
Medea (Seneca) **6**:336, 344-45, 363, 366, 371, 373, 377-81, 404-10, 413-18, 426-27, 432-33, 436, 441
Medicamina Faciei (Ovid) **7**:346
Meditacio de passione Christi (Rolle) **21**:307, 357, 368, 374
Meditation B (Rolle) **21**:393
Meditation on the Passion (Rolle)
  See *Meditacio de passione Christi*
Megalopolis (Demosthenes)
  See *For Megalopolis*
Meghaduta (Kalidasa) **9**:89-90, 92, 95, 102, 107, 113, 115, 125-26, 129
Meister Eckhart: The Essential Sermons, Commentaries, Treatises, and Defense (Eckhart) **9**:67
Melos amoris (Rolle) **21**:283, 287-92, 311, 352-56, 369, 381-82, 386, 389-90, 399
Melum contemplativorum (Rolle)
  See *Melos amoris*
Memoirs (Xenophon)
  See *Memorabilia*
Memorabilia (Xenophon) **17**:329, 331, 335, 337, 340, 341, 342, 343, 344, 345, 349, 362, 374, 375
"A Memorial of Self-Introduction Written for Assistant Director of the Censorate Sung" (Li Po) **2**:173-74
Mending of Life (Rolle)
  See *Emendatio vitae*
Menexenus (Plato) **8**:305-07
Meno (Plato) **8**:206, 218, 250, 264, 283-85, 305-07, 311, 320-22, 328, 356-57, 362
Menon (Plato)
  See *Meno*
Metamorphoses (Apuleius) **1**:3, 7-8, 12-13, 15, 17-24, 26-27, 29-37, 39-43, 45
Metamorphoses (Ovid) **7**:286, 291-92, 298-99, 304-05, 314-16, 322, 324-36, 335-44, 346, 349, 357, 361-63, 365, 368-77, 379, 383-93, 395-96, 398-402, 404, 412-18, 430-32, 434-35, 438, 443-46
Metamorphosis (Ovid)
  See *Metamorphoses*
Metaphysics (Avicenna) **16**:159-60, 164
Meteora (Albert the Great)
  See *De meteoris*
Meteororum (Albert the Great)
  See *De meteoris*
Metrodorus (Epicurus) **21**:119
Middle Commentary on Porphyry's Isagoge and on Aristotle's Categoriae (Averroes) **7**:67

Midiana (Demosthenes)
 See *Against Midias*
"Milun" (Marie de France) **8**:121, 128, 131-34, 147-50, 159, 162-66, 170, 175, 182, 187
Mineralia (Albert the Great)
 See *Liber mineralium*
The Minor Epitome (Epicurus)
 See *Little Epitome*
Minos (Plato)
 See *Meno*
Mirror of Future Times (Hildegard von Bingen)
 See *Pentachronon*
Misoumenos (Menander) **9**:258, 260, 269-70, 276, 287
"Misty Yangtze" (Su Shih) **15**:397
"Modern Music in the Yen Ho Palace" (Su Shih) **15**:385
"The Monkey and Her Baby" (Marie de France) **8**:191
"The Monkey King" (Marie de France) **8**:191
Moral Epistles (Seneca)
 See *Epistulae morales*
Morte Arthure "Alliterative" **10**:375-436
The Mother-in-Law (Terence)
 See *Hecyra*
"A Mouse and a Frog" (Marie de France) **8**:174
Movement of Animals (Albert the Great) **5**:
"Moving to Lin-kao Pavilion" (Su Shih) **15**:410
La Mule sans frein (Chretien de Troyes) **10**:178-79, 232
Multiplication of Species (Bacon)
 See *Tractatus de Mulitiplicatione Specierum*
Murasaki Shikibu nikki (Murasaki) **1**:457
Music (Boethius)
 See *In topica Ciceronis*
Music (Confucius)
 See *Yueh*
"The Muslim Champion and the Christian Damsel" **2**:27
"My Trip in a Dream to the Lady of Heaven Mountain" (Li Po) **2**:150
Myrmidons (Aeschylus) **11**:101, 125, 193
Mystère d'Adam
 See *Ordo Representacionis Ade*
Mystery of Adam
 See *Ordo Representacionis Ade*
Mystical Theology (Albert the Great) **16**:29, 119
N. 4 (Pindar)
 See *Nemean 4*
N. 6 (Pindar)
 See *Nemean 6*
N. 7 (Pindar)
 See *Nemean 7*
N. 9 (Pindar)
 See *Nemean 9*
"Nala and Damayanti"
 See *Nalopakhyana*
Nalopakhyana **5**:188, 206
Natural Questions (Seneca)
 See *Naturales quaestiones*
Naturales quaestiones (Seneca) **6**:344, 348-49, 374, 381, 383, 387, 410-11
The Nature of Love (Rolle) **21**:367-69, 374-75
The Nature of Places (Albert the Great)
 See *De natura locorum*
"Nel dolce tempo de la prima etade" (Petrarch) **20**:281-82
Nem. IV (Pindar)
 See *Nemean 4*

Nem. VIII (Pindar)
 See *Nemean 8*
Nemea (Aeschylus) **11**:192
Nemean Odes (Pindar) **12**:353
Nemean 1 (Pindar) **12**:270, 347-48, 364-65, 378
Nemean 2 (Pindar) **12**:313, 359-60, 362, 378
Nemean 3 (Pindar) **12**:264, 268, 322, 357-58, 365, 369-70, 374, 378, 382-84
Nemean 4 (Pindar) **12**:264, 271, 299-301, 303, 321, 330, 353-54, 357-58, 362, 367, 371, 378, 382-83
Nemean V (Pindar)
 See *Nemean 5*
Nemean 5 (Pindar) **12**:267, 269-70, 272, 304, 307, 309, 311, 325, 357-58, 360, 366, 371, 378-80, 382-84
Nemean 6 (Pindar) **12**:267, 269, 271, 273, 302, 304-05, 323, 357-60, 365, 368, 370, 378
Nemean 7 (Pindar) **12**:276, 288, 299-300, 309, 311, 319, 357-59, 361, 365, 367, 376, 378-79, 383
Nemean 8 (Pindar) **12**:263, 269, 288, 309, 311, 323, 326, 357-59, 362, 365, 367, 371, 376, 379, 382-83
Nemean 9 (Pindar) **12**:296, 307, 321, 353, 364-65, 370, 378, 382
Nemean 10 (Pindar) **12**:270, 274, 321, 348, 353, 355, 362, 365, 368-69
Nemean 11 (Pindar) **12**:272, 315-16, 321, 365-67, 378
Nephelai (Aristophanes) **4**:37, 42, 44-5, 50, 53-4, 58-9, 61-7, 87, 89, 98, 100, 102, 105-06, 110-11, 124-26, 130-32, 137, 143-44, 146, 148, 150, 152-53, 159-60, 162-63, 165-66, 168
Nereïds (Aeschylus) **11**:125
Net Drawers (Aeschylus)
 See *Net-Draggers*
Net-Draggers (Aeschylus) **11**:124, 152
New Kalevala
 See *Kalevala*
New Life (Alighieri)
 See *Vita Nuova*
Nibelung Lay
 See *Book of Chaos*
Der Nibelunge Nôt
 See *Book of Chaos*
Nibelungen Lay
 See *Book of Chaos*
Nibelungen Noth
 See *Book of Chaos*
Nibelungen Song
 See *Book of Chaos*
Das Nibelungenlied **12**:136-255
Nibelungen's Need
 See *Book of Chaos*
"The Nightingale" (Marie de France)
 See "Laüstic"
Nine Books of the Subtleties of Different Kinds of Creatures (Hildegard von Bingen)
 See *Subtilitates naturarum diversarum creaturarum*
Ninfale d'Ameto (Boccaccio)
 See *Ameto*
Ninfale fiesolano (Boccaccio) **13**:28, 32, 63
Ninth Nemean (Pindar)
 See *Nemean 9*
Ninth Paean (Pindar)
 See *Paean 9*

Ninth Pythian (Pindar)
 See *Pythian 9*
Niobe (Aeschylus) **11**:167, 193
Niobe (Sophocles) **2**:348
Njála
 See *Njáls saga*
Njáls saga **13**:322-77
"The Nobleman" (Eckhart) **9**:56-7
Nomothetes (Menander) **9**:203
"Non a tanti animali" (Petrarch) **20**:299
"Non fur ma' Giove" (Petrarch) **20**:241
'*Nostrorum*' (Abelard)
 See *Logica 'Nostrorum'*
Notes for Public Speaking (Hermogenes) **6**:158
"Notice of Hall of Thought" (Su Shih) **15**:399, 403
Nourishment (Albert the Great)
 See *De nutrimento et nutribili*
Novelle (Boccaccio) **13**:13, 15-6
Novelliere (Boccaccio) **13**:22
"Nuptuals of Peleus and Thetis" (Catullus)
 See "Poem 64"
"Nur-Ed-Din and Shems-Ed-Din" **2**:42
O. 1 (Pindar)
 See *Olympian 1*
O. 7 (Pindar)
 See *Olympian 7*
O. 8 (Pindar)
 See *Olympian 8*
O. 9 (Pindar)
 See *Olympian 9*
O. 14 (Pindar)
 See *Olympian 14*
Octavia (Seneca) **6**:336, 342-43, 366, 374-75, 379-81, 389
"Ode to a Beloved Woman" (Sappho)
 See "Ode to Anactoria"
"Ode to Anactoria" (Sappho) **3**:380, 386-87, 396, 416, 436
"Ode to Aphrodite" (Sappho) **3**:381, 385-86, 440
"Ode to Vaucluse" (Petrarch) **20**:228
"Ode to Venus" (Sappho)
 See "Ode to Aphrodite"
Odysseis (Homer)
 See *Odyssey*
Odysses (Homer)
 See *Odyssey*
Odyssey (Homer) **1**: 287, 293, 310, 312, 315-17, 319-20, 329, 338, 354, 362-63, 369-72, 375, 379, 388, 396-97, 400, 407-08
Oeconomicus (Xenophon) **17**:323, 326, 345, 374, 375
Oedipous epi Kolonoi (Sophocles) **2**:289, 292, 296, 298, 300-01, 303-05, 312, 314-16, 318-19, 321, 325, 330, 335-36, 338-39, 342, 345-46, 349-52, 362-63, 367-70, 377, 388, 392, 398, 416-19, 421, 425-28
Oedipous Tyrannos (Sophocles) **2**: 288-89, 292, 296, 300, 304-05, 309-10, 312-16, 319-21, 324-24, 337-40, 343-45,347, 349-51, 353, 355-57, 359-62, 369-78, 382, 384, 387, 389-92, 394, 409-10, 415-21, 423-29
Oedipus (Aeschylus) **11**:122, 124, 138, 159-60
Oedipus (Seneca) **6**:343-44, 366, 369, 373, 379-81, 388-89, 413, 415, 417, 420-22, 428, 432
Oedipus (Sophocles)
 See *Oedipous Tyrannos*
Oedipus at Colonos (Sophocles)
 See *Oedipous epi Kolonoi*

Oedipus Coloneus (Sophocles)
See *Oedipous epi Kolonoi*
Oedipus in Colonos (Sophocles)
See *Oedipous epi Kolonoi*
Oedipus Rex (Sophocles)
See *Oedipous Tyrannos*
Oedipus the King (Sophocles)
See *Oedipous Tyrannos*
"Oenone" (Ovid) **7**:311
Oetaeus (Seneca)
See *Hercules oetaeus*
Of Delight in God (Rolle) **21**:343
Of Natural and Moral Philosophy (Apuleius)
1:12-13
Of the Virtues of the Holy Name of Jesus (Rolle)
21:324
Offices (Cicero)
See *De officiis*
Ol. IX (Pindar)
See *Olympian 9*
Ol. XI (Pindar)
See *Olympian 11*
Old Cantankerous (Menander)
See *Dyskolos*
Old Kalevala
See *Kalevala*
"Old Love Is Best" (Sappho) **3**:396
"Olden Airs" (Li Po) **2**:178
Olympian Odes 1 (Pindar)
See *Olympian 1*
Olympian 1 (Pindar) **12**:263, 269, 295, 298-99,
301, 304-05, 307, 309, 319, 322, 334, 349,
354, 363, 367, 371-72, 377-81, 383
Olympian 2 (Pindar) **12**:264, 271, 293, 298, 304,
319, 321, 351, 358, 363, 365, 367, 379, 383
Olympian 3 (Pindar) **12**:266, 312, 319, 353, 363,
368-69, 378, 383-84
Olympian 4 (Pindar) **12**:321, 354, 362-63, 365,
378, 380, 383
Olympian 5 (Pindar) **12**:321, 353, 363, 365, 370,
377-79, 382-83
Olympian 6 (Pindar) **12**:264, 267, 313, 353, 355,
364, 369, 378-84
Olympian VII (Pindar)
See *Olympian 7*
Olympian 7 (Pindar) **12**:264, 267, 296, 298, 308-
09, 313, 320, 348, 353, 362, 369, 372, 374,
378, 380, 382-83
Olympian 8 (Pindar) **12**:269, 289, 302, 326, 357,
359, 365, 369, 378-80, 382-83
Olympian 9 (Pindar) **12**:289, 300, 352, 355, 365-
66, 368, 370, 372, 378, 381-84
Olympian 10 (Pindar) **12**:272, 304, 309, 322,
352-53, 365-67, 378-79
Olympian 11 (Pindar) **12**:264, 344, 352-53, 380
Olympian 12 (Pindar) **12**:309, 343
Olympian 13 (Pindar) **12**:304, 320, 322, 338,
348, 353, 355-56, 362, 378, 380, 383-84
Olympian 14 (Pindar) **12**:294-95, 297, 301, 323,
325, 348, 352, 378, 383
Olynthiac I (Demosthenes) **13**:145, 148-9, 166,
171, 197
Olynthiac II (Demosthenes) **13**:148, 151, 171,
180, 197
Olynthiac III (Demosthenes) **13**:144, 146, 148-9,
151, 165, 171
Olynthiacs (Demosthenes) **13**:138, 143, 149-51,
165, 169, 183, 189
"On a Picture Screen" (Li Po) **2**:136

"On Anactoria" (Sappho)
See "Ode to Anactoria"
On Ancient Medicine (Thucydides) **17**:253
On Anger (Seneca)
De ira
On Animals (Albert the Great)
See De animalibus
On Armaments (Demosthenes) **13**:158
On Charity (Rolle) **21**:300
On Choice and Aversion (Epicurus)
See *On Choice and Avoidance*
On Choice and Avoidance (Epicurus) **21**:73, 75,
124, 165
On Christian Doctrine (Augustine)
See *De doctrina Christiana*
On Clemency (Seneca)
De clementia
On Consolation (Seneca) **6**:344
On Divination (Cicero)
See De divinatione
On Division (Boethius)
See *Divisions*
On Duties (Cicero)
See *De officiis*
"On Eloquence" (Petrarch) **20**:290
On First Principles (Origen)
See *De Principiis*
On Forms (Hermogenes)
See *On Types of Style*
On Free Will (Augustine)
See *De libero arbitrio voluntatis*
On Friendship (Cicero)
See *De amicitia*
On Gentleness (Seneca) **6**:423
On Giving and Receiving Favours (Seneca)
De beneficiis
On Glory (Cicero) **3**:177
On Good Deeds (Seneca) **6**:427
On Grace (Rolle) **21**:299-300
On Grace and Free Will (Augustine)
See De gratia et libero arbitrio
On Halonnesus (Demosthenes) **13**:165
On His Consulship (Cicero)
See *De consulatu suo*
On Holiness (Epicurus) **21**:142
On Household Economy (Xenophon)
See *Oeconomicus*
On Ideas (Hermogenes)
See *On Types of Style*
On Invention (Cicero)
See *De inventione*
On Invention (Hermogenes) **6**:170-72, 185-86,
188, 191, 198-202
On Justice and the Other Virtues (Epicurus)
21:73, 154
On Kingdom (Epicurus) **21**:109
On Laws (Cicero)
See *De legibus*
"On Leisure and Solitude" (Petrarch) **20**:286
On Lives (Epicurus) **21**:73-5, 124, 165
On Love (Epicurus) **21**:73
On Martyrdom (Origen) **19**:187
On Mercy (Seneca)
De clementia
On Method (Hermogenes)
See On the Method of Deinotes
On Misconduct of Ambassadors (Demosthenes)
See *On the Misconduct of the Embassy*
On Music (Epicurus) **21**:73

On Nature (Epicurus) **21**:72-4, 164-65, 168, 170-
71, 201-02, 204
"On Nourishing Life" (Su Shih) **15**:401
On Old Age (Cicero)
See *De senectute*
"On Oracles" (Petrarch) **20**:286
On Order (Augustine)
See *De ordine*
On Orthography (Bede)
See *De orthographia*
On Peace of Mind (Seneca)
See *De tranquillitate animi*
On Physics (Epicurus) **21**:122, 154
On Piety (Epicurus) **21**:154
On Providence (Seneca)
De providentia
On Qualities of Style (Hermogenes)
See *On Types of Style*
On Sleep and Waking (Albert the Great) **16**:16
On Staseis (Hermogenes)
See *On Stases*
On Stases (Hermogenes) **6**:158, 170-74, 185-86,
191, 196, 198-202
"On Study and Learning" (Petrarch) **20**:286-87
"On Taking Leave of Tzu-yu at Ying-chou: Two
Poems" (Su Shih) **15**:411
On the Activity of God (Hildegard von Bingen)
See *Liber divinorum Operum*
On the Affairs in the Chersonese (Demosthenes)
See *On the Chersonese*
"On the Ages of the World" (Bede) **20**:7
On the Best Kind of Orators (Cicero)
See *De optimo genere oratorum*
On the Blessed Life (Cicero)
See *Tusculan Disputations*
On the Categoric Syllogism (Apuleius) **1**:12-13
On the Categorical Syllogism (Boethius) **15**:27
On the Catholic Faith (Boethius)
See *De fide catholica*
*On the Causes and Properties of the Elements
and of the Planets* (Albert the Great)
See *De causis et proprietatibus elementorum
et planetarum*
On the Chersonese (Demosthenes) **13**:138, 146,
148-9, 152, 161, 166, 193, 195
On the Chief Good and Evil (Cicero)
See *De finibus*
On the Christian Struggle (Augustine) **6**:21
On the City of God (Augustine)
See *De civitate Dei*
On the Computation of Time (Bede)
See *De temporum ratione*
On the Criterion (Epicurus)
See *The Canon*
On the Crown (Demosthenes) **13**:139, 143, 145,
147-52, 162, 166, 172-5, 179, 183-4, 189,
191-5, 197
On the Divine Unity and Trinity (Abelard)
See *Theologia 'Summi boni'*
On the End or Telos (Epicurus) **21**:154
On the False Embassy (Demosthenes)
See *On the Misconduct of the Embassy*
On the Figures and Tropes of the Holy Scripture
(Bede)
See *De schematibus et tropis sacrae scripturae*
On the Fraudulent Embassy (Demosthenes)
See *On the Misconduct of the Embassy*
On the Freedom of Rhodes (Demosthenes)
See *For the Rhodians*

On the Goal (Epicurus) **21**:165
On the God of Socrates (Apuleius) **1**:4, 7, 12-13, 23, 32
On the Gods (Epicurus) **21**:73, 154
On the Greatest Degree of Good and Evil (Cicero)
  See *De finibus*
On the Happy Life (Seneca)
  De vita beata
On the Hypothetical Syllogism (Boethius) **15**: 9, 27,
On the Kinds of Life (Epicurus) **21**:141
On the Lacedaemonian Polity (Xenophon)
  See Constitution of Sparta
On the Measurements of Time (Bede)
  See *De temporibus*
On the Method of Deinotes (Hermogenes) **6**:158, 188, 191, 202
On the Method of Force (Hermogenes)
  See *On the Method of Deinotes*
On the Misconduct of the Embassy (Demosthenes) **13**:138, 147-9, 165, 168, 172, 183-4, 189, 194-5
On the Moral End (Epicurus) **21**:118
On the Nature of Gods (Cicero)
  See *De natura deorum*
On the Nature of Good (Augustine) **6**:9
On the Nature of Things (Bede) **20**:44
On the Orator (Cicero)
  See *De oratore*
On the Pattern for Rhetorical Effectiveness (Hermogenes) **6**:170
On the Peace (Demosthenes) **13**:138, 148-9, 159-60, 165
"On the Red Cliff" (Su Shih)
  See "Rhymeprose on the Red Cliff"
On the Reorganization (Demosthenes) **13**:165
"On the Restoration of the Examination System" (Su Shih) **15**:385
On the Resurrection (Origen) **19**:186
On the Rhodians (Demosthenes)
  See *For the Rhodians*
On the Science of Moral Habits (Avicenna) **16**:164
On the Shortness of Life (Seneca)
  De brevitate vitae
On the Soul (Avicenna) **16**:164
On the State (Cicero)
  See De republica
On the Symmories (Demosthenes) **13**:145, 148, 159, 163-4, 171, 197
On the Treaties with Alexander (Demosthenes) **13**:166
On the Trinity (Augustine)
  See *De Trinitate*
On the Trinity (Bòethius)
  See *De trinitate*
"On the twelfth night" (Su Shih) **15**:398
On the Unity of the Intellect: against Averroes (Augustine) **16**:57
On the Universe (Apuleius)
  See *De mundo*
On the Usefulness of Mathematics (Bacon)
  See *De utilitate mathematicae*
On the Vices Contracted in the Study of Theology (Bacon) **14**:92
On Times (Bede)
  See *De temporibus*
On Types of Style (Hermogenes) **6**:158, 170,

185-92, 196, 200-02, 204
On Vision (Epicurus) **21**:73
"On Wisdom" (Petrarch) **20**:286
One the Art of Metre (Bede)
  See *De arte metrica*
Optics (Bacon) **14**:20
Opus imperfectum contra Julianum (Augustine) **6**:149
Opus Maius (Bacon)
  See *Opus Majus*
Opus Majus (Bacon) **14**:3-5, 7-8, 15, 18, 20, 22-23, 29-31, 34-35, 37, 40, 42, 47, 49-50, 53-54, 59, 61-65, 68-70, 73, 76-77, 80, 82, 84, 86, 92-94, 100, 102, 106-15
Opus Minus (Bacon) **14**:15, 18-20, 29, 40, 48, 52, 54, 62-63, 66-68, 80, 100, 102-03
Opus Sermonum (Eckhart) **9**:57
Opus Tertium (Bacon) **14**:15, 19-21, 29-30, 40, 47-48, 52, 54, 58-59, 62-63, 65, 67-68, 80, 83, 86, 100-05, 108
Opus Tripartitum (Eckhart) **9**:55
The Orator (Cicero)
  See *De optimo genere dicendi*
Orator ad M. Brutum (Cicero)
  See *De optimo genere dicendi*
The Orator: To Marcus Brutus (Cicero)
  See *De optimo genere dicendi*
Ordo Representacionis Ade **4**:182-221
Ordo virtutum (Hildegard von Bingen) **20**:153-54, 176
Oresteia (Aeschylus) **11**:77, 100-01, 105-06, 109, 117-19, 123, 128, 130, 132-34, 136-40, 153-56, 158-59, 160, 162-63, 167-68, 180, 184, 190-91, 193-95, 197-99, 206, 209, 211, 217-19, 222-23
Orestes (Aeschylus) **11**:134
Orge (Menander) **9**:244, 248, 250, 284
Origines (Cato) **21**:3, 20-1, 23-4, 26-7, 29, 39, 41, 47, 49, 54-6
Ornithes (Aristophanes) **4**:44-6, 58, 62-7, 87, 93-6. 100. 110, 114, 124-26. 131-33, 135, 142, 144, 146-49, 155, 159-61, 165-66, 168
Our Daily Life (Rolle) **21**:299
Our Daily Work (Rolle) **21**:300-01, 307
P. 1 (Pindar)
  See *Pythian 1*
P. 2 (Pindar)
  See *Pythian 2*
P. 3 (Pindar)
  See *Pythian 3*
P. 4 (Pindar)
  See *Pythian 4*
P. 5 (Pindar)
  See *Pythian 5*
P. 6 (Pindar)
  See *Pythian 6*
P. 8 (Pindar)
  See *Pythian 8*
"Padre del ciel" (Petrarch) **20**:257
Paean for Ceos (Pindar) **12**:318
Paean for the Abderites (Pindar)
  See *Paean 2*
Paean 1 (Pindar) **12**:355
Paean 2 (Pindar) **12**:321, 351, 360-61
Paean 4 (Pindar) **12**:352, 382
Paean 5 (Pindar) **12**:359
Paean 6 (Pindar) **12**:271, 300, 358-59
Paean 8 (Pindar) **12**:
Paean 9 (Pindar) **12**:266, 308-09, 356

Paeans (Pindar) **12**:318, 320-21, 352
"The Palace of the Grotto of Mists" (Sordello) **15**:391
Paraphrase (Caedmon)
  See "Genesis"
Paraphrase of Genesis (Caedmon)
  See "Genesis"
A Parasite's Brain to the Rescue (Terence)
  See *Phormio*
Parisian Questions and Prologues (Eckhart) **9**:69
Parliament of Women (Aristophanes)
  See *Ekklesiazousai*
Parmenides (Plato) **8**:232, 234, 240, 258-60, 264, 282, 293, 306, 310, 317, 320, 328, 333-34, 338, 340-41, 361, 364
Partheneia (Pindar) **12**:320-21, 351, 356
"The Parting" (Li Po) **2**:138
"A Parting Banquet for the Collator Shu-yün at the Hsieh T'iao Lodge in Hsüan-chou" (Li Po) **2**:163
Partiones oratoriae (Cicero) **3**:201, 218, 259-60, 263
Partitiones (Cicero)
  See *Partiones oratoriae*
Parzival (Wolfram von Eschenbach) **5**:293-94, 296-302, 304-05, 307-10, 312, 314-17, 320-23, 325-26, 333-45, 347, 350-54, 357-58, 360, 362, 366, 369-71, 373, 376, 380-83, 385-86, 390-92, 395-96, 400-01, 403-04, 409, 411, 416-17, 419-23, 425, 429-32
"Passing the Huai" (Su Shih) **15**:413
The Pastorals of Daphnis and Chloe (Longus)
  See *Daphnis and Chloe*
Patrologia Graeca (Origen) **19**:231
"The Pavilion of Flying Cranes" (Su Shih) **15**:382
"The Pavilion to Glad Rain" (Su Shih) **15**:382
Peace (Aristophanes)
  See *Eirene*
The Peace (Demosthenes)
  See *On the Peace*
Pearl **19**:275-407
"A Peasant and a Dung-Beetle" (Marie de France) **8**:174
"The Peasant Who Saw His Wife with Her Lover" (Marie de France) **8**:190
Pedeir Keinc y Mabinogi **9**:144-98
"*Peleus and Thetis*" (Catullus)
  See "*Poem 64*"
Penelope (Aeschylus) **11**:124
Pentachronon (Hildegard von Bingen) **20**:163
Perception (Epicurus) **21**:73
Perceval (Chretien de Troyes) **10**:133, 137, 139, 143, 145-46, 150, 157, 159, 161-66, 169, 178-79, 183, 189-90, 195-96, 199, 206-09, 216-20, 223-26, 228-40
Perceval le Gallois (Chretien de Troyes)
  See *Perceval*
Percevax le viel (Chretien de Troyes)
  See *Perceval*
Peri hermeneias (Apuleius) **1**:24
Perikeiromene (Menander) **9**:207, 210-11, 213, 215, 217, 221, 223, 225, 228, 230, 232, 238-39, 246-48, 250-52, 260, 267, 269-71, 276-77, 281, 288
Perr Archon (Origen)
  See *De Principiis*
Persae (Aeschylus)

Title Index

See *Persians*

Persians (Aeschylus) **11**:77, 85, 88, 96, 102, 112-13, 117-18, 121, 127, 133-35, 139, 151-53, 156, 158-60, 179, 181-84, 191, 193-95, 198, 200, 202-03, 205, 211, 215-20

Perspective (Bacon)
See *De Scientia Perspectiva*

Phaedo (Plato) **8**:204-07, 209, 233, 235-36, 239, 261, 268, 305-07, 312, 320, 322-25, 328, 331, 340-41, 358, 361-62

Phaedra (Seneca) **6**:341, 366, 368-70, 377, 379-81, 389, 403-06, 413-16, 418, 424-26, 432, 448

Phaedrus (Plato) **8**:205, 210, 220, 230, 232-33, 241, 244, 254-55, 259, 262, 264-66, 270, 275, 283, 299, 306-07, 317, 322-25, 331, 334, 355, 359, 362, 364

Philebus (Plato) **8**:248, 260, 264-68, 270, 306, 310, 333, 341, 361, 363-64

Philippic I (Demosthenes) **13**:137, 148-9, 152, 165, 171, 183, 190-2, 195, 197

Philippic II (Demosthenes) **13**:138, 148-9, 151, 160, 165, 172

Philippic III (Demosthenes) **13**:138, 143-5, 148, 161, 166, 172, 177, 180, 192-3, 195

Philippic IV (Demosthenes) **13**:162, 166

Philippics (Cicero) **3**:192-93, 196, 198-99, 229-30, 253, 268, 271-73

Philippics (Demosthenes) **13**:139, 142-3, 149-52, 158, 161-2, 172, 174, 180, 183, 189

Philoctetes (Aeschylus) **11**:125, 140

Philoctetes at Troy (Sophocles) **2**:341

Philoktetes (Sophocles) **2**:289, 294-95, 302-05, 314, 316, 318, 320, 325, 338, 341, 346, 352-54, 357, 367-68, 377, 385-87, 397-408, 415-16, 419, 426

Philomena (Chretien de Troyes) **10**:137

Philosopher (Plato) **8**:259

Phineus (Aeschylus) **11**:159, 174

The Phoenician Women (Seneca)
See *Phoenissae*

Phoenissae (Seneca) **6**:363, 366, 379-80, 402, 413, 421, 432, 437

"Phoenix Song" (Li Po) **2**:152

Phormio (Terence) **14**:303, 306-07, 311, 313-18, 320, 333, 335, 340, 341, 347-49, 352-53, 356-57, 364, 376-80, 383-85, 389-90

Phychostasia (Aeschylus)
See *Weighing of Souls*

"Phyllis" (Ovid) **7**:311

Physica (Albert the Great) **16**:4, 36, 61

Physica (Hildegard von Bingen) **20**:154

Physicorum (Albert the Great) **16**:

Physics (Albert the Great)
See *Physica*

The Pillow Book of Sei Shonagon (Sei Shonagon)
See *Makura no soshi*

Pillow Sketches (Sei Shonagon)
See *Makura no soshi*

Pinakes (Callimachus) **18**: 38, 45-8, 62-4, 68-70

"Pine Wine of the Middle Mountains" (Su Shih) **15**:382

"The Pious Black Slave" **2**:40

Planctus (Abelard) **11**:55, 68

"Planher vuelh en Blacatz" (Sordello) **15**:332, 337, 343, 365, 375, 377

Plants (Albert the Great)
See *De vegetabilibus*

Ploutos (Aristophanes) **4**:44, 46, 62, 67, 76, 90,

94, 111, 115, 124-26, 147-48, 153, 161, 165-68, 174-75, 177-80

"The Plunder of the Home of Salur-Kazan" **8**:97, 103, 109

Plutus (Aristophanes)
See *Ploutos*

"*Poem 1*" (Catullus) **18**: 104, 108, 110-11, 117, 122-23, 130-32, 150, 167-78, 185-93

"*Poem 2*" (Catullus) **18**: 116, 161, 178, 187-93, 196

"*Poem 3*" (Catullus) **18**: 166, 174, 178, 187-88

"*Poem 4*" (Catullus) **18**: 108, 117, 167, 180, 187-88

"*Poem 5*" (Catullus) **18**: 102, 137-38, 141, 159, 166, 179, 186, 188, 196-97

"*Poem 6*" (Catullus) **18**: 99, 106, 122, 125-27, 129-30, 133, 138, 188, 195-96

"*Poem 7*" (Catullus) **18**: 102, 108, 118, 137-38, 140, 150, 160-61, 166, 181, 186, 188, 196-97

"*Poem 8*" (Catullus) **18**: 138, 153, 160-61, 166, 188, 192

"*Poem 9*" (Catullus) **18**: 121, 128, 186, 188

"*Poem 10*" (Catullus) **18**: 99, 107, 122-26, 129-30, 188

"*Poem 11*" (Catullus) **18**: 99, 116, 119, 126, 133, 162, 166-67, 179, 181-82, 185, 187-88, 192, 194

"*Poem 12*" (Catullus) **18**: 122, 181, 188

"*Poem 13*" (Catullus) **18**: 102, 109, 127, 180, 186

"*Poem 14*" (Catullus) **18**: 99-101, 166, 186, 188

"*Poem 14b*" (Catullus) **18**: 122, 193

"*Poem 15*" (Catullus) **18**: 119, 133-34, 188-90, 193-95, 197

"*Poem 16*" (Catullus) **18**: 119, 132, 134, 137, 167, 186, 188-90, 193-97

"*Poem 17*" (Catullus) **18**: 122, 129-30, 181

"*Poem 18*" (Catullus) **18**:127 **18**:127

"*Poem 18*" (Filderman) **18**: 127

"*Poem 21*" (Catullus) **18**: 119, 134, 181, 188

"*Poem 22*" (Catullus) **18**: 100-01, 145

"*Poem 23*" (Catullus) **18**: 99, 119, 133-34, 181, 188

"*Poem 24*" (Catullus) **18**: 99, 132, 134, 188

"*Poem 25*" (Catullus) **18**: 132-33, 166

"*Poem 26*" (Catullus) **18**: 99, 119, 134, 188

"*Poem 28*" (Catullus) **18**: 99, 121, 132, 188

"*Poem 29*" (Catullus) **18**: 99, 118, 144, 166, 181, 187-88

"*Poem 30*" (Catullus) **18**: 99, 125, 169, 171

"*Poem 31*" (Catullus) **18**: 103, 117, 146, 166-67, 186-88

"*Poem 32*" (Catullus) **18**: 115, 122-23, 130, 133, 137-38, 146, 181

"*Poem 33*" (Catullus) **18**: 122, 132-33, 146

"*Poem 34*" (Catullus) **18**: 110-11, 166-67, 176, 181-82

"*Poem 35*" (Catullus) **18**: 93, 99-102, 122, 128, 130, 147, 167, 186

"*Poem 36*" (Catullus) **18**: 100-01, 121, 127, 145, 167, 186

"*Poem 37*" (Catullus) **18**: 118-20, 133

"*Poem 38*" (Catullus) **18**: 99, 181

"*Poem 39*" (Catullus) **18**: 106, 118-19, 131, 133

"*Poem 41*" (Catullus) **18**: 122, 129-30, 146

"*Poem 42*" (Catullus) **18**: 131, 187

"*Poem 43*" (Catullus) **18**: 118, 122-23, 130, 177, 188

"*Poem 44*" (Catullus) **18**: 166

"*Poem 45*" (Catullus) **18**: 122, 126, 130, 166, 181, 188

"*Poem 46*" (Catullus) **18**: 132, 177, 181, 187-88

"*Poem 47*" (Catullus) **18**: 99, 121, 181

"*Poem 48*" (Catullus) **18**: 132, 137-38, 181, 186, 188

"*Poem 49*" (Catullus) **18**: 145, 167, 179, 182

"*Poem 50*" (Catullus) **18**: 99-101, 103, 109, 139, 188-89, 192-93

"*Poem 51*" (Catullus) **18**: 111, 115, 143, 146, 169, 176, 179, 182, 186, 188

"*Poem 52*" (Catullus) **18**: 118, 121, 188

"*Poem 53*" (Catullus) **18**: 139, 188

"*Poem 54*" (Catullus) **18**: 122, 144, 167, 186

"*Poem 55*" (Catullus) **18**: 99, 122, 127, 130, 166, 186, 188

"*Poem 56*" (Catullus) **18**: 99, 109, 130-32, 134, 188

"*Poem 57*" (Catullus) **18**: 132, 144, 188

"*Poem 58*" (Catullus) **18**: 118-19, 133, 179, 182

"*Poem 58b*" (Catullus) **18**: 99, 122, 186

"*Poem 59*" (Catullus) **18**: 99, 130

"*Poem 60*" (Catullus) **18**: 104, 110-11, 117, 123, 130-32, 150, 171, 185-89

"*Poem 61*" (Catullus) **18**: 110-11, 114, 117, 123, 145, 166, 168, 182, 185, 188

"*Poem 62*" (Catullus) **18**: 111, 117, 123, 142, 167-68, 182

"*Poem 63*" (Catullus) **18**: 78, 80, 105, 107-08, 111, 115-17, 123, 135-36, 145, 166, 168, 170, 172, 174, 182-83, 185

"*Poem 64*" (Catullus) **18**: 77-78, 99-101, 104-05, 107-08, 110-11, 113-14, 117, 136, 143, 155, 167-69, 174-75, 177, 183, 189

"*Poem 65*" (Catullus) **18**: 86, 88, 90, 100-01, 110-11, 115-16, 123, 166, 176, 184

"*Poem 66*" (Catullus) **18**: 78, 80, 88-90, 108, 111, 115-16, 123, 166, 176

"*Poem 67*" (Catullus) **18**: 88, 90, 111, 123, 1399, 184

"*Poem 68*" (Catullus) **18**: 74, 84, 86-88, 90, 100-02, 104, 110-11, 113-14, 116, 145, 149, 155, 162, 166-69, 171-72, 175-77, 179-80, 182-85

"*Poem 68a*" (Catullus) **18**: 169

"*Poem 69*" (Catullus) **18**: 78, 104, 117-18, 122, 130, 132, 138, 150, 186-88

"*Poem 70*" (Catullus) **18**: 118, 155, 157, 171, 180

"*Poem 71*" (Catullus) **18**: 118, 122, 132-33, 188-89

"*Poem 72*" (Catullus) **18**: 115, 118, 156-57, 180, 189

"*Poem 74*" (Catullus) **18**: 122-23, 132

"*Poem 75*" (Catullus) **18**: 87, 152, 154, 157

"*Poem 76*" (Catullus) **18**: 86-87, 138-39, 153-56, 158, 161, 171, 175, 177, 180, 183, 189

"*Poem 77*" (Catullus) **18**: 118, 188

"*Poem 78*" (Catullus) **18**: 110, 122, 131-32

"*Poem 79*" (Catullus) **18**: 147

"*Poem 80*" (Catullus) **18**: 133, 185

"*Poem 81*" (Catullus) **18**: 132

"*Poem 82*" (Catullus) **18**: 132

"*Poem 84*" (Catullus) **18**: 81, 117, 139, 185, 188

"*Poem 85*" (Catullus) **18**: 87, 116, 129, 152, 171, 186

"*Poem 86*" (Catullus) **18**: 118, 122-23, 130

"*Poem 87*" (Catullus) **18**: 156-59, 161

"*Poem 88*" (Catullus) **18**: 122, 132, 182

"Poem 89" (Catullus) 18: 132
"Poem 90" (Catullus) 18: 122, 132
"Poem 91" (Catullus) 18: 118, 122-23, 132
"Poem 92" (Catullus) 18: 186
"Poem 93" (Catullus) 18: 185
"Poem 94" (Catullus) 18: 122
"Poem 95" (Catullus) 18: 99-101, 145, 167, 176, 188-89
"Poem 96" (Catullus) 18: 146, 186, 188
"Poem 97" (Catullus) 18: 116, 122, 131-34
"Poem 99" (Catullus) 18: 102, 138
"Poem 100" (Catullus) 18: 118, 122, 132-33, 186
"Poem 101" (Catullus) 18: 146, 185-86, 189
"Poem 102" (Catullus) 18: 186
"Poem 103" (Catullus) 18: 123
"Poem 104" (Catullus) 18: 184
"Poem 106" (Catullus) 18: 133
"Poem 107" (Catullus) 18: 186
"Poem 109" (Catullus) 18: 149, 180, 186
"Poem 110" (Catullus) 18: 123, 131
"Poem 111" (Catullus) 18: 123, 132
"Poem 113" (Catullus) 18: 123, 131, 187-88
"Poem 116" (Catullus) 18: 100-01, 104, 117, 130, 132, 138, 150, 186-87
Poema de mio Cid 4:222-341
"Poignant Grief During a Sunny Spring" (Li Po) 2:132
Politicus (Plato)
   See *Politikos*
Politikos (Plato) 8:249, 258-60, 282, 306, 310, 333-34, 349, 359, 361
Polydectes (Aeschylus) 11:124-25, 193
Pontius Glaucus (Cicero) 3:198
"The Porter and the Ladies" 2:47
Possessed Woman (Menander) 9:211
Posteritati (Boccaccio) 13:66
"Posteritati" (Petrarch) 20:326
"Postscript to the Calligraphy of the Six T'ang Masters" (Su Shih) 15:421
"Postscript to the Paintings of P'u Yung-sheng" (Su Shih) 15:420
Practical Oratory (Hermogenes) 6:204
"The Pregnant Hound" (Marie de France) 8:190
Priestess (Menander) 9:214
"Prince Ahmed and the Fairy Pari Banou" 2:36, 49
Principal Doctrines (Epicurus) 21:73, 154, 161, 164-65, 167, 175, 184, 187-88, 205
Principles of Music (Boethius)
   See *In topica Ciceronis*
Pro Archia (Cicero)
   See *Archias*
Pro Balbo (Cicero) 3:271
Pro Caecina (Cicero) 3:214
Pro Caelio (Cicero) 3:176, 197-99, 269-70
Pro Cluentio (Cicero) 3:197-99, 214, 267-68
Pro Lege Manilia (Cicero) 3:198-99
Pro Ligario (Cicero) 3:272
Pro Marcello (Cicero) 3:198-99, 271-72
Pro Milone (Cicero) 3:198-99, 270-71
Pro Murena (Cicero) 3:198, 203
Pro Plancio (Cicero) 3:198
Pro Quinctio (Cicero) 3:264
Pro Roscio Amerino (Cicero) 3:198, 265-66
Pro Roscio comoedo (Cicero) 3:265
Pro se de magia liber (Apuleius)
   See *Apologia sive oratoria de magia*
Pro Sestio (Cicero) 3:198, 269, 298

Problems (Epicurus) 21:73-4, 188
Processional Hymns (Pindar)
   See *Prosodia*
Los progres e avansaments dei Res d'Aragon (Sordello) 15:330, 338, 344
The Progress and Power of the Kings of Arragon (Sordello)
   See *Los progres e avansaments dei Res d'Aragon*
Progymnasmata (Hermogenes) 6:162, 170, 185, 191, 198, 202
Prometheia (Aeschylus)
   See *Prometheus Bound*
Prometheus Bound (Aeschylus) 11:88, 98-9, 101-02, 105-06, 109-10, 113, 118-19, 123, 128-29, 135-37, 140, 143, 148, 151-55, 157, 166-67, 175, 179, 181, 183, 193-95, 197, 200, 208-09, 217, 219
Prometheus Delivered (Aeschylus)
   See *Prometheus Unbound*
Prometheus the Fire Bringer (Aeschylus)
   See *Prometheus the Firebearer*
Prometheus the Firebearer (Aeschylus) 11:88, 159, 179
Prometheus the Firekindler (Aeschylus) 11:167, 175
Prometheus Unbound (Aeschylus) 11:88, 90, 106, 123, 136, 175, 179
Prometheus Vinctus (Aeschylus)
   See *Prometheus Bound*
Properties of the Elements (Albert the Great)
   See *De causis et proprietatibus elementorum et planetarum*
Prose Treatises (Rolle) 21:278
Prosecution of Aristocrates (Demosthenes)
   See *Against Aristocrates*
Prosodia (Pindar) 12:320-21
Proteus (Aeschylus) 11:162
Protogoras (Plato) 8:219, 232, 247-48, 253-54, 266-68, 283-84, 305-07, 310, 347
Proto-Kalevala
   See *Kalevala*
Psalm Book
   See *Tehillim*
Psalm 1 4:387, 390, 402, 417, 427, 434, 442, 450
Psalm 2 4:355, 357, 364-65, 368, 384, 447, 450
Psalm 3 4:359, 379, 386, 389, 432-33, 439, 446, 448
Psalm 4 4:364, 390, 426, 438, 448
Psalm 5 4:359, 383, 389, 390, 406, 438, 448
Psalm 6 4:359, 370, 373, 387, 390, 418, 432-33, 438, 448
Psalm 7 4:359, 426, 446, 448
Psalm 8 4:357, 361, 368, 373, 385, 390, 395-96, 398, 419, 434, 439, 441, 448, 453
Psalm 9 4:359, 364, 405, 432, 440, 450
Psalm 10 4:359, 364, 379, 450
Psalm 11 4:59, 364, 366, 389, 448
Psalm 12 4:426, 453, 455
Psalm 13 4:359, 432, 434, 448
Psalm 14 4:359, 364, 370, 378-79, 416, 426, 434
Psalm 15 4:357, 367-68, 377, 383, 450
Psalm 16 4:364, 368, 379, 434
Psalm 17 4:359, 364, 387, 391, 426, 448
Psalm 18 4:359, 364, 372, 382, 384, 388-89, 406, 443, 445-47, 449, 454
Psalm 19 4:345, 354, 359, 368, 380, 384, 388, 395, 397, 426, 441-42, 450

Psalm 20 4:345, 357, 365, 368, 373, 384, 388
Psalm 21 4:357, 359, 368, 384, 440
Psalm 22 4:359, 364-66, 368, 373, 382-83, 386-87, 389-90, 392, 419, 427, 434, 448, 450-51
Psalm 23 4:356, 377, 386, 389, 392, 417, 427, 434, 448
Psalm 24 4:345, 357, 373, 375, 378, 380, 383, 406-07, 450
Psalm 25 4:359, 390, 394, 402, 432, 449
Psalm 26 4:359, 364, 376, 378, 382, 387, 391, 406, 426, 448
Psalm 27 4:359, 373, 376, 378, 382, 389-90, 404-06, 432, 434, 441, 448
Psalm 28 4:359, 373, 383, 385, 407, 440
Psalm 29 4:345, 357, 368, 379-80, 384, 395, 401, 434, 439, 441
Psalm 30 4:359, 377, 394, 434, 455
Psalm 31 4:365, 402, 431-33
Psalm 32 4:359, 387, 390, 433-34
Psalm 33 4:359, 371, 381, 427, 434, 440-41, 446, 449
Psalm 34 4:346, 359, 381, 388, 426, 434, 449
Psalm 35 4:350, 359, 378, 382, 434
Psalm 36 4:359, 368, 427
Psalm 37 4:346, 359, 370, 382, 387, 402, 434
Psalm 38 4:383, 390, 392, 433, 448
Psalm 39 4:359, 433, 455
Psalm 40 4:381-82, 386, 389, 393, 433-34, 440, 449-50
Psalm 41 4:350, 359, 368, 439
Psalm 42 4:347, 368, 377-78, 380, 383, 386, 405, 407, 432, 451
Psalm 43 4:368, 377-78, 405, 440
Psalm 44 4:359, 381, 385, 387, 394, 413, 432
Psalm 45 4:357, 365, 368, 384, 440, 443, 450
Psalm 46 4:354, 385, 401
Psalm 47 4:345, 357, 381, 389, 405, 434, 438, 440
Psalm 48 4:357, 389, 407-08, 453
Psalm 49 4:359, 370, 434, 442
Psalm 50 4:357, 362, 364, 370, 384, 387, 395, 405, 434, 440
Psalm 51 4:364, 373, 375, 383, 385, 387, 406-07, 426-28, 431-32, 434, 446
Psalm 52 4:359, 446
Psalm 53 4:389
Psalm 54 4:446, 448, 450
Psalm 55 4:350, 448
Psalm 56 4:446, 450
Psalm 57 4:372, 405, 433, 441, 446, 448-49
Psalm 59 4:359, 446, 450
Psalm 60 4:359, 368, 381, 387, 446, 449
Psalm 61 4:357, 359, 368, 385, 442
Psalm 62 4:354, 359, 401
Psalm 63 4:359, 368, 378, 385, 405-06
Psalm 64 4:359
Psalm 65 4:359, 405, 407, 434
Psalm 66 4:359, 381-82, 387, 389, 406, 413, 434, 441, 450
Psalm 67 4:357
Psalm 68 4:357, 369, 372-73, 377, 395, 404, 406-08, 440-42, 450, 453
Psalm 69 4:351, 359, 365, 382, 386, 394, 427, 432-33, 441, 448, 450
Psalm 70 4:433, 449
Psalm 71 4:359
Psalm 72 4:345, 365, 373, 384, 421, 439
Psalm 73 4:347, 362, 364, 387, 389, 434
Psalm 74 4:381, 385, 432

Title Index

Psalm 76 **4**:357, 362, 400-01
Psalm 77 **4**:354, 440
Psalm 78 **4**:362, 369, 393, 442, 447
Psalm 79 **4**:381, 385, 432, 434
Psalm 80 **4**:369, 381, 385
Psalm 81 **4**:395, 401, 405, 407, 434, 438, 440, 442
Psalm 82 **4**:370, 385
Psalm 83 **4**:385
Psalm 84 **4**:368, 378, 385, 405-06
Psalm 85 **4**:359, 385, 387, 450
Psalm 86 **4**:359, 389, 406, 434, 440
Psalm 87 **4**:357, 368, 373, 408
Psalm 88 **4**:359, 382-83, 386, 432-34, 437, 440, 443, 454
Psalm 89 **4**:368, 381, 384-85, 401, 447
Psalm 90 **4**:356, 368, 374, 377, 389, 411, 434, 440
Psalm 91 **4**:359, 368, 377, 434, 452
Psalm 92 **4**:377, 379
Psalm 93 **4**:353, 369, 409, 434, 450
Psalm 94 **4**:353, 359, 378-79, 381, 386, 391, 451
Psalm 95 **4**:380, 440, 442, 446
Psalm 96 **4**:357, 381, 389, 421, 434, 445, 449
Psalm 97 **4**:353, 387, 405, 434, 454
Psalm 98 **4**:381, 441
Psalm 99 **4**:357, 441
Psalm 100 **4**:380-81, 383, 434, 442
Psalm 101 **4**:357, 384
Psalm 102 **4**:373-74, 382, 440, 448, 450
Psalm 103 **4**:359, 364, 368, 377-78, 381, 385, 387, 390, 427, 434, 449
Psalm 104 **4**:368, 379, 381, 385, 387, 393, 395, 398, 414-16, 434, 441
Psalm 105 **4**:345, 353, 369, 381, 385, 401, 442, 445, 449
Psalm 106 **4**:345, 369, 383, 390, 401, 439, 445, 449
Psalm 107 **4**:345, 377, 383, 450, 453
Psalm 108 **4**:368, 449-50
Psalm 109 **4**:359, 386, 391, 434
Psalm 110 **4**:357, 365-66, 368, 384
Psalm 111 **4**:357, 449
Psalm 112 **4**:434, 449
Psalm 113 **4**:357, 369, 382, 434, 441
Psalm 114 **4**:345, 353, 357, 368, 427, 434
Psalm 115 **4**:359, 443, 449
Psalm 116 **4**:359, 382, 390, 408
Psalm 117 **4**:434
Psalm 118 **4**:345, 347, 359, 369, 377, 383, 406-08, 413, 439, 442, 450
Psalm 119 **4**:359, 367, 376, 390, 393-94, 428, 434, 442, 449-50
Psalm 120 **4**:350, 357, 368, 450, 455
Psalm 121 **4**:368, 373, 387, 418, 452
Psalm 122 **4**:345, 375, 395, 439, 447
Psalm 123 **4**:386
Psalm 124 **4**:434
Psalm 125 **4**:395
Psalm 126 **4**:345, 358, 379, 385, 387
Psalm 127 **4**:357, 373
Psalm 128 **4**:387
Psalm 129 **4**:353, 357, 382
Psalm 130 **4**:386, 434, 440
Psalm 131 **4**:359, 386, 434
Psalm 132 **4**:359, 368, 373, 384, 386, 406, 447
Psalm 133 **4**:356, 392, 428, 434
Psalm 134 **4**:368, 378, 380, 407, 450
Psalm 135 **4**:434, 439, 449-50

Psalm 136 **4**:352, 368, 383
Psalm 137 **4**:358, 393-94, 418, 422, 434, 446
Psalm 138 **4**:359, 382, 450
Psalm 139 **4**:359, 364, 366, 378-79, 393, 411, 437
Psalm 140 **4**:359
Psalm 142 **4**:359, 446
Psalm 143 **4**:434, 455
Psalm 144 **4**:374, 377, 384, 443, 447, 449
Psalm 145 **4**:359, 434, 449
Psalm 146 **4**:369, 391, 434
Psalm 147 **4**:391, 397, 434
Psalm 148 **4**:398, 434, 441
Psalm 149 **4**:372, 385, 391, 434, 440
Psalm 150 **4**:357, 369, 405, 421, 434, 438, 441, 443, 450
Psalms
  See *Tehillim*
"Psalms of David"
  See *Tehillim*
Psalter
  See *Tehillim*
Psophodes (Menander) **9**:203
Psychology (Avicenna) **16**:166-68
Purgatorio (Petrarch) **20**:216
Purgatory (Marie de France)
  See *L'Espurgatoire Saint Patrice*
The Purgatory of St. Patrick (Marie de France)
  See *L'Espurgatoire Saint Patrice*
The Purpose of Life (Epicurus) **21**:72-3, 75
Pyth. III (Pindar)
  See *Pythian 3*
Pyth. X (Pindar)
  See *Pythian 10*
Pyth XI (Pindar)
  See *Pythian 11*
Pythian Odes 10 (Pindar)
  See *Pythian 10*
Pythian 1 (Pindar) **12**:260, 267, 273, 295-96, 298-99, 304-05, 309, 319, 323, 335, 338, 347, 349, 354, 356-57, 359, 361, 364, 366-67, 376, 378-80, 382-84
Pythian 2 (Pindar) **12**:269, 274, 298, 302, 306-07, 317, 319, 352, 355, 360, 364, 366, 378-81, 383-84
Pythian 3 (Pindar) **12**:264, 270, 278, 298-99, 306, 313, 340, 346, 354, 364-65, 367, 369, 376, 378-80, 382-83
Pythian 4 (Pindar) **12**:272, 296, 298-99, 304-05, 312, 320-22, 326, 343, 354, 375-79, 382
Pythian 5 (Pindar) **12**:271, 296-97, 307, 317, 320, 353, 357, 376-80, 382
Pythian 6 (Pindar) **12**:267, 273, 296, 319, 337, 353-54, 363-64, 377, 379
Pythian 7 (Pindar) **12**:317, 325, 353, 359, 361-62, 383
Pythian 8 (Pindar) **12**:272, 288, 297, 300, 304, 309, 314, 320, 323, 326, 337-38, 349, 356, 359-60, 362, 365, 378-80, 382-84
Pythian 9 (Pindar) **12**:264, 283, 313, 320, 322, 356, 366, 368-69, 372
Pythian 10 (Pindar) **12**:263, 270, 303, 312-13, 318, 322, 325, 334, 337, 343, 357, 365-66, 371, 377-79, 383-84
Pythian 11 (Pindar) **12**:263, 270, 274, 322, 326, 347, 352-53, 356, 365-66, 379, 382, 384
Pythian 12 (Pindar
Pythian XII (Pindar)
  See *Pythian 12* **12**:271, 319, 353, 363, 367

Quaestiones evangeliorum (Augustine) **6**:68, 94
Quaestiones Naturales (Seneca)
  See *Naturales quaestiones*
Quaestiones super libros i-vi Physicorum Aristotelis (Bacon) **14**:49, 66
"Quatre Dols" (Marie de France)
  See *"Le Chaitivel"*
Queen Arsinoe (Callimachus) **18**: 5-6
"Quel c'ha nostra natura in se piu degno" (Petrarch) **20**:333
Questions on Aristotle (Bacon)
  See *Quaestiones super libros i-vi Physicorum Aristotelis*
Questions on Aristotle's Physics (Bacon)
  See *Quaestiones super libros i-vi Physicorum Aristotelis*
Raghuvamsa (Kalidasa) **9**:82, 84-5, 89-91, 102, 115, 118-19, 121, 125-26, 138
"Raising a Cup of Wine to Query the Moon" (Li Po) **2**:166
"The Rajah's Diamond" **2**:36
Ransom of Hector (Aeschylus) **11**:125, 193
The Rape of the Locks (Menander)
  See *Perikeiromene*
Razón de amor **16**:336-376
Razón de amor con los denuestos del agua y el vino
  See *Razón de amor*
Rbaiyyat (Khayyam)
  See *Rubáiyát*
"Ready for a Drink" (Li Po) **2**:166
Record of Rites (Confucius)
  See *Li Chi*
Records of Ancient Matters
  See *Kojiki*
"The Red Cliff" (Su Shih)
  See *"Rhymeprose on the Red Cliff"*
Rede der Unterscheidungen (Eckhart) **9**:35, 42
Religion (Epicurus) **21**:73
Remedia Amoris (Ovid) **7**:344-46, 353, 377, 379, 398, 429, 440, 444
Remedia studii (Bacon) **14**:62
Remedies of Love (Ovid)
  See *Remedia Amoris*
The Republic (Cicero)
  See *De republica*
Republic (Plato) **8**:206, 211, 217, 219, 223, 225-28, 232-33, 236, 239, 241, 243-44, 246, 248-50, 252-53, 255, 259-61, 263-68, 270, 276-83, 285, 287, 290-92, 294, 299, 305-06, 308-11, 313, 317, 322, 324-25, 328-29, 331, 339-48, 352, 357-58, 363-64
Rerum memorandarum libri (Petrarch) **20**:256, 286-87, 290
Rerum vulgarium fragmenta (Petrarch)
  See *Canzoniere*
Retractiones (Augustine) **6**:9, 32, 116
Revelation concerning Purgatory (Rolle) **21**:299
Reysen und Wenderschafften duch des Gelobte Land (Mandeville)
  See *Mandeville's Travels*
"Rhapsody of Remorse" (Li Po) **2**:169
Rhetoric (Epicurus) **21**:119
Rhetorica (Cicero)
  See *De inventione*
"Rhymeprose on the Red Cliff" (Su Shih) **15**:382, 385, 398, 419, 421-24
Rime (Petrarch)
  See *Canzoniere*

Rime disperse (Petrarch) **20**:327, 333-34
Rime in vitae e morte Madonna Laura (Petrarch)
    20:214, 217, 249
Rime sparse (Petrarch)
    See *Canzoniere*
Risalat al-Adwiyyah (Avicenna) **16**:147
Rituals (Confucius)
    See *Li Chi*
Rivals (Plato) **8**:305, 311
"Rock of Yen-yu" (Su Shih) **15**:387
Roman
    See *Le Roman de la Rose*
The Roman Calendar (Ovid)
    See *Fasti*
Le Roman de la Rose **8**:374-453
The Romance
    See *Le Roman de la Rose*
The Romance of the Rose
    See *Le Roman de la Rose*
Romanz de la Rose
    See *Le Roman de la Rose*
Rood
    See *The Dream of the Rood*
Rosciana (Cicero)
    See *Pro Roscio Amerino*
Rose
    See *Le Roman de la Rose*
"Rose in Bloom" **2**:23
Rtusamhara (Kalidasa) **9**:89-90, 103-05, 107
Ruba'iyat (Khayyam)
    See *Rubáiyát*
Rubáiyát (Khayyam) **11**:228-309
Ruba'iyat (Rumi) **20**:352-53, 371
*Rycharde Rolle Rolle Hermyte of Hampull in his
    contemplacyons of the drede and loue of god*
    (Rolle) **21**:278
Sacred Treatises (Boethius)
    See *Theological Tractates*
"Saif El-Mulûk" **2**:43
Sakuntala (Kalidasa)
    See *Abhijñana-sakuntala*
"A Salutation of Jesus" (Rolle) **21**:367, 372
Samia (Menander) **9**:205-06, 211, 213, 215, 217,
    220-21, 224, 238, 246, 249, 252-53, 255, 257-
    61, 264, 269-72, 275-78, 281, 287-88
The Samian Woman (Menander)
    See *Samia*
"Satire Against Three Disinherited Lords"
    (Sordello) **15**:276
Satires (Juvenal) **8**:7, 14, 19, 22, 27-8, 59-60, 66,
    68-9, 73-8
"Saying Farewell to the Children at Nanling as I
    Leave for the Capital" (Li Po) **2**:174
"The Scavenger and the Noble Lady" **2**:40
Schionatulander (Wolfram von Eschenbach)
    See *Titurel*
Scipio's Dream (Cicero)
    See *Somnium Scipionis*
Scite Teipsum (Abelard)
    See *Scito Te Ipsum*
Scito Te Ipsum (Abelard) **11**:5, 10, 12, 16, 20,
    24, 49, 51, 53, 54, 57, 68
Scivias (Hildegard von Bingen) **20**:132-33, 135-
    37, 143, 153, 161-63, 168, 172-75, 178, 182-
    86
Scripta Super Sententias (Albert the Great)
    See *Commentary on the Book of the Sentences*
Scriptum Principale (Bacon) **14**:15
The Seasons (Kalidasa)

    See *Rtusamhara*
Second Alcibiades (Plato)
    See *Alcibiades II*
Second Olympian (Pindar)
    See *Olympian 2*
Second Olynthiac (Demosthenes)
    See *Olynthiac II*
Second Philippic (Cicero)
    See *Philippics*
Second Philippic (Demosthenes)
    See *Philippic II*
Second Pythian (Pindar)
    See *Pythian 2*
Secretum (Petrarch) **20**:212, 214, 243-44, 246,
    250, 258, 261-63, 266, 272, 279, 287, 290,
    294, 299, 303, 323, 326-27
"Seeing off Wei Wan, Recluse of Wang-wu
    Mountain, on His Trip Home" (Li Po) **2**:168
"Segrek Son of Ushun Koja" **8**:103
Sei Shonagon ga Makura-no-Soshi (Sei
    Shonagon)
    See *Makura no soshi*
Sei Shonagon's Pillow Book (Sei Shonagon)
    See *Makura no soshi*
"Seizure" (Sappho)
    See "Ode to Anactoria"
Select Apophthegums (Epicurus) **21**:122
Self-Punishment (Terence)
    See *Heautontimoreumenos*
The Self-Tormentor (Terence)
    See *Heautontimoreumenos*
"Senh' En Sordel mandamen" (Sordello) **15**:362
Sentences (Albert the Great)
    See *Commentary on the Book of the Sentences*
Septem (Aeschylus)
    See *Seven against Thebes*
Sermon on St. John the Baptist (Abelard) **11**:66
Seven against Thebes (Aeschylus) **11**:77, 83-5,
    88, 96, 102-03, 107, 111, 113, 117, 119, 124,
    127, 133-35, 137-39, 142, 151-54, 156, 159,
    167, 173, 179, 181, 184, 194, 200, 205, 207,
    217
Seven before Thebes (Aeschylus)
    See *Seven against Thebes*
Seventh Epistle (Plato)
    See *Seventh Letter*
Seventh Isthmian (Pindar)
    See *Isthmian 7*
Seventh Letter (Plato) **8**:222, 305-06, 334, 338-
    41, 349
Seventh Nemean (Pindar)
    See *Nemean 7*
The Sham Eunich (Terence)
    See *Eunuchus*
Shearing of Glycera (Menander)
    See *Perikeiromene*
The Shield (Menander)
    See *Aspis*
Shield of Heracles (Hesiod)
    See *Shield of Herakles*
Shield of Herakles (Hesiod) **5**:74, 82-83, 118,
    174
Shih (Confucius)
    See *Shih Ching*
Shih Chi (Confucius) **19**:21, 84
Shih Ching (Confucius) **19**:6, 19, 21, 29, 31, 34-
    35, 38-39, 46, 51
Shorn Lady (Menander)
    See *Perikeiromene*

Short Treatise in Praise of Dante (Boccaccio)
    See *Trattatello in lode di Dante*
The Short-Haired Lass (Menander)
    See *Perikeiromene*
Shoulder Bite (Chretien de Troyes) **10**:232
Shu (Confucius)
    See *Shu Ching*
Shu Ching (Confucius) **19**:6, 9, 19-20, 28, 34-35,
    38, 46, 67
"Si co'l malaus ge no se sap gardar" (Sordello)
    15:363
Sic et Non (Abelard) **11**:4, 7, 9, 10, 14, 16, 21,
    24, 27, 31, 48, 66
"Signor mio caro" (Petrarch) **20**:334
The Sikyonian (Menander)
    See *Sikyonios*
Sikyonios (Menander) **9**:260, 269-70, 278, 288
Sir Gawain and The Green Knight **2**:181-287
"Sirmio" (Catullus)
    See "Poem 31"
Sisyphus (Aeschylus) **11**:123
Sixth Isthmian (Pindar)
    See *Isthmian 6*
Sixth Nemean (Pindar)
    See *Nemean 6*
Sixth Olympian (Pindar)
    See *Olympian 6*
Sixth Paean (Pindar)
    See *Paean 6*
Sixth Pythian (Pindar)
    See *Pythian 6*
"Sleeper Awakened" **2**:20
Slovo o polku Igoreve **1**:477-530
Soliloquia (Augustine) **6**:53, 62, 68-9, 90, 126
Soliloquies (Augustine)
    See *Soliloquia*
Soliloquy (Abelard) **11**:67
Somnium Scipionis (Cicero) **3**:181, 200, 211,
    289, 293-95
"Song Before Drinking" (Li Po) **2**:140
"Song of Ch'ang-kan" (Li Po) **2**:144
The Song of Ivor's Campaign
    See *Slovo o polku Igoreve*
"A Song of Love-Longing to Jesus" (Rolle)
    21:367-69, 374
"Song of Lu-shan" (Li Po) **2**:144
"Song of Maldon"
    See "The Battle of Maldon"
The Song of Roland
    See *La Chanson de Roland*
Song of Songs **18**: 199-316
"Song of the Cranes" (Su Shih) **15**:382
"Song of the Heavenly Horse" (Li Po) **2**:144-156
Song of the Lord
    See *Bhagavadgita*
Song of the Lord
    See *Bhagavad Gita*
"A Song of the Love of Jesus" (Rolle) **21**:367,
    369, 372
"Song of the Roosting Crows" (Li Po) **2**:140,
    157-58
"Song of the Stone Drums" (Su Shih) **15**:410
Songs for a Chorus of Maidens (Pindar)
    See *Partheneia*
Songs for Dancing (Pindar)
    See *Hyporcemata*
"Songs of the Marches" (Li Po) **2**:132
Sophist (Plato) **8**:258-60, 282, 306, 309-10, 321-
    22, 333-34, 338, 359, 361

Soul Conductors (Aeschylus)
  See *Spirit-Raisers*
"Sparrow Song" (Li Po) 2:138
Sphekes (Aristophanes) 4:44-5, 62, 65, 67, 93-4, 110, 125-26, 130-31, 134, 144, 149, 152, 154, 159, 162, 165-66
Sphinx (Aeschylus) 11:159
Spirit-Raisers (Aeschylus) 11:124
"Spirto gentil" (Petrarch) 20:241
Spring and Autumn (Confucius)
  See *Ch'un Ch'iu*
Spring and Autumn Annals (Confucius)
  See *Ch'un Ch'iu*
St. Patrick's Purgatory (Marie de France)
  See *L'Espurgatoire Saint Patrice*
State (Cicero)
  See *De republica*
"Statement of Resolutions after Being Drunk on a Spring Day" (Li Po) 2:132
Statesman (Plato)
  See *Politikos*
"The Story of Bamsi Beyrek"
  See "Bamsi-Beyrek"
"The Story of Basat Who Killed Depegöz"
  See "How Basat Killed Goggle-eye"
"The Story of Basat Who Kills the One-Eyed Giant"
  See "How Basat Killed Goggle-eye"
The Story of Burnt Njal
  See *Njáls saga*
Story of Calamities (Abelard)
  See *Historia Calamitatum*
"The Story of Deli Dumril"
  See "Wild Dumril Son of Dukha Koja"
"The Story of Emrem" 8:108
Story of His Misfortunes (Abelard)
  See *Historia Calamitatum*
The Story of Igor's Campaign
  See *Slovo o polku Igoreve*
"The Story of Kan Turali"
  See "Kan Turali Son of Kanli Koja"
"The Story of Ma'aruf" 2:39
"The Story of the Captivity of Salur Kazan" 8:108
The Story of the Grail (Chretien de Troyes)
  See *Perceval*
"The Story of the House of SalurKazan"
  See "The Plunder of the Home of Salur-Kazan"
The Story of the Oghuzname—the Oghuz
  See *Kitabi-i Dedem Qorkut*
Stromata (Origen)
  See *Stromateis*
Stromateis (Origen) 19:186, 201, 203, 205, 215
Subtilitates naturarum diversarum creaturarum (Hildegard von Bingen) 20:153, 183
Summa de Bono (Albert the Great) 16:31
Summa de creaturis (Albert the Great) 16:26, 31, 42, 86, 103, 107-08, 112
Summa de homine (Albert the Great) 16:31, 112-13
"Summa Juris" (Sordello) 15:338
Summa Theologiae (Albert the Great)
  See *Summa Theologica*
Summa Theologica (Albert the Great) 16:7, 14, 16, 26, 28, 30, 32, 36, 39, 42, 93-4, 104, 108-11, 121
Super apocalypsim (Rolle) 21:390, 394, 396-97
Super canticum canticorum (Rolle) 21:393, 396-

97
Super lectiones mortuorum (Rolle) 21:389, 392
Super Oratione Dominica (Eckhart) 9:42
Super orationem dominicam (Rolle) 21:389
Super psalmum vicesimum (Rolle) 21:390, 393
Super symbolum apostolorum (Rolle) 21:389
Super symbolum S. Anthanasii (Rolle) 21:389
Super threnos Ieremiae (Rolle) 21:389-90
The Superstitious Man (Menander) 9:214
Suppliant Maidens (Aeschylus)
  See *Suppliants*
Suppliant Women (Aeschylus)
  See *Suppliants*
Suppliants (Aeschylus) 11:88, 101-02, 108, 110-11, 116-18, 123, 127, 133-40, 148, 150, 152-53, 156, 158-60, 175, 178-79, 180-81, 183-84, 190-91, 193-95, 198, 201, 205, 207-09, 211, 216-17
Supplices (Aeschylus)
  See *Suppliants*
"The Swallow and the Other Birds" (Marie de France) 8:174
Symmories (Demosthenes)
  See *On the Symmories*
Symphonia (Hildegard von Bingen) 20:153
Symposium (Epicurus) 21:70, 73-4
Symposium (Plato) 8:210, 234-35, 254-55, 259, 265-66, 270, 280, 283, 305-07, 310, 317, 330-31, 355-56, 358-59, 361, 363-69
Symposium (Xenophon) 17:345, 346
Synaristosai (Menander) 9:270
"The Szechwan Road" (Li Po) 2:138
Tactics (Polybius) 17:168
Tafsir ma ba'd al-tabi'ah (Averroes) 7:64-5, 67
Tahafut (Averroes)
  See *Tahafut al-tahafut*
Tahafut al-tahafut (Averroes) 7:16, 21, 24-6, 30, 42, 68, 71
Tahafut at-tahafut (Averroes)
  See *Tahafut al-tahafut*
The Tale of Genji (Murasaki)
  See *Genji Monogatari*
The Tale of Igor's Campaign
  See *Slovo o polku Igoreve*
Talkhis (Averroes) 7:63-5
Talks of Instruction (Eckhart) 9:56-7
Tao te Ching (Lao Tzu) 7:116-213
Tao-teh ching (Lao Tzu)
  See *Tao te Ching*
The Teachings of Honor (Sordello)
  See *Ensegnamen d'Onor*
Tehillim 4:342-456
"Temple Inscription for Han Wen-kung at Ch'ao-chou" (Su Shih) 15:399
"The Temptation" (Caedmon) 7:91
Tenth Nemean (Pindar)
  See *Nemean 10*
Tenth Olympian (Pindar)
  See *Olympian 10*
Tenth Pythian (Pindar)
  See *Pythian 10*
Tereus (Sophocles) 2:348
"The Terraced Road of the Two-Edged Sword Mountains" (Li Po) 2:132
Teseida (Boccaccio) 13:9, 29, 32-3, 44-5, 62, 65, 87, 102-14
Tetrapla (Origen) 19:184
Thais (Menander) 9:237
Theaetetus (Plato) 8:221-22, 254-55, 259, 264,

284, 306, 309-10, 321, 361
Theages (Plato) 8:305, 311
Thebais (Seneca) 6:339, 342-43
Theogony (Hesiod) 5:70-5, 77-9, 83, 86-7, 92-6, 99-100, 102-05, 108-10, 113-18, 121-23, 128-30, 134-35, 137, 140-43, 145-50, 159-68, 170, 173-74
Theologia Christiana (Abelard)
  See *Christian Theology*
Theologia 'Scholiarum' (Abelard) 11:53, 66
Theologia 'Summi boni' (Abelard) 11:10, 24, 65, 66
Theological Tractates (Boethius) 15:24, 31-33
Theological Treatises (Boethius)
  See *Theological Tractates*
Theology (Abelard)
  See *Christian Theology*
"Thesaurus Thesaurum" (Sordello) 15:329, 338, 377
Thesmophoriazusae (Aristophanes) 4:44, 60-63, 67-68, 94, 105-06, 110, 113, 116, 124-26, 130, 137, 145, 150, 152, 155, 161, 163, 175
Third Nemean (Pindar)
  See *Nemean 3*
Third Olympian (Pindar)
  See *Olympian 3*
Third Olynthiac (Demosthenes)
  See *Olynthiac III*
Third Philippic (Demosthenes)
  See *Philippic III*
Third Pythian (Pindar)
  See *Pythian 3*
Thirteenth Olympian (Pindar)
  See *Olympian 13*
The Thousand and One Nights
  See *Alf Layla wa-Layla*
Thracian Women (Aeschylus) 11:125
The thre Arrows in the Dome (Rolle) 21:275
"The Three Calenders, Sons of Kings, and the Five Ladies of Baghdad" 2:16, 49, 51, 72
Threnoi (Pindar) 12:320
"Thy Joy Be in the Love of Jesus" (Rolle) 21:367-69, 374
Thyestes (Seneca) 6:339-40, 342-43, 366, 368, 377-81, 389-91, 393, 400, 402-04, 406-10, 414-15, 418, 426, 428-29, 431-32, 441, 444-45
"T'ien Mountain Ascended in a Dream" (Li Po) 2:144, 164, 166
Timaeus (Plato) 8:209, 211, 222, 232, 241, 244, 255, 259-61, 265, 306, 310-11, 317-18, 320, 323, 325, 328, 332, 341, 349, 351-53, 361-63
Timocrates (Epicurus) 21:119
Titurel (Wolfram von Eschenbach) 5:301-02, 314, 317, 323, 325-26, 335, 359, 386, 390-91, 429-32
"To a Beautiful Woman on the Road" (Li Po) 2:144
"To Li Yung" (Li Po) 2:169
"To Wang Lun" (Li Po) 2:143
"To Wei Liang-tsai, Prefect of Chiang-hsia—Written on My Exile to Yen-Lang by the Grace of the Emperor after the Uprising to Express Thoughts Arising from Memories of Past Travels" (Li Po) 2:168
Topica (Cicero)
  See *Topica: To Gaius Trebatius*
Topica: To Gaius Trebatius (Cicero) 3:201, 259-60, 263

Topics (Boethius)
  See *De topicis differentiis*
"The Tower of Tranquillity" (Su Shih) **15**:383
The Trachinian Women (Sophocles)
  See *The Trakhiniai*
Trachinians (Sophocles)
  See *The Trakhiniai*
The Trackers (Sophocles)
  See *Ichneutai*
Tractates (Boethius)
  See *Theological Tractates*
Tractatus de astronomia (Llull) **12**:103-10
Tractatus de Mulitiplicatione Specierum (Bacon)
  14:20, 47, 62-63, 80
Tractatus de natura boni (Albert the Great)
  16:31, 66, 72-3, 75, 80
Tractatus expositorius enigmatus alchemiae
  (Bacon) **14**:63-64
Tractatus novus de astronomia (Llull) **12**:110
The Trakhiniai (Sophocles) **2**:289, 294, 296,
  300, 302, 315, 319-20, 322, 324, 338-39, 343-
  45, 349-51, 353, 358, 377, 379, 382, 415-16,
  418-19, 422-23
The Transformation of Lucius Apuleius Madeura
  (Apuleius)
  See *Asinus aureus*
The Transformations (Apuleius)
  See *Metamorphoses*
The Transformation/Transformations (Ovid)
  See *Metamorphoses*
Trattatello in lode di Dante (Boccaccio) **13**:51,
  101
Travels (Mandeville)
  See *Mandeville's Travels*
Travels of John Mandeville (Mandeville)
  See *Mandeville's Travels*
The Travels of Marco Polo the Venetian (Polo)
  15:251-320
Treatise on the Demons (Origen) **19**:203
Tree of Science (Llull)
  See *Arbor scientiae*
The Tree of the Philosophy of Love (Llull)
  12:122, 131-32
"Le Tresor" (Sordello) **15**:339
"Tress of Berenice" (Catullus)
  See *"Poem 66"*
Trionfi (Petrarch) **20**:214, 240, 272-73, 307, 327,
  335
Trionfo del tempo (Petrarch) **20**:295
Trionfo della morte (Petrarch) **20**:215
Trionfo dell'Eternita (Petrarch) **20**:294, 298
Tristan (Chretien de Troyes)
  See *King Mark and Iseut the Fair*
Tristan and Iseult
  See *Tristan und Isolde*
Tristan and Isolde
  See *Tristan und Isolde*
Tristan und Isolde (Gottfried von Strassburg)
  10:247-48, 250, 254-60, 263-64, 267-68, 274-
  79, 282-83, 298, 300-01, 303-06
Tristan und Isolt
  See *Tristan und Isolde*
Tristia (Ovid) **7**:291, 293-94, 300, 306, 320-23,
  332, 341, 343, 346-47, 349, 376-78, 392, 398,
  426, 430, 435, 446
Tristibus (Ovid)
  See *Tristia*
Triumphs (Petrarch)
  See *Trionfi*

Triumphus cupidinis (Petrarch) **20**:334
Troades (Seneca) **6**:340, 342-43, 363, 366-70,
  375-80, 389, 413, 415, 425, 428-29, 431-32
Troas (Seneca)
  See *Troades*
The Trojan Women (Seneca)
  See *Troades*
True Discourse of Celsus the Epicurean (Origen)
  19:189
Tusculan Disputations (Cicero) **3**:177, 183, 193,
  196, 202, 211, 242, 255, 274, 287
Tusculans (Cicero)
  See *Tusculan Disputations*
Twelfth Olympian (Pindar)
  See *Olympian 12*
Twelfth Pythian (Pindar)
  See *Pythian 12*
"The Two Jealous Sisters" **2**:45
"The Two Lovers" (Marie de France)
  See "Les Dous Amanz"
"The Two Wolves" (Marie de France) **8**:192
Tzu Ssu Tzu (Confucius) **19**:20
The Unbridled Mule (Chretien de Troyes)
  See *La Mule sans frein*
Unfinished Work Against Julian (Augustine)
  See *Opus imperfectum contra Julianum*
"The Unfortunate One" (Marie de France)
  See "Le Chaitivel"
"Upon His Returning Home to Pei-hai, I
  Respectfully Offer a Farewell Banquet to
  Reverend Master Kao Ju-Kuei, Gentleman of
  the Tao after He Transmitted to Me a Register
  of the Way" (Li Po) **2**:177
Urvasi Won by Valor (Kalidasa)
  See *Vikramorvasiya*
Uusi Kalevala
  See *Kalevala*
Valiant Woman (Albert the Great) **16**:29
Vanha Kalevala
  See *Kalevala*
Vatican Fragments (Epicurus) **21**:161
"Vergine bella" (Petrarch) **20**:241
Verrines (Cicero) **3**:196-99, 202, 267, 268, 286
Victoria Berenices (Callimachus)
  See *Lock of Berenice*
Vikramorvasiya (Kalidasa) **9**:82, 86-8, 90-1, 96-
  7, 99-100, 102, 125, 131-34, 136-39
"Vinse hanibal" (Petrarch) **20**:333
"Visit to Gold Mountain Temple" (Su Shih)
  15:410
Vita (Hildegard von Bingen) **20**:143, 147-49,
  152-54, 167, 176
Vita (Josephus) **13**:217, 220, 222, 235, 239, 249,
  253, 255, 263, 265, 268, 270-2, 302, 305, 307-
  8, 311, 316-8
Vita di Dante (Boccaccio) **13**:53-4
Vita Nuova (Alighieri) **18**: 317-84
Vita sancti Cuthberti (Bede) **20**:38, 62, 66-7, 71-
  2, 75, 81, 83
"Vogliami sprona" (Petrarch) **20**:241
"Waking from Drunkenness on a Spring Day" (Li
  Po) **2**:141
War (Josephus)
  See *Bellum Judaicum*
Wars of the Jews (Josephus)
  See *Bellum Judaicum*
The Wasps (Aristophanes)
  See *Sphekes*
The Way and Its Nature (Lao Tzu)

  See *Tao te Ching*
Wealth (Aristophanes)
  See *Ploutos*
Weighing of Souls (Aeschylus) **11**:123-24, 193
"The Werewolf" (Marie de France)
  See "Bisclavret"
"When Wilt Thou Come to Comfort Me?"
  (Rolle) **21**:316
"Wild Dumril Son of Dukha Koja" **8**:104, 108-
  09
Willehalm (Wolfram von Eschenbach) **5**:293,
  296, 298-302, 309-14, 317, 322-23, 326, 335-
  37, 343, 350-53, 357-62, 366, 373, 383, 386,
  396-97, 399-400, 420, 429, 431
Willehalm von Oranse (Wolfram von
  Eschenbach)
  See *Willehalm*
William of England (Chretien de Troyes)
  See *Guillaume d'Angleterre*
"Wine Will Be Served" (Li Po) **2**:143
"The Wisdom of Dede Korkut" **8**:103, 107
"A Wolf and a Dung-Beetle" (Marie de France)
  8:174-75
"The Wolf and the Kid" (Marie de France) **8**:193
"The Wolf and the Sow" (Marie de France)
  8:190
"A Wolf as King of the Beasts" (Marie de
  France) **8**:175
"A Woman and Her Hen" (Marie de France)
  8:171
The Woman from Andros (Terence)
  See *Andria*
The Woman from Samos (Menander)
  See *Samia*
Woman of Leucas (Menander) **9**:211
Woman of Thessaly (Menander) **9**:214
Women at the Thesmophoria (Aristophanes)
  See *Thesmophoriazusae*
Women in Assembly (Aristophanes)
  See *Ekklesiazousai*
Women in Parliament (Aristophanes)
  See *Ekklesiazousai*
*Women Keeping the Festival of the
  Thesmophoria* (Aristophanes)
  See *Thesmophoriazusae*
Women of Salamis (Aeschylus) **11**:125
The Women of Trachis (Sophocles)
  See *The Trakhiniai*
The Women's Assembly (Aristophanes)
  See *Ekklesiazousai*
A Women's Lunch-Party (Menander)
  See *Synaristosai*
Works (Hesiod)
  See *Works and Days*
Works and Days (Hesiod) **5**:70, 72-4, 75-7, 79-
  84, 86-101, 103-05, 108, 110-11, 114-16, 121-
  27, 129-51, 153, 156, 160-63, 167-68, 170-74
"The Wretched One" (Marie de France)
  See "Le Chaitivel"
"The Wrong Box" **2**:36
Xantriae (Aeschylus) **11**:124
"Yearning" (Li Po) **2**:159-60
Yes and No (Abelard)
  See *Sic et Non*
Yi (Confucius)
  See *I Ching*
"Yigenek Son of Kazilak Koja" **8**:104
"Yonec" (Marie de France) **8**:114, 116-17, 121-
  23, 127-28, 131, 134, 139-40, 142, 144-45,

147, 149, 154, 161-65, 170, 181
"The Young King of the Black Isles" **2**:72
"The Young Man from Baghdad" **2**:43
Yueh (Confucius) **19**:35, 38
Yvain (Chretien de Troyes) **10**:131, 133-34, 136, 138-39, 141, 143-47, 149, 157, 159-69, 171, 173, 182-90, 194-97, 199, 206, 208, 210, 215-16, 218-21, 223, 225-26, 229-32, 234-35, 237-39

CMLC Cumulative Critic Index

'Abdul Hakim, Khalifa
Rumi, Jalal al-Din **20**:345

Abe Akio
Sei Shonagon **6**:299

Abusch, Tzvi
Epic of Gilgamesh **3**:365

Adams, Charles Darwin
Demoshenes **13**:148

Adams, Henry
The Song of Roland **1**:166

Adcock, F. E.
Thucydides **17**:288

Addison, Joseph
Aeneid **9**:310
Iliad **1**:282
Ovid **7**:292
Sappho **3**:379
Sophocles **2**:293

Adler, Mortimer J.
Plato **8**:342

Adlington, William
Apuleius **1**:6

Aiken, Conrad
Murasaki, Lady **1**:423

Albert, S.M.
Albert the Great **16**:33

Alford, John A.
Rolle, Richard **21**:378

Alighieri, Dante
Aeneid **9**:297
Bertran de Born **5**:4
Seneca, Lucius Annaeus **6**:331
Sordello **15**:323

Ali-Shah, Omar
Khayyam **11**:288

Allen, Archibald W.
Livy **11**:334

Allen, Hope Emily
Rolle, Richard **21**:308

Allen, Richard F.
Njals saga **13**:358

Allinson, Francis G.
Menander **9**:204

Allison, Rev. William T.
The Book of Psalms **4**:371

Al-Nadim
Arabian Nights **2**:3

Alphonso-Karkala, John B.
Kalevala **6**:259

Alter, Robert
The Book of Psalms **4**:451
Song of Songs **18**:283

Ambivius, Lucius
Terence **14**:302

Ames, Roger T.
Confucius **19**:88

Amis, Kingsley
Beowulf **1**:112

Anacker, Robert
Chretien de Troyes **10**:144

Anderson, George K.
Beowulf **1**:98
The Dream of the Rood **14**:245

Anderson, J. K.
Xenophon **17**:342

Anderson, William S.
Juvenal **8**:59

Andersson, Theodore M.
Hrafnkel's Saga **2**:103

Annas, Julia
Epicurus **21**:201

Apuleius, Lucius
Apuleius **1**:3

Aquinas, St. Thomas
Augustine, St. **6**:5
Averroes **7**:3
Plato **8**:217

Arberry, A. J.
Rumi, Jalal al-Din **20**:364

Arendt, Hannah
Augustine, St. **6**:116

Aristophanes
Aeschylus **11**:73

Aristotle
Aeschylus **11**:73
Greek Historiography **17**:13
Hesiod **5**:69
Iliad **1**:273
Plato **8**:202
Sophocles **2**:291

Arnold, E. Vernon
Seneca, Lucius Annaeus **6**:362

Arnold, Edwin
Hesiod **5**:71
Iliad **1**:308
Odyssey **16**:208
Sappho **3**:384

Arnold, Mary
Poem of the Cid **4**:226

Arnold, Matthew
Aeneid **9**:316
Aristophanes **4**:54
Iliad **1**:300
Mabinogion **9**:146
The Song of Roland **1**:162
Sophocles **2**:311

Arnott, Geoffrey
Menander **9**:261

Arnott, W. G.
Menander **9**:253

Arnould, E. J.
Rolle, Richard **21**:350

Arnstein, Adolf
Meister Eckhart **9**:4

Arrowsmith, William
Aristophanes **4**:131

'Arudi, Nizami-i-
Avicenna **16**:147

Ascham, Roger
Cicero, Marcus Tullius **3**:186

Ashe, Geoffrey
Arthurian Legend **10**:2

Asquith, Herbert Henry
Demosthenes **13**:135

Astin, Alan E.
Cato, Marcus Porcius **21**:38

Aston, W. G.
Murasaki, Lady **1**:416
Sei Shonagon **6**:291

Athanasius
The Book of Psalms **4**:344

Atkins, J. W. H.
Aristophanes **4**:104

Atkinson, James C.
Mystery of Adam **4**:207

Auden, W. H.
Iliad **1**:347
Njals saga **13**:330

Auerbach, Erich
Augustine, St. **6**:79
Inferno **3**:72, 95
Mystery of Adam **4**:193
Odyssey **16**:221
Poem of the Cid **4**:251

Augustine, St.
Apuleius **1**:4
Augustine, St. **6**:4
Cicero, Marcus Tullius **3**:177
Epicurus **21**:79
Plato **8**:208
Seneca, Lucius Annaeus **6**:330

Aurobindo, Sri
Bhagavad Gita **12**:32

Austerlitz, Robert
Kalevala **6**:255

Averroes
Plato **8**:212

Avery, Peter
Khayyam **11**:297

Ayscough, Florence
Li Po **2**:132

Bachofen, J. J.
Aeschylus **11**:92
Sappho **3**:382

Bacon, Francis
Plato **8**:219

Bagley, F. R. C.
Khayyam **11**:283

Bailey, Cyril
Epicurus **21**:130

Baker, Donald C.
Beowulf **1**:154

Baldwin, Charles Sears
Sir Gawain and the Green Knight
2:186

Banks, Mary Macleod
Morte Arthure **10**:377

Barber, Richard
Sir Gawain and the Green Knight
2:215

Barbi, Michele
Inferno **3**:87

Barfield, Owen
Bhagavad Gita **12**:71
The Book of Psalms **4**:392

Bargen, Doris G.
Murasaki, Lady **1**:467

Baricelli, Jean-Pierre
Kalevala **6**:280

Barker, E. Phillips
Seneca, Lucius Annaeus **6**:375

Barker, William
Xenophon **17**:318

Barney, Stephen A.
Romance of the Rose **8**:435

Barnstone, Willis
Llull, Ramon **12**:126
Sappho **3**:435

Barolini, Teodolinda
Sordello **15**:368

Barr, William
Juvenal **8**:86

Barron, W. R. J.
Layamon **10**:360
Sir Gawain and the Green Knight
2:261

Barth, John
Arabian Nights **2**:43

Basgoz, Ilhan
Book of Dede Korkut **8**:108

Basore, John W.
Seneca, Lucius Annaeus **6**:374

Bassett, Samuel Eliot
Iliad **1**:329
Odyssey **16**:214

Bates, William Nickerson
Sophocles **2**:336

Batts, Michael S.
Gottfried von Strassburg **10**:293
Hartmann von Aue **15**:183

Bayerschmidt, Carl F.
Njals saga **13**:326
Wolfram von Eschenbach **5**:311

Beare, W.
Terence **14**:343

Bede
Cædmon **7**:77

Beer, Frances
Hildegard von Bingen **20**:175

Bell, Aubrey F. G.
Poem of the Cid **4**:251

Bennett, James O'Donnell
Arabian Nights **2**:27

Bennett, Josephine Waters
Mandeville, Sir John **19**:117

Benson, Eugene
Sordello **15**:33

Benson, Larry D.
Morte Arthure **10**:386
Sir Gawain and the Green Knight
2:227

Bentwich, Norman
Josephus, Flavius **13**:199

Bergin, Thomas G.
Boccaccio, Giovanni **13**:74

Berkeley, George
Plato **8**:221

Berry, Francis
Sir Gawain and the Green Knight
2:194

Berthoud, J. A.
Inferno **3**:116

Bespaloff, Rachel
Iliad **1**:343

Besserman, Lawrence
Sir Gawain and the Green Knight
2:280

Bettelheim, Bruno
Arabian Nights **2**:53

Beye, Charles Rowan
Hesiod **5**:131

Bigg, Charles
Origen **19**:189

Bilde, Per
Josephus, Flavius **13**:302

Billson, Charles J.
Kalevala **6**:233

Bishop, Ian
Pearl **19**:339

Bittinger, J. B.
The Book of Psalms **4**:363

Bixby, James T.
Kalevala **6**:217
Lao Tzu **7**:118

Blair, Hugh
Iliad **1**:289
Sophocles **2**:296

Blair, Peter Hunter
Bede **20**:74

Blamires, David
Wolfram von Eschenbach **5**:342

Bloch, R. Howard
The Song of Roland **1**:240

Blomfield, Joan
Beowulf **1**:85

Blondel, Maurice
Augustine, St. **6**:28

Bloomfield, Morton W.
Sir Gawain and the Green Knight
2:214

Blow, Susan E.
Inferno **3**:42

Bluestine, Carolyn
Poem of the Cid **4**:309

Blum, Rudolf
Callimachus **18**:62

Boatner, Janet W.
The Song of Roland **1**:211

Boccaccio, Giovanni
Boccaccio, Giovanni **13**:3, 17
Inferno **3**:4

Bollard, J. K.
Mabinogion **9**:176

Bolton, W. F.
Hrafnkel's Saga **2**:106

Bonjour, Adrien
Beowulf **1**:105

Bonnard, Andre
Sappho **3**:424

Bonner, Anthony
Llull, Ramon **12**:133

Bonner, Gerald
Bede **20**:86

Boren, James L.
Morte Arthure **10**:415

Borges, Jorge Luis
Anglo-Saxon Chronicle **4**:21
Arabian Nights **2**:29, 37, 67
Inferno **3**:141
Layamon **10**:327

Bosley, Keith
Kalevala **6**:283

Bostock, J. Knight
Hartmann von Aue **15**:163

Botta, Anne C. Lynch
Arabian Nights **2**:8
Cicero, Marcus Tullius **3**:192

Bowra, C. M.
Aeneid **9**:358
Aeschylus **11**:178
Aristophanes **4**:140
Epic of Gilgamesh **3**:313
Iliad **1**:321
Pindar **12**:323
Poem of the Cid **4**:259
Sappho **3**:398, 399
Sophocles **2**:342

Bowring, Richard
Murasaki, Lady **1**:457

Braddock, Joseph
Sappho **3**:438

Braden, Gordon
Seneca, Lucius Annaeus **6**:399

Branca, Vittore
Boccaccio, Giovanni **13**:62

Bowra, C.M.
Odyssey **16**:292
Sordello **15**:353

Bramley, H. R.
Rolle, Richard **21**:276

Branch, M. A.
Kalevala **6**:267

Brandes, Georg
The Igor Tale **1**:478
Iliad **1**:317

Brandon, S. G. F.
Epic of Gilgamesh **3**:314

Brault, Gerard J.
The Song of Roland **1**:256

Braun, Richard E.
Juvenal **8**:67

Brennan, Gerald
Poem of the Cid **4**:256

Brewer, Derek
Sir Gawain and the Green Knight **2**:241, 270

Brewer, J. S.
Bacon, Roger **14**:6

Bridges, John Henry
Bacon, Roger **14**:14

Briscoe, J.
Livy **11**:375

Brodeur, Arthur Gilchrist
Beowulf **1**:112

Bromwich, Rachel
Arthurian Legend **10**:49
Mabinogion **9**:171

Brooke, Christopher
Abelard **11**:28

Brooke, Stopford A.
Beowulf **1**:63
The Dream of the Rood **14**:216

Broshi, Magen
Josephus, Flavius **13**:271

Brothers, A. J.
Terence **14**:385

Brown, Carleton F.
Pearl **19**:278

Brown, George Hardin
Bede **20**:114

Brown, Norman O.
Hesiod **5**:109

Brown, Peter
Augustine, St. **6**:100
Origen **19**:264

Browne, Rev. G. F.
Bede **20**:3

Browning, Robert
Aristophanes **4**:55

Bruce, James Douglas
Arthurian Legend **10**:120

Brueggemann, Walter
The Book of Psalms **4**:434

Bryant, Nigel
Chretien de Troyes **10**:216

Bryant, William Cullen
Iliad **1**:306

Brzezinski, Monica
The Dream of the Rood **14**:288

Buber, Martin
The Book of Job **14**:206
The Book of Psalms **4**:401

Buck, Philo M., Jr.
Aristophanes **4**:86
Inferno **3**:83
Mahabharata **5**:220

Burn, Andrew Robert
Sappho **3**:430

Burnett, Anne Pippin
Pindar **12**:377
Sappho **3**:481

Burrow, J. A.
The Dream of the Rood **14**:238
Sir Gawain and the Green Knight **2**:235, 277

Burshatin, Israel
Poem of the Cid **4**:329

Burton, Richard F.
Arabian Nights **2**:13, 15

Bury, J. B.
Polybius **17**:155
Xenophon **17**:328

Bussanich, John
Hesiod **5**:163

Butler, Samuel
Iliad **1**:311
Odyssey **16**:200, 221

Butterworth, Charles E.
Avicenna **16**:163

Byron, Lord
Aeneid **9**:385

Cadell, Jessie E.
Khayyam **11**:243

Cadiou, Rene
Origen **19**:197

Caesar, Julius
Terence **14**:326

Cairns, Huntington
Cicero, Marcus Tullius **3**:237

Calin, William C.
Mystery of Adam **4**:200

Calvin, John
The Book of Job **14**:118
The Book of Psalms **4**:349
Seneca, Lucius Annaeus **6**:332

Campbell, James
Bede **20**:48, 63

Campbell, Joseph
Arabian Nights **2**:39
Epic of Gilgamesh **3**:319
Mahabharata **5**:238

Campbell, Lewis
Aeschylus **11**:108
Sophocles **2**:313

Campbell, Mary B.
Mandeville, Sir John **19**:161
Polo, Marco **15**:311

Cantarino, Vicente
Averroes **7**:47

Canter, H. V.
Livy **11**:321

Canuteson, John
The Dream of the Rood **14**:276

Carlyle, John A.
Inferno **3**:19

Carlyle, Thomas
Inferno **3**:12
Das Nibelungenlied **12**:138

Carne-Ross, D. S.
Pindar **12**:367

Cassell, Anthony K.
Boccaccio, Giovanni **13**:94
Inferno **3**:151

Cassirer, Ernst
Augustine, St. **6**:52, 77

Cather, Willa
Sappho **3**:388

Catullus, Gaius Valerius
Cicero, Marcus Tullius **3**:174

Cawley, Frank Stanton
Hrafnkel's Saga **2**:83

Caxton, William
Arthurian Legend **10**:27

Chadwick, Rev. H.
Origen **19**:225

Chadwick, Henry
Boethius **15**:53, 58
Origen **19**:214

Chamberlain, Basil Hall
Kojiki **21**:217

Chambers, E. K.
Mystery of Adam **4**:184

Chambers, R. W.
Bede **20**:23
Beowulf **1**:74

Chan, Wing-tsit
Confucius **19**:48, 67

Chandler, Richard E.
Poem of the Cid **4**:266

Chapman, George
Iliad **1**:276
Odyssey **16**:184

Charlesworth, Martin Percival
Josephus, Flavius **13**:220

Charleton, Walter
Epicurus **21**:90

Chateaubriand, Viscount de
Augustine, St. **6**:11
Inferno **3**:7

Critic Index

Chaucer, Geoffrey
Inferno **3**:5

Chaytor, H. J.
Bertran de Born **5**:21
Sordello **15**:332

Chen, Ellen Marie
Lao Tzu **7**:176

Chen, Yu-Shih
Su Shih **15**:417

Ch'en Shou-yi
Li Po **2**:142

Cherniss, Michael D.
Romance of the Rose **8**:431

Chesterton, G. K.
Arabian Nights **2**:18
The Book of Job **14**:188
The Song of Roland **1**:174

Chretien de Troyes
Chretien de Troyes **10**:131, 141,
160

Christine de Pizan
Romance of the Rose **8**:376

Christoph, Siegfried Richard
Wolfram von Eschenbach **5**:386,
409

Chuangtse
Lao Tzu **7**:117

Cicero, Marcus Tullius
Cato, Marcus Porcius **21**:3
Epicurus **21**:61
Plato **8**:205
Terence **14**:305

Cizevskij, Dmitrij
The Igor Tale **1**:501

Clark, Cyril Drummond Le Gros
Su Shih **15**:381, 385

Clark, Donald Lemen
Hermogenes **6**:161

Clark, James M.
Meister Eckhart **9**:45, 54

Clark, John
Poem of the Cid **4**:230

Clark, S. L.
Hartmann von Aue **15**:228

Clarke, H. Butler
Poem of the Cid **4**:229

Clarke, Howard W.
Odyssey **16**:279

Clifton-Everest, J. M.
Hartmann von Aue **15**:202

Cline, Ruth Harwood
Chretien de Troyes **10**:195

Closs, August
Gottfried von Strassburg **10**:255

Cochrane, Charles Norris
Thucydides **17**:243

Cohen, Shaye J. D.
Josephus, Flavius **13**:263, 273

Col, Pierre
Romance of the Rose **8**:380

Coleman, T. W.
Rolle, Richard **21**:323

Coleridge, H. N.
Hesiod **5**:70

Coleridge, Samuel Taylor
Arabian Nights **2**:4
Aristophanes **4**:47
Inferno **3**:10
Pindar **12**:260
Poem of the Cid **4**:224

Colgrave, Bertram
Bede **20**:8, 82

Colish, Marcia L.
Augustine, St. **6**:123

Colledge, Edmund
Meister Eckhart **9**:68

Collinder, Bjorn
Kalevala **6**:247

Collins, Christopher
Longus **7**:251

Colum, Padraic
Arabian Nights **2**:26
Mabinogion **9**:165

Comfort, W. W.
Chretien de Troyes **10**:137

Comparetti, Domenico
Kalevala **6**:219

Comper, Frances M. M.
Rolle, Richard **21**:310

Conant, Martha Pike
Arabian Nights **2**:20

Condren, Edward I.
Hrafnkel's Saga **2**:112

Congreve, William
Pindar **12**:259

Connor, W. Robert
Thucydides **17**:307

Conte, Gian Biagio
Cato, Marcus Porcius **21**:54

Conybeare, John Josias
Beowulf **1**:55

Cook, Albert
Ovid **7**:412

Poem of the Cid **4**:270
Sophocles **2**:404

Cook, Charles W.
Epic of Gilgamesh **3**:352

Cook, Robert G.
Chretien de Troyes **10**:183

Cooper, Arthur
Li Po **2**:145

Copleston, Frederick C.
Abelard **11**:14
Averroes **7**:16

Copleston, Reginald S.
Aeschylus **11**:95

Copley, Frank O.
Livy **11**:363
Terence **14**:349

Corcoran, Thomas H.
Seneca, Lucius Annaeus **6**:436

Cornford, Francis Macdonald
Aristophanes **4**:78
Plato **8**:272
Thucydides **17**:235

Cornwallis, William
Seneca, Lucius Annaeus **6**:334

Cosman, Madeleine Pelner
Gottfried von Strassburg **10**:292

Costa, C. D. N.
Seneca, Lucius Annaeus **6**:413

Courthope, W. J.
Beowulf **1**:59

Courtney, W. L.
Sappho **3**:394

Cowell, Edward Byles
Khayyam **11**:230

Cowley, Abraham
The Book of Psalms **4**:351
Pindar **12**:258

Crabbe, Anna
Boethius **15**:69

Cracroft, Bernard
Arabian Nights **2**:9

Craigie, W. A.
Hrafnkel's Saga **2**:78

Crawford, John Martin
Kalevala **6**:214

Crawford, S. J.
Cædmon **7**:92

Creekmore, Hubert
Juvenal **8**:64

Croce, Benedetto
Inferno **3**:58

Plato **8**:269
Terence **14**:326

Croiset, Maurice
Aristophanes **4**:70

Crombie, A. C.
Bacon, Roger **14**:79

Crump, M. Marjorie
Ovid **7**:314

Cruttwell, Charles Thomas
Cato, Marcus Porcius **21**:22

Cummings, Hubertis M.
Boccaccio, Giovanni **13**:87

Cunliffe, John W.
Seneca, Lucius Annaeus **6**:339

Cunningham, Stanley B.
Albert the Great **16**:43, 65

Curley III, Thomas F.
Boethius **15**:97

Curtius, Ernst Robert
Aeneid **9**:345, 376
Augustine, St. **6**:56
Hermogenes **6**:158
Inferno **3**:98

Dahlberg, Charles
Romance of the Rose **8**:414

Dall, Caroline H.
Sordello **15**:328

D'Alton, Rev. J. F.
Cicero, Marcus Tullius **3**:207

Damon, S. Foster
Marie de France **8**:120

Dandekar, R. N.
Mahabharata **5**:227

Dane, Joseph A.
Mystery of Adam **4**:216

Danielou, Jean
Origen **19**:206

Darrow, Clarence
Khayyam **11**:274

Dashti, Ali
Khayyam **11**:280

Davenport, Guy
Sappho **3**:471

Davenport, W. A.
Sir Gawain and the Green Knight
2:273

David, E.
Aristophanes **4**:174

Davidson, A. B.
The Book of Job **14**:138

Davidson, Herbert A.
Avicenna **16**:147

Davidson, Thomas
Sappho **3**:388

Davies, James
Catullus **18**:73

Davis, J. Cary
Poem of the Cid **4**:260

Davis, Scott
Kalevala **6**:278

Dawson, Christopher
Bacon, Roger **14**:65

De Boer, T. J.
Averroes **7**:7

De Chasca, Edmund
Poem of the Cid **4**:295

De la Mare, Walter
Arabian Nights **2**:35

De Ley, Margo
Razon de Amor **16**:347

De Quincey, Thomas
Arabian Nights **2**:8
Herodotus **17**:54
Iliad **1**:294
Odyssey **16**:197
Sophocles **2**:309

De Sanctis, Francesco
Boccaccio, Giovanni **13**:17
Inferno **3**:23, 31

De Vere, Aubrey
Poem of the Cid **4**:229
The Song of Roland **1**:163

De Vericour, Professor
Poem of the Cid **4**:225

Dean, Christopher
Arthurian Legend **10**:65
Morte Arthure **10**:431

Demetillo, Ricaredo
Murasaki, Lady **1**:429

Den Boer, W.
Thucydides **17**:302

DeWitt, Norman Wentworth
Epicurus **21**:144

Deyermond, A. D.
Poem of the Cid **4**:289

Diamond, Robert E.
The Dream of the Rood **14**:236

Dill, Samuel
Juvenal **8**:26
Seneca, Lucius Annaeus **6**:345

Dimler, G. Richard
Wolfram von Eschenbach **5**:344

Dinsmore, Charles Allen
Iliad **1**:326

Dionysius of Halicarnassus
Sappho **3**:379
Thucydides **17**:209
Xenophon **17**:329

Disraeli, Issac
Beowulf **1**:56

Dobson, J. F.
Demosthenes **13**:141

Dodds, E. R.
Augustine, St. **6**:21

Dole, Nathan Haskell
Petrarch **20**:229

Donner, Morton
Sir Gawain and the Green Knight
2:224

Donohoe, Joseph I., Jr.
The Song of Roland **1**:228

Donovan, Mortimer J.
Marie de France **8**:145

Doolittle, Hilda
Sappho **3**:432

Dorfman, Eugene
Poem of the Cid **4**:271

Dover, K. J.
Aristophanes **4**:147, 159
Demosthenes **13**:185

Dronke, Peter
Abelard **11**:39
Hildegard von Bingen **20**:143

Dryden, John
Aeneid **9**:300
Apuleius **1**:7
Iliad **1**:282
Juvenal **8**:5
Ovid **7**:291
Pindar **12**:258

Ducharme, Leonard
Albert the Great **16**:86

Duckett, Eleanor Shipley
Bede **20**:42
Boethius **15**:23

Duckworth, George E.
Terence **14**:337

Duclow, Donald F.
Meister Eckhart **9**:70

Duff, J. Wight
Cicero, Marcus Tullius **3**:197
Juvenal **8**:34
Livy **11**:336
Terence **14**:305

Duff, Mountstuart E. Grant
Polybius **17**:152

Duggan, Joseph J.
Poem of the Cid **4**:312

Dumezil, Georges
Mahabharata **5**:254

Dunlop, John
Cato, Marcus Porcius **21**:17

Dunn, Charles W.
Romance of the Rose **8**;417

Dunne, M.A.
Sordello **15**:339

Durling, Robert M.
Petrarch **20**:270

Earle, John
Beowulf **1**:57

Easton, Stewart C.
Bacon, Roger **14**:73

Eaton, John H.
The Book of Psalms **4**:438

Ebenstein, William
Cicero, Marcus Tullius **3**:251

Echard, Lawrence
Terence **14**:297

Eckermann, Johann Peter
Longus **7**:217
Sophocles **2**:303

Eckhart, Meister
Meister Eckhart **9**:24

Eckstein, A. M.
Polybius **17**:192

Edgerton, Franklin
Kalidasa **9**:113

Edgren, A. Hjalmar
Kalidasa **9**:87

Edmonds, J. M.
Longus **7**:220

Ehrenberg, Victor
Aristophanes **4**:117

Eide, Elling O.
Li Po **2**:149

Einarsson, Stefan
Hrafnkel's Saga **2**:97

Eliade, Mircea
Bhagavad Gita **12**:74
Epic of Gilgamesh **3**:341
Mahabharata **5**:235

Eliot, George
Sophocles **2**:311

Eliot, T. S.
Aeneid **9**:380
Inferno **3**:67

Pindar **12**:265
Seneca, Lucius Annaeus **6**:371

Elwell-Sutton, L. P.
Khayyam **11**:304

Elyot, Thomas
Ovid **7**:286

Emerson, Oliver Farrar
Beowulf **1**:68

Emerson, Ralph Waldo
The Book of Psalms **4**:360
Plato **8**:235

Engelhardt, George J.
Sir Gawain and the Green Knight
2:204

Enright, D. J.
Murasaki, Lady **1**:447
Sei Shonagon **6**:301

Erasmus, Desiderius
Cicero, Marcus Tullius **3**:184
Seneca, Lucius Annaeus **6**:332

Eusebius
Josephus, Flavius **13**:219
Origen **19**:183

Eustathios
Iliad **1**:274

Evans, J. A. S.
Herodotus **17**:109, 132

Evelyn-White, Hugh G.
Hesiod **5**:83

Everett, Dorothy
Layamon **10**:329
Morte Arthure **10**:378
Pearl **19**:321
Sir Gawain and the Green Knight
2:197

Ewert, Alfred
Marie de France **8**:129

Faber, Ernst
Confucius **19**:12

Falk, Marcia
Song of Songs **18**:297

Fant, Maureen B.
Sappho **3**:481

Fantham, Elaine
Cato, Marcus Porcius **21**:57

Farnell, Ida
Sordello **15**:330

Faris, Wendy B.
Arabian Nights **2**:69

Farnell, Ida
Bertran de Born **5**:18

Critic Index

Farnham, Willard
Boccaccio, Giovanni **13**:62

Farrington, Benjamin
Epicurus **21**:159

Fauriel, C. C.
Bertran de Born **5**:10

Faust, Diana M.
Marie de France **8**:185

Fedotov, George P.
The Igor Tale **1**:491

Feldman, Louis H.
Josephus, Flavius **13**:256

Felson-Rubin, Nancy
Odyssey **16**:321

Feng, Kuan
Lao Tzu **7**:155

Fennell, John
The Igor Tale **1**:521

Ferguson, John
Juvenal **8**:84
Sophocles **2**:408

Ferguson, Margaret W.
Augustine, St. **6**:109

Fergusson, Francis
Sophocles **2**:359

Ferrante, Joan
Marie de France **8**:158

Festugiere, Andre-Jean
Apuleius **1**:24
Epicurus **21**:138

Ficino, Marsilio
Plato **8**:217

Field, P. J. C.
Sir Gawain and the Green Knight
2:258

Fielding, Henry
Aristophanes **4**:41

Finlayson, John
Morte Arthure **10**:391

Finley, John H., Jr.
Pindar **12**:287
Thucydides **17**:251

Finley, M. I.
Greek Historiography **17**:13, 26
Odyssey **16**:253
Xenophon **17**:368

Fiore, Silvestro
Epic of Gilgamesh **3**:325

Fitch, George Hamlin
Arabian Nights **2**:22

Fite, Warner
Plato **8**:280

FitzGerald, Edward
Khayyam **11**:233

Fitzgerald, William
Catullus **18**:189

Flaccus, Statylius
Sophocles **2**:292

Fleming, John V.
The Dream of the Rood **14**:245

Fletcher, Jefferson Butler
Inferno **3**:56

Foley, Helene P.
Aristophanes **4**:169

Ford, J. D. M.
Poem of the Cid **4**:233

Forehand, Walter E.
Terence **14**:381

Fornara, Charles W.
Herodotus **17**:96

Forster, E. M.
Arabian Nights **2**:26

Foscolo, Ugo
Boccaccio, Giovanni **13**:13
Petrarch **20**:194

Fowles, John
Marie de France **8**:157

Fowlie, Wallace
Inferno **3**:144

Fox, Denton
Njals saga **13**:339

Frank, Grace
Mystery of Adam **4**:191, 197

Frank, Tenney
Cicero, Marcus Tullius **3**:211

Frankel, Hermann
Hesiod **5**:99
Ovid **7**:319
Sappho **3**:418

Frappier, Jean
Chretien de Troyes **10**:160

Freccero, John
Inferno **3**:145

Fredericks, S. C.
Juvenal **8**:79

Frese, Delores Warwick
Anglo-Saxon Chronicle **4**:27

Freud, Sigmund
Sophocles **2**:313

Frey, John A.
Marie de France **8**:132

Friberg, Eino
Kalevala **6**:275, 278

Friedlander, Ludwig
Juvenal **8**:20

Friedlander, Paul
Plato **8**:355

Friedrich, Paul
Sappho **3**:457

Friedrich, Rainer
Odyssey **16**:330

Fromm, Erich
The Book of Psalms **4**:416

Fronto, Marcus Cornelius
Cicero, Marcus Tullius **3**:176

Frye, Northrop
Aristophanes **4**:130
The Book of Job **14**:189

Fu, Charles Wei-hsun
Lao Tzu **7**:167

Fung Yu-lan
Confucius **19**:37
Lao Tzu **7**:126

Gadamer, Hans-Georg
Plato **8**:333

Galinsky, G. Karl
Ovid **7**:383

Gantz, Jeffrey
Mabinogion **9**:159, 186

Garci-Gomez, Miguel
Poem of the Cid **4**:335

Gardner, John
Epic of Gilgamesh **3**:340
Morte Arthure **10**:399
Pearl **19**:327
Sir Gawain and the Green Knight
2:233

Garner, John Leslie
Khayyam **11**:262

Gaselee, S(tephen)
Apuleius **1**:17

Gassner, John
Terence **14**:339

Gayley, Charles Mills
Mystery of Adam **4**:186

Geddes, J., Jr.
The Song of Roland **1**:169

Gellius, Aulus
Cicero, Marcus Tullius **3**:176

Geoffrey of Monmouth
Arthurian Legend **10**:18

Gerhardt, Mia I.
Arabian Nights **2**:42

Gerow, Edwin
Kalidasa **9**:130

Ghazoul, Ferial Jabouri
Arabian Nights **2**:61

Gibb, H. A. R.
Arabian Nights **2**:28

Gibbon, Edward
Augustine, St. **6**:10
Boethius **15**:2

Gibbs, J.
Apuleius **1**:13

Gibbs, Marion E.
Wolfram von Eshcenbach **5**:347,
429

Gifford, William
Juvenal **8**:6

Gilson, Etienne
Abelard **11**:17
Augustine, St. **6**:44
Averroes **7**:18, 26
Bacon, Roger **14**:86
Meister Eckhart **9**:42, 60

Gilula, Dwora
Terence **14**:389

Girard, Rene
The Book of Job **14**:191
Sophocles **2**:408

Gladdon, Samuel Lyndon
Hildegard von Bingen **20**:182

Gladstone, W. E.
Iliad **1**:297

Glover, T. R.
Herodotus **17**:67

Godwin, William
Poem of the Cid **4**:225

Goethe, Johann Wolfgang von
Kalidasa **9**:130
Longus **7**:217
Menander **9**:227
Sophocles **2**:303

Goldberg, Harriet
Razon de Amor **16**:360

Goldberg, Sander M.
Menander **9**:276
Terence **14**:372

Goldin, Frederick
The Song of Roland **1**:251

Golding, Arthur
Ovid **7**:287

Goldsmith, Margaret E.
Beowulf **1**:134

Gollancz, I.
Sir Gawain and the Green Knight
2:186

Gollancz, Israel
Pearl **19**:286

Goller, Karl Heinz
Morte Arthure **10**:418

Gombrowicz, Witold
Inferno **3**:131

Gomme, A. W.
Menander **9**:259
Thucydides **17**:261

Good, Edwin M.
The Book of Job **14**:206

Goodell, Thomas Dwight
Aeschylus **11**:112

Goodheart, Eugene
The Book of Job **14**:171

Goodrich, Norma Lorre
Arthurian Legend **10**:100, 108

Goold, G. P.
Catullus **18**:166

Gordis, Robert
The Book of Job **14**:175

Gordon, E. V.
Hrafnkel's Saga **2**:86

Gosse, Edmund
Beowulf **1**:73

Gottfried von Strassburg
Gottfried von Strassburg **10**:246,
249, 258
Wolfram von Eschenbach **5**:291

Gradon, Pamela
Beowulf **1**:138

Grahn, Judy
Sappho **3**:494

Grane, Leifn
Abelard **11**:25

Granrud, John E.
Cicero, Marcus Tullius **3**:205

Gransden, Antonia
Anglo-Saxon Chronicle **4**:21

Grant, Michael
Aeschylus **11**:175
Apuleius **1**:26
Cicero, Marcus Tullius **3**:285, 291
Josephus, Flavius **13**:240
Livy **11**:367
Ovid **7**:405
Polybius **17**:176
Thucycdides **17**:296

Graves, Robert
Aeneid **9**:394
Apuleius **1**:20
Iliad **1**:361
Menander **9**:236
Terence **14**:341

Gray, Vivienne
Xenophon **17**:371

Gray, V. J.
Xenophon **17**:369

Gray, Wallace
Iliad **1**:405

Grayson, Christopher
Xenophon **17**:346

Green, D. H.
Hartmann von Aue **15**:206
Wolfram von Eschenbach **5**:391

Green, Peter
Juvenal **8**:68
Ovid **7**:419
Sappho **3**:438

Greenberg, Moshe
The Book of Job **14**:196

Greene, Thomas
Aeneid **9**:399

Greenfield, Concetta Carestia
Petrarch **20**:265

Greenfield, Stanley B.
Beowulf **1**:119
The Dream of the Rood **14**:243

Greenwood, Thomas
Albert the Great **16**:17

Gregory, Eileen
Sappho **3**:495

Grene, David
Aeschylus **11**:220
Herodotus **17**:113
Thucydides **17**:280

Grierson, Herbert J. C.
Beowulf **1**:90

Grieve, Patricia E.
Razon de Amor **16**:364

Griffin, Jasper
Iliad **1**:392
Odyssey **16**:304

Grigson, Geoffrey
Sei Shonagon **6**:300

Grimm, Charles
Chretien de Troyes **10**:141

Groden, Suzy Q.
Sappho **3**:436

Groos, Arthur
Wolfram von Eschenbach **5**:423

Grossman, Judith
Arabian Nights **2**:57

Grossvogel, Steven
Boccaccio, Giovanni **13**:114

Grube, G. M. A.
Aristophanes **4**:136
Cicero, Marcus Tullius **3**:258

Gruffydd, W. J.
Mabinogion **9**:159

Grundy, G. B.
Thucydides **17**:268

Grunmann-Gaudet, Minnette
The Song of Roland **1**:248

Guardini, Romano
Augustine, St. **6**:95
The Book of Psalms **4**:414

Guarino, Guido A.
Boccaccio, Giovanni **13**:52

Gudzy, N. K.
The Igor Tale **1**:485

Gunkel, Hermann
The Book of Psalms **4**:379

Gunn, Alan M. F.
Romance of the Rose **8**:402

Guthrie, W. K. C.
Plato **8**:321, 360

Hackett, Jeremiah M. G.
Bacon, Roger **14**:99, 110

Hadas, Moses
Aeschylus **11**:150
Apuleius **1**:23
Aristophanes **4**:121
Cato, Marcus Porcius **21**:27
Hesiod **5**:98
Juvenal **8**:45
Plato **8**:304
Sappho **3**:417
Seneca, Lucius Annaeus **6**:378, 385

Hagg, Tomas
Longus **7**:262

Haight, Elizabeth Hazelton
Apuleius **1**:18

Haines, C. R.
Sappho **3**:397

Hainsworth, Peter
Petrarch **20**:324

Haley, Lucille
Ovid **7**:310

Hall, David L.
Confucius **19**:88

Hallam, Henry
Bacon, Roger **14**:16
Poem of the Cid **4**:225

Hallberg, Peter
Hrafnkel's Saga **2**:124
Njals saga **13**:339

Hallett, Judith P.
Sappho **3**:465

Halleux, Pierre
Hrafnkel's Saga **2**:99, 102

Halverson, John
Beowulf **1**:131

Hamilton, Edith
Aeschylus **11**:128
Aristophanes **4**:109
Sophocles **2**:328
Terence **14**:322

Hamori, Andras
Arabian Nights **2**:51

Handley, E. W.
Menander **9**:243, 276

Hanford, James Holly
Razon de Amor **16**:337

Hanning, Robert
Marie de France **8**:158

Hanson-Smith, Elizabeth
Mabinogion **9**:192

Haraszti, Zoltan
Mandeville, Sir John **19**:113

Hardison, O. B., Jr.
Mystery of Adam **4**:203

Hardy, E. G.
Juvenal **8**:17

Hardy, Lucy
Boccaccio, Giovanni **13**:30

Harris, Charles
Kalidasa **9**:81

Harrison, Ann Tukey
The Song of Roland **1**:261

Harrison, Robert
The Song of Roland **1**:220

Harsh, Philip Whaley
Menander **9**:216

Hart, Henry H.
Polo, Marco **15**:309

Hart, Thomas R.
Poem of the Cid **4**:306

Hartley, L. P.
Murasaki, Lady **1**:422

Hastings, R.
Boccaccio, Giovanni **13**:59

Hatto, A. T.
Gottfried von Strassburg **10**:259
Das Nibelungenlied **12**:194

Critic Index

Havelock, E. A.
Catullus **18**:91

Havelock, Eric A.
Hesiod **5**:111, 150
Iliad **1**:382, 386

Hay, John
Khayyam **11**:261

Haymes, Edward R.
Das Nibelungenlied **12**:244

Headstrom, Birger R.
Boccaccio, Giovanni **13**:35

Hearn, Lafcadio
Khayyam **11**:258

Hegel, G. W. F.
Aristophanes **4**:46
The Book of Job **14**:157
Inferno **3**:12
Plato **8**:225
Sophocles **2**:297

Heidegger, Martin
Plato **8**:295
Sophocles **2**:376

Heidel, Alexander
Epic of Gilgamesh **3**:310

Heine, Heinrich
Bertran de Born **5**:10

Heinemann, Frederik J.
Hrafnkel's Saga **2**:120, 123

Heiserman, Arthur
Apuleius **1**:46
Longus **7**:254
Xenophon **17**:351

Herder, Johann Gottfried von
The Book of Psalms **4**:355
Kalidasa **9**:102

Herington, John
Aeschylus **11**:210

Hermann, Frankel
Pindar **12**:305

Herodotus
Hesiod **5**:68

Herriott, J. Homer
Polo, Marco **15**:289

Hesse, Hermann
Arabian Nights **2**:28
Boccaccio, Giovanni **13**:32

Hewlett, Maurice
Hesiod **5**:83

Hickes, George
Cædmon **7**:78

Hieatt, Constance
The Song of Roland **1**:209

Higgins, W. E.
Xenophon **17**:352

Highet, Gilbert
Arabian Nights **2**:41
Beowulf **1**:97
Cicero, Marcus Tullius **3**:232, 241
The Dream of the Rood **14**:243
Juvenal **8**:40, 45
Pindar **12**:279
Romance of the Rose **8**:399

Hillebrandt, A.
Kalidasa **9**:95

Hillgarth, J. N.
Llull, Ramon **12**:112

Hirsch, S. A.
Bacon, Roger **14**:23

Hirsch, Steven W.
Xenophon **17**:361

Hisamatsu, Sen'ichi
Sei Shonagon **6**:292

Hobbes, Thomas
Odyssey **16**:189
Thucydides **17**:214

Hodgson, Geraldine E.
Rolle, Richard **21**:298

Holderlin, Friedrich
Sophocles **2**:297

Hole, Richard
Arabian Nights **2**:4

Hollander, Lee M.
Njals saga **13**:326

Hollander, Robert
Boccaccio, Giovanni **13**:67, 88
Vita Nuova **18**:362

Hollister, C. Warren
Anglo-Saxon Chronicle **4**:19

Holmes, Urban T., Jr.
Chretien de Troyes **10**:150

Holyday, Barten
Juvenal **8**:4

Homann, Holger
Das Nibelungenlied **12**:239

Honko, Lauri
Kalevala **6**:271

Hooper, William Davis
Cato, Marcus Porcius **21**:26

Hopkins, E. Washburn
Mahabharata **5**:192

Horowitz, Irving L.
Averroes **7**:28

Horstman, C.
Rolle, Richard **21**:282

Hough, Lynn Harold
The Book of Psalms **4**:388

Hourani, George F.
Averroes **7**:36

Housman, Laurence
Khayyam **11**:278

Howard, Donald R.
Sir Gawain and the Green Knight **2**:221

Howes, Robert C.
The Igor Tale **1**:517

Hroswitha, Abess
Terence **14**:349

Hsu, Sung-peng
Lao Tzu **7**:182, 190

Huang Kuo-pin
Li Po **2**:164

Hueffer, Francis
Bertran de Born **5**:12

Hugel, Baron Friedrich von
Meister Eckhart **9**:27

Hugill, William Meredith
Aristophanes **4**:107

Hugo, Victor
Inferno **3**:22

Huizinga, Johan
Abelard **11**:6

Hulbert, James R.
Beowulf **1**:90

Hull, Denison Bingham
Iliad **1**:398

Hume, David
Cicero, Marcus Tullius **3**:188

Humphries, Rolfe
Juvenal **8**:58

Hunt, H. A. K.
Cicero, Marcus Tullius **3**:253

Hunt, J. William
Aeneid **9**:433

Huppe, Bernard F.
Augustine, St. **6**:92
Cædmon **7**:105
The Dream of the Rood **14**:278

Hutson, Arthur E.
Das Nibelungenlied **12**:162

Hutton, Richard Holt
Khayyam **11**:271

Huxley, Aldous
Bhagavad Gita **12**:54
Meister Eckhart **9**:68
Sappho **3**:398

Ing, Paul Tan Chee
Lao Tzu **7**:164

Ingalls, Daniel H. H.
Kalidasa **9**:122

Inge, William Ralph
Meister Eckhart **9**:25

Iqbal, Afzal
Rumi, Jalal al-Din **20**:353

Irving, Edward B., Jr.
Beowulf **1**:123
The Dream of the Rood **14**:283

Irwin, Terence
Epicurus **21**:192

Isenberg, M.
The Igor Tale **1**:515

Isherwood, Christopher
Bhagavad Gita **12**:54

Isidore of Seville
Plato **8**:211

Ivanhoe, Philip J.
Confucius **19**:95

Ivry, Alfred L.
Averroes **7**:52

Jackson, F. J. Foakes
Josephus, Flavius **13**:226

Jackson, Holbrook
Khayyam **11**:264

Jackson, W. H.
Hartmann von Aue **15**:188

Jackson, W. T. H.
Chretien de Troyes **10**:218
Gottfried von Strassburg **10**:267, 285, 302

Jacob, Alfred
Razon de Amor **16**:340

Jacobs, Joseph
Longus **7**:217

Jacobsen, Thorkild
Epic of Gilgamesh **3**:342

Jacobson, Howard
Ovid **7**:378

Jaeger, C. Stephen
Gottfried von Strassburg **10**:298, 303

Jaeger, Werner
Aeschylus **11**:133
Aristophanes **4**:96
Demosthenes **13**:152
Hesiod **5**:91
Odyssey **16**:209
Plato **8**:281
Sappho **3**:413
Sophocles **2**:331

Jakobson, Roman
The Igor Tale **1**:499

Janeira, Armando Martins
Sei Shonagon **6**:302

Janson, Tore
Cato, Marcus Porcius **21**:29

Jaspers, Karl
Augustine, St. **6**:69
Lao Tzu **7**:139
Plato **8**:312

Jastrow, Morris, Jr.
The Book of Job **14**:150
Epic of Gilgamesh **3**:303

Jebb, Richard C.
Hesiod **5**:77
Sophocles **2**:322
Thucydides **17**:215

Jenkins, T. Atkinson
The Song of Roland **1**:175

Jenkyns, Richard
Sappho **3**:479

Jevons, Frank Byron
Herodotus **17**:59
Thucydides **17**:226

John, Ivor B.
Mabinogion **9**:148

John of Salisbury
Augustine, St. **6**:4
Plato **8**:211

Johnson, Ann S.
Anglo-Saxon Chronicle **4**:17

Johnson, Leslie Peter
Wolfram von Eschenbach **5**:373

Johnson, Samuel
Aeneid **9**:316

Johnson, Sidney M.
Wolfram von Eschenbach **5**:429

Johnson, W. R.
Aeneid **9**:439
Ovid **7**:401
Sappho **3**:476

Jones, Charles W.
Bede **20**:35

Jones, George Fenwick
The Song of Roland **1**:194

Jones, Gwyn
Beowulf **1**:144
Hrafnkel's Saga **2**:84
Mabinogion **9**:167, 174
Njals saga **13**:323

Jones, Martin H.
Wolfram von Eschenbach **5**:354

Jones, Rufus M.
Meister Eckhart **9**:40

Jones, Thomas
Arthurian Legend **10**:18
Mabinogion **9**:167

Jones, W. Lewis
Layamon **10**:319

Jump, John D.
Pindar **12**:327

Jung, C. G.
Meister Eckhart **9**:30

Juvenal
Cicero, Marcus Tullius **3**:175

Kafka, Franz
Odyssey **16**:208

Kant, Immanuel
Plato **8**:223

Kato, Shuichi
Murasaki, Lady **1**:450
Sei Shonagon **6**:304

Keene, Donald
Murasaki, Lady **1**:432

Keith, A. Berriedale
Kalidasa **9**:96

Kemp-Welch, Alice
Marie de France **8**:114

Kendall, Willmoore
Cicero, Marcus Tullius **3**:274

Kennedy, Charles W.
Beowulf **1**:89
Cædmon **7**:84
The Dream of the Rood **14**:227

Kennedy, George A.
Demosthenes **13**:167
Hermogenes **6**:184, 194
Ovid **7**:376

Kenney, E. J.
Ovid **7**:345, 443

Ker, W. P.
Anglo-Saxon Chronicle **4**:2
Beowulf **1**:59, 64
Boccaccio, Giovanni **13**:42
Chretien de Troyes **10**:131
The Dream of the Rood **14**:229
The Song of Roland **1**:164

Kerenyi, C.
Kalevala **6**:241

Kibler, William W.
Chretien de Troyes **10**:231

Kibre, Pearl
Albert the Great **16**:97

Kieckhefer, Richard
Meister Eckhart **9**:66

Kierkegaard, Søren
Aristophanes **4**:48
The Book of Job **14**:125
Plato **8**:232
Sophocles **2**:305

King, James Roy
Rumi, Jalal al-Din **20**:382

King, K. C.
Hartmann von Aue **15**:171

Kirk, G. S.
Epic of Gilgamesh **3**:331
Iliad **1**:371
Odyssey **16**:273

Kirkby, Helen
Boethius **15**:79

Kirkham, Victoria
Boccaccio, Giovanni **13**:94

Kirkwood, G. M.
Sappho **3**:445
Sophocles **2**:377

Kitto, H. D. F.
Aeschylus **11**:137
Odyssey **16**:287
Sophocles **2**:393

Klaeber, Friederich
Beowulf **1**:69

Klein, Karen Wilk
Bertran de Born **5**:35

Kleiner, Yu. A.
Cædmon **7**:111

Klemp, P. J.
Vita Nuova **18**:367

Knapp, Charles
Aeneid **9**:341

Knapp, Peggy Ann
Sir Gawain and the Green Knight **2**:268

Knight, W. F. Jackson
Ovid **7**:340

Knoche, Ulrich
Juvenal **8**:56

Knowles, Dom David
Rolle, Richard **21**:302

Knowlton, Sister Mary Arthur
Rolle, Richard **21**:366

Knox, Bernard M. W.
Aeschylus **11**:183
Sophocles **2**:371, 397

Koht, Halvdan
Hrafnkel's Saga **2**:82

Konishi, Jin'ichi
Murasaki, Lady **1**:471
Sei Shonagon **6**:322

Konstan, David
Menander **9**:282
Terence **14**:376

Korte, Alfred
Callimachus **18**:3

Kotanski, Wieslaw
Kojiki **21**:260

Kott, Jan
Sophocles **2**:410

Koyre, Alexandre
Plato **8**:284

Kraft, Kent T.
Cicero, Marcus Tullius **3**:293

Kratz, Henry
Hrafnkel's Saga **2**:126
Wolfram von Eschenbach **5**:365

Krishnamoorthy, K.
Kalidasa **9**:114

Kristeller, Paul Oskar
Augustine, St. **6**:64
Plato **8**:326

Krohn, Julius
Kalevala **6**:216

Kroll, Paul W.
Li Po **2**:174

Kupfer, Joseph
Bacon, Roger **14**:95

Kustas, George L.
Hermogenes **6**:175, 178

Laborde, E. D.
Anglo-Saxon Chronicle **4**:7

Lacey, W. K.
Cicero, Marcus Tullius **3**:281

Lactantius, Lucius Caelius Firmianus
Cicero, Marcus Tullius **3**:177

Lacy, Norris J.
Chretien de Troyes **10**:169

Laertius, Diogenes
Epicurus **21**:72

Lagercrantz, Olof
Inferno **3**:134

Laidlaw, W. A.
Cicero, Marcus Tullius **3**:252

Laistner, M. L. W.
Livy **11**:325

Lamberton, Robert
Hesiod **5**:170

Landor, Walter Savage
Seneca, Lucius Annaeus **6**:337

Critic Index

Lang, Andrew
Kalevala **6:**212, 230
Khayyam **11:**266
Layamon **10:**317
Odyssey **16:**204

Lanham, Richard A.
Ovid **7:**395

Lateiner, Donald
Herodotus **17:**126

Latham, Ronald
Polo, Marco **15:**298

Lattimore, Richmond
Herodotus **17:**83
Iliad **1:**344

Lau, D. C.
Lao Tzu **7:**147

Lawrence, William Witherle
Beowulf **1:**75

Lawton, W. C.
Hesiod **5:**79

Layamon
Layamon **10:**311, 314

Leach, Anna
Arabian Nights **2:**16

Leaman, Oliver
Averroes **7:**66

Le Bossu, Rene
Aeneid **9:**298
Iliad **1:**278
Odyssey **16:**187

Lecky, W. E. H.
Bacon, Roger **14:**11

Lee, Alvin A.
Beowulf **1:**140

Lee, Guy
Catullus **18:**185

Leech, Kenneth
Llull, Ramon **12:**124

Leff, Gordon
Abelard **11:**22
Augustine, St. **6:**88

Lefkowitz, Mary R.
Sappho **3:**481

Le Gentil, Pierre
The Song of Roland **1:**203

Legge, James
Confucius **19:**3

Legouis, Emile
Layamon **10:**319

Leibniz, Gottfried Wilhelm
Augustine, St. **6:**8
Averroes **7:**5

Plato **8:**220

Leiter, Louis H.
The Dream of the Rood **14:**256

Leon, Harry J.
Cicero, Marcus Tullius **3:**218

Lerer, Seth
Boethius **15:**124

Lesky, Albin
Aeschylus **11:**158, 190
Demosthenes **13:**162
Hesiod **5:**112
Odyssey **16:**304
Pindar **12:**317
Sophocles **2:**378

Lessing, Gotthold Ephraim
Sophocles **2:**294

Letts, Malcolm
Mandeville, Sir John **19:**108

Lever, Katherine
Aristophanes **4:**123
Menander **9:**227, 233

Levy, G. R.
Epic of Gilgamesh **3:**313

Lewis, C. S.
Aeneid **9:**364
Apuleius **1:**32
Beowulf **1:**87
Boethius **15:**43
The Book of Psalms **4:**403
Chretien de Troyes **10:**147
Layamon **10:**343
Romance of the Rose **8:**387
Sir Gawain and the Green Knight
　2:221

Lewis, George Cornewall
Thucydides **17:**243

Levy, Reuben
Avicenna **16:**180

Lewis, Geoffrey
Book of Dede Korkut **8:**103

Lewis, Rev. Gerrard
Poem of the Cid **4:**228

Liebeschuetz, W.
Boethius **15:**47
Livy **11:**357

Likhachov, Dmitry
The Igor Tale **1:**523

Lindberg, David C.
Bacon, Roger **14:**106

Lindsay, Jack
Bertran de Born **5:**55
Longus **7:**229

Lindsay, Thomas B.
Juvenal **8:**17

Littell, Robert
Murasaki, Lady **1:**419

Liu Wu-chi
Confucius **19:**42
Li Po **2:**143

Livy
Livy **11:**311
Cato, Marcus Porcius **21:**4

Lloyd-Jones, Hugh
Aeschylus **11:**168
Menander **9:**231
Odyssey **16:**321
Pindar **12:**342

Lodge, Thomas
Seneca, Lucius Annaeus **6:**335

Lofmark, Carl
Wolfram von Eschenbach **5:**358

Long, A. A.
Epicurus **21:**163

Long, J. Bruce
Mahabharata **5:**270

Longfellow, Henry Wadsworth
Beowulf **1:**57
Inferno **3:**23

Longinus
Aeschylus **11:**83
Cicero, Marcus Tullius **3:**174
Odyssey **16:**192
Plato **8:**206
Sappho **3:**379
Sophocles **2:**292

Longus
Longus **7:**216

Lonnrot, Elias
Kalevala **6:**208, 210

Loomis, Roger Sherman
Arthurian Legend **10:**57, 90, 110
Layamon **10:**341

Lord, Albert B.
Iliad **1:**363
Odyssey **16:**259

Louth, Andrew
Origen **19:**254

Lowell, Amy
Murasaki, Lady **1:**417

Lowth, Robert
The Book of Psalms **4:**352
Song of Songs **18:**238

Lucas, F. L.
Epic of Gilgamesh **3:**309
Li Po **2:**135
Seneca, Lucius Annaeus **6:**363

Luck, Georg
Ovid **7:**346

Luke, J. Tracy
Epic of Gilgamesh **3:**343

Luscombe, D. E.
Abelard **11:**48, 61

Lu-shih, Lin
Lao Tzu **7:**155

Luther, Martin
The Book of Psalms **4:**347
Cicero, Marcus Tullius **3:**185
Song of Songs **18:**230

Luttrell, Claude
Chretien de Troyes **10:**195

Lyne, R. O. A. M.
Catullus **18:**148

Macaulay, Thomas Babbington
Catullus **18:**99
Greek Historiography **17:**2
Ovid **7:**292

Macdonell, Arthur A.
Mahabharata **5:**185

Mackail, J. W.
Aeneid **9:**327
Cato, Marcus Porcius **21:**25
Iliad **1:**315
Odyssey **16:**243
Sappho **3:**389
Seneca, Lucius Annaeus **6:**344
Sophocles **2:**317
Terence **14:**302

MacKay, L. A.
Apuleius **1:**32

Macrae-Gibson, O. D.
The Dream of the Rood **14:**278

Macrobius, Ambrosius Theodosius
Aeneid **9:**294
Apuleius **1:**3
Cicero, Marcus Tullius **3:**178

Maeterlinck, Maurice
Arabian Nights **2:**17

Magnus, Albertus
Albert the Great **16:**65

Magnus, Leonard A.
The Igor Tale **1:**480

Magnusson, Magnus
Njals saga **13:**332

Magoun, Francis Peabody, Jr.
Cædmon **7:**101
Kalevala **6:**246

Mahaffey, John Pentland
Xeonophon **17:**322

Maier, John
Epic of Gilgamesh **3:**354

Mair, Victor H.
Li Po **2:**168

Maki, J. M.
Murasaki, Lady **1**:426

Makin, Peter
Bertran de Born **5**:56
Sordello **15**:360

Mallery, Richard D.
Polo, Marco **15**:295

Malone, Kemp
Beowulf **1**:92
Cædmon **7**:109

Malory, Sir Thomas
Arthurian Legend **10**:44

Malvern, Marjorie M.
Marie de France **8**:171

Mandal, Paresh Chandra
Kalidasa **9**:137

Mandelstam, Osip
Inferno **3**:74

Manilius
Menander **9**:214

Mann, Cameron
Arabian Nights **2**:19

Marble, Annie Russell
Petrarch **20**:225

March, Andrew L.
Su Shih **15**:395

Margesson, Helen P.
Polo, Marco **15**:273

Marie de France
Marie de France **8**:113

Maritain, Jacques
Augustine, St. **6**:24
Inferno **3**:101

Markman, Alan M.
Sir Gawain and the Green Knight
2:209

Marks, Claude
Bertran de Born **5**:48

Marmura, Michael
Avicenna **16**:165

Marotta, Joseph
Wolfram von Eschenbach **5**:396

Marquardt, Patricia
Hesiod **5**:161

Marrou, Henri
Augustine, St. **6**:60

Marsh, George P.
Polo, Marco **15**:269

Martin, Charles
Catullus **18**:138

Martin, Christopher
Ovid **7**:430

Martin, R. H.
Terence **14**:354

Mascaro, Juan
Bhagavad Gita **12**:57

Mason, Herbert
Epic of Gilgamesh **3**:336

Masters, Edgar Lee
Li Po **2**:137

Matter, E. Ann
Song of Songs **18**:306

Matthews, Caitlín
Mabinogion **9**:186

Matthews, William
Morte Arthure **10**:380

Maxwell, Herbert
Bacon, Roger **14**:14

May, Rollo
Inferno **3**:154

Mayer, Frederick
Bacon, Roger **14**:69

Mayer, J. P.
Cicero, Marcus Tullius **3**:220

Maynadier, Howard
Arthurian Legend **10**:115

Mays, James Luther
The Book of Psalms **4**:443

McCallum, J. Ramsay
Abelard **11**:10

McConnell, Winder
Hartmann von Aue **15**:241

McCoy, Patricia
Das Nibelungenlied **12**:162

McCulloh, William E.
Longus **7**:242

McDonald, William C.
Hartmann von Aue **15**:244

McGregor, James H.
Boccaccio, Giovanni **13**:102

McGuire, Michael D.
Meister Eckhart **9**:60

McKay, K. J.
Callimachus **18**:28

McKeon, Richard
Cicero, Marcus Tullius **3**:241

McKeown, J. C.
Ovid **7**:424

McKenzie, Kenneth
Vita Nuova **18**:325

McLeish, Kenneth
Catullus **18**:144

McNamee, Maurice B., S. J.
Beowulf **1**:116

McNary, Sarah F.
Beowulf **1**:58

Meaney, Audrey L.
Anglo-Saxon Chronicle **4**:31

Mendell, Clarence W.
Seneca, Lucius Annaeus **6**:375

Menocal, Maria Rosa
Vita Nuova **18**:372

Merchant, Frank Ivan
Seneca, Lucius Annaeus **6**:357

Meredith, George
Aristophanes **4**:56
Menander **9**:243
Terence **14**:303

Merimee, Ernest
Poem of the Cid **4**:246

Merriman, James Douglas
Arthurian Legend **10**:35

Merton, Thomas
Meister Eckhart **9**:58

Mew, James
Arabian Nights **2**:11

Meyers, Carol
Song of Songs **18**:292

Michael, Ian
Poem of the Cid **4**:291

Michelangelo
Inferno **3**:6

Michener, Richard L.
Chretien de Troyes **10**:171

Mickel, Emanuel J., Jr.
Marie de France **8**:150

Mill, J. S.
Plato **8**:247

Miller, Barbara Stoler
Bhagavad Gita **12**:85

Miller, Frank Justus
Seneca, Lucius Annaeus **6**:362

Miller, Norma
Menander **9**:284

Miller, Patrick D., Jr.
The Book of Psalms **4**:430, 448

Milman, Henry Hart
Inferno **3**:22

Milton, John
The Book of Psalms **4**:351

Mirsky, Prince D. S.
The Igor Tale **1**:484

Mitchell, John D.
Kalidasa **9**:108

Mittelstadt, Michael C.
Longus **7**:238

Momigliano, Arnaldo
Greek Historiography **17**:36
Polybius **17**:185
Xenophon **17**:336

Mommsen, Theodor E.
Cicero, Marcus Tullius **3**:189
Petrarch **20**:236
Terence **14**:304

Monahan, Michael
Sappho **3**:397

Montaigne, Michel de
Cicero, Marcus Tullius **3**:187
Iliad **1**:275
Seneca, Lucius Annaeus **6**:333
Terence **14**:362

Montgomery, Thomas
Poem of the Cid **4**:331

Mookerjee, Arun Kumar
Mahabharata **5**:276

Moon, Harold
Poem of the Cid **4**:267

Moore, George
Longus **7**:223

Moore, Olin H.
Bertran de Born **5**:29

Moorman, Charles
Iliad **1**:376
Mabinogion **9**:195
Das Nibelungenlied **12**:223
Pearl **19**:314
The Song of Roland **1**:231

Moorman, Frederic W.
Sir Gawain and the Green Knight
2:184

Morgan, Bayard Quincy
Wolfram von Eschenbach **5**:307

Morgan, Wendy
Mystery of Adam **4**:211

Morghen, Raffaello
Inferno **3**:121

Morley, Henry
Layamon **10**:312

Morrall, J. B.
Cicero, Marcus Tullius **3**:295

Critic Index

Morris, George S.
Bacon, Roger **14**:13

Morris, Ivan
Murasaki, Lady **1**:434, 438
Sei Shonagon **6**:303

Morris, Mark
Sei Shonagon **6**:307

Morris, Richard
Pearl **19**:277

Morris, Rosemary
Arthurian Legend **10**:95

Morris, William
Arthurian Legend **10**:81

Morrison, Madison
Lao Tzu **7**:203

Mortimer, Raymond
Murasaki, Lady **1**:417, 423

Moseley, C.W.R.D.
Mandeville, Sir John **19**:148

Motto, Anna Lydia
Seneca, Lucius Annaeus **6**:384, 411

Moulton, Carroll
Menander **9**:272

Moulton, Richard G.
Arabian Nights **2**:22
The Book of Psalms **4**:366

Mowatt, D. G.
Das Nibelungenlied **12**:177, 220

Mowinckel, Sigmund
The Book of Psalms **4**:405

Mudrick, Marvin
Marie de France **8**:166

Mueller, Werner A.
Das Nibelungenlied **12**:179

Muir, Edwin
Odyssey **16**:287

Muir, Lynette R.
Mystery of Adam **4**:204

Mullally, Evelyn
Chretien de Troyes **10**:229

Muller, Herbert J.
Aeschylus **11**:152

Murakami, Fuminobu
Kojiki **21**:264

Murasaki, Lady
Sei Shonagon **6**:291

Murdoch, Iris
Plato **8**:362

Murnaghan, Sheila
Odyssey **16**:310

Murphy, Francis X.
Petrarch **20**:255

Murphy, Mabel Gant
Aeneid **9**:330

Murray, Gilbert
Aeschylus **11**:144
Demosthenes **13**:137
Iliad **1**:312
Ovid **7**:303
Pindar **12**:303
Sophocles **2**:340

Murray, Oswyn
Herodotus **17**:102

Murray, Thomas Chalmers
The Book of Psalms **4**:361

Murry, J. Middleton
Beowulf **1**:69

Musa, Mark
Vita Nuova **18**:355

Muscatine, Charles
Romance of the Rose **8**:407

Musurillo, Herbert
Juvenal **8**:61

Myerowitz, Molly
Ovid **7**:435

Nabokov, Vladimir
The Igor Tale **1**:504

Nadeau, Ray
Hermogenes **6**:170

Nakosteen, Mehdi
Khayyam **11**:295

Naumann, Hans
Wolfram von Eschenbach **5**:304

Needler, George Henry
Das Nibelungenlied **12**:153

Nehamas, Alexander
Plato **8**:364

Nelson, Deborah
Chretien de Troyes **10**:199

Nepaulsingh, Colbert I.
Razon de Amor **16**:366

Nethercut, William R.
Apuleius **1**:38

Newbold, William Romaine
Bacon, Roger **14**:37

Newby, P. H.
Arabian Nights **2**:38

Newman, Barbara J.
Hildegard von Bingen **20**:161, 172

Newman, John Henry Cardinal
Cicero, Marcus Tullius **3**:188, 191

Nichols, James R.
Murasaki, Lady **1**:442

Nichols, Stephen G., Jr.
The Song of Roland **1**:189

Nicholson, Reynold A.
Rumi, Jalal al-Din **20**:352

Niebuhr, H. Richard
Augustine, St. **6**:56

Nietzsche, Friedrich
Aeschylus **11**:98
Aristophanes **4**:57
Inferno **3**:46
Plato **8**:251
Sophocles **2**:312

Niles, John D.
Beowulf **1**:150

Nisbet, R. G. M.
Cicero, Marcus Tullius **3**:263

Nisetich, Frank J.
Pindar **12**:335

Nissen, Christopher
Boccaccio, Giovanni **13**:122

Noble, Peter S.
Chretien de Troyes **10**:210

Nohrnberg, James
Inferno **3**:139

Nordal, Sigurður
Hrafnkel's Saga **2**:91

Norinaga, Motoori
Murasaki, Lady **1**:415

Northcott, Kenneth J.
Wolfram von Eschenbach **5**:403

Norton, Charles Eliot
Khayyam **11**:236
Vita Nuova **18**:318

Norwood, Frances
Apuleius **1**:26

Norwood, Gilbert
Aeschylus **11**:116
Aristophanes **4**:92
Menander **9**:205
Pindar **12**:266
Terence **14**:309, 315

Nothnagle, John T.
Chretien de Troyes **10**:157

Nutt, Alfred
Wolfram von Eschenbach **5**:299

Nyland, Waino
Kalevala **6**:238

Obata, Shigeyoshi
Li Po **2**:133

Obuchowski, Mary Dejong
Murasaki, Lady **1**:444

O'Cleirigh, P.M.
Origen **19**:234

Odenkirchen, Carl V.
Mystery of Adam **4**:205

Ogilvy, J. D. A.
Beowulf **1**:154

Oinas, Felix J.
Kalevala **6**:254

Oldfather, W. A.
Cicero, Marcus Tullius **3**:206

Olschki, Leonardo
Polo, Marco **15**:293

Oppenheim, A. Leo
Epic of Gilgamesh **3**:321

Origen
Song of Songs **18**:200

Ormsby, John
Poem of the Cid **4**:226

Osgood, Charles G.
Boccaccio, Giovanni **13**:37

Osterud, Svein
Hesiod **5**:145

Otis, Brooks
Aeneid **9**:429
Ovid **7**:356

Otto, Rudolph
Meister Eckhart **9**:35

Ovid
Ovid **7**:281

Owen, D. D. R.
Chretien de Troyes **10**:173
The Song of Roland **1**:191, 236

Owen, S. G.
Juvenal **8**:25

Owen, Stephen
Li Po **2**:156

Paden, William D., Jr.
Bertran de Born **5**:51, 61

Page, Denys
Odyssey **16**:300
Sappho **3**:430

Pagels, Elaine
Augustine, St. **6**:140

Palgrave, Francis T.
Ovid **7**:299
Sappho **3**:386

Palsson, Hermann
Hrafnkel's Saga **2**:108

Palumbo, Donald
Arabian Nights **2**:71

Pancoast, Henry S.
Layamon **10**:314

Pandiri, Thalia A.
Longus **7**:265

Pandit, R. S.
Kalidasa **9**:103

Papini, Giovanni
Augustine, St. **6**:37

Park, Katharine
Albert the Great **16**:112

Parker, Douglass
Terence **14**:352

Parry, Adam
Aeneid **9**:421

Parshall, Linda B.
Wolfram von Eschenbach **5**:378

Patch, Howard R.
Boethius **15**:15
The Dream of the Rood **14**:218

Pater, Walter
Apuleius **1**:14
Plato **8**:252

Paterson, John
The Book of Psalms **4**:395

Paton, Lucy Allen
Layamon **10**:315

Patrick, Mary Mills
Sappho **3**:393

Patten, Faith H.
The Dream of the Rood **14**:268

Patterson, Annabel M.
Hermogenes **6**:178

Patton, John H.
Meister Eckhart **9**:60

Paul, Herbert
Cicero, Marcus Tullius **3**:194

Payne, John
Arabian Nights **2**:12

Pearson, C. H.
Juvenal **8**:11

Pearson, Karl
Meister Eckhart **9**:9

Pearson, Lionel
Demosthenes **13**:182

Pease, Samuel James
Xenophon **17**:329

Peck, Russell A.
Morte Arthure **10**:406

Peers, E. Allison
Llull, Ramon **12**:92, 95

Pei, Mario A.
The Song of Roland **1**:178

Pekarik, Andrew
Murasaki, Lady **1**:460

Penwill, J. L.
Apuleius **1**:42

Penzer, N. M.
Polo, Marco **15**:276

Pepler, Conrad
Rolle, Richard **21**:330

Perrier, Joseph Louis
Bertran de Born **5**:24

Perry, Ben Edwin
Apuleius **1**:34

Perry, George G.
Rolle, Richard **21**:272

Perry, Henry Ten Eyck
Menander **9**:214
Terence **14**:333

Perse, St.-John
Inferno **3**:131

Petrarch, Francesco
Augustine, St. **6**:7
Boccaccio, Giovanni **13**:4
Cicero, Marcus Tullius **3**:181, 182

Petronio, Giuseppe
Boccaccio, Giovanni **13**:47

Pfeiffer, Rudolf
Callimachus **18**:43

Philippides, Marios
Longus **7**:260

Philostratus
Hermogenes **6**:158

Pickering, Charles J.
Khayyam **11**:249
Avicenna **16**:156

Pickering, F. P.
Hartmann von Aue **15**:218

Pidal, Ramon Menendez
Poem of the Cid **4**:234

Pinkerton, Percy E.
Wolfram von Eschenbach **5**:293

Piramus, Denis
Marie de France **8**:113

Plato
Aristophanes **4**:38
Iliad **1**:270
Plato **8**:200

Plumptre, E. H.
Bacon, Roger **14**:10

Plutarch
Aeschylus **11**:84
Aristophanes **4**:40
Cato, Marcus Porcius **21**:4
Demosthenes **13**:148, 163, 185
Epicurus **21**:70
Herodotus **17**:50
Menander **9**:203
Sappho **3**:379

Poag, James F.
Wolfram von Eschenbach **5**:400

Podlecki, Anthony J.
Pindar **12**:351
Sappho **3**:491

Poe, Joe Park
Seneca, Lucius Annaeus **6**:389

Poggioli, Renato
The Igor Tale **1**:507
Inferno **3**:123

Polybius
Greek Historiography **17**:25

Pomeroy, Sarah B.
Aristophanes **4**:155

Pope, Alexander
Aeneid **9**:313, 358
Iliad **1**:284
Odyssey **16**:192

Pope, John C.
Cædmon **7**:110

Pope, Marvin H.
The Book of Job **14**:181
Song of Songs **18**:266

Popper, K. R.
Plato **8**:348

Portalie, Eugene
Augustine, St. **6**:17

Portor, Laura Spencer
Arabian Nights **2**:23

Poschl, Viktor
Aeneid **9**:377

Post, Chandler Rathfon
Razon de Amor **16**:338

Post, L. A.
Menander **9**:218

Pound, Ezra
Bertran de Born **5**:22
Inferno **3**:99
Odyssey **16**:279
Poem of the Cid **4**:232
The Song of Roland **1**:173
Sordello **15**:347

Powell, F. York
Hrafnkel's Saga **2**:76

Power, Eileen
Polo, Marco **15**:291

Powys, John Cowper
Iliad **1**:358
Inferno **3**:88

Powys, Llewelyn
Khayyam **11**:275

Prabhavananda, Swami
Bhagavad Gita **12**:54

Pratt, Norman T.
Seneca, Lucius Annaeus **6**:429

Prescott, Henry W.
Aeneid **9**:335

Press, Alan R.
Bertran de Born **5**:48

Pretor, Alfred
Xenophon **17**:322

Price, Arnold H.
Das Nibelungenlied **12**:164

Priest, George Madison
Wolfram von Eschenbach **5**:301

Pritchett, V. S.
Murasaki, Lady **1**:452
Poem of the Cid **4**:263, 264

Proclus
Plato **8**:209

Prothero, Rowland E.
The Book of Psalms **4**:373

Proust, Marcel
Arabian Nights **2**:25

Prowett, C. G.
Apuleius **1**:13

Pruyser, Paul W.
Epic of Gilgamesh **3**:343

Pseudo-Longinus
Demosthenes **13**:134, 175

Puette, William J.
Murasaki, Lady **1**:463

Purser, Louis C.
Ovid **7**:299

Putnam, Michael C. J.
Aeneid **9**:428

Quasimodo, Salvatore
Inferno **3**:113
Sappho **3**:435

Quennell, Peter
Apuleius **1**:22

Quiller-Couch, Sir Arthur
Beowulf **1**:67

Critic Index

Quinn, Kenneth
Aeneid **9**:408
Catullus **18**:99, 116

Quinones, Ricardo J.
Inferno **3**:140

Quintilian
Aeneid **9**:294
Aristophanes **4**:40
Hesiod **5**:69
Menander **9**:203
Ovid **7**:286
Seneca, Lucius Annaeus **6**:403

Rabin, Chaim
Song of Songs **18**:259

Radhakrishnan, Sarvepalli
Bhagavad Gita **12**:14
Mahabharata **5**:195

Radice, Betty
Abelard **11**:56
Terence **14**:363

Rahman, Fazlur
Avicenna **16**:134

Raleigh, Walter
Boccaccio, Giovanni **13**:32

Ralphs, Sheila
Inferno **3**:135

Ramanuja
Bhagavad Gita **12**:3

Ramsay, G. G.
Juvenal **8**:38

Rand, Edward Kennard
Aeneid **9**:350
Boethius **15**:4
Cicero, Marcus Tullius **3**:210, 231

Randall, Dale B. J.
Sir Gawain and the Green Knight
2:212

Raphael, Frederic
Catullus **18**:144

Rapin, Rene
Iliad **1**:276

Rascoe, Burton
Apuleius **1**:17
Boccaccio, Giovanni **13**:42

Rawlinson, Henry
Polo, Marco **15**:267

Reckford, Kenneth J.
Menander **9**:238

Regan, Mariann Sanders
Petrarch **20**:293

Rehder, Robert M.
Rumi, Jalal al-Din **20**:367

Reid, Margaret J. C.
Arthurian Legend **10**:44, 62

Reinhardt, Karl
Sophocles **2**:351

Reiss, Edmund
Boethius **15**:88

Rejak, Tessa
Josephus, Flavius **13**:278

Renan, Ernest
The Book of Job **14**:170
Mabinogion **9**:144

Renard, John
Rumi, Jalal al-Din **20**:389

Renoir, Alain
The Song of Roland **1**:199

Rexroth, Kenneth
Abelard **11**:55
Apuleius **1**:37
Beowulf **1**:118
Bhagavad Gita **12**:73
Epic of Gilgamesh **3**:323
Kalevala **6**:252
Mahabharata **5**:242
Murasaki, Lady **1**:441

Rhodes, Jim
Pearl **19**:393

Rhys, John
Mabinogion **9**:147

Richards, Herbert
Aristophanes **4**:75

Richey, Margaret Fitzgerald
Gottfried von Strassburg **10**:274
Wolfram von Eschenbach **5**:309,
323

Rickert, Edith
Marie de France **8**:113

Rider, Jeff
Layamon **10**:355

Riegel, Jeffrey K.
Confucius **19**:78

Riha, T.
The Igor Tale **1**:515

Rimmer, J. Thomas
Sei Shonagon **6**:325

Robinson, David Moore
Sappho **3**:396

Robinson, Fred C.
Beowulf **1**:153

Robinson, H. Wheeler
The Book of Psalms **4**:377

Roche, Paul
Sappho **3**:434

Roche, Thomas P., Jr.
Petrarch **20**:247

Romilly, Jacqueline de
Aeschylus **11**:192
Hesiod **5**:158

Rose, H. J.
Aristophanes **4**:103

Rosenmeyer, Thomas G.
Aeschylus **11**:196

Rosenthal, Joel T.
Bede **20**:98

Ross, E. Denison
Polo, Marco **15**:284

Rossetti, Dante Gabriel
Vita Nuova **18**:324

Rossi, Paolo
Llull, Ramon **12**:109

Rostovtzeff, Mikhail
Aristophanes **4**:79

Routh, James
Beowulf **1**:64

Rowley, H. H.
Song of Songs **18**:246

Royce, Josiah
The Book of Job **14**:130
Meister Eckhart **9**:14

Ruskin, John
Inferno **3**:14, 19, 21

Russell, Bertrand
Abelard **11**:9
Augustine, St. **6**:53
Averroes **7**:15
Avicenna **16**:171
Bacon, Roger **14**:68
Plato **8**:290

Russell, D. A.
Hermogenes **6**:192

Ryder, Arthur W.
Kalidasa **9**:87

Ryder, Frank G.
Das Nibelungenlied **12**:187

Sabra, A. I.
Averroes **7**:62
Avicenna **16**:156

Sacker, Hughes
Hartmann von Aue **15**:154
Das Nibelungenlied **12**:220
Wolfram von Eschenbach **5**:336

**Saint Palaye, Jean Bapstiste de La
Curne de**
Bertran de Born **5**:4

Saintsbury, George
Aristophanes **4**:69

Longus **7**:221

Saklatvala, Beram
Arthurian Legend **10**:13

Salinas, Pedro
Poem of the Cid **4**:247

Samuel, Maurice
The Book of Psalms **4**:425

Sandars, N. K.
Epic of Gilgamesh **3**:315

Sandbach, F. H.
Aristophanes **4**:156
Menander **9**:259, 268
Terence **14**:367

Sankovitch, Tilde A.
Bertran de Born **5**:61
Marie de France **8**:177

Sansom, George
Sei Shonagon **6**:294

Santayana, George
Inferno **3**:54
Plato **8**:257

Sarasin, Jean Francois
Epicurus **21**:80

Sargeant, Winthrop
Bhagavad Gita **12**:79

Sarna, Nahum A.
The Book of Psalms **4**:421

Sarton, George
Bacon, Roger **14**:61

Sasson, Jack M.
Epic of Gilgamesh **3**:336

Saunders, A. N. W.
Demosthenes **13**:175

Savage, Henry Littleton
Sir Gawain and the Green Knight
2:206

Sayers, Dorothy L.
The Song of Roland **1**:183

Scartazzini, G. A.
Inferno **3**:39

Schach, Paul
Njals saga **13**:374

Schein, Seth L.
Iliad **1**:399

**Schelling, Friedrich Wilhelm Jo-
seph von**
Inferno **3**:8

Scherer, W.
Gottfried von Strassburg **10**:248
Wolfram von Eschenbach **5**:295

Schirmer, Walter F.
Layamon **10**:336

Schlauch, Margaret
The Dream of the Rood **14**:223

Schlegel, August Wilhelm
Aeschylus **11**:84
Aristophanes **4**:42
Seneca, Lucius Annaeus **6**:336
Sophocles **2**:299

Schlegel, Frederick
Wolfram von Eschenbach **5**:293

Schleiermacher, Friedrich Ernst Daniel
Plato **8**:228

Schnyder, Hans
Sir Gawain and the Green Knight **2**:217

Schoenberner, Franz
Das Nibelungenlied **12**:169

Schopenhauer, Arthur
Meister Eckhart **9**:45
Plato **8**:244

Schotter, Anne Howland
Pearl **19**:365

Schreckenberg, Heinz
Josephus, Flavius **13**:299

Schucking, Levin L.
Beowulf **1**:78

Schwartz, Kessel
Poem of the Cid **4**:266

Schwertner, Thomas M.
Albert the Great **16**:19

Scodel, Ruth
Sophocles **2**:426

Scragg, D. G.
Anglo-Saxon Chronicle **4**:25

Scullard, H. H.
Cato, Marcus Porcius **21**:31

Sealey, Rapha l
Kalevala **6**:245

Sedgefield, Walter John
Anglo-Saxon Chronicle **4**:3

Sedgwick, Henry Dwight
Petrarch **20**:219

Segal, Charles
Pindar **12**:375
Sappho **3**:442
Seneca, Lucius Annaeus **6**:447
Sophocles **2**:423

Sei Shonagon
Sei Shonagon **6**:289

Seidensticker, Edward
Murasaki, Lady **1**:455

Selincourt, Aubrey de
Greek Historiography **17**:20
Herodotus **17**:90

Sellar, W. Y.
Aeneid **9**:318
Ovid **7**:293

Seneca, Lucius Annaeus, the Elder
Aeneid **9**:294
Ovid **7**:285

Serafini-Sauli, Judith Powers
Boccaccio, Giovanni **13**:84

Setala, E. N.
Kalevala **6**:235

Sewall, Richard B.
The Book of Job **14**:165
Sophocles **2**:388

Seymour, M.C.
Mandeville, Sir John **19**:128

Shaftesbury, Anthony Earl of
Seneca, Lucius Annaeus **6**:335

Shaw, J. E.
Vita Nuova **18**:331

Shaw, James R.
Albert the Great **16**:81

Shedd, Gordon M.
Sir Gawain and the Green Knight **2**:245

Shelley, Percy Bysshe
Aeschylus **11**:89

Shenoy, Anasuya R.
Mahabharata **5**:247

Shepard, G.
Cædmon **7**:97

Sheppard, J. T.
Aeschylus **11**:126

Sherley-Price, Leo
Bede **20**:60

Shippey, T. A.
Beowulf **1**:146

Shirazi, J. K. M.
Khayyam **11**:268

Shklar, Judith N.
Hesiod **5**:128

Shorey, Paul
Plato **8**:262

Showerman, Grant
Cicero, Marcus Tullius **3**:203

Shumway, Daniel Bussier
Gottfried von Strassburg **10**:250

Shutt, R. J. H.
Josephus, Flavius **13**:235, 267

Sidney, Sir Philip
The Book of Psalms **4**:351
Xenophon **17**:351

Sighart, Joachim
Albert the Great **16**:3

Sikes, E. E.
Aeneid **9**:329

Simmons, Merle E.
Poem of the Cid **4**:310

Simonides
Sophocles **2**:290

Singer, Carl S.
Das Nibelungenlied **12**:211

Singer, Charles
Hildegard von Bingen **20**:131

Singleton, Charles S.
Inferno **3**:102
Vita Nuova **18**:339

Singleton, Mack
Poem of the Cid **4**:254

Siraisi, Nancy G.
Avicenna **16**:171

Sisam, Kenneth
Beowulf **1**:121

Sismondi, J. C. L. Simonde de
Bertran de Born **5**:8

Skinner, John V.
Meister Eckhart **9**:54

Slater, Anne Saxon
Hrafnkel's Saga **2**:104

Small, Stuart G. P.
Catullus **18**:167

Smertenko, Johan J.
Li Po **2**:135

Smiley, Charles N.
Hesiod **5**:85

Smith, Adam
Sophocles **2**:293

Smith, Colin
Poem of the Cid **4**:277, 316

Smith, Huston
Meister Eckhart **9**:66

Smith, J. C.
Beowulf **1**:90

Smith, J. M. Powis
The Book of Psalms **4**:375

Smith, Justin H.
Bertran de Born **5**:18

Smith, Morton
Josephus, Flavius **13**:290

Smith, Robert W.
Origen **19**:230

Smyth, Herbert Weir
Aeschylus **11**:120
Sappho **3**:434

Smythe, Barbara
Bertran de Born **5**:23

Snell, Bruno
Aristophanes **4**:120
Callimachus **18**:21
Pindar **12**:275
Sappho **3**:417

Solomos, Alexis
Aristophanes **4**:153

Sonstroem, David
Khayyam **11**:292

Sørensen, Villy
Seneca, Lucius Annaeus **6**:418

Soulen, Richard N.
Song of Songs **18**:256

Southern, R. W.
Abelard **11**:33
Bede **20**:46

Spearing, A. C.
Pearl **19**:349
Sir Gawain and the Green Knight **2**:248

Speirs, John
Sir Gawain and the Green Knight **2**:188

Spence, Sarah
Aeneid **9**:442

Spender, Stephen
Sophocles **2**:427

Spenser, Edmund
Arthurian Legend **10**:61

Spiegel, Harriet
Marie de France **8**:189

Sponsler, Lucy A.
Poem of the Cid **4**:293

Springer, Otto
Wolfram von Eschenbach **5**:321

St. Bernard of Clairvaux
Song of Songs **18**:217

St. Gregory of Nyssa
Song of Songs **18**:212

Stablein, Patricia H.
Bertran de Born **5**:61

Stace, W. T.
Epicurus **21**:128

Critic Index

Staines, David
Chretien de Troyes **10**:218

Staley, Lynn
Pearl **19**:371

Stanbury, Sarah
Pearl **19**:379

Stanford, W. B.
Odyssey **16**:247
Sappho **3**:415

Stanton, Elizabeth Cady
Song of Songs **18**:245

Stapylton, Robert
Juvenal **8**:3

Starkie, Walter
Poem of the Cid **4**:252

Ste. Croix, G. E. M. de
Thucydides **17**:296

Steele, R. B.
Livy **11**:315

Steele, Robert
Bacon, Roger **14**:45

Stehle, Eva
Sappho **3**:469

Steiner, George
Iliad **1**:368

Steiner, Rudolf
Bhagavad Gita **12**:7

Stendhal
Arabian Nights **2**:6

Steneck, Nicholas H.
Albert the Great **16**:103

Stenton, F. M.
Bede **20**:34

Stephens, Anna Cox
Kalevala **6**:228

Stephens, J. N.
Bede **20**:106

Stephens, Wade C.
Ovid **7**:337

Stephenson, William E.
Apuleius **1**:29

Stevens, John
Marie de France **8**:137

Stewart, Douglas J.
Hesiod **5**:118, 124

Stone, Brian
Arthurian Legend **10**:85

Stone, Charles J.
Mahabharata **5**:179

Stone, Edward Noble
Mystery of Adam **4**:190

Strachan-Davidson, J. L.
Polybius **17**:150

Strahan, James
The Book of Job **14**:144

Strauss, Leo
Xenophon **17**:331

Studer, Paul
Mystery of Adam **4**:186

Stump, Eleonore
The Book of Job **14**:138

Suetonius
Terence **14**:339

Suhm, P. A.
Njals saga **13**:330

Sukthankar, V. S.
Mahabharata **5**:225

Sumer, Faruk
Book of Dede Korkut **8**:98

Suso, Henry
Meister Eckhart **9**:7, 8

Sutton, Dana Ferrin
Aristophanes **4**:162
Terence **14**:393

Suzuki, Daisetz Teitaro
Meister Eckhart **9**:49

Sveinsson, Einar Ólafur
Njals saga **13**:347

Swanton, Michael
Layamon **10**:350

Swinburne, Algernon Charles
Aristophanes **4**:57
Sappho **3**:392

Syme, Ronald
Cicero, Marcus Tullius **3**:222

Symonds, John Addington
Aeschylus **11**:99
Aristophanes **4**:58
Boccaccio, Giovanni **13**:26
Hesiod **5**:74
Pindar **12**:261
Sappho **3**:385

Symons, Arthur
Augustine, St. **6**:16

Syrianus
Hermogenes **6**:158

Tagore, Rabindranath
Kalidasa **9**:92

Taine, H. A.
The Song of Roland **1**:162

TaMaKH, R. Abraham b. Isaac ha-Levi
Song of Songs **18**:226

Tambling, Jeremy
Inferno **3**:158

Tate, Allen
Inferno **3**:112

Tatlock, John S. P.
Layamon **10**:318, 349

Taylor, A. E.
Epicurus **21**:116

Taylor, Beverly
Arthurian Legend **10**:74

Taylor, Henry Osborn
Bacon, Roger **14**:16
Inferno **3**:55
Wolfram von Eschenbach **5**:302

Taylor, Thomas
Apuleius **1**:12

Ten Brink, Bernard
Cædmon **7**:80

Tennyson, Alfred Lord
Aeneid **9**:317
Arabian Nights **2**:6
Arthurian Legend **10**:64, 90

Terrien, Samuel
The Book of Job **14**:162

Thackeray, H. St. John
Josephus, Flavius **13**:206

Thierry, Augustin
Bertran de Born **5**:9

Thomas, Calvin
Gottfried von Strassburg **10**:254
Das Nibelungenlied **12**:160

Thomas, R. George
Hrafnkel's Saga **2**:116

Thompson, Maurice
Sappho **3**:386

Thompson, Raymond H.
Chretien de Troyes **10**:197

Thompson, Wesley E.
Polybius **17**:198

Thoreau, Henry D.
Aeschylus **11**:91
Iliad **1**:296

Thorndike, Lynn
Albert the Great **16**:7
Bacon, Roger **14**:48

Thornley, George
Longus **7**:216

Thorpe, Benjamin
Cædmon **7**:78

Thucydides
Herodotus **17**:90

Ticknor, George
Poem of the Cid **4**:228

Tigay, Jeffrey H.
Epic of Gilgamesh **3**:349

Tillyard, E. M. W.
Aeneid **9**:384
Beowulf **1**:111
Boccaccio, Giovanni **13**:43
Herodotus **17**:/7
Iliad **1**:348
Odyssey **16**:243
The Song of Roland **1**:180

Tobin, Frank J.
Hartmann von Aue **15**:213, 223

Todorov, Tzvetan
Arabian Nights **2**:44, 48

Tolkien, J. R. R.
Anglo-Saxon Chronicle **4**:11
Beowulf **1**:80
Sir Gawain and the Green Knight **2**:201

T
olman, Albert H.
Kalevala **6**:231

Tolstoy, Leo
Odyssey **16**:253

Topsfield, L. T.
Chretien de Troyes **10**:201

Tornay, Stephen Chak
Averroes **7**:10

Toy, C. H.
The Book of Job **14**:138

Toynbee, Arnold J.
Greek Historiography **17**:5

Tracy, H. L.
Aeschylus **11**:147

Trapp, Joseph
Terence **14**:385

Trevelyan, G. Otto
Ovid **7**:292

Trever, Albert Augustus
Hesiod **5**:88

Trible, Phyllis
Song of Songs **18**:275

Trigg, Joseph W.
Origen **19**:245

Trinkaus, Charles
Petrarch **20**:284

Trollope, Anthony
Cicero, Marcus Tullius **3**:192

Trypanis, C. A.
Sappho **3**:474

Tsanoff, Radoslav
Augustine, St. **6**:41

Tu Fu
Li Po **2**:132

Tugwell, Simon
Albert the Great **16**:115

Turbervile, George
Ovid **7**:290

Turner, Eric G.
Menander **9**:257

Turner, Paul
Longus **7**:235

Turunen, Aimo
Kalevala **6**:258

Twomey, Michael W.
Morte Arthure **10**:425

Tyrwhitt, Thomas
Layamon **10**:311

Uhland, Johann
Bertran de Born **5**:10

Uitti, Karl D.
Chretien de Troyes **10**:190
Romance of the Rose **8**:446
The Song of Roland **1**:243

Urwin, Kenneth
Mystery of Adam **4**:191

Usher, Stephen
Greek Historiography **17**:23

Uysal, Ahmet E.
Book of Dede Korkut **8**:98

Vaidya, C. V.
Mahabharata **5**:189

Valency, Maurice
Vita Nuova **18**:349

Valla, Lorenzo
Cato, Marcus Porcius **21**:4
Epicurus **21**:79

Van Antwerp, Margaret
Razon de Amor **16**:353

Van Buitenen, J. A. B.
Mahabharata **5**:267

Van Buskirk, William R.
Lao Tzu **7**:119

Van Doren, Mark
Aeneid **9**:366
The Book of Psalms **4**:425
Iliad **1**:336
Murasaki, Lady **1**:420
Odyssey **16**:231

Van Nooten, Barend A.
Mahabharata **5**:249

Vance, Eugene
The Song of Roland **1**:214

Vannovsky, Alexander
Kojiki **21**:244

Vellacott, Philip
Aeschylus **11**:207

Verdenius, W. J.
Plato **8**:296

Vergil
Aeneid **9**:312, 329

Versenyi, Laszlo
Hesiod **5**:137
Sappho **3**:455

Very, Jones
Homer **1**:292

Vigfusson, Gudbrand
Hrafnkel's Saga **2**:76

Vinaver, Eugene
Arthurian Legend **10**:81
Chretien de Troyes **10**:180
The Song of Roland **1**:234

Vittorini, Domenico
Vita Nuova **18**:346

Vivekananda, Swami
Bhagavad Gita **12**:5

Voltaire, François-Marie Arouet
Aeneid **9**:314
Aristophanes **4**:41
The Book of Job **14**:123
Iliad **1**:288

von Fritz, Kurt
Polybius **17**:160

Vossler, Karl
Inferno **3**:51

Wa, Kathleen Johnson
Lao Tzu **7**:196
Vita Nuova **18**:329

Wailes, Stephen L.
Das Nibelungenlied **12**:231

Walbank, F. W.
Polybius **17**:167

Waldock, A. J. A.
Sophocles **2**:368

Waley, Arthur
Confucius **19**:17
Lao Tzu **7**:128
Li Po **2**:137
Murasaki, Lady **1**:421

Walhouse, Moreton J.
Sappho **3**:385

Waliszewski, K.
The Igor Tale **1**:479

Walker, Roger M.
Razon de Amor **16**:346

Walker, Warren S.
Book of Dede Korkut **8**:98

Wallace, David
Boccaccio, Giovanni **13**:87, 94

Wallace, William
Epicurus **21**:101

Walpole, Horace
Arabian Nights **2**:3

Walsh, George B.
Hesiod **5**:166

Walsh, P. G.
Livy **11**:342, 350

Walshe, M. O'C.
Gottfried von Strassburg **10**:274
Das Nibelungenlied **12**:171
Wolfram von Eschenbach **5**:333

Warburton, William
Apuleius **1**:7

Ward, Benedicta
Bede **20**:102

Warmington, B. H.
Seneca, Lucius Annaeus **6**:395

Warton, Joseph
Inferno **3**:6

Watling, E. F.
Seneca, Lucius Annaeus **6**:387

Watson, Burton
Si Shih **15**:391

Watson, Nicholas
Rolle, Richard **21**:388

Webbe, Joseph
Terence **14**:296

Webbe, William
Ovid **7**:290

Webber, Ruth H.
Poem of the Cid **4**:286

Weber, Alfred
Bacon, Roger **14**:20

Webster, T. B. L.
Callimachus **18**:34
Menander **9**:246

Weigand, Hermann J.
Wolfram von Eschenbach **5**:315, 370

Weil, Simone
Iliad **1**:331

Weiler, Royal W.
Kalidasa **9**:113

Weinberg, Julius R.
Averroes **7**:44
Bacon, Roger **14**:94

Weinberg, S. C.
Layamon **10**:360

Weiss, Paul
The Book of Job **14**:157

Welch, Holmes
Lao Tzu **7**:141

Wellek, Rene
Pearl **19**:299

West, M. L.
Pindar **12**:333

Westcott, John Howell
Livy **11**:312

Westermann, Claus
The Book of Psalms **4**:428

Westlake, John S.
Anglo-Saxon Chronicle **4**:4

Weston, Jessie L.
Arthurian Legend **10**:28
Chretien de Troyes **10**:133
Gottfried von Strassburg **10**:247
Wolfram von Eschenbach **5**:300

Wetherbee, Winthrop
Romance of the Rose **8**:422

Wheeler, Arthur Leslie
Cattullus **18**:82

Whewell, William
Bacon, Roger **14**:3

Whibley, Charles
Apuleius **1**:15

Whigham, Peter
Catullus **18**:109

Whinfield, E. H.
Khayyam **11**:255
Rumi, Jalal al-Din **20**:338

Whitehead, Alfred North
Plato **8**:271

Whitelock, Dorothy
Beowulf **1**:101

Whitman, Cedric H.
Aristophanes **4**:133
Iliad **1**:350
Odyssey **16**:254
Sophocles **2**:362

Wicksteed, Philip H.
Inferno **3**:46

Wiersma, S.
Longus **7**:274

Wilhelm, James J.
Bertran de Born **5**:39

Wilhelmsen, Frederick D.
Cicero, Marcus Tullius **3**:274

Wilkinson, L. P.
Ovid **7**:329

Williams, Harry F.
Chretien de Troyes **10**:225

Willson, H. B.
Gottfried von Strassburg **10**:278
Hartmann von Aue **15**:148, 165, 175, 196

Wilson, B. W. J. G.
Cicero, Marcus Tullius **3**:281

Wilson, Edmund
Sophocles **2**:341

Wilson, H. Schutz
Khayyam **11**:238

Wilson, Harry Langford
Juvenal **8**:23

Wilson, R. M.
Layamon **10**:335

Windelband, Wilhelm
Abelard **11**:3
Augustine, St. **6**:11
Averroes **7**:6

Winkler, John J.
Apuleius **1**:47

Winnington-Ingram, R. P.
Aeschylus **11**:206
Sophocles **2**:415

Winternitz, Moriz
Mahabharata **5**:202

Wiseman, T. P.
Catullus **18**:148

Witte, Karl
Inferno **3**:41

Wittgenstein, Ludwig
Augustine, St. **6**:55

Wolf, Carol Jean
The Dream of the Rood **14**:280

Wolff, Hope Nash
Epic of Gilgamesh **3**:328

Wolfram von Eschenbach
Wolfram von Eschenbach **5**:292, 293

Wolpert, Stanley
Mahabharata **5**:281

Wood, Anthony à
Bacon, Roger **14**:3

Woodman, A. J.
Livy **11**:382

Woodruff, F. Winthrop
Bacon, Roger **14**:66

Woodruff, Paul
Plato **8**:364

Woolf, Rosemary
The Dream of the Rood **14**:230
Rolle, Richard **21**:355

Woolf, Virginia
Aeschylus **11**:126
Murasaki, Lady **1**:418
Sappho **3**:395
Sophocles **2**:326

Wooten, Cecil W.
Demosthenes **13**:189
Hermogenes **6**:202

Wordsworth, William
Arabian Nights **2**:5
Sophocles **2**:304

Wrenn, C. L.
Anglo-Saxon Chronicle **4**:13
Beowulf **1**:107
Cædmon **7**:93

Wright, F. A.
Ovid **7**:304
Sappho **3**:396

Wright, Henry Parks
Juvenal **8**:22

Wright, Thomas
Polo, Marco **15**:261

Wyckoff, Dorothy
Albert the Great **16**:54

Wyld, Henry Cecil
Layamon **10**:320

Wyld, M. Alice
Inferno **3**:50

Wynn, Marianne
Wolfram von Eschenbach **5**:326, 416

Yadin, Yigael
Josephus, Flavius **13**:239

Yaku, Masao
Kojiki **21**:255

Yarmolinsky, Avrahm
The Igor Tale **1**:496

Yates, Frances A.
Cicero, Marcus Tullius **3**:273
Llull, Ramon **12**:103

Yavetz, Zvi
Josephus, Flavius **13**:250

Yoshikawa, Kojiro
Su Shih **15**:410

Young, Karl
Mystery of Adam **4**:190

Yourcenar, Marguerite
Murasaki, Lady **1**:455

Yousofi, Gholam Hosein
Rumi, Jalal al-Din **20**:373

Yutang, Lin
Confucius **19**:25
Lao Tzu **7**:135

Zacher, Christian K.
Mandeville, Sir John **19**:131

Zaehner, R. C.
Bhagavad Gita **12**:67
Mahabharata **5**:243

Zanker, G.
Callimachus **18**:50

Zedler, Beatrice H.
Averroes **7**:22

Zeller, E.
Epicurus **21**:97

Zeydel, Edwin H.
Gottfried von Strassburg **10**:258
Wolfram von Eschenbach **5**:307

Zhirmunsky, Victor
Book of Dede Korkut **8**:96

Zimmer, Heinrich
Arabian Nights **2**:32
Bhagavad Gita **12**:45
Sir Gawain and the Green Knight **2**:187

Zweig, Stefan
Cicero, Marcus Tullius **3**:225

ISBN 0-7876-1125-5

90000

9 780787 611255